BASEBALL TEAM NAMES

BASEBALL TEAM NAMES

A Worldwide Dictionary, 1869–2011

Richard Worth

McFarland & Company, Inc., Publishers
Jefferson, North Carolina, and London

LIBRARY OF CONGRESS CATALOGUING-IN-PUBLICATION DATA

Worth, Richard, 1947–
Baseball team names : a worldwide dictionary,
1869–2011 / Richard Worth.
p.   cm.
Includes bibliographical references and index.

ISBN 978-0-7864-6844-7
softcover : acid free paper ∞

1. Baseball teams— United States— Names— Dictionaries.
2. Baseball players— United States— Terminology.   I. Title.
GV862.3.W67 2013   796.35703 — dc23   2012043795

BRITISH LIBRARY CATALOGUING DATA ARE AVAILABLE

Manufactured in the United States of America

McFarland & Company, Inc., Publishers
Box 611, Jefferson, North Carolina 28640
www.mcfarlandpub.com

To the wonderful librarians, pages, technicians and administrators
of the Northlake Public Library of Northlake, Illinois,
including Erica, Harvey, Kathy, Laura, Lucy,
Mary, Michele, Raleigh, Rob and Tyler

TABLE OF CONTENTS

INTRODUCTION

Nicknames, for both people and groups of people, have been in use since human history began. In the ancient world there were team nicknames, as when Roman Circus Maximus charioteers adopted colored banners to impress their cheering fans, becoming "the Reds," "the Blues," "the Yellows," and so forth. Individuals too had nicknames. Among the gladiators in the Roman coliseum were "Maximus the Merciful" and "Demetrius the Destroyer." The heraldic images used by armies and governments of the Middle Ages were the direct ancestors of the sporting team mascots and logos that we have today. Nicknames appeal to us also because we find them to be fun and entertaining — and oftentimes far easier to remember than an athlete's or team's actual name. In the 1950s Ted Kluszewski of the Reds, Pirates and White Sox was nicknamed "Big Klu" almost certainly because most Americans had trouble pronouncing his surname. The same was true of Carl Yastzremski, beloved Boston Red Sox star of the 1960s and 1970s, who was known simply as "Yaz."

In baseball, team and player nicknames began to appear almost simultaneously with the first organized teams in the 1840s, when team names like Knickerbocker and Gotham were in use and Daniel "Doc" Adams was a star player for the former.

The evolution of team nicknames in baseball has been ongoing for 165 years and had its origin in the names of the social clubs that first played the game using New York rules in the 1840s. One of the first such clubs was the Knickerbocker Club — a social organization of upper-class young men in New York City. The Knickerbocker Club was a social club of as many as 200 members who joined for social fraternization, much like the American Legion, Veterans of Foreign Wars, the Lions Club, Young Men's Christian Association and Young Women's Christian Association of today. Young people in these clubs gravitated towards sports and athletics and the inevitable result was the appearance of sports teams like boxing, rowing, archery, track and field, horse riding, fox hunting, wrestling, ice skating, lacrosse and baseball, not to mention the other ball and stick games, such as cricket, rounders and town ball. Not all of the members of a social club actually joined a sports team. In fact, only a minority of a club's membership played on a sports team and had the skills to qualify for such competition. Herein lies the crucial difference between a "club" and a "team" as defined by 19th-century parameters.

In 1830 the Olympic Club of Philadelphia had a membership of 150 young men and formed a town-ball team to play this ball and stick game. The team consisted of about 30 young men who styled themselves as the "Olympic Town Ball Club." Despite using the word "club" in reference to the social club from which they sprang, the title actually referred to the sporting "team" they had formed. Starting here with the Olympics, this quandary between "club" and "team" would take another 40 years to be resolved with a clear demarcation between social club and sports team. Fifteen years later the "Knickerbocker Baseball Club" was formed as an offshoot from the Knickerbocker Club social society.

By the 1850s all sorts of social clubs had sprung up in the United States and Canada — e.g., the Mutual Club, the Atlantic Club, the Excelsior Club, the Union Club, the Empire Club and so on. But baseball proved to be too popular to be populated merely by the young men of upper-class social clubs. Young men (and young women) of the merchant and labor class also eagerly picked up on the game. In the 1850s the Eckford Club was formed by New York shipbuilder Henry Eckford. He actually had two teams and enlisted his workers at the shipyards, boat builders and dock loaders, to play on them.

The whole original notion of baseball as a genteel, elitist pastime played by carefree upper class young men who cared not whether they won or lost the contest was quickly overthrown by middle and lower class fellows who played the game rough and hard and who played to win. It was this urge to come out on top that not only destroyed baseball's original upper-class status but also paved the way for the professional game that would appear 20 years later in the 1870s.

Baseball's progress was disrupted by the Civil War (1861–65) but by war's end the higher echelon baseball club (of social club origins) had been entirely replaced by the baseball *team*. An increasing number of teams had owners and sponsors who were interested in fielding winning teams that would attract paying fans. (The first admission had been charged at Brooklyn's Union Grounds in 1862.) The logical and inevitable step to semi-professional and then professional baseball, by 1865, was only five or six years away.

As such, the social club motivations of early baseball had been largely disavowed, but, baseball team's often retained the old social club name for the team's official title. The Atlantic Baseball Club of 1865–68 was no longer a social club — playing now strictly as a baseball team — yet it retained its old social club image in its name.

Not only social clubs but even workplace sponsors were falling by the wayside. The Mutual Club of New York (sponsored by the Mutual Firefighter Association in 1857) and the Eckford Club of Brooklyn (sponsored by the Henry Eckford Shipbuilding Company in 1858) were now concentrating exclusively on baseball full-time and their only connection with their sponsors was the money the sponsors were paying out for equipment, uniforms and travel expenses. Indeed, the Mutual Firefighters, the team's original sponsor for the New York Mutuals, had been effectively replaced by New York City politician William "Boss" Tweed and his pals who lavishly funded the team. As such, Mutual Club, Eckford Club, Atlantic Club and other such names no longer referred to social or workplace clubs of athletes and non-athletes, but rather, now to money-sponsored and exclusively athletic teams.

With the image of team in the mind of the sporting public, as opposed to club, it was inevitable that team nicknames would soon be used by fans and reporters to spice up the descriptions, references and game reports. The more obvious *team* nicknames appearing in the period 1868–88 were those based on stocking colors. In 1868 the Cincinnati Baseball Club innovated the knickerbocker pants-leg to replace the full-length pants worn by stick and ball players for the era 1830–1867. In the 18th century men often wore these pants that ended at the knee joint combined with long stockings that covered the ankle and calf reaching to the knee. In the 19th century men started wearing trousers that reached the shoe tops because they were more practical and protected the legs better during hard physical labor. In any case, long trousers were not well-suited to such sports as baseball because they restricted the bending of the knee when running and fielding. If the pants were too long, flowing over the shoe tops, a player could trip and even be injured by the resulting tumble.

The 1868 Cincinnati players appeared on the field in woolen or flannel knickerbocker pants that ended at the knee and long woolen stockings from ankle to knee that were dyed a bright crimson red. The effect on fans and newspaper reporters was electric. The team immediately became known as the "Red Stockings." Almost at once teams began sporting knickerbocker pants with dyed woolen stockings. During hot summer weather players also sported cotton and even silk stockings. The stockings were dyed a bright color: red, green, blue, golden yellow, maroon, orange and black. Some teams wore white stockings.

But the influence of the "social club" had not completely dissipated. The result was an amalgam of an old social club name with the exclusively team-oriented "stocking color" moniker. For example, the players of the Mutual Baseball Club, now playing their home games at the Union Grounds in Brooklyn, wore green stockings. Newspapers soon began calling them the Mutual Green Stockings, a name that would be mostly incomprehensible today but one that made perfect sense to the fans in New York in the 1870s. Unable to be called the New York Green Stockings or New York Green Sox because of the profusion of other pro, semi-pro and amateur clubs in New York, the team maintained its old "Mutual" identity to render it unique to fans and newspapers. The result was such monikers as Mutual Green Stockings, Eckford Orange Stockings, Quaker White Stockings, Lord Baltimore Yellow Stockings and Forest City Blue Stockings.

In today's sporting world, the presence of more than one professional sports franchise per sport in a particular city is uncommon. Indeed only the three biggest U.S. cities, New York, Los Angeles and Chicago, commonly have more than one franchise per sport in town: Yankees–Mets, Giants–Jets, Knicks–Nets, Rangers–Islanders, Cubs–White Sox, Dodgers–Angels, and Lakers–Clippers. Excluding these three exceptional cities, there are practically no cities boasting of two franchises in any particular sport and certainly not at the professional or major league level. The case was entirely different in the 1870s, a situation that tended to perpetuate the old social club designations. However, professional baseball teams in general and National League teams in particular were busy squelching intra-city professional and major league rival presences so that by the 1880s the modern host city–team nickname nomenclature came into vogue.

By 1880, the memory of the social clubs as the original source of baseball teams was waning and such names as Mutual, Eckford, Atlantic and even Knickerbocker were falling by the wayside. Baseball franchises, now professional and owned by profit-minded owners, were sport teams. The modern style of nicknames was now coming into use — e.g., Boston Red Stockings, Chicago White Stockings, Detroit Wolverines, New York Giants, New York Mets, Philadelphia Phillies, St. Louis Browns and Washington Nationals.

For a while the team's stocking colors proved to be so popular that both the National League and American Association, the two major leagues of the 1880s, decreed in April 1882 that each team be assigned its own special stocking color as follows:

National League		American Association	
Club	**Stockings**	**Club**	**Stockings**
Boston	Red	Baltimore	Canary Yellow
Buffalo	Steel Gray	Cincinnati	Scarlet Red
Chicago	White	Louisville	Blue-Gray
Cleveland	Navy blue	Philadelphia	Blue
Detroit	Old Gold	Pittsburgh	Black
Providence	Light blue	St. Louis	Brown
Troy	Green		
Worcester	Ruby red		

However, fans and reporters alike did not want to be restricted to stocking colors to identify their teams. At all levels — major, minor, collegiate, high school and amateur — teams were starting to acquire nicknames based on history, geography, regional animals, state identity and local professions. But there was one significant difference between the baseball team nicknames of the era 1880–1900 and the 20th and 21st century team monikers. That difference was that almost all of the 19th century baseball team nicknames of the professional era 1870–1900 were *unofficial* team names. The marketing concept that would be made possible by newspapers, photography, telegraph, radio and television simply did not exist because there was no technological media to support it.

To be sure, team nicknames were needed so that fans would

not be put to sleep by the constant droning references to the Bostons, Chicagos, New Yorks and Philadelphias in the newspaper. Nevertheless, no one could decide what nickname was to be the sole and official moniker of a baseball franchise. The result was that newspaper reporters were free to choose any team nickname they wanted to describe the hometown players and their exploits. Reporters from cities of opposing teams could do the same. The result was dozens and even scores of nicknames for teams, some of which did not survive more than a few weeks and others that are still used today, some 140 years later.

Every one of the team nicknames of the original 16 franchises of 1901—i.e., the American and National leagues of that season—originated as unofficial team nicknames in the 19th century: the Athletics (1860), Braves (1890), Brewers (1884), Browns (1875), Cardinals (1899), Cubs (1890), Dodgers (1884), Giants (1874), Indians (1877), Phillies (1873), Pirates (1890), Red Sox (1868), Reds (1868), Tigers (1894), White Sox (1870), Yankees (1890) and Senators (1886).

With the advent of the 20th century, nicknames for baseball teams at all levels started to become official. The obvious motive was that teams and their owners wanted a marketable name to help make money in the form of advertising revenue and ticket sales. One by one, professional baseball team nicknames became official and by the 1930s more than half of all professional minor league baseball teams had official nicknames. The trend was gradual: not all teams got their official monikers at once. Indeed, the transformation to official team nicknames took many seasons as a list of the first official team nicknames, by year, for major league teams will show:

    1901—Detroit Tigers and Philadelphia Athletics
    1905—Washington Nationals
    1908—Boston Red Sox and Chicago Cubs
    1911—Cincinnati Reds, Chicago White Sox and
            Pittsburgh Pirates
    1912—Boston Braves
    1913—New York Yankees
    1915—Cleveland Indians
    1921—New York Giants
    1922—St. Louis Cardinals
    1932—Brooklyn Dodgers
    1933—Philadelphia Phillies
    1953—St. Louis Browns
    1957—Washington Senators

In the minor leagues, the pace of official nickname creation was even slower, with only 50 percent of teams displaying official monikers just before World War II. By the postwar 1940s the number of official team nicknames for minor league teams was up to 80 percent and by 1960 it was at 100 percent. Some Class A Mexican baseball teams refused to develop nicknames in the 1970s but that was an exception and a temporary event at that.

In the 1920s the minor league farm system started. Some minor league teams adopted unique nicknames while many others used the moniker of their major league parent club.

Foreign teams in Latin America tended to use their own nicknames, although a few picked up on a major league team name, e.g., the Tokyo Giants (after the NL New York Giants). By the 1990s minor league clubs discovered a cash bonanza in marketing unique team nicknames, logos and mascots for all sorts of merchandise, which prompted them to all but abandon the semi-traditional big league team nicknames they had been using. In today's business age, all professional baseball teams have official and copyrighted nicknames—mostly unique to the one team using the moniker in baseball circles—although such names often appear for teams in other sports, for example, International League Rochester and NHL Detroit Red Wings and International League Columbus and NBA Los Angeles Clippers.

As mentioned, members of the National Association of Professional Baseball Leagues, the governing body established in 1902 to oversee the minor leagues and protect them from player raids by the major leagues, were much slower in procuring official nicknames. Many teams played into the 1920s and 1930s without an official, legal team nickname (and an accompanying logo or mascot). Generally the teams from the larger cities legalized and made official a selected nickname in the teens and 1920s—the Atlanta Crackers, Baltimore Orioles, Buffalo Bisons, Columbus Redbirds, Houston Buffaloes, Hollywood Stars, Indianapolis Indians, Kansas City Blues, Los Angeles Angels, Milwaukee Brewers, Minneapolis Millers, Montreal Royals, Newark Bears, Oakland Oaks, San Diego Padres, San Francisco Seals, Seattle Rainiers and Toronto Maple Leafs.

Teams of the 1920s and 1930s, however, in the lower class circuits—B, C and D—often garnered an unofficial name from local reporters at the start of the season as management of these franchises tended to be quite indifferent to the idea of official team nicknames and their marketing potential. Management realized the need of lighted night games and playoff tournaments to offset the financial troubles caused by the Great Depression but had no realization about the marketing advantages of an official team nickname. By the end of World War II, in 1945-46, however, even the lower class (A, B, C and D) minor league baseball teams realized how crucial it was to market their product by way of nicknames, logos and mascots in order to make enough money to avoid financial failure. Even if the nickname was the moniker of the parent major league team, such a name was essential for proper marketing of the team.

By the 1950s nearly half of all minor league teams chose their parent major league franchise's nickname. The notion of a nickname unique to a minor league team and its host city, a commonplace occurrence in the 1900 to 1940 era, did not again emerge until the 1990s when there was an explosion of new, and sometimes bizarre, nicknames for minor league baseball teams. The choice of a nickname unique to the minor league team allowed for marketing that proved to be highly successful in the sale of tickets, advertising and merchandise.

Foreign baseball teams established nicknames in much the same way as their North American counterparts. However, in foreign baseball circuits, there are two significant differences in the philosophy of team nomenclature.

First, baseball teams in Asia since the 1930s and Italy since 1999 have routinely included their corporate sponsor's (owners') name into their official name by combining it with a mascot nickname, e.g., Tokyo Yomiuri (Yomiuri Newspaper Company) Giants. In the Italian practice, a mascot may be selected but no corresponding nickname invented. Second, baseball franchise owners in Asia, since the 1930s (yes, even in anti–American Japan of 1936–1941) realized the need to market the team nickname in the native language of their country and in English, which is the leading language of worldwide marketing.

In North America, professional and even college sports teams play in stadia that routinely bear the name of a corporate sponsor. The only major league baseball teams to have included the name of a corporate sponsor (i.e., the team gets money from a sponsor for naming their team or ballpark after the company) were the Rochester Hop Bitters (medicinal elixir) of 1879 and the Brooklyn Tip Tops (Tip Top Bread) of 1914–15. In those two instances, the owner of the team superimposed his product name on the team without naming the ballpark in which the team played. This restraint does not mean, however, that the future might not bring forth the likes of the IBM Yankees, McDonald's Cubs or the MGM Dodgers.

Nickname Trends

Professional baseball team nicknames were subject to certain trends and fads that influenced the choice of a moniker. Going in chronological progression, we can start in the 19th century and notice the trends or circumstances that influenced baseball team nicknames as follows:

(1) In the 19th century many cities in the United States were founded. If a town grew fast and constructed beautiful buildings, it was commonly called either the "Gem City" or the "Queen City." In the 19th century, 15 U.S. cities were known as the "Queen City." They were Allentown (Pennsylvania), Bangor (Maine), Buffalo (New York), Charlotte (North Carolina), Cincinnati (Ohio), Clarksville (Tennessee), Cumberland (Maryland), Denver (Colorado), Helena (Montana), Manchester (New Hampshire), Plainfield (New Jersey), Springfield (Missouri), Staunton (Virginia), Virginia (Minnesota) and Seattle (Washington).

(2) In the 19th century, "Infants" meant a young team that was struggling. The terms "Babies" or "Babes" meant an expansion team. "Kids" meant a young team without regard to its performance or its number of years as a member of a league. The tag "Ponies," first used in 1883, also meant a new or expansion team but also indicated it was a "farm" club under the auspices of some other higher-ranked team, or even a league. "Colts" began in 1884, probably a spin-off from "ponies," meaning a "farm team," but quickly changed to referring to a team of young players in general, much like

"kids." The juvenile nature of these monikers was no accident since new teams or farm teams usually had a large number of young players.

(3) Starting in the 1880s, baseball teams playing in cities that enjoyed natural resources such as coal, cotton, gold, iron, lumber, natural gas, oil, silver, sugar, steel, tobacco etc., were sometimes called "Barons" or "Millionaires." These names referred to the tycoons who controlled these lucrative industries. Almost exclusively, it was the owner who became a millionaire, while the workers, under his sway, struggled.

(4) In the era 1875 to 1920, teams that were big winners, usually en route to a pennant, were praised as "Giants." Since the New York Giants won NL pennants in 1888, 1889, 1904, 1905, 1911, 1912, 1913, a Temple Cup in 1894 and the World Series in 1888, 1889 and 1905, the moniker was doubly appropriate.

(5) In the 19th century a "kicker" was a baseball player who argued vehemently with an umpire over a call. Back then as now, the player, who was forbidden to touch the umpire, would kick dirt on the ump's shoes and trousers. Some notorious "kickers" were Cap Anson, John McGraw and Jim "Orator" O'Rourke. Similar terms included "Anarchists" and "Jingoes."

(6) In the era 1885 to 1955, more than thirty teams playing in a state capital, and unaffiliated with any Washington, D.C., Senator team in the big leagues, were known as "Senators." Another ten were named "Capitals."

(7) In the era 1885 to 1920, newspaper reporters sometimes assigned nicknames to teams based on catastrophic events; for example, Flood-Sufferers, Hungarian Rioters, Cyclones, Fever Germs and Insurgents.

(8) Since 1885, minor league teams geographically close to big league city teams started forming loose affiliations that involved getting uniforms and equipment from the "parent club" and occasionally selling a star player's contract to the nearby team. These minor league teams often would adopt the big league team's nickname—Cubs, Giants, Red Sox, White Sox, etc.

(9) The tag "Giants" was also popular for black teams in this era. Black teams in the Northeast and Midwest tended to go with adjective-noun monikers like American Giants, Union Giants, Royal Giants, etc. Meanwhile, black teams in the South and the West simply used "Giants" with a city name (Birmingham Giants, Cleveland Giants, and St. Louis Giants). The back-to-back (1888 and 1889) world champion New York Giants were the most glamorous and successful team at the start of the 1890s. Several teams, both white and black, emulated the New Yorkers by choosing the "Giants" moniker.

(10) As mentioned earlier, the name "Ponies" was a 19th century tag for a farm team. Usually these farm teams had young players, making the term "ponies" appropriate. By the 20th century the moniker changed its meaning, now referring to a young team without reference to its classification. This nickname gave rise to the youth baseball organization known as "Pony League," which was established in 1950.

(11) In the 19th century baseball players were perceived by fans and the press to be much like cowboys and Indians, i.e., rough, rowdy, burly fellows or even primitive savages who were physically violent, much like the denizens of the "Wild West." That perception led to such nicknames as Cowboys, Indians, Warriors, Braves, Broncos, and Rustlers. In the second half of the 19th century, the American public back East was fascinated by the exploits, antics and horrors of the wild, wild West.

(12) Young baseball players in the 19th century were known as the Chicks, Colts, Cubs, Foundlings, Infants, Kids, Nestlings, Youngsters and other such tags. But in 1917, with young American soldiers known as "recruits" shipped by the thousands on ocean liners from the sea ports of the Atlantic Coast to the battlefields of Europe, the nickname for both soldiers and athletes of "rookies" appeared. First coined in 1892 (and thought to be an alteration of "recruits") but little used in sports, the name became so popular that it swept away the aforementioned monikers and tags that had been used for young athletes.

(13) In the era 1890 to 1910, some teams received bird nicknames based on their stocking color, e.g., Blackbirds, Bluebirds, Blue Jays, Cardinals, Crows, Doves, Ravens and Redbirds.

(14) Also in the era 1890 to 1910, teams that played poorly, usually last-place teams, were often branded as Forlorns, Innocents, Misfits and Tramps. When their losing ways forced them onto the road as their fans deserted them, they became known as the Barnstormers, Orphans, Tramps and Wanderers.

(15) Further in that 1890–1910 era, college football and baseball teams at Princeton and Missouri as well as Southern colleges started wearing striped stockings. When Detroit of the Western League began sporting striped hose in 1895, other professional baseball teams picked up on it. The identification between striped hose and the "Tigers" nickname ended abruptly when, in the period 1905–1908, baseball teams universally adopted stirrup stockings, most of which bore multicolor stripes.

(16) Starting around 1900, a team that was in pennant contention was called Boosters because their excited fans would form a "booster club" to cheer the players on to the flag. Teams in the period from 1900 to 1920 that did well in the standings often stimulated their fans to form a "booster club," from which the nickname arose. By the 1920s the fad became passé as radio announcers took over the role of cheering for the home team. The name "booster club" itself was dropped and replaced by "fan club."

(17) In the 1900–1920 era the occasional team would be named "Hustlers" after a manager who encouraged his players "to hustle on the field." It was not until the 1970s that the name — often associated with gambling — became "politically incorrect." Indeed, in this early era, the tag was quite complimentary.

(18) The use of the self-congratulatory term "Champions" and "Champs" was a fad between 1900 and 1920 but became passé as people thought it to be arrogant in an increasingly competitive sport. Occasionally teams that won a pennant in this era were christened as "Champions" at the start of the following season. Although the name might persist for the next season, if the team failed to repeat, the moniker was quietly dropped toward the end of the year.

(19) In the 1920s and especially during the Great Depression, black teams sometimes received donated uniforms from a cross-town white team and simply adopted the letters of the team nickname on the jersey. Thus, these black teams arrived at such monikers as Black Yankees, Brown Dodgers, Black Barons, Black Crackers and Black Senators.

(20) The Branch Rickey farm system began to catch on in the 1930s. Starting around 1925, several hundred minor league teams simply adopted the moniker of their major league parent club. Even today, we have such minor league baseball clubs as the Gwinnett Braves, San Jose Giants, Pawtucket Red Sox, Binghamton Mets, Reading Phillies and Scranton–Wilkes-Barre Yankees.

(21) In the 1900 to 1950 era, there were also minor league "parent clubs." The major league parent club operated a higher classification team (Class AA), which in turn sent and received players from a lower classification (A, B, C or D) team, which assumed the nickname, not of the major league parent team but of the intermediate farm club. This link multiplied the use of such nicknames as Angels, Buffaloes, Orioles, Sports and Stars. Sometimes the lower classification club received donated, or bought on discount, uniforms from the intermediate farm team and then assumed the nickname on the jerseys. This practice was common during the Depression years.

(22) The tag "Trojans" was a popular sports nickname in the 1920 to 1960 era because of the success of the USC Trojans college football team and the introduction of the Trojan Tractor in 1950. By 1949, the college football USC Trojans had won their eighth Rose Bowl. The name comes from antiquity as the Trojans of ancient Troy labored diligently to fight off the invading Greeks during the tenth century B.C. Trojan War. Hard working athletes were often known as "Trojans."

HOW TO READ THE ENTRIES

Baseball Team Names endeavors to list every professional baseball team from every professional baseball league worldwide, and, for all professional teams that played an independent schedule in lieu of league membership worldwide, from 1869 to date.

The teams are listed in alphabetical order by city, with information on the country, league, and league classification provided within the entry.

Under the city heading, nicknames are listed in chronological order, with the team first using the nickname in that locale listed first. For cities with two or more teams, the teams are then listed chronologically by year although always in the same entry by nickname.

Nicknames in foreign languages have their English translation along with the name in the team's country's native language. (Non–Latin alphabets are transliterated.)

A brief history of the nickname is provided, and generally includes its origin and any additional information that explains its adoption. The details in every case were carefully researched and recorded. It was a long, arduous job. Professional baseball has more team nicknames, both official and unofficial, than professional football, basketball (men's and women's), ice hockey, soccer (men's and women's), team tennis, box lacrosse, outdoor lacrosse, volleyball, rugby league football, rugby association football and team boxing *combined.*

A goal of this book is to provide the reader with a comprehensive reference book that is also fun to read. The information following will explain how to read a nickname entry for any baseball team. Here is an example of a team entry in the style used throughout the main text of the book, followed by an explanation of each element of the entry:

Boston, Massachusetts

628 Red Stockings 1871–75 *National Assn. (M)*; 1876–1906, April 1908 *National (M)*; *Players (M)* 1890; *American Assn. (M)* 1891; *New England (ind.)* 1893. Harry and George Wright broke up the 1870 Cincinnati Red Stockings and formed a team in Boston, signing most of the Cincinnati players and dressing them in the same red stockings. At a meeting with Boston team owner Ivers Whitney Adams on January 20, 1871, Harry Wright informed the new owner, "We'll dress the players in white flannel uniforms with red stockings to the knee." Although its use for the Boston Nationals, who had left the NA for the NL in 1876, declined steadily in the 1880s, nonetheless it persisted through the 1906 season and only ended for the Nationals when the Boston Americans declared Red Sox to be their official team nickname in 1908. These other Boston teams all dressed their players in red hose. Although the "sox" spelling appeared as early as 1875, the "stockings spelling" persisted in newspapers as late as 1920.

Nicknames are categorized by the city, in this case, **Boston,** in the state of **Massachusetts,** hence the title **Boston, Massachusetts.** The first team listed in the city category is shown with a heading describing each descriptive entry.

The nickname in bold is preceded by a serial number (**628**). This number does not refer to a single team or nickname but rather to the-nickname-and-a-team in unison. The unique entry here is the **Boston Red Stockings.** Although there are other entries, such as **Boston Red Sox** and **Boston Beaneaters,** they are not the **Boston Red Stockings.**

This entry, standing by itself, is unique, and has four baseball teams that went exclusively by this city-plus-nickname combination. For that reason, this entry stands apart from such entries as **St. Louis Red Stockings** or **Cincinnati Red Stockings.**

Each combination of city and nickname receives a unique serial number. All subsequent teams with the same name under that city are shorn of the nickname, requiring the reader to realize that the city heading (Boston) and team name (Red Stockings) also apply to all subsequent teams listed in the entry.

The reader can readily understand that the second team named Boston Red Stockings played in the National League, the name of which is printed in italics, during the dates 1876–1906 and April 1908. All subsequent teams appearing in the city category will follow the same guidelines.

A league designated by (M) means that this circuit was a major league. The designation "league" is understood and, therefore, omitted. If the circuit identified itself as an "Association," the contraction *Assn.* appears after the circuit's initial name, e.g., *American Assn. (M), Union Assn. (M), American Assn. (AAA),* etc.

After all the Boston teams bearing the nickname of **Red Stockings** have been listed in chronological order, there will appear the origin of the nickname, which is a brief history of how the nickname originated and evolved. This history is a description of the forces that shaped the selection and use of a team nickname. Oftentimes, these historical forces have nothing to do with sports or baseball. There are numerous teams whose nickname is derived from one, two or even three or more historical sources, all of which are included.

One of the charms of baseball team nicknames is the variability of available data about their origin. One nickname will have such a succinct origin that an accompanying history will not even be required, as the following example shows (the "x" after 1936 indicates the team disbanded and the nickname ended that year):

Abbeville, Alabama

1 Red Sox 1936x *Alabama-Florida (D)*. Team disbanded August 10. Players wore red stirrups. Team was not a farm club of the Boston Red Sox.

With regard to the **Abbeville Red Sox**, there is nothing else to say but to note that the players wore red stirrups. This explanation is particularly true for minor league teams that adopted the monikers of their big league parent clubs. The only other information required is a disclaimer that the team was not a farm club of the American League Boston Red Sox. Another nickname, quite to the other extreme, will incorporate a robust amount of information simply because multiple historical events have a bearing on how this nickname arose, as this example shows:

McAlester, Oklahoma

3698 Rockets 1947–56 *Sooner State (D)*. With field manager Bill Nobroak (pronounced *No-brock)* at the helm, local newspapers called the players "Nobroak's Rockets." The team quickly made the nickname official. In 1948, under new manager Vern Hoscheit, the team "rocketed" to first place and a playoff berth. In 1950-51-52-53 the team "rocketed" to four straight pennants. During World War II in 1943, the U.S. Army built an ammunition depot outside the city, including an arsenal of rockets and rocket launchers. After the war, captured V-2 rockets were maintained here.

Sometimes following the history of a team nickname there will be another separate entry of what have been historically called "alternate team nicknames"—one or more team nicknames that served as either a less popular moniker or as an unofficial alternate tag for a baseball franchise. Most minor league teams will not have any alternate team nicknames. However, every major league baseball team has quite a few "alternate team nicknames." Major league baseball, even in the 19th century, vigorously grabbed the attention of fans, providing an incentive for newspaper reporters and others to dream up numerous team monikers as the following example, using the Chicago National League baseball club, demonstrates:

1117 Colts 1887–1907 *National (M)*. The name was first used in 1887 and not 1890, as some baseball historians have reported. After losing the 1886 World Series to the American Association St. Louis Browns, Chicago general manger Al Spalding dumped veteran players King Kelly, George Gore, Jim McCormick and others, who were getting drunk, rowdy and arrested between regular season games in 1887. He replaced these veterans with young players, which Chicago newspapers started to call "Colts." By 1890 Player League raids forced manager Cap Anson to continue to sign younger players, thereby perpetuating the Colt nickname through the 1906 season. In November 1895, Anson reinforced the name by appearing as an actor in a New York theatrical play about the Wild West known as *A Runaway Colt*. Manager Frank Selee (1902–05) preferred Colts over Cubs but his successor, Frank Chance, openly demanded that newspaper reporters refer to his players as "Cubs."

Foreign baseball teams, i.e., all professional franchises that have operated teams outside the territory of the United States and Canada, will have entries identical in format to the U.S. and Canadian teams as follows:

Caracas, Distrito Federal, Vargas, Venezuela

959 Leones 1952–74/75 *Liga Venezolana (W)*; 1976/77 to date *Liga Venezolana (W)*. By 1952 the competition between Cerveceria Caracas and the other teams in the Venezuelan circuit was so intense that opposing fans were refusing to buy beer from the Caracas brewery that owned the club. In desperation the team name was changed to the Caracas Lions with the hope that people would forget the club's connection to the brewer. The ruse worked and there remained a subtle link between the Caracas club and the owner since a lion appeared as a symbol on the brewer's label. "Los Leones" means "lions."

Canadian teams are listed with U.S.–based teams because most have participated in "mixed" leagues wherein each circuit of this type has fielded both U.S. and Canadian teams playing under the same league banner.

Foreign teams whose nickname is written in a foreign language — Spanish, Italian, Mandarin Chinese, Cantonese Chinese, Korean, Dutch or Japanese — will have the corresponding English name presented at the end of the nickname origin history, as follows:

Caracas, Distrito Federal, Vargas, Venezuela

965 Petroleros 1969x *Global (ind.)* The league and all its teams disbanded about a month into the season. Caracas is the major oil refining, storage and shipping center for Venezuela's vast reserves of oil and natural gas. "Los petroleros" means "oilers" in English.

Translations for team nicknames in languages using the Latin alphabet are readily understood. For Asian languages, no attempt is made to display the nickname in pictographic symbols. The Asian language name is spelled out in Latin characters, with its English translation given. An example of this style is as follows:

Tokyo, Tokyo Prefecture, Japan

6417 Kyojin 1936–44 *Japanese Professional (ind.)*. "Kyojin" is the Latin-alphabet Japanese word for "giants."

Asian and Italian teams have had a tendency to include their sponsor's name in their official team titles. These designations are distinct from a team nickname, which usually is accompanied by a mascot and mascot logo. There is a schism between Asian professional baseball teams, which almost always use a nickname, a logo and a mascot, and European professional baseball teams, which seldom use them. Since 1999 when European professional baseball leagues first appeared most professional baseball teams in Italy and the Netherlands have had no nickname and have used their corporate sponsor as their official title. Three examples are presented as follows:

Almere, Netherlands (also spelled Alkmaar)

121 Media Monks Magpies 2007–09; '90 Magpies 2010. *Honkball Hoofdklasse (ind.)*. Team has been owned since 2007 by RCH, i.e. the Racing Club Heemstede Football (soccer) Club, and by Media

Monks Communications. The team logo, derived from the players' black-trim uniforms, is a magpie — a type of crow. The team's name was "Media Monks Magpies." The '90 designation referred to the franchise's founding year of 1990. BSC Corporation held part-ownership in 2006. Not all professional teams in Holland have an official mascot-style team name (i.e., Eagles, Lions, Pirates). Since 1990, when the Dutch Major League turned all-professional, the following Dutch baseball teams have borne a mascot-style name: Amsterdam Expos (1999–2002), Amsterdam Pirates (2003–12), Almere Magpies (2007 only), Heemstede RCH Pinguins (1999–2000), Heemstede RCH Media Monks (2007 only), Hoofdorp KMN Pioniers (1999–2007), Oosterehout Twins (1999, 2003–04). All other Dutch Major League baseball franchises since 1999 have instead been known only by the sponsoring company name.

Ravenna, Italy

5386 DeAngelis-Godo 2006–09 *Italian A1 (ind.)*. Team was owned by DeAngelis-Godo Hotels.

5387 DeAngelis Northeast Knights 2010 *Italian A1 (ind.)*. Ravenna is located in NE Italy. Medieval knights, known as the Condottiere, fought as mercenaries throughout Italy.

5388 Russi DeAngelis Northeast Knights 2011 to date *Italian A1 (ind.)*. Russi Company bought a part-interest in the team.

Haarlem, North Holland, Netherlands (also called Holland)

Corendon Kinheim 1999 to date *Hoofdklasse (ind.)*. The Holland Baseball League became fully professional in 1999. Corendon Airlines own the team, which was originally started by the DPA Kinheim Soccer Club. Team goes by the name of Corendon Kinheim.

Three of the five non–U.S. teams above had no nickname; instead, they were identified by their corporate sponsor name. The capsular summary in these cases lacks a "history" because there is no real origin of the particular team's identity. The Asian baseball teams, in the interest of saving newspaper and Internet space, almost always omit the city name of the franchise. Thus, we have teams like the Yomiuri Giants, who are really the Tokyo Yomiuri Giants. An Asian team entry showing the format of corporate sponsor/mascot-logo-nickname franchises is as follows:

Taipei, Taipei Province, Taiwan

6275 Elephants 1990 to date *Chinese Professional (ind.)* League's official name is the Chinese Professional Baseball League. Brother Hotels, the team's owner, chose in English the nickname of "Elephants." Elephants inhabit Asia and are a historic symbol. The team's title is "Brother Hotels Elephants."

This Taiwanese baseball team has the official name of "Brother Elephants," but is located and identified in this book by its city of residence, Taipei, Taiwan. These teams rarely are identified by the lengthy tag of "Taipei Brother Elephants," with the common identification being "Brother Elephants." A few European professional baseball teams also adopted this nam-

ing model. Such an elimination of the city name is an ironic return to the old style of baseball team nomenclature of the 19th century United States.

Since 1870 there have been several hundred professional baseball teams that never had a nickname. Almost all of these were minor league teams in cities that did not enjoy the 19th century media resources of the larger major league cities. In the 19th century the media consisted of newspapers, the telegraph, the telephone, the mail and wall posters, and many smaller cities and towns were bereft of even these means of communication. Moreover, management of many minor league teams had no incentive to market a team nickname. A significant number of such teams that might have received a nickname didn't because the team disbanded after a short period of existence.

Using the example of Anderson, Indiana (whose first five professional teams were nameless), the listing for nickname-less teams has a format as follows:

Anderson, Indiana

187 Anderson Base Ball Club 1890x *Indiana State (ind.)*. Team disbanded in mid-season; 1895x *Western Interstate (ind.)* Team disbanded in mid-season; 1899x *Indiana-Illinois (ind.)* Team disbanded in mid-season; 1903m *Central (B)* Team moved to Grand Rapids (MI) May 30; 1906x *Interstate Assn. (C)* Circuit and team disbanded July 8. These teams had no nickname.

A special nickname style originated with the 1873 National Association Philadelphia Phillies. Dubbed by the author as the "Phillies-style moniker," it refers to a nickname construct based on the spelling of the host city name. Thus, we have such revealing examples as Beeville Bees, Binghamton Bingos and Corinth Corinthians. Some of the nicknames are meaningless abstractions — Minneapolis Minnies — while others refer to real things, such as the Beeville Bees and Troy Trojans. Generic groups that have a basis in reality are also created, e.g., Drummers (Drumwright, Oklahoma). Other such creations are inappropriate personifications: Green Bay Bays and San Francisco Friscos.

To qualify as a "Phillies-style moniker" the nickname spelling must include a significant number of letters from the city name. For example, the Cairo Egyptians and Philadelphia Quakers are not Phillies-style monikers even though the nickname is intimately associated with the host city and its history and identity. The Henderson Hens is, however, a Phillies-style moniker even though the city of Henderson is not unique among cities in having poultry farms. The Phillies-style monikers are not related to nickname constructs created by host city name pluralizations (like, the Bostons, Chicagos and Detroits). City name pluralization is a technique that was applicable to any and all city names but its actual use ended about 1920.

A surprisingly large number of nicknames in the era 1880 to 1940 were constructed from the name of the manager. These "manager nicknames" include eight different types: (1) A real thing or creature based on the manager's last name, e.g., Pete

Fox's Foxes and Bob Black's Blackbirds. (2) A real thing or creature based on the manager's nickname, e.g., James "Orator" O'Rourke's Orators and A.L. "Snapper" Kennedy's Snappers. (3) A real thing or creature based on the manager's first name, e.g., Jay Andrew's Jays. (4) The addition of "men" as a possessive to the manager's last name, e.g., Mack's Men (Connie Mack), McGraw's Men (John McGraw) and Selee's Men (Frank Selee). (Such possessive forms were often adulterated to Mackmen, McGraw Men and Selee Men.) (5) The addition of the suffix "-ites" to create an individual identity not recognized by English-language dictionaries, e.g., Loftusites (Tom Loftus) and Collinsites (Jimmy Collins). (6) A portion of the manager's surname that creates a real thing or creature, e.g., Ward Buckminster's Bucks and Al Buckenberger's Buckeyes. (7) A mascot-like nickname that is alliterative or consonant with some letters in the manager's surname: Pat Vicks Truckers and Mike "King" Kelly's Killers. (8) A mascot-like nickname based on the first letter of the manager's surname, e.g., Ted Sullivan's Steers, Pat Powers' Pets, and Billy Hamilton's Hustlers.

A widespread style that appears throughout the history of baseball team nicknames is alliteration. There are four types of alliteration as follows: (1) Phillies-style monikers; (2) Nonsensical alliterations like Attleboro Boros, Minnesota Minnies, Petersboro Petes, Winnipeg Peggers; (3) logical alliterations, e.g., Los Angeles Angels, Philadelphia Phillies, Pittsburgh Burghers, and Troy Trojans; (4) manager alliterations, e.g., James Fox's Foxes and Connie Mack's Mack Men.

None of the entries in this book specifically refer to alliteration as the etiology of a nickname but the sharp-eyed reader can easily identify them. Indeed, some nicknames were chosen by newspaper reporters, team officials or fans voting in a name-the-team contest for no apparent reason other than alliteration. Actually, most alliterative nicknames have some other link that gave rise to the tag. For example, the Philadelphia "Phillies" is obviously alliterative but an inhabitant of Philadelphia is also known as a "Phillie." Such nicknames utilize alliteration as an additional impetus for the selection of a particular nickname: the nickname "Phillies" won out over "Quakers" as the official team nickname of the Philadelphia National League Baseball Club.

Since 1950 there has been a trend to bestow geographical names on baseball teams at all levels of play. An example of the so-called "regional" team name is as follows:

Aberdeen, Washington

12 Gray's Harbor Grays 1908-09 *Northwest (B)*. The seaport of Gray's Harbor lies adjacent to the city of Aberdeen. The players also wore gray uniforms and hose.

13 Gray's Harbor Ports 1976 *Northwest (A)*. The regional name refers to the seaport of Gray's Harbor.

14 Gray's Harbor Loggers 1977-78, 1980 *Northwest (A)*. Situated on a peninsula along Gray's Harbor, Aberdeen is known as "Plank Island" because of the factories that manufacture wooden planks from the lumber transported there.

15 Gray's Harbor Mets 1979 *Northwest (A)*. Team was a farm club of the New York Mets.

16 Gray's Harbor Gulls 1995–98m *Western (ind.)*. Team went by the regional name of "Gray's Harbor Gulls." Seagulls are indigenous to the entire Pacific Northwest coastline.

Teams with regional names almost always have a nickname. The regional name replaces not a nickname but rather a *city* name. For example, the state name of Minnesota Twins spares newspapers the agony of having to refer to the team as the Minneapolis–St. Paul Twins.

For the sake of comprehensive presentation this book has three appendices: (1) Barnstorming Teams (those without a home city and who play year round); (2) a list year-by-year of major league team nicknames for the 19th century, 1871–1900; and (3) a similar list for the 20th and 21st centuries, 1901–2012.

In the 19th century there were no official major league baseball team nicknames, allowing reporters and fans to go from nickname to nickname on the basis of team performance, related events in the sports world or non-sports events in the city, county, state, national region, country or world at large. Annual entries of all these "fan-reporter nicknames" for each team are presented in the order of the team standings of a league and not in alphabetical order by city name. A nickname displayed in italics was the most popular moniker in use in any particular season. The 1871 major league season is presented as an example:

1871 National Association Team Nicknames

Philadelphia	Athletic, *Athletics*, Blues, Blue Legs
Chicago	White Legs, Whites, *White Stockings*
Boston	Bostonians, Down-Easters, Reds, Redlegs, *Red Stockings*
Washington	Blues, Blue Legs, Blue Stockings, *Olympics*
Troy	Green Legs, Green Stockings, Haymakers, Trojans, Unions
New York	Green Legs, Green Stockings, Mutes, Mutual, *Mutuals*, Unruly Bad Boys of Baseball (Neil McDonald)
Cleveland	Blues, Blue Legs, Blue Stockings, Forest City, *Forest Citys*
Fort Wayne	Kekinoga, *Kekiongas*
Rockford	Forest City, *Forest Citys*, Green Legs, Green Stockings
Brooklyn	Eckford, *Eckfords*, Orange Legs, Yellow Legs

A 19th century team nickname, coined by an individual, bears that person's name in parentheses immediately following the coined moniker. More information on the "coiner" of the nickname can be found in the main text of the book.

Appendices II and III present only major league team nicknames; a presentation of all the minor league teams' nicknames, year-by-year, would have made for lists so long that they could not be contained in this book.

When a team is named after a field manager, his designation (Mgr.) and his first name appear together in parentheses followed by his last name, in possessive form, followed by the often alliterative nickname. In the early part of the 20th century, official team nicknames had not yet appeared so the most popular nickname in a particular season is presented in italics as in these examples:

1901 National League Team Nicknames

Pittsburgh	Buccaneers (Bucs), (Mgr. Fred) Clarke's Corsairs, *Pirates*, Premiers
Philadelphia	Discards, Nationals, *Phillies*, Quakers, Red Quakers
Brooklyn	Bridegrooms (Grooms), Brooks, Dodgers, So-Called Superbas, (Mgr. Ned) St. Louis *Cardinals*, Maroons, Masqueradors, Nationals, Scarlets, (Mgr. Patsy) Tebeau's Tebeauites, Hanlon's Superbas, Suburbas, Trolley Dodgers
Boston	*Beaneaters* (Beanies), (Mgr. Al) Buckeberger's Galaxy, Nationals, Red Stockings, Redville
Chicago	Colts, *Cubs*, Nationals, Remnant, (Mgr. Frank Selee) Seelites, West-siders, Youngsters
New York	*Giants*, Jints, Nationals
Cincinnati	Lobsters, Queen Citys, *Reds*, Red Legs, Red Stockings, Red Towners, Rhinelanders

1901 American League Team Nicknames

Chicago	Americans, Champions, Comiskeyites, (Mgr. Cal Griffith) Griffith's Go-Go-Sox (David Nemec & Scott Flatow), Griffith Men, Invaders, Lake-shores, Original Go-Go-Sox (Nemec & Flatow), Pennant-Grabbers, Pale Hose, (Mgr. Clark) Griffith's Satellites, White Sox (Sox), *White Stockings*
Boston	Americanos, Americans, (Mgr. Jimmy) Collins' Bostons, Collins' Crew, Invaders, New Englanders, Pilgrims (informal newspaper), Plymouth Rocks (informal newspaper), Puritans (informal newspaper), Somerites, Somersets
Detroit	Bengals, Man-eaters, Michiganders, Rowdies, *Tigers*, Wolverines
Philadelphia	Americans, Athletics (A's), Blue Quakers, Mackites, Mack Men
Baltimore	Birdies, Birdlings, Canaries, (Mgr. John) McGraw's Flock, *Orioles*, McGraw's Roughnecks (Fred Lieb), Roughneck Orioles (Lieb), Yellow Legs
Washington	Capital Citys, Capitals, Griffs, Nationals, *Senators* Capitals, Capitols, Solon
Cleveland	*Blues*, Bluebirds, Blue Jays, Bronchos, Buckeyes, Forest Citys, (Mgr. Jimmy) Infants, McAleer Men, Spiders
Milwaukee	*Brewers*, Beermakers

As the 20th century progressed, official team nicknames started appearing. By the 1930s all major league teams had official nicknames, as the financial rewards of marketing team nicknames, mascots and logos could no longer be ignored by franchise owners. The 1950 season, for example, shows the official names in **BOLD, CAPITAL** letters as follows:

1950 National League Team Nicknames

Philadelphia	Fightin' Phillies, (Mgr. Bill) Carpenter's Kids, **PHILLIES** (Phils), Quakers, Whiz Kids
Brooklyn	Blue Wrecking Crew, Boys of Summer (Roger Kahn), Brooks, Bums, Dem Bums, **DODGERS**, Methodical Maulers, Our Bums

New York	**GIANTS**, Jints
Boston	**BRAVES**
St. Louis	**CARDINALS** (Cards), Redbirds
Cincinnati	Red Legs, **REDS**, Rhinelanders
Chicago	Bruins, **CUBS**, Northsiders, Wrigleys
Pittsburgh	Buccaneers (Bucs), Fifty-Fifty Team, **PIRATES**, (General manager Branch Rickey) Rickey-Dinks

1950 American League Team Nicknames

New York	Bronx Bombers (Bombers), Bronx Juggernaut (h), Damn Yankees (Gilbert & Wallop), Lordly Bombers (h), Men of Autumn (Forker), Magnificent Yankees (Meany), Rampaging Yankees (h), **YANKEES** (Yanks)
Detroit	Bengals, **TIGERS**
Boston	Beantowners, BoSox, Crimson Hose, **RED SOX** (Sox)
Cleveland	**INDIANS**, The Tribe, Wahoos. Chief Wahoo's Tribe (Altherr & Hall)
Washington	Americans, Griffs, **NATIONALS** (Nats), *Senators*, Solons
Chicago	ChiSox, Comiskeys, Pale Hose, Southsiders, **WHITE SOX** (Sox)
St. Louis	Brownies, **BROWNS**
Detroit	Bengals, **TIGERS**
Philadelphia	**ATHLETICS** (A's), (Mgr. Connie Mack) Mack Men, White Elephants

In both Appendices II and III an occasional team nickname will carry an (h) designation, which refers to a historical nickname. Examples above include "Bronx Juggernaut" and "Lordly Bombers." The historical nickname has no specific point of origin or an individual directly responsible for the name. Instead, the moniker seems to have evolved into an appearance in the public consciousness over a period of several months or years. The historical nickname did occur quite a bit in the 19th century but in the 20th century as well. A 19th century example for the reader's scrutiny is as follows:

1897 National League Team Nicknames

Louisville	(Mgr. Jim Barnie's) Boobies, Bourbonville, *Colonels*, Falls Citys, Kings of Losers (h), Loseville, Night Riders, Wanderers

Unofficial nicknames of the 19th and 20th centuries that bear no descriptive designation were monikers dreamed up by fans or newspaper reporters during their team's history. Such designations are different from historical nicknames because they have a specific chronological point of origin. An example would be the Bronx Bombers, which appeared in 1938, whereas Bronx Juggernaut has only a vague placement in the 1950s.

Locating the exact moment when an historical nickname first appeared would seem to be impossible. Yet some *are* possible. For example, the author discovered an Internet entry about the Boston Beaneaters moniker first appearing in print in an April 1880 edition of *Chicago Inter-Ocean* newspaper. This specific use at a specific time spared Beaneaters from being branded by the vague designation of historical (h). In time the name gained popularity, as historical monikers are wont to do, in Boston and around the baseball world to get away from confusion with the Cincinnati Reds.

The main text and Appendix III describe league classifications starting in 1902 when the National Association of Professional Baseball Leagues, the umbrella organization of professional minor league baseball appeared. Renamed Minor League Baseball in 1999, the NAPBL classified its various professional circuits by categories, based on playing talent, as follows: AA, A1, A, B, C, D and E in the 1902–1962 era and then AAA, AA, A, and R (for Rookie) starting in 1963.

League classifications are shown as one of these letters (A, B, C, D, E) or letter multiples (AAA or AA) in parentheses immediately following the league's name. When a league had more than one classification, i.e., moved up or down in classification during its historical run, then the classifications are displayed inside parentheses followed by the years each classification remained in effect. Independent leagues—circuits that had no teams serving as farm clubs for major league baseball teams—bear the designation (ind.).

Major Negro Leagues, all of which appeared and competed in the era 1920–48, are designated not as "Negro" or "Independent" but with an (M), which means they were major leagues, just as all "white" major leagues in the era 1920–48 are also designated with (M).

Indeed, no distinction is made in this book between "white" major leagues and "Negro" major leagues.

Negro leagues that were not major in the 1920–1948 era or that played before 1920 or after 1948 are designated as (ind.). However, unlike the white leagues, which display the categories of M, AAA, AA, A, B, C, D and E, the Negro leagues are designated only as (M) if major and (ind.) if non-major.

All foreign baseball leagues are designated as independent (ind.), except for several professional circuits in Mexico, starting in 1955, which were affiliated with Organized Baseball (the popular designation for the major leagues and their minor league affiliates, 1902 to date).

Foreign professional baseball leagues, other than the Liga Mexicana (Mexican League), the Dominican Summer League and the Venezuelan Summer League, were never members of the minor leagues, even if they had some limited cooperation with Organized Baseball with regard to player contracts.

Winter leagues, whose regular season began roughly in November and terminated in February, are designated with (W). Of all the leagues presented in this book, two are non-professional, but deserve inclusion because their quality of play and level of talent correspond to professional baseball. These two circuits are the Chinese Baseball League of the People's Republic of China (2000 to date) and the Cuban National Series (1961-62 to date). Since 1945-46 athletic teams and players from communist countries have received state subsidies, which spared these players from the need to work at a job, allowing them to devote the same amount of time to training, practice and competition as their professional, salaried counterparts in capitalist countries. These two circuits, therefore, receive the designation of (S), which represents "Subsidized."

Several leagues of the National Association of Professional Baseball Leagues used acronyms (i.e. a name comprised of the first letters of the words in an official title) for league names that were too long for newspapers and guides to easily accommodate. They are as follows: Kansas–Oklahoma–Missouri League (K.O.M.), Kentucky–Illinois–Tennessee League (KITTY), Mississippi–Ohio Valley (M.O.V.), Oklahoma–Arkansas–Kansas League (O.A.K.) and the Pennsylvania–Ohio–New York League (P.O.N.Y.). The Texas–Oklahoma–Missouri (T.O.M.) was an independent Negro league of the 1930s.

Most Negro league teams that competed before 1920 were not members of any league. They were barnstormers who played an independent schedule. As such, this book does not designate them with (ind.) but rather with the designation "Independent Negro team." An example is shown as follows:

Adrian, Michigan

33 Page Fence Giants 1894–98 *Independent Negro team.* Team was sponsored by the Page Fence Company, a manufacturer of chain-link fences. Most of the players worked for this company during the offseason.

The designation of "Independent" is also used for white professional baseball teams that competed in 1870 — the season one year prior to the establishment of baseball's first professional circuit, the National Association. However, starting in 1871 there was a migration of most white professional baseball teams to league membership. Indeed, the last white independent professional baseball teams were the 1880 New York Mets and 1880 Brooklyn Unions. For that reason there was only a handful of league-independent white teams in the years 1871–1880 and almost none thereafter.

Minor league professional baseball teams of the era 1877–1901 are devoid of league classifications for the simple reason that in the 19th century there weren't any. (An attempt to classify minor leagues by players' wages in 1894 was ignored by newspapers.) A National Agreement in 1883 allowed the National League and the American Association to exert strong influence over about half of the professional minor leagues of the 1880s even as another half of all such leagues did not subscribe to the agreement.

In the 1890s, the National League (now baseball's lone king-pin following its merger with the American Association after the 1891 season) maintained its influence over about two-thirds of the minor leagues of the 1890s. Another one-third of the minor leagues were autonomous.

No matter what their status—for instance, National Agreement registrants or non-signatories of this 1883 treaty — the historically available individual teams of these leagues are nevertheless listed in this book but without any parenthetical league classifications.

Minor league teams, starting in 1902 when the NAPBBL was formed and drew up letter classifications for member circuits, have their letter classifications, but the minor leagues of the era 1877–1901 lack it. Starting in 1902 the number of independent professional baseball minor leagues dwindled to a few, but when historically available the teams of these leagues are listed in this book.

With the flowering of independent baseball leagues in 1993, teams of this category are listed as independent and bear the designation (ind.).

Major league teams of the period 1871–1901, however sketchy the classifications of the leagues of the same era, bear the designation of (M) for "major league"; in the 19th century there was already a clear distinction recognized by players, owners, fans and newspapers between major circuits and non-major circuits that were merely professional.

A few professional baseball circuits switched their identity from "league" to "association" and vice versa. This type of change is identified as follows:

Adrian, Michigan

36 Yeggs 1909–11 *South Michigan (D)*. Circuit was designated League (1909) and Association (1910–14)

Rarely, a city entry will also include the county of this city because the baseball team has incorporated the county name into its nickname.

Bartow, Polk County, Florida

440 Polkers 1920 *Florida State (D)*. City of Bartow is located in Polk County.

Salisbury, Rowan County, North Carolina

5502 Rocots 1953 *Tar Heel (D)*. Management combined the beginnings of Rowan and County.

With regard to letter designations describing a change in the franchise status, there are five of which the reader should be informed. The first is "x," which is written immediately after the numerical year in which a team is playing — e.g., "1930x." This letter means the team disbanded in mid-season. The team so listed did not move to another city or take on a new nickname. An example of a team that disbanded in mid-season is as follows:

Bainbridge, Georgia

328 Commodores 1916-17x *Dixie (D)*. Circuit and team disbanded July 4 because of U.S. entry into World War I. City was named in honor of Commodore William Bainbridge, who led the U.S. Navy in battle against the British Royal Navy during the War of 1812.

A declaration of the disbandment date is presented immediately after the league's name and classification letter. The year of disbanding does not accompany the date, i.e. July 4, because the preceding "x" designation identifies the year — e.g., 1916–17x.

Another letter is "m" (for "moved") which means the franchise moved from one city to another in the course of the reg-

ular season. When the letter "m" appears before the numerical year (e.g., "m1920"), that means the team started in another city and then moved to the city under whose heading the entry appears. An example is as follows:

Ballard, Washington

346 Colts m1914 *Northwestern (B)* Team started season as the Portland (OR) "Colts" because of many young players. When the team moved to Ballard July 20 the nickname was retained.

If the letter "m" appears *after* the numerical year, that means the team moved from the city under whose heading it appears to another city before the regular season reached its conclusion. An example of this is:

Beardstown, Illinois

483 Infants 1909-10m *Illinois-Missouri (D)*. Team moved to Jacksonville (IL) July 21, 1910. In the 1890s Infants referred to a young team that played poorly. But this Beardstown bunch did quite well, posting won-lost percentages of .597 and .594. The local newspapers were referring to the many young players on the team.

The letter "t" represents the "transfer" a team underwent when its league and another one merged in mid-season. The in-season merger of leagues, despite the instability of the minor leagues in the era 1877–1944, is fairly rare, having occurred only three times since 1877. However, the letter "t" is used to designate these few teams that have transferred from one circuit to another in mid-season. An example follows:

Muskegon, Michigan

4153 Reds 1926t *Central (C)*; t1926 *Michigan State (B)*. Team started the season in the Class C Central League, which merged with the Class B Michigan-Ontario League in June to form the Class B Michigan State League. Players wore red trim.

The "t" designation is not used for a team that switches leagues during the off-season. For example, after the 1891 season four American Association clubs — Baltimore, Cleveland, Louisville and Washington — transferred to the National League for the start of the 1892 campaign. In this book none of these teams displays a "t" designation because their act of transference took place in the offseason, during the winter of 1891–92.

The letter "b" (for "black") stands for the resignation of a black team from a league in order to assume an independent schedule.

The "b" designation (placed after a year of play) is uncommon (about three listings) and involves black teams resigning — from a white circuit in the 19th century or a Negro league in the 20th — to barnstorm.

An "r" designation (for "revenue"; placed after a year) refers to a team that was forced onto the road because of low attendance (leading to low revenue) at home but managed to finish the season without disbanding or moving. An example of an "r" designated team is as follows:

Muskogee, Oklahoma

4170 Oilers m1933r *Western (A)*. Team started season in Wichita (KS) and then moved to Muskogee June 6. By June 30 the Oilers had become a road team because low attendance left them unable to pay their home park lease leading to their eviction. The Glenn Pools Gusher, near Tulsa, was struck in 1905. Oil rigs were quickly built to transport oil to refineries in both Tulsa and Muskogee. Since 1993, there have been several independent league teams that started the season as road clubs—with no home city at all. These teams have no city designations attached to their years of operation and, as such, are listed with the non-league barnstorming teams in Appendix I.

During World War I and World War II, drafted professional baseball players formed military teams. Such teams are not included in this book because these players received no payment as professionals (other than the standard soldier's pay) while serving in the U.S. Army, Navy, Marines, Coast Guard or Army Air Force.

When a team or league disbands because of a war, it may not be permanent. For instance, many teams suspended operations after 1942 because of the United States' entry into World War II but returned to resume play in 1946. In 1917, several teams and leagues played a war-shortened schedule, but by May 1919 the teams and leagues resumed their regular five-month season. (The deadly Spanish Influenza of 1918–19 caused many baseball teams to wait to resume competition until 1919). In such instances, reasons for the suspension of play are provided:

Miami Beach, Florida

3921 Flamingos 1941-42x *Florida East Coast (D)*. Team and league disbanded May 14 because of U.S. entry into World War II; 1946–52 *Florida International (C 1946–48, B 1949–52)*; 1954m *Florida International (B)* Team began season in Miami Beach (FL) and then moved to Miami (FL) May 22. The red and orange feathered flamingo is indigenous to Florida. With manager Max Rosenfeld at the helm, newspapers called the players "Max Rosenfeld's Flamingos."

Any reader who spots a mistake is encouraged to let the author know; write in care of the publisher.

The author intends for this book to serve as a reference source for the serious student of baseball history in general and for those focused especially on nicknames. It represents the first attempt to present the team nicknames and their origins for the 10,000 professional baseball team nicknames that have been devised since 1869.

ABBREVIATIONS AND INITIALISMS

A = Single A minor league

AA = Double A minor league

AAA = Triple A minor league

A1 = "high A" minor league (equivalent to Adv A)

Adv A = Class A–Advanced minor league (one level below AA)

AL = American League

B = Class B league

C = Class C minor league

D = Class D minor league

E = Class E minor league (The only E league was the 1943 Twin Ports League)

F = Class F minor league

FLAG = Florida–Louisiana–Alabama–Georgia League

h = historical nickname

III (Triple I) = Illinois–Iowa–Indiana League

ind. = independent league

KITTY = Kentucky–Illinois–Tennessee League

KOM = Kansas–Oklahoma–Missouri league

M = major league

m = moved from one city to another during the regular season (1900m = moved *from* this city; m1900 = moved *to* this city)

MINK = Missouri–Iowa–Nebraska–Kansas League

MOV = Mississippi–Ohio Valley League

NA = National Association

NAPBBL/NAPBL = National Association of Professional Base Ball / Baseball Leagues

NL = National League

OAK = Oklahoma–Arkansas–Kansas League

POM = Pennsylvania–Ohio–Maryland League–
PONY = Pennsylvania–Ohio–New York League

R = rookie league

r = played on road because of low attendance at home

S = subsidized by government

t = franchise transferred from one league to another during the regular season (1900t = transferred *from* the indicated league; t1900 = transferred *to* the indicated league)

TOM = Texas–Oklahoma–Missouri League

W = winter league

x = team disbanded during the season

Team Names

Abbeville, Alabama

1 Red Sox 1936x *Alabama–Florida (D)*. Team disbanded August 10. Players wore red-trim hose. Team had a loose affiliation with the Boston Red Sox.

Abbeville, Louisiana

2 Sluggers 1920x *Louisiana State (D)*. Team and league disbanded July 15. Good hitting team. "Sluggers," slang for good hitters, has been a baseball term since 1860. The baseball was "livened," i.e. wound tighter, to boost hitting.

3 Athletics 1935–39 *Evangeline (D)*; 1946–48 *Evangeline (C)*; 1949–50 *Evangeline (D)*; 1952 *Evangeline (C)*. Team had a loose affiliation with the Philadelphia Athletics 1935–38, 1946–50. The team was an official farm club of AL Philadelphia Athletics — but only in 1939.

Aberdeen, Maryland

4 Arsenal 2000 *Atlantic (ind.)*. The Aberdeen Proving Grounds is a testing site for military munitions stored there as part of a great "arsenal" of weapons.

5 Iron Birds 2000 to date *New York–Penn. (A)*. The nickname combines "Birds" from the parent club Baltimore Orioles (who are often called the Birds) and "Iron" after Baltimore Oriole star and team owner Cal "Ironman" Ripken, Jr., who holds the major league record for consecutive games played.

Aberdeen, South Dakota

6 Boosters 1920 *South Dakota (D)*. In the era 1900–30, teams that won pennants or were in the thick of a pennant race were "boosted" by enthusiastic fans. The team didn't win the flag but was in the race for most of the season.

7 Grays 1921–22 *Dakota (D)*; 1923x *South Dakota (D)*. Team and league disbanded July 17. This team wore gray uniforms and hose.

8 Pheasants 1946–71 *Northern (C)*; 1995–97 *Prairie (ind.)*. The wild Golden Pheasant — a popular game bird — is prevalent in the Dakotas.

Aberdeen, Washington

9 Pippins 1903–05 *Southwest Washington (D)*. After the famous Pippin apples that are grown in the area. Orchards in the region transport apples and other fruit to packing houses in the city.

10 Lumbermen 1906 *Northwest (B)*. Washington State has had a vigorous lumber and timber industry for more than 120 years. In honor of the "lumbermen" who cut, haul, and transport timber. The Olympic National Forest is situated about 30 miles north of the city.

11 Black Cats 1907 *Northwest (B)*; 1910 *Washington State (D)*; 1912x *Washington State (D)*. Team disbanded July 10, 1912; 1915x *Northwestern (B)*. Team disbanded August 1; 1918x *Pacific Coast International (B)*. Team and league disbanded July 7 due to the U.S. participation in World War I. Legend has it that mythical black pan-thers roamed the hills outside of Aberdeen, Scotland. Players wore white uniforms with a black cat logo.

12 Gray's Harbor Grays 1908–09 *Northwest (B)*. The seaport of Gray's Harbor lies adjacent to the city of Aberdeen. The players also wore gray uniforms and hose.

13 Gray's Harbor Ports 1976 *Northwest (A)*. The regional name refers to the seaport of Gray's Harbor.

14 Gray's Harbor Loggers 1977–78, 1980 *Northwest (A)*. Situated on a peninsula along Gray's Harbor, Aberdeen is known as "Plank Island" because of the factories that manufacture wooden planks from the lumber transported there.

15 Gray's Harbor Mets 1979 *Northwest (A)*. Team was a farm team of the New York Mets.

16 Gray's Harbor Gulls 1995–98m *Western (ind.)*. Team went by the regional name of "Gray's Harbor Gulls." Seagulls are indigenous to the entire Pacific Northwest coastline.

17 Western Warriors m1998 *Western (ind.)*. By July 5, the team was forced to become a "road warrior" team because of low attendance in Aberdeen.

Abilene, Kansas

18 Red Sox 1909 *Central Kansas (D)*. Team was not affiliated with either the Boston Red Sox or the Cincinnati Reds. By now players were wearing stirrup socks, and many teams favored all-red stirrups or red and white striped stirrups.

19 Reds 1910 *Central Kansas (D)*. Team name was shortened to be newspaper friendly.

Abilene, Texas

20 Eagles 1920–22 *West Texas (D)*. The "Screaming Eagle" railroad locomotive started making its runs out of Abilene in 1909. Express railroad trains of this era were often called Express, Flyers, Rockets or Eagles.

21 Aces 1928–29 *West Texas (D)*. In the 1920s and 1930s Abilene was a popular site for air shows where "aces" would pilot their aircraft in dangerous stunts to thrill the crowds. Team got off to a good start in 1928 and won the first-half title, with local newspapers praising the players for performing like "aces." Newspapers used the tag again in 1929, although the team slumped to fifth place.

22 Apaches 1939m *West Texas–New Mexico (D)*. Team moved to Borger (TX) July 9. The Apache Indians occupied the U.S. Southwest in the era 1750–1850 after being driven there by the savage Comanche, who waged incessant war on them.

23 Blue Sox 1946–54 *West Texas–New Mexico (C)*; 1955 *West Texas–New Mexico (B)*. Abilene players wore blue-trim uniforms and stirrups in the style of big league parent club, the Brooklyn Dodgers. Team was a Brooklyn farm 1946–48, but went independent in 1949–55, although the blue trim and nickname were retained.

24 Prairie Dogs 1995–99 *Texas–Louisiana (ind.)*. Team held a name-the-team contest prior to the 1995, season and Abilene businessman K.O. Long submitted the winning entry. The prairie dog is found throughout the South and Southwest U.S.

Abingdon, Virginia

25 Triplets m1948 *Blue Ridge (D)*. Team started season as the Leaksville–Draper–Spray "Triplets" and then moved to Abingdon on June 18. To save money, the uniforms and the nickname were retained.

Acambro, Guanajuato, Mexico

26 Club de Beisbol de Acambro 1975–76 *Mexican Center (A)*. None of the 11 teams of the 1975–76 Mexican Center League bore any nicknames. League officials apparently saw no need for them.

Acarigua, Portuguesa, Venezuela

27 Los Llaneros de Acarigua 1968/69 *Liga Venezolana (W)*; 1975/76 *Liga Venezolana (W)*. "Llana" is the Spanish word for wool, and "Llaneros" means "Wool-makers." Venezuela has many sheep farms. Both teams playing in the city of Acarigua had the regional name of "Portuguesa" Wool-makers. Portuguesa is the state in which Acarigua is located. "Los Llanos" is pasture land in the central region of Venezuela.

Ada, Oklahoma

28 Herefords 1947–54 *Sooner State (D)*. There are many Hereford dairy cows in Oklahoma. Farms in the region transport dairy products to pasteurization plants.

29 Cementers 1954 *Sooner State (D)*. Tag refers to the local cement industry. Name was switched from "Herefords" to "Cementers" during the 1954 season.

Adelaide, Australia

30 Giants 1989/90–98/99 *Australian (W)*. Team played in Adelaide's suburb of Kensington. Team was owned by Carpet Giants, a manufacturer of carpets.

31 Bite 2010 to date *Australian (W)*. The moniker refers to the powerful biting jaws of the Great White shark that swims off the coast of South Australia. Name also refers to the Great Australian Bight — the curving coastline of Southern Australia.

Adelanto, California

32 High Desert Mavericks 1991 to date. Team president Bill Brett, brother of Kansas City Royals star George Brett, named the club after his favorite TV show *Maverick*. Team is known by the regional name of "High Desert Mavericks." Adelanto is located in the "High Desert" region of California.

Adrian, Michigan

33 Page Fence Giants 1894–98 *Negro independent team*. Players on the team worked for the Page Fence Company — manufacturers of fences and barbed wire — in the off-season. Also, black teams in this era were so fond of the nickname Giants that they made up multiple nicknames, like American Giants, Royal Giants, and Page Fence Giants.

34 Demons 1895 *Michigan State (ind.)*. Newspapers reported the team "played like demons" as the players streaked towards the 1895 pennant with a 57–30 record. Team uniforms apparently had no red trim.

35 Reformers 1895 *Michigan State (ind.)*. Adrian State Prison, located here, was a "reformatory" famous for rehabilitating law-breakers. Moniker was used alternately with "Demon," as neither name was official.

36 Yeggs 1909 *South Michigan League (D)*; 1910 *South Michigan Assn. (D)*; 1911 *South Michigan Assn. (C)*. James Yeggs was a notorious but publicly admired safecracker who was imprisoned at this time in the Adrian State Prison.

37 Lions 1912 *South Michigan Assn. (D)*. Tag was a spin-off from the nearby Detroit Tigers. Team had a loose affiliation with the Detroit Tigers, receiving uniforms and equipment from the big league club.

38 Champs 1913 *South Michigan Assn. (D)*. Team won the 1912 South Michigan Association pennant. Originally "Champions," newspapers shortened it to "Champs."

39 Fencevilles/1914 *South Michigan Assn. (C)*. City is known as "Fenceville" in honor of the local Page Fence Company.

Agua Prieta, Sonora, Mexico

40 Vaqueros 1968 *Mexican Rookie (R)*; 2004–08 *Liga del Norte de Sonora (ind.)*; 2009 to date *Liga Norte de Mexico (ind.)*. In honor of Sonora's cowboys (vaqueros) who round up cattle and herd them to ranches.

Aguadilla, Puerto Rico

41 Tiburones 1941/42 *Liga Puertoriquena (W)*; 1946/47–50/51 *Liga Puertoriquena (W)*. Aguadilla has so many sharks swimming off its coast that it is nicknamed "Shark City" or "Ciudad de los Tiburones" in Spanish.

Aguascalientes, Aguascalientes, Mexico

42 Rieleros 1956–57 *Liga Central de Mexico (C)*; 1975–99 *Liga Mexicana (AAA)*; 2004–07 *Liga Mexicana (AAA)*. Aguascalientes has been a major railroad center in Mexico since the 19th century. Rieleros in English means "Railroad Men."

43 Tigres 1956–57 *Liga Central de Mexico (C)*; 1960–63, 1965 *Liga del Centro de Mexico (C)*. These teams were farm clubs of the Mexico City Tigres (Tigres) of the Mexican League.

44 Broncos 1966–67 *Liga del Centro de Mexico (C)*; 1969–74 *Liga del Centro de Mexico (A)*. These teams were farm clubs of the Reyonosa Broncos of the Mexican League.

Aiken, South Carolina

45 Foxhounds 2007 *South Coast (ind.)*. South Carolina has numerous fox hunting resorts. Fox hunting has been a popular sport there since the 18th century.

Akron, Ohio

46 Acorns 1887 *Ohio State (ind.)*. Ohio is famous for its many oak trees, and the acorn is the nut of the oak. With manager Charles Morton at the team's helm, newspapers called the players "Morton's Acorns."

47 Numatics 1889 *Ohio State (ind.)*; 1890 *Tri-State (ind.)*. In the 1880s Charles Goodrich introduced the use of pneumatic pumps at his Akron tire factory to inflate rubber tires.

48 Summit City 1893 *Ohio–Michigan (ind.)*; 1895 *Eastern Interstate (ind.)*. Akron is called the "Summit City" because it is on an elevated plateau, about 1,200 feet above sea level. Newspapers also used the plural "Summit Citys" and the contraction "Summits."

49 Buckeyes 1905 *Ohio–Pennsylvania (C)*; 1920 *International (AA)*. Ohio is the "Buckeye State." With field manager Art Hoblitzell at the helm in 1920, local newspapers called the players the alliterative "Hoblitzell's Buckeyes."

50 Rubbernecks 1906 *Ohio–Pennsylvania (C)*. Home of the Big Three of tire manufacturing — Goodyear, Firestone, and Goodrich — Akron is nicknamed "The Rubber Capital of the World." "Rubberneck" at the time was a slang for tourist or traveler, which made the name appropriate for endlessly traveling baseball teams.

51 Champs 1907–11 *Ohio–Pennsylvania (C)*. The name was premature, as Akron fans called their 1907 third-place team "Champs" in the hope they would make a late run for the flag that season. The "Champs" played like champions, going 83–53 but falling short — two games behind Youngstown. The disappointment was soon replaced by celebration as the Akron "Champs" won four straight OPL pennants, 1907–11.

52 Rubbermen 1912 *Central (B)*; 1915x *Buckeye (D)*. Team and league disbanded July 5. Tag was a spin-off from "Rubbernecks." With manager Art Newnham at the helm in 1915, newspapers called the players "Art Newnham's Rubbermen." Akron is also known as the "Rubber City."

53 Giants 1913 *Interstate (B)*. In imitation of the successful New York Giants, who were on their way to their third straight NL pennant and fifth since 1904. With manager John Siegle at the helm, newspapers called the players "Siegle's Giants."

54 Tyrites 1928–29 *Central (B)*; 1932m *Central (B)*; 1933 *Negro independent team*. With Goodrich, Goodyear and Firestone making the city the site of their headquarters for the years 1880–1950, Akron became known as the "Tire Capital of the World." Spelling of the nickname is based on the British spelling of tire, i.e. "tyre." Akron is also known as the "Tire Capital of the United States." The 1932 team moved to Canton (OH) June 21.

55 Yankees 1935–41 *Middle Atlantic (C)* Team was a farm of the New York Yankees.

56 Aeros 1997 to date *Eastern (AA)*. In the past 100 years Ohio has become a great aviation state. A more direct connection is with Akron's elevation of 950 feet above sea level, making it the highest point in the 18th century Ohio–Erie Canal region; hence, a spin-off from "Summit City."

Alameda, California

57 Grays 1907 *California (ind.)*. Players wore gray uniforms and hose.

58 Encinals 1908 *California (ind.)*. Team was named after the Encinal oak tree of California.

59 Bracketts 1910m *Central California (D)*. The team began the season in Santa Rosa and moved to Alameda on May 5. Alameda newspapers listed the former team in brackets, i.e. Alameda [Santa Rosa], prompting fans to call the team the "Bracketts."

60 Alerts m1910–11x *Central California (D)*. Team and league disbanded July 9, 1911. The 1910 Alameda Bracketts transferred to Oakland on July 10. A day later the Fruitvale club moved to Alameda, where they went on to win the 1910 league championship because of what the local newspapers called their "alert play."

61 Monday Models m1911 *Central California (D)*. Team started the season as the Fruitvale "Travelers," traveling to and from the Fruitvale ballpark in the popular Model T Fords (of auto manufacturer Henry Ford). When the franchise moved to Alameda on May 28, the entire team drove to its new city in so-called "Monday Model T Fords."

62 Alameda Baseball Club 1915 *California State (D)*. Team had no nickname.

Alamogordo, New Mexico

63 Stealth 2004 *Southwestern (ind.)*. Nearby Alamogordo Air Force Base conducted experimental test flights of the then-secret "Stealth" bomber and "Stealth" jet fighter. The "Stealth" aircraft neutralizes radar, making it "invisible."

64 White Sands Pupfish 2011 *Pecos (ind.)*. Also known as "killifish," these are freshwater fish in streams and rivers of the Western U.S. Team went by the regional desert name of White Sands Pupfish.

Albany, Georgia

65 Albany Baseball Club 1906x *Georgia State (D)*. Team and league disbanded July 9. Team had no nickname.

66 Babies 1911–16x *South Atlantic (C)*. Team disbanded July 23. Albany was an SAL expansion team in 1916. An expansion team, in this era, was known as "Babies." When manager Bernie McCay succeeded previous field manager Harry Mathews in mid-season 1911, newspapers started calling the players "Bernie McCay's Babies."

67 Nuts 1926–28x *Southeastern (B)*. Team disbanded August 12, 1928. With manager George Stinson at the helm starting the 1926 season, newspapers called the players the "Stinson's Nuts." When Sumter Clark took over in mid-season in 1926, the name became "Sumter's Nuts." Georgia is the "Peanut State." Tag was retained through 1928.

68 Travelers 1935–38 *Georgia–Florida (D)*. Team had a loose affiliation with the Class A1 Little Rock Travelers, who donated "Traveler" uniforms to the Albany players.

69 Cardinals 1939–42 *Georgia–Florida (D)*; 1946–58 *Georgia Florida (D)*. These teams were farm clubs of the St. Louis Cardinals.

70 Polecats 1992–95 *South Atlantic (A)*. The owners of the Albany club, Rick Holtzman and Barry Foote, held a fan poll to choose a team nickname. The final four names were Peaches, Pine Cones, Nuts and Pole Cats (entered by the team's announcer). Somehow, the owners agreed to "Pole Cats" even though the fans thought it was crazy.

71 Alligators 2001 *All-American (ind.)*. Name derives from the alligators in nearby Flint River.

72 South Georgia Waves 2002–03 *South Atlantic (A)*. Team went by the regional name of South Georgia Waves. Boats have sailed the waves of the Flint River since 1700.

Albany, New York

73 Capital City 1878 *New York State (M)*; 1879m *National Assn. (M)*. Albany had two NA franchises that started the 1879 season. This team moved to Rochester May 15; 1880 *National Assn. (M)*; 1881 *Eastern Assn. (M)*; 1885 *New York State (ind.)*; 1886 *Hudson River (ind.)*; 1890 *New York State*; m1896m *Eastern Assn. (ind.)*. Toronto played its home games in Albany July 9–31. Albany is the state capital of New York. Albany newspapers immediately shortened the name to **Capitals** and **Caps**. A plural form — **Capital Citys** — was also used.

74 Nolans 1878 *New York State (M)*. In 1878 mayoral candidate Michael Nolan was elected mayor of Albany, New York.

75 Blues 1879 *National Assn. (M)*. Players wore blue stockings. Originally "Blue Stockings," newspapers shortened the name to **Blue Legs** and **Blues**.

76 Senators 1886 *Hudson River (ind.)*; 1891–93 *Eastern Assn. (ind.)*; 1895 *New York State (ind.)*; 1899–1902 *New York State (ind.)*; 1903–16m *New York State (B)*. Albany moved to Reading (PA) August 21; 1920–32x *Eastern (A)*. Team and league disbanded July 17 because of the Great Depression; 1933–36 *International (AA)*; 1937 *New York–Pennsylvania (A)*; *Eastern (AA)* 1938–59. Moniker was originally a spin-off from "Capitals." State senators of New York legislate in the Albany State House.

77 Governors 1886 *Hudson River (ind.)*. Another spin-off, name was used to avoid confusion with the NL Washington Senators.

78 Black Sox 1926–27 *Independent Negro team*. Players wore black stirrups.

79 Giants 1926–35 *Independent Negro team*. Tag was a popular name for black teams.

Albany, Oregon

80 Colts 1896 *Oregon (ind.)*. Team had numerous young players. In the period 1890–1910 young players were known variously as Babes, Chicks, Colts, Cubs, Debutantes, Foundlings, Ponies, Prodigals, and Yearlings.

81 Rollers m1904x *Oregon State (D)*. Team began season in Vancouver (BC) and moved to Albany May 18. Team and league disbanded July 6. A popular game in this timber region has been "log rolling" where two or more contestants "roll" a log, i.e. running on it as it spins seeking to be the last to take a dunking in the water. Logs are also "rolled" down a river to the wood cutting plant. Lumberjacks roll logs down the nearby Calapooya River. With manager E.P. Preble at the helm, newspapers called the players the alliterative "Preble's Rollers."

Albany-Colonie, New York

82 Albany-Colonie Athletics 1983–84 *Eastern (AA)*. Team was a farm club of the Oakland Athletics. Home field was Heritage Park in Colonie, New York.

83 Albany-Colonie Yankees 1985–94 *Eastern (AA)*. Team was a farm club of the New York Yankees. Team continued to play at home in Heritage Park in Colonie, New York.

84 Albany-Colonie Diamond Dogs 1995–98 *Northeast (ind.)*; 1999–2002 *Northern (ind.)*. This team's home field again was Heritage Park in Colonie, New York. With a large population of Dutch and German-Americans in Albany, the team's mascot was a little dachshund, wearing a red baseball cap. "Diamond" refers to the baseball diamond. Diamond, in reference to the baseball field, was coined in newspapers as early as 1856.

Albany-Decatur, Alabama

85 Twins 1921 *Alabama–Tennessee (D)*. Since 1880, numerous baseball teams that represented two cities have been called the "Twins." Team played its home games in Albany but drew fans from nearby Decatur.

Albemarle, North Carolina

86 Rockets 1948 *North Carolina State (D)*. In 1948, the American public was fascinated by the experimental launchings of the captured German V-2 rockets. Also, North Carolina has the nickname of "Sky Land." The moniker soon became sarcastic as local newspapers noted how the team "rocketed its way" into the league cellar (eighth place) with a 32–78 record — 35 games out of first place.

Albuquerque, New Mexico

87 Dukes 1915x *Rio Grande Assn. (D)*. Circuit and team disbanded July 6; 1946–54 *West Texas–New Mexico (C)*; 1955 *West Texas–New Mexico (B)*; 1960–61 *Sophomore (D)*; 1962–64 *Texas (AA)*; 1975–99 *Pacific Coast (AAA)*. Circuit and team disbanded July 6. The historical title "Duke of Albuquerque" was created by King Henry IV of Castile in the 16th century. The Duke of Albuquerque of the early 18th century founded this city — which was then a Spanish fort — in 1706. Albuquerque is known as the "Duke City."

88 Dons 1932x *Arizona–Texas (D)*. Team and league disbanded July 24 because of the Great Depression. "Don" is the Spanish equivalent for the English "lord," and is a title conferred on a Spanish nobleman. The elite in New Spain were also known as "Dons."

89 Cardinals 1937–41 *Arizona–Texas (D)*. Team was a farm club of the St. Louis Cardinals. Team had only a loose affiliation with the St. Louis Cardinals, 1937–38, but then became an official farm club of the St. Louis NL club, starting in 1939.

90 Dodgers 1965–71 *Texas (AA)*; 1972–74 *Pacific Coast (AAA)*. These teams were farm clubs of the Los Angeles Dodgers. In 1971 the Texas and Southern leagues played an inter-locking schedule under the name of the Dixie Association. In 1972 both leagues went back to separate schedules.

91 Isotopes 2003 to date *Pacific Coast (AAA)*. The first atomic bomb was detonated in the desert near Los Alamos, New Mexico, in July 1945. The Los Alamos National Research lab is also located near Albuquerque. But it was a humorous reference on the cartoon TV show *The Simpsons* in a 2002 episode wherein the Springfield (IL) Isotopes baseball team was about to be lured away to Albuquerque — a transfer thwarted by the heroic Homer Simpson — which helped cinch the choice of a nickname for the new PCL franchise.

Alexander City, Alabama

92 Millers 1947–51x *Georgia–Alabama (D)*. Team disbanded in mid-season July 15, 1951. Wheat and corn farms in the region ship grain to mills in Alexander City.

Alexandria, Louisiana

93 White Sox 1907–08x *Gulf Coast (D)*. Circuit and team disbanded June 2, 1908. Players donned white stockings in emulation of the 1906 world champion Chicago White Sox, but the team had no affiliation with the Chicago Americans.

94 Hoo-hoos 1909x *Arkansas State (D)*. Team disbanded June 7. Night owls, which hoot out "hoo-hoo!" are prevalent in the region. Owls apparently flew into the ballpark and perched on seats and fences there. Fans chanted "hoo-hoo" to the players out on the field, which led to this strictly informal moniker.

95 Tigers 1920x *Louisiana State (D)*. Team and league disbanded July 15. Both the Louisiana State college football team and this professional baseball team were named after the famous Louisiana Civil War battalion "Fighting Tigers." Team was not a farm club of the Detroit Tigers.

96 Hubs 1920x *Louisiana State (D)*. Team and league disbanded July 15. The city is the hub of shipping on the nearby Red River. Alexandria is known as the "Hub City" and the "Crossroads of Louisiana on the Red River."

97 Reds 1925–30x *Cotton States (D)*. Team disbanded June 17, 1930, because of the Great Depression. Players wore red-trim uniforms and red stirrups. Team was not a farm club of the Cincinnati Reds or Boston Red Sox.

98 Aces 1934–42x *Evangeline (D)*; 1946–48 *Evangeline (D)*; 1949–57 *Evangeline (C)*; 1972–75 *Texas (AA)*; 1994–2001 *Texas–Louisiana (ind.)*; 2002–03 *Central (ind.)*; 2006–08 *United (ind.)*. Team and league disbanded May 30, 1942, because of U.S. entry into World War II. Inspired by the popular air "aces" who barnstormed across the United States in this era. With manager Art Phelan at the helm 1934–39, newspapers called the players "Art Phelan's Aces." By 1946 the nickname had become traditional.

Alexandria, Virginia

99 Dukes 1978–83 *Carolina (A)*. The 18th century Duke of York, Henry Stuart, helped found the early Virginia settlements.

100 Mariners 1979 *Carolina (A)*. Team was a farm club of the Seattle Mariners.

Algona, Iowa

101 Brownies 1901–03 *Negro independent team*. Players wore brown hose. An amateur team — the Algona Brownies — played in this city in 1883–84.

Allentown, Pennsylvania

102 Dukes 1884 *Eastern Assn. (ind.)*; 1929–30 *Eastern (A)*; 1939 *Interstate (C)*. Name hearkens back to the 17th and 18th century English dukes who ruled the Pennsylvania colony. With manager H.J. Dehlman at the helm, newspapers called the players "Dehlman's Dukes." K.H. Debelle succeeded him in mid-season, changing the name to "Debelle's Dukes."

103 Lumber City 1887x *Pennsylvania State (ind.)*. Team disbanded in mid-season (date unknown). City was a processing center for cedar and oak trees in the 19th century and was nicknamed the "Lumber City." Nickname did not survive into the 20th century.

104 Peanuts 1888 *Central (ind.)*; 1898–1900x *Atlantic (ind.)*. Team and circuit disbanded on June 12, 1900. Nearby peanut farms ship this crop to food processing plants. Team was a farm club of the Philadelphia Phillies. Team was also known as the **Peanut Men**.

105 Queen City 1889 *Eastern Interstate (aka Middle States). (ind.)*. Allentown is known variously as the "Queen City of the Lehigh Valley" and "Queen City of the Lehigh River." Teams here were also known by the plural "Queen Citys."

106 Colts m1890x *Pennsylvania State (ind.)*. Team started season in Lancaster before moving to Allentown in mid-season. Team and league disbanded July 10; 1892–94m *Pennsylvania State*. Team moved to Easton (PA) in mid–1894 (date unknown); m1895m *Pennsylvania State (ind.)*. Team began season as the Pottsville Colts, then moved to Allentown July 27 to replace Allentown Goobers, played 12 games as Allentown's team with the same nickname of "Colts," and then moved again, this time to Reading on August 10. These teams had young players in their lineup, known by the slang of "Colts." With manager John Hanlon at the helm in 1892, newspapers called the players "Hanlon's Colts."

107 Kelly's Killers 1894x *Pennsylvania State (ind.)*. Team disbanded August 16. Former star player Mike King Kelly was the team's field manager after managing a big league team in Cincinnati in 1891 that became known as "Kelly's Killers." With Kelly at the helm in Allentown, the moniker was used again, "Kelly's Killers of Allentown." Kelly, one of the most prominent stars of the major leagues in the 19th century, died on November 8, 1894.

108 Buffaloes m1894m *Eastern (ind.)*. Team played most of its home games in Yonkers (NY) while officially representing Allentown. Team started season in Binghamton (NY) before moving to Allentown/York August 16; 1931–32x *Eastern (A)*. Team and league disbanded July 17. Buffalo Valley, located in Central Pennsylvania, was one of the last "stamping grounds" of the American buffalo (bison). The last bison were killed or driven out at Buffalo Crossroads in 1800. The moniker "buffaloes" was common slang for baseball players.

With King Kelly, who had a buffalo-like physique due to his tall stature and big muscles, as 1894 manager, newspapers called the players "Kelly's Buffaloes." The gothic letter, which prompted Binghamton fans to call their team the "Bingoes," now prompted Allentown/York fans to call the players "Buffaloes." Kelly had also been managing the PSA Allentown "Killers" team, which had disbanded earlier on August 16. No sooner had the Killers disbanded than Kelly was signed to manage the Buffaloes.

109 Goobers 1895x *Pennsylvania State (ind.)*. Team disbanded July 24. "Goober" is a type of peanut grown in Pennsylvania.

110 Allentown Baseball Club 1912–14 *Tri-State (B)*. Team had no nickname.

111 Brooks m1935–36 *New York–Pennsylvania (A)*. Reading Brooks, a farm team of the Brooklyn Dodgers, aka "Brooks," moved to Allentown July 9, 1935. Since the team continued as a Brooklyn farm team, the nickname was retained. With manager Bruno Betzel at the helm in 1936, newspapers called the team "Bruno's Brooks."

112 Fleetwings 1940–43 *Interstate (B)*. During World War II the city, with four airports, was an important aviation center. Nickname was also derived from the St. Louis Cardinals, the team's parent club. Tag was shortened by newspapers to **Wings.**

113 Cardinals 1944–52 *Interstate (B)*; 1954–56 *Eastern (A)*. These teams were farm clubs of the St. Louis Cardinals.

114 Chiefs m1957 *Eastern (A)*. Team started season as the Syracuse (NY) Chiefs before moving to Allentown July 13. The team nickname was retained.

115 Red Sox 1958–60 *Eastern (A)*. Team was a farm club of the Boston Red Sox.

116 Ambassadors 1997–98 *Northeast (ind.)*; 1999–2002 *Northern (ind.)*; 2003 *Northern East*. Management held a contest and the winner was "Ambassadors." Allentown was the hiding place of the Liberty Bell in 1777. Foreign newspapers often depict the U.S. as an ambassador dressed in an Uncle Sam hat — just like the team logo.

117 Lehigh Valley Iron Pigs 2008 to date *International (AAA)*. Moniker is a switch of "pig iron," which refers to crude iron cast in blocks. Allentown, in the 19th century, had iron smelters that were fueled by coal brought in from nearby mines. Eastern Pennsylvania is a major coal mining region.

Alliance-Sebring, Ohio

118 Twins 1912x *Ohio–Pennsylvania (D)*. Team disbanded July 15 due to a players' strike. In professional baseball, a franchise that represents two cities sometimes is known as the "Twins."

Almere, Netherlands (also spelled Alkmarr)

119 Instant Holland of Almere 1999–2006 *Hoofdklasse (ind.)*. Team was owned by Instant Holland Construction Corporation 1999–2006.

120 Penguins 2000–06 *Hoofdklasse (ind.)*. Players wore black-trim uniforms.

121 Media Monks Magpies 2007–09; '90 *Magpies* 2010. *Honkball Hoofdklasse (ind.)*. Team has been owned since 2007 by RCH (Racing Club Heemstede Football Club), and Media Monks Communications. The team logo, derived from the players' black-trim uniforms, is a magpie — a type of crow. The team's name was "Media Monks Magpies." The '90 designation referred to the franchise's founding year of 1990. BSC Corporation held part ownership in 2006. Few professional baseball teams in Italy have an official team nickname although many of them have mascots. Usually the team is known by the sponsoring company's name.

Alpine, Texas

122 Big Bend Cowboys 1959–61 *Sophomore (D)*; 2010 *Continental (ind.)*; 2011 to date *Pecos (ind.)*. Texas is the "Cowboy State." Alpine is located near the "Big Bend" of the Rio Grande River as it "bends" Southwest and then Northwest towards El Paso.

Alton, Illinois

123 Blues 1917 *Three-I (B)*. League ended its regular season on July 8 due to U.S. entry into World War I. Players wore blue-trim uniforms.

Altoona, Pennsylvania

124 Ottawas 1884x *Union Assn. (M)*. The Ottawa Indians inhabited Pennsylvania in the 17th and 18th centuries. The Altoona team, with its five nicknames, disbanded May 31.

125 Mountain City 1884x *Union Assn. (M)*; 1886–87x *Pennsylvania State (ind.)*. Team disbanded in mid-season 1887. 1889–90x *Eastern Interstate* Altoona was built on rolling hills adjacent to the Allegheny Mountains Team disbanded in mid-season 1890. Altoona, built at the base of the Allegheny Mountains. is about 800 feet above sea level and is known as the "Mountain City." The plural **Mountain Citys** was also used. The name "Mountain City" was a generic tag for all 19th-century Altoona baseball teams.

126 Famous Altoonas 1884x *Union Assn. (M)*. Advertising posters at the start of the season proclaimed the players to be the "Famous Aloonas," á la typical marketing style of the era.

127 Pride 1884x *Union Assn. (M)*. Team at the start of the season was billed as the "Pride of Altoona."

128 Unfortunates 1884x *Union Assn. (M)*. Team lost 19 of 25 games, driving the fans away, and then disbanded May 31. Newspapers described the team's performance as "unfortunate."

129 Browns 1886–87x *Pennsylvania State (ind.)*. Team disbanded in mid-season 1887. Players wore brown hose. Originally **Brown Stockings**, it was shortened to "Browns."

130 Altoona Base Ball Club 1892, 1894 *Pennsylvania State (ind.)*. Team moved to Lancaster July 7, 1894.

131 Mud Turtles 1893 *Pennsylvania State (ind.)*. The North American mud turtle inhabits Pennsylvania and often wallows in the mud and silt at the bottom of rivers, streams and lakes. Some baseball infields in this era were shaped like turtle shells. Players often got their uniforms dirty — especially on a wet infield — giving rise to the moniker "Mud Turtles."

132 Mountaineers 1904–06 *Tri-State (ind.)*; 1907–09 *Tri-State (B)*. Tag was a spin-off from Mountain City.

133 Rams 1910–12 *Tri-State (B)*. Team moved to Reading (PA) June 13, 1912. Altoona manager Hank Ramsey led his players to the 1910 pennant with a stellar 73–28 record, prompting fans and the local press to call the team "Ramsey's Rams." Although the team slumped in 1911–12, the nickname was retained. Ramsey left the team after the 1912 season.

134 Engineers m1931m *Middle Atlantic (C)*. Team started season in Jeanette, moved to Altoona May 23, and then moved to Beaver Falls July 18. The engineers of the Altoona-Pennsylvania Railroad have been traveling the "Horseshoe Bend" since 1850. The modern team's "Curve" moniker is a spin-off from "Engineers."

135 Curve 1999 to date *Eastern (AA)*. Before reaching the city, the Altoona-Pennsylvania Railroad travels along the miles-long curving track known as the Horseshoe Bend. A name-the-team contest before the 1999 season chose "Curve." Poll runner-ups included "Fish," "Lake Monsters" and "Ridge-Runners."

Altus, Oklahoma

136 Chiefs 1911x *Texas–Oklahoma (C)*. Team disbanded July 18. Named after the Cherokee Indian tribe that inhabited Oklahoma in the 18th and 19th centuries. Oklahoma is known as the "Indian State."

137 Orphans 1911x *Texas–Oklahoma (C)*. In the era 1895–1915, teams, forced to play on the road due to low attendance at home, were called "Wanderers" and "Orphans." Because of that low attendance, the team gave up on road games and disbanded July 18.

Amarillo, Texas

138 Gassers 1922 *West Texas (D)*; *Panhandle Pecos Valley (D)*. 1923x. Team and circuit disbanded August 15. The city is a supply center for oil and helium gas.

139 Panhandlers 1923x *Panhandle Pecos Valley (D)*. Team and circuit disbanded August 15. Amarillo is located in extreme northwest Texas in the "Texas Panhandle."

140 Broncobusters 1923x *Panhandle Pecos Valley (D)*. Team and circuit disbanded August 15. Amarillo has numerous ranches where cowboys "break the bronco to the saddle," i.e. tame a wild horse. Name was used as an alternate to "Gassers," but newspapers didn't like its length.

141 Texans 1927–28 *Western (A)*. Before 19th century, American pioneer families in Texas called themselves "Texans." In the 18th century, Spaniards born in Texas called themselves "Los Tejicanos." The Spanish word, used by 19th-century Mexicans born in Texas, soon became anglicized into "Texicans" and then to "Texans."

142 Broncs 1928 *Western (A)*. Tag was a contraction of "bronco-buster." Amarillo is noted for its horse ranches and "bucking bronco" rodeos.

143 Black Cats 1938 *Independent Negro team*. Team was also called the "Sudan" Black Cats in reference to the African Sudan Desert, which is similar to the prairie desert surrounding Amarillo where big cats roam.

144 Black Sandies 1938 *Independent Negro team*. This moniker was a spin-off of "Black Cats." The term "Sandies" refers to the Sudan Desert, which is similar to the loams (clay and sand) of the Panhandle prairies.

145 Gold Sox 1939–42x *West Texas–New Mexico (D)*. Team and circuit disbanded July 5, 1942, because of World War II; 1946–54 *West Texas–New Mexico (C)*; 1955 *West Texas–New Mexico (B)*; 1956–58 *Western (A)*; 1959–63 *Texas (AA)*; 1976–82 *Texas (AA)*. Spanish conquistadores of the 16th and 17th centuries searched Texas (in vain) for the mythical "Seven Cities of Gold." "Amarillo" is Spanish for yellow.

146 Sonics 1965–67 *Texas (AA)*. Team was a farm club of the Houston Astros, leading to spin-off name of Sonics. When the NBA Seattle Super Sonics were formed for the 1967–68 pro basketball season, it was decided to change the baseball team's moniker to Giants for 1968.

147 Giants 1968–74 *Texas (AA)*. Team was a farm of the San Francisco Giants.

148 Dillas 1994–2001 *Texas–Louisiana (ind.)*; 2002–04 *Central (ind.)*; 2006–10 *United (ind.)*. The armadillo, an armored burrowing mammal, inhabits the Southern U.S. to South America.

149 Sox 2011 to date *American Assn.(ind.)*. Moniker was a shorter version of the 1982 team name of "Gold Sox."

Americus, Georgia

150 Pallbearers 1906 *Georgia State (D)*. Team was in last place, and newspapers complained that manager Harry Powell's players had "transported the fans' pennant hopes to the cemetery like 'pallbearers.'" "Powell's Pallbearers" eventually ended up in sixth and last place with 13 wins and 32 defeats.

151 Muckalees 1913 *Empire State (D)*; 1914 *Georgia State (D)*; 1915m *Florida–Louisiana–Alabama–Georgia (FLAG). (D)*. Team moved to Gainesville July 31. "Muckalee" is a type of soil used in plantations and farms in the region.

152 Aggies 1913 *Empire State (D)*; Americus is home to Georgia Southwest Agricultural College established in 1906 whose students were called Aggies.

153 Cardinals 1935–38 *Georgia–Florida (D)*. Team was a farm club of the St. Louis Cardinals.

154 Pioneers 1939–42 *Georgia–Florida (D)*. Pioneer families, many of them debtors seeking to escape their creditors, moved into Georgia in the period 1820–50.

155 Phillies 1946–50 *Georgia–Florida (D)*. Team was a farm club of the Philadelphia Phillies.

156 Rebels 1951 *Georgia–Florida (D)*. Georgia was the site of momentous Civil War battles, e.g., Chickamauga in 1863, General William Sherman's March to the Sea in 1864 and the burning of Atlanta in 1865.

157 Arrows 2002x *Southeastern (ind.)*. Team disbanded on July 15. Creek and Cherokee tribes inhabited Georgia in the 17th and 18th centuries.

Americus-Cordele, Georgia

158 Orioles 1954 *Georgia–Florida (D)*. Team was a farm club of the Baltimore Orioles.

Amsterdam, Netherlands (Holland)

159 Expos 1999–2001 *Honkball Hoofdklasse (ind.)*. Amsterdam was the host city of the 1883 Colonial Exposition. Team was not a farm club of the Montreal Expos.

160 L & D Pirates 2002 to date *Honkball Hoofdklasse (ind.)*. Team has been partly owned by the SV Rap Pirates Football Club of Holland. A co-owner, L & D Diagnostic Instruments, bought part interest in the team in 2002 and controlling interest in 2005, but the Pirates nickname was retained.

Amsterdam, New York

161 Amsterdam Base Ball Club 1894 *New York State (ind.)*. Team had no nickname.

162 Reds 1895 *New York State (ind.)*. Players wore red stockings. Originally called **Red Stockings**, newspapers shortened the name to "Reds."

163 Rugmakers 1938–42 *Canadian-American (C)*; 1946–51 *Canadian-American (C)*. Team was owned by the Mohawk Rug Company. Amsterdam, a textile industry center, is nicknamed the "Carpet City."

Anaconda, Montana

164 Serpents 1900 *Michigan State*. Tag is based on a play on words. The city has the same name as the great Anaconda snake found in South America.

Anadarko, Oklahoma

165 Indians 1912x *Oklahoma State (D)*. Circuit and team disbanded June 29. Oklahoma is the "Indian State." With manager Roy Ellison at the helm, newspapers called the players "Ellison's Indians."

Anaheim, California

166 Aces 1941 *California (C)*. With World War II fast approaching for the United States, an air base was built in the area where "ace" pilots trained.

167 Valencias 1947–48m *Sunset (C)*. Team moved to San Bernardino on June 25, 1948. California orchards are famous for their Valencia oranges.

168 Angels 1966 to date *American (M)*. The Los Angeles Angels moved to Anaheim in 1966 and the team nickname was retained. Team was called by the regional name of California Angels, 1965–96; by the city name of Anaheim Angels, 1997–2004; and then by the regional name of Los Angeles Angels of Anaheim, starting in 2005. Angels management wanted the official name of the team to be Los Angeles Angels (to attract fans from Los Angeles County), but the City of Anaheim sued in court to keep the baseball franchise's name the Los Angeles Angels of Anaheim and won.

169 Cherubs 1966 to date *American (M)*. Cherub is an ancient Greek word for angel.

170 Halos 1966 to date *American (M)*. Angel baseball caps since 1961 traditionally have had a golden ring — a halo — embroidered on the crown of the cap.

171 Seraphs 1966 to date *American (M)*. "Seraph" is a biblical word for angel.

172 Cloud Nine Angels 1979 *American (M)*. The 1979 Angels put their fans on "cloud nine" as they won the 1979 A.L. Western Division title with an 88–74 record. The "Cloud Nine Angels" were powered by hitters Rod Carew, Bobby Grich, Don Baylor, Dan Ford, Brian Downing and Carney Lansford, as well as pitcher Nolan Ryan. To be "on cloud nine" means to experience a heavenly type of joy.

173 Glitter Gang 1982 *American (M)*. Some of the "glamorous glittering lights of Hollywood" — usually associated with the nine pennants and five world titles of the Los Angeles Dodgers — rubbed off on the 1982 A.L. Western Division champion Angels (93–69) whom fans and newspapers called the "Glitter Gang."

174 Last Chance Gang 1986 *American (M)*. The 1986 A.L. Western Division champions (92–70) were a veteran team — the oldest in the AL — and were named after a comedy-action "Western" Hollywood movie *The Last Chance Gang*, a movie about aging outlaws on horseback in the Old West who try to rob a train and a bank.

175 Mickey Mouse Club 1996 *American (M)*. Disgruntled Angel fans started calling the team this derogatory name after the Walt Disney Company bought the Angels at the start of the 1996 season. The Angels' pitching staff was so horrible that its team ERA of 6.38 was the worst in the both major leagues since the 1930 Philadelphia Phillies pitchers coughed up 6.71 earned runs per game. In American English slang "Mickey Mouse" means anything that is shoddy and unprofessional.

176 Gaylos 1997 *American (M)*. With the Angels and the Dodgers meeting for the first time in NL–AL interleague play, some Dodger fans referred to the "Halos" as the "Gaylos." "Gay" in modern jargon means something "silly, stupid or hateful." Newspapers shunned the moniker, which — like other insulting baseball team nicknames — is used almost exclusively on the street.

177 Los Angelitos 2000–01 *American (M)*. The franchise underwent a rebuilding phase in 2000–01, prompting fans and newspapers to call the young players "Los Angelitos" — which in Spanish means "Little Angels." Name was dropped because it was confused with the Los Angeles Dodgers.

178 Wings 2002 *American (M)* — Local newspapers praised the Angels in 2002 for "winging their way" through the AL divisional playoff, the AL Championship Series and the 2002 World Series to capture the world championship. The obvious spin-off became the

"Wings" but the moniker was immediately derailed due to confusion with the NHL Detroit Red Wings, who had been known as the newspaper contraction "Wings" since 1934. Name originated with a 2002 team photograph entitled "Earning Their Wings."

179 Los Angeles Angels of Anaheim of Orange County of California of Pacific Time Zone of the United States of the Northern Hemisphere of the Earth of the Solar System of the Milky Way Galaxy of The Universe 2005 *American (M)*. A moniker worthy of *Monty Python* and *Saturday Night Live*, it was a sarcastic pun of the clumsy "Los Angeles Angels of Anaheim" title used by the franchise to quell a lawsuit by the host City of Anaheim against the Angels franchise to thwart a "Los Angeles Angels" team title. Quite funny in 2005, the joke wore off by 2006.

180 Reloaded Halos 2010 *American (M)*. Alliterative moniker coined by *The Sporting News Baseball Magazine* to describe how Angels management made numerous roster changes after the 2009 season to "reload" the team before the 2010 season. The team traded away Vladimir Guerrero, Chone Figgins and pitcher John Lackey, while signing designated hitter–outfielder Hideki Matsui from the Yankees. However, the reloading turned out to be a "misfire" as the Angels skidded to third place behind Texas and Oakland.

Anahuac, Valle de Mexico, Mexico

181 Los Indios de Anahuac 1939 *Liga Mexicana (ind.)*; 1953x *Liga Mexicana* Team disbanded September 15. Name refers to the Aztec Indians. The ancient Aztec capital of Teotitchlan is now Mexico City. Anahuac is a suburb of Mexico City, located in a valley just south of the city. Los Indios is Spanish for "Indians." A semi-professional league began play in Mexico in 1925. By 1937, the all-professional "Liga Mexicana" started competition, although most teams were in Mexico City until 1945.

Andalusia, Alabama

182 Reds 1936 *Alabama–Florida (D)*. Players wore red trim uniforms and red stirrups. Team had a loose affiliation with the Cincinnati Reds.

183 Bulldogs 1937–38 *Alabama–Florida (D)*. Team used the nickname of the University of Georgia "Bulldogs." In 1937 the team "bulldogged" its way to the pennant.

184 Rams 1939 *Alabama–Florida (D)*; 1940–41 *Alabama State (D)*. Sheep farms are found in the area. Moniker was alliterative, vaguely rhyming, and short. With manager Ralph McAdams at the helm in 1941, newspapers called the players "McAdam's Rams."

185 Arrows 1947–50 *Alabama State (D)*. The Creek Indian tribe inhabited the U.S. Southeast in the 17th and 18th centuries. Team was not a farm club of the Cleveland Indians or the Boston Braves.

186 Dodgers m1962 *Alabama–Florida (D)*. Team started season in Ozark (AL) before moving to Andalusia July 10. Team was a farm club of the Los Angeles Dodgers.

Andalusia-Opp, Alabama

187 Indians 1954 *Alabama–Florida (D)*. Tag was a spin-off from the 1950 Andalusia Arrows. Team was not a farm club of the Cleveland Indians or the Milwaukee Braves.

Anderson, Indiana

188 Anderson Base Ball Club 1890x *Indiana State (ind.)*. Team disbanded in mid-season; 1895x *Western Interstate (ind.)*. Team disbanded in mid-season; 1899x *Indiana–Illinois (ind.)*. Team disbanded

in mid-season; 1903m *Central (B)*. Team moved to Grand Rapids (MI) May 30; 1906x *Interstate Assn. (C)*. Circuit and team disbanded July 8. These teams had no nickname.

189 White Caps m1911x *Northern State of Indiana (D)*. Team began season in Logansport (IN) and then moved to Anderson July 2. Team disbanded July 28, forcing the league to disband July 29. Team had a loose affiliation with the Chicago White Sox. Players wore all-white baseball caps and white stirrups over white sanitary hose.

190 Lawmen 1995 only *Mid-America (ind.)*; 1996–98 *Heartland (ind.)*. Name was selected in honor of the Indiana State Police.

Anderson, South Carolina

191 Electricians 1907x *South Carolina (D)*. Team disbanded July 27; 1908–12 *Carolina Assn. (D)*. One of the first hydroelectric plants in the South was constructed at High Shoals near the Rocky River outside of Anderson in 1894 to supply the city with electrical power. In this era a city, upon gaining hydroelectric power, would proudly call itself the "Electric City." With manager Elmer Hines at the helm in 1908, newspapers called the players "Elmer's Electricians." In 1909–11, with Jim Kelly as field skipper, the name became "Kelly's Electricians."

192 Electrics 1931m *Palmetto (D)*. Team moved to Spartanburg June 29. Name was a shorter spin-off of the 1912 Anderson Electricians.

193 Athletics 1946 *Tri-State (B)*. Team was a farm club of the Philadelphia Athletics.

194 Rebels 1947–54 *Tri-State (B)*. Confederate forces, on April 12, 1861, attacked Fort Sumter. South Carolina had been the first state to secede from the Union. Rebel sentiment was so strong that Union troops stayed until 1877. Manager Bob Richards piloted the team through 1950. His charges were known as "Richards' Rebels."

195 Senators 1970–71 *Western Carolinas (A)*. Team was a farm club of the Washington Senators.

196 Giants 1972 *Western Carolinas (A)*. Team was a farm club of the San Francisco Giants.

197 Tigers 1973 *Western Carolinas (A)*. Team was a farm club of the Detroit Tigers.

198 Mets 1974 *Western Carolinas (A)*. Team was a farm club of the New York Mets.

199 Rangers 1975 *Western Carolinas (A)*. Team was a farm club of the Texas Rangers.

200 Braves 1980–84 *South Atlantic (A)*. Team was a farm club of the Atlanta Braves. The Braves were Anderson's sixth major league parent club since 1970.

201 Joes 2007 *South Coast (ind.)*. "Shoeless Joe" Jackson was born in nearby Pickens County (SC). Jackson was a star hitter for the Indians and White Sox until he was banned from Organized Baseball, because of the 1919–20 "Black Sox Scandal." Jackson had the third-highest career major league BA (.356). Legend has it that Jackson didn't accept or receive money from the gamblers but was banned for life by baseball commissioner Kenesaw Landis anyway.

Angier-Fuquay-Varina, North Carolina

202 Bulls 1946 only *Tobacco State (D)*. Tobacco is grown here for the Bull Durham Tobacco Company.

Anniston, Alabama

203 Models 1911–12 *Southeastern (D)*. With the new Model-T Ford sweeping the fancy of the American public, and with Walter

Ford at the helm as field manager, Anniston fans called the players "Ford's Models" in 1911. Although Ford had left the team after the end of the 1911 season, the nickname stuck for the 1912 season.

204 Moulders 1913–17x *Georgia–Alabama (D)*. Circuit and team disbanded May 23 because of U.S. entry into World War I. League pennant was awarded to first-place Anniston. Anniston, near iron-ore mines, had iron factories where "moulders" poured the molten iron into casts. The Woodstock Iron Company started here in 1863, using its blast furnaces to melt and mold iron for weapons for the Confederate Army.

205 Nobles 1928–30 *Georgia–Alabama (D)*. Iron factory industrialist Samuel Noble founded the city in 1872.

206 Rams 1938–42 *Southeastern (B)*; 1946–50 *Southeastern (B)*. Sheep roam the nearby Cheaha Mountains. Sheep farms in the area transport wool to textile mills. Newspapers liked the four-letter moniker.

Ansonia, Connecticut

207 Cuban Giants 1888x *Connecticut State (ind.)*. Team dropped out in mid-season to barnstorm; 1889–90 *Independent Negro club*; 1891 *Connecticut State (ind.)*. The Cuban Giants, who played home games in Babylon, New York, before 1885–87, played home games in Ansonia while members of these leagues and as an independent 1889–90. During these seasons, the team also played some home games in Trenton (NJ).

Anzio, Lazio, Italy

208 Colavito 2000–01 *Italian A1 (ind.)*. Olefici Colavito Oil & Pasta Co. owned the team.

209 Elletron 2004 *Italian A1 (ind.)*. Elletron Electronics owned the team.

Appleton, Wisconsin

210 Papermakers 1891 *Wisconsin (ind.)*; 1909 *Wisconsin–Illinois (D)*; 1910–14 *Wisconsin–Illinois (C)*; 1940–42 *Wisconsin State (D)*. Timber from Wisconsin's Nicolet Forest lumber camps were transported to paper mills here.

211 Crescents 1891 *Wisconsin (ind.)*. Known as the "Crescent City," Appleton was built along the curve of the Fox River, forming a crescent. Newspapers called the team the "Crescents" and "Crescent Citys."

212 Lumber-shorers 1891 *Wisconsin (ind.)*. Lumber-shorers hauled timber at the shores of Green Bay onto trains and wagons to transport to Appleton paper mills.

213 Foxes 1958–61 *Illinois–Indiana–Iowa (B)*; 1962 *Midwest (D)*; *Midwest (A)*. 1963–94. Red and gray foxes attracted 18th-century trappers, who named the area Fox Valley. The river was named Fox River. Team went by the regional name of Fox Cities Foxes for the years 1958–61 because it represented Appleton, Kaukana and Neena, Wisconsin. Team was variously known as the Appleton Foxes (1962, 1964, 1967 and 1971–95) and the Fox Cities Foxes (1963, 1965 and 1968–70).

214 Wisconsin Timber Rattlers 1995 to date *Midwest (A)*. Moniker is a spin-off of Lumber-shorers. When lumberjacks cut down trees, they rattle the ground with a loud, shuddering boom. Team used the state name to attract fans from the entire Fox Cities region. The current logo is a rattlesnake, which is a play-on-words from "tree rattling."

Arandas, Jalisco, Mexico

215 Union de Arandas 1977 *Mexican Center (A)*. In Spanish, Mexico is often referred to as "La Union Mexicana." Following po-litical and religious upheaval here in the era 1890–1930, including the Cristero War of 1926–29, city officials tried to restore a sense of national unity starting in 1930.

Ardmore, Oklahoma

216 Territorians m1904 *Texas (C)*. Team started the season in Paris (TX) and moved to Ardmore August 5. Oklahoma was still a territory in 1904 and did not become a state until 1907.

217 Blues 1911 *Texas–Oklahoma (D)*. Players wore uniforms with blue trim.

218 Giants 1912x *Texas–Oklahoma (D)*. Ironically, the first-place Ardmore club disbanded August 1, forcing league president C.O. Johnson to award the 1912 pennant to first-half winner Wichita Falls; 1913 *Texas–Oklahoma (D)*. In the era 1875–1920 teams that were big winners—usually en route to a pennant—were praised as "Giants." Since the New York Giants won NL pennants in 1911, 1912 and 1913, the moniker was doubly appropriate. Team did not repeat in 1913, finishing in seventh place with a terrible 43–80 record, which goaded fans to use the Giants moniker in sarcastic irony. With manager George McAvoy leading the 1912 team to first place, newspapers and elated fans called the players "George McAvoy's Giants."

219 Indians 1914x *Texas–Oklahoma (D)*. Team disbanded June 11, 1914; 1947–52 *Sooner State (D)*. Although more well known as the "Sooner State," Oklahoma is also called the "Indian State." With manager Brooks Gordon at the helm, newspapers called the players "Gordon's Indians." The team, in 1947–48, was a farm club of the Cleveland Indians and retained the Indians moniker 1949–52 while playing as an independent.

220 Foundlings m1917 *Western Assn. (D)*. Team began the season in Paris and then moved here May 10 because of low attendance in Paris. In the era 1890–1920 teams that faltered because of young and inexperienced players were known as "Foundlings." This team finished in eighth place. Teams that moved to another city in mid-season because of low attendance were called "Orphans" and "Foundlings." In this era children relocated to orphanages were often called "foundlings."

221 Peps 1921 *Oklahoma (D)*. The 1921 club qualified for Oklahoma League championship series as the Ardmore players won 87 games, displaying "lots of pep." With manager Joe Chelette at the helm for a few weeks in mid-season 1921, newspapers called the players "Chelette's Peps." The term "pep" had become popular in American culture with such soft drinks as Pepsi-Cola (first sold 1903) and Dr Pepper (first sold 1904).

222 Producers 1922 *Texas–Oklahoma (D)*. Rich farm country. Farmlands around Ardmore produce wheat, cotton, hay and peanuts. Farm goods are known as "produce."

223 Snappers 1923 *Western Assn. (C)*. With manager Earl "Red" Snapp at the helm, newspapers called the players "Red's Snappers."

224 Bearcats m1924 *Western Assn. (C)*. Team started season as the Bartlesville Bearcats, and then moved here June 8. The "Bearcats" nickname was retained. The name "bearcat" is a misnomer for the North American wolverine.

225 Boomers 1925–26m *Western Assn. (C)*. Team moved to Joplin (MO) July 14. Oil was discovered here in 1920, causing a population and building "boom." A small town that "booms" in population due to the discovery of gold, silver, oil, etc. is known as a "boomtown."

226 Cardinals 1953–57 *Sooner State (D)*. Team was a farm club of the St. Louis Cardinals.

227 Rosebuds m1961 *Texas (AA)*. The Victoria (TX) Rosebuds moved to Ardmore May 27. The nickname was retained.

Arecibo, Puerto Rico

228 Lobos 1961/62–98/99 *Liga Puertoriquena (W)*; 2005/06 to date *Liga Puertoriquena (W)*. The Spanish word for wolf is "lobo," which rhymes with Arecibo. Wolves are not indigenous to the island, but the fans liked this moniker.

Argenta, Arkansas

229 Shamrocks 1908–09x *Arkansas State (D)*. Team disbanded June 7. With Irish-American A.L. James Kerwin managing in 1908, newspapers called the players "Kerwin's Shamrocks." The shamrock is the national symbol of Ireland. There was an influx of Irish immigrants into southeast Arkansas in the years 1900–20.

Arkansas City, Arkansas

230 Arkansas City Base Ball Club 1887 *Kansas State (ind.)*. Team had no nickname.

231 Grays 1909m *Kansas State (D)*. Team started representing both Arkansas City and Winfield (AR) on July 22; 1910 *Kansas State (D)*. Players wore gray uniforms and gray stirrups.

232 Twins 1909m *Kansas State (D)*. Team represented both Arkansas City and Winfield starting on July 22 — prompting newspapers to call the team the "Twins."

233 Osages 1924–26 *Southwestern (D)*. City was built close to the Osage River. Arkansas was once inhabited by the Osage Indians.

Artesia, New Mexico

234 Drillers 1951–53 *Longhorn (C)*. Team was named after the drilling crews of the New Mexico oil fields.

235 Numexers 1954–55 *Longhorn (C)*. Tag was a play on words of New Mexico.

236 Giants 1958–60 *Sophomore (D)*. Team was a farm club of the San Francisco Giants.

237 Dodgers 1961 *Sophomore (D)*. Team was a farm club of the Los Angeles Dodgers.

Aruare, Portuguesa, Venezuela

238 Pastora de los Llanos 2001/02–06/07 *Liga Venezolana (W)*. Sheep farms in the region transport wool to city textile mills. "Los llanos" is the Spanish word for "shepherds." Shepherd evolved from "sheep herder."

Asbury Park, New Jersey

239 Asbury Park Base Ball Club 1897 *New Jersey State (ind.)*. The team had no nickname.

240 Seagulls m1914 *Atlantic (D)*. Team started season in Bloomfield-Long Branch and then moved to Asbury Park July 2. Asbury Park is a summer resort town along the beaches of the Atlantic Ocean. Seagulls inhabit the coastal waters of New Jersey.

241 Sea Urchins m1914 *Atlantic (D)*. Team started season in Bloomfield-Long Branch and then moved to Asbury Park July 2. The sea urchin is a type of starfish. Asbury Park is a summer resort town along the beaches of the Atlantic Ocean. Sea urchins are found in the coastal waters here.

Asheville, North Carolina

242 Moonshiners m1896–97 *Southeastern (D)*. Team started season in Columbus (GA) and then moved here in mid-season; 1910 only *Southeastern (D)*. Prepared in stills, homemade "moonshine" whiskey, usually corn whiskey, was popular in the South in this era when the state and federal governments tried to tax liquor. The corn whiskey was called "moonshine" because it was distilled at night in darkened houses, under the light of the "shining moon," to hide the stills from the authorities.

243 Mountaineers 1913–17x *North Carolina (D)*. Team disbanded May 18, 1917, because of U.S. entry into World War I. Asheville was built just east of the Great Smoky Mountains.

244 Tourists 1915–17x *North Carolina (D)*. Team disbanded May 18, 1917, because of U.S. entry into World War I; 1924–30 *South Atlantic (B)*; 1931–32x *Piedmont (C)*. Team disbanded July 7, 1932, because of the Great Depression; m1934–42 *Piedmont (B)*. Team started 1934 season in Columbia (SC) before moving to Asheville June 7, 1934; 1946–55 *Tri-State (B)*; 1959–63 *South Atlantic (A)*; 1967 *Carolina (A)*; 1968–75 *Southern (AA)*; 1976–79 *West Carolinas (A)*; 1980 to date *South Atlantic (A)*. With the mountains, mild winter weather and a national park nearby, the city built health and tourist resorts to attract visitors. Asheville is the "Tourist City."

Ashland, Kentucky

245 Tri-State Tomahawks 1993x *Frontier (ind.)*. Team disbanded July 12. Team had the regional name of "Tri-State Tomahawks" because Ashland is located near the borders of three states — Kentucky, Ohio and West Virginia. Kentucky was known as the "Dark and Bloody Ground" because of the many wars fought between European settlers and the native tribes — Delaware, Shawnee, Miami and Wyandot — brandishing tomahawks.

Ashland, Pennsylvania

246 Ashland Base Ball Club 1887–88m *Central Pennsylvania (ind.)*. Team moved to Easton (PA) in mid-season; m1894 *Pennsylvania State (ind.)*; m1896x *Central Pennsylvania* Team started season in Mount Carmel before moving to Ashland (date unknown). Team disbanded towards the end of the season (date unknown). These teams had no nickname.

Ashland-Cattlesburg, Kentucky

247 Twins 1910 *Virginia Valley (D)*; 1911–12x *Mountain State (D)*. Team disbanded July 8, helping to force the league to disband. These teams represented both cities.

248 Colonels 1939–41 *Mountain State (D)*; 1942 *Mountain State (C)*. After the War of 1812, former military men and then the Kentucky governor's office, often formally bestowed the deferential title of "Colonel" to men of the upper class, particularly wealthy land owners, politicians, military officers and government officials. Although representing both cities, the team was known simply as the "Ashland Colonels." Team had a loose affiliation with the Southern Association Louisville Colonels, acquiring uniforms and equipment from the higher classification "parent club." During the Great Depression, loose affiliations between minor league teams of different classifications became common.

Aspen, Colorado

249 Aspen Base Ball Club 1889x *Colorado State (ind.)*. Team disbanded in mid-season; 1895–96 *Colorado State (ind.)*; 1898–99 *Colorado State (ind.)*. These teams had no nickname.

Atchison, Kansas

250 Atchison Base Ball Club 1895x *Kansas State(ind.)*. Team disbanded in mid-season; 1896x *Kansas State* Team disbanded in mid-season; 1898x *Kansas State (ind.)*. These teams had no nickname.

Atlanta, Georgia

251 Browns 1885 *Southern (ind.)* Players wore brown hose. Originally, **Brown Stockings**, newspapers shortened it to **Brown Legs** and "Browns."

252 Gate Citys 1886x *Southern (ind.)*; 1889x *Southern (ind.)*. Team disbanded July 6. Atlanta, in the 19th century, became known as the "Gate City" because, as the biggest hub of transportation and commerce in Dixie, it is the "Gateway to the South." The nickname was first used by the 1866 Gate City Baseball Club—Atlanta's first baseball team.

253 Atlanta Base Ball Club 1889m *Southern (ind.)*. Team moved to Charleston (SC) in mid-season; m1889x *Southern (ind.)*. Team began season in Charleston (SC) and moved to Atlanta in mid-season. Team disbanded along with the circuit towards the end of the season. These teams had no nickname.

254 Firecrackers 1892 *Southern (ind.)*. Fans and reporters started calling this team the "Firecrackers," in reference to the Great Fire of Atlanta in 1864, and the term "cracker," which now meant any inhabitant of Georgia. With manager Sam Maskrey at the helm, newspapers called the players "Maskrey's Firecrackers." Although there are some stories reporting fireworks being used at 19th-century baseball games, the first confirmed fireworks shows at a baseball park date to 1909.

255 Windjammers 1893 *Southern (ind.)*. This name has several meanings. It is the large, ironclad 3,000-ton boat that made ocean voyages, 1870–1900, transporting cargo. It also means a bugler, a bugle boy in the Confederate Army. And it also was a synonym for "bondsman," i.e., a slave. Like "cracker" its origin and exact use is obscure. With manager William Murray at the helm, newspapers called the players "William Murray's Windjammers." Since Atlanta is inland and was a Confederate stronghold, the "bugle boy" origin is the most probable—since most minor league baseball players in this era were young men ages 18–25.

256 Crackers m1894x *Southern (ind.)*. Team began season in Mobile (AL) before moving to Atlanta in mid-season and then disbanded August 11; 1895 *Southern (ind.)*; 1896–97 *Southeastern*; 1903–61 *Southern Assn. (A)*. Team and circuit suspended play on June 28, 1918, due to World War I, but the club and league, which never really disbanded, resumed play in 1919; 1962–65 *International (AAA)*. The 1894 moniker was a spin-off from Firecrackers, but the 1895 nickname was based on Dixie history. In any case the origin of the name is vague and controversial. "Crackers" has several meanings. It has a prejudicial bent referring to white people, i.e. "poor white trash" but it also may have stemmed from the black slaves' hatred of the slave-master, i.e. the "whip-cracker." However, by the year 1900 the name had evolved into the neutral meaning of "Southerner," especially an inhabitant of Georgia. The Atlanta franchise (1902–61) won the most games of any Southern Association franchise and has been called the **Yankees of the Minors.**

257 Colts 1898 *Southern (ind.)*. Young players in the era 1890–1910 were often called Babes, Chicks, Colts, Cubs, Debutantes, Fledglings, Foundlings, Ponies, Prodigals and Yearlings. The word "rookie" was not coined until 1917 as slang for "recruit."

258 Firemen 1902 *Southern Assn. (ind.)*. On November 15, 1864, Union forces under General William T. Sherman besieged Atlanta and burned most of the city to the ground. Moniker was a contraction of the 1892 Atlanta Firecrackers.

259 Black Crackers 1938 *Negro American (M)*; 1945 *United States (ind.)*. This team played as an independent in the 1930s except for this single season. Several Negro League teams used white team nickname spin-offs, i.e. Black Yankees, Black Senators, Black Barons, Black Sox and Black Crackers. The USBL played only a few games.

260 Braves 1966 to date *National (M)*. Following the 1965 season the Milwaukee Braves moved to Atlanta. The team nickname was retained. The Braves moniker, used by the franchise in three cities, has been the team's nickname for one hundred years. In the 19th century, "Braves" had been a generic term for "baseball players," or "baseball team."

261 America's Team 1982–2008) *National (M)*. Atlanta Braves owner Ted Turner advertised his 1982 NL Eastern Division champions as "America's Team." The name was strictly a marketing ploy to capitalize on the Braves' NL Eastern Division title run to boost ratings on Turner's TBS Network in imitation of (although some said it was stealing) the informal nickname of the 1977 National Football League's Super Bowl champion Dallas Cowboys, who were known as "America's Team" in the 1970s. Once the Braves started losing by 1985, the gimmick was shunned by Atlanta fans, although it remained on the TBS Network as a marketing tool. When the team started winning big in 1991, the fans picked up on it again.

262 Futile Braves 1987–90 *National (M)*. Tag was coined by baseball writer Joe Strauss to describe the futility of the 1987–90 Atlanta Braves. With the team saddled with three last-place finishes, the name was derived from the old "Futile Phillies" of the 1930s and 1940s. Little did anyone know that the "Futile Braves" were to engage in a miracle ascent to first place and the NL pennant only a year later.

263 Peach State Lemons 1988–90 *National (M)*. From April 1, 1988, to September 3, 1990, the Atlanta Braves lost exactly 300 regular season games—prompting disgruntled fans to call the team the "Peach State Lemons"—a moniker reported by *The Sporting News* in 1990. Georgia is known as the "Peach State" because of its many peach groves and a "lemon" is a car or any other mechanical device that is a "clunker."

264 Bravos 1991 to date *National (M)*. Moniker was coined by baseball broadcaster Ken Harrelson. Harrelson has a knack devising nicknames for teams, i.e. Boston "Carmines," Texas "Wranglers," and for players, i.e. Frank "The Big Hurt" Thomas. Some fans with a prankster's wit use the deflatingly absurd **Barves**, especially when the team is losing.

265 Cinderella Braves 1991 *National (M)*. The Atlanta Braves (along with the 1991 AL Minnesota Twins) became first team since 1890 to jump from last place to first place. Cinderella in the classic fairy tale rose from poverty to royalty and wealth. Only three teams have gone from last place to the pennant: Atlanta NL (1991), Minnesota AL (1991) and Louisville AA (1890).

266 Blessed Braves October 1992 *National (M)*. The Atlanta Braves rallied in the bottom of the ninth inning in Game 7 of the NLCS against the Pirates for three runs to win the game, series and NL pennant. Sportswriters insisted that the players must have been "blessed."

267 Buffalo Bills of Baseball 1994 *National (M)*. At the same time that the Atlanta Braves were winning NL pennants but losing a pair of World Series and another playoff series, the NFL Buffalo Bills appeared in the Super Bowl for four consecutive January attempts to win the world title but were beaten each time. By January 1995 *Beckett's Baseball Card Monthly* magazine described the baseball Braves as the "Buffalo Bills of Baseball." The sour tag was dissolved the next year when the Braves beat Cleveland in the 1995 World Series, 4 games to 2.

268 Pride of the South 1995 *National (M)*. The Atlanta Braves won their third NL pennant in five seasons after winning their fifth straight NL Eastern Division title. The Braves went on to defeat the AL Cleveland Indians in the 1995 World Series, 4 games to 2. The nickname originated from an old Dixie phrase "Pride of the South." When soldiers of the Confederate Army marched off to battle during the Civil War years of 1861–65, people would say "Off to Battle Marches the Pride of the South!"

269 Baby Braves 2005 *National (M)*. Five promising rookies broke through into the Atlanta Braves' starting lineup to help power the team to a 90–72 mark and the NL Eastern Division title: Wilson Betemit, Jeff Francouer, Ryan Langerhans, Brian McCann and Pete Orr. Fans called the entire team the "Baby Braves."

270 Battery Powered Braves 2011 *National (M)*. A good pitching staff (team ERA of 3.58) led by Tim Hudson and Craig Kimbrel, and two good catchers, Brian McCann and David Ross, kept the Braves near .600 and in strong contention for the wild card by September 1. A pitcher and batter are known collectively as "the battery." Tag was coined by sportswriter Ryan Fagan in the August 2011 issue of *The Sporting News*.

Atlantic, Iowa

271 Atlantic Baseball Club 1903 *Southwest Iowa (D)*. Team had no nickname.

Atlantic City, New Jersey

272 Atlantic City Base Ball Club m1885x *Eastern (ind.)*. Team started season in Wilmington (DE) before moving to Atlantic City June 19. Team then disbanded June 24; 1889x *Eastern Interstate (ind.)*. Circuit and team disbanded in mid-season; 1897 *New Jersey State (ind.)*; m1912–13 *Tri-State (B)*. Team started 1912 season in Lancaster (PA) before moving to Atlantic City June 18, 1912. These teams had no nickname.

273 Bacharach Colored Giants 1923–28 *Eastern Colored (M)*; 1929 *American Negro (M)*; 1934 *Negro National (M)*. The 1922–23 independent Jacksonville (FL) Duval Giants moved to Atlantic City for the 1923 season and was named in honor of Atlantic City mayor Michael Bacharach, i.e. the Atlantic City Bacharach Colored Giants.

274 Surf 1998–2006 *Atlantic (ind.)*; 2007–08 *Can-Am (ind.)* Can-Am is short for Canadian-American League. Starting around 1890, Atlantic City started building amusement parks, recreation piers and gambling casinos along its beaches to attract tourists.

Attleboro, Massachusetts

275 Angels 1908 *Atlantic Assn. (D)*. With manager McEleny at the helm, newspapers called the players "McEleny's Angels." The tag "angels" was often ironic as baseball players in this era sometimes engaged in behavior that was anything but angelic.

276 Burros 1928 *New England (B)*. Moniker was used for newspaper headlines, i.e. "Burros edge Hillies, 4–3."

277 Attleboro Baseball Club. 1933m *New England (B)*. Team moved to Lawrence (MA) May 26. Team had no nickname.

Auburn, Nebraska

278 Athletics 1910–13x *Missouri–Iowa–Nebraska–Kansas (MINK). (D)*. Team and league disbanded June 17. Although the team was not a farm club of the AL Philadelphia Athletics, local newspaper reporters chose "Athletics" in emulation of the Philadelphia American Leaguers who were en route to pennants in 1910, 1911 and 1913.

Auburn, Cayuga, New York

279 Auburnians 1877–78 *New York State (M)*; 1878 *Independent* Team was a member of the loosely confederated N.Y. State Championship Assn. both seasons. For stretches both seasons, team played independently. Team rejoined the circuit August 10, 1878. Inhabitants of Auburn are known as "Auburnians." Team aka **New Yorkers**.

280 Auburn Base Ball Club 1888–89 *New York State (ind.)*; 1897 *New York State (ind.)*. These teams had no nickname.

281 Maroons 1898 *New York State*. Players wore maroon hose.

282 Prisoners 1899m *New York State* Team moved to Troy August 1, 1899. Auburn State Prison, one of the oldest prisons in the United States, was built in 1816.

283 Bouleys 1938 *Canadian-American (C)*. The team was purchased by businessman William Bouley, who named the team after himself.

284 Colts 1940 *Canadian-American (C)*. Young players in this era were sometimes called "colts." Most of the players were inexperienced, and it showed as the team finished eighth and last with a 28–93 record. With manager Knotty Lee at the helm, newspapers called the players "Knotty Lee's Colts."

285 Cayugas 1946–50 *Border (C)*. Auburn is located in Cayuga County. Lake Cayuga is located nearby, and the region was once inhabited by the Cayuga Indians.

286 Falcons 1951x *Border (C)*. Team disbanded July 1. Team was sponsored by a local Polish social club whose mascot was a falcon.

287 Yankees 1958–61 *New York–Pennsylvania (D)*. Team was a farm club of the New York Yankees.

288 Mets 1962 *New York–Pennsylvania (D)*; 1963–66 *New York–Pennsylvania (A)*. Team was a farm club of the New York Mets.

289 Twins 1967–71 *New York–Pennsylvania (A)*. Team was a farm club of the Minnesota Twins.

290 Phillies 1972–77, 1980–81 *New York–Pennsylvania (A)*. Team was a farm club of the Philadelphia Phillies.

291 Sunsets 1978 *New York–Pennsylvania (A)*. Team was a farm club of the Hagerstown Suns. Sometimes called **Phillies** this season, the team was not affiliated with the NL Philadelphia Phillies.

292 Red Stars 1979 *New York–Pennsylvania (A)*. Red Star Trucking Company was located in Auburn. Moniker "Red Stars" derives from the red stars of the "Phillies" script name on the jerseys of players of the parent club Philadelphia Phillies.

293 Astros 1982–94 *New York–Pennsylvania (A)*. Team was a farm club of the Houston Astros.

294 Doubledays 1995 to date *New York–Pennsylvania (A)*. Abner Doubleday is the man, named in legend, as having created baseball in 1839 while in school, even though he never mentioned such an act in his memoirs. Although Doubleday (an officer in the Civil War) was a man of considerable achievement, the codification of the rules of baseball (a sport that evolved instead of being "created") must go to lawyer and ball player William Wheaton. He codified rules for a game that was a close cousin of baseball, for his New York Gotham Ball Club of 1837. Alexander Cartwright modified the rules in 1845 for the Knickerbocker Base Ball Club. Another pioneer of the modern game was Daniel "Doc" Adams, who influenced the rules and invented the position of shortstop. Some cynics say the turn-of-the-century (1900–05) wrangling over the "inventor" of the game was politically motivated.

Augusta, Georgia

295 Browns 1885–86x *Southern (ind.)*. Team disbanded August 5. Players wore brown hose.

296 Electricians 1893x *Southern (ind.)*. Hydroelectric stations along the nearby Savannah River brought electric lights and electrical-powered trolleys to the city in the 1890s. With manager George Stallings at the helm, newspapers called the players "Stallings' Electricians." The electrification of America took place over a thirty-year period, from 1880 to 1910.

297 Dudes 1893 *Southern (ind.)*. Players on this team were fancy dressers. "Dude" was coined in 1883 and referred to a young man who dressed too fancy for his own good.

298 Augusta Base Ball Club 1898 *Southern (ind.)*. Team had no nickname.

299 Tourists 1904–11x *South Atlantic (C)*. Team disbanded August 30. Augusta, around 1900, started building resort hotels along the Savannah River to attract winter-weary Northern tourists.

300 Dollies 1919 *South Atlantic (C)*. After field manager Dolly Stark.

301 Georgians 1920–21 *South Atlantic (C)*. Team was named in honor of the State of Georgia.

302 Tygers 1922 *South Atlantic (B)*; 1924–29 *South Atlantic (B)*. Tag was a play on words with Ty Cobb. Baseball star Ty Cobb, a native Georgian, began his professional career in 1904 with the Augusta Tourists.

303 Wolves 1930 *South Atlantic (B)*; 1931x *Palmetto (D)*. Team and league disbanded July 23 because of the Great Depression. Tag was a spin-off from "Tigers." Management decided to avoid confusion with the Detroit Tigers by going from feline to canine.

304 Tigers 1936–42 *South Atlantic (B)*; 1946–52 *South Atlantic (A)*; 1955–58 *South Atlantic (A)*. These teams were farm clubs of the Detroit Tigers.

305 Rams 1953–54 *South Atlantic (A)*. Sheep farms in the region transport wool to city textile mills.

306 Confederate Yankees 1962 *South Atlantic (D)*; 1963 *South Atlantic (AA)*. Team was a farm club of New York Yankees. To placate the Dixie fans who would not "cotton to a Yankee name," Augusta management called the players the "Confederate Yankees," a contradiction in terms. A 1957 TV episode of *You'll Never Get Rich*, starred Phil Silvers as the money-grubbing army sergeant Ernie Bilko, posing as a baseball agent trying to sign a Southern boy "phenom" pitcher to a major league contract. When the pro–South pitcher balked at signing with the New York "Yankees," Bilko dressed up star players Mickey Mantle, Whitey Ford and Yogi Berra in "Kentucky Colonel" garb to convince the fastball hurling Dixie lad to sign with the team.

307 Pirates 1988–96 *South Atlantic (A)*. Team was a farm club of the Pittsburgh Pirates.

308 Green Jackets 1997 to date *South Atlantic (A)*. Augusta is the annual home site of the Masters golf tournament, whose winner gets to wear the victor's green blazer.

Augusta, Maine

309 Kennebecs 1895–96 *New England (ind.)*. Augusta is located in Kennebec County near the Kennebec River. The Kennebec Indians once inhabited the region.

310 Augusta Base Ball Club 1897 *Maine State (ind.)*; 1901 *New England (ind.)*. These teams had no nickname.

Augusta, New Jersey

311 New Jersey Cardinals 1994–2005 *New York–Pennsylvania (A)*. Team was farm club of the St. Louis Cardinals. Team went by the state name of New Jersey Cardinals.

Aurora, Illinois

312 Aurora Base Ball Club 1890–91x *Illinois–Iowa (ind.)*. Team disbanded during mid-season 1891 (date unknown); 1895x *Western Inter-State (ind.)*. Team disbanded during mid-season 1895 (date unknown). These teams had no nickname.

313 Hoo-doos m1892x *Illinois–Iowa (ind.)*. Team started season in Peoria (IL) and then moved to Aurora May 31. Team disbanded July 5. After getting off to a good start in Peoria (won 17, lost 8), the team transferred to Aurora where the players lost 19 of 28 games—prompting fans to say "hoo-doo" which means "bad luck" or "cursed."

314 Islanders 1910 *Wisconsin–Illinois (C)*. Aurora was built on a peninsula along the Fox River in 1850.

315 Blues 1911–12 *Wisconsin–Illinois (C)*. Players wore blue trim. With manager Albert Tebeau at the helm in 1911, newspapers called the players "Tebeau's Blues."

316 Foxes 1915x *Bi-State (D)*. Team disbanded July 5. Foxes are indigenous to the region, hence the name Fox River, which has been used since the 18th century.

Austin, Minnesota

317 Southern Minny Stars 1996–97 *Prairie (ind.)* Minnesota is nicknamed the "North Star State." Team went by the regional name of Southern Minny Stars because Austin is located near the southern border of the state.

Austin, Texas

318 Senators 1888m *Texas (ind.)*. Team moved to San Antonio July 4; 1889, *Texas (ind.)*; 1890x *Texas (ind.)*. Team disbanded June 2; 1895x *Texas-Southern (ind.)*; 1896–98 *Texas-Southern (ind.)*; 1899x *Texas (ind.)* Circuit and club disbanded July 5; 1905x *Texas (D)*. Team disbanded June 6; 1906 *South Texas (C)*; 1907–08 *Texas (C)*; 1911–14 *Texas (B)*; 1925–26 *Texas Assn. (D)*; 1956–67 *Texas (AA)*. City, named after Texas founder Stephen Austin, has been the territorial and state capital of Texas since 1838. No Austin team was a farm club of any Washington Senator team.

319 Beavers 1895x *Texas-Southern (ind.)*. Team disbanded August 6. Beavers are indigenous to the nearby Colorado River. With manager Brennan McBride at the helm, newspapers called the players "Brennan McBride's Beavers."

320 Reps 1915m *Middle Texas (D)*. Team moved to Taylor May 1 when Austin experienced springtime rainstorms that caused flooding. Tag was a spin-off from Senators. Although the team was first known as **Representatives**, newspapers shortened the name to "Reps" for headlines, i.e. "Reps edge Governors, 4–3."

321 Black Senators 1919 *Negro Texas (ind.)*. Moniker was a spin-off from the Austin Senators of the Texas League.

322 Rangers 1923–24 *Texas Assn. (D)*. In honor of the Texas Rangers, who have patrolled Texas since 1840. With manager Rankin Johnson at the helm in 1923, newspapers called the players "Rankin's Rangers." Name was retained under three other managers through 1924.

323 Pioneers 1947–55 *Big State (B)*. American pioneers started settling the region in 1835 while it was still part of Mexico. Pioneer families poured into Texas, allowing it to secede from Mexico in 1838 and then join the United States in 1849.

Avigliano, Potenza, Italy

324 Avigliano Baseball 2007 *Italian A1 (ind.)*. This team had no nickname. Most professional Italian baseball teams use the name of their corporate sponsors in their title.

Avon, Ohio

325 Lake Erie Crushers 2009 to date *Frontier (ind.)*. Granite and coal from nearby mines are sent to factories that utilize rock "crushers" to pulverize these minerals. Avon is located near Lake Erie — hence, the regional name.

Ayden, North Carolina

326 Aces 1937–38 *Coastal Plain (D)*. In the era 1920–40 barnstorming air-shows crisscrossed the United States featuring skydiving, aerial stunts and parachuting performed by "air aces." The Wright Brothers also flew at Kitty Hawk, North Carolina, in December 1903. Actually, "ace" derives from card games and came to baseball to describe famous pitcher Asa "Ace" Brainard of the 1869 Cincinnati Red Stockings. Name evolved to refer to any formidable pitcher who won a lot of games with "great stuff," i.e. an array of hard-to-hit pitches.

Babylon, New York

327 Athletics 1885 *Independent Negro team*. Players worked as waiters at the Argyle Hotel in Babylon, New York. Philadelphia Athletics had recently won a pennant in 1883, and the very first black team decided to emulate them with a name alliterative to "Argyle."

328 Cuban Giants 1886, 1888, 1893–99 *Independent Negro team*. Team played home games in Ansonia (CT) in 1889, 1891 and Harrisburg (PA) in 1890, as well as Hoboken-Trenton 1886–89. This team was the first of the black teams to use an adjective-noun double name including "Giants." Management chose "Giants" to convince black fans that the team was a winner like the NL New York Giants. "Cuban" was added to give white fans the impression that the players were Cubans rather than American blacks in order to dilute the inevitable racial prejudice of the era. One newspaper, wise to the ruse, commented: "The Giants are too dark-skinned for Cubans, and, rather short for Giants, but they played well."

Bainbridge, Georgia

329 Commodores 1916–17x *Dixie (D)*. Team disbanded July 4, 1917, because of U.S. entry into World War I. City was named in honor of Commodore William Bainbridge, who led the U.S. Navy in battle against the British Royal Navy during the War of 1812.

Baker, Oregon
(known as Baker City in 1891)

330 Baker Base Ball Club 1891 *Pacific Interstate (ind.)*. Team had no nickname.

331 Nuggets 1908x *Inland Empire (D)*. Circuit and team disbanded July 12 because of a dangerous heat wave. Gold was discovered at Griffins Creek, Oregon, in 1861, giving rise to the "Second Gold Rush."

332 Gold Diggers 1913x *Western Tri-State (D)*. Team disbanded July 23. Moniker was a spin-off from Nuggets.

333 Miners 1914 *Western Tri-State (D)*. Moniker was a spin-off from Gold Diggers.

334 Kubs 1914 *Western Tri-State (D)*. Team had numerous young players, i.e., "cubs," and the name was changed to "Kubs" to make it alliterative to Baker. There are a lot of bears in Oregon.

Bakersfield, California

335 Bakersfield Base Ball Club 1890–91 *California Winter (W)*. Team had no nickname.

336 Drillers 1910x *San Joaquin Valley (D)*. When league disbanded on September 5, the team, in first place at the time, was awarded the pennant. Nearby oil fields, discovered in 1889, transport crude oil to petrochemical plants. With manager Brick Devereaux at the helm, newspapers called the players "Devereaux's Drillers."

337 Bees 1929x *California State (D)*. Team and circuit disbanded June 17. Nearby honey bee farms ship raw honey to food processing plants. Because of its warm winter climate, California's honey bee farms were successful.

338 Badgers 1941–42 *California (C)*. Circuit and team disbanded June 28, 1942, because of U.S. entry into World War II. The North American badger is found in California. With manager Jack Colbern at the helm in 1942, newspapers called the players "Jack Colbern's Badgers."

339 Indians 1946–55 *California (C)*. Team was a farm club of the Cleveland Indians.

340 Boosters 1956 *California (C)*. The 1956 club was refinanced by a "booster club" of local businessmen.

341 Bears 1957–62 *California (C)*; 1963–67 *California (A)*. The "California Golden Bear" is the state animal and symbol of California.

342 Dodgers 1968–75 *California (A)*; 1984–94 *California (A)*. These teams were farm clubs of the Los Angeles Dodgers.

343 Outlaws 1978–79 *California (A)*. Minor league teams that played as independents, with no big league parent clubs, were sometimes known as "Outlaws." The moniker of "outlaws," in baseball, hearkens back to the days of "outlaw leagues" of the nineteenth century and the first 20 years of the twentieth century. The Baseball Anti-Trust Law of 1922 pretty much put an end to outlaw leagues. Even today's independent leagues cooperate with major league baseball. In the nineteenth century, Bakersfield was plagued by outlaws, bandits, and train robbers.

344 Mariners 1982–83 *California (A)*. Team was a farm club of the Seattle Mariners.

345 Blaze 1995 to date *California (A)*. Every summer dry trees in the San Joaquin Valley ignite, causing brush fires. Newspapers like this alliterative and short moniker. Singular nicknames, which were popularized by the 1974–75 World Football League, are used by some sports teams.

Balboa, Panama

346 Los Cerveceros de Balboa 1951–52–52–53 *Liga de Panama (W)*; 1956–57–67–68 *Liga de Panama (W)*. The owner of these teams was La Cerveceria de Balboa — a beer brewery. The company was named after the city of Balboa. Cerveza is Spanish for beer. In this era, many Latin American teams were sponsored by beer, liquor and tobacco companies.

Ballard, Washington

347 Colts m1914 *Northwestern (B)*. Team started season as the Portland (OR) Colts (because of many young players on the team). When the team moved to Ballard July 20, the nickname was retained. With manager R.L. "Nick" Williams at the helm, newspapers called the players "Nick's Colts."

348 Pippins m1914 *Northwestern (B)*. Team began season in Portland (OR) and moved to Ballard July 20. Nearby apple orchards grow the famous "Pippin" apple.

Ballinger, Texas

349 Bearcats m1921 *West Texas (D)*. Team started season in Mineral Springs (TX) and moved to Ballinger May 19; 1929 *West Texas (D)*. The 1921 team adopted the mascot of Sam Houston State University, which was a bearcat. The North American wolverine is also known as a bearcat. However, the real bearcats are civet-like animals found in Asia. The wolverine is a weasel-like creature. With manager Bill Dean at the helm in 1929, newspapers called the players "Bill Dean's Bearcats."

350 Cats 1947–50 *Longhorn (D)*. A newspaper-friendly contraction of the weasel-like "Bearcats," the new moniker referred to the American mountain lion, which is a decidedly feline creature.

351 Eagles m1953x *Longhorn (C)*. The team started the season in Lamesa (TX) and moved to Ballard June 3. Team represented Winters (TX) as well as Ballinger and went by the name of the Winters-Ballinger Eagles, although home games were played in Ballinger. Team disbanded June 7. The team was a farm club of the Texas League Dallas Eagles.

352 Westerners 1956–57 *Southwestern (B)*. Texas was part of the "Old West," and the "Wild West."

Baltimore, Maryland

353 Maryland Baseball Club 1870 *Independent team*; 1873 *National Assn. (M)*. Team disbanded July 11; 1881 *Eastern Assn. (M)*. These teams represented the State of Maryland. They were also called the "Marylands."

354 Lord Baltimore 1872–74 *National Assn. (M)*; 1881 *Eastern Assn. (M)*; 1882–89 *American Assn. (M)*; 1887x *National Colored (ind.)*. League disbanded May 23 and team barnstormed until disbanding September 10; 1890–91 *American Assn. (M)*; 1892–99 *National (M)*; 1901–02 *American (M)*. George Calvert, the "Lord of Baltimore" in England, established the Maryland colony in the seventeenth century. Maryland was ruled by succeeding "Lords of Baltimore" until 1776. Plural was "Lord Baltimores." The terms "Lord Baltimore" and "Lord Baltimores" was generic for all Baltimore professional baseball teams for the period 1870–1910.

355 Canaries 1872–74 *National Assn. (M)*; 1882 *American Assn. (M)*; 1901–02 *American (M)*. Players on these teams wore canary yellow jerseys and striped black and canary yellow hose.

356 Yellow Stockings 1872–74 *National Assn. (M)*. Players wore canary yellow and black striped hose. Newspapers shortened it to **Yellow Legs.**

357 Mustard Legs 1872–74 *National Assn. (M)*. Players wore canary yellow and black striped hose. Some fans thought the color was less canary yellow and more mustard yellow.

358 Green Stockings 1880x *National Assn. (M)*. Team disbanded June 5. Players wore green hose. Newspapers shortened the name to **Green Legs.**

359 Martyrs 1882 *American Assn. (M)*. Under manager Harry Myer, the 1882 club finished sixth and last with a 19–54 record. Disgruntled Baltimore fans likened the team, which was often slaughtered by opposing teams to the tune of 8–1 and 10–2 scores, with the Christian "martyrs" who were thrown to the lions in the Coliseum in Ancient Rome, hence the tag "Myer's Martyrs."

360 Lambs 1882 *American Assn. (M)*. A spin-off from "Martyrs," fans likened the players to "lambs to the slaughter" as the team lost 54 of 73 games to finish sixth and last in its inaugural season.

361 Orioles 1883–89 *American Assn. (M)*; 1890 *Atlantic Assn. (ind.)*. Team jumped to the AA August 3; m1890–91 *American Assn. (M)*. Team jumped from the Atlantic League to the AA August 3; 1892–99 *National (M)*; 1901–02 *American (M)*; 1903–07 *Eastern (A)*;

1908–45 *International (AA)*; 1946–53 *International (AAA)*; 1954 to date *American (M)*. The 1883 team played in Oriole Baseball Park, which had been named in honor of Oriole District Park, which, in turn, was named in honor of the annual Oriole Parade—a type of Mardi Gras festival held in Baltimore each autumn. The name, in use for 129 years now, has become traditional. Many scientists believe the true "Baltimore oriole" went extinct in the eighteenth century.

362 Birds 1883–89 *American Assn. (M)*; 1890m *Atlantic Assn. (ind.)*. Team switched to AA August 3; m1890–91 *American Assn. (M)*. Team jumped to the AA from the Atlantic League August 3; 1892–99 *National (M)*; 1901–02 *American (M)*; 1903–11 *Eastern (A)*; 1912–45 *International (AA)*; 1946–53 *International (AAA)*; 1954 to date *American (M)*. Used synonymously with "Orioles" since 1883, it has been a favorite of newspapers for 129 years.

363 Birdlings 1883–89 *American Assn. (M)*. Used alternately with "Birds," the moniker fell out of favor by 1890 because newspapers didn't like its nine-letter length.

364 Monumental 1884x *Eastern (ind.)*. Team disbanded May 20; 1884 *Union Assn. (M)*. Baltimore is known as the "Monumental City" because of its Revolutionary War, War of 1812, Mexican-American War and Civil War monuments. The UA team played its home games in Monumental Park. Moniker was also pluralized as **Monumentals.**

365 Baseball's Worst Hitters Ever 1886. The eighth and last place Orioles (48 won, 83 lost) had a team BA of only .204—lowest in major league history. Tag was coined by baseball author Marshall Wright in his book *The Nineteenth Century Baseball Encyclopedia*.

366 Sparrows 1892–93 *National (M)*. The sparrow is a bird noted for its delicate bones. Hence, the 1892–93 Orioles, who had been stripped of their best players by NL owners upon joining the National League from the defunct American Association, were known these two seasons by their fans as the "Sparrows," a spin-off from the more robust Orioles, as their team lost 101 games in 1892 and 70 more games in 1893 for 12th and eighth place finishes, respectively.

367 Hanlon's Tricksters 1892–98 *National (M)*. With manager Ned Hanlon at the helm of the team for seven years (1892–98), he greatly influenced his players to engage in "trick plays," i.e., clever plays, some that were legal but unethical and others that were illegal but hard to enforce. Examples are the "Hidden Ball" trick, the "Spit Ball," the "Baltimore Chop" and the "Hit and Run." Name was coined by editor J. Raymond "Jim" Price in *Baseball Magazine* 1910.

368 Old Orioles 1892–99 *National (M)*. When ex-player and manager Ned Hanlon was felled by a stroke while in a tavern in 1934, he told ambulance attendants on his way to the hospital: "I'm an 'Old Oriole.' I'm too tough to die!" The words were quoted by *New York Times* reporter Joe Kiernan. Baseball writer Fred Lieb coined the name in 1909 in *Baseball Magazine*. The moniker "Old Oriole" applies to any member of the Baltimore National League club of 1892–99.

369 Oysterville 1892–99 *National (M)*. Baltimore has been known as "Oysterville" since the eighteenth century because it has been a major seafood port for fish, crab, shrimp and oysters. "Oysterville" meant both the city of Baltimore and the Baltimore baseball team.

370 Rowdy Orioles 1892–99 *National (M)*. The Baltimore players of the period 1892–99 not only won games on talent but also by "rough play," i.e., sliding with spikes up, "bean balls," barreling over the catcher, and the "brush-back" pitch. The moniker is quite appropriate because an inhabitant of Baltimore is historically known as a "rowdy." Name probably developed in 1892 because the catcher-manager was "Dirty Ned" Hanlon, who got his nickname for being a "dirty player. Name was coined by baseball writer Fred Lieb and quoted by author Steven Riess.

371 Soaring Birds 1894–97 *National (M).* Name was coined by baseball author Michael Gesker in praise of the franchise's three pennants, two Temple Cup titles and six straight winning seasons for an overall .669 won-lost percentage over six seasons.

372 Orioles Juggernaut 1894–99 *National (M).* Tag was coined by baseball author Ted Patterson to celebrate the Orioles' three pennants and two Temple Cup titles in four seasons. The Orioles, in six consecutive winning seasons, posted a record of 538–276 for a stellar .669 won-lost percentage, which would correspond to six straight seasons of 108–54.

373 Battling Orioles 1894–99 *National (M).* Tag was used in the 1924 silent film *The Battling Orioles,* which was a movie about the "Old Orioles" of the Gay Nineties (1892–99).

374 Diamond Thieves 1894–99 *National (M).* Not only did the Orioles "steal" victories with trick plays and deceptive strategy, they also stole 1,790 bases in six seasons, leading the NL in steals 1896–99. Name was coined by author Dennis Purdy.

375 Masters of Inside Baseball 1894–99 *National (M).* The Orioles of the Gay Nineties also invented what today is known as "small ball" or "manufacturing a run, " i.e., the "hit and run," sacrifice bunts, drag bunts, tagging up on a sacrifice fly and hitting to the opposite field. Name was coined by baseball author Fred Lieb.

376 The Team That Gave Birth to Modern Baseball 1894–99 *National (M).* The Orioles perfected such strategies as the bunt, drag bunt, sacrifice bunt, hit and run, sacrifice fly, going with the pitch, hitting to the opposite field, the relay throw, pick-off play, playing the infield up, the brush-back pitch, the spitball and intentional walks. Burt Solomon wrote a book on the Orioles with this tag as its title.

377 Rough 'n Resourceful Orioles 1894–99 *National (M).* Tag was coined by *New York Times* reporter Joe Kiernan in 1934. Name was also quoted in a book about the Orioles by author Jack Kavanaugh.

378 Scrappy Orioles 1894–99 *National (M).* In a review of the 1924 silent movie *The Battling Orioles,* a film about the Old Orioles of the Gay Nineties, the American Film Institute used the term "Scrappy Orioles."

379 Roughnecks 1899 *National (M).* Spin-off from "rowdy," the name has been applied to manager John McGraw's 1899 NL Baltimore Orioles and his AL 1901–02 Baltimore Orioles. McGraw, one of the 1890s "Rowdy Orioles" players, encouraged his teammates to play "rough." "Roughneck" originated as slang for cowboys who needed to be rugged and tough, with a hard head and a strong neck, to endure falls and tumbles from their horses or off a bucking bronco. Tag was coined by baseball author Fred Lieb. Aka **Roughneck Orioles.**

380 Giants 1899 *Independent Negro team;* 1916–19 *Independent Negro team.* Black baseball teams in the nineteenth century lionized the glamorous and wealthy New York Giants.

381 Baltfeds 1914 *Federal (M).* The Federal League owners tried to advertise its teams with "combined" names such as the Baltfeds, Brookfeds, Buffeds, Chifeds, Hoosier-Feds, Pittfeds, and Sloufeds. The tags were amalgams of the city name and "federals." Fans and newspapers didn't take to any of these monikers, and, by 1915, they had all been dropped by the teams in the circuit.

382 Terrapins 1915 *Federal (M).* The terrapin is a sea turtle that swims the waters of the Atlantic coast. The moniker is used today by the athletic teams of the University of Maryland. Newspapers shortened the name to **Terps.**

383 Black Sox 1916–22 *Independent Negro team;* 1923–28x *Eastern Colored (M).* Circuit and team disbanded in mid-season 1928; *American Negro (M);* 1932 *East-West (M);* 1933x *Negro National (M).* Circuit and team disbanded in mid-season. The players wore black stirrups.

384 Stars 1930 *Independent Negro team.* The "Star-Spangled Banner"— the American national anthem — was written in Baltimore by Francis Scott Key during the War of 1812.

385 Pirates 1932–33 *Independent Negro team.* Players wore black-trim uniforms. Pirates sailed the coast of Maryland in the sixteenth and seventeenth centuries.

386 Greys (also **Grays**) 1932–42. Players wore gray uniforms.

387 Silver Moons 1934 *Independent Negro team.* Team represented Baltimore early in the season, but low attendance forced the team out onto extended road trips. Team had been known as the Pirates in 1933, but management dressed players in silver trim that glistened under the lights, and chose "Silver Moons" because the team played many night games.

388 Elite Giants 1938–48 *Negro National (M);* 1940–41 *Southern California (W);* 1943–44 *Southern California (W).* This circuit played all its games in Los Angeles (CA); 1949–52 *Negro American (ind.).* Since about 1890, many black teams have employed the "double name" style using the ever-popular Giants as the noun preceded by a descriptive adjective, i.e., American Giants, Bacharach Giants, Lincoln Giants, Royal Giants and, for this team — Elite Giants.

389 O's 1954 to date *American (M).* A derivation from the old Philadelphia A's newspaper contraction, it is sometimes used by space-conscious newspaper editors, especially in headlines, e.g., "O's beat Yanks."

390 Baby Birds 1954–59 *American (M).* The Oriole teams of 1954–59 were stocked with many young and promising players, e.g., third baseman Brooks Robinson and pitchers Milt Pappas, Steve Barber and Wally Bunker.

391 Orange Birds 1954–59 *American (M).* Tag was a spin-off from the "Redbirds" moniker, used as an alternate by the NL St. Louis Cardinals. Name was used only sporadically, along with the much more popular "Birds." The St. Louis Nationals are never known as the "Birds"— only "Redbirds"— which made the Orange Birds designation awkward and unnecessary by 1960.

392 Paul Richards' Flock 1955–61 *American (M).* Paul Richards, a former catcher who played for the IL Orioles in the 1920s, managed the AL Orioles for seven years (1955–61). The moniker was an obvious spin-off from Birds.

393 O-O-Orioles 1966 *American (M).* When manager **Hank Bauer's Birds** won the city's first big league pennant since 1896, and then won the 1966 World Series in a four-game sweep over the L.A. Dodgers, Baltimore newspapers chortled "O-O-Orioles!" Bauer, in a spin-off from the New York Mets, who were negatively "amazing," called his players the **Amazing Orioles.**

394 Rare Birds 1966 *American (M).* Coined by baseball authors Gary Gillette and Pete Palmer, the moniker describes the prized birds, which won their first AL pennant by a comfortable nine-game margin over Minnesota, and then stunned the favored Los Angeles Dodgers in a 4–0 sweep in the 1966 World Series. The pennant was "rare" because Baltimoreans had waited 70 years for their first big league flag since the 1894–97 National League Baltimore Orioles won three pennants. A "rare bird" refers to a valuable bird, prized for its beauty and scarcity.

395 Big Bad Birds 1969–71 *American (M).* The Orioles, in 1969–71, won three straight American League pennants. Led by sluggers John "Boog" Powell, Frank Robinson and Brooks Robinson and pitchers Jim Palmer, Dave McNally and Mike Cuellar, the Orioles won the 1970 World Series. In 1971, the "Big Bad Birds" won their third straight AL pennant on the arms of *four* 20-game winners, i.e., Cuellar, McNally, Palmer and Pat Dobson.

396 High Flying Orioles 1979, 1983 *American (M).* The Orioles won two AL pennants (1979, 1983) and a World Series title (1983) with the bats of Ken Singleton, John Lowenstein, Eddie Murray, Cal

Ripken and Al Bumbry, and, the hurling arms of Mike Flannagan, Scott MacGregor, Mark Boddicker and Tippy Martinez.

397 Low Flying Orioles 1988 *American (M)*. The 1988 Orioles lost their first 21 games to set a major league record for most consecutive losses starting a season. They eventually finished with a 54–107 record. Baltimore fans berated the players with such nicknames as **Zer-O's**, **Spaghetti-O's** (after a popular brand of canned spaghetti), **Murmurers' Row** (the opposite of the New York Yankees' "Murderers' Row" of the 1920s) and the highly appropriate avian moniker of **Pigeons.**

398 Jurassic Park Orioles 1995–97 *American (M)*. Tag was a gimmick from the hit movie that was directed by Steven Spielberg about dinosaurs—"Jurassic Park." The 1995–97 Orioles, despite making the playoffs twice, had at least eighteen players age 30 or older each year.

Bangor, Maine

399 Millionaires 1894–96 *New England (ind.)*. Captain David Ingram, an English sea captain, guided the first known European ship up the Penobscot River in 1589. When he and his crew later returned to England, they spun a wild tale of a "Lost City of Gold," much like Spanish explorers who dreamed up the "Seven Cities of Gold" in Mexico. These "Golden Cities" were just tall tales.

400 Lumberjacks 1894–96 *New England (ind.)*; 1897 *Maine State*; 2003–04 *Northeast (ind.)*. Maine's forests provide lumber for Bangor's wood products factories. Bangor has been known since the 1870s as the "Lumber City" and the "Greatest Lumber Market in the World."

401 White Sox 1907 *Maine State (D)*. Players wore white stirrups over white sanitary hose. Team had no affiliation with the Chicago White Sox.

402 Maroons 1913x *New Brunswick–Maine (D)*. Team and league disbanded August 23. With George Magoon as manager, team dressed its players in maroon trim, and became known in the newspapers as "Magoon's Maroons."

403 Blue Ox 1996–97 *Northeast (ind.)*. The legendary lumberjack of the timberlands of the American Northeast, Paul Bunyon had as his sidekick and pet a blue ox named "Babe."

Bangor, Pennsylvania

404 Slate-pickers 1949 *North Atlantic (D)*. Mines in the region transport slate to processing factories. Slate is a type of soft rock that can be cut into thin slices suitable for making roof tiles. Deposits of slate are found in the region. Newspapers shortened name to **Pickers.**

Bangor-Berwick, Pennsylvania

405 Slaters 1950 *North Atlantic (D)*. Bangor Slate Pickers of 1949 became the Bangor-Berwick "Slaters" in 1950. A "slater" is not only a miner who drills for this rock but also a craftsman who cuts the slate into tiles. Newspapers preferred this shorter moniker.

406 Bangors 1950 *North Atlantic (D)*. The addition of an "s" to a city name to pluralize it was an old nineteenth-century newspaper style, i.e., Bostons, Chicagos and New Yorks.

Barberton, Ohio

407 Magic Citys 1905x *Ohio–Pennsylvania (C)*. Team disbanded May 20. Barberton became the "Magic City" because of its rapid industrial growth.

Barcelona, Anzoategui, Venezuela

408 Oriente de Anzoategui 1956–57–58–59 *Liga Venezolana (W)*; 1960–61 *Liga Venezolana (W)*; 1963–64 *Liga Venezolana (W)*. Barcelona is located in eastern Venezuela. Oriente in English means "Eastern." These teams went by the state name of "Oriente de Anzoategui."

409 Caribes de Anzoategui 1991–92 to date *Liga Venezolana (W)*. Barcelona is located on the coast of the Caribbean Sea. Caribe is Spanish for Caribbean.

Barquismeto, Lara, Venezuela

410 Cardenales de Lara 1961–62–63–64 *Liga Occidental (W)*; 1965–66 to date *Liga Venezolana (W)*. Team goes by the state name of "Los Cardenales de Lara." Cardinals are found in Venezuela, so the team dressed the players in Cardinal red–trim uniforms and hose.

Barranquilla, Atlantico, Colombia

411 Armco 1948–49 *Liga Colombiana (W)*. Armco Iron Works owned the team.

412 Filtta 1948–52 *Liga Colombiana (W)*. Filtta Silk Company owned the team.

413 Cerveza 1950–51 *Liga Colombiana (W)*; 1981–82–83–84 *Colombian (W)*. Cerveceria Aguila owned the team. Cerveza is Spanish for beer. Cerveceria is Spanish for brewery. Aguila is Spanish for eagle. "Eagle" is a popular name for Latin American sports teams. In the 1940s and 1950s numerous Latin American professional baseball teams were owned by beer, liquor and tobacco companies.

414 Hit 1952 *Liga Colombiana (W)*. Spanish-speaking fans eagerly absorbed English-language baseball terms such as beisbol, jonron (home run), and hit. There is also a Spanish-language baseball magazine entitled *Hit!* The team went by the English "Hit" and not by the Spanish equivalent "Batazo." Spanish-speaking fans often shout both "batazo!" and "hit!" when urging a batter to get a base hit.

415 Willard 1953–54–57–58 *Liga Colombiana (W)*. 1979–80–82–83 *Colombian (W)*. Willard International Batteries owned the team.

416 Vanytor 1953–54–57–58 *Liga Colombiana (W)*. Vanytor Confection Company owned the team.

417 Olimpica 1979–80–80–81 *Liga Colombiana (W)*. "Olympics" (Olimpica in Spanish), based on the ancient Greek and modern (since 1898) Olympic Games, has been a popular nickname for athletic teams since the nineteenth century, not only in English-speaking countries, but also in Romance-language countries.

418 Café Universal 1980–81–83–84 *Liga Colombiana (W)*. Café Universal owned the team.

419 Caimanes 1984–85 *Liga Colombiana (W)*; 1999–2000 *Colombian (W)*; 2001–02 to date *Colombian (W)*. Alligators inhabit the nearby Magdalena River. Liga Colombiana in Spanish.

420 Vaqueros 1999–200 *Liga Colombiana (W)*. Team chose the name to maximize its rivalry with the Cartagena "Indians." The word "vaquero" is Spanish for "cowboy."

421 Electricos 2001–02–02–03 *Liga Colombiana (W)*. Hydro-electric plants along the Magdalena river power the city.

422 Aguilas 2002–03 *Liga Colombiana (W)*. Fan poll chose "Las Aguilas." Eagles (aguilas in Spanish) are found throughout the Americas. Cerveceria Aguila did not own this team.

423 Toros 2003–04 *Liga Colombiana (W)*. The three most popular sports in Colombia are: soccer, baseball and bull-fighting. Team owner Coolechera, a milk and dairy company, altered the milk cow image to the masculine "Toros." Moniker is pleasantly short for newspapers in both English and Spanish.

Bartlesville, Oklahoma

424 Indians 1906 *Kansas State (D)*. Although more well known as the "Sooner State," Oklahoma is also known as the "Indian State." The region was home to the Comanche, Cheyenne, Pawnee and Wichita tribes. Team was not a farm club of the Cleveland Indians, as there was no farm system yet.

425 Boosters 1907 *Oklahoma–Arkansas–Kansas (D)*; 1908 *Oklahoma–Kansas (D)*; 1909–10x *Western Assn. (C)*. Team disbanded July 31, 1910. m1924 *Western Assn. (C)*. After the Bearcats left town in mid-season, the Joplin (MO) club moved here June 16. Starting around 1900, a team that was in pennant contention was called "Boosters" because their excited fans would form a "booster club" to cheer the players on to the flag. Team won 1907 OAK flag with a record of 83–51, nine games in front. With Frank Barbour as 1907 manager, newspapers called the players "Barbour's Boosters." Harry Truby took over in 1908 and the name became "Truby's Boosters." Jake Beckley took over in 1910, making the name "Beckley's Boosters."

426 Braves 1921 *Southwestern (D)*. Tag was a spin-off from the 1906 Indians.

427 Grays 1922 *Southwestern (D)*. Player wore gray trim uniforms. With field manager Ned Pettigrew at the helm, local newspapers called the team "Pettigrew's Grays." In this era, the home team tended to wear white uniforms while the road team wore gray uniforms.

428 Bearcats 1923–24m *Southwestern (C)*. Team moved to Ardmore (TX) June 8. "Bearcat" is an American slang used for wolverines—a weasel-like creature of North America. The true bearcat is a civet-like creature in Asia. With manager Ted Waring at the helm, newspapers called the players "Waring's Bearcats."

429 Bronchos 1931–32 *Western Assn. (C)*; m1933 *Western (C)*. Hutchinson (KS) moved to Bartlesville July 7. The 1932 team had disbanded. Rodeos and ranches in Oklahoma are noted for their "Buckin' Broncos." In 1932 the spelling was changed to **Broncos**.

430 Reds 1934–35 *Western Assn. (C)*. Team was a farm club of the Cincinnati Reds.

431 Mustangs 1936 *Western Assn. (C)*. With manager Bob Morrow at the helm, newspapers called the players "Morrow's Mustangs." Wild mustangs inhabit Oklahoma and Texas. By 1970, the mustang was in danger of extinction, but conservation groups have promoted a rise in their population throughout the Southwestern United States.

432 Bucs 1936 *Western Assn. (C)*; 1948–52m *Kansas–Oklahoma–Missouri (D)*. Team moved to Pittsburgh (KS) July 7. The 1936 team had a loose affiliation with the Pittsburgh Pirates. A newspaper friendly tag, it was a spin-off from Pirates. The 1948 team was formally the "Pirates," but newspapers often shortened it to "Bucs."

433 Blues 1937 *Western Assn. (C)*. This team was farm club of the New York Yankees, whose blue pinstripe uniform style and blue stirrups was adopted for the Bartlesville players.

434 Chiefs 1938 *Western Assn. (C)*. Cherokee, Choctaw and many other tribes inhabited Oklahoma for hundreds of years. Oklahoma is known as the "Indian State."

435 Oilers 1946–47 *Kansas–Oklahoma–Missouri (D)*. In addition to its nearby oil and gas wells, the city manufactures oil-field equipment and has laboratories for oil research.

436 Pirates 1948–52m *Kansas–Oklahoma–Missouri (D)*. Team moved to Pittsburgh (KS) July 7. Team was a farm club of the Pittsburgh Pirates, known as the "Pirates" and the "Bucs."

Bartlett, Texas

437 Bartlett Baseball Club 1914–15 *Middle Texas (D)*. Team had no nickname.

Bartow–Winter Haven, Polk, Florida

438 Polkers 1919 *Florida State (D)*. Team represented two cities going by the name Bartow–Winter Haven Polkers; 1920 *Florida State (D)*. Team represented only Bartow, going by the name of Bartow Polkers. Cities of Bartow and Winter Haven are located in Polk County.

Bassano, Alberta, Canada

439 Boosters 1912 *Western Canada (D)*. Typical to this era, at season's start fans formed a "booster" club, which accrued to the team as a nickname. However, the team struggled to a mediocre 45–46 record.

Bassett, Virginia

440 Furniture-makers 1935–40 *Bi-State (D)*. Bassett is known as "The Furniture City" because of its numerous furniture manufacturers.

441 Statesmen m1950 *Blue Ridge (D)*. Team began season as the Wytheville (VA) Statesmen. When a polio epidemic broke out in the area, the team moved to Bassett July 27 and retained the nickname.

Batavia, New York

442 Red Stockings 1897 *New York State (ind.)*. Players wore red hose. Newspapers shortened the name to **Redlegs** and **Reds**.

443 Clippers 1939–53 *Pennsylvania–Ohio–New York (PONY). (D)*; 1988–97 *New York–Pennsylvania (A)*. With manager William Buckley at the helm, newspapers called the players "Buckley's Clippers." Although Buckley left the team after the 1939 season, fans and newspapers liked the name so much that it became permanent for this franchise. Moniker was appropriate because since the 1930s cargo trucks, traveling to and from Batavia, go "clipping along" Route 50 of the New York State Highway at a 60 mph "clip." The 1988 team revived the moniker.

444 Indians 1957–59 *New York–Pennsylvania (D)*. Team was a farm club of the Cleveland Indians.

445 Pirates 1961–62 *New York–Pennsylvania (D)*; 1963–65 *New York–Pennsylvania (A)*. Team was a farm club of the Pittsburgh Pirates.

446 Trojans 1966–87 *New York–Pennsylvania (A)*. Farm and construction tractors have been built in Batavia since the 1930s. The most famous brand is the hard-working "Trojan" tractor, which was introduced in 1950. These tractors were used by farms on the rich wetlands of the nearby Elbar River. The team had dropped "Pirates" because it played as an independent in 1966 before affiliating with the Philadelphia Phillies in 1967, but Batavia fans liked "Trojans" so much it was retained rather than calling the team the "Batavia Phillies."

447 Muck Dogs 1998 to date *New York–Pennsylvania (A)*. A "Muck Dog" is a type of tractor that can plow through sticky mud, i.e., "muck." Farmers use these tractors to negotiate the "muckland" mud of the nearby Tanawanda and Elbar rivers. Moniker was a spin-off from "Trojan Tractor," which was first manufactured in 1950. In the 1990s "Dogs" and "Cats," inspired, in part, by jazz and rap music, became popular monikers for professional sports teams. Team logo is an angry dog.

Batesville, Arkansas

448 White Sox 1936 *Northeast Arkansas (D)*; 1938 *Northeast Arkansas (D)*. Although not a formal farm club, the team in 1936 had

828 Methodical Maulers 1949–56 *National (M)*. The Dodgers led the NL in home runs in 1949 (152), 1950 (194), 1951 (198), 1952 (195), 1954 (208), 1955 (186), and 1955 (201). In 1956 the Dodgers team hit 179 home runs (good for third in the NL).

829 Boys of Summer 1949–56 *National (M)*. In 1978 baseball author Roger Kahn wrote a book about the Brooklyn Dodgers of the 1950s, which he entitled *The Boys of Summer*.

830 Artful Dodgers 1953 *National (M)*. Baseball writer Tom Meany's 1982 book on the 1953 Brooklyn Dodgers used the title of the Charles Dickens *Oliver Twist* character, Jack Dawkins, *The Artful Dodger*. The 1953 Dodgers were extremely "artful" as they blitzed through the National League pennant race that season, compiling a monster 105–49 record, hitting a league-high 208 home runs, and scoring 955 runs to finish 13 games ahead of second-place Milwaukee. An "Artful Dodger" is a person who lives on the street and hustles for money.

831 Blasters 1955 *National (M)*. The Dodgers won 105 games this season by blasting a major league-high 208 home runs and pounding out a .474 slugging percentage.

832 Cyclones 2001 to date *New York–Pennsylvania (A)*. Although cyclones sometimes lash the Atlantic coast as far north as New York, the team's name was selected after a Coney Island amusement park rollercoaster called the "Brooklyn Cyclone." Name was chosen in a fans' name the team contest. Other entries included Bums, Dodgers, Hot Dogs (i.e., the famous Coney Island Hot Dogs), Mets (the team's parent club) and Sweat Hogs.

Brownsville, Texas

833 Brownies 1910–11 *Southwest Texas (D)*. Moniker was used for newspaper headlines, i.e., "Brownies edge Pelicans, 4–3." The players wore brown-trim uniforms and stirrups. With manager S.H. Bell at the helm, newspapers called the players "Bell's Brownies."

834 Charros 1938 *Texas Valley (D)*; 1949–50 *Rio Grande Valley (D 1949, C 1950)*; 1951–53 *Gulf Coast (B)*. "Charro" (Charo in Spanish spelling) is the Spanish word for "rider" or "horseman." Since Brownsville is right at the U.S.-Mexican border with Matamoros, the moniker is appropriate. With manager Ed Conetchy at the helm in 1938, newspapers called the players "Conetchy's Charros."

835 Toros 2007 *Texas Winter (ind.)*. Name is appropriate because the Brownsville (TX)-Matamoras (MX) area sporting fans do attend bull fights. However, baseball is the more popular spectator sport.

Brunswick, Georgia

836 Brunswick Baseball Club m1906 *Georgia State (D)*. Team began the season in Columbus (GA) and moved to Brunswick June 25. Team had no nickname.

837 Pilots 1913 *Empire (D)*; 1914 *Georgia State (D)*; 1915x *(D)*. Team and league disbanded July 17. The FLAG League represented Florida, Louisiana, Alabama and Georgia. Pilot ships on the St. Andrew's Sound steer freighters into port and out to the Atlantic Ocean at Brunswick. With manager Bert Kite at the helm in 1914, newspapers called the players "Kite's Pilots." With four other managers at the helm, the name was retained through 1915.

838 Pirates 1951–56 *Georgia–Florida (D)*. Team was a farm club of the Pittsburgh Pirates.

839 Phillies m1957–58 *Georgia–Florida (D)*. Team began season in Moultrie (GA) and moved to Brunswick June 1. Team was a farm club of the Philadelphia Phillies.

840 Cardinals 1962–63 *Georgia–Florida (D)*. Team was a farm club of the St. Louis Cardinals.

Bryan, Texas

841 Bombers 1947–48 *Lone Star (C)*; 1949 *East Texas (C)*. During World War II Major Donald Bryan established Bryan Air Field here in 1942 as a training base for bomber pilots. The city of Bryan was named after Major William Bryan, who fought in the Texas Revolution of 1835–36. Donald Bryan is not a descendant of William. With field manager Jess Landrum at the helm in 1948, local newspapers called the players the alliterative "Landrum's Bombers."

842 Sports 1950x *East Texas (C)*. Team disbanded July 20, 1950. In the era 1925–55 minor league teams at a lower classification sometimes had a working agreement with minor league teams at a higher classification, i.e., the Class AA Texas League Shreveport Sports.

843 Majors 1953 *Big State (B)*. Major William Bryan fought in the Texas Revolution in 1835. The city of Bryan (TX) is named after him. Major Donald Bryan (see Bryan Bombers), no relation to William Bryan, established Bryan Air Force Base just outside of the city in 1942. With manager Clyde McDowell at the helm, team was called "McDowell's Majors."

844 Indians 1954m *Big State (B)*. Team moved to Del Rio (TX) July 28, 1954. Team was a farm club of the Cleveland Indians.

Bucyrus, Ohio

845 Bucks 1905 *Ohio–Pennsylvania (C)*. Although deer are common in Ohio, the moniker was more alliterative with the city name than anything else.

Buffalo, New York

846 Bisons 1877 *New York State (M)*; 1878 *International Association (M)*; 1879–85 *National (M)*; 1886–90 *International (ind.)*; 1890 *Players (M)*; 1891–98 *Eastern (ind.)*; 1899 *Western*; 1900 *American (ind,)*; 1901–11 *Eastern (ind. 1901, A 1902–11)*; 1912–70m *International (A 1912, AA 1913–45, AAA 1946 to date)*. Team moved to Winnipeg June 11; 1979–84 *Eastern (AA)*; 1985–97 *American Assn. (AAA)*; *International (AAA)* 1998 to date. Moniker is a spin-off from "buffalo." Bison are found in Asia and Africa while buffaloes are found in North America. An alternate nickname for the IL team, 1998 to date, is **The Herd**.

847 Buffern 1877 *New York State (M)*; 1878 *International Association (M)*; 1879–85 *National (M)*. nineteenth century slang for buffaloes. Name was used by newspapers only in 1877–78.

848 Zephyrs 1877 *New York State (M)*; 1878 *International Association (M)*; 1879–85 *National (M)*. Lazy summer breezes off nearby Lake Erie are known as "zephyrs."

849 Sluggers 1883–84 *National (M)*. In 1883 the Bisons led the NL with 1,058 hits, good for a league-high .284 team batting average. Bison first baseman Dan Brouthers led the NL in 14 offensive categories in 1883 and in another three in 1884. Brouthers led the NL in batting in 1883 with a .374 mark while teammate James "Orator" O'Rourke led the NL in 1884 with a .347 average. In 1883 Brouthers, O'Rourke, Dave Rowe, Deacon White and Hardy Richardson all batted over the .300 mark. The baseball term "slugger" was coined in 1865.

850 Giants 1883–84 *National (M)*. The Buffalo Bisons, led by the "Big Four" of Dan Brouthers, Hardy Richardson, Jim O'Rourke and Jack Rowe, had winning seasons, prompting Buffalo fans to call their teams "Giants"—which, in this era was a generic name for any winning baseball team.

851 Pan-Ams 1900 *American (ind.)*. Owner James Franklin named the team "Pan-Ams" in honor of the Pan-American Exhibition, a sort of World's Fair-type exhibition that was held in Buffalo in 1900–01, but it never caught on with the Buffalo fans. With manager Dan Shannon at the helm, newspapers called the players "Dan Shannon's Pan-Ams."

852 Buffeds 1914 *Federal (M)*. An amalgam of Buffalo and Federal as part of a league marketing gimmick—fans hated it.

853 Blues 1914–15 *Federal (M)*. Players wore blue-trim uniforms and blue stirrups. With Walter Blair at the helm in 1915, newspapers called the players "Blair's Blues."

854 Electrics 1915 *Federal (M)*. Hydroelectric plants in the city are powered by raging river streams from Niagara Falls. These first power plants were built in 1895, leading to Buffalo becoming known as the "Electric City of the Future." With managers Larry Schafly, Walter Blair and then Harry Lord at the helm in 1915, newspapers called the players "Larry Schafly's Electrics," then "Walter Blair's Electrics," and finally "Harry Lord's Electrics."

855 Colored Stars 1917 *Independent Negro team*. After "Giants" the moniker "Stars" was most used by black teams in this era. And in the same fashion, a descriptive adjective was used to precede the noun. The term "colored" was a fashionable alternate to "negro."

856 Pittsburgh Stars of Buffalo 1919–20 *Independent Negro team*. Several players on this 1919 Buffalo team, i.e., player-manager Grant "Home Run" Johnson, Phil Bradley and Chick Meade, had been members of the 1916 Pittsburgh Colored Stars. Therefore, player-manager Thompson called the team the "Pittsburgh Stars of Buffalo."

Burlington, Iowa

857 Babies 1889 *Central (ind.)*. In the era 1885–1905 expansion teams were known as "Baby" or "Babies" whether they had young "baby-face" players or not (they usually did).

858 Lightweights 1889 *Central (ind.)*. Team had many young players who were of slight build.

859 Hawkeyes 1890 *Illinois–Iowa (ind.)*; 1898 *Western Assn. (ind.)*. In the nineteenth century professional baseball teams often took a state nickname years before the more famous college football and basketball teams got around to doing the same. Iowa is the "Hawkeye State."

860 Spiders 1895 *Eastern Iowa (ind.)*. Team had a loose affiliation with the National League Cleveland Spiders. Slowly but surely, starting in 1884, major league teams were becoming aware of the benefits of maintaining a "farm team."

861 Tigers 1895 *Eastern Iowa (ind.)*. Team, already a loose affiliate of the major league Cleveland Spiders, also was a farm team of the Western League Detroit Tigers. Players wore Detroit-style black and orange striped hose.

862 Colts 1895–97 *Western Assn.(ind.)*. Team was a farm club of the Chicago Colts.

863 River Rats 1904 *Iowa State (D)*. In the nineteenth century the Mississippi River had become so polluted with garbage and trash that rats were routinely found swimming in its waters. It wasn't until after World War II that state governments finally got around to cleaning up the river. Contrary to popular belief, the United States in the nineteenth century was polluted by humans in whatever place they congregated in large numbers.

864 Flint Hills 1904 *Iowa State (D)*. The nearby Flint Hills were so named because it contains flint deposits and is the site of flint mines.

865 Pathfinders 1906–07 *Iowa State (D)*; 1908–16 *Central Assn. (D)*. Explorers, known as "Pathfinders," settled in this region in 1832, and founded a town here in 1836. City was also a disembarkation route for "pathfinding" explorers, pioneers and settlers headed west. Iowa is known as the "State Where the West Begins." When the team won pennants in 1906, 1909 and 1915, local newspapers praised the team as "pathfinders" for their fans to "the land of championships." Nearby Fort Madison was a disembarkation point for "pathfinders" desirous of protecting army patrols.

866 Cowboys 1911 *Central Assn. (D)*. Cowboys in the nineteenth century herded cattle drives from Texas to meat-processing centers here. "Cowboys" was a frequent term in this era for baseball players. Burlington newspapers came up with the moniker in its rivalry with fellow league member the Keokuk "Indians."

867 Bees 1924–32 *Mississippi Valley (D)*; 1954–61 *Three-I (B)*; 1962–82 *Midwest (D 1962, A 1963–81)*; 1993 to date *Midwest (A)*. Newspapers called the 1924 team the "B's" to save space because Burlington has ten letters. Newspapers soon switched to a mascot name, which became "Bees." Burlington is the "Orchard City" because of its fruit, especially apple tree orchards and nut trees, which attract bees in the summer. The 1963 team also was sometimes called "B's." In 1963 the use of the name was reinforced when the team became the farm club of the Kansas City Athletics, also known as the "A's," leading to an obvious spin-off.

868 Indians 1947–49 *Central Assn. (C)*. Team was a farm club of the Cleveland Indians.

869 Flints 1952–53 *Three-I (B)*. City was built near the Flint Hills. Flint mining has been ongoing in this region since about 1870.

870 Rangers 1982–85 *Midwest (A)*. Team was a farm club of the Texas Rangers.

871 Expos 1986–87 *Midwest (A)*. Team was a farm club of the Montreal Expos.

872 Braves 1988–90 *Midwest (A)*. Team was a farm club of the Atlanta Braves.

873 Astros 1991–92 *Midwest (A)*. Team was a farm club of the Houston Astros.

Burlington, North Carolina

874 Bees 1942 *Bi-State (D)*. Just as with Iowa's Burlington Bees, the four-letter moniker compensated for the ten-letter city name. Team had a loose affiliation with the Class B Piedmont League Charlotte Hornets. With manager Rube Wilson at the helm, newspapers called the players "Rube's Bees."

875 Indians 1958–64 *Carolina (B 1958–62, A 1963–64)*; 1986–2006 *Appalachian (R)*. Team was a farm club of the Cleveland Indians.

876 Senators 1965–71 *Carolina (A)*. Team was a farm club of the Washington Senators.

877 Rangers 1972 *Carolina (A)*. Team was a farm club of the Texas Rangers.

878 Royals 2007 to date *Appalachian (R)*. Team was a farm club of the Kansas City Royals.

Burlington, Vermont

879 Burlington Base Ball Club 1887 *Northeastern (ind.)*. Team had no nickname.

880 Athletics 1955 *Provincial (C)*. Team was a farm club of the Kansas City Athletics.

881 Vermont Reds 1984–87 *Eastern (AA)*. Team was farm club of the Cincinnati Reds.

882 Vermont Mariners 1988 *Eastern (AA)*. Team was farm club of the Seattle Mariners.

883 Vermont Expos 1994–2005 *New York–Pennsylvania (A)*. Team was a farm club of the Montreal Expos.

884 Vermont Lake Monsters 2006 to date *New York–Pennsylvania (A)*. Just as Loch Ness, Scotland, has "Nessie the Sea Serpent," nearby Lake Champlain has an alleged sea serpent in its waters. Some people are convinced it is a surviving plesiosaur.

Burlington-Elon-Graham, North Carolina

885 Bees 1945–51 *Carolina (C 1945–48, B 1949–51)*. The 1942 moniker was used again as the team regionalized representing three cities but retained the single-city title of "Burlington Bees." Home games were played in Burlington.

886 Pirates 1952–55 *Carolina (B)*. Team was a farm club of the Pittsburgh Pirates. Team was known as the Burlington-Elon-Graham Pirates, 1952–55.

Bussum, Netherlands (Holland)

887 Mr. Cocker HCAW 1999 to date *Holland Honkball (ind.)*. Team was founded by the Allen Weerbaar Soccer Club and is known in Dutch as the Honkball (baseball) Club Allen Weerbaar (H-C-A-W). The team is now owned by the Mr. Cocker chain of restaurants and cafes. The marketing logo of Mr. Cocker Restaurants and Cafes is a cocker spaniel but the team has had no logo or mascot nickname.

Butler, Pennsylvania

888 Bucks 1905 *Ohio–Pennsylvania (C)*. White-tail deer are found in Pennsylvania. The male of the species is a "buck." With manager Ward Buckminster at the helm, newspapers called the players "Buckminster's Bucks." Another team in the circuit this season, the Bucyrus Bucks, had no connection with this team. Their use of the same name was coincidental.

889 Butler Baseball Club 1906 *Pennsylvania–Ohio–Michigan (P.O.M.). (D)*; m1908m *Ohio–Pennsylvania (C)*. The 1908 team started season in Girard (PA) and moved to Butler May 19. Team then moved to Erie June 15 where they acquired the name "Sailors." These teams had no nickname.

890 White Sox 1907 *Western Pennsylvania (D)*. Butler's management outfitted the players in white stirrups in hopes that the 1906 world champion Chicago White Sox's success would rub off on them. Team was not a farm club of the Chicago White Sox.

891 Indians 1935 *Pennsylvania State Assn. (D)*. Team was a farm club of the Cleveland Indians.

892 Yankees 1936–42 *Pennsylvania State Assn. (D)*; 1946–48 *Middle Atlantic (C)*. These teams were farm clubs of the New York Yankees.

893 Tigers 1949–51 *Middle Atlantic (C)*. Team was a farm club of the Detroit Tigers.

Butte, Montana

894 Butte Base Ball Club 1892 *Montana (ind.)*. Team had no nickname.

895 Smoke-Eaters 1898–1900 *Montana State (ind.)*. Starting when an 1860 "Gold Rush" drew settlers here, firefighters have annually battled forest fires in the nearby Beaver Head–Deer Lodge Forest Preserve just northwest of the city. By 1925 these firefighters, who have to battle smoke-inhalation, became known by the term of admiration as the "Smoke-Eaters.

896 Miners 1902 *Pacific Northwest (B)*; 1903–04 *Pacific National (A 1903, B 1903)*; 1906–08 *Northwestern (B)*; 1909x *Inter-Mountain (D)*. Team disbanded July 18; 1911–14x *Union Assn. (D)*. Team August 5, 1914; 1916–17 *Northwestern (B)*. Butte was a boom town that was quickly built after gold, silver and copper deposits were discovered in the 1860s (gold) and the 1880s (silver and copper). Today, copper mines transport copper ore to processing factories.

897 Copper Kings 1978–85 *Pioneer (R)*; 1987–2000 *Pioneer (R)*. With the gold and silver deposits exhausted, copper mining has been Montana's leading industry since 1885. "Copper Kings" was a trendy spin-off from "Miners."

Cabimas, Zulia, Venezuela

898 Petroleros 1954–55–55–56 *Liga Occidental (W)*; 1957–58–59–60 *Liga Occidental (W)*. 1962–63–64–65; *Liga Venezolana* 1991–92–94–95. Oil wells in Cabimas State transport crude oil and natural gas to petrochemical plants. Los Petroleros means "Oilers" in English.

Caborca, Sonora, Mexico

899 Vaqueros 1968 *Mexican Rookie (R)*; 1969 *Liga Mexicana del Norte (A)*. Cowboys herd cattle to ranches in and around the city. "Los vaqueros" is Spanish for "cowboys."

900 Rojos 2006–08 *Liga del Norte de Sonora (W)*; 2009 to date *Liga del Norte de Mexico (ind.)*. Players wore red hose. Rojo is Spanish for "red."

Cadillac, Michigan

901 Chiefs 1910 *West Michigan (C)*; 1911–14 *Michigan State (D)*. Chief Pontiac of the Cadillac Indians led raids against English settlers in Michigan between 1760 and 1790.

902 Chieftains 1914 *Michigan State (D)*. Moniker was a spin-off from "Chiefs."

Caguas, Puerto Rico

903 Los Criollos de Caguas 1941–42 *Liga Puerto Riquena (W)*; 1945–46–95–96 *Liga Puerto Riquena (W)*; For the 1945–46 season the team name was changed to Los Criollos de Caguas y Guayamas as the club officially represented both cities. However, all home games were played in Caguas. For the period 1952–53 to 1960–61 the name was again Los Criollos de Caguas and Guayama but all home games were played in Caguas. 1994–95–2006–07 *Puerto Rican (W)*; 2008–09 to date *Puerto Rican (W)*. "Crillo" (Creole in English) means an inhabitant of Puerto Rico. Originally, the term meant "Spaniard." The league suspended operations for the 2007–08 season because of money problems but then resumed operations in 2008–09.

Cairo, Illinois

904 Egyptians 1897 *Central (ind.)*; 1903 *KITTY (D)*; 1911–14 *KITTY (D)*; 1922–24 *KITTY (D)*; 1946–48 *KITTY (D)*; Cairo, Illinois, is named after the Egyptian city of Cairo because the River Delta region of Southern Illinois closely resembles the Nile Delta Valley of Egypt. The KITTY League represented Kentucky, Illinois and Tennessee.

905 Champions 1904 *KITTY (D)*. The "Champions" moniker was applied to the team for the 1904 season but the team failed to repeat, finishing in second place, one game out. Since the team won 72 games in 1904 and was in the pennant chase to the last day, the nickname was retained. The fad of calling pennant winners "Champions" in defense of their title the following season soon became passé by the 1920s.

906 Giants 1905–06 *KITTY (D)*. When the team won the pennant in 1903 and then persisted in a tight pennant race in 1904, admiring newspapers said the team "played like giants." The moniker was applied to the 1905 team. With manager Dan McCarthy at the helm, newspapers called the players "Dan McCarthy's Giants."

907 Mud Wallopers 1905–06 *KITTY (D)*. Levees were built in the nineteenth century to protect the city from floods. During the flood season, Cairo residents would fill up sacks with mud and fling them into a pile, hence the term "mud-walloper." With manager Dan McCarthy at the helm, newspapers called the team "McCarthy's Mud-Wallopers."

908 Tadpoles 1905–06 *KITTY (D)*. Tadpole is yet another nickname of the era for young players. Others include Babes, Chicks, Colts, Cubs, Debutantes, Duckling, Foundlings, Innocents, Ponies and Yearlings. The name was appropriate because summer floods leave ponds teeming with tadpoles and frogs.

909 Dodgers 1949–50 *KITTY (D)*. Team was a farm club of the Brooklyn Dodgers.

Calais, New Brunswick– St. Stephen, Maine

910 Down-easters 1913 *New Brunswick–Maine (D)*. The team played its home games in Calais but was known by the name of Calais–St. Stephen Down-Easters while representing both cities. All home games were played in Calais. St. Stephens is located in Maine, right across the dividing St. Croix River. Ships sailing the coast of Maine were helped by a "Down East" wind, i.e., an easterly wind at their backs. Inhabitants of Maine soon became known as "Downeasters." With manager Ernest Doyle at the helm, newspapers called the players "Doyle's Downeasters."

Caldwell, Idaho

911 Treasure Valley Cubs 1964–71 *Pioneer (R)*. Team was known by the regional name of "Treasure Valley Cubs" from 1964 through 1966. Treasure Valley is the name given to the region around Caldwell because it has fertile land that produces a "treasure trove" of crops. The team was renamed the Caldwell Cubs in 1967 and had that title through the 1971 season. Team was a farm club of the Chicago Cubs.

Calexico, California

912 Calexico Baseball Club 1915–16 *Southern California (W)*. The team had no nickname.

Calgary, Alberta, Canada

913 Bronchos 1907 *Western Canada (D)*; 1910–14 *Western Canada (D)*; 1920–21 *Western Canada (B)*; 1922 *Western International (B)*. Alberta has had many horse ranches since the nineteenth century. Calgary is host to the annual rodeo known as the Calgary Stampede. With manager William Carney at the helm in 1910, newspapers called the players "Bill Carney's Bronchos." Newspapers often used the more modern spelling of **Broncos** and the shorter **Bronchs**.

914 Eye-Openers 1909 *Western Canada (C)*. "Eye-Openers" referred to players who "opened the eyes" of fans with thrilling plays on the field.

915 Cowboys 1909–14 *Western Canada (C)*. Tag was a spin-off from Bronchos. Nineteenth century Alberta Province was a lot like Texas—vast prairie ranges, ranches and cattle drives led by cowboys on horseback. With manager Charles "Spokane" Crist at the helm, newspapers called the players "Spokane's Cowboys," and "Crist's Cowboys."

916 Stampeders 1953–54x *Western International (A)*. Team disbanded June 21. Every year the "Calgary Stampede" is the highlight of the annual grand rodeo featuring horses stampeding along the Calgary Exhibition Grounds. The Canadian Football League's Calgary "Stampeders" have played Canadian professional football here since 1950.

917 Cardinals 1977–78 *Pioneer (A)*. Team was a farm club of the St. Louis Cardinals.

918 Expos 1979–84 *Pioneer (A)*. Team was a farm club of the Montreal Expos.

919 Cannons 1985–2002 *Pacific Coast (AAA)*. In 1985, Russ and Diane Parker, owners of Calgary Copier Ltd., bought the team and (adding another "n") named the team the "Cannons" in honor of CCL's parent company — Canon Copiers. The moniker is also appropriate because Calgary was founded as a fort in the nineteenth century, replete with cannons.

920 Vipers 2005–07 *Northern (ind.)*; 2008–10 *Golden Baseball (ind.)*; 2010–11 *Arizona Winter (W)*; 2011 to date *North American (ind.)*. The Golden, Northern and United leagues merged to form the North American League. The province of Alberta has numerous wild snakes, including heat-sensitive "vipers" that hunt by sensing the heat of their prey. Team switched circuits in 2008 and again in 2011. The AWL Vipers played their 2010–11 winter schedule with home games in Yuma (AZ).

Cali, Colombia

921 Toros 2010–11 *Liga Colombiana (W)*. Team played as "Los Toros" de Sincelejo in 2009–10 and then moved here in 2010–11. The team nickname was retained. The three most popular spectator sports in Colombia are soccer, baseball, and bullfighting. The Columbian League started play as a professional baseball circuit in the winter of 2004–05.

Calumet, Michigan

922 Redjackets 1890x *Upper Peninsula (ind.)*. Team disbanded July 2; 1891 *Upper Peninsula*. Chief "Red Jacket" (whose real name was Segoyewatha) was the Seneca Indian chief who led his tribe in resistance against the encroachment of their lands by the English and the French in the years 1770–1820.

923 Aristocrats 1905 *Copper Country (D)*; 1906–07 *Northern Copper (C 1906, D 1907)*. The players won pennants—first in 1905 in the Copper Country League and then in 1906 in the Northern Copper Country League — prompting pleased Calumet sportswriters and fans to call them "The Aristocrats of Copper Country Baseball." At this time there was a professional ice hockey team in the city also called the Calumet Aristocrats.

Camaguey, Cuba

924 Club de Beisbol de Camaguey 1946–47 *Cuban Federal (W)*; 1967–68–73–74 *Cuban National(S)*; 1977–78 to date *Cuban National (S)*. The Cuban Federal League was established for the 1946–47 season for players who had been blacklisted by major league baseball from playing in the established Cuban League after the latter joined the National Association of Professional Baseball Leagues in 1946. It played only this season. Team had no nickname.

925 Ganaderos 1974–75 to date. Cattle are herded to ranches near the city. "Los Ganaderos" is Spanish for "cattlemen."

Cambridge, Maryland

926 Canners 1922–28 *Eastern Shore (D)*; 1940–41 *Eastern Shore (D)*. Cambridge has canneries for fish, oysters, crab, fruit and vegetables.

927 Cardinals 1937–39 *Eastern Shore (D)*. Team was a farm club of the St. Louis Cardinals.

928 Dodgers 1946–49 *Eastern Shore (D)*. Team was a farm club of the Brooklyn Dodgers.

Cambridge, Massachusetts

929 Cambridge Base Ball Club 1899m *New England (ind.)*. Team moved to Lowell June 30. Team had no nickname.

930 Cantabs 1934m *Northeastern (A)*. Team started play July 5. Team moved to Wayland (MA) July 17. The word "Cantabrigian" is the nickname of an inhabitant of Cambridge, England, and Cambridge, Massachusetts (which is named after the English city). The Cambridge of England was founded by the Romans in the first century A.D., and was known in Latin as "Cantabrigia" in honor of the Roman conquests of the Cantabri barbarian tribe in Spain at that time. Cambridge newspapers quickly shortened the moniker to "Cantbas."

Cambridge, Ohio

931 Cambridge Base Ball Club 1897m *Ohio–West Virginia (ind.)*. Team moved to Denison-Urichsville in mid-season. Team had no nickname.

Camden, Ouachita, Arkansas

932 Ouachitas 1906 *Arkansas–Texas (D)*. City was built near the Ouachita Mountains. Camden is located in Ouachita County. Camden is "South Arkansas Busy Port City" on the Ouachita River and the "Queen City of the Ouachita."

Camden, New Jersey

933 Merritts 1883x *Inter-State Assn. (ind.* Team disbanded July 20. Wesley Merritt, born in New York City in 1830, was a noted Union army general in the Civil War and led troops in the last of the Indian Wars in the West in the period 1870–90.

934 Camden Baseball Club 1904x *Tri-State (D)*. Team disbanded May 30. Team had no nickname.

935 Riversharks 2001 to date *Atlantic (ind.)*. Camden is located along the Delaware River. Apparently, bull sharks from ocean waters have made their way into Delaware Bay and then to this inland river. In 1916, newspapers reported several shark attacks at beaches in New Jersey. Sharks have been reported in the nearby Potomac River as well.

Campeche, Sonora, Mexico

936 Piratas 1964–67 *Mexican Southeast (A)*; 1969–70 *Mexican Southeast (A)*; 1981 to date *Mexican*. These teams were named after the eighteenth-century pirates who raided the Yucatan coast, forcing the residents of Campeche to build a wall around the city. One of the attackers was the Sea Hawk — Sir Francis Drake of England. Team was not a farm club of the Pittsburgh Pirates.

937 Camaroneros 1968 *Mexican Southeast (A)*. Name is in honor of the city's shrimp-fishing industry. "El camaronero" is Spanish for "shrimp-catcher." "El camaron" means "shrimp."

938 Alacranes 1980 *Liga Mexicana (AAA)*. Los Alacranes de Durango moved to Campeche for the 1980 season. The team nickname was retained. However, by 1981 Campeche fans and newspapers felt the nickname belonged to the "Scorpion City" of Durango. Therefore, the traditional moniker of "Piratas" was revived for the 1981 season.

Canadaigua, New York

939 Canadaigua Base Ball Club 1888–89 *New York State (ind.)*. Team had no nickname.

940 Rustlers 1897–98 *New York State (ind.)*. In the nineteenth century, particularly in the 1890s, the Eastern public in the U.S. was fascinated with the "Wild West." As such, baseball players, a rowdy lot at best, were commonly referred to as Warriors, Braves, Chiefs, Cowboys, Bronchos and Rustlers. Actually, "Rustlers" is also baseball slang, spun-off from "Hustlers." To rustle is to move with energy and speed, i.e., "the team rustled up a couple of runs."

Cananea, Sonora, Mexico

941 Mineros 1954 *Arizona–Texas (C)*; 1955–57 *Arizona–Mexico (C)*; 1968 *Mexican (R)*; 2003x *Arizona–Mexico (ind.)*; 2004–08 *North Sonora (W)*. Team and league disbanded June 17. Gold and copper mines in the region transport mineral ore to processing factories. "El minero" is Spanish for "miner."

Canberra, New South Wales, Australia

942 Bush Rangers 1993–94–94–95 *Australian (W)*. "Bush Ranger" (also spelled Bushranger) refers to the gold rushers, sheepherders, mounted marshals, explorers, pioneers, trackers, settlers and highwaymen and hills bandits of nineteenth century Australia — all of whom "ranged the bush." Nowadays, Australian ranchers keep their sheep herds in line by riding on motorcycles that are called bush-ranging "Jockeroos."

943 Cavalry 2010–11 to date *Australian (W)*. Five thousand Canberry fans participated in a cavalry-like, bugle blowing rally as part of a "Let's Do It Canberra" campaign to convince league officials to award a franchise to Canberry. The rally resulted in the nickname of the "Canberra Cavalry."

Cancun, Quintana Roo, Mexico

944 Langosteros de Quintana Roo 1996–97 *Liga Mexicana (AAA)*; 1998–2005 **Langosteros de Cancun** *Liga Mexicana (AAA)*. Team first went by the state name of "Los Langosteros de Quintana Roo" (1996–97) before going with the city name as "Los Langosteros de Cancun" (1998–2005). Cancun is located in the state of Quintana Roo. Team was named in honor of the lobster fishing industry here.

945 Langosteros 1998–2005 *Mexican (AAA)*. As mentioned in #944, team went by the Quintana Roo state name, 1996–97, before switching to the city name in 1998. Team moved to Poza Rica for 2006 when its home park in Cancun was heavily damaged by Hurricane Wilma. In 2007, the Angelopolis Tigers moved here.

946 Tigres de Quintana Roo 2007 to date *Mexican (AAA)*. Los Tigres de Angelopolis (located in Puebla in 2006) moved to Cancun for the 2007 season. The team, retaining its "Tigers" moniker, chose the state name of "Los Tigres de Quintana Roo." Translated, "El tigre" is Spanish for "tiger." In Mexico where they roam, jaguars and cougars are sometimes called "tigres"(tigers).

Canisteo, New York

947 Canisteo Base Ball Club 1890 *Western New York (ind.)*. Team had no nickname.

Canon City, Colorado

948 Swastikas 1912m *Rocky Mountain (D)*. Team moved to Raton (NM) June 4. The swastika is an ancient sign that was usurped by Adolf Hitler for his Nazi Party in Germany in the 1920s. The Nazi swastika swung clockwise, whereas the ancient symbol swung counter-clockwise. The ancient swastika was a mystical symbol used by the Navajo Indians and by ancient peoples in the Middle East and Central Asia.

Canastota, New York

949 Canastota Base Ball Club 1886 *Central New York (ind.)*. Team had no nickname.

Canton, Illinois

950 Canteens 1908 *Illinois–Missouri (D)*. Tag was used for newspaper headlines, i.e., "Canteens edge Hornets, 4–3." This moniker was strictly a play on words and had nothing to do with water canteens or a food store. Used to get away from the controversial "Chinks," fans didn't like it and the name was dropped after the season.

951 Chinks 1908–11, 1913 *Illinois–Missouri (D)*. The tag was a vulgar epithet for "Chinamen." Although today an ethnic slur, it was used in this era in reference to Chinese immigrant workers when prejudice was more acceptable. Canton, of course, is a prominent city in China. With manager Charles Murphy at the helm in 1908, newspapers called the players "Chuck's Chinks." Such a name, painful to hear today, simply was not objectionable back then.

952 Highlanders 1912 *Illinois–Missouri (D)*. Canton was founded in 1825 by English, Irish, and Scottish settlers led by Isaac Swann. Scotland is famous for its "highland" rolling hills, giving rise to the moniker of Highlander," which means an inhabitant of Scotland. The nearby Dickson Mounds, southwest of the city, were built by prehistoric Indians.

953 Citizens m1952 *Mississippi–Ohio Valley (D)*. Vincennes Velvets moved to Canton June 7. Nickname was retained not only because the Vincennes team had been known as the "Citizens" (before switching to Velvets in mid-season 1952) but also because the new field manager in Canton was Robert Sisk, prompting Canton newspapers to call the players "Sisk's Citizens."

Canton, Mississippi

954 Canton Baseball Club 1904 *Delta (D)*. Team had no nickname.

Canton, Ohio

955 Canton Base Ball Club 1887 *Ohio State (ind.)*; 1888, 1890 *Tri-State (ind.)*; 1915x *Buckeye (D)*. Team disbanded June 11. These teams had no nickname.

956 Nadjys 1889 *Tri-State (ind.)*. The Nadjy is a type of field horse used on Ohio farms.

957 Deubers 1893 Ohio–Michigan; 1910–11 *Ohio–Pennsylvania (C)*. Team was owned by the John Deuber Watch Company.

958 Protectives 1905 *Ohio–Pennsylvania (C)*. In 1905 the Ohio Legislature passed a "protective steel tariff" to safeguard the state iron and steel industry. Many Ohio steelworkers lived in Canton.

959 Reds m1905 *Central (B)*. Team started the 1905 season in Fort Wayne (IN) and moved here July 10. Players wore red-trim hose. Originally **Red Stockings**, local newspapers shortened it to Reds. Team was a farm club of the Cincinnati Reds.

960 Chinamen 1906–07 *Central (B)*. Namesake city in China. City took the name in its founding year of 1854 after the centuries-old city in China.

961 Watchmakers 1908–11 Ohio–*Pennsylvania (C)*. The Hampden Watch Co. owned the team.

962 Statesmen 1912 *Central (B)*. Canton is the birthplace of President William McKinley. McKinley was assassinated in Buffalo, New York, in 1901 and is buried in Canton. Theodore Roosevelt succeeded him. A president, especially in foreign affairs, is often known as "statesman."

963 Senators 1913 *Inter-State (B)*. Tag was a spin-off from "Statesmen," which is actually a misnomer. Before he was elected president, McKinley had been a governor and a member of the House of Representatives but never a senator. Ironically, Ohioans Rutherford Hayes, Benjamin Harrison and William Harrison had all been U.S. senators before each was elected president.

964 Terriers 1928–30 *Central (B)*; m1932x *Central (B)*. Team started season in Akron and moved to Canton June 21. Team disbanded July 21 because of the Great Depression; 1936–42 *Middle Atlantic (C)*. The name was slang for baseball player in the style of bulldogs, rovers, and pets. Baseball players often prance and scratch about the field like dogs. With manager Joe Agler at the helm at the start of the 1928 season, newspapers called the players "Agler's Terriers." Dan O'Leary replaced Agler in mid-season 1928 and the moniker became "O'Leary's Terriers." With manager Floyd Patterson (no relation to boxer Floyd Patterson, whose career spanned the 1950s and 1960s) at the helm in 1936, newspapers called the players "Patterson's Terriers." When the team won pennants in 1937 and 1939, the fans used the moniker with affection. Patterson managed the team for the team's seven seasons of play.

965 Crocodiles 1997–2002 *Frontier (ind.)*. This moniker was the winner of a name-the-team contest. There are no crocodiles in nearby lakes Cable, Mayers and Sippo, although there are a few in the city's Sanders Wildlife Center.

Canton-Akron, Ohio

966 Indians 1989–96 *Eastern (AA)*. Team played its home games in Canton but was known by the regional name of the Canton-Akron Indians. Franchise represented both cities. Ironically, in 1997, the team moved to a new ballpark in Akron and was renamed the "Akron Aeros" while abandoning the Canton name. Team was a farm club of the Cleveland Indians.

Cap de la Madeleine, Quebec, Canada

967 Madcaps m1922 *Eastern Canada (B)*. The team started season in Valleyfield and moved here July 29. Moniker was a newspaper headline, i.e., "Madcaps edge Royals." No account exists that any of the 1922 players lived up (or down) to the team's nickname. Given the nature of baseball players throughout the years, no doubt some of these fellows were rowdy, hard-drinking all-night carousers and skirt-chasers.

Cape Charles, Virginia

968 Northampton Red Sox 1927–28x *Eastern Shore (D)*. Team and league disbanded July 10, 1928. Players wore red-trim hose. Team was not a farm club of the Boston Red Sox. Franchise took the regional name of Northampton Red Sox. Cape Charles, which is a city, is located in Northampton County.

Caracas, Distrito Federal, Vargas, Venezuela

969 Cerveceria 1946–52 *Liga Venezolana (W)*. Team was owned by Cerveceria of Caracas (in English, the Caracas Brewing Company).

970 Vargas 1946–55–56 *Liga Venezolana (W)*. Caracas is located in Vargas State, which is named after Venezuela's first president, Jose Vargas. Before 1960–61, Caracas had six professional teams: Lions, Vargas, Venezuelans, Pamperos, Centaurs, and Rapinos.

971 Venezolanos 1946–52–53 *Liga Venezolana (W)*; 1954–55 *Liga Venezolana (W)*. Inhabitants of Venezuela are known as "Venezuelans"—"Los Venezolanos" in Spanish. There have been teams like the New York Americans (football and ice hockey), Montreal Canadiens (ice hockey), New Jersey Americans (basketball), Rochester Americans (ice hockey), Havana Cubans (baseball) and the Caracas Venezuelans.

972 Leones 1952–74–75 *Liga Venezolana (W)*; 1976–77 to date *Liga Venezolana (W)*. By 1952 the competition between the Cerveceria club and the other teams (in other cities) in the Venezuelan circuit was so intense that fans of the other teams were refusing to buy Cerveceria. In desperation the Caracas club changed the team name to the Caracas Lions to make people forget that the team was owned by a Caracas-based beer company in hopes that the fans would buy a glass of their suds at a game! The ruse worked and there remains a subtle link between the Caracas club and the owner — a lion appears as a symbol on the Cerveceria beer bottle's label.

973 Pamperos 1955–56 *Liga Venezolana (W)*; 1957–58 *Liga Venezolana (W)*. Name means "Winds of the Pampas." The Pampas are prairies of South America (most extensive in Argentina) where a strong wind, known as the "Pampero," blows across these plains.

974 Centauros 1957–58 *Liga Venezolana (W)*. Cerveceria Centauro (Centaur Beer Company) owned the team. Centauro is Spanish for centaur.

975 Rapinos 1957–58–59–60 *Liga Venezolana (W)*. In Europe and Latin America, a baseball team will sometimes adopt the moniker of an established soccer team, i.e., Rapinos de Caracas. In the U.S. in the 1930s and 1940s, NFL teams often took the nicknames of MLB teams, i.e., Giants, Dodgers, Pirates, Yankees, etc.

976 Petroleros 1969x *Global (ind.)*. League and all its teams disbanded about a month into the season. Caracas is the major oil refining, storage and shipping center for Venezuela's vast reserves of oil and natural gas. "Los petroleros" means "oilers" in English.

977 Tibuleones 1975–76 *Liga Venezolana (W)*. For this one season the Caracas and LaGuiara franchises merged. The nickname of "Leones" and "Tiburones" were also merged, forming the combined name of "Tibuleones." Leon means lion and tiburon means shark. A similar event happened in the NFL during World War II when the Chicago Cardinals and Pittsburgh Steelers merged to form the "Card-Pitt" team, called "Carpets" by the fans in the two cities when the team finished fifth and last in its division. Another NFL team example was the Philadelphia Eagles–Pittsburgh Steelers hybrid called "Steagles." Although there are "Tiger-sharks," there is no such creature as a "Lion-shark." The following season (1976–77) the two franchises returned to the Caracas Lions and LaGuiara Sharks.

978 Metros 1979x *Inter-American (AAA)*. Team and league disbanded June 30. Like New York, where the New York Mets play, Caracas is a great metropolis of 8 million people.

Carbondale, Pennsylvania

979 Carbondale Base Ball Club 1895–96m *Pennsylvania State (ind.)*. Team moved to Pottsville in mid-season of 1896. Team had no nickname.

980 Pioneers 1946 *North Atlantic (D)*; 1948–50 *North Atlantic (D)*. Pennsylvania of the eighteenth and nineteenth centuries was explored and settled by Quaker "pioneer families." Quakers promoted religious tolerance to encourage immigrants to make their homes in Pennsylvania. Team was also called **Pioneer Blues** (1946. 1948–50) because the players wore blue-trim uniforms.

981 Blue Sox 1947 *North Atlantic (D)*. Players wore blue stirrups. Carbondale newspapers didn't like 1946 "Pioneer Blues" moniker because it was too long; the moniker was shortened to "Blue Sox" and **Sox** in 1947.

Carlisle, Pennsylvania

982 Carlisle Base Ball Club 1884 *Keystone Association (ind.)*; 1895–96 *Cumberland Valley (ind.)*. These teams had no nickname.

Carlsbad, New Mexico

983 Potashers 1953–55 *Longhorn (C)*; 1956–57 *Southwestern (B)*; 1958–61 *Sophomore (D)*. Nearby potash mines transport potassium carbonate to processing plants. With manager Pat McLaughlin at the helm in 1953, newspapers called the players "Pat McLaughlin's Potashers."

984 Bats 2011 *Pecos (ind.)*. Carlsbad is the "Cavern City" because of nearby Carlsbad Caverns National Park where tens of thousands of bats roost.

Carmen, Campeche, Mexico (Ciudad de Carmen)

985 Camaroneros 1967–70 *Liga del Sureste de Mexico (A)*. Carmen is a maritime city of the Bay of Campeche where shrimp-catching boats sail in and out of port. "El camaron" means "shrimp." "El camaronero" means "shrimp-catcher."

Carrington–New Rockford, North Dakota

986 Twins 1923 *North Dakota (D)*. Team represented the "Twin Cities" of New Rockford (ND) and Carrington. Home games were played in Carrington. Team was called the "New Rockford–Carrington Twins."

Carrollton, Georgia

987 Carrollton Baseball Club 1920–21 *Georgia State (D)*. Team had no nickname.

988 Frogs 1928 *Georgia–Alabama (D)*. Circuit was Association in 1928. River frogs inhabit the nearby Tallapoosa River. With Paul Fittery at the helm as the team's manager, newspapers and fans, delighted at the team's successful run to the GAL pennant, called the players the affectionate "Fittery's Frogs."

989 Champs 1929–30x *Georgia State (D)*. Team disbanded August 14, 1930, because of the Great Depression. Circuit was League 1929–30. Team won the 1928 and 1929 league pennants.

990 Hornets 1946–50 *Georgia–Alabama (D)*. Team was a farm club of the Class B Charlotte Hornets. Georgia Institute of Technology sports teams, whose fans wear yellow, have been called the "Yellow Jackets" since 1905. With manager Luther Gunnell at the helm in 1946, newspapers called the players "Luther Gunnell's Hornets."

Cartagena de la India, Bolivar, Colombia

991 Torices 1948–54–55 *Liga Colombiana (W)*; 1979–80–83–84 *Liga Colombiana (W)*; 1987–88 *Liga Colombiana (W)*. Manuel Rodriguez Torices was elected as the first president of the Republic of Colombia in 1812.

992 Indios 1948–57–58 *Liga Colombiana (W)*; 1979–80–84–85 *Liga Colombiana (W)*; 1987–88 *Liga Colombia (W)*; 1999–2000 *Liga Colombiana (W)*; 2001–02 *Liga Colombiana (W)*. When the Spaniards arrived here in the sixteenth century they named the region Cartagena de la India, wrongfully believing, as Christopher Columbus had also done in 1492, that they had arrived in India and the East Indies. They called the native peoples "Los Indios." The complete, official name of the city is "Cartagena de la India."

993 Kola Roman 1955–56–57–58 *Liga Colombiana (W)*. Kola Roman Beverage Company owned the team. "Kola Roman" is a popular soft drink in Latin America.

994 Café Universal 1984–85 *Liga Colombiana (W)*. Café Universal de Colombia owned the team.

995 Caimanes 1997–98–99–2000 *Liga Colombian (W)*. Alligators are found in the Magdalena, Cauca, Andes, Orinoco and Vapues rivers. With the name in disuse, another league team, the Baranquilla Toros, switched to Gators (Caimanes) at the start of the 2003–04 season.

996 Tigres 1999–2000 *Liga Colombiana (W)*; 2002–03 to date *Liga Colombiana (W)*. Players wore striped stirrups. Jaguars and pumas of the Colombian jungles are sometimes called "tigres" in Spanish. "Tigers" is a popular name for Latin American sports teams.

997 Aguilas 2002–03 *Liga Colombian (W)*. Team was owned by Ceverceria Aguila, i.e., Eagle Beer Company.

Carthage, Missouri

998 Carthage Base Ball Club 1891 *Southwestern (ind.)*. Team had no nickname.

999 Pirates 1938–40x *Arkansas–Missouri (D)*. Team and league disbanded July 1, 1940. Team was a farm club of the Pittsburgh Pirates.

1000 Browns 1941 Western Association *(C)*. Team began season in St. Joseph (MO) and moved here June 3. Team was a farm club of St. Louis Browns.

1001 Cardinals 1946–48 *Kansas–Oklahoma–Missouri (K.O.M.) (D)*. Team was a farm club of the St. Louis Cardinals.

1002 Cubs 1949–51 *K.O.M. (D)*. Team was a farm club of the Chicago Cubs.

Caruthersville, Missouri

1003 Caruthersville Baseball Club 1910 *Northeast Arkansas (D)*. Team had no nickname.

1004 Pilots m1936–40m *Northeast Arkansas (D)*. Team started 1936 season in West Plains (WI) and moved here June 10. Team moved to Batesville (AR) July 7, 1940. Pilot boats have been sailing the nearby Mississippi River since the eighteenth century.

Caserta, Caserta, Italy

1005 Auriga 1999–2005 *Italian A1 (ind.)*. Auriga Fiber Optics owned the team.

Casper, Wyoming

1006 Rockies 2001–07 *Pioneer (R)*. Team was a farm club of the Colorado Rockies.

1007 Ghosts 2008 to date *Pioneer (R)*. Moniker is inspired by the popular TV cartoon character "Casper the Friendly Ghost." While Casper is a friendly, young kid-ghost, the logo for this team displayed an angry, adult ghost, probably to avoid copyright infringement.

Cassville, Missouri

1008 Tigers 1935 *Arkansas State (D)*. Team had a loose affiliation with the Detroit Tigers. Team was also named Tigers in emulation of the University of Missouri Tigers athletic teams.

1009 Blues 1936 *Arkansas–Missouri (D)*. Team was a farm club of the Brooklyn Dodgers and wore Brooklyn Dodger-style blue-trim uniforms and blue stirrups.

Cantania, Sicily, Italy

1010 Warriors 2010 *Italian A1 (ind.)*. Ancient Roman soldiers and gladiators were the most renowned "warriors" of the ancient world.

Catskill, New York

1011 Catskill Baseball Club m1903 *Hudson River (D)*. Team moved from Ossining to Catskill August 2. Team had no nickname.

1012 Cougars 1995–96 *North Atlantic (ind.)*; 1997–98 *Northeast (ind.)*. Mountain Lions, i.e., cougars, inhabit the Catskill Mountains.

Cavalier, North Dakota

1013 Cavalier Baseball Club 1902x *Northern (ind.)*. Team disbanded July 21. Team had no nickname.

Cedar Rapids, Iowa

1014 Kickers 1890 *Illinois–Iowa (ind.)*. In the nineteenth century players and managers who were argumentative with umpires were known as "kickers." Apparently, this 1890 team engaged in more than its share of heated arguments with the umpires. "To kick" means to argue or complain.

1015 Canaries 1891 *Illinois–Iowa (ind.)*. Players wore canary yellow stockings.

1016 Pork Packers 1891 *Illinois–Iowa (ind.)*. Nearby farms transported pigs and hogs to slaughterhouses and meat packing plants.

1017 Cedar Rapids Base Ball Club 1895 *Eastern Iowa (ind.)*. Team had no nickname.

1018 Bunnies 1896–98 *Western Assn. (ind.)*; 1914 *Central Association (D)*; 1922–32 *Mississippi Valley (D)*; 1922–32 *Mississippi Valley (D)*. Tag was a spin-off from "Rabbits."

1019 Rabbits 1896–99 *Western Association (ind.)*; 1901–09 *Three-I (ind.* 1901, *B* 1902–09); 1913, 1915–17m *Central Association (D)*. Team moved to Clear Lake (IA) July 27; 1920–21 *Three-I (B)*. The 1906 team, which finished first with a 79–43 record "raced to the pennant like rabbits." There are plenty of rabbits in Iowa. The "rapids" of the nearby Iowa and Shell Rock rivers led to Iowa's state nickname of "Rapid City," which led tongue-in-cheek reporters to call the team the "Rapid City Rabbits."

1020 Raiders 1934–37 *Western (A)*; 1938–42 *Three-I (B)*; 1955–57 *Three-I (B)*. Iowa was a land of strife in the period 1750–1850 with wars, first between the French and the Saux and Fox Indians, and then the Black Hawk War of the 1820s. The Sioux tribes continuously raided the settlements and the supply wagons of Iowa's pioneers right up to the Civil War era. With manager Bubbles Hargraves at the helm in 1934, newspapers called the players "Hargraves' Raiders." When Clarence "Pops" Crossley took over as manager in 1935 and again in 1938, newspapers switched to "Clarence Crossley's Raiders." In 1939, Oliver Marquardt took over, resulting in "Marquardt's Raiders."

1021 Rockets 1949 *Central Association (C)*. After World War II ended, the city had numerous factories that manufactured electronic equipment, some of which was used by the U.S. Army for its V-2 rocket program. A nickname trend for Cedar Rapids baseball teams was **R** nicknames, i.e., Rabbits, Raiders and Rockets. With manager Sam "Packy" Rogers at the helm, newspapers called the players "Packy's Rockets" and "Roger's Rockets."

1022 Indians 1950–54 *Three-I (B)*. Team was a farm club of the Cleveland Indians.

1023 Braves 1958–61 *Three-I (B)*. Team was a farm club of the Milwaukee Braves.

1024 Red Raiders 1962–64 *Midwest (D 1962, A 1963–64)*. Team in 1962–63 was a farm club of the Milwaukee Braves sporting red-trim uniforms and red stirrups. In 1964 the team became a farm club of the Cincinnati Reds, again using the red-trim uniform and red stirrups of the parent Cincinnati club. Mississippi River "raiders" (i.e., river pirates) attacked all types of shipping in the seventeenth and eighteenth centuries.

1025 Cardinals 1965–72 *Midwest (A)*. Team was a farm club of the St. Louis Cardinals.

1026 Astros 1973–74 *Midwest (A)*. Team was a farm club of the Houston Astros.

1027 Giants 1975–79 *Midwest (A)*. Team was a farm club of the San Francisco Giants.

1028 Reds 1980–92 *Midwest (A)*. Team was a farm club of the Cincinnati Reds.

1029 Kernels 1993 to date *Midwest (A)*. Moniker was chosen in a name-the-team contest. Cedar Rapids is a major corn-processing center. Iowa farms transport corn to packing plants.

Cedartown, Georgia

1030 Cedars 1920–21 *Georgia State (D)*. Moniker was used for headlines, i.e., "Cedars edge Pepperels, 4–3." In the nineteenth century, the city fathers lined the streets with cedar trees.

1031 Sea Cows 1928–29 *Georgia–Alabama (D)*. The fans in Cedartown, which is land-locked, started using this clever nickname, spun-off from the city name. The only real cows in Cedartown have four legs, stand in a pasture, and graze on grass. The sea cow is a type of ocean-swimming walrus called the manatee. With manager Sherrod Smith at the helm 1928–29, newspapers called the players "Sherrod Smith's Sea Cows."

1032 Braves 1930 *Georgia–Alabama (D)*. Creek and Cherokee inhabited the U.S. Midwest since pre–Columbian times. Iowa is named after the famous Sioux chief "Hawkeye." Team was not a farm club of the Boston Braves.

Celaya, Queretaro, Mexico

1033 Cajeteros 1960–61 *Mexican Center (D)*; 1975 *Mexican Center (A)*. Cajeta is Spanish for sweets, i.e., fruit snacks and fruit candy. In Mexico, the "Cajeteros" make jelly and jams out of fruits like strawberries, raspberries, peaches, etc. Cajetero means literally "jelly-maker."

Celeron, New York

1034 Acme Colored Giants 1898x *Iron & Oil (ind.)*. Team owner Henry Curtis called this black team the Acme Colored Giants. "Acme" means "the best" and Giants was a popular moniker among black teams in this era, which was often preceded by an adjective, i.e., American, Union, Elite, Royal etc. Actually, this name had two adjectives preceding the noun.

1035 Acme Giants 1898x *Iron & Oil (ind.)*. When the Acme Colored Giants lost 41 of 49 games in league play, team owner Henry Curtis disbanded the club (firing all the players) and formed an all-white team with players from the Louisville Eclipse of the recently disbanded Southern League. Both this new team and the Iron & Oil League disbanded on July 20. The Acme Colored Giants' players were the last Negro players in Organized Baseball until 1947.

Celeron-Chatqua, New York

1036 Celeron-Chatqua Base Ball Club 1893x *New York State (ind.)*. Team and circuit both disbanded in mid-season. Team had no nickname.

Central City, Kentucky

1037 Reds m1954 *Kentucky–Illinois–Tennessee (KITTY) (D)*. Team started in Jackson (TN) and moved to Central City July 5. Team was a farm club of the Cincinnati Reds.

Central de Antonio Gutieras

1038 Centrales 1965–/66–66–67 *Liga National Cubana (S)*. City was named after a hero of the 1898 Cuban Revolution, Antonio Gutieras. Central is Spanish for "central," which means a municipality. The Cuban National League (name in English) is a state-subsidized league.

Central Islip, New York

1039 Long Island Ducks 2000 to date *Atlantic (ind.)*. The name is a revival of the Long Island Ducks of the Eastern Hockey League, starting in the 1933–34 season. The hockey team had been sponsored by a duck farm on Long Island.

Centralia, Illinois

1040 White Sox 1907 *Eastern Illinois (D)*. The Centralia club management maintained a loose affiliation with the Chicago White Sox. In this era, minor league teams, geographically close to a big league city, sometimes formed a loose affiliation with the major league club, which donated or sold uniforms and equipment to the minor leaguers. Team was also known as the **White Stockings**.

1041 Cubs 1947–48 *Illinois State (D)*; 1949 *Missouri Ohio Valley (M.O.V.) (D)*. Team was a farm club of the Chicago Cubs in 1948–49. The 1949 team played as an independent but retained the newspaper-friendly Cubs moniker.

1042 Sterlings 1950 *Missouri Ohio Valley (M.O.V.) (D)*. "Sterling" not only refers to silver but also to "excellent work" done by a person or a group. Fans and newspapers praised the team in winning the 1950 co-championship with a "sterling" 83–40 record. With manager Lou Bekeza at the helm, newspapers called the players "Lou Bekeza's Sterlings."

1043 Zeros 1951–52 *Missouri Ohio Valley (M.O.V.) (D)*. Centralia was home to the famous Zero Candy Bar Company. Starting in a Minneapolis candy factory, which manufactured the Double Zero candy bar, the company moved here in 1934 and renamed their product the Zero Candy Bar. With Lou Bekeza at the helm, newspapers called the players "Bekeza's Zeros." Hershey Foods bought the company in 1996.

Centralia, Washington

1044 Midgets 1903–04 *Southwestern Washington (D)*. Team, which played in a league with an abbreviated 18-game schedule each season, finished third both years with 7–11 and 6–12 records, respectively. In this era "Giants" was a generic name for a team that won, and, conversely, "Midgets" was a sarcastic barb against a team that was a loser. Team also had very young players of boyish stature, prompting newspapers to call them the "Midgets."

1045 Pets 1911 *Washington State (D)*. The moniker "Pets" referred to a field manager's baseball players, i.e., Connie Mack's "Pets" or John McGraw's "Pets." Some managers pampered their players like a cocker spaniel. Managed by W. R. Patton, newspapers called the players "Patton's Pets."

1046 Rail-Roaders 1912x *Washington State (D)*. An important deport for the Pacific Northwest Railroad, the city became known as the "Hub of Southwest Washington."

Centreville, Queen Anne, Maryland

1047 Colts 1937–38 *Eastern Shore (D)*. Maryland is famous for horse racing, i.e., the Preakness Stakes in Baltimore (since 1873). Newspapers liked the four-letter "Colts" in comparison to the 11-letter Centerville. Team was also called by the county name of "Queen Anne Colts" in 1937.

1048 Red Sox 1939–41 *Eastern Shore (D)*. Team was a farm club of the Boston Red Sox.

1049 Orioles 1946 *Eastern Shore (D)*. Team was a farm club of the Baltimore Orioles. In the period 1920–60, some of the higher classification (AAA and AA) minor league teams had their own farm teams. With manager Jim McLeod at the helm, newspapers called the players "Jim McLeod's Orioles."

Cerro Azul, Mexico

1050 Club de Beisbol de Cerro Azul 1978 *Mexican Center (A)*. Team had no nickname.

Chambersburg, Pennsylvania

1051 Chambersburg Base Ball Club 1884 *Keystone Association (ind.)*. Team had no nickname.

1052 Maroons 1915–17m *Blue Ridge (D)*. Team moved to Cumberland (MD) June 30, 1917; 1920, 1922–28 *Blue Ridge (D)*. Players wore maroon-trim uniforms and maroon stirrups. With manager Eddie Hooper at the helm in 1920, newspapers called the players "Hooper's Maroons." Newspapers in 1922–23 called the players "Mowrey's Maroons" after new field manager Mike Mowrey. Red McDermott took over in 1924 and the name became "McDermott's Maroons," followed by "Ramey's Maroons" after skipper Buck Ramsey. Mickey Keliher became manager in 1927–28, leading to "Mickey's Maroons."

1053 Marooners 1921 *Blue Ridge (D)*. The moniker was a clever but grammatically clumsy spin-off from "Maroons." Newspapers did not like the nine-letter moniker.

1054 Young Yanks 1929–30 *Blue Ridge (D)*. City had been occupied by General Robert E. Lee in July 1863 and was used as a staging area for the Battle of Gettysburg. Later, Lee burned the city down. Chambersburg was the classical "Yankee" city during this era. "Yankee" meant anyone who was a Northerner. With manager Leo Mackey at the helm, newspapers called the players "Mackey's Young Yanks." Team was not a farm club of the New York Yankees.

Champaign, Illinois

1055 Clippers 1889 *Illinois–Indiana (ind.)*. Small clipper ships, loaded with cargo, sailed the winding Salt Creek out of Lake Springfield.

Champaign-Urbana, Illinois

1056 Velvets 1911–14 *Illinois–Missouri (D)*. The home field was in Champaign but the team also represented Urbana and played as the Champaign-Urbana Velvets. The name is from the old saying "Champagne and Velvet." Team manager was Fred "Blackie" Wilson, giving rise to the moniker "Blackie's Velvets" after the "Black Velvet" drink — a mix of champagne and stout beer. Fred "Blackie" Wilson took over as manager in 1913–14, leading newspapers to call the players "Blackie's Velvets." Black velvet is also an expensive, luxurious type of velvet. The home field was in Champaign but the team also represented Urbana.

1057 Twins 1911–14 *Illinois–Missouri (D)*. Team represented both cities with home games in Champaign. Tag was an alternate moniker, preferred by newspapers to "Velvets."

1058 Champaign-Urbana Bandits 1994x *Great Central (ind.)*. Team and league disbanded August 17. Management chose a nickname derived from the city name but were embarrassed when they realized the moniker was also the nickname of an infamous sexual predator, Michael Kenyon, alias the "Champaign 'Enema' Bandit," who robbed and sexually assaulted a dozen women in the years 1966–75, before being caught and sent to prison in 1975. Team represented both cities. Some cynical fans said management deliberately chose the name to generate "shock" interest.

Chandler, Arizona

1059 Cardinals 1992–94 *Arizona (R)*. Team was a farm club of the St. Louis Cardinals.

1060 Brewers 1992–95 *Arizona (R)*. Team was a farm club of the Milwaukee Brewers.

1061 Diamondbacks 1992–96 *Arizona (Fall)*. Team was a farm club of the Arizona Diamondbacks.

1062 Rockies 1994–97 *Arizona (R)*. Team was a farm club of the Colorado Rockies. The Arizona Rookie League routinely had two, three or even four teams in a single city playing "complex baseball," i.e., several rookie teams sharing a home field. The same pattern occurs in Florida in the Rookie-level Gulf Coast League.

Chanute, Kansas

1063 Chanute Base Ball Club 1896 *Kansas State (ind.)*. Team had no nickname.

1064 Oilers m1902 *Missouri Valley (D)*. Team began season in Coffeyville (KS) and then moved here June 23. Oil was discovered here in 1880. With manager Jack Jamison at the helm, newspapers called the players "Jamison's Oilers."

1065 Browns 1906 *Kansas State (D)*. Team had a loose affiliation with the St. Louis Browns. Players wore brown hose. These loose affiliations began as early as 1884 and continued until 1950.

1066 Athletics 1946–47, 1949–50 *Kansas–Oklahoma–Missouri (K.O.M.) (D)*. Team had a loose affiliation with the Philadelphia Athletics interrupted by one season as a N.Y. Giants farm club.

1067 Giants 1948 *Kansas–Oklahoma–Missouri (K.O.M.) (D)*. Team was a farm club of the New York Giants.

Chapman, Kansas

1068 Chapman Baseball Club m1910 *Central Kansas (D)*. Team started in Beloit (KS) and moved here July 20, 1910. Team had no nickname.

Charleroi, Pennsylvania

1069 Charleroi Baseball Club 1902 *Pennsylvania State (D)*; m1906–07 *Pennsylvania–Ohio–Michigan (D)*. Team started season in Butler, moved to Piedmont July 14, and then moved to Charleroi Aug. 6; 1909m *Pennsylvania–West Virginia (D)*. Team moved to Parkersburg June 30, 1909. These teams had no nickname.

1070 Cherios 1908 *Pennsylvania–West Virginia (D)*. Moniker was used for newspaper headlines, i.e., "Cherios edge Cokers, 4–3." The abstract nickname does not refer to the British English drinking salute of "cheery oh!"

1071 Babes 1927–28 *Middle Atlantic (C)*. Players were young and inexperienced and it showed as the 1927 team finished eighth and last with a 42–75 record. In 1928 manager Bill Phillips got the team to a winning 62–60 record, prompting fans and newspapers to affectionately call the players "Bill's Babes."

1072 Governors 1929–31 *Middle Atlantic (C)*. John K. Tener was born in Charleroi in 1863. As a young man he played professional baseball with Haverhill in 1885 and major league baseball with the Baltimore Orioles that same season. He then went into politics and was elected governor of Pennsylvania in 1911.

1073 Tigers 1934–36 *Pennsylvania State (D)*. Team was a farm club of the Detroit Tigers.

Charles City, Iowa

1074 Tractorites m1917 *Central Association (D)*. Team started season in Dubuque and moved to Charles City July 4. City has a vehicle company that builds farm tractors.

Charleston, Illinois

1075 Broome Corn Cutters 1906 *Kentucky–Illinois–Tennessee (KITTY). (D)*; 1907 *Eastern Illinois (D)*. Illinois farmers, i.e., "corn cutters," grow a breed of corn with coarse stalks used to manufacture brooms. The stalks were shipped to factories where the brooms were manufactured.

1076 Evangelists 1908 *Eastern Illinois (D)*. This region of Illinois was settled in the nineteenth century by Methodist Evangelicals. With Mr. Madden at the helm as manager, newspapers called the players "Madden's Evangelists."

Charleston, South Carolina

1077 Fultons 1886 *Southern League of Colored Baseballists (ind.)*. Robert Fulton, who was born in Pennsylvania, invented the steamboat in 1815. "Fulton" steamboats were sailing in and out of Charleston in this era. The "Best Friend of Charleston" was the first steam locomotive built in the U.S. It was based on a Fulton design.

1078 Sea Gulls 1886–87x *Southern (ind.)*. Team and league disbanded August 21, 1887; 1888x *Southern (ind.)*. Team and league disbanded July 4, 1888; 1889m *Southern (ind.)*. Team moved to Atlanta July 6, 1889; 1893 *Southern (ind.)*; 1894 *Southern (ind.)*; 1898 *Southern (ind.)*; 1904–09m *South Atlantic (C)*. Team moved to Knoxville July 5, 1909; 1911x *South Atlantic (C)*. Team disbanded August 30 when storms destroyed the team's ballpark; 1913–17x *South Atlantic (C)*. League ended its season on July 4 due to U.S. entry into World War I. Sea gulls are coastal birds that have thrived in North America. Newspapers often shortened the name to "Gulls." With manager James Powell at the helm 1886–87, newspapers called the players "James Powell's Sea Gulls." Moniker became traditional for the next twenty years.

1079 Palmettos 1892 *South Atlantic (ind.)*; 1920 *South Atlantic (C)*. South Carolina is nicknamed the "Palmetto State." A Palmetto is a type of palm tree, which is prolific in South Carolina. Newspapers shortened the moniker to "**Pals**."

1080 Gulls 1919 *South Atlantic (C)*. For earlier Charleston teams, "Sea gulls" and "Gulls" were used interchangeably. This time, local newspapers went exclusively with "Gulls."

1081 Pals 1921–23m *South Atlantic (B)*. Team moved to Macon (GA) May 28, 1923. Newspapers went exclusively with "Pals" for headlines, i.e., "Pals edge Hornets, 4–3." Charleston is known s the "Palmetto City."

1082 Rebels m1940–42 *South Atlantic (B)*. Team started 1940 season in Spartanburg (SC) and moved here July 15, 1940; 1946–53 *South Atlantic (A)*. It was at Fort Sumter, just outside of Charleston, in April 1861 that city garrison shore batteries opened fire on Union ships trying to get supplies to the fort. These hostilities started the Civil War. Charleston, which issued the first ordinance of secession, is the "City of Secession." With manager Cecil Rhodes at the helm (1940–42), newspapers called the players "Rhodes Rebels" and "Cecil's Rebels."

1083 White Sox 1959–61 *South Atlantic (A)*. Team was a farm club of the Chicago White Sox.

1084 Pirates 1973–78 *Western Carolinas (A)*. Team was a farm club of Pittsburgh Pirates.

1085 Royals 1980–84 *South Atlantic (A)*. Team was a farm club of the Kansas City Royals.

1086 Rainbows 1985–93 *South Atlantic (A)*. Rainbows appear over the nearby Albemarle Point, Ashley River, Charleston Harbor and the coast of the Atlantic Ocean. Charleston is the "City by the Sea."

1087 River Dogs 1994 to date *South Atlantic (A)*. In the 1990s, the nicknames "Dogs" and "Dawgs" had become a style due to rap and hip-hop music. "River" referred to the nearby Ashley and Cooper rivers. Chosen in a fan poll, "River Dog" is a spin-off from "Sea Dog," which is an old English slang for sailor. The notable rock band "The River Dogs" was founded in 1990.

Charleston, West Virginia

1088 Statesmen 1910 *Virginia Valley (D)*; 1911–12x *Mountain States (D)*. Team disbanded July 1, 1912. Charleston is the capital of West Virginia. A president or senator who avoids partisanship and leads with patriotism is known as a "statesman."

1089 Senators 1910 *Virginia Valley (D)*; 1911–12x *Mountain States (D)*. Team disbanded July 1, 1912; 1913–16m Team moved to Chillicothe (OH) July 13, 1916. *Ohio State (D)*; 1931–42 *Mid-Atlantic (C)*; 1949–51 *Central (A)*; m1952–60 *American Assn. (AAA)*. Team started season in Toledo (OH) and then moved to Charleston June 23, 1952. Moniker was a spin-off from "Statesmen." The West Virginia state senators convene in Charleston at the state capitol. With manager John Benny at the helm, newspapers called the players "Benny's Senators." None of these teams was a farm club of the AL Washington Senators.

1090 Marlins m1961 *International (AAA)*. When the San Juan Marlins (named after the fish) moved to Charleston May 19, the nickname was retained but had a new meaning—conveniently linked to West Virginia history—referring to the "Marlin Rifles" used by West Virginia hunters.

1091 Indians 1962–64 *Eastern (A 1962, AA 1963–64)*. Team was a farm club of the Cleveland Indians.

1092 Charlies 1971–83 *International (AAA)*. Team owner Bob Levine called the team "Charlies" not only because the home city was Charleston but also in honor of his father, Charles Levine.

1093 Wheelers 1987–94 *South Atlantic (A)*. "Sternwheeler" boats have sailed the nearby Kanawha River since 1855. The "sternwheeler" is a steamboat driven by a single paddle at the stern.

1094 Alley Cats 1995–2004 *South Atlantic (A)*. People were confusing this team with the franchise in Charleston (SC) (renamed River Dogs in 1994). Team owner Dennis Bastien held a name-the-team Contest and the fans chose the nickname "Alley Cats" to distinguish the West Virginia team from the South Carolina "River Dogs." Team logo was a jazz hep cat with sunglasses. Jazz has been popular in Charleston since the 1920s.

1095 West Virginia Power 2005 to date *South Atlantic (A)*. City has hydro-electrical plants at the Elk and Kanawha rivers and is a distribution center for coal, natural gas and oil. Team owner Tom Dickson renamed the team from "Charleston Alley Cats" to "West Virginia Power," explaining to reporters: "West Virginia is and will continue to be recognized as one of the leading energy providers for the country. The energy production from coal, natural gas and hydroelectric sources, combined with the fact that Charleston serves as the center for the state's political and economic powers, leads us to the name of the team. We felt it was extremely important that the name reflect the entire region and are excited about the tremendous marketing opportunities that will go along with the name."

Charlestown, New Hampshire see Springfield-Charlestown

Charlotte, Michigan

1096 Giants m1926 *Michigan State (B)*. Team started season in Flint (MI) before moving to Charlotte July 22. Disgruntled fans sarcastically called the team "Giants" as the team went 14–37 en route to the league cellar. Ray Dunn was the manager, prompting newspapers to tag the losers as "Dunn's Giants."

Charlotte, North Carolina

1097 Charlotte Base Ball Club 1892 *South Atlantic (ind.)*; 1905x *Virginia–North Carolina (D)*. Team and league disbanded August 19. These teams had no nickname.

1098 Presbyterians 1900 *Virginia–North Carolina (ind.)*. Charlotte was settled, starting in 1750, by three immigrant groups: the Irish (who were Catholic), the Germans (who were Lutheran), and the Scottish, who were Presbyterian. Charlotte is known as the "City of Churches."

1099 Hornets m1901 *Virginia–North Carolina (ind.)*. Team started season in Portsmouth and moved to Charlotte June 21, 1901; 1902x *North Carolina (D)*. New franchise in a new league. Team disbanded July 9; 1908–12 *Carolina Assn. (D)*; 1913–17x *North Carolina State (D)*. Team and league disbanded May 30, 1917 because of U.S. entry into World War I; 1919–30 *South Atlantic Assn. (A 1919–20, B 1921–30)*; 1931–35 *Piedmont (C 1931–32, B 1933–35)*; 1937–42 *Piedmont (B)*; 1946–53 *Tri-State (B)*; 1954–63 *South Atlantic (A 1954–62, AA 1963)*; 1964–72 *Southern (AA)*. During the Revolutionary War of 1776–1781, British General Charles Cornwallis bitterly complained to King George that the city of Charlotte was a "Hornet's Nest" because so many British troops were being killed and wounded by colonial snipers and guerrilla fighters when the British tried to occupy the city in 1780. Charlotte, henceforth, has been known as the "Hornets' Nest."

1100 Twins 1972 *Western Carolinas (A)*.Team was a farm club of the Minnesota Twins.

1101 Orioles 1976–86 *Southern (AA)*. Team was a farm club of the Baltimore Orioles.

1102 Knights 1986–92 *Southern (AA)*; 1993 to date *International (AAA)*. Charlotte is the Queen City. "Knights" was chosen in a fan poll as a logical spin-off from Queen City, Charlotte's nickname. The team's home field is called Knights' Castle.

Charlottesville, Virginia

1103 Tuckahoes 1914x *Virginia Mountain (D)*. Team and league disbanded July 25. The Algonquin Indians, of this region, made a paste from Tuckahoe mushrooms, which was then baked into a bread. This bread was also called by the more famous name of "Virginia Truffles."

Chaska, Minnesota

1104 Chaska Valley Buccaneers 1995 *North Central (ind.)*. Team went by the regional name of Chaska Valley Buccaneers. Pirates sailed Lake Superior and the Mississippi River from at least as far back as 1700 until well into the nineteenth century. They attacked frontier settlements, flatbeds, keel boats, and rafts to steal anything and everything, i.e., livestock, cargo and slaves. The last of the "Great Lakes Pirates" was "Roaring Dan" Seavey, 1900–31. Team was not a farm club of the Pittsburgh Pirates.

Chatham, Ontario, Canada

1105 Babes 1898 *Canadian (ind.)*. In this era, "Babes" meant an expansion team, while "Infants" meant a young team that struggled on the field. This team was an expansion team in the Canadian League in 1898. Expansion teams usually have young players, i.e., "baby faces."

1106 Reds 1899 *Canadian (ind.)*; 1900 *International (ind.)*. Players wore red hose.

Chattanooga, Tennessee

1107 Lookouts 1885–86 *Southern (ind.)*; 1889 *Southern (ind.)*; 1892–93x *Southern (ind.)*; 1897 *Southeastern (ind.)*; 1898 *Southern (ind.)*; 1901–02 *Southern Assn. (ind. 1901, A 1902)*; 1909 *South Atlantic (C)*; 1910–43m *Southern Assn. (A 1910–35, A1 1936–43)*. Team moved to Montgomery July 11, 1943; 1944–61 *Southern Assn. (A1 1944–45, A1 1946–62)*; 1963 *South Atlantic (AA)*; 1964–65 *Southern (AA)*; 1976 to date. Soldiers, both Union and Confederate, used Lookout Mountain to survey troop movements during the Battle of Chattanooga in September–November 1863. In a very early 1909 name-the-team contest, the fans voted for the old standby of "Lookouts."

1108 Chatts 1892 *Southern (ind.)*. Tag was used in headlines, i.e., "Chatts edge Blues, 4–3."

1109 Warriors 1893 *Southern (ind.)*; 1895x *Southern (ind.)*. Team moved to Mobile (AL) July 19. The Cherokee, Chickasaw, Creek and Shawnee inhabited Tennessee and North Carolina.

1110 Chattanooga Baseball Club 1913 *Dixie (ind.)*. Team had no nickname.

1111 Black Lookouts 1920 *Southern Negro (ind.)*; 1926 *Independent Negro team*; Tag was spin-off moniker. Black teams in this era often used major league team nicknames added the adjective "black," i.e., Black Barons, Black Yankees, Black Crackers, Black Senators and Black Lookouts.

1112 Choo-Choos 1945 *Negro Southern (ind.)*. Name was in honor of the Western & Atlantic Railroad that started in 1850. Passengers referred to the train as the "Chattanooga Choo-Choo." So inspired, the "Chattanooga Choo-Choo" was the title of a jazz song from the 1940s.

Chehalis, Washington

1113 Gophers 1910 *Washington State (D)*. With manager Fielder Jones at the helm, newspapers called the players "Jones' Gophers." Gophers are found mostly in the western U.S., the southern U.S. and Central America.

1114 Protoges 1911 *Washington State (D)*. In this era, before the popularization of the word "rookie," (1917), young players were known as Babes, Chicks, Colts, Cubs, Debutantes, Ducklings, Foundlings, Innocents, Ponies, Protoges and Yearlings. With manager Lenny Taylor at the helm, newspapers called the players "Taylor's Proteges."

Cheon-Chu, North Cholla, South Korea (also spelled Chonchu)

1115 Sangbang Wool Raiders 1983–96 *Korean (ind.)*. During the Korean War, the 41st British Commando "Raiders" distinguished themselves in the fight against the Communist Chinese. The Sangbang Wool Company, the team owner, desirous to market the team in English with a winning image, also went with "Raiders" in emulation of the two-time NFL Super Bowl champion Oakland Raiders.

Cherryvale, Kansas

1116 Boosters m1906 *Kansas State (D)*. Team started the season in Iola and then moved to Cherryvale June 15. Cherryvale fans immediately formed a booster club. In the era 1890–1910 fans often formed "booster clubs," to cheer the players on. When a team found itself in pennant contention, newspapers called the players the "Boosters." The team, managed by William Burris, finished second and was called "Burris' Boosters."

Chester, Pennsylvania

1117 Blue Stockings 1884 *Keystone Association (ind.)*. Players wore blue hose.

1118 Chester Baseball Club m1912 *Tri-State (B)*. Team started season in Johnstown (PA) and then moved to Chester August 2. Team had no nickname.

Chester, South Carolina

1119 Chester Baseball Club 1908 *South Carolina (D)*; m1912 *Tri-State (B)*. The 1912 team started the season in Johnstown and moved to Chester August 2. These teams had no nickname.

Chetumal, Quintana Roo, Mexico

1120 Los Mayas de Quintana Roo 1998–99 *Mexican (AAA)*. Team went by the state name of "Los Mayas de Quintana Roo." Team was named after the Maya Mountains of nearby Belize. Archaeologists believe the pre–Columbian Mayan Empire probably extended into Southern Mexico.

Cheyenne, Wyoming

1121 Indians m1912 *Rocky Mountain (D)*. Team began season in Trinidad (CO) and then moved here June 28; 1941 *Western (D)*. With manager Ira Bidwell at the helm in 1912, newspapers called the players "Ira's Indians." The 1941 team was not a farm club of the Cleveland Indians.

Chiayi-Tainan, West Central, Taiwan (aka Republic of China and Formosa)

Note: City name also spelled Chiai and Chiayi.

1122 Luka 1997–2002 Taiwan Major team went by the amalgamated name of Chianan, i.e., Chiayi and Tainan. Home games are split between stadia in Chiayi and Tainan, which are about 50 miles apart. Name refers to the ancient gods of the aboriginal Taiwanese people who lived on the island 2,000 years ago. One of their gods was the god of bravery or courage.

Chiba, Honshu, Japan

1123 Marines 1991 to date *Pacific (ind.)*. The team goes by the company name of Lotte Marines. The Lotte Baking Company of South Korea owns the team. Chiba, located along Tokyo Bay, is a major fishing port. Team logo is a sea gull, which refers to the team's alternate moniker of **Gulls** (Komome in Japanese).

1124 Fighters 2004–08 *Eastern (Japan)*. Team, which played in Tokyo in 2003, moved to Chiba for the 2004 season. Nippon Ham owned the team for 2004–05 seasons, making the team's name "Nippon Ham Fighters." Tamagawa Company bought the team in 2006, making the team's name the "Tamagawa Nippon Ham Fighters." Team moved to the Chiba suburb of Kamagaya in 2008.

Chicago, Illinois

1125 White Stockings 1870 *Independent*; 1871, 1874–75 *National Assn. (M)*; 1876–87 *National (M)*; 1890 *Players (M)*; 1900 *American (M)*; 1901–10 *American (M)*. The fame (if not the financial success of a team that merely broke even) of the 1869 Cincinnati Red Stockings prompted Chicago businessmen to form a team that dressed its players in white hose as a gesture of respect and rivalry to the Cincinnati players. Hence, the team became known as the "White Stockings." The nickname first appeared in print in the *Cleveland Herald* on May 2, 1870, which explained: "The snowy purity of the hose has suggested the name of 'White Stockings' for the nine, and it is likely to become as generally accepted, not to say as famous, as that of the sanguinary extremities." Captain Jimmy Wood designed the team's uniform and color. Alternate nicknames included **White Socks, White Sox, White Legs** and **Whites**— all newspaper contractions.

1126 The Mighty Nine 1876 *National (M)*. Name was another moniker of praise for the dominating pennant winners. The "Mighty Nine" led the 1876 NL in hits (926), doubles (131), batting average (.337), on-base percentage (.353), and slugging percentage (.417). The team batting average of .337 was an amazing 70 points above Hartford's team batting average of .267 for the 1876 campaign.

1127 Tulips 1876 *National (M)*. Management provided caps of a different color by position, i.e., red, light blue, dark blue, white, violet, maroon, yellow, magenta and green to the derisive guffaws of the fans. The *Chicago Daily Tribune* described the players as a "bed of Dutch tulips." The experiment was dropped after the season ended.

1128 Westerners 1876 *National (M)*. In 1876 , the Chicago "Westerners" and St. Louis "Pilgrims" were the two most western cities in the new National League. Indeed, in this era, the expanse of land from Minnesota to Oklahoma and Indiana to Iowa was not known as the Midwest but rather the "West." St. Louis made 1,000-mile train "pilgrimages" to New York.

1129 Big White Machine 1876–86 *National (M)*. Coined by baseball writer and author David Nemec, the name referred to the Chicago teams of the first 11 seasons of the National League. The moniker was a spinoff of the Cincinnati "Big Red Machine" teams of 1969–76 in the National League. The "Big White Machine" won six of the first 11 National League pennants in 1876, 1880, 1881, 1882, 1885 and 1886. Strangely, although the team dominated the NL, the Chicagoans lost the World Series to Washington in 1880, to the New York Mets in 1881, to St. Louis in 1886, tying Cincinnati in 1882 and St. Louis in 1885, and winning only over the Mets in 1882.

1130 Giants 1876–86 *National (M).* Led by hitters Cap Anson, Ross Barnes, Cal McVey and pitcher Al Spalding, Chicago dominated the NL in its inaugural 1876 season as they rolled to a first-place, pennant-winning 52–14 record. "Giants" in this era referred not necessarily to tall and muscular players but to a team that was "winning big" or "playing like giants." Subsequent pennants in 1880, 1881, 1882, 1885 and 1886 kept the "Giants" moniker bandied about the Chicago press until the NL New York Giants grabbed a monopoly on the name with their first NL pennant in 1888.

1131 The Original Hitless Wonders 1877 *National (M).* Coined by baseball writer David Nemec as a spinoff of the Chicago American League "Hitless Wonders" of 1905–07, the 1877 Chicagoans became the first and only major league baseball team to hit no home runs in a regular season — this year 60 games. The team's BA was .270 but with nary a round-tripper.

1132 Cap Anson's Juggernaut 1880–86 *National (M).* Name was coined by baseball author Warren Wilbert to celebrate the White Stockings' run of five NL pennants in seven campaigns. In 1885–86 the Chicagoans became the first MLB team to reach 87 (in 1885) and 90 (in 1886) regular season victories.

1133 Rough'n Toughs 1884 *National (M).* Manager Cap Anson's 1884 players were scrappy and mean-tempered who got into numerous fistfights with players on opposing teams and bullied umpires. Moreover, several of the players were as brawny as lumberjacks.

1134 Gold Stockings 1884 *Union Association (M).* The players wore golden yellow hose. Newspapers shortened the name to **Old Golds.** When frequent washings faded the gold to brown, newspapers called the team the **Browns.**

1135 Brewers 1884 *National (M).* The players of this team had a reputation for frequenting saloons in Chicago and other cities. "Brewers" was a generic name for players who were hard drinkers.

1136 Babes 1884 *Reserve (ind.).* The word "rookie" would not be coined until young U.S. Army recruits, i.e., "rookies," started boarding ships to sail for Europe across the Atlantic Ocean. Although generic in baseball in 1884–86, by 1887 the moniker began to gravitate to Chicago for the period 1887–1907. Similarly, the generic terms Giants (winning players), Cubs (young players), and Braves (baseball players in general) began to gravitate to New York (1885), Chicago (1901), and Boston (1912), respectively.

1137 Cap Anson's Kickers 1885–86 *National (M).* Cap Anson was a notorious umpire-baiter and chronic complainer who encouraged his players to bitch, moan and kick seemingly every play. All baseball players in the nineteenth century were occasional "kickers," but Anson's charges were the nastiest. "Kick" originates from a furious man or woman angrily kicking his or her foot during a dispute with another person.

1138 Terrors 1885–86 *National (M).* The Chicago White Stockings "terrorized" NL opponents, finishing first in the NL standings both seasons with fantastic 87–25 and 90–34 records. The Chicago "Terrors" were led by a veritable all-star lineup of hitters Cap Anson, Tom Burns, Fred Pfeffer and Jim Ryan and pitchers Larry Corcoran, Fred Goldsmith and John "Dad" Clarkson.

1139 Colts 1887–1907 *National (M).* The name was first used in 1887, and not 1890 (as some baseball historians have reported). After losing the 1886 World Series to the American Association St. Louis Browns, Chicago general manger Al Spalding dumped veteran players King Kelly, George Gore, Jim McCormick and others, who

were getting drunk and rowdy (and arrested) between regular season games in mid-season 1887. He replaced these veterans with young players whom Chicago newspapers started to call the "Colts." By 1890 Player League raids swiped ten players from the Chicago Nationals, forcing manager Cap Anson sign more young players, thereby perpetuating the "Colt" nickname through the 1906 season. In November 1895, manager Cap Anson reinforced the name by appearing as an actor in a New York theatrical play about the Wild West, *A Runaway Colt.*

1140 Maroons 1888 *Western Assn. (ind.).* Players wore maroon hose. Team was a farm club of the NL Chicago Black Stockings. Maroon hose was a spin-off from the black hose of the Chicago Nationals.

1141 Black Stockings 1888–91 *National (M).* The hot, humid summer of 1887 prompted management to dress players in cooler silk stockings that were dyed black. Newspapers, displaying a sense of humor, called the team the **Dickey Birds** and **Swallowtails.**

1142 Pirates 1890 *Players League (M).* Although the Chicago franchise and the other seven clubs of the Players League "pirated" away scores of players from the National League, the "Pirates" moniker for the Chicago Brotherhood team (PL teams were known as "Brotherhood" teams) came about in mid-season because the Chicago players rallied in the late innings to "pirate away" victories in games where the fans thought they were sure to lose.

1143 Comiskey's White Stockings 1890 *Players League (M).* Ten years before the American League Chicago club donned the white hosiery discarded by the Chicago Nationals after the 1887 season, the Chicago Brotherhood players wore white stockings. Newspapers shortened the moniker to **White Socks** and **White Sox.**

1144 All-Stars 1890 *Players League (M).* Field manager Charles Comiskey and club management succeeded in signing a veritable "all-star" team, including hitters Hug Duffy, Tip O'Neil, Jimmy Ryan, Fred Pfeffer, Arlie Latham, Charlie Bastian, and Duke Farrell as well as Mark Baldwin, Silver King, Charlie Bartson and Frank Dwyer.

1145 Cubs 1890, 1901 to date *National (M).* In 1901, the American League raided NL teams, including the Colts, forcing the Chicago NL team to sign numerous younger players who became known as "Cubs." Briefly used and quickly discarded in 1890, this time the name soared in popularity, eclipsing "Colts," and became the official team nickname in 1908. Apparently a Chicago newspaper held a name-the-team Contest in April 1900 with "Cubs" emerging as the winner. Chicago sportswriters Fred Hayner and George Rice popularized the nickname in 1901. Manager Frank Selee (1902–05) preferred Colts over Cubs, but his successor, Frank Chance, openly demanded of newspaper reporters that they refer to his players as "Cubs," and issued coats to the Chicago players during the 1907 World Series with a white bear logo on the front. The Chicago NL franchise made "Cubs" the team's official name in April 1908.

1146 Cap Anson's Anarchists 1893 *National (M).* In the era 1870–1900 Chicago was a cauldron of labor disputes and workers' strikes, which culminated in the 1883 Haymarket Riot. The American public was fearful of Communist and Socialist "anarchists" who proliferated during capitalism's "Gilded Age." Cap Anson's 1893 Chicago Colts were especially nasty in fist fighting, umpire baiting and "kicking" (i.e., complaining).

1147 Unions 1897–99 *Independent Negro team.* Team was a semi-professional outfit from 1888–96. After the Civil War ended, any name that was associated with the Northern states—where civil rights were more prevalent—was favored by black baseball team managements. Hence, the names of Unions, American Giants, Lincoln Giants and Union Giants were in vogue.

1148 Rainmakers 1898 *National (M).* Tongue-in-cheek moniker as the team did its spring training in rainless Arizona. By May the moniker was discarded.

1149 Orphans 1898–99 *National (M)*. After 22 years with the Chicago Nationals as player and manager, Cap Anson left the team following the 1897 season, prompting the Chicago press to call the 1898 players the "Orphans." "Orphans" was used primarily for minor league teams that went on the road in mid-season when home attendance plummeted so much that the fans had "abandoned" their players. With new manager Tom Burns at the helm, newspapers called the players "Burns' Orphans." A variant was the **Ex-Colts**.

1150 Bronchos 1899 *National (M)*. The team did its 1899 spring training in Arizona. Moniker was a spin-off from "Colts." Teams doing "spring training" in the South and Southwest was in vogue. The nickname faded away by May.

1151 Cowboys 1899 *National (M)*. The team did its 1899 spring training in Arizona. The Chicago players got into shape doing a regimen that included riding horses.

1152 Desert Rangers 1899 *National (M)*. With the players riding horses to help get them in shape, Chicago newspapers called them the "Desert Rangers."

1153 Ranchers 1899 *National (M)*. This moniker was the fourth of five such "spring training" nicknames the Chicago Nationals were assigned by newspapers. Arizona's desert sun helped the players "sweat their way" into shape.

1154 Roughriders 1899 *National (M)*. Here was another Arizona spring training nickname. This one paid homage to Teddy Roosevelt's "Rough Riders" soldiers fighting in the 1898 Spanish-American War in Cuba. Some of the Chicago players actually rode horses to get in shape.

1155 Columbia Giants 1899–1900 *Negro independent team*; 1931 *Negro National (M)*. This was a new team that revived the 1900 name. In the era 1890–1920 of Black baseball, Giants, the most popular team nickname for black clubs, was chosen with an adjective in front of it, i.e., American Giants, Royal Giants, Cuban Giants, etc. "Columbia" was chosen because it was a spin-off of "America." A black social organization, known as the Columbia Club, sponsored the team. The team merged with the Chicago Unions to form the Chicago Union Giants in 1901.

1156 White Sox 1900 *American (ind.)*; 1901 to date *American (M)*. When owner Charlie Comiskey moved his St. Paul team to Chicago in March 1900, owner James Hart of the Chicago Colts of the National League allowed him the opportunity to play in the Windy City on the condition that the name "Chicago" be omitted from the players' jerseys and that the team play in a ballpark on the South Side near the foul-smelling Chicago Stockyards. Comiskey agreed but in a clever ruse got around that edict by dressing his players in white hose and naming his team the "White Stockings"— the nickname dropped by the Chicago Nationals back in 1888—but still forcefully identified with Chicago baseball by Chicago's fans. Newspapers quickly shortened the moniker to **White Socks, White Sox** and **ChiSox**. (Boston newspapers did the same with the 1908 Boston Americans going with Bosox.) Chicago sportswriters Carl Green and Irving "Si" Sanborn, realizing Comiskey's ruse, eagerly started using "White Stockings" and "White Sox" in news print. White Sox had been printed in newspapers all the way back to 1870 but it was in 1901 that the nickname exploded in popularity. In 1904, team scorer Christopher Hynes started writing "White Sox" instead of "White Stockings" on the scorecards he provided to reporters, who jumped on the shorter moniker to please their editors. By 1911 the name "White Sox" appeared on the players' jerseys. The Chicago Americans were also called White Stockings but by the start of the 1912 season, **White Sox** became the official nickname of the franchise. Indeed, the Spalding Baseball Guide of 1912 declared the franchise's

official nickname to be the White Sox. **White Socks** was also used for a few years but was dropped by 1911.

1157 Loftus' Legion 1900–01 *National (M)*. When field manager Tom Loftus took the helm, Chicago newspapers started to call the players "Loftus' Legion." Baseball players in this era were generically known as "Gladiators," making "Legion" a predictable spin-off from it.

1158 Bruins 1901 to date *National (M)*. This logical spin-off of Cubs has lasted an amazing 111 years. The tag is unofficial, and is not to be confused with the National Hockey League Boston Bruins.

1159 Remnants 1901 *National (M)*. The American League signed so many Chicago Colts players prior to the 1901 season that manager Frank Selee and management were left with the 1900 benchwarmers and discards not signed by other major league teams.

1160 ChiSox 1901 to date *American (M)*. First used in 1900, the abbreviation was newspaper-friendly (much like Bosox in Boston) and has been used continuously for 111 years.

1161 Pale Hose 1901 to date *American (M)*. First used in 1900, the moniker is an alternate employed by newspapers. The name has been in use now for more than 110 years. In 1908 Boston newspapers started calling their AL team the "Crimson Hose" and the "BoSox" in imitation.

1162 Original Go-Go-Sox 1901 *American (M)*. The 1959 "Go-Go White Sox" stole 113 bases in a "slow-foot slugging" era—a number which paled in comparison to the 280 bases swiped by the 1901 AL champion Chicagoans. Tag was coined by baseball authors David Nemec and Scott Flatow. Team was also known as (manager Clark) **Griffith's Go-Go Sox**.

1163 Union Giants 1901–04 *Negro independent team*. The team was formed from the merger of the Chicago Unions and the Chicago Columbia Giants. The adjective "Columbia" was dropped in favor of "Union" to precede the noun "Giants."

1164 West Siders 1901–15 *National (M)*. Team played in Westside Park until it moved to Weeghman Park on Chicago's Northside in 1916.

1165 Microbes 1902 *National (M)*. Depleted by AL player raids, the team signed young players, several of whom were rather short and slight in build, prompting some newspaper reporters to dub the team the "Microbes." With the team playing mediocre ball (68–69) the moniker was sometimes applied as a sarcastic tag. The American public, finally aware of the "germ theory," became paranoid about "microbes."

1166 Recruits 1902 *National (M)*. The 1902 team was again forced to sign young players and came up with three marvelous recruits—Frank Chance (age 24), Joe Tinker (age 21) and Johnny Evers (age 20). The name "recruit" eventually gave rise to the term "rookie" in 1917 when newly recruited soldiers—called "rookies"—boarded ships to sail to the war in Europe.

1167 Panamas 1903 *National (M)*. The team did its 1903 spring training in sunny Los Angeles where the players bought popular "Panama hats." The team did not play in the Central American country of Panama. A variant was **Panamahatmas**. Both monikers were discarded by May.

1168 Southsiders 1903 to date *American (M)*. Team played at Southside Park near the stockyards (1900–09) and then moved into Comiskey Park at 35th and Shields on Chicago's Southside in the Bridgeport neighborhood in April 1910. Team then moved into new Comiskey Park (now U.S. Cellular Field) at 35th and Shields in 1991.

1169 Zephyrs 1905 *National (M)*. Chicago is the "Windy City." In summertime gentle lake breezes, known as "zephyrs," flow from Lake Michigan into the city.

1170 Bare Cubs 1905 *National (M)*. Coined by the website "Dressed to the Nines: A History of the Baseball Uniform," it referred to the Chicago Nationals uniforms of 1905, which were the last major league baseball uniforms to be completely bare of any jersey letters, cap letter, and/or logo on the cap, breast or sleeve. The jerseys and pants were white and the caps and stockings were blue. Incidentally, blue became the traditional team color in 1892 when it replaced the ill-advised black stockings style (1888–91).

1171 Spuds 1905–06 *National (M)*. Team owner Charles Murphy was of Irish descent. Chicago was home to many Irish immigrants who began immigrating to Chicago in the 1840s because of the Great Potato Famine of Ireland. The moniker was used mostly by the *Chicago Tribune* newspaper. Irish potatoes back then had the nickname of "Murphy's Spuds"— Murphy being slang for "Irishman."

1172 Hitless Wonders 1905–06 *American (M)*; 1959 *American (M)*. Coined October 7, 1905, by Edward Nichols of *The Sporting News*, as the White Sox won 92 games with a flimsy .237 team batting average, the moniker was most notably used in 1906 as the White Sox won the AL pennant with a major league-low .230 team batting average. Like their 1959 descendants, the "Hitless Wonders" parlayed excellent pitching, sure defense and speed on the base paths to generate a 19-game winning streak in August and September to jump over previous AL leader New York. The only two players to hit over .250 were shortstop George Davis (.295) and outfielder Fielder Jones (.284). The term was first used in 1905 by Chicago sports reporters Charles Dryden and Hughie Fullerton. The 1959 team won the AL flag despite batting .250 and hitting only 97 home runs (lowest in the league).

1173 Leland Giants 1905–12 *Negro independent team*. Team was named in honor of manager Frank Leland.

1174 Giant-Killers 1906 *National (M)*. In this era "Giant Killers" became a spin-off from "Giants," as it was obvious that the latter was monopolized by the New York Nationals. From the legend "Jack the Giant Killer" Chicago newspapers praised the 1906 Chicago NL club for dethroning the 1905 NL and world champion New York Giants en route to major league baseball's greatest season as the "Giant Killers" won an astounding 116 games with only 36 defeats. The second-place Giants won 96 games and finished 20 games behind the Cubs. The "Giant Killers" were led by hitters Frank Chance, Joe Tinker and John Evers as well as pitchers Mordecai "Three Finger" Brown, Jack Pfiester, Orval Overall and Andy Coakley.

1175 Not-Quite Hitless Wonders October 1906 *American (M)*. Batting a league-low .230 in the regular season and only .160 in the first four games of the 1906 World Series against the cross-town rival Cubs, the White Sox erupted for 8–6 and 8–3 victories to clinch the 1906 World Series championship. The tag was coined by baseball authors Pete Palmer and Gary Gillette.

1176 Warriors 1906–09 *National (M)*. With Frank Chance at the managerial helm the Cubs won three pennants and two World Series before finishing second to the 110-victory Pittsburgh Pirates with 104 wins of their own. In this era "Warriors" was generic for any baseball team and even more so for championship teams. "Chance's Warriors" were led by hitters Frank Chance, Joe Tinker, Johnny Evers, Vic Saier, Frank Shulte, Solly Hoffman, Heinie Zimmerman and pitchers Jack Pfiester, Leo Cole and Lew Richie.

1177 Chance Men 1906–09 *National (M)*. In the era 1890–1920 newspaper sometimes resorted to clumsy "manager nicknames" for their teams and even created nicknames from team owners. Thus, we have such awkward monikers as Seleeites (Frank Selee), Somersets (William Somers), Stalwarts (Lee Stahl) and Loftusites (Tom Loftus).

1178 Big Bad Bears 1906–10 *National (M)*. Not at all like the losing "Cubbies" of the 1970s and 1980s, the Big Bad Bears won four NL pennants and two World Series in six seasons. Newspaper sports cartoons often depicted the team not as a cute little bear cub but a big and frightful grizzly bear. The image played on the mind of football coach George Halas when he named his 1922 NFL team the Chicago Bears. People tend to forget that between 1906 and 1945 — a period of only 39 years — the Cubs won *ten* National League pennants.

1179 The Greatest Baseball Machine of All Time 1906–12 *National (M)*. With 713 wins in seven years, the Cubs averaged 102 victories per season as they clinched four NL pennants and two World Series titles, prompting sportswriter Gerald Cohen of the *San Francisco Bulletin* on February 21, 1913, to grace the Chicagoans with the opulent title "The Greatest Baseball Machine of All Time."

1180 Cubbies 1908 to date *National (M)*. The popular "watering hole" (i.e., saloon) known as the Cubby Inn opened on Clark Street near Weegham Park in April 1916. The owner of the inn placed a live bear cub in a cage to hang outside the tavern. The mascot's name was "Joa the Cubbie Bear." The saloon name was inspired by the occasional use of "Cubbies" by reporters to describe the Chicago Nationals, starting in 1908 when the "Cubs" moniker became official. Indeed, the team's uniform logos and newspaper cartoons often used a cute, little mischievous "cubbie" to depict the team. By the 1980s the name, used only sporadically the previous 65 years, become controversial as some fans tired of the Cubs' losing ways, which included no winning record in the 1950s, eleven straight non-winning seasons in the period 1973–83 and nine of ten losing seasons in the period 1985–94. The moniker again became popular when new Cubs TV broadcaster Harry Caray started the tradition of singing "Take Me Out to the Ball Game" to the Wrigley Field fans during the Seventh-Inning Stretch in 1981. Caray invariably would sing the line "So let's root, root, root for the *Cubbies*!" and the name quickly caught on with fans and the press to the point that it surpassed "Bruins" as the franchise's "second nickname." Diminutive nicknames like Birdie, Brownie, Kittie and Cubbie have been commonly employed by newspaper reporters from since the nineteenth century.

1181 Nate Harris' Giants 1910 *Negro independent team*. In the era 1890–1920 the nickname "Giants" was the most popular nickname for black clubs. Harris was the field manager this year.

1182 American Giants 1911–19 *Negro independent team*; 1912–13 *Southern California (W)*; 1920–30 *Negro National (M)*; 1932 *Southern (M)*; 1934–35 *East–West (M)*; 1936 *Negro independent team*; 1937–48 *Negro American (M)*; 1949–54 *Negro American (ind.)*. This franchise chose the most popular nickname for black teams of the era, "Giants," and placed a patriotic adjective in front of it; hence, the "American Giants."

1183 Green Sox 1912 *United States (ind.)*. Players wore green-trim hose. Team was never known as the "Green Stockings." The shorter "Sox" had replaced "Stockings" in newspaper bylines.

1184 Trojans 1913 *National (M)*. When Cub player Johnny Evers, a native of Troy, New York, took the helm as manager for the Chicago team, newspapers called the players the "Trojans." When Evers left the team at the close of the 1913 season, the nickname was dropped.

1185 Chifeds 1914 *Federal (M)*. The Federal League tried amalgamated nicknames for its various clubs, such as Baltfeds, Brookfeds, Buffeds, Chifeds, Hoosier Feds, Pittfeds and (the worst) Sloufeds. Fans in FL cities gagged on the names and all were dropped by 1915 FL teams, including Chicago. The 1914 uniforms displayed a C-Feds logo on the left breast, which eventually resulted in the famous C-Cubs logo on the left breast of Cubs jerseys, starting in 1915.

1186 Whales 1915 *Federal (M)*. As the Chicago team battled for the 1915 FL pennant (which they won), this nickname, chosen in a name-the-team contest in April, soared in popularity. Chicagoan D.J. Eichoff submitted the winning entry, explaining that the team played on the Northside of town and the best commercial whales were found in Northern waters. Moreover, "to whale" means to lash, thrash or drub — something the team did winning the 1915 FL pennant.

1187 Cupboard of Hitters 1917 *American (M)*. The AL and world champion White Sox of 1917 were led offensively by steady hitters Joe Jackson, Happy Felsch, Swede Risberg, Fred McMullen and Chick Gandil, whom local newspapers praised as a "Cupboard of Hitters." "Shoeless Joe" Jackson, playing the middle of the "Dead Ball" era, produced a robust .356 batting average in 1917.

1188 Dynasty Sox 1917–20 *American (M)*. Baseball writer Richard Lindberg, speculating about how the White Sox had some of the best players in major league baseball these four years, called the team the "Dynasty Sox." Losing players in 1918 to the military draft and then suspending the nucleus of the 1920 team on September 10 because of the Black Sox scandal, the franchise was denied a potential four consecutive AL pennants.

1189 Black Sox 1918–20 *American (M)*; 1990 *American (M)*. Ironically, the team was called "Black Sox" in 1918, because apparently team owner Charlie Comiskey was so stingy with "per-diem" money for his players, they couldn't wash their uniforms after every game and were forced to don soiled jerseys, pants, caps, sanitary hose and stirrups before many games. It was Comiskey's penurious ways, i.e., low salaries and insufficient per-diem cash, that provoked the 1919 players to throw the World Series for gambler bribes. In response to news about the scandal, newspapers started using the "Black Sox" label only in 1920 as an investigation of the "thrown" 1919 World Series, between the "Black Sox" and the NL champion Cincinnati Reds, led to court proceedings. White Sox hitters Joe Jackson, Chick Gandil, Swede Risberg, Happy Felsch, and Fred McMullin were accused of striking out on easy pitches, making wild throws for errors and booting easy ground balls and pop-ups while White Sox pitchers Ed Cicotte and Lefty Williams allegedly tossed easy pitches to batters of the opposing Cincinnati Reds after getting bribe money from gamblers, intent on making a windfall by betting on the underdog Reds. Although these players were found not guilty in a court trial in 1920, they were banned from Organized Baseball for life by baseball commissioner Kenesaw Mountain Landis. Sporting new silver and black uniforms, with black stirrups, in the style of the white and black White Sox uniforms of the Go-Go-1950s and featuring new players like slugger Frank Thomas and pitcher Jack McDowell, the 1990 team jumped from seventh to second place with 94 victories in the American League Western Division. Only the "Black Sox" challenged the powerful Oakland A's for the AL Western Division title.

1190 Aggressive & Intelligent Bunch 1919 *American (M)*. Just as the NL pennant winners this year were the "Brainy Bunch" (Cincinnati), so the 1919 AL champions knew how to use the hit and run, the delayed steal, the relay, the squeeze bunt and the clutch hit to win the team's fourth pennant in 20 years—a run of success that the franchise never again duplicated (only two AL pennants in 93 years).

1191 Bleak Sox 1921–24 *American (M)*. Coined by baseball reporter Jerome Holtzman in his history book of the White Sox, the moniker lamented the unraveling of the 98-win 1920 team to increasing defeats culminating in an eighth-place finish in the American League in 1924. Except for a few winning seasons under manager Jimmy Dykes in the 1930s and 1940s, the White Sox would not be competitive again until 1951.

1192 Bears 1921–29 *National (M)*. Tag was a favorite moniker of the *Chicago Tribune* in the 1920s, which called both the baseball team and the professional football Chicago Bears by the same name. Indeed during the baseball season the *Chicago Tribune* used the names "Cubs" and "Bears" almost interchangeably.

1193 Wrigleys 1927 to date *National (M)*. Chewing gum owner Phil Wrigley purchased the Cubs and Weegham Field at the start of the 1927 season. He named the ballpark after himself, i.e., Wrigley Field. Chicago newspapers started calling the team the "Wrigleys." When the Wrigley family sold the Chicago Cubs to the *Chicago Trib-*

une in 1981, the name Wrigley Field was retained and local newspapers went right on calling the team the "Wrigleys."

1194 Comeback Cubs 1935 *National (M)*. Mired in fourth place on September 1, 1935, the Cubs reeled off 21 consecutive victories to leap into first place and win the NL pennant with a splendid 100–54 record. Also known as the **Rampaging Cubs**, the team was led by consistent hitters like Babe Herman, Stan Hack, Phil Cavaretta, Chuck Klein, Frank Demaree and Augie Galan.

1195 Glowing Cubs 1938 *National (M)*. Baseball authors Gary Gillette and Pete Palmer, citing Cub catcher Gabby Hartnett's exciting "homer in the gloamin'" on September 28 at dusk—which hardly any fan, player, umpire or reporter could see flying into the stands—to clinch the 1938 NL pennant, called the 1938 NL champions the "Glowing Cubs."

1196 Brown Bombers 1943–49 *Independent Negro*; 1945 *United States (ind.)*. In honor of boxing great Joe Louis, who was known as the "Brown Bomber." The USL was a paper league devised by Brooklyn Dodger GM Branch Rickey to sign the best available black talent in 1945–46. The USL played a few games in 1945 and none in 1946.

1197 Northsiders 1916 to date *National (M)*. When the Cubs moved to Weegham Park on Chicago's Northside, local newspapers started to call them the "Northsiders" to distinguish them from the Southside Chicago White Sox. The name has been used for nearly a century.

1198 I Don't Think Either of Them Can Win 1945 *National (M)*. When Chicago sportswriter Warren Brown was asked by people just before the 1945 Cubs-Tigers World Series began about which team would win, he replied, "I don't think either team can win!" Brown was referring to the World War II rosters of the two teams that were filled with 4F draft rejects, minor leaguers and over-the-hill veterans. Some historians refer to the 1945 Cubs and Tigers as the "Neither Can Win Cubs" and "Neither Can Win Tigers."

1199 Surprise Team of 1945 1945 *National (M)*. With a team roster depleted by the wartime military draft, the 1944 Cubs finished in fourth place with a losing 75–79 record. Most newspapers in the spring of 1945 figured the Cubs would finish about the same, but hitter Phil Cavaretta had an MVP season and the Cubs signed Hank Borowy from the Yankees (where he was 10–5), who won 11 of 13 decisions in Chicago. That powered the Cubs to a 98–56 record and the 1945 NL pennant.

1200 Hibernating Bruins 1946 to date *National (M)*. With only a wartime pennant (1945) on their mantle, the Cubs had eight losing seasons in the 1940s, no winning seasons in the 1950s, six straight winning seasons (1967–72) under manager Leo Durocher, and twenty losing seasons since 1980, with 22 playoff game defeats since 1984 and no pennants in 66 years. Frustrated Cub fans and newspapers often dismiss the franchise as the "Hibernating Bruins."

1201 Basement Bruins 1948–49, 1951, 1956, 1966, 1974, 1980–81, 1999–2000, 2006 *National (M)*. The franchise's eleven last-place finishes since 1945 have prompted some newspapers to call these cellar dwellers the "Basement Bruins."

1202 Go-Go-Sox 1951–67 *American (M)*. General manger Frank Lane realized after the 1950 season that cavernous Comiskey Park needed a team with good pitching, solid defense and lots of speed on the base paths and set out to sign players suited for this "pitchers' park." Starting in 1951 fans started chanting "Go, go, go!" urging speedy base runners like Minnie Minoso, Chico Carrasquel, Jim Busby, Jim Rivera, Luis Aparicio, Jim Landis and Don Buford to steal bases. Chicago led the AL in team steals for eleven straight seasons, 1951–61, and again in 1966.

1203 Comiskeys 1951–2002 *American (M)*. Coined by sportswriter Edgar Munzel, the name honors team founder and owner Charles A. Comiskey (a star player himself in the 1880s). In 1910 the

White Sox moved into Comiskey Park on the Southside. When new Comiskey Park (built in 1991 to replace old Comiskey Park) was re-named U.S. Cellular Field in 2003, the long-term moniker was discontinued.

1204 Lame Horses 1957–62 *National (M)*. Legendary WGN-TV and radio broadcaster Jack Brickhouse, contemplating the great potential of fire-balling pitchers Bob Anderson, Moe Drabowski, Dick Drott and Glen Hobbie, who all suffered arm injuries that shortened their careers, told reporters in 1964, "The Cubs had the horses. But they all came up lame."

1205 Lost Contenders 1957–64 *National (M)*. In this eight-year period, the Cubs had top-flight talent like hitters Ernie Banks, Dale Long, Tony Taylor, Billy Williams, George Altman, Ron Santo, George Altman and pitchers Dick Ellsworth, Moe Drabowski, Dick Drott, Glenn Hobbie, Jim Brewer, Don Elston, Lindy McDaniel, Larry Jackson and Ron Perranowski. However, the team had only one winning season (82–80 in 1963). Name was coined by George Castle in his 2000 book *The-Million-to-One-Team*.

1206 So-So-Sox 1960–62 *American (M)*. After winning the 1959 AL pennant, the White Sox cooled off to finish third, fourth and fifth place in the 10-team American League. Owner Bill Veeck blundered by trading away future stars. Name was coined by baseball writer Michael LeBlanc.

1207 Hitless Wonders II 1967 *American (M)*. This 1967 team amazed Chicagoans by staying in first place in the American League Western Division for five consecutive months despite the lowest team batting average in the major leagues—an amazingly weak .225 batting average. Second baseman Don Buford was the only White Sox regular to bat as high as .240 (he batted .241)! The White Sox were buoyed by the AL's best pitching staff with a league-best 2.45 ERA. Unfortunately, the team ran out of gas, losing its last five games to allow the Cinderella Boston Red Sox to finish first out of a pack of four contending teams.

1208 Eddie Stanky's Vultures 1967 *American (M)*. White Sox field manager called his team the "Vultures" for their amazing tenacity in hanging onto first place in the American League Western Division for five consecutive months until the last week of the regular season. Stanky explained to the press: "If you beat this team and think they are gone away from first place, they always, while you're not expecting it, quietly return to first place when you're not looking … just like vultures!" When the White Sox were eliminated on the final weekend of the season, a tearful Stanky told reporters, "All year long the more powerful teams feared **The Mouse**."

1209 Durocher's Dandies 1967–72 *National (M)*. By far the Chicago NL franchise's most underrated field manager was Leo Durocher. Leo "The Lip" (He was a notorious complainer with umpires.) led the Cubs to six consecutive winning seasons, a feat no Cub field manager has since accomplished. A spin-off tag of **Leo's Lion Cubs** was species-incorrect and ignored.

1210 The Greatest Team That Didn't Win 1967–72 *National (M)*. Moniker was coined by baseball writer David Claerbaut in his 2000 book of the same name. Claerbaut both praises and laments for Cub manager Leo Durocher, who did something no other Cub manager has been able to do for 70 years—lead the Cubs to six consecutive winning seasons. Team had marvelous hitters (Ernie Banks, Billy Williams, Ron Santo), steady fielders (Glen Beckert, Don Kessinger, Adolfo Phillips and Randy Hundley), and formidable pitchers (Ferguson Jenkins, Ken Holtzman, Milt Pappas, Bill Hands, Joe Niekro and Phil Regan), Durocher won no flag. Banks, Williams, Jenkins and Santo are in the Hall of Fame.

1211 Nearly Gone Sox 1968 *American (M)*. In a melancholy spin-off from "Go-Go Sox," newspapers complained that the team was losing, Comiskey Park was experiencing a high crime rate, which frightened fans from attending games, and that team owner Art Allyn blundered by leaving popular WGN-TV to broadcast games on low-ratings cable television. When Allyn scheduled eight home games to be played in Milwaukee, the media openly speculated about the franchise moving to Milwaukee.

1212 Sagging Sox 1968–70 *American (M)*. After 17 consecutive winning seasons, the White Sox lost 303 games in the next three years. The 1968 team scored a major league low 438 runs and the 1970 team lost 106 games, pushing team owner Art Allyn to consider moving the franchise to Milwaukee.

1213 Big Bad Bears II 1969 *National (M)*. The *New York Daily Herald* called the Chicagoans the "Big Bad Bears" until the Mets caught and passed Chicago in September to win the NL Eastern Division title with a 100–62 mark. The Cubs slipped back to a 92–70 mark and a second-place finish.

1214 Grizzly Bears 1977 *National (M)*. Manager Herman Franks led the 1977 Cubs to a roaring start with a major league best 47–22 record up to All-Star break, prompting fans and newspapers to use the spin-off "Grizzly Bears." However, the team had a miserable record of 34–59 in the second half of the season to wind up 81–81 and 20 games behind the eventual NL Eastern Division champion Phillies.

1215 Southside Hitmen 1977 *American (M)*. Used by Chicago newspapers to hearken images of Gangster Era Chicago, "hitmen" (i.e., machine gun-toting assassins), the moniker referred to White Sox hitters like Richie Zisk, Oscar Gamble, Eric Soderholm, Ralph Garr and Chet Lemon. With offense leading the way (the team hit 192 home runs in cavernous Comiskey Park), the team led the American League Western Division for the first 20 weeks of the regular season until the streaking Kansas City Royals overtook them in September to clinch the AL Western Division title. The "Southside Hitmen" eventually finished third with a 90–72 record.

1216 Little White Machine 1977 *American (M)*. Used by Chicago newspapers as a spin-off of Cincinnati's famous "Big Red Machine " of the 1970s, the tag honored the amazing staying power of the team in occupying first place in the AL Western Division for five consecutive months until the Kansas City Royals roared past the "Little White Machine" in September.

1217 Spiders 1981 *National (M)*. In 1981, before the baseball strike in August mercifully made it mathematically impossible to do so, the Cubs were actually on a pace in April, May and June to approach the 20–134 mark of the infamous Cleveland Spiders of the 1899 National League. Inevitable comparisons, i.e., the "Chicago Spiders," were being made until the team managed to win enough games in the second half of the season (after the strike was settled) to wind up with a 38–65 record.

1218 Flubs 1981, 1987, 1999–2000, 2006 *National (M)*. A sarcastic, pejorative tag applied to the horrible 1981 Cubs team, used mostly by hostile St. Louis Cardinal and Chicago White Sox fans. The name pops up in any year that the Cubs finish in last place in their division (see the years listed in the first line of this entry). The epithet is shunned by newspapers, TV and radio. Variations also used are **Scrubs, Scrubbies, Flubbies, Chubbies, Drubs** and **Drubbies**.

1219 Loveable Losers 1981 to date *National (M)*. As TV ratings soared in the 1980s with the popularity of Cubs TV broadcaster Harry Caray and the extension of Cubs TV broadcasts on the WGN-TV super station throughout the United States, and even into foreign lands, more people began to view the exploits of a gaily marketed but usually dismally performing team. Cynical fans started calling the team, which generated high TV ratings and drew capacity crowds of adoring fans only to lose year in and year out—the "Loveable Losers." Some critics claimed the new owner—the *Chicago Tribune*—deliberately projected the image of "Loveable Losers" to stimulate ticket and merchandise sales without any intention of spending enough money to improve the team.

1220 Winning Ugly Sox 1983 *American (M).* After his Texas Rangers lost a game to the White Sox in June in which the Sox played "sloppy," i.e., errors, base running gaffes, balks and wild pitches, frustrated Texas manager Doug Rader complained to reporters, "Those guys win ugly!" The nickname immediately stuck in the newspapers and with White Sox fans, as the "Winning Ugly" White Sox played near .700 ball in the second half of the season to win the AL Western Division by a then-record 20 games over second-place Kansas City. Notable players on the team that "won ugly" were hitters Ron Kittle, Carlton Fisk, Greg Luzinski, and Harold Baines and pitchers Lamar Hoyt, Floyd Bannister and Rich Dotson.

1221 America's Team 1984–2003 *National (M).* While the NFL Dallas Cowboys of the 1970s and the 1982 Atlanta Braves used this moniker as a marketing ploy, the 1984–2003 Chicago Cubs were idolized by millions of adoring fans as "America's Team" via the WGN-TV super station and because of the "Mecca of Baseball"— Wrigley Field. After an agonizing NLCS playoff meltdown against the Florida Marlins in 2003, the "America's Team" image was discredited. As the team started losing again in 2009, the "America's Team" status was replaced by the "Loveable Losers" image as attendance declined at Wrigley Field.

1222 Black and Blue Bears 1985 *National (M).* The defending NL Eastern Division champions got off to a good start by winning 30 of their first 50 games and reaching first place by May 15. The team then suffered so many injuries that they tumbled to a 77–85 record to finish 23 and one-half games behind the NL Eastern Division– winning Cardinals. Cub uniforms have blue trim.

1223 Bruins-in-Ruins 1985 *National (M).* After nearly getting to the 1984 World Series, the Cubs were ruined by injuries in 1985 as hitters Bob Dernier and Gary Matthews as well as pitchers Dennis Eckersley, Steve Trout and Rick Sutcliffe were disabled for extended periods of times drop the Cubs from 96 victories in 1984 to only 77 wins in 1985.

1224 Little Bears 1986 *National (M).* With the 1984 NL Eastern Division championship roster aging, general manager Dallas Green signed a lot of young players for 1986 in the hope that the young blood would spark the team but their inexperience doomed them to a 70–90 record, landing them in sixth and last place in the National League Eastern Division.

1225 Strange Sox 1986 *American (M).* Ex-ballplayer and TV broadcaster Ken Harrelson was hired as the club's general manager and proceeded to make weird trades (there were 20 bench players and 18 pitchers this year) and moves, i.e., putting catcher Carlton Fisk in left field. These moves undermined field manager Tony LaRussa, who was fired in June as the team skidded to a 72–90 record.

1226 Team Chaos 1986 *American (M).* Ken Harrelson's one-year run as the team's GM threw the franchise into a resulting chaos that led to four consecutive losing seasons.

1227 Runless Hose 1986 *American (M).* The White Sox this season scored only 644 runs—lowest in the American League. The team batting average of .247 was also lowest of the 14 American League teams.

1228 Harrelson's Circus 1986 *American (M).* With such stunts as veteran catcher Carlton Fisk playing in left field and the signing of 18 pitchers and 21 position pitchers, local newspapers started to call GM Ken Harrelson's team a "circus."

1229 Swoon Sox 1987 *American (M).* The team lost 21 games in 1987 in the traditional "June Swoon" that White Sox fans have experienced and dreaded since the 1920s. Name was coined by baseball writer Dave Van Dyck.

1230 Smurfs 1987–88 *National (M).* In cynical imitation of the popular "Blue Smurf" dolls that were a big seller in the 1980s, Cubs fans started calling the losing, blue-trim uniformed players of the 1987 and 1988 seasons "The Smurfs." A smurf is some kind of harmless, pixie-like elf that some angry Cubs fans confirmed as accurately describing their non-competitive players.

1231 Fregosi's Forlorns 1988 *American (M).* With field manager Jim Fregosi at the helm, the team lost 90 games in 1988. More than forlorn—the White Sox were just plain lousy with a .247 team batting average and 4.12 earned run average.

1232 St. Petersburg Sailors 1988 *American (M).* The excitement of new ownership by Jerry Reinsdorf (who bought the team in 1981) following the 1983 AL Western Division title had worn off. The team was in its fourth losing season in five years, complaints returned about the crime-ridden Comiskey Park neighborhood, and Ken Harrelson's one-year tenure as club GM ruined the franchise's farm system. When Reinsdorf threatened to move the franchise to Tampa-St. Petersburg, local newspapers started to mock the franchise as the "St. Petersburg Sailors" and the **St. Petersburg Sox.** In a midnight move, the Illinois senate voted funds for the construction of a publically owned stadium, which eventually became U.S. Cellular Field.

1233 Boys of Zimmer 1989 *National (M).* In a play-on-word spin-off of Roger Kahn's famous book on the Brooklyn Dodgers of the 1950s—*The Boys of Summer,* the 1980 Chicago Cubs, champions of the National League Eastern Division and led by field manager Don Zimmer, were known as the "Boys of Zimmer." Although the "Boys of Zimmer" lost the NLCS to San Francisco, 4 games to 1, manager Zimmer had some glamorous players, including hitters Ryne Sandberg, Mark Grace, Andre Dawson, Dwight Smith, Shawon Dunston and pitchers Rick Sutcliffe, Mile Bielecki and Mitch Williams.

1234 Good Chemistry Cubs 1989 *National (M).* Coined by baseball writer Dave Van Dyke, the moniker referred to field manager Don Zimmer's NL Eastern Division–winning players (93–69) that had a good "chemical mix" of hitting (leading the NL in BA at .261), good basepath work (leading NL in runs scored at 702), fielding (.980 fielding average, which was fourth-best in the league) and decent pitching (a 3.43 team ERA and a league-high 55 saves).

1235 Struggling Sox 1989 *American (M).* The team's fourth straight losing season saw them drop into seventh and last place in the American League Western Division with a 69–93 mark. Tag was coined by *The Sporting News.*

1236 Good Guys in Black 1993–94 In an ironic twist from the Hollywood movie cliché where "the bad guys always wear black," the White Sox players wore NFL Oakland Raider–like silver and black uniforms as they won the 1993 AL Western Division title with a 94–68 record. The "Good Guys in Black" were led by hitters Frank Thomas, Bo Jackson, Robin Ventura and Ozzie Guillen, as well as pitchers Jack McDowell, Alex Fernandez, Wilson Alvarez and Jason Bere. The 1994 "Good Guys in Black" were also in first place in August in the AL West when the players' strike hit. Team was also styled as the "Good Guys Who Wear Black." TV broadcaster Ken Harrelson occasionally refers to the home team players as the **Good Guys**—a somewhat chauvinistic but mildly endearing name.

1237 Titanics 1995 *American (M).* After two consecutive American League Central Division first-place finishes, the 1995 White Sox sank to a 68–76 record, 32 games behind AL Central champ Cleveland, mostly due to a pitching staff meltdown as the team's ERA soared to a 4.85 mark. Tag was coined by ex-player and baseball editor Bill Mazeroski.

1238 Keystone Kubs 1996 *National (M).* The 1996 squad hit the skids with a seven-game losing streak in September with the players throwing the ball away on routine throws, over-slides on the bases, and letting pop-ups drop between three fielders, reminiscent of the

"Keystone Cops" 1920s silent movies about wild-eyed, bumbling, building-destroying policemen.

1239 Gilligan's Islanders 1997 *National (M)*. The Cubs started the 1997 season losing two games in Atlanta and then two games against the Florida Marlins before getting stranded in Miami because of rainstorms. When baseball writer and reporter Mike Kiley noted how weary Cubs fans were already becoming cynical about the bungling players, he humorously called them "Gilligan's Islanders" after the popular 1965–70 TV show "Gilligan's Island" starring Bob Denver, Alan Hale, Tina Louise and Jim Backus about a crew of inept bunglers trying to survive on a rainy tropical island following their tour boat's shipwreck.

1240 Team Tribune 1997 *National (M)*. This tag was pinned on the 1997 team, which finished with a cruddy 68–94 record to finish fifth and last in the Central Division, by *Chicago Sun Times* baseball writer Jay Mariotti, who was complaining about the stingy fiscal policies of the rival newspaper and owner of the team, the *Chicago Tribune*. For years, Cub fans had griped about the miserly Wrigley family (which owned the team from 1926–80) that refused to spend enough money to get good pitchers that were desperately needed in a home run haven "pillbox" like Wrigley Field. When the *Chicago Tribune* bought the team in 1981, Cubs fans hoped that "The Trib" would spend more money on the team, especially for pitching, and install lights to prevent day-game August "burnouts" of the players (as happened in 1969 when the gasping Cubs let the Miracle Mets rocket by them in the NL Eastern Division). The *Tribune* did spend more money (adjusted for inflation) than the Wrigley family ever did, which resulted in NL Eastern Division titles in 1984 and 1989, NL Central Division titles in 2003, 2007–08 and a wild-card berth in 1998, but never could countenance moving the franchise away from the dilapidated Wrigley Field (the masochistic fans' "Cash Cow") into a state-of-the-art sliding-roof domed stadium somewhere else in Chicago to increase the number of night games from a paltry 20 nocturnal contests to the 70 home night games every other major league team schedules. By the time the *Tribune* sold the club to billionaire Sam Zell in 2008, the franchise's World Series drought had reached 100 years.

1241 Riggleman's Rigglers 1998 *National (M)*. With field manager Jim Riggleman at the helm and Sammy Sosa slamming a Ruthian 66 home runs, the 1998 Cubs "wriggled" their way up and down the National League Central Division standings until they grabbed a playoff berth on the last day of the regular season.

1242 The Million-to-One-Team 2000 *National (M)*. A moniker coined by Las Vegas sports bookie John Avello, when interviewed in 1992 by baseball writer George Castle, who was doing research for his eventual 2000 book of the same title. The tag refers to the Cubs, who are the only National League club from the "Old Eight" franchises of 1945, to have failed to win the NL pennant in the past 67 seasons.

1243 Monsters of Baseball 2000 *American (M)*. The 2000 White Sox jumped into first place in the AL Central Division in April and started playing .650 baseball. When the team won seven straight road games against the New York Yankees and Cleveland Indians in June, the *Chicago Sun-Times* held a fan poll to give the players an unofficial alternate moniker. The winning entry was "Mob"—ostensibly in reference to the legendary Chicago mafia—but it was also an acronym for "Monsters of Baseball." When the White Sox were swept in three games in the first round of the AL playoffs by the Seattle Mariners, the "Mob" moniker was dropped.

1244 Cinderella White Sox 2000 *American (M)*. The *Baltimore Sun* on May 6, 2001, quoted impatient Cleveland manager Charlie Manuel's rebuke of a reporter who kept talking about the "Cinderella" teams of 2000 (White Sox) and 2001 (the Minnesota Twins). Manuel

huffed, "I'm getting tired of hearing about the Cinderella story coming out of the AL Central every year. Last year it was the Cinderella White Sox and now it's the Cinderella Twins." The White Sox jumped from 76 wins in 1999 to 95 wins in 2000 to clinch the AL Central Division.

1245 Completely Useless By September, i.e., C.U.B.S. 2002 *National (M)*. A clever acronym dreamed up by some Cub fans that found its way into home and rival city newspapers. The term was a historical observation on the mythical failings of the franchise in Septembers and Octobers as evidenced by the wrenching ordeals of Cub fans, regardless of whether it was a competitive Cubs team melting down in a pennant chase or a nowhere outfit approaching 100 regular season defeats. The name didn't catch on perhaps because it was too cruel.

1246 The Wizards of Ozzie 2005 *American (M)*. In a spin-off from the 1939 movie *The Wizard of Oz*, some Chicago newspapers referred to the surprise AL and World Series champion as the "Wizards of Ozzie" after colorful field manager Ozzie Guillen, whose loose mouth and chronic obscenities prompted reporters to dub him the "Blizzard of Oz." Ozzie's "Wizards" went 99–63 and then won 11 of 12 post-season games to capture Chicago's first baseball world title in 88 years. To utter a "blizzard of words" means to speak rapidly and loudly.

1247 Say It Is So White Sox 2005 *American (M)*. A *Chicago Tribune* story of September 28, 1920, described a small boy approaching White Sox star and accused bribe-taker "Shoeless Joe" Jackson in front a Chicago courthouse, where Jackson and six other Sox players were brought to trial in the infamous Black Sox scandal. The young lad tearfully beseeched Jackson, "Say it ain't so, Joe." Jackson allegedly said, "Yes, kid, I'm afraid it is." Subsequent reports over the last 90 years denied such an exchange took place and relegated it to the realm of legend. In any case, when the 2005 White Sox won their first AL pennant in 46 years and the city's first World Series title in 88 years, joyous White Sox fans called the team the "Say It Is So White Sox." Phil Rogers wrote a book, *Say It's So*, describing the White Sox's championship year.

1248 Right Sox 2005 *American (M)*. A tag assigned to the 2005 American League champions by baseball writer Phil Rogers in his 2006 book *Say It's So*.

1249 Surprising Sox 2005 *American (M)*. Baseball authors Gary Gillete and Pete Palmer astutely noted that most baseball magazines in the spring of 2005 predicted that the White Sox would win only "75 to 80 games and finish 3rd in the AL Central behind Minnesota and Cleveland." However, the White Sox surprised the pundits with a pitching staff that, one through ten, was the best in baseball this season. That, combined with a powerful offense, energized the White Sox to the world title.

1250 Hibernating Cubs 2009 *National (M)*. Used sporadically to describe losing Cub seasons in the pennant-less era of 1945–2008, *The Sporting News* used it for the 2009 Cubs, who were tied with the Cardinals in the NL East on August 5, and, then "fell asleep" with erratic hitting and bad fielding to skid to 10 games behind St. Louis by August 31.

1251 British Petroleum Cubs 2010 *National (M)*. In reference to the messy British Petroleum oil rig disaster in the Gulf of Mexico during the spring and summer of 2010, Steve Rosenblum, sports broadcaster of Chicago's WSCR radio, described both Chicago teams—Cubs and White Sox—to be the British Petroleum Cubs and British Petroleum White Sox for the cruddy losing records both teams were sporting in June. The Cubs went on to lose 90 games and finish fifth in the NL Central Division. In a stroke of supreme irony, a sponsor was procured for the annual Cubs–White Sox inter-league competition, a sponsor that would donate a sterling silver cup bearing its name starting in 2010 to be awarded to the team winning the six-game series. That sponsor was British Petroleum. When the BP Cup was introduced at the height of the BP oil spill, both Cub and White Sox fans hooted in derision.

1252 Sad Sox 2010 *American (M)*. Coined by *Chicago Sun-Times* reporter Toni Ginneti to describe a team that went 24–33 in its first 57 games and then slumped in September, losing 12 of 14 games to allow the torrid Minnesota Twins (who played .700 ball from the All-Star break to their September 20 clinching date) to seize the AL Central Division title. Only a 25–5 hot streak just before the All-Star break and a 9-of-11 closing kick allowed the "Sad Sox" to finish second with a winning 88–74 record.

1253 Schizophrenic Sox 2010 *American (M)*. After a bad start in April and May, the team won 25 of 30 games to vault into the AL Central lead by the end of July, only to play under–.500 ball in August, allowing Minnesota to take the AL Central lead. An eight-game September losing streak handed the division crown to the Twins only to be followed by a season-ending hot streak of nine wins in 11 games. Name was coined by *Chicago Sun-Times* writer Joe Cowley.

1254 Dow-Jones Sox 2010–11 *American (M)*. Like the wild undulations of the Dow-Jones stock market, the White Sox played .400 ball in the spring and then .700 ball in June and July (25 wins in 30 games) only to skid to .400 ball in August and a September eight-game loss streak that knocked them out of the 2010 AL Central Division title race. With nothing to play for, the team got hot again, winning 9 of 11 contests, to finish with an 88–74 mark and second place in the division. Tag was coined by ESCR radio broadcaster Les Grobstein.

1255 Ground Hogs 2011 *National (M)*. Chicago's WSCR sports broadcaster Les Grobstein lamented that the Cubs' 23–34 record on June 6 was proving that they, once again, were spiraling into yet another losing season, and likened these repeated failures, extending all the way back to 1946, to the funny 1990 Bill Murray movie *Ground Hog's Day*, where every day Murray woke up in his bed, it was Ground Hog's Day, again!

1256 Dead-Ass Cubs 2011 *National (M)*. WGN-TV broadcaster Bob Brenly, who won the 2001 World Series managing the Arizona Diamondbacks, harshly criticized the 2011 Cub players, who fell as low as 41–65 in July, for "lacking hustle and emotion," while also committing too many mental mistakes. Never one for mincing his words, Brenly called the club "dead-ass." A non-obscene vulgarity, both noun and adjective, refers to a person who is both careless and lazy.

1257 Sox-a-tanics 2011 *American (M)*. A spin-off from the 1909 *Titanic* sinking, sportswriter Joe Cowley used this moniker to describe the White Sox's April decline as the team lost 14 of 18 games to sink to a season-threatening 11–22 record by May 10. The team fought its way up the standings by going 62–49 only to be torpedoed by Detroit (who swept the Sox, 6–0, in two crucial series) and sink to a third-place finish with a losing record.

1258 Cockroaches 2011 *American (M)*. Noting how the White Sox (and the Cleveland Indians) "refused to die" when it came to their AL Central Division title hopes as of September 1, WSCR broadcaster Les Grobstein, on his August 30 radio show, branded these two teams, both five games behind the Detroit Tigers, as the "cockroaches of the AL Central Division." In September the Tigers played at a .700 clip and pummeled both Chicago and Cleveland in showdown series to finally kill off these bugs.

1259 Slopfest Sox 2011 *American (M)*. In a typical September Sox skid, the team lost six games in a row to the Detroit Tigers and then blew seven consecutive games, prompting Rick Tellander of the *Chicago Sun-Times* to describe the error-prone and mental mistake-committing play of the team a "slopfest." Tag is a play on words from the franchise's annual winter fan festival called "Sox Fest." Some fans noted how the "All-In White Sox" slogan of the season had now become the **All-Out** White Sox.

1260 Thorny Sox 2011 *American (M)*. When the White Sox blew an 8–1 lead to lose to the Tigers, 9–8, on two ninth-inning home runs in Detroit on September 3, to push them seven games behind Detroit, a *Chicago Sun-Times* reporter complained, "When you embrace the White Sox, they leave you embedded with thorns." The next night, the Sox were destroyed, 18–2.

1261 Jekyll & Hyde Sox Tag was used, August 1, 2011, by controversial radio show host Mike North to describe a White Sox team that started this season 11–22 then bounced back to post a 41–29 mark, only to lose six in a row and then surge to six wins in seven decisions to stay in the race in this season's woeful American League Central Division.

Chickasha, Oklahoma

1262 Indians m1904m *Southwestern (A)*. Team started season in Shawnee and then moved here June 30 before moving back to Shawnee August 3. Team was named after the Chickasaw Indians. The term "Chickasha" is a Chickasaw word that means "rebel." With Mr. Van Ness at the helm, newspapers called the players "Van Ness' Indians."

1263 Chicks 1920–21 *Western Assn. (D)*; 1922 *Oklahoma State (D)*. The name is a spin-off from "Chickasha," which means "rebel" in the Chickasaw language. Team was a farm club of the Class A Southern Association Memphis Chickasaws. In this era, higher classification minor league teams sometimes had a farm club of the lower classifications.

1264 Chiefs 1948–52 *Sooner State (D)*. Name was chosen in honor of the Chickasaw Indians and other tribes. Oklahoma is known as the "Indian State" and the "Land of the Red Men." With Ray Honeycutt at the helm in 1948, newspapers called the players "Honeycutt's Chiefs."

Chico, California

1265 Heat 1997–2002 *Western (ind.)*. The city experiences hot California summers.

1266 Outlaws 2005 to date *Golden Baseball (ind.)*; 2011 *North American (ind.)*. Outlaws plagued Chico from its founding in 1860 until 1900 when marshals, sheriffs and their posses, previously on horseback, started using automobiles to track down the bad guys. With owner Kevin Outcalt in charge of the franchise, the team was known as "Outcalt's Outlaws." In baseball, teams and leagues that were not members of Organized Baseball, i.e., the major leagues and the National Association of Professional Minor Leagues, were known as "outlaws."

Chihuahua, Chihuahua, Mexico (aka Ciudad de Chihuahua, Chihuahua City)

1267 Los Dorados 1940 *Mexican (ind.)*; 1946 *Mexican National (ind.)*; 1952 *Arizona–Texas (C)*; 1956–57 *Central Mexican (C)*; 1958 *Arizona–Mexico (C)*; 1973–82 *Mexican (AAA)*; 2007 to date. Old tales have it that there was a legendary "City of Gold" in the region. Spanish conquistadors searched for it in vain. Ironically, the Spaniards discovered silver in the region around 1700. The Spaniards brutally forced the natives to work the silver mines.

1268 Centauros 1973–82 *Mexican (AAA).* The legendary Pancho Villa, who used Chihuahua as a home base, was known as "El Centauro" (The Centaur) because he was always photographed riding on a horse. In mythology the centaur is half man and half horse.

Chillicothe, Ohio

1269 Logans 1884 *Ohio (ind.).* Benjamin Logan was a settler who established Fort Logan in this area in 1775 to protect settlers from attacks by the Shawnee Indians. The fort was renamed Chillicothe in 1796 when the city was founded. "Chillicothe" is the Shawnee word for "town."

1270 Chillicothe Base Ball Club 1894x *Tri-State.* Team disbanded in mid-season. Team had no nickname.

1271 Infants 1910–12 *Ohio State (D).* Team had numerous baby-faced young players. The youth and inexperience of the 1910 players showed as the team finished sixth and last in 1910 and again in 1912. "Infants" was a term describing a young team that was struggling on the field. With manager W. Cochran at the helm, newspapers called the players "Cochran's Infants."

1272 Babes 1913–15m *Ohio State (D).* Team moved to Huntington (WV) July 13. Fans and newspapers switched from the more pitying "Infants" to the affectionate "Babes" as the team jumped from last to first to win the 1913 Ohio State League pennant.

1273 Paints 1993–2008 *Frontier (ind.).* Name also refers to the Paint Horse, i.e., "Pinto," which Spaniards brought over to North America starting in the sixteenth century and the riding of which was mastered by the Indians. Team logo is a "painter" horse.

Chinandega, Chinandega, Nicaragua

1274 Los Tigres 2004–05–07–08 *Liga Professional de Nicaragua (W);* 2009–10 to date *Liga Professional de Nicaragua (W).* Jaguars and pumas, found in the jungles of Nicaragua, are sometimes known in the Spanish language as "tigres."

Chiriqui-Bocas, Bocas del Toro, Archipelago, Panama

1275 Los Campesinos 1962–63 *Liga de Panama (W).* Nearby sugar plantations transport sugar cane to processing plants. Campesino is the Spanish word for peasant or farmer.

1276 Los Cigarrelleros 1963–64–68–69 *Liga de Panama (W).* Nearby plantations transport tobacco to processing plants. Cigarillo means cigarette, and, cigarrelleros means cigarette-makers.

Chongju, North Choalla, South Korea (old spelling Zenshu)

1277 Raiders 1991–99 *Korean (ind.).* The 41st British Commando "Raiders" distinguished themselves during the Korean War in 1950. The Ssangbangwool Clothing Company. owner of the team, also chose "Raiders" to emulate the 1976 and 1980 NFL Super Bowl champion Oakland Raiders.

1278 SK Wyvern 2000 to date *Korean (ind.).* New owner SK Company chose "Wyvern," which refers to the heraldic dragon, used in Britain in the Middle Ages, to get away from the overused symbol of "Dragon"—a historic Asian symbol. Name includes the letters SK after team owner Son-Kil-seung. Sangbang Wool Company (1991–99) sold the team to Son Kil-seung in 2000.

Ciego de Avila, Ciego de Avila, Cuba (Ciudad de Ciego Avila)

1279 Club de Beisbol Ciego de Avila 1977–78 to date *Cuban National (S).* Team had no nickname.

Cienfuegos, Cienfuegos, Cuba (Ciudad de Cienfuegos)

1280 Petroleros 1928–29–30–31 *Liga Cubana (W);* 1939–40–44–45 *Liga Cubana (W).* City is a port for oil ships. Petrolero means "oiler."

1281 Elefantes 1945–46–60–61 *Liga Cubana (W);* 1977–78 to date *Liga Cubana (W).* The 1945–46 Cuban League encouraged fan name-the-team contests in each of the four baseball cities of the circuit to chose a mascot for each team. Cienfuegos became the "Elephants," while Havana became the "Lions," Almendares was the "Scorpions," and Matanzas became the "Tigers." Years earlier Santa Clara had been the "Leopards." With World War II ended, many players returned to the winter leagues, prompting club managements to more vigorously market their teams.

1282 Camaroneros 1977–78 to date *Nacional Cubana (S).* Fishing boats bring in seafood, including shrimp, for cleaning and packing in warehouses. "El camaron means shrimp. "El camaronero" means "shrimp-fisher."

Cincinnati, Ohio

1283 Red Stockings 1869–70 *Independent;* 1876–80 *National (M);* 1881 *Independent;* 1882–89 *American Assn. (M);* 1884 *Union Assn. (M);* 1890–1912 *National (M).* The 1868 Cincinnati amateur team introduced Knickerbocker pants, which ended at the knee, not so much to allow more flexibility at the knee than to avoid tripping over one's pant cuffs. The lower legs were covered with bright red woolen stockings—giving rise to the nickname. The style was ridiculed at first and even regarded as "obscene" because "the manly shape of their legs could be observed by the fair sex." Newspapers immediately shortened the name to "Reds." But in three short years, the style became universal and lasted 125 years. In 1876, the new NL team revived the old "Reds" name by dressing the players in red stockings. Cincinnati newspapers immediately called the team **Redlegs** and **Reds**, although there was not as yet any prejudice against the lengthy Red Stockings. In 1882, the American Association declared red to be the official stocking color of the Cincinnati team. By 1913, newspaper editors were dropping Red Stockings in favor of Reds, Red Sox and Redlegs. In 1913, both *The Sporting News* and *Spalding's Baseball Guide* disavowed the use of "Red Stockings" and declared "Reds" to be Cincinnati's official team nickname.

1284 Buckeyes 1876 *National (M).* Ohio is the Buckeye State. Moniker was dropped in 1877 to avoid conflict with the neighboring Columbus Buckeyes.

1285 Ponies 1876–80 *National (M).* Although "Ponies" in this era could mean young players, the designation here referred to Cincinnati's status as a new team in the 1876 National League, i.e., an "expansion team." In the nineteenth century, "colts" meant young players, whereas "ponies" meant an expansion team. The 1876 National league consisted of six "returnees" from the 1875 National Association plus two expansion "pony teams" in Cincinnati and Louisville.

1286 Porkopolitans 1876–80 *National (M);* 1890–1912 *National (M).* Cincinnati has remained an important meat-packing center to the present day. When the Cincinnati club established "Reds" as its official team nickname in 1912, the 13-letter long "Pokorpolitans" began to lose favor with newspaper editors, although it did sporadically appear in print until the 1920s. Newspapers almost always contracted the moniker to **Porkers.**

1287 Queen City 1876–80 *National (M)*; 1890–1912 *National (M)*. Cincinnati is known as the "Queen City of the Ohio River." In the nineteenth century Cincinnati grew fast, built many beautiful buildings, and became the economic hub of the Ohio River, prompting the nickname of "Queen City." The baseball team was known by the singular "Queen City" and the plural "Queen Citys." Cincinnati is also known as the "Queen City of the West."

1288 Si Keck's Stinker Nine 1877 *National (M)*. Team owner Josiah "Si" Keck also owned a waste-burning plant, a fertilizer factory and a meat-packing plant, creating an unsavory stench (similar to the notorious Southside Chicago Stock Yards). As the season progressed, the 1877 team sank to sixth and last place. Newspapers and fans, especially when they started to get tipsy in the National League's only "wet" ballpark, complained, "This team stinks!"

1289 Pioneers 1879 *National (M)*; 1884, 1889 *National (M)*. As on the 10th anniversary of the "pioneer" Red Stockings of 1869, the moniker was used for the fifteenth and twentieth anniversaries of the advent of baseball's first all-professional nine.

1290 Zebra Stockings 1882 *National.* In a cacophony of colors, major league teams (in both the NL and AA) made players wear specially designated stocking colors for each team and designated colors for jerseys based on a player's field position. The system was such a mess that it was dropped in June, with teams in both leagues reverting to white uniforms at home and grays on the road. Name was derived from the team's red, white and black-striped hose.

1291 Maroons 1882–89 *National (M)*. Players wore red stockings, which some people described as maroon or scarlet.

1292 Scarlets 1882–89 *National (M)*. Players wore red stockings, which some people described as maroon or scarlet.

1293 Outlaw Reds 1884 *Union Association (M)*. Players wore red hose. The Union Association was regarded by the National League and American Association as an "outlaw" league for failing to honor the reserve clause established in 1882. As the UA "stole" players from the NL/AA, the NL/AA teams spent money to "steal them back," effectively running the UA into bankruptcy.

1294 Avengers 1884 *Union Assn.(M)*. According to David Nemec in his *The Beer and Whiskey League*, Messrs. Justus Thorne and John McLean were angry at the Cincinnati American Association franchise that had forced them to sell their stock as part-owners of that team in 1883. To "avenge themselves," the two men gained ownership of the Cincinnati Unions and then raided teams of Organized Baseball for players. Their target eventually turned out be not the AA Reds, but rather the NL Cleveland Blues. Thorne and McLean, unhappy with their UA team's slow start, decided to raid the NL Cleveland Blues for hitters John Glasscock and "Fatty" Briody as well as pitcher Jim McCormick. Signed to the Outlaw Reds by July, the three new players helped the UA team play at a .650 pace in the second half of the UA season to mount the only challenge against the first-place St. Louis Maroons. En route to a 69–36 record (good for second place, although still 20 games behind the high-atmospheric St. Louis Maroons), Cincinnati newspapers praised the team for "playing like avengers."

1295 O'Leary's Grabs 1884 *Union Assn. (M)*. Messrs. Thorne and McLean authorized field manager Dan O'Leary to talk to and convince the "Cleveland Three" to join the Outlaw Reds. Cleveland newspapers complained that O'Leary was trying "to grab our big three players."

1296 Cincinnati Base Ball Club 1884 *Reserve (ind.)*. Team had no nickname. The Reserve League functioned as a "farm" league for the major league clubs of the NL and AA.

1297 Caylor's Crabs 1886 *National (M)*. With Opie Caylor at the helm, the team sunk to seventh place by June. A local newspaper — the *Cincinnati Enquirer*—complained the team was "crawling around like lowly crabs on the sandy bottom of the ocean."

1298 Reds 1890 to date *National (M)*. Between 1890 and 1910, newspapers used **Red Stockings, Redlegs,** and **Reds** interchangeably but by 1911 "Reds" had become the team's official nickname. *Spalding's Baseball Guide* for 1911 declared the franchise's official nickname to be the "Cincinnati Reds." Indeed, a "Reds" logo appeared on the jersey.

1299 Baby 1890 *National (M)*. "Baby" and "Babies" in the era 1885–1900 did not mean young players but rather new *teams,* i.e., expansion teams. Having left the American Association following the 1889 season, the Cincinnati franchise was a "baby" in their new circuit — the National League. The name seemed to cling to Ohio teams, as the Cleveland "Baby" had joined the NL a year earlier and the Columbus "Baby" replaced Cincinnati in the American Association for the 1890 season. A new Kansas City team was also called "Baby."

1300 Dealers 1890 *National (M)*. With the war between the Players League and the NL-AA establishment in full fury, players joined and left teams in dizzying fashion, forcing Reds management to scramble for players, like poker players flinging cards onto the gaming table. Even today the trading of athletes is known as a "player deal."

1301 Rhinelanders 1890 to date *National (M)*. Between 1850 and 1900 many German immigrants arrived in Cincinnati. At the ballpark they insisted on drinking beer, which led management of the 1876 Reds to serve beer and play games on Sunday. Moreover, the Ohio River Valley closely resembled Germany's Rhineland. As a result, a "Rhinelander" came to mean an inhabitant of Cincinnati. By the 1920s, Opening Day in Cincinnati was known locally as "Der Tag" (The Day!), which means an excitingly festive occasion. The name was popular until the Big Red Machine of the 1970s squeezed it off the newspaper pages, but it is still used sporadically. German immigrants of the nineteenth century flocked to cities like Cincinnati, Milwaukee and St. Louis where liberal laws allowed the consumption of beer and liquor at public events and on Sundays.

1302 Kelly's Killers 1891m *American Assn. (M)*. When Mike "King" Kelly signed on as player-manager, Cincinnati newspapers started calling the team **Kelly's Klippers.** But Kelly's long-standing reputation for rowdy play, evading the rules, and arguing with the umpires soon bestowed on the team the moniker of "Kelly's Killers." When Kelly left the team in August, attendance dropped, forcing management to move the franchise to Milwaukee to finish out the season. Sometimes Cincinnati newspapers called the team **King Kelly's Royals** but the name never caught on.

1303 Red Towners 1901–30 *National (M)*. The Reds were so popular in Cincinnati by 1900 — even though they had last won a pennant 18 years earlier in 1882 — that the city acquired the nickname of "Red Town" and "Redtown." "Also known as **Redville,** the fad declined in the 1930s when Reds fans suffered through nine consecutive losing seasons (1929–37). The team was also named **Redlanders** after their home park of Redland Field (1912–32).

1304 Lobsters 1902–08 *National (M)*. With field managers Joe Kelley (1902–05), Ned Hanlon (1906–07) and John Ganzel at the helm, local newspapers referred to their players as the alliterative "Kelley's Lobsters," "Hanlon's Lobsters," and "Ganzel's Lobsters." The tint of the Cincinnati players' hose was lobster red.

1305 Cuban Stars 1913–19 *Negro independent team*; 1920–30 *Negro National (M)*. Using Cincinnati as their home city, this team had such Cuban stars as Bernardo Baro, Juan Guerra, Helidoro Hidalgo, Cristobal Torriente, Manuel Villa and pitchers Bombin Pedroso, Pastor Pareda and Julio LeBlanc. Aka Western Cuban Stars since another team, the Eastern Cuban Stars, played in New York City in the same era.

1306 Well Oiled Machine 1919 *National (M)*. Ironically, the 1919 and 1970s Cincinnati teams were both identified as "machine." This earlier "Machine" went 96–44 for the best record in the major leagues in 1919 and then defeated the AL champion Chicago White Sox, 5 games to 3, in the 1919 World Series. When it came out in 1920 that eight White Sox players "threw" the Series, defenders of the Reds declared that the team was the match of Chicago and would have won the 1919 Series even if the Sox players had played straight.

1307 Brainy Bunch 1919 *National (M)*. A contemporary moniker complimenting the 1919 Reds players for having baseball "smarts." These players knew how to run the bases, when to bunt, when to make and take a cut-off throw, and on what count to swing or take a pitch. Some of these "brains" included hitters Heinie Groh, Edd Roush, Jake Daubert and pitchers Ray Fisher, Slim Sallee and Dutch Reuther.

1308 Depression Era Reds 1931–34 *National (M)*. Just as the stock market crashed in 1929, the Reds started "crashing," finishing eighth and last in the National League four consecutive seasons— 1931, 1932, 1933 and 1934. Name was coined by baseball author Lee Allen.

1309 Roughhouse Reds 1935 *National (M)*. Cincinnati newspapers, hoping to capitalize on the famous "Gashouse Gang" 1934 pennant winners in St. Louis, tried calling the Cincinnati players the "Roughhouse Reds." The gimmick fizzled out as the Reds finished sixth with a 68–85 mark, 31 and a half games behind the first-place Chicago Cubs.

1310 Tigers 1936 *Independent Negro team*; 1937 *Negro American (M)*. Players wore striped hose.

1311 Queen City Renaissance 1939–40 *National (M)*. After wondering around the National League in a 20-year-long "Dark Age," the Reds entered the light of a veritable fifteenth century Italian "Renaissance" by winning back-to-back NL pennants in 1939 and 1940 and then besting the AL champion Detroit Tigers in a seven-game World Series for the team's first title since 1919. Cincinnati is known as the "Queen City." Moniker was coined by baseball authors Gary Gillette and Pete Palmer. Team was aka the **Renaissance Reds**.

1312 Vine Street Victors 1939–40 *National (M)*. Playing at Crosley Field on the corner of Vine Street and Deacon Avenue, the Reds won two consecutive NL pennants, in 1939–40. The "Vine Street Victors" were led by hitters Frank McCormick, Ernie Lombardi, Ival Goodman and Lonny Frey as well as pitchers Bucky Walters, Paul Derringer, Junior Thompson, Jim Turner and Joe Beggs.

1313 Dismukes 1940 *Independent Negro team*. Team was named in honor of manager William "Dizzy" Dismukes.

1314 Buckeyes 1942–45 *Negro American (M)*. Ohio is the "Buckeye State." In 1876, the Cincinnati Reds of the National League were sometimes called "Buckeyes." The name "Buckeyes" was a generic tag, used by baseball teams in Cincinnati, Cleveland and Columbus.

1315 Clowns 1943–45 *Negro American (M)*. A barnstorming team called the "Ethiopian Clowns" (a moniker that would be "politically incorrect" today) started play in 1930. With players in short supply by 1943 at the height of the fighting in World War II, the Negro American League invited the Clowns to join the league using Cincinnati as their home city. In 1944 the team played a few home games in Indianapolis (IN).

1316 Redlegs 1944–45, 1953–59. For the years 1953–59, the official nickname of the Cincinnati club was changed from Reds to **Redlegs** to avoid any association with the hated and feared "Reds" of the Russian Communist Party as the "Cold War" (1944–90) developed following the end of World War II. In 1961, the club went back to Reds. When the Pennsylvania Supreme Court criticized the use of Reds as unpatriotic, Lou Smith, the sports editor of the *Cincinnati Enquirer* and his reporter, Tom Swope, noting Cincinnati baseball had used the moniker since 1867, some 50 years before the 1917 Russian Revolution, happily replied: "Let the Russians change their name. We had it first!" Even while the Soviet Union was America's ally in the war years 1944–45, some newspapers refused to use the moniker "Reds," switching to "Redlegs" because their editors were sensitive to a growing anti–Communist feeling in the American public due to Joseph Stalin's monstrous crimes and a growing dread about what the Russians planned to do once Hitler and the Japanese were defeated. The hatred of Communism, which gathered force early in the twentieth century, was unabated simply because the Allies had a common foe in Nazi Germany. "Redlegs" survives to this day as an alternate moniker to Reds. Indeed, the team mascot is known as "Mr. Redleg."

1317 Big Red Machine 1969–81 *National (M)*. The Reds got this nickname from 1969 manager Dave Bristol when he realized that players like Johnny Bench, Pete Rose and Tony Perez were going to propel this team to great success in the 1970s. Sparky Anderson took over the managerial of the helm in 1970. When the Reds started losing in 1982, the name was dropped. The Big Red Machine won four NL pennants and two World Series titles and produced thirteen consecutive winning seasons.

1318 Sparky Anderson's Destroyers 1975–76 *National (M)*. The 1975 Reds won 108 games and destroyed the NL Western Division champion Pittsburgh Pirates in a three-game sweep, before fighting off the spunky Boston Red Sox in seven games. In 1976 the Reds destroyed the AL champion New York Yankees in a four-game sweep in the 1976 World Series. Name coined by baseball author Warren Wilbert.

1319 Distracted Reds 1989 *National (M)*. The team had numerous injuries, and players, fans and the media were distracted by the Pete Rose betting scandal that eventually forced Rose to resign as Red's field skipper on August 23 with Tommy Helms succeeding him. The "Distracted Reds" finished with a mediocre 75–87 record, plopping them in fifth place. Name was coined by sports writer Hal McCoy.

1320 Red October Reds 1990 *National (M)*. When the Reds, surprise winners of the NL pennant, stunned the heavily favored Oakland Athletics in a 4–0 sweep in the 1990 World Series, a popular Sean Connery spy movie, *Red October*, was playing in theaters. The name was put on the cover of the October issue of the popular magazine *Sports Illustrated*.

1321 Little Red Machine 1990 *National (M)*. The moniker was a spin-off of the "Big Red Machine" of the 1990s. Unlike the slugging Reds of the 1970s the "Little Red Machine" only hit 125 home runs and mustered a .265 team batting average. But the team was boosted by excellent pitching (team ERA 3.35) and steady fielding, which allowed the "Little Reds" to best the Pirates, 4 games to 2, in the NLCS prior to sweeping the A's in the Fall Classic. The "Little Red Machine" did have steady hitters, i.e., Eric Davis, Barry Larkin, Chris Sabo, Paul O'Neill and Hal Morris as well as solid starters Jose Rijo, Tom Browning and reliever Randy Myers.

1322 Upstart Reds 1999 *National (M)*. Coined by baseball writer Mark Schmetzer, the 1999 Reds, expected to finish at the bottom of the NL Central Division, were surprising "upstarts," going 96–66 to tie for a playoff berth (before losing a one-game playoff to Houston).

1323 Sheriffs 2010 *National (M)*. In September of this season, Chicago's WGN Radio broadcaster David Kaplan, noting that manager Dusty Baker's Reds were dethroning the 2009 NL Central Division champion St. Louis Cardinals, called Baker's first-place team the "new sheriff in town," i.e., "town" meaning the NL Central Division.

1324 Comeback Kids 2011 *National (M)*. With a roster of young players, manager Dusty Baker's "Kids" won an impressive number of come-from-behind victories, which allowed them to come from behind in September to overtake the summer-time leading Cardinals and win their first NL Central Division title. Moniker was coined by baseball writers Mark Schmetzer and Joe Jacobs for their 2011 book of the same title.

Circleville, Ohio

1325 Circleville Base Ball Club 1894 *Tri-State (ind.)*. Team had no nickname.

Cisco, Texas

1326 Scouts 1920–21x *West Texas (D)*. Team disbanded July 6. Comanche and Ute horse riders served as scouts for themselves and occasionally for the U.S. Army during the period 1850–1900. With managers Jack York and then Tom Carson at the helm in 1920, newspapers called the players "York's Scouts," and then "Carson's Scouts." Josh Billings took over in 1921 and the name became "Josh's Scouts."

Ciudad Alianza, Distrito Federal, Venezuela

1327 Red Sox–Padres 2005 *Venezuelan Summer (R)*. Team was a farm club of the Boston Red Sox and San Diego Padres.

Ciudad de Trujillo, Dominican Republic

1328 Dragones 1937 *Dominican (ind.)*. Players wore Red dragon uniform trim and stirrups. The Dominican League of 1937 was a four-team professional circuit, the country's first. There would not be another professional baseball league in the Dominican Republic until 1951.

Ciudad Juarez, Chihuahua, Mexico

1329 Indios 1946 *Mexican National (B)*; 1956–57 *Liga Central Mexicana (C)*; 1973–84 *Liga Mexicana (AAA)*. Benito Juarez, born in Oaxaca, Mexico, known as "El Indio" (The Indian), became an anti–French activist, revolutionary, and statesmen in this city in 1865. He eventually was elected to the Mexican presidency. City was renamed from El Paso del Norte to Ciudad Juarez in 1888.

1330 Indians 1947–50 *Arizona–Texas (C)*; 1951 *Southwest International (C)*; 1952–54 *Arizona–Texas (C)*; 1958 *Arizona–Mexico (C)*. It was possible for these teams located in Mexico to play in U.S. leagues because Juarez is located at the U.S.-Mexican border. The team name in English was "Indians" and in Spanish "Los Indios" in honor of statesmen Benito "El Indio" Juarez.

1331 Los Vaqueros 2004 *Southwestern (ind.)*. Tag was a spin-off from Indians. Cowboys—Spanish, Mexican, Texan, and American—have herded cattle in this region since at least 1690.

1332 Los Indios Rojos 2004–08 *Norte de Sonora (ind.)*. Farm club of SWL Indians. The players were dressed in red-trim uniforms and red stirrups.

Ciudad Madero, Veracruz, Mexico

1333 Bravos 1968–70 *Mexican Center (A)*. Francisco Madero, the first president of the Mexican Revolution of 1910–20, bravely opposed the regime of Porfirio Diaz and his wealthy backers in favor of landless peasants, giving rise to men like Pancho Villa and Emiliano Zapata. Bravo!—both in English and Spanish—is a cry of approval when an individual or group has performed well, i.e., an opera singer, bullfighter, or baseball player. Team was not a farm club of the Atlanta Braves.

Ciudad Mante, Tamaulipas, Mexico

1334 Broncos 1969–70 *Mexican Center (A)*. Team was a farm club of the Reynosa Broncos of the Class AAA Mexican League.

1335 Los Caneros 1971 *Mexican Center (A)*. Nearby sugar plantations transport sugar cane to factories for processing and packing. Caneros means sugar-cane farmers.

1336 Los Azucarereos 1973–74 *Mexican Center (A)*. The city is located in a valley between the Eastern Sierra Madre Mountains and the Atlantic Coast.

1337 Club de Beisbol de Cd. Mante 1977 *Mexican Center (A)*. Team had no nickname.

Ciudad Obregón, Sonora, Mexico

1338 Los Yaquis *Mexican Pacific Coast (W)*. 1945–46–1957–58x. Team disbanded January 5, 1958; 1958–59 to date *Mexican Pacific (W)*; *Mexican Pacific (A)*. The Yaqui Indians have inhabited northwest Mexico and Arizona since pre–Columbian times. Mexican Pacific Coast League in Spanish is La Liga de la Costa Mexicana. After the MPCL disbanded in 1958, a new circuit, called the Sonora-Sinoloa League, operated before renaming itself the Mexican Pacific League for the 1970–71 season. The Mexican Pacific League in Spanish is La Liga del Pacifico de Mexico. The MPL tried summer games in 1976 but attendance was too low to continue.

Ciudad Valles, San Luis Potosí, Mexico

1339 Valles 1974 *Mexican Center (A)*. Team had no nickname. Los valles means the valleys.

1340 Club de Cd. Valles 1978 *Mexican Center (A)*. Team had no nickname. The 13 franchises of the 1978 Mexican Center League had no team nicknames.

Ciudad Victoria, Tamaulipas, Mexico

1341 Club de Beisbol de Cd. Victoria 1971 *Mexican Center (A)*; 1976–78 *Mexican Center (A)*. These teams had no nickname. In 1971, Ciudad Victoria was the league's only franchise without a team nickname. In 1978 none of the teams in the league had nicknames.

1342 Henequerneros 1973–74 *Mexican Center (A)*. The henenquen (derived from a Mayan word) plant is a fibrous that grows in this region and is used to make ropes, cords and rugs. It is also used to make tattoo and hair dyes and is known as the Henna plant in English.

Clarinda, Iowa

1343 Clarinda Baseball Club 1903 Southwest Iowa *(D)*. Team had no nickname.

1344 Antelopes 1910–11 *M.I.N.K. (D)*. The regional Pronghorn Deer of Iowa are sometimes called American Antelopes. With manager Rudy Kling at the helm, newspapers called the players "Kling's Antelopes." After Kling left the team following the 1910 season, moniker was retained.

Clarksburg, West Virginia

1345 Bees 1907 *Western Pennsylvania (D)*; 1909 *Pennsylvania–West Virginia (D)*; *West Virginia (D)*. West Virginia has many honeybee farms. With manager Tom Essler at the helm, newspapers called the players "Essler's Bees." Bull Smith took over later in the season and the name became "Bull's Bees."

1346   Drummers 1908 *Pennsylvania–West Virginia (D)*. With Ferdinand Drumm as field manager in 1908, local newspapers called the players "Drumm's Drummers."

1347   Generals 1925–32 *Middle Atlantic (C)*. Clarksburg, ironically used as a supply depot for Union troops during the Civil War, was the birthplace of General T.J. "Stonewall" Jackson.

1348   Ghosts 1925–32 *Middle Atlantic (C)*. Legend has it that the ghost of "Stonewall" Jackson walks the battlefields of the Civil War. Jackson was shot by friendly fire on May 2, 1863, lost an arm, and then died on May 10 due to pneumonia.

1349   Cirians 1925–32 *Middle Atlantic (C)*. A clever reporter constructed the amalgam "Cirians" as follows: C-1-AR-k-S-bu-R-g we-S-t v-IR-g-INA CIRIANS.

Clarksdale, Mississippi

1350   Clarksdale Baseball Club 1904 *Delta (D)*. Team had no nickname.

1351   Swamp Angels 1913 *Cotton States (D)*. In summertime at night, the swamp banks of the Big Sunflower River exude vapors, which local legend describes as angelic spirits, i.e., "swamp angels." The "Swamp Angels" legends, based on sightings, have been spun by people who make their home in swampy regions throughout the United States, i.e., the Alabama River, the Missouri River and the Ohio River. With manager Carlos Smith at the helm, newspapers called the players "Carlos Smith's Swamp Angels."

1352   Cubs 1921 *Mississippi State (D)*; 1922–23x *Cotton States (D)*. Team and league disbanded July 24. "Cubs" was used to describe young players, although the term "rookie" was gaining in popularity. These teams were not a farm club of the Chicago Cubs.

1353   Ginners m1934–35 *East Dixie (C)*; 1936 *Cotton States (C)*. Team started 1934 season in Baton Rouge (LA) and moved to Clarksdale June 11, 1934; 1936–41m. The cotton gin was invented by Eli Whitney in the U.S. in 1796. Mississippi has been a major producer of cotton since 1750. Clarksdale is the "Golden Buckle on the Cotton Belt." Mississippi is the "Cotton Kingdom." With manager Josh Billings at the helm, newspapers called the players "Billings' Ginners."

1354   Red Sox 1937–41m *Cotton States (C)*. Team moved to Marshall July 10, 1941. Team was a farm club of the Boston Red Sox. Originally **Little Red Sox**, newspapers shortened it to **Red Sox**.

1355   Planters 1947–51 *Cotton States (C)*. Mississippi not only produces cotton but also has soybean and grain farms. Clarksdale is the "Golden Buckle on the Cotton Belt."

Clarksville, Tennessee

1356   Villagers 1903 *Kentucky–Illinois–Tennessee (KITTY) (D)*. Inhabitants of Clarksville are known as "Villagers."

1357   Grays 1904 *Kentucky–Illinois–Tennessee (KITTY) (D)*. Players wore gray uniforms.

1358   Volunteers 1910 *Kentucky–Illinois–Tennessee (KITTY) (D)*; 1916 *KITTY (D)*. Tennessee is the "Volunteer State." Originally **Volunteers**, local newspapers shortened it to **Vols.**

1359   Billies 1911 *Kentucky–Illinois–Tennessee (KITTY) (D)*. "Hill-Billy" and "Hill-Billies" are usually ingratiating (although sometimes disparaging) terms describing inhabitants of the rural South. It derives from the mountain goats, i.e., "billies" and "billy goats," that inhabit hilly regions of the South. With manager Johnny Siegle at the helm, newspapers called the players "Siegel's Billies."

1360   Rebels 1912 *Kentucky–Illinois–Tennessee (KITTY) (D)*. Tennessee was the site of four major Civil War battles: Shiloh, Chattanooga, Stones River and Nashville. With manager Senter Rainey at the helm, newspapers called the players "Rainey's Rebels" and "Senter's Rebels."

1361   Boosters 1913–14x *Kentucky–Illinois–Tennessee (KITTY) (D)*. Team disbanded July 10. Fans formed a booster club, cheering the team into a heated pennant race and on to a credible 78 wins for second place in 1913. Nickname retained in 1914, although team skidded to fifth place. With manager William McAndrews at the helm in 1913, newspapers called the players "Bill's Boosters."

1362   Owls 1946 *KITTY (D)*. Owls inhabit Tennessee's Cherokee National Forest. With manager Dick Luckey at the helm, newspapers called the players "Luckey's Owls."

1363   Colts 1947–49 *KITTY (D)*. "Colts" was slang for young players. This young team showed its inexperience by finishing eighth with a 40–83 record. With manager Harley Boss at the helm, newspapers called the players "Harley Boss' Colts."

1364   Coyotes 1994 *Mid-South (ind.)*; 1996 *Big South (ind.)*; 1997 *Heartland (ind.)*. Coyotes are found in the nearby White Rock Wildlife Management Area. Driven out of the state by 1850, coyotes today have been migrating eastward in the southern U.S.

Clarksville, Texas

1365   Clarksville Base Ball Club 1905x Team disbanded July 31, 1905. *North Texas (D)*. Team had no nickname.

Clay Center, Kansas

1366   Cubs 1909–11 *Central Kansas (D)*; 1913 *Kansas State (D)*. Team had many young players known in the jargon of the era as "cubs." During the era 1890–1920, young baseball players were known as Babes, Chicks, Colts, Cubs, Debutantes, Foundlings, Proteges, Yearlings and so on.

Clay Center, Nebraska

1367   Clay Center Base Ball Club 1887 Nebraska State. Team had no nickname.

Clear Lake City, Iowa

1368   Rabbits m1917 *Central Association (D)*. Team began season as the Cedar Rapids Rabbits and moved to Clear Lake July 27. The nickname of "Rabbits" was retained. With manager Harry Shanley at the helm, newspapers called the players "Harry's Rabbits."

Clearwater, Florida

1369   Pelicans m1924 *Florida State (C)*. Team started season in Daytona Beach and moved to Clearwater July 15. Pelicans inhabit the coastal waters of Louisiana, Alabama, and Florida. With manager Tom McMillan at the helm, newspapers called the players "McMillan's Pelicans."

1370   Phillies 1985–2005 *Florida State (A)*; 1999 to date *Gulf Coast (R)*. These teams were farm clubs of the Philadelphia Phillies.

1371   Threshers 2006 to date *Florida State (A)*. Thresher sharks, which have a flexible tail that allows them to "thrash" their prey, are common in the waters off the Florida coast.

Cleburne, Texas

1372 Railroaders 1906 *Texas (C)*; 1911 *Texas–Oklahoma (D)*; 1912 *South Central (D)*. City, 30 miles south of Dallas–Fort Worth, has been an important depot of the Southern Texas Railroad. In 1911, with manager Will Reed at the helm, newspapers called the team "Reed's Railroaders." In mid-season 1911, Dad Ritter took over changing the tag to "Ritter's Railroaders." Ritter returned in 1912.

1373 Generals 1921–22x *Texas–Oklahoma (D)*. Team disbanded July 22. City was named in honor of General Patrick Cleburne, a Confederate Army general. Texas was a member of the Confederacy during the Civil War.

1374 Scouts 1922x *Texas–Oklahoma (D)*. Team disbanded July 22. Both U.S. Army and Indian scouts (the latter hired by the army) patrolled the vast plains, deserts and river valleys of nineteenth-century Texas. With manager Lindy Hiett at the helm, newspapers called the players "Hiett's Scouts."

Cleveland, Mississippi

1375 Bengals m1935 *East Dixie (C)*. Team began season as Columbus (Ga.) Bengals and moved to Cleveland June 18. After the team moved to Cleveland, the Bengals nickname was kept. With manager Slim Brewer at the helm, newspapers called the players "Brewer's Bengals."

1376 Athletics 1936 *Cotton States (C)*. Team was a farm club of Philadelphia Athletics.

Cleveland, Ohio

1377 Forest Citys 1870 *Independent*; 1871–72 *National Assn. (M)*; 1878 *Independent*; 1879–84 *National (M)*; 1885 *Western (ind.)*; 1898–99 *National (M)*; 1901–14 *American (M)*. Starting in 1836, apple and cherry trees were planted in Cleveland's city streets, leading to the city's nickname of "Forest City." In the eighteenth century, the Cuyahoga River region was heavily forested. Cleveland mayor William Case coined the nickname of "Forest City" for his city in 1850.

1378 Blue Stockings 1879–84 *National (M)*; 1887–88 *American Assn. (M)*; 1889, 1891–99 *National (M)*; 1890 *Players (M)*; 1900 *American (ind.)*; 1901–02 *American (M)*. Players wore blue hose. Cleveland newspapers shortened it to **Blue Legs** and **Blues**.

1379 Colts 1884 *Reserve (ind.)*. The team had all young players, known in this era as "colts." The Reserve League was a farm system that emphasized the signing of young players.

1380 Spiders 1887 *American Assn. (M)*; 1889–99 *National (M)*; 1915 *American Assn. (AA)*. Cleveland got its Spiders nickname during spring training when team owner George House and field manager Jimmy Williams stood together on the field watching the Cleveland players engaged in batting and fielding practice. Their conversation turned to the subject of a name for the ball club, with Loftus turning to the owner and saying, "You know, Mr. House, these fellows are so tall and skinny and spindly that they look like ... spiders!" House brightened up and said, "You know, Jim, we might as well call these fellows 'Spiders' and be done with it!" House dressed his players in uniforms with blue stripes that looked like spider webs, which accentuated the "spider" look of the tall and gangly players. In 1889, the players were dressed in black and red pinstriped uniforms, which made them look even more like spiders.

1381 Baby 1887 *American Assn. (M)*; 1889 *National (M)*. Baby and Babies were terms in the period 1880–1900 for new teams, i.e., expansion teams in baseball leagues. After Pittsburgh jumped to the National League following the 1886 season in the American Association, the Cleveland "Baby" team joined the American Association as a new franchise. The name was appropriate because nine of the sixteen players on the new team were baby-faced youngsters. The NL added Cleveland as a "baby" expansion team. "Baby" and "Babies" in this era referred not to young players but rather to new *teams*, i.e., "expansion" teams. Several teams that were newcomers to a baseball circuit were known as "Baby" or "Babies," i.e., Cleveland, Columbus and Kansas City.

1382 Remnants 1887 *American Assn. (M)*. Seven players on the 1887 roster of the Cleveland team had been released from other teams. The lack of experience showed as the club finished eighth and last in the American Association with a horrendous 39–92 record, 54 games behind first-place St. Louis.

1383 Ice Carts 1888 *American Assn. (M)*. A spin-off from "Ice Wagon Gang," the phrase also referred to a baseball team of slow-footed players. Coined by baseball writer Gerald Cohen of the *New York World* on April 19, 1888 to describe the plodding Cleveland Spiders in a spring game.

1384 Rebels 1889 *National (M)*. The Civil War was still fresh in the minds of most Americans and a person who was "hard-nosed" and fought hard and often skirted the rules was called a "rebel." Athletes of the nineteenth century, baseball players included, were sometimes called "rebels" because they liked to break team rules by staying out late at night to carouse and drink in "rebellion" against the manager.

1385 Black Stockings 1890 *National (M)*. The Cleveland Blues Brotherhood team of the 1890 Players League dressed its players in the traditional Cleveland blue uniform stripes and blue stockings, forcing the Cleveland Nationals to switch to black stockings.

1386 Schmelz' Kids 1890 *National (M)*. So many of Cleveland's veteran players had been raided by Players League teams that the front office and field manager Gus Schmelz were forced to sign 14 youngsters, prompting newspapers to call these players Schmelz' Kids. One of the new kids was pitcher Cy Young.

1387 Infants 1890 *National (M)*. Not only did the Players League team sign away scores of National League and American Association players, they even seized team nicknames from two NL clubs, i.e., Cleveland Spiders and New York Giants. The "Infants," which meant a young team that was struggling, did indeed labor, finishing seventh with a shoddy 55–75 record. The team signed a 16-year-old pitcher, Willie McGill, on May 8. McGill led the pitching staff in victories with 11. Team was aka the **Babes**.

1388 Tebeau's Tartars 1893–98 *National (M)*. By 1893, the team consisted of a bunch of fierce-looking, whiskered fellows who played rough and got their uniforms dirty so much that they resembled the old Mongol-like Tartar barbarians of the 10th century. The team played well, too, enjoying six straight winning seasons, two playoff berths and one Temple Cup championship (in 1895). The team's manager was Patsy Tebeau, prompting newspapers to call the players "Tebeau's Tartars."

1389 Scrappy Spiders 1893–98 *National (M)*. Coined by baseball writer David Nemec, and much like their contemporaries, the Roughneck Orioles, the "Scrappy Spiders" enjoyed six straight winning seasons (1893–98) powered by hitters Ed McKean, Clarence Childs, George Davis, Jack O'Connor, Patsy Tebeau and Hall of Famers Jesse Burkett and Cy Young.

1390 Indians 1897–98 *National (M)*; 1915 to date *American (M)*. Native American of the Penscobot tribe Lou Sockalexis, an outfielder, made a big splash in 1897 when he batted .331 in 66 games, prompting Cleveland fans and newspapers to dub the team the Cleveland Indians. Unfortunately, Sockalexis had a bad drinking problem that adversely affected his play. In 1898 he had a poor year and by 1899 he was out of baseball. But Sockalexis did make his mark as sportswriter Bill Deane of *The Sporting News* on March 27, 1897, declared:

"There is one feature of the signing of Sockalexis more gratifying than the fact that his presence on the team will result in relegating to obscurity the title of 'Spiders' by which the team has been handicapped for several seasons to give place to the more significant name of 'Indians.'" In January 1915 team owner Charles Sommers held a news reporters' poll after star player and team namesake (i.e., Cleveland Naps) Nap Lajoie was signed by the Philadelphia Athletics. The reporters finally settled on "Indians" but not in honor of the 1897–98 player, Lou Sockalexis, but rather because Sommers wanted a spin-off from the Boston "Braves," who had won the World Series a year earlier (in 1914). Sommers hoped that Cleveland fans would regard the name as a "winning" moniker. The Indians moniker also was appropriate because the Cleveland teams of 1903–11 were sometimes known as "Lajoie's Braves"—a generic name for "baseball players" until the Boston Nationals made it their official nickname in 1912. Some of the other entries submitted by the newspaper reporters included Commodores, Forest Citys, Grays, Harponics, Hustlers, Napless Naps, Sixers, Rangers, Some Runners, Speeders, Spiders and Tornadoes.

1391 Misfits 1899 *National (M).* The most infamous of losing team nicknames was the fault of neither Cleveland fans nor players but was caused by "syndicate baseball." Brothers Charles and Frank Robison obtained controlling financial interest in both the Cleveland Spiders and the pitiful St. Louis Browns. Sensing they could make more money in St. Louis than Cleveland, the Robison brothers cannibalized the Cleveland team by sending players like future Hall of Famer Cy Young, George Cupp, Lave Cross (the player-manager), John Heidrick, Jesse Burkett (a future Hall of Famer who batted .402 in 1898), John McKean and Rhodie Wallace to the Browns (who were renamed the Cardinals in 1899). The Spiders were forced to field a minor league lineup for the 1899 season; the result was a historical disaster as the Spiders lost in bunches forcing them to become a road team in July (Cleveland fans refused to attend home games by June) en route to an astounding 20–134 record. Early on in the season, manager Cross pleaded with owner Frank Robison as follows:

> Cross: "Mr. Robison, I could field a good team here in Cleveland. If you could get me a center fielder, one pitcher, and a good shortstop, we could win some games here." Robison (with an angry stare): "Your job here in Cleveland is … to play out the schedule!"

Other nicknames were dumped on the 1899 Spiders by fans, newspapers and historians and were as follows: **Barnstormers** (team played road games by July); **Castoffs** (team signed players cut by other teams); **Exiles** (Cleveland fans refused to attend games, forcing the team onto the road); **Forlorns** and **Wanderers** (team playing road games starting in July). Team also continued to be known as the **Spiders**.

1392 Lake Shores 1900 *American (ind.).* Cleveland is located along the shores of Lake Erie.

1393 Bluebirds 1901–02 *American (M).* Players wore blue trim and hose. Management dressed the players in blue stockings. Blue had been traditional color for Cleveland stockings since 1870. Team was aka **Blue Jays**.

1394 Bronchos 1902 *American (M).* Before the first game of the regular season, the players held a poll amongst themselves and decided on "Bronchos" because they wanted a "Wild West" nickname. Players were probably influenced by the old Chicago Colts moniker.

1395 Naps 1903–11 *American (M);* 1915 *American (M).* At the start of the 1903 season, the team held a name-the-team contest. The winning entry was "Naps"—in honor of star player Nap Lajoie. Other entries in the poll included Buckeyes, Cyclones, Emperors, Giants (already used in New York) and Mets. When the 1915 Indians failed

miserably to gain some of the charm of the "Boston Braves" and finished in eighth and last place with a horrible 51–102 record, one disgruntled Cleveland fan expressed his opinion to a newspaper as follows: "Indians? They should call 'em the Naps again. After all, they're sleeping through the season, aren't they?"

1396 Cleveland Colored Baseball Club 1908 *Independent Negro (ind.).* Team had no nickname.

1397 Napkins September 1908 *American (M).* On September 28, 1908, the Naps had a one game lead over Detroit with two games to play but lost contests to the White Sox and Browns while the Tigers won their last two games. Angry Cleveland fans called the team the "Napkins" (an obvious spin-off from "Naps") because "they folded."

1398 Molly McGuires 1909–11 *American (M).* When player-manager Nap Lajoie relinquished his duties as skipper in mid-season 1909, Irishman Deacon McGuire took the helm. Newspapers used the clever but overlong moniker of "Molly McGuires." The "Molly McGuires" were an infamous nineteenth century Irish terrorist group who sought the total independence of Ireland from Great Britain. When McGuire was fired and replaced by George Stovall in mid-season 1911, the tag was dropped.

1399 Green Sox 1913 *Federal (ind.).* Team chose green for the players' uniform trim and stirrups because Cleveland is nicknamed the "Forest City."

1400 Bearcats 1914 *American Assn. (AA)* "Bearcats" is slang for the North American wolverine. The true bearcat is a canine-like creature indigenous to Asia. With manager Herman Bronkie at the helm, newspapers called the players "Bronkie's Bearcats." Moniker was a spin-off from the University of Cincinnati "Bearcats" sports teams, who adopted the name in 1912.

1401 The Tribe 1915 to date *American (M).* Tag is one of the more famous and long-time unofficial nicknames of major league baseball teams. Connie Mack's 1901–14 Philadelphia Athletics sometimes had been called "Mack's Tribe," but starting in 1915 the name became monopolized by Cleveland as an unofficial, alternate team nickname to "Indians."

1402 Squaws 1915 *American (M).* When the team announced its new name, i.e., the "Cleveland Indians," the *Cleveland Press* warned: "If this team loses, our fans are going to call the players squaws!" It turned out the newspaper was right as the team finished seventh with a most un-warrior-like 57–95 record.

1403 Mighty Warriors 1920 *American (M).* Baseball writer Mike LeBlanc called the 1920 AL and world champion Cleveland Indians the "Mighty Warriors." The Warriors were powered by hitters Bill Wambsganss, Ray Chapman (who was tragically killed on August 17, 1920, by a blow to the head from a Carl Mays pitch), Larry Gardner, Joe Sewell, Tris Speaker, Steve O'Neill, Charlie Jamieson and Elmer Smith as well as pitchers Stan Coveleski, Ray Caldwell and Jim Bagby.

1404 World Champions 1921 *American (M).* Like the 1906 New York Giants, the Cleveland players sported jerseys for the 1921 season emblazoned with the title "World Champions." Perhaps the jerseys were a little bit too boastful (neither the Giants nor the Indians repeated) because no other professional baseball team has repeated the practice.

1405 Tate Stars 1922 *Negro National (M);* 1927–28 *Southern California (W).* Team was first known as "Taylor's Stars," after manager "Candy Jim" Taylor. It soon became the easier-to-pronounce "Tate Stars" because, coincidentally, the home field was known as Tate Park. Team played winter ball in Los Angeles in 1927–28 under the moniker **Stars**.

1406 Browns 1924 *Negro National (M).* Players wore brown-trim hose.

1407 Elite Giants 1926 *Negro National (M).* Using the popular

"Giants" noun, the team chose "Elite" as its preceding adjective because it advertised to fans that the team would be very talented. The team, however, was quite pedestrian, finishing eighth and last in the circuit with a terrible 5–32 record.

1408 Hornets 1927 *Negro National (M).* Players wore yellow and black striped hose. With manager Pete Duncan at the helm, newspapers called the players "Duncan's Hornets."

1409 Tigers 1928 *Negro National (M).* Players wore yellow and black striped hose. Team decided to switch from yellow and black "Hornets" to yellow and black "Tigers."

1410 Giants 1928–29 *Southern California (W);* 1933 *Negro National (M).* Moniker was a spin-off from the 1926 "Elite Giants."

1411 Stars 1932 *East–West (M).* Moniker was a contraction of the 1922 Tate Stars.

1412 Red Sox 1934 *Negro National (M).* Players wore red stirrups.

1413 Bears 1939–40 *Negro American (M).* Tag was a spin-off of the 1914 American Association "Bearcats" name.

1414 Crybabies 1940 *American (M).* The 1940 Cleveland players did not like their manager Ossie Vitt. They complained to team owner Alva Bradley that Vitt was "too sarcastic" with them. Sportswriters, realizing the players were distracting themselves from a heated three-team pennant race involving the Tigers, Yankees and themselves, called the players "Crybabies." The "Crybabies" just missed the AL pennant, finishing second, a single game behind the Detroit Tigers, thereby preventing an "All-Ohio" World Series against the NL champion Cincinnati Reds.

1415 White Sox 1941 *Independent Negro team.* Players wore white stirrups over white sanitary hose.

1416 Buckeyes 1943–48 *Negro American (M);* 1950 *Negro American (ind.).* Ohio is the Buckeye State.

1417 Clippers 1946 *United States (ind.).* Clipper ships have sailed Lake Erie since the eighteenth century. The USBL was a "paper league" devised by Brooklyn Dodgers GM Branch Rickey to allow him to sign the best black baseball talent available in 1945–46.

1418 Wahoos 1946–67 *American (M).* Also called **Chief Wahoo's Tribe,** the name coincided with the appearance of the most modern version of the mascot Chief Wahoo. By the late 1960s and 1970s, in an era of "political correctness," Native American started to protest "Chief Wahoo" and the NFL Washington "Redskins" team nickname. Although the moniker was abandoned, the Chief Wahoo logo has appeared prominently on the players caps and jerseys every season since then, making money and fueling controversy to the present day.

1419 Chief Wahoo's Tribe 1947–67 *American (M).* The player uniforms sported a "Chief Wahoo" logo patch on the left sleeve of the 1947 uniforms. By 1950 Chief Wahoo was also on the baseball caps as well. By 1970 as the U.S. moved to more politically sensitive attitudes about ethnic slurs, newspapers stopped mentioning old Chief Wahoo.

1420 The Boys of the Summer of '48 1948 *American (M).* A spin-off of the Brooklyn Dodger "Boys of Summer," this is the title of a book by Russell Schneider of the 1948 AL and world champion Cleveland Indians.

1421 Al Lopez Limited 1954 *American (M).* Managed by Al Lopez, the Indians raced like a speeding train to a 154-game American League–record 111 victories with only 43 defeats to beat out the mighty New York Yankees by eight games for the 1954 American League pennant.

1422 Subdued Indians 1957 *American (M).* Under new manager Kerby Farrell the team went 76–77 as Indians fans suffered through their team's first losing season since 1946.

1423 Mistake by the Lake 1960–93 *American (M).* A historical tag that referred to Lake Erie's nearby Cleveland Stadium, the city of Cleveland itself, and the Indians team in its "Dark Age" of 1960–93 when they were chronic losers.

1424 Featherheads 1967–93 *American (M).* A "featherhead" means a bumbling fool, and some baseball writers started to designate the Indians of the era 1967–93 with this epithet because the franchise had 22 losing seasons in 27 years, including seven last-place finishes and three 100+ loss seasons. Name was emphasized in those years in which the Indians finished last. Tag was aka **Featherbrains.** American Indians wore feathers in their hair as a ceremonial headdress.

1425 The Lost Tribe 1969–93 *American (M).* Like a legendary lost tribe wandering deserts and snow plains, the Indians had only five winning seasons in 27 years and finished last in the American League Eastern Division seven times. Team is aka the **Wandering Tribe.**

1426 Torborg's Tumblers 1977–78 *American (M).* After an encouraging 81–78 record in 1976, the Indians began to "tumble" in 1977, costing manager Frank Robinson his job. Coming to the helm in mid-season 1977, Jeff Torborg could not halt the team's descent as the Indians lost 90 games in both the 1977 and 1978 seasons.

1427 Fighting Braves of the Cuyahoga 1980 *American (M).* After the popular baseball movie *Major League* in which the Cleveland baseball team was known by this title. In real life that year, the Indians were more often surrendering, posting a losing 79–81 record.

1428 Erie Sensation 1987 *American (M).* The Indians, playing in Municipal Stadium on the shores of Lake Erie, went 61–101 to finish seventh and last in the AL Eastern Division, giving Cleveland fans an "eerie sensation."

1429 Jndians 1994 to date *(American).* The script lettering on the jersey uses a script "I" which many people mistake for a "J." Mischievous fans call the players "Jin-dians."

1430 Oakland Raiders of Baseball 1995 *American (M).* With flashy uniforms and rowdy players, the Indians rampaged the AL Central Division, winning 100 of 144 games to win by a major league baseball–record 30 games over second-place Kansas City. Their swaggering style was reminiscent of the old AFL and NFL Oakland Raiders football team, who strutted with often justifiable braggadocio onto the gridiron. The Indians won their first AL pennant in 41 years on the offense of Albert Belle, Manny Ramirez, Jim Thome and Eddie Murray as well as the pitching of Charles Nagy, Orel Hershiser and Jose Mesa. The "Raiders" moniker was coined by Cleveland general manager John Hart.

1431 Lost Tribe by the Lake 2009–10 *American (M).* Tag was coined by sportswriter Mike Payne to describe the team that "lost its way" from the 2007 AL Central Division title to 81 victories in 2008 and a "sinking in Lake Erie" 65–97 record in 2009.

1432 Incredible Indians 2011 *American (M).* After finishing fourth in the 2010 AL Central with a crummy 69–93 record, manager Manny Acta led the Indians to a rousing start by winning 30 of their first 45 games in 2011 to take a comfortable five-game lead in the AL Central by May 23. Although cooling off in the summer, the team was still only five games behind Detroit by Labor Day. Name was coined by baseball writer Anthony Witrado.

1433 Cockroaches 2011 *American (M).* Noting how the Indians (and the Chicago White Sox) "refused to die" when it came to their AL Central Division title hopes as of September 1, Chicago WSCR broadcaster Les Grobstein, on his August 30 radio show, branded these two teams, both five games behind the Detroit Tigers, as the "cockroaches of the AL Central Division." In September the Tigers played at a .700 clip and pummeled both Cleveland and Chicago in showdown series to finally kill off these two bugs.

Cleveland, Tennessee

1434 Counts 1911–13m *Appalachian (D)*. Team moved to Morristown (TN) June 9, 1913. Pioneer and settler John Counts (born 1765) founded the city in 1838. City was named Cleveland after landowner John Cleves Symes. In a coincidence, the 1913 team was managed by "Count" Zimeski.

1435 Manufacturers 1921–22 *Appalachian (D)*. Numerous businesses here were engaged in the manufacture of textiles, furniture and chemicals. To promote business, Cleveland called itself "The Good City to Aim For."

Clifton Forge, Virginia

1436 Railroaders 1914x *Virginia Mountain (D)*. Team and league disbanded July 25. City is the midway stop for the Alleghany Railroad traveling between Richmond (VA) and Charleston (WV).

Clinton, Illinois

1437 Champs 1910–12 *Illinois–Missouri (D)*. Team won 1911 pennant. Clinton fans called the players "Charley's Champs" (after manager Charley Cline) in the hopes of a pennant in 1910 as they pursued league-leader Pekin. The Clinton team finished second. The team earned the "Champs" name by winning the 1911 pennant under manager Jack Carter, i.e., "Carter's Champs." Nickname stuck with the team in 1912 even though they did not repeat as flag-winners. In baseball, "Champs" sometimes survived one complete season after winning a pennant but without a repeat pennant, the moniker was always dropped. By the 1920s the style was dropped because fans considered it to be arrogant.

Clinton, Iowa

1438 Clinton Base Ball Club 1895 *Eastern Iowa*. Team had no nickname.

1439 Miners m1906 *Iowa State (D)*. Team started season in Boone as the Boone Miners and moved to Clinton July 14. Nickname was retained. Moniker was appropriate because of Iowa's gypsum mines.

1440 Infants 1907–08 *Three-I (B)*. Three-I League represented Illinois, Indiana and Iowa. Many young players were on this team. The word "rookie" was coined around 1917. Before then young players were known variously as Babes, Chicks, Colts, Cubs, Debutantes, Foundlings, Infants, Proteges and Yearlings. With field manager Monte McFarland at the helm, local newspapers called the players the alliterative "McFarland's Infants." City name, i.e., Clinton Infants, was also alliterative.

1441 Teddies 1910 *Northern Assn. of Baseball (D)*. Nickname was an obvious spin-off of the successful Chicago Cubs (on their way to their fourth pennant in five years) and ex-president but still popular Theodore "Teddy" Roosevelt. However, the direct origin of the name was the team's field manager Ted Sullivan, i.e., "Ted Sullivan's Teddies"

1442 Pilots 1914–15x *Central Assn. (D)*. Team disbanded July 5; 1916–17x *Central Assn. (D)*. Team disbanded July 17; 1966–76 *Midwest (A)*. "Pilot" boats are ships that guide river traffic up and down the Mississippi River.

1443 Owls 1937–38 *Three-I (B)*. Although owls are plentiful in Iowa, the moniker was chosen because it was short and alliterative, i.e., Clinton Owls. Then, with manager Oliver Marquardt at the helm in 1938, newspapers called the players the obvious "Ollie's Owls."

1444 Giants 1939–41 *Three-I (B)*. Team was a farm club of the New York Giants.

1445 Cubs 1947–48 *Central Association (C)*. Team was a farm club of the Chicago Cubs.

1446 Steers 1949 *Central Association (C)*. Team was a farm club of the Dallas Steers.

1447 Pirates 1954–55 *Missouri–Ohio Valley (D)*; 1956–59 *Midwest (D)*. Team was a farm club of the Pittsburgh Pirates, except in 1959 when it played as an independent (keeping the "Pirates" moniker that year).

1448 C-Sox 1960–65 *Midwest (D 1960–62, A 1963–65)*. Team was a farm club of the Chicago White Sox. In the style of "ChiSox" and "BoSox," team was identified as the "C-Sox," the "C" standing for Clinton.

1449 Dodgers 1977–79 *Midwest (A)*. Team was a farm club of the Los Angeles Dodgers.

1450 Giants 1980–93 *Midwest (A)*. Team was a farm club of the San Francisco Giants.

1451 Lumber Kings 1994 to date *Midwest (A)*. In the nineteenth century logging companies transported timber on boats down the Mississippi River to lumber mills in Clinton where the more moderate weather allowed year-round production of processed wood. In the years 1850–1900, Clinton was known as the "Lumber Capital of the World."

Clinton, Sampson, North Carolina

1452 Blues 1946–48 *Tobacco State (D)*. Players wore blue-trim uniforms. Team was not a farm club of the blue-trimmed Brooklyn Dodgers, playing instead as a loose affiliation in 1946–47 with and as an official farm club of the blue-trimmed Detroit Tigers 1948.

1453 Sampson Blues 1949–50 *Tobacco State (D)*. Clinton is located in Sampson County. Players wore blue-trim uniforms and blue stirrups.

Clinton, Oklahoma

1454 Bulldogs 1922–23 *Oklahoma State (D)*. A "Bulldogger" is a cowboy who wrestles a steer to the ground after jumping on it from his horse for the entertainment of rodeo fans. Newspapers chose the shorter "Bulldogs" in their stories.

Clovis, New Mexico

1455 Buzzers 1922 *West Texas (D)*. With manager "Buzz" Wetzel at the helm, newspapers called the players the "Buzzers."

1456 Cubs 1923 *Panhandle Pecos Valley (D)*. Although there are bears in New Mexico, the name referred to young players on the team. With manager Clarence "Pop Boy" Smith at the helm, newspapers called the players "Clarence's Cubs." Team was not a farm club of the Chicago Cubs.

1457 Pioneers 1938–42 *West Texas–New Mexico (D)*; 1946–55 *West Texas–New Mexico (B)*; 1956 *Southwestern (B)*; 2004 only *Southwestern (ind.)*. Some of the last of the pioneer families of America founded the city in 1907. The 1868 Taos Gold Rush and the construction of railroads brought thousands of homesteaders into the state.

1458 Redlegs 1957 *Southwestern (B)*. Team was a farm club of the Cincinnati Redlegs. The parent club was known as the "Redlegs" from 1953–59 before switching back to "Reds" in 1960.

Coalinga, California

1459 Savages 1910–11 *San Joaquin Valley (D)*. In the period 1750–1850, the Yuma, Umqua and Comanche Indian tribes periodically attacked California settlers, resulting in several massacres causing settlers and later U.S. soldiers to refer to the Indians as "savages." The historical right-or-wrongness aside, today the term, which was permitted in 1910, is "politically incorrect." Baseball players in this era were often regarded as "uncouth savages" for their rowdy misbehavior, spitting tobacco, rank body odor, drunkenness, yellow-toothed smoking and womanizing.

Coatzacoalcos, Veracruz, Mexico

1460 Portenos 1966–70 *Mexican Southeast (A)*. Team known by the regional name of Port Mexico Ports, i.e., Los Portenos de Puerto Mexico in Spanish. The city is located by the Coatzacoalcos River and receives shipping from as far away as the Bay of Campeche. Los portenos is Spanish for port men or dockworkers.

1461 Azules 1979–83 *Mexican (AAA)*. Players wore blue-trim uniforms and blue stirrups. Local newspapers wanted a short nickname because the city name has 13 letters.

Cobbleskill, New York

1462 Giants 1890 *New York State (ind.)*. Team had a loose affiliation with the New York Giants. In the era 1885–1920, some minor league teams in close proximity to New York City had a loose affiliation with the NL Giants—i.e., buying uniforms and equipment from the big leaguers and selling an occasional player contract to the New Yorkers.

Cocoa, Florida

1463 Fliers 1941–42x *Florida East Coast (D)*. Team disbanded April 21, 1942, because of World War II. Cocoa was the site of Patrick Army–Air Force Base and Eastern Test Range during World War II.

1464 Indians 1951–58 *Florida State (D)*. Team was a farm club of the Cleveland Indians.

1465 Colt .45's 1964 *Florida Rookie (R)*. Team was a farm club of the Houston Colt .45s.

1466 Mets 1964 *Florida Rookie (R)*. Team was a farm club of the New York Mets.

1467 Tigers 1964 *Florida Rookie (R)*. Team was a farm club of the Detroit Tigers.

1468 Astros 1965–71 *Florida State (A)*; 1972 *Florida East Coast (R)*; 1977 *Florida State (A)*. These teams were farm clubs of the Houston Astros.

Cocoa-Melbourne, Florida

1469 Astros 1972 *Florida East Coast (R)*. Team was a farm club of the Houston Astros.

1470 Expos 1972 *Florida East Coast (R)*. Team was a farm club of the Montreal Expos.

1471 Reds 1972 *Florida East Coast (R)*. Team was a farm club of the Cincinnati Reds.

1472 Twins 1972 *Florida East Coast (R)*. Team was a farm club of the Minnesota Twins.

Codogno, Milano, Italy

1473 Semex 2002–07 *Italian A1 (ind.)*. The Semex Livestock Company owned the team. Italian professional baseball teams usually have lacked a nickname, using instead the corporate sponsor's title as its team name. Sometimes these teams have a mascot.

Coffeyville, Kansas

1474 Coffeyville Base Ball Club 1896 *Kansas State (ind.)*. Team had no nickname.

1475 Indians 1902m *Missouri Valley (D)*. Team moved to Chanute June 23. Team was named after the Kansa Indian tribe. Squatters, who settled on Kansas land without authorization, started arriving in Kansas in 1854 and were attacked by Indians.

1476 Bricks 1906 *Kansas State (D)*. In 1906, the city was noted for three brick manufacturers—Standard, Vitrified, and Yoke. With manager Harry Barndollar at the helm, newspapers called the players "Barndollar's Bricks."

1477 Glassblowers 1907 *Oklahoma–Arkansas–Kansas (O.A.K.) (D)*. The regular season was shortened to September 15, but the league did not disband. The Vitrified Brick Company also manufactured glass products.

1478 White Sox 1911x *Western Assn. (D)*. Team disbanded June 14. Players wore white hose. As some other minor league teams had in this era, Coffeyville had a loose affiliation with the Chicago White Sox.

1479 Refiners 1921–24x Southwestern Assn. *(D 1921, C 1922–24)*. Team disbanded July 5, 1924. Oil wells and gas fields in Northeast Oklahoma transported crude oil and natural gas to petrochemical plants here.

Coleman, Texas

1480 Bobcats 1928–29 West Texas *(D)*. Bobcats and cougars are large cats that inhabit Texas. With manager Bob Couchman at the helm in 1928, newspapers called the players "Bob's Bobcats." After Couchman left the team after the 1928 season, nickname was retained in 1929.

College Park, Maryland

1481 Indians 1931–35 *Independent Negro team*. Algonquin Indians inhabited Maryland in the seventeenth and eighteenth centuries.

Collinsville, Illinois

1482 Gateway Grizzlies 2001 to date *Frontier (ind.)*. Team represents the cities of Collinsville and Sauget, Illinois. Collinsville is only 20 miles east of St. Louis (MO), which is the "Gateway to the West." Grizzly bears routinely roamed the Missouri region until 1850.

Colon, Colon, Panama

1483 Club de Beisbol de Colon 1962–63 *Panamanian (W)*. Team had no nickname.

1484 Canaleros 2001–02 Panamanian *(W)*. The Panama Canal was built in Panama from 1898–1910. "Los Canaleros" is Spanish for "canalers."

Colonial Heights–Petersburg, Virginia

1485 Generals 1951 *Virginia (C)*. Generals Ulysses S. Grant and George Meade besieged Petersburg for 10 months, starting in June 1864. By April 1865 the Confederates surrendered at Appomattox.

1486 Colts 1954 *Piedmont (B)*. Local newspapers used this short nickname because the club went by the twenty-five-letter double name of Colonial Heights–Petersburg.

Colorado Springs, Colorado

1487 Colorado Springs Base Ball Club 1889 *Colorado State (ind.).* Team had no nickname.

1488 Millionaires 1901–04 *Western (1901 ind., 1902–04 A)*; 1912 *Rocky Mountain (D)*; m1916 *Western (A).* Team started season in Wichita (KS) before moving to Colorado Springs on September 10. Gold was discovered at Cripple Creek in 1870, causing a "gold boom." The only people who became millionaires, however, were the owners of the mining companies. With field manager Billy Hulen at the helm in 1901, local newspapers called the players "Billy's Millionaires." Bill Everett took over for 1902–03 and newspapers continued with "Bill's Millionaires." Moniker was also alliterative with the city name, i.e., Colorado Springs Millionaires.

1489 Sky Sox 1950–58 *Western (A)*; 1988 to date *Pacific Coast (AAA).* The 1950–58 team was a farm club of Chicago White Sox. "Sky" became part of the nickname because of the Rocky Mountains and the nearby United States Air Force Academy. The team, established in 1988, has been a farm club of neither the Chicago White Sox nor the Boston Red Sox.

Columbia, Missouri

1490 Mid-Missouri Mavericks 2003–05 *Frontier (ind.).* Sam Maverick was a nineteenth-century Texas rancher who refused to brand his cattle. His name was coined in reference to an unbranded steer or calf. The term evolved into a "free-thinker," i.e., an individualist. Such an individualist was pioneer Daniel Boone, who settled in this region. Missouri is also the "Show-Me" State, and Missourians are the paragon of individualist skepticism. Name also evolved to mean "cowboy."

Columbia, South Carolina

1491 Columbia Base Ball Club 1892 *South Atlantic (ind.)*; 1896 *Southeastern (ind.).* These teams had no nickname.

1492 Skyscrapers 1904 *South Atlantic (C).* The Piedmont Hills city was built near hilly terrain, i.e., Horrell and Liberty Hills and Sligh's Little Mountain.

1493 Gamecocks 1905–10 *South Atlantic (C)* 1916 *South Atlantic (C).* Team was named after the University of South Carolina Fighting "Gamecocks" teams. With managers Win Clark and Ed Granville at the helm, newspapers went with "Clark's Gamecocks" and "Granville's Gamecocks." The 1916 team revived the moniker.

1494 Commies 1911 *South Atlantic (C).* Tag was used for newspaper headlines, i.e., "Commies edge Peaches, 4–3." With managers Frederick Cavender and then William Clark leading the team to the 1911 pennant, newspapers called the players the alliterative "Cavender's Commies" and "Clark's Commies." The anti–Communist term, "Commie," was coined in 1940 and came into vogue in the Cold War era of 1946–90.

1495 Comers *South Atlantic Assn. (C 1919–20, B 1921–23).* Team moved to Gastonia (NC) July 26, 1923. Because of U.S. entry into World War I, the regular season ended July 4, 1917; *South Atlantic Assn. (B) 1925–30.* The term "comers" is sports slang for an athlete or a team that was excelling in competition, i.e., the "team is coming on!" The ultimate origin is the fan exhortation "Come on!" With manager William Clark at the helm in 1914, newspapers called the players "Clark's Comers." The 1915 players were quoted in newspapers as "real comers" as they won the league pennant with a 76–44 record. Under manager Connie Lewis, the 1915 team was known as "Connie's Comers." The 1917 players, managed by John Corbett, were known as "Corbett's Comers." Tom Clarke took over in 1919,

and the players became "Clarke's Comers." Zin Beck took over in 1920–22, changing the name to "Beck's Comers" as the team won the 1920 pennant. Scott Alcock took over in 1923, changing the name to the fan-snickering, risqué "Alcock's Comers." The sexual innuendo convinced the 1934 team to discourage the moniker.

1496 Sandlappers 1934m *Piedmont (B).* Team moved to Asheville (NC) June 7. Birds, fish, frogs and turtles that inhabit the nearby Congaree River are called sandlappers. With manager Bill Laval at the helm, newspapers called the players the "Laval's Sandlappers" and "Laval's Lappers."

1497 Senators 1936–37 *South Atlantic (B).* Capital of South Carolina for 225 years. The city was founded in 1786 to succeed Charleston as the state capital. Team was not a farm club of the Washington Senators.

1498 Reds 1938–42 *South Atlantic (A)*; 1946–55 *South Atlantic (A)*; 1960–61 *South Atlantic (A).* Team was a farm club of the Cincinnati Reds.

1499 Gems 1956–57 *South Atlantic (A).* Between 1786, when it was founded, and 1854 when it became a municipality, the city grew rapidly and built beautiful buildings, leading to the nickname of "Gem City. Written by David Shaw in 1862, the song "Columbia, Gem of the Ocean" was sometimes used as the national anthem of the United States until 1930 when the "Star Spangled Banner" became the official national anthem of the United States.

1500 Mets 1983–92 *South Atlantic (A).* Team was a farm team of the New York Mets.

1501 Capital City Bombers 1993–2004 *South Atlantic (A).* Team went by the city nickname of Capital City Bombers. Columbia is the "Capital City" because it is the state capital of South Carolina. General William Sherman shelled the city in 1865 before entering it. The nickname is related to the construction of B-17 and B-25 bombers in city factories during the war years 1941–45, which were then stationed at South Carolina's wartime air base in nearby Fort Jackson.

Columbia, Tennessee

1502 Mules 1921 *Alabama–Tennessee (D)*; 1996 *Big South (ind.)*; 1997 *Heartland (ind.).* The region, irrigated by the Duck River, is farm country with farm mules. "Mule" is also baseball slang for a baseball player, particularly one whose play is not very distinguished. Moniker was short and alliterative, i.e., Columbia Mules.

Columbus, Georgia

1503 Columbus Base Ball Club 1885 *Southern (ind.).* Team had no nickname.

1504 Babies 1896 *Southern (ind.)*; 1897 *Southeastern (ind.).* Team had several young, baby-faced players. The terms "Babies" and "Baby" not only meant young, baby-faced players; it also meant a new team in an established league, i.e., an "expansion team." Although an expansion team may have had veteran players, most teams in this era (1885–1915) usually had young players.

1505 River Snipes 1906m *Georgia State (D).* Team moved to Brunswick (GA) June 25. The River Snipe frequents the marshy shores of the nearby Chattahoochee River.

1506 Black Tourists 1908 *Independent Negro (ind.).* While the white-player Augusta Tourists played in the Class C South Atlantic League, the "Black Tourists," with their home field in Columbus (GA), barnstormed across the South.

1507 Foxes 1909–17x *South Atlantic (C).* Team disbanded May 19, 1917 due to U.S. entry into World War I; 1926–30 *Southeastern (B)*; 1932x *Southeastern (B).* Team and league disbanded May 21 because of the Great Depression; 1956–57 *South Atlantic (A)*. Before 1800 wild foxes hunted along the nearby Chattahoochee River. Also, the 1915 team was managed by James Fox, which reinforced the name. With manager Bobby Lennox at the helm in 1930, newspapers called the players "Lennox' Foxes."

1508 Redbirds 1936–42 *South Atlantic (B)*. Tag was a spinoff from "Cardinals." Team was a farm club of the NL St. Louis Cardinals. The St. Louis NL club is oftentimes called the "Redbirds," which some St. Louis Cardinals farm teams have used to avoid confusion with the big league club.

1509 Cardinals *South Atlantic (A)* 1946–55. Team was farm club of the St. Louis Cardinals.

1510 Pirates 1959m *South Atlantic (A)*. Team moved to Gastonia (NC) July 6. Team was a farm club of the Pittsburgh Pirates.

1511 Confederate Yankees 1964–66 *Southern (AA)*. Team was a farm club of the New York Yankees. Team management naively chose "Yankees" as the team's moniker, only to hurriedly modify it to "Confederate Yankees" as the team's Dixie fans were in near-rebellion (no pun intended). Even so, Columbus fans gagged on the oxymoron of "Confederate Yankees" for three seasons. A 1965 SL pennant did assuage them a little. In a funny episode of the old "You'll Never Get Rich" TV show (aired in 1957) starring Phil Silvers (as Sgt. Ernie Bilko), Bilko, maneuvering to be paid an agent's fee, tries to recruit and sign a Southern boy soldier with a "golden arm" to the New York Yankees. When the pro–Dixie young man balks at joining a team called the "Yankees," Bilko dresses up the likes of Mickey Mantle, Whitey Ford and Yogi Berra as Southern "colonels" to con the young man into signing.

1512 White Sox 1969 *Southern (AA)*. Team was a farm club of the Chicago White Sox

1513 Astros 1970–88 *Southern (AA)*. Team was a farm club of the Houston Astros.

1514 Mudcats 1989–90 *Southern (AA)*. Schools of mudcat fish are indigenous to the Chattahoochee River.

1515 Indians 1991–2002 *South Atlantic (SALLY)*. *(A)*. Team was a farm club of the Cleveland Indians.

1516 Red Stixx 1992–2002 *(SALLY)*. *(A)*. The Red Sticks tribe, in the eighteenth and nineteenth centuries, had this name because they used red-painted poles to mark the boundaries of their territory. As a tribute to four predecessor teams named "Foxes," the team logo is a mischievous red fox.

Columbus, Mississippi

1517 Discoverers 1907–08 *Cotton States (D)*. City was named in honor of Italian explorer Christopher Columbus. Columbus "discovered" the Caribbean Islands in 1492. Moniker had been used by the Columbus Discoverers of the American Association of 1883–84 and 1889–91.

1518 Joy Riders m1912–13 *Cotton States (D)*. Team started the 1912 season in Hattiesburg (MS) before moving to Columbus June 5. With the automobile age here, the term "joy-rider" meant someone who would cruise in a car strictly for fun, especially without permission of the owner. Falling short of auto theft, it implied someone who was rowdy, slightly drunken, and certainly a rule-breaker and a creature of nighttime saloons and dance halls—a perfect description of baseball players of this era. In this era when a team shifted cities in mid-season, as this team did in 1912, players sometimes traveled by car (as opposed to a bus) to their new home, receiving the name of "Joy Riders." Previously, teams that had switched cities in mid-season were called "Orphans" and "Wanderers."

1519 Bengals 1935m *East Dixie (C)*. Team moved to Cleveland (TN) June 18. City was founded as a U.S. Army base known as Fort

Benning. The soldiers there over the years became known as the "Bengals." Moreover, there was a popular Hollywood movie released in 1935 about the British Army in India called *Lives of a Bengal Lancer*. With field manager Slim Brewer at the helm, local newspapers called the players the alliterative "Brewer's Bengals." A rival in the league were the El Dorado Lions, i.e., Lions v. Bengals. Team was not a farm club of the AL Detroit Tigers (who were then sometimes known as the "Bengals").

Columbus, Nebraska

1520 Discoverers 1910–13 *Nebraska State (D)*. Actually there were three cities that employed this name: Columbus, Ohio (1883–84, 1888–91), Columbus, Mississippi (1907–08), and, here in Nebraska. "Discoverers" refers to Christopher Columbus' "discovery of the New World." With manager Joe Dolan at the helm, newspapers called the players "Dolan's Discoverers."

1521 Pawnees 1914–15x *Nebraska State (D)*. Team disbanded June 4. In pre-colonial times, the region was inhabited by Pawnees and Creeks. Newspapers wanted a shorter name—Discoverers had eleven letters—so reporters chose "Pawnees."

Columbus, Ohio

1522 Buckeyes 1876 *Independent*; 1877 *International Assn. (M)*; 1883–84 *American Assn. (M)*; 1887 *Ohio State (ind.)*; 1889–91 *American Assn. (M)*. Ohio is the Buckeye State. The 1883 team's official title was the Buckeye Baseball Association, one of the earliest professional teams to use a nickname of sorts in its formal title. Buck West was manager of the 1887 team, i.e., "Buck's Buckeyes." Al Buckenberger was the manager of the 1889–91 Columbus team, changing the name to "Buckenberger's Buckeyes." The contraction **Bucks** was used by newspapers to save space.

1523 Senators 1883–84 *American Assn. (M)*; *Tri-State* 1888; 1889–91 *American Assn. (M)*; 1896–99m *Western (ind.)*. Team moved to Grand Rapids July 17, 1899; m1899m *Inter-State (ind.)*. City got another team when Grand Rapids ISL franchise moved to Columbus July 20, 1899. Team moved to Anderson July 30, 1899; 1900 *Inter-State (ind.)*; 1902–39 *American Assn.* (A 1902–07, AA 1908–39). Columbus is the state capital.

1524 Solons 1883–84 *American Assn. (M)*; *Tri-State* 1888; 1889–91 *American Assn. (M)*; 1896–99m *Western (ind.)*. Team moved to Grand Rapids July 17, 1899; m1899m *Inter-State (ind.)*. City got another team when Grand Rapids ISL franchise moved to Columbus July 20, 1899. Team moved to Anderson July 30, 1899; 1900 *Inter-State (ind.)*; 1902–39 *American Assn.* (A 1902–07, AA 1908–39). "Solons" is a spin-off of Senators. Solon was a ancient Greek ruler noted for his harsh laws. By the seventeenth century his name meant a "senator" or "legislator." Newspapers often preferred "Solons" because it was shorter and avoided confusion with the NL and AL Washington Senators.

1525 Discoverers 1883–84 *American Assn. (M)*; 1889–91 *American Assn. (M)*; 1901 *Western Assn. (ind.)*. Team was named after Christopher Columbus, who "discovered" America in 1492.

1526 Bad Actors 1889–90 *American Assn. (M)*. Field manager Bucky Buckenberger's "Bad Actors" often over-dramatized their protests to umpires on disputed plays with a chorus of intentional, melodramatic "bad acting," i.e., grimaces, angry pointing, flailing arms, and, of course, kicking dirt—theatrics which not only grated on the opposing teams but also on the fans, including the Columbus patrons at home games.

1527 Colts 1889–91 *American Assn. (M)*. Many young players were on the team. In this era, "colt" was slang for a young player. Newspapers used it for headlines, i.e., "Colts edge A's."

1528 Red Stockings 1892 *Western (ind.)*. Team was a farm club of the Cincinnati Reds. Newspapers shortened the name to **Reds**.

1529 Statesmen 1895 *Inter-State (ind.)*. Tag was a spinoff from Senators.

1530 Buckeyes 1916 *Independent Negro (ind.)*. Ohio is the "Buckeye State." In this era, the "Buckeyes" moniker was used by the athletic teams of Ohio State University.

1531 Carter's Baseball Club 1925 *Independent Negro team*. Team was owned and managed by a baseball promoter named Mr. Carter.

1532 Redbirds 1940–54 *American Assn. (AA 1940–45, AAA 1946–54)*. Team was a farm club of the St. Louis Cardinals, who were also known by the unofficial name of "Redbirds." Several St. Louis Cardinal farm teams chose "Redbirds" to dilute any confusion with the St. Louis parent club.

1533 Jets 1955–70 *International (M)*. Aircraft manufacturing started here in 1941 to build fighters and bombers for the coming war effort.

1534 Clippers 1977 to date *International (AAA)*. Columbus' 1492 "fleet" consisted of three boats— the *Nina, Pinta* and *Santa Maria*— which were actually "caravels"— a type of "clipper" ship that was smaller than the larger clipper ships of future centuries. Moniker is also alliterative, i.e., Columbus Clippers.

Comstock Park, Michigan

1535 West Michigan White Caps 1994 to date Midwest *(A)*. Team goes by the regional name of West Michigan White Caps. Comstock is located next to stormy Lake Michigan. Team's logo depicts white-foamed storm waves.

Concord, New Hampshire

1536 Marines 1902–05 New England *(B)*. New Hampshire is nicknamed the "Mother of Rivers." The state is noted for shipbuilding (Portsmouth) and the "New Hampshire Privateers," who helped defeat the British Royal Navy during the Revolutionary War. With manager John Carney at the helm in 1901–02, newspapers called the players "Carney's Marines."

Concord, North Carolina

1537 Weavers 1939–42 North Carolina State *(D)*; 1945–48 *North Carolina State (D)*. Cotton textile mills operated in the city during the era 1870–1920.

1538 Nationals 1949–50 *North Carolina State (D)*. Team was a farm club of the Washington Nationals.

1539 Sports 1951 *North Carolina State (D)*. Team was a farm club of Shreveport Sports. In the era 1920–60, some lower classification minor league teams, i.e., A, B, C, D, were affiliates of higher classification minor league teams, i.e., AA and AAA.

Concordia, Kansas

1540 Boosters 1910 *Central Kansas (D)*. Team won 1910 pennant. In the era 1900–30, teams that won pennants or were in pennant contention were cheered on by their fans, who formed "booster" clubs. Sometimes the name was then switched over to the players. With manager Harry Short at the helm, newspapers called the pennant-winning players "Short's Boosters."

1541 Travelers 1911x *Central Kansas (D)*. Team and league disbanded July 23. When the Little Rock Travelers became the Chat-

tanooga Lookouts in 1910, the "Travelers" moniker was picked up the following year by Concordia newspapers to praise the players who were "traveling to the pennant" by playing at a .600 percentage. When the league and all four teams disbanded on July 23, league president Roy Gafford awarded the pennant to Concordia on the basis of its 44–27 first-place record. With manager Harry Short at the helm, newspapers called the players "Harry Short's Travelers."

Connellsville, Pennsylvania

1542 Cokers 1907 *Western Pennsylvania (D)*; 1908–09 *Pennsylvania–West Virginia (D)*; 1912x *Ohio–Pennsylvania (D)*. Team disbanded June 18. Coke is the solid residue left by burning petrol. City iron mills produce coke from the burning of coal. Connellsville is known as the "Bituminous City."

Connersville, Indiana

1543 Connersville Base Ball Club 1896 Indiana State *(ind.)*. Team had no nickname.

Constableville, New York

1544 Constableville Base Ball Club 1886 *Central New York*. Team had no nickname.

Cooleemee, North Carolina

1545 Weavers 1937–38 *North Carolina (D)*. In the era 1870–1940 North Carolina had many textile mills for the weaving of wool, cotton and linen.

1546 Cools 1939 *North Carolina (D)*. Moniker was used for newspaper headlines, i.e., "Cools edge Moors, 4–3."

1547 Cardinals 1940–41 *North Carolina (D)*. Team was a farm club of the St. Louis Cardinals.

Cordele, Georgia

1548 Cordele Baseball Club 1906 *Georgia State (D)*. Team had no nickname.

1549 Babies 1913 *Empire State (D)*. Team had many young baby-faced players. By 1917–20 "rookie" had replaced the many previous names, i.e., "Babes, Colts, Cubs" for a young player. The moniker was now more applied to individual players, i.e., "Babe" Ruth. With manager Eddie Reagan at the helm, newspapers called the players "Eddie Reagan's Babies."

1550 Ramblers 1914 *Georgia State (D)*. Under the reins of manager Ed Reagan, the players "rambled to the league pennant," finishing first with a 57–44 record. Newspapers called them "Reagan's Ramblers."

1551 Reds 1936–38, 1941–42 *Georgia–Florida (D)*. Team was a farm club of the Cincinnati Reds.

1552 Bees 1939–40 *Georgia–Florida (D)*. Team had a loose affiliation with the Boston Bees. Bee farms near the city transport raw honey to plants for processing. With manager William Taylor at the helm in 1940, newspapers called the players "Bill's Bees."

1553 White Sox 1946 *Georgia–Florida (D)*. Team was a farm club of the Chicago White Sox.

1554 Indians 1947–49 *Georgia–Florida (D)*. Team was a farm club of the Cleveland Indians.

1555 Athletics 1950–53 *Georgia–Florida (D)*. Team was a farm club of the Philadelphia Athletics.

1556 Orioles 1955 Georgia–Florida *(D)*. Team was a farm club of the Baltimore Orioles.

Cordele-Americus, Georgia

1557 Orioles 1954 *Georgia–Florida (D)*. Team represented both cities but played its home games in Cordele. Team was a farm club of the Baltimore Orioles.

Cordoba, Veracruz, Mexico

1558 Cafeteros 1937–39 *Mexican (ind.)*; 1972–79 *Mexican (AAA)*; 1984–86 *Mexican (AAA)*; 1991–92 *Mexican (AAA)*; 1998–2003 *Mexican (AAA)*. Nearby coffee farms transport coffee beans to city processing and packing plants.
1559 Petroleros 2006 *Mexican (AAA)*. Team started season in Poza Rica, the Poza Rica Oilers, and then moved to Cordoba in mid-season where the nickname was retained, i.e., the "Cordoba Oilers"—"Los Petroleros de Cordoba" in Spanish.

Corinth, Mississippi

1560 Corinthians 1925–26 *Tri-State (D)*. An inhabitant of any city named Corinth is known as a "Corinthian"—whether it be Corinth, Mississippi, or Corinth, Greece. With manager M.R. Striplin at the helm, newspapers called the players "Striplin's Corinthians."

Corning, New York

1561 Athletics 1951–52 *Pennsylvania–Ohio–New York (P.O.N.Y.) (D)*. Team was a farm club of the Philadelphia Athletics.
1562 Independents 1953 *Pennsylvania–Ohio–New York (P.O.N.Y.) (D)*. Team was the only one in the PONY League this season to play without a major league parent club. With manager Tony Lupien at the helm, newspapers called the team "Lupien's Independents." Paul O'Dea took over in mid-season, and the name became "O'Dea's Independents."
1563 Red Sox 1954–56 *Pennsylvania–Ohio–New York (P.O.N.Y.) (D)*; 1957–60 *New York–Pennsylvania (D)*. Team was a farm club of the Boston Red Sox.
1564 Cor-Sox 1958–59 *Pennsylvania–Ohio–New York (P.O.N.Y.) (D)*. Newspaper used an amalgam of city and nickname to come up with "Cor-Sox" for headlines, i.e., "Cor-Sox edge Reading, 5–4."
1565 Royals 1968–69 *New York–Pennsylvania (A)*. Team was a farm club of the Kansas City Royals.

Cornwall, Quebec, Canada

1566 Bisons 1938 *Canadian–American (C)*. Team was a farm club of the Buffalo Bisons. A few lower classification minor league teams, i.e., A, B, C, D, were affiliated with higher classification minor league teams, i.e., AA and AAA, in the era 1925–40. Buffalo was a Class AA International League team.
1567 Maple Leafs 1939 *Canadian–American (C)*. Team was a farm club of the Toronto Maple Leafs. A few lower classification minor league teams were affiliated with higher classification minor league teams in the era 1910–55. Toronto was a Class AA International League team.
1568 Canadiens 1951x *Border (C)*. Team disbanded June 26. An inhabitant of Canada is a "Canadian." In French, it is "Le Canadien." Ten professional baseball teams, located in Canada, have been known as the "Canadians."

Coronado, California

1569 Arabs m1929x *California State (D)*. Team started season in Santa Ana (CA) and Pomona (CA) before moving to Coronado May 15. Team and league disbanded June 17. In the sixteenth century Francisco Vazquez de Coronado explored the American Southwest in search for the fabled "Seven Cities of Gold." His followers consisted of soldiers, their families, priests and Zuni Indian guides. Bringing along farm animals and poultry for food, they wandered the dry plains and deserts of the region for years, much like wandering "Arabs" in the Sahara Desert. In fact, Coronado was nicknamed "the Arab," i.e., "El Arabe."

Corpus Christi, Texas

1570 Pelicans 1910–11x *Southwest Texas (D)*. Team disbanded July 17, 1911. Team had a loose affiliation with the Class A New Orleans Pelicans. The Brown Pelican inhabits the coastline along the Gulf of Mexico.
1571 Sea Hawks 1926 *Gulf Coast (D)*; 1927 *Texas Valley (D)*; 1931m *Rio Grande Valley (C)*. Team moved to La Feria–Harlingen (TX) June 5. Pirates and privateers, known as the Seahawks, sailed the Gulf of Mexico, Corpus Christi Bay and the Nueces River in this area from about 1550 to 1850. With manager Chick Brandon at the helm, newspapers called the players the alliterative "Chick's Seahawks."
1572 Spudders 1938 *Texas Valley (D)*. Farms in the region ship potatoes to cleaning and packing plants.
1573 Aces 1951–53 *Gulf Coast (B)*. Air aces have been flying U.S. Navy planes at the Kingsville Naval Air Station, just southwest of the city, since 1940. Newspapers liked the four-letter name.
1574 Clippers 1954–57 *Big State (B)*. Navy clipper planes regularly flew in and out of the U.S. Navy base located here. Also clipper boats hauled cargo in and out of the seaport at Corpus Christi in the era 1700–1900. A "clipper" boat is one that travels at a "fast clip," i.e., one designed for speed. Corpus Christi is "The City Where Texas Meets the Sea."
1575 Giants 1958–59 *Texas (AA)*. Team was a farm club of the San Francisco Giants.
1576 Sea Gulls 1976 *Gulf States (A)*; 1977 *Lone Star (A)*. Sea gulls inhabit the coastlines of Texas, Louisiana and Alabama.
1577 Barracudas 1994–95 *Texas–Louisiana (ind.)*. The city has fishing resorts where barracuda swim the waters of Corpus Christi Bay.
1578 Hooks 2005 to date *Texas (AA)*. A maritime city since 1800, Corpus Christi has been a port for freighters transporting oil and farm products. Boats, replete with nets and fishhooks, sail in and out of the Corpus Christi Bay fishing for crab fish, trout, snapper, catfish, perch and oysters. The Naval Air Station of Corpus Christi is located just outside the city. Corpus Christi is the "Sparkling City by the Sea." Team mascots are "Sammy the Seagull" and "Rusty the Hook."

Corsicana, Texas

1579 Oil Citys 1902–04 *Texas (D 1902–03, C 1904)*. Oil was discovered in the region in the 1890s and the city enjoyed a "boom" greatly increasing its population and leading to the construction of oil wells and refineries here. By 1900, the Corsicana was known as "Oil City."
1580 Oilers 1905 *Texas (C)*; 1907 *North Texas (D)*; m1917x *Central Texas (D)*. Team started season in Temple and moved to Corsicana June 1. League and team disbanded June 6 because of U.S. entry into World War I; 1923–26 *Texas Assn. (D)*; 1927–28 *Lone Star (D)*. In 1905, Corsicana newspapers decided "Oil Citys" was too abstract, so they started calling the team the "Oilers," which also used a little less print space. The 1923 team took the moniker after newspapers rebelled against "Gumbo-busters." The 1927 team played at Oil City

Park. Corsicana was home to the Oil City Textile Company, which manufactured petro-textiles, i.e., plastic and synthetic fibers. With manager Con Lucid at the helm in 1905, newspapers called the players "Con Lucid's Oilers." Moniker then became traditional for the next four Corsicana teams.

1581 Desperados 1907 *North Texas (D)*. Like any boomtown in the Old West that attracted people because of gold, silver or oil, honest folk arrived to seek their fortune, and a whole array of bandits and outlaws arrived to steal a fortune. These "Desperados" raided trains, riverboats, stagecoaches, and banks quite frequently until about 1915. Baseball players in the era 1870–1920 had an image among fans of being uncouth and rowdy, giving rise to such names as Cowboys, Indians, Gladiators, Bronchos, Rustlers and Desperados. With manager Dee Poindexter at the helm, newspapers called the players "Dee Poindexter's Desperados."

1582 Athletics 1914–15x *Central Texas (D)*. The 1914 regular season was shortened to July 25 but the league did not disband. Team and league disbanded July 24, 1915; m1917x *Central Texas (D)*. Team started season in Temple and moved to Corsicana June 1. League and team disbanded June 6 because of U.S. entry into World War I. Although the team was not a farm club of the Philadelphia Athletics (there was no farm system yet), newspapers used "Athletics" to place its contraction in newspaper headlines, i.e., "A's edge Buffaloes, 4–3." Name also emulated the successful Philadelphia Athletics, who had won the 1913 World Series and were favorites to win the 1914 AL pennant.

1583 Gumbo-busters 1922 *Texas–Oklahoma (D)*. By 1920 farmers in the region were using gasoline-motorized tractors to haul away mud after rains and floods. This mud was as thick and sticky as "gumbo soup," leading to the nickname of "gumbo-busters" for these tractors. When manager Harvey Grubb took over for Charles Miller in mid-season, newspapers started calling the players "Grubb's Gumbo-busters."

Cortazar, Guanajuato, Mexico

1584 Club de Beisbol de Cortazar 1975 *Mexican Center (A)*. Team had no nickname.

Cortland, New York

1585 Cortland Base Ball Club 1886 *Central New York (ind.)*. Team had no nickname.

1586 Wagon-Makers 1897–1901m New York State *(ind.)*. Team moved to Waverly (NY) July 11. Team was owned by Lawrence Fitzgerald, who also owned the Cortland Wagon Company.

Coshocton, Ohio

1587 Coshocton Base Ball Club 1898x Ohio State *(ind.)*. Team and league disbanded in mid-season. Team had no nickname.

Coudersport, Pennsylvania

1588 Giants 1905 *Inter-State (D)*. In the era 1870–1910, any team that won a lot of games, contended for the pennant and/or won the flag was credited by newspapers as having "played like giants." These players did perform "like Giants" as they won the league pennant with a 59–38 record. Also, minor league teams of this time often chose nicknames in emulation of successful big league clubs, i.e., the New York Giants, who were en route to the 1905 NL pennant. With manager Ray Knight at the helm, local newspapers called the players "Knight's Giants."

Council Bluffs, Iowa

1589 Bluffers 1903m *Iowa–South Dakota (D)*. Team moved to Sheldon-Primghar (IA) June 20. Moniker was used for newspaper headlines, i.e., "Bluffers edge Blackbirds, 4–3."

1590 Rails m1935x *Western (A)*. Team began season in Omaha (NE) and moved here June 25. Team disbanded August 27. The Union Pacific Railroad built a major station here in 1863 because it was an important outfitting point for pioneers, explorers, soldiers, settlers, and gold rushers.

Covington, Kentucky

1591 Blue Sox 1913m *Federal (ind.)*. Team moved to Kansas City (MO) June 26. Players wore blue stirrups.

Covington, Virginia

1592 Paper-makers 1914x *Virginia Mountain (D)*. Paper mills are located in the city.

1593 Red Sox 1966 *Appalachian (R)*. Team was a farm club of the Boston Red Sox.

1594 Astros 1967–76 *Appalachian (R)*. Team was a farm club of the Houston Astros.

Crawfordsville, Indiana

1595 Hoosiers 1888m *Central Inter-State (ind.)*. Team moved to Terre Haute (IN) July 2. Franchise had the only Indiana team in the league playing in Crawfordsville, and then in Terre Haute. An inhabitant of Indiana is called a "Hoosier." Crawfordsville is known as the "Hoosier Athens" because of the presence of Wabash College.

1596 Orphans m1899 *Indiana–Illinois (ind.)*. Team started season in Muncie (IN) and then moved to Crawfordsville June 4. In the era 1890–1910 when a team was forced to move to another city in mid-season — usually because of poor attendance — the players were often referred to as "Orphans," i.e., the original city's fans had "abandoned" them as "unwanted orphans." Circuit also known as the Two-I League.

Creston, Iowa

1597 Cyclones 1903x *Southwest Iowa (D)*. Team disbanded August 29. Iowa is in the middle of the so-called "Tornado Alley" that extends from Texas to Minnesota where spring and summer tornadoes strike between the months of April and September.

Crestview, Florida

1598 Braves 1954–56 *Alabama–Florida (D)*. Originally inhabitants of Alabama and Georgia in the eighteenth century, the Seminole Indians were resettled in Florida and Oklahoma. Moniker was also alliterative, i.e., Crestview Braves. Team was not a farm club of the Milwaukee Braves, playing as an independent in 1954–55 and affiliating with the Chicago Cubs in 1956.

Crestwood, Cook County, Illinois

1599 Cook County Cheetahs 1998 *Heartland (ind.)*; 1999–2003 *Frontier (ind.)*. Fan poll chose "Cheetahs" as part of a regional name — the "Cook County Cheetahs." Crestwood is located in Cook County. Franchise switched circuits, going to the Frontier League for the 1999 season.

1600 Windy City Thunderbolts 2004 to date *Frontier (ind.)*. Chicago is not only the "Windy City," but the Chicago-land area is subjected to thunder and lightning storms in the spring and summer.

Crisfield, Maryland

1601 Crabbers 1922–28x *Eastern Shore (D)*. Team and league disbanded July 10, 1928; 1937 *Eastern Shore (D)*. The city is a major port and processing center for crab and oyster fishing. Crisfield, located on Chesapeake Bay's Tangier Sound, is the "Seafood Capital of the World." With manager Jack Ryan at the helm, newspapers called the players "Jack Ryan's Crabbers."

Crockett, Texas

1602 Crocket Baseball Club 1916x *East Texas (D)*. Team disbanded July 15. Team had no nickname.

Crookston, Minnesota

1603 Crookston Base Ball Club 1891 *Midwest (ind.)*. Team had no nickname.

1604 Crooks 1902–05 *Northern (ind. 1902, D 1903–05)*. Moniker was used for newspaper headlines, i.e., "Crooks edge Maroons, 4–3." With names in Minnesota, like "Thief River" and "Thief River Falls," the "Crooks" moniker was appropriate. People know all about ocean pirates, but few know that "river pirates" terrorized the Great Lakes region for nearly 200 years, starting in 1700. They attacked flat boats, keelboats and even rafts. And they stole anything, i.e., livestock, stores and slaves. These river pirates sailed up and down the Mississippi River.

1605 Pirates 1933–40 *Northern (A 1933–39, C 1940)*. Team was an independent 1933–35, 1939–40, then a farm club of the AL White Sox 1936, NL Cardinals 1937, and AL Red Sox 1938 but never was a farm team of the NL Pittsburgh Pirates. About 150 miles northwest of the city is Thief Lake and the Thief River, which runs to Crookston. River pirates attacked shipping in the Great Lakes and on the Mississippi and Ohio rivers, ranging from Minnesota to Missouri and Kentucky.

Crowley, Louisiana

1606 Rice Birds 1908x *Gulf Coast (D)*. Team and league disbanded June 2. Birds, including sparrows and the Bobolink, feed off the grains in the fields of the rice farms of this region. Crowley is the "Rice City of America" and the "Rice Capital of the World."

1607 Millers 1950 *Gulf Coast (C)*; 1951–57 *Evangeline (C)*. The city has milling factories for the corn, rice and wheat crops of surrounding farms. Crowley is the "Rice Center of America."

Culiacan, Sinoloa, Mexico

1608 Los Tomateros 1945–46–57–58 *Mexican Pacific Coast (W)*; 1958–59–69–70 *Sinoloa–Sonora (W)*. Circuit was known as the Sinoloa–Sonora League through the 1969–70 season before being renamed the Mexican Pacific League at the start of the 1970–71 season; 1970–71 to date *Mexican Pacific (W)*. Farms in the region ship tomatoes to packing plants. "El tomatero" is Spanish for tomato farmer.

Cumberland, Maryland

1609 Rooters 1906 *Pennsylvania–Ohio–Maryland (P.O.M.) (D)*; m1907m *Western Pennsylvania (D)*. Team started season in Latrobe (PA) and then moved here May 28. Team then moved to Piedmont (WV) June 27. Site of the first federal road, construction began in 1811 with the road eventually reaching St. Louis, Missouri. "Rooter" is slang for "route."

1610 Colts 1916x *Potomac (D)*. Team and league disbanded August 16; m1917–18x *Blue Ridge (D)*. Team started 1917 season in Chambersburg and moved to Cumberland June 13, 1917. Team and league disbanded in June 16, 1918 because of U.S. participation in World War I; 1925–32 *Middle Atlantic (C)*. Horseracing, i.e., the annual Preakness Race, is popular in Maryland. Moreover, the players on the team were mostly young "colts," i.e., slang for young players used in the era 1883–1916.

Cushing, Oklahoma

1611 Oilers m1921 *Southwestern (D)*. Team started season in Parsons (KS) and moved to Cushing July 27. Oil was discovered in the region and by 1920 Cushing had become a "boom town" complete with oil wells, natural gas wells and refineries.

1612 Refiners 1923–24 *Oklahoma State (D)*; 1925 *Southwest (D)*. City has petrochemical plants to refine crude oil. With manager Ned Pettigrew at the helm in 1923–24, newspapers called the players "Pettigrew's Refiners." Frank Thompson managed the 1925 team, which became "Frank's Refiners."

Cynthiana, Kentucky

1613 Merchants 1922 *Blue Grass (D)*. A suburb of Lexington, Cynthiana grew during the 1920s with an influx of people who wanted to shop locally rather than travel to Lexington. Located along the South Licking River, the city has been a mercantile center since its founding in 1793. With manager Sprouts McIlvain at the helm, newspapers called the players "McIlvain's Merchants."

1614 Cobblers 1923–24 *Blue Grass (D)*. Although there are shoe manufacturers in the city, the moniker was a local newspaper gimmick. With field manager Bill Schumaker at the helm, local newspapers called the players "Schumaker's Cobblers." Schumaker is German for "shoemaker." Baseball manager Schumaker is no relation to the famous horse racing jockey Bill Shoemaker.

Daegu, South Korea see
Taegu, South Korea

Daejeon, South Korea see
Taejeon, South Korea

Dale City–Woodbridge,
Prince William, Virginia

1615 Prince William Pirates 1984–86 *Carolina (A)*. Team was a farm club of the Pittsburgh Pirates.

1616 Prince William Yankees 1987–88 *Carolina (A)*. Team was a farm club of the New York Yankees.

1617 Prince William Cannons 1989–2004 *Carolina (A)*. Team went by the county name of Prince William Cannons 1989–98. Team went by the river name of **Potomac Cannons** 1999–2004. Many Civil War battles took place in Virginia, i.e., Bull Run, Fredericksburg and Appomattox.

1618 Potomac Nationals 2005 to date *Carolina (A)*. Team was a farm club of the Washington Nationals.

Dallas, Texas

1619 Hams 1888 *Texas (ind.)*. Regional farms ship pigs and hogs to slaughterhouses and meat packing plants. A baseball player, much like an actor in a theatrical display of anger, when arguing with an umpire is known as a "ham." Such players were known as Actors, Kickers, Rag Chewers and Hams.

1620 Tigers 1889x *Texas (ind.)*. Team disbanded August 9; 1890x *Texas (ind.)*. Team and league disbanded June 10. In imitation of Princeton University's athletic teams, the 1889 Dallas team dressed their players in striped stockings, leading to the tag of "Tigers." With manager Doug Crouthers at the helm in 1889, newspapers called the players "Doug Crouther's Tigers"

1621 Steers 1895 *Texas–Southern (ind.)*; 1897 *Texas (ind.)*. With manager Ted Sullivan at the helm, newspapers called the players "Sullivan Steers." In this era, Dallas had become the biggest cattle center in Texas.

1622 Navigators 1896x *Texas–Southern (ind.)*. Team disbanded August 2. Boats have sailed on the nearby Trinity River since at least 1840. The Trinity Rivers empties into Galveston Bay, which empties into the Gulf of Mexico. With manager Henri Blackburn at the helm, newspapers called the players "Henri Blackburn's Navigators."

1623 Colts 1898x *Texas (ind.)*. Team and circuit disbanded May 15. Young players on team were known as "colts," a typical slang of the era. In the era 1890–1910 young players were called Babes, Chicks, Colts, Cubs, Debutantes, Foundlings, Innocents, Ponies, Prodigals and Yearlings.

1624 Scrappers 1898x *Texas (ind.)*. Team and league disbanded May 15. In the era 1880–1910, baseball players were perceived as rowdy "scrappers" who often fought other players, umpires, reporters and even fans. "Scrap" is slang (coined 1889) for a fight—usually a fist fight. It applied to cowboys, who were "rough, tough hombres ready for a scrap." With manager Ted Sullivan at the helm, newspapers called the players "Sullivan's Scrappers."

1625 Griffins 1902 *Texas (D)*. With manager Les Dawkins at the helm, newspapers called the players "Dawkin's Griffins." Baseball players of this era were always likened to imposing and powerful creatures, i.e., Bisons, Eagles, Elephants, Lions, Tigers, Wolverines and Griffins. The Griffin is a mythological creature—half eagle and half lion.

1626 Giants 1903–18 *Texas (D 1903 & 1906, C 1904–05 & 1907–10, B 1911–18)*; 1919 *Negro Texas (ind.)*. Starting in 1903, the New York Giants played spring training games in Dallas for the next 25 years, prompting the Dallas team to choose "Giants." The nickname was reinforced when the Dallas club won the 1903 pennant. "Playing like giants" was a phrase in this era, which referred to players who won games, contended for the pennant, or who won a pennant. With manager Charles Moran at the helm 1903–04, newspapers called the players "Moran's Giants." After Moran left the team following the 1904 season, the popular moniker was retained. When the Dallas "Giants" of the Texas League dropped the name in favor of "Marines," for the 1919 season, this black Negro Texas League team chose it as their nickname.

1627 Dallas Baseball Club 1908–11 *Independent Negro* team; 1917–18 *Negro Texas (ind.)*. These teams had no nickname.

1628 Marines 1919 *Texas (B 1920, A 1921)*. Although inland, Dallas is located near the Trinity River and the White Rock Lake—a man-made lake constructed in 1900. City is also surrounded by Bachman, Mount Creek and North lakes. With manager Hamilton Patterson at the helm, newspapers called the players "Hamilton Patterson's Marines."

1629 Submarines 1920–21 *Texas (B)*. The Dallas–Fort Worth area was subjected to frequent flooding in 1920. With Patterson back

again but unable to stop a sixth-place finish with a "submerging" 63–85 record, 45 games out of first place, disgruntled fans and newspapers changed the team nickname from "Marines" to "Submarines." The team in 1921 had a winning 81–78 record but the unhappy fans persisted with Submarines. The U.S. Navy established a base here in 1929.

1630 Steers 1922–38 *Texas (A 1922–35, A1 1936–38)*. In the era 1900–30, the Dallas–Fort Worth area had the largest livestock and processing center south of Kansas City. With manager Walter Morris at the helm in 1922, newspapers called the players "Walter Morris' Steers." Morris left the team after the 1924 season but the moniker was retained because newspapers liked it.

1631 Texas Giants 1929–31 *Independent Negro team*. Team used the 1919 Dallas "Giants" moniker with the state name of "Texas."

1632 Rebels 1939–42 *Texas (A1)*; 1946–47 *Texas (AA)*. Although Texas was part of the Confederacy during the Civil War, the moniker actually refers to the American rebels, known as "Los Rebeldes" to the Mexican Army, who fought against Mexico in the 1847–49 Mexican-American War.

1633 Eagles 1948–57 *Texas (AA)*. With the Civil War fading into history and the Cold War arriving, management decided on a less polemic, pro–American nickname. Team was named in their honor. The nickname was official and the team logo was a bald eagle.

1634 Rangers 1958 *Texas (AA)*; 1959 *American Assn. (M)*; 1964 *Pacific Coast (AAA)*. The Texas Rangers, the mounted police of Texas, were formed by Texas military hero Stephen Austin in 1823.

Dallas–Fort Worth, Texas

1635 Dallas–Fort Worth Base Ball Club 1892 *Texas (ind.)*; m1898 *Southwestern (ind.)*. Team started season in Sherman (TX) and then moved to Dallas–Fort Worth in mid-season; m1899 *Southern (ind.)*. Team started season in Montgomery (AL) and then moved to Dallas–Fort Worth in mid-season. These teams had no nickname. The 1898 team is not to be confused with the 1898 Texas League Dallas Colts/Scrappers.

1636 Rangers 1960–62 *American Assn. (AAA)*; 1963 *Pacific Coast (AAA)*; 1972 to date *American (M)*. The 1959 Dallas Rangers team regionalized to represent Dallas and Fort Worth. The new 1972 A.L. team picked up the moniker used by four teams since 1958. Because the 1972 team represented both Dallas and Fort Worth, management decided to use the regional name of "Texas Rangers" to placate nervous newspaper editors over the prospect of a team called the "Dallas–Fort Worth Rangers"—a name with 22 letters that had been the title of the 1963 PCL club. The formal title of "Texas Rangers" was chosen by team owner Robert Short.

1637 Spurs 1965–71 *Texas (AA)*. In 1971, the Texas and Southern leagues played an interlocking schedule under the banner of the Dixie Association. The arrangement ended after only this one season. When management of this new team decided to go with the title Dallas–Fort Worth, local newspaper editors were ready to rebel until "Spurs" was chosen. Even so, the full name had 19 letters. Although used by nineteenth century American cowboys, spurs were first used by medieval mounted knights.

1638 Worst Baseball Team in History 1972 *American (M)*. Notwithstanding the 1899 Spiders and 1962 Mets, baseball author Mike Shropshire branded the 1972–73 Texas Rangers with this title for somehow managing to lose 205 games in these two seasons after the franchise arrived in Texas from Washington, D.C., in April 1972. For several seasons, the franchise struggled as though it were an expansion team.

1639 Strangers 1972–2009 *American (M)*. When the team started playing spring training games in March 1972 after leaving Washington, Dallas–Fort Worth fans, looking at box scores in the newspaper, were befuddled by the unknown players on the team. The non-identity of hitters like Dick Billings, Ted Ford, Joe Lovito, Dave Nelson, Lenny Randle, and pitchers Pete Broberg, Bill Gogolewski and Jim Panthers astonished Texas fans as newspapers called the new team the Texas "Strangers." Indeed, about the only "name" player on the 1972 team was slugger Frank Howard. The *Dallas Morning News* reported on April 22, 1972, "The home crowd appeared to be feeling its way down the lineup of the mostly unknown Texas team — which has been referred to as the 'Strangers' as much as 'Rangers.'" Starting in 1973, impatient Texas fans branded *losing* Rangers teams as the "Strangers" for the seasons 1973, 1982–85, 1987–88, 1992 whether they had marquee players or not. When major league baseball owners toyed with the idea of replacement players as the 1994–95 strike dragged into April 1995, Texas fans, with jeering sarcasm, called the proposed Texas team the "Texas Strangers" (after the 1972 moniker). The 1994 team was mocked as the "Strangers" for being in first place in the AL Western Division while sporting a record (52–62) ten games under .500! The name abruptly stopped when the Rangers won the 2010 AL pennant, although future losing seasons figure to hasten its return. Also spelled st–Rangers.

1640 Corralled Rangers 1973 *American (M)*. After a Washington Senator–like 54–100 season in 1972, the Rangers were "corralled" again posting a un–Texas like 57–105 mark for another sixth and last place finish in the AL Western Division.

1641 Wranglers 1990 to date *American (M)*. Tag was coined by ex–baseball player and sportscaster Ken Harrelson. A "wrangler" is a ranch hand who takes care of the saddle horses. The meaning now includes cowboys.

1642 Dangers 1994 to date *American (M)*. The light hitting, decent pitching Rangers of the 1970s gave way to an offense powered by strong hitters like Larry Parrish, Ruben Sierra, Juan Gonzalez, Dean Palmer, Jose Canseco, Rafael Palmeiro and Ivan Rodriguez while pitchers struggled in the bandbox known as Arlington Stadium. When the franchise moved into the hitter-friendly Ball Park at Arlington, the offense got stronger (.293 team BA and 230 HR in 1999) while the pitching degenerated into batting practice quality with seven consecutive seasons resulting in team ERAs over 4.50 and three 5.00 plus campaigns at 5.45, 5.07 and 5.52! Newspapers started to call the team the "Dangers" because the pitching staff was always in danger of blowing a big lead. Powered by a strong offense, the Rangers won their first American League pennant in 2010.

1643 Power Rangers 1994 to date *American (M)*. The inevitable and clever spinoff from the very popular kids' TV series applied to Rangers teams of the 1990s that spent most of its money on hitters, resulting in a potent offense and abhorrent pitching. Texas fans sighed in dismay at a seemingly endless stream of 10–8 and 9–7 defeats during losing seasons but were electrified by the slugging in the franchise's three playoff seasons of 1996, 1998–99 and the AL pennant campaign of 2010.

1644 Lamers 2005 *American (M)*. When Houston beat out the Rangers for the State of Texas' first World Series appearance, Houston fans began to taunt the Dallas–Fort Worth team as the "Lamers" for 34 seasons of pennant-less futility. An obviously mean-spirited moniker, it has been pretty much shunned by the media but it is no worse an insult than those appearing in other major league cities.

1645 Yard-bangers 2010 *American (M)*. The Texas Rangers won their first A.L. pennant as the team was powered by hitters Vladimir Guerrero (29 HR, 115 RBI), Josh Hamilton (.359 BA, 32 HR, 100 RBI) and Mike Young (21 HR, 91 RBI). Moniker was coined by ESPN broadcaster Mark Kestiger.

1646 Monsters 2011 *American (M)*. A White Sox fan, who had attended a August 22 game between the Rangers and Chicago, called

into a sports show, hosted by WSCR broadcaster Les Grobstein, and described the tall and muscular Ranger hitters, i.e., Vladimir Guerreo, Josh Hamilton, Mike Young and the others in the batting lineup, as "Monsters."

Danbury, Connecticut

1647 Hatters 1887 *Eastern (ind.)*; 1898 *Connecticut (ind.)*; 1913 *New York–New Jersey (D)*; 1914 *Atlantic (D)*. Danbury is "The Hat City" because hats have been manufactured there since about 1740.

Danville, Illinois

1648 Danville Browns 1888 *Central Inter-State (ind.)*; 1889 *Indiana–Illinois (ind.)*. Players wore brown hose.

1649 Champions 1899 *Indiana–Illinois (ind.)*; 1900 *Central (ind.)*. Team won 1899 pennant. Occasionally teams that won a pennant in this era were christened as "Champions" at the start of the following season. Although the name might persist for the next season, if the team failed to repeat, the moniker was quietly dropped toward the end of the year.

1650 Old Soldiers 1906 *Kentucky–Illinois–Tennessee (KITTY). (D)*. Danville had a rest home built in 1905 for veterans of the Civil War. Dayton (OH) had previously built a similar rest home in 1895. Both Union and Confederate veterans were welcome.

1651 Speakers Team moved to Staunton (IL) July 17, 1908m *Eastern Illinois (D)*; 1910–14m *Three-I (B)*. Team moved to Moline (IL) July 14, 1914. The Three-I League represented Illinois, Indiana and Iowa. In the 1840s Abraham Lincoln opened a law office and started making public speeches in this city.

1652 Veterans 1922–32m *Three-I (B)*. Team and league disbanded July 15, 1932, because of the Great Depression. Tag was a spin-off from the 1906 Dayton Old Soldiers.

1653 Dodgers 1946–50 *Three-I (B)*. Team was a farm club of the Brooklyn Dodgers.

1654 Dans 1951–54 *Missouri–Ohio Valley (M.O.V.). (D)*. Moniker was used for newspaper headlines, i.e., "Dans edge Kings, 4–3." An inhabitant of Danville is not a "Dan."

1655 Warriors 1970–74 *Midwest (A)*. Kickapoo Indians inhabited Iowa in the eighteenth and nineteenth centuries.

1656 Dodgers 1975–76 *Midwest (A)*. Team was a farm club of the Los Angeles Dodgers.

Danville, Pennsylvania

1657 Danville Base Ball Club m1886 *Pennsylvania State (ind.)*. Team started season in Lancaster before moving to Danville in midseason; 1887 *Central Pennsylvania (ind.)*; 1892–93m *Pennsylvania State (ind.)*. Team moved to Reading July 7; 1896 *Central Pennsylvania (ind.)*; 1898 *Central Pennsylvania (ind.)*. These teams had no nickname.

Danville, Virginia

1658 Tobs 1905x *Virginia–North Carolina (D)*. Team and league disbanded August 19; *Piedmont* 1920–24 (D 1920, C 1921–24); Regional tobacco market. Originally called "Tobacconists," newspapers immediately shortened name to Tobs.

1659 Red Sox 1906–10, 1912x *Virginia (C)*. Team disbanded June 15. Players wore red hose. Team was not a farm club of the Boston Red Sox.

1660 Bugs 1911 *Virginia (C)*. June Bugs (aka lady bugs and May bugs) are so prevalent in the spring in Danville that the 1911 team had a "June Bug" mascot logo drawn for its advertising posters. Unfortunately, the team played so poorly, going 50–70 and finishing in eighth place, that local newspapers indignantly reported the players in numerous one-sided losses got "squashed like bugs!" With manager Joseph Laughlin at the helm, newspapers called the players "Laughlin's Bugs."

1661 Leafs m1925–26m *Piedmont (C).* Team started 1925 season in High Point (NC) before moving to Danville June 18, 1925. Team moved back to High Point May 12, 1926; 1934–38 *Bi-State (D);* 1946–58 *Carolina (C 1946–48, B 1949–58).* Tag was a spin-off from "Tobs."

1662 Braves 1993 to date *Appalachian (A).* Team is a farm club of the Atlanta Braves.

1663 97's 1998 *Carolina (A).* Franchise was created in 1997 and a fan poll decided upon the " 97's." The franchise moved to Danville from Durham for one year while a ballpark was built for the team in Myrtle Beach, SC. Team logo of a steam locomotive honored Virginia's railroad history.

Danville-Schoolfield, Virginia

1664 Leafs 1939–42 *Bi-State (D).* Team, using the 1938 "Leafs" moniker, assumed the dual-city name of "Danville-Schoolfield Leafs," although it played its home games in Danville.

Darby, Pennsylvania

1665 Hilldales 1924 *Independent Negro team.* The Philadelphia Hilldales played some home games in Darby, a suburb of Philadelphia. Team did not go by any regional or dual-city name and was listed in Darby newspapers simply as the "Hilldales."

1666 Daisies 1930 *Independent Negro team.* The Philadelphia Hilldales played as an independent in 1930 with most of its home games in Darby. Team went by its stadium name of Hilldale Daisies. Players wore daisy yellow-trim uniforms and stirrups.

1667 Phantoms 1948 *Independent Negro team.* Darby is a suburb of Philadelphia, but the team did not go by the title of Philadelphia. The Darby "Phantoms" dressed their players in black-trim uniforms and black stirrups.

Darlington, South Carolina

1668 Fiddlers 1907 *South Carolina (D).* Team moved to Florence (SC) July 27. In this era Darlington hosted an annual "Fiddlers' Convention" in the local social hall and on the street replete with music, square dancing, band shells, fireworks and concerts. With Mr. Russell at the managerial helm, newspapers called the players "Russell's Fiddlers."

Davenport, Iowa

1669 Browns 1879 *Northwestern (ind.);* 1888x *Central Interstate (ind.).* Team disbanded July 5. Players wore brown hose. Originally **Brown Stockings** for both teams, newspapers shortened the name to Browns.

1670 Hawkeyes 1879 *Northwest (ind.);* 1891 *Illinois–Iowa (ind.).* Iowa is the "Hawkeye State."

1671 Onion-weeders m1888 *Western Assn.(ind.).* Team started season in Minneapolis and moved to Davenport August 25. Farms in the region transported onions and other vegetables and grains to packing houses.

1672 River Rats 1901–04 *Three-I (ind. 1901, B 1902–04).* By 1900, the Mississippi River had become so polluted that rats were swimming in the floating garbage. State and federal cleanup laws became effective in the 1930s.

1673 Riversides 1905 *Three-I (B).* City fathers and team officials were so embarrassed by the team's nickname of "River Rats" that they pressured local newspapers to change the moniker to something more attractive for the sake of the tourist industry.

1674 Knicks 1906 *Three-I (B).* Dutch families who had settled in New York State in the eighteenth century and became known as the "Knickerbockers" because of their "knickerbocker pants" (which reached to the knee) continued westward in the nineteenth century, settling in the Midwest, including Iowa and Davenport. With manager A.L. "Snapper" Kennedy at the helm, newspapers called the players "Kennedy's Knickerbockers." Originally **Knickerbockers**, newspapers shortened it to "Knicks."

1675 Prodigals 1909–12 *Three-I (B).* New team had young players. Although meaning "abundant," i.e., farm produce, the name also means "son" and refers to the young players on the team. Baseball players were sometimes called "prodigals" (recklessly extravagant) because they wasted money smoking, drinking and chasing women and got into fist fights and bar-room brawls, costing the team a good deal of money.

1676 Blue Sox 1913–16 *Three-I (B);* 1929–33 *Mississippi Valley (D 1929–32, B 1933);* 1934–37 *Western (A).* Players wore blue stirrups. The 1913–26 team was not a farm club of the Brooklyn Dodgers but the 1915 team did have a loose affiliation with the Chicago White Sox (hence, the blue color spin-off from white). The 1929–33 team had a loose affiliation with the Brooklyn Dodgers, purchasing blue-trim uniforms from the big league team. The 1934–37 team, loosely affiliated with NL Brooklyn 1934–35, became an official Dodgers farm club in 1936. All these teams wore blue-trim uniforms and blue stirrups. The Brooklyn Dodgers wore blue-trim.

1677 Cubs 1946–47 *Three-I (B).* Team was a farm club of the Chicago Cubs.

1678 Pirates 1947–48 *Three-I (B).* Team was a farm club of the Pittsburgh Pirates.

1679 Quads 1950 *Three-I (B).* Team went by the regional name of "Quad Cities Quads" but also the city name of "Davenport Quads." Davenport is the largest of the four so-called "Quad Cities," which also includes Bettendorf (IA), Moline (IL) and Rock Island (IL).

1680 Tigers 1951–52 *Three-I (B).* Team went by the regional name of "Quad Cities Tigers" but also by the city name of "Davenport Tigers." Team was a farm club of Detroit Tigers.

1681 Dav-Sox 1957–58 *Three-I (B).* Team was a farm club of the Chicago White Sox. Sometimes a team will combine a portion of its city name with Sox. Thus we have BoSox, ChiSox, Knox-Sox, Paw-Sox and Dav-Sox.

1682 Braves 1960–61 *Midwest (D).* Team was a farm club of Milwaukee Braves.

Davenport-Bettendorf, Iowa, and Moline–Rock Island, Illinois

1683 Quad Cities Braves 1961 *Midwest (D).* Team was a farm club of the Milwaukee Braves.

1684 Quad Cities Angels 1962–78 *Midwest (D 1962, A 1963–78);* 1985–90 *Midwest (A).* These teams were farm clubs of the L.A. (1961–64) and California (1965–78, 1985–90) Angels.

1685 Quad Cities Cubs 1979–84 *Midwest (A).* Team was a farm club of the Chicago Cubs.

1686 Quad Cities River Bandits 1991–2003, 2008 to date *Midwest (A).* Management held a name-the-team contest with 1,000 entries submitted, including 800 suggested names. The winner was Davenport resident Bob Heimer. Team owner Rick Holtzman, upon choosing "River Bandits," said:

> We thought about the Mighty Mississippi and the mystery and flair of bandits. We wanted to develop a name that was marketable, both internally and nationally, and I think we found it in River Bandits. When people think about the Angels, they think about the California Angels. We wanted to give the franchise more of a Quad City identity.

Ironically, Heimer said he wasn't thinking about river pirates but rather about the "one-arm bandits," i.e., slot machines of riverboat gambling. River pirates plagued shipping on the Mississippi River in the eighteenth and nineteenth centuries.

1687 Quad Cities Swing 2004–07 *Midwest (A)*. Bix Biederbeck, a native son of Davenport, is a noted musician who specializes in 1940s "Swing Music."

Davenport–Haines City, Florida

Note: All these teams have played at a complex known as Baseball City, midway between Davenport (FL) and Haines City (FL).

1688 Indians 1988 *Gulf Coast (R)*; 1990 *Gulf Coast (R)*. These two teams, playing in the sports complex known as Baseball City, went by the complex name of "Baseball City Indians." These teams were farm clubs of the Cleveland Indians.

1689 Royals 1988–92 *Gulf Coast (R)*; 1999–2002 *Gulf Coast (R)*. Teams were called the "Baseball City Royals." These teams were farm clubs of the Kansas City Royals.

Dawson, New Mexico

1690 Stags m1912 *Rocky Mountain (D)*. Team started season in Colorado Springs (CO) and moved to Dawson June 15. Red deer inhabit New Mexico. The stag is the male of the species. With Mr. Brammell at the helm, newspapers called the players "Brammell's Stags."

Dawson Springs, Kentucky

1691 Dawson Springs Baseball Club 1916x *Kentucky–Illinois–Tennessee (KITTY) (D)*. Team and league disbanded August 4. Team had no nickname.

Dayton, Ohio

1692 Gems 1884 *Iron & Oil (ind.)*. Dayton is nicknamed "The Gem City" not because there are any diamond mines there, but because it grew quickly and constructed many beautiful buildings. "Gem City" was a nickname used by several nineteenth century U.S. cities. With manager Ben Shade at the helm, newspapers called the pennant-winning team "Ben's Gems."

1693 Reds 1889–90 *Tri-State (ind.)*; 1891 *Northwest (ind.)*. Players wore red hose. Originally **Red Stockings**, local newspapers shortened it to Reds. Team was a farm club of the Cincinnati Reds.

1694 Old Soldiers 1897–99 *Inter-State (ind.)*; 1901 *Western Assn. (ind.)*. In 1895 the city built a rest home for Civil War veterans. By 1900 the Civil War rest home was also used for soldiers injured in the Spanish-American War.

1695 Veterans 1900 *Inter-State (ind.)*; 1903–17 *Central (B)*. Spin-off from the Old Soldiers moniker.

1696 Marcos *Independent team* 1910–17; 1918–19 *Independent Negro team*; 1920 *Negro National (M)*; 1931–32 *Independent Negro team*. Team owner, Moses Moore, also owned Dayton's San Marco Hotel. A black realtor, Moore built Dahomey Park for his "Marcos" team. Newspapers called the players "Moses Moore's Marcos."

1697 Giants 1917–18 *Independent Negro team*; 1920 *Independent Negro team*. Tag was a popular name for black teams.

1698 Chappies 1925 *Independent Negro team*. Team was named in honor of player-manager George "Chappie" Johnson. Johnson was a catcher and first baseman.

1699 Aviators 1928–30 *Central (B)*. Dayton is the birthplace of Wilbur and Orville Wright and the site of Wright-Paterson Air Force base. The city also has a center for aviation and aeronautical research. With field manager Everett Booe at the helm in 1928, local newspapers called the players the alliterative "Everett's Aviators." Merido Acosta took over and the name became "Acosta's Aviators." The name was retained in 1930 under manager Nick Cullop.

1700 Ducks 1932 *Central (D)*; 1933–38 *Middle Atlantic (C)*. With field manager Howard "Ducky" Holmes at the helm in 1932–38, the team was the "Ducks." Moniker was appropriate because many wild ducks and geese inhabit Ohio.

1701 Wings 1939–40 *Middle Atlantic (C)*. As war loomed, Dayton's factories converted to the building of bombers and fighter airplanes. Moniker was also a spin-off from Aviators and Ducks.

1702 Indians 1946–47 *Ohio State (D)*; 1948–51 *Central (A)*. These teams were farm clubs of the Cleveland Indians.

1703 Dragons 2000 to date *Midwest (A)*. Winner in fan poll. In the 1990s Hollywood produced a half-dozen fantasy movies that featured dragons while several video games highlighted these creatures. Moniker was also alliterative.

Daytona Beach, Florida

1704 Islanders 1920–24m *Florida State (D 1920, C 1921–24)*. Team moved to Clearwater (FL) July 15; 1928 *Florida State (D)*; 1936–41 *Florida State (D)*; 1946–66 *Florida State (D 1946–62, A 1963–66)*; 1977, 1985–86 *Florida State (A)*. Region was settled in 1870 on a peninsula between the Halifax River and the Atlantic Ocean. City was founded in 1926.

1705 Dodgers 1968–73 *Florida State (A)*. Team was a farm club of the Los Angeles Dodgers.

1706 Astros 1978–84 *Florida State (A)*. Team was a farm club of the Houston Astros.

1707 Admirals 1987 *Florida State (A)*. U.S. Navy ships sail the nearby inter-coastal waterway of the Halifax River. The Daytona Beach Naval Air Station was established here in 1941. An "admiral" is a sea commander, roughly equivalent to the army general. Daytona Beach is a peninsula between the Halifax River and the ocean, ideal for navy ships to anchor.

1708 Cubs 1993 to date *Florida State (A)*. Team was a farm club of the Chicago Cubs. Team goes by the curtailed city name of Daytona Cubs.

Decatur, Alabama

1709 Twins 1911 *Southeastern (D)*. The team represented both Decatur (AL) and Albany (AL), although the team's name was the single-city "Decatur Twins."

Decatur, Alabama–Albany, Alabama

1710 Twins 1921 *Alabama — Tennessee (D)*. Team was known as the Albany-Decatur Twins, although home games were played in Decatur. The 1911 name was used again.

Decatur, Illinois

1711 Decatur Base Ball Club 1888 *Central Inter-State (ind.)*; 1889 *Illinois–Indiana (ind.)*. These teams had no nickname.

1712 Commodores 1900 *Central (ind.)*; 1901–09 *Illinois–Iowa–Indiana (Three-I). (ind. 1901, B 1902–09)*; 1910x *Northern Assn. (D)*. Team and league disbanded July 19; 1922–32 *Three-I (B)*; 1935 *Three-I (B)*; *Three-I (B)* 1937–42; *Three-I (B)* 1946–50; *Missouri Ohio Valley (M.O.V.)(D)* 1952–55; 1956–74 *Midwest (D 1956–62, A 1963–74)*. City was named in 1812 in honor of war hero Commodore Stephen Decatur. The 1900 baseball team named itself after his military rank. Over the years Decatur newspapers constantly shortened the by-now traditional name to **Coms** and **Commies**, which sometimes sparked controversy during the Cold War era of 1946–89. Most fans knew better and tolerated the name. No less than nine Decatur teams used the "Commodores" nickname.

1713 Nomads m1911–15 *Three-I (B)*. Team started 1911 season in Springfield (IL) and moved to Decatur May 31. In the era 1890–1910 teams that transferred from one city to another in mid-season were sometimes called "Wanderers" and "Nomads." By 1912, the team stabilized in Decatur, but the nickname was retained for four more years. With manager Richard Smith at the helm, newspapers called the players "Richard Smith's Nomads."

Deerfield Beach, Florida

1714 Sun Sox 1966m *Florida State (A)*. Team moved to Winter Haven (FL) June 27. Team was a farm club of the Chicago White Sox. Team nickname was an amalgam of "White Sox" and "sunshine." Florida, of course, is "The Sunshine State." Deerfield is the "Heart of the Gold Coast."

DeLand, Florida

1715 Reds 1936–38 *Florida State (D)*. Team was a farm club of the Cincinnati Reds in 1937 and loosely affiliated with them in 1936. In 1938, the team became a farm club of the Chicago White Sox but kept the "Reds" moniker, wearing red-trim uniforms and red stirrups.

1716 Red Hats 1939–41 *Florida State (D)*; 1942x *Florida East Coast (D)*. Team and league disbanded May 14 because of U.S. entry into World War II; 1946–54 *Florida State (D)*. John Stetson, a Philadelphia hat manufacturer of the nineteenth century, donated money to De Land College in 1902 in the city of the same name, where he had a winter home, prompting the school to rename itself Stetson University in his honor and to take up the nickname of "Hatters" for its athletic teams. The baseball team became a farm club of the Cincinnati Reds, who gave the 1939 team red-trim uniforms and red stirrups. Local newspapers combined "red" with "Hatters" to call the team the "Red Hats." Deland is known as the "Home of Stetson University" and, because of the school's academic fame, the "Athens of Florida."

1717 Sun Sox 1970 *Florida State (A)*. Team was a farm club of the Chicago White Sox. As with Deerfield Beach (see above), nickname was an amalgam of "sunshine" and "White Sox." DeLand is known as the "Land of Sunshine."

Del Rio, Texas

1718 Cowboys 1948 *Longhorn (D)*; 1949–50 *Rio Grande Valley (C)*. City has been a ranching and livestock center since 1880. Cowboys, in southwest Texas, herded cattle in drives to ranches and stockyards along the Rio Grande to water the herd. Because of its lucrative cattle industry, Del Rio became known as the "Queen City of the Rio Grande."

1719 Indians m1954 *Big State (B)*. Team began season as the Bryan Indians and moved to Del Rio July 28 as the Del Rio Indians. Team was a farm club of the Cleveland Indians.

Demorest, Pennsylvania

1720 Demorest Base Ball Club 1887 *Pennsylvania State (ind.)*. Team had no nickname.

1721 Denison-Urichsville Base Ball Club m1897 *Ohio–West Virginia (ind.)*. Team started season in Cambridge (OH) and moved to Denison-Urichsville in mid-season. Although the team represented both cities, home games were played in Denison. Team had no nickname.

Denison, Ohio

1722 Denison Base Ball Club 1897 *Ohio–West Virginia (ind.)*. Team had no nickname.

Denison, Texas

1723 Tigers 1896x *Texas (ind.)*. Team disbanded August 2; 1897 *Texas–Southern (ind.)*. Players wore striped hose. In the era 1890–1910, college football and baseball teams at Princeton, Missouri and Southern colleges started wearing striped stockings. When Detroit of the Western League started wearing striped hose in 1895, other professional baseball teams picked up on it.

1724 Katydids 1912 *Texas–Oklahoma (D)*. Katydids are a type of grasshopper that inhabits the forested Hagerstown National Wildlife Preserve and the State Historical Park in the vicinity of the city. The insects give off a chirp that sounds like "katy … did, katy … did, katy … did!" With manager Hart McCormick at the helm, newspapers called the players "Hart McCormick's Katydids."

1725 Blue Sox 1913 *Texas–Oklahoma (D)*. Players wore blue-trim hose.

1726 Champions 1914 *Texas–Oklahoma (D)*. Team won 1913 pennant.

1727 Railroaders 1915–17 *Western Assn. (D)*. Since 1890, Denison has been an important railroad center linking commercial traffic between Texas and Midwest. Denison is known as "Texas' First Stop."

Denver, Colorado

1728 Browns 1885–86, 1889–91 *Colorado State (ind.)*. Players wore brown hose.

1729 Mountain Lions 1886 *Western (ind.)*. Circuit was League 1886–88 and Association 1889–92. In the Western U.S. mountain lions are also called cougars, panthers and pumas. With W.W. Wallace at the helm, newspapers called the players "Wallace's Lions."

1730 Mountaineers 1887–88 *Western (ind.)*. Denver is located in the Rocky Mountains. With manager William McLintock at the helm, newspapers called the players "McLintock's Mountaineers."

1731 Daisies 1887–88 *Western (ind.)*. The players wore striped black and daisy-yellow stockings, the same color as the yellow Gerber daisies found in the Rocky Mountains.

1732 Solis 1887–88 *Western (ind.)*. The moniker, which means "of the sun" in Latin, was a spin-off name. Athletic teams in the nineteenth century occasionally used ancient Greek and Latin names.

1733 Carbonates 1891 *Western (ind.)*. Nearby carbonate mines transported this and other minerals to processing plants. Carbonate, sulfur and calcium make gunpowder.

1734 Sluggers 1891 *Western (ind.).* The 1891 team had some good hitters, but ineffective pitching brought the team down to a losing 53–63 record. With manager Sim Cantrell at the helm, newspapers called the players "Sim Cantrell's Sluggers."

1735 Grizzlies m1895m *Western Assn. (ind.).* Team began the season in Omaha (NE) and moved to Denver July 5. Team moved to Dubuque (IA) August 25; 1900–12 *Western (ind.* 1900–01, *A* 1902–12). Grizzly bears are indigenous to the region. With manager Joe Cantillon at the helm in 1895, newspapers called the players "Cantillon's Grizzlies." With manager George Tebeau at the helm in 1900, newspapers called the players "George's Grizzlies." Fans liked the name and it was retained after Tebeau left the team following the 1901 season.

1736 Gulfs 1898 *Colorado State (ind.).* Denver sometimes was called the "Gulf City" because of the Rocky Mountains. "Gulf" not only means a deep ocean but also a deep mountain chasm or ravine.

1737 Teddy Bears 1900–12 *Western (ind.* 1901–02, *A* 1902–12). Denver newspapers also called the players "Teddy Bears" in honor of U.S. President Theodore Roosevelt, who inspired the popular "Teddy Bear" toy dolls of the era. It was "Teddy Bears" that gradually evolved into "Bears" in 1913.

1738 Bears 1913–17 *Western (A);* 1922–32 *Western (A);* 1941 *Western (D);* 1947–54 *Western (A);* 1955–62 *American Assn. (AAA);* 1963–68 *Pacific Coast (AAA);* 1969–83 *American Assn. (AAA).* Tag was a shorter spin-off from Grizzlies. Billy Gilbert managed "Billy Gilbert's Bears" in 1923. With field manager Joe Berger at the helm 1924–27, the team was "Berger's Bears." In 1931 John Butler managed "Butler's Bears."

1739 Zephyrs 1984–92 *American Assn. (AAA).* Mountain breezes from the West, known as "zephyrs," stream from the Rocky Mountains into Denver. With too many team using Bears, i.e., Chicago Bears (football), Brown University, Washington University, University of California, Hershey Bears (ice hockey), etc., management held a fan poll to choose a different name.

1740 Rockies 1993 to date *National (M).* Team went by the state name of Colorado Rockies. The moniker was chosen by team owner John Antonucci despite the fact that Denver fans preferred "Denver Bears" after the long-time minor league club and disliked using the moniker of a defunct hockey team that averaged only 19 victories per season during its seven years in the National Hockey League. Antonucci defended the choice, saying, "I think for us to be compared to a failed hockey franchise from ten years ago is nonsense. We feel very strongly that 'Colorado Rockies' might become one of the strongest names in all of professional sports. 'Rockies' is strong, enduring and majestic."

1741 Rocks 1993 to date *National (M).* This tag, and its shorter spelling of **Rox**, are contractions used almost exclusively by Denver newspapers. The latter is a contraction, like BoSox (Boston) and ChiSox (Chicago). A "cute" tag is **Pebbles**, inspired, in part, by the baby character of "Pebbles" from the popular Hanna-Barbera TV cartoon *The Flintstones.*

1742 Blake Street Bombers 1993 to date *National (M).* As the team moved into new Coors Field, located on Blake Street, for the 1994 season (after drawing 3 million fans in Mile High Stadium in 1993), the team was led by sluggers Andres Galarraga, Dante Bichette, Vinny Castilla, and Larry Walker, who contributed 200 home runs during the team's playoff-berth season in 2005. In 1996, the "Bombers" hit an NL-leading 221 home runs and a league-high 239 four-baggers in 1997. Slugging first baseman Todd Helton joined the team in 1997 and the Bombers led the NL again in homers in 1999 with 223 round-trippers. In the 2000s, as the team faded into mediocrity, the moniker was used less often.

1743 Blake Street Bullies 1995–2000 *National (M).* An obvious spinoff from the "Broad Street Bullies" used by the 1974–75–75–76 National Hockey League Philadelphia Flyers ice hockey Stanley Cup champions. Unlike the hockey players who administered punishing checks into opponents, the tag referred to the Rockies hitters "bullying" opposing pitchers.

1744 Todd and the Toddlers 2005–06 *National (M).* Team captain Todd Helton was a nine-year veteran when the Rockies surrounded him with peach-fuzz youngsters in a youth movement. Newspapers called the players "Todd and the Toddlers." Fortunately, the youth movement brought dramatic improvement from 65 (in 2005) to 76 (in 2006) and then 90 wins in the surprise pennant season of 2008.

1745 Roktober 2007 *National (M).* The Rockies roared back from near non-contention with 14 victories in their last 15 regular season games and then blitzed their way through the NL playoffs (3–0 over Philadelphia in the semifinals, and 4–0 over Arizona in the NLCS) to make frenzied Colorado fans think they were attending a rock concert. Although swept by Boston in the 2007 World Series, the mere playing of two World Series games in Denver only 14 seasons after the Rockies was enfranchised generated great excitement in the Centennial State of Colorado. The moniker is really a slogan and not a nickname. By 2011, Roktober was a faded memory as the team wound up with a poor 73–89 record, finishing fifth in the NL Western Division.

De Quincy, Louisiana

1746 Railroaders m1932m *Cotton States (D).* Team began season in Port Arthur (TX) before moving to De Quincy June 19. De Quincy then moved to Opelousas July 7. De Quincy has been an important railroad stop for the Texas-Louisiana Railroad since 1890. With manager Cecil Jones at the helm, newspapers called the players "Cecil Jones' Railroaders."

Derby, Connecticut

1747 Derby Base Ball Club 1888 *Connecticut State (ind.);* 1891 *Connecticut State (ind.);* 1897–98 *Connecticut State (ind.).* These teams had no nickname.

1748 Lushers 1899–1901 *Connecticut State (ind.).* With field manager Billy Lush at the helm, local newspapers called the players "Billy's Lushers." These players drank their share but none were drunks. In nineteenth century baseball, players were notorious for abusing alcohol. Some derogatory monikers applied to them included "Brewers" and "Lushers."

1749 Angels 1900 *Connecticut State (ind.).* In the swamp regions of nineteenth-century America, pioneers and settlers sometimes thought they saw ghosts and spirits in the vaporous steam rising from swamp waters, i.e., "swamp angels." The nearby Peat Swamp Reservoir, about 20 miles northwest of the city, is one such site. With manager Jeremiah Denny at the helm in 1897 and 1898, newspapers called the players "Jeremiah's Angels." Jeremiah was a prophet of the Old Testament. Players were also known as "Denny's Angels."

Derby-Ansonia, Connecticut

1750 Derby-Ansonia Base Ball Club 1888 *Connecticut State (ind.).* Team had no nickname.

Des Moines, Iowa

1751 Hawkeyes 1887 *Northwestern (ind.)* 1888–90m *Western Assn. (ind.).* Team moved to Lincoln (NE) August 1; 1900–01 *Western (ind.).* Iowa is the "Hawkeye State."

1752 Colts 1888–90m *Western Assn.* Team moved to Lincoln (NE) August 1. Team had many young players. In the era 1885–1915 young players were known as Babes, Chicks, Colts, Cubs, Debutantes, Foundlings, Ponies, Prodigals and Yearlings.

1753 Indians 1894–96 *Western Assn. (ind.)*; 1900–37 *Western (ind.)*1901, *(A 1902–37)*. Sac and Fox Indians inhabited Iowa in the eighteenth and nineteenth centuries.

1754 Prohibitionists 1894–97 *Western Assn. (ind.)*; 1900, 1904 *Western (ind. 1900, A 1904)*. The Prohibition Party was started to elect politicians who would ban liquor for moral reasons. This party became popular with Iowa farmers, not because Iowans were teetotalers, but because a ban on hops and barley brewing on eastern farmers might put many of them out of business to the advantage of Iowa farms. Milwaukee's "Brewers" were their moniker opposites.

1755 Capitals 1894–97 *Western Assn. (ind.)*. Des Moines has been the state capital of Iowa since 1857.

1756 Midgets 1902 *Western (A)*. The team had a loose affiliation with the Chicago Nationals, who had been called this season the "Midgets," because some the Chicago players were of slight build. Some of the players on the Des Moines team this season were also minuscule, prompting local newspapers to call the team "Midgets." The 1902 team finished seventh of eight teams with a poor 54–83 record. The 1901 team also had a losing record. Impatient fans and newspapers complained the team was "playing like midgets." With manager Joe Quinn at the helm, newspapers called the players "Quinn's Midgets."

1757 Undertakers 1903 *Western (A)*. In the era 1890–1910 disgruntled fans and newspapers, saddled with losing and especially with last-place teams, called them Pallbearers, Undertakers and Gravediggers because their losing ways rendered "dead and buried" the pennant hopes of their fans. The 1903 team finished seventh of eight with a 55–76 record. With Joe Quinn as manager, newspapers called the team "Quinn's Undertakers."

1758 Underwriters 1905 *Western (A)*. Des Moines is the largest insurance center of the West, with about 50 insurance companies. Some local newspaper reporter in April 1905 may have lost his job when he decided to replace "Undertakers" with "Underwriters" just to maintain a consistent alliteration from one name to the next.

1759 Champs 1906–07 *Western (A)*. The team won pennants in 1905–06. In the era 1895–1915, when a minor league team won a pennant, they were often labeled "Champions" or "Champs."

1760 Boosters 1908–24 *Western (A)*. The moniker "Boosters" lasted 17 years because the team won three pennants in this time (1909, 1915 and 1917) and usually had winning teams in non-pennant years. The moniker was reinforced by some of the field managers, i.e., "Isbell's Boosters" (Frank Isbell), "Bill's Boosters" (Bill Dwyer) and "Breen's Boosters" (Dick Breen).

1761 All-Nations 1912–14 *Independent Negro team.* Team had players who were white Americans, black Americans, Cubans, Asians and Native Americans. Carrie Nation, baseball's first professional female baseball player, played on this team.

1762 Demons 1925–37 *Western (A)*; 1959–61 *Three-I (B)*. The 1925 and 1926 teams "played like demons" en route to consecutive flags. Newspapers liked the name and kept using it. The team also won the pennant in 1931. The 1959 team revived the moniker. Alternate names include **Devils** and **Imps**.

1763 Bruins 1947–58 *Western (A)*. Team was a farm club of the Chicago Cubs. The parent Chicago Cubs are sometimes referred to as the "Bruins."

1764 Oaks 1969–89 *American Assn. (AAA)*. Team went by the state name of "Iowa Oaks" to save newspaper space. The oak tree is the state tree of Iowa.

1765 Cubs 1990–97 *American Assn. (AAA)*; 1998 to date *Pacific Coast (AAA)*. Team has been a farm club of the Chicago Cubs. Team went by the state name of "Iowa Cubs" to save newspaper space.

Detroit, Michigan

1766 Old Golds 1881–82 *National (M)*. Detroit players wore old gold stockings. Golden yellow stockings was the standard for the Detroit Nationals for its NL tenure of 1881–88.

1767 Wolverines 1881–88 *National (M)*; 1889–90 *International (ind.)*; 1891 *Northwestern (ind.)*; 1894 *Western (ind.)*. Michigan has been known as the "Wolverine State" since 1836, not because there are any real wolverines there (the animal is found in the Western U.S.), but because, for the period 1700–1850, thousands of wolverine pelts were imported to Michigan by fur traders to sell to Michigan ladies who wanted wolverine fur coats. The traders who came to Michigan with their supply of pelts were themselves called "Wolverines."

1768 Straits Citys 1881–88 *National (M)*. Detroit, known as the "Strait City," was built along the shores of the Detroit Strait between Lake Erie and Lake St. Clair.

1769 Wolves 1881–88 *National (M)*; 1932 *East–West (M)*. Tag was a contraction of "Wolverines." Ironically, there *are* wolves in Michigan.

1770 Ponies 1883 *National (M)*. Team had many young players on the roster. Young players in this era were known as "Colts" and "Ponies." The tag "ponies" was a spin-off of "Colts."

1771 Daisies 1886 *National (M)*. In 1882, Detroit players had worn old gold yellow hose. This season, the players wore daisy-yellow stockings.

1772 Sluggers 1886–87 *National (M)*. Detroit signed four talented hitters from the Buffalo Bisons after the Buffalo franchise disbanded at the close of the 1885 season. With Dan Brouthers (a future Hall of Famer), John Rowe, Art "Hardy" Richardson and Deacon White, who were named by Buffalo newspapers "The Big Four," now playing for Detroit, the Wolverines went 87–36 in 1886 (good for second place behind Chicago) and then captured the 1887 NL pennant with a 79–45 mark. The "Big Four" then powered the Wolverines to victory in the 1887 World Series, defeating the AA champion St. Louis Browns, 10 games to 5.

1773 Giants 1886–87 *National (M)*. A generic name used to describe a winning team, even if the players were only of ordinary size, the Detroit "Giants" won 166 games, losing 81, in the 1886–87 seasons, which culminated in the 1887 NL pennant and a World Series title in October 1887.

1774 Tigers 1892 *Western Assn. (ind.)*; 1895–99 *Western (ind.)*; 1900 *American (ind.)*; 1901 to date *American (M)*. There are no local accounts of the players of the 1892 team wearing striped hose, they were called "Tigers" by newspapers. Three years later, manager Dan Strouthers proudly called his 1895 players "My Tigers" as described by reporter Philip Reid in the April 16, 1895, *Detroit Free Press*. However, management didn't dress the team in orange and black striped hose until a year later, in April 1896. The *Detroit Free Press* on April 16, 1895, printed a headline "Strouther's Tigers Showed Up Very Nicely" (apparently they lost the game). The team's box scores started to be listed under the heading of "Detroit Tigers of 1895." In 1900, baseball writer Richard Bak reports that the new AL franchise actually asked permission from the Detroit Light Guard "Tigers" to use their nickname for their charter AL baseball team. This military unit, a brigade that fought in the Civil War (1861–65) and again in the Spanish-American War (1897–98), granted permission to use the name, which the baseball team then used. By 1901 the moniker "Tigers" was already traditional, prompting management to put a red tiger logo on the players' caps. Name first appeared on Detroit player jerseys in 1928 as the nickname became official.

1775 Creams 1894–95 *Western (ind.)*. To field a competitive team in 1894 management of the new Detroit entry raided the California League, signing away players whom California newspapers complained were the "The Cream of the California League."

1776 Bengals 1901 to date *American (M)*. As major league baseball teams acquired official team nicknames in the era 1900–20, fans and newspapers liked to assign the club with an alternate, unofficial nickname, i.e., Indians (Tribe), Nationals (Senators), Orioles (Birds), Pirates (Buccaneers), Reds (Rhinelanders), Red Sox (Crimson Hose), White Sox (Pale Hose) and Tigers (Bengals). When the Cincinnati Bengals started play in the American Football League in 1968, the baseball "Bengals" moniker was used less frequently, but it still appears in newspaper print.

1777 Jungle Towners 1901–27 *American (M)*. The Detroit Tigers were so popular in 1901 (home attendance this year was 260,000, which was good in this era) that newspapers started to call the city of Detroit "Jungle Town." In 1907, Hugh Jennings took over the reins as field manager, which prompted newspapers to call the Detroit players "Jennings' Jungle Towners." By 1928 the tag was pretty much spent as newspapers preferred the official "Tigers" or the shorter "Bengals."

1778 Man Eaters 1901–27 *American (M)*. Tag was a clever Detroit Tigers spin-off from "Jungle-towners" that never caught on because it was too long (nine letters). With manager George Stallings at the helm, newspapers called the players "George Stallings' Maneaters."

1779 Wranglers 1906 *American (M)*. Just as the Chicago Nationals was called Broncos, Cowboys, Rainmakers, Ranchers, and Roughriders while training in Arizona in March of 1898, the Detroit Tigers were called the Wranglers in April, May and June of 1906 after having also played spring training games in Arizona in March.

1780 Stars 1919 *Independent Negro team*; 1920–31 *Negro National (M)*; 1925–26 *Southern California (W)*; 1933 *Negro National (M)*; 1937 *Negro American (M)*; 1937–38 *Southern California (W)*; 1951–55 *North American (ind.)*. In 1919, team owner Tenny Blount wanted Detroit fans to know his team had superior talent, so he called the team the "Stars." Team started league play in 1920 and played winter ball in Los Angeles twice.

1781 Destroyers 1935 *American (M)*. Coined by baseball authors Gary Gillette and Pete Palmer to describe the 1935 AL champion Detroit Tigers, who led the league runs scored (919) and batting average (.290) and then won the franchise's first World Series, 4 games to 2, over the Chicago Cubs.

1782 Good Ol' Boys 1940 *American (M)*; 1968 *American (M)*. Detroit Tigers pitcher Dizzy Trout liked to tell stories about the "good ol' boys" of his farm and fishing hole days in Indiana to his teammates—some who had been with the team for years, i.e., Rudy York, Charlie Gehringer, Dick Bartell, Pinky Higgins, Hank Greenberg, Birdie Tibbetts, Bobo Newsom. Schoolboy Rowe, Tommy Bridges, and Al Benton. This veteran crew, as they won the 1940 AL pennant, became known in the Detroit press as the "Good Ol' Boys." In 1968, another group of veteran "Good Ol' Boys," i.e., Al Kaline, Norm Cash, Dick McAuliffe, Jim Northrup, Willie Horton, Bill Freehan, Denny McClain, Earl Wilson, Mickey Lolich and Joe Sparma won the 1968 A.L. pennant to the accolades of Detroit newspapers who called them, as the AL champions of 1940, the "Good Ol' Boys."

1783 Black Sox 1941–42 *Independent Negro team*. Players wore black stirrups.

1784 Motor City Giants 1945 *United States (ind.)*. The circuit was a "paper-league" invented by Brooklyn Dodger GM Branch Rickey to sign up black players for the NL Dodgers anticipating the arrival of the integration of Organized Baseball. The USL played only a few games in 1945, and, apparently, none in 1946. Popular name for black teams. Team chose a customary preceding adjective—

"Motor City" to be paired with Giants—a technique used by black teams for 60 years.

1785 Senators 1946–47 Negro independent team.1946–47. Detroit had once been the capital of the Michigan Territory, 1805–37, and the state of Michigan, 1837–47.

1786 Jungle-landers 1934–40 *American (M)*. With the Detroit Tigers winning three AL pennants and the 1935 World Series title amidst seven straight winning seasons, Detroit fans jubilantly called the Motor City "Jungle Land."

1787 Sock-It-to-'Em Tigers 1968 *American (M)*. Coined by baseball author Mark Pattison who was referring to the popular TV show *Laugh-In* of the "Psychedelic Era," wherein pretty but besieged comedienne Judy Carne was splashed with a pail of water every time she uttered the line "Sock it to me!" The Tigers socked it to A.L. pitchers with a league-leading 185 home runs and a league-best .385 slugging percentage in what was otherwise a "pitchers' year."

1788 Runaway Tigers 1968 *American (M)*. Like a sprinting tiger, the Detroiters ran away with the 1968 AL pennant by winning 35 of their first 40 games, allowing them to win 104 games and the flag by 15 games. In 2011, the name was reapplied to the team as the Tigers "ran away" with the AL Central Division race by playing at a .700 pace to post a 95–67 record.

1789 Baseball's Last Real Champions 1968 *American (M)*. Baseball writer, George Cantor, in his 1997 book of the same title, observed that the 1968 World Series was major league baseball's last competition between pennant winners whose accomplishments were not watered down by division play, imbalanced schedules and interleague play. The Tigers played nine AL opponents, 18 games each, for a 162-game schedule in which the regular season sent only the first-place team to the Fall Classic, which the Tigers won over the Cardinals, 4 games to 3. In 1969 the two major leagues split into East and West division with unbalanced schedules. In 1994 each major league realigned into three divisions, and, then, in 1997 interleague play was adopted.

1790 Billy Martin's Half-Game Champs 1972 *American (M)*. Baseball author Todd Masters' book (2010) describes the exploits of the 1972 AL Western Division champion Tigers, who got this tag by winning the West title by a half-game over Boston in a season with an uneven schedule because of a 10-day players' strike at the start of the season. The Tigers played 156 games, posting an 86–70 record while Boston went 85–70 in 155 games played.

1791 Bless You Boys 1984 *American (M)*. Not a nickname but a slogan (much like "Beat 'em Bucs") bestowed on the players of the championship 1984 season by Detroit Tigers broadcaster Al Ackerman following each Tiger victory.

1792 Declawed Tigers 1994–2005 *American (M)*. Coined by Wikipedia to describe the twelve consecutive losing seasons the Detroit Tigers struggled through, 1994–2005. Inconsiderate White Sox and Twins fans degraded the slang-for-cat **Pussies** into the vulgar **Pussys**.

1793 Motor City Kitties 2003 *American (M)*. Detroit's version of the Chicago "Cubbies" while Motor City fans suffered through the worst season in franchise history as the "Kitties" went 43–119, only two games better than the modern 162-game record low of the 1962 New York Mets (40–120). When the Tigers improved to 72 wins in 2004, the moniker was quickly dumped by grizzled Detroit fans.

1794 Tabbies 2004 *American (M)*. Rarely used in the dim mists of Detroit Tigers baseball history, the "Tabbies" moniker described the much-improved but still-weak Tigers of 2004. Both "Kitties" and "Tabbies," whose origins go back to the 1920s, never caught on because blue-collar Tiger fans have always shunned "cute little animal" monikers and mascots.

1795 Tiggs 2005 *American (M)*. A diminutive in the style of Phils

(Phillies), Cards (Cardinals), Yanks (Yankees), Injuns (Indians), 'Stros (Astros), Pads (Padres), Jays (Blue Jays) and Nats (Nationals) that simply did not catch on with grizzled blue-collar Detroit Tiger fans.

1796 Team of Destiny 2006 *American (M)*. After six straight losing seasons, including the team's worst record in franchise history in 2003, Detroit fans sensed the Tigers, in a season-long three-team race with the Twins and White Sox, were a "Team of Destiny." The team realized the fans' hopes with the 2006 AL pennant — the first for the franchise since 1984. The team slogan this year was "Restore the Roar!"

1797 Tamed Tigers 2009 *American (M)*. Coined by *The Sporting News* for the 2009 team, which blew a seven-game lead over the Minnesota Twins in the AL Central to finish in a first-place tie with Minnesota and then lost a tie-breaker game to the Twins, leaving the Tigers out of the playoffs after having led the AL Central Division for the first 161 games of the regular season.

Devil's Lake, North Dakota

1798 Devil's Lake Baseball Club 1902x Team disbanded July 21. *Northern (ind.)*. Team had no nickname.

Diaz Ordaz, San Luis Potosi, Mexico

1799 Club de Beisbol de Diaz Ordaz 1978 *Mexican Center (A)*. Team had no nickname. Many of the teams of the Mexican Class A leagues of the 1970s lacked a nickname.

Dominion, Nova Scotia, Canada

1800 Hawks 1937–38 *Cape Breton Colliery (D)*. Hawks are small falcons found in North America.

Donaldsonville, Louisiana

1801 Jones BBC 1907 *Independent Negro team*. Team was named after Mr. Jones, the club owner. Independent black teams in the South in this era often lacked a team nickname.

1802 Indians 1955 *Alabama–Florida (D)*. The Seminole Indians inhabited Louisiana. With manager Charles Grant at the helm, newspapers called the players "Grant's Indians." Team was not a farm club of the Cleveland Indians.

1803 Seminoles 1956 *Alabama–Florida (D)*. The Seminoles were a historic tribe of Louisiana. With manager Nesbit Wilson at the helm, newspapers called the players "Nesbit Wilson's Seminoles."

Donna, Texas

1804 Cardinals 1949m *Rio Grande Valley (C)*. Team was a farm club of the St. Louis Cardinals.

1805 Twins 1949m *Rio Grande Valley (C)*. Team moved to Robstown (TX) June 6. Team represented Donna and Welasco (TX). Team went by the single-city name of "Donna Twins." The "Twins" moniker, long before the Minnesota Twins of 1961, was has been used by baseball teams since 1887.

Donna-Welasco, Texas

1806 Twins 1950x *Rio Grande Valley (C)*. Team disbanded on May 4. Franchise went to a dual-city title, i.e., the "Donna-Welasco Twins."

Dothan, Alabama

1807 Dothan Baseball Club 1915 *Florida–Louisiana–Alabama–Georgia (F.L.A.G.) (D)*; 1916–17x *Dixie (D)*. Team and league disbanded July 4, 1917, due to U.S. entry into World War I. These teams had no nickname.

1808 Boll Weevils 1936 *Alabama–Florida (D)*. The boll weevil — a cotton-gobbling beetle — is the scourge of cotton farmers. With manager Bobby Murry at the helm, newspapers called the players "Bobby Murry's Boll Weevils."

1809 Browns 1937–39 *Alabama–Florida (D)*; 1940–41 *Alabama State (D)*; 1942 *Georgia–Florida (D)*; 1946–50 *Alabama State (D)*; 1951–52 *Alabama–Florida (D)*. Cash-strapped team had a loose affiliation for five seasons with the AL St. Louis Browns, receiving donated uniforms and equipment from the big league club. The team became an official farm club of the Browns big league team in 1942. The 1946–50, 1951–52 teams were independent, again wearing brown-trim uniforms and brown stirrups.

1810 Rebels 1953–54 *Alabama–Florida (D)*. The government of the Confederate States of America was organized in Montgomery (AL) on February 4, 1861.

1811 Cardinals 1955–56, 1960 *Alabama–Florida (D)*; 1958–60 *Alabama–Florida (D)*. Team was a farm club of the St. Louis Cardinals.

1812 Phillies 1961–62 *Alabama–Florida (D)*. Team was a farm club of the Philadelphia Phillies.

Douglas, Arizona

1813 Smeltermen 1915 *Rio Grande Valley (D)*. Mines in the region transport copper ore to copper-smelting factories.

1814 Miners 1915 *Rio Grande Valley (D)*. Newspaper editors balked at "Smeltermen," and started using "Miners." With manager William Quigley at the helm, newspapers called the players "William Quigley's Smeltermen."

1815 Copper Kings 1956–58 *Arizona–Mexico (C)*. Arizona leads the U.S. in copper production.

Douglas, Georgia

1816 Rebels 1948 *Georgia State (D)*. Georgia was in the Confederacy 1861–65 and was the site of major Civil War battles. Georgia is the "Yellowhammer State" because Georgia's Confederate Army soldiers wore yellow uniforms. With manager Bill Barnes at the helm, newspapers called the players "Bill Barnes' Rebels." John Humphries was at the helm mid-season, changing the name to "Humphries' Rebels." Emil Ray took over later and the name became "Ray's Rebels."

1817 Trojans 1949–55 *Georgia State (D)*. The tag "Trojans" was a popular sports nickname in the era 1920–60 because of the success of the USC Trojans college football team and the introduction of the "Trojan Tractor" in 1950. With manager Fred Tschudin at the helm in 1950, newspapers called the players "Tschudin's Trojans." Van Davis took the helm in 1952, making the name "Van's Trojans." Charles Bledsoe, taking over for 1953–54, managed "Charles Bledsoe's Trojans." Bob Wellman in 1955 managed "Wellman's Trojans."

1818 Reds 1957 *Georgia State (D)*. Team was a farm club of the Cincinnati Reds.

Dover, Delaware

1819 Senators 1923–24, 1926 *Eastern Shore (D)*. Baseball teams located in state capitals often go by the name of Senators, Solons, Capitals, Capitols and Governors. Dover has been the state capital of Delaware since 1777. Manager Jigg Donahue managed here in 1923–24 and 1926 and played for the Washington Senators in 1909. Newspapers called the players "Jiggs Donahue's Senators."

1820 Dobbins 1925 *Eastern Shore (D)*. The Dobbin is a farm horse used on Delaware farms. With Jiggs Donahue at the helm as manager, newspapers called the players "Jiggs Donahue's Dobbins."

1821 Orioles 1937–40 *Eastern Shore (D)*. Team was a farm club of the Class AA Baltimore Orioles. In the era 1910–50 minor league teams at lower classifications sometimes were farm clubs of minor league teams at a higher classification. With manager Jiggs Donahue at the helm, newspapers called the players "Donahue's Orioles."

1822 Phillies 1946–48 *Eastern Shore (D)*. Team was a farm club of the Philadelphia Phillies.

Dover, New Hampshire

1823 Dover Base Ball Club 1888 *New England Inter-State (ind.)*; 1893 *New England (ind.)*; 1902 *New England (B)*. These teams had no nickname.

Dowagiac, Michigan

1824 Dowagiac Baseball Club 1910 *Indiana–Michigan (D)*. Team had no nickname.

Drummondville, Quebec, Canada

1825 Tigers 1940x *Quebec Provincial (B)*. Team disbanded July 8 because of Canada's entry into World War II. Team had a loose affiliation with the Detroit Tigers. In the period 1930–50, Canadian teams often had a loose affiliation with major league teams without actually being an official farm club.

1826 Cubs 1950–52 *Provincial (C)*. Team was a farm club of the Chicago Cubs.

1827 Royals 1953 *Provincial (C)*. Team was a farm club of the Montreal Royals. Name was doubly appropriate because Queen Elizabeth II's coronation took place this same year.

1828 Athletics 1954 *Provincial (C)*. This circuit was also known as the Quebec Provincial League. Team was an official farm club of the Philadelphia Athletics.

Drumright, Oklahoma

1829 Drummers 1920 *Western Assn. (D)*. Moniker was used for newspaper headlines, i.e., "Drummers edge Huskers, 4–3." With manager Dick Crittenden at the helm, newspapers called the players "Dick Crittenden's Drummers."

1830 Oilers 1921 *Western Assn. (D)*. Drumright benefitted from the oil boom of the 1920s. The Glenn Pool Gusher of 1905, located midway between Tulsa and Drumright, converted the city into an oil refinery site by 1920. Drumright is the "Pipeline Capital of the World."

1831 Boosters 1923m *Oklahoma State (D)*. After a year without a team, enthusiastic fans formed a booster club for the new club. However, the team fared poorly on the field with an 11–21 record and moved to Ponca City June 7 because of poor attendance. Booster clubs, usually consisting of adult males, gave way in the 1920s to the "fan club." whose members were children, teenagers and females.

Dublin, Georgia

1832 Trojans 1949–52 *Georgia State (D)*. By 1949, the college football USC Trojans had won their eighth Rose Bowl. The Trojan Tractor came out in 1950 and was used to haul lumber here. With manager David Coble at the helm in 1949, newspapers called the players "Coble's Trojans." With manager Fred Tschudin at the helm in 1950, newspapers called the players "Tschudin's Trojans."

1833 Green Sox 1951–52 *Georgia State (D)*. Since the city is named after Dublin, Ireland, whose symbol is the green shamrock, management decided to outfit the players in green-trim uniforms with green and white striped stirrups.

1834 Irish 1953–56 *Georgia State (D)*. Team switched to this spin-off from "Green Sox." Name was inspired by the Notre Dame Fighting Irish, which was a successful and popular college football team.

1835 Orioles 1958 *Georgia–Florida (D)*. Team was a farm club of the Baltimore Orioles.

1836 Braves 1962 *Georgia–Florida (D)*. Team was a farm club of the Milwaukee Braves.

DuBois, Pennsylvania

1837 Miners m1905–07 *Inter-State (C)*. Team began 1905 season in Jamestown (NY) and moved to DuBois July 12, 1905. Coal mines in the region ship coal to processing plants. With manager Menzo Sibley at the helm, newspapers called the players "Menzo Sibley's Miners."

Dubuque, Iowa

1838 Rabbits 1879 *Northwest (ind.)*. Although there are rabbits in Iowa, newspapers commented that the Dubuque players "ran the base paths like rabbits." Tom Loftus batted .308 and scored 40 runs in 47 games. Dan Sullivan batted .417 and scored 39 runs in 47 games. Jack Gleason batted .344 and scored 38 runs in 43 games. Even pitcher Charles ("Old Hoss" when he was older) Radbourne batted .367 and scored 37 runs in 47 games. The team "raced to the lead" with a 19–6 record when the circuit disbanded July 15. The "Rabbits" scored 277 runs in only 25 games for an average of nearly twelve runs scored per game.

1839 Reds 1879 *Northwest (ind.)*. Players wore red hose. Originally **Red Stockings**, Dubuque newspapers shortened it to **Reds**.

1840 Dubuque Base Ball Club 1888x *Central Inter-State (ind.)*. Team disbanded July 9; m1895–97 *Western Assn.(ind.)*. Team began season in Omaha (NE) then moved to Denver (CO) and then moved to Dubuque in mid-season; m1899x *Western Assn. (ind.)*. Team started season in Quincy (IL) before moving to Dubuque May 19. Team disbanded June 13. None of these three teams had a nickname.

1841 Giants 1890 *Illinois–Iowa (ind.)*. The back-to-back (1888–89) world champion New York Giants were the most glamorous and successful team at the start of the 1890s. Several teams, both white and black, emulated the New Yorkers by choosing the "Giants" moniker.

1842 Champs 1895 *East Iowa (ind.)*. Team won the 1895 East Iowa League pennant.

1843 Colts 1895 *East Iowa (ind.)*. Team had numerous young players who were called "Colts."

1844 Shamrocks 1903–05 *Three-I (B)*. Matias Loras, the nineteenth century Bishop of Dubuque, invited Irish immigrants to settle here. Dubuque's "Southend" neighborhoods were known as "Little Dublin" because of the arrival of several thousand Irish immigrants in the period 1900–20. The shamrock is the symbol of Ireland. Irish-American manager Clarence "Pants" Rowland was at the helm in 1903 and newspapers called the players the "Rowland's Shamrocks." The Shamrock Import Company has operated in Dubuque since 1894.

1845 Dubs 1906–10, 1912–15 *Three-I (B)*; 1917m *Three-I (B)*.

Team moved to Charles City (IA) July 4; 1924, 1927–28 *Mississippi Valley (D)*. Moniker was used for newspaper headlines, i.e., "Dubs edge Bloomers, 4–3."

1846 Hustlers 1911 *Three-I (B)*. "Hustlers" was slang in this era for a baseball player. The term meant a hustling player and had no connotation of gambling. With manager Clarence "Pants" Rowland at the helm, newspapers called the players "Clarence Rowland's Hustlers."

1847 Climbers 1922–23 *Mississippi Valley (D)*. "Climbers" was the moniker for a team that got off to a good start early in the season. The Dubuque team, managed by Larry Mullen and called "Mullen's Climbers," was in first place for a while but then skidded to sixth place of six teams with a 44–84 record. Disgruntled fans and newspapers began to use the "Climbers" name in sarcastic irony. The sarcasm switched the next year to praise as the 1923 team leapt from last place in 1922 to first place and the league championship in 1923 with a 78–50 record. The "Climbers" nickname was well earned.

1848 Iron Men 1925–28 *Mississippi Valley (D)*. With Hall of Fame pitcher "Iron Man" Joe McGinnity at the managerial helm, local newspapers called the players the "Iron Men."

1849 Speasman 1928 *Mississippi Valley (D)*. When McGinnity left in mid-season 1928, Bill Speas took over, but the awkward "Speasmen" never caught on. Naming a team directly after a manager's surname, i.e., Mackmen, McGraw Men, Loftusites, Collinsites, Seleeites, Griffmen, Armourites and Chance Men, was a fad that began around 1900 but faded by the 1920s. Teams were even named after the franchise owner, i.e., Somersets, Doves, Rustlers and Heps.

1850 Tigers 1929–32 *Mississippi Valley (D)*. Players wore striped hose. As the team contended for and won the 1929 pennant, newspapers praised them for "playing like Tigers." With manager Lester "Pat" Patterson at the helm in 1929, newspapers called the players "Patterson's Tigers." Team had a loose affiliation with the Detroit Tigers.

1851 Packers 1954–55 *Missouri Ohio Valley (M.O.V.) (D)*; 1956–57 *Midwest (D)*; 1974–76 *Midwest (A)*. Regional farms transport produce to city factories where the food is processed and packed for transport to market. Iowa is the "Food Market of the World."

1852 Royals 1968 *Midwest (A)*. Team was a farm club of the Kansas City Royals.

Dulles, Louden, Virginia

1853 Louden County Hounds 2011 to date *Atlantic (ind.)*. Team held a name-the-team contest and the winner was "Hounds." Team CEO and president Bob Farron explained, "Hound-dogs are part of the history of this region as hunting dogs, herding dogs and beloved pets."

Duluth, Minnesota

1854 Zeniths 1886–87 *Northwestern*. Duluth is called the "Zenith City" because it is the hub between Great Lakes shipping and Western railroads, allowing it to reach a zenith of prosperity. Duluth, built at the base of Spirit Mountain to the north, is also called the "City on a Mountain."

1855 Jayhawkers m1891x *Western Assn*. Team began season in St. Paul (MN) and then moved to Duluth June 8. Team disbanded August 20. Remnants of Confederate raider William Quantrill's "Jayhawks" worked their way up to Minnesota during the Civil War after these Confederate raiders sacked and burned Lawrence, Kansas, in 1863. The "Jayhawk" is a mythical mix of blue jays and hawks — both of which inhabit Kansas.

1856 Whalebacks m1891x *Western Assn*. Team began season in St. Paul (MN) and then moved to Duluth June 8. Team disbanded August 20. Steamships that sailed in and out of Duluth to and from Lake Superior had an unusual "whaleback" shape — a "spoon" bow and a convex main deck — hence the name for these ships: "Whalebacks."

1857 Cardinals 1903 *Northern (D)*. Team had a loose affiliation with the St. Louis Cardinals, who supplied them with Cardinal red-trim uniforms and red stirrup socks. Loose affiliations between major league teams and nearby minor league teams was not uncommon in this era.

1858 White Sox 1904–05 *Northern (D)*; 1906–07 *Northern Copper Country (D 1906, C 1907)*; 1908 *Northern (D)*; 1909–11 *Minnesota–Wisconsin (D 1909, C 1910–11)*; 1912 *Central–International (C)*; 1913–16 *Northern (C)*. The 1904 team severed its loose ties with the St. Louis Cardinals and formed a loose affiliation with the Chicago White Sox. Team bought uniforms and equipment from the Chicago AL club, which included white stirrups and socks. Duluth teams maintained a loose affiliation with the AL White Sox for fifteen seasons.

1859 Dukes 1934–42 *Northern (D 1934–40, C 1941–42)*; 1946–55 *Northern (C)*; 1993–2002 *Northern (ind.)*. French Duke of Luth (Sieur de Luth), Daniel Greysolon, explored the region of present-day Duluth in 1659. The city is named after him and the team was named after his title.

Duluth-Superior, Minnesota

1860 Dukes 1943 *Twin Ports (E)*; 1993–2002 *Northern (ind.)*. The 1942 Duluth Dukes regionalized into the dual city title of "Duluth-Superior Dukes."

1861 Heralds 1943 *Twin Ports (E)*. The name was a spin-off from "Dukes." A herald is an armorial or military representative of a king, duke or baron.

1862 Marine Iron 1943 *Twin Ports (E)*. During World War II Duluth was an important shipbuilding site for the U.S. Navy.

1863 White Sox 1956–70 *Northern (C)*. Team was a farm club of the Chicago White Sox.

Duncan, Oklahoma

1864 Oilers 1922–24x *Oklahoma State (D)*. Team disbanded July 6. An oil boom started here in 1920. Not only were oil rigs constructed, but city factories began to manufacture rigs and machinery for drilling. There are also petrochemical plants here that refine oil into gasoline.

1865 Cementers 1947–48 *Sooner State (D)*. After oil, the city's major industry is cement and concrete. Regional mines transported aluminum, lime, iron, and magnesium to city cement factories. With manager Otto Utt at the helm, newspapers called the players "Otto Utt's Cementers." Jess Welch managed briefly in 1948 and the name was "Jess Welch's Cementers."

1866 Uttmen 1949–50m *Sooner State (D)*. Team moved to Shawnee (OK) August 18. Some of the players on the team had played baseball for the University of Texas State "Uttmen." With manager Otto Utt (a coincidence) at the helm 1947–48, the team was known as the "Cementers." Utt then became general manager in 1949, and the team was named after him, i.e., the Duncan "Uttmen."

Dunedin, Florida

1867 Blue Jays 1978–79 *Florida State (A)*; 1987 to date *Florida State (A)*; 1993–95 *Gulf Coast (R)*; 2007 to date *Gulf Coast (R)*. Teams were farm clubs of the Toronto Blue Jays.

Dunkirk, New York

1868 Dandies 1890 *New York–Pennsylvania (ind.)*. English King Charles II sent his best troops, known as "Charles Dandies," to join with French forces and combined they defeated the Spanish forces on June 4, 1658, in the famous "Battle of the Dunes" at Dunkirk (then known as Dunkerque).

1869 Dunkirk Base Ball Club 1898 *Iron & Oil (ind.)*. Team had no nickname.

Dunn-Erwin, North Carolina

1870 Twins 1946–49 *Tobacco State (D)*. The team represented both cities. Home games were played in Dunn.

Durango, Durango, Mexico

1871 Alacranes 1956–57 *Central Mexican (C)* 1965–67 Team took double city name of Durango-Laguna Scorpions in 1957. Home games were played in Durango; *Mexican Center (A)*; 1976–79 *Mexican (AAA)*; 1982–83 *Nacional de Mexico (ind.)*. Regional, poisonous arachnids found in the southwestern United States and Mexico, especially in desert regions. Durango is known as the "Scorpion City." In Spanish Durango is "La Ciudad de los Alacranes."

1872 Algodoneros 1972–74 *Mexican Center (A)*; *Mexican Center (A)*. Nearby cotton plantations transport cotton to city processing and packing houses.

Durant, Oklahoma

1873 Educators 1911 *Texas–Oklahoma (D)*. The city is home to Southeastern Oklahoma State University. Several of the players, on the professional team, played college baseball here.

1874 Choctaws 1912–14 *Texas–Oklahoma (D)*. Choctaw Indians inhabited Oklahoma since the eighteenth century. Oklahoma is the "Land of the Red Man."

1875 Hustlers 1912–14 *Texas–Oklahoma (D)*. With Hettie Green and then Bill Harper at the helm as field manager, local newspapers called the players "Hettie's Hustlers" and "Harper's Hustlers." "Hustler" was a common nickname for a baseball player in this era.

Durham, North Carolina

1876 Bulls 1902 *North Carolina (C)*; 1913–17 *North Carolina State (D)*; 1920–33 *Piedmont (D 1920, C 1921–30, B 1931–33)*; 1936 *Piedmont (B)*; 1945–67 *Carolina (C 1945–62, A 1963–67)*; 1980–97 *Carolina (A)*; 1998 to date *International (AAA)*. Durham is home of the Bull Durham Tobacco Company. With manager Jim Kelly at the helm 1913–15, newspapers called the players "Kelly's Bulls." The name became traditional.

1877 Red Bulls 1936 *Piedmont (B)*. Uniforms used the red-trim style of the parent club St. Louis Cardinals.

Dyersburg, Tennessee

1878 Forked Deers 1923 *Kentucky–Illinois–Tennessee (KITTY) (D)*. City is located near the Forked Deer River. With manager Dutch Quellmalz at the helm, newspapers called the players "Dutch's Deer."

1879 Deers 1924 *(KITTY). (D)*; 1925 *Tri-State (D)*. Newspapers preferred this shorter spin-off.

East Chicago, Indiana

1880 Conquistadors 1995 *Mid-America (ind.)*. Management wanted a marketable moniker and chose "Conquistadors." Team logo was a Spanish conquistador. As with the American Basketball Association San Diego Conquistadores (1975), the team's management shortened the name to Q's for the sake of newspapers.

East Grand Forks, Minnesota

1881 Colts 1933 *Northern (D)*. The nickname "Colts," used to describe young players in the era 1880–1915, began to fall out of vogue after 1920. Grand Forks (NE) and East Grand Forks (MN) were founded in 1871. Horse ranches here raised colts.

1882 Grand Forks Chiefs 1935 *Northern (D)*. Waves of French, English and American settlers came into conflict with Cree, Chippewa, Dakota and Sioux Indian tribes in this region during the seventeenth and eighteenth centuries.

East Liberty, Ohio

1883 Stars 1884 *Iron & Oil Assn. (ind.)*. Baseball teams in this era often chose patriotic names like Unions, Young Americans, Robert E. Lees, Rebels and Stars. The U.S. flag is also called the "Stars and Stripes" while the Confederate flag was known as the "Stars and Bars." The moniker "Stars" is also a spin-off from "Liberty."

East Liverpool, Ohio

1884 East End All-Stars 1893 *Ohio State (ind.)*. "All-Stars" was used by teams on its advertising posters to entice fans to attend a game. The team's ballpark was situated at the "East End" district of the city near the Ohio River. Team did have one "star"—outfielder Curt Welch, who played ten years, batting a career .263 in the major leagues. With manager Jack Darragh at the helm, newspapers called the players "Darragh's All-Stars."

1885 East Liverpool Baseball Club 1906–07 *Pennsylvania–Ohio–Michigan (P.O.M.) (C)*. Team had no nickname.

1886 Potters 1908–12 *Ohio–Pennsylvania (C 1908–11, D 1912)*. City had one of the leading ceramic industries in the nineteenth century giving rise to nickname of "Ceramic City." The "Potter's Museum" is located in the city and displays ceramic items going back to 1800. East Liverpool is also nicknamed "The Pottery Center of America."

East Saginaw, Michigan

1887 Greys 1888 *Saginaw Valley (ind.)*. The players wore gray uniforms. Moniker's spelling was both "Greys" and "Grays."

Eastlake, Ohio

1888 Lake County Captains 2003–09 *South Atlantic (A)*; 2010–12 *Midwest (A)*. Captains of exploring, commercial and military ships have sailed Lake Erie since 1669.

Eastland, Texas

1889 Judges 1920 *West Texas (D)*. Inspired by "The Hanging Judge," Isaac Parker, northern Texas had its own system of judges, marshals, deputy marshals and Texas Rangers to control and capture the outlaws of the era 1870–1900. With manager James Maloney at the helm, newspapers called the players "James' Judges."

Eastman, Georgia

1890 Dodgers 1948–53 *Georgia State (D)*. Team was a farm club of the Brooklyn Dodgers.

Easton, Maryland

1891 Farmers 1924–28x *Eastern Shore (D)*. Circuit and team disbanded July 10, 1928. Easton has numerous dairy, corn, fruit and vegetable and poultry farms.
1892 Browns 1937 *Eastern Shore (D)*. Team was a farm club of the St. Louis Browns.
1893 Cubs 1938 *Eastern Shore (D)*. Team was a farm club of the Chicago Cubs.
1894 Yankees 1939 *Eastern Shore (D)*; 1946–49 *Eastern Shore (D)*. Each team was a farm club of the New York Yankees.

Easton, Pennsylvania

1895 Easton Base Ball Club 1879 *Pennsylvania (ind.)*; m1888 *Central Pennsylvania (ind.)*. Team began season in Ashland (PA) before moving to Easton in mid-season; 1889 *Atlantic Assn.(ind.)*; 1889 *Inter-State (ind.)*; 1889 *Middle States (ind.)*; 1893 *Pennsylvania State (ind.)*. These teams had no nickname.
1896 Gorhams 1890 *Pennsylvania State (ind.)*. The team was founded as the "Gorham Baseball Club" in 1884 in Gorham (NY), a city in western New York State.
1897 Colts 1894 *Pennsylvania State (ind.)*. Many young players, known as "colts" in this era, were on the team.
1898 Triple Citys 1896 *Pennsylvania State (ind.)*. Although the team played its home games in Easton, it also represented Phillipsburg (NJ) and Wilson (PA), which collectively are known as the "Triple City."

Eau Claire, Wisconsin

1899 Eau Claire Base Ball Club 1886–87 *Northwest (ind.)*. Team had no nickname.
1900 Tigers 1907 *Wisconsin State (D)*. Team had a loose affiliation with the Detroit Tigers.
1901 Commissioners 1909–12 *Minnesota–Wisconsin (C)*. 1909–11, *(D)*. 1912. Eau Claire is home to the National Association of Insurance Commissioners. Name was shortened by newspapers to **Coms** for headlines, i.e., "Coms edge Roosters, 4–3."
1902 Puffs 1909 *Minnesota–Wisconsin (C)*. Like Duluth (MN), i.e., the Duluth Freeze, the city of Eau Claire is subjected to harsh winter winds that last into April. Hardy local residents downplay them as mere "puffs of cool air." Local newspapers gagged on "Commissioners" and insisted on "Puffs." When "Commissioners" became more or less official in 1910, local newspapers shortened it to "Coms."
1903 Cardinals 1933 *Northern (D)*. Team was a farm club of the St. Louis Cardinals.
1904 Bears 1934, 1936–42 *Northern (D 1934, 1936–40, C 1941–42)*; 1946–53 *Northern (C)*. Although there are bears in Wisconsin, the name was an obvious rhyme to "Claire." The 1934 team had a loose affiliation with the Chicago Cubs. The 1936 team used the moniker while playing as an official farm club of the Boston Red Sox in 1936 and then switched to the Chicago Cubs, 1937–39. Wartime money troubles reduced the Chicago–Eau Claire relationship to a loose affiliation 1940–42.
1905 Muskies 1935 *Northern (D)*. Muskies, a freshwater fish, swim in the nearby Mississippi and Flambeau rivers.
1906 Braves 1954–62 *Northern (C)*. Team was a farm club of the Milwaukee Braves.

Eau Claire–Chippewa Falls, Wisconsin

1907 Orphans 1906 *Wisconsin State (D)*. In the era 1895–1915, teams that suffered poor attendance (usually because of a losing record) were forced to play on the road. Such teams were often called "Wanderers" and "Orphans." Sometimes, these road travelers would disband before season's end. This team, with a poor 44–71 record that put them sixth and last in the league, made it to the end of the 1906 season without disbanding. Team represented both cities with home games in Eau Claire. With manager Andy Porter at the helm, team was called "Andy Porter's Orphans."

Ebano, San Luis Potosi, Mexico

1908 Los Rojos 1971–74 *Mexican Center (A)*. Team was a farm club of the Mexico City Reds. Actually, the parent club in Mexico City is officially "Los Diablos Rojos," i.e., "Red Devils," but fans and newspapers have called this Mexico City team "Rojos" and "Reds" to save newspaper space.
1909 Club de Beisbol de Ebano 1977 *Mexican Center (A)*. Team had no nickname.

Edenton, North Carolina

1910 Colonials 1951 *Virginia (D)*; 1952 *Coastal Plain (D)*. City was the capital of North Carolina until 1792. The "Edenton Tea Party" was a ladies' rebellion in October 1774 against the English Tea Tax. It was a peaceful boycott of English tea and clothing. Edenton, founded 1750, is known as the "Cradle of the Colony."

Edgewater, New Jersey

1911 Giants 1941 *Independent Negro* team. The name "Giants" was popular with black teams. Black teams in the New York area in this era sometimes received used and donated uniforms from the New York Yankees and New York Giants.

Edinburg, Texas

1912 Bobcats m1926 *Gulf Coast (D)*. Team started season in Victoria (TX) before moving to Edinburg August 24; 1927 *Texas Valley (D)*. Bobcats inhabit Texas. Manager Cam Hill's 1926–27 players were known as "Cam's Cats" and "Cam's Bobcats."
1913 Roadrunners 2001 *Texas–Louisiana (ind.)*; 2002–05 *Central (ind.)*; 2009 to date *United (ind.)*; 2011 to date *North American (ind.)*. The Golden, Northern and United leagues merged to form the North American League. The roadrunner is a fast-running, terrestrial cuckoo-like bird found in the southwestern U.S. and Mexico.
1914 Coyotes 2006–08 *United (ind.)*; 2007 *Texas Winter (W)*. The Texas Winter League was a winter circuit for UL teams. Coyotes, both gray and red, inhabit the southwestern U.S. and Mexico.

Edmonton, Alberta, Canada

1915 Grays 1907 *Western Canada (D)*. The gray goose and the gray bird inhabit Canada. Team also wore gray uniforms.
1916 Eskimos 1909–11, 1914 *Western Canada (D)*; 1921 *Western Canada (B)*; 1922x *Western International (B)*. League disbanded June 18 with Edmonton and Calgary meeting in a pennant playoff after the circuit broke up; 1953–54 *Western International (B)*. Eskimos not only inhabit Alaska but also Eastern Siberia, Greenland, and Northern Canada. By 1955, the nickname identity had swung to the Edmonton Eskimos of the Canadian Football League. With Dennis

McGuire at the helm in 1909, newspapers called the players "Dennis McGuire's Eskimos."

1917 Gray Birds 1912–13 *Western Canada (D)*. Moniker was a spin-off from "Grays." In 1913, manager Ray Whisman led "Ray's Graybirds." Players wore gray uniforms.

1918 Les Esquimos 1920 *Western Canada (B)*. Newspapers used the French spelling. With manager Pete Stanridge, team was called "Pete Stanridge's Esquimos."

1919 Trappers 1981–96 *Pacific Coast (AAA)*. The Hudson Bay Company established a fort here in 1795 where soldiers protected fur trappers. Trappers hunted badgers, bear, deer, elk, fox, and wolverines.

1920 Cracker Cats 2005–07 *Northern (ind.)*; 2008–10 *Golden (ind.)*; 2011 to date *North American (ind.)*. The Golden, Northern and United leagues merged to form the North American League. Chosen in a fan poll in 2005, the name derives from "cracker jack," which means an individual or group who are skilled in what they do. Mountain lions also are found in Alberta. Putting the two together creates "Cracker Cats."

1921 Capitals 2011 *North American (ind.)*. Edmonton is the provincial capital of Alberta.

Eindhoven, Northbrandt, Netherlands (aka Holland)

1922 PSV Eindhofen 1990–2003 *Hoofdklasse (ind.)*. Team was owned by PSV Soccer Team and went by the name of PSV Eindhoven. PSC stands for Phillips Sport Voreniging (i.e., Phillips Sports Club).

Elberon, Pennsylvania

1923 Elberon Base Ball Club m1895 Team began the season in Sharon (PA) and then moved to Elberon in mid-season. Team had no nickname.

El Centro, Imperial, California

1924 El Centro Baseball Club 1909–10 *Southern California (W)*; 1914-15-15-16 *Southern California (W)*. Neither team had a nickname.

1925 Imperials 1947–50 *Sunset (C)*; 1951 *Southwest International (C)*. El Centro is located in Imperial County.

1926 Imps 1952 *Southwest International (C)*. Local newspapers in 1952 shortened the name to "Imps."

El Dorado, Arkansas

1927 Lions 1929–32x *Cotton States (D 1929–30, C 1931–32)* Circuit and team disbanded July 13 because of the Great Depression; 1933 *Dixie (C)*; 1934–35 *East Dixie (C)*; 1936–40 *Cotton States (C)*. The city name of El Dorado, which means "golden" in Spanish, sometimes refers to regional mountain lions whose tawny color resembles gold. The direct origin of the name is manager Hickory Jackson, whose players were called "Hickory Jackson's Lions." Clyde Glass took over in mid-season 1932, and the name became "Clyde Glass' Lions."

1928 Oilers 1941 *Cotton States (C)*; 1947–55 *Cotton States (C)*. El Dorado became a boom-town when oil was discovered here in 1921. El Dorado is the "Oil Capital of Arkansas."

Eldorado, Illinois

1929 Eldorado Baseball Club 1910–11 *Southern Illinois (D)*. Team had no nickname.

El Dorado, Kansas

1930 Crushers 1911 *Kansas State (D)*. Wheat is transported from surrounding farms to city factories here where it is milled into flour. The milling machines are called "crushers." With manager Walter Sizemore at the helm, newspapers called the players "Walter Sizemore's Crushers."

Elgin, Illinois

1931 Kittens 1910 *Northern Assn. (D)*. With manager Matt Kittridge at the helm, newspapers called the players "Kittridge's Kittens," which was appropriate since most of the players were very young.

1932 Watchmakers 1915 *Bi-State (D)*. In the nineteenth century, Elgin had numerous watch-making factories and shops. The best known of these companies is the Elgin Watch Company, makers of the widely advertised "Elgin Watch." With manager Dennis Blake at the helm, newspapers called the players "Blake's Watchmakers."

Elizabeth, New Jersey

1933 Resolutes 1873 *National Assn. (M)*. In 1865, the Resolute Firehouse Company of New York City formed an amateur baseball team. The name was popular and spread to New Jersey in 1866 where the amateur Resolute Base Ball Club of Elizabeth team picked it up. The team turned professional in 1873 and joined the National Association but was outclassed, losing 23 of 25 games. The team played as a semi-professional nine in 1874–78 and then disbanded.

1934 Growlers 1873 *National Assn. (M)*. The Resolute players were notoriously argumentative with umpires. The *New York Clipper* said they "growled with umpires." Baseball players in the nineteenth century often physically kicked and punched umpires.

1935 Jersey Nine 1873 *National Assn. (M)*. Baseball teams in the nineteenth century were often known as "nines." Baseball teams have had "nine to a side" since 1837.

1936 Elizabeth Base Ball Club 1892 *Central New Jersey (ind.)*. Team had no nickname.

Elizabeth City, North Carolina

1937 Albemarles 1950–51 *Virginia (D)*. The city was built on the shore of the Albemarle Sound. The U.S. Navy defeated the Confederates here in an 1862 sea battle.

Elizabethton, Tennessee

1938 Betsy Red Sox 1937, 1939–42 *Appalachian (D)*. Team was a farm club of Boston Red Sox. "Betsy" was added to the name to avoid confusion with the Boston AL club. The city's nickname is "Betsy Town" and "Betsy."

1939 Red Sox 1938 *Appalachian (D)*. Newspapers this year didn't like "Betsy Red Sox," considering too long, and shortened it to "Red Sox." In 1939 the longer name was used again.

1940 Betsy Cubs 1945–47 *Appalachian (D)*. Team was a farm club of the Chicago Cubs. Elizabethton is known as the "Betsy Town."

1941 Betsy Local 1949–50 *Appalachian (D)*. The "Betsy Local" was a New Jersey railroad line of the LaGrange & Memphis Railroad.

The city was founded in 1772 by the Watauga Local Government Association. Elizabethton is known as the "Betsy Town."

1942 Phillies 1951 *Appalachian (D)*. Team was a farm club of the Philadelphia Phillies.

1943 Twins 1974 to date *Appalachian (A)*. Team was a farm club of the Minnesota Twins.

Elkhart, Indiana

1944 Elkhart Base Ball Club 1888 *Indiana State (ind.)*; 1890 *Indiana State (ind.)*. These two teams had no nickname.

1945 Blue Sox 1910x *Indiana–Michigan (D)*. Team and league disbanded August 21. Players wore blue stirrups. Team had a loose affiliation with the Chicago White Sox. The players stirrup color of blue was a spin-off from the white stirrups of the Chicago Americans.

Elkin, North Carolina

1946 Blanketeers 1949–50 *Blue Ridge (D)*; m1951–52 *North Carolina (D)*. Team began 1951 season in Landis (NC) before moving to Elkin July 18, 1951. Textile mills in the city specialized in manufacturing blankets, sheets, and pillow cases. The textile industry in the Carolinas led the nation in the era 1870–1920 but then was all outsourced.

Ellsworth, Kansas

1947 Ellsworth Baseball Club 1905 *Kansas State (D)*. Team had no nickname.

1948 Blues 1908, 1910 *Central Kansas (D)*. Team was a farm club of the Kansas City Blues. In the era 1900–40, lower classification minor league teams sometimes were farm teams of higher classification minor league teams.

1949 Worthies 1909 *Central Kansas (D)*. Moniker was used for newspaper headlines, i.e., "Worthies edge Minnies, 4–3."

Elmhurst, California

1950 Elmhurst Baseball Club m1910–11m *Central California (D)*. Team began 1910 season in Petaluma (CA) before moving to Elmhurst June 5, 1910. Team began 1911 season in Elmhurst before moving to Oakland (CA) June 4, 1911. Team had no nickname.

Elmira, New York

1951 Colonels 1885x *New York State (ind.)*. Franchise joined the league July 6 and disbanded July 16; *New York State (B)*. 1908, 1911–13, 1915–17 Team began 1908 season in Johnstown (NY) and then moved to Elmira July 22; 1924–31 *New York–Pennsylvania (B)*; 1937 *New York–Pennsylvania (A)*. The Battle of Chemung River was fought here on August 29, 1779, led by Colonels John Sullivan and James Clinton who defeated a combined force of British troops and pro-Tory Indians. Colonel Thomas Tracy, who distinguished himself by leading the 109th Volunteer Infantry during the Civil War was also the controversial commandant of the notorious Elmira Prison Camp where Confederate soldiers were interned in brutal conditions, i.e., cold, disease and filth.

1952 Elmira Base Ball Club 1889 *New York State (ind.)*. Team had no nickname.

1953 Gladiators 1891 *New York–Pennsylvania (ind.)*; 1892 *Eastern (ind.)*. Baseball players of the nineteenth century, like football players in the twentieth and 21st centuries, were perceived as the modern equivalent of the gladiators of Rome. With manager J. C. Velder at the helm in 1891, newspapers called the team "Velder's Gladiators." Moniker was retained in 1892.

1954 Maple Citys 1895 *New York State (ind.)*. Elmira has several factories that produce maple syrup. The city also sponsors "The Maple Syrup Festival" every year. Elmira is known as the "Maple City."

1955 Pioneers m1900 *New York State (ind.)*. Team started season in Oswego and then moved here July 30; 1909; 1914 *New York State (B)*; 1935–36 *New York–Pennsylvania (B)*; 1938–55; 1958–61 *New York–Pennsylvania (D)*; 1963–70, 1973, 1979–80, 1984–95; 1972 *Eastern (AA)*; 1996–98 *Northeast (ind.)*; 1999–2004 *Northern (ind.)*; 2005 *Canadian–American (ind.)*. Captain Abraham Miller resigned from the Continental Army in 1776 to build a log cabin in the present site Elmira — the first of many pioneer families to settle here in this era. With manager Abner Powell at the helm for the team in 1900, newspapers called the players "Powell's Pioneers." Bill Conroy led the 1914 team to the pennant as newspapers called the players "Conroy's Pioneers." By 1963 moniker became traditional. Team logo is a covered wagon and a raccoon cap.

1956 Colonials 1910 *New York State (B)*. Tag was a spin-off from Colonels. Elmira was an important colonial town. With manager Michael O'Neill at the helm, newspapers called the players "O'Neill's Colonials."

1957 Red Jackets 1923 *New York–Pennsylvania (B)*. Chief Red Jacket was a war chief of the Seneca in the War of 1812, siding with the Americans but later demanding rights for his people. He habitually wore a red British army jacket. With manager John Riley at the helm, newspapers called the red-trim uniformed players "Riley's Red Jackets."

1958 Red Wings 1932–34 *New York–Pennsylvania (A)*. Team was a farm club of the St. Louis Cardinals. Some of the Cardinal farm teams in this era used the spinoff monikers of "Redbirds" and "Red Wings."

1959 Dodgers Eastern 1950–55 Team was a farm club of the Brooklyn Dodgers.

1960 Royals 1971 *Eastern (AA)*. Team was a farm club of the Kansas City Royals.

1961 Red Sox 1974–76, 1978 *New York–Pennsylvania (A)*. Team was a farm club of the Boston Red Sox.

1962 Pioneer Red Sox 1977 *New York–Pennsylvania (A)*. Management tried a stunt — a double nickname. Elmira newspapers didn't like it. Tag was replaced by Red Sox the following year.

1963 Suns 1981–83 *New York–Pennsylvania (A)*. Philadelphia businessman Clyde Smoll, who also owned the Quakertown Blazers of the Atlantic Collegiate League, bought this franchise to play in Elmira and named it "Suns" as a spin-off from his Atlantic Collegiate League team — the "Blazers." The nickname had nothing to do with the NBA Phoenix Suns. However, fans got confused, and by 1984, "Pioneers" was brought back.

El Paso, Texas

1964 Mack Men 1915 *Rio Grande Assn. (D)*. Just as Connie Mack's Philadelphia Athletics were often called the "Mack Men," 1915 El Paso field manager John McCloskey's players were also known as the "Mack Men."

1965 Texans 1930 *Arizona State (D)*; 1931–32 *Arizona–Texas (D)*; 1937–41 *Arizona–Texas (D 1937–39, C 1940–41)*; 1946x *Mexican National (B)*. Circuit and team disbanded May 27; 1947–50 *Arizona–Texas (C)*; 1951 *Southwest–International (C)*; 1952–54 *Arizona–Texas (C)*; 1955 *West Texas–New Mexico (B)*; 1956–57 *Southwestern (B)*. Derived from the Spanish "Tejano," name means an inhabitant of

Texas. Newspapers used Texans, Cowboys and Longhorns. The name "Texans" has been used by fifteen professional sports teams hailing from Texas.

1966 Cowboys 1930 *Arizona State (D)*. City was settled in 1827 and became an important route for cowboys to herd cattle. Newspapers used Cowboys, Texans and Longhorns.

1967 Longhorns 1930 *Arizona State (D)*. Texas has the largest livestock industry in the United States. The Texas Longhorn steer is especially prized. Fort Bliss, established in 1848, sent soldiers out to protect the cattle drives. The Texas Longhorn is a special breed of the Spanish Longhorn.

1968 Sun Kings 1961 *Sophomore (D)*; 1962–70 *Texas (AA)*; 1973 *Texas (AA)*. A city noted for its sunny weather, El Paso is the "Host City of the Sunland Empire." The name "Kings" is a spin-off from empire.

1969 Sun Dodgers 1972 *Texas (AA)*. Team was a farm club of the Los Angeles Dodgers with an amalgamated name. Newspapers didn't care for it.

1970 Diablos 1974–2004 *Texas (AA)*; 2005 *Central (ind.)*; 2006 to date *American Assn. (ind.)*. The appropriately named "Diablo Sierra" and Devil Ridge Eagle Mountains, both about 150 miles southwest of the city, are devilishly hot and diabolically sunny in summer. Spanish has been spoken in the city since 1659 when the Spaniards settled the region.

1971 Coastal Kingfish 2009–10 *Continental (ind.)*. The Continental, Golden and United leagues merged into the North American League for the 2011 season. The Kingfish franchise disbanded after the 2010 season. The Kingfish is a small, silvery food and sport fish of inshore waters, i.e., the Rio Grande.

1972 Desert Valley Mountain Lions 2010 to date *Continental (ind.)*. The Continental, Golden and United leagues merged into the North American League for the 2011 season. The Mountain Lions franchise disbanded after the 2010 season. Mountain lions once inhabited Texas in great numbers. They were hunted to near extinction but, fortunately, they have made a comeback in large part due to the efforts of wildlife protection agencies.

El Reno, Oklahoma

1973 Railroaders 1922–23 *Oklahoma State (D)*. Since 1889, trains of the El Paso–Western Railroad bring produce to the city for processing and packing before picking up the goods for shipment into Oklahoma City. With manager Virgil Moss at the helm in 1923, newspapers called the players "Virgil Moss' Railroaders." Harry Burge took over in 1923 and the name became "Harry Burge's Railroaders."

Elwood, Indiana

1974 Elwood Base Ball Club 1896 *Indiana State (ind.)*; 1900 *Indiana State (ind.)*. These teams had no nickname.

Empalme, Sonora, Mexico

1975 Rieleros 1958–59 *Liga del Pacifico Mexicano (W)*; 1968 *Mexican Rookie (R)*. Trains of Nacional de Mexico Railroad travel through the Sonora Desert to reach the city. Los Rieleros is Spanish for "railroadmen."

Emporia, Kansas

1976 Emporia Base Ball Club 1887x *Western (ind.)*. Team joined the league August 13 and then disbanded September 9. Team had no nickname.

1977 Maroons 1895–96 *Kansas State (ind.)*. Players wore maroon hose.

1978 Bidwells 1914 *Kansas State (D)*. Team was named in honor of manager Ira Bidwell.

1979 Traders 1924 *Southwestern (D)*. The city is a processing center and distribution point for farm products, wheat and salt. With manager Tom Oran at the helm, newspapers called the players "Tom Oran's Traders." Oran left the team in mid-season but the name was retained under three other managers.

Emporia, Virginia

1980 Nationals 1948–50 *Virginia (D)*. Team was a farm club of the Washington Nationals. Local newspapers immediately shortened the name to **Nats**.

1981 Rebels 1951 *Virginia (D)*. Fans didn't like the "union" name of Nationals, so the obvious opposite choice was selected. Many desperate battles were fought in Virginia during the Civil War. Virginia is the "Battlefield of the Civil War."

Enid, Oklahoma

1982 Evangelists 1904 *Southwestern (D)*. The Bible Belt are those areas of the Southern and Midwest U.S.(and Western Canada), where Protestant fundamentalism is practiced, emphasizing evangelism, i.e., the authority of the Bible and public preaching. With manager Walter Frantz at the helm, newspapers called the players "Frantz' Evangelists."

1983 Railroaders 1908–10 *Western Assn. (C)*. Starting in 1893, the city became a processing and packing center for dairy, poultry and meat products, and wheat. In the 1920s oil was discovered in the region. These goods were transported by train. The railroad made Enid the "Queen City of the Cherokee Strip." With manager Red Wright at the helm, newspapers called the players "Red Wright's Railroaders." Wright left the team after 1908, but the name was retained.

1984 Harvesters 1920–23 *Western Assn. (D 1920–21, C 1922–23)*; 1924–25m *Southwestern (D)*. Team moved to Shawnee (OK) June 17, 1925. Farmland around the city produces poultry, meat and wheat, which is sent by train to the city for processing and redistribution. With manager Ted Waring at the helm in 1920, newspapers called the players "Waring's Harvesters." Barney Cleveland took over in 1921, making the name "Barney's Harvesters." Name was retained 1922–23 with manager Tom Downey.

1985 Boosters 1926 *Southwestern (D)*. When the team won the first-half pennant, happy Enid fans formed a "booster club." The name was applied to the team, i.e., "Boosters." The team finished second to clinch a playoff berth against first-place Salina in a pennant playoff. Although Enid lost 3 games to 1, their fans "boosted" them.

1986 Giants 1950 *Western Assn. (C)*. Team was a farm club of the New York Giants.

1987 Buffaloes 1951 *Western Assn. (C)*. Team was a farm club of the Houston Buffaloes. In the period 1910–50 some higher-level classification (i.e., AAA and AA) minor league teams had their own farm clubs from the ranks of lower-level classification (i.e., A-B-C-D) minor league teams.

Ennis, Texas

1988 Tigers 1914–15x *Central Texas (D)*. Team and league disbanded July 24, 1915; 1916–17x *Central Texas (D)*. Team and league disbanded June 6, 1917, due to U.S. entry into World War I. Team had a loose affiliation with the Class B Texas League Fort Worth Panthers — hence, the feline moniker. The Enid baseball players also sported striped orange and black stirrups, after the Oklahoma State University sports teams, who were known at this time (1901–24) as the "Tigers." With manager Ed Wicker at the helm, newspapers called the players "Ed Wicker's Tigers." Team had no affiliation with the Detroit Tigers.

Ensenada, Baja California, Mexico

1989 Tigres 1968–69 *Mexican Northern (A)*. Team was a farm club of the Mexico City Tigers. In the 1960s and 1970s, the Mexico City Tigers had a fairly extensive farm system with about five farm teams in the Class A Mexican Leagues of this era. "Los Tigres" in English is "Tigers."

1990 Marineros 2004–08 *Norte de Sonora (ind.)*; 2009 to date *Norte de Mexico (ind.)*. This new league, renamed in 2009, is a profesional circuit. Ensenada, about 60 miles south of Tijuana, is a port city along a crescent bay leading out into the Pacific Ocean. Tourists visit this port city for recreational and deep sea fishing. Local fishing boats head to sea to catch tuna and shrimp. Cotton, from the Mexicali Valley, is also shipped out by boat to market. "Los marineros" is Spanish for "sailors."

Enterprise, Alabama

1991 Browns 1936 *Alabama–Florida (D)*. Although not a formal farm club of the St. Louis Browns, the team did have a loose working agreement with this big league club.

1992 Boll Weevils 1947–50 *Alabama State (D)*; 1951–52m *Alabama–Florida (D)*. Team began season in Enterprise before moving to Graceville (FL) July 5, 1952. Since cotton was first harvested in the South around 1700, the dreaded boll weevil, also known as the Cotton Beetle, has plagued the cotton crops. Edenton is the "Home of the Boll Weevil Monument." This monument was dedicated in 1919. With manager Ben Catchings at the helm in 1947, newspapers called the players "Ben's Boll Weevils." Richard Bixby took over in 1948 and the name became "Bixby's Boll Weevils."

Erie, Pennsylvania

1993 Olympics 1885 *Inter-State (ind.)*. The first ball club to use this moniker was the 1830 "Philadelphia Olympics." Up to 1859, the Olympics played town ball and then switched to baseball in 1860. The Erie team was named after the Philadelphia Olympics. The nineteenth century American public was very much enamored of the Ancient Greek Olympic Games. Numerous sports teams in the era (1850–1900) used the name.

1994 Erie Base Ball Club 1890–91 *New York–Pennsylvania (ind.)*. The team had no nickname.

1995 Blackbirds 1893–94 *Eastern (ind.)*. Players wore black hose. Several teams in the 1890s had bird names after their stocking color, i.e., Blackbirds, Bluebirds, Blue Jays, Cardinals, Crows, Doves, Ravens, and Redbirds.

1996 Fishermen 1905, 1908 *Interstate (D)*. The city is a seaport of Lake Erie. Commercial and recreational fishing has been here since the site was first settled in 1795. Erie, the only lake port in Pennsylvania, is the "Harbor City."

1997 Sailors 1906–07 *Interstate (D)*; m1908–11 *Ohio–Pennsylvania (C)*. Team began the 1908 season in Butler (PA) before moving to Erie June 15, 1908, replacing the ISL Sailors who had disbanded 10 days earlier; 1912 *Central (D)*; 1912 *Central (D)*; 1913 *Inter-State (D)*; 1915 *Central (B)*; 1916x *Inter-State (D)*. Team disbanded August 9; 1928–30 *Central (B)*. 1932 *Central (D)*; 1938–39 *Middle Atlantic (C)*; 1941–42 *Middle Atlantic (C)*; 1944–45 *Pennsylvania–Ohio–New York*

(P.O.N.Y.)(D); 1946–51 *Middle Atlantic (C)*; 1954 *Pennsylvania–Ohio–New York (P.O.N.Y.)(D)*; 1957–59, 1961–63 *New York–Pennsylvania (D 1957–59, S 1961–62, A 1963)*; 1990–93 *New York–Pennsylvania (A)*; 1994 *Frontier (ind.)*. The city served as the headquarters of Commodore Oliver Perry during the War of 1812. The city is a major harbor for military and civilian commercial shipping. Erie is the "Gem City of the Lakes."

1998 Yankees 1914 *Canadian (B)*. The Erie team, playing in the eight-team Canadian League this season, was the only U.S. entry in the circuit. Hence, the moniker of "Yankees" was used by newspapers. With manager Frank Gygli at the helm, newspapers called the players "Frank Gygli's Yankees."

1999 Senators 1955–56 *Pennsylvania–Ohio–New York (P.O.N.Y.) (D)*; 1960 *New York–Pennsylvania (D)*. Team was a farm club of the Washington Senators.

2000 Tigers 1967 *New York–Pennsylvania (A)*. Team was a farm club of the Detroit Tigers.

2001 Cardinals 1981–87 *New York–Pennsylvania (A)*. Team was a farm club of the St. Louis Cardinals.

2002 Orioles 1988–89 *New York–Pennsylvania (A)*. Team was a farm club of the Baltimore Orioles.

2003 Sea Wolves 1995–98 *New York–Pennsylvania (A)*; 1999 to date *Eastern (AA)*. Tag was a spin-off from "Sailors." Pirates, known as "sea wolves," sailed the waters of Lake Erie from as early as 1700. These "sea wolves" besieged the coast so much that the French built Fort Presque on the isle of the same name in 1753.

Erwin, Tennessee

2004 Mountaineers 1940 *Appalachian (D)*. The city is located near the North Carolina border to the west of the Appalachian Mountain range. Erwin is the "Gateway to the Smoky Mountains."

2005 Aces 1943 *Appalachian (D)*. The Johnson City–Erwin area was an airplane manufacturing center during World War II. Local newspapers wanted a very short nickname to avoid printing "Mountaineers."

2006 Cubs 1943 *Appalachian (D)*. Team was a farm club of the Chicago Cubs.

Eufaula, Alabama

2007 Eufala Baseball Club 1916–17 *Dixie (D)*. Team had no nickname.

2008 Millers 1952–53 *Alabama–Florida (D)*. Farms in the region transport grain and peanuts to mills.

Eugene, Oregon

2009 Blues 1904x *Oregon State (D)*. Team disbanded July 6. League, down to two teams, also disbanded. Players wore blue hose.

2010 Larks 1950–51 *Far West (D)*. Mountain larks are indigenous to the Pacific Northwest. With manager Louis Vezilich at the helm, newspapers called the players "Louis' Larks" and "Vezilich's Larks." Vezilich left the team after 1950 but the name was retained.

2011 Emeralds 1955–68 *Northwest (B 1955–62, A 1963–68)*; 1969–73 *Pacific Coast (AAA)*; 1974 to date *Northwest (A)*. Nickname was appropriate because Oregon has rich emerald-green fir trees in the Williamette National Forest to the east and the Suislaw National Forest to the west.

Eureka, Kansas

2012 Oilers 1924 *Southwestern (D)*; m1926 *Southwestern (D)*. Team began the season in Ponca City (OK) and then moved here

June 22. Oil was discovered in Kansas in 1892 (Neodosha), 1915 (El Dorado) and 1936 (western Kansas). Crude oil is transported to Eureka for refining. With field manager Ross Crawford at the helm, local newspapers called the players the alliterative "Ross' Oilers" and "Crawford's Oilers." Ironically, the city was so-named after "Eureka!"—the cry of gold prospectors when they struck it rich. Since oil is "Black Gold," the name "Oilers" is quite appropriate.

Evansville, Indiana

2013 Riversides m1884 *Northwestern (ind.)*. Team began season in Bay City (MI) and then moved to Evansville July 30. The city was built at the confluence of the Ohio and Wabash rivers. Portsmouth of the Ohio State Association also was known as "Riverside" this year.

2014 Evansville Base Ball Club 1889 *Central Inter-State (ind.)*; 1892 *Illinois–Indiana*. Team had no nickname.

2015 Black Stockings 1891 *Northwest (ind.)*. Players wore black hose. Originally "Black Stockings," newspapers shortened it to **Black Sox**.

2016 Blackbirds 1895 *Southern (ind.)*; 1897 *Central (ind.)*. Players wore black hose.

2017 River Rats 1901–02 *Three-I (ind. 1901, B 1902)*; 1903–10 *Central (B)*; 1913–14 *Central (B)*. The city is built on the convergence of the Ohio and Wabash rivers, which by 1900 were so polluted that rats were swimming amidst the floating trash and garbage. The river pollution continued unabated. Fortunately, attempts were made to clean up the Ohio and Wabash rivers starting in 1950.

2018 Punchers 1911m *Central (B)*. Team moved to South Bend (IN) August 11, 1911. Team was named in honor of manager Charles "Punch" Knoll.

2019 Strikers 1911m *Central (B)*. Team moved to South Bend (IN) August 11, 1911. In April 1894 coal miners in Illinois, Indiana, Ohio, Pennsylvania and western Pennsylvania staged a series of strikes, protesting low wages and dangerous working conditions, against "scab" (non-union) workers, and strike-busters sent out onto the streets by management. With manager Angus Grant at the helm, newspapers called the players "Grant's Strikers." Moreover, "striker" is baseball slang for a batter or hitter.

2020 Yankees 1912 *Kentucky–Illinois–Tennessee (KITTY) (D)*. The city was the northernmost team of the KITTY League's member clubs, the rest of which played in home cities south of this Indiana team. "Yankee" is slang for Northerner.

2021 Evas 1915–17 *Central (B)*; 1919–24 *Three-I (B)*. Moniker was used for newspaper headlines, i.e., "Evas edge Sailors, 4–3."

2022 Little Evas 1924 *Three-I (B)*. Local newspapers didn't like the name because it sounded "girly" and was unnecessary. ("Evas" alone was sufficient.)

2023 Pocketeers 1925 *Three-I (B)*. Evansville is located in southwest Indiana — a region known as the "Little Pocket of Indiana." In 1924 a local company, the Pocketeer Toy Company, started to manufacture a billiard ball game table called "The Pocketeer" that became popular nationwide. However, Evansville fans couldn't relate to this marketing name, and local newspapers hated the length of the nickname.

2024 Hubs 1926–31 *Three-I (B)*. The receiving point of six highways, three states and the Ohio River, Evansville is nicknamed the "Hub of North Central America." The city also has an airport. Evansville newspapers welcomed a nickname only four letters long after suffering with the ten-letter moniker of "Pocketeer" the previous year.

2025 Colored Braves 1938–39 Independent Negro team. Indiana was nicknamed the "Land of the Indians" by the U.S. Congress in 1800. Using the spin-off "Braves," management combined it with the adjective "colored" to come up with "Colored Braves." Moniker was available because the Boston Nationals had abandoned it in 1936. Many black teams used this style of adjective/noun for a team nickname.

2026 Bees 1938–39, 1941–42 *Three-I (B)*. Team was a farm club of the Boston Bees. In 1941, the parent club had switched to its old nickname of "Braves," but Evansville newspapers insisted on continuing with the shorter "Bees."

2027 Braves 1940 *Three-I (B)*; 1946–57 *Three-I (B)*. Team went to the 1935 nickname of the Boston Bees—the Braves. The next season the team reverted to "Bees" while the parent club ironically re-adopted "Braves." Team was a farm club of the Boston Braves (1946–52) and the Milwaukee Braves (1953–57).

2028 White Sox 1966–68 *Southern (AA)*. Team was a farm club of the Chicago White Sox.

2029 Triplets 1970–84 *American Assn. (AAA)*. Evansville is located at the junction of three states—Illinois, Indiana and Kentucky. Name was chosen in a name-the-team contest.

2030 Otters 1995 to date *Frontier (ind.)*. Weasels swim in the nearby Wabash and Ohio rivers and are known as "river otters."

Evart, Michigan

2031 Evart Base Ball Club 1887 *Northern Michigan (ind.)*. Team had no nickname.

Everett, Washington

2032 Smoke-stackers 1905 *Northwestern (B)*. With lumber mills, fisheries, paper mills, fruit-packing plants all working nearly round-the-clock, the smoke stacks of these places spewed smoke, causing significant air pollution. By 1900 the city was nicknamed "The City of Smokestacks." As in many U.S. cities, anti-pollution measures were slow to be instituted, but by the 1950s clean air laws were in effect here.

2033 Giants 1984–94 to date *Northwest (A)*. Team was a farm club of the San Francisco Giants.

2034 AquaSox 1995 to date *Northwest (A)*. Team, a farm club of the Seattle Mariners, adopted the parent club's aquamarine uniforms, prompting the moniker of "AquaSox." The team logo is a green frog with a baseball cap. Frogs inhabit the nearby Snohomish River.

Evergreen, Alabama

2035 Greenies m1937–38 *Alabama–Florida (D)*. Team started 1937 season in Ozark (AL) before moving to Evergreen June 29, 1937. Moniker was used for newspaper headlines, i.e., "Greenies edge Trojans, 4–3."

Fairbury, Jefferson, Nebraska

2036 Shaners 1915x *Nebraska State (D)*. Circuit and team disbanded July 18. Team was named after manager Bert Shaner.

2037 Jeffersons 1922–23 *Nebraska State (D)*; 1928–30 *Nebraska State (D)*. Fairbury is located in Jefferson County.

2038 Jeffs 1936x *Nebraska State (D)*. Team disbanded July 16; 1937 *Nebraska State (D)*. Newspapers shortened "Jeffersons" to "Jeffs," i.e., "Jeffs edge Omaha, 5–4."

Fairmount, West Virginia

2039 Champions 1907 *Western Pennsylvania (D)*; 1909 *Pennsylvania–West Virginia (D)*; 1910x *West Virginia (D)*. Team won 1907 pennant and the 1909 first half-season title, though losing in the 1909 playoffs to Uniontown, 4 games to 3. The 1910 team was in first place when the league disbanded July 5. League president Thomas Haydon awarded pennant to Fairmount.

2040 Baddies 1908 *Pennsylvania–West Virginia (D)*. When the 1909 team skidded to fifth place (of six) with a 55–64 record, disgruntled fans and reporters started calling them the "Baddies" in stark contrast to Champions. With the team losing, Reddy Mack replaced Tom Haymond as manager. But as the team continued to struggle, local newspapers started calling the team "Reddy's Baddies."

2041 Fairies m1912 *Ohio–Pennsylvania (D)*. Team started season in Salem (OH) before moving to Fairmount July 9. Name was a Phillies-style moniker.

2042 Maroons 1925 *Middle Atlantic (D)*. Players wore maroon trim.

2043 Black Diamonds 1926–31 *Middle Atlantic (D)*. Coal-mining region. "Black Diamond" is the nickname for coal. "Black Gold" is the nickname for oil. When the players performed well en route to a 68–44 first-place finish and the pennant, local newspapers said the team's play "sparkled like diamonds." West Virginia is the "Fuel State."

Fall River, Massachusetts

2044 Cascades 1877 New England. The Taunton River, which flows inland from Mt. Hope Bay, ends in a waterfall near the city. Cascade is a synonym for "waterfall." Fall River is named the "City of Falling Water."

2045 Blue Stockings 1877 *New England Assn. (M)*. Players wore blue hose. Aka **Blue Legs** and **Blues**.

2046 Braves 1877 *New England Assn. (M)*. In an obvious reference to the Sioux Indians, who massacred General George Custer's army brigade a year earlier in 1876, it is the first known newspaper reference to baseball players as "braves." The *New York Clipper* described manager Jim Mutrie's Fall River team as "Mutrie's Braves."

2047 Gentlemen 1877 *New England Assn. (M)*. *New York Clipper* of September 15 cited the players' "gentlemanly demeanor on the field."

2048 Indians 1893–98 *New England (ind.)*; 1902–10 *New England (B)*. 1946–49 *New England (B)*. No less than 10 tribes lived in Massachusetts in pre-colonial times. Indians fought settlers here in King Phillip's War (1675–76) and the French-Indian War (1704–13). An Indian appears on the Massachusetts state seal. The 1946–49 team was not a farm club of the Cleveland Indians.

2049 Brinies 1911–12 *New England (B)*. Manager John O'Brien. Newspapers called the players "O'Brien's Brinies." "Brinies," which derives from brine and means salt water, is a very old slang for "sailors." Though not directly on the Atlantic shore, Fall River is a maritime city.

2050 Adopted Sons 1913 *New England (B)*. Only five of the 25 players on the roster were from Massachusetts, so they were given the patriotic moniker "Adopted Sons," which stems from the patriotic phrase "Adopted Sons of the Republic" used during the Revolutionary War. Sometimes an American city will honor a war hero as an "adopted son" of that community. An example is the French General Lafayette, who was made an "Adopted Son of the United States" by George Washington in 1782.

2051 Spindles 1914–15 *Colonial (A 1914, ind. 1915)*. New England cities Fall River, Lowell and Manchester are known as the "Spindle Cities" because of their textile industries that began in eighteenth century. A spindle is a threading machine. Ironically, the textile industry of New England all but disappeared in the 1920s and 1930s. With field manager John Kiernan at the helm, local newspapers called

the players the alliterative "Kiernan's Spindles." Kiernan left the team after 1914 but the name was retained in 1915.

Falls City, Nebraska

2052 Colts 1910–13x *Missouri–Iowa–Nebraska–Kansas (M.I.N.K.) (D)*. Team and league disbanded June 17, 1913. For the period 1870–1917, young players were known variously as Babes, Chicks, Colts, Cubs, Debutantes, Foundlings, Ponies, Prodigals and Yearlings. By 1917 these names had been supplanted by "rookie," which comes from "recruit," i.e., a young American soldier headed to Europe to fight in World War I. Moniker was short and alliterative, i.e., Falls City Colts.

Fargo, North Dakota

2053 Fargo Base Ball Club 1887 *Dakota (ind.)*; 1891 *Dakota (ind.)*; 1902–05 *Northern (ind. 1902, D 1903–05)*; 1906 *Northern Copper Country (C)*. These teams had no nickname.

2054 Browns 1908 *Northern (D)*. Players wore brown trim.

2055 Athletics 1922 *Dakota (D)*. Local newspapers insisted on a short nickname since the double-city name, Fargo-Moorhead, contained 13 letters. Management chose "Athletics," which traditionally can be shortened to "A's." With field manager Ed Whiting at the helm, local newspapers called the players the alliterative "Whiting's Athletics." Team was not a farm club of the Philadelphia Athletics. In 1922 only Branch Rickey's St. Louis Cardinals were constructing a farm system. The team's title was "Fargo-Moorhead A's," although the team played its home games in Fargo.

Fargo, North Dakota– Moorhead, Minnesota

2056 Graingrowers 1914–17 Northern *(A 1914–16, D 1917)*. North Dakota has more than 40,000 wheat farms. The city is known as the "Breadbasket of the World." With field manager Bob Unglaub at the helm, local newspapers called the players the alliterative "Unglaub's Graingrowers."

2057 Twins 1917 Northern *(D)*; 1933–42 *Northern (D 1933–40, D 1941–42)*; 1946–60 *Northern (C)*. Team represented both Fargo and Moorhead (MN). Long before the advent of the Minnesota Twins in 1961, numerous teams, which represented two cities of close proximity, were named "Twins."

2058 Red Hawks 1996–2010 *Northern (ind.)*; 2011 to date *American Assn. (ind.)*. The players wear red-trim uniforms and hose. Hawks fly into the region to hunt fish in the many lakes in the state.

Farnham, Quebec, Canada

2059 Pirates 1950–51 *Provincial (C)*. Pittsburgh Pirates affiliate. Teams of the Provincial League of the 1950s were not farm clubs of ML teams but they did loosely affiliate with them.

Fayetteville, Arkansas

2060 Educators 1934 *Arkansas State (D)*. The University of Arkansas was founded here in 1871. With field manager Fred Hawn at the helm, local newspapers called the players the alliterative and rhyming "Fred's Educators."

2061 Bears 1935 *Arkansas State (D)*. Nearby Southwest Missouri University college teams were going by the name of "Bears" at the time. Also, local newspapers wanted a short moniker and the not-too-far-away Chicago Cubs were en route to their third pennant in seven years.

2062 Angels 1937–40 *Arkansas–Missouri (D)*. "Angels" rhymed somewhat with "Fay" in the city name. Moniker was also alliterative, Fayetteville Angels. Manager Fred Hawn prompted newspapers in 1937 to use "Hawn's Angels." When Ken Blackman took over in mid-season, newspapers switched to "Blackman's Angels." In 1939 Frank Oceak managed "Frank's Angels." Team was not a farm club of the P.C.L. Los Angeles Angels.

Fayetteville, North Carolina

2063 Highlanders 1909–10 *Eastern Carolina (D)*; 1928–29 *Eastern Carolina (D)*. The city was founded by Scottish colonists in 1739. Because of the rolling hills of Scotland, people from Scotland are known as "Highlanders." The Carolina Hills near the city also closely resemble the Scottish "Highlands." With field manager Charles Clancy at the helm in 1909–10, local newspapers called the players "Clancy's Highlanders."

2064 Cubs 1946 *Coastal Plain (D)*; 1947–48 *Tri-State (B)*. Farm club of the Chicago Cubs.

2065 Scotties 1949 *Tobacco State (D)*. Newspaper friendly spin-off from "Highlanders." "Scottie" is a slang for the Scottish terrier dog but also means an inhabitant of Scotland.

2066 Generals 1987–96 *South Atlantic (A)*. Nearby Fort Bragg is one of the largest army bases in the United States. General Marquis de Lafayette (city was named after him) led troops here during the American Revolution and General William Sherman's Union troops occupied the city in 1865.

2067 Crocs 1997–2000. Team went by the nearby river name of Cape Fear Crocs. Alliterative moniker was chosen in a fan poll.

Federalsburg, Maryland

2068 Little A's 1937–41 *Eastern Shore (D)*. Farm club of the Philadelphia Athletics. "Little" was used to distinguish the Federalsburg team from its parent club. Newspapers soon dropped it.

2069 Athletics 1946–48 *Eastern Shore (D)*. Team was a farm club of the Philadelphia Athletics.

2070 Feds 1949 *Eastern Shore (D)*. Phillies-style moniker.

Fergus Falls, Minnesota

2071 Fergus Falls Base Ball Club 1887x *Dakota (ind.)*. Team disbanded in mid-season; 1891x *Dakota (ind.)*. Team disbanded in mid-season. These teams had no nickname.

Fieldale, Virginia

2072 Virginians 1934 *Bi-State (D)*. Inhabitant of Virginia. Since 1884 sports teams have occasionally used the names of the inhabitants of their state, i.e., Texans, Hoosiers (Indiana), Floridians, Numexers (New Mexico), Utes (Utah) and Virginians. With field manager D. L. Hodge at the helm, local newspapers called the players the alliterative "Hodge's Virginians."

2073 Towlers 1935–37 *Bi-State (D)*. The textile industry was prominent in the Mid-Atlantic states from 1850 to 1950. Nicknames from this industry included Blanketeers (Elkin, NC), Blanket-Makers (Springfield, TN) and Towlers (shortened from Towel-makers and Towelers) in Fieldale.

Findlay, Ohio

2074 Natural Gassers 1895 *Inter-State (ind.)*. Natural gas deposits were discovered here in 1884. The natural gas deposits were exhausted by 1900, but oil was discovered here in 1920. By 1960 the oil reserves ran out and the city built factories to refine imported oil.

2075 Browns 1937–38, 1941 *Ohio State (D)*. Team was a farm club of the St. Louis Browns.

2076 Oilers 1939–40 *Ohio State (D)*. City was established as a "boom town" after oil was discovered in the region in the 1880s.

Firenze, Tuscany, Italy

2077 Faiero-Sarti-Sigli 2002–05 *Italian A1 (ind.)*. FFS Textile Company owns the team.

Fishkill, New York

2078 Renegades 1994 to date *New York–Pennsylvania (A)*. Team went by the regional name of Hudson Valley Renegades. For the period 1664–1840 the region suffered numerous wars, i.e., English-Dutch, French & Indian (vs. the English & Dutch), Revolutionary and the War of 1812. Although it was the Europeans who broke most of the treaties made with the Mohawks, Iroquois, Delaware and Seneca Indians, the latter were often called "renegades" for their attacks and raiding against colonials.

Fitchburg, Massachusetts

2079 Trilbies 1895 *New England Assn.(ind.)*. The "Trilby" was the popular hat style worn by men in this region during colonial times. It was made of felt with a narrow brim and indented crown. With field manager Lawrence Thyne at the helm, local newspapers called the players the alliterative "Thyne's Trilbies."

2080 Fitchburg Base Ball Club 1899m *New England (ind.)*. Team moved to Lawrence (MA) May 24; 1922m *Eastern (A)*. Team moved to Worcester (MA) July 30. These teams had no nickname.

2081 Burghers 1914m *New England (B)*. Team moved to Manchester (NH) July 30; 1915 *New England (B)*. Phillies-style moniker. With field manager Hugh McCune at the helm in 1915, local newspapers called the players the alliterative "Hugh's Burghers."

2082 Foxes 1919 *New England (B)*. Although foxes are found in the region, moniker was chosen mostly because it was alliterative and short. Local newspapers liked it. Fox hunting is a popular sport in New England.

2083 Wanderers m1929m *New England (B)*. Team started season in Haverhill (MA) and moved to Fitchburg July 28, only to move again to Gloucester (MA) August 25. Teams that transferred cities in mid-season were sometimes called "Wanderers" and "Orphans."

Fitzgerald, Georgia

2084 Pioneers 1948–52 *Georgia State (D)*; 1953–54 *Georgia-Florida (D)*. Oglethorpe and his followers were the first pioneers in Georgia, 1733–43. More pioneers flooded Georgia during the Northern Georgia Gold Rush of 1829. In 1895 Fitzgerald became the "Colony City" as Union Army veterans and their families settled here. Moniker was alliterative, i.e., Fitzgerald Pioneers.

2085 Redlegs 1954 *Georgia-Florida (D)*. Team was a farm club of the Cincinnati Redlegs. Cincinnati switched to "Redlegs," 1953–60, before returning to "Reds" in 1961.

2086 Athletics 1956 *Georgia-Florida (D)*. Team was a farm club of the Kansas City Athletics.

2087 Orioles 1957 *Georgia–Florida (D)*. Team was a farm club of the Baltimore Orioles.

Flandreau, South Dakota

2088 Indians 1902 *Iowa–South Dakota (D)*. Dakota and Sioux Indians inhabited the northern Mississippi Valley. Moniker was alliterative, i.e., Flandreau Indians.

Flint, Michigan

2089 Flyers 1889–90 *Michigan (ind.)*. When the city was built in 1855, the "Flyer" of the Detroit–New Buffalo Railway started arriving at the local railroad station here. Moniker was also alliterative.

2090 Flint Base Ball Club m1897 *Michigan State (ind.)*. Team had no nickname.

2091 Vehics 1906x *Inter-State (D)*. Team and league disbanded July 8. General Motors established the United States' first automobile factory here in 1904. Flint became known as "Vehicle City." Newspapers called this team the "Vehics" but not "Vehicles."

2092 Vehicles 1907–15 South Michigan *(A 1907–10, 1912, C 1911, 1914–15)*; 1921–26t *Michigan–Ontario (B)*. M.O.L. merged with the Central League June 14 to form the Michigan State League. Flint was a charter member of the new circuit. At this time Flint became known as the "Automobile Center" with Buick and Chevrolet setting up factories here. Just as Detroit became known as the "Motor City" in this era, Flint became known as the "Vehicle City" because of GM and other auto plants in the city.

2093 Halligans 1919–20 *Michigan–Ontario (B)*. Named after the Halligan Electric Company.

2094 Gems 1940 *Michigan State (C)*. Chosen as the nickname by team owner Maurice Winston, a Dearborn, Michigan, jeweler who also owned the Detroit "Gems" of the National Basketball League.

2095 Arrows 1941 *Michigan State (C)*; 1948–51 *Central (D)*. The 1941 team was a farm club of Cleveland Indians. Sometimes called **Indians**, the team was formally the **Arrows**—a spin-off from Indians. Flint arrowheads dating back to 5,000 B.C. have been found in this region. The 1948–51 team was not a farm club of the Cleveland Indians.

Florence, Kentucky

2096 Freedom 2003 to date *Frontier (ind.)*; *Atlantic (ind.)*. Because its home field in Florence wasn't completely built, team played its 2003 home games in Hamilton, Ohio. Moniker was alliterative and patriotic.

Florence, South Carolina

2097 Fiddlers m1907 *South Carolina (D)*. Team was known as the Darlington-Florence Fiddlers. Darlington is a suburb of Florence. In the nineteenth century, South Carolina was home to Blue Grass Fiddle and Spirit Fiddle music. Fiddler band square dances are common today, and fiddlers concerts were common in the Carolinas and Virginia in the post–Civil War era and are held annually in these areas. The Fiddler Crab inhabits the coastal waters of the Carolinas.

2098 Pee Deans 1931x *Palmetto (D)*. Team and league disbanded July 23 because of the Great Depression. The Pee Dee River was named after the original inhabitants—the Pee Dee Indians. Newspapers shortened it to **Deans** for personification, rhyming and space-saving. Also, apparently too many fans snickered over use of the word "pee" in the team's name.

2099 Steelers 1948–50 *Tri-State (B)*. Local steel is manufactured in the area. Moniker was alliterative, i.e., Florence Steelers.

2100 Blue Jays 1981–86 *South Atlantic (A)*. Team was a farm club of the Toronto Blue Jays.

2101 Flame 1995x *Atlantic Coast (ind.)*. Team and league disbanded June 30, 1995. Short and alliterative moniker.

Florence, South Carolina–Sheffield, Alabama–Tuscumbia, Alabama

2102 Triplets 1921 *Alabama–Tennessee (D)*. Collectively, Florence, Sheffield and Tuscumbia are known as the "Tri-Cities." The team was known as the Tri-Cities Triplets. Home games were played in Florence.

Follansbee, West Virginia

2103 Stubs m1912 *Ohio–Pennsylvania (D)*. Team began season as the Steubenville Stubs and then moved here in mid-season. The "Stubs" nickname was retained and was alliterative because of manager Gene Curtis, i.e., "Curtis' Stubs."

Fond du Lac, Wisconsin

2104 Mudhens 1891 *Wisconsin (ind.)*. Mudhens and ducks inhabit nearby Lake Winnebago.

2105 Webfeet 1891 *Wisconsin (ind.)*. Slang for duck. Used alternately with Mudhens.

2106 Webfooters 1907 *Wisconsin State (D)*. Ducks inhabit nearby Lake Winnebago. With field manager Tom Fletcher at the helm in 1907, local newspapers called the players the alliterative "Tom Fletcher's Webfoots."

2107 Fondies 1907 *Wisconsin State (D)*. Phillies-style moniker.

2108 Cubs 1908 *Wisconsin State (D)*. Young players. Not only were there numerous young players on the team, known as "Cubs" in this era, but management sought to emulate the successful Chicago Cubs, who were en route to their third straight NL pennant and second straight World Series title. Minor league teams sometimes chose the moniker of a nearby and successful big league team. In the era 1885–1920, minor league teams geographically close to a big league city sometimes formed a very loose affiliation with the major league team, i.e., buying used uniforms and equipment at a discount and selling an occasional player contract to a big league club.

2109 Giants 1909–10 *Wisconsin State (D)*. Moniker was alliterative, i.e., fo-N du l-A-c gi-AN-ts. Giants was also a major league nickname often emulated by minor league teams hoping the prestige and success of the New York Giants might rub off on them.

2110 Mud Hens 1911 *Wisconsin State (D)*. The mud hen is actually a water bird—similar to but not the same as a duck. Mud hens inhabit most of the Midwest along the shores of the Great Lakes and rivers. With field manager Bobby Lynch at the helm, local newspapers called the players the alliterative "Lynch's Mud Hens."

2111 Molls m1913 *Wisconsin–Illinois (C)*. Team started season in Milwaukee (WI) and the moved to Fon du Lac June 28. Supposedly Al Capone, complete with an entourage of his "gun molls," came up to Fond-du-Lac during the summer of 1913 to check on his "bootleg whiskey" operations in Wisconsin. Even at this early date, Capone had a reputation in the public eye. "Molls" was appropriate because baseball players during this era were viewed by the public as rowdy virtual-gangsters. Indeed, their girlfriends, mistresses and wives who attended games at the ballpark were sometimes called the "Molls." With field manager Marty Hogan at the helm, local newspapers called the players the alliterative "Marty's Molls."

2112 Panthers 1940–42 *Wisconsin State (D)*; 1946–53 *Wisconsin State (D)*. With field manager Harry Rice at the helm 1940–41, local newspapers called the players the alliterative "Harry Rice's Panthers." Ray Powell took over in 1943, making the name "Ray Powell's Panthers." Following the end of World War II, official nicknames for minor league professional baseball teams became the rule. Radio was universal, newspapers all used photographs, and television was spreading across the country. An official team nickname was now a marketing necessity.

Forest City, North Carolina

2113 Owls 1948 *Western Carolina (D)*. The Forest Owl inhabits woodlands near the city. With field managers Jess Hill and later in the season Gene Hollifield at the helm, local newspapers called the players the alliterative "Hill's Owls" and "Hollifield's Owls."

Forest City–Spindale, Rutherford, North Carolina

2114 Owls 1949–52 *Western Carolina (D)*; 1953–54 *Tar Heel (D)*; 1960 *Western Carolinas (D)*. Teams of 1949–52 and 1960 went by the county name of Rutherford County Owls. Teams of 1953–54 went by the single city "Forest City Owls." Management chose the four-letter "Owls" to prevent open rebellion by local newspaper editors.

Fort Collins, Colorado

2115 Fort Collins Base Ball Club 1898x *Colorado State (ind.)*. Circuit and team disbanded in mid-season (July 5). Team had no nickname.

Fort Dodge, Iowa

2116 Gypsum-eaters 1904 *Iowa State (D)*. Nearby gypsum mines transported gypsum to processing factories in the city. "Gypsum-eater" is a slang for a gypsum miner.

2117 Gypsumites 1905–06 *Iowa State (D)*. Spin-off moniker. Hydrated calcium sulfate is gypsum, which is used to make "Plaster of Paris." Such names as "Gypsum-eaters" and "Smoke-eaters" were concessions to the dangerous inhalations to which miners and firefighters of this era were exposed. Fort Dodge is nicknamed the "Gypsum City." With field manager Frank Boyle at the helm 1904–06, local newspapers called the players the alliterative "Boyle's Gypsum-eaters" and "Boyle's Gypsumites."

2118 Dodgers 1916–17 *Central Assn. (D)*. Phillies-style moniker. With field manager Paul Turgeon at the helm, local newspapers called the players the alliterative "Turgeon's Dodgers." When Babe Towne took over in mid-season, the name was retained because it was alliterative with the city name, i.e., "Fort Dodge Dodgers," and kept for 1917 as well under manager Charles Stis. Team was not a farm club of the Brooklyn Dodgers.

Fort Lauderdale, Florida

2119 Tarpons 1928m *Florida State (D)*. Team moved to St. Petersburg (FL) May 24; 1940–42x *Florida East Coast (D)*. Team disbanded April 25 because of U.S. entry into World War II. The Tarpon is a herring-like game fish found in the waters off the Florida coast. With field manager Tom Leach at the helm in 1928, local newspapers called the players the alliterative "Tom's Tarpons." With field manager Herb Thomas at the helm in 1940–42, local newspapers called the players "Thomas' Tarpons." When Buster Kinard took over in mid-season 1941 (succeeding Thomas, who would return in 1942) the name became "Kinard's Tarpons."

2120 Braves 1947–52m *Florida International (C 1948, B 1949–52)*. Team moved to Key West June 20, 1952. Farm club of Boston Braves. Team played as an independent in 1949 but kept the Braves name.

2121 Lions 1953 *Florida International (B)*. The only lions in Fort Lauderdale are in the zoo, which means this name was chosen because it was alliterative and short (the city name has 14 letters).

2122 Yankees 1962–92 *Florida State (D 1962, A 1963–92)*. Farm club of New York Yankees.

2123 Red Sox 1963 *Florida State (A)*. Farm club of Boston Red Sox.

Fort Myers, Lee County, Florida

2124 Palms 1926 *Florida State (D)*. The state tree of Florida is the Sabal Palmetto Palm, actually a cabbage palm. Fort Myers is known as the "City of Palms."

2125 Royals 1978–87 *Florida State (A)*; 1996 *Florida State (A)*. Team was a farm club of the Kansas City Royals.

2126 Sun Sox 1989–91x *Senior Assn. (ind.)*. Circuit's full name was the Senior Professional Baseball Association — a circuit for players age 35 or older (catchers could be as young as 30). It was a gimmick that didn't catch on. Florida is the "Sunshine State."

2127 Twins 1989 to date. Team went by the county name of Lee County Twins for the 1993–95 seasons. Farm club of Minnesota Twins.

2128 Miracle 1992 to date *Florida State (A)*. After the 1991 season, new owner Marvin Goldklang moved the Miami "Miracle" to Fort Myers. The team nickname was retained. The moniker continued to be appropriate because Fort Myers is known as the "Jewel City of the Florida West."

2129 Lee County Royals 1992–95 *Gulf Coast (R)*. Team went by the county name of Lee County Royals. Team was a farm club of the Kansas City Royals.

2130 Red Sox 1993 to date *Gulf Coast (R)*. Team is a farm club of the Boston Red Sox.

2131 Cubs 1995–96 *Gulf Coast (R)*. Team was a farm club of the Chicago Cubs.

2132 Twins 1996–99 *Gulf Coast (R)*. Team was a farm club of the Minnesota Twins.

Fort Pierce, Florida

2133 Bombers 1940–42 *Florida East Coast (D)*. With World War II raging in Europe, the U.S. Government began to fund the construction of numerous army, army-air and naval bases along the Florida coast, including the Fort Pierce Army Air Base. City factories started building B-17 bombers for Fort Pierce.

Fort Scott, Kansas

2134 Kickers 1891 *Southwestern (ind.)*. In the nineteenth century a "kicker" was a ball player who argued vehemently with an umpire over a call. Back then as now, the player — forbidden to touch the umpire — would kick dirt on the ump's shoes and trousers. Some notorious "kickers" were Cap Anson, John McGraw and Jim "Orator" O' Rourke.

2135 Giants 1902–04 Missouri Valley *(D 1902–03, C 1904)*; 1906x *Kansas State (D)*. Team disbanded July 5. The team went 80–44 in a hot three-team race for the pennant and grateful fans and newspapers praised the team for "playing like Giants" despite finishing in third place. With field skipper Fred Hornady at the helm 1902–03, local newspapers referred to the players at the alliterative "Hornady's Giants." In the era 1870–1920 teams that won a lot of games were often praised as "Giants." Sometimes, a team that was a "big loser" was also called "Giants" as a term of sarcastic derision. This 1904 squad finished eighth (of eight) with a terrible 36–89 mark, prompting "Giants" to change from a term of endearment to one of contempt. The 1906 team was "playing like Giants," getting off to a hot 35–18 start when the franchise, beset by financial problems, disbanded July 5.

2136 Hay-diggers 1902–04 *Missouri Valley (C)*. Nearby farms produce hay. A "hay-digger" is a slang for farmer.

2137 Jayhawkers 1902–05 Missouri Valley (D 1902–03, C 1904–05). Both blue jays and sparrow hawks fly over the skies of Kansas. Somehow, settlers created a mythical amalgam called the "Jay Hawk." It was this symbol that Colonel Doc Jennison used for his "Jayhawk Battalion" of the Union Army.

2138 Scotties 1906x *Kansas State (D)*. Phillies-style moniker.

Fort Smith, Arkansas

2139 Indians 1887 *Southwestern (ind.)*; 1897 *Arkansas (ind.)*. In 1673, the Quapaw tribe warned explorers Lewis & Clark about hostile tribes to the South, forcing them to turn back. In 1818 the Quapaw were forced by settlers to abandon their land. The "Five Civilized Tribes," i.e., Osage, Cherokee, Chickasaw, Choctaw and Quapaw, were forced out of the state by 1835. Site was a U.S. Army post in 1817 and became a city in 1851.

2140 Electrics 1897 *Arkansas (ind.)*. In the era 1890–1910 hydroelectric power stations were built throughout the United States. In this city a hydroelectric power plant was built along the confluence of the Arkansas and Poteau rivers.

2141 Giants m1905 *Missouri Valley (C)*. As the South McAlester (OK) club skidded into eighth and last place with an losing record, disgruntled fans and reporters there sarcastically called the players "Giants." Franchise then moved here in mid-season and continued to lose, eventually posting a brutal 33–63 record, prompting fans to also deride the players with the sarcastic tag of "Giants." In this era "Giants" was a generic nickname for a winning team but was also used as a term of sarcastic derision for "big losers."

2142 Razorbacks 1906 *South Central (D)*. Arkansas is the "Razorback State." The "Razorback" is a forest hog with a ridge-like back found mostly in the South. The name has been popularized by University of Arkansas collegiate basketball and football teams.

2143 Soldiers 1907x *Oklahoma–Arkansas–Kansas (O.A.K.) (D)*. Team disbanded August 6. City began as an 1835 army base known as Fort Smith.

2144 Scouts 1911 *Western Assn. (D)*. In the nineteenth century Old West "scouts" could be either Indian scouts or U.S. Army scouts. With field manager Arthur Riggs leading the team to a pennant, local newspapers called the players the alliterative "Arthur's Scouts."

2145 Twins 1920–32m Western Assn. (D 1920–21, C 1922–26, B 1927, C 1927–32). Team moved to Muskogee (OK) July 1, 1932. Team represented Fort Smith and Van Buren (AR).

2146 Giants 1938–42 *Western Assn. (C)*; 1946–49 *Western Assn. (C)*. Team was a farm club of the New York Giants. Team resumed operations in 1946 after World War II ended.

2147 Indians 1951–52 *Western Assn. (C)*. Team was a farm club of the Cleveland Indians.

Fort Smith–Van Buren, Arkansas

2148 Twins 1914–17 *Western Assn. (D)*. Team represented Fort Smith and Van Buren (AR).

2149 Indians 1953m *Western Assn. (C)*. Team was a farm club of the Cleveland Indians.

Fort Walton (Beach), Florida

2150 Jets 1953–62 *Alabama–Florida (D)*. Team went by the regional name of Fort Walton Beach Jets. Eglin Air Force Base is nearby.

Fort Wayne, Indiana

2151 Kekiongas 1871 *National Assn. (M)*. Team was named after the Kekionga Indian tribe.

2152 Hoosiers 1883–84 *Northwest (ind.)*. Indiana is the "Hoosier State." The nickname "Hoosiers" was used by several Indiana professional baseball teams in the nineteenth century. By the twentieth century it had become used exclusively by the University of Indiana collegiate and basketball teams.

2153 Corn Sailors 1883–84 *Northwest (ind.)*. Name was coined by the newspaper, the *Bloomington Eye*. A "corn sailor" is slang for a farmer, i.e., "walking through a sea of corn."

2154 Summit Citys 1888 *Indiana State (ind.)*. Fort Wayne became known as the "Summit City" because of its rapid economic development after it was established as a city in 1840. Akron (OH) is known as the "Summit City" because of its elevation above sea level.

2155 Fort Wayne Base Ball Club 1890 *Indiana State (ind.)*; m1892x *Western (ind.)*. Team began season in St. Paul (MN) and moved to Fort Wayne May 25. Team disbanded July 7. These teams had no nickname.

2156 Warriors 1891 *Northwestern (ind.)*. Indiana is the "Land of the Indians." Unfortunately, there was a long history of strife and warfare—the Battle of Fort Miami (1791), Battle of Fallen Timbers (1794), the Battle of Tippecanoe (1811), the Pigeon Root Massacre (1812) and the Expulsion of the Potawatomi (1838).

2157 Jewels 1895 *Interstate (ind.)*. In the nineteenth century cities that enjoyed rapid economic growth, including the construction of beautiful buildings, were sometimes nicknamed the "Gem City" and the "Jewel City." "Summit City"—Fort Wayne's other nickname—usually refers to a city built in the hills or mountains, i.e., Akron (OH). But in the case of Fort Wayne, like "Zenith City" of Duluth (MN), the moniker meant economic success.

2158 Farmers 1896 *Interstate (ind.)*. The city receives produce from the rural farms that is then processed, packed and shipped out. Fort Wayne is known as the "Hub of the Great Northern Central Industrial and Agricultural America."

2159 Indians 1897–1900 *Inter-State (ind.)*. A spin-off from "Kekiongas," and "Warriors."

2160 Railroaders 1901 *Western Assn. (ind.)*; 1903–04 *Central (B)*. By 1855, no less than eight railroad lines had reached Indiana, and by 1900 and all these lines were traveling through Fort Wayne, which soon became a major railroad center. The railroad helped Fort Wayne become the "Gateway to the Northern Indiana Lake Region."

2161 Billikens 1908–10 *Central (B)*. Horsman Dolls, Ltd. Chicago manufactured a popular doll called the "Billiken"—an impish pixie-like elf which along with the "Teddy Bear" were the two best-selling dolls of the era. Fans couldn't relate to the name and local newspapers loathed it. Influenced by the popularity of the "Teddy Bear," a stuffed bear doll patented in honor of popular President Theodore "Teddy" Roosevelt, Florence Petz of St. Louis (MO) created and patented the "Billiken Lucky Charm" doll, which was then manufactured by Horsman Doll Incorporated. The "Billiken," a rather chubby "genie," was inspired by the heavy-set president William

Howard Taft. The Billiken fad lasted only about 10 years whereas "Teddy Bears" are popular to this day. With field manager Jack Hendricks at the helm 1908–09, local newspapers, mindful of the popular Billiken doll fad of the last two years, called the players the alliterative "Jack's Billikens" and "Hendrick's Billikens." James Burke took over in 1910, changing the name to "Burke's Billikens."

2162 Brakies 1908–10 *Central (B)*. Actually the "brakie" was the name given to the fellow who operated the train's brakes, usually from the caboose. The term was originally "brakeman." Team was owned by Fred Zollner's Piston and Brake Company. Zollner later went on to establish the famous Fort Wayne Zollners Pistons pro basketball team in the 1930s, 1940s and 1950s. With field manager Doc Casey at the helm, local newspapers called the players the rhyming and alliterative "Casey's Brakies." Newspapers had given up on the "Billikens" moniker because the fad was subsiding and a shorter name was desired.

2163 Railroaders 1912, 1914 *Central (B)*. By 1860 Indiana had 37 railroad lines operating on Indiana railways. Reporters used the moniker to the consternation of their editors.

2164 Champs 1913 *Central (B)*. Team won the 1912 flag.

2165 Cubs 1915 *Central (B)*. In this era, minor league teams close to a major league city sometimes chose the nickname of the big league team, in this case the Chicago Cubs. In the era 1900–30, minor league teams close to big league cities sometimes established a loose affiliation that involved obtaining used equipment and uniforms and the occasional sale of a player contract.

2166 Chiefs 1917 *Central (B)*; 1928–30 *Central (B)*; 1932 *Central (B)*; 1934 *Central (B)*; 1935 *Three-I (B)*. Pontiac, chief of the Ottawa tribe, wrested control of the fort away from the British in 1790. By 1794 the British had regained the site and built a new fort. With field manager Carl Vandergrift at the helm, local newspapers called the players the alliterative "Carl's Chiefs" and "Vandergrift's Chiefs." None of the four teams of the 1930s were farm clubs of the Cleveland Indians or Boston Braves.

2167 Generals 1948 *Central (D)*. After regaining control of the region back from Chief Pontiac in 1793, British General Anthony Wayne had his troops rebuild Fort Wayne in 1794.

2168 Daiseys 1954 *All-American Girls (ind.)*. Moniker was rhyming, i.e., WAY-DAI- and alliterative, i.e., Fort Wayne Daiseys.

2169 Wizards 1993–2008 *Midwest (A)*. Prior to the inaugural 1993 season, management held a name-the-team contest in which 20,000 entries and 1,500 suggestions were submitted. A Fort Wayne resident submitted the winning name of "Wizards." Other entries included Cavalry, Kekiongas and Sand-baggers.

2170 Tin Caps 2009 to date *Midwest (A)*. The legendary "Johnny Appleseed" was actually a real man named John Chapman (born in 1774 and died in 1845). Chapman was a farmer who pioneered the use of apple tree "nurseries" to spread the planting of apple trees throughout Ohio, Indiana and Illinois. As a quirk, he often wore a tin pot on his head as protection from falling debris and the sun. Nineteenth century Americans admired him so much that they spun yarns about him, calling him "Johnny Appleseed."

Fort William, Ontario

2171 Canadians 1914–15 *Northern (C)*. Nine baseball teams playing in Canadian cities have been known as the "Canadians" or "Canadiens."

2172 Canucks 1914–15 *Northern (C)*. Preferred by newspapers. First coined in 1835, the name originally meant "French Canadian," but today refers to any inhabitant of Canada.

Fort William–Port Arthur, Ontario

2173 Canadians 1916x *Northern (C)*. Team disbanded July 10. The 1915 team went regional in 1916. Team went by the double-city name of Fort Williams–Port Arthur Canadians.

Fort Worth, Texas

2174 Panthers 1888–90 *Texas (ind.)*; 1892 *Texas (ind.)*; 1895 *Texas–Southern (ind.)*; 1896x *Texas–Southern (ind.)*. Team disbanded August 2; 1897–98 *Texas (ind.)*; 1902–33 *Texas (D 1902–05, C 1906–10, B 1911–20, A 1921–33)*. Fort Worth is known as the "Panther City." One legend has it that mountain lions would wander into town looking for food. Another legend describes the "Panther's Den" as an area in town in the 1880s where thieves, bandits and robbers would congregate. "Panther" was a slang for bandit or thief.

2175 Jackrabbits 1889 *Texas (ind.)*. The jackrabbit inhabits western North America from Texas and the plains to the Pacific Coast. Baseball slang for fast-running players. In this era there was a strong emphasis on fast base runners.

2176 Fort Worth Base Ball Club 1890–91 *Texas (W)*; 1903–04 *North Texas (D)*; 1929–31 *Texas–Oklahoma–Louisiana (T.O.L.) (ind.)*. These teams had no nickname.

2177 Wonders 1909 *Independent Negro team*. Alliterative name, i.e., Fort Worth Wonders.

2178 Cats 1932–42 *Texas (A 1932–35, A1 1936–42)*; 1946–58 *Texas (AA)*; 1959 *American (AAA)*; 1964 *Texas (AA)*; 2001 *All-American (ind.)*; 2002–05 *Central (ind.)*; 2006 to date *American Assn. (ind.)*. Newspaper friendly spin-off.

2179 Rangers 1963 *Pacific Coast (AAA)*. After the city was settled in 1849, Texas Rangers started coming into town in the 1870s to look for the "Panthers," i.e., cattle-rustlers, thieves, bandits, bank robbers and murderers who frequented the "Panther's Den."

2180 Blue Thunder 2007–08 *Continental (ind.)*. Team went by the county name of Tarrant County Blue Thunder. Team moved to suburban McKinney (TX) for the 2008 season. McKinney is a suburb of the greater Dallas–Fort Worth metropolitan area. City is a major aircraft manufacture site. Certain military jets, i.e., the Blue Angels, perform in Dallas–Fort Worth, and the helicopter from the 1985 Roy Scheider action movie of the same name is called the "Blue Thunder." A fan poll determined the name.

Fostoria, Ohio

2181 Cardinals 1936 *Ohio State (D)*. Team was a farm club of St. Louis Cardinals.

2182 Redbirds 1937–41 *Ohio State (D)*. "Redbirds" is a popular spin-off from Cardinals.

Frankfort, Indiana

2183 Frankfort Base Ball Club 1885 *Inter-State (ind.)*; 1888 *Indiana State (ind.)*. These teams had no nickname.

Frankfort, Kentucky

2184 Frankfort Base Ball Club 1885x *Inter-State (ind.)*. Circuit and team disbanded June 1. Team had no nickname.

2185 Statesmen 1908–11 *Blue Grass (D)*. State capital of Kentucky. Frankfort is known as the "Blue Grass Capital" and the "Capital City."

2186 Lawmakers 1912 *Blue Grass (D)*. Spin-off from Statesmen. The city has been the state capital of Kentucky since 1792.

2187 Old Taylor 1915–16x *Ohio State (D)*. Team disbanded July 6, 1916. The Old Taylor Whiskey Company ran a distillery in the city.

Franklin, New Hampshire

2188 Franklin Baseball Club 1907 *New Hampshire (ind.)*. Team had no nickname.

Franklin, Pennsylvania

2189 Franklin Baseball Club 1884 *Iron & Oil Assn. (ind.)*. Team had no nickname.

2190 Millionaires 1908x *Inter-State (D)*. Team and league disbanded June 5. Since 1850 wealthy "Coal Barons" have run the coal mines of Pennsylvania. "Millionaires" was an occasional nickname of teams in a city that prospered because of a natural resource like gold, silver, oil, natural gas, lumber or coal. Of course, it was usually the owner who became a millionaire while the workers struggled. With field manager William Smith at the helm, local newspapers called the players the alliterative "Bill's Millionaires."

Franklin, Virginia

2191 Cubs 1948–51 *Virginia (D)*. Young players. Team was not a farm club of the Chicago Cubs. Moniker was conveniently short and alliterative.

2192 Kildees 1949–51 *Virginia (D)*. The Kildee is a shorebird, similar to a seagull, though not the same, that inhabits the Mid-Atlantic shoreline. Also known as a "Plover." Moniker was alliterative, i.e., Franklin Kildees.

Frederick, Maryland

2193 Hustlers 1915–17 *Blue Ridge (D)*; 1920–28 *Blue Ridge (D)*. The 1915 players "hustled their way" to a 53–23 record and a first-place pennant. In the era 1900–30 "Hustlers" was a common slang for a baseball team. In this era it was a complementary tag — i.e., "players who hustled." It wasn't until the 1970s that the name, often associated with gambling, became politically incorrect. Managed by George "Buck" Ramsey 1920–22, the name was "Buck's Hustlers" — especially when the team won the 1921 pennant. Ramsey left the team after 1922 but the name was retained. Under the guidance of field manager Herb Armstrong, the 1924 team, called by local newspapers as "Herb's Hustlers," won the pennant. Buck Ramsey returned in 1925. The 1926 team "hustled" its way into the league playoffs. Henry Sherry took over in 1927–28, leading "Henry's Hustlers."

2194 Warriors 1929–30 *Blue Ridge (D)*. The Nanticoke, Conoy, Powhattan, Shawnee and Susquehannock tribes had been in the region since at least 1500. Between 1634 and 1744 the colonists warred on them and pushed the surviving tribes out of Maryland. The direct origin of the moniker was field manager Bob Wells. Local newspapers dubbed the team "Well's Warriors."

2195 Keys 1989 to date *Carolina (A)*. Francis Scott Key, the composer of "The Star Spangled Banner," maintained his residence in this city. Management held a name-the-team contest just prior to the 1989 season with Frederick resident Bob Reed submitting the winning entry of "Keys." Other entries included Falcons, Flames, Flintstones and Flyers.

Fredericton, New Brunswick, Canada

2196 Fredericton Base Ball Club 1890 *New Brunswick (ind.)*. Team had no nickname.

2197 Pets 1913 *New Brunswick–Maine (D)*. In the era 1885–1915 players were sometimes called the "pets" of the field manager. Thus we have "McGraw's Pets" (John McGraw) and "Mack's Pets" (Connie Mack). But, in cities like Fredericton and Pendleton (OR), the motive was a short and alliterative moniker to compensate for a city name of 10 letters or more. For this team, local newspapers wanted a name that was short and alliterative, i.e., Fredericton Pets.

Freeport, Illinois

2198 Pretzels 1905–06 *Wisconsin State (D)*. Circuit was designated Association in 1905 and League in 1906; 1907 *Wisconsin State (D)*; 1908–09 *Wisconsin–Illinois (D)*; 1910 *Northern Assn. of Baseball (D)*; 1915 *Bi-State (D)*. With numerous pretzel factories, Freeport is nicknamed the "Pretzel City." Moniker was also alliterative, i.e., Freeport Pretzels.

2199 Come-Ons 1915 *Bi-State (D)*. From seemingly time immemorial, fans would yell to players "Come On!" sometimes in expectant cheering, although just as often in disgusted reproof, i.e., "Oh! … the ball went between his legs … come on!" As such, the term referred to players for the period 1900 to about 1930. But the direct origin of "Come-Ons" was that the moniker was used by local newspapers for 1915 field manager Doug Cummings, i.e., "Cummings' Come-Ons."

Fremont, Nebraska

2200 Freaks 1892 *Nebraska State (ind.)*. No, the moniker has nothing to do with 1960s hippies. But baseball players in the Nineteenth century were often "freakish"-looking individuals — scruffy, unshaven, hairy, pot-bellied, unwashed, liquor-smelling rowdies. The nickname was an obvious rhyme.

2201 Pathfinders 1910–13 *Nebraska State (D)*. Meriwether Lewis and William Clark, exploring the Louisiana Territory in 1806, explored Nebraska along the Mississippi River. Fur traders and steam boats soon thereafter explored and settled the region. By winning the 1910 pennant, the players were "pathfinders," leading their happy fans to "pennant-land." Led by manager Dad Bennett, newspapers called the players the alliterative "Dad Bennett's Pathfinders." Name was retained.

Fremont, Ohio

2202 Reds 1936–38m *Ohio State (D)*. Team was a farm club of the Cincinnati Reds.

2203 Green Sox 1938m *Ohio State (D)*. Trim colors were changed in mid-season 1938. Color switch was done to avoid confusion with the nearby parent club Cincinnati Reds and to give the team its own identity.

French Lick, Indiana

2204 Plutos 1913–14 *Independent Negro team*. Because of nearby sulfur springs, the city became a resort city in this era. The sulfur springs emit a yellowish vapor that invokes images of the Greco-Roman God Pluto's fabled *Underworld*. Moniker was also alliterative, i.e., French Lick Plutos.

Fresnillo, Zacatecas, Mexico

2205 Mineros 1956 *Central Mexican (D)*. Founded in 1554, silver was discovered here in the eighteenth century. The city has a school of mining to train future miners. Minero is Spanish for miner.

2206 Rojos 1957 *Central Mexican (D)*; 1962 *Mexican Center (D)*. The teams were farm teams of the Mexico City Reds. Rojo in Spanish means red.

2207 Charos 1964 *Mexican Center (A)*. Zacatecas has numerous cattle ranches where cowboys herd the steers.

2208 Mineros 1965–66 *Mexican Center (A)*. Nearby silver mines transport silver ore to processing factories in the city.

2209 Tuzos 1967–68 *Mexican Center (A)*; 1976–78 *Mexican Center (A)*. In Spanish "El Tuzo," which literally means a gopher, is a slang for a "miner."

Fresno, California

2210 Corkers 1891–92 *California (W)*. Fresno is noted for its wine industry. A "corker" is slang for a wine maker. Also, in the nineteenth century, the word meant a remarkable feat, i.e., "That catch the center fielder made was a corker!" Fresno is known as the "Sweet Wine Capital of the World." Moniker was alliterative, i.e., Fresno Corkers.

2211 Republicans 1898 *California (ind.)*. In the Nineteenth century, an inhabitant of California was known as a "Republican" because the state's official name is the "Republic of California." The name had nothing to do with the national Republican Party.

2212 Tigers 1898 *California (ind.)*; 1908–09 *California (ind.)*; 1910x *California State (D)*. Team and league disbanded June 24; 1913–14x *California State (D)*. The Fresno players wore striped hose. Inspired by the striped stockings of the 1890 Princeton University football team, striped stockings became fashionable as dozens of sports teams copied the design. The invariable name that followed the hosiery was "Tigers."

2213 Raisin Eaters 1906 *Pacific Coast (A)*; 1908–09 *California (ind.)*. Raisin farms in the surrounding area routinely transport the dried fruit to be packed in city plants prior to national distribution. Fresno is the "Raisin Center of the World." Aka **Raisin Growers** in 1909.

2214 Packers 1913 *California State (D)*. Although raisins dried from California grapes is the most prevalent produce, other fruits are packed in warehouses in the city, i.e., oranges, lemons, limes, grapefruit, etc.

2215 Sun Maids 1918–19 *So. California (W)*. The Sun Maid Raisin Company owned the team. "Sun Maids" was a nickname given to the women who worked the vineyard fields picking grapes and raisins.

2216 Cardinals 1941–42 *California (C)*; 1946–56 *California (C)*. Teams were farm clubs of the St. Louis Cardinals.

2217 Tigers 1946 *West Coast Baseball Assn. (ind.)*. Players wore striped stockings.

2218 Sun Sox 1957 *California (C)*. Sunny California. Team played as an independent in 1957, which required a different nickname. Some "sox" nicknames are amalgams, i.e., Bay Sox, BoSox, ChiSox, PawSox, Sky Sox and Sun Sox.

2219 Giants 1957 *California (C 1957–62, A 1963–87)*. Farm club of the San Francisco Giants.

2220 Suns 1988 *California (A)*. California is noted for its sunny weather. The standing joke is that "it never rains in California!"

2221 Grizzlies 1998 to date *Pacific Coast (AAA)*. The state flag displays the California golden bear, which is actually the North American brown bear and is the state symbol of California. The brown bear, also called the grizzly bear, inhabits California's national parks and forests, i.e., Klamath, Modoc, Lassen, Yosemite, Sequoia, Los Padres and the northwest Marble Mountains.

Frisco, Texas

2222 Roughriders 2003 to date *Texas (AA)*. Long before "Teddy Roosevelt's Roughriders" of 1898, Texas roughriders worked at ranches breaking horses by riding these bucking broncos until they became tame. Eventually the term evolved into referring to any "hard riders," i.e., cowboys, outlaws, pioneers, settlers, explorers, wanderers, Pony Express riders, army scouts, army patrols and posses on the harsh Texas plains. Team is a farm club of the Texas Rangers and the nicknames are related, as both refer to mounted forces under the auspices of the federal government.

Frostburg, Maryland

2223 Demons 1916x *Potomac (D)*. Demons who lurk about in fiery brimstone and hellish flames might not play baseball in the frost. But this bunch "played like demons" en route to a 33–25 first-place finish when the league disbanded on August 16. Moniker originally was an ironic play on words that soon became appropriate as the team reached first place.

Fruitvale, California

2224 Fruitvale Baseball Club m1910–11m *Central (C 1910, D 1910–11)*. Team had no nickname.

Fujidera, Shizuoka, Japan

2225 Buffaloes 1962 to date *Japanese Eastern (ind.)*. Farm club of the Kintetsu Buffaloes.

Fukuoka, Fukuoka, Japan

2226 Lions 1973–74, 1976–78 *Japanese Pacific (ind.)*. The Taiheiyo Cement Company bought the Tokyo Nishitetsu Lions franchise after the 1972 season and moved the team to Fukuoka for the 1973 season, where the team became the Fukuoka "Taiheiyo Lions." In 1977, Crown Lighter Company bought the team and kept the "Lions" moniker. Two years later, Seibu Department Stores bought the franchise and moved the team to the city of Tokorozawa for the 1979 season as the Tokorozawa "Seibu Lions." The nickname originated in 1950 with the first publication of the Japanese comic book—*Kimba the White Lion*. By the 1960s, *Kimba the White Lion* became a TV cartoon series that remains a popular to this day.

2227 Flyers 1975 *Japanese Pacific (ind.)*. The venerable Lions name was replaced this one season by "Flyers," making the team's official title "Taiheiyo Flyers." Fans much preferred "Lions," and its trendy logo/mascot, so it was switched back to "Lions" in 1976.

2228 Hawks 1989 to date *Japanese Pacific (ind.)*; 2005 to date. *Japanese Western (ind.)*. The Osaka Nankai Hawks moved to Fukuoka for the 1989 season. The team became the Fukuoka Daiei Hawks. Changes in ownership dictated new formal titles as follows: Daiei Hawks, 1989–97, and the Softbank Hawks, 1998 to date. The Western League team moved to Gannosu, a suburb of Fukuoka for 2006 to play as a farm club of Pacific League Hawks. The minor league team is run by Softbank, 2005 to date.

Fullerton, California

2229 Flyers 2005–10 *Golden (ind.)*; 2011 to date *North American (ind.)*. Team goes by the county name of Orange County Flyers. The Golden, Northern and United leagues merged to form the North American League for 2012. After the 2006 season team switched to the county name of Orange County Flyers. The city has manufactured airplanes here since 1940. However, the team logo depicts a train "Flyer" hearkening back to the 1890s when western railroads arrived in Southern California cities. Express trains in the Nineteenth century, including those in California, were often given romantic nicknames such as Chief, Comet, Eagle, Flyer, Mogul, Rocket and Super-Chief.

Fulton, Kentucky

2230 Colonels 1911 *Kentucky–Illinois–Tennessee (KITTY). (D).* After the famous "Kentucky Colonels," an honorary title bestowed by the state governor on its leading citizens since 1815. Moniker was also alliterative, i.e., Fulton Colonels.

2231 Railroaders 1922–24 *Kentucky–Illinois–Tennessee (KITTY) (D)*; 1949–51 *Kentucky–Illinois–Tennessee (KITTY) (D)*. The city is an important stop for the Lexington & Ohio and Louisville & Nashville railroads. With manager Ralph Works at the helm, newspapers called the players "Ralph's Railroaders." In mid-season Works left the team, which was handed to Senter Rainey, prompting the papers to call the players "Rainey's Railroaders." Nickname was retained 1923–24 and used again 1949–51.

2232 Eagles 1936–38 *Kentucky–Illinois–Tennessee (KITTY) (D)*. The symbol of Franklin Roosevelt's National Recovery Act work program was an eagle that was used by baseball teams (i.e., Newark Eagles) and football teams (i.e., Philadelphia Eagles) as well as the Fulton Eagles. The direct origin of the nickname was field manager Norman Elberfeld. Newspapers called the players "Elberfeld's Eagles." Nickname was retained 1937–38.

2233 Tigers 1939–42x *Kentucky–Illinois–Tennessee (KITTY) (D)*. Team and league disbanded June 19, 1942, because of U.S. entry into World War II. Farm club of Detroit Tigers.

2234 Bulldogs 1946 *Kentucky–Illinois–Tennessee (KITTY) (D)*. Moniker was alliterative with "Fulton." Also four Southern colleges were using bulldog mascots at the time—North Carolina, James Madison, North Carolina A &T and South Carolina State.

2235 Chicks 1947–48 *Kentucky–Illinois–Tennessee (KITTY) (D)*. Young players.

2236 Lookouts 1952–55 *Kentucky–Illinois–Tennessee (KITTY) (D)*. Team was a farm club of the Chattanooga Lookouts. In the period 1910–60 some lower classification (A, B, C, D) minor league teams were farm clubs of a higher classification (AA, AAA) minor league team.

Gadsden, Alabama

2237 Steelmakers 1910–12 *Southeastern (D)*; 1913–14r *Georgia–Alabama (D)*. Team, due to low attendance at home, became a road club August 3. City is an iron and steel processing center that receives shipments of iron ore from nearby mines that were discovered when the city was established in 1840. With manager Paul Stevenson at the helm in 1910, newspapers called the players "Stevenson's Steelmakers." John Siegel became manager in 1912 and the name became "Siegel's Steelmakers."

2238 Pilots 1938–41r *Southeastern (B)*. Team, due to low attendance as people became distracted by the war, became a road club July 8; 1946–48, 1950 *Southeastern (B)*. Team disbanded August 1, 1950. Pilot boats have directed traffic on the nearby Coosa River since 1870. Gadsden is home to the Alabama Aviation College since 1937. With field manager Bill Morell at the helm in 1938, local newspapers called the players the alliterative "Morell's Pilots." After Morell left the team, following the 1938 season, the nickname was retained.

2239 Chiefs 1949 *Southeastern (B)*. In the Battle of Mauvilla on October 18, 1540, Hernando De Soto's Spanish forces defeated Chief Tuscaloosa's Talladega Indians. Tuscaloosa was killed in battle. It was one of the first battles of the wars between Europeans and Native Americans.

Gainesville, Florida

2240 Gainesville Base Ball Club 1890–91 *Florida Winter (W)*. Team had no nickname.

2241 Sharks m1915 *Florida–Louisiana–Alabama–Georgia (F.L.A.G.). (D)*. Team started season in Americus (GA) and moved to Gainesville May 31. Sharks swim in the coastal waters of the region. With manager Oscar Baker at the helm for the team, local newspapers called the players the alliterative "Oscar Baker's Sharks."

2242 G-Men 1936–41 *Florida State (D)*; 1946–52x *Florida State (D)*. Team disbanded June 2; 1955–58 *Florida State (D)*. In the 1930s there was a popular radio show called *Tales of the G-Men*. "G-Men" was a nickname for government (federal) agents, who battled everything from organized crime and bootleggers to spies and saboteurs during the 1920s and 1930s.

Gainesville, Texas

2243 Gainesville Base Ball Club 1892 *Texas (ind.)*. Team had no nickname.

2244 Blue Ribbons 1911x *Texas–Oklahoma (D)*. Team disbanded June 14, 1911. Gainesville sponsors an annual livestock show where winners receive a blue ribbon. In this era "blue ribbon" described baseball teams that played well. Players wore blue-trim uniforms and blue stirrups. With manager John Stone at the helm, newspapers called the players "John Stone's Blue Ribbons." George Morris took over in mid-season and the name became "George Morris' Blue Ribbons."

2245 Owls 1947–51 *Big State (B)*; 1953–55m *Sooner State (D)*. Team moved to Ponca City (OK) May 19. Owls inhabit the numerous forested state parks of Northern Texas. With manager Leroy Gilchrist at the helm, newspapers called the players "Leroy Gilchrist's Owls."

Galax, Virginia

2246 Leafs 1946–50 *Blue Ridge (D)*. Tobacco farms in the region transport tobacco leaves to city processing and packing houses. Just as ice hockey teams are called "Leafs," i.e., Toronto Maple Leafs, six professional baseball teams were known as Leafs, i.e., "tobacco" leafs.

Galesburg, Illinois

2247 Galesburg 1890 *Illinois–Iowa (ind.)*. The circuit was also known as the *Central Interstate and Western Interstate*; 1895 *Indiana State (ind.)*. These teams had no nickname.

2248 Hornets 1908 *Illinois–Missouri (D)*. With manager Clyde Horne at the helm, newspapers called the players "Horne's Hornets."

2249 Boosters 1909 *Illinois–Missouri (D)*. "Boosters" and "Giants" were nicknames associated with winning teams in this era. Fans here formed a booster club hoping for a winning season and even pennant contention, but they could not "boost" the players, as they played poorly, going 47–83 and winding up in last place. Future Hall of Fame pitcher Grover Cleveland Alexander was a member of the Galesburg pitching staff this season.

2250 Pavers 1910–12 *Central Assn. (D)*; m1914 *Central Assn. (D)*. Team started season in Ottumwa (IA), then moved to Rock Island (IL) July 17. Because of a territorial dispute, they moved back to Galesburg July 24. City was home to the Purington Paving Brick Company. With manager Bert Hough at the helm 1910–11, newspapers called the players "Bert's Pavers." Ducky Eberts took over in 1912 and the name became "Ebert's Pavers."

Galt, Ontario, Canada

2251 Galt Base Ball Club 1896 *Canadian (ind.)*. Team had no nickname.

Galveston, Texas

2252 Giants 1888 *Texas (ind.)*. At the time the New York Giants were probably the best known baseball team in the world en route to two consecutive world titles. Numerous teams in this era emulated the New Yorkers by adopting their moniker.

2253 Sandcrabs 1889–90 *Texas (ind.)*; 1892 *Texas (ind.)*; 1895–96 *Texas (ind.)*; 1898–99 *Texas (ind.)*; 1903–06 *South Texas (C)*; 1907–17x *Texas (C 1907–10, B 1911–12)*; 1922–24 *Texas (A)*. Sand crabs inhabit the sandy beaches and dunes along Galveston Bay and the Texas shores along the Gulf of Mexico. Newspapers often shortened the name to **Crabs**.

2254 Galveston Base Ball Club 1890–91 *Texas Winter (W)*. Team had no nickname.

2255 Pirates 1912–17x *Texas (B)*. Team was forced to drop out August 14, 1915, when a hurricane destroyed its ballpark. However, the franchise did not disband and returned to play in 1916. Team disbanded May 18 due to U.S. entry into World War I; 1919–21 *Texas (B)*; 1931–37 *Texas (A 1931–35, A1 1936–37)*. Pirates and buccaneers sailed the Caribbean and the Bay of Galveston as far back as the seventeenth century. In the years 1817–21, French buccaneer Jean Lafite, using this region as a rendezvous point, led his lads in the ship known as the *Baratari Bay* on numerous raids of ships and cities.

2256 Buccaneers 1931–37 *Texas (A 1931–35, A1 1936–37)*. Moniker was a spin-off from Pirates. Newspapers, to avoid confusion with the NL Pittsburgh Pirates, switched to "Buccaneers," which could easily be shortened to "Bucs." Team was not a farm club of the Pittsburgh Pirates. With Del Pratt at the helm in 1931–32, players were called "Del Pratt's Buccaneers." Bill Webb took over in 1933 and the name became "Bill Webb's Buccaneers." Name was retained through 1937.

2257 White Caps 1950–53 *Gulf Coast (C 1950, B 1951–53)*; 1954–55x *Big State (B)*. Team disbanded June 12. In 1900 a hurricane struck Galveston, killing an estimated 6,000 people. Other severe hurricanes hit here in 1961 and in the 1980s. These storms create the proverbial "white caps" as turbulent waves appear. Players wore all-white caps. Since 1967, Galveston College teams have also been known as the "White Caps."

Gary, Indiana

2258 Sand Fleas 1910 *Indiana–Michigan (D)*. Every summer, sand flies are found at the nearby beaches of the Indiana Dunes and Miller Beach on the shores of Lake Michigan. With manager F. E. Copeland at the helm, newspapers called the players "F. E. Copeland's Sand Fleas."

2259 Southern Shore Rail Cats 2002–10 *Northern (ind.)*; 2011 to date *American Assn. (ind.)*. The city is located on the shores of the Southern tip of Lake Michigan. Gary was an important rail city. Cats was a popular tag in this era.

Gastonia, North Carolina

2260 Comers m1923 *South Atlantic (B)*. Team started season as the Columbia "Comers," before transferring to Gastonia July 26. The nickname was retained.

2261 Cardinals m1938 only *North Carolina (D)*; 1939–40 *Tar Heel (D)*. Team started season as Shelby Cardinals and moved to Gastonia where the team, still a St. Louis NL farm club, retained the name of Cardinals.

2262 Browns 1950 *Western Carolina (D)*. The cash-strapped AL St. Louis Browns formed a loose affiliation with Gastonia. In this era, with televised games, teams like the Boston Braves, Philadelphia Athletics and St. Louis Browns could not remain solvent in what were once two-team metropolitan areas.

2263 Rockets 1952–53 *Tri-State (B)*. Gastonia was the site of the Rocket Tire Company. Name became appropriate when the players "rocketed" to an 89–50 record, good for first place. In the period 1947–52 Rockets became a popular nickname because of the U.S. public's fascination with the German V-2 and UFO's, i.e., "Flying Saucers."

2264 Pirates m1959 *South Atlantic (A)*. Team began season in Columbus (GA) before moving to Gastonia July 6; 1963–70 *Western Carolinas (A)*; 1972 *Western Carolinas (A)*. Teams were farm clubs of the Pittsburgh Pirates.

2265 Rippers 1960 *Western Carolinas (A)*. An old legend tells of Rip Van Winkle, who fell asleep seated against a tree, only to wake up 20 years later and find out how things had changed. North Carolina is nicknamed the "Rip Van Winkle State" since this legend originated here. "Ripper" is a baseball slang describing a strong hitter who "rips" long drives. Local newspapers complained the players were asleep on the field "like Rip Van Winkle" as the team "sleepwalked" to a somnolent 36–62 eighth-place finish. The Deere Moving Equipment Company of Gastonia manufactures "The Ripper," a very large two-ton vehicular digger for construction sites.

2266 Rangers 1973–74 *Western Carolinas (A)*; 1987–92 *South Atlantic (A)*. Teams were farm clubs of the Texas Rangers.

2267 Cardinals 1977–82 *Western Carolinas (A)*. Team was a farm club of the St. Louis Cardinals.

2268 Expos 1983–84 *Western Carolinas (A)*. Team was a farm club of the Montreal Expos.

2269 Jets 1985 *Western Carolinas (A)*. The city has several factories that manufacture airplane engines. Name was a spin-off from the 1953 "Rockets" nickname as well. Name was dropped over fear of a possible lawsuit by the NFL New York Jets.

2270 Tigers 1986 *Western Carolinas (A)*. Team was a farm club of the Detroit Tigers.

2271 Gastonia County King Cougars 1995x *Atlantic Coast (ind.)*. In the nineteenth century cougars were often mistaken for bears because they grew so big. The "King Cougar" is an exceptionally big mountain lion, much like the "King of the Beasts" of North America. Moniker was a revival of the American Basketball Association Carolina Cougars of 1969–70–73–74 and a spin-off of the NFL Carolina Panthers.

Gate City, Virginia

2272 Pioneers 1990 *Pioneer (R)*. Pioneer Daniel Boone explored this region from 1769–71, establishing the Cumberland Gap Trail. Virginia, the first state settled in 1609, attracted so many pioneers that it became known as the "Beckoning Land."

Geneva, Alabama

2273 Redbirds 1946–50 *Alabama State (D)*. The 1946 team was a farm club of the Boston Red Sox, who provided the Geneva players with red-trim uniforms, including red stirrups. But management refused to call the Geneva players "Red Sox," instead going with "Redbirds" in anticipation of an affiliation with the NL St. Louis Cardinals.

In 1947 the team formed a loose affiliation with the NL Cardinals before becoming an official farm club of the team in 1950.

Geneva, Kane, Illinois

2274 Kane County Cougars 1991 to date *Midwest (A)*. Mountain lions inhabited Illinois until about 1850. Since the 1970s, cougar sightings in Illinois have increased. The *Chicago Tribune* of November 2, 1990, reported that management chose the name for the team. Also, the World Hockey Association Chicago Cougars played professional ice hockey in Chicago from 1972–73–73–74.

Geneva, New York

2275 Red Stockings 1897 *New York State (ind.)*. Player wore red hose. Originally "Red Stockings," local newspapers quickly shortened it to **Reds**.

2276 Redbirds 1947 *Border (C)*. Players wore red-trim uniforms and red stirrups. Tag was a spin-off from 1897 "Red Stockings" name. Team was not a farm club of the St. Louis Cardinals.

2277 Robins 1948–51x *Border (C)*. Team disbanded June 26, 1951. Team was a farm club of the Brooklyn Dodgers. Although there are plenty of robins in New York State, the moniker hearkens back to the old Brooklyn "Robins" of 1914–31, managed by Wilbert Robinson, before the parent club was renamed Dodgers in 1932.

2278 Redlegs 1958–62 *New York–Pennsylvania (D 1958–62, A 1963–72)*. Team was a farm club of the Cincinnati Redlegs.

2279 Senators 1963–68, 1970–72 *New York–Pennsylvania (A)*. Team was a farm club of the Washington Senators.

2280 Pirates 1969 *New York–Pennsylvania (A)*. Team was a farm club of the Pittsburgh Pirates.

2281 Rangers 1972 *New York–Pennsylvania (A)*. Team was a farm club of the Texas Rangers.

2282 Twins 1973 *New York–Pennsylvania (A)*. Team was a farm club of the Minnesota Twins.

2283 Cubs 1977–93 *New York–Pennsylvania (A)*. Team was a farm club of the Chicago Cubs.

Georgetown, Texas

2284 Collegians 1914 *Middle Texas (D)*. Southwestern University was built here in 1840. With manager James Callahan at the helm, newspapers called the players "Callahan's Collegians." Some of the players on the professional team also played baseball with Georgetown's college team.

2285 Pedagogues 1914 *Middle Texas (D)*. Tag was a spin-off from "Collegians." Pedagogue refers to a teacher, usually a college-level professor. Newspaper editors hated both monikers. Although this Middle Texas League team was Georgetown's only foray into professional baseball, the name continued to be used by the Georgetown college baseball team.

Gettysburg, Pennsylvania

2286 Patriots 1915 *Blue Ridge (D)*. Battle of Gettysburg, in which Meade's Union troops turned back Lee's Rebel forces, was fought here July 1–3, 1863. Reporters decided to use a moniker than honored both sides' patriotism to their respective causes. With manager Ira Planck at the helm, newspapers called the players "Planck's Patriots." Name also was influenced by the looming U.S. entry into World War I.

2287 Ponies 1916–17 *Blue Ridge (D)*. Manager Ira Planck was at the helm and newspapers, dropping "Patriots," called this team's

players "Planck's Ponies." In 1917, the word "rookie" (first appearing in the English language in 1892) became popular, replacing all other baseball slang for a young player, i.e., Babes, Colts, Cubs, etc. This nickname gave rise to the youth baseball organization known as "Pony League," which was established in 1950.

Gezer Modi'in, Israel

2288 Miracle 2007 *Israeli Professional (ind.)*. Biblical legend has it that oil lamps miraculously burned, even after their oil ran out, allowing the Israelites to cook food and forge weapons to battle the Assyrians for their freedom in the fifth century B.C. The team and the circuit disbanded after the 2007 season.

Gillette, Colorado

2289 Gillette Base Ball Club 1896x *Colorado State (ind.)*. Team had no nickname.

Girard, Pennsylvania

2290 Sailors 1908m *Ohio–Pennsylvania (C)*. Team moved to Butler (PA) May 19. Naval Commander Stephen Girard, after whom the city was named, led the Colonial Navy in battle against the British Royal Navy during the Revolutionary War of 1776–81. The city is also a shipping port of Lake Erie. With manager Daniel Koster at the helm, newspapers called the players "Daniel Koster's Sailors."

Glace Bay, Nova Scotia, Canada

2291 Miners 1937–39 *Cape Breton Colliery (D)*. 1937–38, (C). 1939. Colliery is an Old English word for "Coal Town." Hence, this circuit was a "Coal Miners'" League. Glace Bay is a coal mining town. With manager Fred Maguire at the helm in 1937, newspapers called the players "Maguire's Miners." Maguire left the team following the 1937 season but the nickname was retained. Ray Moore took over in 1939, making the name "Moore's Miners."

Gladewater, Texas

2292 Bears m1935 *West Dixie (C)*. Team started the season in Shreveport (LA) and then moved to Gladewater June 4; 1936 *East Texas (C)*; 1948 *Lone Star (C)*; 1949–50 *East Texas (C)*. Grizzly and brown bears continue to inhabit Texas. These teams picked up the moniker of Baylor University "Bears." With manager Neal Rabe at the helm in 1935, newspapers called the players the alliteratively perfect "Rabe's Bears."

Glendale, California

2293 Glendale Baseball Club 1923–24–24–25 *Southern California (W)*. Team had no nickname.

Glens Falls, New York

2294 White Sox 1980–85 *Eastern (AA)*. Team was a farm club of the Chicago White Sox.

2295 Tigers 1986–88 *Eastern (AA)*. Team was a farm club of the Detroit Tigers.

2296 Redbirds 1993 *New York–Pennsylvania (A)*. Team was a farm club of the St. Louis Cardinals.

Glens Falls–Saratoga Springs, New York

2297 Tri-Countys 1906 *Hudson River (C)*. Team went by the name of Glens Falls–Saratoga Tri-Countys. All home games were played in Glens Falls. Team represented three counties: Washington, Saratoga and Warren.

2298 Glens Falls–Saratoga Springs Baseball Club 1906 *Hudson River (C)*. Team's official title was used at the season's start.

2299 Rams 1906 *Hudson River (C)*. With field manager Henry Ramsey at the helm, newspapers called the team players Ramsey's Rams.

2300 Adirondack Lumberjacks 1995–98 *Northeast (ind.)*; 1999–2002 *Northern (ind.)*. Even before the city was established in 1908, the lumber industry in the nearby Adirondack Mountains, had been thriving since settlers first arrived in the region in 1760. Glens Falls is the "Gateway to the Adirondacks." Management chose the title because of the obvious rhyme.

Glenwood, Colorado
(known as Glenwood Springs today)

2301 Glenwood Baseball Club 1898x *Colorado State (ind.)*. Team disbanded in mid-season (c. July 5). Team had no nickname.

Globe, Arizona

2302 Bears 1929–31 *Arizona State (D)*. There are some wild bears in Arizona. With manager Mickey Shader at the helm, newspapers called the players "Shader's Bears."

Globe-Claypool-Miami, Arizona

2303 Browns 1947–50 *Arizona–Texas (C)*. Team was a farm club of the St. Louis Browns. The Globe-Miami team played independently in 1950 because the AL Browns were cash-strapped. However, the players continued to wear old St. Louis Browns home uniforms.

2304 Miners 1955 *Arizona–Mexico (C)*. No other U.S. city has so many types of mineral mines, i.e., silver, gold, asbestos, manganese, vanadium, tungsten and copper. Nearby Gila County copper mines transport copper ore to city factories for processing. Globe is the "Capital City of the County with a Copper Bottom." Team, representing all three cities, went by the dual city name of "Globe-Miami Miners" and played its home games in Globe.

Gloucester, Massachusetts

2305 Hillies m1929 *New England (B)*. Team began season in Haverhill (MA) as the Haverhill "Hillies," then moved to Fitchburg (MA) June 28 to play as the "Wanderers" before moving to Gloucester August 25. When the team arrived in Gloucester, the "Hillies" moniker was restored because the city was built near the Cape Anne Hills. Led by manager Jack Driscoll, newspapers called the players "Driscoll's Hillies."

Gloversville, New York

2306 Gloversville Base Ball Club m1890 *New York State (ind.)*. Team began season in Johnstown (NY) before moving to Gloversville July 2. Team had no nickname.

2307 Mitten Makers 1895 *New York State (ind.)*. The city got its name because the first big industry was glove manufacturing, including mittens. The city was named in 1760 by its founder, Sir William Johnson, as "Glove's Ville."

2308 Hyphens 1903–04 *New York State (B)*. Newspaper editors, tired of using precious space with a team named the Johnstown-Amsterdam-Gloversville Baseball Club, jokingly called the team the "Hyphens." The nickname worked for two years. With manager William Hazleton at the helm in 1903, newspapers called the players "Hazleton's Hyphens." Howard Earl took over in 1904 and the name became "Howard's Hyphens." Team played in JAG Park (aka Parkhurst Field) in Gloversville.

2309 Cuban Giants 1908 *Independent Negro team*. After the old Cuban Giants disbanded following the 1900 season, this new team picked up the moniker. Team also played home games in York (PA) and Ansonia (CT), which were once home cities of the Cuban Giants.

2310 Glovers 1937 *Canadian–American (C)*. Moniker was a shorter spin-off from "Mitten-makers." City got its name in 1760 because of its numerous glove-manufacturing shops.

Gloversville-Johnstown, New York

2311 Glovers 1938–42 *Canadian–American (C)*. Team went by the dual-city name of Gloversville-Johnstown Glovers. Moniker was used for newspaper headlines, i.e., "Glovers edge Blue Sox, 4–3."

Gold Coast City, Queensland, Australia

2312 Dolphins 1990–91–92–93 *Australian (W)*. Dolphins swim along the coastal waters of Queensland.

2313 Cougars 1993–94–98–99 *Australian (W)*. Team went by the regional name of "East Coast Cougars" in 1993–94–94–95 and then went back to the city name of "Gold Coast Cougars" in 1995–96–98–99. Although there are no cougars indigenous to Australia, the name was chosen because it was energetic and had an attractive tawny gold mascot.

Goldsboro, North Carolina

2314 Giants 1908–10 *Eastern Carolina (D)*. Circuit was designated League 1908–09 and Association in 1910. In the period 1890–1920, "Giants" was a popular choice for teams. With manager H. E. Kling at the helm in 1908–09, newspapers called the players "Kling's Giants." King Kelly took over in 1910, making the alliteration "King's Giants."

2315 Manufacturers 1928 *Eastern Carolina (D)*. Raw tobacco from nearby farms was shipped to the city be processed for cigarettes and cigars.

2316 Goldbugs 1929 *Eastern Carolina (D)*. Moniker was used for newspaper headlines, i.e., "Goldbugs edge Hornets, 4–3." There is an insect in the South called the "Golden Beetle." Jim Teague managed "Teague's Goldbugs."

2317 Cardinals 1950–51 *Coastal Plain (D)*. The team was a farm club of the St. Louis Cardinals.

2318 Jets 1952 *Coastal Plain (D)*. The city is home to Seymour Air Force Base, which was established in 1946.

Gomez Palacio, Union Laguna, Mexico

2319 Algodoneros de Union Laguna 1970–74 *Mexican (AAA)*. Local cotton farms transport cotton to city processing and packing houses. "Los algodoneros" is Spanish for cotton-pickers, cotton farmers, or cotton-growers.

Goodyear, Arizona

2320 Indians 2009–10 *Arizona (R)*. Team was a farm club of the Cleveland Indians. Team moved to Phoenix (AZ) for the 2011 season.

2321 Reds 2010 *Arizona (R)*. Team was a farm club of the Cincinnati Reds. Team moved to Phoenix (AZ) for the 2011 season.

Gorman, Texas

2322 Buddies 1920 *West Texas (D)*. With manager Bert Hise at the helm, newspapers called the players "Bert Hise's Buddies." Moniker was a less-condescending spin-off from "Pets" and "Favorites." Baseball players of the twentieth century were beginning to be less subservient to managers and team officials.

Graceville, Florida

2323 Boll Weevils m1952 *Alabama–Florida (D)*. Team began season in Enterprise (AL) and then moved to Graceville July 5. The boll weevil is the scourge of the Dixie cotton crop since cotton was first cultivated in the region around 1700. The insect also ravages Florida's citrus fruit crop. With manager Ed Mitchell at the helm, newspapers called the players "Mitchell's Boll Weevils."

2324 Oilers 1953–58 *Alabama–Florida (D)*. Team had a loose affiliation with the Class AA Tulsa Oilers. Although there is no oil in this region, oil and natural gas from Texas, Oklahoma and the Gulf of Mexico are shipped here for processing in petrochemical refineries. With manager Holt "Cat" Milner at the helm in 1953–54, newspapers called the players "Holt Milner's Oilers." Name was retained through 1958.

Grafton, West Virginia

2325 Wanderers m1908 *Pennsylvania–West Virginia (D)*. Team started season in Scottsdale (PA) and moved to Grafton July 31. In this era, when a team was forced to move to another city in mid-season, it was almost always due to low attendance. The players then became known as "Wanderers" or "Orphans."

2326 Grafton Baseball Club 1909 *Pennsylvania–West Virginia (D)*; 1910 *West Virginia (D)*. These teams had no nickname.

Graham, Texas

2327 Hijakers 1921m *Texas–Oklahoma (D)*. Team moved to Mineral Wells (TX) May 27. Fans started calling the players "Highjackers"— shortened to "Hi-Jakers"— because the team lost 24 of its first 29 games causing them to "high-jack" the fans' pennant hopes. Then, management skipped town like a "high-jacked truck" moving the franchise May 27. In the 1920s and 1930s, gangsters often "highjacked" a truck, carrying a valuable haul, by first greeting the truck driver with the cordial "Hi, Jack!" A variation of the term's origin, designed to frighten the driver into raising his hands in the air, is the pistol-wielding gangster's shout, "Keep 'em high, Jack!" The term "hijack" was coined in 1920. With manager Alex Boggus at the helm, newspapers called the players "Alex' Hijakers."

Granada, Granada, Nicaragua (Ciudad de Granada)

2328 Los Orientales 1957–58–66–67 *Liga de Nicaragua (W)*. Although the team's home city of Granada is located in the southwest part of the country, it was the eastern-most city in the league since all the other teams of the Nicaraguan Winter League played in cities located along the west coast of Nicaragua, i.e., Managua and Leon. The Nicaraguan Winter League of this era was a professional circuit.

Granby, Quebec, Canada

2329 Red Socks 1940 *Quebec Provincial (B)*. Since the team was not a formal farm club of the Boston Red Sox, maintaining a loose affiliation with the AL Bostonians instead, management decided to spell the nickname as "s-o-c-k-s" to avoid confusion with "s-o-x." Canadian-based teams of the era 1930–50 often took a major league baseball team nickname to emulate a northeastern big league team, or because the Canadian team had a loose affiliation with an AL or NL club.

2330 Red Sox 1946 *Border (C)*; 1948–51 *Provincial (ind. 1948–49, (C). 1950–51)* This circuit was also known alternately as the Quebec Provincial League. Players wore red stirrups. Team maintained a loose affiliation with the Boston Red Sox. The 1940 "Red Socks" spelling fell into disfavor.

2331 Phillies 1952–53 *Provincial (C)*. This circuit was also known alternately as the Quebec Provincial League. Team was a farm club of the Philadelphia Phillies.

Grand Canyon, Arizona

2332 Rafters 1992–96 *Arizona Fall (W)*. Water rafting is a popular sport done on the waters of the nearby Little Colorado River that flows near the city.

Grand Forks, North Dakota

2333 Grand Forks Baseball Club 1902 *Northern (D)*. Team had no nickname.

2334 Forkers 1903–05 *Northern (D)*; 1906x *Northern Copper Country (C)*. Team disbanded July 29. Moniker was used for newspaper headlines, i.e., "Forkers edge Crooks, 4–3." The city was built along the Red River, which has a fork in it, formed by the junction of the Otter Tail and Bois de Sioux rivers. French explorers of the seventeenth century called the River "Les Grandes Fourche," which means "Grand Fork."

2335 Flickertails 1912 *Central International (C)*; 1913–15 *Northern (C)*. The Flickertail fox inhabits the region. With manager Sam Foster at the helm, newspapers called the players "Foster's Flickertails." William Fox took over as manager in 1915 and the name became "Fox' Flickertails." Team was never known as the "Foxes" however.

2336 Chiefs 1934–35 *Northern (D)*; 1938–42 *Northern (D 1938–40, C 1941–42)*; 1946–64 *Northern (C 1946–62, A 1963–64)*. On May 11, 1876, Chief Sitting Bull led the Sioux and Dakota in an attack that wiped out the federal troops of General George Armstrong Custer at the Little Big Horn.

2337 Varmints 1996–97 *Prairie (ind.)*. In their trek across the continent, settlers called the fauna of these regions "varmints," which was a variation of "vermin." Many of these animals were not only predators but also carried disease. The team mascot is a coyote.

Grand Island, Nebraska

2338 Sugar Citys 1892 *Nebraska State (ind.)*. Grand Island is known as the "Sugar City" because it has numerous flour and sugar mills as well as packing houses for these foodstuffs.

2339 Collegians 1910–13 *Nebraska State (D)*. The city is home to Grand Island College. Several players on the professional team played college baseball there. With manager Buck Beltzer at helm in 1910, newspapers called the players "Buck Beltzer's Collegians." Under James Cockman in 1913, the name was "Cockman's Collegians."

2340 Islanders 1914 *Nebraska State (D)*; 1924 *Tri-State (D)*; 1929–32 *Nebraska State (D)*. Moniker was used for newspaper headlines, i.e., "Islanders edge Kapitalists, 4–3." City is built on a peninsula of the Platte River. A peninsula is an island on a river or lake that is connected to the main body of land by an isthmus. With manager Harry Claire at the helm, newspapers called the players "Harry Claire's Islanders."

2341 Champions 1915 *Nebraska State (D)*; 1922–23 *Nebraska State (D)*; 1924 *Tri-State (D)*; 1928–31 *Nebraska State (D)*. Team won 1914 pennant. With manager Henry Claire at the helm in 1915, newspapers called the players "Claire's Champions." The 1922 team finished last, prompting use of the nickname sarcastically. In 1923 they improved to third place, but impatient fans continued to brand them as "champions" with sarcastic disdain. Danny Claire, Henry's brother, managed the 1928 team, which prompted local newspapers to once again call the players "Claire's Champions." Team won the pennant in 1931, reinforcing the tag. City hosted an annual "Champions Livestock Show" where a blue ribbon was awarded to the champion of various categories. In this era, when a baseball team won a pennant, it was sometimes called "Champions" at the start of the next season.

2342 Redbirds 1937 *Nebraska State (D)*. Team was a farm club of the St. Louis Cardinals. This alternate tag to Cardinals was used to avoid confusion with the parent club.

2343 Cardinals 1938 *Nebraska State (D)*. Team was a farm club of the St. Louis Cardinals.

2344 Athletics 1956–59 *Nebraska State (D)*. Team was a farm club of the Kansas City Athletics.

Grand Prairie, Texas

2345 Air Hogs 2008 to date *American Assn.(ind.)*. Grand Prairie, a suburb of the Dallas–Fort Worth metropolitan area, has meat packing plants and hog farms. Back in the 1920s and 1930s, air shows were popular in Texas. During World War II, local factories built bombers and fighters. After the war, jet fighters were built here. The term "air hog" is slang for a military jet pilot. Grand Prairie is known as the "Center of the Aircraft Industry."

Grand Rapids, Michigan

2346 Grays 1883–84 *Northwestern (ind.)*. Players wore gray uniforms and gray hose. Team won the 1884 NWL pennant with a 48–15 record.

2347 Grand Rapids Base Ball Club 1889–90 *Michigan State (ind.)*; 1891x *Northwestern* Team and league disbanded June 13; 1893 *Michigan State (ind.)*. These teams had no nickname.

2348 Shamrocks m1890x *International (ind.)*. Team began season in Buffalo and moved to Grand Rapids June 11. Team and league disbanded July 10. Many Irish immigrants settled in Grand Rapids during the nineteenth century. Team wore shamrock green stockings. With Irish-American Louis Bacon at the managerial helm, newspapers called the players "Louis Bacon's Shamrocks."

2349 Rustlers 1894 *Western (ind.)*. In an era when the American public was fascinated with the "Wild West," baseball players who were perceived to be a "wild and wooly" lot, much like cowboys and Indians were often called Indians, Broncos, Braves and Rustlers. With manager Rasty Wright at the helm, newspapers called the team "Rasty Wright's Rustlers."

2350 Rippers 1894 *Western (ind.)*. Player-manager Rasty Wright led the team, whose players newspapers called "Rasty Wright's Rippers." Clashing tides, known as "rip-tides," form in the nearby Grand River and Lake Michigan during storms. Slugging baseball players are said to "rip the ball."

2351 Blackbirds 1895 *Western (ind.)*. Players started the season wearing black stockings. In the era 1890–1910, some teams took the nicknames of birds based on the player's stocking color, i.e., Blackbirds, Bluebirds, Blue Jays, Cardinals, Crows, Doves, Ravens and Redbirds. With manager George Ellis at the helm, newspapers called the players "Ellis' Blackbirds."

2352 Goldbugs 1895–97 *Western (ind.)*. Players switched to yellow hose. With manager George Ellis at the helm 1895–06, newspapers called the yellow-legged players "George's Goldbugs." Bob Leadley took over in 1897 and the name became "Bob Leadley's Goldbugs." With the Panic of 1893, the U.S. went into a five-year depression, prompting many people, Michiganders included, to become "goldbugs," i.e., gold hoarders.

2353 Yellowjackets 1896 *Western (ind.)*. Players continued to wear yellow hose. Moniker alternated with "Goldbugs" this season. With manager G.E. Ellis at the helm, newspapers called the players "G.E. Ellis' Yellow Jackets."

2354 Bobolinks 1897 *Western (ind.)*. The bobolink is a songbird found in North America around the Great Lakes. With manager Bob Leadley at the helm, newspapers called the players "Bob Leadley's Bobolinks."

2355 Cabinetmakers 1898 *Inter-State (ind.)*; m1899 *Western (ind.)*. After the city was founded in 1850, it became a major lumber center. By the 1880s the city had numerous furniture manufacturing factories that led to the city's nickname of "Furniture Capital of America." Local newspaper editors loathed the 13-letter name.

2356 Furnituremakers m1899 *Western (ind.)*. Team started season in Columbus (OH) and then moved to Grand Rapids July 17; 1910–11m *Central (B)*. Team moved to Newark (OH) June 27. Tag was a spin-off from "Cabinetmakers." Grand Rapids' newspaper editors absolutely loathed both nicknames, which is why they seized upon "Boers" the following season. Grand Rapids is the "Furniture City."

2357 Boers 1900x *International (ind.)*. Team disbanded July 3. The Boer War of 1899–1902 was fought between the British overlords and South African colonials of Dutch descent who were nicknamed the "Boers." Since many Dutch immigrants had settled in Grand Rapids in the nineteenth century, the pro–Dutch, anti–British moniker of "Boers" was applied to the team. "Boer" comes from the Dutch word "Boor" or "Boer," which means farmer. Politically charged nicknames, i.e., Boers, Highlanders, Hungarian Rioters, Night Riders, Yankees, Young Turks, etc., were quite the fad for baseball teams in this era. With manager E.W. Dickerson at the helm, newspapers called the players "Dickerson's Boers."

2358 Woodworkers 1901 *Western Assn. (ind.)*. Tag was a spin-off from the 1899 name. Local newspapers found no solace in this replacement moniker. The team actually had a team mascot and logo—a woodpecker! Grand Rapids had a third city nickname, the "Furniture Center of the World," because factories here made high quality—though very expensive—furniture.

2359 Colts 1902x *Michigan State (D)*. Team disbanded July 20; 1941 *Michigan State (C)*. In 1902 the team had a loose affiliation with the National League Chicago Colts. The team also had many young players, known in the slang of the era as "colts." By the spring of 1941, baseball players were being drafted into the army, forcing minor league clubs to sign younger players. With manager Charles Lucas at the helm in 1941, newspapers started calling the players "Charlie Lucas' Colts."

2360 Orphans m1903–05 *Central (B)*. Team started the season in Anderson (IN) but low attendance forced the team onto the road as "Orphans." The team finally moved to Grand Rapids May 30. Team was the "Orphans" for two reasons. First, the team transferred to another city because the Anderson fans had "abandoned" the players due to low attendance even though the Anderson team had a winning record (15–12). Teams in this era that transferred cities in mid-season due to low attendance were typically known as "Orphans." Second, the Chicago Nationals were still called the "Orphans" six years after star player and team manager Adrian "Pop" Anson left the team after the 1897 season, prompting newspapers to call the "fatherless" players "orphans."

2361 Wolverines 1906–09 *Central (B)*. Michigan is the "Wolverine State." The nickname was already in use by the University of Michigan college football and basketball teams, but "the team played like ferocious wolverines" on their way to the 1906 CL pennant. Also, the team had a loose affiliation with the AL Detroit Tigers, whose ancestor franchise was the "Wolverines."

2362 Raiders 1909–10 *Central (B)*. With field manager Joe Raidy at the helm, local newspapers called the players "Raidy's Raiders." "R" nicknames were usual for Grand Rapids teams, i.e., Rustlers, Rippers and Raiders. Newspapers were anxious to get away from Wolverines because it was 10 letters long and already being used by the University of Michigan college teams.

2363 Grads m1911 *Central (B)*. Team started the season in South Bend (IN) and moved to Grand Rapids July 13 to replace the Furniture-makers. By 1911 the city had four colleges: Davenport Business College, Calvin College, Calvin Theological Seminary and Grand Rapids Community College. Newspapers liked the name but the fans did not.

2364 Colored Athletics 1906–20 *Independent Negro (ind.)*. In emulation of the 1905 world champion Philadelphia Athletics, players wore a gothic A on their jerseys.

2365 Black Sox 1912, 1915–16 *Central (B)*; 1926t *Central (C)*; t1926 *Michigan State (B)*. The Central and Michigan Ontario Leagues merged June 15 to form the Michigan State League. The players on all three teams wore black stirrups.

2366 Bill-Eds 1913 *Central (B)*. The Bill-Ed is a North American songbird that inhabits the Great Lakes region. The Bill-Ed is similar to the North American Bob-O-Link — another songbird. With field manager Ed Smith at the helm, newspapers called the players the "Bill-Eds."

2367 Champs 1914 *Central (B)*. Team won the 1913 pennant.

2368 Joshers 1920–21 *Central (B)*. The team was named after field manager Josh Devore.

2369 Wolverines 1921 *Central (B)*. When field manager Louis Wolfe took over for Devore in July 1921, newspapers started calling the team "Wolfe's Wolverines."

2370 Billbobs 1922 *Central (B)*; 1923–24 *Michigan–Ontario (B)*. Moniker is an amalgam of the names of two birds found in Michigan — the "Bill-Ed" and the "Bob-O-Link." Hence, there is the moniker "Bill-Bob." Local newspapers printed it "Billbobs." With manager Bob Wells at the helm in 1922–23, newspapers started calling the players the alliterative "Bob Well's Bill-bobs."

2371 Homoners 1924 *Michigan–Ontario (B)*. Grand Rapids became known as the "Home Owner City" at this time because of a housing construction boom, influenced by the abundant wood-making industry. Newspapers didn't like the nickname's length.

2372 Tigers 1934x *Central (B)*. Team and league disbanded June 10 because of the Great Depression. Team had a loose affiliation with the Detroit Tigers. By the 1930s minor league teams often started out as a loose affiliate of a nearby big league team before becoming a formal farm team a few years later.

2373 Dodgers 1940 *Michigan State (C)*. Team was a farm club of the Brooklyn Dodgers.

2374 Chicks 1943–54 *All-America Girls (ind.)*. Young players. For men's baseball "chick" had previously meant a young player,

often a rookie. For women's baseball, "chick" was a jazz-oriented 1940s slang for a young woman, somewhat sexist but usually complimentary.

2375 Jets 1948–51 *Central (A)*. Car manufacturer Henry Ford started the Stout Air Service here on July 31, 1926, for passenger plane flights between Detroit and Grand Rapids, one of the earliest regular scheduled domestic air travel services in the United States. Starting in 1941 the city became an important site for the manufacture of airplane engines and other parts, especially those components made out of aluminum. After the war, components for jet engines were made here. In 1978, John Jetts established the Grand Rapids Pizza Company which, in honor of the city's aviation history, introduced the "Jet Pizza."

2376 West Michigan White Caps 1994 to date *Midwest (A)*. Team goes by the regional name of West Michigan White Caps. Grand Rapids is 25 miles east of stormy Lake Michigan, whose waves lash western Michigan. Both Lake Michigan and the nearby Grand River form "white caps" during storms.

Granite Falls, North Carolina

2377 Graniteers 1951 *Western Carolina (D)*. Phillies-style nickname. Granite quarries, just outside the town, transport quartz, orthoclase and microcline ore to factories for the manufacture of cement and concrete.

Great Bend, Kansas

2378 Big Benders 1905 *Kansas State (D)*. Team joined the league July 6. Moniker was used for headlines, i.e., "Benders edge Millers, 4–3." Team went an excellent 19–9, prompting fans and newspapers to praise the players as the "Big Benders."

2379 Millers 1905 *Kansas State (D)*; 1909–11x *Kansas State (D)*. Team and league disbanded July 11 due to drought and a crop failure; 1912 *Central Kansas (D)*; 1913–14 *Kansas State (D)*. Farms near the city transport wheat to grain mills. Great Bend is known as the "The Oil Capital in the Heart of the Wheat Belt." With field manager Carl Moore at the helm in 1905, local newspapers called the players the alliterative "Moore's Millers." When Mr. Stillings took over for Rudy Kling as manager in July 1909, local newspapers called the players the alliterative "Stillings' Millers." Stillings left the team after the 1909 season, but the name was retained in 1910. Affie Wilson and then William Luhrsen managed the team in 1911, leading to the alliterative names "Wilson's Millers," and "Bill's Millers." Affie Wilson returned as skipper to manage "Wilson's Millers" to the 1912 CKL pennant. Affie Wilson was again at the helm for both seasons as "Wilson's Millers" won the 1913 KSL pennant before slumping to fourth place in 1914.

2380 Benders 1909–11x *Kansas State (D)*. This name was shorter for newspaper headlines, i.e., "Benders edge Millers, 4–3."

Great Falls, Montana

2381 Great Falls Base Ball Club 1892 *Montana State (ind.)*; 1911–12 *Union Assn. (D)*; 1916 *Northwestern (B)*. These teams had no nickname.

2382 Indians 1900 *Montana State (ind.)*. The Blackfeet were the dominant military force in Montana until they were decimated by a small pox epidemic in 1837. With Mr. Kinsella at the managerial helm, newspapers called the players "Kinsella's Indians."

2383 Electrics 1913 *Union Assn. (D)*; 1917 *Northwestern (B)*. Regular season schedule ended July 15, 1917, because of U.S. entry into World War I; 1948, 1951–63 *Pioneer (C)*. In 1913, a hydroelectric plant was built at the Great Falls of the Missouri River to generate electricity for the region. The city soon became known as the "Electric City." With field manager Harry Hester at the helm in 1913, local newspapers called the players the alliterative "Hester's Electrics." By 1917, Great Falls had become known as the "Niagara of the West" because of the hydroelectric plants along the Great Falls of the Missouri River. Skipper Herb Hester was back, guiding the alliterative "Hester's Electrics" to the 1917 Northwest League pennant.

2384 Selectrics 1949–50 *Pioneer (C)*. Moniker was an amalgam of two names. In 1949 the Select Beer Company bought the team and combined "Select" with "electric" (after Electric City) to come up with "Selectrics."

2385 Giants 1969–83 *Pioneer (R)*. Team was a farm club of the San Francisco Giants.

2386 Dodgers 1984–2002 *Pioneer (R)*. Team was a farm club of the Los Angeles Dodgers.

2387 White Sox 2003–07 *Pioneer (R)*. Team was a farm club of the Chicago White Sox.

2388 Voyagers 2008 to date *Pioneer (R)*. French traders and trappers first explored here in the seventeenth century. French explorers Louis-Joseph and Francois Verendrye discovered the Rocky Mountains here in 1743. Lewis and Clark arrived here in 1803 and Sacagawea, a Shoshoni Indian girl, led Lewis and Clark northward into the Dakotas.

Green Bay, Wisconsin

2389 Dock Wallopers 1891–92 *Wisconsin (ind.)*. "Dock Walloper" is a term for dock workers who unloaded timber from boats bringing it to harbor. The wood beams would "wallop" the docks with a thunderous sound. Lumber boats have brought wood to city factories here for manufacture into paper since 1850.

2390 Colts 1905–06 *Wisconsin State (D)*. With manager W. Kennelly at the helm of a young team, newspapers called the 1905 players the alliterative "Kennelly's Colts." Kennelly left the team after the 1905 season but the newspaper-friendly name was retained.

2391 Orphans 1907 *Wisconsin State (D)*. Team was managed by John Corrigan. As attendance sagged because of a losing record, the team left town to play on the road for most of the second half of the season as "Corrigan's Orphans." In this era, such homeless squads were called either "Orphans" or "Wanderers." The team wound up seventh (of eight) with a forlorn 48–73 mark.

2392 Tigers 1908 *Wisconsin–Illinois (D)*. Players wore striped hose. Team had a loose affiliation with the Detroit Tigers. With managers John Corrigan and then John Pickett at the helm, newspapers called the players "Corrigan's Tigers," and "Pickett's Tigers."

2393 Bays 1909–14 *Wisconsin–Illinois (D 1909, C 1910–14)*. Moniker was used for newspaper headlines, i.e., "Bays edge Malted Milks, 4–3."

2394 Blue Jays 1940, 1942 *Wisconsin State (D)*; 1946–53 *Wisconsin State (D)*; 1958–59 *Three-I (B)*. With field manager Otto Bluege (pronounced "blu-jee") at the helm, local newspapers called the team "Bluege's Blue Jays." Management dressed the players in blue-trim uniforms and hose. After Bluege left the team following the 1940 season, the moniker and blue-trim uniforms and blue stirrups were retained. Fans decided they preferred "Blue Jays" over "Blue Sox" for the 1942 season, so the bird nickname was restored for manager Dick Smith's 1942 club. By coincidence, the Philadelphia Blue Jays placed a farm team here for the 1946 season. When the parent club switched back to the Phillies in 1950, the farm club retained "Blue Jays" to foster its own identity.

2395 Blue Sox 1941–42 *Wisconsin State (D)*. Players wore blue stirrups. When Otto Bluege did not return as skipper in 1941, management was left with blue-trim uniforms and blue stirrups. "Blue Jays" was no longer a relevant tag, so the team switched the name to "Blue Sox."

2396 Dodgers 1960 *Three-I (B)*. The Three-I League represented Illinois, Indiana and Iowa. The Green Bay club was the only team from Wisconsin in the circuit. Team was a farm club of the Los Angeles Dodgers.

2397 Sultans 1996 *Prairie (ind.)*; 1997 *Heartland (ind.)*. At first the name of the team was going to be the Green Bay "Genies"—a folded-arm genie mascot logo had already been designed—but fan response was cool so it was dropped. After the Springfield (IL) Sultans of the Midwest League disbanded at the end of the 1995 season, Green Bay's management decided to pick up the nickname. The somewhat-inappropriate genie mascot was retained. The new nickname was appropriate because Babe Ruth was the "Sultan of Swat," and baseball home run hitters are known as "swatters." With the moniker, the sultans of Old Baghdad-by-the-Bay could now be the "Sultans of Green Bay."

Greensboro, North Carolina

2398 Farmers 1902 x *North Carolina (D)*. Team and league disbanded July 15; 1905x *Virginia–North Carolina (D)*. Team and league disbanded August 19; Greensboro has been home to North Carolina State Agricultural and Technical University since 1891. Nearby farms transport sweet potatoes, peanuts, grapes, pecans, apples, tomatoes, and soybeans to city processing plants where the produce is cleaned, packed and shipped to market.

2399 Champs 1908–10 *Carolina Assn. (D)*. The team won league championships in 1908 and 1909. The nickname carried over to the 1912 season. Naming a team "Champions" because of a pennant the previous year was a trend of this era (1900–20) that fans eventually grew disenchanted with.

2400 Patriots 1911–12 *Carolina Assn. (D)*; 1913–17 *North Carolina (D)*. Circuit was League in 1913 and State League in 1914–17; 1920–26 *Piedmont (D)*. 1920 (C). 1921–26; 1928–34 *Piedmont (C)*. 1928–31 (B). 1932–34; 1945–57 *Carolina (C 1945–48, B 1949–57)*. General Nathaniel Greene led American Continental Army troops into combat against the British at the Battle of Guilford Court House on March 15, 1781. The city of Greensboro was named in his honor. With manager Charles Carroll at the helm in 1920–24, newspapers called the players "Caroll's Patriots." After Carroll left the team following the 1924 season, the moniker was retained. Charles Carroll returned for two seasons to lead "Carroll's Patriots." Carroll left again following the 1929 season but the name was retained.

2401 Red Sox 1941–42 *Piedmont (B)*. Team was a farm club of the Boston Red Sox.

2402 Red Wings 1948–50 *Negro American Assn. (ind.)*. Players wore red-trim uniforms and red stirrups.

2403 Yankees 1958–67 *Carolina (B 1958–62, 1963–67)*.

2404 Astros 1968 *Carolina (A)*. Team was a farm club of the Houston Astros.

2405 Hornets 1980–93 *South Atlantic (A)*. After the Southern League Charlotte Hornets disbanded following the 1971 season, the nickname was available and the new Greensboro team picked it up for its inaugural 1980 campaign.

2406 Bats 1994–2004 *South Atlantic (A)*. The Virginia Big-Eared Bats inhabit caves and rocky ridges all along the Mid-Atlantic.

2407 Grasshoppers 2005 to date *South Atlantic (A)*. Although local newspapers loved the four-letter "Bats" that provided relief from the ten-letter name of Greensboro, management chose in a fan poll this moniker, i.e., the "Greensboro Grasshoppers." Newspapers shorten it to **Hoppers** and **Hops**.

Greensburg, Pennsylvania

2408 Red Sox 1907 *Western Pennsylvania (D)*. Players wore red hose. Team was not a farm club of the Boston Red Sox. The farm system would not arise until 1925–30.

2409 Trojans 1934 *Pennsylvania (D)*. Team was named in part after the popular USC Trojans, who had just finished winning three Rose Bowls in four years—1930, 1932 and 1933. Local newspapers recounted that the players "worked as hard as Trojans" to a 57–45 first-place finish. To "work like a Trojan" is an expression meaning to work hard and diligently. The phrase comes from antiquity as the Trojans of Ancient Troy labored diligently to fight off the invading Greeks during the tenth century B.C. Trojan War. Greensburg is known as the "Tunnel City" because of the nearby coal tunnels from which coal is hauled and sent to city factories. Coal miners there "worked like Trojans" to perform the back-breaking labor.

2410 Red Wings 1935–36 *Pennsylvania (D)*. Team was a farm club of the St. Louis Cardinals.

2411 Green Sox 1937–38 *Pennsylvania (D)*. Team was a farm club of the Brooklyn Dodgers. The team changed colors to Brooklyn green. In the 1930s the NL Dodgers abandoned their traditional blue-trim to experiment with green trim. By the 1940s the Brooklyn NL club had returned to blue trim. The 1938 team was an independent but retained the green-trim uniforms and green stirrups.

2412 Senators 1939 *Pennsylvania State (D)*. Circuit was known as the Pennsylvania State Association. Team was a farm club of the Washington Senators.

Greeneville, Tennessee

2413 Burley Cubs 1921–25x *Appalachian (D)*. Team and league disbanded July 15, 1925; 1937–42x *Appalachian (D)*. Team disbanded June 14 because of U.S. entry into World War II. Burley tobacco is a type of leaf that is thinner and lighter than many other tobacco types. Greenville is "One of the Country's Leading Burley Markets." Team had many young players—hence the tag of Cubs. Unlike the 1921–25 team, which was independent, the 1937–42 team was a farm club of the Chicago Cubs.

2414 Astros 2004 to date *Appalachian (R)*. Team is a farm club of the Houston Astros.

Greenville, Alabama

2415 Lions 1939 *Alabama–Florida (D)*; 1940–41 *Alabama State (D)*; 1946–47 *Alabama State (D)*. The Florida panther inhabits Alabama and the Southeast. Large North American predator cats are known variously as cougars, panthers, pumas, and mountain lions.

2416 Pirates 1948–50 *Alabama State (D)*. Team was a farm club of the Pittsburgh Pirates.

Greenville, Michigan

2417 Greenville Base Ball Club 1887 *Northern Michigan (ind.)*; 1889 *Michigan State (ind.)*. These teams had no nickname.

Greenville, Mississippi

2418 Greenville Base Ball Club 1894 *Mississippi (ind.)*. Team had no nickname.

2419 Cotton-pickers 1902, 1904–05 *Cotton States (D)*. Cotton farms in the region transport cotton to textile mills. With manager Bell Hebron at the helm, newspapers called the players "Hebron's Cotton-pickers." Greenville is the "Port City of the Delta" where cotton was transported by boat. Mississippi is known as the "Cotton Kingdom."

2420 Grays 1903 *Cotton States (D)*. Players wore gray uniforms and gray hose.

2421 Bucks 1922 *Cotton States (D)*; 1936–38 *Cotton States (C)*; 1947–53, 1955 *Cotton States (C)*. With manager Bud Stapleton at the helm in 1922, newspapers called the players "Bud's Bucks." Name was appropriate because white-tailed deer inhabit the Southeast. Newspapers liked the name's five-letter length.

2422 Swamp Angels 1923 *Cotton States (D)*. American legend has it that swamp lands along the Mississippi River give rise to the specter of "swamp angels" that materialize out of the swampy vapors and mist rolling over the nearby Mississippi Delta. With manager Harold Irelan at the helm, guiding the team to a first-place finish (league disbanded July 24, prompting league president Frank Scott to award the pennant to Greenville), newspapers called the players "Harold Irelan's Swamp Angels."

2423 Buckshots 1934–35 *East Dixie (C)*; 1936–38 *Cotton States (C)*; 1953 *Cotton States (C)*. Tag was a spin-off from Bucks. Mississippi has several forest preserves for deer hunting. With field managers Bill Eisemann and then Frank Brazill at the helm in 1934, local newspapers called the players "Bill's Buckshots" and "Brazill's Buckshots." Glen Bolton took over in 1935, changing the name to "Bolton's Buckshots." Hunters used shotguns that fired "scattershot," which when used to hunt deer became known as "buckshot." Moniker was used once more in 1953.

2424 Tigers 1954 *Cotton States (C)*. Team was a farm club of the Detroit Tigers.

2425 Bluesmen 1994 *Mid-South (ind.)*; 1996–97 *Big South (ind.)*; 1998–2001 *Texas Louisiana (ind.)*. The nearby Blue Ridge Mountains are part of the Appalachian Mountain Range. Blues musicians born in Mississippi include Charlie Patton, Big Bill Broonzy, Howlin' Wolf, Muddy Waters, John Lee Hooker and B.B. King. The team logo was a saxophone.

Greenville, North Carolina

2426 Tobs 1928–29 *Eastern Carolina (D)*. With managers Taylor Jolliff and then Tom Abbott at the helm, newspapers called the players "Taylor's Tobacconists" and "Abbott's Tobacconists." Both managers had left by 1929, but the nickname was retained. Originally **Tobacconists**, local newspapers shortened it to "Tobs."

2427 Greenies 1937–41 *Coastal Plain (D)*; 1946–49 *Coastal Plain (D)*. Moniker was used for newspaper headlines, i.e., "Greenies edge Eagles, 4–3."

2428 Robins 1949 *Coastal Plain (D)*. With manager Randy Heflin at the helm, newspapers called the players "Randy Heflin's Robins."

Greenville, South Carolina

2429 Edistoes 1907x *South Carolina (D)*. Team disbanded July 27. The city was built along the Edisto River, which flows southeast into the Atlantic Ocean.

2430 Eskimos 1907 *South Carolina (D)*. Name was a play on words from "Edistoes." As the city sweltered in the hot summer of 1907, local fans and reporters jokingly called the players the "Eskimos." In this era baseball players sometimes hitched a ride to the ballpark on ice wagons.

2431 Mountaineers 1907 *South Carolina (D)*. Greenville is situated near the Blue Ridge Mountains. The city is a tourist resort in the Piedmont region. With manager Thomas Stouch at the helm, newspapers called the players "Thomas Stouch's Mountaineers."

2432 Spinners 1908–12 *Carolina Assn. (D)*; 1919–30 *South Atlantic (C 1919–20, B 1921–30)* Circuit designated Association 1919–20 and League 1921–30; 1931 *Palmetto (D)*; 1938–42 *South Atlantic (A)*; 1946–50 *South Atlantic (A)*; 1951–52 *Tri-State (B)*; 1953–54 *Tri-State (B)*. With factories for textile "finishing" and garment production, Greenville became known as the "Textile Center of the World."

2433 Tobs 1928–29 *Eastern Carolina (D)*. Regional tobacco farms transport tobacco to city packing houses. Originally **Tobacconists,** local newspapers quickly shortened it to **Tobs.**

2434 Braves 1963–64 *Western Carolinas (A)*; 1984–2004 *Southern (AA)*. Teams were farm clubs of the Milwaukee Braves (1963–64) and the Atlanta Braves (1984–2004).

2435 Mets 1965–66 *Western Carolinas (A)*. Team was a farm club of the New York Mets.

2436 Red Sox 1967–71 *Western Carolinas (A)*. Team was a farm club of the Boston Red Sox.

2437 Rangers 1972 *Western Carolinas (A)*. Team was a farm club of the Texas Rangers.

2438 Bombers 2005 *South Atlantic (A)*. After the Class AA Braves moved to Pearl (MS) at the close of the 2004 season, the Class A Columbia (SC) Bombers moved here in 2005. The nickname was retained.

2439 Drive 2006 to date *South Atlantic (A)*. Greenville is the transportation hub of western South Carolina with a dozen highways and railroad lines leading in and out of the city.

Greenville, Hunt, Texas

2440 Hunters 1905 *North Texas (C)*; 1907 *North Texas (D)*; 1924–26 *East Texas (D)*. City is located in Hunt County. Moniker is doubly appropriate because the county allows game hunting.

2441 Midlands 1906 *Texas (C)*. Greenville is located in Central Texas, called by locals "Midland." With managers William Owen, Richard Bendel and Cy Mulkey successively at the helm, team was called "William Owen's Midlands," "Richard Bendel's Midlands," and "Mulkey's Midlands."

2442 Independents 1922 *Texas–Oklahoma (D)*. General Thomas Green led American troops against Santa Ana's Mexican forces in the Texas War of Independence in 1835–36. The city is named in his honor. Skipper Bennie Brownlow led "Bennie's Independents."

2443 Togs 1922 *Texas–Oklahoma (D)*. City had a cotton textile industry noted for manufacturing "togs"—a long, white cotton coat popular with Texans in the 1920s. The players wore similar togs while sitting on the bench on cold April and September days.

2444 Staplers 1923 *East Texas (D)*. Staplers are machines that sort cotton out by the length and fineness of its fibers, i.e., long-staple and short-staple cotton.

2445 Majors 1946 *East Texas (C)*; 1947–50 *Big State (B)*; 1953m Team moved to Bryan (TX) June 25; 1957 *Sooner State (D)*. General Thomas Green led American troops against Santa Ana's Mexican forces in the Texas War of Independence in 1835–36. The city is named in his honor. Before rising to the rank of general, Thomas Greene was a U.S. Army major.

Greenwood, Mississippi

2446 Chauffeurs 1910 *Cotton States (D)*. The year 1910 was the dawning of America's Automobile Age and the team's management drove the players to their home ballpark—Wright's Field—in a bus. Players would take turns driving the bus as if they were chauffeurs.

2447 Scouts 1911 *Cotton States (D)*. With field manager Orth Collins at the helm, local newspapers called the players "Orth Collins' Scouts."

2448 Indians 1921 *Mississippi State (D)*; 1922–23x *Cotton States (D)*. Team and league disbanded July 24, 1923. In pre-settler times, the Choctaw and Muskohegan Indians lived here.

2449 Chiefs m1934–35 *East Dixie (C)*. Team started season in Shreveport (LA) and moved to Greenwood July 13, 1934; 1936 *Cotton States (C)*. The French destroyed the Natchez Indians in the 1729–30 war. The Choctaws and Chickasaws were driven west by British and then American soldiers over the next 100 years, eventually signing a treaty and settling in Oklahoma by 1832. The tags "Indians" and "Chiefs" were used interchangeably.

2450 Giants 1937 *Cotton States (C)*. Team was a farm club of the New York Giants.

2451 Dodgers 1938 *Cotton States (C)*; 1947–52 *Cotton States (C)*. Teams were farm clubs of the Brooklyn Dodgers.

2452 Crackers 1939 *Cotton States (C)*. Team was a farm club of the Atlanta Crackers. In the era 1920–50 minor league teams at a lower classification (A, B, C, D) sometimes were affiliated with a minor league team at a higher classification (AA and AAA).

2453 Choctaws 1940 *Cotton States (D)*. Named in honor of the Choctaw Indians.

2454 Pirates 1981–83 *South Atlantic (A)*. Team was a farm club of the Pittsburgh Pirates.

Greenwood, South Carolina

2455 Tigers 1951 *Tri-State (B)*. Team had a loose affiliation with but was not an official farm club of the Detroit Tigers.

2456 Braves 1968–79 *Western Carolinas (A)*. Team was a farm club of the Atlanta Braves.

2457 Pirates 1981–83 *South Atlantic (A)*. Team was a farm club of the Pittsburgh Pirates.

2458 Grizzlies 1995x *Atlantic Coast (ind.)*. Team and league disbanded June 30. Black Bears, i.e., grizzly bears, still inhabit state parks and forests along the Mid-Atlantic Coast.

Griffin, Georgia

2459 Lightfoots 1915–16 *Georgia–Alabama (D)*. Team had several agile players. Lightfoots, Speed Boys and Quicksteps were period nicknames for speedy and agile baseball players, not only on the base paths but also defensively on the field. Colonel Harry "Lighthorse" Lee, leading the Continental Army in Georgia, captured nearby Augusta from the British in 1781. His soldiers were "nimble a' foot."

2460 Griffs 1917 *Georgia–Alabama (D)*. Team and league disbanded May 23 due to U.S. entry into World War I. Moniker was used in newspaper headlines, i.e., "Griffs edge Romans, 4–3."

2461 Griffin Baseball Club 1920–21 *Georgia State (D)*. Team had no nickname.

2462 Red Sox 1935 *Independent Negro team*. Players wore red stirrups.

2463 Pimientos 1947–49, 1951 *Georgia–Alabama (D)*. Nearby farms transport pimiento peppers to city factories where the peppers are cleaned, packed and shipped to market. Griffin is the "Pimiento Center of the World."

2464 Tigers 1950 *Georgia–Alabama (D)*. With manager Adel White at the helm, newspapers called the players "White's Tigers." Team was not a farm club of the Detroit Tigers. The players wore striped stirrups.

Grosseto, Tuscany, Italy

2465 Papalini 1999–2000 *Italian A1 (ind.)*. The Papalini Football (soccer) Club owned this baseball team.

2466 My Space 2001 *Italian A1 (ind.)*. My Space website owned the team.

2467 Orioles 2002, 2008 to date *Italian A1 (ind.)*. Local newspapers liked the short and alliterative moniker. Team is not a farm club of the Baltimore Orioles. The so-called Old World Oriole is a species of bird found in Europe. Team is known officially as the Montespachi Orioles after franchise owner Montespachi di Siena Bank.

2468 La Gardenia 2003 *Italian A1 (ind.)*. La Gardenia Hotels owned the team.

2469 Prink 2004–05 *Italian A1 (ind.)*. Prink Printers owned the team.

Guadalajara, Jalisco, Mexico

2470 Charos 1949–52 *Mexican (ind.)*; 1964–65 *Mexican (AA)*; 1982–83 *Nacional de Mexico (ind.)*; 1988 *Mexican (AAA)*; 1991–95 *Mexican (AAA)*. Cattle herds and ranches are common in Jalisco State. Like the "Chappies" in the United States, the Mexican "Charos" are cowboys who wear leather chaps to protect their legs while herding cattle. These teams went by the state name of "Los Charos de Jalisco," i.e., the "Jalisco Cowboys" in English.

Guamuchil, Sinaloa, Mexico

2471 Tomateros 1976 *Mexican Pacific (A)*. Tomato farms in the region transport tomatoes to city plants where they are cleaned and packed. The English translation of "Los Tomateros" can be Tomato Growers, Tomato Pickers, Tomato Farmers and Tomato Men.

Guanajuato, Central, Mexico

2472 Tuzos 1960–67 *Liga Central de Mexico (D 1960–62, A 1963–67)*. The gopher (tuzo in Spanish) is found throughout North and Central America, especially in Central Mexico. In Spanish "El Tuzo"—which literally means a gopher—is slang for a "miner." In Central Mexico there are gold, silver and coal mines.

2473 Club de Beisbol de Guanajuato 1975–76 *Mexican Center (A)*; 1978 *Mexican Center (A)*. Neither team had a nickname.

Guangzhou, Guangdong, China

2474 Hunting Leopards 2005 to date *Chinese (S)*. The Chinese Baseball League functions like a professional league, as its players are subsidized by the Chinese Communist government. The Cuban National Series League engages in the same type of subsidy. Nickname was a spin-off from the Beijing Vicious Lions and Tianjin Fierce Tigers to create a three-way mascot rivalry. Chinese and English-speaking newspapers often shorten the name to "Leopards."

Guantanamo, Guantanamo, Cuba

2475 Indios 1977–78 to date *Cuban National (S)*. The Cuban National Series functions like a professional league as its players are subsidized by the Cuban government. The pre–Columbian Indians tribes on the island of Cuba were the Arawaks and Ciboney. The United States maintains a military base in nearby Guantanamo Bay, the only American presence in Cuba.

Guasave, Sinoloa, Mexico

2476 Algodoneros 1950–51–57–58 *Liga Pacifica Mexicana (W)*; 1958–59–69–70 *Sonora–Sinoloa (W)*; 1970–71–72–73 *Liga Pacifica Mexicana (W)*. Circuit was known as the Sonora–Sinoloa League through 1969–70 and then was reorganized into a new circuit that was renamed the Mexican Pacific League starting the 1970–71 season; 1974–75–79–80 *Mexican Pacific (W)*; 1976 *Mexican Pacific (A)*. In 1976 owners of the Mexican Pacific League teams tried out a summer schedule but attendance was low, prompting them to play exclusively in winter; 1986–87–87–88 *Mexican Pacific (W)*; 1989–90 to date *Mexican Pacific (W)*. Cotton farms in the region transport cotton to textile mills. The English translation of "Los Algodoneros" can be "Cotton growers" or "Cotton pickers."

Guayama, Puerto Rico

2477 Brujos 1941–42 *Puerto Rican (W)*. When African slaves were first brought to Puerto Rico in the sixteenth century, they resisted conversion to Christianity and practiced voodoo, which is still practiced today. "El brujo" is Spanish for "witch doctor."

Guayamas, Sonora, Mexico

2478 Ostioneros 1976 *Mexican Pacific (A)*; 1986–87 to date *Mexican Pacific (W)*; 2004–08 *Norte de Sonora (ind.)*; 2009 to date *Norte de Mexico (ind.)*. The Liga del Norte de Sonora reorganized after the 2008 season, changing its name to the Liga del Norte de Mexico for the 2009 season. Fishing ships in the Gulf of California sail into port in this city to unload their catches of fish, shrimp, lobsters and oysters. "El ostionero" means "oyster catcher."

Guelph, Ontario, Canada

2479 Maple Leafs 1877 *International Assn. (M)*; 1884 *Ontario (ind.)*; 1885 *Canadian (ind.)*; 1896–97 *Canadian (ind.)*; 1899 *Canadian (ind.)*; 1908m *International (D)* Team began season in Guelph and then moved to St. Thomas (ONT) June 12; 1911–13 *Canadian (C 1911, D 1911, C 1912–13)*; 1915 *Canadian (B)*. The national tree of Canada is the maple tree. The symbol of Canada is the maple leaf. The 1877 team played in 1876 under the title of "Maple Leaf Baseball Club."

2480 Biltmores 1930 *Ontario (C)*. The Biltmore Hat Company, est. 1897, moved its headquarters to Guelph in 1923.

Gulfport, Mississippi

2481 Crabs 1906–07 *Cotton States (D)*. City is a seaport on the Gulf of Mexico. Seafood catches are delivered to port and transported to city factories to be cleaned, processed and canned.

2482 Tarpons 1926–28 *Cotton States (D)*. City has a beach resort for renting boats to go marlin and tarpon fishing. Gulfport is the host of the annual "Deep Sea Fishing Rodeo," a fishing contest.

Gulfport-Biloxi, Mississippi

2483 Crabs 1908 *Cotton States (D)*. The 1907 Gulfport Crabs represented both Gulfport and Biloxi in 1908, although all home games were played in Gulfport.

Guthrie, Oklahoma

2484 Senators 1904 *Southwestern (D)*; 1905 *Western Assn. (C)*; 1906x *South Central (D)*. Team disbanded July 21; 1909–10 *Western*

Assn. (C); m1914m *Western Assn. (D)*. Team began the season in Joplin–Webb City and moved to Guthrie July 10. Team then moved to Henryetta July 22. City was the territorial and state capital of Oklahoma, 1889–1910.

2485 Blues 1904 *Southwestern (D)*. Players wore blue hose.

2486 Legislators 1909 *Western Assn. (C)*. To avoid confusion with the AL Washington Senators, reporters used this name. Local newspaper editors loathed it, and Senators was used as an alternate.

2487 Guthrie Baseball Club 1912x *Oklahoma State (D)*. Team and league disbanded June 29; 1922–24m *Oklahoma State (D)*. Team moved to McAlester (OK) May 24. These two teams had no nickname.

2488 Monarchs 1926 *Independent Negro team*. Team was a farm club of the Kansas City Monarchs.

Haarlem, North Holland, Netherlands (also called Holland)

2489 Corendon-Kinheim 1999 to date *Hoofdklasse (ind.)*. The Dutch Hoofdklasse League became fully professional in 1999. Corendon Airlines own the team, which was originally started by the DPA Kinnheim Soccer Club. Team goes by the name of Corendon-Kinnheim. Professional baseball teams in Holland and Italy often lack a nickname mascot and use the sponsoring corporation in their official team name.

Hagerstown, Maryland

2490 Hagerstown Base Ball Club 1889 *Middle States (ind.)*; 1896 *Cumberland Valley (ind.)*. These teams had no nickname.

2491 Blues 1915 *Blue Ridge (D)*. Hagerstown is some 100 miles from the Blue Ridge Mountains for which the circuit was named as well as inspiring the players' uniform color, i.e., blue-trim uniforms and blue stirrups.

2492 Hubites 1916–17 *Blue Ridge (D)*. Hagerstown is the site of four highways coming into the city and is a river port of the Potomac River. The city is the farm products center for the Antietam Creek region.

2493 Terriers 1916–18 *Blue Ridge (D)*; 1922–23 *Blue Ridge (D)*. Just like Dogs and Dawgs today, Terriers, Bulldogs and Rovers was slang for baseball players in this era. With manager Bert Weeden at the helm in 1916, newspapers called the players "Bert's Terriers." In 1917 Charles Dysert took over in mid-season for Jack Hurley and led "Dysert's Terriers" to the 1917 pennant. Doc Ferris took over in 1918, managing "Ferris' Terriers." When Tony Walsh took over in mid-season 1922, the name became "Tony's Terriers."

2494 Champs 1920–21 *Blue Ridge (D)*. Team won the 1920 pennant. Use of the tag "Champions" was popular in the era 1900–25 for pennant winners and for the season following the flag year, but it became passé by 1930. The 1920 team skidded to sixth place in 1921, fomenting the use of "Champions" as sarcasm by fans and newspapers.

2495 Hubs 1924–30 *Blue Ridge (D)*; 1931m *Middle Atlantic (C)*. Team moved to Parkersburg (WV) June 28. Hagerstown is the "Hub of Northwest Maryland."

2496 Owls 1941–49 *Interstate (B)*. Team owner Owen Sterling used the motto "Winning and Luck" for the team, and that phrase, along with the initials of his name, spelled out O-W-L-S, i.e., Owen-Win-Luck-Sterling. Owls are found in Maryland.

2497 Braves 1950–52 *Interstate (B)*; 1953 *Piedmont (B)*. Teams were farm clubs of the Boston Braves (1950–52) and the Milwaukee Braves (1953).

2498 Packets 1954–55 *Piedmont (B)*. River boats called "packets"

have been transporting goods on the Potomac River to and from the city since at least 1830. When coach Zeke Bonura took over for manager Paul Campbell in mid-season, newspapers constructed "Packets" from their names. Name was retained in 1955.

2499 Suns 1981–88 *Carolina (A)*; 1989–92 *Eastern (AA)*; 1993 to date *South Atlantic (A)*. A fan poll in 1981 chose "Suns" because newspaper editors wanted a short name. Maryland is the "Star-Spangled State," and "Suns" is a spinoff from "Stars." Also, weather in the hilly Piedmont Plateau of western Maryland is quite sunny.

The Hague, North Holland, Netherlands (Den Haag in Dutch)

2500 ADO 1999 to date *Holland Hoofdklasse (ind.)*. Team is owned by the Hague Sport Company (Vereeniging). ADO stands for the motto "Alles Door Oefening" which means "All Through Training."

Haines City, Florida see Davenport—Haines City

Hamilton, Ohio

2501 Hamilton Base Ball Club 1884 *Ohio State Assn. (ind.)*. Team had no nickname.

2502 Mocking Birds 1889x *Tri-State (ind.)*. Team disbanded August 28. The mocking bird, found in the Midwest, got its name because it can mimic, i.e., "mocks," the cries of other bird species.

2503 Maroons 1911 *Ohio State (D*; 1913 *Ohio State (D)*. Players of the 1911 and 1913 teams wore maroon-trim uniforms and maroon stirrups.

2504 Mechanics 1911 *Ohio State (D)*. Some players on the team worked as mechanics in the off-season. "Mechanics" was slang for baseball players with dirty uniforms.

Hamilton, Ontario, Canada

2505 Clippers 1886 *International Assn. (ind.)*; 1924–25 *Michigan–Ontario (B)*. Clipper ships have sailed in and out of Hamilton's ports along Lake Ontario since 1820. With managers Charles Collings and then Thomas Crooks at the helm in 1886, newspapers called the players the alliterative "Charles Collings' Clippers" and "Crook's Clippers." With manager Frank "Buzz" Wetzel at the helm in 1924, newspapers called the players "Wetzel's Clippers."

2506 Hams 1886–90m *International Assn. (ind.)*. Team moved to Montreal (QUE) June 23. Circuit was League 1886–87 and Association 1888–90; 1900 *International (ind.)*; 1908x *International (D)*. Team and league disbanded July 31; 1913–15 *Canadian (C 1913, B 1914–15)*. Moniker was used for newspaper headlines, i.e., "Hams edge Bisons, 4–3."

2507 Mountaineers 1888,1890m *International Assn. (ind.)*. Team moved to Montreal (QUE) June 23. City was built near Mount Hope. Newspaper editors hated the twelve-letter name and used "Hams" as an alternate name.

2508 Blackbirds 1899 *Canadian (ind.)*. Players wore black hose. Some teams in this era had bird nicknames according to their stocking colors.

2509 Kolts 1911–12 *Canadian (D 1911, C 1912)*. Team had young players. With manager George "Knotty" Lee at the helm, newspapers called the young players "Knotty Lee's Kolts."

2510 Tigers 1915 *Canadian (B)*; 1919–23 *Michigan–Ontario (B)*; 1930x *Ontario (C)*. Team disbanded July 3 because of the Great Depression. The players wore striped stirrups. Team had a loose affiliation with the Detroit Tigers, using the nickname, which was pioneered in Canada by the National Hockey Association's Hamilton Tigers.

2511 Red Wings 1939–42 *Pennsylvania–Ohio–New York (P.O.N.Y.) (D)*. These teams were farm clubs of the St. Louis Cardinals.

2512 Cardinals 1946–56 *Pennsylvania–Ohio–New York (P.O.N.Y.) (D)*. Team was a farm club of the St. Louis Cardinals.

2513 Redbirds 1988–92 *New York–Pennsylvania (A)*. Team was a farm club of the St. Louis Cardinals.

Hamlin, Texas

2514 Pipers 1928m *West Texas (D)*. Team moved to Big Spring (TX) July 3. A famous legend from the Middle Ages describes how the "Pied Piper" of Hamlin, England, tunefully entranced the rats of the city with his enchanted flute to follow him on a road out of the city and to their destruction in a nearby river.

Hammond, Indiana

2515 Hammond Base Ball Club 1895x *Western Inter-State (ind.)*. Team and league disbanded June 15; 1923–24 *Southern California (W)*. Black team of players from Hammond, Indiana, played pro winter ball 1923–24, calling themselves the Hammond Baseball Club, using Los Angeles as their home city. Team went back to Indiana to play semi-professional ball in the spring. These teams had no nickname.

Hammond, Louisiana

2516 Berries 1946–51 *Evangeline (D 1946–48, C 1949–51)*. Farmers in the region grow strawberries, blueberries, raspberries and mulberries, which are then transported to packing houses in the city. Hammond is the "Strawberry Capital of America."

Hampton, Virginia

2517 Hampton Base Ball Club m1896 *Virginia (ind.)*; 1897x *Southeast Virginia (ind.)*. These teams had no nickname.

2518 Shipbuilders 1900 *Virginia (ind.)*. Newport News, by 1896, had become a major ship-building center and seaport. Team had the single-city name of "Newport News."

Hampton–Newport News, Virginia

2519 Hampton–Newport News Base Ball Club 1894 *Virginia (ind.)*. Team had no nickname.

2520 Shipbuilders 1901 *Virginia–North Carolina (ind.)*. This club was a new team with the same name. Although this team represented both cities, its formal name was "Newport News," just as it was in 1900.

2521 Peninsula Senators 1963 *Carolina (A)*. Team went by the regional name of Peninsula Senators. Team was a farm club of the Washington Senators.

2522 Peninsula Grays 1964–68 *Carolina (A)*. Team went by the regional name of Peninsula Grays. Rebel pride, albeit a desperate one, was manifested in 1861 by the residents of Hampton, who burned the city rather than allow it to be occupied by Union troops.

2523 Peninsula Astros 1969–70 *Carolina (A)*. Team went by the regional name of Peninsula Astros. The team was a farm club of the Houston Astros.

2524 Peninsula Pilots 1971 *Carolina (A)*; 1976–78 *West Carolinas (A)*. Both teams went by the regional name of the Peninsula Pilots. Pilot ships have guided cargo ships and freighters in the Chesapeake Bay and James, Elizabeth and Nansemond rivers since at least 1700.

2525 Peninsula Whips 1972–73 *International (AAA)*. After the 1971 season, the Winnipeg Whips moved to Hampton–Newport News (VA). The nickname was retained.

2526 Peninsula Pennants 1974 *Carolina (A)*. Alliterative moniker was a spin-off from "Whips." In the nineteenth century a baseball pennant was often called a "whip-pennant" because it whipped about in a strong breeze.

2527 Peninsula White Sox 1986–87 *Carolina (A)*. Team was a farm club of the Chicago White Sox.

Hancock, Michigan

2528 Hancock Base Ball Club 1890 *Upper Peninsula (ind.)*. Team had no nickname.

2529 Infants 1905 *Copper Country Soo (D)*; 1906x *Northern Copper Country (C)*. Team disbanded July 29. Team in both seasons struggled, using young players. With manager John Condon at the helm, newspapers called the young players "Condon's Infants." The youthful team was overmatched, posting a 38–58 record in 1905 and a 29–34 mark in 1906.

Hanford, California

2530 Braves 1911 *San Joaquin Valley (D)*. With manager Sydney Jehl (pronounced "jail") at the helm, newspapers called the players the rhyming "Jehl's Braves." In this era "Braves" was a generic term for "baseball players."

Hannibal, Missouri

2531 Cannibals 1908 *Illinois–Missouri (D)*; 1909–12 *Central Assn. (D)*. In 1895, the professional San Antonio Missionaries (later Missions) stopped off in Longview (TX) to play an exhibition game with the local team. When the local boys ripped the pros by a 10–5 score, jubilant local newspapers boasted, "Locals cannibalize the Missionaries!" That team became known as the Longview Cannibals. When Hannibal was awarded a franchise in 1908 (Longview had disbanded years earlier), the rhyming (and available) nickname became an obvious choice.

2532 Eagles 1909 *Central Assn. (D)*. Name of Central College of Fayette (MO)—whose sports teams were the "Eagles"—was applied to the 1910 professional baseball team here. Newspapers preferred it, but the name was dropped to avoid confusion with the college team.

2533 Mules 1916–17x *Three-I (B)*. League shortened its season, ending it on July 8, 1917, due to U.S. entry into World War I. Although there are plenty of mules on Missouri farms, the nickname refers to a team that struggles on the field, i.e., "They played like mules." Teams in this era that played poorly were known variously as Midgets, Misfits, Innocents and Mules. Indeed, newspapers and the public often likened baseball players to mules, i.e., "mule-headed."

2534 Pilots 1947–48 *Central Assn. (C)*. Pilot boats have guided river traffic on the Mississippi River in and out of the city port since at least 1850.

2535 Stags 1952 *Mississippi–Ohio Valley (D)*. The white-tail deer inhabits Illinois.

2536 Cardinals 1953–54 *Mississippi–Ohio Valley (D)*. Team was a farm club of the St. Louis Cardinals.

2537 Pepsies 1955 *Mississippi–Ohio Valley (D)*. Management failed to meet the players' payroll on August 20, forcing the team onto the road. Team declared bankruptcy. Fans started to call the team the "Hannibal Bankruptcies," which was mirthfully shortened to the "Hannibal Pepsies." The tag has nothing to do with the Pepsi-Cola soft drink.

2538 Citizens 1955 *Mississippi–Ohio Valley (D)*. The city is the boyhood home of its "First Citizen" Mark Twain (his real name is Samuel Clemens). The team's home field was Samuel Clemens Field. With field managers Jim Granneman and then Allan Shinn at the helm, local newspapers called the players the alliterative "Jim's Citizens" and "Shinn's Citizens."

Hanover, Pennsylvania

2539 Hanover Base Ball Club 1896 *Cumberland Valley (ind.)*. Team had no nickname.

2540 Hornets 1915–16 *Blue Ridge (D)*. Moniker was alliterative, i.e., Hanover Hornets.

2541 Raiders 1917 *Blue Ridge (D)*; 1920–29 *Blue Ridge (D)*. Confederate general Jeb Stuart led his horse-mounted "Raiders" against Union cavalry at the Battle of Hanover in 1863. These teams had a loose affiliation with the Pittsburgh Pirates, hence the spin-off moniker of "Raiders." World War I ended in February 1919 but then the Spanish Influenza struck, forcing the franchise and the league to postpone operations until 1920. With manager Bert Weeden at the helm, newspapers called the players "Bert's Raiders." Joe Miller took over in 1922 and the name became "Miller's Raiders." Roy Clunk took over in 1925 and the name became "Roy's Raiders." Buck Ramsey took over in 1926 and the name became "Ramsey's Raiders." The name was retained through 1929.

Harlan, Kentucky

2542 Smokies 1948–54 *Mountain States (D 1948–53, C 1954)*; 1961–62 *Appalachian (D)*. Team was a farm of the Knoxville Smokies. In the era 1900–60, some lower classification (A-B-C-D) minor league teams were farm clubs of higher classification (AAA and AA) minor league teams. Higher classification minor league teams in the 1950s often sold equipment and uniforms to lower classification teams on a discount. In the 1950s, television was causing minor league baseball to lose lots of money.

2543 Yankees 1963 *Appalachian (A)*. Team was a farm club of the New York Yankees.

2544 Red Sox 1965 *Appalachian (R)*. Team was a farm club of the Boston Red Sox.

Harlingen, Texas

2545 Ladds 1931x *Rio Grande Valley (D)*. Team and league disbanded July 30 because of the Great Depression. E.P. Ladd was a railroad owner who founded the St. Louis, Brownsville & Mexico Railway in 1918. One of the important depots along the route was Harlingen.

2546 Hubs 1938 *Texas Valley (D)*. City is a transport point for three highways. Harlingen is known as the "Hub of the Rio Grande Valley."

2547 Capitals 1951–53 *Gulf Coast (B)*; 1954–55 *Big State (B)*. Harlingen is known as the "Economic Capital of the Rio Grande Valley" because it is the financial, trade and shipping center of south Texas. Team name was also spelled "Capitols."

2548 Rio Grande Valley Giants 1960–61 *Texas (AA)*. Team went by the regional name of Rio Grande Valley Giants. The team was a farm club of the San Francisco Giants.

2549 Rio Grande Valley White Wings 1976 *Gulf States (R)*; 1977 *Lone Star (A)*; 1994–2001 *Texas–Louisiana (ind.)*; 2002–04 *Central*

(ind.); 2006–10 *United (ind.)*; 2007 *Texas Winter (W)*. The Texas Winter League was affiliated with the United League with some UL franchises fielding teams in this circuit to play a winter schedule. The circuit lasted only this one season; 2011 to date *North American (ind.)*. The Golden, Northern and United leagues merged to form the North American League. All these clubs went by the regional name of Rio Grande Valley White Wings. The dove is a white-winged pigeon that is common in the South. It first migrated to the region in 1870 and multiplied in the millions, causing the city to legalize dove hunting in 1920. By 1990 the bird was nearly extinct but conservation laws have fostered its population growth.

Harriman, Texas

2550 Boosters 1914x *Appalachian (D)*. Team and circuit disbanded June 17. A team in the era 1900–20 that found itself in the thick of a pennant race often won the support of enthusiastic fans who formed a "booster club." Although the team played fairly well (14–13 and a mere half-game out of first place) — which encouraged the formation of a booster club — both the team and league disbanded in mid-season. With the onset of radio broadcasts of minor league games in the 1920s, booster clubs became passé as, in their stead, enthusiastic radio announcers "boosted" the home team. With manager Pit Pasini at the helm, newspapers called the players "Pit Pasini's Boosters."

Harrisburg, Pennsylvania

2551 High Bays 1883 *Interstate Assn.(ind.)*; 1884 *Eastern (ind.)*. The nearby Susquehanna River is called the "High Bay" because it flows at an elevated altitude from the Blue Mountains northwest of the city.

2552 Olympics 1884 *Eastern (ind.)*. Sports and athletics of the nineteenth century espoused fervent feelings for the ancient Greek Olympic Games, making "Olympics" a popular name. With manager R.M. Sturgeon at the helm, newspapers called the players "Sturgeon's Olympics."

2553 Ponies 1889 *Middle States (ind.)*; 1890 *Atlantic Assn. (ind.)*. When Jersey City disbanded July 22, a new team in Harrisburg joined the circuit, taking up Jersey City's slot, on July 24; 1911 *Tri-State (B)*. Fans and newspapers called the 1890 team the "Ponies," which was nineteenth-century baseball slang for "expansion team." Harrisburg newspapers in 1911 preferred "Ponies" because it was short and avoided confusion with the AL Washington club, which went by three names — Senators, Nationals and Capitals.

2554 Capital Citys 1890 *Pennsylvania State (ind.)*; 1904–14 *Tri-State (1904–06 D, B 1904–14)*. Starting in 1904, Capital Citys and Capitals became alternate names to avoid confusion with the AL Washington Senators. Local newspapers shortened the tag to "Caps" for headlines. Harrisburg has been the state capital of Pennsylvania since 1812.

2555 Hustlers 1893–94 *Pennsylvania State (ind.)*. "Hustlers" was an early slang for baseball players. In this era, the moniker referred to players who showed "hustle" on the field. The connotation with gambling did not arise until the "politically correct" 1970s.

2556 Senators 1894–95 *Pennsylvania State (ind.)*; 1904–14 *Tri-State (D 1904–06, (B). 1907–14 Tri-State (D)*; m1915 *International (AA)*. Team began season in Newark (NJ) and moved to Harrisburg July 2; 1924–35 *New York–Pennsylvania (B 1924–32, A 1933–35)*; 1940–42 *Inter-State (B)*; 1946–52 *Inter-State (B)*; 1987 to date *Eastern (A)*. In 1894 the moniker was a spin-off of the 1883 tag of "Capitals." Albert Selbach managed in 1910 and the team was "Selbach's Senators." In 1915, Harry Smith was manager, making the name "Smith's Senators."

2557 Harrisburg Baseball Club m1900x *Atlantic (ind.).* Franchise started season in Philadelphia, and moved to Harrisburg in mid-season. Team and league disbanded June 12. Team had no nickname.

2558 Capitals *(ind.).* 1904–14 *Tri-State (1904–06 D, B 1904–14).* The 1883 name was used again. Capitals became an alternate moniker to avoid confusion with the AL Washington Senators. Albert Selbach managed in 1910 and the team was "Selbach's Senators."

2559 Giants 1909 *Independent Negro team.* The tag "Giants" was a popular nickname for black teams, 1885–1955.

2560 Islanders m1916–17 *New York State (B).* Team began the season in Troy and moved to Harrisburg on June 20. The city was built on the East Bank peninsula of the Susquehanna River. A peninsula is a piece of land jutting into a body water, as though it were an island, but connected to the land mass by an isthmus.

2561 Stars 1943 *Negro National (M).* Team went by the dual-city name of Harrisburg-St. Louis Stars. With money tight and war-time travel restrictions in place, the 1942 St. Louis Stars played half their home games in Harrisburg (PA) in 1943, especially on the way to dates with East Coast clubs, to reduce travel expenses.

Harrisonburg, Virginia

2562 Lunatics m1914x *Virginia Mountain (D).* Team began season in Staunton and moved to Harrisonburg July 1. Team and league disbanded July 25. Just like the baseball cities of Jacksonville (IL) and Nevada (MO), whose teams also were named "Lunatics" after local mental hospitals, Harrisonburg's teams were labeled this way.

2563 Turks 1939–41 Virginia *(D 1939–40, C 1941).* Team won 1939 pennant. Student radicals, known as the "Young Turks," disrupted Turkish society in the period 1850–1900 in the old Ottoman Empire (today the country of Turkey) in order to foment revolution. By 1900, the term "Turk" or "Young Turk" meant any young man who was energetic and aggressively out-spoken, i.e., a political revolutionary. In baseball circles, a team that was in pennant contention usually consisted of aggressive players who were called "Young Turks" or "Turks." This baseball edition of "Turks" finished first in the regular season (although they lost in the playoffs). With manager Hank Hulvey at the helm, newspapers called the players "Hank Hulvey's Young Turks." Ironically, once the Ottoman Empire started to decline in the period 1848–1918, it became known as the "Tired Old Man of Europe."

Hartford, Connecticut

2564 Dark Blues 1874–75 *National Assn.(M);* 1876 *National (M);* 1886 *Eastern (ind.).* Team disbanded July 10, 1887. Players wore dark blue hose. Team switched leagues in 1876. Originally **Blue Stockings,** newspapers shortened name to "Dark Blues" and **Blues.**

2565 Nutmegs 1874–75 *National Assn.(M);* 1876 *National (M).* Connecticut is also known as the "Nutmeg State." Nutmeg is a spice found in the evergreen tree seed.

2566 Yankees 1874–75 *National Assn.(M);* 1876 *National (M).* Inhabitants of New England have been known as "Yankees" since 1700. The term originally meant "Dutchman," then "New Yorker," and now means "New Englander."

2567 Charter Oaks 1874–75 *National Assn.(M);* 1876 *National (M);* 1878 *International Assn. (M).* Connecticut is the "Charter Oak State." In 1687 Connecticut colonists placed their constitution, first drawn up in 1639, in an oak tree to hide it from soldiers of the pro-British governor Edmund Andros. The event became known as the "Charter Oak Incident." This constitution, the oldest in colonial America, was known as the "Fundamental Orders of Connecticut."

2568 Capital Citys 1884 *Connecticut (ind.).* Hartford has been the state capital of Connecticut since 1876. For the period 1701–1875, the city was the state co-capital along with New Haven. Originally "Capital Citys," the nickname was shortened by local newspapers to **Capitals.**

2569 Oaks 1885 *Southern New England (ind.).* Name was a contraction of "Charter Oaks," previously used by the 1878 Hartford team.

2570 Hartford Colored Base Ball Club 1885 *Independent Negro team.* Team had no nickname. Team was reportedly semi-professional but may have paid several players a salary under the table.

2571 Yankees 1886–87x *Eastern (ind.);* 1890x *Atlantic Assn. (ind.).* Team disbanded August 25; 1901x *Eastern (ind.).* Team disbanded September 10. The name refers to any inhabitant of New England. The state song is "Yankee Doodle Dandy." The moniker was popularized by Mark Twain's story *A Connecticut Yankee in King Arthur's Court,* which was first published in 1889. Moniker wound up in New York in 1903 with the New York American League franchise.

2572 Nutmeggers 1889 *Atlantic Assn. (ind.).* Because the state was forested with evergreen (aka nutmeg) trees (and oak trees as well), the inhabitants of seventeenth and eighteenth century Connecticut soon became known as "Nutmeggers."

2573 Bluebirds 1896–98 *Atlantic (ind.).* Players wore blue hose.

2574 Cooperatives 1898–99 *Atlantic (ind.).* By 1895 Hartford has become known as the "Insurance City." In this era, a "cooperative" referred to an insurance business. In the 1870s, a sports cooperative referred to a professional baseball team. Hartford newspapers immediately shortened the name to **Co-ops** but Hartford fans didn't like it.

2575 Indians 1899–1901x *Eastern (ind.).* War erupted between the colonists and native Pequot Indians in the seventeenth century. The fight led to King Phillip's War (1675–76), ending the hold on the region by the Pequot and Wampanoag Indians. With manager Billy Barnie at the helm 1899–1900, newspapers called the players "Barnie's Indians." Bill Shindle took over in July 1900 and the name became "Shindle's Indians."

2576 Wooden Nutmegs 1901 *Eastern (ind.).* The nearby Meshomasic Forest Preserve, southwest of the city, has thousands of oak and nutmeg trees.

2577 Senators 1902–12 Connecticut *(D 1902–04, B 1905–12);* 1913–14 *Eastern Assn. (B);* 1915 *Colonial (ind.);* 1916–30x *Eastern (B).* 1916–18, *(A).* 1919–30 Team disbanded June 30 because of the Great Depression; 1931–32x *Eastern (A).* Team and league disbanded July 17 because of the Great Depression; 1934 *Northeastern (B).* Hartford has been the state capital of Connecticut since 1876. With manager William Kennedy at the helm in 1904–05, newspapers called the players "Kennedy's Senators."

2578 Laurels 1938, 1944 *Eastern (A).* Since the cities Hartford and Boston openly proclaim their ties to ancient Greek culture and learning, the 1938 team was known as "Onslow's Laurels." The laurel wreath was a crown placed on the heads of athletes who won a sporting contest in the ancient Olympic Games. However, no laurels were in store for the 1938 team, which finished fourth with a 66–67 record. Name was also appropriate because Connecticut has forests of laurel oak trees. The 1944 team captured league "laurels" by finishing first in the regular season (although they lost in the playoffs) under manager Del Bisonette, prompting newspapers to call the players "Del's Laurels."

2579 Bees 1939–43, 1945–46 *Eastern (A).* Even though the Boston parent club switched back to Braves in 1941, the Hartford management kept "Bees" because it avoided confusion with the parent club, and Hartford newspapers relished its four-letter name length.

2580 Chiefs 1947–52 *Eastern (A)*. Management dropped Bees, which had become passé, and went to "Chiefs," a spin-off of Braves that was fairly short to satisfy Hartford newspaper editors.

Hastings, Nebraska

2581 Reds 1887 *Western (ind.)*; 1914–15 *Nebraska State (D)*. Players wore red hose. Originally "Red Stockings," local newspapers shortened it to Reds. The 1914–15 team was not a farm club of the Cincinnati Reds, as there would be no farm system in existence for another ten years.

2582 Hustlers 1892 *Nebraska State (ind.)*. The term "hustler" was complimentary, admiring baseball jargon for a disciplined player who "hustled on the field." The negative connotation with gambling did not arise until the "politically correct" 1970s.

2583 Brickmakers 1910 *Nebraska State (D)*. City was noted for its brick-making industry. By the turn of the century brick-making was exceeded only by farm products as the city's leading industry. By the 1920s, however, farm machine manufacturing took over as brick-making faded because bricks were now machine produced and could be manufactured across the country.

2584 Third Citys 1911–13 *Nebraska State (D)*. By 1910, Hastings was known as the "Third City of Nebraska" because it ranked third in population behind Omaha (first) and Lincoln (second).

2585 Cubs 1922–23 *Nebraska State (D)*; 1924x *Nebraska State (D)*. Team and league disbanded July 17. These teams entered into a loose affiliation with the Chicago Cubs, purchasing old Cubs uniforms and equipment at a discount.

2586 Giants 1956–59 *Nebraska State (D)*. Team was a farm club of the New York Giants in 1956–57 and the San Francisco Giants in 1958–59.

Hattiesburg, Forrest, Mississippi

2587 Hattiesburg Baseball Club 1904 *Delta (D)*. Team had no nickname.

2588 Tar Heels 1905x *Cotton States (D)*. Team disbanded July 17. Lumber mills produced wood tar by distillation. Workers in lumber mills here were known as "tar heels." Moniker has nothing to do with the "Tar Heel State" of North Carolina.

2589 Timberjacks 1910 *Cotton States (D)*. Around the turn of the century lumber was the leading city industry. By 1920 textiles and chemical manufacturing had taken the lead. Because of the nearby pine forests and lumber industry, the surrounding county was named Forrest County. With manager Link Stickney at the helm, newspapers called the players "Link Stickney's Timberjacks."

2590 Woodpeckers 1910–11 *Cotton States (D)*. Team moved to Columbus (MS) June 5. In summer and winter woodpeckers are found in great numbers in nearby DeSoto National Forest, which is about 20 miles southwest of the city. With manager Link Stickney at the helm, newspapers called the players "Link Stickney's Wood-peckers."

2591 Hubmen 1923–24 *Cotton States (D)*. The city is at the convergence of six major highways and four railroads. In the 1920s trucks transported raw materials into town and then textiles and refined chemicals out of the city. In the era 1870–1930 numerous baseball teams in the cities that were major transportation hubs were known as the "Hubs" and "Hub Men." With manager Herschel Bobo at the helm, newspapers called the players "Herschel's Hubmen."

2592 Hubbers 1925 *Cotton States (D)*. Herschel Bobo returned to the helm as manager, prompting newspaper reporters to call the players "Herschel Bobo's Hubbers."

2593 Pine-toppers 1925–29 *Cotton States (D)*. Team moved to Baton Rouge (LA) May 30. The nearby DeSoto National Forest has thousands of pine trees. Nickname was appropriate as the team won the 1925 pennant with a 77–46 record to finish first "atop the pines" of the league's eight teams.

Havana, Distrito Federal, Cuba (La Habana in Spanish)

2594 Club de Cuba 1898 *Cuban (ind.)*; 1947–48 *Nacional (W)*. Each team represented Cuba. The 1947–48 circuit was an outlaw league for those Cuban players who refused to return to the old Cuban League once the Mexican Outlaw League signings were forgotten and the blacklist against the "outlaw players" was lifted. In essence, it was the successor of the 1946–47 outlaw "Federacion." The Cuban League in Spanish is La Liga Cubana.

2595 Azules de Almendares 1898–99 *Cuban (W)*; 1901–16 *Cuban (W)*; 1918–33 *Cuban (W)*; 1934–35–60–61. Players wore blue hose. Team, playing in El Estadio Almendares, went by the ballpark name of Almendares "Blues." Los Azules is Spanish for "Blues." The Cuban League is the Liga Cubana in Spanish.

2596 Cubanos 1898–1902 *Liga Cubana (W)*; 1946–53 *Florida–International (C)*. 1946–48, *(B)*. 1949–53; 1954–60m *International (AAA)*. Each team represented Cuba. "Los Cubanos" means "Cubans." The IL team was formally known as "Sugar Kings" but was also called "Los Cubanos" because it was the only Cuban team in the International League.

2597 Fe 1900 *Liga Cubana (W)*; 1905–16 *Liga Cubana (W)*. Cuba was the first new world land to receive the Roman Catholic faith. Fe is the Spanish word for "Faith."

2598 Carmelitas de San Francisco 1901–02 *Liga Cubana (W)*; 1904 *Liga Cubana (W)*. These teams went by the city district name of "Los Carmelitas de San Francisco." In the twelfth century Palestine, during the Crusades, a Christian religious order was established by building a church on Mount Carmel. The order's adherents were known as the "Carmelites." Carmelite friars came to Cuba starting in the sixteenth century.

2599 Rojos 1901–16 *Cuban (W)*; 1918–33 *Cuban (W)*; 1934–35–60–61 *Cuban (W)*. Players wore red-trim uniforms, red stockings (through 1906) and red stirrups (beginning in 1907). Starting in 1876, the team mascot was a lion — a nickname that would surface in 1946.

2600 Leones 1901–16 *Cuban (W)*; 1918–33 *Cuban (W)*; 1934–35–60–61 *Cuban (W)*; 1946–47 *Federacion (W)*. When the franchise was founded as a semi-professional team in 1878, Havana fans praised the players for being "aggressive and fiery" much like a lion, which became the team mascot in 1876. From 1878 until 1945, the team went by two monikers—"Leones" and "Rojos." The name "Leones" was chosen as the team's official nickname in a name-the-team contest at the start of the 1945–46 season to better market the team. By 1946–47 there was a schism in Cuban baseball that resulted in two circuits: the Cuban League and the Cuban Federation. The latter league was formed to sign ostracized players of the old Cuban League who had been illegally acquired by Jorge Pascual to play in the outlaw Mexican League of 1946. The Havana FL club simply "appropriated" the 1945–46 CL Havana team's nickname of "Lions" while the CL team, in response, used its other moniker of Havana "Reds." By 1948–49 the blacklisted players were allowed to return to the Cuban League. The CL team had a "Lions" mascot logo but, as for the previous 68 years, Lions and Reds (Rojos) were used interchangeably.

2601 Lincoln Giants 1914–15 *Cuban (W)*. The New York Lincoln Giants played this winter season in the Cuban League and represented Havana.

2602 Red Sox 1917 *Cuban (ind.)*. A spin-off from Reds (Rojos), the moniker (Los Medias Rojas in Spanish) was marketed in both English and Spanish.

2603 White Sox 1917 *Cuban (ind.)*. The circuit this year played its schedule of games in the summer. To reproduce the Havana-Almendares red and blue rivalry of old, this team chose white stirrups to rival the all-red stirrups of the other Havana team. The moniker was marketed in both English and Spanish. White Sox in Spanish is "Los Medias Blancas."

2604 Estrellas Cubanos 1918–19 *Cuban (W)*. Team advertised itself as having star players. The team's uniform logo was the Cuban flag, which has red, white and blue colors with a single star in the center. "Las Estrellas Cubanos" means Cuban Stars in English.

2605 America 1919–20x *Cuban (W)*. The New World was named in honor of Italian explorer and cartographer Amerigo Vespucci and not Christopher Columbus. Cuba was the first land of the New World discovered by Columbus.

2606 Bacharach Giants 1919–20 *Cuban (W)*. The Atlantic City Bacharach Giants, like the Lincoln Giants five years earlier, joined the Cuban Winter League this season and represented Havana.

2607 Regla 1931–32 *Cuban (W)*. This team played at a baseball park located in the Regla District of Havana.

2608 Alacranes 1945–46–60–61 *Cuban (W)*. The Cuban League sponsored fan polls to choose "strong and powerful" mascots for each of the four teams in the league. Havana fans chose Lions (los Leones), Marianao chose Tigers (los Tigres), Cienfuegos chose Elephants (los Elefantes) and Almendares chose Scorpions (los Alacranes). Scorpions are arthropods that inhabit the warm, moist climate of Cuba's jungles.

2609 Sugar Kings 1954–60m *International (AAA)*. Cuban sugar plantations transport sugar cane to processing factories in Havana for processing and packing. The team's official name was the English "Havana Sugar Kings." Some Cuban newspapers called the players "Los Reyes de Azucar" but preferred "Los Cubanos."

2610 Club de Beisbol de la Habana 1961–62 *Cuban National (S)*; 1967–68–73–74 *Cuban National (S)*; 1977–78 to date *Cuban National (S)*. These teams had no nickname.

2611 Azucareros 1961–62–63–64 *Cuban National (S)*; 1967–68–76–77 *Cuban National (S)*. Cuba is the world's largest exporter of sugar. Sugar has been Cuba's largest crop since 1850, surpassing even tobacco. Sugar plantations in central and western Cuba transport sugar by truck and train to Havana's sugar-processing factories. "Los Azucareros" means "sugar-planters." It does not mean "Sugar Kings."

2612 Occidentales 1961–62–66–67 *Cuban National (S)*. Havana is located in western Cuba. "El occidental" means "western." Name in English can mean "Westerners" or "Westerns."

2613 Industriales 1962–63 to date *Cuban National (ind.)*. Once he consolidated power in 1960, Fidel Castro ordered industrialization of the Cuban economy much the way Stalin in the 1930s and Mao Tse-Tung in the 1950s ordered the industrialization of the Soviet Union and China, respectively. Although copper and gypsum were mined in Havana Province, most early industrialization in Castro's Cuba required the importation of raw materials and machinery from the USSR, China and Eastern Europe.

2614 Constructores 1962–63–76–77 *Cuban National (S)*. Starting in 1963, Fidel Castro ordered state-sponsored building construction in Cuba's largest cities. "Los constructores" is Spanish for "builders."

2615 Mineros 1967–68–76–77 *Cuban National (S)*. Cuban manganese, iron, nickel and copper mines ship metal ore to factories in Havana and other cities for smelting. "Los mineros" means "miners."

2616 Metropolitanos 1974–75 to date *Cuban National (S)*. With a city population of 2.5 million and a metro population of 4 million, Havana is the "Great Metropolis of Cuba," i.e., "La Gran Metropolis de Cuba."

2617 Agricultores 1974–75–76–77 *Cuban National (S)*. Havana Province has many citrus fruit, rice and tobacco farms. Los Agricultores means farmers.

2618 Arroceros 1974–75–76–77 *Cuban National (S)*. Rice farms to the west of the city transport rice to Havana factories to be processed and packed for shipping to market. "Los arroceros" means "rice farmers."

2619 Vaqueros 1977–78 to date *Cuban National (S)*. Although Cuba is a tropical island, the cattle industry does require cowboys on horseback to herd cattle to ranches and meat-packing factories, especially in central and eastern Cuba. Havana is the island's leading meat-packing center. "Los vaqueros" means "cowboys."

Havana, Illinois

2620 Perfectos 1908 *Illinois–Missouri (D)*. After the 1899 St. Louis "Perfectos" signed away the best players of the 1898 Cleveland Spiders (ruining that team), the moniker "Perfectos" was used as self-promotion by management when it signed a slew of players with designs on winning a pennant. This team was a long way from "perfect," finishing third of six teams with a mediocre 58–61 record.

Haverhill, Massachusetts

2621 Reds 1885–86 *Eastern (ind.)*; m1887 *New England (ind.)*. Team began season as the Boston Reds and then moved to Haverhill July 11 to replace the nameless Haverhill club that had disbanded earlier that same day. Players on both teams wore red hose. Team had a loose affiliation with the NL Boston Red Stockings (aka Beaneaters). Originally **Red Stockings**, newspapers shortened the name to "Reds" and **Redlegs**.

2622 Colts 1886 *Eastern (ind.)*. Team had many young players. Of the plethora of names for young players, i.e., Babes, Chicks, Cubs, Ponies and so on, "Colts" was by far the most popular in the nineteenth century. All these names were replaced by "rookie" in 1917.

2623 Haverhill Base Ball Club 1887x Team disbanded July 11; 1888 *New England Inter-State (ind.)*; 1894 *New England (ind.)*. These teams had no nickname.

2624 Duffers m1895x *New England Assn. (ind.)*. Team started season in Fitchburg (MA) and moved to Haverhill June 20. Team disbanded July 8. Led by manager W.T. Dwyer, the team finished sixth and last with a 12–26 record, prompting newspapers to sarcastically call the players "Dwyer's Duffers." A "duffer" means a person who is awkward and clumsy, especially in a sport like baseball or golf.

2625 Hustlers 1901–12 *New England (ind. 1901, B 1902–12)*; 1914 *New England (B)*. Hustlers first appeared in the 1880s as slang for "baseball players." The name, politically incorrect today because it provokes uneasy feelings about gambling, was strictly complimentary, i.e., "players who hustled on the field." The nickname was reinforced when the 1904 team "hustled its way" to a pennant with an 82–41 record. In 1907 manager Billy Hamilton guided his players, known in newspapers as "Hamilton's Hustlers." Hamilton managed the team in 1902–04 and 1907–08.

2626 Orphans 1919x *New England (B)*. Team and league disbanded August 2. In the era 1895–1920, teams that were young and inexperienced often started losing in bunches, prompting home city fans to stay away. Invariably, such a team was forced to extended stays on the road to reduce revenue losses. Teams in this dilemma were known as "Wanderers" and "Orphans," the latter term used because the home fans stayed away from the ballpark "abandoning the players as though they were orphans."

2627 Climbers 1919x *New England (B)*. Team and league disbanded August 2 because of health concerns caused by the Spanish Influenza. "Climbers"—along with "Comets"—was baseball slang for a team that got off to a hot start in the pennant race in April and May. In this case the moniker more directly is in reference to the city's Ayer's Hill, which is 340 feet in height. The team never "climbed" in the standings but rather plummeted to a 27–40 record, sixth and last place, a road schedule in July and disbandment on August 2.

2628 Hillies 1926–29m *New England (B)*. Team moved to Fitchburg (MA) July 28, 1929. The highest site in the city is Ayer's Hill. The name was used in newspaper headlines, i.e., "Hillies edge Blue Sox, 4–3." The city elevation is about 108 feet along the Merrimac River.

Haverstraw, New York

2629 Haverstraw Base Ball Club 1888 *Hudson River (ind.)*. Team had no nickname.

Hayward, California

2630 Hayward Baseball Club m1910m *Central California (ind.)*. Team began the 1910 season in San Rafael (CA) before moving to Hayward June 12 and then moved to Fruitvale (CA) July 10. Team had no nickname.

2631 Cubs 1911x *Central California (D)*. Team and league disbanded July 9. Along with Giants, "Cubs" was the favorite moniker of several minor league teams of this era seeking to emulate a big league club by choosing their team name. This team also had young players, making the newspaper-friendly name desirable.

Hazard, Kentucky

2632 Bombers m1948–52 *Mountain States (D)*. Team started 1948 season as the Oak Ridge "Bombers" and moved to Hazard June 10, where the nickname was retained. The Oak Ridge team got the name because that city was the site of a research laboratory, for the 1940–45 Manhattan Project, to develop an atomic bomb. Manager Hobe Brummit was at the helm for the entire season, prompting newspapers in both cities to call the players "Hobe's Brummit's Bombers."

Hazlehurst-Baxley, Georgia

2633 Red Socks 1949 *Georgia State (D)*. Players wore red stirrups.

2634 Red Sox 1950–51 *Georgia State (D)*. Tag was a spin-off of Red Socks. Team was not a farm club of the Boston Red Sox.

2635 Cardinals 1952–55 *Georgia State (D)*. Team was a farm club of the St. Louis Cardinals.

2636 Tigers 1956 *Georgia State (D)*. Team was a farm club of the Detroit Tigers.

Hazleton, Pennsylvania

2637 Hazleton Base Ball Club 1887 *Central Pennsylvania (ind.)*; 1889 *Middle States (ind.)*. These teams had no nickname.

2638 Pugilists 1888 *Central (ind.)*. The "Big Three" sports of this era were baseball, horse racing and boxing. Argumentative and fist-swinging baseball players were known as "Kickers" and "Pugilists." The nineteenth century was also the Golden Era of Boxing with such champions as John L. Sullivan, Jim Corbett and Jack Johnson.

2639 Quakers 1894–96 *Pennsylvania State (ind.)*. Pennsylvania is the "Quaker State." In 1681 King Charles II of England gave Quaker proprietor William Penn most of modern-day Pennsylvania to found a colony there. For the next 200 years there was a steady influx of Mennonite Quakers into the region. Alternate spelling was: **Quaykers**.

2640 Barons 1894–96 *Pennsylvania State (ind.)*. Coal barons established mines here shortly after the city was established in 1851.

2641 Mountaineers m1929–32 *New York Pennsylvania (B)*. Team began the 1929 season in Syracuse (NY) and then moved to Hazleton June 16; 1934–36 *New York–Pennsylvania (A)*; 1939–40m *Inter-State (C 1939, B 1940)*. Team moved to Lancaster (PA) June 12; 1949 *North Atlantic (D)*. Known as "Pennsylvania's Highest City," Hazleton is located on the slopes of the Nescopeck Mountains. With manager Irvin "Kaiser" Wilhelm at the helm, newspapers called the players "Irvin Wilhelm's Mountaineers."

2642 Red Sox 1938 *Eastern (A)*. Team was a farm club of the Boston Red Sox.

2643 Dodgers 1950 *North Atlantic (D)*. Team was a farm club of the Brooklyn Dodgers.

Headland, Alabama

2644 Dixie Runners 1950 *Alabama State (D)*; 1951–52 *Alabama–Florida (D)*. During the Civil War, Confederate boats known as "Runners" often attempted to "run the blockade" set up by the Union Navy on the Mississippi River and in the Gulf of Mexico.

Healdsburg, California

2645 Grapevines 1910m *Central California (C)*. Team moved to San Leandro (CA) April 24. Vineyards in the region transport grapes to wineries in the city.

Heemstede, North Holland, Netherlands

2646 Pinguins 1999–2001 *Hoofdklasse (ind.)*; 2010 to date *Hoofdklasse (ind.)*. The Racing Club of Heemstede, a boat racing team of 1900 with the water bird penguin as its mascot, sponsored a soccer team in 1930 known as the RCH Penguins. In 1999 the soccer club sponsored this professional baseball team that plays in Heemstede to date. In 2001 the PC Zone — a Dutch computer company — bought the team, which became known as PC Zone RCH "Pinguins." In 2010, team owner decided to drop the 10-letter "Media Monks" in favor of the old and popular "Pinguins."

2647 Media Monks 2007–09 *Hoofdklasse (ind.)*. The team owner became the "Media Monks" Interactive Marketing Company, which manufactures video tapes and games.

Helena, Arkansas

2648 Hellions 1908–09x *Arkansas State (D)*. Since a "hellion" means a "disorderly, troublesome and rowdy" person, it was a perfect match for the baseball players of this era who were rarely "genteel." Newspapers continued calling this team "Hellions," as the players battled "hellaciously" for the 1909 pennant, situating them in second place with a fine 39–25 record and only a half-game out of the lead when the team and the circuit disbanded on July 7 due to financial woes.

2649 Helena Base Ball Club 1911 *Northeast Arkansas (D)*. Team had no nickname.

2650 Sea-porters 1935 *East Dixie (C)*; 1936–41 *Cotton States (C)*; 1947–49 *Cotton States (C)*. The city, built along the Mississippi River, is the only riverport, i.e., "seaport," in Arkansas. Helena is nicknamed "Arkansas's Only Seaport." With manager Riggs Stephenson at the helm in 1938, newspapers called the players "Riggs Stephenson's Sea-porters."

Helena, Montana

2651 Helena Base Ball Club 1892 *Montana State (ind.)*. Team had no nickname.

2652 Senators 1900 *Montana State (ind.)*; 1902 *Pacific Northwest (B)*; 1903x *Pacific National (A)*. Team disbanded August 16; 1909x *Inter-Mountain (D)*. Team and league disbanded July 25; 1911–14 *Union Assn. (D)*. Helena has been the state capital of Montana since 1894. City was also the territorial capital of Montana from 1875–93. Danny Shay managed the 1913 team known as "Shay's Senators."

2653 Phillies 1978–83 *Pioneer (R)*. Team was a farm club of the Philadelphia Phillies.

2654 Gold Sox 1984–86 *Pioneer (R)*. Gold was discovered at the Last Chance Gulch, near the city's present site in 1864, giving rise to "The 1864 Gold Rush." The mining camps grew into today's city of Helena, which was incorporated in 1881.

2655 Brewers 1987–2000 *Pioneer (R)*; 2003 to date *Pioneer (R)*. These teams were farm clubs of the Milwaukee Brewers.

Henderson, Kentucky

2656 Henderson Base Ball Club 1896–97x *Kentucky–Indiana (ind.)*. Team and circuit disbanded July 7; 1916x *Kentucky–Illinois–Tennessee KITTY (D)*. Team and league disbanded August 4. These teams had no nickname.

2657 Bluebirds 1903–04 *Kentucky–Illinois–Tennessee KITTY (D)*. Players wore blue hose. In the era 1890–1910, bird names were sometimes used to reflect the stocking color, i.e., Blackbirds, Bluebirds, Blue Jays, Cardinals, Doves, Ravens and Redbirds.

2658 Hens 1905 *Kentucky–Illinois–Tennessee KITTY (D)*; m1911–14 *Kentucky–Illinois–Tennessee KITTY (D)*. Team began 1911 season in McLeansboro (TN) and then moved to Henderson June 20. Moniker was used in newspaper headlines, i.e., "Hens edge Hoppers, 4–3." With numerous chicken farms in the vicinity, the name was appropriate.

Henderson, North Carolina

Note: Not to be confused with Hendersonville, NC.

2659 Bunnies 1929 *Piedmont (C)*. With field manager Bunn Hearn at the helm, local newspapers called the players "Bunn's Bunnies." There are plenty of rabbits in North Carolina.

2660 Gamecocks 1930–31 *Piedmont (C)*. Gamecocks are roosters trained for fighting—a betting activity in the Carolinas that started in the seventeenth century. The nearby University of South Carolina "Fighting Gamecocks" have used the moniker since 1903. Gamecocks have been used in North America for "cock-fighting" since at least 1700. The bloody sport has started to be outlawed in the last 40 years. Perhaps to atone for this past, Henderson established bird sanctuaries, a refuge where predation is prevented and hunting prohibited. For that reason, Henderson is now known as the "Bird Sanctuary."

Henderson, Texas

2661 Oilers 1931x *East Texas (D)*. Team and league disbanded May 7; 1933 *Dixie (D)*; 1934–35 *West Dixie (C)*; 1936–40 *East Texas (C)*; 1946 *East Texas (C)*; 1947–48 *Lone Star (C)*; *East Texas (C)*. 1949–50. In 1931, the East Texas Oil Fields, i.e., the "Black Giant"

and enormous oil rig, was built 43 miles from the city after oil had been discovered in the region in 1930.

Hendersonville, North Carolina

Note: Not to be confused with Henderson, NC.

2662 Skylarks 1948–49 *Western Carolina (D)*. Skylarks are the mountain larks of the nearby Blue Ridge Mountains.

Henryetta, Oklahoma

2663 Boosters m1914 *Western Assn. (D)*. Team started season in Webb City (OK), moved to Guthrie (OK) July 10, and then moved to Henryetta July 22. "Boosters" was a name not only given to pennant-contending and pennant-winning teams of this era but also to teams transferring to a new city in mid-season. In a mid-season franchise transfer, fans of the new city would sometimes enthusiastically welcome the transferring team, no matter what its previous won-lost record, and form booster clubs, even if the team went on to fare poorly on the field in the second half of the season. The new team fared disastrously, going 11–44 for their time in Guthrie.

2664 Hens 1920–23x *Western Assn. (D 1920–21, C 1922–23)*. Team disbanded July 21. Moniker was used in newspaper headlines, i.e., "Hens edge Chicks, 4–3."

Herkimer, New York

2665 Trailbusters 2007 *New York State (ind.)*. General Nicholas Herkimer led American troops along difficult trails against the British here in the Battle of Oriskany in 1777. City was settled in 1725 by German immigrants who "blazed a trail" south of the Adirondack Mountains. Trails here were used by soldiers (who built Fort Herkimer in 1730), settlers, and Mohawk Indians during battles in the French and Indian War (19750–70). "Trailbuster" is another term for "trailblazer." Note: Team played its 2007 schedule in Utica (NY). Circuit disbanded after the 2007 season. The term "trail-busters" also means "trailblazers" and "trailbreakers."

Hermosillo, Sonora, Mexico

2666 Presidentes 1945–46 *Liga de la Costa de Mexico (W)*. Team was owned by Ron El Presidente, a liquor company producing rum, tequila, mescal and other liquors. "Ron" is Spanish for "rum." The Spanish "Los Presidentes" means the "Presidents."

2667 Naranjeos 1948–49–57–58 *Mexican Pacific Coast (W)*; 1958–59–69–70 *Sonora–Sinoloa (W)*. The Mexican Pacific Coast League reorganized and became the Sonora–Sinola League with the "Naranjeros" as a charter team in 1958–59; 1970–71 to date *Mexican Pacific (W)*; 1976 *Mexican Pacific (A)*. The winter league tried to play a summer schedule but low attendance halted the experiment following the 1976 season. Oranges and other citrus fruit from nearby groves are transported to city factories for cleaning, packing and shipment to market. The team's name in Spanish—"Los Naranjeros"—can be translated into English as Orange Men, Orange-farmers, Orange-Growers and Orange-Packers.

Herrin, Illinois

2668 Herrin Base Ball Club 1910x *Southern Illinois (D)*. Team and league disbanded July 11. Team had no nickname.

Hiawatha, Kansas

2669 Boosters 1910 *Eastern Kansas (D).* Hiawatha fans were so happy to get a team — even though the club eventually wound up a mediocre 44–44 for a third-place finish — that they formed a booster club. A team that was winning enough to get involved in a heated pennant race often spurred its fans to form booster clubs, which sometimes was applied as a nickname for the team. Booster clubs was the term used for organized fan clubs of the era 1900–20. After that the term became "fan club."

2670 Athletics 1912 *Missouri, Iowa, Nebraska and Kansas (M.I.N.K.) (D).* Moniker was alliterative, i.e., Hiawatha Athletics. Team was not a farm club of the Philadelphia Athletics as the farm system was still 15 years away.

Hibbing, Minnesota

2671 Minnesota Skeeters 1995 *North Central (ind.).* Surrounded by forests, rivers and lakes in all directions in a 50-mile radius, the city is invaded by mosquitoes in spring and summer. "Skeeters" is slang for mosquitoes.

Hickory, North Carolina

2672 Rebels 1939–40 *Tar Heel (D)*; 1942 *North Carolina State (D)*; 1945–50 *North Carolina State (D)*; 1952 *Western Carolina (D)*; 1953–54 *Tar Heel (D)*; 1960 *Western Carolina (D).* North Carolina was ravaged by war at the Battle of Fort Macon, Battle of Fort Fisher in 1862, and again in 1865 at the Battle of Bentonville in 1865.

2673 Crawdads 1993 to date *South Atlantic (A).* North Carolina's fishing industry includes Menhaden, Blue Fish, Flounder, Mackerel, Red Lobster and small lobsters known as crawfish and "Crawdaddys."

High Point, North Carolina

2674 Furniture Makers 1920–22 *Piedmont (D 1920, C 1921–22).* Since the city was founded in 1859, lumber from the Pisgah and Uwharrie National Forests has been imported here to city factories to manufacture finished wood and furniture. High Point is the "Furniture City" and the "Furniture City of the World." Over the years, the city has been home to about ninety furniture factories.

2675 Pointers 1923–25m *Piedmont (C).* Team moved to Danville (VA) June 18; m1926–32x *Piedmont (C 1926–31, B 1932).* Team started 1926 season in Danville (VA) and then moved to High Point May 12. Team disbanded July 7, 1932, and was replaced by a new franchise in 1932; m1932 *Piedmont (B).* Team started season in Winston-Salem (NC) before moving to High Point August 20, replacing the 1926–32 franchise that had disbanded a week earlier. Moniker was used for newspaper headlines, i.e., "Pointers edge Bulls, 4–3."

Hilldale, Pennsylvania see Philadelphia, PA

Hillsboro, Texas

2676 Hillsboro Baseball Club 1914 *Central Texas (D).* Team had no nickname.

Hilo, Hawaii

2677 Stars 1993–97 *Hawaii Winter (W).* Because Hawaii has clear skies, the Mauna Kea Observatory of the University of Hawaii was built in 1967 to observe the stars. Newspapers liked its five-letter length.

Hiroshima, Honshu, Japan

2678 Toyo Carp 1950 to date *Japanese Central (ind.).* The carp is a freshwater fish native to Asia. It is a popular food in Japan. Both teams are owned by Toyo Kogyo, which is the parent company of Mazda Motors, an automobile and tire manufacturer.

2679 Yuu Carp 1962 to date *Western (ind.).* In the era 1962–99, the 12 minor league teams of the Japanese Eastern and Western Leagues were more like NFL taxi squads, playing in the same city and same stadium while the parent club was on the road, with players called up and down based on the needs of the parent club — with all players on the official roster of the parent club. Since 2000 more of the Japanese minor league teams are playing in their own stadia with some moving to different (although usually nearby) cities or suburbs. The CL team owner since 2006 is Yuu Toyo.

Hobbs, New Mexico

2680 Drillers 1937 *West Texas–New Mexico (D).* Founded in 1909, the city became a boom-town when oil was discovered in the vicinity in 1928–29. City now manufactures oil-well supplies and equipment.

2681 Boosters 1938 *West Texas–New Mexico (D).* By the 1930s, the Boosters nickname was losing popularity because booster clubs had become passé. Adults were too distracted by the Great Depression, leaving their children to form "fan clubs." Night games helped attendance, but many more fans stayed at home to listen to the game on the radio. By the time adults had more money and time after World War II, starting in 1946, the very name "booster club" had been changed to "fan club."

2682 Sports 1955 *Longhorn (C)*; 1956–57 *Southwestern (B).* Shreveport Sports owner Bonneau Peters developed his own farm system, including Hobbs this season, to develop raw talent — albeit white players only because of Shreveport segregation laws — for eventual promotion to the Shreveport roster.

2683 Pirates 1958–61 *Sophomore (D).* Team was a farm club of the Pittsburgh Pirates.

Hoboken, New Jersey

2684 Hoboken Base Ball Club 1886 *Inter-State (ind.).* Team had no nickname.

2685 Cuban Giants 1886–88 *Independent Negro* team m1889 *Middle States (ind.).* The Cuban Giants, who played their home games in 1885 in Babylon (NY), played their home games split between Hoboken (NJ) and Trenton (NJ) in 1886–89. Actually, in 1889, the team played its home games in four cities: New York City, Johnston (PA), Trenton (NJ) and Hoboken. Team is listed under Hoboken because it played most of its home games here. See Trenton (NJ).

Hoisington, Kansas

2686 Hoisington Baseball Club m1905 *Kansas State (D).* Team began season in Kingman (KS) and then moved to Hoisington July 24. Team had no nickname.

Holden, Missouri

2687 Tennessee Rats 1912–14 *Independent Negro team.* Team went by the state name of "Tennessee Rats." Rivers of America at the turn of the century, i.e., Mississippi, Ohio and Missouri, were so polluted with garbage that rats regularly swam in them. America in the nineteenth century was just as polluted as it was in the twentieth century when government regulations finally started to clean up by the 1950s. Sometimes a team would go by anti-heroic or unwholesome nicknames to debase themselves, on purpose, as a marketing ploy, i.e., Burglars, Kickers, River Rats, Savages, Chinks and Rats. Even today amateur teams go by such self-deprecating tags as "Field Rats" (baseball and soccer) and "Gym Rats" (basketball).

Holdenville, Oklahoma

2688 Villies 1912x *Oklahoma State (D)*. Circuit and team disbanded June 29. Moniker was used for newspaper headlines, i.e., "Villies edge Miners, 4–3." With manager Al Vorhees at the helm, newspapers called the players Vorhee's Villies."

2689 Hitters 1912x *Oklahoma State (D)*. Circuit and team disbanded June 29. With manager John Hendley at the helm, newspapers called the players "Hendley's Hitters."

Holdrege, Nebraska

2690 White Sox 1956–59 *Nebraska State (D)*. Team was a farm club of the Chicago White Sox.

Holland, Michigan

2691 Wooden Shoes 1910 *West Michigan (D)*; 1911 *Michigan State (D)*. City's namesake, the European country of Holland (officially the Netherlands), was famous for its carved wooden shoes for centuries.

Hollywood, California

Note: Hollywood is a district in Los Angeles, California
2692 Hollywood Baseball Club 1918–19 *Southern California (W)*. Team had no nickname.

2693 Stars 1926–35 *Pacific Coast (AA)*; 1938–57 *Pacific Coast (AA 1938–45, AAA 1946–57)*. As early as 1910, Hollywood, because of its spring-like weather throughout the year, became the premier moviemaking site in the United States.

2694 Twinklers 1926–35 *Pacific Coast (AA)*; 1938–57 *Pacific Coast (AA 1938–45, AAA 1946–57)*. A spin-off from the tag was first used by the 1876–79 Syracuse Stars. Team was aka **Twinks**.

2695 Sheiks 1926–35 *Pacific Coast (AA)*. The team was named after actor Rudolph Valentino, the indisputably most popular actor of the 1920s, who starred in the 1921 movie *The Sheik*.

Hollywood, Florida

2696 Chiefs 1940 *Florida East Coast (D)*. The Seminole Indians, original inhabitants of Georgia and Alabama, warred with settlers in the period 1835–42 and were eventually pushed into Florida reservations by 1860.

Holquin, Holquin, Cuba

2697 Sabuesos 1977–78 to date *Cuban National (S)*. The "Sabueso" is a greyhound-like hunting dog brought by the Spaniards to the island of Cuba in the sixteenth and seventeenth centuries.

2698 Cachorros 1977–78 to date *Cuban National (S)*. Los Cachorros is Spanish for "Cubs." Holquin fans use the moniker when the team has many young players. "Cubs" originated in the nineteenth century (c. 1890) to describe young baseball players.

Holton, Kansas

2699 Holton Baseball Club 1910m *Eastern Kansas (D)*. Team moved to Blue Rapids (KS) August 25. Team had no nickname.

Holton-Whiting, Kansas

2700 Holton-Whiting Base Ball Club 1895 *Kansas State (ind.)*. Team had no nickname.

Holyoke, Massachusetts

2701 Green Stockings 1878 *International Assn. (M)*. Players wore green hose. Originally "Green Stockings," newspapers shortened it to **Green Legs** and **Green Sox**.

2702 Gentlemen 1878 *International Assn. (M)*. In an era when most players were rowdy, teams whose players were well-mannered were praised by newspapers as "Gentlemen."

2703 Hard Hitters 1879 *National Assn. (M)*. The Holyoke club led the circuit in team batting average and featured four .300 hitters in Abner Powell (.371), Roger Connor (.367), Pete Gillespie (.352) and Mike Dorgan (.301).

2704 Holyoke Base Ball Club 1884x *Massachusetts State (ind.)*. Team disbanded in mid-season (c. June 20). Team had no nickname.

2705 Paperweights 1903–06 *Connecticut (D 1903, B 1904–06)*. Known as the "Paper City," Holyoke has had paper mills since 1870. Nickname was an affectionate play on words, as the team won pennants in 1903 and 1905. Local newspapers would gush, "These 'paperweights' are playing like heavyweights!" Newspapers praised the hitters for swinging "heavy lumber" despite their moniker. Usually, in sports, "paperweight" means an athlete who is short, small, light, weak and ineffectual. With manager Jesse Freysinger at the helm in 1905, newspapers called the players "Freysinger's Paperweights." After Freysinger left the team following the 1905 season, name was retained for 1906. Boxing has a "paperweight" classification for fighters weighing less than 100 pounds.

2706 Papermakers 1907–11x *Connecticut State (B)*. Team disbanded June 26; 1912 *Connecticut (B)*; 1913m *Eastern Assn. (B)*. Team moved to Meriden (CT) July 11. Since the founding of the city in 1850, boats have transported lumber on the nearby Connecticut River to be processed into paper products here. With two pennants already captured by the immediate predecessor, this new team eschewed "Paperweights" in favor of "Paper-makers."

2707 Millers 1977–82 *Eastern (AA)*. Not only does Holyoke have paper mills but also wheat mills, which made this shorter spin-off name attractive for local newspapers.

Homestead, Pennsylvania

2708 Blue Ribbons 1899–1913 *Independent Negro team*. Players wore blue-trim uniforms. In the nineteenth century, show competitions, i.e., dog shows, livestock expositions, carnival contests, etc., were popular. Contests winners were traditionally awarded a blue ribbon. Winning baseball teams were sometimes called the "Blue Ribbons."

2709 Steel Workers 1905 *Ohio–Pennsylvania (D)*. City had a turbulent steel mill history punctuated by violent strikes in 1892 and 1967 (statewide this year) and 1986 (again statewide). The coal industry of Pennsylvania gave rise to iron and steel mills by the 1880s. The coal industry has survived but the iron and steel mills have moved away.

2710 Grays 1912–28 *Independent Negro team*; 1929 *American Negro (M)*; 1930–31 *Independent Negro team*; 1932x *East–West (M)*.

Team disbanded in mid-season, c. July 7; 1933 *Independent Negro team*; 1934–42 *Negro National (M)*. Team moved to Washington, D.C., for the 1943 season; 1949–50 *Independent Negro* team. Players wore gray trim. Team began its history as the semi-professional Murdock Grays in 1906.

Honolulu, Hawaii

2711 Buffalo Wreckers 1917 *Independent Negro team*. Team won 52 games, "wrecking the opposition" along the way. The players came from Buffalo, New York.

2712 Hawaii Islanders 1961–87 *Pacific Coast (AAA)*. Team played its home games in Honolulu. An inhabitant of the Hawaiian Islands is known as an "Islander."

2713 Sharks 1993–96 *Hawaii Winter (W)*; 2006–08 *Hawaii Winter (W)*. Sharks swim along the coast of Oahu. Both teams went by the city name of Honolulu Sharks.

Hoofdoorp, North Holland, Netherlands

2714 Pioniers 1999 to date *Hoofdklasse (ind.)*. Konica Minolta, the owner of the team, runs a certification program for its technicians and researchers known as the "Pioneer Program." The company considers itself a "pioneer" in printing and document imaging technology. Team goes by the name of Konica Minolta Pioneers (Pioniers in Dutch). The Holland Baseball League became fully professional in 1999.

Hope, Arkansas

2715 Hope Baseball Club m1905x *North Texas (D)*. Team began season in Paris (TX) and moved to Hope July 20. Team and league disbanded August 6. Team had no nickname.

Hopewell, Virginia

2716 Hopewell Baseball Club 1900 *Virginia (ind.)*. Team had no nickname.

2717 Powder Puffs 1916x *Virginia (C)*. Team disbanded July 22. Local newspapers complained that the team "played like powder-puffs" as the players skidded to a sixth- and last-place finish with a 30–52 record. A "powder puff" is a small ball of cotton to apply talcum powder to the skin. Since it is so soft, it developed a secondary meaning as "weak and non-threatening," i.e., a sports team or athlete who poses no real challenge to the opponent.

2718 Blue Sox 1949–50 *Virginia (D)*. Players wore blue stirrups. Team was a farm club of neither the blue-stirrup Brooklyn Dodgers nor the Philadelphia Blue Jays.

Hopkinsville, Kentucky

2719 Browns 1903–04 *Kentucky–Illinois–Tennessee (KITTY) (D)*. Players wore brown hose. Team had a loose affiliation with the St. Louis Browns.

2720 Hoppers 1905 *Kentucky–Illinois–Tennessee (KITTY) (D)*. Team disbanded July 18; 1910–14x Team disbanded July 10; 1916x *KITTY (D)*. Team and league disbanded August 4; 1922–23 *KITTY (D)*; 1935–42x *KITTY (D)*. Team and league disbanded June 19 due to U.S. entry into World War II; 1946–54 *KITTY (D)*. Moniker was used for newspaper headlines, i.e., "Hoppers edge Bluebirds, 4–3."

Hoquiam, Washington

2721 Perfect Gentlemen 1903–04 *Southwest Washington (D)*. Although baseball players of the era 1870–1920 were notoriously rowdy, there were some exceptions. Three teams went by the sobriquet of "Gentlemen": Holyoke (MA), 1878; Springfield (MA), 1879; and Hoquiam (WA). The Hoquiam nickname also referred to the 1903 pennant-tie and the outright 1904 pennant the team won, as the newspapers said the team played like "perfect gentlemen."

2722 Loggers 1905 *Southwest Washington (D)*; 1910x *Washington State (D)*. Team disbanded July 15. Since 1860, lumber from Washington State forests has been transported to wood mills that manufacture shingles, plywood, veneer, pulp, wooden furniture and paper.

2723 Cougars 1912x *Washington State (D)*. Team and league disbanded July 14. The cougar, once inhabiting all of North America, now inhabits the western U.S., especially in the Rocky and Olympic mountains.

Hornellsville, New York
(renamed Hornell in 1888)

2724 Hornells 1877x *Independent*; 1878 *International Assn. (M)*. Tag was an early use of a headline moniker, i.e., "Hornells defeat Stars, 7–5." When the city name changed to Hornell in 1888, subsequent nineteenth century baseball teams here were known by the typical plural form of the city name, i.e., the "Hornells."

2725 Railroaders 1877x *Independent Assn. (M)*. Team disbanded June 22; 1878 *International Assn. (M)*. City has been a railroad center for the Erie Railroad since 1850. Aka **Railroad Men, Railroaders.**

2726 Hornellsville Base Ball Club 1890 *Western New York (ind.)*. Team had no nickname.

2727 Pygmies 1906m *Inter-State (D)*. Team moved to Patton (NY) August 6. In the era 1890–1915, teams that had losing records were sometimes called "Midgets" and "Pygmies"— in contradistinction to "Giants," i.e., teams with winning records. In 1906, Hornell fans complained that while the New York Nationals were "playing like Giants" en route to 96 victories, "Our team is playing like pygmies!" These particular baseball Pygmies were not terrible (a won-lost record of 53–56) but low attendance forced the franchise to move to Patton (NY) August 6. The American public in this era was fascinated about the expeditions of Stanley and Livingston in Africa and the discovery of Pygmy tribes. The terms "pygmies" and "midgets" also referred to players of short stature, often teenaged players who had not yet reached their adult height.

2728 Green Sox 1914 *Inter-State (D)*. Players wore green stirrups.

2729 Maple Leafs 1915 *Inter-State (D)*; 1948–49 *Pennsylvania–Ohio–New York (P.O.N.Y.) (D)*. The maple syrup industry is located here. Maple trees proliferate in New York State.

2730 Pirates 1942, 1945–47 *Pennsylvania–Ohio–New York (P.O.N.Y.) (D)*. Team was a farm club of Pittsburgh Pirates.

2731 Maples 1943–44 *Pennsylvania–Ohio–New York (P.O.N.Y.) (D)*. Tag was a spin-off of the 1915 name.

2732 Dodgers 1950–56 *Pennsylvania–Ohio–New York (P.O.N.Y.) (D)*. Team was a farm club of the Brooklyn Dodgers.

2733 Redlegs m1957 *New York–Pennsylvania (D)*. Team began season in Bradford (PA) and then moved to Hornell May 28. Team was a farm club of the Cincinnati Redlegs.

Horton, Kansas

2734 Horton Baseball Club 1910x *Eastern Kansas (D)*. The franchise disbanded September 1. The team had no nickname.

Hot Springs, Arkansas

2735 Blues 1887 *Southwestern (ind.)*. Players wore blue hose. Originally known as the **Blue Stockings**, newspapers shortened the name to **Blue Legs**, **Blue Sox** and "Blues."

2736 Sluggers 1887 *Southwestern (ind.)*. A common nineteenth century slang for a baseball player, specifically a hitter, was "slugger." Of course, not all baseball players were sluggers or even good hitters.

2737 Vapor Citys 1897x *Arkansas State (ind.)*. The city was founded in 1807. In the nineteenth century it became a resort and health spa because of the region's 47 thermal springs, which are heated by subterranean lava flows. By 1900, the city became a major resort center in the U.S. where people came to bathe in the vaporous hot waters, which gave rise to the city nickname of "Vapor City."

2738 Vapors 1906x *Arkansas–Texas (D)*. Team and league disbanded August 26. Tag was a newspaper friendly spin-off from Vapor Citys.

2739 Vaporites 1908 *Arkansas State (D)*. Moniker is a variation of Vapor Citys.

2740 Hot Springs Baseball Club 1909 *Arkansas State (D)*. Team had no nickname.

2741 Bathers 1938–41 *Cotton States (C)*; 1947–55 *Cotton States (C)*. Hot Springs National Park, in suburban Hot Springs, boasts of 47 thermal springs. Millions of visitors each year bathe in the warm spring waters for therapeutic benefits or for pleasure. Bottled mineral water from these springs is sold throughout the United States and the world.

Houghton, Michigan

2742 Houghton Base Ball Club 1890–91 *Upper Peninsula (ind.)*; 1895 *Upper Peninsula (ind.)*. These teams had no nickname.

2743 Giants 1906–07 *Northern Copper Country (C)*. The 1906 team "played like Giants," finishing second (of eight teams) with a fine 56–35 record. The 1907 team skidded to a 47–55 record, finishing next-to-last in the league and prompting fans and newspapers to use the tag sarcastically. In the era 1885–1910, teams that were winning often were called "Giants." Losing teams were sarcastically called "Giants."

Houma, Louisiana

2744 Buccaneers 1940m *Evangeline (D)*. Team moved to Natchez (MS) June 27. Jean Paul Laffite and his brother, Pierre, led the Barratarra Pirates in raids against Louisiana shipping in the period 1800–1820. Engaged in contraband, smuggling, slave trade and black market trade, these pirates not only fought against the British in the War of 1812 but actually stimulated the Louisiana economy.

2745 Indians 1946–52 *Evangeline (C)*. Between 1550 and 1800 waves of Spanish, French, English and American settlers and soldiers eventually destroyed the Caddo and Natchez Indians, who had lived here in pre–Columbian times. Team was not a farm club of the Cleveland Indians.

2746 Hawks 2003 *Southeastern (ind.)*. A fan poll chose this short and alliterative name that hearkens back to the eighteenth and nineteenth century "Sea Hawk" privateers that sailed the Louisiana coast.

Houston, Texas

2747 Babies 1888 *Texas (ind.)*. Team joined the Texas League as an expansion team. "Baby" and "Babies" was a nineteenth century slang for an expansion team.

2748 Reds 1888 *Texas (ind.)*. Players wore red hose. Originally "Red Stockings," newspapers shortened the tag to "Redlegs" and "Reds."

2749 Mudcats 1889 *Texas (ind.)*; 1898 *Texas Assn. (ind.)*. Team and circuit disbanded May 15; 1899 *Texas Assn. (ind.)*. Team and circuit disbanded July 5. Mudcats are fish that swim in the Buffalo Bayou, the river that runs through the city. "Mudcat" is actually a slang or nickname for the creature's real name—the Flathead Catfish.

2750 Colts 1892 *Texas (ind.)*. Young players on the team were called "colts." This moniker from 1892 has nothing to do with the Houston Colt .45's of 1962–64, whose nickname was often shortened by local newspapers to "Colts." The 1962 Houston NL expansion team stocked its roster with mostly veteran players. The 1962–64 Colts was a reference to the "Gun That Won the West" and not young players or young horses.

2751 Magnolias 1895–96 *Texas–Southern (ind.)*. Houston became known as the "Magnolia City" because starting around 1860, the streets were lined with hundreds of magnolia trees.

2752 Gladiators 1895–97 *Texas–Southern (ind.)*; 1899 *Texas Assn. (ind.)*. Team and circuit disbanded July 5. Used earlier (1890) by Brooklyn of the American Association, "Gladiators" was a nineteenth century slang for baseball players. A hundred years later the name has been used for football players. Baseball players of this time, like their gladiatorial forbearers, often got quite bloodied up on the field, i.e., vicious sliding, sliding with spikes up, fisticuffs on the field, getting "skulled" with the ball, catchers without shin guards getting broken shins and ankles, outfielders getting hit in the face with ground balls on uneven fields, and outfielders spraining and breaking ankles in rough outfields.

2753 Buffaloes 1897 *Texas Assn. (ind.)*; 1898 *Texas Assn. (ind.)*. Team and circuit disbanded May 15; 1899 *Texas Assn. (ind.)*. Team and circuit disbanded July 5; 1903–05 *South Texas (C 1903, D 1904, C 1904–05)*; 1907–42 *Texas (C 1907–10, B 1911–20, A 1921–35, A1 1936–42)*; 1946–58 *Texas (AA)*; 1959–61 *American Assn. (AAA)*. The Buffalo Bayou is a river that runs through the city and flows into the Houston Ship Canal. Although there have been buffalo herds in Texas for centuries, the moniker refers, strictly speaking, to the river. Newspapers shortened the name to **Buffs**.

2754 Marvels 1903 *South Texas (C 1903, D 1904, C 1904–05)*. With field manager Wade Moore at the helm, local newspapers called the players "Moore's Marvels." Nicknames related to the manager in this era were often alliterative, i.e., Pat Powers' Pets, Cap Anson's Colts, Dave Foutz' Fillies, Jim Mutrie's Mules and John M. Ward's Wonders. Over-complimentary nicknames were a fad in this era, i.e., Superbas, Perfectos, Wonders, and Marvels.

2755 Wanderers 1904 *South Texas (D)*. The team had a winning record (66–59), so it was not low attendance that plagued the club but rather no home attendance. The team had no home field at the start of the 1904 season and was forced to play as a road team until mid-season, when West End Park had been built for them. "Wanderers" was a contemporary moniker for teams with a home field that were forced onto the road due to low attendance.

2756 Black Buffaloes 1918, 1920–25 *Independent Negro team*; 1919 *Negro Texas (ind.)*; 1929–31 *Texas–Oklahoma–Louisiana T.O.L. (ind.)*. Tag was a spin-off from Buffaloes. Team received donated uniforms from the Texas League Houston Buffaloes. In this era black teams often used the nicknames from donated white uniforms, i.e., Black Yankees, Black Senators, Black Barons and Black Crackers.

2757 Eagles 1949–50 *Negro American (ind.)*. By 1949 the NAL was no longer a major league circuit due to player defections to Organized Baseball's major and minor leagues. Tag was a spin-off from the Dallas Eagles. The Dallas Eagles were an independent Negro team.

2758 Colt .45's 1962–64 *National (M)*. The famous pistol, the

Colt .45, was named after inventor Samuel Colt. It is a revolver pistol that uses a 45-caliber cartridge. Caliber refers to the diameter of the gun bore. Houston management chose the name for the 1962 NL expansion team. Ironically, the Samuel Colt Firearms manufacturing company filed a copyright infringement lawsuit against the Houston team in 1964 for having a team logo that was a direct copy of the gun manufacturer's emblem. When some people complained that the nickname was a "symbol of violence," the baseball team simply chose a new nickname to end the threatened litigation and the ethical complaints. **Colts** was a newspaper contraction.

2759 Astros 1965 to date *National (M)*. Team was named after the new domed stadium, the Houston Astrodome. The stadium was named after the National Aeronautics and Space Administration (NASA), which monitors the activities of astronauts in outer space after their rockets launch into orbit from Cape Canaveral (FL).

2760 Disastros 1975 to date *National (M)*. Houston fans were tolerant of the team in the 1960s because it can take a good ten years for an expansion team to get competitive. But six years of steady improvement (1969–74) ended with a disastrous 64–97 sixth- and last-place finish in the NL West in 1975. Moniker was applied to the players every time the team played disastrously, i.e., 1975, 1978, 1982, 1991, 2007 and 2010.

2761 Lastros 1975, 1991 *National (M)*. Management held a fire sale after the 1990 season, trading away first baseman Franklin Stubbs (23 HR), second baseman Bill Doran (.288), and pitchers Danny Darwin (11–4) and Dave Smith (23 SV, 2.39 ERA) which plunged the team into sixth and last place in the NL Western Division in 1991 with a 65–97 record. Name used for cellar-dwelling Houston clubs, i.e., 1995, 1991.

2762 Yellow 'Stros of Texas 1975–91 *National (M)*. From the song the "Yellow Rose of Texas." "Stros" is not only a play on words with "rose," but also with the Stroh's Beer Company, which serves beer at Houston sports games.

2763 Rainbows 1975–93 *National (M)*. Players wore "rainbow" jerseys with yellow, red and orange stripes. Most fans and media thought the uniforms to be garishly unpleasant. At first, the stripes were around the waist of the jersey (1975–90) but then sewn only onto the shoulders (1991–93). In 1994 blue trim on white uniforms was introduced.

2764 The Orange 1980 *National (M)*. Players wore orange and yellow jerseys. The trend to assign a special jersey color to a sports team in the form of a color was a spill-over from the NFL, i.e., Denver "Orange Crush," and the Oakland "Silver and Black."

2765 Bill Virdon's No-names 1980–81 *National (M)*. Manager Bill Virdon led a group of little-known hitters, i.e., second baseman Jose Cruz (.302), outfielder Cesar Cedeno (.309), second baseman Enos Cabell, first baseman–outfielder Denny Walling and outfielder Terry Puhl and pitchers Joe Niekro (20–12), Vern Ruhle (12–4), Joe Sambito (8–4 2.20) and Frank LaCorte (8–5, 2.82) to the 1980–81 NL Western Division titles. The only two well-known players were aging second baseman Joe Morgan and pitcher J. R. Richard, who was 10–4 when his career was ended by a stroke.

2766 Stars 2000 *National (M)*. The shoulder rainbow design (1991–93) and then a blue-trim uniform style (1994–99) bore a blue star on the jersey breast. Never the "Blue Stars," the simple "Stars" tag name never caught on because it conflicted with the moniker of the NHL Dallas Stars. The alternate logo of a red star appeared on the uniform sleeve in 2002 and the alternate moniker became "Red Stars," but it is strictly a local tag, not used outside Houston.

2767 Fatros 2000 to date. A tag applied to the team, usually by Texas Rangers fans, or Houston fans, unhappy with the team's losing ways, when the city of Houston was voted "America's Fattest City" three years in a row, starting in 2000.

2768 Houston's Minor League Ball Club 2011 Controversial sports radio host Mike North, never one to shy away from indiscreet comments, on his July 31 radio show branded the Astros, on their way to a 56–106 season, as Houston's "Minor League team." The franchise had won its first-ever National League pennant in 2005, but declining attendance forced them sell, release and trade numerous talented players.

Hsinchuang, Taipei County, Taiwan

Note: Hsinchuang (also spelled Hsinjuang) is a suburb of Taipei.

2769 China Trust Whales 1997 to date *Chinese Professional (ind.)*. Team represents Taipei County, although it plays its home games in Hsinchuang. Circuit goes by the name of Chinese Professional Baseball League and should not be confused with the Chinese Baseball League of mainland People's Republic of China. Many sea mammals swim off the coastal waters of Taiwan, i.e., whales, dolphins and seals. Moniker is alliterative in English with team owner's name China Trust Bank, i.e., China Trust Whales.

2770 Taipei County Gida 1997–2002 *Taiwan Major (ind.)*. Team went by the county name of Taipei County Suns but played its home games in Hsinchuang. The aboriginal Taiwanese — probably from Indonesia or Malayo-Polynesia — worshiped a sun god. Taiwan folk religion derives from animism and Shamanism.

2771 Macota Cobras 2003 to date *Chinese Professional (ind.)*. Team represents Taipei County, although it plays its home games in Hsinchuang. Team goes by the company name of "Macota Cobras." Team owner, Macota Bank, chose a name that it felt would be marketable in English, i.e., Macota Cobras. Since the 1930s, most professional baseball team owners in Asia realized the urgency to market their teams in English. That includes even Japanese owners in the years (1936–41), leading to World War II.

Hudson, New York

2772 Hudson Base Ball Club 1885 *Hudson River (ind.)*. Team had no nickname.

2773 Marines 1903–07x *Hudson River (D 1903, C 1904–07)* Circuit and team disbanded June 18. "Marine" in this era referred to a sea-faring ship. The city has been a major ocean-trade port since it was founded in 1783 by whalers and maritime merchants. English explorer Henry Hudson explored this region in 1520. Hudson Bay and the Hudson River were named in his honor.

Hugo, Oklahoma

2774 Hugoites m1913 *Texas–Oklahoma (D)*. Team started season in Wichita Falls (TX) and then moved to Hugo July 7. An inhabitant of Hugo is called a "Hugoite."

2775 Scouts 1914x *Texas–Oklahoma (D)*. Team disbanded June 11. With field manager Lon Ury at the helm, newspapers called the players the alliterative "Lon Ury's Scouts." In the "Wild West" years of the nineteenth century, Oklahoma, like Texas, was a vast expanse of prairies and valleys where the U.S. cavalry and Indian scouts would lead the way for soldiers and settlers.

Humacao, Puerto Rico

2776 Grises Orientales 1941–42 *Liga Puertoriquena (W)*. Humacao is a city in eastern Puerto Rico about 28 miles southeast of San Juan. The players wore gray uniforms with gray-trim stockings. Team, known as the Eastern Grays (Los Grises Orientales), played semi-pro games from 1938–39 through the 1940–41 season. Team and league became professional for the 1941–42 campaign.

Humboldt, Nebraska

2777 Infants m1911–13 *Missouri–Iowa–Nebraska–Kansas (M.I.N.K.)*. Team started season in Maryville (KS) and moved to Humboldt July 10. With manager A.F. Bridges at the helm, newspapers called the mostly young players "Bridges' Infants." In the period 1890–1920, "Infants" meant a young team that stumbled on the field, mustering a losing record. In this case, these Infants were "intrepid" as they won the 1911 MINK League pennant.

Huntington, Indiana

2778 Miamis 1908 *Indiana–Ohio (D)*. Miami war chief Little Turtle defeated American troops on November 4, 1791, near Fort Miami (present day Fort Wayne). On August 20, 1794, the Miami were defeated at the Battle of Fallen Timbers.

2779 Johnnies 1909–11 *Northern State League of Indiana (D)*. General John "Johnnie" Hunt Morgan led the Confederate cavalry in a raid of southern Indiana July 8–13, 1863. Indiana enlisted 196,363 men into the Union Army. Union soldiers were known as "Johnnies" (after the song "When Johnny Comes Marching Home"). Confederate soldiers were known as "Johnny Rebs." With field manager Johnnie Strands at the helm, team was known as the "Johnnies."

2780 Indians 1912 *Northern State League of Indiana (D)*. Tag was a spin-off from Miami Indian tribe nickname of the 1908 team.

Huntington, DuBois, Indiana

Note: Not to be confused with Huntington, West Virginia.

2781 DuBois Dragons 1996–98 *Heartland (ind.)*; 1999–2002 *Frontier (ind.)*. Team, jumping circuits in 1999, went by the county name of DuBois Dragons. Moniker, alliterative with the county name, was chosen in a name-the-team contest.

Huntington, West Virginia

Note: Not to be confused with Huntington, Indiana.

2782 Huntington Base Ball Club 1894x *Tri-State (ind.)*. Team disbanded in mid-season (date unknown); 1910 *Virginia Valley (D)*; m1915m *Ohio State (D)*. Team started season in Chillicothe (OH) and moved to Huntington July 13. Team then moved to Maysville (OH) July 19. These teams had no nickname.

2783 Blue Sox 1911–12x *Mountain States (D)*. Team disbanded July 8, 1912; 1913–14x *Ohio State (D)*. Team disbanded July 22; 1916x *Ohio State (D)*. Team disbanded July 6. Team had a loose affiliation with the Cincinnati Reds. Players wore blue-trim uniforms and blue stirrups as a spin-off from the red stirrups of the parent Cincinnati team.

2784 Boosters 1931–33 *Middle Atlantic (C 1931,D 1932–33)*; 1937x *Mountain States (D)*. Team disbanded August 1; 1939 *Mountain States (D)*. With manager Johnny Stuart at the helm 1931–33, newspapers called the players the rhyming "Stuart's Boosters." Joe Watson took over in 1937, and the name became "Joe Watson's Boosters." Mike Broski took over in mid-season 1937 and the name became "Broski's Boosters." Ellis "Mike" Powers was at the helm in 1939, and the name became "Powers' Boosters."

2785 Redbirds 1934–36 *Middle Atlantic (C)*. Team was a farm club of the St. Louis Cardinals.

2786 Bees 1938 *Mountain States (D)*. Team had a loose affiliation with the NL Boston Bees but was not a formal farm club.

2787 Aces 1940 *Mountain States (D)*. Newspaper editors at the start of the 1938 season wanted a short nickname for the team. With manager Pee Wee Wanninger at the helm, reporters were faced with a ten-letter city name and nine-letter surname from the manager. Reporters resorted to "Aces"—as an "A-B" spin-off from the 1938 name of "Bees"—to placate the wrath of their editors. Ezra Midkiff took over in mid-season and the name became "Ezra's Aces." Fred Blake took over in 1941 and the name became "Blake's Aces." Robert Larsen took over in mid-season 1941 and the name became "Larsen's Aces." The 1940 team skidded to eighth and last place in the league with a terrible 33–87 record, prompting newspapers and fans to sarcastically call the players "Aces." The moniker "aces" is used in several sports, i.e., baseball, golf and tennis, to describe a talented and winning player, although it can also be a sarcastic barb for a bumbling, losing team. In the 1920s and the 1930s "Aces" had become a popular nickname for baseball teams because of barnstorming air shows, which also were staged in West Virginia. By 1940, Aces was used by teams to honor Army Air Force pilots training at local air bases in preparation for World War II.

2788 Jewels 1942 *Mountain States (D)*. With manager Charles Lucas at the helm in 1942, team got off to a winning start, prompting newspapers to call players "Lucas' Jewels." Lucas left in mid-season with At Scharein taking over and leading the team to the playoffs. Players were so talented that they made many plays that were "jewels."

2789 Cubs 1990–94 *Appalachian (R)*. Team was a farm club of the Chicago Cubs.

2790 River City Rumblers 1995 *Appalachian (R)*. Team went by the city nickname of "River City Rumblers." Subterranean coal mining and natural gas drilling causes the earth in the vicinity to "rumble." Located next to the Ohio River, Huntington is known as the "River City." The term "rumble" means a street fight, especially between gangs. Baseball players, who often fight, were sometimes known as "rumblers."

2791 Rail Kings m1998x *Heartland (ind.)*. Team began the season as the Altoona (PA) Rail Kings and then transferred to Huntington (WV) July 31. The nickname was retained, which was appropriate because Huntington, like Altoona, started out as a railroad town in 1870. It was founded by railroad magnate Collis Huntington, whose Chesapeake & Ohio Railroad had reached the Ohio River.

Huntsville, Alabama

2792 Westerns 1911 *Southeastern (D)*. Although three league cities were further west than Huntsville, newspapers came up with "Watkins' Westerns" after manager W.H. Watkins. Newt Horn took over in mid-season and the name became "Newt Horn's Westerns." Although Alabama is in the Deep South, Americans in this era were being exposed to motion pictures for the first time. One of the most popular of these silent films was *The Great Train Robbery* starring Tom Dix. The movie industry and Western pulp novels re-ignited the popular interest in the "Old West."

2793 Mountaineers 1912 *Southeastern (D)*. Team moved to Talladega (AL) July 9, 1912. Monte Sano and the Monte Sano State Park are just northeast of the city.

2794 Springers 1930 *Georgia–Alabama (D)*. When the region was first settled, the town was called Big Spring because of the springs that flowed from the Tennessee River as it emptied into nearby Lake Wheeler. City was renamed Huntsville in 1811. With manager Bill Pierre at the helm, newspapers called the players "Pierre's Springers." Name was retained under four other managers this season.

2795 Stars 1985 to date *Southern (AA)*. Huntsville is home to the Marshall Space Flight and Rocket Center (est. 1959), which designed, built and tested America's first space rocket—the Jupiter-C. City has been known since 1960 as the "Space Capital of America." Since the

Houston NBA team was already known as the "Rockets," the moniker of **Stars** became the team's official nickname.

Huntsville, Arkansas

2796 Redbirds 1935 *Arkansas State (D)*. Team had a loose affiliation with the NL St. Louis Cardinals although, it was not a formal farm team. In the 1930s, Cardinals GM Branch Rickey.

Huron, South Dakota

2797 Packers 1920 *South Dakota (D)*. Huron is a shipping center for the farm produce of fifteen counties—particularly meat packing. With manager Bill Shipke at the helm, newspapers called the players "Shipke's Packers."

2798 Huron Baseball Club 1921 *Dakota (D)*. Team had no nickname.

2799 Phillies 1965–68 *Northern (A)*. Team was a farm club of the Philadelphia Phillies.

2800 Cubs 1969–70 *Northern (A)*. Team was a farm club of the Chicago Cubs.

2801 Heaters 1994 *North–Central (ind.)*. Wintry springs here require ballplayers to play "hot" and win games. Back in 1886 the St. Paul (MN) "Freezers" played games in April with the daytime highs barely reaching 20 degrees Fahrenheit. Spring weather in South Dakota can be wintry.

Hutchison, Kansas

2802 Blues 1887x *Kansas State (ind.)*. Team disbanded in mid-season (date unknown). Team had a loose affiliation with the Western League Kansas City Blues. Players wore blue hose.

2803 Giants 1887x *Kansas State (ind.)*. Team disbanded in mid-season (date unknown). Although the New York Giants (so-named in 1885) had not yet won their first NL pennant, their nickname quickly became the most popular in baseball. This popularity prompted local reporters to call the team the "Giants" in the hope that they would "play like giants" and win the pennant. No record of the regular season is currently available.

2804 Hutchison Base Ball Club 1888x *Western (ind.)*. Team and league disbanded June 21; 1898 *Kansas State (ind.)*. These teams had no nickname.

2805 Salt Miners 1905 *Kansas State (D)*. Salt from nearby mines is transported to city processing plants. With extensive salt beds underlying the city, Hutchison is known as the "Salt City."

2806 Salt Packers m1906, 1908 *Western Assn.(C)*. Team began the 1906 season in St. Joseph (MO) and moved to Hutchison June 12, 1906; 1909–11 *Kansas State (D)*; m1917–18m *Western (A)*. Team started the 1917 season in St. Joseph (MO) and then moved to Hutchison July 24, 1917. Team moved to Oklahoma City June 2, 1918. Tag was a spin-off from "Salt Miners." The city is surrounded by extensive salt beds. Salt is mined and then transported into the city where it is processed, packed and shipped for distribution. With manager Bill Zink at the helm in 1909, newspapers called the players "Zink's Salt Packers."

2807 White Sox 1907 *Western Assn.(C)*. Although known for his tightwad ways, Chicago White Sox owner Charles Comiskey was smart enough to know that he needed to spend some money to gather young talent from minor league teams in the Midwest, which prompted him to establish loose affiliations with minor league teams in Rockford (IL), Saginaw (MI), South Bend (IN), Leavenworth (KS), Duluth (MN), Topeka (KS), Kalamazoo (MI), Centralia (IL), Coffeyville (KS) and Hutchison (KS)—all of whom were nicknamed

White Sox. The result was four AL pennants and two World Series championships in a 20-year period for the Chicagoans, a feat the White Sox have never come close to doing again. The practice of having a loose affiliation between a major league baseball team and a geographically close minor league team goes back to 1884 with the so-called Reserve League. Comiskey got the idea from fellow owner John Brush, who established a loose affiliation of "farm" clubs for his NL Cincinnati Reds in Indianapolis (IN), Youngstown (OH), Muskegon (MI) and Canton (OH). In this era the minor league teams were known as "subsidiary clubs" and "friendly clubs."

2808 Packers 1914 *Kansas State (D)*. Tag was a shorter version of Salt Packers. Team was not a farm club of the FL Kansas City Packers.

2809 Wheat Shockers *Southwestern (C)*. 1922–23; 1924 *Western Assn.(C)*; m1932x *Western Assn. (C)*. Team began season in Muskogee (OK) and then moved to Hutchinson June 8. Team disbanded July 18 because of the Great Depression and dust storms; 1933m *Western (A)*. Team moved to Bartlesville (OK) July 7. In the era 1870–1940, Hutchinson was the most important wheat-growing region in the state of Kansas. With field manager Emmett Rodgers at the helm, local newspapers called the players "Emmett Rodgers' Wheat Shockers." Red Harriott took over in mid-season 1922 and the name became "Harriott's Shockers." The name was retained under Marty Purtell in 1923. Kansas is the "Wheat State of the Nation."

2810 Larks 1934–38 *Western Assn. (C)*. The Western *League* (1902–37) and the *Western Association* (1922–32 & 1934–42) were two completely different circuits and not a single circuit undergoing name changes. Mountain Larks inhabit the Western U.S. With field manager Bob Morrow at the helm 1934–35, local newspapers called the players "Morrow's Larks." Dick Goldberg took over in 1936 and the name became "Goldberg's Larks." Dick Klinger took over in mid-season 1937 and the name became "Klinger's Larks." Hugh McMullen then took over in 1937 and the name became "McMullen's Larks." With Hutchison having nine letters in its name, local reporters were mindful to choose a short nickname to soothe the editor, hence the five-letter "Larks."

2811 Pirates 1939–42 *Western Association (C)*. Team was a farm club of the Pittsburgh Pirates.

2812 Cubs 1946–48m *Western Assn. (C)*. Team moved to Springfield (MO) July 21, 1948. Team was a farm club of the Chicago Cubs.

2813 Elks 1949–54 *Western Assn. (C)*. A regional animal, the elk is the North American Red Deer. Local newspapers were delighted with the four-letter moniker that eased the jitters regarding a 10-letter city name in print.

Idaho Falls, Idaho

2814 Spuds 1926–28x *Utah–Idaho (C)*. Team disbanded July 5, 1928. Potato farms in the surrounding vicinity ship them into the city where they are cleaned, processed, packed and shipped.

2815 Russets 1940–42 *Pioneer (C)*; 1946–61 *Pioneer (C)*. The famous Russet apple is grown in Idaho.

2816 Yankees 1962–63 *Pioneer (C 1962, R 1963)*. Team was a farm club of the New York Yankees.

2817 Angels 1964–81 *Pioneer (R)*. Team was a farm club of the California Angels.

2818 Athletics 1982–85 *Pioneer (R)*. Team was a farm club of the Oakland Athletics.

2819 Braves 1986–91 *Pioneer (R)*. Team was a farm club of the Atlanta Braves.

2820 Gems 1992 to date *Pioneer (R)*. Idaho is an Indian word for "Gem of the Mountains." Although there are no jewel mines in the region, gold was discovered in 1860 and silver in 1880. Idaho is known as the "Gem State."

Ilion, New York

2821 Typewriters 1901–04 *New York State (ind.* 1901, *B* 1902–04*)*. Christopher Latham invented the typewriter in 1873, and then contracted E. Remington & Sons—gunsmiths—to factory produce the typewriter in Ilion (NY) in 1874. The Remington Typewriter was the first practical typewriter. With field manager Timothy Shinnick at the helm in 1901, local newspapers called the players the alliterative "Timothy's Typewriters." The nickname was retained through 1904.

Inchon, Kyong-gi, South Korea

Note: Not to be confused with Jeonju, South Korea

2822 Super Stars 1982–84 *Korean (ind.)*. South Korean baseball owners realized the need to market their teams in English. "Superstar" entered the Korean language intact because Korean baseball fans were enamored of such "superstars" like Mickey Mantle, Sandy Koufax and Roberto Clemente.

2823 Pintos 1985–87 *Korean (ind.)*. Chongbo Company bought the team and wanted an English-language moniker not previously used by professional teams, i.e., "Chongbo Pintos. "

2824 Dolphins 1988–2005 *Korean (ind.)*. TPY Company bought the team and named it "Dolphins" after the aquatic mammals that swim in the waters near the Korean coast.

2825 Unicorns 1996–2007 *Korean (ind.)*. Samsung bought the team and chose a new English-language alliterative moniker, i.e., the "Samsung Unicorns."

Independence, Kansas

2826 Independence Base Ball Club 1896 *Kansas State (ind.)*. Team had no nickname.

2827 Coyotes 1906 *Kansas State (D)*; 1907 *Oklahoma–Arkansas–Kansas (O.A.K.). (D)*; 1908 *Oklahoma–Kansas (D)*. The North American coyote is found mostly in the central and western U.S. With field managers Charles McLinn and then Mr. Crutcher at the helm in 1906, local newspapers called the players the alliterative "McLinn's Coyotes" and "Crutcher's Coyotes." The name was used again in 1907.

2828 Oilers 1906 *Kansas State (D)*; 1907 *Oklahoma–Arkansas–Kansas (O.A.K.). (D)*; 1908 *Oklahoma–Kansas (D)*. Oil was discovered in Neodesha (KS), about 15 miles outside of Independence, in 1892, turning the city into a "boomtown." Numerous companies built oil and natural gas rigs in the area, starting in 1894. Oil refineries in the city refine crude oil.

2829 Champs 1907 *Oklahoma–Arkansas–Kansas (O.A.K.). (D)*. Team won 1906 KSL pennant.

2830 Jewelers 1908 *Oklahoma–Kansas (D)*. Kansas City was home to the Hurst Diamond Company of Kansas City (est.1908). With manager Harry Truby at the helm, newspapers called the players "Truby's Jewelers." Because of the natural gas (1881) and oil (1903) booms, Independence boasted the presence of more oil millionaires than the rest of the U.S. combined. These wealthy people spared no expense in purchasing fancy jewels from jewelry stores that sprung up in the city.

2831 Packers 1911x *Western Assn. (C)*. Team disbanded June 14. Farms in the region transport wheat to city factories for packing.

2832 Producers 1921–24x Southwestern *(D* 1921, 1924; *C* 1922–23*)*. Team disbanded July 5; 1925 *Western Assn. (C)*; 1928–32m *Western Assn. (C)*. Team moved to Joplin (MO) May 23. The state of Kansas not only produces oil but also leads the nation in wheat production. Farm cash receipts for wheat since 1900 are in the top three in the United States since 1900. Manager Pat Mason led his team to a first place 45–21 record, prompting newspapers and fans to call the players "Pat's Producers," but the team lost money and disbanded July 5, 1924. With manager Jimmy Payton at the helm in 1928, newspapers called the players "Payton's Producers." Mark Purtell took over 1929–32 and the name changed to "Purtell's Producers."

2833 Yankees 1947–50 *Kansas–Oklahoma–Missouri (K.O.M.) (D)*. Team was a farm club of the New York Yankees.

2834 Browns 1952 *Kansas–Oklahoma–Missouri (K.O.M.) (D)*. Team was a farm club of the St. Louis Browns.

Indianapolis, Indiana

2835 Blues 1877 *League Alliance (ind.)*. The League Alliance was a "farm system" not for any one National League team but collectively for all six NL teams of 1877; 1878 *National (M)*; 1884 *American Assn. (M)*; 1887–89 *National (M)*. The League Alliance Indianapolis Blues, whose players wore blue hose, joined the National League in 1877. The players continued to wear blue stockings. Name appeared in the *New York Clipper* May 12, 1877. Originally **Blue Stockings**, newspapers shortened the name to **Blue Legs** and "Blues."

2836 Capital Citys 1877 *League Alliance (ind.)*; 1878 *National (M)*. City has been the state capital of Indiana since 1816. Newspapers often shortened the name to **Capitals**.

2837 Hoosiers 1878 *National (M)*; 1884 *American Assn. (M)*; 1885 *Western (ind.)*; 1887–89 *National (M)*; 1892, 1894–99 *Western (ind.)*; 1900 *American (ind.)*; 1901 *Western Assn. (ind.)*; 1913 *Federal (ind.)*; 1914 *Federal (M)*. Indiana is nicknamed the "Hoosier State." The 1877 team was also called **Hoosier Blues** (*New York Clipper*, June 2, 1877). By 1901, the name gravitated to Indiana University college teams. The 1913 team went with "Hoosiers" to avoid confusion with the American Association's Indianapolis Indians.

2838 Indians 1878 *National (M)*; 1884 *American Assn. (M)*; 1887–89 *National (M)*; 1902–62 *American Assn. (A* 1903–07, *AA* 1908–45, *AAA* 1946–62*)*; 1963 *Pacific Coast (AAA)*; 1964–68 *International (AAA)*; 1969–97 *American Assn. (AAA)*; 1998 to date *International (AAA)*. The tag was one of the earliest used for newspaper headlines, i.e., "Indians edge Reds, 4–3." The U.S. Congress bestowed the sobriquet "Land of Indians" on Indiana territory in 1800.

2839 Browns 1878 *National (M)*. Players wore brown hose. Team was not related to the 1877 St. Louis Browns, whose only player who moved to Indianapolis was first baseman–outfielder Art Croft.

2840 Homeless Browns 1878 *National (M)*. Low attendance forced the team to start playing exclusively on the road by August 10.

2841 Green Stockings 1887–89 *National (M)*. By July of each season the repeated washings of the blue hose faded the blue dye to green so that by August the players were known as the "Green Stockings" and "Green Legs."

2842 Hapless Hoosiers 1887–89 *National (M)*. The Indianapolis franchise was abominable, finishing no higher than seventh in the eight-team NL while losing 249 games in three senior circuit seasons.

2843 Blue Licks 1887–89 *National (M)*. Team led the 1889 NL in hits (1,356) and doubles (228) for a .278 team batting average (second in the NL), prompting newspapers to call the blue-hosed Indy players the "Blue Licks." A "lick" is a slang meaning to hit or swing at something, i.e., throw a punch at somebody's face or a hit a baseball with a bat. A batter walks up to the plate to "take his licks."

2844 Indianapolis Base Ball Club 1890 *Western Inter-State (ind.)*. Team had no nickname.

2845 Hoofeds 1914 *Federal (M)*. Federal League team owners encouraged the use of hideous amalgams of a city name and "Feds." Thus fans were confronted with such monstrosities as "Baltfeds,

Brookfeds, Buffeds, Chifeds," the awful "Hoofeds," the "Pitfeds" and the worst team nickname of all-time — the "Sloufeds."

2846 ABC's 1914–19 *Independent Negro*; 1920–26 *Negro National (M)*. 1920–26; 1931, 1933 *Negro National (M)*; 1932 *Negro Southern (M)*; 1938–39x *Negro American (M)*. Team disbanded June 10. The 1914 team was owned by the American Brewing Company, a manufacturer of beer. The company's initials, A-B-C, were used on the player jerseys.

2847 Genuine ABC's 1916 *Independent Negro*. Several players of the 1915 ABC's franchise left the team over a salary dispute and formed another club, which they claimed was the legitimate black baseball team in Indianapolis and called themselves the "Genuine ABC's."

2848 Athletics 1937 *Negro American (M)*. Management decided to shorten the jersey letters from "ABC'S" to "A's."

2849 Crawfords 1940 *Negro American (M)*. Toledo Crawfords (originally Pittsburgh) transferred to Indianapolis in 1940. Team was owned by bookie king and boxing promoter Gus Greenlee, who also owned the Crawford Bathhouse in Pittsburgh.

2850 Clowns 1944 *Negro–American (M)*; 1946–48 *Negro–American (M)*; 1949–54 *Negro–American (ind.)*; *Independent Negro team* 1955–88. The 1943 Cincinnati Clowns played nearly half of their 1944 home games in Indianapolis to generate a little more revenue. With World War II winding down in 1945, the team reverted to an all–Cincinnati home schedule. With attendance low in Cincinnati in 1945, the team moved its home games to Indianapolis in 1946 and the nickname was retained. The NAL was no longer a major league in 1949, having lost its best players to Organized Baseball. The nickname derived from the players "comic acts" on the field, a la the Harlem Globetrotters.

2851 The Tribe 1969–97 *American Assn. (AAA)*; 1998 to date *International (AAA)*. "Tribe," like Braves, Gladiators, Warriors, Rustlers, etc. was a generic nineteenth-century moniker for "baseball players" or "baseball team." When the Cleveland AL club declared its official nickname to be Indians in 1915, "The Tribe" became its traditional alternate moniker. However, Indianapolis fans and local newspapers conferred the same tag on their 1969 Indianapolis Indians, which has since become Indy's traditional alternate nickname.

2852 Arrows 1997 *National (M)*. "Arrows" was the name of a proposed National League expansion franchise for the upcoming expansion of 1998. The NL awarded a franchise to Phoenix (AZ) but not to Indianapolis. The moniker was a spin-off from "Indians."

Ingersoll, Ontario, Canada

2853 Ingersoll Baseball Club 1905 *Canadian (D)*. Team had no nickname.

Iola, Kansas

2854 Gasbags 1902, 1904 *Missouri Valley (D 1902–03, C 1904)*. Major helium gas deposits were discovered in the Iola-Dexter region of the state in 1903. Companies quickly moved in and built rigs and processing factories here. Iola soon became known as the "Gas City." Helium was an ideal buoyant gas for balloons and dirigibles because, unlike hydrogen, it is not flammable.

2855 Gaslights 1903 *Missouri Valley (D)*. Fans snickered a little too much at the undignified "Gas-bags," so newspapers went "with "Gas-lights." Ironically, at this time the city of Iola was being electrified along with hundreds of other U.S. cities, so the newspapers went back to "Gas-bags" in 1904.

2856 Grays 1906 *Kansas State (D)*. Players wore gray trim.

2857 Cubs 1946–47 *Kansas–Oklahoma–Missouri (K.O.M.) (D)*. Team was a farm club of the Chicago Cubs.

2858 Indians 1948–52 *Kansas–Oklahoma–Missouri (K.O.M.) (D)*; 1954 *Western Assn. (C)*. These teams were farm clubs of the Cleveland Indians.

Ionia, Michigan

2859 Ionia Base Ball Club 1887 *Northern Michigan (ind.)*. Team had no nickname.

2860 Mayors m1921–22 *Central (B)*. Team began 1921 season in Jackson (MI) and moved to Ionia July 20. Ionia has been the site of an annual Michigan Mayors' Convention since 1900. Team was also named after long-term (1914–26) Ionia mayor Fred Green.

Ironton, Ohio

2861 Ironton Base Ball Club 1884 *Ohio State Assn.* Team had no nickname.

2862 Nailers 1911 *Mountain States (D)*; 1913–14x *Ohio State (D)*. Team disbanded July 5, 1914. With large deposits of coke and iron ore, the city upon its founding in 1848 began to construct coke furnaces to smelt iron. The smelted iron was used to manufacture nails, spikes and tools of iron. By 1870 the city gained the nickname of "Nail City."

2863 Forgers 1912 *Mountain States (D)*. Pig iron furnaces were built here by John Campbell and others. Steel and iron mills here manufacture metal castings and fabricated metals by forging, i.e., heating and hammering.

2864 Orphans m1912 *Ohio State (D)*. Team started 1912 season in Marion (OH) and moved to Ironton July 15. In this era when a team was forced to move to another city in mid-season (almost always due to low attendance), fans and newspapers sympathetically — or sarcastically — called the players the "Orphans." "Orphans" meant that the players had been "orphaned" by their heedless fans who would stay away from the ballpark in droves rather than watch losing baseball.

Ishpeming, Michigan

2865 Ishpeming Base Ball Club 1891x *Upper Peninsula (ind.)*. Team disbanded in mid-season (date unknown); 1895x *Upper Peninsula (ind.)*. Team disbanded in mid-season (date unknown). Neither team had a nickname.

Ishpeming-Negaunee, Michigan

2866 Unions 1892 *Michigan–Wisconsin (ind.)*. "Unions" (and the more prevalent "Twins") was sometimes used when a baseball team represented two cities.

Italy, Texas

2867 Italy Baseball Club 1914 *Central Texas (D)*. Regular season was shortened, ending July 25. Team had no nickname.

Iwakuni, Yamaguchi, Japan

2868 Toyo Carp 2011 to date *Japanese Western (ind.)*. Team was a farm club of the Hiroshima Toyo Carp.

Jackson, Michigan

2869 Jaxons 1888 *Tri-State (ind.)*; 1889 *Michigan State (ind.)*; m1895 *Michigan State (ind.)*. Team started 1895 season in Battle

Creek (MI) and moved to Jackson July 8. Moniker was used for newspaper headlines, i.e., "Jaxons edge Kazoos, 4–3."

2870 Wolverines 1896 *Inter-State (ind.)*; 1897x *Michigan State (ind.)*. Team disbanded in mid-season (date unknown). As the only Michigan team in the circuit, the Jackson players were known as the "Wolverines." Michigan is the "Wolverine State."

2871 Jackson Baseball Club m1902x *Michigan State (D)*. Team began season in Saginaw (MI) and moved to Jackson July 20. Team and league disbanded August 20; 1921m *Central (B)*. Team moved to Ionia (MI) July 20. These teams had no nickname.

2872 Convicts 1906–07x *Southern Michigan (D)*. Team disbanded July 15; 1908–13 *Southern Michigan (D 1908–10, C 1911–13)*. Jackson was the home of the South Michigan Correctional Facility.

2873 Yeggs 1912 *Southern Michigan (C)*. John Yeggs was a professional "safecracker" who was imprisoned at the Michigan State Penitentiary in Jackson, Michigan. Notorious lawbreakers, i.e., Billy the Kid, Jessie James, Al Capone, John Dillinger, Bonnie and Clyde, Ma Barker, etc., were often idolized by the public in this era. The name was also appropriate because news stories about baseball players in trouble with the law were eagerly consumed by the public.

2874 Chiefs 1914 *Southern Michigan (D)*. The French and Indian War was partly fought in Michigan. Michigan was inhabited by Algonquin, Iroquois, Ottawa and Potawatomi tribes who resisted successive waves of French, England and American settlers and troops.

2875 Vets 1915 *Southern Michigan (D)*. Circuit designated Association 1908–10, 1912–15 and League 1911 . Civil War and Spanish-American War veterans were patients and residents at the Michigan's Soldiers Home in nearby Grand Rapids. "Vet" and "Vets" were coined to fit in newspaper headlines during the Mexican-American War 1847–48.

Jackson, Mississippi

2876 Senators 1904 *Delta (D)*; 1906–08 *Cotton States (D)*; 1912 *Cotton States (D)*; 1921 *Mississippi State (D)*; 1936 *Cotton States (C)*; 1937–42 *Southeastern (B)*; 1946–50 *Southeastern (B)*; 1953 *Cotton States (C)*; 2002–05 *Central (ind.)*. Jackson has been the state capital of Mississippi since 1821.

2877 Blind Tigers 1905x *Cotton States (D)*. Well before national prohibition was enacted in 1919, Southern states like Georgia, Alabama and Mississippi enacted a regional liquor prohibition law in 1907. However, the law was barely enforced, as local authorities acted like "blind tigers" in allowing these saloons to operate, enforcing the law with only occasional raids (about once a month) to extort money via legal fines to the saloon operators. These saloons, the equivalent of the northern "speak-easies" of the 1920s and 1930s, became known as "Blind Tigers." Mississippi newspapers, i.e., *Leslie's Weekly*, openly declared that Jackson's "Blind Tigers" operated with impunity, "selling beer and whisky all over the state." With manager Tom Reynolds at the helm, newspapers called the players "Tom Reynolds' Blind Tigers."

2878 Tigers 1910 *Cotton States (D)*. Tag was a spin-off from the 1905 name.

2879 Drummers 1911 *Cotton States (D)*. City parades, replete with drummers, have commemorated the fierce battles in and around the city during the Civil War when it was twice taken by Union forces and almost completely burned down by fire. With manager Frank Norcum at the helm, newspapers called the players "Norcum's Drummers."

2880 Lawmakers 1913–14 *Cotton States (D)*. Team was named in honor of Andrew Jackson. Not only was he a general in the U.S. Army, Jackson was a lawyer, governor of Florida, United States

senator and U.S. president (1828–36). The city was named in his honor. A U.S. president and senator are "lawmakers."

2881 Red Sox 1921 *Mississippi State (D)*. Players wore red stirrups. Team was not a farm club of the Boston Red Sox. (The farm system was still ten years away.)

2882 Mississippians 1932x *Southeastern (B 1932, C 1933)*. Team and league disbanded May 21; 1934–35 *East Dixie (C)*. Inhabitants of the state of Mississippi are known as "Mississippians."

2883 Mets 1975–90 *Texas (AA)*. Team was a farm club of the New York Mets.

2884 Generals 1991–99 *Texas (AA)*. Andrew Jackson (for whom the city is named) was a major general in the Tennessee Militia, defeated the Creeks in the Battle of Horseshoe Bend in 1814, and won the Battle of New Orleans in January 1815 to end the War of 1812. He also fought the Seminole Indians in 1818.

Jackson, Tennessee

2885 Railroaders 1903 *Kentucky–Illinois–Tennessee (KITTY) (D)*. The musical ballad "Casey Jones" honors railroad engineer and Jackson native John Luther "Casey" Jones, who was a pioneering railroad engineer in the 1840s. Jackson is the "Home of Casey Jones." By 1850, Tennessee had two railways — the Western Atlantic and the Memphis–LaGrange line.

2886 Jackson Baseball Club m1911 *KITTY (D)*. Team began the season in Harrisburg (IL) and moved to Jackson August 13. Team had no nickname.

2887 Blue Jays 1924 *KITTY (D)*. The blue-feathered crested jay is a regional bird of eastern North America. In this era, teams in cities starting with the letter "J" were sometimes called "J's" by their local newspapers. After a few weeks, the name would evolve into "Jays." Since blue jays are found in Tennessee, the name further evolved into a bird mascot.

2888 Giants 1925 *Tri-State (D)*. "Giants" was a nickname of admiration for winning teams and sarcastic criticism for losing teams. The latter came in play here as the team finished fifth (of six teams) with a crummy 40–63 record.

2889 Jays 1926 *KITTY (D)*. Tag was a shorter version of the 1924 moniker.

2890 Generals 1935–42x *KITTY (D)*. Team disbanded in July 17 because of U.S. entry into World War II; 1950–54x *KITTY (D)*. Team disbanded June 1; City was named after Andrew Jackson, who was a general in the Creek wars and in the War of 1812. Jackson later became president. With manager Tom Leidl at the helm, newspapers called the players "Leidl's Generals."

2891 Diamond Jaxx 1998 to date *Southern (AA)*. Moniker combines the city name of Jackson with the baseball "diamond" to come up with Diamond Jaxx. Spelling alterations, i.e., Jaxx for Jacks and Starzz for Stars, was a trend in the 1990s. These spelling changes were popularized by rap music and video games. Historically, football is known as the "gridiron game," and baseball, the "Diamond Game."

Jackson, Texas

2892 Diamond Kats 2000 *Texas–Louisiana (ind.)*. Moniker was a spin-off of the Texas League Jackson "Diamond Jaxx." In the 1990s minor league teams started to market their teams by dropping parent club nicknames and selecting their own. In this era, dog (also "dawg") and cat names — made popular by rap and hip-hop music — were sometimes used. The team logo displays a wildcat. Wildcats are found throughout the Southwest and Texas. Baseball is the "diamond game."

Jacksonville, Duval, Florida

2893 Athletics 1886 *Southern League of Colored Baseballists*. Black newspaper reporters noted that the players on the team were "very athletic." Editors shortened the name to A's.

2894 Florida Clippers 1886 *Southern League of Colored Baseballists*. Team went by the state name of "Florida Clippers," one of the earliest sports teams to use a state name. Clipper ships have sailed the nearby St. John's River and along the Atlantic coast of Florida since at least 1840.

2895 Macedonians 1886 *Southern League of Colored Baseballists*. Some nineteenth-century teams used athletic names of the ancient Greco-Roman world i.e., Olympics, Trojans, Spartans, Athenians, Gladiators, and Macedonians. Team was sponsored by the Macedonia Baptist Church of Jacksonville. Team was a rival, on the field and in name, of the Jacksonville Roman Citys.

2896 Roman Citys 1886 *Southern League of Colored Baseballists*. Occasionally, two rival teams in a sports league will choose opposing nicknames, i.e., Trojans v. Spartans, Lions v. Tigers, Yankees v. Rebels and Macedonians v. Romans. The biggest European empire, before the Roman Empire, was the Macedonian Empire of Alexander the Great of 336–323 B.C. Team was sponsored by a Roman Catholic church as a rival to the Jacksonville Macedonians, who were sponsored by the Macedonia Baptist Church.

2897 Jacksonville Base Ball Club 1890–91–91–92 *Florida (W)*. The Florida Winter League is the oldest professional winter circuit in the eastern U.S.; 1892 *Florida State (W)*. These teams had no nickname.

2898 Jays 1904–05, 1907–10 *South Atlantic (C)*. Although there are blue jays in Florida, the name was derived from the habit of local newspapers to call the team the "J's" to compensate for a 12-letter city name. After a few weeks, it became "Jays." In a similar fashion, Burlington teams went from the newspaper contraction "B's" to "Bees." With managers George Kelly and then Jack Robinson at the helm, newspapers called the players "George's Jays" and "Jack's Jays."

2899 Jax 1906 *South Atlantic (C)*. Moniker, only four letters long, was used for newspaper headlines, i.e., "Jax edge Seagulls, 4–3." Even in this era, the use of "X" names was becoming popular, i.e., Jax and Sox. Actually, "Jax" was a newspaper abbreviation for Jacksonville.

2900 Tars 1911–16 *South Atlantic (C)*; 1926–30 *Southeastern (D)*; 1946–52 *South Atlantic (A)*. Moniker is an abbreviation of a regional fish, the tarpon. Local newspapers sometimes shortened the name to "Tars." Tag has nothing to do with the "Tar Heel State" of North Carolina.

2901 Duval Giants 1915 *Independent Negro team*. Black teams that selected the nickname of "Giants" almost always placed a modifying adjective in front of it. For this team, the modifying adjective was "Duval." Jacksonville is located in Duval County.

2902 Roses 1917 *South Atlantic (C)*. The schedule was shortened, ending July 4, because of U.S. entry into World War I. Team was owned by Randolph Rose and played in a ballpark named after the owner — Rose Field.

2903 Red Caps 1920 *Southern Negro (ind.)*; 1923 *Independent Negro team*; 1934 *Independent Negro team*; 1938 *Negro American (M)*; 1941–42 *Negro American (M)*. Players wore red caps.

2904 Scouts 1921 *Florida State (C)*. With field manager Dominick Mullaney at the helm, local newspapers called the players "Dominick's Scouts." Name was appropriate because the Osceola, Creek and Seminole Indians sometimes served as scouts for settlers in the eighteenth and nineteenth centuries.

2905 Indians 1921 *Florida State (C)*. The Osceola and Creek Indians inhabited northern Florida in pre–Columbian times. By 1750, the Creeks became known as the "Seminoles."

2906 Braves 1953–60 *South Atlantic (A)*. Team was a farm club of the Milwaukee Braves.

2907 Jets 1961 *South Atlantic (A)*. Named after the Jacksonville Naval Air Station and the Jacksonville International Airport, local newspapers loved the name considering Jacksonville has 12 letters.

2908 Suns 1962–67 *International (AAA)*; 1970–84 *Southern (AA)*; 1991 to date *Southern (AA)*. Florida is the "Sunshine State," giving rise to this newspaper-friendly four-letter name. When the NBA Phoenix Suns started play in 1967–68, the baseball team switched to Mets in 1968 but the "Suns" moniker was so popular with Jacksonville fans that the 1970 team revived it.

2909 Mets 1968 *International (AAA)*. Team was a farm club of the New York Mets.

2910 Expos 1985–90 *Southern (AA)*. In 1971 the Texas and Southern leagues played an inter-locking schedule under the banner of the Dixie Association. In 1972 the two circuits returned to separate schedules. Team was a farm club of the Montreal Expos.

Jacksonville, Illinois

2911 Jacksonville Base Ball Club 1892 *Illinois–Iowa (ind.)*. Team had no nickname.

2912 Jacks 1894–95m *Western Assn. (ind.)*. Team moved to Springfield (IL) in mid-season 1895; 1910x *Northern Assn. (D)*. Team and league disbanded July 19; m1910x *Illinois–Missouri (D)*. This IML team started season in Beardstown (IL) and moved to Jacksonville July 21, picking up the "Jacks" moniker abandoned by the NA team. Team disbanded August 17.

2913 Reds m1900x *Central (ind.)*. Team started season in Springfield (IL) as the Springfield Reds and then moved to Jacksonville May 21. Players continued to wear red hose and the nickname was retained. Team disbanded July 8.

2914 Braves 1906 *Kentucky–Illinois–Tennessee (D)*; 1907 *Iowa State (D)*; 1908–09 *Central Assn. (D)*. Creek tribes settled in Northern Florida in 1750 and become known as the Seminoles. In this era, "Braves" was common jargon for baseball players or a baseball team.

2915 Lunatics 1906 *Kentucky–Illinois–Tennessee (D)*; 1907 *Iowa State (D)*; 1908–09 *Central Assn. (D)*. The city built the Jacksonville State Mental Hospital here in 1847. Just as in our era, fans and scandal newspapers had a fascination with celebrities who had mental problems.

Jacksonville, Texas

2916 Tomato-growers 1916x *East Texas (D)*. Team joined the league June 29 but after only playing nine games, disbanded July 13. Farms in the region transport tomatoes and other vegetables to packing houses in the city.

2917 Jax 1934–35 *West Dixie (C)*; 1936–40 *East Texas (C)*; 1946 *East Texas (C)*; 1947 *Lone Star (C)*; 1950 *Gulf Coast (D)*. Moniker was used for newspaper headlines, i.e., "Jax edge Pals, 4–3." All Jacksonville teams (in Florida, Illinois and Texas) have chosen short names, i.e., "Gems, Jays, Jets, Suns" and "Jax."

Jacksonville Beach, Florida

2918 Seabirds 1952–54 *Florida State (D)*. Also known as marine birds, seagulls, terns, auks, skuas and skimmers inhabit the coastal waters of Florida.

Jalapa, Veracruz, Mexico

Note: Xalapa was the English spelling, which has now fallen into disuse.

2919 Chileros 1955–56–1958–59 *Veracruzana (W)*. Farms produce a hot pepper so famous it is known as "jalapenos" or "jalapeno chili peppers" after the city. Chili peppers grown in surrounding farms are transported into the city for processing, packing and shipping. Known in English as the Veracruz League, the Liga Veracruzana meant literally the "True Cross League." The "True Cross" was a symbol of Roman Catholic Mexico and did not refer to the actual city or state of Veracruz (although the Chili Farmers represented Jalapa, Veracruz in league play). "Los chileros" means "chili farmers."

Jamestown, New York

2920 Jamestown Base Ball Club 1890–91 *New York–Pennsylvania (ind.)*. Team had no nickname.

2921 Hill Climbers 1905m *Interstate (D)*. Team moved to DuBois (PA) July 12. Although there was no farm system in the era 1883–1923, some minor league teams in cities close to a major league city formed a loose affiliation with the big league franchise, including emulating the ML club's nickname. The Jamestown club had a loose affiliation with the AL New York Hilltoppers. The New York Hilltoppers were also known as the New York Highlanders.

2922 Oseejays 1906m *Inter-State (D)*. Team represented both Oil City (PA) and nearby Jamestown (NY). Nickname is an acronym O-C-J, which, when spoken, sounds like some kind of bird, i.e., "oseejay." The team played 28 home games in each city.

2923 Giants 1914 *Interstate (D)*. In the era 1900–30 some minor league teams close to a big league team formed a loose affiliation with the big league club. The 1905 Jamestown "Hill-climbers" had a loose affiliation with the AL New York "Hilltoppers." In 1914 the Jamestown "Giants" had a loose affiliation with the NL New York "Giants." The tag "Giants" was also bestowed on teams that were winners. The 1914 team won the pennant, finishing first with a 59–40 record. As was the custom, the nickname was retained in 1915 even though the team failed to repeat.

2924 Rabbits 1915x *Interstate (D)*. Team disbanded August 14. With manager William Webb at the helm, newspapers called the players "Webb's Rabbits." In this, the "dead ball" era, speedy players on the base paths known as "rabbits" were highly prized.

2925 Falcons 1939 *Pennsylvania–Ohio–New York (P.O.N.Y.) (D)*; 1941–56 *P.O.N.Y. (D)*; 1957x *New York–Pennsylvania (D)*; 1970–73 *New York–Pennsylvania (A)*. Although there are falcons flying in the skies of New York, the nickname was selected because the team played its home games in suburban Falconer (NY).

2926 Ponies 1939 *Pennsylvania–Ohio–New York (P.O.N.Y.) (D)*; 1941–56 *P.O.N.Y. (D)*; 1957x *New York–Pennsylvania (D)*. "Ponies" in the nineteenth century referred to a team, usually an expansion team, with lots of young players and rookies, i.e., "young colts." This team used the nickname as a spin-off from the Pennsylvania–Ontario–New York League, i.e., P.O.N.Y. League.

2927 Jockeys 1939 *Pennsylvania–Ohio–New York (P.O.N.Y.) (D)*; 1957x *New York–Pennsylvania (D)*. Tag was a spin-off from "Ponies." Tag was also spelled **Jockies** in 1957.

2928 Tigers 1961–65 New York–Pennsylvania *(D)*. 1961–62, *(A)*. 1963–65. Team was a farm club of the Detroit Tigers.

2929 Dodgers 1966 New York–Pennsylvania *(A)*. Team was a farm club of the Los Angeles Dodgers.

2930 Braves 1967–69 *New York–Pennsylvania (A)*. Team was a farm club of the Atlanta Braves.

2931 Expos 1977–93 *New York–Pennsylvania (A)*. Team was a farm club of the Montreal Expos.

2932 Jammers 1994 to date *New York–Pennsylvania (A)*. Fruit farms grow strawberries, raspberries, apples, peaches and grapes that are transported into the city where jams and jellies are produced. Management held a name-the-team contest and the winner was "Jammers." From 1994 through 2005 the team had no mascot logo for what was then an abstract headline tag. In 2006 the team got an anthropomorphic logo, i.e., a "grape man" holding a bat. The poor fellow has boil-like grapes all over his face and body. Other entries in the contest were All-Americans, Furniture-makers, Jimmies, Lakers, Lucys (comedienne Lucille Ball was born here), Muskies and Stompers (grape-stromping). Team now has a wildcat logo. Wildcats inhabit New York State.

Jamestown, North Dakota

2933 Jimkotans 1922 *Dakota (D)*; 1923 *North Dakota (D)*. In a hybrid of two names, the nickname derives from "James" and "Dakota," combining to form "Jimkotan." Actually, "Jim" is the nickname of James.

2934 Jamestown Baseball Club 1934 *Independent Negro team*. Team had no nickname.

2935 Jimmies 1936–37 *Northern (D)*. Moniker was used for newspaper headlines, i.e., "Jimmies edge Colts, 4–3." Jamestown is nicknamed "Jimtown."

Janesville, Wisconsin

2936 Mutuals 1877 *League Alliance (ind.)*. Teams in the LA were farm clubs of the entire senior circuit rather than any one NL team. An amateur club in 1876, the "Mutual Baseball Club of Janesville" was named after the famous "New York Mutuals." The club turned professional in 1877 and joined the League Alliance.

2937 Cubs 1941–42 *Wisconsin State (D)*. Team was a farm club of the Chicago Cubs.

2938 Bears 1946–53 *Wisconsin State (D)*. Team was a farm club of the Chicago Cubs. "Bears" was a spin-off from "Cubs."

Jeanerette, Louisiana

2939 Blues m1934–39 *Evangeline (D)*. Team began 1934 season in Lake Charles (LA), then moved to Jeanerette May 29, 1934. Players wore blue trim uniforms and blue stirrups in the style of the parent club Detroit Tigers, whose own uniforms had navy blue trim.

Jeanette, Pennsylvania

2940 Jays 1926–31m *Middle Atlantic (C)*. Team moved to Altoona (PA) May 23. Although there are plenty of blue jays in Pennsylvania, the name came about from local newspapers calling the team the J's, which soon became "Jays." Others examples are B's becoming Bees and OCJ's becoming Oseejays. With manager Jack Snyder at the helm in 1926, newspapers called the players "Jack's Jays." Jim Ferguson took over in 1927 and the name became "Jim's Jays." Lee Strait came next (1927–29), making the name "Strait's Jays." Leo Hanley took over next, making the name "Hanley's Jays." The name was retained through 1931.

2941 Reds 1934–35 *Pennsylvania State (D)*. Team was a farm club of the Cincinnati Reds.

2942 Pirates 1936 *Pennsylvania State (D)*. Team was a farm club of the Pittsburgh Pirates. When farm teams became the rule around 1935–36, several added the adjective "Little" to modify the parent club's nickname, i.e., **Little Pirates**. This fad proved to be unpopular with fans and newspapers, and it was dropped by 1940.

2943 Bisons 1937 *Pennsylvania State (D)*. Team was a farm club of the Buffalo Bisons. In the era 1900–55, and especially in the 1930s and 1940s, lower classification (i.e., A-B-C-D) minor league teams sometimes were farm clubs of higher classification (i.e., AA and AAA) minor league teams.

Jefferson City, Missouri

2944 Capitolites 1902 *Missouri Valley (D)*. Jefferson City has been the state capital of Missouri since 1821.

2945 Convicts 1902 *Missouri Valley (D)*. The Missouri State Penitentiary was built here in 1850. With manager A.B. Carey at the helm, newspapers called the players "Carey's Convicts."

2946 Senators 1911x *Missouri Valley (D)*. Team disbanded June 2. Tag was a spin-off from the 1902 name. By the turn of the century, the word "capitolite"—meaning a resemblance to a senate building—had become archaic.

Jenkins, Kentucky

2947 Cavaliers 1948–51 *Mountain State (D)*. Robert Cavalier, the Duke of LaSalle, claimed the Louisiana Territory for his sovereign King Louis XIV. Kentucky was part of the Louisiana Territory at this time. The name was also appropriate because starting in the sixteenth century, gentlemen trained in arms and horsemanship as well as mounted soldiers in England and France were known as "Cavaliers."

Jersey City, New Jersey

2948 Browns 1878–79 *Independent*. Team in 1878 was nominally affiliated with the International Association but played an independent schedule, compiling a 46–12 record mostly against semi-professional and amateur opponents. Team started the 1879 season as an independent and then joined the National Association September 5. Players wore brown hose.

2949 Blues 1885m *Eastern (ind.)*. Team moved to Trenton (NJ) June 23; 1886–87 *Eastern (ind.)*. Players wore blue hose.

2950 Skeeters 1885m *Eastern (ind.)*; 1888 *Central (ind.)*; 1902–15 *Eastern (A 1902–07, AA 1912–15)*; 1918–21 *International (AA)*; 1923 *International (AA)*; 1925–33 *International (AA)*. Term is slang for "mosquito," insomuch as New Jersey is the "Mosquito State." Inhabitants of New Jersey are called "Skeeters," a slang coined in 1839. It was around 1900 that the mosquito-ridden Meadowland Swamps of northern New Jersey were finally drained to reduce the danger of malaria.

2951 Jerseys 1885m *Eastern (ind.)*; m1960–61 *International (AAA)*. Team began the season in Havana (Cuba) and then because of Fidel Castro's Communist Revolution moved to Jersey City June 13, 1960. Moniker was used for newspaper headlines, i.e., "Jerseys edge Blue Hens, 4–3."

2952 Giants 1888 *International (ind.)*; 1937–50 *International (AA)*. 1937–45, *(AAA)*. 1946–50). Both **teams** were farm clubs of the New York Giants.

2953 Lads 1888 *Central (ind.)*. Team was named after manager Pat Powers. Sometimes teams were named as an alliteration or rhyme after their field manager, i.e., McGraw Men, Kennedy's Kids, Mack Men, Loftus' Orphans and **Pat's Lads**.

2954 Gladiators 1889 *Atlantic (ind.)*. Today a nickname for football players, back in the period 1880–1910 the nickname was used to describe baseball players who were perceived to be brawny and brutal men, much like the gladiators of Ancient Rome. Pat Powers managed the team and local newspapers called the players "Pat's Gladiators" and "Powers' Gladiators."

2955 Jersey City Baseball Club 1900 *Atlantic (ind.)*. Team had no nickname.

2956 Cubans 1916 *Independent Negro team*. Black Cubans played on this team. In the era 1900–50, Cuban players would play winter ball on the island and summer ball in the States. During the summer, a few white Cubans played in the majors and in the U.S. minor leagues, but all the black Cubans were forced to play on U.S. Negro teams.

2957 Colts 1922 *International (AA)*; 1924 *International (AA)*. Team had many young players. By the 1920s, "colts" no longer was a generic baseball tag for "rookie" or for a young player. Instead, the moniker had become a team nickname with an "Old West" motif.

2958 Little Giants 1937–50 *International (AA)*. 1937–45 *(AAA)* (1946–50). This style of using "Little" before the major league parent club's nickname was not well received by fans, who found the style condescending, and newspaper editors, who wanted shorter team nicknames.

2959 Indians 1977–78 *Eastern (AA)*. Team was a farm club of the Cleveland Indians.

Jesup, Georgia

2960 Bees 1950–53 *Georgia State (D)*. The state insect of Georgia is the honeybee. Honey farms in the rural areas transport raw honey into the city where it is processed, packaged and shipped. The home ballpark was named Jesup Bees Field.

Johnson City, Tennessee

2961 Soldiers 1910 *Southeastern (D)*; 1911–13 *Appalachian (D)*; 1921–24 *Appalachian (D)*; 1937–38 *Appalachian (D)*. Tennessee got its nickname as the "Volunteer State" not during the Civil War but during the Mexican-American War of 1847–49 when the federal government asked for 2,000 volunteers from Tennessee to enlist and more than 14,000 men volunteered. The Johnson City branch of the National Home for Disabled Volunteer Soldiers was built here in 1910 and opened in 1911. Reinforcing the name, no less than seven major battles were fought in Tennessee during the Civil War from 1862 to 1865.

2962 Taylorites 1910 *Southeastern (D)*. With field manager Nat Taylor at the helm, newspapers called the players "Taylorites."

2963 Old Soldiers 1910 *Southeastern (D)*; 1911–13 *Appalachian (D)*. Many retirees at the National Home were elderly Civil War veterans.

2964 Cardinals 1939–55 *Appalachian (D)*; 1961 *Appalachian (D)*; 1975 to date *Appalachian (R)*. These teams were farm clubs of the St. Louis Cardinals.

2965 Phillies 1957–60 *Appalachian (D)*. Team was a farm club of the Philadelphia Phillies.

2966 Yankees 1964–74 *Appalachian (R)*. Team was a farm club of the New York Yankees.

Johnsonburg, Pennsylvania

2967 Johnnies 1916 *Inter-State (D)*. Moniker was used for newspaper headlines, i.e., "Johnnies edge Sailors, 4–3." With manager Thomas "David" Jones at the helm, newspapers called the players "Tommy Jones' Johnnies."

Johnstown, New York

2968 Buckskins 1894–95 *New York State (ind.)*. Dressed in buckskins, pioneers from England, France and Holland explored and settled the Johnstown region from 1640 until 1760. City was founded in 1762. The first trackers to wear buckskins were not Europeans but the native Iroquois. An ideal costume for tracking and hunting, the Europeans copied this attire. "Buckskin" was also a slang for a soldier of the Continental Army during the Revolutionary War of 1776–81. City leather factories manufactured buckskin gloves and mittens.

2969 Foundlings 1898 *New York State (ind.)*. In the era 1885–1910 expansion teams invariably were very young teams, with lots of rookies and otherwise inexperienced players, leading to such tags as Baby, Babies, Ponies and Foundlings. When the word "rookie" (coined in 1892) became popular in 1917 as a designation for young "recruits" of the U.S. Army on their way to fight in Europe, the other terms for a new and young player were swept away.

2970 Johnnies 1902–08 *New York State (B)*; 1909 *Eastern (AA)*. Moniker was used for newspaper headlines, i.e., "Johnnies edge Townies, 4–3."

Johnstown-Amsterdam-Gloversville, New York

2971 Jays m1890 *New York State (ind.)*. Although blue jays and green jays are found in Pennsylvania, the name was derived from the newspaper technique of calling the team the J's. After a few weeks the name became a more mascot-like Jays. Team was called the "Johnstown-Gloversville Jays," playing its home games in Johnstown.

2972 Jags 1902–08m *New York State (B)*. Team moved to Elmira (NY) July 22, 1908. Playing its home games in Gloversville, the team represented the three cities of Johnstown (NY), Amsterdam (NY) and Gloversville (NY), whose first initials spell out J-A-G.

Johnstown, Pennsylvania

2973 Johnstown Base Ball Club m1884 *Iron & Oil (ind.)*. Team began season in New Brighton (PA) and moved to Johnstown August 2; 1887 *Mountain (ind.)*. These teams had no nickname.

2974 Johnnies 1892 *Pennsylvania State (ind.)*; 1905–08 *Tri-State (ind.)*. 1905–06, *(B)*. 1907–08; 1910–12m *Tri-State* Team moved to Chester (PA) August 2; 1925–38 *Middle Atlantic (C)*; 1939–42 *Pennsylvania State Assn. (D)*; 1946–50 *Middle Atlantic (C)*; m1955–56 *Eastern (A)*. Team began the 1955 season in Wilkes-Barre (PA) and then moved to Johnstown July 1; 1998–2002 *Frontier (ind.)*. Moniker was for newspaper headlines, i.e., "Johnnies edge Barons, 4–3." The team of 1998–2002 had a little red fox as its logo and mascot. Foxes inhabit Pennsylvania.

2975 Flood Sufferers 1892–93 *Pennsylvania State (ind.)*. On May 31, 1889, the Southport Dam at Lake Conemaugh and the Little Creek River burst during a rainstorm, causing a flood that drowned 2,209 people and destroyed most of the city of Johnstown. Johnstown became known as the "Flood City," and later, due to dam construction, the "Flood-Free City." Nineteenth century sports teams (baseball included) sometimes took up nicknames based on turmoil in the world, i.e., Flood-Sufferers, Boers, Hungarian Rioters, and Young Turks.

2976 Terrors 1893 *Pennsylvania State (ind.)*. "Terrors" was an occasional nickname for a baseball team, especially in a city whose spelling started with a "T" or was guided by a manager whose first or last name started with a "T." Hence, with manager Thayer Torreyson at the helm, newspapers called the players "Torreyson's Terrors." In this era, "Terrors" meant a formidable opponent and may have been, in this case, based on the "terrifying flood" of May 31, 1889.

2977 Genuine Cuban Giants 1900 *Independent Negro team*. The Cuban Giants (est. 1885) changed their name to Genuine Cuban Giants to avoid confusion with a new, rival team — the Cuban-X Giants. For this season this black team played home games in Johnstown (PA), Hoboken (NJ), Trenton (NJ) and New York City.

2978 Jawns 1909 *Tri-State (B)*. Moniker was used for newspaper headlines, i.e., "Jawns edge Dutchmen." Tag was a spin-off from Johnnies. The name "Jawn" is an archaic slang for "John."

2979 Red Sox 1961 *Eastern (A)*. Team was a farm club of the Boston Red Sox.

2980 Steal 1995–97 *Frontier (ind.)*. The team logo portrays a Cincinnati-style baseball-head player stealing a base as a play on words between "steel" and "steal." Johnstown has traditionally been a steel industry city. The Columbia Iron Company (est. 1852), Bethlehem Steel Company (est. 1890) and Cambria Iron Company (1900) operated in this city.

Joliet, Illinois

2981 Convicts 1890–91 *Illinois–Iowa (ind.)*. Alton Prison was built here in 1833. The Joliet Correctional Center opened here in 1853 and closed in 2002.

2982 Cyclones 1890–91 *Illinois–Iowa (ind.)*. A series of tornadoes struck the Midwest in 1890, killing hundreds of people. The Joliet Cyclones and the Louisville Cyclones used this nickname for the 1890 season.

2983 Stone Citys 1892 *Illinois–Iowa (ind.)*. City got the nickname of "Stone City" because of its burgeoning cement and concrete industry.

2984 Joliet Base Ball Club 1895 *Western Inter-State (ind.)*. Team had no nickname.

2985 Standards 1903 *Three-I (D)*. Standard Oil built refineries in the city to process crude oil and natural gas. With manager Albert Tebeau at the helm, newspapers called the players the "Albert Tebeau's Standards."

2986 Jollyites 1910m *Northern Assn. (D)*. Team moved to Sterling (IL) June 21. Moniker was used for newspaper headlines, i.e., "Jollyites edge Jacks, 4–3."

2987 Jackhammers 2002–10 *Northern (ind.)*. Moniker is a spin-off from "Stone Citys." The "Jackhammer" is a drill used to break up blocks of cement and granite.

2988 Slammers 2011 to date *Frontier (ind.)*. Team held a name-the-team contest and the winning entry was "Slammers." The moniker is a spin-off from the 1891 "Joliet Convicts" and is a reference to the famous phrase, i.e., "jail door being slammed." The term "slammer" is slang for "jail."

Jonesboro, Arkansas

2989 Jonesboro Baseball Club 1909x *Arkansas State (D)*. Team and league disbanded July 7. Team had no nickname.

2990 Zebras 1909–11 *Northeast Arkansas (D)*. The N.E. Arkansas League began play July 26 after the Arkansas State League disbanded July 7. Players wore striped hose. When athletes started wearing striped stockings, starting around 1890, many of these teams started calling themselves the "Tigers." This team went with "Zebras" to be a little more unique. As the team went on to win the pennant with a first-place 30–23 record, the fans would roar the rally cry of "Go Zebras!" The nickname has been used by Jonesboro College baseball teams since 1911, although the professional baseball teams here did not continue with it.

2991 Buffaloes 1925–26 *Tri-State (D)*. Team was a farm club of the Houston Buffaloes. In the era 1900–50 a few minor league teams at a lower classification (A-B-C-D) would sometimes serve as farm clubs for minor league franchises at a higher classification. With manager Buck Stapleton at the helm, newspapers called the players "Buck Stapleton's Buffaloes."

2992 Giants 1936–38 *Northeast Arkansas (D)*. Team had a loose affiliation with the New York Giants. During the Depression years of 1930–39, major league teams often donated uniforms to minor league teams.

2993 White Sox 1939–41 *Northeast Arkansas (D)*. Team was a farm club of the Chicago White Sox. With factory production exploding because of the inevitable specter of U.S. involvement in World War II, the Great Depression ended and major league baseball teams had more cash to maintain formal ties with minor league farm teams.

Joplin, Missouri

2994 Joplin Base Ball Club 1887 *Southwestern (ind.)*; 1891 *Southwestern (ind.)*. These teams had no nickname.

2995 Miners 1902–04 *Missouri Valley (D)*. 1902–03, *(C)*. 1904; 1905–09m *Western Assn. (C)*. Team moved to El Reno (OK) July 4, 1909; 1910–11x *Western Assn. (C 1910, D 1911)*. Team disbanded May 10. 1917–21 *Western (A)*; 1922–24m *Western Assn. (D 1922, C 1923–24)*. Team moved to Bartlesville (OK) June 16; m1927–32m *Western Assn. (C)*. Team started season in St. Joseph (MO) to Joplin July 7, 1927. Team moved to Topeka (KS) May 6, 1932; 1933 *Western (A)*; 1934–42 *Western Assn. (C)*; 1946–53 *Western Assn. (C)*. City was settled in 1838. By 1850 lead and marble deposits had been discovered. By the time the city was chartered in 1873, zinc deposits had also been encountered. With manager Claude Marcum at the helm in 1902, newspapers called the players "Marcum's Miners." With manager Elmer Meredith at the helm in 1910, newspapers called the players "Meredith's Miners." With manager Runt Marr at the helm in 1933, newspapers called the players "Marr's Miners." Marr returned as manger in 1934–35. Ted Meyer took over in 1938 to lead "Meyer's Miners." The nickname was retained through 1942.

2996 Ozarks m1926 *Western Assn. (A)*. Team began season in Ardmore (TX) and moved to Joplin July 14. City was built at the foot of the nearby Ozark Mountains. Joplin is the "Gateway to the Ozarks."

2997 Cardinals 1954 *Western Assn. (C)*. Team was a farm club of the St. Louis Cardinals.

Joplin–Webb City, Missouri

2998 Joplin–Webb City Baseball Club 1914m *Western Assn. (D)*. Team moved to Guthrie (OK) July 10. Team had no nickname.

Junction City, Kansas

2999 Junction City Base Ball Club 1896–97 *Kansas State (ind.)*; m1898m *Kansas State (ind.)*. Team started the 1898 season in Salina (KS) and moved to Junction City June 4, where they played about a month before returning to Salina July 5 for the second half of the season. These teams had no nickname.

3000 Soldiers 1909–12 *Central Kansas (D)*; 1913x *Kansas State (D)*. Team disbanded July 9. In 1860 city was originally Fort Riley — home of the 9th and 10th Horse Cavalry Regiments of the U.S. Army. These troops were called "Buffalo Soldiers." With manager Louis Armstrong (no relation to the famous trumpet musician) at the helm in 1909, newspapers called the players the "Louis Armstrong's Soldiers."

Jupiter, Florida

3001 Expos 1997–2001 *Gulf Coast (R)*. Team was a farm club of the Montreal Expos.

3002 Hammerheads 1998 to date *Florida State (A)*. The "hammerhead shark," with a hammer-shaped snout, swims off the coast of Florida.

3003 Marlins 2002 to date *Gulf Coast (R)*. Team was a farm club of the Florida Marlins.

3004 Cardinals 2007 to date *Gulf Coast (R)*. Team was a farm club of the St. Louis Cardinals.

Kalamazoo, Michigan

3005 Kazoos 1887 *Ohio State (ind.)*; 1889 *Michigan (ind.)*; 1894–95 *Michigan State (ind.)*; 1897 *Michigan State (ind.)*; 1909–10 *Southern Michigan (C)*; 1913–14 *Southern Michigan (D)*; 1924 *Michigan-Ontario (B)*; 1926 *Central (C)*. The 1908–14 circuit was designated League 1908 and 1910–14 and Association 1906–07 and 1909. Moniker was used for newspaper headlines, i.e., "Kazoos edge Buckeyes, 4–3." By 1926 Kalamazoo newspaper editors were fed up with such lengthy names as Celery-Pickers Celery Champs and Celery-Eaters.

3006 Kalamazoo Base Ball Club 1888 *Tri-State (ind.)*. Team had no nickname.

3007 White Sox 1906–08 *Southern Michigan (D 1906–07, C 1908)*. Team had a loose affiliation with the Chicago White Sox. In the era 1900–30, before the farm system was instituted, minor league teams, in the vicinity of a big league city, sometimes formed a loose affiliation with the major league club located nearby.

3008 Celery-Eaters 1911 *Southern Michigan (C)*. Numerous farms in the region sent celery and other vegetables into the city to be washed, processed, packed and shipped. The city became known at this time as the "Celery City."

3009 Celery Champs 1912 *Southern Michigan (C)*. Noted for its celery farms, the city was known as the "Celery City." Newspapers combined that nickname with "Champs" since the team had won the 1911 flag.

3010 Celery Pickers 1920–22 *Central (D)*; 1923 *Michigan-Ontario (B)*; 1926 *Michigan State (D)*. Name was a spin-off from the 1911 team's name. The moniker for this 1926 MSL team was used to avoid confusion with the 1926 CL Kazoos. Attendance was split between the two franchises, causing both teams to lose money and disband at season's end.

3011 Lassies 1950–54 *All-American Girls Professional Baseball League (ind.)*. Tag is a Scottish name for girl.

3012 Kodiaks 1996–98 *Frontier (ind.)*. Although there are no Alaskan "Kodiak" bears in Michigan, the moniker was appropriate because Kalamazoo's weather in April can be wintry. The Kodiak brown bear, which was used as the team's logo, inhabits southern Alaska and the Aleutian Islands.

3013 Kings 2001–10 *Frontier (ind.)*. Management sponsored a name-the-team contest and the winner was "Kings." Franchise disbanded after the 2010 season.

Kanagawa, Japan

3014 Bay Stars 2011 to date *Japan Western (ind.)*. Team was a farm club of the CL Yokohama Bay Stars.

Kane, Pennsylvania

3015 Mountaineers 1905–07 *Interstate (D)*. "Appalachia," the Eastern U.S. regions occupied by the Appalachian Mountains, includes Kane (PA). Kane, at an elevation of 2,013 feet above sea level, is known as the "Summit City." In the seventeenth and eighteenth centuries, Swedish, Dutch and English settlers explored the Appalachian Mountains.

Kankakee, Illinois

3016 Kays 1910 *Northern Assn. of Baseball (C 1910, D 1910)*. Local newspapers first called the team the "K's." The name was then changed to Kays—an imaginary equivalent of "Jays." Team nick-names of one letter, i.e., B's, J's, OCJ's, and K's were lengthened to Bees, Jays, Oseejays and Kays, respectively.

3017 Kanks m1912–14 *Illinois–Missouri (D)*. Moniker was used for newspaper headlines, i.e., "Kanks edge Abes, 4–3."

Kannapolis, North Carolina

3018 Towelers 1939–41 *North Carolina (D)*. Kannapolis is home to the Cannon Textile Mills whose most famous product is the "Cannon Towel." Kannapolis is known as the "Towel City."

3019 Piedmont Phillies 1995 *South Atlantic (A)*. The Piedmont is a region of the foothills of the Blue Ridge and Appalachian Mountains, in which Kannapolis is located. Team was a farm club of the Philadelphia Phillies.

3020 Piedmont Bollweevils 1996–2000 *South Atlantic (A)*. Also known as the "gray weevil," the "boll weevil" is an insect pest of cotton plants in the South.

3021 Intimidators 2001 to date *South Atlantic (A)*. Famous NASCAR auto racer Dale "The Intimidator" Earnhart became a part-owner of the team in 1995. When Earnhart was tragically killed in a car crash at the Dayton 500 in February 2001, fans asked management to name the team the "Intimidators."

Kansas City, Missouri

3022 Cowboys 1884 *Union Assn. (M)*; 1885 *Western (ind.)*; 1886 *National (M)*; 1887 *Western (ind.)*; 1888 *Western Assn. (ind.)*; 1888–89 *American Assn. (M)*; 1890–93x *Western (ind.)*. Team and league disbanded in mid-season June 20. Circuit was designated League 1890 and 1892–93 and Association 1891; 1894–99 *Western (ind.)*; 1900 *American (ind.)*; 1901 *Western (ind.)*; 1902–03 *American Assn. (ind. 1902, A 1903)*. Kansas City is "Cow Town." As the population grew, the city became known as the "Overgrown Cow Town." Although "Cowboys" was not an official moniker, the players of the 1888 Kansas City team posed for a team photograph wearing a ten gallon hat on their heads. By 1900, the city was the largest meat-packing city south of Chicago. As early as 1850, cowboys herded cattle here. In 1902–03, newspapers called the American Association team the "Cowboys," and the Western League team, the "Blues." The names Blues and Cowboys were used interchangeably for K.C. teams 1885–1901. When the WL Blues disbanded after the 1903 season, the 1904 AA team went to Blues, and Cowboys was dropped.

3023 Red Lions 1885 *Western (ind.)*. Players wore red hose. With manager Ted Sullivan at the helm, newspapers called the players "Ted Sullivan's Red Lions."

3024 Baby 1886 *National (M)*. Name was a baseball slang that referred to a new franchise—either an expansion franchise or an existing franchise joining a new league. A team could jump up to a major league from a minor league and sign major league players, or a team sometimes was formed from scratch to join the National League or the American Association. With manager Dave Rowe at the helm, newspapers called the players "Dave's Baby." Such a team was aka **Babies**.

3025 Stormy Petrels 1886. The team suffered through a "stormy" losing season, going 30–91 and finishing seventh in the eight-team NL. A "petrel" is a seabird—similar to a seagull—that endures stormy weather in its search for food.

3026 Rowe's Revengers 1886. With field manager Dave Rowe at the helm, newspapers called the players "Rowe's Revengers." Moniker was probably a spin-off of the UA Cincinnati Avengers of 1884.

3027 Blues 1887 *Western (ind.)*; 1888 *Western Assn. (ind.)*; 1888–89 *American Assn. (M)*; 1894–99 *Western (ind.)*. 1890–93x *Western (ind.)*. Team and league disbanded June 20. Circuit was designated League 1890 and 1892–93 and Association 1891; 1894–99 *Western (ind.)*; 1900 *American (ind.)*; 1901 *Western (ind.)*; *American Assn.* 1904–54 (A 1904–07, AA 1908–45, AAA 1946–54.) Players wore blue hose. Occasionally **Blue Stockings**, newspapers shortened it to **Blues**, which took over completely by 1910.

3028 Ice Wagon Gang 1888–89 *American Assn. (M)*. Term was a nineteenth-century baseball slang—coined by the *Philadelphia North American* August 4, 1886, and appearing in Richard Miller's *Pucks Library Vol. I*—described a slow-footed runner or a slow-footed team. Ironically, the tag could be applied to a speedy team that stole a lot of bases, like an "out-of-control ice wagon racing down the street." Kansas City this year stole only 257 bases, lowest in the American Association, in an era when the stolen base was emphasized (the home run was hard to come by in this era). Unhappy K.C. fans and reporters branded the team as the "Ice Wagon Gang" because the 257 steals contributed to the team's eighth and last-place finish. In the nineteenth century, horse-pulled, slow-moving ice wagons plodded along, delivering ice blocks to homes and businesses. Baseball players in this era sometimes hitched a ride on ice wagons with as many as ten grown men perched precariously on the bouncing wagon, which must have made for a comic scene for baseball fans milling outside the park waiting to be admitted to the game. Strangely, the 1889 K.C. team led the majors with 472 stolen bases.

3029 Manning's Men 1894–99 *Western (ind.)*. Tag was used in honor of manager Jim Manning.

3030 Westerns 1894–99 *Western (ind.)*. Kansas City was the western-most team in the league. Kansas City is also known as the "Gateway to the West."

3031 Gate Citys 1894–99 *Western (ind.)*. Kansas City is known as "The Gate City to the West."

3032 Manning's Kindergarden 1900 *American (ind.)*; 1901–03 *Western (ind. 1901, A 1902–03)*. Tag was used for manager Jim Manning's 1900 team, which signed mostly young players. Kindergarden comes from the German "kindergarten," which is pre-school for children.

3033 Kaws 1901–03 *Western (ind. 1901, A 1902–03)*; *American Assn. (A 1904–07, AA 1908–32)*. The Kawnee Indians inhabited the Midwest since pre–Columbian times. Used as an alternate to the bland "Blues," newspapers liked its four-letter length and fans happily screamed the crow chant "caw! caw!" as the team won back-to-back WL pennants, 1901–02. With manager Kid Nichols at the helm, 1902–03, newspapers called the players "Kid's Nichol's Kaws."

3034 Giants 1908–15 Independent Negro team. Moniker was popular for black teams in this era.

3035 Royal Giants 1909–10 *Independent Negro team*; 1925 *Independent Negro team*. In the era 1890–1950, black teams using "Giants" invariably modified the noun with a descriptive adjective, i.e., American, Black, Columbia, Cuban, Elite, Leland, Quaker, Union and Royal. "Royal," used for this team to distinguish it from the cross-town Kansas City Giants, eventually evolved into the AL Kansas City Royals in 1969.

3036 Monarchs 1910 *Independent Negro team*; 1920–31 *Negro National (M)*. Team barnstormed in 1929 and 1931; 1932–36 *Independent Negro team*; 1937–49 *Negro American (M)*. 1950–59 *Negro American (ind.)*. The 1950–59 circuit was a professional minor league. Name is a spin-off from "Royals." Historians retroactively call the 1910 team the "Original Monarchs." Pitcher John Donaldson conferred the moniker of "Monarchs" on the 1920 squad because, as a kid, he had watched the old 1910 Monarchs play in Kansas City.

3037 Pullman Colts 1911 *Independent Negro team*. Team had many young players who were known, in baseball slang, as "colts." Team was sponsored by the Pullman Railroad Company and several of the players worked during the off-season as porters on its trains.

3038 Kawfeds 1914 *Federal (M)*. Unmercifully, Kansas City was yet another Federal League team that gagged its fans with the "Feds" amalgam style of team nickname in 1914, i.e., Baltfeds, Buffeds, Chifeds, Hoosierfeds, Newfeds, Pitfeds and the truly hideous Sloufeds. In this case, it was **Kawfeds**— a combination of the Kawnee Indians and "Federals."

3039 Packers 1914–15 *Federal (M)*. In the nineteenth century, meat-packing factories sprung up in Oklahoma City, Kansas City and Chicago. Kansas City became a "Cow Town" just as railroads were replacing the cowboy-on-horseback cattle drives. As the K.C. population grew in the 1880s the city became known as the "Overgrown Cow Town" and the "Steak Center of the Nation."

3040 Colored Giants 1917 *Independent Negro team*. Another descriptive adjective for black "Giants" teams, the term was respectful of black people in this era and persisted into the 1960s before it was replaced by the more self-respectful "black" and "African American."

3041 Royals 1944–45 *Southern California (W)*; 1947 *Southern California (W)*; 1969 to date *American (M)*. The 1944–45 and 1947 teams had players from the Kansas City Monarchs— hence the spin-off nickname. These teams played their home games at Pirrone Stadium in Los Angeles. As for the 1969 nickname origin, the American Royal Livestock and Horse Show is held in Kansas City every year. The name has a historical link with the blue-hosed Kansas City Cowboys teams of yesteryear, and the royal blue-trimmed American Association Kansas City Blues of 1904–54. The moniker also has a link with the famous Negro League Kansas City Monarchs and the 1909–10 Kansas City Royal Giants. The name was the winning entry in a name-the-team contest, submitted by Sanford Porte (his submission had the earliest postmark date of 547 "Royals" entries). Porte explained his chose the name because "Royals stands for the best." Other entries included Eagles, Mokans, Hearts and Zoomers as 17,000 fans participated.

3042 Yankees' Farm Club 1955–62 *American (M)*. Team owner Arnold Johnson (1955–62), constantly strapped for cash, resorted to selling and trading good player after good player to the wealthy New York Yankees for less talented (and less expensive) players and cold, hard cash. Some of the more notable A's who became Yankees and helped the New Yorkers to seven pennants in those eight seasons were hitters Roger Maris, Hector Lopez and Enos Slaughter and pitchers Bud Daley, Art Ditmar, Ryne Duren, Duke Maas, Bobby Schantz and Ralph Terry. When Charlie Finley bought the club in 1963, he embarked on a five-year building program, shunning trades with the Bronx Bombers, which resulted in competitive Oakland Athletics teams, starting in 1968.

3043 Athletics 1955–67 *American (M)*. The Philadelphia Athletics moved to Kansas City in 1955. The nickname was retained.

3044 A's 1955–67 *American (M)*. Baseball's oldest single-letter contraction, it has been the only one that has become popular and universally known. Any team with the **A's** tag is the "Athletics." Minor league teams in Burlington in Iowa and North Carolina have sometimes been known as "B's." The Baltimore Orioles are sometimes identified as the "O's" and the Seattle Mariners the "M's" but these latter designations have not been much used except by space-conscious newspaper editors.

3045 White Elephants 1955–67 *American (M)*. Pretty much abandoned by the losing Philadelphia Athletics of the 1930s, 1940s and 1950s, the moniker was revived by K.C. owner Arnold Johnson, who moved the team to Kansas City in 1955. The white elephant reappeared on the left sleeve of the uniform's jersey.

3046 Underdog Athletics 1955–67 *American (M)*. From 1955 through the 1967 season (the franchise's last season in Kansas City), the Athletics did not have a winning season — the only major league franchise of at least ten years in duration to fail to have a winning season. In 1955 K.C. fans rooted for "Our Underdogs" in such numbers, the A's led the AL in attendance with no less than 1,339,000 fans after drawing only 366,000 fans in Philadelphia the previous season in 1952. But the A's never had a winning season in K.C. and attendance was so low by 1967 that team owner Charlie Finley got permission from AL president Joe Cronin to move the franchise to Oakland for the 1968 season.

3047 Flashy Athletics 1963–67 *American (M)*. Some four years before the "Psychedelic Fashion Revolution" of 1967–68, team owner Charlie Finley broke with the dull tradition of "whites at home and grays on the road" when he dressed his K.C. players in Kelly green and gold uniforms. In an era that was conservative (before the psychedelic colors of the Beatles), many people condemned the flashy colors as too gaudy, but by the 1970s baseball uniforms became universally "psychedelic." In the pre-hippie, pre–Cultural Revolution era, intolerant people considered flashy colors in man's clothing to be an indication of homosexuality, leading to the occasional epithet of **Faggots** for the team.

3048 Boys in Blue 1969–76 *American (M)*. A play on words of the phrase that originally referred to policemen, it became passé when the Toronto Blue Jays joined the American League in 1977. Team GM Dayton Moore coined a team slogan in 2007 "True. Blue. Tradition"— but the slogan rang hollow with Kansas City fans jaded from years of losing. The team has never been called the "True Blues."

3049 R's 1969–2001 *American (M)*. This single-letter tag was yet another dopey spin-off from the classic A's "team letter" of Philadelphia–Kansas City–Oakland. Like the Baltimore O's and Seattle M's, it served strictly as a newspaper contraction, which fans have mostly ignored. When the team dropped the letter "R" from its shield logo in 2002, the single-letter tag was dropped.

3050 Middle America's Team 1975–89 *American (M)*. In a spin-off from the NFL Dallas Cowboy's "America's Team" marketing title of the 1970s, the very successful Kansas City Royals of 1975–89 (two pennants, one World Series title, six division titles and 12 winning seasons out of 15) were praised by delighted K.C. fans as "Middle America's Team," led by hitters George Brett, Willie Wilson, Frank White, Hal McRae, Cookie Rojas and Amos Otis as well as pitchers Paul Splittorf, Dennis Leonard and Steve Busby. Its use faded as the team started to lose.

3051 Blue Thunder 1983–89 *American (M)*. Baseball writer Steve Cameron called the Royals of this era "Blue Thunder" after a popular 1983 movie (starring Roy Scheider) entitled *Blue Thunder* about a law enforcement "super helicopter." The K.C. players, decked out in Royal blue uniforms, with capable pitchers and "thunderous" home runs won six division titles, two pennants and the 1985 World Series while producing 12 winning seasons in 15 years.

3052 Men in Blue 1985 *American (M)*. Tag was a spin-off of the Kansas City "Boys in Blue" of the 1970s. The 1985 AL and world champion Royals were a veteran team led by George Brett (age 32), Frank White (age 34), Jim Sundberg (age 36) and pitcher Dan Quisenberry (age 32).

3053 Relentless Royals 1985 *American (M)*. The Royals "relentlessly" outlasted California and Chicago to win the AL Western Division title, and "relentlessly" overcame a 3-to-1 games deficit in the ALCS to edge out Toronto for the AL pennant and then "relentlessly" came back from a seemingly hopeless 3-to-1 deficit to defeat the NL champion St. Louis Cardinals to win the 1985 World Series championship. Team was aka the **Remarkable Royals**.

3054 Resilient Royals 1985 *American (M)*. Coined by baseball author Jeff Spivak to describe how the Royals trailed the Angels by one game following a three-game Royals losing streak and then met the Angels in a season-ending four-game series and won three of four to clinch the AL Western Division title.

3055 Royal Finishers 1985 *American (M)*. Coined by baseball writer Alan Eskew, the Royals capped their second consecutive 3-to-1 deficit comeback against a frustrated Cardinals group in Game 7 of the World Series—an 11–0 Royals blowout over St. Louis where several Cardinal players were thrown out for arguing trivial calls in an obvious reference to the Game 6 call. What made the feat all the more impressive was that the Royals lost their first two World Series games *at home* and became the first team in the World Series to overcome such a 3-to-1 deficit.

3056 Gamers 1985 *American (M)*. When the Royals beat the Cardinals, 11–0, in Game 7 to win the 1985 World Series, Royals catcher Jim Sundberg told reporters that the Royals were a team of "'gamers." A "gamer" is an athlete who is spunky, energetic and optimistic and who redoubles his or her efforts in the face of adversity.

3057 Never-Say-Die-Royals 1985 *American (M)*. Coined by sportswriter Tracy Ringolsby of *Baseball America* to describe the Royals' successive comebacks from 3-to-1 deficits—first in the AL championship series with Toronto and then in the 1985 World Series with the Cardinals. No other professional baseball team, before or since, has accomplished this feat.

3058 Baseball's Most Successful Expansion Team 1985 *American (M)*. Although the Mets won the World Series in only their eighth season in existence, the Royals overall were the most successful of the expansion teams of 1961–62, 1969 and 1977. Starting in 1971 the Royals had 11 winning seasons in 14 years, won seven AL Western Division titles, two AL pennants and the 1985 World Series. The name was coined by sportswriter Tracy Ringolsby.

3059 Missouri's Finest 1985 *American (M)*. Wikipedia describes the 1985 world champion Kansas City Royals as "Missouri's Finest" because the KC's won the first and only (to date) All-Missouri World Series, 4 games to 2, against the cross-state rival and NL champion St. Louis Cardinals.

3060 No-Quits 1985, 2011 *American (M)*. The 1985 Royals fell behind to the Toronto Blue Jays in the 1985 A.L. Championship Series, 3 games to 1, but rallied to win the next three contests to win the playoff and the A.L. pennant, 4 games to 3. In the 1985 All-Missouri World Series—against the cross-state St. Louis Cardinals—the Royals again fell behind the Cardinals, 3 games to 1, only to rally again winning the next 3 games, including a controversial Game 6 when an umpire blew a crucial call on an apparent ground ball out at first base in favor of the Royals, to capture the 1985 World Series championship. In 2011, manager Ned Yost praised his struggling team, saying, "We may lose a game, but my players never quit."

3061 Bulls 1999 *American (M)*. Used 121 years earlier by the young, strong Milwaukee "Bulls" of the 1878 National League, the moniker was coined by baseball writer Alan Eskew to describe the 1999 Royals' strong, young hitters like Carlos Beltran, Mike Sweeney and Jermaine Dye. But the Royals floundered to a 64–97 record as the pitching staff produced a gruesome 5.35 ERA.

3062 Rock-bottom Royals 2002–07 *American (M)*. Except for a surprise 83–79 winning season in 2003, the Royals of this five-year period were terrible, going 62–100 in 2002, 58–104 in 2004, 56–106 in 2005 and 62–100 in 2006 for three fifth- and last-place finishes and one fourth-place finish in the AL Central. Term was coined by Wikipedia.

3063 True Blue Royals 2003 *American (M)*. Team marketed the team this season with the slogan "True Blue Royals." When the team skidded to a 69–93 record, the slogan was discarded.

3064 T-Bones 2003–10 *Northern (ind.)*; 2011 to date *North American (ind.)*. Kansas City has been a major meat-packing center since 1870. The "T-bone" is a style of cooked steak using a T-bone tenderloin.

3065 Trey's Boys 2010 *American (M)*. Moniker was coined by *The Sporting News* after Kansas City field manager Trey Hillman.

Kao-Hsiung / Ping-tung, Southwest, Taiwan

Note: Taiwan is also known as Formosa and the Republic of China.

3066 Thundergods 1997–2002 *Taiwan Major (ind.)*. Team played home games in both cities and was called Kao-Ping Thunder Gods. Kao-Ping is an amalgamation of Kao-Hsiung, and Ping-tung. Fala is the Chinese word for thundergod. Moniker was also alliterative with the team owner, i.e., Fala of First Financial Savings Bank. Before the introduction of Buddhism (fourth century) and Confucianism (seventh century), the gods of Shamanism were worshipped by the Koreans. Some of these deities were "Thunder Gods" much like the Greek Zeus and the Nordic Odin.

3067 Bears 2003 to date *Chinese Professional (ind.)*; 2003 to date *Chinese Pro Minor (ind.)*. Team owner, La New Shoe Company, chose a nickname alliterative in English, i.e., La New Bears, for the parent and farm clubs. Farm club aka **Second Team Bears**.

Kauai, Hawaii

3068 Emeralds 1993–94 *Hawaii Winter (W)*. The city is noted for the "emerald" waters of its beaches.

Kaufman, Texas

3069 Kings 1915x *Central Texas (C)*. Team and league disbanded July 24.

Kawasaki, Kanagawa, Japan

3070 Whales 1955–77 *Japanese Pacific (ind.)*; 1955 *Japanese Eastern (ind.)*. Both the PL and EL team were owned by the Taiyo Fishing Company, which hunts whales as well as fish. The Eastern League "Whales," using the name of its parent club, was a farm club of the Pacific League Whales.

3071 Orions 1969–91 *Japanese Western (ind.)*. 1976–89 *Japanese Pacific (ind.)*. Lotte Confectionary, which manufactures pastries, named the team with the English alliterative "Lotte Orions." The central office is located not in Japan but rather in Seoul, South Korea. People in Asia, when they look up in the sky, see the constellation of Orion (aka "Tropic of Orion"). "Orion" means Eastern. When Lotte Confectionaries bought the CL Tokyo Orions in 1969, they established this WL farm club for the CL Orions in 1969.

3072 Giants 2006 to date *Japanese Eastern (ind.)*. Team was a farm club of the Central League Giants. The Yomiuri "Young Giants," after playing in Tokyo 1962–2005, moved to Kawasaki for the 2006 season. Team is also known as the "Junior Giants."

Kearney, Buffalo, Nebraska

3073 Lambs m1892 *Nebraska State (ind.)*. Team started season in Lincoln (NE) and moved here in mid-season (date unknown). "Lambs" was a nineteenth century baseball slang for young players, especially on a struggling team. Before the coining of the word "rookie" in 1917 (newly enlisted American soldiers—known as recruits—were being called "rookies"), young baseball players were called a whole litany of names, i.e., Babes, Chicks, Colts, Cubs, Debutantes, Foundlings, Lambs, Ponies, Prodigals and Yearlings.

3074 Kapitalists 1912–14 *Nebraska State (D)*. To fend off the abuses of the Gilded Age (1850–1900), local farmers in Nebraska formed their own marketing groups to improve the sale of their crops. Kearney's free market system excelled, making the city the economic center of Platte Valley, which garnered the nickname of "Hub of the Nation."

3075 Buffaloes 1915 *Nebraska State (D)*. City is located in Buffalo County. In pre–American times the region was populated by buffalo herds.

3076 Yankees 1956–59 *Nebraska State (D)*. Team was a farm club of the New York Yankees.

Keene, New Hampshire

3077 Champs 1911 *Twin States (D)*. In this era, teams that won a pennant were sometimes called "Champions" for the following season. Occasionally, a team contending for a flag also got the name. This team finished in second place, two games behind first-place Brattleboro. Newspapers called field manager Tom Leonard's players the alliterative "Tom's Champs."

Kelso, Washington

3078 Kelso Base Ball Club 1897 *Washington State (ind.)*. Team had no nickname.

Kennewick-Richland-Selma, Washington

3079 Tri-Cities Braves 1950–54 *Western International (B 1950–51, A 1952–54)*; 1955–60, 1962–63 *Northwest (B 1955–60, A 1962–63)*. Teams were known by the regional name of "Tri-Cities Braves." Teams were farm clubs of the Boston (1950–52) and Milwaukee (1953–60, 1962–63) Braves.

3080 Tri-Cities Atoms 1961, 1965–68 *Northwest (B 1961, A 1965–68)*. Team went by the regional name of "Tri-Cities Atoms." North of the city is the U.S. Department of Energy which does atomic energy research. Site of the Hanford Engineer Works, which does atomic research, Richland became known as the "Town the Atom Built." The Tri-Cities collectively are known as "The Nuclear Capital of the World."

3081 Tri-Cities Angels 1964 *Northwest (A)*. Team went by the regional name of "Tri-Cities Angels." Team was a farm club of the California Angels.

3082 Tri-Cities Athletics 1969 *Northwest (A)*. Team went by the regional name of "Tri-Cities Athletics." Team was a farm club of the Oakland Athletics.

3083 Tri-Cities Padres 1970–72 *Northwest (A)*. Team was a farm club of the San Diego Padres.

3084 Tri-Cities Triplets 1973 *Northwest (A)*; 1983–86 *Northwest (A)*. Team went by the regional name of "Tri-Cities Triplets." Name is a Phillies-style moniker. Kennewick, Pasco and Richland are known as the "Tri-Cities." Throughout baseball history, teams representing two cities have sometimes been called the "Twins" (i.e., Minnesota). Any team representing three cities (about four of them since 1900) has occasionally gone by the moniker of "Triplets."

3085 Tri-Cities Ports 1974 *Northwest (A)*. Team went by the regional name of Tri-Cities Ports. Kennewick (along with Richland and Pasco) is a riverport for boat traffic on the Columbia and Snake rivers.

Kenosha, Wisconsin

3086 Comets 1943–51 *All-American Girls Professional Baseball League (ind.)*. Moniker was alliterative.

3087 Twins 1985–92 *Midwest (A)*. Team was a farm club of the Minnesota Twins.

3088 Mammoths 2003 *Frontier (ind.)*. Baseball teams in the Upper Midwest have received such nicknames as "Duluth Freeze" and "Kenosha Mammoths" because of "Ice Age" winters. Fossilized bones of Ice Age wooly mammoths have been discovered in Wisconsin. The team's logo was a "wooly mammoth."

Kent, Ohio

3089 Kenties 1895–96 *Ohio State (ind.)*. Name was a Phillies-style moniker.

3090 Kings 1905 *Ohio–Pennsylvania (D)*. Moniker was alliterative and short.

Keokuk, Iowa

3091 Westerns 1875 *National Assn. (M)*. In 1865, the state of Iowa was considered to be "Out West." Hence, the team named itself the "Western Club" in 1865. The team played 10 years of amateur ball before turning professional and joining the NA in 1875.

3092 Hawkeyes 1885 *Western (ind.)*. Iowa is the "Hawkeye State." With field manager Bill Harrington at the helm, newspapers called the players the alliterative "Harrington's Hawkeyes."

3093 Indians 1904–07 *Iowa State (D)*; 1908–15 *Central Assn. (D)*; 1929–33 *Mississippi Valley (D)*. *(1929–32, B 1933)*; 1935 *Western (A)*. In 1805, some 8,000 Indians remained in Iowa. Chief Blackhawk led the Saux and Fox tribes in attacks against settlers in 1813. During the War of 1812, the British allied themselves with Chief Blackhawk, who, after 20 years of fighting, was defeated in 1832, and the Indian tribes were pushed west of the Mississippi. Tribes that have lived in Iowa include the Illinois, Saux, Fox, Winnebago, Iowa and Sioux. The 1929–33 teams were not farm clubs of the Cleveland Indians.

3094 Pirates 1947–49 *Central Assn.(C)*. Team was a farm club of Pittsburgh Pirates.

3095 Kernals 1952–57 *Three-I (B)*. Farms transport corn into city factories, where it is cleaned, packed and shipped out to stores.

3096 Cardinals 1958–62 *Midwest (D)*. Team was a farm club of the St. Louis Cardinals.

Kewanee, Illinois

3097 Boilermakers 1908–13 *Central Assn. (D)*. This region of Illinois and Indiana had numerous boiler factories where locomotive and factory boilers were built. Workers who built and repaired such boilers were known as "Boiler-Makers." Team's name emulated the college football team Purdue "Boilermakers." With manager Bill Connors at the helm (1909–10), newspapers called the players "Bill's Boilermakers."

3098 Athletics m1948–49 *Central Assn. (C)*. Team began season in Moline (IL) before moving to Kewanee June 18, 1948. Team was a farm club of the Philadelphia Athletics.

Key West, Florida

3099 Conchs m1952–53 *Florida–International (B)*; Team began 1952 season in Fort Lauderdale before moving to Key West June 20, 1952; 1972–74 *Florida State (A)*. The Spanish word for seashell is "concha." "Conch" is the English form of "concha." The name has come to mean an inhabitant of Key West.

3100 Padres 1969–70 *Florida State (A)*. Team was a farm club of the San Diego Padres.

3101 Sun Caps 1971 *Florida State (A)*. Florida is the "Sunshine State." Players wore San Diego–style yellow caps.

3102 Cubs 1975–76 *Florida State (A)*. Team was a farm club of the Chicago Cubs.

Kibutz Gezer, Israel

Note: see Bet Shemish, Israel.

3103 Blue Sox 2007 *Israel Baseball (ind.)*. Team was scheduled to move to Bet Shemish, Israel, in 2008 but the league disbanded. League operated only in 2007 and then disbanded due to financial problems. Manager Ron Blomberg is a former New York Yankee. Management therefore dressed the team in blue Yankee pinstripes and blue-trim stockings.

3104 Miracle 2007 *Israel Baseball (ind.)*. Team was scheduled to move to Modi'in, Israel, in 2008 but the league disbanded. League operated only in 2007 and then disbanded due to financial problems. Team manager Art Shamsky is a former New York "Miracle" Met. Players are dressed in the blue and red uniforms. Judaism celebrates the "Oil Lamp Miracle" during the Babylonian Captivity of the fifth century B.C.

Kilgore, Texas

3105 Gushers 1931 *East Texas (D)*. Petrochemical plants in Kilgore receive crude oil and natural gas from the East Texas Oilfield. Oil was discovered in this region on October 3, 1930, prompting the construction of rigs.

3106 Braves 1936–40 *East Texas (C)*. Team was a farm club of the Boston Bees. The recently discarded parent-club nickname of "Braves" was picked up by the Kilgore team.

3107 Rangers 1937–38 *East Texas (C)*. Alliterative moniker was used in honor of the Texas Rangers, who patrolled the nearby oil fields to protect them from vandalism, con men, prostitutes and Nazi sabotage.

3108 Boomers 1939–40 *East Texas (C)*. By 1938, the city had become an oil "boom town." A "boom town" is a city that enjoys an economic "boom," i.e., rapid growth in population and construction because of the discovery of gold, silver, oil, natural gas, coal, granite, minerals, etc.

3109 Drillers 1947–48 *Lone Star (C)*; 1949–50 *East Texas (C)*. The moniker is a spinoff from "Boomers" and "Gushers." East Texas Oil field drilling sites transport crude oil and natural gas to city petrochemical plants.

Kingman, Kansas

3110 Kingman Baseball Club 1905m Team moved to Hoisington (KS) July 22. Team had no nickname.

Kingsport, Tennessee

3111 Indians 1921–25 *Appalachian (D)*. Team was named after the Cherokee Indians. In the eighteenth century, they established the Cherokee Nations East in the western Carolinas, eastern Kentucky, eastern Tennessee and northern Georgia.

3112 Cherokees 1938–41, 1943–47, 1949–52 *Appalachian (D)*; 1953–54 *Mountain States (D)*; 1955 *Appalachian (D)*. The Cherokees, who dominated the region in the seventeenth century, were decimated by disease (small pox) and war and eventually left Tennessee, traveling along the "Trail of Tears" to Oklahoma, starting in 1838. Name today is used by the Kingsport High School "Cherokees."

3113 Dodgers 1942 *Appalachian (D)*. Team was a farm club of the Brooklyn Dodgers.

3114 White Sox 1948 *Appalachian (D)*. Team was a farm club of the Chicago White Sox.

3115 Orioles 1957 *Appalachian (D)*. Team was a farm club of the Baltimore Orioles.

3116 Pirates 1960–63 *Appalachian (D 1960–62, A 1963)*. Team was a farm club of the Pittsburgh Pirates.

3117 Royals 1969–73 *Appalachian (A)*. Team was a farm club of the Kansas City Royals.

3118 Braves 1974–79 *Appalachian (A)*. Team was a farm club of the Atlanta Braves.

3119 Mets 1980–82 *Appalachian (A)*; 1984 to date *Appalachian (A)*. Team was a farm club of the New York Mets.

Kingston, New York

3120 Kingston Base Ball Club 1886 *Hudson River (ind.)*; 1888 *Hudson River (ind.)*. These teams had no nickname.

3121 Colonials 1903–06 *Hudson River (D)*. 1909 *Eastern Assn. (B)*; 1913 *New York–New Jersey (D)*; m1948–50x *Colonial (B)*. Team started 1948 season in New Brunswick (NJ) before moving to Kingston July 10. Circuit and team disbanded July 16; 1951 *Canadian–American (C)*. Kingston is the "Colony City" and "Colonial City" because, after being taken over by the British in 1669, it became the first capital of New York State in 1777.

3122 Colonial Colts 1907x *Hudson River (C)*. Team disbanded June 1. City was founded by the Dutch in 1615. The team was known as the "Colony City Colts," which local newspapers shortened to "Colonial Colts." In the era 1884–1917, young baseball players were known as "Colts." Kingston is the "Colony City" and "Colonial City" because, after being taken over by the British in 1669, it became an important colonial city and then the first state capital of New York State in 1777.

3123 Dodgers 1947 *North Atlantic (D)*. Team was a farm club of the Brooklyn Dodgers.

Kingston, Ontario

3124 Kingston Base Ball Club 1888 *Eastern International (ind.)*. Team had no nickname.

3125 Ponies 1946–51x *Border (C)*. Circuit and team disbanded July 16, 1951. Mounted troops on horseback, known as "Pony Soldiers," were stationed at Fort Frontenac, which was built here in 1673. The region's Cataraqui Indians also rode ponies. The Royal Military College of Canada was founded here in 1876, where student soldiers learned to ride horses.

Kingsville, Texas

3126 Jerseys 1926m *Gulf Coast (D)*. Team moved to Mission (TX) July 9. Nearby farms raise Jersey dairy cows. Raw milk is transported to dairies for pasteurization.

Kinston, North Carolina

3127 Kinston Baseball Club 1908x *Eastern Carolina (D)*. Team disbanded July 15. Team had no nickname.

3128 Eagles 1925–27 *Virginia (B)*; 1928–29 *Eastern Carolina (D)*; 1937–41 *Coastal Plains (D)*; 1946–52 *Coastal Plains (D)*; 1956–57m *Carolina (B)*. Team moved to Wilson (NC) May 11; 1962–68, 1970–73 *Carolina (B 1962, A 1963–74)*; 1978–81, 1986 *Carolina (A)*. With manager John Nee at the helm in 1925, newspapers called the players

"Nee's Eagles." After Nee left the team in mid-season 1926, the moniker proved to be so popular that it was used on-and-off for 61 years. Eagles perch on the cliffs of Neuse State Park 15 miles west of the city.

3129 Yankees 1969 *Carolina (A).* Team was a farm club of the New York Yankees.

3130 Expos 1974 *Carolina (A).* Team was a farm club of the Montreal Expos.

3131 Blue Jays 1982–84 *Carolina (A).* Team was a farm club of the Toronto Blue Jays.

3132 Indians 1987 to date *Carolina (A).* Team was a farm club of the Cleveland Indians.

Kirksville, Missouri

3133 Osteopaths 1911 *Missouri State (D).* Missouri State University, founded here in 1867, has a school of osteopathy. Osteopaths are doctors who specialize in treating the back. Some of the players on the team were students at the school. The college was the birthplace of osteopathic medicine in the U.S. Baseball players with back problems often consult osteopaths and chiropractors, as well as physicians.

Kissimmee, Osceola, Florida

3134 Braves 1976–96 *Gulf Coast (R).* Team was a farm club of the Atlanta Braves.

3135 Osceola Astros 1985–89 *Florida State (A);* 1988–98 *Gulf Coast (R).* Teams went by the county name of Osceola Astros. Teams were farm clubs of the Houston Astros.

3136 Osceola Dodgers 1988–91 *Gulf Coast (R).* Team went by the county name of Osceola Dodgers. Team was a farm club of Los Angeles Dodgers.

3137 Astros 1990–98, 2009 to date *Gulf Coast (R).*

3138 Osceola Marlins 1992–93 *Gulf Coast (R).* Team went by the county name of Osceola Marlins. Team was a farm club of the Florida Marlins.

3139 Cubs 1994 *Gulf Coast (R).* Team was a farm club of the Chicago Cubs.

3140 Cobras 1995 to date *Florida State (A).* A fan poll selected the alliterative "Cobras." Cobras are native to Asia and Africa and are not found in North America except in zoos or medical clinics. Team GM Tim Bawmann, mindful of marketing revenue, declared, "This (the switch to Cobras) seemed to be an opportunity to make ends meet and it's been great so far! We've had to reorder hats and T-shirts." Team, dropping the county name of Osceola, changed to the city name of Kissimmee Cobras, 1995 to date.

3141 Braves 2001–07 *Gulf Coast (R).* Team moved to Lake Buena Vista (FL) for the 2008 season. Team was a farm club of the Atlanta Braves.

Kitchener, Ontario, Canada

3142 Beavers 1919–21 *Michigan–Ontario (B).* With field manager Jack Beatty at the helm, local newspapers called the players "Beatty's Beavers." The nickname was appropriate because beavers are found throughout Ontario in its numerous rivers and lakes.

3143 Terriers 1922 *Michigan–Ontario (B).* Moniker was alliterative, i.e., Kitchener Terriers. Terriers were brought by the British to North America, where they became popular hunting dogs in Canada. Baseball players in this era were sometimes called "Terriers" because they bounced around the field like frisky dogs and scratched themselves.

3144 Kolts 1925 *Michigan–Ontario (B).* Team signed many young players. "Colt" was a popular slang for a young player in the era 1884–1917. Local newspapers changed the name from "Colts" to "Kolts" as an alliterative gimmick. The inexperience of the young players showed as the team finished eighth and last in the league with a terrible 35–103 record.

Kittaning, Pennsylvania

3145 Infants 1907 *Pennsylvania State (D).* In this era of baseball, "Infants" and "Innocents" referred to a young team that was overmatched by more experienced opponents. "Babes" referred to an expansion team. "Colts" and "Kids" simply meant young players without considering their talent or franchise history.

Klamath Falls, Oregon

3146 Gems 1948–51 *Far West (D).* Established in 1867, the city grew quickly and built beautiful edifices, giving it the name of "Gem City." With manager Joe Gantenbein at the helm in 1948, newspapers called the players "Gantenbein's Gems." In the nineteenth century any U.S. city that enjoyed speedy economic growth and constructed beautiful buildings became known as the "Gem City."

Knoxville, Tennessee

3147 Indians 1896–97 *Southeastern (ind.).* The Cherokee tribes of Tennessee were attacked by the Spanish in 1540, lost half their population in a smallpox epidemic 1736–38, fought the French, British and Americans, and then were forced to emigrate along the "Trail of Tears" to Oklahoma 1838–40.

3148 Appalachians m1909 *South Atlantic (C).* Team began season as Charleston Seagulls before moving to Knoxville July 5; 1910 *Southeastern (D);* 1911 *Appalachian (D). Appalachian (D).* Knoxville is the "Queen City of the Mountains."

3149 Reds 1912–14x *Appalachian (D).* Team and league disbanded June 17. Players wore red stirrups. When the fans and reporters called the team the "Appalachians" once again at the start of the 1912 season, newspaper editors finally rebelled and started printing the team name as "Reds." The league was already called "Appalachian," which created confusion.

3150 Black Giants 1920–24 *Independent Negro team.* Numerous black teams of the era 1890–1950 lionized the "Giants" nickname, typically adding a descriptive adjective in front of it, i.e., American, Bacharach, Elite, Royal, etc.

3151 Pioneers 1921–24 *Appalachian (D).* The city was founded in 1794 and by 1800 became a depot for settlers traveling into Appalachia. Fort White sent soldiers to protect the pioneers.

3152 Smokies 1925–29 *South Atlantic (B);* m1931–44 *Southern Assn. (A).* Team began 1931 season in Mobile (AL) before moving to Knoxville July 22, 1931; 1945 *Independent Negro team;* 1946–52 *Tri-State (B);* 1953 *Mountain States (D);* 1954 *Tri-State (B);* m1956–63 *South Atlantic (A).* Team began 1956 season in Montgomery (AL) before moving to Knoxville June 18; 1964–67 *Southern (AA);* 1993–99 *Southern (AA).* City was built near the Smoky Mountains. Knoxville is the "City of the Great Smokies" and the "Gateway to the Smokies."

3153 Giants 1931 *Independent Negro team.* A few black teams used the "Giants" moniker with the city name, not using the usual descriptive adjective. This team's formal name was the "Knoxville Giants."

3154 Red Sox 1940–41 *Independent Negro team.* Players wore red caps, red-trim uniforms and red stirrups. Black teams of the era

1920–46 did not have farm ties with major league teams but by 1947 all of the more-talented black players signed with Organized Baseball. Team was aka the **Red Caps.**

3155 Grays 1945 *Independent Negro team.* Players wore gray uniforms and hose.

3156 White Sox 1972–79 *Southern (AA).* Team was a farm club of the Chicago White Sox. Aka **Knox Sox** in the style of the BoSox, ChiSox, PawSox, etc.

3157 Blue Jays 1980–92 *Southern (AA).* Team was a farm club of the Toronto Blue Jays. Aka **K-Jays.**

Kobe, Hyogo, Japan

3158 Orix Braves 1989–90 *Japanese Pacific (ind.);* 1989–90 *Japanese Western (ind.).* The Osaka Hankyu Braves were purchased by the Orix Corporation, which moved the team to Kobe for the 1989 season. The team nickname was retained. The citizens of Kobe have been historically courageous, working hard to dominate the Hyogo region by 1900, surviving the U.S. bombing of 1943–45 that destroyed the city, and overcoming the devastation of the January 1995 earthquake. Hence, the "Braves" moniker was appropriate. The JWL team was a farm club of the JPL Braves.

3159 Blue Wave 1991–2004 *Japanese Pacific (ind.).* Franchise merged with the Osaka Kintetsu Buffaloes for 2005. By 2008 the merged team — the Orix Buffaloes — started playing all their home games in Osaka, opening the way for the Tigers to move to Kobe. In essence, the Kintetsu Buffaloes and Hanshin Tigers swapped cities; 1991–2004 *Japanese Western (ind.).* Team colors are blue and green because Kobe is a major seaport on Honshu Island. Team is formally known as the Orix Blue Wave. Orix Company owns the team.

3160 Surpass 2005–08 *Japanese Western (ind.).* The new owner, Orix, followed a Japanese tradition of using lofty nicknames and phrases of achievement, i.e., diligence, energy, excellence, excitement, loyalty, superior, teamwork, undaunted, and surpass.

3161 Tigers 2008 to date *Japanese Central (ind.).* The team nickname was retained since Hanshin maintained ownership. The Nishinomiya Hanshin Tigers transferred to Kobe after the 2007 season.

3162 Buffaloes 2009 to date *Japanese Western (ind.).* Team revived the old moniker of the parent club Osaka Kintetsu Buffaloes to become the "Kobe Orix Blue Wave." The parent club splits its games between Osaka and Kobe. The WL team plays all home games in Kobe.

Kodak, Tennessee

3163 Tennessee Smokies 2000 to date Southern (AA). Knoxville Smokies moved to Kodak for the 1998 season and now go by the state name of Tennessee Smokies.

Kokomo, Indiana

3164 Kokomo Base Ball Club 1890 *Indiana State (ind.);* 1900 *Indiana State (ind.).* The teams had no nickname.

3165 Combines 1907 *Ohio–Indiana (D).* A "combine" is a machine that harvests and threshes grain. Kokomo farms were using these machines by 1900.

3166 Wildcats 1909 *Northern Indiana State (D).* After U.S. Steel opened steel and iron plants in Gary, Kokomo and other Indiana cities, "wildcat" worker strikes occasionally flared up as workers demanded higher pay, better hours and better working conditions. "Wildcat" oil rigs are also found in Indiana. Standard Oil established the first oil drilling rigs in the state in Whiting in 1889. Name was also influenced by the 1909 AL champion Detroit Tigers.

3167 Giants 1955 *Missouri–Ohio Valley (M.O.V.) (D).* Team was a farm club of the New York Giants.

3168 Dodgers 1956–61 *Midwest (D).* Team was a farm club of the Brooklyn–L.A. Dodgers.

Kumagaya, Saitama, Japan

3169 Fighters 2006 to date *Japanese Eastern (ind.).* Team was a farm club of CL Fighters. The owner is Nippon Ham. Team is known as Ham Fighters Kyuj, which is Japanese for "farm club." In English the phrase would be the Nippon Ham Fighters Farm Club.

Kwang-Ju, South Choalla, South Korea
(Also spelled Gwang-ju)

3170 Tigers 1982 to date *Korean (ind.).* The team's original owner, Hatai, wanted an English-language marketable nickname. The moniker was appropriate because, in ancient Korea, the tiger was a heraldic symbol of nobility and military power. Kia Motors bought the team and kept the "Tigers" moniker.

La Barca, Jalisco, Mexico

3171 Potros 1978 *Mexican Center (A).* The city has ranches where young horses are raised and trained. Los Potros is the Spanish word for colts.

La Crosse, Wisconsin

3172 LaCrosse Base Ball Club 1887 *Northwestern (ind.).* Team had no nickname.

3173 Pinks 1905–06 *Wisconsin State (D);* 1908 *Wisconsin–Illinois (D).* Manager Pink Hawley was at the helm both times.

3174 Badgers 1907 *Wisconsin State (D).* There are no badgers indigenous to Wisconsin. The state of Wisconsin nickname of "Badger State" started in 1824 when miners at the Hazel Green lead mines took to living in burrows cut out of the sheer rock walls nearby. People said the miners were "holed up like badgers."

3175 Outcasts 1910–12 Minnesota–Wisconsin *(C 1910–11, D 1912).* Team signed a lot of players that had been released by other teams after the 1908 season, i.e., "outcasts." Yet the 1909 squad played fairly well, posting a winning 60–56 record, good for a third-place tie. With manager Joe Safford at the helm in 1910, newspapers called the players "Safford's Outcasts." Name was retained through 1912.

3176 Colts m1913 *Northern (C).* Team started season in St. Paul (MN) and moved to La Crosse July 23. For the era 1885–1920 young players were known as Babes, Chicks, Colts, Cubs, Debutants, Foundlings, Ponies, Prodigals and Yearlings. The word "rookie" was popularized in 1917 (first appeared in 1892) and replaced all these monikers soon thereafter. With manager Frank Kurke at the helm, newspapers called the players "Kurke's Colts."

3177 Infants 1917x *Central Assn. (D).* Team disbanded July 17 due to U.S. entry in World War I. Team finished in eighth (of eight) place with a 29–43 record. In the era 1890–1920, last-place teams — usually loaded with younger players — were often called "Infants." With manager Jay Andrews at the helm, newspapers called the players the "Andrews' Infants."

3178 Blackhawks 1940–42 *Wisconsin State (D).* In 1832 Chief Blackhawk led Sauk and Fox warriors in the Battle of Bad Axe, near Lacrosse on August 2. The Illinois State Militia won the battle and then shamefully massacred the Saux and Fox survivors. By 1840 the Saux and Fox had been pushed to lands west of the Mississippi River.

Lafayette, Indiana

3179 Lafayette Base Ball Club m1888x *Central Interstate (ind.)*. Team started season in Decatur (IL) and moved to Lafayette June 13. Team disbanded July 9; 1889 *Illinois–Indiana (ind.)*; 1890m *Western Indiana* Team moved to Anderson (IN) in mid-season (date unknown); 1895m *Western Inter-State (ind.)*. Team moved to Anderson (IN) in mid-season (date unknown). These teams had no nicknames.

3180 Wets 1909 *Northern State of Indiana (D)*. "Wets" is short for "wetlands," referring to the banks of the nearby Wabash River.

3181 Farmers 1910–11 *Northern State of Indiana (D)*. Neighboring wheat farms ship the grain into the city where it is processed, packed and shipped out.

3182 Chiefs 1955 *Missouri–Ohio Valley (M.O.V.) (D)*. The Battle of Tippecanoe was fought outside the city in 1811. General William Henry Harrison (later U.S. president) defeated Chief Tenskwatawa and his Shawnee warriors. Tenskwatawa was the brother of Chief Tecumseh.

3183 Red Sox 1956–57 *Midwest (D)*. Team was a farm club of the Boston Red Sox.

3184 Leopards 1994x *Great Central (ind.)*. Team disbanded August 10; 1995 *Mid-America (ind.)*; 1996–98 *Heartland (ind.)*. Fans chose the moniker because of the Lafayette University Leopards in Easton (PA). Moniker was alliterative, i.e., Lafayette Leopards.

Lafayette, Louisiana

3185 Browns 1907 *Gulf Coast (D)*. Players wore brown stirrups.

3186 Hubs 1920 *Louisiana State (D)*. The city is the market and distribution center for cotton, cottonseed oil, sugar, oil and natural gas for southern Louisiana. Lafayette has five highways that travel into the city and Lafayette Regional Airport is a mile east of the city. Freighters on the nearby Vermillion River also bring cargo into the city. Lafayette is known as the "Hub City of Southwestern Louisiana."

3187 White Sox 1934–42x *Evangeline (D)*. Team disbanded May 22, 1942 because of U.S. entry into World War II. Team had a loose affiliation with the Chicago White Sox in 1934–35 before becoming an official farm club of the St. Louis Browns 1936–41. Team then played as an independent in 1942. Players wore white stirrups over white sanitary socks and never took the name "Browns."

3188 Brahman Bulls 1948–49 *Evangeline (D 1946–48, C 1949)*. Brahman cattle — indigenous to Asia — were first imported to the city in the 1850s. This breed soon became popular. Lafayette cattle ranchers import and raise Brahman bulls on their ranches.

3189 Bulls 1948–53 *Evangeline (D 1946–48, C 1949–53)*, Management shortened the name to placate local newspapers.

3190 Oilers 1954–57x *Evangeline (C)*. Team disbanded June 20. The city has factories that manufacture the rigs and equipment for the oil and natural gas wells located in Louisiana. The Heyman Oil Center manages the business affairs of the local oil companies.

3191 Drillers 1975–76 *Texas (AA)*. Moniker was a spin-off from Oilers.

LaFeria, Texas

3192 Nighthawks 1931x *Rio Grande Valley (D)*. Actually, the name is a spinoff. The team began the season as the Corpus Christi Seahawks and then moved to LaFeria June 5, changing its name to "Nighthawks." Since the home jerseys displayed the letters "H-A-W-K-S," there was no need to purchase costly new uniforms. Team and league disbanded July 30 because of the Great Depression. The "Nighthawk" is a predatory owl that is common to the region. It hunts mostly at night.

Lagoon, Utah

3193 Lagoon Baseball Club 1901x *Inter-Mountain (ind.)*. Team disbanded June 17. Team had no nickname.

Lagos de Moreno, Jalisco, Mexico

3194 Caporales 1975–77 *Mexican Center (A)*. In Mexico, the leader of a cattle drive is known as the "caporal" (literally "corporal"). The word roughly translates into English as "chief." Cattle ranches have been in Jalisco since the eighteenth century.

La Grande, Oregon

3195 La Grande Base Ball Club 1891 *Pacific Inter-State (ind.)*. Team had no nickname.

3196 Babes 1908x *Inland Empire (D)*. Team and league disbanded July 12 due to a dangerous heat wave. With manager Billy O'Brien at the helm of a team of mostly youngsters, newspapers called the players "Billy O'Brien's Babes." The term "babes" in this era usually meant an expansion team or a charter team in a new league.

3197 Pippins 1912 *Western Tri-State (D)*. Farms in the region transport Pippin apples to city packing houses where they are cleaned, packed and shipped out.

3198 Spuds 1913x. Team disbanded June 22, 1913. Farms in the region transport potatoes to city factories where they are cleaned, processed, packed and shipped out.

LaGrange, Troup, Georgia

3199 Terrapins 1913–15 *Georgia–Alabama (D)*. Team was a farm club of the Federal League Baltimore Terrapins. With manager Jim Lafitte at the helm, newspapers called the players "Lafitte's Terrapins." The freshwater Terrapin turtle is found inland, i.e., the fresh waters of West Point Lake near LaGrange, and is distinct from the saltwater Atlantic terrapin.

3200 Grangers 1916–17 *Georgia–Alabama (D)*. Moniker was used for newspaper headlines, i.e., "Grangers edge Cowetas, 4–3." The name had a secondary meaning from England. A "granger" is a "gentleman farmer." Since the region has numerous farms, the moniker was appropriate. With manager Grady Bowen at the helm in 1916, newspapers called the players "Grady's Grangers." Bowen left the team after the 1916 season but the name was retained in 1917.

3201 LaGrange Baseball Club 1920–21 *Georgia State (D)*. Team had no nickname.

3202 Troupers 1946–51 *Georgia–Alabama (D)*. LaGrange is located in Troup County. "Troupers" were medieval singers, dancers and actors who traveled from town to town in the Middle Ages, hence the name sometimes was applied to baseball players in this era. With manager Newton Parker at the helm in 1946, newspapers called the players "Newton's Troupers." With manager Bill Cooper at the helm in 1949–51, newspapers called the players "Cooper's Troupers." Cooper led his troops to the 1950–51 pennants.

3203 Rebels 1946–51 *Georgia–Alabama (D)*. This shorter tag was preferred by newspapers. The site of many Civil War battles, i.e., Chickamauga (1863) and Atlanta (1865), Georgia refused to ratify the 14th Amendment (to return it to the Union) in 1867 and was under Union military rule until 1870.

La Guiara, Santa Marta, Venezuela

3204 Santa Marta 1954–55 *Liga Venezolana (W)*. Team was named after the state of Santa Marta whose capital and largest city is La Guiara.

3205 Orientales 1956–57–61–62 *Liga Venezolana (W)*. In the 1950s, Venezuela had two leagues—the Western (Liga Occidental), which had teams in the Western states of Lara, Portuguesa and Zulia, and, the Venezuelan League (Liga Venezolana), comprising teams in Caracas and Valencia, which was also called the "Eastern" League, i.e., Liga Oriental. "Oriental" is Spanish for "Eastern."

3206 Tiburones 1962–63–63–64 *Venezolana Assn. (W)*; 1964–65–2007–08 *Liga Venezolana (W)*. Franchise moved to Porlamar, Nuevo Espana, for 2008–09 and was renamed "Los Bravos de Margarita." LaGuaira is on the northern coast of Venezuela and there are sharks in the off-shore waters. LaGuaira is a suburb of Caracas and the team plays its home games in Caracas while going by the name of LaGuaira. "El tiburon" is the Spanish word for "shark."

3207 Tibuleones 1974–75–75–76 *Venezuelan (W)*. For the 1974–75 and 1975–76 seasons, team merged with the Caracas Lions—with home games in Caracas—as the Caracas-LaGuaira Lions-Sharks (Tibu-Leones) before the two franchises separated for the 1976–77 season. Fans in both cities loathed the "Tibuleones" nickname, which is reminiscent of the ludicrous 1914–15 Federal League team nicknames and the National Football League "Card-Pitt" and "Steagles" monikers during World War II.

Laguna, Mexico

3208 Club de Beisbol de Laguna 1957 *Central Mexican (C)*. Team had no nickname.

Lake Buena Vista, Florida

3209 Braves 2008 to date *Gulf Coast (R)*. Team was a farm club of Atlanta Braves.

Lake Charles, Louisiana

3210 Creoles 1906 *South Texas (C)*; 1907–08 *Gulf Coast (D)*. Louisiana was a French Colony from 1682 to 1762 and again 1800 to 1803. The French settlers here were known as "Creoles," which comes from the French dialect they spoke, i.e., the Creole language. The "Cajuns" are French settlers from Nova Scotia in Canada who were expelled by the British from there in 1755, and who then migrated to Louisiana. With manager Dan Collins at the helm in 1907, newspapers called the players "Collins' Creoles." L.A. McCoy took over as skipper in 1908 and the name became "L.A. McCoy's Creoles."

3211 Newporters m1929–30x *Cotton States (D)*. Team began the 1929 season in Meridian (MS) and then moved to Lake Charles June 17. Team disbanded June 17, 1930, because of the Great Depression. When the area was settled in 1780, it was originally called "Newport" because it is a lake port of Lake Calcasieu. Today it is the fourth-largest port in the U.S. Newport became the city of Lake Charles in 1867. With manager Al Nixon at the helm in 1930, newspapers called the players "Nixon's Newporters."

3212 Skippers 1935–42x *Evangeline (D)*. Team and league disbanded May 30 because of U.S. entry into World War II. Merchant, recreational and military ships have sailed nearby Lake Calcasieu and the Calcasieu River since at least 1700. Originally meaning "flying fish," the term "skipper" soon became slang for the captain of a ship. Lake Charles is the "Seagate to Southwest." This maritime city is a port for rice cargo boats. These boats are called "rice ships." With manager Josh Billings at the helm in 1935, newspapers called the players "Billing's Skippers." Name was retained through 1942.

3213 Lakers 1950–53 *Gulf Coast (C 1950, B 1951–53)*; 1954–55 *Evangeline (C)*. Moniker was used for newspaper headlines, i.e., "Lakers edge Seahawks, 4–3."

3214 Giants 1956–57 *Evangeline (C)*. Team was a farm club of the New York Giants.

Lake Elsinore, California

3215 Storm 1994 to date *California (A)*. Although California is famous for its sunny weather, the region around Lake Elsinore quite frequently endures violent rainstorms.

Lake Linden, Michigan

3216 Lakes 1905 *Copper County Soo (C)*; 1906–07 *Northern Copper Country (C)*. Moniker was used for newspaper headlines, i.e., "Lakes edge Aristocrats, 4–3." The league cities were located next to Lake Superior.

Lakeland, Florida

3217 Highlanders 1919–24x *Florida State (D 1919–20, C 1921–24)*. Team and circuit disbanded August 8; 1925–26 *Florida State (D)*. The team's home field was built on a hill. Moniker was alliterative. The region is somewhat hilly, hence the name of nearby Highland City. The name was appropriate because many of the city residents were of Scotch and Irish descent whose European ancestors lived in the rolling hills of Scotland and Ireland and were known historically as "Highlanders."

3218 Pilots 1946–50, 1952–55 *Florida International (C 1946–48, B 1949–50, B 1952)*; m1953–55 *Florida State (D)*. Team started 1953 season in Palatka and moved to Lakeland. Although not a sea-coast city, the city is near many lakes and the Withlacoochee River on which cargo boats transport citrus fruits and phosphates—the region's two leading products. The cargo boats are guided by pilot boats. Lakeland is known as the "City of Lakes." Nickname also was derived from Lakeland Municipal Airport, which opened in 1935.

3219 Patriots 1951 *Florida International (B)*. The Republic of Florida was established by the Florida "Patriots" who stormed and occupied the Spanish Fort of Fernandina in northeast Florida during the War of 1812.

3220 Indians 1960 *Florida State (D)*. Team was a farm club of the Cleveland Indians.

3221 Giants 1962 *Florida State (A)*. Team was a farm club of the San Francisco Giants.

3222 Tigers 1963–64 *Florida State (A)*; 1967–2006 *Florida State (A)*; 1992 to date *Gulf Coast (R)*. These teams were farm clubs of the Detroit Tigers.

3223 Flying Tigers 2007 to date *Florida State (A)*. Named after the famous "Flying Tigers"—the American pilots based in China in 1940–41, who battled Japanese Zeros in their outclassed P-40s on which they painted Tiger fangs. Team is a farm club of the Detroit Tigers. Serving the Chinese Air Force after 1942, the Flying Tigers received the P-51 Mustang, which destroyed Japanese Zeroes by the hundreds.

Lakewood Township, New Jersey

3224 Lakewood Blue Claws 2001 to date *South Atlantic (A)*. Team goes by the regional and alliterative name of Lakewood Blue Claws. Fishing boats bring seafood catches to port, which are transported to city factories for cleaning, processing, packing and transport to market. The North American Blue Crab is found in the coastal waters of the Atlantic Coast.

Lamesa, Texas

3225 Lobos 1939–41 *West Texas–New Mexico (D)*; 1946–52 *West Texas–New Mexico (C)*; 1953m *Longhorn (C)*. Team moved to Winters-Ballinger (TX) June 3. The Spanish name for wolf is "lobo" and management used it because it was short and a fierce tag. Lobo refers to the gray wolf, which is found in North America.

3226 Dodgers 1942x *West Texas–New Mexico (D)*. Team and league disbanded July 5 because of U.S. entry into World War II. Team was a farm club of the Brooklyn Dodgers.

3227 Indians m1957 *Southwestern (D)*. Team started season in Midland (TX) and moved to La Mesa August 1. Indian inhabitants of Texas have included Apache, Comanche, Yaqui and many other tribes. Team was not a farm club of the Cleveland Indians.

Lampassas, Texas

3228 Resorters 1914 *Middle Texas (D)*. Regular season ended August 8 but the league did not disband, although this team did not return in 1915. With the establishment of Colorado State Park and the fishing at Buchanan Lake started drawing visitors to the region by 1910; the visitors then stayed at resort hotels in the city. With manager Luke Roberts at the helm, newspapers called the players "Roberts' Resorters."

Lancaster, California

3229 Jethawks 1996 to date *California (A)*. The city is 25 miles southwest of Edwards Air Force Base. Eagles, hawks, falcons and condors inhabit the Pacific coast. Moniker is an amalgam of "jets" and "hawks."

Lancaster, Ohio

3230 Lanks 1905–07 *Ohio–Pennsylvania (C)*; 1908–09x *Ohio State (D 1908–10, C 1911)*. Team disbanded August 23; 1910–11 *Ohio State (D 1910, C 1911)*. The moniker was used for newspaper headlines, i.e., "Lanks edge Steels, 4–3." The moniker was simply abstract as the players on the team were not necessarily "lanky."

3231 Red Roses 1908 *Ohio State (D)*. The coat of arms of the English House of Lancaster of the fifteenth century displayed a red rose. The name had been more associated with Lancaster, Pennsylvania, baseball teams, prompting local newspapers to switch back to "Lanks."

Lancaster, Pennsylvania

3232 Ironsides m1884–85m *Eastern (ind.)*. Team started 1884 season in Baltimore (MD) before moving to Lancaster in July 22. Team moved to Bridgeport (CT) August 4, 1885. During the Revolutionary War the American warship, the *Lancaster*, was nicknamed "Old Ironside" because of the protective iron plating along its hull.

3233 Lancaster Base Ball Club 1884 *Keystone Assn. (ind.)*; 1886m *Pennsylvania State (ind.)*. The 1886 team moved to Danville (PA) June 5. These teams had no nickname.

3234 Giants 1887 *Independent Negro* team. This team was the second black team to emulate the New York Giants, the first being the Cuban Giants of Babylon (NY). By 1950 more than 50 black professional teams had used the "Giants" moniker.

3235 Red Roses 1889x *Middle States (ind.)*. Team disbanded June 15; 1905–12m *Tri-State (ind.1905–06, B 1907)*; m1914 *Tri-State (B)*. Team began season in York (PA) before moving to Lancaster July 8; m1940–52 *Interstate (B)*. Team began 1940 season in Hazleton (PA) before moving to Lancaster June 12; 1954–55 *Piedmont (B)*; 1958–61 *Eastern (A)*. Circuit was also known as Eastern Interstate League. The fifteenth century "War of Roses" (1455–85) was fought between the House of Lancaster (heraldic symbol was the Red Rose) and the House of York (heraldic symbol was the White Rose) to claim the throne of England. The nearby baseball cities of Lancaster and York (both in Pennsylvania) became rivals, picking up as their nicknames—the Red Roses and White Roses. Founded in 1730 after the English city, colonial Lancaster adopted the English city's heraldic symbol—the Red Rose. City goes by the nickname of the "Red Rose City."

3236 Chicks 1894–95 *Pennsylvania State (ind.)*. Team signed many young players. In the era 1880–1920 young players were variously known as Babes, Chicks, Colts, Cubs, Debutantes, Foundlings, Ponies, Prodigals and Yearlings.

3237 Maroons m1896–99 *Atlantic (ind.)*. Team started 1896 season in New Haven (CT) before moving to Lancaster July 3. Players wore maroon hose.

3238 Lanks 1912 *Tri-State (B)*. Team moved to Atlantic City (NJ) June 18. Moniker was used for newspaper headlines, i.e., "Lanks edge Chicks, 4–3." With Red Roses at eight letters, newspapers preferred this five-letter name.

3239 Red Sox 1932x *Interstate (D)*. Team disbanded June 17. Players wore red-trim hose. Team had a loose affiliation with the Boston Red Sox. Moniker was also a spin-off from Red Roses.

3240 Scouts 1993–94 *Frontier (ind.)*. Founded in 1730, the city was an important strategic site during the French and Indian wars of the 1750s where many pioneer and Indian scouts provided information for the French against British troops. The team logo was a colonial pioneer scout holding a telescope.

3241 Barnstormers 2005 to date *Atlantic (ind.)*. "Barnstorm" is a nineteenth-century word that means to travel the countryside making speeches, giving lectures, performing plays, appearing at fairs, and by 1880, playing in sporting events, including baseball. By the 1920s stunt pilots and parachute jumpers barnstormed across the U.S., as well. In baseball "to barnstorm" meant to play as an independent team outside the auspices of a league. This team, however, is a member of the Atlantic Association.

Landis, North Carolina

3242 Senators 1937–39, 1941 *North Carolina State (D)*. Team was a farm club of the Washington Senators.

3243 Dodgers 1940 *North Carolina State (D)*. Team was a farm club of Brooklyn Dodgers.

3244 Millers 1942 *North Carolina State (D)*; 1945–47 *North Carolina State (D)*. Farms outside Landis transport corn to milling factories in the city.

3245 Spinners 1949–51m *North Carolina State (D)*. Team moved to Elkin (NC) July 18. North Carolina's leading industry was cotton until tobacco surpassed it in 1920.

Lannett, Alabama

3246 Lannett Valley Rebels 1951 *Georgia–Alabama (C)*. Team went by the regional name of Lannett Valley Rebels. The first Confederate capital was in Montgomery (AL); many battles were fought in Alabama, including the Battle of Mobile Bay (1864) and the Union invasions of December 1864 and the Battles of Mobile and Montgomery (April 1865). Federal troops stayed in Alabama until 1876 to quell smoldering rebelliousness.

Lannett–Langdale–Fairfax–Shawmut–West Point, Georgia

3247 Valley 1946–50 *Georgia–Alabama (C).* The team represented five cities. These five cities occupy a region known as "Appalachian Valley." Team went by the name of Valley Rebels and did not use a city name, although home games were played in Lannett. Same franchise went by name of "Lannett Valley Rebels" in 1951.

Lansdale, Pennsylvania

3248 Dukes 1948 *North Atlantic (D).* The Marquis Duquesne led French Huguenots exploring and settling eastern Pennsylvania, 1710–30. Actually, "marquis" in French means "nobleman" but falls short of the rank of "duke." Duquesne is a French surname that rhymes with the English "duke." It is the rhyme that gives rise to the nickname of "Dukes" currently used by Pennsylvania college teams at Duquesne (Pittsburgh) and James Madison University (Harrisburg).

Lansing, Michigan

3249 Lansing Base Ball Club 1889–90x *Michigan State (ind.).* Circuit and team disbanded in mid-season (date unknown); 1897x *Michigan State (ind.).* Team disbanded in mid-season (date unknown); 1902x *Michigan State (D).* Team disbanded August 20, which caused the league to disband as well. The teams had no nickname.

3250 Senators 1895 *Michigan State (ind.);* 1907–14m Southern Michigan *(D 1909–10, C 1911–12, D 1912–14).* Team moved to Mount Clemens (MI) July 10; 1921–22 *Central (B);* 1940–41 *Michigan State (D 1940, C 1941).* Lansing has been the state capital of Michigan since 1847. The 1940–41 team was not a farm club of the Washington Senators.

3251 Colored Capital All-Americans 1895–99 *Independent Negro team.* Tag was a spin-off from Senators. As Civil War resentments lingered, black teams often chose pro–Union names like Americans, Lincolns, Unions and All-Americans.

3252 Lugnuts 1996 to date *Midwest (A).* A "lug nut" is a nut that fits on a bolt to fix a wheel onto a car. Lansing, like Detroit, has been an automobile manufacturing center since 1910. Some fans, however, didn't like management's predilection to the "quirky" nickname style that seems to have infected numerous minor league franchises.

Lansingburg, New York

3253 Union 1870 *Independent.* The team, officially known as the "Union Club," started play as an amateur nine in this city in 1865 and then became all-professional in 1870. The plural form of "Unions" was also used. Lansingburg, a suburb of Syracuse, changed its name to Lansing in 1900.

Laredo, Texas

Note: Laredo (TX) and Nuevo Laredo (MX) are the "Twin Cities."

3254 Bermudas 1910–11 *Southwest Texas (D).* Citrus fruits and vegetables, including Bermuda onions, are important crops of the farms near the city.

3255 Oilers m1926 *Gulf Coast (D);* 1927 *Texas Valley (D).* Team began season in Beeville (TX) and moved to Laredo May 29. The Spindletop Oil Field was discovered in 1901. By 1920 Laredo had become a "boomtown." With manager George "Tex" Wisterzil at the helm in 1927, newspapers called the players "Wisterzil's Oilers."

3256 Apaches 1949–50 *Rio Grande Valley (D 1949, C 1950);* 1951–53 *Gulf Coast (B);* 1995 *Texas–Louisiana (ind.).* The Apaches were driven into Texas by the Comanche in the eighteenth century and then battled Americans and Mexicans in the nineteenth century, gaining a great reputation as brave warriors.

3257 Broncos 2006–10 *United (ind.);* 2007 *Texas Winter (W).* The Golden, Northern and United leagues merged to form the North American League in 2011. The Laredo franchise was not included and disbanded. Texas Winter League played November–December 2007 and then disbanded. City has numerous horse ranches and rodeos featuring "bucking broncos." Name is a spin-off from the 1953 "Apaches" team because "Bronco Apaches" learned how to tame wild horses.

Larned, Kansas

3258 Cowboys m1909–10 *Kansas State (D).* Team started 1909 season in Twin Cities (KS) and then moved to Larned July 12. With manager Buck Weaver at the helm in 1909–10, newspapers called the players "Buck Weaver's Cowboys." Harry McClean took over in mid-season 1910 and the name became "Harry McClean's Cowboys."

3259 Wheat Kings m1909–11 *Kansas State (D).* Team started 1909 season in Twin Cities (KS) and moved to Larned July 12. Outlying farms send wheat to city factories for cleaning, processing, packing and shipping. With manager Buck Weaver at the helm, 1909–10, newspapers called the players "Buck Weaver's Wheat Kings." Harry McClean took over in mid-season 1910 and the name became "Harry McClean's Wheat Kings." Harry Berte took over in 1911 and the name was "Harry Berte's Wheat Kings."

La Romana, La Romana, Dominican Republic (Ciudad de la Romana in Spanish)

3260 Azucareros 1984–85–97–98 *Dominican (W);* 2000–01 to date *Dominican (W).* Sugar cane is grown in outlying farms and then transported to city factories where it is refined, packed and shipped out. "Azucareros" in English means "Sugar-packers."

LaSalle, Illinois

3261 Blue Sox 1914 *Illinois–Missouri (D).* Players wore blue stirrups. Moniker was a spin-off from White Sox because the team had a loose affiliation with the Chicago White Sox.

Las Choapas, Veracruz, Mexico

3262 Diablos Rojos 1967–69m *Liga del Sureste Mexicana (A).* Team moved to Las Choapas in mid-season. Team moved to Minatitlan (VZ) May 16, 1969. Team was a farm club of the Mexico City Red Devils. The name "Red Devils" in Spanish is "Los Diablos Rojos."

Las Cruces, New Mexico

3263 Farmers 1915x *Rio Grande Assn. (D).* Team disbanded May 24, 1915. By 1900 numerous farms for wheat, fruit, sorghum, legumes, hot peppers, and even cotton had been established in New Mexico. With field manager William Hurley at the helm, local newspapers called the players the alliterative "Hurley's Farmers."

3264 Dust Devils 2004 *Southwestern (ind.).* A four-year drought drove about 150,000 homesteaders and farmers out of the state. By 1920, irrigation techniques allowed New Mexico farmers to return and produce wheat, sorghum, legumes, hot peppers and fruit. Non-irrigated areas often give rise to "Dust Devils," which are whirlwinds that whip dust high into the sky.

3265 Vaqueros 2010 *Continental (ind.)*; 2011 to date *Pecos (ind.)*. Name is Spanish for "cowboys." Team chose the Spanish "Vaqueros" to avoid confusion with league rival the Big Bend Cowboys. The annual Pan-American Fiesta features a rodeo with cowboys on horseback.

Las Vegas, Nevada

3266 Wranglers 1947–50 *Sunset (C)*; 1951 *Southwest (C)*; 1957 *Arizona–Mexico (C)*. Area was settled by the Mormons 1855–57, and almost immediately became a stock-raising region, with cowboys driving cattle herds to ranches. The 400,000-acre T-Lazy Ranch was established in this area in 1870. Cowboys were rough fellows who often argued, yelled and shouted, i.e., "wrangling." By 1880 a "wrangler" meant "cowboy." Northern Nevada's Great Basin is known as "Cattle Country."

3267 Pirates m1958 *California (C)*. Team started the season in San Jose (CA) before moving to Las Vegas May 26. Team was a farm club of the Pittsburgh Pirates.

3268 Stars 1983–2000 *Pacific Coast (AAA)*. Around 1950 numerous gambling casinos were built in the city. They featured Hollywood-style entertainment, which attracted Hollywood stars to perform there.

3269 51's 2001 to date *Pacific Coast (AAA)*. Following the infamous Roswell incident of 1947, the U.S. military constructed a secret base in the Nevada desert outside of Las Vegas where artifacts of a supposed UFO are secretly maintained in a special building called "Area 51." Name was coined in 2001 by Aaron Artman, the team's director of creative services. The team's mascot is a green-skinned, big-eyed alien.

Las Villas, Las Villas, Cuba

3270 Club de Las Villas 1966–67–73–74 *Cuban National (S)*. Team had no nickname.

Latrobe, Pennsylvania

3271 Latrobe Base Ball Club 1889x *Eastern Inter-State (ind.)*. Circuit was also known as Middle States League. Team disbanded in mid-season (date unknown); 1907m *Western Pennsylvania (D)*. Team moved to Cumberland (PA) May 28. Neither team had a nickname.

Laurel, Delaware

3272 Blue Hens 1922–23 *Eastern Shore (D)*. The state bird of Delaware is the Blue Hen. Team took its name from the Delaware University "Fighting Blue Hens." During the Revolutionary War, American soldiers used blue hen cocks to for cock fighting. Delaware's blue-coated American soldiers (to distinguish themselves from the British "Redcoats") were known as the "Blue Hens."

Laurel, Mississippi

3273 Lumberjacks 1923–27 *Cotton States (D)*. Lumber saw mills have been in the city since 1881, fostering the city's nickname of "Lumber Town." Factories in the city process lumber into boards.

3274 Cardinals 1928–29 *Cotton States (D)*. Team was a farm club of the St. Louis Cardinals. One of the earliest farm clubs, the 1928 team was also called the "Junior Cardinals."

Lawrence, Alabama

3275 Bullfrogs 1998–2000 *Texas–Louisiana (ind.)*. City is located at the Bayou Stream near the Mississippi River where bullfrogs like to swim.

Lawrence, Kansas

3276 Orioles 1892 *Kansas–Missouri (ind.)*. Orioles are found throughout North America. Players wore orange and black striped hose, which gave rise to "Orioles." Team had no affiliation with the National League Baltimore Orioles.

3277 Farmers 1893 *Western Assn. (ind.)*. Kansas wheat farms lead the nation in production of this grain. Other crops include oats, barley and rye.

3278 Collegians 1893 *Western Assn. (ind.)*. The University of Kansas was founded in this city in 1866. Some of the players on the professional team were on the college team.

Lawrence, Massachusetts

3279 Lawrence Base Ball Club 1884 *Massachusetts (ind.)*. Circuit went by the formal title of Massachusetts State Association; 1885 *Eastern New England*; 1886–87m *New England* Team moved to Salem (MA) July 26; 1888 *New England Inter-State (ind.)*; m1892x *New England (ind.)*. Team started season in Manchester and moved to Lawrence July 2. Team then disbanded later in the season (date unknown); m1899x *New England (ind.)*. Team began the season in Fitchburg and moved to Lawrence May 24. Team disbanded June 1; 1919x *New England (B)*. Team disbanded July 12. These teams had no nickname.

3280 Indians 1895 *New England Assn. (ind.)*. With manager John Irwin at the helm, newspapers called the players "Irwin's Indians." Around the year 1000 A.D. the Vikings landed on the Massachusetts coast, and encountered the "Seven Tribes" of the Algonkians. In 1621 friendly tribes taught the Pilgrims to plant corn and beans. By 1675 King Phillip's War breaks out as settlers fight the tribes. The conflict dragged on, leading to the French and Indian War 1704–05.

3281 Colts 1902–04 *New England (B)*; m1905–10 *New England (B)*. Team started season in Manchester and moved to Lawrence (MA) July 20. The inexperience of youth showed as the team finished eighth (out of eight) in 1907 and 1909 with 40–74 and 41–82 records, respectively. Newspapers liked the short five-letter name. Team signed many young players, who in the slang of the era were called "colts." With manager Will Clark at the helm, newspapers called the players "Clark's Colts."

3282 Barristers 1911–15 *New England (B)*; 1916–17 *Eastern (B)*. The first legal code in the colonies was Massachusetts' Body of Liberties of 1641. Colonial lawyers were known as "barristers," i.e., "Men of the Bar." Lawrence is home to the Massachusetts University Law School, established here in 1720. Abbot Lawrence, a wealthy merchant who later became a lawyer and a Congressman, bought land here in 1845 and helped found the city, named after him, in 1853. The 1911–17 teams were managed by Jesse Burkett, prompting newspapers to call the players "Burkett's Barristers."

3283 Merry Macks 1926–27 *New England (B)*. Lawrence is located near the Merrimac River. "Merry Mack" vaguely refers to "Merry-maker," i.e., a person who "makes merry" at a festival or party. Baseball players have always been notorious for being wild "party animals," i.e., drinking, fighting and womanizing in bars.

3284 Weavers 1933 *New England (B)*. Since 1853, the city has had a reputation for the manufacture of fine-quality worsted wool. Lawrence is the "Worsted Mill Capital of the World."

3285 Millionaires 1946 *New England (B)*. The city's founder, Abbot Lawrence, was one of the country's first "millionaires." Millionaire textile barons so underpaid their employees that it fomented a textile workers strike here in 1912. With manager George Kissell at the helm, newspapers called the players "Kissell's Millionaires."

3286 Orphans 1947m *New England (B)*. The team moved to Lowell (MA) July 15. Teams that move to another city (almost always due to low attendance in the first city) were called "Orphans." The name "orphans" was used because the fans had "abandoned" the players in their now empty ballpark, forcing the cashless management to move to another city. This was the last historical use of "Orphans" as a nickname for a team in Organized Baseball.

Lawrenceburg, Kentucky

3287 Lawrenceburg Baseball Club 1908 *Blue Grass (D)*. Team had no nickname.

Lawrenceville, Gwinnett, Georgia

3288 Gwinnett Braves 2009 to date *International (AAA)*. The Richmond Braves moved to Lawrenceville for the 2009 season. The team, a farm club of the Atlanta Braves, retained its nickname and went by the county name of "Gwinnett Braves."

Lawrenceville, Virginia

3289 Cardinals 1948 *Virginia (D)*. Team was a farm club of the St. Louis Cardinals.

3290 Robins 1949 *Virginia (D)*. The robin is a North American thrush. With manager Garland Braxton at the helm, newspapers called the players "Braxton's Robins."

Lawton, Oklahoma

3291 Medicine Men 1911 *Texas–Oklahoma (D)*. Although the many Indian tribes of Oklahoma historically had "medicine men," this moniker refers to the white "medicine man" who sold snake oil, potions, and elixirs in the many "Tent City" and "Shack City" sites that sprung up after the state was opened up to settlement in 1889. By 1920, the state government put a stop to these "potion sellers." Treaty of Medicine Lodge was signed in Oklahoma in 1890 to stop "gold-rushing" and "silver-rushing." Near to the city are the Medicine Bluffs, landmarks sacred to the Comanche and Kiowa. Lawton is known as the "Rollicking, Hilarious Tent and Shack City."

3292 Giants 1947–51 *Sooner State (D)*. Team was a farm club of the New York Giants.

3293 Reds 1952–53 *Sooner State (D)*. Team was a farm club of the Cincinnati Reds.

3294 Braves 1954–57 *Sooner State (D)*. Team was a farm club of the Milwaukee Braves.

Lead, South Dakota

3295 Grays 1891–92 *Black Hills (ind.)*. Gold was discovered at the Homestake Mine in 1876, leading to founding of the city. When the gold ran out in the 1890s, lead mining commenced. The players wore lead gray uniforms and hose.

Leadville, Colorado

3296 Magic Citys 1885 *Colorado (ind.)*. When gold was discovered here in 1860, the few camps were built into a city. In the nineteenth century such cities were called "Magic City," i.e., the city appeared "like magic." Leadville is called the "Magic City."

3297 Mountaineers 1885–86 *Colorado (ind.)*. City is located near the Rocky Mountains. City was founded in 1860 as a gold camp. Silver, lead, zinc, copper, bismuth, manganese and molybdenum were discovered, bringing several thousand "mountain miners" into the region. Leadville (named after the lead mines) has an altitude of more than 10,152 feet and is the highest city in the U.S.

3298 Blues 1887 *Colorado (ind.)*. Circuit was designated Colorado State League in 1885 and Colorado League in 1886–87; 1889 *Colorado (ind.)*. Players wore blue hose.

3299 Angels 1896 *Colorado State (ind.)*. At an elevation of 10,152 feet, the city is the highest populated region in the United States. About 25 miles northwest of the city is the Mount of the Holy Cross at 14,005 feet. And 100 miles to the south of the city is a mountain peak known as the "Angel of Shavano." Because of its elevation, Leadville is known as the "Cloud City." Angels inhabit the clouds.

League City, Texas

3300 Bay Area Toros 2007–09 *Continental (ind.)*. League City is a suburb midway between Houston (TX) and Galveston (TX). The city is built right along Galveston Bay. The greater Houston-Galveston metropolitan area is known as the "Bay Area." "Toro" is the Spanish word for bull.

Leaksville, North Carolina

3301 Triplets 1948 *Blue Ridge (D)*. Although officially known as the "Leaksville Triplets" with all home games in Leaksville, the team represented the Tri-City region of Leaksville, Spray and Draper (NC).

Leaksville-Spray-Draper, North Carolina

3302 Tri-City Triplets 1934–42 *Bi-State (D)*; 1945–47 *Carolina (C)*. Both teams went by the regional name of "Tri-City Triplets." The Bi-State League represented North Carolina and Virginia. Although home games were played in Leaksville, the city represented the Tri-City region of Leaksville, Spray and Draper (NC).

Leavenworth, Kansas

3303 Woodpeckers 1886–87 *Western (ind.)*. The woodpecker is found throughout North America. Leavenworth is the "Cottonwood City." The cottonwood tree, a type of poplar, flourishes in Kansas, and attracts woodpeckers by the thousands.

3304 Soldiers 1886–88x *Western (ind.)*. Team and circuit disbanded June 21; 1889m *Western (ind.)*. Team moved to Hastings (NE) in mid-season 1889 (date unknown). Fort Leavenworth, one of the oldest military outposts west of the Mississippi River, was established here in 1827. The city is home to the U.S. Army Command and General Staff College since 1870. An Old Soldiers Home was built in the city in 1885 for disabled and aging Civil War veterans. With manager Michel Hurley at the helm in 1886, newspapers called the players "Hurley's Soldiers." Charles Hall took over in mid-season and the name became "Charlie Hall's Soldiers." Name was retained 1888–89.

3305 Maroons 1886–89m *Western (ind.)*. Players wore maroon hose.

3306 Lions 1892 *Kansas (ind.)*. Newspaper editors demanded of their reporters a short nickname and the reporters chose "Lions." The team had a loose affiliation with the 1892 Western League Kansas

City Blues, a city in which a previous team played in the 1885 Western League as the "Red Lions."

3307 Reds 1895 *Kansas State (ind.)*. Players wore red hose. Originally **Red Stockings**, newspapers shortened it to **Redlegs** and "Reds."

3308 Orioles 1903 Missouri Valley *(D)*; 1905 *Western Assn. (C)*. Somewhat different from the Eastern Baltimore Oriole, this "Western Oriole" is also known as the "Golden Robin." With managers Eli Cates and then Elmer Smith at the helm in 1903, newspapers called the players "Eli's Orioles" and "Elmer's Orioles." With manager Louis Armstrong (no relation to the jazz trumpeter) at the helm in 1905, newspapers called the players "Louis Armstrong's Orioles."

3309 White Sox 1904 Missouri Valley *(C)*. Players wore white hose. In the era 1900–20, some minor league teams established a loose affiliation with a nearby major league team to buy uniforms and equipment at a discount, or even for free. This team had such an arrangement with the Chicago White Sox.

3310 Old Soldiers 1906 *Western Assn. (C)*. Name is a spin-off from the 1889 moniker. An Old Soldiers Home was built in the city in 1885 for disabled and aging Civil War veterans. Armstrong returned and the team name was "Louis Armstrong's Old Soldiers."

3311 Convicts 1906–07 *Western Assn. (C)*. The Leavenworth Federal Penitentiary was built here in 1865. In 1906, managers George Pennington, Bill Zink and then Nick Kahl took over, prompting names of "Pennington's Convicts," "Zink's Convicts," and "Nick Kahl's Convicts." John Ray took over in 1907 to lead "John's Convicts."

3312 Braves 1946–49 *Western Assn.(C)*. Team was a farm club of the Boston Braves.

Lebanon, Pennsylvania

3313 Pretzel Eaters 1889 *Eastern Inter-State (ind.)*; 1890x *Pennsylvania State (ind.)*. Team and league disbanded July 21; 1891 *Eastern Assn. (ind.)*; 1892 *Pennsylvania State (ind.)*. J.T. Adams established bakeries in the three Pennsylvania cities of Lancaster, Lebanon and Reading in 1873. The snack became so popular that each of these cities became known as the "Pretzel City." Local newspapers quickly shortened the moniker to "Pretzels."

3314 Lebanon Base Ball Club 1889 *Middle States (ind.)*; 1904 *Tri-State (ind.)*. The teams had no nickname.

3315 Miners m1890 *Atlantic Assn. (ind.)*. Team began season in Worcester (MA) and moved to Lebanon July 28; 1896 *Schuylkill Valley (ind.)*. City was founded in 1756 after hematite (iron ore) deposits were discovered here in 1742. The Cornall Ore Mines shipped iron ore to city factories, where it was smelted into iron and steel. Lebanon is known as the "Iron Mountain City."

3316 Cedars 1891 *Eastern Assn. (ind.)*. Cottonwood and cedar trees were hewn down in western Pennsylvania and transported to Lebanon for processing and carving.

3317 Chix 1949–50 *North Atlantic (D)*. Team was a farm club of St. Louis Cardinals. With more than twenty St. Louis NL farm teams known as "Cardinals" and "Redbirds" from about 1930, management decided to call this youthful team the "Chix." Originally "Chicks," newspapers shortened the moniker to "Chix." With manager Harold Contini at the helm, newspapers called the youthful players "Contini's Chicks."

Leesburg, Lake, Florida

3318 Gondoliers 1937–38 *Florida State (D)*. City is located on three lakes—Lisbon, Sumter and Tangerine—where Italian-style gondolas transport people for travel and pleasure cruises. Leesburg is located in Lake County. New manager Nelson Leach led "Nelson's Gondoliers" to the 1938 pennant.

3319 Anglers 1939–41 *Florida State (D)*; 1946 *Florida State (D)*. Recreational fishing of shell-crackers and blue gills is popular here. An "angler" is another name for fisherman. Newspapers wanted a shorter name than Gondoliers. With manager Nellie Leach at the helm, newspapers called the players "Nellie Leach's Anglers." Emil Yde took over in 1940, making the name "Emil's Anglers." Wilbur Good Jr. took over in 1941 (and again in 1946), making the name "Wilbur Good's Anglers."

3320 Pirates 1947–48 *Florida State (D)*. Team was a farm club of the Pittsburgh Pirates.

3321 Dodgers 1949 *Florida State (D)*. Team was a farm club of the Brooklyn Dodgers.

3322 Packers 1950–52 *Florida State (D)*. Citrus fruit grown in outlying farms is shipped to city factories to be cleaned, processed, packed and transported to grocery stores and supermarkets. With manager Frank Piet at the helm in 1950, newspapers called the players "Frank Piet's Packers." Name was retained through 1952.

3323 Lakers 1953 *Florida State (D)*. Leesburg is located in Lake County.

3324 Braves 1956–57 *Florida State (D)*. Team was a farm club of the Milwaukee Braves.

3325 Orioles 1960–61 *Florida State (D)*. Team was a farm club of the Baltimore Orioles.

3326 Athletics 1965–68 *Florida State (D)*. Team was a farm club of KC-Oakland Athletics.

Leesville, Alabama

3327 Angels m1950 *Gulf Coast (D)*. Team started season in Lufkin (TX) as the Lufkin "Angels" and then moved to Leesville July 15. The team nickname was retained. The team was not a farm club of the Los Angeles Angels.

LeMars, Iowa

3328 Blackbirds 1902–03 *Iowa–South Dakota (D)*. With manager Bob Black at the helm, newspapers called the players the "Blackbirds." Moniker was apt because crows are attracted to the region's corn fields. Management dressed the players in black hose. In the era 1890–1910, several teams used a bird nickname based on their players' hose or stirrup colors, i.e., Blackbirds, Bluebirds, Canaries, Cardinals, Crows, Doves, Orioles, Ravens, and Redbirds. Even today, several major league teams have bird names with matching stirrup colors, i.e., Cardinals (red), Blue Jays (blue) and Orioles (orange).

Lemoore, California

3329 Cubs 1911 *San Joaquin Valley (D)*. Team signed many young players, who in the slang of the day were known as "cubs." Name was also appropriate because the golden bear is the state animal of California. With manager Frank Blakley at the helm, newspapers called the players "Blakley's Cubs."

Lenoir, North Carolina

3330 Indians 1939 *Tar Heel (D)*. The Algonquin, Iroquois and Cherokee inhabited the Carolinas. The team was not a farm club of the Cleveland Indians.

3331 Reds 1940 *Tar Heel (D)*. Team was a farm club of the Cincinnati Reds.

3332 Red Sox m1946–47 *Blue Ridge (D)*. m1946–47 Team began the season in Salem (VA) and moved to Lenoir June 25; 1948–51 *Western Carolina (D)*. The teams wore red stirrups. The 1946–47 and 1948–51 teams were not farm clubs of the Boston Red Sox.

Leon, Guanajuato, Mexico

3333 Diablos Rojos 1960 *Mexican Center (D)*. Team was a farm club of the Mexico City Red Devils.

3334 Aguila 1961 *Mexican Center (C)*. Team was a farm club of the Veracruz Eagle.

3335 Zapateros 1962 *Mexican Center (C)*. City is noted for its shoe-making industry.

3336 Diablos Verdes 1963, 1965–67 *Mexican Center (A)*. Tag was a spin-off from "Red Devils." (Diablos Rojos). Players wore green-trim uniforms and green stirrups.

3337 Broncos 1964 *Mexican Center (A)*. Team was a farm club of the Reynosa Broncos.

3338 Aguilichas 1968–70 *Mexican Center (A)*. Team was a farm club of the Veracruz Eagle (Aguila). "Los Aguiichas" is Spanish for little eagles.

3339 Bravos 1971 *Mexican Center (A)*; 1983–91 *Mexican (AAA)*. Bullfighting, soccer, and baseball fans in Mexico shout "bravo!" Originally meaning a hired assassin (sixteenth century), the name evolved to mean desperado, i.e., bandits, thieves, pirates and highwaymen, of which there were plenty in seventeenth and eighteenth century Mexico.

3340 Lechugeros 1975 *Mexican Center (A)*. Nearby farms transport lettuce, cabbage and other leafy vegetables to city packing houses where the produce is cleaned and packed. "Los lechugeros" is Spanish for "lettuce growers" or "lettuce farmers."

3341 Cachorros 1979 *Mexican (AAA)* Leon means "Lion" in English. Since many of the players on the 1979 team were young, the fans started calling the team "Cubs." In Spanish, "Los Cachorros" means "Cubs." Team was not a farm club of the Chicago Cubs. In any case, lion cubs had no relation to bear cubs.

3342 Club de Beisbol de Leon 1975 *Mexican Center (A)*. Team had no nickname.

Leon, Leon, Nicaragua
(Ciudad de Leon)

3343 Leones 1956–57–66–67 *Nicaraguan (W)*; 2004–05–05–06 *Nicaraguan (W)*; 2009–10 to date *Nicaraguan (W)*. Pumas are found in Central America. Puma is the Spanish name for "mountain lion." Team is a rival of "Los Tigres" de Chinandega.

Lethbridge, Alberta, Canada

3344 Miners 1907 *Western Canada (D)*; 1909–10 *Western Canada (D)*. Coal mining began here in 1870 in the town of Coalbanks. The city was renamed Lethbridge in 1885.

3345 Expos 1975–76 *Pioneer (R)*. Team was a farm club of the Montreal Expos.

3346 Dodgers 1977–78 Pioneer (*Summer A* 1977–78, *R* 1979–83). Team was a farm club of the Los Angeles Dodgers.

3347 Mounties 1992–95 *Pioneer (A)*. Founded as a coal-mining settlement around 1870, the region became notorious for its whiskey trade, leading to its name of "Fort Whoop-Up," forcing the government to send in "Mounties," i.e., the Royal Canadian Mounted Police, to restore order.

3348 Black Diamonds 1996–98 *Pioneer (A)*. Name is a spin-off from "Miners." "Black Diamond" is a nickname for coal.

Lewiston, Idaho

3349 Broncos 1937 *Western International (B)*; 1952–54 *Western International (A)*; 1971–74 *Northwest (A)*. When the city was founded

in 1863, there were already several horse ranches where horses were tamed and rodeos where cowboys rode "buckin' bronchos." With manager Bill Brenner at the helm 1952–53, newspapers called the players "Brenner's Broncos." Larry Barton took over in 1954, changing the name to "Barton's Broncos."

3350 Indians 1939 *Pioneer (C)*. The Nez Perce tribe, led by Chief Joseph, refused to sign the 1855 Reservation Treaty and were forced to flee pursuing federal troops through Iowa before surrendering in Montana. The team was not a farm club of the Cleveland Indians.

3351 Broncs 1955–68 *Northwest (B 1955–62, A 1963–68)*. Tag was a spin-off from "Broncos."

Lewiston, Maine

3352 Lewsiton Base Ball Club 1891–96 *New England (ind.)*; 1897 *Maine State (ind.)*; 1901 *New England (ind.)*; 1908 *Atlantic Assn. (D)*. None of these teams had a nickname.

3353 Cupids 1914–15 *New England (B)*. Legend has it that a Lewiston sea captain went to sea without presenting his new bride a wedding cake. He built a house for her, in the shape of a wedding cake, and adorned it with wedding cake decorations every time he went to sea. There is an actual house in the vicinity called the "Wedding Cake House."

3354 Red Sox 1919x *New England (B)*. Team disbanded July 12. The team had a loose affiliation with the Boston Red Sox.

Lewiston-Augusta, Maine

3355 Twins 1919 *New England (B)*; 1926–30x *New England (B)*. Team disbanded June 16 because of the Great Depression. Team represented two cities. Team went by the alliterative name of "Lewiston Twins." The 1968 team changed its name to the "Lewis-Clark Broncos" for 1969–70 to represent Lewiston (where home games were played) and nearby Clarkston. The explorers Meriwether Lewis and William Clark explored Idaho in 1805. The two cities were named after them — hence the hyphenated name. Local newspapers didn't like the lengthy name so the team went back to Lewiston Broncos in 1971. Some 1969–70 newspapers simply went with Lewiston Broncos.

Lewiston, Pennsylvania

3356 Independents 1886x *Pennsylvania (ind.)*. An independent club was a typical name in this era for a small town team not affiliated with any league. The Declaration of Independence was signed in Philadelphia (PA) on July 4, 1776.

Lewisville, Texas

3357 Lizards 2007 *Continental (ind.)*. Lewisville is a suburb of Dallas (TX). Desert lizards are found throughout Texas.

Lexington, Kentucky

3358 Colts 1908–11 *Blue Grass (D)*; 1913–16x *Ohio State (D)*. Team disbanded July 16. City is the home of the Kentucky Horse Park where thoroughbred horses are raised for competition. Teams also had young players who were known in the slang of the day as "colts." Three teams in the circuit used young player nicknames — Chillicothe Babes, Maysville Cubs and Lexington Colts. Field skipper Jack Reynolds managed "Reynold's Colts." Lexington is the "Capital of the Horse World."

3359 Reds 1922–23 *Blue Grass (D)*. Players wore red trim. Team was not a farm club of the Cincinnati Reds as the farm system had not yet begun.

3360 Studebakers 1924 *Blue Grass (D)*. City was the home of the Studebaker Automobile Company in the 1920s. With manager Jesse Young at the helm, newspapers called the players "Jesse Young's Studebakers."

Lexington, Nebraska

3361 Red Sox 1956–58 *Nebraska State (D)*. Team was a farm club of the Boston Red Sox.

Lexington, North Carolina

3362 Indians 1937–42 *North Carolina (D)*; 1945, 1947–49, 1951–52 *North Carolina (D)*; 1953 *Tar Heel (D)*; 1960–61 *Western Carolina (D)*. Algonquin, Iroquois and Cherokee Indians inhabited the pre-Columbian Carolinas. These teams were not farm clubs of the Cleveland Indians. It was a farm club of the 1938–39 Philadelphia Athletics and independent in 1937 and 1940–42.

3363 Athletics 1946, 1950 *North Carolina (D)*. Team was a farm club of the Philadelphia Athletics.

3364 Giants 1963–66 *West Carolinas (A)*. Team was a farm club of the San Francisco Giants.

3365 Red Sox 1967 *West Carolinas (A)*. Team was a farm club of the Boston Red Sox.

3366 Legends 2001 to date *South Atlantic (A)*. North Carolina is home to such favorite legendary sons as boxer Floyd Patterson, NASCAR driver Richard Petty, football quarterbacks Sonny Jurgenson and Roman Gabriel, baseball pitchers Gaylord Perry and Jim "Catfish" Hunter and basketball players Meadowlark Lemon and Michael Jordan.

Lexington, Tennessee

3367 Giants 1935–38 *Kentucky–Illinois–Tennessee (KITTY) (D)*. With manager John Antonelli (no relation the 1950s N.Y. Giants pitcher Johnny Antonelli) at the helm in 1935, newspapers called the players "Antonelli's Giants." Team was not a farm club of the New York Giants, although the tag did emulate the 1932 and 1936–37 NL champions.

3368 Colts 1954x *Mountain States (D)*. Team disbanded July 7. Like its namesake city in Kentucky, this city also has horse farms. Local newspapers liked the four-letter nickname because the city name has nine letters. With manager Zeke Bonura at the helm, newspapers called the players "Zeke Bonura's Colts."

Ligonier, Indiana

3369 Ligonier Baseball Club 1910x *Indiana–Michigan (D)*. Team disbanded June 30. Team had no nickname.

Lima, Ohio

3370 Beaneaters 1888 *Tri-State (ind.)*. Team was not a farm club of the Boston Beaneaters but did have one of baseball's earliest minor-major league team affiliations with the Chicago Black Stockings. The American tropical Sieva bean, known popularly as the lima bean, is cultivated on U.S. farms.

3371 Lushers 1888 *Tri-State (ind.)*. "Lushers" (along with "Brewers") was a not-so-subtle nineteenth century slang for baseball players, who in this era were notorious heavy drinkers. There is no record that these Lima players caused trouble with "the brew" or "the bottle," but the moniker raises suspicions. The players must have been sober on the field, though, as they played with sharpness, compiling a splendid 74–35 record to win the 1888 Tri-State League pennant.

3372 Farmers 1895 *Eastern Inter-State (ind.)*. Regional farms transported corn and soy beans to city packing houses.

3373 Lima Base Ball Club 1896 *Ohio State (ind.)*. Team had no nickname.

3374 Lees 1905 *Ohio–Pennsylvania (C)*. With manager Eddie Bailey at the helm, newspapers called the players "Bailey's Lees."

3375 Lima Baseball Club 1906x *Interstate Assn. (C)*. Team and circuit disbanded July 8. Team had no nickname.

3376 Cigar-makers 1908–12 *Ohio State (D)*. Team was owned by the Pearle-Hume Cigar Company.

3377 Buckeyes 1934x *Central (B)*. Team disbanded May 26 because of the Great Depression. Ohio is the "Buckeye State."

3378 Pandas 1939–41 *Ohio State (D)*. About this time, there was a touring zoo exhibition of a Tibetan panda bear, captured by explorer and hunter Ruth Harkness in 1936. With manager Otis Brannon at the helm in 1941, newspapers called the players "Brannon's Pandas."

3379 Redbirds 1944 *Ohio State (D)*. Team was a farm club of the St. Louis Cardinals.

3380 Reds 1945 *Ohio State (D)*. Team was a farm club of the Cincinnati Reds.

3381 Terriers 1946–47 *Ohio State (D)*; 1948 *Ohio–Indiana (D)*. The Manchester English terrier was brought to Pennsylvania in the eighteenth century and became popular as a pet as well as a hunting dog. With Charlie Moore at the managerial helm in 1946, newspapers called the players "Charlie Moore's Terriers." Merle Settlemire took over in 1947 and the name became "Settlemire's Terriers."

3382 Chiefs 1949 *Ohio–Indiana (D)*. The Miami, Shawnee, Wyandot and Delaware tribes numbered about 15,000 in 1740. By 1782 conflict began as settlers massacred 96 Delaware at Gnadenhutten on March 8. The tribes killed 96 U.S. soldiers at Blue Licks on August 19. The Battle of Fallen Timbers was won by General Anthony Wayne on August 20, 1794, breaking the tribes' power in the state. Between 1825 and 1847 the tribes were forced to leave or were expelled from Ohio.

3383 Phillies 1950–51 *Ohio–Indiana (D)*. Team was a farm club of the Philadelphia Phillies.

Lincoln, Illinois

3384 Babes 1910 *Illinois–Missouri (D)*. With the team roster including numerous rookies and young players under the helm of manager Bill Salliard, newspapers called the players "Bill's Babes." The inexperience showed as the team went 43–71.

3385 Blackhawks 1910–11 *Illinois–Missouri (D)*. Chief Blackhawk led the Saux and Fox tribes against settlers in the Battle of Western Illinois 1831–32. The settlers and U.S. Army troops drove the Saux and Fox out of Illinois. With manager Bill Salliard at the helm 1910–11, newspapers called the players "Bill Salliard's Blackhawks."

3386 Abes 1910–14x *Illinois–Missouri (D)*. Team disbanded July 3. When the city became the state capital in 1867, it was decided to rename the city Lincoln, in honor of the president who had been assassinated in April 1865. Although born in Kentucky, Lincoln had spent much of his early life in Illinois. Illinois is known as the "Land of Lincoln."

3387 Champions 1913–14 *Illinois–Missouri (D)*. Team won flags in 1912 and 1913.

Lincoln, Nebraska

3388 Farmers 1886 *Western (ind.)*. Nearby farms transport grain to city packing houses. Nebraska is the "Cornhusker State." Harry Durfee led "Durfee's Farmers."

3389 Treeplanters 1886–88x *Western (ind.)*. Team disbanded June 6; m1890–91 *Western Assn. (ind.)*. Team began the 1890 season in Des Moines (IA) and then moved to Lincoln August 1; 1894–95 *Western Assn.(ind.)*; 1906 *Western (A)*. Starting around 1880, state authorities started planting trees to create forest preserves. No less than eight forest preserves were created encircling the city, i.e., Branched Oak, Pioneer, Memphis, Wagon Train, Stagecoach, Olive Creek, Blue-stern and Conestoga. By 1890, Nebraska had become known as the "Tree-Planter State." With manager Harry Durfee in 1886, newspapers called the players "Durfee's Tree-planters." Durfee left the team in mid-season 1886 but the name was retained.

3390 Warriors 1887 *Western (ind.)*. With manager Dave Rowe at the helm in 1887, newspapers called the players "Rowe's Warriors."

3391 Senators m1890–91 *Western Assn. (ind.)*. Team began the 1890 season in Des Moines (IA) and moved to Lincoln August 1, 1892, *Nebraska State (ind.)*. In the era 1880–1920 many teams playing in a state capital were known as Senators, Capitals, Governors, Legislators and Solons.

3392 Giants 1890–91x *Independent Negro team*. The tag "Giants" was a popular nickname for Negro teams in the nineteenth century. Several of these players moved to New York to found the New York "Lincoln Giants" in 1911.

3393 Missing Links 1895 *Western Assn. (ind.)*. Name was a play on words. In the nineteenth century, the baseball-viewing public regarded baseball players much as we view professional football players today — hulking, dim-witted Neanderthal types. Moreover, at this time, the U.S. public was fascinated with the anthropological declarations of Charles Darwin about monkeys, man and "missing links." Local newspapers shortened the name to "Links."

3394 Ducklings 1906 *Western (A)*. Newspapers tagged the players with this moniker in honor of field manager James "Ducky" Holmes.

3395 Greenbacks 1908 *Western (A)*. Newspapers invented this tag in honor of field manager Guy Green. "Greenbacks" were government dollars based on U.S. sterling silver deposits while privately produced bank notes were based on banking gold reserves. The Nebraska Progressive "Greenback" Party supported the introduction of "greenbacks."

3396 Greenbackers 1908–09, 1913 *Western (A)*. With manager Guy Green at the helm, newspapers called the players "Green's Greenbackers." The "Greenback Party" (which was popular in Nebraska) was a post–Civil War party that favored government money over private bank money. Ironically, it was Abraham Lincoln who tried to print greenbacks to fund the Union's Civil War effort. The name used again in 1913.

3397 Sterlings 1909 *Western (A)*. With manager James Sullivan at the helm, newspapers called the players "Sullivan's Sterlings." The Greenback Party was a midwestern political movement of this era that was prominent in Nebraska. It supported "sterlings," i.e., green-ink paper money based on silver, aka "greenbacks."

3398 Railsplitters 1910–12 *Western (A)*. With the city surrounded by Cottonwood trees and a major railroad center by 1890, "rail-splitters" — men who chopped up logs, i.e., "rails" — were in great demand. The team nickname more likely originated from the old legend of Abraham Lincoln winning a "rail-splitting" contest as a young man in Illinois around 1845 or 1846. With manager James Sullivan at the helm in 1910–11, newspapers called the players "Sullivan's Rail-splitters." Sullivan left the team after 1911, but the name was retained.

3399 Tigers 1914–16 *Western (A)*. When the players showed up for their first game in 1914 dressed in striped stockings, newspaper editors pounced on the moniker of "Tigers" to get away from 12- and 13-letter nicknames. With manager Charlie Mullen at the helm in 1914, local newspaper editors called the players "Charlie's Tigers." Matty McIntyre took over in 1915 and the name became "McIntyre's Tigers." McIntyre was out by 1916, but the name was retained because new manager James "Ducky" Holmes had been a star outfielder for the Detroit Tigers in 1901–02.

3400 Links 1917 *Western (A)*; 1924–27 *Western (A)*; 1929–35 *Nebraska State (D)*; 1938 *Nebraska State (D)*; 1939 *Western (D)*. Tag was a spin-off of the 1895 "Missing Links" name. When the striped stockings were abandoned in 1917, local newspapers went to "Links" to trounce any return of "Rail-splitters" and "Tree-planters." With manager James "Ducky" Holmes at the helm in 1917, newspapers called the players "Ducky Holmes' Links." Howard Wakefield managed in 1924 and the name was "Wakefield's Links." Josh Clarke and Frank Hanley took over in 1925 and the names were "Frank Hanley's Links," and "Clarke's Links." Dutch Zwilling managed in 1926 and the name became "Zwilling's Links." John Lavan managed in 1927 and the name was "Lavan's Links." By 1929 the moniker was traditional and preferred by newspapers.

3401 Browns 1928 *Nebraska State (D)*. Newspapers sometimes called the team the "Browns" in honor of field manager Bob Browne. The team was not a farm club of the AL St. Louis Browns.

3402 Red Links 1936 *Nebraska State (D)*. Team was a farm club of the Cincinnati Reds. The old "Links" moniker was combined with the parent club nickname of "Reds."

3403 Chiefs 1953–58 *Western (A)*. The 1953–58 team was a farm club of the Milwaukee Braves; 1959–61 *Three-I (B)*. Crazy Horse, chief of the Sioux, was killed in a battle against federal troops at Fort Robinson on September 7, 1877. "Chiefs" is a spin-off from Braves. The team became a farm club of the Pittsburgh Pirates in 1955 but the Chiefs moniker was retained. The 1959–61 team was not a farm club of the Milwaukee Braves (the parent club was now the Chicago White Sox) but retained the nickname.

3404 Salt Dogs 2001–05 *Northern (ind.)*; 2006 to date *American Assn. (ind.)*. City is built on a basin on Salt Creek. Since 1990 sports team nicknames using "dog" and "cat" have become popular.

Lincolnton, North Carolina

3405 Cardinals 1948–52 *Western Carolina (D)*; *Tar Heel (D)*. 1953m Team moved to Statesville (NC) July 12. With manager Red Mincy at the helm in 1948, and because the state bird of North Carolina is the cardinal, management dressed the players in red-trim uniforms, prompting newspapers to call the team "Cardinals." Carl Miller took over to lead "Carl's Cardinals." Miller left after 1949 but the red-trim uniforms and the name was retained. Moniker was alliterative, i.e., Lincoln Cardinals. The 1948–52 team was never a farm club of the St. Louis Cardinals; the 1953 was a farm of the St. Louis Cardinals.

Lindale, Georgia

3406 Pepperells 1920–21 *Georgia State (D)*; 1930 *Georgia–Alabama (D)*. In 1926, the Pepperell Cotton Company (est. 1900) made donations to the city government to help build grammar and high schools, which became known as "Pepperell Schools."

3407 Dragons 1928 *Georgia–Alabama (D)*. With field manager Earl Donaldson at the helm, local newspapers called the players the alliterative "Earl Donaldson's Dragons."

3408 Collegians 1929 *Georgia–Alabama (D)*. Lindale is home to Shorter College, established in 1873.

Linton, Indiana

3409 Linton Baseball Club m1908x *Eastern Illinois (D)*. Team began season in Pana (IL) and moved to Linton July 17. Team and league disbanded August 20. Team had no nickname.

Little Falls, Minnesota

3410 Little Falls Baseball Club 1930 *Independent Negro team*. Team had no nickname.

Little Falls, New Jersey

3411 Jackals 1998 *Northeast (ind.)*; 1999–2004 *Northern (ind.)*; 2005–07 *Can–Am (ind.)*. Picking up from the NFL Jacksonville Jaguars, a fan poll chose the alliterative state name of New Jersey Jackals.

Little Falls, New York

3412 Mets 1977–78 *New York–Pennsylvania (A)*. Team was a farm club of the New York Mets.

3413 Mohawk Valley Landsharks 1995 *Northeast (ind.)*. Sharks have been reported swimming in both the Hudson and Mohawk rivers. A river in New Jersey is named the "Shark River." A "landshark" literally means a cartoon-character shark that has legs and runs about on the dry ground. The team's logo/mascot was a shark with arms and legs holding a bat. Today, the name is slang for a dragon.

Little River, Kansas

3414 Little River Baseball Club 1908 *Central Kansas (D)*. Team had no nickname.

Little Rock, Arkansas

3415 Giants 1887 *Southwestern (ind.)*. Preceding the 1885 New York Giants, the moniker "Giants" referred to a winning team. But because the 1885–89 New York Giants were in the country's biggest market (and because they won back-to-back world titles 1888–89), numerous minor league teams sought to emulate them by choosing their "Giants" identity.

3416 Rosebuds 1895 *Southern (ind.)*. In the nineteenth century the city had so many rose gardens that it was nicknamed the "Rose City."

3417 Travelers 1895 *Southern (ind.)*; 1901–10 *Southern Assn. (A)*; 1915–61 *(A)* 1915–34 *(A1)* 1935–45, *(AA)* 1946–61 In 1956, the team played several home games in June–July in Montgomery (AR); 1963 *International (AAA)*; 1964–65 *Pacific Coast (AAA)*; 1966 to date *Texas (AA)*. In 1971, the Texas and Southern leagues played a combined schedule under the banner of the Dixie Association. In 1972 the two circuits split up and played separate schedules. Starting in 1957, Little Rock baseball teams went by the state name of **Arkansas** Travelers. The region has a legend about the "Arkansas Traveler"—a poor minstrel who roamed the Ozark Mountains, singing songs to entertain prospective buyers while he sold them his trinkets for money to sustain himself. With manager Frank Thyne (the H is silent) at the helm, newspapers called the players "Thyne's Travelers."

3418 Senators 1897 *Arkansas (ind.)*. Little Rock has been the state capital of Arkansas since 1836. It was also the Arkansas Territorial capital, 1821–35.

3419 Capitals 1898 *Southwestern (ind.)*. Tag was a spin-off from Senators.

3420 Black Travelers 1931–32 *Independent Negro team*; 1945 *Negro Southern (ind.)*. In the era 1900–50, black teams often received donated uniforms from white teams and simply used the nicknames on the jerseys as their own, adding adjectives like "Black" and "Colored."

3421 Grays 1932 *Independent Negro team*. Players wore gray trim uniforms and gray stirrups.

Littlestown, Pennsylvania

3422 Browns 1884 *Keystone Assn. (ind.)*. Players wore brown hose. Originally **Brown Stockings**, local newspapers shortened it to "Browns."

Livingston, Montana

3423 Livingston Baseball Club m1909x *Inter-Mountain (D)*. Team started season in Salt Lake City and moved to Livingston July 10. Team and league disbanded July 25. Team had no nickname.

Lock Haven, Pennsylvania

3424 Lock Haven Base Ball Club m1885x *New England (ind.)*. Team started season in Bridgeport and then moved to Lock Haven in mid-season. Circuit and team disbanded July 25; m1897–98 *Central Pennsylvania (ind.)*. Team started 1897 season in Shamokin (PA) and then moved to Lock Haven in mid-season (date unknown). The teams had no nickname.

Lockport, New York

3425 White Sox 1942 *Pennsylvania–Ohio–New York (P.O.N.Y.) (D)*. Team was a farm club of the Chicago White Sox.

3426 Cubs 1943–44, 1946 *Pennsylvania–Ohio–New York (P.O.N.Y.) (D)*. Team was a farm club of the Chicago Cubs in 1943–44 and used the "Cubs" tag in 1946 while playing as an independent.

3427 White Socks 1945 *Pennsylvania–Ohio–New York (P.O.N.Y.) (D)*. Team was a farm club of the Chicago White Sox. Management altered the spelling to give the team its own identity. The spelling of "Socks" for baseball teams goes all the way back to 1870, but by 1900 it had been abandoned in favor of "Sox."

3428 Reds 1947–50 *Pennsylvania–Ohio–New York (P.O.N.Y.) (D)*. Team was a farm club of the Cincinnati Reds.

3429 Locks 1947–50 *Pennsylvania–Ohio–New York (P.O.N.Y.) (D)*; 1951 *Middle Atlantic (C)*. Phillies-style moniker. Moniker was appropriate because of the nearby New York State Barge Canal. "Locks" are canal gates/elevators used to raise and lower ships.

Lodi, California

3430 Crushers 1966–69, 1984 *California (A)*. Grapes from nearby vineyards are transported to city factories, where wine-presses "crush" the grapes into juice for fermentation into wine.

3431 Padres 1970 *California (A)*. Team was a farm club of the San Diego Padres.

3432 Orions 1971 *California (A)*. Team was a farm club of the Tokyo Orions. The team was a mix of American and Japanese players.

3433 Lions 1972–73 *California (A)*. Newspapers liked the short moniker chosen by the unaffiliated team, but management worried about a "copyright infringement" lawsuit by the NFL Detroit Lions. When the Orioles took over, the "Lions" name was dropped.

3434 Orioles 1974–75 *California (A)*. Team was a farm club of the Baltimore Orioles.

3435 Dodgers 1976–83 *California (A).* Team was a farm club of Los Angeles Dodgers.

Logan, Utah

3436 Collegians 1926–27 *Utah–Idaho (D).* 1926–27. City has been the home of Utah State University since 1888.

Logan, West Virginia

3437 Indians 1937–42 *Mountain State (D 1937–41, C 1942).* Team was a farm club of the Cleveland Indians. Team was a Cleveland Indians affiliate 1937–38, then became a formal farm of the Cleveland Indians in 1939 but returned to a loose affiliation with the Cleveland AL club 1940–42.

Logansport, Indiana

3438 Oilers 1888x *Indiana State (ind.).* Team disbanded in mid-season (date unknown). Standard Oil built its first refinery in Whiting (IN) in 1889. Another refinery was built in Logansport in 1895. Oil was first discovered in Indiana in 1887.

3439 Logansport Base Ball Club 1890 *Indiana State (ind.).* Team had no nickname.

3440 Whitecaps 1911m *Northern State (ind.).* Team moved to Anderson (IN) July 2. City is built alongside the Wabash River, which displays "whitecaps" during stormy weather. Players also wore all-white caps with no stripes or logos.

Lonaconing, Maryland

3441 Giants 1916x *Potomac (D).* In the era 1885–1920 teams that were winners were said to be "playing like Giants." This team won the first-half flag with a good 26–18 won-lost record for a league-best .590 percentage when it disbanded July 23 due to money troubles.

London, Ontario, Canada

3442 Tecumseh 1876 *Independent team.* The 1876 team played an independent schedule of 90 games, winning 40 and losing 50. Newspapers reported this 1876 team as variously professional and semi-professional, sharing gate-receipt money with their players; 1877–78 *International Assn.(M)*; 1885 *Eastern (ind.)*; 1888–90 *International (ind.)*; 1898 *Canadian (ind.).* Chief Tecumseh was the Shawnee chieftain who fought with the British against the United States in the War of 1812. The team joined the IA in 1877. The name was sometimes pluralized as "Tecumsehs." Team was aka the **Canadian Indians.**

3443 Indians 1876 *Independent*; 1877–78 *International Assn. (M)*; 1925 *Michigan–Ontario (B).* Tag was a spin-off from Tecumseh of the Shawnee Indian tribe.

3444 Canadians 1876 *Independent team*; 1877–78 *International Assn.(M).* Canada's first professional team, the Tecumseh, thoroughly reported in the U.S. press, which called them the "Canadians."

3445 Solid Boys 1878 *Independent team*; 1877–78 *International Assn. (M).* "Solid boy" was a nineteenth-century slang for a competitive athlete. The 1878 Londoners had such "solid boys" as Archie Hall, Mike Burke, Ross Barnes and pitcher Fred Goldsmith, all of whom went on to play in the National League.

3446 Alerts 1896–97 *Canadian (ind.).* "Alerts" was a popular nineteenth century "action" moniker. Nineteenth century "action" names included Active, Alert, Athletic, Eureka, Fleet-foot, Flyaway, Olympic, Quickstep, Resolute, and Rough'n Ready.

3447 Cockneys 1899 *Canadian (ind.)*; 1908x *International (D).* Team and league disbanded July 31; 1911 *Canadian (D).* An inhabitant of the East End of London is known as a "Cockney." It also refers to the typical English accent of East End London. People in London, Canada, speak with a "cockney" accent. "Cockney" comes from the term "Cock's egg," which meant a pampered child. Since cocks don't lay eggs (they're male!), it meant something or someone so special that they merited pampering. With manager Joe Keenan at the helm in 1911, newspapers called the players "Keenan's Cockneys."

3448 Pirates 1940–41 *Pennsylvania–Ohio–New York (P.O.N.Y.) (D).* Team was a farm club of the Pittsburgh Pirates.

3449 Tigers 1989–93 *Eastern (AA).* Team was a farm club of the Detroit Tigers.

3450 Werewolves 1999–2001 *Frontier (ind.).* A fan poll named the team "Werewolves" after the popular 1993 movie *An American Werewolf in London.* London, Ontario, settled in 1826, was named in honor of London, England.

Long Beach, California

3451 Clothiers 1910 *Southern California (D).* Highcliffe Clothiers sponsored the team.

3452 Beachcombers 1913 *Southern California (D).* Long Beach has miles of bathing beaches. The city owns a marina that accommodates 2,000 boats. The city also has a shipyard and a maritime port. The city is home to the Los Angeles–Long Beach Naval Station. "Beachcomber" originally meant a drifter or loafer living at a beach and searching for seashells and beach debris to sell for money. Now it means a moneyed tourist or a person who strolls along a beach. Long Beach is the "Resort Metropolis of the Pacific" and the "Year-round Playground of the Pacific." With Louis manager "Bull" Durham at helm, newspapers called the players "Bull Durham's Beachcombers."

3453 Barracudas 1995 *Western (ind.).* Fishing resorts provide recreational boats for barracuda fishing. The barracuda is a large, predatory, warm-water fish.

3454 Riptide 1996 *Western (ind.).* The city is a Pacific Ocean harbor and beach resort. A riptide is a strong, wind-blown surface wave returning to shore. Long Beach is the "City by the Sea."

3455 Breakers 2001–02 *Western (ind.).* After oil was discovered in the region, the city became a beach-front tourist resort. A "breaker" is a wave that breaks onto shore. Long Beach is the "Gem of Beaches" and the "Queen of the Beaches."

3456 Armada 2005–09 *Golden (ind.)*; *Arizona Winter (W).* Once the city was founded in 1897, it became a site for commercial and recreational fishing. By 1917 factories here began to build boats and larger naval ships. An "armada" of boats sails in and out of this port city. In 1533 the Spanish "Armada" (Spanish for "armed force") fought the British in the English Channel and eventually were defeated. When not at war, ships of the Spanish Armada often explored the California coast. Long Beach was part of New Spain from 1784 to 1820.

Long Branch, New Jersey

3457 Cubans 1913 *New York–New Jersey (D)*; m1914 *Atlantic (D).* Team began season in Newark (NJ) as the Newark Cubans and moved to Long Branch July 22. The team nickname was retained; 1915–16 *Independent Negro team.* In this era, white-skinned Cuban players signed with this team. Black Cuban players were barred from Organized Baseball but did join U.S. Negro teams, i.e., the 1915–16 Long Branch Cubans, or barnstormed with other independent Negro teams throughout the U.S.

Longview, Texas

3458 Cannibals 1912 *South Central (D)*; 1923–25 *East Texas (D)*; 1927x *Lone Star (D)*. Team disbanded May 22; 1931x *East Texas (D)*. Team and league disbanded May 7 because of the Great Depression; m1932 *Texas (A)*. Team began season in Wichita Falls (TX) and then moved to Longview May 20; 1933 *Dixie (C)*. With manager Joe Cantrell at the helm in 1933, newspapers called the players "Cantrell's Cannibals;" 1934–35 *West Dixie (C)*; 1936–39 *East Texas (C)*. In 1895, the professional San Antonio Missionaries (aka Missions) visited Longview to play an exhibition game against the Longview amateur team. When Longview upset the visiting professionals by a 17–0 score, Longview newspapers crowed out the headline "Cannibals devour Missionaries!" Fans so liked the name that it stuck until 1939. Professional teams in Hannibal (MO), starting in 1900, used the moniker as well, but this was only because the nickname rhymed with the city name. In any case, Longview had it first.

3459 Long Cats 1925 *East Texas (D)*. The Mount Pleasant Cats and the Longview Cannibals merged June 7. The "Cannibals" nickname was dropped and the new team adopted the nickname of "Long Cats." From June 8 to July 11, home games were split between Longview and Mount Pleasant. Starting July 12, all home games were played in Longview until the end of the season.

3460 Browns m1932 *Texas (A)*. Team was a farm club of the St. Louis Browns.

3461 White Sox 1939 *East Texas (C)*. Team was a farm club of the Chicago White Sox.

3462 Texans 1940 *East Texas (C)*; 1947–48 *Lone Star (C)*; 1949–50 *East Texas (C)*. With manager "Tex" Jeanes at the helm in 1940, newspapers called the players "Texans." When Al Costello took over in mid-season, the Texans moniker was retained.

3463 Cherokees 1952 *Big State (B)*. The Cherokee originally inhabited Tennessee and North Carolina but were driven westward into Texas in the nineteenth century by relentless pressure from American settlers and the U.S. Cavalry as well as the Apache and Comanche.

3464 Pirates m1953 *Big State (B)*. Team started season in Waco (TX) and moved to Longview May 22. A tornado had destroyed Katy Park in Waco, forcing the team to move. Team was a farm club of the Pittsburgh Pirates.

Los Angeles, California

3465 Los Angeles Base Ball Club 1889–90 *Southern Winter (W)*; 1890–91 *California (W)*. The teams had no nickname.

3466 Giants 1892 *California (ind.)*; 1908–09 *Southern Calif. (W)*. The 1892 team won the pennant with an 80–57 record, nine games ahead of second-place San Francisco. In the era 1870–1910 winning teams were praised for "playing like Giants."

3467 Southerns 1892 *California (ind.)*. Team was the southernmost team in the league.

3468 Angels 1892–93x *California (ind.)*. Team disbanded in midseason 1893 (date unknown); 1901 *California (ind.)*; 1903–57 *Pacific Coast (ind. 1903, A 1904–11, AA 1912–45, AAA 1946–51, Open 1952–57)*; 1961–65 *American (M)*. Although the team was renamed the California Angels in 1965 (in anticipation of moving to Anaheim in 1966), home games were played in Los Angeles through the 1965 season. Starting in 1892, moniker was used for newspaper headlines, i.e., "Angels edge Friscos, 4–3." Founded in 1781 by Mexican settlers, the city was named El Pueblo de la Reina de los Angeles. "Los Angeles" is Spanish for "Angels." Los Angeles is nicknamed the "Angel City."

3469 Lulus 1903–15 *Pacific Coast (ind. 1903, A 1904–11, AA 1912–15)*. Team won four PCL flags in six seasons. Newspapers praised the players as "lulus." "Lulu" (coined in 1886) is slang for something terrific and successful, i.e., "The catch he made was a 'lulu!'" In 1903, the team went an amazing 133–78 under manager Frank "Cap" Dillon, prompting newspapers to call the players "Dillon's Lulus." Overall, Dillon led his "Lulus" to PCL flags in 1903, 1905, 1907 and 1908.

3470 Seraphs 1903–57 *Pacific Coast (ind. 1903, A 1904–11, AA 1912–45, AAA 1946–51, Open 1952–57)*; 1961–65 *American (M)*. Name is a spin-off from Angels. The term "Seraphim" is a biblical word for "angels."

3471 Occidentals 1909–10 *Southern Calif. (W)*. The Southern California league was an early all-professional winter circuit. Occidental means "Western."

3472 Maires 1910 *Southern California Trolley (ind.)*. The Maier Machine Company owned the team.

3473 McCormicks 1910 *Southern California (ind.)*; 1912–13 *Southern Calif. (W)*. The McCormick Tractor Company, named after inventor Cyrus McCormick, owned these teams.

3474 Leland Giants 1910–11 *Southern Calif. (W)*. The Chicago Leland Giants came west to play their home games in L.A. while competing in this winter circuit. Over the years, many East Coast and Midwest teams used Los Angeles as their "home city" while playing in this circuit.

3475 Tufts-Lyons 1912–13 *Southern Calif. (W)*. In the 1890s, baseball teams of Tufts College of Massachusetts and Lyons College of Arkansas played semi-professional baseball in Los Angeles during the winter. For the 1912–13 winter season, players from both schools formed a professional team, playing for pay as a member of this league.

3476 Hoegees 1913–14 *Southern Calif. (W)*. The Hoegee Trail Camp was established near Hoegee Falls for campers and tourists. Team was sponsored by the Hoegee Trail Camp.

3477 Los Angeles Baseball Club 1913–14 *Southern California (W)*; 1916–17 *Southern California (W)*; 1918–19 *Southern Calif. (W)*. These teams had no nickname.

3478 White Sox 1916–20 *Southern California. (W)*; 1946 *Western Colored Baseball Assn. (ind.)*. Circuit was also known as the West Coast Negro League and the Pacific Coast Negro League. Players wore white stirrups over their white sanitary hose. These black teams were not farm clubs of the Chicago White Sox.

3479 Submarine Base 1917–18 *Southern Calif. (W)*. The first submarine base in the U.S. was established in San Pedro in 1913. During World War I, the base studied captured German U-boats and eventually built such "submarines" for the U.S. Navy.

3480 Fisher's All-Stars 1920–21 *Southern Calif. (W)*. Team was sponsored by the Fisher Automobile Company. After Giants, the most popular team nickname for black or integrated teams was "All-Stars," which also reminded Los Angelinos of the "Stars of Hollywood."

3481 Lincoln Alexander Giants 1920–21 *Southern Calif. (W)*. For winter play in Los Angeles, the black New York Lincoln Giants signed white players, including Grover Cleveland Alexander, who was their player-manager.

3482 Rall's All-Stars 1920–21 *Southern Calif. (W)*. Noted college baseball coach Ed Rall managed this team. Newspapers used the moniker of "Rall's All-Stars."

3483 Pirrone's All-Stars 1920-21-39-40 *Southern Calif. (W)*. Local night-club owner Joe Pirrone sponsored this team starting in 1920–21 and then built Pirrone Park in Los Angeles in 1924 for his "All-Stars" team.

3484 Colored All-Stars 1921–22 *Southern California (W)*. This team signed several "colored stars" from Eastern Negro teams.

3485 Meusel's All-Stars 1921–22 *Southern Calif. (W)*. Major leaguer Bob Meusel was player-manager of an integrated "all-star" team for winter play this year.

3486 Buick All-Stars 1923–24 *Southern Calif. (W)*. The Buick Automobile Company sponsored the team. The team boasted of "colored stars" from the Negro Leagues.

3487 Universal 1923–24 *Southern Calif. (W)*. Universal Studios, an up-and-coming motion picture studio, sponsored the team.

3488 Gilmore Oil 1924–25 *Southern Calif. (W)*. Team was owned by the Gilmore Oil Company.

3489 White Kings 1924–25–28–29. *Southern California (W)*; 1933–34–39–40 *Southern California (W)*; 1946 *Western Colored Baseball Assn. (ind.)*. Circuit was also known as the West Coast Negro League and the Pacific Coast Negro League. The teams of 1924–29 and 1933–40 were owned by White King Soap Makers. Players of the 1946 team wore white stirrups over their white sanitary hose.

3490 Shell Oil 1924–25–30–31 *Southern Calif. (W)*. Team was owned by the Shell Oil Company.

3491 Commercial 1925–26–27–28 *Southern California (W)*; 1930–31 *Southern California (W)*. Teams were owned by Commercial Oil.

3492 Pacific Electric 1925–26 *Southern Calif. (W)*. Team was owned by Pacific Electric.

3493 Wilson's Elite Giants 1925–26–26–27 *Southern Calif. (W)*; 1929–30 *Southern Calif. (W)*; 1933–34–39–40 *Southern Calif. (W)*. Tom Wilson was the owner of the black Nashville Elite Giants and the Brooklyn Royal Giants. Starting in 1925–26, he brought his players out west three times for ten seasons of winter play. Moniker was appropriate because Wilson signed "elite" players like hitters Mules Suttles, Turkey Stearnes and Larry Brown and pitchers Satchel Paige, Steel Arm Davis and Cannonball Willis.

3494 Wilson's Royal Giants 1925–26–26–27 *Southern Calif. (W)*; 1935–36–42–43 *Southern California (W)*. Tom Wilson, a white businessman, owned the Nashville Elite Giants and the Brooklyn Royal Giants. Both teams looked to make extra money playing winter ball.

3495 Marion 1926–27 *Southern Calif. (W)*. Team was sponsored by the Marion Company.

3496 Kelly Kars 1929–30–30–31 *Southern Calif. (W)*. Team was owned by the Kelly Car Company.

3497 California Stars 1930 *Independent Negro team*. Team went by name of Los Angeles Stars and also California Stars. Los Angeles is home to the "Hollywood movie stars."

3498 MGM 1930–31 *Southern Calif. (W)*. Team was owned by MGM Studios.

3499 Dizzy Dean's All-Stars 1935–36 *Southern Calif. (W)*. Pitcher Dizzy Dean recruited Major and Negro League "stars" to compete in this winter circuit.

3500 Giants 1935–36 *Southern Calif. (W)*. The Philadelphia Giants played in this winter circuit using Los Angeles as its home city.

3501 Dodgers 1958 to date *National (M)*. The Brooklyn Dodgers moved to Los Angeles for the 1958 season. The nickname was retained.

3502 Hollywood Heroes 1959 *National (M)*. After being known as the Brooklyn "Bums" from 1938 to 1957, the 1959 Los Angeles Dodgers won the NL pennant and then defeated the Chicago White Sox in the 1959 World Series, 4 games to 2. On October 5, TV comedian Steve Allen invited the Dodgers players on his Burbank, California, TV show, and hailed them as "Bums no longer, but now the 'Heroes of Hollywood!'" The team was led by hitters Duke Snider, Gil Hodges, Wally Moon, Norm Larker, Charlie Neal, Johnny Roseboro and Jim "Junior" Gilliam as well as pitchers Roger Craig, Don Drysdale, Johnny Podres and 1959 World Series MVP Larry Sherry, who won two games and saved two others against Chicago. Sherry was touted by L.A. newspapers as the "Hero of the 1959 World Series." After appearing on TV with Allen, the Dodgers lost Game 5

to the White Sox, 1–0, but then proved their heroics by blitzing Chicago, 9–3, in Game 6 at Chicago to win the 1959 World Series.

3503 Sun-kissed Dodgers 1959 *National (M)*. With the old Brooklyn Dodger players enjoying sunny California weather in April and September–October, the team rebounded from the 1958 seventh-place misstep and won the 1959 NL pennant in a 2–0 playoff victory over the Milwaukee Braves and the 1959 World Series, 4 games to 2, over the AL champion Chicago White Sox. Tag was coined by baseball authors Gary Gillette and Pete Palmer.

3504 Lords of Flatbush 1959–1988 *National (M)*. Phrase was an affectionate use of the Brooklyn tag, used by non-nostalgic but grateful Dodger fans for the team's nine NL pennants and five World Series titles in its first 30 years in La-la land. Los Angeles is just as much flatland as Brooklyn.

3505 Roger Dodgers 1963 *National (M)*. In this era when jet pilots or astronauts accomplished a difficult aerial task, ground control would acknowledge the feat with a hearty "Roger that!" The "Roger Dodgers" staved off the pesky St. Louis Cardinals en route to a splendid 99–63 record, which was prelude to an unanticipated 4–0 sweep of the AL champion New York Yankees in the 1963 World Series. The moniker was coined by baseball authors Gary Gillette and Pete Palmer and had nothing to do with former Dodger pitcher Roger Craig.

3506 Sandy Koufax & Company 1963–66 *National (M)*. The Dodgers, led by the overwhelming hurling power of Sandy Koufax, won NL pennants in 1963, 1965 and 1966 and defeated the New York Yankees in 1963 and Minnesota Twins in 1965 in World Series competition. Koufax was accompanied by pitchers Don Drysdale, Claude Osteen, Phil Regan and Ron Perranoski. Batters who backed up Koufax included Frank Howard, Wally Moon, John Roseboro, Tommy Davis, Willie Davis, Ron Fairly, Jim Lefebvre, Lou Johnson and Maury Wills. Shortstop Maury Wills set numerous base-stealing records in this era. Unfortunately, Koufax was forced to retire at the age of 30 after the 1966 season because of an arthritic elbow.

3507 Babes of Summer 1974–81 *National (M)*. In a take-off from Roger Kahn's book *The Boys of Summer* (which dealt with the Brooklyn Dodgers of the 1950s), this moniker applied to the usually very young Dodger players who won NL pennants in 1974, 1977, 1978 and 1981 and the 1981 World Series over the New York Yankees. The "Babes of Summer" included hitters Steve Garvey, Davey Lopes, Ron Cey, Bill Russell, Jim Wynn, Dusty Baker, Bill Buckner, Rick Monday, Pedro Guerrero and Reggie Smith as well as pitchers Tommy John, Fernando Valenzuela, Andy Messersmith, Don Sutton and Burt Hooton.

3508 Little Blue Wrecking Crew 1974–81 *National (M)*. The dependable Dodger hitters led the NL in home runs with 139 in their 1974 pennant year. The 1977 pennant-winners hit a league-high 191 home runs. In 1978 the Dodgers again led the NL with 149 homers to win their third NL flag in five seasons. In the strike-shortened season of 1981 the Dodgers led the NL with 89 homers en route to their first world title since 1965. The tag for the blue-trimmed L.A. hitters was a spinoff from the blue-trimmed Brooklyn "Blue Wrecking Crew" Dodgers of the 1955 and 1956 seasons.

3509 Bluebloods 1977 to date *National (M)*. When Tommy Lasorda, who had been a player, coach and minor league manager in the Dodger organization since 1955, was hired as manager for the L.A. Dodgers, he proudly announced to reporters, "I bleed Dodger Blue!" as an expression of his loyalty to the franchise. Avid Dodger fans sometimes are called **Bleeding Dodger Blue** fans.

3510 Blue Crews 1977 to date *National (M)*. Tag is a spin-off from Bluebloods and the Milwaukee "Brew Crew." The moniker is used exclusively by local newspapers. For fans in the rest of the country, the only baseball "crew" are the Milwaukee Brewers.

3511 Traffic Dodgers 1980 *National (M)*. From a 1980 joke by comedian Bob Hope about the dangerous and sometimes life-threatening Los Angeles traffic, it was a throwback moniker because, back in the Brooklyn era, the Brooklyn fans were called "Trolley Dodgers" because they had to "dodge" electrified trolleys—literally for their lives—on the streets in front of the Brooklyn ballpark. Hope's wisecrack was: "You know, with the traffic these days in L.A., you're either a Dodger ... or an Angel!" Hope was referring to the nearby California Angels.

3512 Rat Pack 1981 *National (M)*. The Los Angeles Dodgers emerged from the chaos of the 1981 players strike and split-season playoffs as NL champions and then ran over the AL champion New York Yankees, 4 games to 2, winning four straight contests after dropping the first two games. Dodger outfielder Davey Lopes described his team's exploits as "scrambling around on the field like rats" as the Dodgers fielded well with good range like mice going after cheese, stole bases, and initiated hit-and-run plays to scamper around the bases.

3513 Artful Dodgers 1988 *National (M)*. Based on the Charles Dickens novel and coined by baseball writer Gordon Verrell, the "Artful Dodgers" refers to the 1988 Los Angeles Dodgers who seemed to win the NL Eastern Division, the 1988 NL pennant and the 1988 World Series using smoke and mirrors. Actually, it was the Dodger pitchers who were "artful," compiling a splendid 2.96 team ERA for the regular season. Despite only hitting .210 in the NL Championship Series, the Dodgers somehow edged the New York Mets to win the 1988 NL pennant. Heavy underdogs to the powerful AL champion Oakland A's, the Dodgers hurlers "artfully" held the Oakland hitters to a minuscule .177 team batting average while Kirk Gibson hit a memorable pinch-hit two-run home run in the bottom of the ninth in the first game to convert a 4–3 deficit into a 5–4 victory. Gibson hobbled around the bases on not one but two gimpy legs!

3514 Top Dogs 1988 *National (M)*. Tag was coined by baseball writer Tracy Ringolsby to celebrate the Dodgers' 1988 NL pennant and world championship season. Ringo got the idea from Dodger ace Orel "Bulldog" Hershiser (23–8, 2.26 ERA) who hurled 59 consecutive scoreless innings to establish a major league record. Hershiser was indeed a "bulldog" as he tossed six consecutive shutouts in his last six starts of the regular season. The Dodgers had been heavy betting "underdogs" at the start of the season, throughout the playoffs and at the start of the World Series. By 1990, California Angel fans began to resent haughty Dodger fans, who often referred to the Anaheim team as "Gaylos," thereby rubbing in the nine Dodger pennants into their Orange County faces. Therefore, with scatological words becoming ever more prevalent in previously "polite" English (thanks to the "hippie liberation" of the 1960s), the California Angels fans spewed out the vulgarity of **Dog-turds** in reference to the Los Angeles "Top Dogs."

3515 Punchless Dodgers 1989 *National (M)*. The 1989 batted only .240 as a team with a major league-low 89 home runs, causing the team to drop from the world championship to a losing 77–83 record. The team was shut out an NL-high 17 times in 1989. The term was coined by baseball writer Gordon Verrell.

3516 Los Doyers 2005 to date *National (M)*. With 4 million Spanish-speaking residents in the greater Los Angeles metropolitan area, it was inevitable that the English-Spanish amalgam would appear. Spanish-speakers have trouble pronouncing the hard "D-G" of English.

3517 The Azul 2005 to date *National (M)*. An obvious spin-off from one of Mexico's most famous soccer teams—Cruz Azul—the blue-trimmed Dodgers are referred to in Spanish as "El Azul," i.e., "The Blue."

3518 Bums 1958–61, 1989 to date *National (M)*. The "Bums" moniker arose in the 1930s in Brooklyn when the old Dodgers teams were chronic losers. In the team's first 31 years in Los Angeles, the Dodgers enjoyed 23 winning seasons, nine NL pennants and five World Series titles. When the team moved to Los Angeles in 1958, cartoonist Willard Mullin drew the famous Brooklyn Bum character as a tanned Hollywood type luxuriating in shorts, sandals and a Hawaiian shirt with a straw hat and sun glasses on a reclining chair by a swimming pool. When the Dodgers finished seventh in their first season in California, Los Angelinos grumbled, "They're still bums!" The moniker became affectionate when the Dodgers won the World Series in 1959. By 1962 the name had become passé as the L.A. team had its own winning identity, and Brooklyn fans turned their attention to the New York Mets. But starting in 1989, when the team skidded from the 1988 world championship and went tumbling to a 77–83 record, spoiled Dodger fans barked "Bums" in describing their charges in those seasons in which the team played poorly, i.e., 1989, 1992, 1999 and 2009–10. As the 1988 championship season has faded over the last 24 years, the old "Bums" tag is being used more frequently. However, this Los Angeles version is strictly local, and is never heard outside of L.A.

3519 Unexpected Dodgers 1988 *National (M)*. With Kirk Gibson adding some needed offensive power and Orel Hershiser pitching 6 consecutive shutouts, the Dodgers surprised their NL Western Division with a 94–67 record to finish 1st, 7 games ahead of Cincinnati. Tag coined by David Neft.

3520 Damned Dodgers 2011 *National (M)*. The opposite of "Damn Yankees," this tag was coined by baseball writer Lee Jenkins in *Sports Illustrated* to describe the franchise's woes: (1) loss of revenue, putting the team $500 million in debt; (2) incidents of fan violence; (3) declining TV ratings; and (4) team owner Frank McCourt, fighting off a multi-million dollar divorce case, being forced to declare bankruptcy. The franchise's failure to win an NL pennant for the past 24 years also has hurt the team.

Los Mochis, Sinoloa, Mexico

3521 Caneros 1955–56–1957–58 *Mexican Pacific Coast (W)*; 1958–59–69–70 *Sonora–Sinoloa (W)*. This circuit was known as the Sonora–Sinoloa League through the 1969–70 season and was renamed the Mexican Pacific League starting with the 1970–71 season. *Mexican Pacific (W)*. 1970–71 to date. Nearby sugar plantations transport sugar cane to city plants where the sugar is processed and packed. Los caneros is Spanish for Sugar Men, sugar-harvesters and sugar-caners.

Louisville, Kentucky

3522 Kentuckys 1870 *Independent*. In the nineteenth century, baseball teams occasionally would adopt their state name, i.e., Baltimore Marylands, Louisville Kentuckys, New Orleans Louisianas, Providence Rhode Islands, Richmond Virginias and San Francisco Californias.

3523 Gateway Citys Louisville is the "Gateway City" to the Ohio River.

3524 Grays 1876–77 *National (M)*. The players started the season wearing blue stockings, which after several washings faded to gray. In this era teams didn't have the money to buy new uniforms, stockings, spikes and caps, which had to last the entire season.

3525 Giant Team of the West 1876–77 *National (M)*. The *New York Clipper* used this title, noting several of the 1876 Louisville players were "six foot tall heavyweights."

3526 Kentuckians 1876–77 *National (M)*. Numerous teams were referred to by their home state name, i.e., Manchester New Hampshirites, Richmond Virginians, Providence Rhode Islanders, and Louisville Kentuckians.

3527 Kentucky Cracks 1876–77 *National (M)*. "Cracks" was baseball slang for skilled baseball players. The term probably originated from the term "crack shot," referring to an accurate firearms shooter.

3528 Kentucky Leaguers 1876–77 *National (M)*. Name used to distinguish the Louisville NL club from amateur teams in Louisville. Tag first appeared in the *New York Clipper* May 5, 1877.

3529 Blues 1876–77 *National (M)*; 1882–91 *American Assn*. The 1876 team dressed the players in blue hose. After numerous washings the hose faded to gray. The same problem occurred in 1877. The American Association team in Louisville simply sidestepped the problem by using non-color names like Eclipse and Colonels. Fading of hose color in the 19th century was a chronic problem that would not be alleviated until white sanitary hose was introduced around 1906 and colorfast dyes came into vogue around 1980.

3530 Colonels 1882–91 *American Assn. (M)*; 1892–99 *National (M)*; 1903–62 *American Assn. (A 1902–07, AA 1908–45, AAA 1946–62)*; 1968–72 *International (AAA)* Following the War of 1812, heroic soldiers, politicians, successful businessmen and prominent citizens received a special, honorary title from the governors of Kentucky, starting in 1815. When the Kentucky Militia, which had fought valiantly in the War of 1812, disbanded in 1815, then–Kentucky Governor Isaac Shelby drew from their ranks several men to work as aides in his administration and awarded them the honorary title of "colonel." By the twentieth century, the term "Colonel" meant any inhabitant of Kentucky, although the cliché image was always one of a white-haired, goateed gentleman in a white suit.

3531 Eclipse 1882–91 *American Assn. (M)*. Solar Eclipse was an eighteenth century race horse owned by the Duke of Cumberland of England. Between 1769 and 1771 Solar Eclipse won 18 races in England, prompting the motto "Eclipse first and the rest nowhere." American colonists followed the horse's exploits in colonial newspapers and the term came to mean "sporting excellence." When the Louisville baseball team formed in Louisville as an independent team in 1881, the team was christened "Eclipse" because Louisville, a major horse racing city, had fans that remembered the exploits of Solar Eclipse more than 100 years earlier.

3532 Kaintucks 1882–91 *American Assn. (M)*. Tag was an amusing period moniker that never caught on. Southern slang and pronunciation reached its most influential period in the nineteenth century. Newspapers used it to avoid the 11-letter "Kentuckians."

3533 Falls Citys 1882–91 *American Assn. (M)*; *Independent Negro team* 1883–86; 1887 *National League of Colored Baseballists*; 1892–99 *National (M)*. Louisville is known as the "Falls City" because the city was built on the shores of the Ohio River and its nearby waterfalls.

3534 Blue Jays 1889 *American Assn. (M)*. Players wore blue stockings.

3535 Record-breakers 1889 *American Assn. (M)*. The 1889 Louisville club lost a then-record 111 games (winning only 27), prompting fans to call the team the "Record Breakers." In this era any big league team that broke the then-existing record for most victories or most defeats was known as the "Record-Breakers." Ironically, despondent Louisville fans could not anticipate that the team would become the first major league team to rise from last to first place in a single season — a feat that would not be duplicated until 102 years later.

3536 Louisville Liables 1889 *American Assn. (M)*. Newspaper reporters laughed in their opinion columns that the Louisville players were "liable for court room proceedings" for their almost "criminal

misconduct" on the field for producing a horrendous 27–111 record.

3537 Loseville 1889 *American Assn. (M)*. As the 1889 team spiraled down to last place with 111 defeats, newspapers in other cities started to call this team the rather ungracious moniker of "Loseville." The 1982–83 NHL Winnipeg Jets hockey team, when they went a hideous 9–57–14 (won-lost-tied), were also called "Lose-peg" by fans and newspapers. Louisville and Winnipeg are the only two cities where this play on words works.

3538 Lillies 1889 *American Assn. (M)*. As the team went on to lose 111 games, newspapers sniffed that the players were about as competitive as a "bunch of lilies."

3539 Clan Na-Gaels 1889–90 *American Assn. (M)*. Team captain Dennis O'Kelly was of Irish descent — a fact that pleased the many residents of Louisville who were of Irish descent and whose parents and grandparents immigrated to Kentucky to escape the "Irish Potato Famine" of the 1840s. "Clan Na-Gaels" was an Irish Republican social-political organization.

3540 Cyclones 1890 *American Assn. (M)*. In the same summer that Louisville rose from an eighth and last place finish in 1889 to a first-place finish for the 1890 American Association pennant, a terrible tornado struck the city and surrounding regions, killing 78 people. Although perhaps insensitive to the loss of life, the moniker stuck in 1890 but was discontinued in 1891.

3541 Kentucky Colonels 1890 *American Assn. (M)*. Team flew a pennant banner proclaiming themselves as the "Kentucky Colonels."

3542 Distillery Delegates 1890–91 *American Assn. (M)*. The state government of Kentucky sent "delegates" to monitor the manufacture of whiskey and bourbon in Kentucky's many distilleries. However, the Louisville players were not drunkards, in distinction to the sarcastic "Brewers," i.e., players who drank heavily.

3543 Sour Mashes 1891 *American Assn. (M)*. Tag is in honor of Kentucky's famous sour mash whiskey.

3544 Wanderers 1892–93 *National (M)*. The team had losing seasons (63–89 in 1892 and 50–75 in 1893), which kept Louisville fans away in droves, forcing the players to become "Wanderers" in increasingly long road trips where Louisville home games were transferred to the home parks of opponents.

3545 Loserville 1892–97 *National (M)*. After the lone success of the surprise 1890 pennant, Louisville teams started to lose again after joining the National League in 1892. In their defense the four American Association exiles that joined the NL in 1892 were subjected to a player draft by the eight returning NL teams that stripped the four newcomers of their best players.

3546 King of Losers 1892–97 *National (M)*. In this six-year period the Louisville Nationals lost 556 games while finishing 11th, 12th, 12th, 12th and 11th in the twelve-team National League.

3547 Bourbonville 1892–99 *National (M)*. Louisville is nicknamed "Bourbonville" because of its numerous bourbon whiskey distilleries.

3548 Night Riders 1892–99 *National (M)*. In the years 1880–1900, raiders on horseback in nocturnal attacks burned the crops of Kentucky farmers who sided with big tobacco companies that were establishing a tobacco industry monopoly.

3549 Barnie's Boobies 1893–97 *National (M)*. Jim Barnie managed this hapless club, which is the only major league baseball team ever to finish in 12th place three straight years. In 1897 the Boobies soared to 11th place. The name derives from the "Booby," a penguin-like bird that waddles as it walks. The name soon was applied to the so-called "Booby Prize," which is a joke prize for a terrible performance.

3550 Bourbon Club 1899 *National (M)*. The name appeared in *The Sporting News* this year. Louisville is known as the "Bourbon City."

3551 Cubs 1910–13 *Independent Negro team*. Team also signed young players, who in the slang of the era were known as "cubs."

3552 White Sox 1915–19 *Independent Negro team*; 1930 *Independent Negro team*; 1931 *Negro National (M)*. Players wore white stirrups over their white sanitary hose.

3553 Black Caps 1920 *Negro Southern (ind.)*; 1921 *Southeast Negro (ind.)*; 1932 *Negro Southern (M)*. Players wore black caps.

3554 Zulu Cannibals 1932–42 *Independent Negro team*. Using a nickname that would be "politically incorrect" today, this team used Louisville as an occasional home base while barnstorming for most of its yearly schedule. The nickname gimmick worked because enough fans— white as well as black — attended games to keep the team financially solvent for 11 years. In this era, Negro stereotypes were often used.

3555 Red Caps 1933–34 *Independent Negro team*. Players wore red caps.

3556 Black Colonels 1938 *Independent Negro team*; 1954 *Negro American (ind.)*. Moniker was a spin-off from Colonels. The American Association Louisville Colonels donated old "Colonel" uniforms and equipment to this black team, which used the nickname sewn on the jerseys.

3557 Buckeyes 1949 *Negro American (ind.)*. The 1948 Cleveland Buckeyes moved to Louisville for the 1949 season. The nickname was retained as management could not afford new uniforms.

3558 Redbirds 1982–97 *American Assn. (AAA)*. Team was a farm club of the St. Louis Cardinals.

3559 Bats 1988 to date *International (AAA)*. Although the team's mascot is a little flying bat with a baseball cap on its head, the name actually refers to the famous Louisville Slugger baseball bat that was first manufactured here in 1886. Originally **River Bats**, the name was shortened to Bats because of the displeasure of Louisville newspaper editors, who wanted a short four-letter name to compensate for Louisville's ten letters. Management held a name-the-team contest and a 12-year-old girl submitted the winning entry of "River Bats," which was then pared down to "Bats." Other entries included the traditional Colonels and Sluggers. Jeff Hollis, director of media relations for the team, declared "River Bats" to be the winning name. In 1968 Kansas City Athletics owner Charlie Finley asked major league baseball to allow him to move his K.C. team to Louisville where they would play as the Louisville "Sluggers." However, the major league baseball owners refused his petition because at the time Louisville was much too small as a TV market.

Lowell, Massachusetts

3560 Ladies' Men 1877 *New England Assn. (M)*. Lowell was one of the very first teams to sponsor a "Ladies' Day," i.e., free admission for women and girls. Hence, Lowell fans included ladies who sometimes attracted the attention of the Lowell players on the field. The 1876 amateur Lowell team was called the "Lions"— but this name was not used for the Lowell professional teams of 1877–78. The name was reported by the *New York Clipper* on July 9, 1877.

3561 Spindle Citys 1877 *New England Assn. (M)*; 1878 *International Assn. (M)*; 1888 *New England (ind.)*; 1892x *New England (ind.)*. Team disbanded July 2. Lowell has been a major textile producer since 1840. Textile mills using water-driven "power looms," invented by Francis Lowell, were built here. Using the currents of the nearby Merrimack and Concord rivers, the looms were so effective that Lowell became a major textile center and soon became known as the "City of Spindles." There have been nine cotton mills in the city since 1835. By the 1920s, the changing economy forced the mills to close. The name first appeared in the *New York Clipper* on April 28, 1877.

3562 Magicians 1887 *New England (ind.)*. Incorporated as a town in 1826, Lowell grew so quickly that by 1836 it became incorporated as a city and was known as the "Magic City." The burgeoning textile industry was largely responsible for this building spurt. Any nineteenth century U.S. city that grew quickly was said to have "sprung up like magic," leading to nicknames such as Gem City, Jewel City and Magic City.

3563 Browns 1887 *New England (ind.)*. Players wore brown hose.

3564 Chippies 1888 *New England (ind.)*. A "Chippie" is a type of sparrow or songbird found in the Eastern U.S. It is actually a tree finch, hence the name "Chippie."

3565 Indians 1891 *New England (ind.)*. Vikings, exploring the New England coast in the 11th century, encountered the Algonkians. Indians befriended the Pilgrims in 1620. Indians and British attacked colonists in King Phillip's War 1675–76. Indians and French attacked colonists in the French and Indian War 1704–13. Six of eight tribes were expelled from this region by 1800. Nipmuc and Wampanoags live in small reservations.

3566 Lowell Base Ball Club 1895 *New England Assn. (ind.)*. Team had no nickname.

3567 Tigers 1901–05m *New England (ind. 1901, B 1902–05)*. Team moved to Taunton (MA) August 3, 1905; 1906–10 *New England (ind.)*. Starting around 1890, when Princeton University's football players started wearing striped stockings (the team nickname became "Tigers"), baseball teams started picking up on the fad. The nickname was solidified in 1903, when the team "played like Tigers" en route to the 1903 New England League pennant. By 1908, striped stirrups had become the fad for most baseball teams. However, the Lowell team kept the "Tigers" moniker because both newspapers and fans liked it. With Fred Tenney at the helm in 1910, newspapers called the team "Tenney's Tigers." In 1911 the team again "played like Tigers" en route to winning the 1911 pennant.

3568 Grays 1911–15 *New England (ind.)*; 1916x *Eastern (B)*. Team disbanded September 4; 1919m *New England (B)*. Team moved to Lewiston (ME)-Auburn (ME) July 14. With the big league Detroit Tigers having won three AL straight pennants (1907–09), the "Tigers" moniker was becoming monopolized by the Detroiters, prompting Lowell newspapers to switch to "Grays" because the Lowell fans were happy with manager James Gray for having led the Lowell team to the 1911 New England League pennant. The name was reinforced when Gray again led the team to the 1913 New England League pennant. Gray did not return as skipper in 1916, however the Grays moniker was retained this year and in 1919 because the players continued to wear gray uniforms.

3569 Highwaymen 1926m *New England (B)*. The team played only 14 games (including seven home games) before transferring to Salem (MA) June 3. Local newspapers, paying no heed to fan disinterest and their willful low attendance for a .500 team, reported that the now ex–Lowell players had "stolen away in the night like highwaymen." "Highwayman" originated in the seventeenth century, meaning a thief who assaults and robs travelers along a highway. In baseball lexicon, it meant a team forced to take to the road, or even transfer to another city in mid-season, because of low attendance at home games. With Tom "Poke" Whalen at the helm, newspapers called the players "Tom Whalen's Highwaymen."

3570 Millers 1929m *New England (B)*. Team moved to Nashua (NH) June 19. The city, known as the "Spindle City," had cotton mills here from 1835 to about 1920. With manager Bill Merritt at the helm, newspapers called the players "Merritt's Millers."

3571 Lauriers 1933 *New England (B)*. Laurier Jewelry Company owned the team. With manager Buster Yarnell at the helm, newspapers called the players "Buster Yarnell's Lauriers."

3572 Hustlers 1934 *Northeastern (B)*. With manager Bill Hunnefeld at the helm, newspapers called the players "Hunnefield's Hustlers" and "Hunnefield's Honeys." Both fans and newspapers praised the team "for hustling" to the 1934 pennant.

3573 Orphans m1947 *New England (B)*. Team started season in Lawrence but poor play provoked low attendance, forcing the team to move to Lowell July 15 as the Lawrence fans abandoned these "Orphans." The usage was about the last time a professional baseball team has been branded "Orphans." Lawrence fans had stayed away as the team stumbled to an 29–38 record. Then, Lowell fans shunned the team as it continued losing with a grisly 11–49 mark for an overall 40–87 record, dropping them into last place. The franchise seems to have had no official team nickname, one of the last such nameless professional baseball teams in the United States. By the 1950s a baseball franchises saw the marketing need of an official team nickname.

3574 Spinners 1996 to date *New York–Pennsylvania (A)*. During the era 1850–1920, the city was a major textile producer. Today, Lowell produces electronics and chemicals. The cotton textile mills of old were first sent to Dixie, and in today's global economy, they've been outsourced overseas.

Lowville, New York

3575 Lowville Base Ball Club 1886 *Central New York (ind.)*. Team had no nickname.

Lubbock, Texas

3576 Hubbers 1922 *West Texas (D)*; 1923x *Panhandle Pecos (D)*. Team and league disbanded August 15; 1928 *West Texas (D)*; 1938–42x *West Texas New Mexico (D)*. Team and league disbanded July 5 because of U.S. entry into World War II; 1946–55 *West Texas–New Mexico (C 1946–54, B 1955)*; 1956m *Big State (B)*. Team moved to Texas City (TX) July 8. In the period 1901–20 oil was discovered in the region, causing Lubbock to become a "boomtown" and the "Hub of the South Plains." Also known as the "Hub of Northwest Texas," the city produced cotton and cottonseed oil and was the transport center for six highways by 1920. Lubbock is also known as the "Hub of Texas Livestock." When Ray "Red" Hill took over in mid-season 1928, local newspapers started calling the players the alliterative "Hill's Hubbers." With manager James "Hack" Miller at the helm in 1938, newspapers called the players "Hack's Hubbers." Moniker became traditional and was used through the 1956 season.

3577 Bobcats 1928 *West Texas (D)*. The alliterative nickname is a spin-off from "Wildcat" oil rigs. The moniker is also appropriate because the American Lynx, i.e., the "bobcat" is found in Texas and the Southwest. With manager Bennie Bronlow at the helm at season's start, newspapers called the players "Bennie Bronlow's Bobcats."

3578 Crickets 1995–98 *Texas–Louisiana (ind.)*. The alliterative moniker is appropriate because crickets are found along the Yellow House Draw (a small river adjacent to the city) and nearby Buffalo Springs Lake (about 10 miles southeast of the city).

Ludington, Michigan

3579 Mariners 1912–14 *Michigan State (D)*; 1920–22 *Central (B)*. The city has been a lake port receiving shipping on Lake Michigan since 1850. Boat ferries run from here to ports in Milwaukee (WI) and Manitowoc (WI). With Frank Warrender at the helm in 1912, newspapers called the players "Warrender's Mariners." Bob Grogan took over in 1913, making the name "Grogan's Mariners." Harry Arndt took over in mid-season 1913 and the name became "Harry Arndt's Mariners." Grogan returned to the helm in 1914. After James Sharpe led "James Sharpe's Mariners" to the 1921 pennant, two more

skippers led the team to the 1922 playoffs under the banners of "Ambrose McConell's Mariners" and "Andy Wohre's Mariners."

3580 Tars 1926t *Central (C)*. Team transferred to the Michigan State League June 15; 1926 *Michigan State (B)*. The circuit began play June 15 as the Michigan State League, following the merger of the Central League and Michigan Ontario League. Lumber from the Manistee National Forest, about 35 miles southeast of the city, is transported to city factories where it burns coal to produce coal tar and wood tar.

Lufkin, Angelina, Texas

3581 Lumbermen m1934 *West Dixie (D)*. Team started season in Paris (TX) and then moved to Lufkin June 27. The city is situated between Davey Crocket (to the west) and Angelina (to the east) national forests. Lumber is transported on four highways leading into the city where it is processed. The city has newsprint and woodworking plants.

3582 Foresters 1946 *East Texas (C)*; 1947–48 *Lone Star (C)*. Name was a spin-off from Lumbermen.

3583 Angels 1950m *Gulf Coast (C)*. Team moved to Leesville (LA) July 15. The city is located in Angelina County. In 1968 the city became the home of Angelina College, whose baseball team is known as the "Angels." Team was not a farm club of the Los Angeles Angels.

Lumberton, North Carolina

3584 Cubs 1947–48 *Tobacco State (D)*. Team was a farm club of the Chicago Cubs.

3585 Auctioneers 1949 *Tobacco State (D)*. The city has hosted tobacco auctions here since 1700. One of the most famous is Lloyd Meekins and Sons Auctioneers.

Lynchburg, Virginia

3586 Hill Climbers 1894–96m *Virginia (ind.)*. The city was built along the James River in the foothills of the Blue Ridge Mountains. Because of its geography, Lynchburg is known as the "Hill City."

3587 Shoemakers 1906–12 *Virginia (C)*; 1917x *Virginia (C)*. Team and league disbanded May 15 due to U.S. entry into World War I. Lynchburg was noted for its shoe manufacturing in the era 1870–1920.

3588 Grays 1939 *Virginia (D)*. Players wore gray uniforms, but the name actually referred to the gray uniforms of the Confederate Army of 1861–65. Virginia is known as "The Battlefield of the Civil War."

3589 Senators 1940–42 *Virginia (D)*; 1959 *Appalachian (D)*. The 1940–42 team maintained a loose affiliation with the AL Washington Senators but was not a formal farm team. The 1959 team was an official farm club of the AL Washington Senators.

3590 Cardinals 1943–55 *Piedmont (B)*. Team was a farm club of the St. Louis Cardinals.

3591 White Sox m1962–63 South Atlantic (A 1962, AA 1963). The team began the season in Savannah (GA) and moved to Lynchburg August 26; 1966–69 *Carolina (A)*. Both teams were farm clubs of the Chicago White Sox. Team was also known by the newspaper contraction **LynSox**.

3592 Twins 1970–74 *Carolina (A)*. Team was a farm club of the Minnesota Twins.

3593 Rangers 1975 *Carolina (A)*. Team was a farm club of the Texas Rangers.

3594 Mets 1976–87 *Carolina (A)*. Team was a farm club of the New York Mets.

3595 Red Sox 1988–94 *Carolina (A)*. Team was a farm club of the Boston Red Sox.

3596 Hillcats 1995 to date *Carolina (A)*. Large cats such as cougars and bobcats inhabit the foothills of the Blue Ridge Mountains.

Lynn, Essex, Massachusetts

3597 Live Oaks 1877 *New England Assn. (M)*; 1878 *International Assn. (M)*; m1886–87 *New England (ind.)*. Team began the season in Newburyport (MA) and moved to Lynn August 14; m1901x *New England (ind.)*. Team began the season in Augusta (ME) and moved to Lynn June 30. Team disbanded July 6. Although the American Elm is the state tree of Massachusetts, the Evergreen Oak, aka the "Live Oak," was imported to the city from California, the Southwest and Mexico, to line the city's streets. With manager Jack Leighton at the helm in 1901, newspapers called the players "Leighton's Live Oaks." Lynn became known as the "Live Oak City." Newspapers often shortened the name to **Oaks**.

3598 Yankees m1886–87 *New England (ind.)*. Team began the season in Newburyport (MA) and moved to Lynn August 14. First coined in the eighteenth century, the name referred to an inhabitant of New England. Mark Twain's *A Connecticut Yankee in King Arthur's Court* (written about this time) and the eighteenth century song "Yankee Doodle Dandy" helped popularize the moniker. In baseball circles, the nickname was used by New England teams in Boston, Hartford, Lynn and other places long before the New York Yankees of 1903.

3599 Shoemakers m1886–88x *New England (ind.)*. Team began the 1886 baseball season in Newburyport (MA) and moved to Lynn August 14. Team disbanded July 25, 1888; 1891 *New England (ind.)*; 1905–10, 1913 *New England (B)*. Shoe manufacturing began in Lynn around 1635. By 1770 the city made most of the footwear used by the Colonies. Lynn is known as the "Shoe City." With managers Frederick Lake and then Frank Leonard at the helm, newspapers called the players "Frederick Lake's Shoemakers" and "Frank Leonard's Shoemakers." Leonard managed in the years 1905–08. The name was retained through 1910 and used again in 1913. Newspaper editors hated the name and often used "Oaks" instead. By 1920, machine-made shoes, manufactured countrywide, killed the shoe industry of New England.

3600 Lions 1888x *New England (ind.)*. Team disbanded July 25. Used by Lynn newspaper reporters, the moniker was a spin-off of the 1876 Lowell (MA) Lions.

3601 Essex m1901x *New England (ind.)*. Team began the season in Augusta (ME) and moved to Lynn June 30. Team disbanded July 6. Lynn is located in Essex County.

3602 Leonardites 1911–12 *New England (B)*. Team was led by manager Frank Leonard.

3603 Fighters 1914 *New England (B)*. With manager Pat Flaherty at the helm, newspapers called the players "Flaherty's Fighters."

3604 Pirates 1915 *New England (B)*. Legend has it that pirates of the seventeenth, eighteenth and even nineteenth centuries hid out near the city, storing their booty in nearby Dungeon Rock Cave. Historically, pirates raided the New England coastline until 1840. With manager Louis Piper at the helm, newspapers called the team "Piper's Pirates." Team was not a farm club of the Pittsburgh Pirates as there would be no farm system for another 10 years.

3605 Pipers 1916 *Eastern (B)*. Name was doubly appropriate because of the Saugus Iron Works in neighboring Saugus (Lynn, originally known as Saugus, divided into Lynn and Saugus in 1637), where iron pipe manufacture went on for 200 years (1650–1850)

3606 Ocean Parkers 1916 *Eastern (B)*. Beaches of the city include Lynn, Nahant, Black Rock and Kings, collectively known as "Ocean Park." The team was owned by the Ocean Park Inn.

3607 Papooses 1926–30x *New England (B)*. Team and league disbanded June 22, 1930, because of the Great Depression. The 1926 team was the first minor league farm club of the Boston Braves (a loose affiliation in 1926–27), prompting local newspapers to call these young Braves, the "Papooses." From the old Narragansett Indian word for "baby," it came into English in 1634. With manager Poke Whalen at the helm in 1927, newspapers called the players "Poke's Papooses." Name became popular as "Poke's Papooses" won consecutive pennants, 1927–28, and made the playoffs in 1929.

3608 Tigers 1949x *New England (B)*. Team disbanded July 19. Team was a farm club of the Detroit Tigers.

3609 Sailors 1980–83 *Eastern (AA)*. The city is located along Lynn Harbor and Nahant Bay. The twin cities of Lynn-Saugus were founded in 1631 as maritime cities for shipping and traveling in and out of Massachusetts Bay.

3610 Massachusetts Mad Dogs 1996 *North Atlantic (ind.)*; 1997–98 *Northeast (ind.)*; 1999 *Northern (ind.)*. Largely due to the influence of Rap music, which uses "dog" and "dawg" much the way Jazz has used "cat" and "cool cat," sports team nicknames, using these canine terms, sprouted up everywhere in the 1990s. Hence, there were such teams as Surf Dogs, RiverDogs, Diamond Dogs, Steel Dogs and Mad Dogs.

3611 North Shore Spirit 2003–04 *Northeast (ind.)*; 2005–07 *Can–Am (ind.)*. The team is located on the coast, the North Shore of Boston Harbor. Settled in 1629, the city has a long history and experienced the "Spirit of '76" during the Revolutionary War.

Lyons, Kansas

3612 Lions 1909–11 *Kansas State (D)*; 1912 *Central Kansas (D)*; 1913 *Kansas State (D)*. Moniker was used for newspaper headlines, i.e., "Lions edge Millers, 4–3." Team "played like Lions" as manager Cecil Bankhead guided "Cecil's Lions" to the 1909 pennant. Bankhead left in mid-season 1910 but the name was retained. In 1912 the team was named "Wilson's Lions" after new manager Fred Wilson. The 1913 team was named the "William Nelson's Lions" after manager William Nelson.

Lyons, New York

3613 Lyons Baseball Club 1897–98 *New York State (ind.)*. Team had no nickname.

Macomb, Illinois

3614 Potters 1908–10x *Illinois–Missouri (D)*. Team disbanded August 17. Sandstone mines near the city provide aluminum silicate, i.e., clay, which is transported to city factories for pottery manufacture. The city's biggest ceramic store was Haeger Potteries. Macomb is known as the "World's Largest Art Pottery City."

Macon, Georgia

3615 Blacklegs 1885 *Southern (ind.)*. Players wore black hose. Originally **Black Stockings**, newspapers shortened it to **Black Sox** and "Black Legs."

3616 Central Citys 1886 *Southern (ind.)*; 1891–93 *Southern (ind.)*. Macon is nicknamed the "Central City" and the "Heart of Georgia" because it is six miles from Georgia's geographical center.

3617 Hornets 1894x *Southern (ind.)*. Team disbanded June 27. With manager Bill Hoggins at the helm, newspapers called the players

"Hoggins' Hornets." Management then dressed the players in yellow and black striped hose. When Hoggins left in mid-season, he was replaced by John Hill, prompting reporters to alter the moniker to "Hill's Hornets."

3618 Macon Base Ball Club 1898 *Texas–Southern (ind.)*. Team had no nickname.

3619 Acmes 1903–05 *Independent Negro team*. "Acme" is an ancient Greek word meaning "high." In English it means "excellence." Tag was an occasional sports team nickname of the nineteenth century. Acme is alliterative with Macon.

3620 Highlanders 1904 *South Atlantic (C)*. People who lived in the "Highlands," i.e., hilly regions of Scotland, Ireland and Germany, were known as "Highlanders" ("Hochlander" in German). These immigrants settled in Georgia and in Macon in the eighteenth and nineteenth centuries. The team's ballpark was located near Macon Hill, aka Falls Lines Hill, the highest points in the city. The nearby Ocmulgee National Monument has several prehistoric mounds built by the Mound Builder Indians of antiquity.

3621 Brigands 1905–07 *South Atlantic (C)*. "Blackbeard" and his pirates, aboard their vessel, *Queen Anne's Revenge*, raided the coastlines of the Carolinas from 1690 to 1718. A military force from Fort Macon (near present-day Macon) sunk his ship in 1718. In an ensuing battle near Ocracoke Island, Blackbeard (real name Edward Teach) was killed on November 22, 1718. With manager William Smith at the helm, newspapers called the players "Bill's Brigands."

3622 Peaches 1908–15 *South Atlantic (C)*; m1923–30 *South Atlantic (B)*. Team began the 1923 season in Charleston (SC) and then moved to Macon May 28. Circuit was League 1923–25, Association 1926–30; 1932 *Southeastern (B)*; 1946–55 *South Atlantic (A)*; 1961 *Southern Assn. (AA)*; 1962–63 *South Atlantic (D 1962, A 1963)*; 1964 *Southern (AA)*; 1966–67 *Southern (AA)*; 1980–83 *South Atlantic (A)*; 2003 *Southeastern (ind.)*. Outlying farms transport peaches to factories where the fruit is cleaned, packed and shipped to market. The state of Georgia is known as the "Peach State."

3623 Tigers 1916–17x *South Atlantic (C)*. Team disbanded May 19, 1917, due to U.S. entry into World War I. Macon is located near Tiger Mountain by the lowlands inhabited by a Cherokee tribe led by Chief Tiger-Tail. Settlers started a town in this region in 1822, which they named Tiger Town. Years later the city was renamed Macon. Not to be outdone by the Cherokee chief, the leader of the 1822 settlers, William Jenkins, took the nickname of "Tiger" Jenkins. With manager George Stinson at the helm, newspapers named the players the alliterative "Stinson's Tigers." The players wore striped stirrups.

3624 Black Peaches 1931–38 *Independent Negro team*. Tag was a spin-off from "Peaches." Sometimes, black teams received donated uniforms from their white counterparts and assumed the nickname on the jerseys, adding the adjective "black" or "colored."

3625 Dodgers 1956–60 *South Atlantic (A)*. Team was a farm club of the Brooklyn (1956–57) and Los Angeles (1958–60) Dodgers.

3626 Pirates 1984–87 *South Atlantic (A)*. Team was a farm club of the Pittsburgh Pirates.

3627 Braves 1991–2002 *South Atlantic (A)*. Team was a farm club of the Atlanta Braves.

3628 Music 2007 *South Coast (ind.)*. Circuit disbanded after the 2007 season. In the era 1900–30, black and later white Jazz and Blues musicians played in Macon nightclubs, cafes and street festivals.

Macon, Missouri

3629 Athletics 1911x *Missouri State (D)*. Circuit and team disbanded June 4. At this time, owner-manager Connie Mack ran his Philadelphia Athletics team, who sometimes were referred to as the Philadelphia "Macks" in the newspapers. Macon newspapers first called the local team the emulative "Macon Macks," which logically gave rise to "Macon Athletics." The names emulated the 1910 AL and World Series champion Philadelphia Athletics. The team, however, was not a farm club of the Philadelphia Athletics.

Madison, South Dakota

3630 Greys 1920 *South Dakota (D)*. Dakota is the "Coyote State." The coyote is a buff-gray to red-gray North American canine, smaller than a wolf, that inhabits the plains of North America. Players also wore gray uniforms and gray stirrups.

3631 Madison Baseball Club 1921 *Dakota (D)*. Team had no nickname.

Madison, Wisconsin

3632 Senators 1907 *Wisconsin State (D)*; 1908–14 *Wisconsin–Illinois (D 1908–09, C 1910–14)*. City has been the territorial and state capital of Wisconsin since 1836. Madison is known as the "Capital City." With manager Howard Cassibone at the helm 1908–10, newspapers called the players "Howard Cassibone's Senators." Smiley Smith took over as skipper in 1911–12, changing the name to "Smiley's Senators" and "Smith's Senators." Name was retained in 1913–14 under manager Harry Bay.

3633 Stars 1920 *Independent Negro team*. Following Giants, the moniker was the second most popular nickname for black baseball teams in the era 1885–1955.

3634 Colored Giants 1922–25 *Independent Negro team*. In the era 1890–1950, more than 25 black professional teams used Giants in some combination with a descriptive adjective, i.e., American, Bacharach, Colored, Royal and Union.

3635 Blues 1940–42 *Three-I (B)*. Team was a farm club of the Chicago Cubs. Team wore blue-trimmed Chicago Cubs–style uniforms. Team had a loose affiliation with the NL Cubs in 1940–41 before becoming an official farm club of the Chicago Nationals in 1942. World War II ended the team and league by 1943.

3636 Muskies 1982–93 *Midwest (A)*. The Madison area is noted for its recreational fishing at nearby Lake Mendota and Lake Menona. Muskies abound in these waters. The muskie is actually a large pike, often over 60 pounds in weight.

3637 Hatters 1994 *Midwest (A)*. Moniker was a spin-off from "Mad Hatter" of the Lewis Carroll *Alice in Wonderland* story. Actually, the team logo was not the Mad Hatter himself, but rather the drunken little mouse at the tea party.

3638 Black Wolf 1996–2000 *Northern (ind.)*. Players wore black-trim uniforms and all-black calf stirrups. Wolves still roam Wisconsin's colder, rural areas. In the 1990s "calf" stirrups began to take over in place of "string" stirrups. Moreover, these new wider stirrups that covered the entire lower leg — both shin and calf — were only one solid color, with stripes now banished.

Madisonville, Kentucky

3639 Madisonville Base Ball Club 1896x *Kentucky–Indiana (ind.)*. Team disbanded in mid-season (date unknown). Team had no nickname.

3640 Miners 1916x *Kentucky–Illinois–Tennessee (K.I.T.T.Y.) (D)*. Circuit and team disbanded August 4; 1922 *K.I.T.T.Y. (D)*; 1946–55 *K.I.T.T.Y. (D)*. Coal and gravel from nearby mines is trucked to city processing factories. The city is located in western Kentucky near the Western Coal Fields.

Magdalena, Sonora, Mexico

3641 Membrilleros 2004–08 *Norte de Sonora (ind.)*. Prickly pears from nearby fruit farms are transported to city processing plants where they are cleaned and packed.

Mahanoy City, Pennsylvania

3642 Mahanoy City Base Ball Club 1887–88x *Central Pennsylvania (ind.)*. Team had no nickname.

3643 Bluebirds 1946–47 *North Atlantic (D)*. Team had a loose affiliation with the NL Philadelphia Blue Jays and wore blue-trim uniforms. With manager George "Bulk" Boyle at the helm, newspapers called the players "Bulk's Bluebirds" and "Boyle's Bluebirds."

3644 Brewers 1948–50 *North Atlantic (D)*. Mahanoy City was home to Bergner & Engel Brewers and the Kaiser Beer Company. Team was not a farm club of Milwaukee Brewers.

Malone, New York

3645 Malone Base Ball Club 1887x *Northeastern (ind.)*. Team had no nickname.

Managua, Distrito Federal, Nicaragua

3646 Indios de Boer 1956–57–66–67 *Nicaraguan (W)*. An early soccer team in Nicaragua was the 1902 Boer Football Club, which was named after "Boers" (white settlers of Dutch descent in South Africa). The name "Los Indios" refers to the Mayas and Chunichis who inhabited Central America for at least 1,000 years. The baseball team was founded in 1904 by U.S. counsel Carter Donaldson, who named the diamond nine the "Boer Baseball Club." The tag "Indians" was added in the 1920s.

3647 Five Stars 1957–58–66–67 *Nicaraguan (W)*. Team was owned by the Cinco Estrellas (Five Stars) Bus Company.

3648 Indios 2004–05–07–08 *Nicaraguan (W)*. The Nicaraguan League suspended operations in 2008–09 but resumed play for the 2009–10 season; 2009–10 to date *Nicaraguan (W)*. The team dropped "Boer" as too antiquated and "politically incorrect."

Manati, Puerto Rico

3649 Atenienses 2004–05–06–07 *Puerto Rican (W)*. Management named the team after "El Ateneo" (The Athenian), which is a cultural society that has built and run public libraries in San Juan, Manati and other cities in Puerto Rico. The title of the team was "Los Atenienses de Manati." The name "El Ateniense" is Spanish for "Athenian."

Manchester, New Hampshire

3650 Reds 1877 *New England Assn. (M)*; 1877–78 *International (M)*. In 1877 Manchester was a member of both the NEA and the IA. 1879 *National Assn. (M)*. The International Association changed its name to National Association in 1879 when its 1878 Canadian entry—the London Tecumsehs—dropped out. Players wore red hose. Originally **Red Stockings**, newspapers shortened it to **Redlegs** and "Reds."

3651 New Hampshirites 1877 *New England Assn. (M)*; 1877–78 *International (M)*. In 1877 Manchester was a member of both the NEA and the IA. 1879 *National Assn. (M)*. The International Association changed its name to National Association in 1879 when its 1878 Canadian entry—the London Tecumsehs—dropped out. Some team

nicknames, in the nineteenth century, referred to the state, i.e., Baltimore Marylands, Providence Rhode Island, Richmond Virginians, San Francisco Californias and Manchester New Hampshirites. Team was aka **New Hampshire Men** and **New Hampshire Boys**. Moniker first appeared in the *New York Clipper* on May 5, 1877.

3652 Maroons 1886 *New Hampshire (ind.)*; 1887–88x *New England (ind.)*. Players wore maroon hose.

3653 Farmers 1887 *New England (ind.)*. Dairy and poultry farms in the surrounding Merrimack Valley transport poultry and dairy products to city processing plants. With manager Frank Leonard at the helm, newspapers called the players "Frank Leonard's Farmers."

3654 Amskoegs 1891–92m *New England (ind.)*. Team moved to Lawrence (MA) July 2. City was built near the Amskoeg Falls of the nearby Merrimac River. The Amskoeg Textile Mill was established in 1809. At the time it was the world's largest textile factory. With manager Louis Bacon at the helm, newspapers called the players "Bacon's Amskoegs."

3655 Manchester Base Ball Club 1894 *Tri-Staten (ind.)*; 1899 *New England (ind.)*; 1901–04 *New England (ind. 1901, B 1902–05)*. These teams had no nickname.

3656 Colts 1905m *New England (B)*. Team moved to Lawrence (MA) July 20. With manager Win Clark at the helm, newspapers called the players "Clark's Colts." The name was appropriate as the team had many young players, known in this era as "colts."

3657 Textiles 1906 *New England (B)*; 1914–15 *New England (B)*. The Amskoeg Textile Mill was located in Manchester. The name was a more generic spin-off from the 1892 Amskoegs moniker. Cotton and wool mills were the principal industry in the city until the 1920s. With manager Frederick Lake at the helm, newspapers called the players the "Frederick Lake's Textiles." Name was retained under new manager John Kiernan in 1915.

3658 Blue Sox 1926–30x *New England (B)*. Circuit and team disbanded June 22 due to the Great Depression. Players wore blue stirrups, whose color was a spin-off from the red stirrups of the Boston Red Sox, with whom the Manchester team had a loose affiliation.

3659 Indians 1934 *Northeastern (B)*. With manager Chief Were at the helm, newspapers called the players "The Chief's Indians." Team was not a farm club of the Cleveland Indians.

3660 Giants 1946–48 *New England (B)*. Team was a farm club of the New York Giants.

3661 Yankees 1949 *New England (B)*; 1969–71 *Eastern (AA)*. Teams were farm clubs of the New York Yankees.

3662 New Hampshire Fisher Cats 2004 to date *Eastern (AA)*. On November 3, 2003, management announced a new team nickname of "Primaries" in honor of New Hampshire's status as the site of the first presidential election primary every four years. The fans, however, so disliked the name that they signed a 1,200-name petition for another name. Management relented and held a name-the-team contest. The winner was "Fisher Cats." The fisher cat is a type of weasel that hunts fish in the nearby Merrimack River. Other entries in the contest were Manchester Millers, Granite State Mountain Men and New Hampshire Granite.

Manchester, Ohio

3663 Manchester Base Ball Club 1894x *Tri-State (ind.)*. Team had no nickname.

Manhattan, Kansas

3664 Elks 1909, 1912 *Central Kansas (D)*; 1913 *Kansas State (D)*. Elks, also known as Red Deer, are found in Kansas. With Earle Bryant as manager in 1909, newspapers called the players "Earl's Elks." With manager Nick Kohl at the helm in 1912 and 1913, newspapers called the players "Nick Kohl's Elks."

3665 Maroons 1909–12 *Central Kansas (D)*. Players wore maroon trim. With manager Earl Bryant at the helm, newspapers called the players "Earl Bryant's Maroons." With manager Nick Kohl at the helm, newspapers called the players "Kohl's Maroons."

Manistee, Michigan

3666 Manistee Base Ball Club 1890x *Michigan State (ind.)*. Circuit and team disbanded June 10; 1893–94 *Michigan State (ind.)*. The teams had no nickname.

3667 Colts 1911 *Michigan State (D)*. Team had many young players known in the slang of the era as "colts."

3668 Champs 1912–14m *Michigan State (D)*. Team moved to Belding (MI) September 9. Team won the Michigan State League championships in 1911, 1912 & 1913.

Mankato, Minnesota

3669 Mets 1967–68 *Northern (A)*. Team was a farm club of the New York Mets.

Mannington, West Virginia

3670 Mannington Baseball Club 1910x *West Virginia (D)*. Team and league disbanded July 5. Team had no nickname.

Mansfield, Ohio

3671 Mansfield Base Ball Club 1887 *Ohio (ind.)*; 1888–90 *Tri-State (ind.)*. The teams had no nickname.

3672 Electricians 1893x *Ohio–Michigan (ind.)*. Team and league disbanded July 4. The nearby Ohio River Basin was chosen as a site in 1890 to build the region's first hydroelectric power plant. Today the city manufactures electrical appliances. Between 1890 and 1910 the United States become "electrified" as electrical plants and power lines were built throughout the country. Occasionally, a baseball team would assume the moniker "Electricians" as its home city gained electrical services.

3673 Kids 1895 *Western Inter-State (ind.)*. Team had many young players known in the slang of the day as "kids."

3674 Haymakers 1897–1900 *Interstate (ind.)*. Mansfield is located in fertile farm country, which gave rise to the county name of Richland. Haymaker was a nineteenth-century slang for "farmer." By 1912 the name became a boxing term, meaning a "terrific blow." Farmers would throw bales of hay onto wagons and later onto trucks with a resounding thud, hence the boxing term.

3675 Giants 1906 *Ohio–Pennsylvania (C)*. Team played poorly, compiling a 59–77 record (finishing seventh of eight), provoking local newspapers and fans to sarcastically call the players "Giants." Losing teams were also called the direct epithet of "Midgets."

3676 Pioneers 1907 *Ohio–Pennsylvania (C)*; 1908–09 *Ohio State (D)*; 1910 *Ohio — Pennsylvania (C)*. In 1748, the Ohio Land Company was established, which attracted French, Moravians, English, Germans and, later, Americans to fight off the Indians and settle in Ohio. Zane's Trail, built in 1796, encouraged more settlements. City was named after Jared Mansfield, the U.S. Surveyor General, who ordered surveys of the area to help make it suitable for pioneer families to settle here, starting in 1808. The "Johnny Appleseed" legend (symbolic of American farmer-pioneers) began in this region. Johnny Appleseed was a real man named John Chapman. Chapman was a pioneer-farmer who popularized the planting of apple orchards throughout the Midwest. Chapman rode a horse 30 miles at night to summon troops to defend the town against an Indian attack.

3677 Reformers 1910 *Ohio–Pennsylvania (C)*. The Ohio State Reformatory was founded just outside the city in 1870. In this era, baseball teams in cities with noted prisons were sometimes called "Prisoners" and "Reformers." With manager George Fox at the helm, newspapers called the players "George Fox' Reformers."

3678 Brownies 1911 *Ohio–Pennsylvania (C)*; 1912 *Ohio State (D)*. Team had a loose affiliation with the Cincinnati Reds. The players wore red hose at the start of the season. After a few weeks, repeated washing faded the color of the hose to brown. Because the team was a young farm club, newspapers called the players the diminutive "Brownies."

3679 Tigers 1936x *Ohio State (D)*. Team disbanded May 26. Players wore striped stirrups. Team was not a farm club of the Detroit Tigers.

3680 Red Sox 1937 *Ohio State (D)*. Team was a farm club of the Boston Red Sox.

3681 Braves 1939–41 *Ohio State (D)*. Team was a farm club of the Cleveland Indians. Rather than call the team Indians, management chose the alliterative spin-off of Braves, which had been available since 1936 when the Boston NL club dropped it in favor of Bees. When the Boston Nationals went back to Braves in 1941, this club retained the moniker for its third and final year of play.

Maracaibo, Zulia, Venezuela

3682 Lecheros de Pastora 1946–51–52 *Liga Venezolana (W)*; 1953–54 *Liga Venezolana (W)*; 1954–55–62–63 *Liga Occidental (W)*. Starting with the 1954–55 season, the Venezuelan League expanded to eight teams and then divided into two regional leagues—the *Venezuelan League* in and around Caracas and the *Western League* in and around Maracaibo. This Maracaibo team went by the regional name of Pastora Milkers (Los Lecheros de Pastora). Although Maracaibo is an oil city, dairy farming is also a major industry here. "El Pastora" is the Spanish word for shepherd. After the city was founded in 1571, shepherds tended goats and cows for their milk and to make cheese. The patron saint of the state of Lara is "La Divina Pastora." The Divine Shepherd of the Santa Rosa Church is located in Barquismeto.

3683 Centauros 1954–55 *Liga Occidental (W)*. The Centaur Beer Company owned the team. Centauros is Spanish for "centaur."

3684 Rapinos 1954–55 *Liga Occidental (W)*; 1957–58–60–61 *Western (W)*; 1962–63–63–64 *Western (W)*. Team disbanded January 5, 1964. The teams were sponsored by the Rapinos Soccer Club.

3685 Gavilanes 1954–55–59–60 *Liga Occidental (W)*. Originating in Europe, the "Gray Sparrow Hawk" was brought to the New World and became indigenous in South America. "Gavilan" is the Spanish word for sparrow hawk.

3686 Espadon 1955–56 *Liga Occidental (W)*. Swordfish swim in the coastal waters near Maracaibo.

3687 Occidentales 1960–61x *Liga Occidental (W)*. Team disbanded November 30, 1960. Maracaibo is the western-most major city in Venezuela. The Western League in Spanish is La Liga Occidental.

3688 Aguilas de Zulia 1969–70 to date *Liga Venezolana (W)*. Team goes by the state name of Zulia Eagles (Las Aguilas de Zulia). Cerveceria Aguila (the Eagle Beer Company) owns the team. The famous eagle on a cactus symbol is found on the Mexican flag.

3689 Petroleros de Zulia 1979 *Inter-American (AAA)*. Team went by the state name of Zulia Oilers (Los Petroleros de Zulia in Spanish). Oil fields were discovered here in 1917. Since then the Maracaibo oil industry not only drills and processes oil, but also ships it by freighter boat because the city is a seaport for the Gulf of Venezuela and the Caribbean Sea.

Maracay, Aragua, Venezuela

3690 Tigres de Aragua 1965–66–83–84 *Liga Venezolana (W)*; 1986–87 to date *Liga Venezolana (W)*. Management chose the nickname in rivalry with the Caracas Lions, i.e., "Leones" de Caracas vs. "Tigres" de Aragua. The team's name in English is the "Aragua Tigers." Maracay is located in Aragua State (El Estado de Aragua).

3691 Club de Maracay 2008 to date *Venezuela Summer (R)*. Team had no nickname.

Marianao, Distrito Federal, Cuba

3692 Monjes Grises 1922–23–24–25 *Liga Cubana (W)*; 1931–32–32–33 *Liga Cubana (W)*; 1934–35–37–38 *Liga Cubana (W)*. Monks of the first Christian churches of sixteenth century Cuba began the tradition of wearing gray robes. The Marianao players wore gray uniforms. "Los Monjes Grises" is Spanish for "Grey Monks." Roman Catholicism is traditional in Cuba.

3693 Tigres 1943–44–60–61 *Liga Cubana (W)*. When the franchise started up again in 1943, management decided to call the team "Tigers" as a spin-off to the long-established Havana "Lions." Tigres in English is "tigers."

Marianna, Arkansas

3694 Brickeys 1909 *Northeast Arkansas (D)*. League began play July 26. Team represented the cities Marianna and Brickeys, Arkansas, both located in Lee County. With Mr. McAdams at the managerial helm, newspapers called the players "McAdam's Brickeys."

Marinette, Wisconsin

3695 Indians 1890 *Upper Peninsula (ind.)*. Chief Blackhawk led Sauk and Fox Indians in the Battle of Bad Axe near Lacrosse August 2, 1832. American forces defeated and massacred them. The Sauk, Fox and Menominee were forced to cede land until they finally left the state in 1848. Marinette is the "Queen City" in honor of Queen Marinette of the Menominee Indian tribe.

3696 Log Rollers 1891 *Wisconsin (ind.)*. Originally, "logrollers" referred to people who rolled logs into a pile for burning. The term in the nineteenth century began to describe lumberjacks who rolled logs into streams and rivers by treading on them. This log "treading" gave rise to the sport of "log-rolling," whereby opponents try to outlast each other treading on logs floating on a river or lake before spectators.

3697 Lumber-shorers 1892 *Wisconsin–Michigan (ind.)*. By 1870, the state was still 80 percent covered with trees. Lumber from Nicolet National Forest, about 200 miles northwest of the twin cities of Marinette (WI) and Menominee (MN), are transported to these two cities for cutting and processing in numerous sawmills there. By 1900 Wisconsin led the nation in lumber production. "Lumber-shorers" is a nineteenth-century term for men who transported timber on rafts and then set them ashore near lumber factories.

Marinette-Menominee, Wisconsin

3698 Twins 1914 *Wisconsin–Illinois(C)*. Since 1880 "Twins" has been a traditional nickname for a team that represented two adjacent or nearby cities. Team's official title was the Marinette-Menominee Baseball Club, which forced newspapers to use "Twins" in its headlines, i.e., "Twins edge Bays, 4–3."

3699 Twin Cities Molls 1914 *Wisconsin–Illinois(C)*. Newspapers used "Twin Cities Molls" because editors rebelled against the name "Marinette-Menominee Twins." Chicago gangsters and their "gun molls" frequented the Marinette Train Depot as they traveled from Chicago to Wisconsin transporting stolen goods. Young Al Capone and his "molls" were seen at the Marinette Train Depot numerous times in 1914–15.

Marion, Illinois

3700 Indians 1947–48 *Illinois State (D)*. With manager Melvin Ivy at the helm, newspapers called the players "Ivy's Indians." The team was not a farm club of the Cleveland Indians.

3701 Southern Illinois Miners 2007 to date *Frontier (ind.)*. Nearby mines produce bituminous coal, known as "soft coal," which is transported to city coal processing plants where it is burned to produce asphalt and tar.

Marion, Indiana

3702 Marion Base Ball Club 1888 *Indiana State (ind.)*; 1890m *Indiana State (ind.)*. Team moved to Logansport (IN) in mid-season (date unknown); 1906 *Inter-State Assn. (C)*. These teams had no nickname.

3703 Glassblowers 1900–01 *Indiana State (ind.)*. Miners excavate nearby sandstone deposits that are transported to city factories to be heated into glass for the manufacture of glass products.

3704 Oil Workers 1903–m04m *Central (B)*. During the 1904 season, team moved to Peoria (IL) June 1, but then returned to Marion July 31. After oil fields were discovered in the state in 1885, Standard Oil built an oil refinery in Whiting (IN). By 1895 a refinery was built in Marion. Marion is the "Queen City of the Gas Belt" because natural gas and oil deposits were discovered here in the 1880s.

3705 Boosters 1909, 1911x *Northern State League of Indiana (D)*. Circuit and team disbanded July 29, 1911, with the pennant going to Marion. "Boosters" was a nickname used in this era for a team in the pennant chase or for a new team welcomed by the fans. This team, though welcomed, skidded to a 38–67 record and a fifth-place finish (out of six). At season's start in 1911, the team had no nickname and no booster club, but when the team leapt into first place in May, a booster club was formed, cheering the players all the way to their first-place pennant finish with a splendid 46–24 record. League president C.A. Clunk awarded the 1911 pennant to Marion when the league disbanded July 29.

Marion, North Carolina

Note: Not to be confused with Marion, South Carolina.

3706 Marauders 1948–52 *Western Carolina (D)*; 1953–54 *Tar Heel (D)*. Blackbeard the Pirate (Edward Teach) led his buccaneers abroad *Queen Anne's Revenge*, raiding the Carolina coast from 1690 to 1718 when he was killed in a battle against a colonial militia. Pirates, buccaneers, seahawks and privateers marauded the Carolinas coastlines in the seventeenth and eighteenth centuries.

Marion, Ohio

3707 Marion Baseball Club 1901 *Western Assn. (ind.)*. Team had no nickname.

3708 Moguls m1906–07 *Ohio–Pennsylvania (C)*. Team began season in Zanesville and then moved to Marion August 28. John D. Rockefeller started the Standard Oil Company in Cleveland in 1870. B.F. Goodrich started his automobile tire company in Akron in 1891.

These men, as well as Ohio's railroad owners and the Ohio rubber manufacturer, Charles Goodyear, were known as "moguls." "Mogul," whose modern meaning is "rich and powerful," came from the Persian-Arabic word, i.e., "mogul" for a Mongolian warrior.

3709 Swamp Foxes 1907 *Ohio–Pennsylvania (C)*. The midwestern red fox hunts along the swampy shores of the Scioto River.

3710 Diggers 1908–12m *Ohio State (D 1908–10 & 1912, C 1912)* The team moved to Ironton (OH) in mid-season July 15; 1944 *Ohio State (D)*. Iron ore (hematite) and coal mines send raw material to city factories where they are processed and shipped out. Swamps outside the city along the shores of the nearby Olentangy and Little Scioto rivers have peat mosses that are dug out for fertilizer and fuel. To excavate all the iron ore, coal and peat, the first steam shovel in the U.S. was used here in 1874. Soon, Marion became known as the "Shovel City of the World." With manager Charles O'Day at the helm 1908–09, newspapers called the players "O'Day's Diggers." O'Day left the team after the 1909 season but the name was retained. The team was a farm club of Cleveland AL.

3711 Marion Baseball Club 1915x *Buckeye (D)*. Team disbanded June 11. Team had no nickname.

3712 Presidents m1937 *Ohio State (D)*. Team began season in Sandusky (OH) and moved to Marion June 22. Warren G. Harding, the 29th president of the U.S., was born and raised and is buried here. He became editor of the town newspapers, the *Marion Star*, before entering politics. The story of his boyhood in the city is now recounted in a museum in downtown Marion. Harding was born in nearby Blooming Grove (OH), about 40 miles northwest of Marion.

3713 Cardinals 1945–47 *Ohio State (D)*. Team was a farm club of the St. Louis Cardinals.

3714 Cubs 1948 *Ohio State (D)*. Team was a farm club of the Chicago Cubs.

3715 Red Sox 1949–51 *Ohio State (D)*. Team was a farm club of the Boston Red Sox.

Marion, Virginia

3716 Athletics m1955 *Appalachian (D)*. Team began season in Welch (WV) and moved to Marion July 14. Team was a farm club of the Kansas City Athletics.

3717 Mets 1965–76 *Appalachian (R)*. Team was a farm club of the New York Mets.

Marlin, Texas

3718 Marlins 1916–17x *Central Texas (D)*. Team and league disbanded June 6 due to U.S. entry into World War I. Tag was a Phillies-style moniker. The only body of water anywhere near the city is the Brazos River. The Marlin nickname is strictly a play on words. Team apparently had no marlin fish mascot. The marlin is an ocean fish found in the Gulf of Mexico and the Pacific Ocean. With manager Bob Tartleton at the helm in 1916, newspapers called the players "Tartleton's Marlins." Bob Murray took over later in the season and the name became "Murray's Marlins." Mr. Sinclair took over in 1917 and the name became "Sinclair's Marlins."

3719 Bathers 1923–24 *Texas Assn. (D)*. Marlin is the "Southwest's Greatest Health Resort." Hot Artesian wells (a water well formed by drilling through rock) were discovered during a search for oil in 1892. The hot mineral waters spurred the construction of spas and health resorts to attract tourists to enjoy the curative miracle waters.

Marquette, Wisconsin

3720 Marquette Base Ball Club 1891–92 *Upper Peninsula (ind.)*. Team had no nickname.

3721 Kittens 1892x *Michigan–Wisconsin (ind.)*. Team had mostly young players and rookies. "Kittens," like colts, babes and chicks, was one of a dozen nineteenth century monikers describing young players.

Marshall, Minnesota

3722 Mallards 1994 *North Central (ind.)*. The mallard is a wild duck with green feathers about the head and neck. It is indigenous to the many lakes of Minnesota.

Marshall, Texas

3723 Athletics 1912 *South Central (D)*. In the era 1900–20, minor league teams sometimes chose alliterative nicknames of successful and popular big league teams. The Philadelphia Athletics were winning four AL pennants in five years at this time, i.e., 1910, 1911, 1913 and 1914.

3724 Indians 1923–26 *East Texas (D)*; 1927x *Lone Star (D)*. Team disbanded May 22. Texas was once home to 27 Indian tribes, the most famous of which are the Apache and the Comanche. The earliest tribe here were the Caddo. Today, only the Shawnee and Alabama (relocated to Texas in 1910) reside in the state.

3725 Snappers 1926 *East Texas (D)*. Team was named after manager "Red" Snapp. The team had no snapping turtle or snapper fish mascots. Although snapping turtles are found in Texas, the snapper is an ocean fish.

3726 Orphans 1936 *East Texas (C)*. Low attendance at home forced the losing team (59–90 and seventh of eight) onto extended road trips. In the era 1895–1945, such teams were called "Orphans" and "Wanderers." Unlike most such franchises, the team managed to avoid moving to another city.

3727 Tigers 1936–40 *East Texas (C)*; m1941 *Cotton States (C)*. Team began season in Clarksdale (MS) and then moved to Marshall July 10; 1948 *Lone Star (C)*. With manager Tex Nugent at the helm in July 1936, the team switched names, from "Orphans" to "Tex's Tigers." Players wore striped stirrups. The 1938 team "played like Tigers" en route to making the league playoffs this year. The name was retained through 1940. The teams were not farm clubs of the Detroit Tigers.

3728 Comets 1947 *Lone Star (C)*. Playing in the Lone Star League, the team chose the name of "Comets." Getting off to a slow start under manager Jerry Feille, management replaced him with Paul Kardow. With the team winning steadily, "Kardow's Comets" got into a heated four-team pennant race and qualified for the league playoffs.

3729 Rockets 1948 *Lone Star (C)*. After World War II, the U.S. Army established the nearby McAlester Ammunitions and Rocket Depot. Captured German V-2 rockets were tested here. Marshall is known as the "Industrial Rocket Center." Moniker was a spin-off from "Comets." Known as "Tigers" at season's start, the name switched when manager Harry Davis, i.e., "Harry Davis' Tigers," was replaced by Red Jones, prompting the name switch to "Red Jones' Rockets." Team was not a farm club of the Detroit Tigers.

3730 Browns 1949–50 *East Texas (C)*. Team was a farm club of the St. Louis Browns.

Marshalltown, Iowa

3731 Grays 1904–05 *Iowa State (D)*. Players wore gray uniforms.

3732 Brownies 1906 *Iowa State (D)*. Team's manager was Rollo Brown. Players wore brown hose. Team had a loose affiliation with the St. Louis Browns.

3733 Snappers 1907 *Iowa State (D)*. Team's field manager was A.L. "Snapper" Kennedy.

3734 Ansons 1914–17 *Central Assn. (D)*; 1922–28 *Mississippi Valley (D)*. The nineteenth century baseball star, Cap Anson, was born in Marshalltown in 1853 and played for the semi-professional Marshalltown club here in 1870 before joining the Philadelphia Athletics in 1871 and then the Chicago White Stockings in 1876. With manager Frank Richardson at the helm 1914–15, newspapers called the players "Richardson's Ansons."

Martinsburg, West Virginia

3735 Champs 1915 *Blue Ridge (D)*; 1923–25 *Blue Ridge (D)*. When a team got off to a good start, local newspapers and fans sometimes started calling the players "Champions" and "Champs." The phrase of the day was, "They're playing like champs!" The team played well most of the season, but faltered in the stretch to finish second, eight games out, but with a nevertheless credible 44–30 record. With manager W.J. "Country" Morris at the helm, newspapers called the pennant-contending players "Country's Champs." Unlike the 1915 team, this 1923–25 franchise won three straight Blue Ridge League pennants in 1922, 1923 and 1924.

3736 Blue Sox 1916–17 *Blue Ridge (D)*; 1922–29 *Blue Ridge (D)*. Players on both teams wore blue stirrups, which were a color spin-off from the red stirrups worn by the Cincinnati Reds, with whom these Martinsburg teams had a loose affiliation.

3737 Mountaineers 1918x *Blue Ridge (D)*; 1920–21 *Blue Ridge (D)*. Team and league disbanded June 16 due to U.S. entry into World War I. Located in the Allegheny Mountains, West Virginia is known as the "Mountain State." City is located in the Blue Ridge Mountains of the Allegheny Range. With W.J. "Country" Morris at the managerial helm in 1918, the team was known as "Morris' Mountaineers." With manager William Louden at the helm 1920–21, newspapers called the players "William Louden's Mountaineers."

Martinsville, Virginia

3738 Manufacturers 1934–41 *Bi-State (D)*. Known as the "Furniture City" after its founding in 1793, the city manufactures furniture, paper, pulp and wood products. The city is also known as the "Sweatshirt Capital of the World" and manufactures clothing. The city also had ten cigar manufacturing plants here by 1882. With manager James Sanders at the helm in 1934 and 1936, newspapers called the players "James Sanders' Manufacturers."

3739 Athletics 1945–49 *Carolina (C)*. Team was a farm club of the Philadelphia Athletics.

3740 Phillies 1988–98 *Appalachian (R)*. Team was a farm club of the Philadelphia Phillies.

3741 Astros 1999–2003 *Appalachian (R)*. Team was a farm club of Houston Astros.

Marysville, California

3742 Braves 1948–49 *Far West (D)*. Team was a farm club of the Boston Braves.

3743 Peaches 1950 *Far West (D)*. Peach groves outside the city transport the peaches to city factories where they are cleaned, packed and shipped to market. With so many peach groves in the area, the city became known as the "Peach Bowl of the United States."

3744 Feather River Mud Cats 2000 *Western (ind.)*. Team went by the regional name of "Feather River Mudcats." Mudcats, also known as catfish, swim in the nearby Feather River.

3745 Feather River Fury 2000 *Western (ind.)*. Team went by the regional name of "Feather River Fury." The Carolina Mudcats baseball team threatened a copyright infringement lawsuit against the team unless management changed the nickname, which they did to the "Feather River Fury." During rainstorms the Feather River turns "furious," causing regional flooding.

Marysville, Kansas

3746 Marysville Baseball Club 1910x *Eastern Kansas (D)*. Team disbanded September 1. Team had no nickname.

Maryville, Missouri

3747 Comets 1910–11m *Missouri–Iowa–Nebraska–Kansas M.I.N.K. (D)*. When "Haley's Comet" appeared in North American skies in 1910, the moniker "Comets" was commonly used in this era to describe a team on a winning tear. Teams off to a good start in April and May or who zoomed to an eight-, nine- or 10-game winning streak were sometimes called the "Comets. "With manager Joe Wentz at the helm in 1910, newspapers called the players "Joe Wentz' Comets." The tag was used again in 1911.

Maryville-Alcoa, Tennessee

3748 Twins 1953–54m *Mountain States (D 1953, C 1954)*. Team moved to Morristown (TN) June 19. Team represented the Twin Cities of Maryville-Alcoa (TN).

Masaya, Nicaragua

3749 Ferias 2004–05–07–08 *Liga Nicaraguense (W)*. The Nicaraguan League suspended play for the 2008–09 season because of financial problems. The league reorganized and resumed operations in 2009–10; 2009–10 to date *Liga Nicaraguense (W)*. The hills, swamps, lakes, rivers and jungles of Nicaragua are home to many exotic creatures, i.e., jaguars, cougars, eagles, falcons, hawks, snakes, piranhas, scorpions, tarantulas and lizards. The city is on the western border of Masaya Volcano National Park where many of these creatures are now protected by law. "Las Ferias" is Spanish for "wild animals."

Mason City, Iowa

3750 Clay-diggers 1915–17 *Central Assn. (D)*. After the region was settled in 1853, clay, calcium and limestone deposits were discovered nearby. By 1881, when the city was founded, the chief industry was cement and brick manufacturing. Cement is a mixture of calcium, clay, limestone and water. Brick is kiln-baked clay. With manager Harry Bay at the helm 1915–16, newspapers called the players "Bay's Clay-diggers." Name was retained in 1917 under manager Dan O' Leary as "O'Leary's Clay-diggers." Although the city was named in honor of the religious order of Free Masons, the stone masonry of cement and brick construction here also led to the team nickname.

3751 Bats 1994x *Great Central (ind.)*. Team and league disbanded August 10, 1994. Fan poll chose a newspaper-friendly (only four letters) nickname. At this time Hollywood had released two popular *Batman* movies and several vampire movies over the past ten years that created a new interest in bats.

Maspeth, New York

3752 Long Island Athletics 1886 *Eastern (ind.)*. Team went by the regional name of "Long Island Athletics," which was the first time a professional baseball team assumed a regional name instead of a city name. In the nineteenth century, "Athletic Club" was a popular name for baseball teams.

Massillon, Ohio

3753 Massillon Base Ball Club 1898x *Ohio State (ind.)*. Team had no nickname.

3754 Farmers 1905 *Ohio–Pennsylvania (D)*. The region around Canton-Massillon produces wheat, fruit, vegetables, dairy cattle, hogs and poultry. Farm products are transported to city factories to be processed, packed and shipped out to market.

Matamoros, Tamaulipas, Mexico

3755 Perforadores 1978 *Mexican Center (A)*. The Tamaulipas Pneumatic Drill Company owned the team. Los Perforadores is the Spanish word for "drillers."

3756 Castros 1978 *Mexican Center (A)*. Colonel (Coronel in Spanish) Cesareo Castro was a hero of the Battle of Matamoros in 1913 during the Mexican Revolution.

Matanzas, Matanzas, Cuba

3757 Club de Matanzas 1901–02 *Cuban (W)*; 1908–09 *Cuban (W)*; 1918–19 *Cuban (W)*; 1924–25 *Cuban (W)*; 1946–47 *Federal (W)*; 1967–68–73–74 *Cuban National (S)*. These teams had no nickname.

3758 Henenquereros 1967–68–91–92 *Cuban National (S)*. The tough fibers of the henenquera plant — which was brought to Cuba from Europe by the Spaniards — are used to make rope and its pigment is used to make tattoo and hair dye. Name in English is the henna plant. Henenquerors in English is "henna plant growers."

3759 Citricultores 1974–75–91–92 *Cuban National (S)*. Citrus fruits, i.e., oranges, grapefruit, lemons and limes, are grown in plantations and shipped to city factories for cleaning and packing. Citricultores is Spanish for "citrus fruit growers."

3760 Crocodilos 1992–93 to date *Cuban National (S)*. Many people believe crocodiles are found in Africa and Asia while alligators are found in the Americas. Actually, crocodiles swim in tropical waters of Cuba and Latin America.

Mattoon, Illinois

3761 Broom Corn-raisers m1899 *Indiana–Illinois (ind.)*. Broom corn is a type of corn called sorghum with stalks so fibrous they are used to manufacture brooms and brushes. Mattoon is known as the "Center of Agriculture."

3762 Giants 1907–08x *Eastern Illinois (D)*. Team disbanded July 30. In the era 1871–1910, teams that won pennants or at least contended for a flag were sometimes called Giants because they "played like Giants" even if their players were not big, strapping fellows. This Mattoon team had an excellent 74–44 record en route to a first-place finish in 1907.

3763 Comers 1907–08x *Eastern Illinois (D)*. Team disbanded July 30, 1908. "Comers" was an alternate to Giants in describing a pennant-contending or pennant-winning team. The name derives from the excited fan exclamation "Come on!" Newspapers called manager Charles O'Day's 1907 pennant-winning team "Charley's Comers." Mr. Russell started 1908 as the manager making the name "Russell's

Comers." Then, George Kizer took over in mid-season 1908, changing the name to "George's Giants." An athlete who excelled was known as a "comer," i.e., "That young Ty Cobb is a real comer!" A team making its move in the pennant race was said to be "coming on!" The name also derives from Mattoon's city nickname, i.e., "The Center of Commerce."

3764 Indians 1947–48 *Illinois State (D)*; 1949–52 *Missouri–Ohio Valley (M.O.V.D)*. Strife between settlers and Kaskaskia, Sauk and Fox Indians led to the 1831–32 Blackhawk War that was won by the settlers. By 1833 the Kaskaskias, Saux, Fox, Chippewa, Potawatomi, and Ottawa had left Illinois. With manager Melvin Ivy at the helm, newspapers called the players "Ivy's Indians." The team had a loose affiliation with the AL Cleveland Indians in 1947 before becoming a formal Cleveland AL farm club in 1948. In 1952, the team became a formal farm club of the Cincinnati Reds while retaining the Indians moniker.

3765 Phillies 1953–55 *M.O.V. (D)*; 1956 *Midwest (D)*. These teams were farm clubs of the Philadelphia Phillies.

3766 Athletics 1957 *Midwest (D)*. Team was a farm club of the Kansas City Athletics.

Mattoon-Charleston, Illinois

3767 Hyphens 1906 *Kentucky–Illinois–Tennessee (KITTY) (D)*. "Hyphens" was a rather lame naming gimmick of this era for a team representing two cities. "Hyphens" was used by four teams: Bay City-Saginaw, Johnstown-Amsterdam-Gloversville, Springfield-Charleston and Mattoon Charleston. Not counting Minnesota AL farm teams, the far more popular "Twins" has been used as an independent moniker by more than thirty professional baseball teams.

3768 Canaries 1906 *Kentucky–Illinois–Tennessee (KITTY) (D)*. Players wore canary yellow hose. Bob Berryhill opened the season as manager of "Berryhill's Canaries." Jack McCarthy took over in mid-season to lead "McCarthy's Canaries."

Maud, Oklahoma

3769 Chiefs m1929 *Western Assn. (C)*. Team began season as the Muskogee (OK) Chiefs and transferred to Maud August 22 where the nickname was retained. The state seal of Oklahoma depicts the "Five Civilized Tribes"—Chickasaw, Choctaw, Seminole, Creek and Cherokee.

Mayaguez, Puerto Rico

3770 Indios 1941–42 to date *Liga Puertoriquena (W)*. The team and the Puerto Rican League operated as a semi-professional circuit from 1938–39 through 1940–41. The Arawak Indians called themselves the Boriquen in the fifteenth century when Christopher Columbus arrived in Puerto Rico in 1493. For the next 300 years the Arawaks suffered terribly from war, European diseases, and forced labor, imposed on them by the Spaniards.

Mayfield, Kentucky

3771 Pants-makers 1922–24x *Kentucky–Illinois–Tennessee (KITTY) (D)*. Team disbanded August 26. Mayfield Clothiers owned the team. In the era 1880–1920, the city had numerous wool mills that manufactured garments, i.e., men's pants.

3772 Cardinals 1936 *Kentucky–Illinois–Tennessee (KITTY) (D)*. Team was a farm club of the St. Louis Cardinals.

3773 Clothiers 1936–38 *(KITTY) (D)*; 1946–55 *KITTY (D)*. Moniker was a spin-off of the 1924 name, although the team was no longer sponsored by Mayfield Clothiers. The team was a 1936 farm of the Brooklyn Dodgers, and then switched to the St. Louis Browns 1937–41.

3774 Browns 1939–41 *(KITTY) (D).* Team was a farm club of the St. Louis Browns.

Mayodan, North Carolina

3775 Senators 1934 *Bi-State (D);* 1937 *Bi-State (D).* Team had a loose affiliation with Washington AL in 1934 but was not a formal farm club. In the era 1925–35 some minor league teams formed a loose affiliation with major league "parent clubs" prior to becoming official farm clubs.

3776 Mills 1934 *Bi-State (D).* City was home to the Mayo Mills Textile Company and the Washington Mills Textile Company.

3777 Orphans 1936 *Bi-State (D).* Team suffered through a hideous 35–83 season, dropping into last place, forcing extended road trips. Teams in this era, forced to go onto extended road trips because of fans being driven away by chronic losing, were sometimes branded as "orphans" because the home fans abandoned them.

3778 Millers 1938–41 *Bi-State (D).* Team disbanded July 18 because of U.S. entry into World War II. Personified moniker was a spin-off from "Mills."

Maysville, Kentucky

3779 Maysville Base Ball Club 1894x *Tri-State (ind.).* Team and league disbanded in mid-season (date unknown); 1913–14x *Ohio State (D).* Team disbanded July 22. These teams had no nickname.

3780 Rivermen m1910–12 *Blue Grass (D).* Team began the season in Shelbyville (KY) and moved to Maysville August 24. When the city was founded in 1787, it was known as Limestone (KY) because transport boats would carry limestone from nearby limestone quarries to factories in Louisville. By the 1850s, limestone started to be transported by train.

3781 Angels 1915 *Ohio State (D).* Team began season as the Chillicothe (OH) "Babes," moved to Huntington July 13 and then moved to Maysville July 19. The Chillicothe "Babes" had numerous cherubic-faced young players who were still with the team in Maysville, prompting Maysville newspaper reporters to call the players of the new team in town the "Angels." Cherubs are baby-faced, winged angels.

3782 Burley Cubs 1916x *Ohio State (D).* Team and league disbanded July 19. Burley tobacco is a thin-leaf tobacco, grown mostly in Kentucky, that is used for cigarettes. The 1916 team had numerous young players, i.e., "cubs." This moniker is an early example of a white team adding a modifying adjective to distinguish its identity from a big league team, i.e., the Chicago Cubs.

3783 Cardinals 1922–23 *Blue Grass (D).* The Kentucky Cardinal is the state bird of Kentucky. It is a finch with dark-red feathers, somewhat different from other lighter-hued cardinals of North America. The team was not a farm club of the St. Louis Cardinals.

Mazatlan, Sinoloa, Mexico

3784 Venados 1945–46–57–58 *Liga de la Costa Pacifica Mexicana (W);* 1958–59–69–70 *Liga de Sinora–Sinoloa (W);* 1970–71 to date *Liga Pacifica Mexicana.* Circuit was known as the Sinoloa–Sonora League 1958–59–1969–70 before it was renamed the Mexican Pacific League for the 1970–71 season; 1976 *Liga Pacifica Mexicana (A).* The club owners of the Mexican Pacific League teams played a summer schedule in 1976, but attendance was too low to justify continued summer play in 1977. The North American deer is found in Alaska,

Canada, the U.S. and Mexico. "El Venado" is the Spanish word for deer. A famous Aztec dance is known as "Dance of the Deer."

McAlester, Oklahoma

3785 Miners 1907x *Oklahoma–Arkansas–Kansas (O.A.K.) (D).* Team disbanded June 2; 1908x *Oklahoma–Kansas (D).* Team disbanded July 5; 1912 *Oklahoma State (D);* 1914–17 *Western Assn. (D);* 1922 *Western Assn. (C);* m1924m *Oklahoma State (D).* Team began season in Guthrie (OK) before moving to McAlester May 24. Team moved to Wewoka (OK) in June 8; 1926x *Western Assn. (C).* Team disbanded July 20. Region was settled around 1870 because of large coal deposits. The city got its name from the McAlester Coal and Mining Company. There were also mines that produced selenite, a crystalized form of gypsum.

3786 Diggers 1923x *Western Assn. (C).* Team disbanded July 19. With the Joplin Miners already using the moniker, McAlester newspapers switched to "Diggers."

3787 Rockets 1947–56 *Sooner State (D).* With manager Bill Nobroak (pronounced No-brock) at the helm, newspapers called the players "Nobroak's Rockets." In 1948, under new manager Vern Hoscheit," the team "rocketed" to first place and a playoff berth. In 1950–51–52–53 the team "rocketed" to four straight pennants. During World War II in 1943, the U.S. Army built an ammunition depot outside the city including an arsenal of rockets and rocket launchers. After the war, captured V-2 rockets were maintained here.

McAllen, Hidalgo, Texas

3788 Palms 1931x *Rio Grande (D).* Team and league disbanded July 30 because of the Great Depression; 1949–50 *Rio Grande Valley (D 1949, C 1950).* The city is a semi-tropical river port along the Rio Grande with palm trees, fruit groves and vegetable farms. The city has fruit and vegetable canneries and is a shipping center for canned foods. McAllen is known as the "City of Palms."

3789 Packers 1938 *Texas Valley (D).* Farms in the region transport fruit and vegetables to city factories for canning, packing and shipping to market. Cotton and sugar also are processed and packed in city factories.

3790 Giants 1949–50 *Rio Grande Valley (D 1949, C 1950).* Newspaper editors wanted a forceful name and used letters from the city name of "McAllen" and the county name of "Hidalgo" and the state name of "Texas" to come up with "Giants." The team was not a farm club of New York Giants. McAllen is the largest city, i.e., "the giant" of Hidalgo County.

3791 Dusters 1977 *Lone Star (A).* Texas is known as the "Blizzard State" because of its dust and windstorms. In the 1930s, the region was hit hard by the 1936–37 drought, known as the "Dust Bowl." Since the 1920s, crop-dusting pilots have flown over the fruit and vegetable farms surrounding the city.

McCook, Nebraska

3792 Generals 1928–32 *Nebraska State (D).* City was named after Nebraskan Alexander McCook, who was a brigadier general for the Union Army in the Civil War. After participating in many battles, he was a U.S. Army general in the West during the Indian Wars of 1870–90. With manager Elmer "Doc" Bennett at the helm in 1928–31 newspapers called the players "Elmer Bennett's Generals." The name used again in 1932.

3793 Braves 1956–59 *Nebraska State (D).* Team was a farm club of the Milwaukee Braves.

McKeesport, Pennsylvania

3794 McKeesport Base Ball Club 1890 *Tri-State (ind.)*. Team had no nickname.

3795 Colts 1905 *Ohio–Pennsylvania (C)*. In the era 1870–1917, young players were often known as "colts." Ed Crawford managed "Crawford's Colts." He was replaced by Frank Metz in mid-season who then led "Metz' Colts."

3796 Tubers 1907 *Pennsylvania–Ohio–Michigan (P.O.M.) (D)*; 1908–10 *Ohio–Pennsylvania (C)*; 1912x *Ohio–Pennsylvania (D)*. Team disbanded July 17; 1934, 1936–37 *Pennsylvania (D)*. Team disbanded June 10; 1938 *Pennsylvania (D)*. Circuit was known as the Pennsylvania State Association. Bethlehem Iron (1862) and Bessemer Steel (1867) established factories throughout the state, including McKeesport. Iron and steel tubes and pipes were manufactured in these factories for machines, motors, oil rigs and electrical wiring. A "tuber" is a steel and iron worker who smelts metals to produce tubes and pipes. By 1900, McKeesport was known as the "Tube City." The city was home to the National Tube Company.

3797 Braves 1935 *Pennsylvania (D)*; 1940 *Pennsylvania (D)*. Circuit was known as the Pennsylvania State Association. Teams were farm clubs of the Boston Bees (nee Braves). Actually, several Boston Bees' (nee Braves) farm teams went by the old nickname of "Braves," which had been abandoned by the big league club after the 1935 season. Boston fans never liked "Bees," prompting Boston management to return to "Braves" in 1941. Team was aka the **Little Braves**.

3798 Pirates 1939 *Pennsylvania (D)*. Team was a farm club of the Pittsburgh Pirates. The team was aka the **Little Pirates**—an example of a 1930s fad—the diminutive nickname—for minor league farm clubs, i.e., "Little Giants, Little Athletics, Little Braves" and "Little Pirates," that soon was rejected by fans and newspapers.

McKinney, Texas

3799 McKinney Baseball Club 1912x *Texas–Oklahoma (D)*. Team disbanded June 7. Team had no nickname.

McLeansboro, Illinois

3800 Merchants 1910t *Southern Illinois (D)*. Team joined the KITTY League on July 24 after the Southern Illinois League disbanded July 11. The city was a vacation center for tourists, visiting the local fish and wildlife areas nearby. The tourists patronized local merchants for food, fishing and hunting gear and hotel rooms.

3801 Billikens t1910 *Kentucky–Illinois–Tennessee KITTY (D)*. Team, starting the season in the Southern Illinois League, joined the KITTY July 24 after the SIL disbanded July 11. With field manager Ollie Gfroerer at the helm, local newspapers called the players "Ollie's Billikens." Name referred to a popular lucky charm doll of the era, i.e., the "Billiken," which was manufactured by the Holman Toy Company.

3802 Miners 1911m *Kentucky–Illinois–Tennessee KITTY (D)*. Team moved to Henderson (KY) June 20. The Cosgrove-Meehan Coal Company opened the Stiritz Mine here in 1900. On December 20, 1927, a natural gas explosion killed seven miners.

McPherson, Kansas

3803 Merry Macks 1908 *Central Kansas (D)*; 1909–11 *Kansas State (D)*. Moniker was used in newspapers, i.e., "Merry Macks rally to defeat Minnies, 4–3." In headlines the result was "Macks edge Minnies, 4–3." Teams in cities or led by managers with Scottish "Mc" or Irish "Mac" prefixes in their names sometimes were known as

"Macks" or "Merry Macks." Merry Mack is a medieval term for "merry-maker," and since baseball players of this era certainly knew how to party, the moniker was quite appropriate.

Meadville, Pennsylvania

3804 Meadville Base Ball Club 1890–91 *New York–Pennsylvania (ind.)*; 1898 *Iron & Oil (ind.)*. These teams had no nickname.

Medford, Oregon

3805 Dodgers 1948 *Far West (D)*; 1971 *Northwest (A)*. The 1948 team was a farm club of the Brooklyn Dodgers. The 1971 team was a farm club of the Los Angeles Dodgers and went by the city name of "Medford Dodgers" after being known by the regional name of "Rogue Valley Dodgers" in 1969–70.

3806 Nuggets 1949 *Far West (D)*. In 1853, gold was discovered in the nearby Rogue River Valley. California prospectors flooded the region only to be confronted by the Rogue River Indians, whom they defeated after several weeks of savage fighting.

3807 Rogues 1950–51 *Far West (D)*. Medford is located near to the Rogue River.

3808 Giants 1967–68 *Northwest (A)*. Team was a farm club of the San Francisco Giants.

3809 Rogue Valley Dodgers 1969–70 *Northwest (A)*. Team went by the regional name of Rogue Valley Dodgers. Team was a farm club of the Los Angeles Dodgers.

3810 Athletics 1979–87 *Northwest (A)*. Team went by the city name of "Medford Athletics," and then was renamed as the regional "South Oregon Athletics" in 1988. The team was a farm club of the Oakland Athletics.

3811 South Oregon Athletics 1988–94 *Northwest (A)*. Team went by the regional name of Southern Oregon Athletics, starting in 1988. The team was a farm club of the Oakland Athletics.

3812 South Oregon Timberjacks 1995–99 Team went by the regional name of "Southern Oregon Timberjacks." The first steam-driven lumber mill was built in 1850 in Oregon. Lumber from Oregon's twelve national forests was transported on the Rogue River and later on six highways leading into Medford.

Medicine Hat, Alberta, Canada

3813 Hatters 1907 *Western Canada (C)*; 1913–14 *Western Canada (D)*. Moniker was used in newspaper headlines, i.e., "Hatters edge Bronchos, 4–3."

3814 Mad Hatters 1909–10m *Western Canada (D)*. Team moved to Saskatoon (SK) July 23. Moniker was a spin-off from "Hatters." In Lewis Carroll's fantasy story *Alice in Wonder Land*, the "Mad Hatter" was a demented rabbit in a top hat who hosted a bizarre tea party for Alice. Since baseball players turn into "mad hatters" when they swig a little bit too much liquor, the moniker was appropriate. With manager William Hamilton at the helm, newspapers called the players "Hamilton's Hatters."

3815 Athletics 1977 *Pioneer (R)*. Team was a farm club of the Oakland Athletics.

3816 Blue Jays 1978–2002. Team was a farm club of the Toronto Blue Jays.

Melbourne, Victoria, Australia

3817 Monarchs 1989–90–90–91 *Australian (W)*. Since Australia is part of the British Commonwealth, a fan poll chose the alliterative name of "Monarchs" in honor of Queen Elizabeth II of England.

3818 Bushrangers 1989–90–92–93 *Australia (W)*. Tasmanian settlers, who founded the city in 1835, and prospectors of the 1850 Gold Strike, became known as "Bush Rangers" for their ability to traverse forest and the nearby Australian Alps.

3819 Aces 2010–11 to date *Australian (W)*. The professional Australian Baseball League was revived after disbanding following the 1998–99 season. This professional team is named after the semi-professional Melbourne "Aces."

Melbourne, Brevard, Florida

3820 Twins 1972 *Florida East Coast (R)*. Team was a farm club of the Minnesota Twins.

3821 Brevard County Manatees 1994–96 *Florida State (A)*. Team went by the county name of "Brevard County Manatees." The manatee is a sea mammal with paddle-like flippers found in the waters of the Caribbean and the Gulf of Mexico.

3822 Marlins 1994–97 *Gulf Coast (R)*. Team was a farm club of the Florida Marlins.

3823 Expos 2002–04 *Gulf Coast (R)*. Team was a farm club of the Montreal Expos.

3824 Nationals 2005 to date *Gulf Coast (R)*. Team is a farm club of the Washington Nationals.

Memphis, Tennessee

3825 Reds 1877 *League Alliance (ind.)*. This league was a farm system to the National League; 1887–89 *Southern (ind.)*. Players wore red hose. Memphis newspapers shortened the original **Red Stockings** to "Reds."

3826 Browns m1885 *Southern (ind.)*; 1885 *Southern (ind.)*. Players wore brown hose.

3827 Grays 1886 *Southern (ind.)*. Players wore gray uniforms and gray hose.

3828 Eclipse 1886 *Southern Colored (ind.)*. The Southern League of Colored Baseballists was a professional circuit that preceded the National Colored League of 1887. "Eclipse" was a famous racehorse of eighteenth century England. By 1850, U.S. racehorses in Kentucky and Tennessee were sometimes called "Eclipse." The name came to represent athletic skill. The name was a pick-up from the American Association Louisville Eclipse.

3829 Eurekas 1886 *Southern Colored (ind.)*. The Southern League of Colored Baseballists was a professional circuit that preceded the National Colored League of 1887. After gold was discovered in California in 1848, thousands of people streamed west to hunt for gold, silver, natural gas and oil. From the ancient Greek "heureka,"—"I have found it!"—this exclamation was used by prospectors when they discovered gold, silver, oil and natural gas. Moniker spread to baseball when players would yell "Eureka" after winning a game or making a great play in the field or hitting a home run. By 1900 the moniker had become passé.

3830 Giants 1892–94 *Southern (ind.)*. Local fans and newspapers sarcastically called the 1892 last-place club (with a 46–76 record) the "Giants." In the nineteenth century, "Giants" was applied to a winning and/or pennant-clinching team as a term of admiration, or a sarcastic brand against a losing team. With manager Frank Graves at the helm 1892–94, newspapers called the players the alliterative "Graves' Giants." But by 1894, the Giants moniker became a term of endearment when the team posted a 42–23 record, missing first place and the pennant by only a half-game.

3831 Fever Germs 1892–94 *Southern (ind.)*. The worst Yellow Fever epidemic in any U.S. city hit Memphis in 1878. More than 19,000 people contracted the infection, with 5,000 fatalities. Previous outbreaks occurred in 1855 and 1867. The Aedes mosquito in Southern swamps transmits the Yellow Fever virus to humans, which causes high fever and jaundice, hence the name. A smaller Yellow Fever outbreak occurred in Memphis in 1892–93. By draining swamps in the 1890s, health authorities reduced the extent of the epidemic. Manager Frank Graves' players were sometimes called "Frank Graves' Fever Germs."

3832 Lambs 1895x *Southern (ind.)*. Team disbanded July 5. With manager Charles Levi at the helm in 1895, newspapers called the 1895 team, which had young players, "Levi's Lambs." The moniker "Lamb" was a nineteenth-century slang to describe a rookie or a young player.

3833 Egyptians 1901–08 *Southern Assn. (ind. 1901, A 1902–08)*. Settled in 1819 and a city by 1849, Memphis was named after its counterpart in Egypt. Ancient Memphis was the capital of the Old Kingdom of Egypt as far back as 3100 B.C.

3834 Turtles 1909–11 *Southern Assn. (A)*. The Red Elm ballpark in Memphis in 1909 was one of the first baseball fields to install both grass and sand in the infield area, creating a "turtle shell" design when seen from above. Today the turtle-shell infield is used almost everywhere except Japan.

3835 Chickasaws 1912–38 *Southern Assn. (A 1912–35, A1 1936–38)*. Although credited to the Chickasaw Indians, the nickname comes directly from the Chickasaw Military Guard, which was a famous military drill team of the era 1870–1940. The drill team marched up and down the field before games in Memphis.

3836 Claybrook Tigers 1936 *Independent Negro team*. Team owner John Claybrook, a black businessmen, invested $4,000 signing players and building Claybrook Stadium. Players wore striped hose.

3837 Chicks 1939–60 *Southern Assn. (A1 1939–45, AA 1946–60)*; 1978–97 *Southern (AA)*. Name was a shorter tag for newspapers.

3838 Blues 1968–73 *Texas (AA)* In 1971 the Southern and Texas leagues played a common schedule under the banner of the Dixie Association. By 1972 the leagues went back to separate schedules; 1974–76 *International (AAA)*. Players wore blue-trim uniforms and blue stirrups. Moniker was inspired by the "Dixie Blues" music popular in Tennessee since 1900.

3839 Redbirds 1998 to date *Pacific Coast (AAA)*. Team was a farm club of the St. Louis Cardinals. "Redbirds," an alternate, unofficial moniker used in St. Louis, became the official nickname of the Memphis team.

Menominee, Michigan

3840 Menominee Base Ball Club 1892 *Michigan–Wisconsin (ind.)*. Team had no nickname.

Merced, California

3841 Fig Growers m1910x *California State (D)*. Team began season in Oakland (CA) and moved to Merced June 7. Team and league disbanded June 24. Figs grown in nearby farms are transported to the city where they are cleaned, packed and shipped to market.

3842 Bears 1941 *California (C)*. When the U.S. defeated Mexico in 1849 in the Mexican-American War, American settlers established the Republic of California with the golden bear as its flag symbol. A regional animal, the golden bear is the state animal of California.

Merida, Yucatan, Mexico

3843 Leones de Yucatan 1954–58 *Mexican (AA)*; 1964–74 *Mexican (AA 1964–66, AAA 1967–74)*; 1979 to date *Mexican (AAA)*. Team went by the state name of Yucatan. Mountain lions (aka cougars, panthers and pumas) inhabit the Yucatan Peninsula.

Meriden, Connecticut

3844 Meriden Base Ball Club 1884 *Connecticut (ind.)*; 1885 *Southern New England (ind.)*; 1886x *Eastern (ind.)*. Team disbanded July 13; 1888 *Connecticut State (ind.)*; 1891 *Connecticut State (ind.)*. These teams had no nickname.

3845 Bulldogs 1897–98 *Connecticut State (ind.)*. City is near Yale University (in New Haven), whose sports team mascot is the bulldog. Occasionally throughout baseball history, a professional baseball team in or near a college town will use the college sports team's nickname. Examples include Buckeyes, Hawkeyes, Hoosiers, Wolverines, and Bulldogs.

3846 Silverites 1899–1905 *Connecticut State (D)*. First settled in 1661, by the time it became founded as a city in 1867, Meriden had numerous silver shops where silver jewelry and cutlery was manufactured. The city became known in the nineteenth century as the "Silver City of the World" because of its silver jewelry and silverware. The city was home to the International Silver Company and other silverware manufacturers.

3847 Meriden Base Ball Club 1908 *Connecticut State (B)*. Team had no nickname.

3848 Doublins m1910x *Connecticut Assn. (D)*. Team began the season in Norwich (CT) and then moved to Meriden July 15. Team disbanded July 24. The "Silver City" of Meriden also manufactured silver coins, which became known as silver doubloons and later the anglicized silver doublins. Gold doubloons were the coins used by the upper classes in Spain and in Spanish America from the fifteenth century to nearly the twentieth century. Irish immigrants settled in Connecticut between 1850 and 1910. The capital of Ireland, Dublin, is sometimes spelled Doublin.

Meridian, Mississippi

3849 White Ribboners 1905–08 *Cotton States (D)*. White ribbon and blue ribbon trout, aka "bull trout," swim in nearby Lake Okatibbee and the Buckatoona and Chunky rivers.

3850 Ribboners 1906 *Cotton States (D)*. Newspapers shortened name to "Ribboners" to use in newspaper headlines, i.e., "Ribboners edge Crabs, 4–3."

3851 White Ribbons 1910–11 *Cotton States (D)*. This second version of "White Ribboners" frustrated newspaper editors because it was insufficiently short. The white ribbon trout is a popular game fish at the nearby Lake Okatibbee, Lake Water Park and the Long Creek Reservoir.

3852 Mets 1912x *Cotton States (D)*. Team disbanded August 3; 1913 *Cotton States (D)*; 1921 *Mississippi State (D)*; 1922–23 *Cotton States (D)*; 1925–26 *Cotton States (D)*. Although the city population never exceeded 44,000, newspaper editors, exasperated by the likes of White Ribboners, Ribboners and White Ribbons, pounced on "Mets" this season to save print space. The region, city and suburbs are known as the "Meridian Metro."

3853 Metros 1927–29m *Cotton States (D)*. Team moved to Lake Charles (LA) June 17. Tag was a spin-off from "Mets." Local newspapers wanted to get away from Mets, which historically belonged to the old New York Mets teams of the 1880s.

3854 Scrappers 1937–39 *Southeastern (B)*. Baseball players in this era were known as "scrappers" because they always seemed to get involved in fist-fighting on the field and brawls outside of their favorite saloon. "Scrappy" is a complimentary term for a hard-nosed athlete who plays hard to win. The city was a Confederate military camp. When General Sherman's Union troops besieged the city in 1864, Confederate troops there became known as "Scrappers" for their fierce resistance. Sherman's troops overwhelmed the resistance and destroyed the city. Iron and steel mills manufactured structural steel, aluminum, automobile parts, weighing scales and aircraft assemblies. "Scrappers" in the mills were workers who produced and disposed of scrap metal. With manager Emmett Lipscomb at the helm, newspapers called the players "Lipscomb's Scrappers."

3855 Bears 1940 *Southeastern (B)*. Newspaper editors, tired of "Scrappers," instructed their reporters to use a name that was short and fierce. Bears used to roam nearby farm lands until the city was settled in 1831. With manager Clarence Mitchell and then Bernie DeViveiros at the helm, newspapers called the players "Clarence's Bears" and "Bernie's Bears."

3856 Eagles 1941–42 *Southeastern (B)*. With World War II looming, newspaper editors wanted a patriotic moniker. With manager Bennie Tate at the helm, newspapers called the players "Bennie Tate's Eagles." Mississippi is the "Border Eagle State" and the "Eagle State." An eagle is depicted on the Mississippi coat of arms.

3857 Peps 1946–48 *Southeastern (B)*. The Pepsi-Cola soft drink company opened a bottling plant here in 1919. Newspaper editors wanted the 1946 team's management to choose another four-letter nickname like "Mets" (used for three earlier Meridian teams), so the choice became the homonymous "Peps." With manager Papa Williams at the helm in 1946, newspapers called the players "Papa's Peps."

3858 Millers 1949–50 *Southeastern (B)*; 1952–54 *Cotton States (C)*; m1955 *Cotton States (C)*. Team began the season in Pine Bluff (AR) and moved to Meridian June 16. Farms in the region transport oat and wheat to city factories for processing, packaging and shipping. With manager Jack Maupin at the helm 1949–50, newspapers called the players "Maupin's Millers."

3859 Brakemen 1994 *Mid-South (ind.)*; 1996–97 *Big South (ind.)*. Musician, guitar player and singer Jimmy Rodgers, a Meridian native, wrote and sang the blues song "The Brakeman" in 1925. The Mississippi-Louisiana Railroad started running in 1831 with Meridian as an important stop along the line. The "brakeman" operated, inspected and repaired the brakes on nineteenth-century trains.

Merrillville, Indiana

3860 Mud Dogs 1995 *Mid-America (ind.)*. An occasional baseball team playing in the "Farm Belt" sometimes chose a tractor name, i.e., Trojans, Gumbo-busters and Mud Dogs. Farms in the Merrillville area get muddy in the spring, requiring "Mud Dogs" to plow. "Dogs" and the spelling variation "Dawgs" were a popular team nickname in the 1990s.

Mesa, Arizona

3861 Jewels 1929x *Arizona State (D)*. Team disbanded July 24. Settled by Mormons in 1878, the city soon became known as the "Gem City of the Sun Valley." Mesa is a suburb of Phoenix, which is the "Crown Jewel of Arizona."

3862 Orphans m1947 *Arizona–Texas (C)*. Team began season as Juarez (TX) Indians before moving to Mesa June 27. In the era 1890–1920 Orphans referred to a team, usually a big loser that was "abandoned by its fans." Low attendance forced the club to go on extended road trips and then, almost always, transfer to another city in midseason. With manager Manuel Fortes at the helm, newspapers called the players "Fortes' Orphans." The nickname was not official but the "Indians" moniker of the Juarez team was not used in Mesa. The Mesa club had no official nickname. This team was the last one in Organized Baseball ever to be named "Orphans."

3863 Angels 1989–96 *Arizona (R)*. Team was a farm club of the California Angels.

3864 Rockies/Cubs 1992 *Arizona (R)*. Team was a farm club of the Colorado Rockies and Chicago Cubs.

3865 Saguaros 1992–98 *Arizona Fall (W)*. The Saguaro—also known as the "Giant Cactus" (Carneigiea gigantea)—that sprouts white flowers and edible red fruit is found in the southwestern United States and northern Mexico.

3866 Rockies 1993 *Arizona (R)*; 1997–99 *Arizona (R)*. Teams were farm clubs of the Colorado Rockies. The Chicago Cubs severed its affiliation with the team after the 1992 season, leaving the Colorado Rockies as the sole parent club.

3867 Cubs 1997 to date *Arizona (R)*. Team was a farm club of Chicago Cubs.

3868 Angels 2001 to date *Arizona (R)*. Team is a farm club of the Los Angeles Angels of Anaheim.

3869 Miners 2005 *Golden (ind.)*. Mines transport copper to smelting plants in the city. Arizona leads the U.S. in copper production. Mining in Arizona also includes gravel, molybdenum, uranium, zinc and gold. Arizona is known as the "Copper State."

Mexia, Texas

3870 Gassers 1915x *Central Texas (D)*. Team and league disbanded July 24; 1916–17 *Central Texas (D)*. The Spindletop Oil and Natural Gas Fields were discovered in Texas in 1901. By 1915 the city had built natural gas rigs and a gas refinery factory. With Grady White at the helm in 1916, newspapers called the players "Grady's Gassers."

3871 Gushers 1922 *Texas–Oklahoma (D)*; 1923–26 *Texas Assn. (D)*; 1927–28 *Lone Star (D)*. By 1920, oil rigs and an oil refinery factory had been built in and around the city. Moniker was a spin-off from "Gassers."

Mexicali, Baja California, Mexico

3872 Aguilas 1948–50 *Sunset (C)*; 1951–52 *Southwest International (C)*; 1953–54 *Arizona–Texas (C)*; 1955–58 *Arizona–Mexico (C)*; 1958–59–69–70 *Sonora–Sinoloa (W)*. Circuit was the Sonora–Sinoloa League 1958–59 through 1969–70 and became the Mexican Pacific League in 1970–71; 1968–69 *Mexican Northern (A)*; 1970–71 to date *Mexican Pacific (W)*. The Mexican flag bears the famous symbol of an eagle devouring a snake perched on a cactus.

3873 Azules 2004–08 *Norte de Sonora (ind.)*. Players wore blue trim and blue stirrups.

Mexico City, Distrito Federal, Mexico

3874 Agraria 1937 *Liga Mexicana (ind.)*. The inaugural professional season of the Mexican League included eight teams playing in Mexico City. These teams represented five government departments, i.e., Agricultura, Agraria, Comintra, Petroleros and Transito as well as three Mexico City suburbs—Nexaca, Rio Blanco and Santa Rosa. This team represented the Department of Agriculture.

3875 Agricultura 1937 *Liga Mexicana (ind.)*. This was another team that represented the Department of Agriculture.

3876 Nexaca 1937 *Liga Mexicana (ind.)*. Team's home field was in Nexaca, a suburb of Mexico City.

3877 Petroleros 1937 *Liga Mexicana (ind.)*. The Mexican Department of Energy sponsored the oil industry, known as PEMEX, i.e., Petroleos Mexicanos. It was in 1937 that Mexico nationalized its oil industry, leading to the creation of PEMEX.

3878 Santa Rosa 1937 *Liga Mexicana (ind.)*. Team played its home games in Santa Rosa, a suburb of Mexico City.

3879 Transito 1937 *Liga Mexicana (ind.)*. Team represented the Department of Transportation.

3880 Rio Blanco 1937–38 *Liga Mexicana (ind.)*. Rio Blanco is a suburb of Mexico City.

3881 Comintra 1937–39 *Liga Mexicana (ind.)*. Team represented the Department of Commerce.

3882 Diablos Rojos 1940 *Liga Mexicana (ind.)*; 1955 to date *Liga Mexicana (AA 1955–66, AAA 1967 to date)*; 1955–56–57–58x *Veracruz (W)*. Team disbanded January 5, 1958. The team played a winter schedule in the Veracruz League for three seasons. Players wore red-trim uniforms and red stirrups. "Diablos Rojos" is Spanish for "Red Devils."

3883 Aztecas 1946 *Liga Nacional Mexicana (B)*. In the pre–Columbian epoch, Mexico City was known as Tenochtitlan, capital of the ancient Aztec Empire.

3884 Azules 1954 *Liga Mexicana (AA)*. Players wore blue-trim uniforms and blue stirrups. "Azul" is the Spanish word for "blue."

3885 Tigres 1955–2002 *Liga Mexicana (AA 1955–66, AAA 1967–2002)*. Team owners Don Alejo Peralta and Diaz Cevallos wanted a team to rival Latin America's most popular team of the era—the Havana "Lions." They dressed the players in striped stirrup stockings and called the club "Los Tigres." Jaguars and pumas, found in Mexico, are sometimes called "tigres" in Spanish.

3886 Metros 1982–83 *Liga Natconal de Mexico (ind.)*. The "Liga Nacional de Mexico" signed players who had not returned to the Liga Mexicana following the Mexican League Players Strike of 1980. The circuit disbanded after the 1983 season. With a population of 20 million people, Mexico City is a "great metropolis."

Miami, Arizona

3887 Miners 1928–30 *Arizona State (D)*. Nearby copper mines transport copper ore to city smelting plants.

Miami, Florida

3888 Giants 1924–26 *Independent Negro team*; 1934–36 *Independent Negro team*. Between 1890 and 1950 there were more than 20 professional black teams with "Giants" as their nickname. Southern black teams tended to simply link the city name with Giants, whereas Northern black teams adopted the style using a preceding adjective before Giants, i.e., American, Bacharach, Cuban, Leland, Lincoln, Royal, Union etc.

3889 Hustlers 1927–28 *Florida State (D)*. With manager Bill Holloway at the helm, newspapers called the players "Holloway's Hustlers." In this era, "hustler" was a complimentary term for an athlete who "hustled on the field." The negative gambling connotation would not appear until the 1970s.

3890 Ethiopian Clowns 1935–42 *Independent Negro team*. A name, horrendously and politically incorrect today, was used without embarrassment to describe these black players who were allegedly from Ethiopia and who also clowned on the field like other black teams, i.e., the baseball Harlem Globetrotters. During the 1930s the African nation of Ethiopia was in the news as its president Haile Selassie went to the League of Nations to plead for protection against its invasion by the armed forces of Benito Mussolini's Italy. Actually, these players were no more "Ethiopian" than the nineteenth-century Cuban Giants were "Cuban." Both teams attempted to diffuse the racial hostility of white fans by "internationalizing" these obviously American blacks.

3891 Wahoos 1940–41 *Florida East Coast (D)*. The wahoo tree is an elm tree found in the Southeast, a brush with purple flowers and a tropical fish of the mackerel family.

3892 Seminoles 1942 *Florida East Coast (D)*. Creek Indians migrated from Georgia to Florida in 1750 and were renamed the Seminoles. Tensions with settlers sparked a seven-year (1835–42) Seminole War. By 1870 the Seminoles were confined to three reservations.

3893 Sun Sox 1946, 1949–54x *Florida International (C 1946–48, A 1949–54)*. Team disbanded May 5. They were replaced by the Greater Miami Flamingos on May 22. Florida is the "Sunshine State." Miami is the "Sunshine Capital of the World." Players wore golden yellow stirrups over white sanitary socks. Team was not a farm club of the Boston Red Sox or the Chicago White Sox.

3894 Tourists 1947–48 *Florida International (C)*. As the first railroads reached Miami in 1896, the city became America's leading resort area for tourists and vacationers. Miami is known as the "World's Greatest Resort" and the "Sun and Fun Capital of the World."

3895 Greater Miami Flamingos m1954x *Florida International (B)*. Team started season in Miami Beach (FL) and moved to Miami May 22, replacing the Miami Sun Sox, who had disbanded May 5. Team replaced the Miami Sun Sox in mid-season. Team management chose the regional name of Greater Miami Flamingos because the team represented Miami and nearby Fort Lauderdale. The flamingo is a tropical wading bird with red and orange feathers.

3896 Marlins 1956–60 *International (AAA)*; 1962–70, 1982–87 *Florida State (A)*. The marlin is a game fish of tropical waters. It is large and has a spear-like upper jaw.

3897 Orioles 1971–81 *Florida State (A)*. Team was a farm club of the Baltimore Orioles.

3898 Amigos 1979 *Inter-American (AAA)*. With more than a million Spanish-speaking Cuban immigrants arriving in Miami after Fidel Castro took power in Cuba in 1959, management used the Spanish moniker of "Amigos." Miami is the "U.S. Gateway to Latin America."

3899 Miracle 1988–91 *Florida State (A)*. The downtown shopping area of Miami is located in Coral Gables and is known as the "Miracle Mile." When the Miami franchise after the 1988 season was in danger of going bankrupt, a "miraculous" purchase of the team was made by comedian Bill Murray, businessman Jimmy Buffet, and other investors to save the franchise.

3900 Florida Tropics 1989–90 *Senior (W)*. Team went by the state name of "Florida Tropics" because "Miami–Fort Lauderdale Tropics" was too long for local newspapers. The circuit was known as the Senior Professional Baseball Association — a league for players age 35 and over and for catchers age 30 and over. Fans were bemused by the circuit's gimmick in 1989–90 but by 1990–91 attendance dropped like a rock and the circuit disbanded January 4, 1991. Miami is located in the tropical zone of the western hemisphere.

Miami–Fort Lauderdale, Florida

3901 Florida Marlins 1993 to date *National (M)*. Management decided to use the state name of "Florida Marlins" instead of the overly long "Miami–Fort Lauderdale Marlins." The same situation occurred in 1961 with the Minnesota Twins instead of the "Minneapolis–St. Paul Twins." The tag "Marlins" had been used by AAA and A teams for the previous 35 years, prompting team owner Wayne Huizenga to chose the formal title of "Florida Marlins." He explained, "I chose 'Marlin' because the Marlin is a fierce fighter and adversary that tests your mettle."

3902 Fish 1993 to date *National (M)*. Just as the 12-letter Arizona "Diamondbacks" immediately were tagged the newspaper-friendly "Snakes," the Marlins were referred to by the newspaper contraction of "Fish."

3903 Fins 1993 to date *National (M)*. Tag was a shorter newspaper contraction that many Florida fans used to be almost "hip" and "chic." Moniker was used in newspaper headlines, i.e., "Fins edge Bucs, 4–3."

3904 Fighting Fish 1993 to date *National (M)*. Tag was the inevitable moniker that touches every jokester's heart. But once appearing in newspaper print, "Fighting Fish" immediately became popular. There is nary a fisherman or fisherwoman who has hooked an apparent easy catch that didn't battle like a "fighting fish" to escape.

3905 Men of Teal 1997 *National (M)*. When the five-year-old Florida Marlins leapt "in a single bound" to a playoff berth, the NL pennant and a World Series triumph over the AL Cleveland Indians, fans and newspapers called the players, who wore uniforms of blue and teal (a dark green characteristic of Florida's Teal duck), the "Men of Teal" in a spin-off from the comic book character Superman's "Man of Steel."

3906 Millionaire Marlins 1997 *National (M)*. Team owner Wayne Huizenga, who also owned Blockbuster Video, signed the best players he could find on the free agent market, causing the team payroll to soar to $65 million in 1997, which paid for the talent needed to boost the Marlin to the world championship.

3907 Fire-sale Marlins 1998 *National (M)*. After winning the 1997 World Series, team owner Huizenga reversed himself and traded or released all of the big-name, big-bucks stars on the team causing the Marlins to crash from a playoff spot to last in the NL Eastern Division, becoming the first World Series winner ever to lose 100 or more games the following year.

3908 Jack McKeon's Fighting Warriors 2003 *National (M)*. When the Marlins won an unexpected NL pennant and World Series title in 2003, field manager Jack McKeon, holding the World Series trophy before TV cameras and reporters, proudly announced, "My players are fighting warriors!"

3909 Miami Marlins 2012 to date *National (M)*. For ten years, the franchise threatened to leave southern Florida if no sliding-roof domed stadium was built to shield fans from rain and humidity. A dome has finally been constructed and it opened for the 2012 season. Management decided to go to with the traditional city name of "Miami Marlins" to avoid confusion with the cross-state Tampa Bay Rays. With the metropolitan population of the Miami–Fort Lauderdale area at five million people, there was enough of a fan base to draw on to support the team, making the state name no longer necessary. Although the team is called the single city "Miami Marlins," the team represents the entire Miami–Fort Lauderdale metropolitan area.

Miami, Oklahoma

3910 Indians 1921 *Southwestern (D)*; 1946 *Kansas–Oklahoma–Missouri (K.O.M.) (D)*. The state seal of Oklahoma is a star depicting on each of its points a symbol for each of the "Five Civilized Tribes" of Oklahoma — Chickasaw (warrior), Choctaw (bow and arrow and a tomahawk), Seminole (a rider in a canoe), Creek (plow and a wheat sheaf) and Cherokee (seven-pointed star with oak leaves). Indians have lived in Oklahoma for 15,000 years, including 52 tribes from 1541 to date.

3911 Blues 1946 *(K.O.M.) (D)*. Team was a farm club of the Brooklyn Dodgers. Several Brooklyn farm clubs of the era 1930–55 wore blue-trim uniforms and blue stirrups in the style of the parent club. Several of these teams were known as "Blues" and "Blue Sox."

3912 Owls 1947–49 *(K.O.M.) (D)*. The night owl is common in this region. Newspapers preferred its four-letter length. With manager Omar Lane at the helm in 1949, newspapers called the team "Omar's Owls."

3913 Eagles 1950–52 (*K.O.M.*) (*D*). Team was a farm club of the Dallas Eagles. In the era 1900–50, higher classification (AAA and AA) minor league teams sometimes had their own farm clubs, affiliating with teams in the lower classification leagues (A, B, C, D and E). With manager Jack Hodges at the helm, team was called "Jack Hodges' Eagles."

Miami Beach, Florida

3914 Tigers 1940 *Florida East Coast (D)*. Players wore striped stirrups. The team was not a farm club of the Detroit Tigers.

3915 Flamingos 1941–42x *Florida East Coast (D)*. Team and league disbanded May 14 because of U.S. entry into World War II; 1946–52 *Florida International (C 1946–48,(B 1949–52*); 1954m *Florida International (B)*. Team began season in Miami Beach (FL) and then moved to Miami (FL) May 22. The red and orange feathered flamingo is indigenous to Florida. With manager Max Rosenfeld at the helm, newspapers called the players "Max Rosenfeld's Flamingos."

Michigan City, Michigan

3916 White Caps 1956–59 *Midwest (D)*. City is a lake port on Lake Michigan. Storms on the lake cause "white caps." Storm-wave "white caps" roll ashore at the Washington Park beach. Management provided the players with all-white caps.

Middleport-Pomeroy, Ohio

3917 Middleport-Pomeroy Baseball Club m1911–12m *Mountain States (D)*. Team began season in Point Pleasant–Gallipolis (OH) and moved to Middleport-Pomeroy July 1, 1911. Team moved to Montgomery (WV) June 16, 1912. Team had no nickname. Newspapers sometimes used the abbreviation "MP's" in headlines, i.e., "MP's edge Miners, 4–3." However, the abbreviation was not a "nickname."

Middlesboro, Kentucky

Note: Alternate spelling is Middlesborough.

3918 Colonels 1913–14x *Appalachian (D)*. Team and league disbanded June 17. After the Civil War, the state of Kentucky sometimes awarded the honorary title of "Colonel" to some of its leading citizens. The name soon became synonymous with the state of Kentucky.

3919 Athletics 1949–54 *Mountain States (D 1949–53, C 1954)*. With league rivals, the Morristown Red Sox and Norton Braves using big league team nicknames, Middlesboro chose "Athletics" as its team nickname. Team had a loose affiliation with the AL Philadelphia Athletics.

3920 Senators 1961–62 *Appalachian (D)*. Team was a farm club of the Washington Senators.

3921 CubSox 1963 *Appalachian (D)*. Team in 1963 had two parent clubs—the Chicago Cubs and Chicago White Sox. Management decided upon an amalgam of "CubSox." Players wore caps with an "M" on the front to represent the city name.

Middletown, Connecticut

3922 Mansfields 1872 *National Assn. (M)*. Team, which was established as an amateur nine in 1865, was named in honor of General Joseph Mansfield, who perished in the Battle of Antietam in Sharpsburg (MD) September16–17, 1862. More than 23,000 Union and Confederate soldiers were killed or wounded in the Battle of Antietam.

3923 Blues 1872 *National Assn. (M)*. Players wore blue hose. Originally **Blue Stockings**, local newspapers shortened it to "Blues."

3924 Jewels 1910 *Connecticut Assn. (D)*. In the era 1870–1910, cities that grew quickly and constructed beautiful buildings were sometimes nicknamed Jewel City, Gem City and Magic City. Settled in 1650 and founded as a city in 1784, Middletown became a major shipping center, which led to its growth and wealth. When the team won the league's second-half title, the player were the "Jewels of Baseball." With manager Walter Bellis at the helm, newspapers called the players "Walter Bellis' Jewels."

3925 Middies 1913 *New York–New Jersey (D)*; 1914 *Atlantic (D)*. Moniker was used for newspaper headlines, i.e., "Middies edge Cubans, 4–3." Originally known by the Indian name of Matabaseck when it was founded in 1650, the city was renamed Middle Town because of its location halfway between Hartford and Saybrook (CT). By 1900, the spelling became the modern version of "Middletown." The moniker has nothing to do with the U.S. Naval College nickname of "Middies," which means "Midshipmen."

Middletown, Ohio

3926 Red Sox 1944 *Ohio State (D)*. Team was a farm club of Boston Red Sox.

3927 Rockets 1945–46 *Ohio State (D)*. Tag was a spin-off from "Red Sox." Seeking a spin-off from Red Sox, the team went with "Rockets." The name worked well because the U.S. public was fascinated with captured German V-2 rockets. The name worked perfectly, as the 1945 team "rocketed to first place" with a flag-winning 89–50 mark. However, the Rockets "crashed" to last place in 1946 with a 56–83 record.

Midland, Michigan

3928 Great Lakes Loons 2007 to date *Midwest (A)*. Team goes by the regional name of Great Lakes Loons. Michigan is bordered by Lake Michigan to the west and Lake Huron to the east. The loon is a North American fish-eating diving bird that hunts along rivers and lakes.

Midland, Texas

3929 Colts 1928–29 *West Texas (D)*. City became a cattle-shipping center when the railroad arrived in 1881. Cowboys herded steers, calves, horses and colts to ranches. In 1928 manager Jimmy Maloney guided "Maloney's Colts," and then was replaced by skipper James "Snipe" Conley, who led "Conley's Colts." Kal Segrist took over in 1929 and led "Kal's Colts" before being replaced by John King, who guided "King's Colts" to the 1929 West Texas League pennant.

3930 Cardinals 1937–38 *West Texas–New Mexico (D)*. Team was a farm club of the St. Louis Cardinals.

3931 Cowboys 1939–40 *West Texas–New Mexico (D)*. Settled in 1884, the region was used for cattle drives. Numerous cattle ranches in and around Midland were built and cowboys drove the herds to these ranches. The cattle industry gave rise to the founding of the city of Midland in 1906. With manager Jimmy Kerr at the helm in 1939, city newspapers called the players the "Kerr's Cowboys." Name was retained in 1940 under manager Sammy Hale.

3932 Indians 1947–55 *Longhorn (D 1947–50, C 1951–55)*; 1956–57m *Southwestern (B)*. Team moved to Lamesa (TX) August 1. No fewer than 28 tribes have lived in Texas since the seventeenth century. The most famous are the Apaches and the Comanche. Teams were not farm clubs of the Cleveland Indians.

3933 Rock Hounds 1999 to date *Texas (AA)*. Many prehistoric fossils are located in central Texas. A "rock hound" is a geologist or an amateur rock and mineral collector. The team has a "bloodhound" logo. The Texas Rangers and posses of the Old West used bloodhounds as search dogs because of their excellent sense of smell. Geologists are supposed to have "a nose" for hidden geological treasures.

Miguel Aleman, Mexico

3934 Club de Miguel Aleman 1978 *Mexican Center (A)*. Team had no nickname. In the era 1956–78, Mexico had four lower-classification (A, C & R) leagues: the Central Mexican, Mexican Center, Northern, Rookie and Southeast Leagues. By 1980, economic problems precluded the continued operation of these circuits.

Milano, Lombari-Milano, Italy (Milan in English)

3935 Saim Rho & Ambrosiana 2004 *Italian A1*. Team was owned by both SAIM Rho Business Management and Ambrosiana Chemicals. Since 1999, many Italian professional baseball teams use their sponsor/owner name as their nickname.

Milford, Delaware

3936 Sandpipers 1923x *Eastern Shore (D)*. Team disbanded July 14. The sandpiper is a wading bird that feeds in mud and sand for insects and inhabits much of the shore of the Atlantic Coast. These birds are not seagulls.

3937 Giants 1938–41 *Eastern Shore (D)*. Team was a farm club of the New York Giants.

3938 Red Sox 1946–48 *Eastern Shore (D)*. Team was a farm club of the Boston Red Sox.

Miller, South Dakota

3939 Climbers 1920 *South Dakota (D)*. Usually used for a team on a win streak, allowing it to "climb in the standings," here the name was used by angry fans taunting the players on their "climb right into the cellar" with a free-fall 28–65 record.

3940 Jugglers 1920 *South Dakota (D)*. Team had a porous defense, i.e., fielders "juggling the ball," which contributed to the 28–65 record that plopped the team into last place. With manager Frank Gurney at the helm, newspapers called the players "Gurney's Jugglers."

Millville, New Jersey

3941 Millville Base Ball Club 1897x *New Jersey State (ind.)*. Team had no nickname.

Milton, Pennsylvania

3942 Milton Base Ball Club 1887–88x *Central Pennsylvania (ind.)*. Team had no nickname.

Milwaukee, Wisconsin

3943 Cream Citys 1877 *League Alliance (ind.)*. The League Alliance was a 13-club minor league affiliated with the National League; 1878 *National (M)*; 1884 *Union Assn. (M)*; 1885 *Western (ind.)*; 1886–87 *Northwestern (ind.)*. In the early years of the city (1836–76), many buildings were built with cream-colored bricks that soon became a Milwaukee trademark. The 1877 LA team joined the NL in 1877. Milwaukee is known as the "Cream City" and the "Cream White City of the Unsalted Seas."

3944 Bulls 1878 *National (M)*. Coined by the *New York Clipper* May 6, 1878, the moniker is sports slang for big, strapping players, i.e., "He's a 'bull' of a man!"

3945 Chapman's Grays 1878 *National (M)*. Former Louisville "Grays" field player Jack Chapman signed on as skipper for the Milwaukee 1878 club. Management apparently chose gray uniforms and gray stockings for the players, although Milwaukee was a brand-new team with no players from the 1877 Louisville club.

3946 Brewers 1884m *Northwestern (ind.)*; m1884 *Union Assn. (M)*. The NWL team joined the UA September 27; 1888–91 *Western Association (ind.)*; 1891 *American Assn. (M)*; 1892 *Western (ind.)*; 1894–1900 *Western (ind.)*; 1900 *American (ind.)*; 1901 *American (M)*; 1902–52 *American Assn. (A 1903–07, AA 1908–45, AAA 1946–52)*; 1970–97 *American (M)*; 1998 to date *National (M)*. The city of Milwaukee, along with Cincinnati and St. Louis, attracted German immigrants in the era 1840–1900. These immigrants soon started numerous breweries here. Beer drinking at festivals is a traditional pastime in German culture. Milwaukee by the 1880s had become known as the "Beer City" and the "Beer Capital of America."

3947 Greys 1884 *Union Assn. (M)*. Players wore gray hose.

3948 Chicks 1884 *Reserve (ind.)*; 1944 *All-American Girls Professional Baseball League (ind.)*. Although a "baseball" circuit, league played softball 1943–47, then baseball 1948–54. "Chick" was a nineteenth century slang for a young baseball player. "Chick" is slang for "girl."

3949 Creams 1889–91 *Western Association (ind.)*; 1896–97 *Western (ind.)*; 1902–03 *Western (A)*; 1913 *Wisconsin–Illinois (D)*. Tag was a newspaper contraction. Originally "Cream Citys," local newspapers shortened the moniker to "Creams." The 1902–03 Western League Milwaukee club was forced to choose "Creams" to avoid confusion with the new American Association Milwaukee "Brewers." The 1913 Class D team was also forced to use the "Creams" to avoid confusion with the 1913 American Association Milwaukee Brewers.

3950 Lame Duck Brewers 1901 *American (M)*. When a team is slated to move to a new city the following season, it is branded as "lame duck." AL president Ban Johnson considered Milwaukee to be too small to support a major league team and also wanted to battle the National League in St. Louis for the 1902 season. The Brewers moved to St. Louis to become the St. Louis Browns. The tag was coined by baseball author Marc Okkonen.

3951 Miracle Boys 1953 *National (M)*. Name was coined by baseball writer William Sunners praising the exploits of hitters Eddie Mathews, Joe Adcock, Johnny Logan, Andy Pafko, Bill Bruton, Sid Gordon and Del Crandall along with pitchers Warren Spahn, Lew Burdette, Bob Buhl and Johnny Antonelli in elevating the 64–89 Boston Braves of 1952 into the 92–62 Milwaukee Braves of 1953.

3952 Miracle Braves 1953 *National (M)*. Name was coined by author Tom Meany in his book of the same title to describe the miraculous rebirth of the old Boston Braves (who had drawn only 287,000 fans while going 64–89 in 1952) into the Milwaukee Braves (who drew 1,827,000 fans while going 92–62 to finish a credible second behind the meteoric 105-game winning Brooklyn Dodgers).

3953 Braves 1953–65 *National (M)*. The Milwaukee Braves franchise moved to Atlanta for the 1966 season and the team nickname was retained. Moniker was appropriate because Wisconsin was the home of many Algonkian Indian tribes. Cartoonist Willard Mullin drew a witty Milwaukee Braves caricature of an Algonkian Indian with a German accent. Although politically incorrect today, the gag back then was very funny.

3954 Lame Duck Braves 1965 *National (M)*. After excellent attendance (nearly two million a year in a country with a population of 150 million people) in Milwaukee's County Stadium in the 1950s, support for a winning team declined in the 1960s, dropping to a franchise-low 767,000 in 1962. By 1964 team owner John McHale was determined to move the franchise to Atlanta, and the Braves played a "lame duck" season in 1965, playing before only 555,000 Milwaukee fans. The team was also known as **Vagabond Braves.**

3955 Alcoholics 1971–77 *American (M).* Milwaukee fans were so happy to have a major league team in 1970 that they restrained themselves when the Brewers played as miserably as the 1969 Seattle Pilots. By 1971 when the Brewers dropped to last place in the AL West, disgruntled fans laughed when newspapers called the team the "Alcoholics." The moniker was used sporadically during Milwaukee's losing era 1971–77, and then "dried out" when the Brewers started winning 1978–83. Although baseball players are notorious drinkers, there was no insinuation of any player being a drunk.

3956 Bambi's Bombers 1978–80 *American (M).* Moniker was a predecessor to "Harvey's Wallbangers." The team prior to the 1982 pennant year already had a heavy-hitting lineup, i.e., Cecil Cooper, Larry Hisle, Sixto Lezcano, Paul Molitor, Ben Ogilve, Gorman Thomas and Robin Yount. Led by manager George "Bambi" Bamberger, the players were known as "Bambi's Bombers," hitting 178 homers in 1978 (1st in AL), 185 homers in 1979 (2nd in AL) and 203 homers in 1980 (1st in AL).

3957 Wrecking Crew 1978–80 *American (M).* Tag was a variation of "Bambi's Bombers" and "Harvey's Wallbangers." Tag was used before in Brooklyn in 1955.

3958 Harvey's Wallbangers 1982 *American (M).* After a well-known alcoholic drink, manager Harvey Kuenn's "Wallbangers" banged the walls of Milwaukee's County Stadium with an AL-leading 216 home runs en route to the 1982 American League pennant. Gorman Thomas (39 HR), Ben Ogilvie (34 HR), Cecil Cooper (32 HR) and Robin Yount (29 HR) led the offense while Pete Vuckovich (18 wins), Mike Caldwell (17 wins) and Rollie Fingers (29 saves) led the pitching.

3959 True Blue Brew Crew 1982 *American (M).* Tag was a clumsy, hard-to-pronounce moniker that never caught on.

3960 Beermakers 1982 *American (M).* Tag was an alternate moniker that didn't catch on because it was ten letters long.

3961 Milwaukee's Best 1982 *American (M).* Baseball writer Andy Maraniss cleverly praised the 1982 AL champion Milwaukee Brewers as "Milwaukee's Best," after a popular brand of home-brewed beer known by the same name.

3962 Brew Crew 1982–97 *American (M);* 1998 to date *National (M).* A likeable, newspaper-friendly moniker used by fans, newspapers and sports broadcasters. It is attributed to baseball broadcaster Ken Harrelson sometime in the 1980s when the franchise was in the American League.

3963 Suds City Streakers 1987 *American (M).* Tag was coined by baseball writer Tom Flaherty—in a humorous reference to the "Streaking Fad" of the 1970s, i.e., a person, usually a drunken youth, would "streak" stark naked before hundreds or even thousands of people in attendance at an sporting or entertainment event before quickly disappearing (either escaped or arrested)—it described the team's 13-game winning streak to open the season (April 6–20) only to be followed by a 12-game losing skid May 3–19. Milwaukee, famous for its beer brewing industry, is known affectionately as "Suds City." "Suds" is a slang for beer foam and, hence, a glass of beer. Name was also **Team Streak.**

3964 Termites 1997 *American (M).* Tag was coined by Chicago White Sox slugger Frank Thomas, after his team finished a tough series with the Brewers during the 1997 season. Thomas said of the Brewers: "They are industrious and persistent in each game. They remind me of termites."

3965 Budget Brewers 1997 *American (M).* Bill Mazeroski, former Pirates second basemen and editor of a baseball magazine, complained in his publication at the start of the 1997 season that the Milwaukee management was too budget-conscious after trading away high-priced players like Greg Vaughn, Pat Listach, Kevin Seitzer and Graeme Lloyd.

3966 Traders 2002–04 *National (M).* Because of low attendance and low revenue, GM Doug Melvin traded away his best players, causing the Brewers to plunge from 73 to 68 to 56 victories (with 106 defeats in the 2002 season), plunging the team into the NL Central cellar three seasons in a row.

3967 Home of the Prince 2005 to 2011. The franchise's greatest offensive star, Prince Fielder, exploded onto the scene in 2005. He slammed 50 home runs in 2007 and 46 round-trippers and 141 RBIs in 2009. Admiring fans started calling the Milwaukee team "Home of the Prince."

3968 Young'ens 2005 *National (M).* Younger players started to jell, boosting the team to .500 (81–81) in 2005. By 2008 the "Youngen's" (a Dixie slang for young people) had improved enough to win 90 games and clinch the team's first playoff berth since 1982.

3969 Cerveceros 2006 to date *National (M).* With an influx of Spanish-speaking immigrants to Milwaukee since 1990, Spanish language TV and radio broadcast now cover the exploits of "Los Cerveceros" (Brewers). Milwaukee players wore "Cerveceros" letters uniforms for Hispanic Appreciation Night, July 29, 2006, and Hispanic Heritage Month, September 6, 2008.

3970 Brewhas 2008 *National (M).* With the Brewers winning 90 games to reach the playoffs for the first time since the 1982 AL pennant year, ESPN broadcasters assigned the lame moniker of "Brewhas" to the Milwaukee team as a play on words with "brouhaha," which means a fist fight or an angry jostling or wrestling of people. The tag was discarded.

3971 Milwaukee's Worst 2009 *National (M).* A spin-off on "Milwaukee's Best"—a popular brand of beer—the name was coined by *The Sporting News* to describe the team's unsavory pitching staff that wound up with a 4.83 team ERA (fifteenth in the NL) and held down the team to an 80–82 mark.

3972 Strange Brew Crew 2011 *National (M).* Playing at .600 ball as the season approached September 1, the team gained a 10-game lead over St. Louis in the NL Central with their first playoff berth since 1982 looming. Moniker was coined by sportswriter Lee Jenkins in *Sports Illustrated*, who invoked a slang from the psychedelic 1960s. A "strange brew" back then was a cocktail of psychedelic drugs used by the hippies to "get high." The team is typically known as the "Brew Crew," and "brew" is slang for "beer." Tag was a spin-off from Kool Aid, which is a fruit drink spiked with LSD supposedly used by fans with unrealistic pennant expectations.

3973 High Life Millers 2011 *National (M).* Another moniker coined by baseball writer Lee Jenkins in the August edition of *Sports Illustrated* describing the Milwaukee Brewers players and their fans enjoying the "high life" in the NL Central, i.e., first place with a ten-game lead over St. Louis as Labor Day approached. Moniker is a play on words of one of the team's sponsors, Miller Beer, whose famous brand of beer is known as "Miller High Life" beer. The Brewers play in Miller Park. Since the franchise's only pennant in 1982, Milwaukee fans have suffered through mostly losing seasons while waiting for the "high life" of a playoff berth.

Minatitlan, Veracruz, Mexico

3974 Petroleros 1968 *Liga del Sureste Mexicana (A);* 1992–95 *Liga Mexicana (AAA);* 2007 to date *Liga Mexicana (AAA).* Oil refineries, built here by Standard Oil in the 1920s, were nationalized by Mexico in 1939 when PEMEX, the national oil company, took control. The largest oil refinery in Latin America is located here.

3975 Rojos 1969 *Liga del Sureste Mexicana (A)*. Team was a farm club of the "Diablos Rojos" de Mexico. "Los Rojos" is Spanish for "Reds."

3976 Potros 1996–97 *Liga Mexicana (AAA)* Numerous horse ranches in the region raise colts. "Los potros" is the Spanish word for "ponies."

Mineral Wells, Texas

3977 Resorters 1920–21m *West Texas (D)*. Team moved to Ballinger (TX) in May 19; m1921 Team started season in Graham (TX) and then moved to Mineral Wells May 27. By 1910 the city used mineral water wells, fed by the Possum Kingdom Lake and the Palo Pinto Creek Reservoir, to attract tourists to newly constructed resort lodges and the Baker Hotel, which opened in 1929.

Minersville, Pennsylvania

3978 Minersville Base Ball Club 1887 *Central Pennsylvania (ind.)*. Team had no nickname.

Minneapolis, Kansas

3979 Minneapolis Base Ball Club 1896 *Kansas State (ind.)*. Team had no nickname.

3980 Minnies 1905 *Kansas State (D)*; 1908–09 *Central Kansas (D)*; m1912 *Central Kansas (D)*. Team started season in Newton (KS) and then moved to Minneapolis July 12. Moniker was used for newspaper headlines, i.e., "Minnies edge Millers, 4–3."

Minneapolis, Minnesota

3981 Brown Stockings 1877 *League Alliance (ind.)*. Players started the season wearing blue stockings that became dirty and turned brown with frequent washings. Newspapers shortened it to **Browns**.

3982 Millers 1884 *Northwestern (ind.)*; 1886–87 *Northwestern (ind.)*; 1888m *Western Assn.(ind.)*. Team moved to Davenport (IA) August 18; 1889–91 *Western Assn. (ind.)*; 1892–99 *Western (ind.)*; 1900 *American (ind.)*; 1901 *Western (ind.)*; 1902–60 *American Assn. (ind. 1902, A 1903–08, AA 1908–45, AAA 1946–60)*; 1994x *Great Central (ind.)*. During the Civil War, the city became a major flour milling center for breadstuffs for both civilians and soldiers in the Union Army. Minneapolis is known as the "Mill Town" and the "Flour Milling Capital of the World."

3983 Minnies 1888m *Western Assn.* Team moved to Davenport (IA) August 18; 1892–99 *Western (ind.)*; 1913 *Northern (C)*. Moniker was used for newspaper headlines, i.e., "Minnies edge Saints, 4–3." Tag was used as an alternate to "Millers."

3984 Millerettes 1944 *All-American Girls Professional Baseball League (ind.)*. League played softball 1943–47, baseball 1948–54. In the English language the suffix "-ette" feminizes a noun.

3985 Loons 1994 *Northern Central (ind.)*; 1995 *Prairie (ind.)*. The loon is a cold-weather bird that dives into water to catch fish. The North American loon is found in the northern U.S., Canada and Alaska. Loons inhabit Minnesota's many lakes.

Minneapolis–St. Paul, Minnesota

3986 Twins 1961 to date *American (M)*. After the 1960 season, Washington Senators owner Cal Griffith moved the franchise to the "Twin Cities" of Minneapolis–St. Paul (MN). After false starts with "Minneapolis–St. Paul Twins" (which put local newspaper editors into a state of rebellion) and "Twin Cities Twins" (which was redundant), Griffith settled on "Minnesota Twins," which was appropriate since the team played in suburban Bloomington, halfway between Minneapolis and St. Paul. In 1982 the team moved to the Hubert Humphrey Metrodome in Minneapolis but kept the Minnesota Twins moniker. The franchise was the first major league team to use a state name. Since then there has been the California Angels, Colorado Rockies, Florida Marlins and Texas Rangers.

3987 Win! Twins! 1961 to date *American (M)*. The original Minnesota Twins logo displays the phrase "Win! Twins!" Baseball writer Tracy Ringolsby praised the 1987 AL and world champions as the "Win! Twins!" Tag is used more as a slogan than a nickname.

3988 The Minnesota Lumber Company 1963–64 *American (M)*. Led by sluggers Harmon Killebrew, Bob Allison, Jim Lemon, Earl Battey, Don Mincher, Rich Rollins, Jim Hall and steady hitters Zoilo Versalles, Tony Oliva and Rod Carew, the Twins had a winning record in seven of their first 10 seasons in the Twin Cities, and won the AL pennant in 1965 and two AL Western Division titles, in 1969–70. Named after an old lumber company in a state where lumber is a leading industry, the " Minnesota Lumber Company" also led the AL in homers with 225 in 1963 and 221 in 1964.

3989 The Minnesota Lumber Company II 1973–78 *American (M)*. By the 1970s the Twins had a new generation of dependable singles hitters and home run sluggers with the likes of Lyman Bostock, Rod Carew, Bobby Darwin, Dan Ford, Larry Hisle, Tony Oliva, Roy Smalley and Butch Wynegar. Although the team hit well, the Twins' pitching in this era was mediocre and the team won no division titles.

3990 Twinkies 1982 to date *American (M)*. When the Twins skidded to last place in the AL Western Division in 1982 with a horrible record of 60–102, disenchanted Minnesota fans started calling the team the "Twinkies" after the popular brand Hostess snack cake "Twinkies" because the players reminded them of "cream puffs" (an old sporting slang referring to a team or athletes who performed poorly). The moniker stuck, but when the Twins started winning again in 1987, the nickname became a term of endearment, much like "Bums" in Brooklyn and "Cubbies" in Chicago. Some of the "Twinkies" who helped Minnesota win the 1987 World Series were hitters Chili Davis, Greg Gagne, Brian Harper, Kent Hrbek, Chuck Knobaluch and Shane Mack as well as pitchers Rick Aguilera, Scott Erikson, Jack Morris and Kevin Tapani. Alternates **Twinks** (used for the 1877–79 Syracuse Stars) and **Twinkers** are seldom used.

3991 Kelly's Heroes 1991 *American (M)*. Named after the popular Clint Eastwood 1970 war movie "Kelly's Heroes," the 1991 Twins, managed by Tom Kelly jumped from 7th and last place in the AL Western Division in 1990 to the division title in 1991. Finishing with a 95–67 (won-lost) record "Kelly's Heroes" were led by hitters Chili Davis, George Gagne, Brian Harper, Kent Hrbek, Chuck Knobaluch, Shane Mack and Kirby Puckett as well as pitchers Rick Aguilera, Scott Erickson, Jack Morris and Kevin Tapani.

3992 Cinderella Twins 1991 *American (M)*. The Twins (along with the 1991 NL Atlanta Braves) became the first team to go from last place (with a 74–88 mark) in one season (1990) to first place and a league pennant the next (1991) since the 1889–90 Louisville Cyclones of the old American Association.

3993 Piranhas 2006 to date *American (M)*. A great farm system compensated for the team's small TV market dilemma and provided players perfectly tailored for the controversial Metrodome. The result was a Minnesota franchise that produced six consecutive winning seasons (2001–06) and four AL Central Division titles, much to the chagrin of White Sox manager Ozzie Guillen, who called manager

Ron Gardenhire's 2006 Twins players the "Piranhas" for their ability "to bite their opponents until they are torn apart … just like piranhas!" The Twins were experts at bunting, the hit and run, taking the extra base, double steals, escaping rundowns, hitting to the opposite field and turning double plays. Guillen complained, "All those piranhas … a blooper here, a blooper there, hit a home run … and they're up by four!"

3994 Sharks 2008 to date *American (M)*. Chicago manager Ozzie Guillen complimented the Twins' "killer instinct" at beating opponents guilty of mental mistakes and physical errors by exclaiming, "Those guys over there … if you make a mental mistake, they smell blood … they're sharks." In the summer of 2010 *Chicago Sun-Times* writer Joe Cowley also started using the name for the Minnesotans.

3995 Killer Bees 2010 to date *American (M)*. Chicago manager Ozzie Guillen, impressed by the Twins' opportunism to beat an opponent making mental and physical errors, called the Minnesotans the "Killer Bees."

3996 Big Bad Fish 2011 to date. Utilizing a spinoff from White Sox manager Ozzie Guillen's deep-sea monikers of "Piranhas" and "Sharks," *Sports Illustrated* reporter Albert Chen praised the 2010 AL Western Division champions as the "Big Bad Fish" in his spring training report about the team.

3997 Who Are These Guys? 2011 to date *American (M)*. When the Twins dumped the White Sox three of four games in a July series this season, they completed a streak of winning 27 of 36 games against the Chicagoans over three seasons. Chicago radio broadcaster Les Grobstein expressed his exasperation on July 8 by asking about the Twins: "Who are these guys!?" The question was a humorous reference to actor Paul Newman's similar question in the famous 1969 movie *Butch Cassidy and the Sundance Kid*, when Butch (Newman) and the Sundance Kid (Robert Redford) were hunted by a relentless posse. Playing with mostly anonymous lineups, the Twins won six AL Central titles.

Minot, North Dakota

3998 Why-Nots 1917x *Northern (D)*. Team and league disbanded July 4 due to U.S. entry into World War I. Newspaper reporters, with tongue planted firmly in cheek, came up with this tag, which was a rhyming moniker, i.e., "Minot Why-Nots."

3999 Magicians 1923 *North Dakota (D)*. Minot, home of the annual North Dakota State Fair, is nicknamed the "Magic City." Also this season, newspapers applauded the players' "magical play" as the team streaked to a 48–21 first-place record and the pennant. The city was established in farm country and when the railroads arrived in the 1870s it grew so fast that it became known as the "Magic City." U.S. towns and cities in the nineteenth century that enjoyed rapid economic and architectural growth were known variously as Magic City, Gem City and Jewel City.

4000 Mallards 1958–60 *Northern (C)*; 1962 *Northern (C)*; 1995–97 *Prairie (ind.)*. The mallard is the wild duck from which domestic ducks were bred.

Mission, Texas

4001 Grapefruiters m1926 *Gulf Coast (D)*. Team began season in Kingsville (TX) and then moved to Mission July 9; 1927 *Texas Valley (D)*. Citrus fruits, i.e., the Ruby Red grapefruit, grown in surrounding farms are transported to the city for processing and packing. Packed fruits are then shipped out by highway trucks and boats on the nearby Rio Grande River. Mission is known as the "Home of the Texas Grapefruit."

Mission Viejo, California

4002 Vigilantes 1997–98 *Western (ind.)*. By 1870, the Los Angeles area was plagued by outlaws, rustlers and thieves. Vigilante committees were formed to chase down the bad guys.

Missoula, Montana

4003 Missoula Base Ball Club 1892 *Montana State (ind.)*; 1911–13 *Union Assn. (C 1911, D 1912–13)*. These teams had no nickname.

4004 Timberjacks 1956–60 *Pioneer (C)*. Lumber from the nearby Bitter-Root and Lolo national forests are shipped to the city for processing.

Mitchell, South Dakota

4005 Kernels 1920 *South Dakota (D)*; 1921–22 *Dakota (D)*; 1923 *South Dakota (D)*; 1936–37 *Nebraska State (D)*; 1939 *Western (D)*. Farms in the region transport corn to city packing houses. In 1934, the city built the Corn Palace — a corn-farming museum to attract tourists. Mitchell is "The Home of the World's Only Corn Palace." With manager Hank Scharnweber at the helm in 1920, newspapers called the players "Hank's Kernels."

Miyaga-Yamagata, Japan

4006 Golden Eagles 2011 to date *Japanese Western (ind.)*. Team was a farm club of the Pacific League Tohoku Golden Eagles.

Mobile, Alabama

4007 Swamp Angels 1887x *Southern (ind.)*. Team disbanded May 17. Watered by Mobile Bay and the Mobile and Tensaw rivers, the region has numerous swamps whose hot vapors fueled legends of misty ghostlike apparitions known as "Swamp Angels."

4008 Bears m1889x *Southern (ind.)*. Team began season in Birmingham and then transferred to Mobile June 5. Team and league disbanded July 6. Although bears had been driven out of Alabama by 1840, local newspapers and fans relished the short moniker after a reporter first used it in July 1889.

4009 Blackbirds 1892–93 *Southern (ind.)*; 1896 *Southern*; 1898–99 *Southern*. Players wore black hose. In the era 1890–1910 some teams used bird names reflective of their stocking colors, i.e., Bluebirds, Blue Jays, Canaries, Cardinals, Doves, Ravens, Redbirds and Blackbirds.

4010 Bluebirds 1894m *Southern (ind.)*. Team moved to Atlanta (GA) June 2; m1895 *Southern (ind.)*. Team began season in Chattanooga and then transferred to Mobile July 19. Players wore blue hose.

4011 Sea Gulls 1905–07 *Cotton States (D)*; 1908–17 *Southern Assn. (A)*. Although the Yellowhammer is the state bird of Alabama, sea gulls inhabit the entire Gulf of Mexico and Mobile Bay coastline of Alabama.

4012 Bears 1918–30 *Southern Assn. (A)*; m1944–61 *Southern Assn. (A1 1944–45, AA 1946–61)*. Team began the 1944 season in Knoxville (TN) and moved to Mobile July 5; 1997 to date *Southern (AA)*. In 1917, the Seagulls went a horrendous 34–117 to finish 62.5 games out of first place. Before the start of the next season, local newspapers tried to create a new image for the 1918 team by switching to a new nickname of "Bears."

4013 Tigers 1921 *Negro Southeastern (ind.)*. Players wore striped stirrups.

4014 Marines 1931m *Southern Assn. (A)*. Team moved to Knoxville (TN) July 22. In August 1864 Union Admiral David Farragut's

Union Navy repulsed the Confederate Navy and captured numerous coastal forts in the Battle of Mobile Bay. Mobile is Alabama's only seaport, adjacent to the Mobile River and the Gulf of Mexico. The city is known as the "Port City." When the 1930 Mobile Bears went a horrendous 40–112 to finish 57.5 games out of first place, newspapers tried to create a new image for the team in 1931 by switching to a new nickname, i.e., "Marines."

4015 Red Warriors 1932x *Southeastern (B)*. Team and league disbanded May 21 because of the Great Depression. Players wore redtrim uniforms and red stirrups because the team was a farm club of St. Louis Cardinals. The four historical Indian tribes of Alabama were the Creek, Chickasaw, Choctaw and Cherokee. Settlers expelled them westward by 1835.

4016 Shippers 1937–42 *Southeastern (B)*. Shipping boats have traveled Mobile Bay since 1702. Mobile is known as the "Gulf City" because it is a major seaport by the Gulf of Mexico.

4017 Athletics 1966 *Southern (AA)*. Team was a farm club of the Kansas City Athletics.

4018 White Sox 1970 *Southern (AA)*. Team was a farm club of the Chicago White Sox.

4019 Mobile Bay Sharks 1994–95 *Texas–Louisiana (ind.)*. Team went by the regional name of "Mobile Bay" Sharks. Sharks sometimes swim into Mobile Bay.

4020 Mobile Bay Bears 1997 to date Southern (AA). Team, based in Mobile, is known as the Mobile Bay Bears— in the style of the Tampa Bay Rays. Mobile, the "Port City," is situated on the northernmost coast of Mobile Bay.

Modena, Emilia-Romagna, Italy

4021 GB Ricambi 1999–2003 *Italian A1(ind.)*. GB Ricamni Tractor Company owned the team.

4022 Fiume Costruzioni 2004–05 *Italian A1(ind.)*. Fiume Costruzioni Company owned the team.

4023 Comcor 2006 *Italian A1(ind.)*. Comcor, a communications company, owned the team.

Modesto, California

4024 Reds 1914x *California State (D)*. Team and league disbanded June 1; 1915x *California State (D)*. Team and league disbanded May 30 due to rain storms; 1946–61 *California (C)*; 1966–74 *California (A)*. Players wore red-trim uniforms, red caps, and red stirrups. Team was never a farm club of the Cincinnati Reds, although in 1968 the team became a farm club of the St. Louis Cardinals whose own uniforms sport red-trim.

4025 Colt .45's 1962–64 *California (C 1962, A 1963–64)*. Team was a farm club of the Houston Colt. 45's.

4026 Athletics 1975–2004 *California (A)*. Team was a farm club of the Oakland Athletics

4027 Nuts 2005 to date *California (A)*. Modesto is the "Peach Capital of the World," but farms near Modesto also grow nuts and other fruits. These farms transport fruit and nuts to city packing houses.

Moline, Illinois

4028 Plowboys m1914–17 *Three-I (B)*. Team began 1914 season in Danville (IL) before transferring to Moline July 14, 1914. League ended its regular season July 8, 1917, because of U.S. entry into World War I; 1919–23 *Three-I (B)*; 1924–32 *Mississippi Valley (D)*; 1937–41 *Three-I (B)*. Industrialist John Deere established his plow-making business in this city in 1847. City is nicknamed the "Farm Implement

Capital of the World." Moline is also known as the "Plow City." Team was aka the **Plows**.

4029 Athletics 1947–48m *Central Assn. (C)*. Team moved to Kewanee June 18. Team was a farm club of the Philadelphia Athletics.

Monahans, Texas

4030 Trojans 1937 *West Texas–New Mexico (D)*. With manager Paul Trammel at the helm, newspapers called the players "Trammel's Trojans." "Trojans" was a generic slang for baseball players in the 1930s and 1940s, i.e., the warriors of Ancient Troy trained hard and were athletic. The tag was a spin-off from "Gladiators," which was common in the nineteenth century. The University of Southern California Trojans was a successful and popular college football team during the 1920s and 1930s.

Monclova, Coahuila, Mexico

4031 Acereros 1980 *Liga Mexicana (AAA)*; 1982 to date *Liga Mexicana (AAA)*. Monclova is the site of a steel mill. "Los Acererors" is Spanish for "Steelers."

Moncton, New Brunswick, Canada

4032 Moncton Base Ball Club 1890 *New Brunswick (ind.)*. Team had no nickname.

Monessen, Pennsylvania

4033 Indians 1934, 1936 *Pennsylvania State Assn. (D)*. Team was a farm club of the Cleveland Indians.

4034 Reds 1935 *Pennsylvania State Assn. (D)*. Team was a farm club of the Cincinnati Reds.

4035 Cardinals 1937 *Pennsylvania State Assn. (D)*. Team was a farm club of the St. Louis Cardinals.

Monett, Missouri

4036 Redbirds 1936–39 *Arkansas–Missouri (D)*. Team had a loose affiliation with the NL St. Louis Cardinals, 1936–37, before becoming a formal farm club with the NL Cardinals 1938–39.

Monmouth, Illinois

4037 Maple Citys m1889 *Central Inter-State (ind.)*. Team began season in Davenport (IA) before moving to Monmouth (IL) September 14. An important business here was the Western Stoneware Company, a producer of ceramics. The company logo was a maple leaf. The nickname soon became the city's nickname, i.e., the "Maple City." In the nineteenth century reporters would often name a baseball team after its home city's nickname.

4038 Browns 1908–09 *Illinois–Missouri (D)*; 1910–13 *Central Assn. (D)*. The Monmouth teams of 1908–13 had a loose affiliation with the AL St. Louis Browns, i.e., buying uniforms and equipment and selling an occasional player contract to the big league club.

Monroe, Louisiana

4039 Hill Citys 1903–04 *Cotton States (D)*. Monroe is the "Hill City." City was built in 1785 amidst the rolling hills of northern Louisiana.

4040 Municipals 1907 *Gulf Coast (D)*; 1908 *Cotton States (D)*; 1909m *Arkansas State (D)*. Monroe moved to Newport-Batesville

July 1. City's official name is the "Municipality of Monroe." Moniker was also alliterative, i.e., "Monroe Municipals."

4041 Drillers 1924–30 *Cotton States (D)*. Oil and natural gas fields were discovered near the city in 1907. The Standard Oil Company built oil rigs and long-distance pipelines here in 1909. Oil and natural gas are shipped to petrochemical refineries in the city. With manager Bill Wise at the helm in 1924, newspapers called the players "Bill's Drillers." When Paul Trammell succeeded Wise during the 1925 season, the team became "Trammell's Drillers." With manager Charles Caroll at the helm for the 1926 season, newspapers called the players "Caroll's Drillers." With Eddie Palmer at the helm as manager for the 1927 team, newspapers called the players "Palmer's Drillers." With manager Tillie Meeter at the helm for the 1929 team, newspapers called the players "Tillie's Drillers."

4042 Twins 1931–32x *Cotton States (D)*. Team and league disbanded July 13 because of the Great Depression; 1937 *Cotton States (C)*; 1956 *Evangeline (C)*. The teams represented the "Twin Cities" of Monroe–West Monroe, Louisiana.

4043 Monarchs 1932 *Negro Southern (ind.)*. Team was a farm club of the Kansas City Monarchs.

4044 White Sox 1938–41 *Cotton States (C)*. Team maintained a loose affiliation with the AL Chicago White Sox, i.e., White Sox uniforms, via the Dallas Texas League club with whom the Modesto club operated as a farm club.

4045 Sports 1950–55 *Cotton States (C)*. Team was a farm club of the Shreveport Sports. By 1950, the Shreveport Sports, shunned by potential major league "parent clubs" and in order to remain competitive, were forced to maintain and stock their own farm teams with white players because Shreveport city statutes forbade the use of Shreveport's baseball park by Negro players who might have been farmed to Shreveport by a potential major league team. Aka **Twin Cities Sports** 1954–55 (representing Monroe and West Monroe).

Monroe, North Carolina

4046 Indians m1969 *Western Carolinas (A)*. Team began season in Statesville and then transferred to Monroe June 20. Team was a farm club of the Cleveland Indians.

4047 Pirates 1971 *Western Carolinas (A)*. Team was a farm club of the Pittsburgh Pirates.

Montclair, New Jersey

4048 New Jersey Jackals 1998 *Northeast (ind.)*; 1999–2002 *Northern (ind.)*; 2005 to date *Can–Am (ind.)*. Team went by the state name of New Jersey Jackals. Fan poll chose "Jackals" because it is alliterative to the team's state nickname of New Jersey. Jackals are canine-like wild dogs found in Asia and Africa. The closest relative to the jackal in North America is the coyote.

Montebello, California

4049 Montebello Baseball Club 1925–26 *California Winter (W)*. Team had no nickname.

Monteria, Colombia

4050 Cardenales de Comfacor 2004–05–07–08 *Lia Colombiana (W)*. Team was known as "Los Cardenales de Comfacor," after the franchise's new owner, in the franchise's last two seasons of play in 2006–07 and 2007–08. Monteria players wore red-trim uniforms similar to the St. Louis Cardinals.

Monterrey, Nuevo Leon, Mexico

4051 Carta Blanca 1938 *Liga Mexicana (ind.)*. Team was owned by the Carta Blanca beer company. In Spanish the company's name is Cerveceria Carta Blanca.

4052 Industriales 1940–48 *Liga Mexicana (AAA)*; 1989–94 *Liga Mexicana (AAA)*. Steel and iron factories were first built here in 1903. Natural gas was discovered in the nearby Reynosa Fields in the 1950s. Lead smelting and glass blowing factories also are here. Monterrey is known as the "Industrial Sultan of Northern Mexico." The 1989–94 franchise was a second club in the city and in competition with the Monterrey Sultans.

4053 Sultanes 1949 to date *Mexican (ind.1949–54, AA 1955–66, AAA 1967 to date)*. City is known as the "Sultan of Northern Mexico" because of its size and industry. "Los Sultanes" means "sultans" in English. Previously called "Industriales" (1940–48), the team is not to be confused with the 1989–94 Monterrey "Industriales."

4054 Indios 1970–71 *Mexican Center (A)*. When the Spaniards arrived in the región in the 1520s, they subjugated the native Acoma Indians, who fell prey to small pox and slavery.

4055 Sultancitos 1972 *Mexican Center (A)*. Team was a farm club of the Class AAA Mexican League Sultanes. Fans called the team "Los Sultancitos," i.e., the "Little Sultans."

Montesano, Washington

4056 Farmers 1905 *Southwest Washington (D)*; 1910 *Washington State (D)*. The league played six times a week, but only the weekend games counted in the standings for a 36-game schedule. Dairy farms in the region transport raw milk to city processing plants for pasteurization and the production of dairy products.

Montgomery, Alabama

4057 Lambs 1892 *Southern (ind.)*. In this era, teams with young players were known variously as Babes, Chicks, Colts, Cubs, Debutantes, Foundlings, Lambs, Ponies and Prodigals. With manager Charles Levi at the helm, newspapers called the players "Levi's Lambs." The term "rookie," coined in 1892, would not become popular until 1917.

4058 Colts 1893 *Southern (ind.)*. Team had young players, known as "colts." With field manager John McCloskey at the helm, local newspapers called the players the alliterative "McCloskey's Colts."

4059 Grays 1895–96 *Southern (ind.)*; 1952–53 *South Atlantic (A)*. Players in 1895–96 wore gray uniforms and gray hose. With manager Jack Hayes the helm, newspapers called the players "Hayes' Grays." Rich Gorman took over in 1896 and the name became "Gorman's Grays." In the Civil War, Confederate Army "rebel" troops wore gray uniforms and were known as the "Grays" in contradistinction to the blue uniforms of the Union Army "Blues" soldiers. The 1952–53 players wore gray-trim uniforms.

4060 Senators 1898–99m *Southern (ind.)*. Team moved to Dallas–Fort Worth (TX) July 5; 1904–08 *Southern Assn. (A)*. Montgomery has been the state capital of Alabama since 1847. With manager William Stickney at the helm in 1904, newspapers called the players "Stickney's Senators." Stickney left the team after 1904 but the name was retained through 1908.

4061 Black Sox 1903 *Southern Assn. (B)*. Players wore black hose.

4062 Climbers 1909–10 *Southern Assn. (A)*. The 1909 team got off to a good start, prompting the tag "Climbers," before cooling off to a 76–60 and a third-place finish. In 1910, unhappy Montgomery fans sarcastically called the players the "Climbers" as the team sunk to a last-place finish (59–80 record). Teams in this era that got off to hot starts (usually getting them to first place) were sometimes called "Climbers." With field manager Ed Gremlinger at the helm 1909–10, local newspapers called the players "Gremlinger's Climbers."

4063 Billikens 1911, 1914 *Southern Assn. (A)*. No less than five players on this team were named Bill — Bill Bailey, Bill Elwert, Bill Kay, Bill Levilet and Bill McAlester. Another player was Joseph Bills. With the "Billiken doll" craze sweeping the nation, newspapers called the players, guided by manager Johnny Dobb, "Dobb's Billikens." With manager Robert Gilks at the helm in 1914, the "Billikens" name returned as the team was known as "Bob's Billikens" and "Gilk's Billikens." The "Billiken" was a genie-looking doll for little girls.

4064 Rebels 1912–13 *Southern Assn. (A)*; 1939–42 *Southeastern (B)*; m1943 *Southern Assn. (A1)*. Team began season in Chattanooga (TN) and moved to Montgomery July 11; 1946–50 *Southeastern (B)*; 1951, 1954–56m *South Atlantic (A)*. Team moved to Knoxville (TN) June 18. 1957–62 *Alabama–Florida (D)*; 1965–80 *Southern (AA)* In April 1861, Montgomery was named capital of the Confederate States of America. The Confederate White House was built here for Confederate President Jefferson Davis. City is nicknamed the "Cradle of the Confederacy." Montgomery fans and newspapers gagged on "Billikens" as overlong and silly and started calling the team the more dashing "Johnny Rebels" after manager Johnny Dobbs.

4065 Grey Sox 1920 *Negro Southern (ind.)*; 1921 *Southeastern Negro (ind.)*; 1932 *Negro Southern (ind.)*. Players wore gray-trim uniforms and gray stirrups.

4066 Lions 1926–30 *Southeastern (B)*. With managers Joe Brennan and then Nig Leonard at the helm in 1926, newspapers called the players "Brennan's Lions" and "Leonard's Lions." Bill Pierre took over in mid-season 1927 and the name became "Bill's Lions." Roy Ellam took over for 1929–30 and the name became "Ellam's Lions."

4067 Capitals 1932x *Southeastern (B)*. Team and league disbanded May 21 because of the Great Depression. Montgomery has been the state capital of Alabama since 1847.

4068 Bombers 1937–38 *Southeastern (B)*. 1937–42. Gunter and Maxwell Air Force Bases were built just outside the city in 1940 as the Army Air Corps prepared for World War II. With manager Bud Connolly at the helm in 1937–38, newspapers called the players "Bud's Bombers."

4069 Wings 2001 *All-American (ind.)*. Montgomery is home to Maxwell Air Force Base. Moniker is a spin-off from the 1937–38 Bombers nickname.

4070 Biscuits 2004 to date *Southern (AA)*. Management held a name-the-team contest hoping for a moniker that would be a tie-in to the ballpark food, which included "Southern fried chicken and biscuits." The winning entry turned out to be "Biscuits." The team logo is Monty, an anthropomorphized buttermilk biscuit. The ballpark's souvenir store is called the "Biscuit Basket."

Montgomery, West Virginia

4071 Miners 1910 *Virginia Valley (D)*; 1911 *Mountain States (D)*; m1912x *Mountain States (D)*. Team began season in Middleport-Pomeroy before transferring to Montgomery June 16. Team then disbanded June 29. Coal mining is so extensive in West Virginia that its nickname is the "Fuel State."

Montpelier, Vermont

4072 Capital Citys 1887 *Northeastern (ind.)*. Montpelier has been the state capital of Vermont since 1805, and is known as the "Capital City."

4073 Goldfish 1924x *Quebec–Ontario–Vermont (B)*. Team dis-

banded July 15. Players wore gold-trim uniforms after the gold-leaf dome of the state capitol building.

Montreal, Quebec, Canada

4074 Canadians m1890x *International (ind.)*. Team began season in Hamilton (ONT) and moved to Montreal June 23. Team and league disbanded July 7. Later used more famously by the pro ice hockey franchise, Canadians refers to an inhabitant of Canada. With manager Jimmy Dean at the helm, newspapers called the players "Dean's Canadians." Team's name in French was "Les Canadiens."

4075 Montreal Base Ball Club 1895 *Eastern International (ind.)*. Team had no nickname.

4076 Jingos m1897–1900 *Eastern (ind.)*. Team began the 1897 season in Rochester (NY) and moved to Montreal July 16. The British Royal Guards of this era were known as "Jingos." Canada was and is a British Commonwealth nation. "Jingos" gave rise to the word "jingoistic," which like "chauvinistic" means "fanatically patriotic."

4077 Royals m1897–1900 *Eastern (ind.)*. Team began the 1897 season in Rochester (NY) and moved to Montreal July 16; m1903–05, 1907–11 *Eastern (A, 1903–05, 1907–11)*. Team began the 1903 season in Worcester (MA) and moved to Montreal July 21; 1912–17 *International (AA)*; 1922–23 *Eastern Canada (B)*; m1923 *Eastern Canada (B)*. Team started the 1923 season in Trois Rivieres (Three Rivers) and moved to Montreal July 5; 1924 *Quebec–Ontario–Vermont (B)*; 1928–60 *International (AA 1928–45, AAA 1946–60)*. The city is built around Mount Royal.

4078 Canucks 1906 *Eastern (A)*. Coined in 1835 and at first a slang for French Canadians, term now refers to a western Canada "pioneering trapper" type. James Bannon managed the 1906 "Bannon's Canucks," and then later in the same season, Matt Kittridge led "Kittridge's Canucks."

4079 Black Royals 1928 *Independent Negro team*. Tag was a spin-off from the Montreal Royals of the International League.

4080 Expos 1969–2004 *National (M)*. Montreal hosted a World's Fair in the summer of 1967 called Expo '67. Expo '67 celebrated Canada's Centennial (1867–1967). Management held a name-the-team contest and "Expos" was the winner. Other entries included Nationals, Royals and Voyageurs.

4081 Red, White & Blue 1969–2004 *National (M)*. The traditional colors of the Expos uniform were "red, white and blue." Because these tints were the colors of the United States flag, the moniker never was used much and usually only by Montreal newspapers.

4082 Les Expos 1969–2004 *National (M)*. French language newspapers in the city referred to the Montreal players as "Les Expos" — much in the style as the NHL "Les Canadiens."

4083 Les Tres Colores 1969–2004 *National (M)*. Tag was a French language spin-off from the team's uniform colors. It was used principally in French-speaking newspapers in Quebec.

4084 Bon Voyage Expos 1995–2004 *National (M)*. A moniker of condemnation hurled by Canadian fans against the team's management following the splendid 1994 season (74–40 until the players strike ended the season in August), when the franchise almost systematically traded or sold every star player the then-productive farm system was presenting to the big league team. Some of the top-notch players that Expo management let get away included hitters Moises Alou, Andres Galarraga, Mark Grudzielanek, Henry Rodriguez and Larry Walker and pitchers Omar Daal, Pedro Martinez, Ugueth Urbina, Dave Veres and John Wetteland.

4085 Royales 2003x *Canadian (ind.)*. Circuit and team disbanded July 20. In the last 20 years there has been an emphasis on French becoming of equal importance to English in both the city of Montreal and the province of Quebec.

Moorhead, Minnesota

4086 Moorhead Base Ball Club 1897 *Red River Valley (ind.)*. Team had no nickname.

Mooresville, North Carolina

4087 Moors 1937–42 *North Carolina State (D)*; 1946–52 *North Carolina State (D)*; 1953 *Tar Heel (D)*. Moniker had no connection to the Arab and Berber warriors of the Middle Ages. With manager Jim Poole at the helm, newspapers called the eventual 1937 pennant winners "Jim Poole's Moors." Poole left the team after the 1937 season but the newspaper-friendly moniker was retained through 1942.

4088 Braves 1945 *North Carolina State (D)*. Team was a farm club of the Boston Braves.

Moose Jaw, Saskatchewan, Canada

4089 Robin Hoods 1909–11 *Western Canada (D)*; 1913–14 *Western Canada (D)*; 1919–20 *Western Canada (C 1919, B 1920–21)*. Originally a wheat milling company in the 1880s, the Robin Hood Wheat Milling Company, owned by Francis Bean, soon diversified and became the Robin Hood Bakery by 1909. The baseball team was named after this company. The name was appropriate because the Provincial Crown Forests of Saskatchewan cover 50 percent of the entire territory of Saskatchewan. According to legend, Robin Hood and his Merry Band made camp in England's Sherwood Forest.

4090 Millers 1921 *Western Canada (B)*. Local newspapers preferred this spin-off from Robin Hood Bakery that was shorter than "Robin Hoods." Manager Nick Williams led "Williams' Millers" and, then was succeeded by field skipper Elmer Leifer, who managed "Elmer Leifer's Millers." City has large grain storage facilities to store wheat shipped into the city from Saskatchewan farms.

4091 Diamond Dogs 1995–97x *Prairie (ind.)*. Team disbanded July 27, 1997. Chosen in a fan poll, Diamond Dog was a 1990s slang for "baseball player." "Dogs" (and its spelling variant "Dawg") derived from Rap and Hip-Hop music, and "Cats" derived from jazz music, were in popular use for songs in the 1990s. Sports teams then picked them up as team nicknames. Name was also appropriate because there are wild prairie dogs in Saskatchewan.

Morgan City, Louisiana

4092 Oyster Shuckers 1908 *Gulf Coast (D)*. Offshore fishing boats transport shrimp and oysters to city seafood processing factories to be processed, packed and shipped.

4093 South Louisiana Pipeliners 2009 *Continental (ind.)*. Offshore oil rigs transport crude oil to the city's petrochemical plants via pipelines that run from the Gulf of Mexico into Atchafalaya Bay directly to the city.

Morganton, North Carolina

4094 Aggies 1948–52x *Western Carolina (D)*. Team disbanded August 3. City is home to Western Piedmont College, which includes an Agricultural College. The school's sports teams are nicknamed the "Aggies"—short for Agriculturals. With manager Les McGarity at the helm in 1948, newspapers called the players "Les McGarity's Aggies." Moniker was retained through mid-season 1952 under seven other managers.

Moroleon, Mexico

4095 Club de Moroleon 1975 *Mexican Center (A)*. Team had no nickname.

Morristown, Tennessee

4096 Jobbers 1910 *Southeastern (D)*; 1911–12 *Appalachian (D)*; m1913–14x Team began the 1913 season in Cleveland (TN) and moved to Morristown June 9. Team and league disbanded June 17, 1914. With farming, furniture and textiles as the three leading industries, middle-men known as "jobbers" have bought merchandise from manufacturers and sold it to retailers in city markets here since 1870. As such, the city is known as the "Home of the Tennessee Valley Industrial District." Also, baseball players were known in this era as "jobbers" because they had off-season jobs before resuming play in spring training.

4097 Roosters 1923–25x *Appalachian (D)*. Circuit and team disbanded July 15. Farms near the city transport poultry to city food factories to be cleaned, packed and shipped. With manager James Barton at the helm in 1923, newspapers called the players "James Barton's Roosters." In 1924 Roy Clunk took over, changing the name to "Roy's Roosters." Hack Henderson took over in 1925, changing the name to "Henderson's Roosters."

4098 Red Sox 1948–54x *Mountain States (D)*. Team disbanded May 15. Team had a loose affiliation with the AL Boston Red Sox.

4099 Twins m1954 *Mountain States (D)*. Team started the season as the Maryville-Alcoa "Twins" and then moved to Morristown in mid-season. The Twins nickname was retained.

4100 Cubs 1959–61 *Appalachian (D)*. Team was a farm club of the Chicago Cubs.

Moultrie, Georgia

4101 Packers 1916–17x *Dixie (D)*. Team and league disbanded July 4 due to U.S. entry into World War I; 1936–42 *Georgia–Florida (D)*; 1946–47 *Georgia–Florida (D)*. Farms near the city transported peanuts, pecans, peaches, cotton and tobacco to city factories to be processed, packed and shipped.

4102 Steers 1935 *Georgia–Florida (D)*. Team was a farm club of the Class A Dallas Steers. Between 1910 and 1950 minor league teams sometimes had their own farms clubs. Examples included the Los Angeles Angels, Shreveport Sports and Dallas Steers. The Great Depression of 1929–40 forced loose affiliations between teams at all levels of Organized Baseball.

4103 Athletics 1948–49 *Georgia–Florida (D)*. Team was a farm club of the Philadelphia A's.

4104 Cubs 1950 *Georgia–Florida (D)*. Team was a farm club of the Chicago Cubs.

4105 Tobaks 1951 *Georgia–Florida (D)*. Right after World War II there was a boom in tobacco production here, which then declined in the 1970s as federal warnings about cigarette smoking were issued. Plantations in the region transported tobacco leaves to city packing houses.

4106 Giants 1952 *Georgia–Florida (D)*. Team was a farm club of the New York Giants.

4107 Reds 1956 *Georgia–Florida (D)*. Team was a farm club of the Cincinnati Reds.

4108 Phillies 1957m *Georgia–Florida (D)*. Team moved to Brunswick (GA) June 1. Team was a farm club of the Philadelphia Phillies.

4109 Colt .22's 1962–63 *Georgia–Florida (D 1962, A 1963)*. Team was a farm club of the Houston Colt .45's. The caliber .22 is a pistol that is smaller than a caliber .45 pistol. "Caliber" refers to the diameter of the bore of a gun.

Mound City, Illinois

4110 Blues 1916 *Independent Negro team.* Players wore blue-trim uniforms and stirrups.

Mount Airy, North Carolina

4111 Graniteers 1934, 1939–41 *Bi-State (D)*; 1946–50 *Blue Ridge (D).* Granite quarries have been mined in the nearby Blue Ridge Mountains since 1889. North Carolina is "Nature's Mineral Specimen Case" (300 different minerals have been discovered in the state). With manager Cecil Harris at the helm in 1934, newspapers called the players "Cecil Harris' Graniteers." Guy Lacy managed in 1939 and the name was "Guy's Graniteers." Edwin Morgan in 1946 led "Edwin Morgan's Graniteers." In 1948 Noel Casbier led "Casbier's Graniteers." In 1949 Eurice Trece led "Eurice's Graniteers."

4112 Reds 1935–38 *Bi-State (D).* Players wore red-trim uniforms. Team had a loose affiliation with the Cincinnati Reds.

Mount Carmel, Pennsylvania

4113 Reliance 1887–88 *Central Pennsylvania (ind.).* Team was the amateur "Reliance Club of Mount Carmel" (est. 1880). Reliance was a popular nineteenth-century team nickname for baseball teams in the style of stability and dependability, i.e., Enterprise, Equity, Excelsior, Independent, Perseverance, Reliance, Resolute and Star.

4114 Mount Carmel Base Ball Club 1896 *Central Pennsylvania (ind.).* Team had no nickname.

Mount Clemens, Michigan

4115 Bathers 1906–07 *Southern Michigan Assn. (D)*; 1912–13x *Border (D).* Circuit and team disbanded July 12. City is located on the west coast of Lake St. Clair. Around 1900, the city built health resorts to attract tourists to enjoy baths of mineral water found in nearby springs. With manager D. Trembly at the helm in 1906, newspapers called the players "Trembly's Bathers." Trembley left the team after the 1906 season, but the name was used again in 1907. Mount Clemens is known as "America's Bath City."

Mount Pleasant, Texas

4116 Cats 1923–25m *East Texas (D).* The Mount Pleasant Cats and the Longview Cannibals merged June 7. The "Cannibals" nickname was dropped and the new team adopted the nickname of "Long Cats." Nickname combined "Cats" with "Long" (from Longview) to form "Long Cats." All home games for the merged team were played in Longview. The team played home games in both cities June 8–July 11. Starting on July 12 all home games were played in Longview until the end of the season. The team was a farm club of the Class A Fort Worth Panthers. In the 1920s and 1930s several higher class minor league teams (AAA and AA) maintained farms teams in the lower classification leagues (A, B, C and D).

Mount Sterling, Kentucky

4117 Orphans m1912 *Blue Grass (D).* Team began season in Winchester (KY), moved to Nicholasville (KY) and then moved to Mount Sterling June 26. Teams that switched cities in mid-season due to low attendance were sometimes called "Orphans," i.e., "abandoned" by the fans of the initial city.

4118 Essex 1922–23 *Blue Grass (D).* With manager Hod Eller at the helm local newspapers called the players "Eller's Essex." Robert Devereux, the 2nd Earl of Essex, was a sixteenth century English nobleman who was a favorite of Queen Elizabeth I. Noblemen of this era were often quite athletic, i.e., horse riding, archery, fencing and hawking. Essex found its way into baseball jargon as referring to "athletic men"—hence a team of baseball players became known as the "Essex."

Mount Vernon, Illinois

4119 Merchants 1910x *South Illinois (D).* Another team in the circuit, McLeansboro, was also known as the "Merchants." Team disbanded June 30. City was built in 1820 and quickly became a market center for farm produce. Local newspaper reporters started using "Merchants" to reflect the city's farming merchant trade.

4120 Braves 1947–48 *Illinois State (D).* Team had a loose affiliation with the NL Boston Braves in 1947 before becoming an official farm team of the NL Braves in 1948.

4121 Kings 1949–54 *Mississippi–Ohio Valley (M.O.V.) (D).* Surrounded by rich farm land, Mount Vernon is known as the "King of Diversified Farming of Illinois."

Mount Vernon, Ohio

4122 Clippers 1905 *Ohio–Pennsylvania (D).* Since 1880 small clipper boats have sailed the nearby North Fork Licking, Sycamore and Wahlhondling rivers. "Clipper" trains traveled the Baltimore & Ohio and Cleveland-Akron-Columbus railroads in this era. With manager Bill Goodrich at the helm, local newspapers called the players "Bill's Clippers."

Mountaindale, New York

4123 Sullivan County Mountain Lions 1995 *Northeast (ind.).* Team went by the county name of "Sullivan County Mountain Lions." Although most mountain lions, i.e., cougars, were driven away by settlers in the eighteenth and nineteenth centuries, a few mountain lions inhabit the nearby Catskill Mountains. Cougar sightings in New York State have increased in the last few years.

4124 Catskill Cougars 1996 *North Atlantic (ind.)*; 1997–98 *Northeast (ind.).* Team went by the regional name of "Catskill Cougars." Mountain Lions, i.e., cougars, inhabit the nearby Catskill Mountains. "Cougars" was a newspaper-friendly spinoff from "Mountain Lions."

Muncie, Indiana

4125 Muncie Base Ball Club 1890 *Indiana State (ind.)*; 1900–01 *Indiana State (ind.).* These teams had no nickname.

4126 Hoosiers 1899x *Indiana–Illinois (ind.).* Team disbanded July 5. Indiana is known as the "Hoosier State."

4127 Fruit Jars 1906 *Inter-State Assn. I*; 1908 *Indiana–Ohio (D).* Fruit farms in the vicinity shipped fruit to city processing centers to be cleaned, packed and shipped. With manager Frederick Paige at the helm in 1906, newspapers called the players "Fred's Fruit Jars." With manager J.F. "Dick" Baird at the helm in 1908, newspapers called the players "Baird's Fruit Jars."

4128 Reds 1947 *Ohio State (D)*; 1949–50 *Ohio–Indiana (D).* Team was a farm club of the Cincinnati Reds.

4129 Packers 1948 *Ohio–Indiana (D).* Surrounding fruit farms transport fruit to the city for processing, packing and shipping.

Murray, Utah

4130 Infants 1914x *Union Assn. (D)*. Team disbanded July 20. Team had many young players and their inexperience showed as they were unable to get out of last place when the franchise disbanded July 20. With manager Cliff Blankenship at the helm, newspapers called the players "Cliff's Infants."

Muscatine, Iowa

4131 Pearl Finders 1910 *Northern Assn. of Baseball (C 1910, D 1910)*. City is home to three pearl button manufacturers—the J.F. Boeppel Button Company (since 1884), McKee Button Company (since 1902) and Weber & Sons Button Company (since 1915). Because of this industry, Muscatine became the "Pearl Button Capital of the World." Pearl divers and oyster fishermen are sometimes called "pearl finders."

4132 Camels 1911 *Central Assn. (D)*. Later used by the city's Muscatine College athletic teams, starting in 1929, the moniker derives from the city name's spelling. With manager Harry C. Blake at the helm, newspapers called the players "Blake's Camels."

4133 Wallopers 1912–13 *Central Assn. (D)*. During flood seasons, the banks of the Mississippi River overflow, prompting city officials to hire people known as "Mud Wallopers" to sand-bag the river banks. With manager Joe Wall at the helm in 1912, newspapers called the players "Wall's Wallopers." Frank Boyle took over in 1913 and the name became "Boyle's Wallopers."

4134 Button Makers 1914 *Central Assn. (D)*. Tag was a spin-off from "Pearl-finders." Frank Boyle returned as manager and the team nickname became "Boyle's Button-makers."

4135 Muskies 1915–16 *Central Assn. (D)*. The Muskie fish is found in lakes, rivers and bays of the Great Lakes throughout the Midwest. The muskie also inhabits the nearby Mississippi River.

Muskegon, Michigan

4136 Muskegon Base Ball Club 1884x *Northwestern (ind.)*. Team disbanded August 2; 1890x *Michigan State (ind.)*. Team disbanded in mid-season (date unknown). These teams had no nickname.

4137 Lumber Citys 1902x *Michigan State (D)*. Muskegon has been a lumbertown since 1860. Team and league disbanded August 20.

4138 Reds 1902x *Michigan State (D)*. Team and league disbanded August 20; 1911 *Michigan State (D)*; 1916 *Central (B)*; 1926t *Central (C)*; t1926 *Michigan State (B)*. Team started the season in the Class C Central League, which merged with the Class B Michigan–Ontario League in June to form the Class B Michigan State League; 1934x *Central (B)*. Team disbanded May 30 because of the Great Depression; 1940–41 *Michigan State (C)*. Players wore red hose (1902) and red stirrups (1916, 1926, 1934, 1940–41). The 1902 team was a farm club of the Cincinnati Reds, but the other teams were not.

4139 Speed Boys 1910 *West Michigan (D)*; 1912 *Michigan State (D)*. Moniker, which was a contemporary slang for baseball players, was actually a spin-off from "speeders" and "speedsters," which were slang for automobiles. People in this era were amazed at how speedy automobiles were in comparison to horses. With manager Arthur DeBaker at the helm in 1910 and 1912, newspapers called the players "DeBaker's Speed Boys."

4140 Speeders 1910 *West Michigan (D)*; 1912–13 *Michigan State (D)*. Moniker has two origins. Ford, Buick, General Motors and Oldsmobile, after building factories in Detroit and Flint, built automobile factories in Muskegon by 1909. In this era automobiles were known as "speedsters" and "speeders." Cars were so fast in com-

parison to horse-drawn carriages that people were amazed at these "speeders." Eventually the term evolved into the driver of a car who exceeded the speed limit and, in doing so, broke the law. In this era, "speeder" also meant a "baseball player." In this Dead Ball era, great emphasis was placed on speedy base runners. Teams that won with team speed were called "Speed Boys" and "Speeders." With manager Arthur DeBaker at the helm in 1912, newspapers called the players "DeBaker's Speed Boys." Manager Peg Bemis took over, leading "Peg Bemis' Speeders," and then Sandy Murray succeeded him, guiding "Sandy Murray's Speeders."

4141 Muskies 1917 *Central (B)*; 1920–22 *Central (B)*. Muskies swim in the nearby Muskegon River, which drains into Houghton Lake. Newspapers used the tag for headlines, i.e., "Muskies edge Evas, 4–3."

4142 Daniels 1922 *Central (B)*. The field manager this year was Dannie Claire.

4143 Anglers 1923–24 *Michigan–Ontario (B)*. With manager George "Red" Fisher at the helm, newspapers called the players "Fisher's Anglers." Fishing is available at nearby White Duck Lake and the Muskegon River. Jack Ryan took over in mid-season 1924 and the name became "Ryan's Anglers."

4144 Lassies 1946–50 *All-American Girls (ind.)*. This league played softball 1941–47 and baseball 1948–54. Scottish slang for girl was appropriate for this all-female team.

4145 Clippers 1948–51 *Central (A)*. Commercial, recreational boats and clipper boats have sailed the Muskegon River, Muskegon Lake and Lake Michigan since 1840.

Muskogee, Oklahoma

4146 Reds 1905x *Missouri Valley (D)*. Team disbanded September 1; 1917 *Western Assn. (D)*; 1937–42 *Western Assn. I*; 1946–50 *Western Assn. I*. Players wore red hose in 1905 and red-trim uniforms with red stirrups in 1917. Team was a farm club of the Cincinnati Reds, 1937–42 and 1946–50.

4147 Indians 1906x *South Central (D)*. Team and league disbanded in August; 1912 *Oklahoma State (D)*. Explorers and settlers encountered the "Five Civilized Tribes" of Oklahoma—the Cherokee, Chickasaw, Choctaw, Creek and Seminole—who had been expelled from Georgia to travel the "Trail of Tears" (4,000+ died along the way) from 1865 to 1885. Skirmishes, battles, massacres and war (the tribes allied themselves with Confederate troops) were numerous. With homesteaders flooding Oklahoma starting in 1889, a military headquarters was established in this city in 1898 to govern and tend to the needs of the survivors. With manager Nixey Callahan at the helm, newspapers called the players "Nixey Callahan's Indians." The team had no affiliation with the Cleveland Indians. Oklahoma is the "Land of the Red Men."

4148 Redskins 1907 *Oklahoma–Arkansas–Kansas (O.A.K.) (D)*; 1911 *Western Assn. (D)*. Circuit and team disbanded June 19. Tag was a spin-off from Indians. Oklahoma is the "Land of the Redmen." A "politically incorrect" name today, "redskins" caused no stir in a society of that time when racism was commonplace. With manager Lon Ury at the helm in 1911, newspapers called the players "Ury's Redskins."

4149 Navigators 1909–10x *Western Assn. I*. Team disbanded July 22. Muskogee is a port city along the Arkansas and Verdigris rivers where commercial and recreational boats have sailed since 1820.

4150 Mets 1914–16 *Western Assn. (D)*; 1921–23 *Southwestern (D 1921, C 1922–23)*. With manager George McAvoy at the helm in 1914, newspapers called the players "McAvoy's Mets." McAvoy left the team after 1914, but the newspaper-friendly Mets name was retained.

4151 Athletics 1924–26x *Western Assn.(C).* Team disbanded July 20, 1926. With field manager Gabby Street at the helm, local newspapers called the players "Gabby's Athletics." Street never played for the Philadelphia Athletics, nor was the team ever a farm club of this big league team. Walt Kreuger and then George Armstrong managed the team in 1926, hence the names "Walt's Athletics" and "Armstrong's Athletics."

4152 Chiefs 1927–29m *Western Assn. I.* Team moved to Maud (OK) August 22; 1930–32m *Western Assn. I.* Team moved to Hutchinson (KS) June 8. The Shawnee leader, Chief Tecumseh, convinced the Muskogee-Creek to become involved in the War of 1812. By the 1830s the Muskogee-Creek had been forced onto reservations in Oklahoma.

4153 Nighthawks 1932 *Western Assn. I.* Team moved to Hutchinson (KS) June 8. "Nighthawks," also known as "Whip-poor-wills," inhabit the region.

4154 Oilers m1933r *Western (A).* Team started season in Wichita (KS) and then moved to Muskogee June 6. By June 30 team had become a road team because low attendance left them unable to pay their home park lease, leading to their eviction. The Glenn Pools Gusher, near Tulsa, was struck in 1905. Oil rigs were quickly built to transport oil to refineries in both Tulsa and Muskogee.

4155 Tigers 1934–36 *Western Assn. I.* Players wore striped stirrups. With manager Conrad Fisher at the helm in 1934, newspapers called the players "Fisher's Tigers." With manager David Miner at the helm in 1935, the name became "Miner's Tigers." When Carl Kentling succeeded him in mid-season, the name became "Kentling's Tigers." The team was never a farm club of the Detroit Tigers.

4156 Seals 1936 *Western Assn. I.* Team was a farm club of the New York Giants, who sometimes optioned players from the Giants' Class AAA affiliate, the San Francisco Seals. Fans didn't like the name and it was used only sporadically this season.

4157 Giants 1951–54 *Western Assn. I*; 1955–57 *Sooner State (D).* Team was a farm club of the New York Giants.

Myrtle Beach, South Carolina

4158 Blue Jays 1987–90 *South Atlantic (A).* Team was a farm club of the Toronto Blue Jays.

4159 Hurricanes 1991–92 *South Atlantic (A).* During the summer and autumn months hurricanes sometimes travel up along the Atlantic coast and reach South Carolina.

4160 Pelicans 1999 to date *Carolina (A).* Pelicans are semi-tropical and tropical fisher-birds that inhabit the temperate coasts of the Southeast.

Nacogdoches, Texas

4161 Cogs 1916 *East Texas (D).* With manager Tom Cherry at the helm, newspapers called the players "Cherry's Cogs."

Nagoya, Japan

4162 Kinkos 1936–40 *Japanese Professional (ind.).* Team owner, the Kinnosachihiko Company, used the first three and last two letters of its name to form the abbreviation of "Kinko." The company was also known as Kinachihiko as well as "Kinko."

4163 Golden Dolphins 1936–40 *Japanese Professional (ind.).* The players wore gold trim uniforms, which gave rise to the monikers of "Golden Dolphins" and "Goldfish." Dolphins swim the coastal waters of Japan.

4164 Goldfish 1936–40 *Japanese Professional (ind.).* Players wore gold trim uniforms. Goldfish ponds are popular in Japan. Team was

also known as **Dragon Fish**, which eventually evolved into "Dragons" for the franchise in 1947.

4165 Nagoya Baseball Club 1936–43 *Japanese Professional (ind.).* This franchise is a different one from the Nagoya Kinko. In the years 1936–40, the city of Nagoya had two teams. The team had no nickname.

4166 Sangyo 1944 *Japanese Professional (ind.).* Team was owned by the Kato Sangyo Foodstuffs Company.

4167 Chubu Nippon 1946 *Japanese Professional (ind.).* Team was owned by the Chubu Nippon Broadcasting Company.

4168 Nippon Dragons 1947 *Japanese Professional (ind.).* Team was purchased by newspaper tycoon Toranosuke "The Dragon" Sagiyama. He got his nickname because he had been born in the "Year of the Dragon." The team adopted his nickname for its own.

4169 Chunichi Dragons 1948–49 *Japanese Professional (ind.).* Team has been owned by Chunichi-Chimbum Newspapers 1946–50 and 1953 to date. Nippon, which is the Japanese word for "Japan," was dropped.

4170 Chunichi Dragons 1950, 1953 to date *Japanese Central (ind.).* After the Japanese Professional League disbanded, the team joined the new Japanese Central League in 1950.

4171 Dragons 1951–52 *Japanese Central (ind.)*; 1959 to date *Japanese Western (ind.).* The sponsor name was dropped as the team was known as the "Nagoya Dragons" in 1951–52. The Western League team is a farm club of the Central League Chunichi Dragons.

Napa, California

4172 Napa Baseball Club 1910x *Central California (D).* Team disbanded May 29. Team had no nickname.

Naranjos, Mexico

4173 Valles 1972–73 *Mexican Center (A).* City is located in Orange Valley (Valle de Naranjas).

Narrows-Perrisburg, Virginia

4174 New River Rebels 1946–50 *Appalachian (D).* Team went by the regional name of "New River Rebels." In May 1861, Robert E. Lee became commander of the Confederate Army of Northern Virginia. Most battles of the Civil War were fought in Virginia. Virginia is the "Battlefield of the Civil War."

Nashua, New Hampshire

4175 Nashua Base Ball Club 1886 *New Hampshire State (ind.)*; 1888 *New England Interstate (ind.)*; 1901–05 *New England (ind. 1901, B 1902–05).* These teams had no nickname.

4176 Rainmakers 1895 *New England Assn. (ind.).* In the era 1890–1910, teams that had numerous postponed games because of rainy weather, particularly at the start of the season, were sometimes called "Rainmakers."

4177 Millionaires 1926–27 *New England (B)*; m1929–30 *New England (B).* Team began the 1929 season in Lowell (MA) and then moved to Nashua June 19; m1933m *New England (B).* Team began season in Quincy (MA) and then moved to Nashua in June 6. Team moved to Brockton (MA) August 8. Settled in 1653, the city became the "Gate City of New Hampshire," and by 1900 was a textile, manufacturing and shipbuilding center. Owners of such industries quickly became millionaires. Team was owned by millionaire Frank Murphy, who owned Tom McAn Shoes, and later become governor of New Hampshire. Name quickly turned sarcastic as the 1926 team skidded to eighth place, finishing with a 37–56 record. With manager John Mitchell at the helm in 1927, as the team sunk into last place, newspapers started sarcastically calling the players "Mitchell's Millionaires." With manager Bill Merritt at the helm in 1929, newspapers called the players "Bill Merritt's Millionaires." Tom DeNoville took over as manager in mid-season 1929, leading to "DeNoville's Millionaires." Shano Collins took over as manager in 1930, and the team became "Collins' Millionaires. With new manager Billy Flynn at the helm in 1933, Nashua newspapers called the players "Billy Flynn's Millionaires." New Hampshire has silver mines and is known as the "Silver State," which contributed to the "Millionaires" moniker.

4178 Dodgers 1946–49 *New England (B)*. Team was a farm club of the Brooklyn Dodgers.

4179 Angels 1983 *Eastern (AA)*. Team was a farm club of the California Angels.

4180 Pirates 1984–86 *Eastern (AA)*. Team was a farm club of the Pittsburgh Pirates.

4181 Hawks 1995–96 *North Atlantic (ind.)*. Management held a name-the-team contest and the fans chose "Hawks."

4182 Pride 1998–2005 *Atlantic (ind.)*; 2006–08 *Canadian–American (ind.)*. In 1997 *Money Magazine* declared Nashua as the "Best Place to Live in America." The new Nashua team responded by calling themselves the "Pride." The jersey blouse uniform bore the insignia "Pl." Eventually a lion was portrayed as the team logo/mascot, suggesting a "pride of lions."

4183 American Defenders of New Hampshire 2009 *Canadian–American (ind.)*. On August 17, 1777, Vermont brigadier General John Stark led 1400 Vermont Continental Army soldiers in a defense against British troops. More directly, the team was owned by the Nacona Athletic Goods Company, which manufactures a line of baseball gloves with the marketing name of "American Defenders."

Nashville, Tennessee

4184 Americans 1885–86 *Southern (ind.)*. During the Civil War, eastern Tennessee was pro–Union while western Tennessee seceded and joined the Confederacy. Moniker honored both groups. The Battle of Nashville, December 15–16, 1864, resulted in the Union Army seizing the city. After the war, Tennessee experienced no occupying U.S. Army because loyalty to the Union was quickly reestablished.

4185 Blues 1887 *Southern (ind.)*. Players wore blue hose. Originally **Blue Stockings**, newspapers shortened the name to "Blues."

4186 Tigers 1893–94 *Southern (ind.)*. Players wore striped hose. Popularized by the striped jerseys and stockings of the Princeton University Tigers football (and baseball) teams of the 1890s, numerous baseball teams started wearing striped hose. With manager Ted Sullivan at the helm, newspapers called the 1893 players "Ted's Tigers." In 1894 George Stallings, a Princeton alumnus, became field manager and the team became "Stallings' Tigers." Stallings resigned to manage the Western League Detroit Tigers.

4187 Seraphs 1895 *Southern (ind.)*. With manager George Stallings at the helm, newspapers called the team "Stalling's Seraphs." In this era, "seraphs" was a common, ironic slang for drinking, smoking, spitting, brawling, womanizing baseball players who were anything but "angelic."

4188 Vols 1901–61 Southern Assn. *(ind. 1901, A 1902–34, A1 1935–45, AA 1946–61)*. With the outbreak of war against Mexico in 1847, Tennessee Governor Aaron Vail Brown, on May 26, 1847, made a public plea for 2,800 Volunteers from his state to join the military. An astonishing 30,000 volunteers responded to enlist in the army, navy and marines, and Tennessee became known as the "Volunteer State." Nashville newspapers immediately shortened the name of **Volunteers** to "Vols."

4189 Fishermen 1904 *Southern Assn. (A)*. The field manager this season was Jack Fisher.

4190 Finnites 1906 *Southern Assn. (A)*. The field manager this season was Michael Finn.

4191 French Lick Plutos 1916 *Independent Negro* team. Team went by the regional name of "French Lick Plutos." Sulfur swamps, known as the "French Lick" or "Big Salt Lick," just outside the city give off hellish sulfur fumes. In Roman mythology, Pluto was the God of the sulfur and brimstone underworld known as "Hades."

4192 Standard Giants 1918–19 *Independent Negro team*; 1920 *Southern Negro (ind.)*. The 1920 Southern Negro League was a professional but not major league. Combining the ever-popular "Giants" with an adjective denoting quality was a common practice for black teams of this era. "Standard" means a "model of excellence."

4193 Elite Giants 1921–25 *Independent Negro team*; 1926–29 *Negro Southern Negro (M)*. The 1920 Southern Negro League was a minor league. The 1926–29 Negro Southern League was a major league; 1930 *Negro National (M)*; 1930–31, 1932–33, 1934–35 *California Winter (W)*; 1932 *Negro Southern*. This Negro Southern League was a minor league; 1933–34 *Negro National (M)*; 1951 *Negro American (ind.)*. After the 1948 season this circuit was no longer a major league. Moniker was a newspaper-friendly spinoff from "Standard." The new adjective of "Elite" also refers to top echelon ability.

4194 Black Vols 1947 *Independent Negro team*. Tag is a spin-off from Vols. In the 1930s and 1940s, black teams strapped for cash received donated uniforms from white teams and simply adopted the nickname appearing on the jersey, i.e., Black Barons, Black Crackers, Black Senators, Black Yankees, Brown Dodgers and Black Vols.

4195 Sounds 1978–84 *Southern (AA)*; 1986–97 *American Assn. (AAA)*; 1998 to date *Pacific Coast (AAA)*. The American Association was disbanded after the 1997 season. Four teams joined the PCL, while the other four teams joined the International League. Known as the "Music City" and the "Country Music Capital of the World," Nashville hosts the Grand Ole Opry and is the site of the Country Music Hall of Fame, Ryman Auditorium, and several recording studios. Blues and jazz music has been prevalent here since at least 1920. In the 1930s a style of music known as the "Nashville Sound" sprung up in clubs and concerts.

4196 X-Press 1993–94 *Southern (AA)*. The Louisville & Nashville Railroad (est. 1855) provides the city with transport to and from the North while the Memphis & Charleston Railroad (est. 1860) links the city to the East. Some of these trains were known as "The Express." Trains that travel at high speed with few or no stops prior to the destination are known as "express trains."

Natchez, Mississippi

4197 Indians 1902–03 *Cotton States (D)*; 1948–53 *Cotton States I*. Settlers, resorting to warfare and enslavement, drove the now-extinct Natchez Indians out of Mississippi in the eighteenth century. A French colony was wiped out in 1729 by the Natchez Indians, led by Chief Great Sun. In 1730 a French Army from New Orleans destroyed the Natchez tribes. There was no farm system in 1902–03, and the 1948–53 teams were not farm clubs of the Cleveland Indians.

4198 Hill Climbers 1904–05m *Cotton States (D)*. Team moved to Mobile (AL) June 26. Mississippi was inhabited by the mound-building Plaquemine Culture Indians, who built mounds in the region from 1200 to 1450 A.D. The Natchez Indians arrived next and continued to build mounds. The city was built on rolling hills of the Eastern Plains near the Mississippi River. When the French arrived in 1716, they used the hills to build fortified settlements.

4199 Pilgrims m1940–41 *Evangeline (D)*. Team began 1940 season in Houma (LA) and moved to Natchez June 27. In the era 1930–50, teams that transferred in mid-season were occasionally called "Pilgrims." The "Natchez Trail" was a route used by Rene Robert Cavalier and his French Catholic "pilgrims" in 1682. The town was established in 1716. English Baptist "pilgrims" settled in Natchez during the eighteenth century. In 1932, tours of nineteenth-century mansions and plantations commenced. These tours have been known as the "Natchez Pilgrimage Tours" and continue to this day.

4200 Giants 1942x *Evangeline (D)*; 1946–47 *Evangeline (D)*. The 1942 team was a farm club of the New York Giants. By 1946 the team played as an independent, using the 1942 moniker. The team was not a farm club of the New York Giants in 1946–47.

Navajoa, Sonora, Mexico

4201 Caneros 1945–46 *Liga de la Costa Pacifica Mexicana (W)*; 1955–56–57–58 *Liga de la Costa Pacifica Mexicana (W)*. Sugar is transported from nearby plantations to city factories to be processed, packed and shipped. "Los Caneros" in English means variously sugarcaners, sugar harvesters and sugar cane growers.

4202 Mayos 1950–51–54–55 *Liga de la Costa Pacifica Mexicana (W)*; 1959–60 *Liga de Sonoroa–Sinoloa (W)*; 1962–63–1966–67 *Liga de Sonora–Sinoloa*; 1970–71 to date *Liga Mexicana del Pacifico(W)*; 1976 *Liga Mexicana del Pacifico (A)*. Mexican Pacific League, a winter circuit, experimented with a summer schedule in 1976. Low attendance prompted league officials to discontinue summer play. The Mayo Indians are a tribe of northern-central Mexico, i.e., Sinoloa and Sonora. They are not to be confused with the Maya Indians of southern Mexico, Central America and South America.

Nazareth, Pennsylvania

4203 Cement Dusters 1946 *North Atlantic (D)*. More than 90 percent of Pennsylvania's non-fuel mineral production consists of crushed stone, i.e., lime, cement (for porcelain and masonry), construction sand and gravel. Non-fuel minerals are excavated in nearby sites and then shipped to city factories for processing. Cement companies in the city include CoPlay Cement, Hercules Cement and Penn-Dixie Cement.

4204 Tigers 1947 *North Atlantic (D)*. Team was a farm club of the Detroit Tigers.

4205 Barons 1948–50 *North Atlantic (D)*. With manager Bill Burich at the helm, newspapers called the players "Burich's Barons." Pennsylvania is noted for its coal and mineral and oil deposits, giving rise to the terms "coal barons, oil barons, steel barons, retail barons and big business barons, i.e., Pennsylvania's Andrew Carnegie, Charles Schwab, Frank Woolworth (stores) and Milton Hershey (chocolate candies)."

Nebraska City, Nebraska

4206 Forresters 1910–13x *Missouri–Iowa–Nebraska–Kansas (M.I.N.K.) (D)*. City and team disbanded June 17. The city is the birthplace of Sterling Morton, who originated Arbor Day. In 1872 Morton and government officials encouraged tree planting in Nebraska, a prairie state barren of forests. In 1913, ironically, the field manager was Jack Forrester.

Negaunee, Michigan

4207 Unions 1892 *Michigan–Wisconsin (ind.)*. "Unions" was a popular team nickname for northern states' athletic clubs for the pe-

riod 1865–1900 because of lingering hostile feelings toward the South due to the Civil War. The moniker also derives from the spelling of the city's name.

4208 Negaunee Base Ball Club 1895x *Upper Peninsula (ind.)*. Circuit and team disbanded in mid-season (date unknown). Team had no nickname.

Neosho, Missouri

4209 Nighthawks 1937 *Arkansas–Missouri (D)*. The nighthawk, also called the whip-poor-will and the American nightjar, is found throughout North America. The moniker "Nighthawks" became the traditional name for the city's high school and college teams.

4210 Yankees 1938–40 *Arkansas–Missouri (D)*. Team was a farm club of the New York Yankees.

Nettuno, Italy

4211 Caffe Danesi 1999 to date *Italian A1 (ind.)*. Team is owned by the Caffe Danesi coffee company.

Nevada, Missouri

4212 Lunatics 1902–03x *Missouri Valley (D)*. Nevada is the site of the Missouri State Institute for the Criminally Insane. In this era many people thought professional baseball players were "crazy." With manager Bill Driscoll at the helm, newspapers called the players "Driscoll's Lunatics."

New Bedford, Massachusetts

4213 Whalers 1878 *International Assn. (M)*; 1879 *National Assn. (M)*; 1895–98m *New England (ind.)*. Team moved to Worcester (MA) June 14; m1903–13 *New England (B)*. Team began 1903 season in Brockton (MA) and transferred to New Bedford June 27; 1914–15 *Colonial (C 1914, ind. 1915)*; 1933 *New England (B)*; 1934 *Northeastern (B)*. New Bedford is known as the "Whaling City" and the "Whaling Capital of the World." Founded in 1760, the city soon became a shipping and whaling center.

4214 Blues 1878 *International Assn. (M)*; 1879 *National Assn. (M)*. Players wore blue hose. Originally **Blue Stockings**, newspapers shortened it to **Blue Legs** and "Blues."

4215 Browns 1896 *New England (ind.)*. Players wore brown hose.

4216 Millmen 1929 *New England (B)*. Apart from whaling and fishing, the city in the nineteenth century had many textile mills and clothing stores.

New Bern, North Carolina

4217 Truckers 1902 *North Carolina (D)*. Settled in 1710, the city was a center of commerce and farm goods and became a resort area by 1900. "Truckers" were peddlers who transported goods by wagon and carriage, and by 1900 the first motorized automobile for transport appeared, i.e., "trucks." In the nineteenth century, boats transported freight to Pimlico Port where it was "trucked" off in wagons for market. State was nicknamed the "Good Roads State" after new roads were built for the infant trucking industry. The city of New Bern is known as the "Hub of Coastal Carolina" where goods are trucked in and out by boat and land vehicles.

4218 New Bern Baseball Club 1908x *Eastern Carolina (D)*. Team disbanded July 15. Team had no nickname.

4219 Bears 1937–41 *Coastal Plain (D)*; 1946–52 *Coastal Plain (D)*. City was named in honor of Bern, Switzerland. The city crest of Bern portrays a bear.

New Brighton, Beaver, Pennsylvania

4220 New Brighton Base Ball Club 1884 *Iron & Oil Assn. (ind.)*. Team had no nickname.

New Britain, Connecticut

4221 New Britain Base Ball Club 1885 *Connecticut State (ind.)*; 1891x *Connecticut (ind.)*. These teams had no nickname.

4222 Perfectos 1908–12m *Connecticut (B)*. Team moved to Waterbury (CT) June 15. White Cuban League stars Armando Marsans, Rafael Alameida, Alfredo Cabrera and pitcher Luis Padron were signed by New Britain for the 1908 season. Enthused local newspapers gushed that the signings were reminiscent of the 1899 St. Louis "Perfectos" signings of star pitcher Cy Young and numerous other talented ex–Cleveland Spiders players. Despite the high hopes, the 1908 team disappointed its fans with a 61–64 record. The era 1895–1910 brought forth some quite boastful nicknames, i.e., Superbas, Perfectos, Champions, Wonders and Premiers.

4223 Sinks 1914 *Eastern Assn. (B)*. With a worldwide economic empire since the seventeenth century, Great Britain maintained what was known as the "Unsinkable British Empire." Unfortunately, for New Britain fans, the 1914 team sank like a rock to the bottom the Eastern Association standings with an ocean-floor dwelling 27–97 record.

4224 Red Sox 1984–94 *Eastern (AA)*. Team was farm club of the Boston Red Sox.

4225 Rock Cats 1995 to date *Eastern (AA)*. In the 1990s, dogs and cats and its Hip-Hop music slang of Dawgs and Katz became popular for sports team nicknames. Settled in 1668, the city became a metal-working center. By 1850 the city had numerous shops and factories for the manufacture of tools, locks and other hardware. City acquired the nickname of "Hardware City." Accordingly, the team played under the title of "Hardware City Rock Cats" 1995–96 because it got financial backing from the Stanley Tools Factory. However, team owner Joe Buzas feared that out-of-town and out-of-state fans would be confused about "Hardware City" and changed the name back to New Britain Rock Cats. The "Rock Cats" logo is a "cool" cat playing a rock 'n' roll guitar.

New Brunswick, New Jersey

4226 Hubs 1948m *Colonial (B)*. New Brunswick, located in central New Jersey, is the hub of five highways, i.e., the Jersey Turnpike, and the Delaware and Raritan canals for ships that lead in and out of New York Bay. City is known as the "Industrial and Cultural Center of New Jersey." Two-thirds of New Jersey's state population resides in the New Brunswick metropolitan area.

New Castle, Pennsylvania (also spelled Newcastle)

4227 Neshannocks 1884 *Iron & Oil Assn. (ind.)*. The team was named after the Neshannock Indians, who inhabited this region when European settlers arrived here in 1650. The city was built near the Shenango River and Neshannock Creek.

4228 Yanigans 1896 *Interstate (ind.)*. Team signed many young players. "Yanigan" was a nineteenth-century slang for a young player. With manager Jay Faatz at the helm, newspapers called the young players "Jay's Yanigans."

4229 Quakers 1896–1900 *Interstate (ind.)*. Pennsylvania, settled by William Penn and his Quaker Colony in 1680, soon became known as the "Quaker State."

4230 Outlaws 1906 *Ohio–Pennsylvania (C)*. With manager Percy Stetler at the helm, newspapers called the players "Stetler's Outlaws." Baseball players in this era were sometimes known as Cowboys, Rustlers and Outlaws because they were dirty, illiterate, tobacco-spitting rowdies as far as many fans were concerned.

4231 Nocks 1907–11m *Ohio–Pennsylvania (C)*. Team moved to Sharon (PA) August 12; 1912x *Ohio–Pennsylvania (D)*. Team disbanded June 18. Newspapers used a shorter version of Neshannocks.

4232 Alliance 1909 *Ohio–Pennsylvania (C)*. Team owned by the Alliance Steel Company. In this era, Pennsylvania was a world leader in iron, steel and coal production.

4233 Chiefs 1948 *Middle Atlantic (C)*. Moniker refers to the Neshannock Indians.

4234 Nats 1949–50 *Middle Atlantic (C)*. Team was a farm club of the AL Washington Nationals.

4235 Indians 1951 *Middle Atlantic (C)*. Like "Neshannocks" (1884) and "Chiefs" (1948), the moniker refers to the Neshannock Indians. Team was not a farm club of the Cleveland Indians.

4236 Knights 1995–96x *North Atlantic (ind.)*. This city was named after New Castle, England, which was founded by Robert II, the Duke of Normandy in the 11th century. Robert II was a soldier, landowner and knight. His fortress was the "The New Castle."

New Cumberland, Pennsylvania

4237 New Cumberland Base Ball Club 1891 *Ohio Valley (ind.)*. Team had no nickname.

New Haven, Connecticut

4238 Elm Citys 1875 *National Assn. (M)*; 1876 Independent team; 1878m *International Assn. (M)*. Team moved to Hartford (CT) May 20; 1889–90 *Atlantic Assn. (ind.)*. In the nineteenth century, city residents planted elm trees along city streets, which gave rise to the nickname of "Elm City." The 1876 "Elm Citys" had a loose affiliation with National League teams playing a semi-regular schedule (12–26–1 won-lost-tied) with them. The results of the games did not count in the NL standings. Local newspapers shortened the name to **Elms**.

4239 Connecticut Crackers 1878m *International Assn. (M)*. In the nineteenth century, talented and competitive sports teams were known as a "crack club." In baseball, a good hitter makes such forceful contact with the ball that the fans hear the "crack of the bat." Hence, "crackers" meant a competitive team. The tag was one of the earliest regional nicknames.

4240 Nutmeg Nine 1878m *International Assn. (M)*. Connecticut is the "Nutmeg State." In the nineteenth century, a baseball synonym for club and team was "nine."

4241 Professionals 1878m *International Assn. (M)*. In the 1870s, baseball as a professional game was still alien to many sport fans who only knew it as an amateur pastime. New Haven newspapers emphasized this team as a play-for-pay franchise by referring to them as the "Professionals" and the shorter **Pros**.

4242 Nutmegs 1891–92 *Eastern (ind.)*. The state nickname of Connecticut is the "Nutmeg State." The nutmeg is a seed from the Evergreen tree, which is used to make a spice. Team was also known as the **Nutmeggers**, i.e., an inhabitant of Connecticut.

4243 Texas Steers 1896m *Atlantic (ind.)*. With manager Ted Sullivan at the helm, after his one-year stint as manager of "Sullivan's Steers" of the 1895 Dallas club of the Texas League, local newspapers called the players on this 1896 New Haven club "Ted Sullivan's Texas Steers."

4244 Students 1896m *Atlantic (ind.)*. New Haven is home to Yale University. Several of the players on the team were also students at

Yale. With manager Ted Sullivan at the helm, newspapers called the players "Sullivan's Students."

4245 Blues 1899–1908 Connecticut *(ind. 1899–1901, D 1902–04, B 1905–12)*. Players wore blue hose (1899–1906) and blue stirrups (1907–08).

4246 Bluebirds 1899–1908 Connecticut *(ind. 1899–1901, D 1902–04, B 1905–12)*. In the era 1890–1910, teams often used a bird name corresponding to their stocking/stirrup color, i.e., Blackbirds, Black Crows, Bluebirds, Blue Jays, Canaries, Cardinals, Ravens and Redbirds.

4247 Black Crows 1909 *Connecticut (B)*. Players wore black trim. With field manager George Bone at the helm, newspapers called the black-hosed players the alliterative "George Bones' Black Crows."

4248 Prairie Hens 1910 *Connecticut (B)*. Prairie Hens are red and blue pheasants found in North America. With field manager Bill Carrick at the helm, local newspapers called the players "Carrick's Prairie Hens." In this era, reporters were willing to call baseball players anything to get an interesting nickname into print.

4249 White Wings 1911–12 *Connecticut (B)*. Circuit was known as both League and Association; 1913–14 *Eastern Assn. (B)*. These teams had a loose affiliation with the NL Boston Doves (renamed Braves in 1912). Players on both teams wore all-white uniforms (with dark stirrups) and maintained a loose affiliation with the Boston Doves, who also wore all-white uniforms. Doves, the bird, are sometimes called "white wings."

4250 MaxFeds 1915 *Colonial (ind.)*. Moniker has a double origin. The manager was Bert Maxwell, and the team was a farm club of the Federal League Brooklyn Tip Tops, aka "Brookfeds." Using a naming style prevalent in the FL, the moniker was an amalgam of Maxwell and Federal, i.e., MaxFeds.

4251 Murlins 1916–18 *Eastern (B)*. Ex–big league player and team owner Danny Murphy took over the managerial reins and local newspapers called the players the alliterative "Murphy's Murlins." During the team's 1917 successful pennant run, local newspapers exclaimed that the team "played like Merlin the Magician."

4252 Weissmen 1919–20 *Eastern (B)*. George Weiss, who played baseball at Yale University in New Haven and later became the general manager of the New York Yankees, owned the team.

4253 Indians 1921–22 *Eastern (A)*. With former big league pitcher "Chief" Bender the manager for the 1921 team, newspapers called the players "Chief Bender's Indians." Bill Donovan took over in 1922, making the name "Donovan's Indians."

4254 Profs 1923–30x *Eastern (A)*. Team disbanded July 18. New Haven is home to Yale University. Several players on the team were also students at the college. Management wanted to get away from Indians to avoid confusion with the Cleveland Indians. "Prof" is a newspaper-friendly contraction of "professor."

4255 Bulldogs 1931–32 *Eastern (A)*. The nickname for the sports teams at Yale University is "Bulldogs." This professional baseball team assumed the moniker since several of the players on the team had attended Yale and played on the school's baseball team.

4256 Ravens 1994 to date *Eastern (AA)*. Tag was a spin-off from the 1909 "Black Crows."

New Iberia, Louisiana

4257 Sugar Boys 1920 *Louisiana State (B)*. Louisiana farms transport sugar cane to city factories to be processed and shipped. Louisiana is known as the "Sugar State."

4258 Cardinals 1941–42x *Evangeline (D)*. Team disbanded May 22; 1946–47, 1949, 1953 *Evangeline (D 1946–47, C 1949, 1953)*. Team maintained a loose affiliation with the St. Louis Cardinals 1941–42, 1947, 1949 and 1953. The team was never a formal farm club with St.

Louis, though it was a formal farm club of Boston AL (1948) and Pittsburgh NL (1949).

4259 Rebels 1941–42 *Evangeline (D)*; 1950 *Evangeline (C)*. Louisiana seceded from the Union in 1861. Union forces attacked and occupied New Iberia in April 1862 and New Orleans in May 1862.

4260 Pelicans 1948, 1951–52, 1954–55 *Evangeline (D 1948, C 1951–52, 1954–55)*. Team was a farm club of the Class AA Southern Assn. New Orleans "Pelicans" and assumed the parent club's nickname. In the era 1920–50, some lower class (A, B, C, D) minor league teams were farm clubs of higher class (AAA and AA) minor league teams.

4261 Indians 1956x *Evangeline (C)*. Team disbanded May 19. Atakaba and Choctaw Indian tribes were confronted by waves of Spanish, French, English and American settlers. These tribes allied themselves with the British in the War of 1812 but were defeated and scattered while the Natchez tribes were wiped out. The team was not a farm club of the Cleveland Indians.

New London, Connecticut

4262 Colts 1898 *Connecticut State (ind.)*. Team had numerous young players, who in this era were known by the slang of "colts."

4263 Whalers 1899–1907 *Connecticut State (ind.)*; 1910 *Connecticut Assn. (D)*. Like nearby New Britain, the city became a whaling port from 1784 to 1850. New London is known as the "Whaling City."

4264 Planters 1913–14 *Eastern Assn. (B)*; 1916–18x *Eastern (B)*. Team disbanded July 22 because of U.S. entry into World War I. An arboretum is a greenhouse for trees, shrubs and plants for scientific study and education. The Connecticut Arboretum was built at Connecticut College in 1911. With manager Eugene McCann at the helm 1913–14 and 1916–17, newspapers called the players "McCann's Planters." John Flynn took over in 1918 and the name became "Flynn's Planters." New London is known as the "All Seasons City" because in the nineteenth century it planted oak, elm and pine trees on its city streets. Pioneer settlers became known as "planters" in the seventeenth century as they tried to establish farms in this region. After battling the Pequot Indians, they established the Pequot Colony and became known as the "Pequot Planters."

4265 Raiders 1947 *Colonial (B)*. On September 6, 1781, Benedict Arnold, commander of British navy ships, raided the port of New London and destroyed American privateer boats moored there and then burned the port and the city.

New Martinsville, West Virginia

4266 New Martinsville Baseball Club 1912 *Ohio–Pennsylvania (D)*. Team had no nickname.

New Orleans, Louisiana

4267 Expos 1885 *Independent team*. New Orleans hosted the "World's Industrial and Cotton Centennial Exposition" in 1884–85.

4268 Acid Iron Earth 1886 *Gulf (ind.)*. Team was owned by Charles Mohr, who patented supplemental iron tablets and a tonic called "Acid Iron Earth."

4269 Robert E. Lee 1886 *Gulf (ind.)*. After the Civil War, at least ten baseball teams in the South were named in honor of the commander of the Armies of the Confederate States of America — Robert E. Lee. Resentment of the North persisted in Louisiana in part because the state economy was devastated by the Civil War for at least 20 years.

4270 New Orleans Base Ball Club 1886 *Gulf (ind.)*. Team had no nickname.

4271 Unions 1886 *Southern League of Colored Baseballists (ind.).* Despite persistent bitter feelings between the North and South, these black players chose a pro–North moniker. Although "Unions" was a tag that was popular for Northern black teams, white baseball fans here resented the name.

4272 Pelicans 1887–88 *Southern (ind.)*; 1888 *Texas (ind.)*; 1892–96 *Southern (ind.)*; 1898–99 *Southern* The 1898 circuit was also known as the Texas–Southern League; 1901–59 *Southern Assn. (A 1902–34, A1 1935–45, AA 1946–59)*; 1977 *American Assn. (M).* The Brown pelican is the state bird of Louisiana and is found as far west as Texas and as far east as Florida. The 1977 team was slated to be named "Masqueraders" (after the annual New Orleans' Mardi Gras), but local newspapers gagged on the 12-letter name. The team held a quick fan poll and the old stand-by of "Pelicans" won.

4273 Eclipse 1907 *Independent Negro* team. Named after a eighteenth century English race horse, this nickname was first used in professional baseball by the 1882 Louisville Eclipse.

4274 Black Rappers 1907 *Independent Negro team (ind.).* The "rap" music of the 1990s actually originated 90 years earlier in the rural South, where black musicians combined singing and chanting with rhyming lyrics accompanied by rhythmic drum beats. This sound often overlapped with "blues" and "jazz" music. When a batter hits the ball hard, the fans shout, "He rapped that ball!"

4275 Blue Rappers 1907 *Independent Negro team (ind.).* The players on this team, a rival to the "Black Rappers," wore blue-trim uniforms and stirrups.

4276 Black Pelicans 1907–08 *Independent Negro team (ind.)*; 1920 *Independent Negro team*; 1926 *Negro Independent team*; 1938 *Negro Independent team*; 1951 *Negro American (ind.).* Starting in 1949 this circuit was no longer a major league. The NAL lasted through the 1954 season. Between 1900 and 1950 several black teams combined the adjective "Black" with a major league or high minor league team nickname, i.e., Black Yankees, Black Senators and Black Pelicans. Oftentimes, these black teams received donated or low-cost uniforms from Organized Baseball teams and simply adopted the team name on the jersey.

4277 Little Pels 1912m *Cotton State (D).* Team moved to Yazoo City May 9. Team was a farm club of the Class AA New Orleans Pelicans. In the era 1900–50, some Class AA and AAA minor league clubs organized a farm team among the ranks of Class A, B, C and D minor league teams. With manager Gene DeMontreville at the helm, newspapers called the players "DeMontreville's Little Pels." "Pels" is a newspaper abbreviation for "pelicans."

4278 Eagles 1915–16 *Independent Negro team.* Numerous black teams of this era chose pro–North monikers like Unions, Americans, Abraham Lincolns and Eagles. While safe to choose in the North, Southern white fans were sometimes hostile to these names.

4279 Crescent Stars 1921–22 *Independent Negro team*; 1932–37 *Independent Negro team.* New Orleans is nicknamed the "Crescent City." Settled in 1718, the city was laid out in a crescent-shape along the Mississippi River. "Stars" was after "Giants" the most popular nickname for black teams. The adjective "Crescent" placed in front of the noun "Stars" was a typical naming technique used by black baseball teams 1885–1955.

4280 New Orleans–St. Louis Stars 1940 *Independent Negro team*; 1941 *Negro American (M).* The St. Louis Stars, strapped for cash, played half their home schedule these two years in New Orleans, where expenses were lower.

4281 Creoles 1949 *Independent Negro team.* The original French settlers of eighteenth century Louisiana were known as "Creoles," which means "indigenous people."

4282 Zephyrs 1993–97 *American Assn. (AAA)*; 1998 to date *Pacific Coast (AAA).* The Denver Zephyrs moved to New Orleans for

the 1997 season. The team nickname was retained. Zephyrs—named after the cold winds of the Rocky Mountains—was also appropriate because of the lake breezes which sweep over New Orleans from Lake Pontchartrain in the north. "Zephyr" (from ancient Greek) means a gentle wind, i.e., a breeze, usually coming from the West.

New Philadelphia, Ohio

4283 Redbirds 1936 *Ohio State (D).* Team was a farm club of St. Louis Cardinals. The St. Louis Cardinals are known unofficially as the "Redbirds"—an alternate moniker.

New Rochelle, New York

4284 Owls 1994 *Northeast (ind.).* A name-the-team contest produced a newspaper friendly moniker. The North American owl are found in the Catskill Mountains and numerous state parks and forests throughout the Northeast.

New Rockford–Carrington, North Dakota

4285 Twins 1923m *North Dakota (D).* Team moved to Valley City (ND) July 17. The team represented two cities. With home games played in New Rockford, the team also drew fans from Carrington.

New Waterford, Nova Scotia

4286 Dodgers 1937–39 *Cape Breton Colliery (D 1937–38, C 1939).* Team had a loose affiliation with the Brooklyn Dodgers. In the era 1935–50, several Canadian professional baseball teams maintained a loose affiliation with major leagues teams playing in the Northeast.

New Westminster, British Columbia, Canada

4287 Frasers 1974 *Northwest (A).* Explorer Simon Fraser (b. 1776) discovered this region and its river, which was named in his honor. The city was built in 1858 some 16 miles from the mouth of the Fraser River.

New York, New York (aka New York City, New York)

4288 Mutual 1870 Independent Team went semi-professional in 1869 and then turned all-professional in 1870; 1871–75 *National Assn. (M)*; 1876 *National (M).* The amateur Mutual Baseball Club, sponsored by the Manhattan Mutual Hook and Ladder Company, was founded in 1857. Team joined the NA in 1871 and then transferred to the NL in 1876. It was at this time that newspapers were starting to transform the old, singular "club" name into plural "team" nicknames. Pleural monikers in print included **Mutuals** and the abbreviated **Mutes**, the latter used in headlines, i.e., "Mutes edge A's, 4–3."

4289 Green Stockings 1871–75 *National Assn. (M).* The players wore green hose. Newspapers shortened the moniker to Green Legs, Green Sox and Greens.

4290 New Yorkers 1871–75 *National Assn. (M).* Tag was soon to become a generic nineteenth-century nickname for any sports team from New York City.

4291 Browns 1871–75 *National Assn. (M).* Frequent washings of the originally green socks and dust particles that became embedded in their fabric produced a brown hue that prompted newspapers by mid-season to identify the team as "Browns" and "Brown Stockings."

4292 Giants from the East 1871–75 *National Assn. (M)*. The moniker referred to the "big cities of the East," i.e., the "giant" cities of the Atlantic coast — New York, Brooklyn, Philadelphia and Boston. Since New York was the largest U.S. city in the 1870s, the Mutual players, regardless of their stature and build, were dubbed "Giants from the East."

4293 Unruly Bad Boys of Baseball 1871–75 *National Assn. (M)*. The Mutuals in their amateur period in the 1860s were owned by New York politician and businessman Boss Tweed, who was notorious for his illegal money deals. The Mutual players themselves were routinely accused of fixing games. When the team turned professional in 1870, the players continued to be suspect in their play on the field and their questionable business practices. Moniker was coined by baseball author Neil McDonald in his book about the National League entitled *The League That Lasted*.

4294 Mutes 1876 *National (M)*. A newspaper contraction using a name that became popular with fans and the media, the disbandment of the 20-year-old Mutual franchise after the 1876 season erased "Mutuals" and "Mutes" from baseball history.

4295 Reds 1876 *National (M)*. By the inaugural year of the National League, the use of stocking colors to identify a baseball team was still quite generic. The Cincinnati Reds/Red Stockings would not gain a monopoly on this team moniker until the 1880s. Even so, the Mutual team, despite wearing red hose, was only infrequently referred to as Red Stockings, Redlegs and Reds in newspaper stories.

4296 Chocolate Sox 1876 *National (M)*. Starting the season with bright red stockings, the players washed their crimson, scarlet hose so many times that by June they had faded to a dirt-stained brown, which newspapers started calling the "Chocolate Sox." The moniker is one of the earliest uses of the abstract "sox" spelling as opposed to "stockings" and "socks."

4297 Mets 1880 *Independent team*; 1881 *Eastern Championship Assn. (M)*; *League Alliance (ind.)* 1882; 1883–87 *American Assn. (M)*; 1896m *Atlantic (ind.)*; 1962 to date *National (M)*. Team's official name was the Metropolitan Exhibition Company. Team took its nickname from the amateur Metropolitan Baseball Club of New York that played from 1857 to 1860. New York City has the nickname of "Metropolis." Originally printed as **Metropolitan** and **Metropolitans**, newspapers quickly shortened the moniker to "Mets." In 1962, the NL expansion team chose a moniker used by the amateur Metropolitans (1857–60) and the professional Mets (1880–87). The newspaper-friendly nickname of "Mets" won out in a fan poll. The name-the-team contest produced 9,163 suggestions involving 644 different names. The runners-up were Empires (second) and Islanders (third and later used by the NHL franchise on Long Island). Other entries were Avengers, Burros (after Queensborough), NYB's, and, the best of all, "Moles" (The submitter explained, "They'll probably down at the bottom anyway!"). Newspapers liked the four-letter "Mets" name and baseball purists preferred the name because it was historic, i.e., the New York Mets of 1880–87. Owner Joan Payson, who originally wanted "Meadowlarks" (after the Meadowlands region in which Shea Stadium had been built), selected Mets, explaining it is "short, historical and reflective of our great metropolis." Starting around 1990, "politically hip" reporters and broadcasters sometimes use the lengthy, old-time appellation of "Metropolitans," although newspaper editors, horrified at the prospect, never do.

4298 Browns 1881 *Eastern Championship Association (M)*. Players wore brown hose.

4299 Quicksteps 1881 *Eastern Assn. (M)*. Circuit's formal title was the Eastern Championship Association. Agile, sure-footed and speedy players of nineteenth-century baseball were known as "Quicksteps."

4300 Ponies 1883–85 *American Assn. (M)*. The origin of the term "Pony League" occurred in 1883–84 when the National League and American Association formed a minor league called the Reserve League with teams in Chicago, Cincinnati, Cleveland, Milwaukee, Pittsburgh and St. Louis in 1883. In 1884 teams in Akron, Boston, New York and Pittsburgh were added. The RL was less a farm system as it was a reserve circuit for replacement in the event of injuries on the roster of parent National League teams. Players in the RL were known as "Colts" and "Ponies." With Giants-Mets syndicate owner John B. Day starting to transfer the better Mets players to the Giants, disgusted Mets fans started calling the remaining, less-talented players on the AA Mets the "Ponies."

4301 Gothams 1883–84 *National (M)*. Name was first used in 1837 by the "Gotham Ball Club," whose players used the Gotham Inn, an eatery and tavern a couple of blocks from their playing field in New York, as a clubhouse before and after games. In 1857 the team became the "Gotham Base Ball Club." The team disbanded in 1865, but the nickname sprang up again with the 1883 New York National League club.

4302 Giants 1883–1957 *National (M)*. When the 1885 team won 16 of its first 20 games, field manager Jim Mutrie exulted about his players "My Boys! My Giants!" Some historians, i.e., Peter Mancuso, call this exclamation historical lore, but the June 8, 1885, *Rocky Mountain News* described the New Yorkers as the "maroon-stocking giants." Sportswriter P.J. Donahue of the *New York World* called the New York players the "Gotham Giants" and "Mutrie's Giants." The name actually preceded Mutrie, because *Chicago Daily News* sportswriter Richard Hershberger on August 3, 1883, called the New York Nationals the "Gotham Giants." "Giants" was a nineteenth-century generic term for a team that was winning. It meant that a team was playing "like Giants" rather than players with a tall and burly appearance. Nevertheless, New York Nationals teams of 1883–89 were noted for signing six-foot tall and muscular players, which influenced reporters to call the team "Giants." Moniker was de facto official when a song, "The New York Giants' March," was published in 1895, and became legally official in 1918 when the nickname first appeared on the players' jerseys. With Roger Connor, Danny Richardson, Art Whitney, George Gore, Jim O'Rourke, Buck Ewing, Tim Keefe, Ed "Cannonball" Crane and Hank O'Day all leaving the NL Giants to join the 1890 New York PL team, New York newspapers and fans started calling this new team the "real Giants," and "Buck Ewing's Giants," while the New York Nationals were now "Mutrie's Mules."

4303 Jints 1883–1957 *National (M)*. Tag was a five-letter, appealing, almost charming newspaper contraction that was in occasional use for 74 years. In New York City–style "English" the name rhymes with "pints"—but not with "mints."

4304 New York Base Ball Club 1884 *Reserve (ind.)*. Team had no nickname.

4305 Mutrie Men 1885–91 *National (M)*. Manager Jim Mutrie led the New York Nationals to two NL pennants (1888, 1889), two World Series championships (1888, 1889) and six winning seasons out of seven with such hitters as Roger Connor (Hall of Fame), Buck Ewing (Hall of Fame), Pete Gillespie, Mike Dorgan, Pat Deasley, George Gore, Mikey O'Rourke, Mike Tiernan, John Montgomery Ward (Hall of Fame) and pitchers Mickey Welch (Hall of Fame) and Tim Keefe (Hall of Fame).

4306 Staten Island Indians 1886–87 *American Assn. (M)*. Unable to compete with the NL Giants in New York, the Mets moved to Staten Island for the 1886 season where hooting fans and sarcastic newspapers called them the alliterative "Staten Island Indians." Fans of the team were angry at syndicate ownership, i.e., John B. Day, who owned both the Giants and Mets, for shunting talented Mets players to the Giants, i.e., hitters Roger Connor (Hall of Fame), Mike Dorgan, Tom Esterbrook, Buck Ewing (Hall of Fame), and Pete Gillespie, as well as pitchers Tim Keefe (Hall of Fame) and Mickey Welch (Hall of Fame). At the start of the 1886 season, Day, wanting to concentrate solely on the Giants, sold the Mets to the Staten Island Amusement Company and Transit System, which moved the team to St. George's Park on Staten Island, giving rise to the "Indians" moniker as a tongue-in-cheek spin-off from the Manhattan Indians, who were swindled by English settlers into selling Manhattan Island for beads and trinkets.

4307 Gorhams 1887–91 *Independent Negro team*; 1887 *National League of Colored Baseballists (ind.)*. Team played as a semi-professional outfit in Gorham (NY) in 1887, turned all-professional in 1888 under the name "New York Gorhams," and joined this circuit (which disbanded May 23). Team then moved to Philadelphia, later in the 1888 season, to play as the "Philadelphia Gorham Giants." Team played home games in New York City in 1889–91, again becoming the "New York Gorhams." During the Dutch colonial period, two towns sprung up — Gotham and Gorham. Gotham became New York City while Gorham, in western New York, remained a small town. The team became known as the New York **Big Gorhams** in 1891 after signing six Cuban Giants players. "Big" in this era meant "big time," i.e., "New York is a 'big time' city."

4308 Coney Island Dudes 1888 *National (M)*. A sarcastic jab against the New Yorkers made by the *Indianapolis Sentinel* noting the Giants dirty uniforms while playing a game against hometown Indianapolis on July 4, 1888.

4309 Staten Islanders 1889 *National (M)*. New team owner Nick Engel moved the Giants to St. George's Park on Staten Island in May and June 1889 while the new Polo Grounds was being built in Manhattan. When the Polo Grounds was completed in June, the Giants returned to Manhattan to play in their new park.

4310 Nickels 1889 *National (M)*. Moniker was in honor of team owner Nick Engel. It never caught on.

4311 Nickel Platers 1889 *National (M)*. A spinoff of Nickels and a clever reference to "nickel plating" — a new industrial process in the manufacture of nickel-iron and nickel-steel alloys — the moniker was a newspaper gimmick that was quickly abandoned.

4312 Braves 1890 *Players (M)*. Name was a generic moniker for "baseball players." With manager Buck Ewing at the helm, newspapers called the players "Buck's Braves."

4313 Warriors 1890 *Players (M)*. With player-manager Buck Ewing at the helm, the team was called by newspapers "Ewing's Warriors."

4314 Charley Horses 1890 *Players (M)*. Despite five regulars hitting over .300, the PL Giants pitching staff of Hank O'Day (22–13, 4.21 ERA), John Ewing (not Buck Ewing) (18–12, 4.24 ERA), and Tim Keefe (17–11, 3.38 ERA) made the team's overall performance quite "lame," prompting unhappy New York PL fans to brand them with a "Mutrie's Mules" spin-off — the "Charley Horses." A "Charley Horse" originally meant a lame farm horse (named Charley) — an appropriate moniker for the New York PL team that fell out of the pennant race in September and limped home with an unimpressive 74–57 record, eight games behind the first-place Boston Reds. Actually, "Charley Horse" previously referred to an individual player who pulled up lame with a muscle pull in his groin, hip, leg, ankle or foot. Legend ascribes the baseball origin to a ball player named Charlie who often pulled up lame running the bases.

4315 Mutrie's Mules 1890 *National (M)*. Field manager Jim Mutrie lost Giants hitters Roger Connor, Danny Richardson, Art Whitney, George Gore, Jim O'Rourke, and Buck Ewing as well as pitchers Tim Keefe, Cannonball Crane and Hank O'Day to Players

League raids, leaving the team to limp home in 6th place in the 1890 NL standings with a 63–68 record. Newspapers and fans dismissed the team as "Mutrie's Mules."

4316 Cuban-X — Giants 1897–1909 *Independent Negro team*. When the team formed in 1897, management tried to call the players the "Cuban Giants" to usurp publicity away from the original Cuban Giants (who were still operating in 1897). When the original Cuban Giants protested, the team added an X to the name to acknowledge their status as a new team.

4317 All-Cubans 1899–1905 *Independent integrated team*. Team consisted of both white and black native Cuban players. Although a touring club, they played their "home" games in New York.

4318 Genuine Cuban Giants 1900 *Independent Negro team*. After the Cuban Giants disbanded following the 1899 season, a new team was formed at the start of the 1900 season and called itself the "Cuban Giants." The Cuban-X-Giants, who had formed in 1897, complained that they were the proper successors to the pioneering Cuban Giants (1885–99), but the new team insisted they were the "real" Cuban Giants, and to reinforce that image started calling themselves the "Genuine" Cuban Giants. The team lasted only this one year.

4319 McGraw Men 1902–32 *National (M)*. Under the direction of Hall of Fame player and manager John McGraw, the New York Giants, during his 31-year tutelage, won ten National League pennants, four World Series, and enjoyed 27 winning seasons in 30 years. Hall of Fame players who played for McGraw were Casey Stengel, Frankie Frisch, Christy Mathewson and Joe McGinnity.

4320 Burglars 1903 *American (M)*. The new team "burglarized" such National League star players as hitters Willie Keeler, John Ganzel, Wid Conroy, Lefty Davis and Jack O'Connor and pitcher Jack Chesbro, which prompted the moniker "Burglars."

4321 Porch Climbers 1903 *American (M)*. For home games at Highland Park/Hilltop Park, fans had to struggle up steep roads to get to the ballpark. Moniker also was a slang for "burglar," i.e., a thief who scales a porch in order to break into the second story of a house or hotel. This definition was appropriate because the New Yorkers as well as the other seven teams of the American League were all "burglarizing" National League rosters for players. Newspapers balked at using this thirteen-letter moniker.

4322 Greater New York Baseball Club 1903–04 *American (M)*. As part of the NL-AL truce agreed upon in the winter of 1902–03, the new AL team in New York was allowed by NL president Nick Young and Giants owner to play in New York City under the name of Greater New York Baseball Association. The new team's club president Joseph Gordon opportunistically called the franchise the Greater New York Baseball Club to attract suburban fans in addition to inner city Gothamites. By 1905 newspapers dropped the lengthy designation in favor of "Yankees" and "Yanks." Highlanders and Hilltoppers — which were never official designations of the franchise — were used, but by 1913 Yankees became the official team nickname.

4323 Invaders 1903–04 *American (M)*. Tag was a generic name that National League circles used to describe AL teams that were "invading" sacred National League territory, i.e., Boston, Chicago, New York, Philadelphia and St. Louis. Once the last vestiges of the AL-NL "Interleague War" (1901–02) ended, the "Invaders" animosity faded by 1905 when Phillies owner John T. Brush, a leading "Hawk" against AL president Ban Johnson's junior circuit, convinced all 16 MLB owners to make the World Series compulsory and permanent. The name was coined by the *New York Evening Journal*.

4324 Quaker Giants 1903–05 *Independent Negro team*. Team played as the independent Philadelphia "Quaker Giants" in 1902, and then moved to New York, where the moniker was retained.

4325 Cuban-X-Stars 1903–05 *Independent Negro team*; 1906 *Independent International (ind.)*. Circuit was known as the Independent

League of International Players. Team, as formed in 1903, consisted of ex–Cuban Giant players—hence the moniker of "Cuban-X-Giants."

4326 Griffmen 1903–08 *American (M)*. Clark Griffith was the field manager of the New York Americans 1903–08.

4327 Hilltoppers 1903–12 *American (M)*. The team's home park was known as both Highlander Park and Hilltop Park.

4328 Highlanders 1903–12 *American (M)*. Since the team's general manager was James Gordon and because the team played at Highland Park (aka Hilltop Park) located in Washington Heights, and as there was famous British military regiment called "Clan Gordan's Highlanders," the team became known as the "Highlanders." At once, New York fans rebelled against the moniker as "too British" and started calling the team "Yankees." Newspapers much preferred Yankees, which could be shortened to Yanks. Although Highlanders was the official team nickname, Yankees was so popular that it became the franchise's official nickname in 1913. In the years 1903–12, the George Cohan Broadway Street (in New York City) musical *Little Johnny Jones* was best known for its popular song "Yankee Doodle Dandy."

4329 Yankees 1903–12 *American (M)*. When Hilltop Park burned down prior to the 1913 campaign, the team was forced to move to the Polo Grounds at the start of the season. Consequently, the "Highlanders" moniker was conveniently dropped in favor of the popular "Yankees," the latter tag which has become the franchise's official moniker for the next 100 seasons. Moniker was first used in print by Harry Beecher and Sam Crane in the *New York Evening Journal* and Mark Roth in the *New York Globe* March 20, 1904.

4330 Famous Cuban Giants 1906 *Independent Negro team*. Tag was yet another spin-off from Cuban Giants. Some of the players on the team from Cuba and other players, who had actually played for the old Cuban Giants before 1900, were becoming well known in the U.S.

4331 Havana Stars 1906x *Independent International (ind.)*. League disbanded in July but the team continued to play as a barnstorming outfit; 1906–07 *Independent Negro team*. Several players on the team played winter ball in Havana and Almendares.

4332 Quaker Giants 1906x *Independent International (ind.)*. Team disbanded July 5. Team played the 1905 season as the semiprofessional Philadelphia Quaker Giants.

4333 Stars of Cuba 1906 *International Independent (ind.)*; 1907–14 *Independent Negro team*; 1915–29 *Independent Negro team*; 1930–31 *Independent Negro team*. In 1915, a new franchise with the same name started play. These teams signed several of the star players of the Cuban Winter League. Teams were each also known as the **Cuban Stars**.

4334 Colored Giants 1908–10 *Independent Negro team*. Tag was another "Giants-style" nickname. Black teams used such as adjectives as Black, Brown and Colored.

4335 Black Sox 1910–18 *Independent Negro team*; 1912–13x *Independent Negro team*. The 1912–13 Black Sox were a different team using the same nickname. Players wore black stirrups.

4336 Pinstripers 1911 *American (M)*. Although baseball teams had worn pinstripe uniforms going back to the 1880s (i.e., Cleveland 1887–89), it was the Yankees who made the style famous in the 1920s, making the moniker synonymous with their franchise. The name is used so sporadically that it barely qualifies as a nickname, most especially since many other teams have adopted the pinstripe design.

4337 Lincoln Grays 1911–15 *Independent Negro team*. The players wore gray-trim uniforms. Moniker was a spin-off from the Lincoln Giants. Like the Lincoln Giants, this team honored Abraham Lincoln. This team never played in Lincoln, Nebraska.

4338 Lincoln Giants 1911–23 *Independent Negro team*; 1923–26 *Eastern Colored (M)*; 1927 *Independent Negro team*; 1928 *Eastern Colored (M)*; 1929 *American Negro (M)*. The 1910 Lincoln (Nebraska) Giants, who started playing as early as 1890, moved to New York, where the name was retained but whose meaning was modified to honor Abraham Lincoln. Team alternated play as an independent and a league team.

4339 Cubans 1911–27 *Independent Negro team*; 1939–48 *Negro National (M)*. These teams had native Cuban players from the Cuban Winter League.

4340 Havana Red Sox 1913 *Independent Negro team*. Most of the players on the team were members of the Cuban Winter League Havana Reds (Los Rojos de la Habana).

4341 Chance Men 1913–14 *American (M)*. With Frank Chance at the helm as Yankees' field manager, the name was an obvious spin-off from the "McGraw Men" of the cross-town Giants. However, the name faded as the Yankees posted losing records both seasons that Chance managed the team.

4342 Lincoln Stars 1914–17 *Independent Negro team*; 1925–30 *Independent Negro team*. Moniker was a spin-off from "Lincoln Giants," and "Lincoln Grays." Black teams in this era tended toward pro–American and pro–Union names. This team used the name of the "Great Emancipator" of slaves in America, i.e., Abraham Lincoln.

4343 Knickerbockers 1915 *American (M)*. The Knickerbocker Beer Company was finalizing plans to buy the New York AL club and rename it the "Knickerbockers" (the name coincidentally used by baseball's first team in 1845) but the deal fell through. The name was never used by the team.

4344 Union Giants 1915–34 *Independent Negro team*. This team used a pro–North, pro–American Union adjective with the popular Giants.

4345 Cuban Giants 1916 *Independent Negro team*; 1934 *Independent Negro team*. This 1916 team was the first one bearing the name of "Cuban Giants" that played in New York City. The old-time Cuban Giants played in Babylon (NY), Hoboken (NJ), Ansonia (CT) and York (PA).

4346 Meteoric Giants 1916 *National (M)*. When the Giants won 21 games in a row during the 1916 season, the *New York Times* called the team "Meteoric Giants." But the Giants started their major league longest winning streak from too far back in the standings to catch eventual NL champion Brooklyn, as the "Meteors" finished fourth with an 86–66 record.

4347 Havana Cubans 1917 *Independent Negro team*; 1935 *Independent Negro team*. Players on these teams came from the Havana-based clubs—the Havana Reds and Almendares Blues.

4348 Murderers' Row 1918–28 *American (M)*. Like a row of scary homicidal convicts in their cells or murderers and thieves in the "Murders' Row" in the "Darktown" slums of nineteenth-century New York, the Yankees of 1926–28 "murdered" the ball off opposing pitchers while racking up three consecutive American League pennants and two World Series championships. Babe Ruth, Lou Gehrig, Tony Lazzeri, Walt Koenig, Earle Combs and Joe Dugan were a lineup that was a nightmare for opposing teams' pitchers. The 1927 Yankees had a team slugging percentage of .489, which has never been equaled to date. Actually, the name was coined by Peter Morris in the *Boston Globe*, August 11, 1918, when the Yankees started signing such good hitters as Wally Pipp, Frank "Home Run" Baker, Frank Gilhooey, Roger Peckinpaugh, Ping Bodie, Del Baker, Bob Meusel and Babe Ruth (who joined the Yankees in 1920).

4349 Hugmen 1918–29 *American (M)*. Manager Miller Huggins presided over the transformation of the Yankees from a mediocre "second team" in New York to major league baseball's most glamorous and most dominant team. Huggins took ill and died in September 1929.

4350 Red Caps 1919–35 *Independent Negro team*. Team played in 1918 as the Pennsylvania Red Caps of New York — a name that was retained by the New York–based team. Most local newspapers simply used the name "New York Red Caps." Players wore red caps.

4351 Philadelphia Giants 1920–28 *Independent Negro team*. The 1919 Philadelphia Giants transferred to New York in 1920. Team assumed the formal title of "Philadelphia Giants of New York" to avoid confusion with the National League New York Giants. In any case the players, with not enough money to buy new uniforms, continued to wear uniforms with the "Philadelphia" name on their jerseys.

4352 All-Cubans 1921 *Independent Negro team*. Team sported an all–Cuban lineup.

4353 Bacharachs 1921 *Independent Negro team*. Most of the players of this team were former members of the Atlantic City Bacharach Giants.

4354 Rupert's Rifles 1921–24 *American (M)*. Team owner Rupert Murdoch signed the best hitters in the game in this period, i.e., Babe Ruth, Lou Gehrig, Bob Meusel, Wally Pipp, Whitey Whitt, Wally Schang and Joe Dugan — all of whom were able to "rifle" the ball all over the field and over the fence. In 1921 Babe Ruth had literally the greatest individual season of all time — G-152, AB-540, R-177, HR-59, RBI-171, 2B-44, 3B-16, BB-144, SO-81, BA-.378, SA-.846 and then batted .313 in the 1921 World Series.

4355 Sluggers 1921–29 *American (M)*. Although used by other teams back as early as 1869, the Yankees of 1921–23 were the most deserving recipients of this moniker. Babe Ruth alone in 1920 (54 HR) and 1921 (59) hit more home runs than other major league *teams* were able to hit in the same year! Variation was **Huggins' Sluggers**. Huggins died in the spring of 1929 but the team continued to be known as Sluggers that year. By the 1930s "sluggers" had become a generic moniker for any team with home run power. "Slugger" had become a generic name for any player who could hit with power.

4356 Cuban Stars East 1923–28 *Eastern Colored (M)*; 1929 *American Negro (M)*. Alex Pompez, who made his fortune in cigars, banking and the numbers racket, chose the name of "Cuban Stars" for his players. Both the New York Cuban Stars (East) and the Cincinnati Cuban Stars (West) had Cuban players on the team. Pompez did not own the Cincinnati franchise.

4357 Harlem Globetrotters 1926–48 *Independent Negro team*. Nickname was derived from the basketball "Harlem Globetrotters," who as a traveling basketball show only occasionally played in New York City. The baseball team also mostly barnstormed but did play several games in New York City.

4358 Eradicators 1927 *American (M)*. Coined by baseball authors Pete Palmer and Gary Gillette to describe how the Yankees "eradicated" all opposition, compiling a 114–40 record (including the World Series) en route to the AL pennant and the World Series championship of 1927. The *team* slugged .489 in the regular season.

4359 Steamrollers 1927 *American (M)*. Baseball writer Larry Ritter called the 1927 Yankees the "Steamrollers" as they won a then–AL record 110 games to finish a then-record 19 games ahead of second-place Philadelphia before sweeping the NL champion Pittsburgh Pirates, 4 games to none, in the 1927 World Series.

4360 Gehrig & Ruth, Inc. 1927 *American (M)*. Baseball author Warren Wilbert, in his book of the same title, noted that Babe Ruth and Lou Gehrig together hit 107 home runs — a total that equaled the HR totals of the next two teams with most team homers, the Athletics (56) and the Tigers (51) — combined!

4361 Window-Breakers 1927–32 *American (M)*. Boys and girls have been breaking windows with batted balls at least since 1781 when a newspaper reported the prohibition of baseball playing near

a church, lest the church windows are broken. The Yankees led the American League in home runs for five straight seasons with 158 (1927), 133 (1928), 142 (1929), 152 (1930), 155 (1931) with a second-highest total of 160 four-baggers in 1932.

4362 Harlem Stars 1930–35 *Independent Negro team*. Moniker was a spin-off from the "Harlem Globetrotters." Like the Globetrotters, this team was also a barnstorming team that played only a few games in New York.

4363 McCarthy Men 1931–46 *American (M)*. With Joe McCarthy at the helm as Yankee field manager, the "McCarty Men" won eight American League pennants in 1932, 1936, 1937, 1938, 1939, 1941, 1942 and 1943. McCarthy's seven Yankee pennants placed him just ahead of Miller Huggins (6) and second to Casey Stengel (10).

4364 Black Yankees 1932–35 *Independent Negro team (ind.)*; 1936–48 *Negro National (M)*; 1949–50 *Independent Negro team (ind.)*. With black teams strapped for cash during the Great Depression, they often asked major league teams for donated uniforms and equipment. Nickname was then based on the jersey lettering. By the 1940s Negro League teams had enough money to buy uniforms from major league teams, although they almost always got a discount.

4365 Terry Men 1933–41 *National (M)*. In the same style of John McGraw, player-manager Bill Terry led his "Terry Men" to pennants in 1933, 1937 and 1938 with hitters Lefty O'Doul, Mel Ott (Hall of Fame), Travis Jackson, Mark Koenig, Dick Bartell, Gus Mancuso, Jim Ripple, and Terry himself (Hall of Fame) as well as pitchers Carl Hubbell (Hall of Fame), Adolfo Luque, Clydell Castleman, Hal Schumacher and Cliff Melton.

4366 Tigers 1935 *Independent Negro team (ind.)*. Players wore striped hose.

4367 Cubans 1935–36 *Negro National (M)*. Team signed numerous native Cuban players, some of whom were white, who were regulars in the Cuban Winter League. The balance of the player roster consisted of black Americans.

4368 Dominators 1936 *American (M)*. Coined by baseball writers Gary Gillette and Pete Palmer, the moniker was a name of praise for the "dominating" New York Yankees, who went 102–51 to finish 19-and-a-half games over second-place Detroit. The Yankees then beat a strong New York Giants team in the 1936 World Series, including a "dominating" 18–4 victory in Game 2.

4369 Bronx Bombers 1936 to date *American (M)*. Tag is the second most famous unofficial baseball team nickname — after the Brooklyn "Bums." The Yankees were playing in Yankee Stadium, located in the Bronx district of New York City, with a powerful offensive team, including Lou Gehrig, Joe DiMaggio, Bill Dickey, Tony Lazzeri, Red Rolfe, George Selkirk and Jake Powell. In the 1930s Joe Louis, "The Brown Bomber," came to prominence as a boxer, winning the heavyweight championship and inspiring the baseball nickname of "Bronx Bombers." First used by the *New York Post* on June 18, 1936, the moniker has been used now for the last 75 years.

4370 Snow White & The Seven Dwarfs 1937–39. Shortly after the release of Walt Disney's popular feature movie *Snow White and the Seven Dwarfs*, reporters started referring to the four straight pennant-winning, four straight World Series winning Yankees of 1936–39 and the other seven AL also-rans as "Snow White and the Seven Dwarfs."

4371 Crushers 1939 *American (M)*. The Yanks won their fourth straight AL flag with a 106–45 record, 17 games ahead of second-place Boston. The New Yorkers led the league in six offensive categories, including a league-high 161 home runs. From July 1 to August 31, 1939, the Yanks went 48–13 to blow Boston and Cleveland out of contention.

4372 Cuban Stars 1940–44 *Independent Negro team (ind.)*. Team signed star players from the Cuban Winter League. Three previous teams, known as the "Stars of Cuba," sometimes were called the "Cuban Stars." However, this 1940–44 team was never known as the "Stars of Cuba."

4373 Magnificent Yankees 1949–52 *American (M)*. Named after the title of a Hollywood movie, the moniker was coined by baseball writer Tom Meany for the 1949–53 New York Yankees, who are the only team to win *five* consecutive World Series. The "Magnificent Yankees," managed by Casey Stengel, were led by hitters Mickey Mantle, Joe DiMaggio, Yogi Berra, Hank Bauer, Billy Martin and Gil McDougald and pitchers Allie Reynolds, Ed Lopat, Vic Raschi, Whitey Ford, Johnny Kucks, Bob Grim and Johnny Sain. Meany's original edition was published in the summer of 1953 before the Yankees won their fifth straight AL and World Series titles. A second edition of Meany's book also covered the 1955–58 Yankee pennant-winners.

4374 Men of Autumn 1949–53 *American (M)*. In a twist from the title of Roger Kahn's book *The Boys of Summer* (about the Brooklyn Dodgers of the 1950s), baseball author Dom Forker came out with a 1989 book entitled *The Men of Autumn* about the 1949–53 New York Yankee dynasty.

4375 Damn Yankees 1949–64 *American (M)*. The tag was the title of a successful Broadway theatrical play and a popular 1958 Hollywood movie (starring Tab Hunter, Ray Walston and Gwen Verdon). The name was given to the Yankees by frustrated fans and newspaper reporters from other American League cities as the "Damn Yankees" seemed to never lose — winning an unbelievable 14 AL pennants in 16 seasons. "Damn Yankees" had its origin in the Civil War as bitter Southerners branded victorious Union troops as the "Damn Yankees."

4376 Rampaging Yankees 1949–64 *American (M)*. With historic pennant streaks of five (1949–53 including five straight World Series titles), four (1955–58) and another five (1960–64), the Yankees rampaged over their American League opponents in the greatest sustained dynasty in major league baseball history. Without the aid of playoffs, which often allows a team with less than the best won-lost record in the regular season to win the flag, the Yankees feat was amazing. The moniker was particularly apt on September 15, 1960, when the Yankees broke open a hard-fought three-team race with the Orioles and White Sox when they "rampaged" to 15 consecutive victories. Baseball writer Roger Kahn reports the name was first used in 1949.

4377 Bronx Juggernaut 1949–64 *American (M)*. The Yankees won an unprecedented 14 pennants in 16 American League seasons during this period. The franchise also won nine World Series championships, as well. Baseball writer Roger Kahn notes that the name was first used by the media in 1949 when the Yankees already had 15 AL pennants and 10 World Series championships.

4378 Lordly Bombers 1949–64 *American (M)*. The tag was another description of the dominant New York American League franchise. The Yankees lost out in the American League pennant race only twice — in 1954 to the Cleveland Indians and in 1959 to the Chicago White Sox. Baseball writer Roger Kahn reports the name was first used in the media in 1949.

4379 Willie Mays & Company 1951–57 *National (M)*. Led by superstar Willie Mays, the Giants won NL pennants in 1951 and 1954, losing to the Yankees in the 1951 World Series and sweeping the Cleveland Indians in the 1954 Fall Classic. With manager Leo Durocher at the helm (1951–55), Mays led such hitters as Alvin Dark, Bobby Thomson, Don Mueller, Dusty Rhodes, Eddie Stanky, Hank Thompson, and Monte Irvin (Hall of Fame) and was supported by the excellent hurling of pitchers Johnny Antonelli, Sal Maglie, Ruben Gomez and Hoyt Wilhelm (Hall of Fame).

4380 Rooting for U.S. Steel 1953 *American (M)*. With the Yankees winning their fifth consecutive World Series championship,

New York Herald Tribune sportswriter Red Smith recounted a remark made by one of his friends — an unemployed actor — at a party in 1953. Smith reported that the actor exclaimed: "How can you root for the Yankees!? It's like rooting for U.S. Steel!" U.S. Steel has been a powerful and influential corporate business for a hundred years.

4381 Incredible Giants 1954 *National (M)*. Tom Meany's book with the same title described the Giants "incredible run" to the 1954 NL pennant led by Willie Mays (41 HR and a .345 BA). The Giants then engineered an equally incredible four-game sweep over the favored Cleveland Indians to win the 1954 World Series.

4382 Black Stockings 1953 *American (M)*. After winning their fifth consecutive World Series, newspapers called the team the "Lordly Yankees."

4383 Awesome Machine 1961 *American (M)*. Name was coined by baseball author Peter Golenbeck in his 2000 book *Dynasty*. The awesome machine went 109–53, and hit a major league–high 240 home runs (including Roger Maris' 61 round-trippers) to easily topple the Cincinnati Reds in the World Series, 4 games to 1.

4384 Bronx B-52's 1961–64 *American (M)*. The premier United States Air Force jet bomber of the Cold War era (1951–91) was the B-52 Stratofortress bomber that could carry more explosive power in the form of nuclear weapons than the entire explosive output of all the bombers in World War II. Similarly, the 1961–64 Yankees boasted Mickey Mantle, Roger Maris, Yogi Berra, Bill "Moose" Skowron, Elston Howard, Clete Boyer, Johnny Blanchard, Tom Tresh and Joe Pepitone. The "Bronx B-52's" hit 193 (1st in 1960), 240 (1st in 1961), 199 (2nd in 1962), 188 (2nd in 1963) and 162 (1964) home runs in American League regular season play.

4385 High Altitude Bombers 1961–64 *American (M)*. Tag was a spin-off from the Bronx B-52's. The B-52 Stratofortress is a high-altitude jet bomber that has been so valuable that it has been used by the United States Air Force for nearly 60 years.

4386 Babies 1962 *National (M)*. Cartoonist Willard Mullins depicted the new NL expansion team in New York as a little one-year-old baby dressed in a baseball uniform. The name did not catch on and was dropped by 1963. It is the last time a major league expansion team was called "Baby" or "Babies." Ironically, the 1962 Mets were a veteran team with such experienced players as Richie Ashburn, Charley Neal, Frank Thomas, and Gene Woodling and pitcher Roger Craig.

4387 Casey's Loveable Losers 1962–65 *National (M)*. Used again for the NL Chicago Cubs in 1981, the name was coined for Casey Stengel's abominable New York Mets of 1962–65 — a team that lost 552 games in these four seasons.

4388 Amazin' Mets 1962 to date *National (M)*. When during spring training field manager Casey Stengel first observed his new team, i.e., a collection of kids and veterans missing bunt signals, getting picked off first base, throwing the ball on steal attempts into center field, over-sliding bases, knee-buckling on curveballs that crossed the plate for a strike, and falling down as pop flies dropped to the turf, he commented to a reporter who asked how his charges were doing with the gently sarcastic, "They're just amazin!" The moniker immediately stuck — used more as a term of endearment rather than hostile sarcasm. Tag is often shortened by newspapers to the **Amazin's**.

4389 Baseball's Roman Empire 1964 *American (M)*. The greatest sustained winning "empire" in sports was that of the Yankees of 1921–64, who during this era produced 43 winning seasons in 44 years while capturing 28 AL pennants and winning 20 World Series titles. The Roman Empire lasted 1,000 years while conquering the known Western world.

4390 Fallen Empire 1965 *American (M)*. When the New York

Yankees unexpectedly declined to a losing 77–85 record in 1965, baseball pundits described their descent as the "fall of an empire." It was the Yankees first losing season since 1925, and the pennant drought lasted 12 years, until 1976. By 1976 the Yankees established a "mini-empire" in 1976–81.

4391 Bronx Bunnies 1965–66 *American (M)*; 1990–92 *American (M)*. Baseball author Roger Angell in his 1972 book *The Summer Game* described the 1965–66 New York Yankees, who declined from the 1964 AL pennant to a last-place finish in 1966, as the "Bronx Bunnies." Twenty-three years later, with free agency making it much harder to monopolize the player market, the Yankees stumbled in the four years of 1989–92 with four losing seasons in a row, causing impatient Yankee fans to again barb the players with "Bronx Bunnies," a spin-off from "Bronx Bombers." But by 1994 the New Yorkers were building for another mini-dynasty for the period 1996–2003.

4392 Miracle Mets 1969 *National (M)*. The Mets, who had never finished higher than ninth place out of 10 clubs in the National League, parlayed good fielding, clutch singles hitting and the best pitching in the league to play a torrid .700 ball in August and September, jumping from a .500 team to a 100-game divisional winner, outstripping the ill-fated Chicago Cubs in the process. The Mets then swept Atlanta in the N.L. Championship Series and stunned the heavily favored Baltimore Orioles, 4 games to 1, in the 1969 World Series, prompting Mets field manager Gil Hodges to exclaim to reporters after the clinching victory in Game 5 of the Fall Classic, "If a man can walk on the moon (Neil Armstrong in July 1969) and if the Jets can win the Super Bowl (who had beaten the NFL Baltimore Colts in January 1969), then the Mets can win the World Series." The moniker was coined by sportswriter Barry Popik in the *New York Times* October 17, 1969.

4393 Magical Mystery Mets 1969 *National (M)*. In a spin-off from the Beatles' *Magical Mystery Tour* 1967 album, which contained music that practically defined the so-called "Hippie Era" state of joyous bliss and exaltation, the 1969 Mets, under manager Gil Hodges, traveled along in their own "Magical Mystery Tour" as they unexpectedly won the 1969 NL Eastern Division title, the NL pennant and the 1969 World Series—sending millions of Mets fans into ecstasy.

4394 Quarreling Yankees 1976–81 *American (M)*. Not to be outdone by the strife of the Oakland A's of 1972–74, the Yankees had their share of arguments, screaming matches and fisticuffs amongst themselves, the most noted the in the dugout shouting match between then-manager Billy Martin and star hitter Reggie Jackson in 1977.

4395 Steinbrenner's Millionaires 1976–81 *American (M)*. Flamboyant team owner George Steinbrenner spent millions to sign high-priced players like hitters Reggie Jackson, Thurman Munson, Mickey Rivers, Bucky Dent, and Graig Nettles and pitchers Jim "Catfish" Hunter, Don Gullet and Sparky Lyle. The results paid off as "Steinbrenner's Millionaires" won four AL pennants and two World Series titles over the course of six seasons to revive the then-dormant (1965–75) Yankee dynasty.

4396 Damnable Yankees 1976–81 *American (M)*. Hearkening back to the 1950s "Damn Yankees," baseball writers Bill Madden and Moss Klein called Steinbrenner's boisterous and winning team of 1976–81 the "Damnable Yankees."

4397 Bronx Zoo 1976–78 *American (M)*. At first glance, it may seem that the 1979 book, entitled *Bronx Zoo* and written by then Yankee pitcher Sparky Lyle and author Peter Golenbeck, might be about a losing team. Instead, all the dissension and pandemonium of the Yankee teams of 1976–78 were actually about a club that won three consecutive American League pennants. The title was inspired by players, from both the Yankees and visiting clubs, who complained that Yankee fans were so rowdy and unruly that Yankee Stadium re-

sembled a zoo. In 1978, sportswriter Tom Dalzell coined the term August 11 to describe the wild Yankee Stadium scene of fans, managers, reporters and owner George Steinbrenner. The name was derived from the actual New York City animal zoo known as the Bronx Zoo.

4398 Steinbrenner's Brownshirts 1977 *American (M)*. A hostile March 2 tag, coined by Bill "Spaceman" Lee, then a pitcher with arch-rival Boston who got the nickname for his own share of "spacy" remarks, was a response to the verbal insults hurled at Lee in 1976 by the Yankee bench and New York manager Billy Martin. Lee complained, "Last year (1976), I was assaulted by (Yankee owner) George Steinbrenner's Nazis, his brownshirts. He (Steinbrenner) brainwashes those kids over there (in New York) and they're led by 'Herman Goering the Second.' They got a convicted felon running the club. What do you expect?"

4399 October Men 1978 *American (M)*. In a follow-up to his 1972 book *The Boys of Summer* about the Brooklyn Dodgers of the 1950s, baseball author Roger Kahn wrote another book in 2003 — entitled *October Men*—about the 1978 New York Yankees, who defeated the Los Angeles Dodgers in the 1978 World Series to capture back-to-back world titles.

4400 Kings of Queens 1986 *National (M)*. When the Mets, who played in Shea Stadium in Queen's County, were winning the NL pennant and the 1986 World Series, local newspapers sometimes called them the **Kings of Queens**. The name never caught on, but was revived by the success of the popular Kevin James *Kings of Queens* TV comedy in 1998. Since 2005, the name's use has declined again as the Mets started struggling.

4401 Miraculous Mets 1986 *National (M)*. Coined by baseball writer Tracey Ringolsby, the moniker was a spin-off of the 1969 "Miracle Mets." Of course, this 1986 edition of the team had been carefully crafted to be a Yankee-style powerhouse so it wasn't that much of a "miracle" except for Games 6 and 7 of the World Series when the Boston Red Sox blew these last two games.

4402 Methodical Mets 1986 *National (M)*. Tag was coined by baseball writer Tracy Ringolsby, who noted that the 1986 Mets were much like the methodical New York Yankees of 1949–64, i.e., leading the NL in BA (.263), slugging average (.401), 783 runs scored, 730 runs batted in and best ERA (3.11) en route to a superior 108–54 record and a 21-and-a-half game lead over second-place Philadelphia.

4403 The Bad Guys Who Won 1986 *National (M)*. General manager Frank Cashen and field manager Davey Johnson assembled an intimidating roster for the 1986 season with hitters Lenny Dykstra, Wally Backman, Tim Teufel, Keith Hernandez, Darryl Strawberry, and Gary Carter and pitchers Dwight Gooden, Ron Darling, Bob Ojeda, Sid Fernandez, Rick Aguilera, Roger McDowell and Jesse Orosco. When field manager Johnson said to reporters in spring training: "We don't just want to win. We want to dominate." The aggressive attitude generated a "Bad Guy" image, much like the "Big Bad Yankees" of the 1950s. When the Mets defeated Boston in the World Series, manager Johnson told reporters that his team were the "Bad Guys Who Won." It is also the title of a book by baseball author Jeff Pearlman.

4404 Pondscum 1986 *National (M)*. Bitter Cardinal fans, with their team skidding to 28-and-a-half games behind the NL Eastern Division champion Mets, ungraciously called the New Yorkers the "Pondscum." Tag was strictly an on-the-street remark that faded when the Cardinals replaced the Mets as NL champions the following season.

4405 Bronx Bummers 1988 *American (M)*. Coined by sportswriter Mike Downey to lament the Yank's decline from 40–28 under manager Billy Martin to only 45–48 under new manager Lou

Piniella, who was saddled with an ineffective pitching staff. "Bummer" was a Hippie word from the 1960s meaning unpleasant or disappointing.

4406 Fall-Short Mets 1989 *National (M).* Tag was coined by baseball writer Dan Castellano to describe the 1989 Mets, who trailed Don Zimmer's Chicago Cubs all summer for the NL Eastern Division title before slumping in the last two weeks of the season to finish six games behind Chicago.

4407 Steinbrenner's Sputterers 1989 *American (M).* Tag was coined by sportswriter Bill Madden to describe the 74–87 1989 Yankees who skidded to the team's first losing season since 1982 and the lowest won-lost percentage since 1967.

4408 Bronx Bomb 1990 *American (M).* In the second year of a four-year slump, the Yankees dropped into last place in the AL Eastern Division with a 67–95 mark, their worst winning percentage since 1913! To "Lay a Bomb" is an old Broadway theatrical expression meaning to produce a displeasing show for the audience.

4409 Mutts 1991–96, 2002–04 *National (M).* Mets fans, who were tolerant of the expansion team of 1962–68 and the struggling club of 1977–83 following two NL pennants and a world's championship, lost patience with the team during its "Dog Days" era of 1991–96 and 2002–04, calling these bad Mets teams the "Mutts." A "mutt" refers to an alley dog.

4410 Mess 1991–96, 2002–04, 2011 *National (M).* Abrasive tag flung onto these losing teams by irate Mets fans. In 2011, team owner Fred Wilpon informed *Sports Illustrated* that the franchise was in danger of losing $70 million this season. Moreover, the team had a losing record and was falling out of the NL East Division title race. Tag was revived by sportswriters Andrew Brill and Gordon Wittenmyer.

4411 My Entire Team Sucks 1991–96, 2002–04 *National (M).* When the Mets slumped in the 1990s, enterprising Yankee and Phillies fans stuck this insulting acronym on the New York Nationals, i.e., M.E.T.S. Use gradually faded as the Yankees and Phillies' subsequent successes (eight pennants between the two of them) distracted their fans back to their own team's exploits. The word "suck"—a horrific vulgarity before 1970—has evolved into an almost acceptable and indeed genteel term, meaning to "perform terribly."

4412 The Worst Team That Money Could Buy 1992 *National (M).* In a twist of the phrase "The best team that money could buy," baseball authors Bob Klapisch and John Harper wrote a book with this phrase as a title describing the 1992 Mets who spent $45 million (a big sum at that time) for hitters Bobby Bonilla, Vince Coleman and Howard Johnson and pitcher Bret Saberhagen for a Mets team that stumbled to a 72–90 record and fifth place in the NL Eastern Division. The team batted .233 and was disabled by injuries.

4413 Battlers 1996 *American (M).* When the New York Yankees overcame a two games-to-none deficit against the Atlanta Braves in the 1996 World Series to win the next four games to claim the 1996 world's championship, proud manager Joe Torre told reporters that his players were "battlers."

4414 Steinbrenner's Warriors 1998 *American (M).* When the 1998 Yankees won 114 games in the regular season to approach the 116 major league record of the 1906 Chicago Cubs and outstrip second-place Boston's 92 victories by 22 games, and then win 11 of 13 post-season games—including a four-game sweep of NL champion San Diego in the World Series—team owner George Steinbrenner hailed his players (who went 125–50 overall) to the media as his "Warriors."

4415 Team of the Century 1999 *American (M).* When the Yankees closed out the twentieth century with their 37th American League pennant and 26th World Series championship, the media hailed the franchise as the "Team of the Century."

4416 Evil Empire 2002 *American (M).* When Yankee owner George Steinbrenner signed long ball hitter Jose Canseco to deny the Boston Red Sox the chance to do the same, Red Sox CEO Larry Luchino decried Steinbrenner's Yankees in a 2002 TV interview as the "Evil Empire"—a spinoff of the "Evil Empire" of movie producer George Lucas' *Star Wars* flicks and Ronald Reagan's characterization of the Soviet Union in 1982. The Yankees with 40 AL pennants and 27 World Series titles in 89 years of the era 1921–2009 are "Baseball's Empire." The gimmick moniker caused a few grins but then fans dismissed it as uninteresting, although newspapers continue to use the tag about from time to time. Baseball writer Mike Vaccaro claims the moniker started up in the summer of 1977, immediately after the smash hit movie *Star Wars* debuted in movie theaters.

4417 Winners 2003 *American (M).* The Yankees won their 40th American League pennant this year, prompting fans and media to use this concessionary term.

4418 Emperors 2005 *American (M).* (2005). Coined by sportswriter Mike Vaccaro, the name was a spin-off of "Roman Empire of Baseball" and "Evil Empire." At the time the Yankees had won 39 AL pennants and 26 World Series titles in 85 seasons dating to 1921. The "Emperors" had also completed 13 consecutive winning seasons, which included 11 consecutive playoff appearances.

4419 Los Mets 2005–06 *National (M).* During this two-year period, team GM Omar Minaya signed Latin players Carlos Beltran, Pedro Martinez, Carlos Delgado, Julio Franco and Jose Valentin, prompting English-speaking Mets fans to call the players "Los Mets." Moreover, the franchise began radio broadcasting games in Spanish where the announcers routinely referred to the team as "Los Mets."

4420 Bankees 2007 *American (M).* When the Yankee player payroll reached $200 million in 2007, some newspapers referred to them as the "Bankees." Though amusing, the moniker did not catch on.

4421 Skankees 2008 *American (M).* Yet another uncouth "street slur" that were introduced in the 2000s. A "skank" is slang for a prostitute. Inelegant spin-offs include **Spank-mees** (a sexual innuendo) and **Stankees**. These "slur names," which have been coined in every big league city, have been shunned by the media and are merely part of common street language, mostly used by hostile Boston Red Sox and New York Mets fans. The Café Press T-Shirts Company specializes in derogatory sports team names, declaring in an advertisement: "The 'Evil Empire' now has a new name. Our T-shirts call them the 'New York Stankees.'"

4422 The Team America Loves to Hate 2009 *American (M).* With their 41st AL pennant and 27th World Series titles won by 2009, the Yankees reinforced the dislike, borne of envy, directed towards them by many baseball fans outside of New York City. Many non–New York fans have disliked Babe Ruth's womanizing, Reggie Jackson's antics and George Steinbrenner's imperial swagger, not to mention the Yankees' "Bronx Zoo" fans.

4423 The Bottomless Pit Yankees 2010 *American (M).* *The Sporting News* referred to the New York American League franchise's endless money reserves allowing them to maintain a $200 million player payroll.

Newark, New Jersey

4424 Domestics 1884–85 *Eastern (ind.).* Team began in 1880 as an amateur nine — the Domestic Club. Team was called "Domestic" because all the players were from the Newark area.

4425 Little Giants 1886 *Eastern (ind.);* 1889–90 *Atlantic Assn. (ind.).* Team had a loose affiliation with the NL New York Giants. In the era 1880–1920, minor league cities geographically close to big league cities, i.e., Newark–New York and Jersey City–New York, maintained a very loose affiliation with nearby major league teams.

"Little" meant the players were not only young but that the team was also a minor league outfit.

4426 Mosquitoes 1886 *Eastern (ind.)*. New Jersey is the "Mosquito State" because of the many swamps in the region that bred malaria-carrying mosquitoes. The swamps were finally drained by 1900.

4427 Jugglers 1886 *Eastern (ind.)*. Tag was a complimentary term for a skilled, winning team, such as this one, which compiled a 68–26 record, winning the pennant by eleven games. A juggler is deft and agile in the performance of tricks, i.e., "juggling balls."

4428 Kids 1886–86 *Eastern (ind.)*. Team had numerous young players. With manager Charles Hackett at the helm, newspapers called the players "Hackett's Kids."

4429 Giants 1887 *International (ind.)*. The diminutive "Little" was sometimes applied to a major league team nickname used by a minor league team in the 1880s (and again in the 1930s). The fans thought it was pretentious, and by 1940 the usage stopped. In this case, newspapers editors dropped the "Little" adjective to save space.

4430 Hustlers 1887 *International (ind.)*. This moniker was baseball slang for a good team and good players. These players "hustled" on the field, compiling a very competitive 59–39 record.

4431 Trunk Makers 1887 *International (ind.)*. A leather-maker named Saeth Bayden arrived in Newark in 1815 where he invented "patent leather," which is a glossy leather used for shoes, clothing accessories and baggage. By 1830, Bayden had invented malleable iron. By 1850, patent leather and malleable iron were used to manufacture baggage, i.e., suitcases and trunks. Newark became known for the manufacture of baggage, i.e., Peddie's Trunk Company and the Morrison Trunk Company.

4432 Colts 1896–1900x *Atlantic (ind.)*. Team disbanded June 2. The team signed many young players.

4433 Sailors 1902–07 *Eastern (A)*. Settled by the Puritans in 1666, the city became a major eastern maritime port located along the Passaic River and Newark Bay. A famous U.S. war vessel in the 1890s was the *U.S.S. Newark*.

4434 Indians 1908–11 *Eastern (A)*; 1912–15m *International (AA)*. Team, unable to compete with the FL Newark Peppers, moved to Harrisburg (PA) July 2; 1915–16 *International (AA)*. The Delaware Indians arrived in the region around 4000 B.C. Successive waves of Dutch, English and American settlers forced the Delaware to surrender and sell their territory in 1750. The tribes then retired to reservations. With manager George Stallings at the helm, newspapers called the players "Stallings' Indians." Joe McGinnity took over in 1909 and the name became "McGinnity's Indians." Joe McGinnity returned in 1912 to lead "McGinnity's Indians." Harry Smith led "Smith's Indians" to the IL pennant in 1913.

4435 Cubans 1914m *Atlantic (D)*. Team moved to Long Branch (NJ) July 22. For the 1914 season, the team signed four players from Cuba—all of them white. In this era big league teams, desperate for talent because of the Federal League player raids, tried to sign Cuban players, including some "morenos," who were somewhat darker than Caucasian.

4436 Peppers 1915 *Federal (M)*. Baseball players are energetic young men who have a lot of pep. Moreover, about this time the pre-game exercise of "pepper" was introduced where three or four fielders gently toss the ball to a batter, positioned about 10 feet away, who repeatedly bunts the ball to the fielders to sharpen their reflexes. With manager Bill Phillips at the helm, newspapers called the players "Phillip's Peppers." Bill McKechnie took over in mid-season and the name became "McKechnie's Peppers." A "pepper" in this era was slang for an energetic player. Eating pepper or some other spicy food tends to make a person energetic and alert as they make a mad dash for water.

4437 Bears 1917–19 *International (AA)*; 1921–25m *International (AA)*. Team moved to Providence May 16; 1926–49 *International (AA 1926–45, AAA 1946–49)*; 1998 to date *Atlantic (ind.)*. With Indians now monopolized by the Cleveland American Leaguers, local newspapers wanted a new moniker. A 1917 fan poll chose "Bears."

4438 Stars 1926x *Eastern Colored (M)*. After Giants, "Stars" was the most popular black baseball team nickname. Management wanted a name similar to "Bears."

4439 Grizzlies 1926–45 *International (AA)*. Tag was an alternate moniker that did not catch on.

4440 Browns 1931–32 *Independent Negro team*. Players wore brown-trim uniforms and brown stirrups.

4441 Dodgers 1933 *Independent Negro team*; 1934–35 *Negro National (M)*. During the Great Depression of 1930–40, black teams strapped for cash often asked big league teams for their old uniforms. Teams like the Newark Dodgers and New York Black Yankees simply adopted the nickname on the big league jerseys. After the 1933 season, the team joined this major circuit in 1934.

4442 Eagles 1936–48 *Negro National (M)*. The Newark Dodgers and Brooklyn Eagles merged after the 1935 season to form the Newark Eagles.

Newark–Jersey City, New Jersey

4443 New Jersey Titans 1969x *Global (ind.)*. Team and circuit disbanded July 5. Tag was a spin-off of the NL and NFL New York Giants and the AFL New York Titans. The league was the brainchild of baseball owner Charlie Finley but failed financially.

Newark, New York

4444 Co-Pilots 1968–79 *New York–Pennsylvania (A)*. Team was a 1968 farm club of the expansion Seattle "Pilots," who established a farm club there, one year before starting play in the American League in 1969. When the Pilots moved to Milwaukee to play there as the "Brewers," the "Co-Pilots" moniker was retained for the farm club. Newark International Airport is located just outside the city. In aviation terms, the co-pilot is subordinate to the pilot, making the name for a farm team quite appropriate. Ironically, the team logo was the helmsman's wheel on a boat.

4445 Orioles 1983–87 *New York–Pennsylvania (A)*. Team was a farm club of Baltimore Orioles.

4446 Barge Bandits 1995–96 *North Atlantic (ind.)*. Barges have sailed the Erie Canal since 1895. Baseball teams, in cities near bodies of water, sometimes use the monikers of Pirates, Buccaneers, Marauders, Raiders, Sea Wolves and Bandits. Starting around 1720, river pirates and barge bandits plagued shipping on American lakes and rivers for more than a hundred years. The team logo is a masked "bandit horse."

Newark, Ohio

4447 Newark Base Ball Club 1889 *Ohio State*; 1900 *Ohio–Pennsylvania (ind.)*. These teams had no nickname.

4448 Idlewilds 1905 *Ohio–Pennsylvania (C)*. "Idlewild" is an archaic term that refers to any land that is barren of cultivated plants. The city was settled in an "idlewild" near the Licking River and Raccoon Creek. Farms sprung up, converting the "idlewild" into wheat fields and fruit groves. With manager Jack Doyle at the helm, newspapers called the players "Doyle's Idlewilds."

4449 Cotton Tops 1906 *Pennsylvania (D)*. To combat the summer heat, this year's players wore cotton jerseys. With manager Billy

Bottenus at the helm in 1906, newspapers called the cotton-clad players "Bottenus' Cotton Tops."

4450 Newks 1907 *Pennsylvania (D).* Newspapers used this tag to save space.

4451 Skeeters m1911 *Central (D).* Team began season in Grand Rapids (MI) and moved to Newark (OH) June 27; 1915 *Buckeye (D).* Mosquitoes infested the nearby Licking River and Raccoon Creek, causing swarms of these monsters to infest the Newark ballpark. Name first was used by the Newark (NJ) "Mosquitoes" in the 1886 season. The same problem was occurring in Jersey City, where the Jersey City "Skeeters" played.

4452 Moundsmen 1944–47 *Ohio State (D).* Team was a farm club of the AL St. Louis Browns. St. Louis is known as the "Mound City." Missouri and Ohio (Newark in particular) are sites of the mounds built by the pre-historic Hopewell Culture "Mound Builders" who occupied the Midwest from Missouri to Ohio some 3,000 years ago.

4453 Yankees 1948–51x *Ohio–Indiana (D).* Team disbanded July 17. The team was a farm club of the New York Yankees.

4454 Buffaloes 1994 *Frontier (ind.).* Ohio was the site of large buffalo herds in the seventeenth century but the encroachment of settlers, soldiers and migrating Indian tribes resulted in a high attrition rate that all but eliminated them from Ohio by 1800.

4455 Bisons 1995 *Frontier (ind.).* Tag was a shorter name for newspapers.

Newburgh, New York

4456 Cobblestone Throwers 1886 *Hudson River (ind.).* In the nineteenth century, numerous brickyards were established in this city along the nearby Naugatuck River. These brickyards manufactured "Belgium Bricks," which were granite cobble stones. In this era baseball players were sometimes known as "cobblestone throwers." The baseball itself was likened to such round objects as apple, pill, potato and cobblestone.

4457 Taylor-mades 1903–05 *Hudson River (D).* Fred Taylor was the team captain (1903–04) and 1904–05 manager of the team. City was also a textile and clothing manufacturing center. Moniker was a play on words on "tailor-made."

4458 Hill Climbers 1906 *Hudson River (D);* 1914m *Atlantic (D).* Team moved to Long Branch July 22. Newburgh was built in the Litchfield Hills. With manager Andrew Marshall at the helm in 1914, newspapers called the players "Marshall's Hill Climbers." When William Todd Waterman took over in mid-season 1914, the name became "William's Hill Climbers."

4459 Hillies 1907 *Hudson River (D).* This tag was shorter for newspapers. Team had a loose affiliation with the AL New York Highlanders.

4460 Dutchmen 1913 *New York–New Jersey (D).* Starting in 1709, the region was settled by Dutch colonists. With field manager Archie Marshall at the helm, local newspapers called the players "Archie's Dutchmen."

4461 Hummingbirds 1946m *North Atlantic (D).* Team moved to Walden (NY) May 23. The ruby-throat hummingbird is found in North America and in the nearby Appalachian Plateau Hills.

Newburgh, Pennsylvania

4462 Nighthawks 1995–96 *Northeast (ind.).* Also known as the American nightjar and the whippoorwill, the American nighthawk is found in the eastern U.S.

4463 Lehigh Valley Black Hawks 1998 *Atlantic (ind.).* Team went by the regional name of "Lehigh Valley Black Hawks." The name is a combination of "Nighthawks" and "black," the latter word referring to coal mining.

4464 Lehigh Valley Black Diamonds 1998 *Atlantic (ind.).* Mines in the region transport coal to city petrochemical factories. Pennsylvania is known as the "Coal State."

Newburyport, Massachusetts

4465 Yankees 1885 *New England (ind.).* In 1815 a Dutch settler arrived in New Amsterdam. His name was Jean Kaase — John Cheese in English. He was a successful businessman, but jealous English colonists used his name to describe any Dutchman as a buffoon. The name "Jean Kaase" evolved into "Yankee." Ironically, when the British seized New Amsterdam from the Dutch colonists and renamed it New York, the term "Yankee" soon referred to any colonist, Dutch and English. Newburyport is known as the "Yankee City."

4466 Clam-diggers 1886 *New England (ind.).* The city is an oceanport where fishing boats catch fish, lobsters, oysters, crab, shrimp and clams, which are transported to city factories to be cleaned, processed, packed and shipped. The city was also a shipbuilding and whaling center.

Newnan, Coweta, Georgia

4467 Cowetas 1913–16 *Georgia–Alabama (C).* City is located in Coweta County. Occasionally, a team will take its county as a nickname after its city name.

4468 Brownies 1946–50 *Georgia–Alabama (D).* Team named after team captain and star pitcher Lloyd Brown. When manager George Nix left the team in mid-season, Brown became player-manager. When Brown left the team after the 1946 season, the nickname was retained. The team was not a farm club of the St. Louis Browns but the players did wear brown-trim uniforms starting in 1947.

Newport, Arkansas

4469 Pearl Diggers 1908 *Arkansas State (D);* 1909 *Northeast Arkansas (D).* City was built along the White River. Fishing boats net the fat pocketbook pearly mussel for its pearls. In 2000 the Arkansas Game and Fish Commission declared the fat pocketbook pearly mussel to be an endangered species.

4470 Cardinals 1936–38 *Northeast Arkansas (D).* Team was a farm club of the St. Louis Cardinals.

4471 Tigers 1939 *Northeast Arkansas (D).* Team was a farm club of the Detroit Tigers.

4472 Dodgers 1940 *Northeast Arkansas (D).* Team was a farm club of the Brooklyn Dodgers.

Newport, Kentucky

4473 Newport Brewers 1914m *Ohio State (D).* Team joined the league May 26 and moved to Paris (OH) June 16. Newport is the home Wiedemann's Brewery, which was established in 1890.

Newport, Rhode Island

4474 Colts 1897–99 *New England (ind.).* Team had many young players, known as "colts" in the slang of the era.

4475 Ponies 1908 *Atlantic Assn. (D).* Tag was a spin-off from the 1899 "Colts" team. In the nineteenth century, "ponies" was slang for an expansion team. With manager Ben Anthony at the helm, newspapers called the players "Anthony's Ponies."

Newport, Tennessee

4476 Canners 1937–42x *Appalachian (D)*. Team disbanded June 26 due to U.S. entry into World War II; 1948–50 *Mountain States (D)*. City was home to a factory of the Alcoa Canning (later Alcoa Aluminum). When war came in 1942 the factory switched from canning to manufacture of airplane parts. Alcoa Aluminum's first factory was named after and built in neighboring Alcoa (TN) in 1939. After the war Alcoa Canning Company renamed itself Alcoa Aluminum.

Newport News, Virginia

4477 Shipbuilders 1900 *Virginia (ind.)*; 1901m *Virginia–North Carolina (ind.)*. Team moved to Charlotte June 21; 1912–17x *Virginia (B)*. Circuit and team disbanded May 15 due to U.S. entry into World War; 1918x *Virginia (C)*. Circuit and team disbanded June 25 because of World War I; 1919–22 *Virginia (B)*. Settled in 1621 because of its waterways, the region became a city in 1882. Because it was an important embarkation point off Hampton Roads, which consists of the James, Elizabeth and Nansemond rivers into Chesapeake Bay, the city became militarily important during the Civil War and the Spanish American War. The city's strategic naval importance stimulated the establishment of shipbuilding factories here in the 1890s. With manager W.H. Richardson at the helm in 1900, newspapers called the players "Richardson's Shipbuilders." With Ed Ashenback at the helm in 1901, newspapers called the players "Ed Ashenback's Shipbuilders." Newport News is known as the "City of Ships and Shipbuilding." Moniker was shortened for newspapers to "Builders," i.e., "Builders edge Colts, 4–3." Moniker was used by five different franchises from 1900 through the 1922 season. Ships were built here for World War I and World War II.

4478 Pilots 1941–42 *Virginia (C)*. Pilot ships have guided commercial, recreational and military boats through the Hampton Roads since 1750. Newport News, along the James River, is known as the "World's Greatest Harbor." Early air pilots Thomas Baldwin, Carl Batts, Victor Carlstrom, Ted Hequembourg and Jimmy Johnson perfected the "Flying Boat"—a Curtiss tractor bi-plane capable of landing on the water. They practiced taking off and landing on water off the Virginia coast in 1915.

4479 Dodgers 1944–55 *Piedmont (B)*. Team was a farm club of the Brooklyn Dodgers.

Newport News–Hampton, Virginia

4480 Newport News–Hampton Base Ball Club 1894 *Virginia (ind.)*. Team had no nickname.

4481 Peninsula Senators 1963 *Carolina (A)*. Team went by the regional name of "Peninsula Senators" because Newport News–Hampton was too long. City was built on a peninsula at the mouth of the James River. Team was a farm club of the Washington Senators.

4482 Peninsula Grays 1964–68 *Carolina (A)*. In a sea battle off the coast here, the Confederate *Virginia* (nee *Merrimac*) destroyed two Union ships—the *Cumberland* and the *Congress*—and then fought the *Monitor* to a stand-off. When local newspapers wanted a short, pro–South name, management dressed the players in uniforms with gray trim and called them the "Grays" because Peninsula has nine letters.

4483 Peninsula Astros 1969–70 *Carolina (A)*. Team went by the regional name of "Peninsula Astros." Team was a farm club of the Houston Astros.

4484 Peninsula Phillies 1971 *Carolina (A)*. Team went by the regional name of "Peninsula Phillies." The team was a farm club of the Philadelphia Phillies.

4485 Peninsula Whips 1972–73 *International (AAA)*. Team went by the regional name of "Peninsula Whips." The Winnipeg Whips moved to Newport News–Hampton after the 1971 season and the nickname was retained.

4486 Peninsula Pennants 1974 *Carolina (A)*. Team went by the regional name of "Peninsula Pennants." The moniker was a spin-off from the previous year's team name of "Whips." Commercial, recreational and military ships have been flying "whip pennants" on their vessels for more than 250 years. A whip pennant is also a type of baseball flag celebrating a special occasion or a league championship. A pennant is a celebratory flag, usually an elongated triangle that "whips in the wind."

4487 Peninsula Pilots 1976–85 *Carolina (A)*; 1989–92 *Carolina (A)*. Both teams went by the regional name of "Peninsula Pilots." Local newspapers wanted a shorter name so the 1942 Virginia League "Pilots" team nickname was used.

4488 Peninsula White Sox 1986–87 *Carolina (A)*. Team went by the regional name of "Peninsula White Sox." The team was a farm club of the Chicago White Sox.

4489 Virginia Generals 1988 *Carolina (A)*. Team went by state name of "Virginia Generals." George Washington and Robert E. Lee were both born in Virginia.

Newton, Kansas

4490 Newton Base Ball Club 1888x *Western (D)*. Team and league disbanded June 21. Team had no nickname.

4491 Browns 1908 *Central Kansas (ind.)*; 1909 *Kansas State (D)*. These teams had a loose affiliation with the St. Louis Browns, who donated old "Browns" uniforms to them.

4492 Railroaders 1909–11x *Kansas State (D)*. Team and league disbanded July 11; 1912m *Central Kansas (D)*. Team moved to Minneapolis (KS) July 12; 1912m *Central Kansas (D)*. Team moved to Minneapolis (KS) July 12; m1924m *Southwestern (D)*. Team, after its home park was damaged by wind storms, moved to Blackwell (OK) July 26 and then moved to Ottawa (KS) August 5 before moving back to Newton once again on August 28 following completion of repair of the Newton park. By 1872 the Kansas-Pacific (now Union Pacific) and Santa Fe (now Burlington Northern–Santa Fe) railroads reached the towns of Ellsworth, Newton, Caldwell, Wichita, Dodge City and Abilene.

Newton-Conover, North Carolina

4493 Twins 1937–38 *North Carolina (D)*; 1939–40x Team disbanded July 19; 1948–51 *Western Carolina (D)*; 1960–62 *Western Carolina (D)*. These teams represented two cities. The "Twins," playing home games in Newton, also drew fans from Conover.

Niagara Falls, New York

4494 Niagara Falls Baseball Club 1908x *International (D)*. Team and league disbanded in July. Team had no nickname.

4495 Rainbows 1939 *Pennsylvania–Ohio–New York (P.O.N.Y.) (D)*. Water mists from the nearby Niagara Falls often create beautiful rainbows.

4496 Frontiers 1946–47 *Middle Atlantic (C)*. Niagara Falls was built at the U.S.–Canadian border. The eastern half of the city is in New York State while the western half is in Ontario.

4497 Citizens 1950–51 *Middle Atlantic (C)*. Moniker honors both American and Canadian citizens of the two cities and two countries. With managers Michael Ulisney and then Walter Chipple at the helm, newspapers called the teams "Ulisney's Citizens" and "Chipple's Citizens." Starting in 1946, more and more minor league teams started to adopt formal, official team nicknames. However, the process was not uniform. Some teams continued to rely on reporters to coin an unofficial team nickname well into the 1950s. By 1960, the switch-over to formal team nicknames had become complete.

4498 Pirates 1970–79 *New York–Pennsylvania (A)*. Team was a farm club of the Pittsburgh Pirates.

4499 White Sox 1982–85 *New York–Pennsylvania (A)*. Team was a farm club of the Chicago White Sox.

4500 Rapids 1989–93 *New York–Pennsylvania (A)*. Stormy weather churns the Niagara River into rapids.

4501 Mallards 1995 *North Atlantic (ind.)*. Mallards, i.e., the North American green-headed wild duck, inhabit the watery regions of the Niagara River, Lake Erie and Lake Ontario.

Niagara Falls–Jamestown, New York

4502 Rainbows 1940 *Pennsylvania–Ohio–New York (P.O.N.Y.) (D)*. The 1939 team changed its name to the two-city name of "Niagara Falls–Jamestown Rainbows." Home games were played in both cities.

Nicholasville, Kentucky

4503 Nicholasville Baseball Club m1912m *Blue Grass (D)*. Team began season in Winchester (KY) and moved to Nicholasville June 8. The team moved to Mt. Sterling (KY) June 26. The team had no nickname.

Niles, Michigan

4504 Blues 1910x *Indiana–Michigan (D)*. Team and league disbanded August 21. Players wore blue stirrups.

Niles, Ohio

4505 Crowites 1905 *Ohio–Pennsylvania (D)*. Moniker was in honor of manager Charles Crowe.

Nishinomiya, Japan

4506 Orix Braves 1989 to date *Japanese Pacific (ind.)*; 1989–99 *Japanese Western (ind.)*. The franchise was the Osaka Hankyu Braves through the 1988 season. Orix Financial Services purchased the team and moved it to Nishinomiya for the 1989 season. The nickname of Braves was retained. The Western League team, a farm club of the Pacific League Braves, was purchased by Surpass, who renamed the team "Surpass" for the 2000 season.

4507 Hanshin Tigers 1991–2007 *Japanese Central (ind.)*; 1991 to date *Japanese Western (ind.)*. Hanshin Railway Company owns the team. Osaka Hanshin Tigers and its farm team moved to the city of Nishinomiya for the 1991 season. Nishinomiya is part of the greater Osaka metropolitan area. Hanshin decided to maintain the Tigers moniker. Players wear striped hose with yellow and black uniform trim. Because of the team colors, Japanese newspapers have called the team the "Detroit Tigers of Japan." The WL is also known as the **Junior Tigers.**

Nogales, Arizona, USA

4508 Internationals 1931 *Arizona–Texas (D)*. City was built along the U.S.-Mexican border. After the end of the Mexican-American War in 1849, the northern section has been part of Arizona while the southern section has been in Sonora, Mexico.

4509 Yaquis 1954–55 *Arizona–Texas (C)*. The Yaquis were an Indian tribe that occupied Sonora and Arizona in pre–Columbian times and into the nineteenth century.

4510 Red Devils 1956 *Arizona–Mexican (C)*. Although playing in a U.S. city, the team was a farm club of the Mexico City Red Devils (Diablos Rojos in Spanish). Even so, the name was also influenced by the University of Arizona Sun Devils athletic teams. Both nick-names, i.e., "Red Devils" (English) and **Diablos Rojos** (Spanish), were used.

4511 Mineros 1958 *Arizona–Mexico (C)*. With the discovery of gold and silver, miners rushed into the region and founded the city in 1880. Later, copper and molybdenum deposits were discovered.

4512 Cowboys 2003x *Arizona–Mexico (ind.)*. Team played in War Memorial Park in Nogales, Arizona. Circuit and team disbanded July 17. American cowboys and Mexican charos have herded cattle in the region since 1880. The team was also known by the Spanish name of **Los Charos.**

4513 Charos 2003x *Arizona–Mexico (ind.)*. Team played in War Memorial Park in Nogales, Arizona. Circuit and team disbanded July 17. American cowboys and Mexican charos have herded cattle in the region since 1880. The team was also known, in English, as the **Cowboys.**

Nogales, Sonora, Mexico

4514 Mineros 1958 *Arizona–Mexico (C)*. This team played in Mexico's Nogales. With the discovery of gold and silver, miners rushed into the region and founded the city in 1880. Later, copper and molybdenum deposits were discovered.

4515 Internacionales 1968–69 *Mexican Northern (A)*; 2006–07 *Norte de Sonora*. These teams, playing in Sonora, Mexico, used the Spanish form of the 1931 Nogales team nickname (see above).

4516 Club de Beisbol de Nogales 1969 *Mexican Northern (A)*. Team had no nickname in 1969.

Norfolk, Nebraska

4517 Drummers 1914–15x *Nebraska State (D)*. Team disbanded June 28. Nebraska's "Percussion Day," which originated at Concordia University, is celebrated annually in Norfolk on March 1 and is cel-ebrated with parades featuring drummers. With manager Warren Cummings at the helm in 1914, newspapers called the players "Cum-mings' Drummers." The name was retained in 1915.

4518 Elk Horns 1922–23 *Nebraska State (D)*; 1924 *Tri-State (D)*; 1928–36, 1938 *Nebraska State (D)*; 1939 *Western (D)*. Name refers to the red deer, which is found in North America. The male red deer sports large and heavy antlers—as long as 12 inches. The North American red deer is also called the North American elk. With man-ager Ernest Adams at the helm in 1922, newspapers called the players "Ernest's Elk Horns." Clifton Marr took over in mid-season 1922 and the name became "Clifton Marr's Elk Horns." Ed Reichle took over in 1923 and the name became "Ed Reichle's Elks." With manager Elmer "Nig" Lane at the helm in 1924, newspapers called the players "Elmer Lane's Elk Horns." With manager J. Lefty Wilkus at the helm in 1928–29, newspapers called the players the "Lefty Wilkus' Elks Horns." Hal Brokaw took over in 1930, making the name "Hal Brokaw's Elkhorns." The name was used through 1938.

4519 Elk 1937 *Nebraska State (D)*; 1939 *Western (D)*. With Elmer "Doc" Bennett at the helm both seasons, newspapers called the players "Elmer's Elks." This shorter version of "Elk Horns" had been used starting in 1922 in newspaper headlines, i.e., "Elks edge Canaries, 4–3." In 1937 and 1939, "Elk Horns" was not used at all.

4520 Yankees 1940–41 *Western (D)*. Team was a farm club of the New York Yankees.

Norfolk, Virginia

4521 Norfolk Base Ball Club 1885m *Eastern (ind.)*; 1885–86x *Virginia (ind.)*. Team and circuit disbanded in mid-season (date unknown). These teams had no nickname.

4522 Oystermen 1894 *Virginia (ind.)*. Fishing boats have sailed in and out of Hampton Roads Port since at least 1700. With manager Camden Sommers at the helm, newspapers called the players "Camden Sommers' Oystermen." Norfolk is known as the "Seafood Shopping Center."

4523 Crows 1895 *Virginia (ind.)*. Players wore black hose. With manager Camden Sommers at the helm, newspapers called the players "Camden Sommer's Crows." In the era 1890–1910, teams often adopted a bird name corresponding to stocking color, i.e., Bluebirds, Blue Jays, Cardinals, Doves, Ravens, Redbirds and Crows.

4524 Clams 1895–96 *Virginia (ind.)*. Fishing boats catch fish, oysters and clams that are transported to city factories for cleaning, processing, packaging and shipping. With manager Camden Sommers at the helm in 1895, newspapers called the players "Camden's Clams." Claude McFarland was at the helm in 1896 and the name became "Claude McFarland's Clams." Originally **Clam-diggers**, newspapers shortened it to "Clams."

4525 Jewels 1897–98 *Atlantic (ind.)*. Team was managed by W.A. Jewell.

4526 Mary Janes 1900 *Virginia (ind.)*. "Mary Jane Shoes" were popular girls shoes in the U.S. at this time. Reporters for the arch-rival Portsmouth team often derided the Norfolk players as "Mary Janes," i.e., insinuating that the Norfolk fellows "played like girls." Norfolk newspapers then used the name as a badge of honor, as the "Mary Janes" compiled a superlative 43–15 record to win the pennant by a whopping 14 games over second-place Portsmouth.

4527 Phenoms 1900 *Virginia (ind.)*. Team won pennant going away. After becoming known as the "Mary Janes" because of taunts by rival Portsmouth newspapers, Norfolk fans and hometown reporters tried to be more positive, praising the Norfolk players as "phenomenal" when they played at .741 percentage to win the league pennant going away with a 14-game advantage over second-place Portsmouth and that city's abashed newspaper reporters. "Phenom" was a popular nineteenth-century slang for a rookie who excelled at the game.

4528 Reds 1900–05 *Independent Negro team*. Players wore red hose. Originally **Red Stockings**, newspapers quickly shortened the tag to "Reds." In this era, the lengthy "Stockings" was quickly being overtaken by "Sox."

4529 Skippers 1901 *Virginia–North Carolina (D)*. Built along the shores of Chesapeake Bay and Hampton Roads, the city has been a major seaport of the Atlantic coast since 1700. "Skipper" is slang for sea captain.

4530 Tars 1906–17 *Virginia (C)*; 1921–28x *Virginia (B)*. Team and league June 3; 1931–32x *Eastern (A)*. Team and league disbanded July 17 due to the Great Depression; 1934–55x *Piedmont (B)*. Team disbanded July 14. For centuries, sailors have applied tar to their ships to render it water-proof, and they have covered their ships with canvas tarpaulins. "Tars" was a nineteenth-century slang for the sailors who worked the "wharves and currents" of the nearby Elizabeth River Harbor. With manager Win Clark at the helm in 1906, newspapers called the players "Clark's Tars." Robert Pender took over 1907–08 and the name became "Robert's Tars." Win Clark returned 1909–10. Charles Babb took over in 1911 and the name became "Charles' Tars." Charles Shaffer took over 1912–13 and the name

was again "Charles' Tars." Name was retained through 1917. With manager Jack Warhop at the helm, newspapers called the players "Warhop's Tars." Win Clark returned 1922–24, making the name "Clark's Tars." The name was retained through 1928. Win Clark returned as field skipper 1931–32.

4531 Stars 1919 *Independent Negro team*; 1920 *Negro Southern (ind.)*; 1921 *Southeast Negro (ind.)*. After Giants, the newspaper-friendly moniker of "Stars" was the most popular of black baseball team nicknames. The moniker was a spin-off from the Norfolk "Tars."

4532 Giants 1920 *Negro Southern (ind.)*; 1921 *Southeast Negro (ind.)*. "Giants," used by Northern black teams since 1885, was also popular as a nickname for black teams in the South.

4533 Tidewater Tides 1969–92 *International (AAA)*. Tides roll onto the beaches of Norfolk from Chesapeake Bay, Hampton Roads, Lafayette Bay, Willobough Bay and Elizabeth Bay. Just prior to the start of the 1969 season, the team owner William McDonald held a name-the-team contest. The winning entry was "Mariners," but *Norfolk News* editor Robert Mason preferred the shorter "Tides" and McDonald acceded to him as the team became the "Tidewater Tides."

4534 Tides 1993 to date *International (AAA)*. Team went by the city name of "Norfolk Tides."

Norfolk–Newport News, Virginia

4535 Royals 1934 *Independent Negro team*. The Colony of Virginia was named after her royal majesty Queen Elizabeth I — the Virgin Queen. Newport News and Norfolk are located near to the "Royal Front," which is that region of Virginia in the state's northeast that was occupied by the English in the seventeenth century from a land grant by English King Charles II. French settlers near Norfolk called the British frontier "Le Front Royal."

Norfolk-Portsmouth, Virginia

4536 Tidewater Tides 1966–68 *Carolina (A)*. Team represented both cities, but home games were played in Norfolk. Tides roll onto the beaches of Norfolk from Chesapeake Bay, Hampton Roads, Lafayette Bay, Willobough Bay and Elizabeth Bay.

Normal, Illinois

4537 CornBelters 2010 to date *Frontier (ind.)*. Because of the many corn farms in the region, the Middle States, ranging from Illinois and Iowa to the north to Nebraska and Missouri to the south, are known collectively as the "Corn Belt."

Norristown, Pennsylvania

4538 Norristown Base Ball Club 1889 *Middle States (ind.)*; 1896 *Schuylkill Valley*; 1932m *Interstate (D)*. Team moved to St. Clair (PA) May 28. These teams had no nickname.

North Bend–Coos Bay, Oregon

4539 Athletics 1970–72 *Northwest (A)*. Team was a farm club of the Oakland Athletics.

North Platte, Nebraska

4540 Buffaloes 1928–32 *Nebraska State (D)*. William "Buffalo Bill" Cody, with money he earned from his famous Wild West shows, bought a 4,000-acre ranch in 1886 in North Platte. Since then, North

Platte has been known as the "Home of Buffalo Bill." Buffaloes roamed the plains of Nebraska well into the nineteenth century.

4541 Indians 1956–59 *Nebraska State (D)*. Team was a farm club of the Cleveland Indians.

North Wilkesboro, North Carolina

4542 Flashers 1948–50 *Blue Ridge (D)*. With player-manager Henry "Flash" Lohman leading the team, management named the team the "Flashers."

North Yakima, Washington

4543 Braves 1913–14 Western Tri-State *(C 1913, D 1914)*. Clashes between settlers and the Yakima, Nisqualli and Cayuga led to war and the November 29, 1847, Waiilatpu Massacre that drove these tribes into reservations by 1858.

Northampton, Massachusetts

4544 Meadowlarks 1909–11x *Connecticut State (B)*. Northampton is nicknamed the "Meadow City." The Meadowlark is a yellow and black songbird of North America.

Northampton, Virginia

4545 Red Sox m1927 *Eastern Shore (D)*. Players wore red stirrups. The team had a loose affiliation with the Boston Red Sox.

Norton, Kansas

4546 Jayhawks 1929–30 *Nebraska State (D)*. The two regional birds of Kansas are the Nighthawk and the Blue Jay. The University of Kansas college sports teams of the 1890s combined the two monikers into "Jay Hawks."

Norton, Virginia

4547 Braves 1951–53 *Mountain States (D)*. Team had a loose affiliation with the Boston Braves (1951–52) and then the Milwaukee Braves (1953).

Norwalk, Connecticut

4548 Clam-eaters 1888–89x *Atlantic Assn. (ind.)*. Team disbanded June 1. Fishing boats sail in and out of the Thames River to and from the Long Island Sound. Norwalk is known as the "Clam Town" and the "World's Oyster Capital."

4549 Norwalk Base Ball Club 1889 *Middle States (ind.)*. The MSL was also known as the Eastern Interstate League. Team had no nickname.

Norwich, Connecticut

4550 Norwich Base Ball Club 1888 *Connecticut State (ind.)*. Team had no nickname.

4551 Witches 1899–1901 *Connecticut (ind.)*. Reporters, in a humorous bent, derived this moniker from the city name. Connecticut, in addition to Massachusetts, had its share of witchcraft trials in the seventeenth century.

4552 Reds 1902–03 *Connecticut (D)*; m1904 *Connecticut (B)*. Team began season in Worcester (MA) before moving to Norwich June 21; 1906–07 *Connecticut (B)*. Players wore red hose. Team was a farm club of the Boston Beaneaters, who also wore red hose.

4553 Bonbons 1910m *Connecticut Assn. (D)*. Connecticut hosts an annual "Norfolk-Norwich Festival." The festival, first held in 1772, is a 16-day celebration that is held every summer. Jelly beans, lemon sherbet, bonbons (candy inside chocolate) and "bonbon" coffee is served to attendees.

4554 Navigators 1995–2005 *Eastern (AA)*. Commercial and recreational boats sail the nearby Quinebaug River. Shipbuilding, cargo shipping to and from the West Indies, slave trading, and whaling were all conducted from 1750 to 1800.

4555 Connecticut Defenders 2006–09 *Eastern (AA)*. During the Revolutionary War (1776–81), Connecticut sent 3,600 men into early battles and became the "Arsenal of the Nation." The state manufactured munitions, which were sent to George Washington's troops throughout the war. The Nokona Athletic Goods Company, the producer of a line of baseball gloves known as the "American Defenders," owned both the Connecticut Defenders (Norwich, CT) of the Eastern League and the American Defenders of New Hampshire (Nashua CT) of the Can-Am League.

4556 Connecticut Tigers 2010 to date *New York–Pennsylvania (A)*. Team was a farm club of the Detroit Tigers. Oneonta Tigers moved to Norwich (CT) for the 2010 season and assumed the state name of "Connecticut Tigers."

Norwich, New York

4557 Norwich Base Ball Club 1886 *Central New York (ind.)*. Team had no nickname.

Novara, Sicily, Italy

4558 United 2011 to date *Italian A1 (ind.)*. Novara is an Italian city that was the site of the Battle of Novara in 1849 — a conflict, which historians say, set into motion the Italian unification movement. The Cantanina (Sicily) Warriors moved to Novara for the 2011 season.

Nueva Gerona, Isla de Juventud, Cuba

4559 Toronjeros 1978–79 to date *Cuban National (S)*. Citrus fruits are grown on groves on the Isla de Juventud. The fruit is then shipped to packing factories in the city of Nueva Gerona.

Nuevo Laredo, Tamaulipas, Mexico

4560 Tecolotes 1940 *Liga Mexicana (ind.)*; 1943–46 *Mexican (ind.)*; 1949–59 *(ind. 1949–54, A 1955–59)*; 1968 *Mexican Center (A)*; 1976–2003 *Mexican (AAA)*. This Nuevo Laredo team was the first franchise in the Mexican league to install electric lights at its home stadium to play night games. Local newspapers and fans immediately started calling the players Los Tecolotes (Owls) after the wide-eyed bird that hunts by night.

Nuevo Laredo, Tamaulipas, Mexico — Laredo, Texas, USA

4561 Tecolotes de Los Laredos *Mexican (AAA)* 1985–2003. Team, officially representing both cities, tried to attract fans from Laredo (TX) just north of the border while playing its home games in Laredo, Mexico. The team name in English was the "Two Laredos Owls."

Nyack, New York

4562 Rocklands 1946–48 *North Atlantic (D)*. City was built in the Hudson River Uplands near the Taconic Mountains, which consists of extremely rocky terrain.

4563 Rockies 1946–48 *North Atlantic (D)*. Tag was a newspaper contraction from "Rocklands."

Oak Ridge, Tennessee

4564 Bombers 1948m *Mountain States (D)*. Team moved to Hazard (KY) June 10. The Manhattan Project built a nuclear research laboratory here in 1941 and continued do research work after World War II ended. With manager Hobe Brummit at the helm, newspapers called the players "Hobe's Brummit's Bombers." Oak Ridge is the "Atomic Capital of the World."

4565 Pioneers 1954 *Mountain States (D)*. Daniel Boone explored this region in the 1760s, helping to establish the Wilderness Road. It was along this pioneer trail the city was built. The Daniel Boone National Forest is 100 miles north of the city.

Oakdale, Louisiana

4566 Lumberjacks 1920 *Louisiana State (D)*. Logging companies in Kistache National Forest (northwest of the city) sent lumber to city factories for processing. With manager Lew Bremerhoff at the helm, newspapers called the players "Lew's Bremerhoff's Lumberjacks."

Oakland, California

4567 G & M's 1886–87 *California State (ind.)*; 1888 *California (ind.)*. Team was owned by the Greenhood & Moran Clothing Store. The team's owners were Jacob Greenwood and James T. Moran.

4568 Colonels 1889–91, 1893 *California (ind.)*. The 1889 star player Danny Long (league-leading 116 runs scored and 118 steals) had played the 1888 season with the Louisville Colonels. The team was named after owner-manager "Colonel" Tom Robinson.

4569 Stars 1892 *California (ind.)*. Team's formal name was the "Star Base Ball Club of Oakland." However, the tag was used sarcastically by Oakland fans as the team produced a shoddy 34–57 record, i.e., "The 'Stars' lost again!"

4570 Clam-diggers 1898 *California State (ind.)*. Fishermen and tourists find clams along California's beaches. With manager Cal Ewing at the helm, newspapers called the players "Cal Ewing's Clam-diggers."

4571 Colts 1898 *Pacific Coast (ind.)*. Team had many young players who were known in the slang of the era as "colts."

4572 Reliances 1898 *Pacific States (ind.)*. Enterprise, Excelsior, Intrepid, Perseverance, Valiant and Reliance were nineteenth-century team nicknames that emphasized high quality performance as a goal.

4573 Haberdashers 1899 *California State (ind.)*. As soon as the moniker "Haberdashers" was used in print in April, newspapers editors quickly transformed it into "Dudes." Haberdasher meant a men's clothing store. A previous franchise had been owned by Greenhood & Moran Clothiers—also known as Greenhood & Moran Haberdashers.

4574 Outlaws 1899 *California State (ind.)*. The rowdy, ruffian image of baseball players in this era gave rise to such monikers as Rustlers, Cowboys, Indians, Kickers, Gladiators, Braves, Warriors and Outlaws. With manager Cal Ewing at the helm, newspapers called the players "Cal Ewing's Outlaws."

4575 Dudes 1899–1902 *California State (ind.)*. Baseball players who dressed in fancy "duds" were in this era known as "Dudes." The Oakland players dressed in fancy civilian duds replete with a haberdasher hat. With manager Cal Ewing at the helm, local newspapers called the players "Ewing's Dudes.

4576 Papas 1902–05 *Pacific Coast (A)*. Some newspapers called the veteran team "Los Papas," which is Spanish for "Fathers." With manager Pete Lohman at the helm 1902–05, newspapers called the players "Pete's Papas."

4577 Acorns 1902–05 *Pacific Coast (A)*; 1997 *Pacific Coast (AAA)*. The city of Oakland was named after the abundant oak trees of the region. The acorn is the nut of these trees. With manager Pete Lohman at the helm, 1902–05, newspapers called the players "Lohman's Acorns." As the 1997 team, guided by field skipper Art Howe, stumbled through its fifth consecutive losing season, disgruntled Oakland fans and newspaper editors, hearkening back to the awful Oakland "Acorns" of the Pacific Coast League, i.e., 72–136 in 1916 and 65–113 in 1938, started calling the players "Art's Acorns."

4578 Oaks 1903–55 *Pacific Coast (A 1903–07, AA 1908–45, AAA 1946–51, Open 1952–55)*. Spanish explorers who visited here in the seventeenth century called this place "Land of the Oaks" because of the extensive oak tree forests in this region.

4579 Commuters 1907–08 *California (ind. 1907–08, D 1909)*; 1915x *California State (D)*. Team and league disbanded May 30 due to rain storms. With the construction of ferry boats (1851), railroads and the introduction of trolley cars, many Oakland residents commuted to jobs and schools in San Francisco and other nearby cities. With manager Walt McMemony at the helm 1907–08 and again in 1915, newspapers called the players "McMenomy's Commuters."

4580 Invaders 1909 *California (D)*. Name had two origins: 1) team was a rival to the PCL Oakland Oaks "invading" the PCL territory in Oakland; and, 2) team won the 1909 pennant, decimating their opponents in local newspaper accounts like "marauding invaders." With manager Cy Moreing at the helm, newspapers called the players "Moreing's Invaders."

4581 Basches m1910m *California State (D)*. Team started season in Santa Rosa and then moved to Oakland July 10. Team then moved to Berkley July 31. Basche-Sage Hardware Company owned the team.

4582 Emery Arms m1911 *Central California (D)*. Team began the season in Elmhurst (CA) and then moved to Emeryville, a suburb of Oakland, June 4. The team played in Emeryville Park near Emory University and the Holton-Arms School.

4583 Larks 1946 *West Coast Assn. (ind.)*. An Old World songbird, the lark was introduced into the New World and now inhabits North America, including the western U.S.

4584 Casey Stengel's Nine Old Men 1948 *Pacific Coast (A)*. All nine of manager Casey Stengel's players in the Oakland starting lineup were age 30 and over. Their age didn't hamper them as the team won the 1948 PCL pennant.

4585 Athletics 1968 to date *American (M)*. Team nickname was retained when the Kansas City Athletics moved to Oakland for the 1968 season. At the time, team owner Charlie Finley made "Oakland A's" the official name of his team, but "Oakland Athletics" was used almost interchangeably by fans and newspapers. When Walter Haas bought the team from Finley in 1981, he designated "Oakland Athletics" as the team's official name, although A's continued to be used interchangeably with that moniker. Apparently, Finley didn't want "Athletics" because it was associated with the old Philadelphia Athletics of 1901–55. The abbreviation of "A's" also hinted at the old Pacific Coast League Oakland "Acorns."

4586 Green & Gold 1968–76 *American (M)*. Even though the psychedelic "Age of Aquarius" hippie revolution was in full swing by the time the Athletics arrived in Oakland in 1968, the A's owner

Charlie Finley were still the only team with colorful uniforms. Finley took the "Green and Gold" look one step further by putting the players in dye-fast California golden yellow sanitary socks— the first time sanitary socks that had been anything other than white since they were introduced in 1908. With the "Hippie Era" fading by the late 1970s and with other teams in all sports adopting colorful uniforms, the moniker lost its verve by the time the A's skidded into last place in 1977.

4587 Swinging A's 1972–74 *American (M)*. The moniker had a triple meaning: (1) the A's were excellent hitters, swinging their bats with vigor; (2) the A's players were "swingers," a 1960s slang for wild party goers; and (3) the players often fought amongst themselves in the clubhouse, even talking swinging punches at each other. Despite all this "swinging," the Athletics became the first major league baseball team since the 1951 New York Yankees to win three consecutive World Series titles.

4588 Fighting A's 1972–74 *American (M)*. Reminiscent of an old "collegiate" tag, i.e., the "Fighting Irish," the moniker was a spin-off of the "Swinging A's." However, in addition to fighting opponents, the moniker also referred to dugout and clubhouse disputes that took hold of A's players on occasion. Aka **Angry Athletics**.

4589 Moustache Brigade 1972–74 *American (M)*. Tag was coined by baseball authors David Neft, Richard Cohen and Michael Neft. The moniker cited the "hippie moustaches" that Oakland players sported during their championship years of 1972–74. Pitcher Rollie Fingers grew an elegant, barbershop-style "handlebar" moustache.

4590 Moustache A's 1972–74 *American (M)*. The era of long hair, beards and moustaches that arose in the period of 1967–71, when young men sought to rebel against the establishment, militarism and regimentation, finally arrived in professional sports by 1971–72. The Athletics were a bunch of individualistic, extroverted, and outspoken personalities in any case, so it was natural that they would sport moustaches and beards that had last been in vogue in the nineteenth century.

4591 Champagne and Baloney A's 1972–74 *American (M)*. Baseball author Tom Clark wrote a book entitled **The Champagne and Baloney A's** in 1975 describing the ups and downs of the three-time world champion Athletics. Led by hitters Reggie Jackson (Hall of Fame), Sal Bando, Joe Rudi, Dave Duncan, Bert Campaneris, Gene Tenace, Mike Epstein, Dave Johnson and Bill North and pitchers Jim "Catfish" Hunter, (Hall of Fame), Ken Holtzman, John "Blue Moon" Odom, Vida Blue, Rollie Fingers (Hall of Fame), Bob Locker and Darold Knowles, the A's, who sometimes seemed to be "full of baloney" to fans and the media, also popped the champagne bottles nine times as they won three division titles, three pennants, and three World Series championships.

4592 Sprinters 1974 *American (M)*. Coined by baseball authors Gary Gillette and Pete Palmer, the moniker referred to the Oaklanders finishing kick in beating out second-place Texas by five games in the AL West and then "sprinting" to their third consecutive world title by winning seven of nine post-season contests, 3 games to 1 over Baltimore in the AL Championship Series, and 4 games to 1 over the NL champion Los Angeles Dodgers in the World Series. The A's also led the AL in stolen bases with 164 swipes due in large part to base "sprinters" Billy North (56 SB), Bert Campaneris (34 SB), Herb Washington (29 SB) and Reggie Jackson (25 SB).

4593 Over-30 Gang 1975 *American (M)*. The byword for young people of the hippie generation was "Don't trust anyone over thirty!" With an aging veteran team, the Athletics powered their way to their fifth consecutive American League Western Division title with grizzled veterans Reggie Jackson, Joe Rudi, Gene Tenace, Billy Williams (traded here from the Cubs), Vida Blue and Rollie Fingers.

4594 Oakland F's 1977–79 *American (M)*. Charley Finley decided to hold a "fire sale" in the winter of 1976–77 that disemboweled the previously highly competitive A's of 1968–76. The 1977 team, stocked with youngsters and rejects, "flunked" itself right into sixth place in the seven-team AL Western Division with a "failing" 63–98 record. In 1978 the "Oakland F's" hit rock-bottom in last place with a horrible 54–108 record. The team resorted to hiring manager Billy Martin, who guided the 1980 team to a winning 83–79 record and a half-season division title in 1981 (with the players playing what came to be known as "Billy Ball"), but by 1982 the team scored more "F's" with 94 defeats and did not have another winning season until Tony LaRussa led the 1988 team to an AL Western Division title. In the American school system letter grades (unlike the number grades used in schools in other countries) are used, i.e., A, B, C, D and F.

4595 Oakland Triple A's 1977–79 *American (M)*. Tag was a clever spin-off describing the 1977–79, 1982 losers as a team only about as good as a Triple-A minor league baseball team. Name was occasionally written as the **Oakland AAA's**.

4596 Straight A 1988 *American (M)*. Tag was coined by baseball writer Tim Kurkjian in *Baseball America* to describe the consistent 1988 AL champion Oakland Athletics, who blended a decent offense with the best pitching staff in the American League. Starters Dave Stewart, Storm Davis, Mike Moore and Bob Welch won a combined 76 games and Dennis Eckersley saved 56 games with a 1.56 ERA. The A's then easily downed Toronto, 4 games to 1, to win the 1988 AL pennant.

4597 White Elephants 1988 to date *American (M)*. In 1988 Oakland management added the previously abandoned "White Elephant" mascot as a sleeve patch on the players' uniforms. Previously used by the franchise during its seasons in Philadelphia and Kansas City, the mascot logo was well received by fans and the moniker has been used ever since. The current logo displays a fashionable elephant wearing sun glasses in front of a bright California sun.

4598 Rugged A's 1988–90 *American (M)*. Baseball writers called the 1988–90 Oakland Athletics the "Rugged A's" because of strong hitters and hard-throwing pitchers who powered the Athletics to three consecutive American League pennants. The team was led by rugged hitters like Mike McGwire, Jose Canseco, Dave Henderson, Dave Parker, Harold Baines and Rickey Henderson and tough pitchers like Bob Welch, Scott Sanderson, Dave Stewart, Dennis Eckersley (Hall of Fame), Storm Davis and Mike Moore.

4599 Bay Area Bashers 1988–90 *American (M)*. Led by Mark McGwire (32, 33 and 39 HRs in 1988–90), Jose Canseco (42, 17 and 37 HRs in 1988–90), Dave Henderson (32, 15 and 20 HRs in 1988–90), Dave Parker (22 HRs in 1989) and Rickey Henderson (28 HRs in 1990), the Athletics bashed their way to three consecutive American League pennants and a four-game sweep of the San Francisco Giants in the 1989 "Earthquake" World Series. San Francisco, Oakland and San Jose are all part of the Bay Area metropolitan area that surrounds San Francisco Bay.

4600 Assletics 2000 to date *American (M)*. With bitter feelings lingering from the historic, earthquake afflicted "Across the Bay" World Series of 1989, a battle of words was waged between Giants and A's fans, utilizing rather tepid vulgarities such as "Gay Area Giants" and "Assletics." The liberation of obscene language, begun in the hippie 1960s, was re-energized in the 1990s by the arrival of "rap" and "hip hop" music.

4601 Unathletics 2007–09 to date *American (M)*. Although management professed to be "rebuilding" as a justification for three straight losing seasons (76–86 in 2007, 75–86 in 2008 and 75–87 in 2009), *Sports Illustrated* baseball writer Peter Gammons was unimpressed, branding these teams as the "Un-Athletics."

Oakland County, Michigan

4602 San Jose Athletics 2006 to date *American (M)*. Cash-strapped A's owner Lewis Wolff has been negotiating with Fremont (CA), Sacramento and San Jose to move his team to a proposed new stadium in each city. Disgruntled Oakland fans started calling the team the "SanJose" Athletics.

4603 Canaries 2010 *American (M)*. New player uniforms including a canary yellow jersey were introduced. Manager Billy Beane referred to his players as "canaries." A's relief pitcher Jerry Blevins commented, "We'll be noticed now."

Oaxaca, Oaxaca, Mexico

4604 Guerreros 1996 to date *Liga Mexicana (AAA)*. Team was named after the Zapotec warriors of sixteenth century Oaxaca. Management heavily markets the team name in English, i.e., the "Oaxaca Warriors."

Ocala, Florida

4605 Ocala Base Ball Club 1890–91 *Florida Winter (ind.)*; 1892 *Florida State (ind.)*. These teams had no nickname.

4606 Yearlings 1940–41 *Florida State (D)*. The team signed first-year professionals for both seasons. With managers Wilbur Good and then Gibbs Miller at the helm, newspapers called the players "Wilbur's Yearlings" and "Miller's Yearlings." Alan Mobley took over in 1941 and the name became "Mobley's Yearlings."

Oconto, Wisconsin

4607 Lumbermen 1891 *Wisconsin State (ind.)*. Timber hewn from the Nicolet National Forest was transported to city lumber mills.

4608 Log-Drivers 1891 *Wisconsin State (ind.)*. Tag was an alternate moniker for "Lumbermen."

4609 Loggers 1891 *Wisconsin State (ind.)*. Newspaper editors hated both "Lumbermen" and "Log-drivers," and insisted that their reporters use "Loggers" in their stories. Moniker was used in headlines, i.e., "Loggers edge Mud Hens, 4–3." League rival Marinette was known as the "Lumber-shorers," which created confusion, prompting the switch to "Loggers."

Odessa, Texas

4610 Oilers 1937x *West Texas–New Mexico (D)*. Team disbanded June 17; m1940 *West Texas–New Mexico (D)*. Team started season in Big Spring (TX) and moved to Odessa June 20; *Longhorn* 1947–54 *(D 1947–50, C 1951–54)*. Petroleum was discovered in 1927 in nearby Crane County. Oil was discovered in 1928 in nearby Ector County. Penn Field was opened in 1929 and Crowden Field opened in 1930.

4611 Eagles 1955 *Longhorn (D)*. Team was a farm club of the Dallas Eagles. In the era 1910–55, some higher classification (AAA, AA) minor league teams had their own farm clubs among the lower classification (A, B, C and D) leagues.

4612 Dodgers 1959–60 *Sophomore (D)*. Team was a farm club of the Los Angeles Dodgers.

O'Fallon, Missouri

4613 River City Rascals 1999 to date *Frontier (ind.)*. Team went by the city nickname of "River City Rascals." Team owner Ken Wilson chose the name and presented a logo mascot of the dog that appeared in the beloved *Little Rascals Our Gang* comedy shorts of the 1930s.

Ogden, Utah

4614 Ogden Baseball Club 1901 *Inter-Mountain (ind.)*. Team had no nickname.

4615 Canners 1912–14 *Union Assn. (D)*. City factories produce canned fruit, vegetables and dog food. With John McCloskey at the helm, newspapers called the players "McCloskey's Canners."

4616 Gunners 1926–28 *Utah–Idaho (C)*. The city is a military supply center, i.e., the Ogden Arsenal & Defense Depot, Hill Air Force Base and the Naval Supply Base. With manager Guy Cooper at the helm, newspapers called the players "Guy's Gunners."

4617 Reds 1939–42 *Pioneer (C)*; 1946–55 *Pioneer (C)*. These teams were farm clubs of the Cincinnati Reds.

4618 Dodgers 1966–73 *Pioneer (R)*. Team was a farm club of the Los Angeles Dodgers.

4619 Spikers 1974 *Pioneer (R)*. Ogden was established in 1851 and serves as an important railroad city for the Union Pacific, Southern Pacific, Denver & Rio Grande Western, Pacific Fruit Express and Amtrak. A ceremonial golden spike was hammered into the last rail-track at certain special sites when a railroad line was completed and became a symbol for railroads in general. "Spikers" are railway construction workers.

4620 Athletics 1979–80 *Pacific Coast (AAA)*. Team was a farm club of Oakland Athletics.

4621 Raptors 1994 to date *Pioneer (R)*. Archaeologists have discovered the fossilized remains of the carnivorous Velociraptors that inhabited Utah some 70 million years ago.

Ogdensburg, New York

4622 Colts 1936–39 *Canadian–American (C)*. Team took the regional name in mid-season 1940 of Ogdensburg-Ottawa, although no home games were played in Ottawa. The team had many young players on the team, who in the jargon of the era were known as "colts." With manager Knotty Lee at the helm 1936–40, newspapers called the players the "Knotty Lee's Colts."

Oil City, Pennsylvania

4623 Oil City Base Ball Club 1884 *Iron & Oil Assn. (ind.)*; 1898m *Iron & Oil (ind.)*. Team moved to Dunkirk (NY) in mid-season (date unknown). These teams had no nickname.

4624 Hitters 1885 *Iron & Oil (ind.)*. With manager Guy Hecker at the team, newspapers called the players "Hecker's Hitters." Even at this early date players were categorized as pitchers and hitters (non-pitchers).

4625 Oilers 1907 *Interstate (D)*; m1940–42 *Pennsylvania State (D)*. Team began 1940 season in McKeesport (PA) and moved to Oil City July 1; 1946 *Middle Atlantic (C)*. Titusville (PA) was the site of the first oil strike in the U.S. For the next 50 years Pennsylvania led the country in oil production. With manager James Collopy at the helm in 1907, newspapers called the players the "Collopy's Oilers." With manager Elmer Klump at the helm in 1940, local newspapers called the players "Elmer Klump's Oilers." George Norton took over in 1941 changing the name to "George Norton's Oilers." Frank Oceak took over in 1942 and the name changed to "Oceak's Oilers."

4626 Cubs 1908x *Interstate (D)*. Circuit and team both disbanded June 5. The team had many young players, known in the jargon of the era as "cubs."

4627 Refiners 1947–50 *Middle Atlantic (C)*. Moniker was a spin-off from "Oilers."

4628 Athletics m1951x *Middle Atlantic (C)*. Team started season in Youngstown (OH) and moved to Oil City June 2. Team disbanded August 6. Team was a farm club of the Philadelphia Athletics.

Oil City–Jamestown, Pennsylvania

4629 Oseejays 1906m *Interstate (D)*. To save space, newspapers referred to the team in bylines and headlines as the "OJC's." Since blue jays inhabit Pennsylvania, the name quickly evolved into "oseejays."

Oklahoma City, Oklahoma

4630 Mets 1904 *Southwestern (D)*; 1905–08 *Western Assn. (C)*; 1910 *Texas (C)*. With manager Emmett Rogers at the helm in 1904, newspapers called the players "Emmett's Mets." After Rogers left the team, the four-letter nickname was retained by newspapers.

4631 Giants 1906 *Independent Negro team*; 1910 *Independent Negro team*. Between 1890 and 1950 more than thirty professional black baseball teams used the "Giants" moniker. The 1910 team went by the state name of "Oklahoma Giants."

4632 Oklahoma Monarchs 1909 *Independent Negro team*. Team went by the state name of Oklahoma Monarchs. The team was a farm club of the Kansas City Monarchs. Oklahoma City native Wilbur "Bullet Joe" Rogan played here and then was signed by the KC Monarchs.

4633 Indians 1909, 1911 Texas *(C 1909–10, B 1911)*; m1918–32 *Western (A)*. Team started season in Hutchinson (KS) and then moved here June 2; 1933–57 *Texas (A 1933–35, A1 1936–42, AA 1946–57)*. The Plains Indian tribes—Kiowa, Comanche and Apache as well as the lodge-dwelling Pawnee and Wichita—inhabited Oklahoma in the seventeenth and eighteenth centuries. Between 1815 and 1840 the U.S. government moved the Five Civilized Tribes to Oklahoma—the Cherokee, Chickasaw, Choctaw, Creek and Seminole. With manager Lee Garvin at the helm in 1911, newspapers called the players "Garvin's Indians." With manager Jack Holland at the helm in 1918–19, newspapers called the players "Holland's Indians." The nickname was retained through 1932 under 13 other managers. Except for 1941 when this latest franchise's team *was* a farm club of the Cleveland Indians, the team was not a farm club of any major league club during its 25 years of competition.

4634 Senators 1912 *Oklahoma State (D)*; 1915–16 *Oklahoma State (D)*. Oklahoma City has been the state capital of Oklahoma since 1910. With manager Heinie Magg at the helm in 1915, newspapers called the players "Heinie Magg's Senators." Earl "Red" Snapp took over in 1916 and the name became "Earl Red Snapp's Senators." Oklahoma City is the "Capital of Soonerland."

4635 Runts 1912 *Oklahoma State (D)*. Team had a number of slender and short players whom the fans tagged as "runts." The team, managed by Bill Reukauff, tied for seventh place with an anger-inducing 15–33 mark, prompting fans to brand the team "Reukauff's Runts." One of the team's best players was "Runt" Marr. The tag "Runts" was a synonym for "Midgets," with both terms describing a losing team that was at or near the league cellar. With manager Bill Reukauff at the helm, newspapers called the players "Reukauff's Runts." Outlaw Al "Runt" Jennings and his gang robbed banks and trains in Oklahoma in 1897. When captured, newspaper photographs prompted reporters to describe the rather puny-looking gang members as "runts." After he got out of jail, he acted in a 1913 movie about his exploits and actually ran for Oklahoma governor in 1914.

4636 Boosters 1914, 1917 *Western Assn. (D)*. Winning teams often had fan "booster" clubs and took this tag as their nickname. The 1914 team won the league's first-half title. The 1917 team disappointed their boosters with a losing 72–80 record. The Henryetta team, also playing in the Western Association this season, had the same nickname of "Boosters." By the 1920s, booster clubs became known as "fan clubs."

4637 Oklahoma City Baseball Club 1929–31 *Texas–Oklahoma (ind.)*. The Texas–Oklahoma League was a regional black professional baseball circuit in this era. Team had no nickname.

4638 89ers 1962 *American Assn. (AAA)*; 1963–68 *Pacific Coast (AAA)*; 1969–97 *American Assn. (AAA)*. At noon on April 22, 1889, the territory of Oklahoma was opened to white settlement. More than 10,000 people in wagons, stagecoach, on horseback and by train staked claims to land in and around the region.

4639 Horse Soldiers 1994 *American Assn. (AAA)*. The "Horse Soldiers" of the U.S. Cavalry protected settlers from renegade Indians, cattle-rustlers and bandits in the nineteenth century. Team was aka the **Cavalry**. Neither tag caught on and was dropped after this one year. Oklahoma is the "Horse Pistol Town."

4640 Red Hawks 1998 to date *Pacific Coast (AAA)*. The hawk inhabits the Southwest. Red hearkens to the word "Oklahoma," which is the Choctaw word for "Red People." Team went by the state name of Oklahoma Red Hawks 1998–2008, but then switched to the city name of Oklahoma City Red Hawks 2009 to date. However, there is also an actual "red hawk"—the red-tailed chicken hawk that inhabits all of North America.

Okmulgee, Oklahoma

4641 Glassblowers 1912 *Oklahoma State (D)*. In this era, Okmulgee had numerous glass-making factories. With manager Frank Garner at the helm, newspapers called the players "Garner's Glassblowers." The city's nickname is the "Glass Glow City."

4642 Drillers 1920–27 *Western Assn. (D 1920–21, C 1922–26, B 1927, C 1927)*. The Tulsa-Okmulgee Oil Fields were discovered in 1900. By 1901 commercial oil production began. Oil is transported to city refiners for conversion into petroleum products. Okmulgee is the "City Where Oil Flows."

Old Orchard Beach, Maine

4643 Maine Guides 1984–87 *International (AAA)*. Maine is known as the "Dirigo State," which is Latin for "guide." The state nickname in English is the "Old Guide State." Maine has many lighthouses on its Atlantic coast, which serve to guide recreational, commercial and military boats.

4644 Maine Phillies 1988 *International (AAA)*. Team was a farm club of the Philadelphia Phillies.

Olean, New York

4645 Olean Base Ball Club 1890–91 *New York–Pennsylvania (ind.)*; 1898 *Iron & Oil (ind.)*. These teams had no nickname.

4646 Refiners 1905–07 *Interstate (D)*; 1914 *Interstate (D)*. With manager Paul Wrath at the helm in 1905, newspapers called the players "Wrath's Refiners." John Ziegler took over in 1906 and the name became "Ziegler's Refiners." With manager Joe Reynolds at the helm in 1914, newspapers called the players "Reynolds' Refiners." The moniker was retained after Reynolds left the team following the 1914 season.

4647 Candidates 1908x *Interstate (D)*. Circuit and team disbanded June 5. In addition to Cubs, Babes, Kids, Rustlers, Braves, etc., baseball players were sometimes known as a field manager's "Candidates." With manager Percy Stetler at the helm, newspapers called the players "Stetler's Candidates." Politics in this era was a rough and rowdy endeavor—much like professional baseball. In 1908 the city voted for candidates to oppose the state's Tammany Hall Machine.

4648 White Sox 1915–16 *Interstate (D)*. Players wore white hose. The team had a loose affiliation with the Chicago White Sox.

4649 Oilers 1939–51, 1955–56 *Pennsylvania–Ohio–New York (P.O.N.Y.) (D)*; 1957–58 Tag was a spin-off from Refiners. With manager Jake Pitler at the helm 1939–43, newspapers called the players the "Pitler's Oilers." The name was retained through 1951. In 1951 Orval Cott managed "Orval's Oilers." With manager Paul Owens at the helm in 1957, newspapers called the players "Owen's Oilers."

4650 Yankees 1952–53 *Pennsylvania–Ohio–New York (P.O.N.Y.) (D)*. Team was a farm club of the New York Yankees.

4651 Giants 1954 *Pennsylvania–Ohio–New York (P.O.N.Y.) (D)*. Team was a farm club of the New York Giants.

4652 Athletics 1959 *New York–Pennsylvania (D)*. Team was a farm club of the Kansas City Athletics.

4653 Red Sox 1961–62 New York–Pennsylvania *(D)*. Team was a farm club of the Boston Red Sox.

Olympia, Washington

4654 Senators 1903–05 *Southwest Washington (D)*. City became the territorial capital in 1853. When Washington territory became a state in 1881, the city became the state capital. With manager Jessie Mill at the helm, newspaper s called the players "Jessie's Senators."

Omaha, Nebraska

4655 Green Stockings 1879 *Northwestern (ind.)*. Players wore green hose. All four league members used stocking colors to identify themselves, i.e., Rockford (white), Dubuque (red), Davenport (brown) and Omaha (green). Originally "Green Stockings," newspapers shortened it to **Green Legs.**

4656 Mashers 1879 *Northwestern (ind.)*. Mash is a mixture of different ground feeds for livestock. A "masher" is a cattle farmer who feeds the mash to livestock. The team owner was William Paxton, a rancher and cattleman. "Masher" means a man who makes unwanted advances on a woman. In the nineteenth century numerous baseball players were notorious flirts, womanizers and mashers. "Masher" was slang for a strong hitter, i.e., "he mashed the ball off the fence." Newspapers called the players "William's Mashers." Nebraska is the "Tall Corn State."

4657 Omahogs 1885 *Western (ind.)*; 1887 *Western (ind.)*; 1888–89, 1892 ; 1894–95m *Western Assn. (ind.)*. Team moved to Denver July 5; m1898 *Western (ind.)*. Team started season in St. Joseph (MO) and moved to Omaha July 7; 1900–03 Omaha was a "Hog Town," i.e., a nineteenth-century tag for a meat-packing center. Reporters blended the city name of Omaha and hog together to form the amalgam of "Omahog." Omaha had become a major meat-packing center by 1883. Omaha is the "World's Largest Livestock and Meatpacking Center."

4658 Union Pacifcs 1887 *Western (ind.)*. The Union Pacific Railroad was built in and around Omaha (the city was founded in 1857) in the 1860s.

4659 Omahosses 1888–92 *Western Assn. (ind.)*. "Hoss" was a Western slang for "horse." Baseball players, brawny and perceived to be dimwitted, were sometimes called "Horses" and "Hosses," especially as the charges of the field manager, i.e., "Leadley's Hosses." The suffix of Omaha blended with the suffix or horse to form "Omahoss." In the nineteenth century, Omaha was a "horse town" where much transport was by done by drawn wagons and carriages; farm produce, meat, flour and grain were transported from arriving trains to city factories by horse-driven wagons.

4660 Black Snakes 1889–90 *Western Assn. (ind.)*. Players wore black jerseys and black stirrups. Name was appropriate because the North American black snake is found in the Southwest and Midwest. With manager Frank Selee at the helm 1889–90, newspapers called the players "Frank Selee's Black Snakes." Black jerseys had become a fad with some baseball teams in this era.

4661 Ghosts 1891 *Western Assn. (ind.)*. With manager Dan Shannon at the helm, newspapers called the all-white clad, white-hosed players "Shannon's Ghosts."

4662 Lambs 1891 *Western Assn. (ind.)*. With manager Bob Leadley at the helm, newspapers called the players "Leadley's Lambs" because they were quite young, and because their all-white caps, uniforms and stockings were "fleece as white as snow" (from the folkloric "Mary Had a Little Lamb" song).

4663 Gate Citys 1891 *Western Assn. (ind.)*. Omaha is the "Gate City to the West."

4664 Indians 1895m *Western Assn. (ind.)*. Team moved to Denver July 5; 1900–03 *Western (ind. 1900–01, A 1902–03)*. The Omaha, Pawnee, Oto, Missouri and Sioux Indians inhabited this region but were eventually forced to reservations by 1854. With manager Joe Cantillon at the helm, newspapers called the players the "Cantillon's Indians."

4665 Babes m1898 *Western (ind.)*. Team started season in St. Joseph (MO) and moved here July 7. The team had many young players, known in the jargon of the era as "babes." With manager "Pa" Rourke at the helm, newspapers called the players, appropriately, "Pa's Babes."

4666 Kidnappers 1900–03 Western *(ind. 1900–01, A 1901–02)*. In Omaha in 1900, 16-year-old Edward Cudahy Jr. was kidnapped by career criminal Pat Crowe, who demanded and received a ransom of $10,000 from meat packing magnate Edward Cudahy Sr. Crowe was caught several years later but was acquitted because Nebraska had no law against kidnapping. Crowe actually became a folk hero for his robberies and the kidnapping. In this era baseball players were regarded as rowdy, scrubby-bearded louts who were likened to bandits, brigands, pirates, cattle rustlers and kidnappers.

4667 Rangers 1904 *Western (A)*. With manager Pa Rourke at the helm, newspapers called the players "Rourke's Rangers." Cowboys and Indian team nicknames were popular in this era. The 1904 team "rode like rangers" to the WL pennant with a 90–60 record. Explorers LaSalle, Lewis and Clark, fur traders, and U.S. army horse soldiers (from Fort Atkinson, est. 1819) ranged across Nebraska. By the 1840s the Oregon and Mormon Trails went through Nebraska for westward-traveling pioneers. Forest rangers patrol the Nebraska and Blaine National Forests in the state.

4668 Rourkes 1905–20 *Western (A)*. Field manager Pa Rourke was the team's skipper 1904–14. Instead of "Rangers," newspapers used Pa's actual last name until 1920. Marty Krug took over 1915–17 and the name became "Krug's Rourkes." Pa Rourke returned in mid-season 1917. Bill Jackson took over 1918–19 and the name became "Jackson's Rourkes." Jack Lelivelt took over in 1920 and the name became "Jack's Rourkes."

4669 Rods 1921–22, 1926–27 *Western (A)*. A "birch rod" is a bundle of birch tree twigs tied together and used for whipping, i.e., cattle or a horse. Moniker was a play on words of the name of the team's owner Barney Burch. Newspapers used it for headlines, i.e., "Rods edge Boosters 4–3."

4670 Burchers 1921–22, 1926–27 *Western (A)*. A vulgarization of "butcher," name was a cowboy slang for meat cutters and meat cooks. The team was led by owner-manager Barney Burch 1921–22 and 1926–27. Omaha is the "Steak Capital of the World."

4671 Buffaloes 1921–27 *Western (A)*. In eighteenth century Nebraska, Pawnee Indians hunted great herds of buffaloes. With manager Jack Lelivet at the helm in 1921, team was "Jack Lelivet's Buffaloes." Team owner-manager Barney Burch, who played for the Houston Buffaloes in 1910, took over in mid-season 1921 and for 1922 (and again 1926–27) as the name became "Barney Burch's Buffaloes."

Petey Brausen took over as manager in mid-season 1927 and the name became "Brausen's Buffaloes." In 1922 team did its spring training in Texas and played the Houston Buffaloes in several games.

4672 Crickets 1928–29 *Western (A)*. In the 1890s a series of grasshopper infestations decimated the crops of most Nebraska farms.

4673 Packers 1930–35m *Western (A)*. Team moved to Council Bluffs (IA) June 25. Slaughterhouses transport meat to packing houses in the city. With manager Pug Griffin at the helm 1931–33, newspapers called the players "Pug's Packers." Malcom Pickett took over in mid-season 1934 and the name became "Pickett's Packers." Pickett left after the 1934 season, but the name was retained in 1935. Omaha is the "World's Largest Meat Packing Center."

4674 Black Packers 1935 *Independent Negro team*. Moniker was a spin-off from Packers. The Black Packers, strapped for cash during the Great Depression, received donated items from the Western League Omaha Packers.

4675 Robin Hoods 1936m *Western (A)*. Team moved to Rock Island (IL) August 18. Arbor Day tradition was established in Nebraska in 1872 after one million trees had been planted in the state.

4676 Cardinals 1947–54 *Western (A)*; 1955–59 *American Assn. (AAA)*. These teams were farm clubs of the St. Louis Cardinals.

4677 Dodgers 1961–62 *American Assn. (AAA)*. Team was a farm club of Los Angeles Dodgers.

4678 Royals 1969–97 *American Assn. (AAA)*; 1998, 2003–10 *Pacific Coast (AAA)*. These teams were farm clubs of the Kansas City Royals.

4679 Golden Spikes 1999–2002 *Pacific Coast (AAA)*. When the Union Pacific Railway was completed at Summit, Utah rail workers and public officials hammered in a golden spike as a symbol during a ceremony in May 1865. The Union Pacific Railroad traveled through Omaha. The fans didn't like the name and it was replaced by the old moniker of Royals in 2003.

4680 Stormchasers 2011 to date *Pacific Coast (AAA)*. For several years, meteorologists have "chased storms" in the "Tornado Alley" states of Iowa, Texas and Nebraska to study them with electronic instruments. TV documentaries and a Hollywood movie have demonstrated how these "Storm-chasers" travel about in cars and vans, getting within a few hundred yards of dangerous and deadly tornadoes before speeding away from them in a near panic. Although an interesting moniker, some Omaha fans have openly preferred a return of "Royals."

Oneida, New York

Note: Not to be confused with Oneonta, New York.

4681 Oneida Base Ball Club 1886 *Central New York (ind.)*; 1889x *New York State (ind.)*. Team was expelled from the league July 12 and then disbanded. These teams had no nickname.

4682 Barge Bucs 2007 *New York State (ind.)*. Team played its 2007 home games in Utica (NY). Circuit disbanded after the 2007 season. The lake serves as a link for the New York State Barge Canal System for shipping to and from Lake Ontario, the Oswego Canal and Lake Oneida. Barges are large transport flat-tops used mostly in harbors, canals and rivers. Pirate ships often sailed Lake Ontario, starting around 1600 until about 1830.

Oneonta, New York

Note: Not to be confused with Oneida, New York.

4683 Indians 1890 *New York State (ind.)*; m1924 *New York–Pennsylvania (B)*. Team began season in Utica (NY) and moved to Oneonta August 7; 1940–42 *Canadian–American (C)*. In the eigh-

teenth century settlers encountered the Iroquois, Mohawk, Mohican, Oneida and Tuscarora tribes. The team of 1940–42 was not a farm club of Cleveland Indians.

4684 Red Sox 1946–51 *Canadian–American (C)*; 1966 *New York–Pennsylvania (A)*. Teams were farm clubs of the Boston Red Sox.

4685 Yankees 1967–88 *New York–Pennsylvania (A)*. Team was a farm club of the New York Yankees.

4686 Tigers 1989–2009 *New York–Pennsylvania (A)*. *Team* was a farm club of the Detroit Tigers. Franchise moved to Norwich (CT) with the name Connecticut Tigers in 2010.

Ontario, California

4687 Orioles 1947 *Sunset (C)*. The Baltimore Oriole is found more in the eastern U.S. while the Western Oriole — usually called the "Golden Robin" — is found in the Midwest and California.

Opelika, Alabama

4688 Opelicans 1913 *Georgia–Alabama (D)*. Name was appropriate because the pelican is found all along the Gulf of Mexico coast. Moniker was a play on words: a blending of Opelika and Pelicans. Fans didn't like it.

4689 Pelicans 1914 *Georgia–Alabama (D)*. Local newspapers decided to chose the literal name of the bird to avoid fan confusion, which prompted the question, "Just what is an Opelican?!?"

4690 Owls 1946–51x *Georgia–Alabama (D)*. Team disbanded July 1. This short, four-letter moniker of a bird found in Georgia and Alabama eliminated the conflict with the neighboring New Orleans Pelicans.

Opelousas, Louisiana

4691 Indians 1907 *Gulf Coast (D)*; 1934–41 *Evangeline (D)*. The Atakapa, Caddo, Chitimacha and Tunica Indian tribes inhabited the region into the eighteenth century. The 1934–41 franchise was a farm team of the Cleveland Indians.

4692 Orphans m1932x *Cotton States (D)*. Team began season in Port Arthur (TX), then moved to De Quincy (LA) and later transferred to Opelousas July 7. Team and league disbanded July 13. Teams in the era 1895–1955 that transferred to another city in mid-season because of poor attendance in the original host city's ballpark were sometimes known as the "Orphans." Team had no official nickname.

Orange, Texas

4693 Hoo-hoos 1907–08x *Gulf Coast (D)*. Team, in 1907, got off to a losing start en route to a poor 50–65 mark, prompting disgruntled fans to "hoot" the team with the owl-like yelp of "hoo! hoo!" Moniker stuck in 1908, even though the team did better with a 15–14 record when the franchise and league disbanded June 2, 1908. With manager Tim Cook at the helm, newspapers called the players "Cook's Hoo-hoos."

Orangeburg, South Carolina

4694 Cotton-pickers 1907–08 *South Carolina (D)*. Regional plantations transported cotton to city textile mills.

4695 Cardinals 1973 *Western Carolinas (A)*. Team was a farm club of the St. Louis Cardinals.

4696 Dodgers 1974 *Western Carolinas (A)*. Team was a farm club of the Los Angeles Dodgers.

Orem, Utah

4697 Owlz 2005 to date *Pioneer (R)*. Starting in the 1990s, some teams whose nicknames ended in "S" started spelling them with a "Z," i.e., Utah Starzz (basketball), Ottawa Rapidz (baseball), Zion Pioneerzz (baseball) and Orem Owlz. The Great Horned Owl inhabits the mountains, forests and national parks of Utah.

Orizaba, Mexico

4698 Cerviceros 1966 *Liga del Sureste Mexicana (A)*. The Orizaba Brewery brews a dozen brand names of Mexican beer.

4699 Charos 1967 *Liga del Sureste Mexicana (A)*. Team was a farm club of the Mexican League Jalisco Charos. With manager Minnie Minoso at the helm in 1967, newspapers called the players the "Los Charros de Minoso." "Charo" in English means "horseman."

Orlando, Florida

4700 Caps 1919–20 *Florida State (D)*. Lakes Monroe Jessup, Harney, Apopka, Hart, Tohopekaliga, East Tohopekaliga and Mary Jane — the eight lakes of Orlando — form white caps during stormy weather.

4701 Tigers 1921 *Florida State (D)*. With manager Joe Tinker at the helm, management dressed the players in striped hose, leading local newspapers to call the players "Tinker's Tigers." As the team "roared" to the 1921 FSL pennant with an excellent 73–42 record, newspapers reported the team "played like Tigers." The team was not a farm club of the Detroit Tigers as there was no farm system yet.

4702 Bulldogs 1922–23 *Florida State (D)*. With manager Ernie Burke at the helm, newspapers called the players "Burke's Bulldogs." In 1922, local newspapers wanted to get away from "Tigers," which they felt properly belonged to Detroit and Princeton. They wanted a name praising the ferocity and tenacity of the 1921 pennant winners, so they went with "Bulldogs."

4703 Colts 1926–28x *Florida State (D)*. Team and league disbanded July 4. The team had many young players, who were known in the jargon of the era as "colts."

4704 Gulls 1937 *Florida State (D)*. Seagulls inhabit the coastal waters of Texas, Louisiana, Georgia and Florida.

4705 Senators 1938–41 *Florida State (D)*; 1946–53 *Florida State (D)*. Team had a loose affiliation with the AL Senators in 1938 before becoming a formal farm club of Washington 1939–41 and 1946–53.

4706 Nationals 1942 *Florida East Coast (D)*; *Florida State (D)*. Team was a farm club of the AL Washington Nationals. Although the official nickname of the Washington AL franchise was "Nationals," fans and newspapers almost universally called the D.C. team the "Senators."

4707 C.B.'s 1954–55 *Florida State (D)*. Orlando is nicknamed "The City Beautiful." Moniker was also appropriate because the "Sea Bees" Naval Commandos trained here at the Orlando Naval Training Center during World War II.

4708 Seratomas 1956 *Florida State (D)*. Orlando is headquarters for the Seratoma Club, an international service club similar to the Lion's Club. "Serai" means a travel resort (from the ancient Persian word "serai," which means "palace"). The logo of the Seratoma Club is a mermaid.

4709 Flyers 1957 *Florida State (D)*. The Orlando Naval Training Center was established here in 1940. Moniker was appropriate because the "Sea Bees" — the Navy's aquatic commando unit that distinguished itself in World War II — train here. U.S. Navy pilots train at the base here.

4710 Twins 1963–72 *Florida State (A)*; 1973–89 *Southern (AA)*. Teams were farm clubs of the Minnesota Twins.

4711 Sun Rays 1990–92 *Southern (AA)*. Florida is nicknamed the "Sunshine State." Fans did not like the team nickname.

4712 Cubs 1993–96 *Southern (AA)*. Team was a farm club of the Chicago Cubs.

4713 Braves 1997 to date *Gulf Coast (R)*. Team was a farm club of the Atlanta Braves.

4714 Rays 1997–2003 *Southern (AA)*. Team was a farm club of the Tampa Bay Devil Rays. To save newspaper space this farm club went by the shorter "Rays." Presaging the 2008 Tampa Bay name change, the team in 1997 wore jerseys with the "Sun Rays" name but fans didn't like it.

Oroville, California

4715 Red Sox 1948 *Far West (D)*. Team was a farm club of Boston Red Sox.

Osaka, Shizuoka, Japan

4716 Tigers 1935–39 *Japanese Professional (ind.)*; 1946–49 *Japanese Professional (ind.)*; 1950–60 *Japanese Pacific (ind.)*; 1952–53 *Japanese Western (ind.)*; 1957–90 *Japanese Western (ind.)*. The first professional Osaka baseball team was named after the 1934–35 pennant-winning Detroit Tigers. The team owner, the Hanshin Electric Railway Company, chose a logo almost identical to the Detroit Tigers team logo. In this somewhat friendly era, before war winds arrived, the Hanshin Tigers and Detroit Tigers were declared to be "sister teams," just as Detroit and Osaka were "sister cities." Team colors were yellow, black and white — including yellow and black striped stirrups. Resuming play, after being inactive in 1945, management again chose Tigers in emulation of the 1945 world champion Detroit Tigers. The franchise switched to the Pacific League in 1950. The Japanese Western League franchise was a farm team of the Pacific League Tigers. The players wore striped yellow and black stirrups.

4717 Nankai 1938–43 *Japanese Professional (ind.)*. Team was owned by Nankai Railroad Company and went by the corporate name of the Nankai Baseball Club.

4718 Hanshin 1940–44 *Japanese Professional (ind.)*. With hostilities near, the Japanese government, now controlled by the Japanese army, forced the team to abandon its Western-style nickname and logo and simply call the team "Hanshin."

4719 Nihon 1944 *Japanese Professional (ind.)*. Japan in the Japanese language is known as Nippon and Nihon. Sports teams during the war resorted to company names and patriotic tags.

4720 Great Ring 1946 *Japanese Professional (ind.)*. Team, owned by the Kinki Nippon Railway Company, played at a ball park in the downtown area of the city, which is known as the "Great Ring" of railroads.

4721 Nankai Hawks 1947–49 *Japanese Professional (ind.)*; 1950–88 *Japanese Pacific (ind.)*; 1962–87 *Japanese Eastern (ind.)*. Team was owned by the Nankai Railroad Company, which chose the English name "Hawks" for marketing purposes. The franchise switched leagues for the 1950 season. The Eastern League Hawks were a farm club of the Pacific League Hawks.

4722 Kintetsu Pearls 1950–58 *Japanese Pacific (ind.)*. Team went by the company name of "Kintetsu Pearls" after the Kintetsu Railway Company. Osaka was built along Osaka Bay and the Inland Sea on which fishing boats catch oysters — many of which have pearls. The team owner was Kintetsu Railways. The team moved to a stadium in suburban Fujiidera in 1952.

4723 Braves 1950–88 *Japanese Pacific (ind.)*; 1955–88 *Japanese*

Western (ind.). The teams were owned by Hankyu Railway Company, which chose "Braves" in honor of the sixteenth century feudal Lord Toyotomi Hideyoshi, who built Osaka Castle here that became the governing palace of the Kyoto-Osaka region. Actually, the team's logos were first an American Indian "brave" and then one of an ancient Greek warrior. Both teams moved to the city Kobe for the 1989 season.

4724 Taiyo-Shochiku Robins 1953–54 *Japanese Central.* Joint owners Taiyo and Shochiku transferred the Tokyo Taiyo Shochiku Robins to Osaka for the 1953 season. The team title of "Taiyo-Shochiku Robins" was retained.

4725 Jaguars 1954–56 *Japanese Western (ind.).* Moniker was a spin-off from Osaka "Tigers." The name was chosen to avoid confusion with the parent club, but, curiously, the fans didn't care for it.

4726 Kintetsu Buffalo 1959–61 *Japanese Pacific (ind.).* The Asian "Water Buffalo" is found throughout Asia and is used as a domesticated beast of burden. The team played its home games in a stadium in suburban Fujiidera.

4727 Hanshin Tigers 1961–90 *Japanese Pacific (ind.).* Team was owned by the Hanshin Electric Railway Company and went by the company name of Hanshin Tigers (1961–90). The team was known by the city name of Osaka Tigers 1950–60.

4728 Kintetsu Buffaloes 1962–2004 *Japanese Pacific (ind.);* 1962–2004 *Japanese Western (ind.).* Team owner Kintetsu Railways decided to pluralize the name. The city name of Osaka, not used in the team's title 1962–98, was added to the team's title in 1999. The Western League Buffaloes were a farm team of the Pacific League Buffaloes. The Pacific League team regionalized to the dual cities of Osaka and Kobe in 2005. The team played its home games in a stadium in suburban Fujiidera, 1962–96.

Osaka, Honshu-Kobe, Hyogo, Japan

4729 Buffaloes 2005 to date *Japanese Pacific (ind.).* Before the start of the 2005 season, the Orix Company, owner of the Kobe Orix Blue Wave, purchased the Osaka Kintetsu Buffaloes and merged them with the Blue Wave. They scheduled the new team to split its home games between Osaka and Kobe under the name of "Osaka-Kobe Orix Buffaloes."

Osceola, Arkansas

4730 Indians 1936–37 *Northeast Arkansas (D).* Team was named in honor of Chief Osceola, who led the Seminoles against American troops in the Second Seminole War of 1835–42. The chief was stricken with a fatal attack of malaria in 1838. With manager Royce Williams at the helm, newspapers called the players "William's Indians." Emil Kirchoff took over in 1937, and the name became "Emil Kirchoff's Indians." The team was not a farm club of the Cleveland Indians.

Osceola, Florida see Kissimmee, FL, of the FSL (1985 to date)

Osceola, Iowa

4731 Osceola Baseball Club 1903 *Southwest Iowa (D).* Team joined the league June 29. Team had no nickname.

Oshkosh, Wisconsin

4732 Indians 1886–87 *Northwestern (ind.);* 1891 *Wisconsin (ind.);* 1892 *Michigan–Wisconsin (ind.);* 1905–07 *Wisconsin State (D);* 1908– 14 *Wisconsin–Illinois (D 1908–09, C 1910–14).* City, established in 1840, was named after Chief Oshkosh of the Menominee Indians. With manager William Harrington at the helm in 1886, newspapers called the players "Harrington's Indians." Frank Selee took over in 1887 and the name became "Frank Selee's Indians." John Lavie (1905), Chip Hanford (1906) and Kid Nichols (1908), Frank Cassiboine (1911) and Joseph Killian (1912–14) perpetuated the use of the Indians name.

4733 Giants 1941–42 *Wisconsin State (D);* 1946–53 *Wisconsin State (D).* The 1941 team had a loose affiliation with the New York Giants before becoming a formal farm team of the New Yorkers in 1942.

Oskaloosa, Iowa

4734 Quakers 1904–07 *Iowa State (D);* 1908 *Central Assn. (D).* Quaker settlers reached Iowa in the nineteenth century in the period 1850–60. Daniel Boone, who was a Quaker, traveled extensively throughout Iowa. With A.L. Kennedy at the helm in 1908, newspapers called the players "Kennedy's Quakers." Taylor Kensel took over in mid-season 1908 and the name became "Kensel's Quakers."

Ossining, New York

4735 Ossining Baseball Club 1903m *Hudson River (D).* Team moved to Catskill (NY) August 2. Team had no nickname.

Oswego, New York

4736 Sweegs 1885 *New York State (ind.).* Moniker was used for newspaper headlines, i.e., "Sweegs edge Bingos, 4–3."

4737 Starchboxes 1886–87x *International (ind.).* Team disbanded May 31. The Oswego Starch Company owned the team.

4738 Starch-makers 1898–99 *New York State (ind.).* City was home to the Oswego Starch Company.

4739 Oswegos 1899 *New York State (ind.).* Oswego is situated along the Oswego River. With manager George Sayers at the helm in 1899, newspapers called the players "George's Oswegos."

4740 Grays 1900m *New York State (ind.).* Team moved to Elmira (NY) July 30.

4741 Netherlands 1936–40 *Canadian–American (C).* Team was owned by the Netherlands Milk and Ice Cream Company. The city was established by Dutch traders in 1660.

Ottawa, Ontario, Canada

4742 Wanderers m1898 *Eastern (ind.).* Franchise started season in Rochester (NY) and transferred to Ottawa July 7. Teams that shifted cities in mid-season were sometimes in this era called "Wanderers."

4743 Senators 1912–15 *Canadian (C 1912–13, B 1914–15);* 1922 *Eastern Canada (B);* 1936, 1939 *Canadian–American (C);* 1948–49 *Border (C).* Ottawa has been the national capital of Canada since 1857 by order of Queen Victoria. With manager Frank Shaughnessy at the helm 1913–15, newspapers called the players "Frank Shaughnessy's Senators." With manager Dick Dawson at the helm in 1922, newspapers called the players "Dawson's Senators." The 1948–49 team was not a farm club of the Washington Senators.

4744 Canadians 1923 *Eastern Canada (B).* Although officially representing Ottawa, team played its home games in Montreal as the "Montreal Canadians" until a ballpark was completed in Ottawa in the month of July. When the team moved into the Ottawa park, the nickname "Canadians" was retained. The team nickname in French was "Les Canadiens."

4745 Braves 1937–38 *Canadian–American (C)*. The 1936 and again in 1938, the team maintained a loose affiliation with the Boston Bees, who had been known as the "Braves" for the years 1912–35. In 1937 the team was a formal farm club of the Boston Nationals. The Ottawa Indians, led by Chief Pontiac, sided with the French in the French and Indian War but continued to raid the British after the 1763 peace treaty, which led to Pontiac's Rebellion of 1763–65.

4746 Nationals 1947, 1950 *Border (C)*. Ottawa is the national capital of Canada. Almost all baseball teams playing in Washington, DC, and Ottawa (ONT) have used the monikers of Capitals, Nationals, and Senators, oftentimes interchangeably. The team was *not* a farm team of the Washington Senators.

4747 Giants 1951 *International (AAA)*. Team was a farm club of the New York Giants.

4748 Athletics 1952–54 *International (AAA)*. Team was a farm club of the Philadelphia Athletics.

4749 Lynx 1993–2007 *International (AAA)*. The Lynx is a wildcat found in North America and is sometimes called the "Canadian Wildcat." Team was a farm club of the National League Montreal Expos, whose nickname contained an "x."

4750 Rapidz 2008 *Canadian–American (ind.)*. Team disbanded after the 2008 season. The Ottawa River rushes so fast that it made possible the construction of Canada's first hydroelectric plant in 1882. At the start of the season the team was purchased by the Zip.ca, a telecommunications company that introduced the "Z" gimmick name of Rapidz. Moniker in French was "Les Rapides," which phonetically ends with a "Z" sound. Since the 1990s, influenced by rap music lyrics that substitute a Z for an S in certain names, several teams have used the "Z" fad, i.e., Utah Starzz, Zion Pioneezz, Zion-St. George Pioneerzz and the Ottawa Rapidz.

Ottawa, Ontario-Hull, Quebec, Canada

4751 Senators 1924 *Quebec–Ontario–Vermont (B)*. Team, in a spin-off from the 1922 "Ottawa Senators," went by the twin-city name of Ottawa-Hull Senators.

Ottawa, Illinois

4752 Crows 1890 *Illinois–Iowa (ind.)*. Crows inhabit the Midwest feeding on the corn and wheat crops of the region. Players wore black hose. Teams in the era 1890–1910 sometimes chose a bird nickname to correspond to the players stocking color, i.e., Blackbirds, Bluebirds, Blue Jays, Canaries, Cardinals, Crows, Doves, Ravens and Redbirds.

4753 Modocs 1891 *Illinois–Iowa (ind.)*. At 1890s carnivals a "Modoc" was a dummy used as a target in baseball-throwing games. Baseball players in this era had a reputation of being dullards—hence, "modoc" meant a baseball player.

4754 Indians 1914 *Illinois–Missouri (D)*; 1915 *Bi-State (D)*. The Bi-State League represented Illinois and Wisconsin. The Ottawa Indians inhabited Illinois, Michigan and southern Ontario. With manager Chuck Fleming at the helm, newspapers called the players "Fleming's Indians."

Ottawa, Kansas

4755 Ottawa Base Ball Club 1898 *Kansas State (ind.)*. Team had no nickname.

4756 Gassers m1924m *Southwestern (D)*. Team began season in Newton (KS), moved to Blackwell (OK), and then moved to Ottawa August 5. Team played in Ottawa August 6–27 and then moved back

Newton August 28. Natural gas from nearby Ottawa Wells is transported to city refineries.

Ottawa, Ontario– Ogdensburg, New York

4757 Senators 1940 *Canadian–American (C)*. The team played half its home games in Ogdensburg and the other half in Ottawa, the capital of Canada, hence the Senators moniker was picked up. The team was a farm club of the Philadelphia Phillies and not the Washington Senators.

4758 Maples 1946–51x *Border (C)*. Team and league disbanded July 16. The city was founded as a fort and fur-trading post in a region with many maple trees.

Ottumwa, Iowa

4759 Coal Palace Kings 1890–91 *Illinois–Iowa (ind.)*. First settled in 1843, the city became a processing center for coal deposits discovered in the region. The city became known as the "Coal Palace of the Midwest." A king resides in his palace.

4760 Coal Barons 1890–91 *Illinois–Iowa (ind.)*; 1895 *Eastern Iowa (ind.)*. Newspapers shortened the tag even further to **Barons**. Moniker was used in newspaper headlines, i.e., "Barons edge Modocs, 4–3."

4761 Coal-heavers 1890–91 *Illinois–Iowa (ind.)*. Reporters used this tag along with "Coal Palace Kings" and "Coal Barons" to provide variety in their game stories.

4762 Giants 1898–99 *Western Assn. (ind.)*. Moniker was a spin-off from "Coal Palace Kings." In this era, "Kings" and "Giants" were equivalent descriptions of winning or dominant teams. Originally called the **Coal Palace Giants**, local newspapers quickly switched to Giants. Although predominantly a nickname-style used by black teams, a few white teams combined Giants with an adjective to produce a compound name.

4763 Stand-patters 1904 *Iowa State (D)*. With manager A.L. "Snapper" Kennedy at the helm, newspapers called the players "Snapper Kennedy's Stand-patters." The term "stand-pat" is used in poker when a player has very good cards and doesn't need to call for new cards, i.e., he "stands-pat" or he's got "pat-hand." With the "right" players the team complied, coming up with a "pat-hand"—a first-place 70–36 record.

4764 Snappers 1905–07 *Iowa State (D)*. With "Snapper" Kennedy returning to manage the 1904 champions, newspapers called the players the "Snappers." The moniker was appropriate since the red snapper fish swims in the nearby Des Moines River.

4765 Champs 1906 *Iowa State (D)*. Team won 1904–05 pennants. In this era teams that won a pennant the preceding season sometimes called themselves "Champions" or "Champs" at the start of the new season. This fad ended in the 1920s when players, now well-known because of radio, considered the use of this tag as too arrogant.

4766 Packers 1908–10, 1913 *Central Assn. (D)*; m1916 *Central Assn. (D)*. Team began season in Burlington (IA) and then moved to Ottumwa July 20. Surrounding farms transport produce to city factories to be cleaned, processed, packed and shipped out. With manager Chuck Fleming at the helm in 1908, newspapers called the players "Chuck's Packers." Fleming left the team after 1908 but the name was retained.

4767 Speed Boys 1911–14m *Central Assn. (D)*. Team moved to Rock Island (IL) July 17. Name was first used by the American League Bostons (before they were "Red Sox" in 1903–04). That team emphasized team speed to win games in the "Dead Ball" era when home run power was minimal. This Ottumwa team won consecutive Central League pennants 1911–12 by also emphasizing team speed. Because "Speed Boys" also referred to winning teams, local newspapers reported that the players "sped to the pennant." With manager Ned Egan at the helm, newspapers called the pennant-winning players "Ned Egan's Speed Boys."

4768 Cardinals 1922–25 *Mississippi Valley (D)*. Players wore red-trim uniforms and hose. The state bird of Iowa is the cardinal. With manager Jim Droham at the helm, newspapers called the players "Drohan's Cardinals." Carl Bond took over in mid-season 1922, changing the name to "Carl's Cardinals." Although both sippers left the team after the 1922 season, the nickname proved to be popular with the fans. The team was not a farm club of the St. Louis Cardinals as the farm system was not yet established.

4769 Packers 1926–28 *Mississippi Valley (D)*. With manager Pat Harkins at the helm in 1926–27, newspapers called the players "Pat Harkins' Packers." Preston Gray took over in 1928 and the name became "Preston Gray's Packers."

Outremont, Quebec, Canada

4770 Canadians 1924 *Quebec–Ontario–Vermont (B)*. With manager Pete Farrand at the helm, newspapers called the players "Pete Farrand's Canadiens." The name in French is "Les Canadiens."

Owensboro, Kentucky

4771 Owensboro Base Ball Club 1896x *Kentucky–Indiana (ind.)*. Team had no nickname

4772 Distillers 1903x *Kentucky–Illinois–Tennessee (KITTY) (D)*. Team disbanded June 1; 1913–14 *KITTY (D)*; 1916x *KITTY (D)*. Team and league disbanded August 4. City has had whiskey distilleries here since 1860. With manager William Long at the helm 1913–14, newspapers called the players "Bill's Distillers." Ollie Pickering took over in mid-season 1914 and the name became "Ollie's Distillers." The 1916 team also used the name.

4773 Pirates m1936 *KITTY (D)*. Team began 1936 season in Portageville (MO) and moved to Owensboro July 17. The team was a farm club of the Pittsburgh Pirates.

4774 Oilers 1937–42x *KITTY (D)*. Team and league disbanded June 19. Settled in 1800, oil and natural gas deposits were discovered here in the 1890s. Crude oil and natural gas are transported to refineries for conversion into petro-chemicals.

4775 Oilers 1946–55 *KITTY (D)*. Team returned after World War II ended.

Owosso, Michigan

4776 Owosso Base Ball Club 1893x *Michigan State (ind.)*. Team disbanded in mid-season 1893 (date unknown). Team had no nickname.

4777 Colts 1895x *Michigan State (ind.)*. Team had a many young players, known in the jargon of the era as "colts." The team had a loose affiliation with the National League Chicago "Colts."

Oxnard, California

4778 Oxnard Baseball Club 1913–14 *California Winter (W)*. Team had no nickname.

4779 Pacific Suns 1998 *Western (ind.)*. Team went by the regional name of Pacific Suns. The city is located in "Sunny California." California is also known as the "Sunshine Empire."

Ozark, Alabama

4780 Cardinals 1936–37m *Alabama–Florida (D)*. Team moved to Evergreen (AL) June 29. The cardinal is a red-feathered finch that inhabits not only the Atlantic coast and Midwest but also the South. The team had a loose affiliation with the NL St. Louis Cardinals but was not a formal farm club. With manager Edward Porter at the helm in 1936, newspapers called the players "Edward's Cardinals." In 1937 Monroe Mitchell took over and the name became "Monroe Mitchell's Cardinals."

4781 Eagles 1946–50 *Alabama State (D)*; 1951–52 *Alabama–Florida (D)*. Fighter pilots trained at Ozark's nearby Fort Rucker Army Aviation Center and Cairms Army Air Force Base during World War II. Several of these pilots joined the famous Royal Air Force "Eagle Squadron" in England. With manager Chase Riddle at the helm in 1951, newspapers called the players "Chase Riddle's Eagles." Walter Jones took over in mid-season in 1951 and the name became "Walter's Eagles." Chase Riddle returned in 1952 and led "Riddle's Eagles" to the league championship.

4782 Dodgers 1962m *Alabama–Florida (D)*. Team moved to Andalusia (AL) July 10. The team was a farm club of the Los Angeles Dodgers.

Ozark, Missouri

4783 Mountain Ducks 1999 *Texas–Louisiana (ind.)*. The Ozark Mountains, which range through Arkansas, Missouri and Oklahoma, has five rivers — Arkansas, Osage, White, Casconade and Black — which sustain these mountain ducks.

Ozark-Springfield, Missouri

4784 Ducks 2000–01 *Texas–Louisiana (ind.)*; 2002–04 *Central (ind.)*. With the team formally renamed the "Springfield-Ozark Ducks" (home games remained only in Ozark), management dropped Mountain to save newspaper space.

Paducah, Kentucky

4785 Paducah Base Ball Club 1897 *Central (ind.)*. Team had no nickname.

4786 Chiefs 1903–06 *Kentucky–Illinois–Tennessee KITTY (D)*; 1912–13 *KITTY (D)*; 1949–50 *Missouri–Ohio Valley (D)*; 1951–55 *KITTY (D)*. Explorer and city founder William Clark named the city, established in 1827, Paducah in honor of the Chickasaw Indian chief by the same name.

4787 Indians 1910, 1914 *KITTY (D)*; 1922–23 *KITTY (D)*; 1936–41 *KITTY (D)*. Tag was a spin-off of Chiefs. The 1923 team had a loose affiliation with the Cleveland Indians.

4788 Polecats 1911 *KITTY (D)*. With manager Ollie Pickering at the helm in 1911, newspapers called the players "Pickering's Polecats." The polecat, a type of skunk, inhabits regions around the nearby Ohio and Tennessee rivers. Numerous baseball players in this era seldom bathed and reneged at wearing clean clothes. They more often smelled of booze, sweat and dirty clothes, both on the field in their uniforms and off the field in their civilian garb.

4789 Redbirds 1935 *KITTY (D)*. Team was a farm club of the St. Louis Cardinals, whose fans sometimes refer to them with the alternative moniker of "Redbirds." The cardinal is the state bird of Kentucky.

Paintsville, Kentucky

4790 Hilanders 1978 *Appalachian (R)*. City was built on the Cumberland Plateau along the Knobs Hills.

4791 Yankees 1979–82 *Appalachian (R)*. Team was a farm club of the New York Yankees.

4792 Brewers 1983–84 *Appalachian (R)*. Team was a farm club of the Milwaukee Brewers.

Paintsville-Pikeville, Kentucky

4793 Kentucky Rifles 1993–94 *Frontier (ind.)*. Home games were played in Paintsville (KY). A rifle in eighteenth-century Pennsylvania, known as the "Pennsylvania Rifle," made its way into nineteenth-century Kentucky, where it was modified and saw heavy use during the War of 1812, so much so that there was a song about this firearm called the "Kentucky Rifle."

Palatka, Florida

4794 Azaleas 1936–39 *Florida State (D)*; 1946–53m Team moved to Lakeland (FL) May 15. The Azalea is a shrub flower found in the southern U.S.

4795 Tigers 1956 *Florida State (D)*. Team was a farm club of the Detroit Tigers.

4796 Red Legs 1957–61 *Florida State (D)*. Team was a farm club of the Cincinnati Redlegs.

4797 Cubs 1962 *Florida State (D)*. Team was a farm club of the Chicago Cubs.

Palestine, Texas

4798 Athletics 1916 *East Texas (D)*. Newspaper reporters started using the name because it could be shortened to the space-saving "A's." The team was not a farm club of the Philadelphia Athletics; the farm system had not yet been established.

4799 Browns 1916 *East Texas (D)*. Players wore brown-trim hose. The team was not a farm club of the St. Louis Browns.

4800 Pals m1925–26 *Texas Assn. (D)*. Team started 1925 season in Marlin (TX) and moved to Palestine May 13; 1927–29 *Lone Star (D)*; 1927–29 *Lone Star (D)*; 1934–35 *West Dixie (C)*; 1936–40x *East Texas (C)*. Team disbanded June 5.

Palm Beach, Florida

4801 Cardinals 2003 to date *Florida State (A)*. Team was a farm club of St. Louis Cardinals.

Palm Desert, California

4802 Coyotes 2009–10 *California Winter (W)*. Gray and red coyotes, smaller than wolves, are found mostly in the central plains and the southwest U.S.

Palm Springs, California

4803 Angels 1986–93 *California (A)*. Team was a farm club of the California Angels.

4804 Pacific Suns 1995–96 *Western (ind.)*; 1998 *Western (ind.)*. Circuit was known officially as the Western Baseball League. Palm Springs is the "Capital of Sunshine."

4805 Chill 2008–09 *Arizona Winter (W)*. Tag is an ironic play on words spin-off from "Suns." The team mascot is "Tundra" the Yeti. The Yeti is the "Abominable Snowman of Tibet." Palm Springs is the "Capital of Sunshine" and the "Oasis in the Desert."

4806 Canada Athletics 2010 to date *California Winter (W)*. Team played its home games at Palm Springs Stadium. Players on the team are from Canada.

4807 Coachella Valley Snowbirds 2010 to date *California Winter (W)*. Palm Springs is located in Coachella Valley. The snowbirds are owls that inhabit the snowy ridges of the San Jacinto, Little San Bernardino and Chocolate mountains.

4808 Palm Desert Coyotes 2010 to date *California Winter (W)*. Coyotes roam the nearby Mojave Desert. The Palm Desert, part of the Mojave Desert, is northwest of the city.

Palmyra, New York

4809 Mormons 1897–98x *New York State (ind.)*. Joseph Smith founded the Mormon Church here in 1830.

Pampa, Texas

4810 Plainsmen 1939 *West Texas–New Mexico (D)*. The Great Plains extends from Texas to the Rocky Mountains. "Pampa" is a Spanish word for "plains." The "Pampas" are the grassy plains of Argentina.

4811 Oilers 1940–42 *West Texas–New Mexico (D)*; 1946–55 *West Texas–New Mexico (C)*; 1956–57m *Southwestern (B)*. Team moved to San Angelo (TX) May 16. The Panhandle Oil Field was discovered near Pampa in 1921. The discovery made Pampa an oil "boom-town." The city has numerous oil-field supply houses. Pampa is the "City Where Oil Flows."

Pana, Illinois

4812 Coal Miners 1907–08m *Eastern Illinois (D)*. Team moved to Linton (IL) July 17. Coal deposits, discovered in central Illinois in 1880, are transported to city factories for processing.

Panama City, Florida

4813 Pilots 1935 *Georgia–Florida (D)*; 1938 *Alabama–Florida (D)*. City is built on the shore of St. Andrew's Bay where pilot boats guide civilian and commercial ships along the Apalachicola River, in and out of the Gulf of Mexico. City is known as the "City in Beautiful Bay County." With managers Bill Snyder and then Harry Snyder at the helm, newspapers called the players "Snyder's Pilots."

4814 Papermakers 1936 *Alabama–Florida (D)*. In the era 1880–1945, lumber from the Appalachicola National Forest was transported to wood and paper mills in the city.

4815 Pelicans 1937, 1939 *Alabama–Florida (D)*. Team was a farm of the Class A1 New Orleans Pelicans. Pelicans are found all along the Southeast.

4816 Fliers 1951–61 *Alabama–Florida (D)*. Tyndall Air Force Base is located halfway between Panama City and Tallahassee (FL).

Panama City, Provincia de Panama, Panama

4817 General Electric 1946–47 *Liga de Panama (W)*. Team was owned by General Electric de Panama.

4818 Cigarilleros de Chesterfield 1946–47 *Liga de Panama (W)*; Chesterfield Tobacco Company de Panama owned the team. "Cigarellero" means "cigarette-maker."

4819 Cigarilleros de Marlboro 1946–47 *Liga de Panama (W)*. Team was owned by Marlboro Tobacco Company de Panama. "Cigarellero" means "cigarette-maker."

4820 Carta Vieja 1946–47–52–53 *Liga de Panama (W)*. Team was owned by Carta Vieja Beer, i.e., Cerveceria Carta Blanca, in Spanish.

4821 Cinco Estrellas 1946–47–52–53 *Liga de Panama (W)*. Team was owned by Los Hoteles de Cinco Estrellas de Panama.

4822 Spur Cola 1946–47–55–56 *Liga de Panama (W)*. Spur Cola, a soft drink company, owned the team.

4823 Yanquis 1946–47–58–59 *Liga de Panama (W)*. In March 1946, the New York Yankees played several spring exhibition games in Panama City. The team was owned by Cerveza Carta Vieja (Carta Vieja Beer Company), who chose the nickname of "Yanquis" for the team. Yanqui in English is "Yankee."

4824 Ramblers 1949 *Liga de Panama (W)*. British buccaneer Henry Morgan destroyed the city in 1671. Pirates have also been called Buccaneers, Corsairs, Invaders, Raiders, Rovers and Ramblers.

4825 Cerveza Balboa 1956–57–68–69 *Liga de Panama (W)*; 1970–71–71–72 *Liga de Panama (W)*; 2001–02 *Liga de Panama (W)*. The Balboa Beer Company owned the team. The company's name in Spanish was Cerveceria de Balboa.

4826 Comercio 1959–60 *Liga de Panama (W)*. Banco Comercio, S.A. owned team.

4827 Central 1962–63 *Liga de Panama (W)*. Panama City is located in center of the country.

4828 Club de Beisbol de Panama 1962–63 only *Liga de Panama (W)*. Team had no nickname.

4829 Novatos 1963–64 *Liga de Panama (W)*. Team had many young players. "Novato" is the Spanish word for rookie.

4830 Panalit 1963–64 *Liga de Panama (W)*. The Panalit Construction Company owned the team.

4831 Ron Santa Clara 1964–65–68–69 *Liga de Panama (W)*; 1970–71–71–72 *Liga de Panama (W)*. Ron Santa Clara owned team. "Ron" is Spanish for "rum."

4832 Banqueros 1979 *Inter-American (ind.)*. Team owned by Banco de Panama.

4833 Ronners 2001–02 *Liga de Panama (W)*. This circuit played the full season but then disbanded because of financial problems. The team was owned by Carta Vieja. Ronners is Spanish for Rum-makers. Team owner Carta Vieja is most famous for beer but also makes rum.

4834 Estrellas 2001–02 *Liga de Panama (W)*. Moniker was a spin-off from the 1953 Cinco Estrellas team.

4835 Canaleros 2001–02 *Liga de Panama (W)*. Team was named in honor of the Panama Canal.

Paoli, Pennsylvania

4836 Black Diamonds 1999–2002 *Atlantic (ind,)*. Nearby coal mines ship coal to processing factories. Pennsylvania is the "Coal State." "Black Diamond" is slang for "coal."

Paragould, Arkansas

4837 Scouts 1909–11 *Northeast (ind.)*. During the Indian Wars of the 1880s, the U.S. Army employed Seminole scouts to monitor the movements of the Cherokee Indians. Baseball players in this era were often referred to by Wild West names, i.e., Braves, Broncos, Cowboys, Indians, Rustlers and Scouts. Arkansas is the "Bowie State," in honor of explorer and scout Jim Bowie. With manager Howard Schaff at the helm, newspapers called the players "Schaff's Scouts."

4838 Rebels 1936–38 *Northeast Arkansas (D)*. The Battle of Pea Ridge took place in July 1863 and led to the Union Army taking Little Rock by 1863. With manager Orlin Collier at the helm in 1936, newspapers called the players "Collier's Rebels." Rip Fanning took over later in the season and the name became "Rip's Rebels." Royce Williams took over in 1937 and the name became "Royce's Rebels." Bobby Schleicher took over in 1938 and the name became "Bobby Schleicher's Rebels." Paul Rucker took over in mid-season 1938, changing the name to "Rucker's Rebels."

4839 Broncos 1939 *Northeast Arkansas (D)*. In the era 1880–1940, baseball players were often identified with Wild West name, i.e., Cowboys, Braves, Rustlers and Broncos. With manager Elmer Kirchoff at the helm, newspapers called the players "Kirchoff's Bronchos."

4840 Browns 1940–41 *Northeast Arkansas (D)*. Team was a farm club of the St. Louis Browns.

Paris, Illinois

4841 Paris Base Ball Club 1898x *Southwestern (ind.)*. Team and circuit disbanded in mid-season (date unknown). Team had no nickname.

4842 Colts m1907 *Eastern Illinois (D)*. Team began season as the Centralia "White Sox" and had a loose affiliation with the AL Chicago White Sox. When it relocated to Paris June 20, the 1907 team established a loose affiliation with the NL Chicago Colts, who would become the Cubs the next year.

4843 Parisians 1908 *Eastern Illinois (D)*. Team began season in Centralia (IL) and moved to Paris June 20. An inhabitant of any city named Paris is known as a "Parisian."

4844 Lakers 1950–55 *Missouri–Ohio Valley M.O.V. (D)*; 1956–59 *Midwest (D)*. The Walnut Point Lake and Wildlife Area, 10 miles northwest of the city, is a recreational site for swimming, fishing, boating, ice skating and picnics. The West Lake Reservoir was created by a dam here in 1895 to be used as a boating lake for tourists. The resort is known as Twin Lakes Park.

Paris, Kentucky

4845 Bourbonites 1909–12 *Blue Grass (D)*. The first distillery in the United States was built in this city in 1785. With Mr. Barnett at the helm as field manager in 1909, local newspapers called the players "Barnett's Bourbonites." Ed McKernan took over 1910–11 and the name became "McKernan's Bourbonites." The name was retained in 1912 under two other managers.

4846 Paris Baseball Club m1914x *Ohio State (D)*. Team started the season in Newport (OH) and moved to Paris June 16. Team disbanded July 5. Team had no nickname.

4847 Bourbons 1922–24 *Blue Grass (D)*. Newspapers shortened the 1912 "Bourbonites" to "Bourbons." With manager B. Goodman at the helm, newspapers called the players "B. Goodman's Bourbons." Kentucky is known as the "Bourbon State" because of its many distilleries of bourbon whiskey.

Paris, Tennessee

4848 Travelers 1922 *Kentucky–Illinois–Tennessee K.I.T.T.Y. (D)*, Team was a farm club of the Little Rock Travelers. In the era 1900–57, higher classification (AAA and AA) minor league teams sometimes had farm clubs in the ranks of lower classification (A, B, C, D) minor leagues.

4849 Parisians 1923–24 *Kentucky–Illinois–Tennessee K.I.T.T.Y. (D)*. An inhabitant of a city named Paris (France, Texas, Illinois, Kentucky, etc.) is known as a "Parisian."

Paris, Texas

4850 Midlands 1896 *Texas–Southern (ind.)*. After the Sherman team disbanded on June 10, league president John Ward traveled to Paris (TX) and convinced the Texas Midland Railroad to finance a team there.

4851 Home-seekers 1902 *Texas (D)*. Team got off to a losing start, which caused fans to stay away, forcing owner-manager C.W. Eisenfelder to send the team on extended road trips. Newspapers started calling the team "Eisenfelder's Home-seekers." The team avoided last place but finished with a 42–65 record.

4852 Parasites 1903m *Texas (D)*; 1904m *Texas (C)*. Team moved to Waco (TX) June 26; 1904m *Texas (C)*. Team moved to Ardmore (TX) August 5. Vaudeville was live, variety entertainment, presented in theaters throughout the United States for the era 1860–1940. A well-known joke of Vaudevillian comedy went "I visited Paris and saw the parasites." The correct term for an inhabitant of Paris is Parisian.

4853 Athletics 1907 *North Texas (D)*. With manager Robert Shelton at the helm, newspapers called the players "Shelton's Athletics." Everett Sheffield took over in mid-season 1907 and the name became "Everett's Athletics." The team was not a farm club of the Philadelphia Athletics as there was no farm system in this era.

4854 Boosters 1912 *South Central (D)*; 1913 *Texas–Oklahoma (D)*. With high expectations in 1912, fans formed a booster club, which prompted local newspapers to call the players "Boosters." However, the team disappointed with a 46–63 record. With manager Jack Jutze at the helm in 1912–13, newspapers called the players "Jutze's Boosters." The 1913 team went a splendid 80–45 before finishing second to Denison. In response, fans set up another booster club.

4855 Snappers 1914 *Texas–Oklahoma (D)*; 1921–22 *Texas–Oklahoma (D)*; 1927 *Lone Star (D)*. Snapping turtles are found in Texas and inhabit North America from eastern Canada to Mexico. Baseball man Earl "Red" Snapper was part-owner and general manager of this 1914 team. With manager Johnny Fillman at the helm, newspapers called the players "Fillman's Snappers." Red Snapper returned to manage the team in 1920–21.

4856 Red Snappers 1915 *Western Assn. (D)*. With team owner and now field manager Earl "Red" Snapp controlling the club, local newspapers called the players the Red Snappers.

4857 Survivors 1916 *Western Assn. (D)*. While the team was "under siege" by the rest of the league en route to a last-place 56–83 finish, the city of Paris was under siege by the German army as World War I raged in Europe. When Paris survived the German siege, the namesake baseball team was named the Paris "Survivors." With manager Dick Speer taking over in mid-season 1916, local newspapers called the remaining players and coaches that had not been released "Speer's Survivors."

4858 Athletics 1917m *Western Assn. (D)*. Team moved to Ardmore (TX) May 10. When the team got off to a 16–12 record, by virtue of the players "athletic performances" local reporters started calling the players the "Athletics," which editors happily shortened to A's. The team was not a farm club of the AL Philadelphia Athletics. After moving to Ardmore, the team disintegrated, going 41–86 to finish last in the league standings.

4859 Grays 1923 *East Texas (D)*. Players wore gray trim.

4860 North Stars 1924 *East Texas (D)*. Paris was the northernmost city of the eight-team circuit. Texas is the Lone Star State.

4861 Bearcats 1925–26 *East Texas (D)*. The so-called North American "bearcat" is actually the wolverine—a member of the weasel family. The true bearcat is found only in Asia.

4862 Colts 1928 *Lone Star (D)*. With manager Abe Bowman at the helm at the start of the 1928 season, local newspapers called the team with mostly young players "Bowman's Colts." With manager Ewell "Turkey" Gross at the helm in mid-season 1928, newspapers called the player "Ewell Turkey Gross's Rustlers." Baseball players in the era 1880–1930 were often referred by Wild West names, i.e., Braves, Bronchos, Cowboys, and Rustlers.

4863 Rustlers 1928 *Lone Star (D)*. City, founded in 1840, was in the nineteenth century often the scene of cattle rustling just outside of town. With manager Ewell "Turkey" Gross at the helm in mid-season 1928, newspapers called the players "Ewell Turkey Gross's Rustlers." The tag "rustlers" was slang for "baseball players."

4864 Pirates 1934 *West Dixie (C)*. Team moved to Lufkin (TX) June 27. Local newspapers started using "Pirates" as a convenient moniker. The team was not a farm team of the Pittsburgh Pirates.

4865 Red Peppers 1946 *East Texas (C)*; 1947 *Big State (B)*. Red and green peppers, grown in nearby farms, are transported to city factories to be cleaned, processed, packaged and shipped out.

4866 Rockets 1948 *Big State (B)*. With the American public fascinated by German V-2 rockets and the appearance of UFOs (Unidentified Flying Objects), numerous sports teams in the years 1946–50 started calling themselves the "Rockets." With manager Homer Peel at the helm in 1948, newspapers called the players "Homer's Rockets."

4867 Panthers 1949–50 *East Texas (C)*. Team was a farm club of the Fort Worth Cats. The Fort Worth franchise had abandoned "Panthers" in favor of "Cats." Mountain lions, also called panthers, inhabit Texas. With manager Jimmy Walkup at the helm, local newspapers called the players "Walkup's Panthers."

4868 Indians 1952–53 *Big State (B)*. With manager John "Red" Davis at the helm in 1952–53, newspapers called the players "Red's Indians." Today such a name would be "politically incorrect," but back then nobody seemed to care. Newspapers also used "Davis' Indians." The team was not a farm club of the Cleveland Indians.

4869 Orioles 1955–57 *Sooner State (D)*. Team was a farm club of the Baltimore Orioles.

Park City, Utah

4870 Park City Baseball Club 1901 *Inter-Mountain (ind.)*. Team had no nickname.

Parkersburg, West Virginia

4871 Parkersburg Base Ball Club 1897 *Ohio–West Virginia (ind.)*. Team had no nickname.

4872 Parkers m1909x *Pennsylvania–West Virginia (D)*. Team started season in Charleroi (PA) and moved to Parkersburg June 30. Team disbanded July 10; 1910 *Virginia Valley (D)*; m1931m *Middle Atlantic (C)*. Team started season in Hagerstown (MD) then moved to Parkersburg (WVa) June 28, and then moved to Youngstown (OH) July 12. Local reporters simply abbreviated the city name so that it would fit into headlines, i.e., "Parkers edge Bees, 4–3."

4873 Ohio Valley Red Coats 1993–98 *Frontier (ind.)*. British soldiers, i.e., Red Coats, used the region as a staging area during the Revolutionary War. The city was established here in 1810.

Parksley, Virginia

4874 Spuds 1922–28x *Eastern Shore (D)*. Potatoes were grown in subsistence farms here in the seventeenth century. Potatoes were a New World food that caused a sensation in Europe.

Parma, Emilia-Romagna, Italy

4875 C.V.S. Carpiparma 1999, 2007 *Italian A1 (ind.)*; 2008 to date *Italian Baseball (ind.)*. Team owner is the Cariparma Credit Agricole, and CVS Security Services. Team represented the nearby cities of Carpi and Parma.

4876 Cantine Ceci 2000–03 *Italian A1 (ind.)*. Team was owned by Cantine Wines and the Ceci Energy Company.

4877 Ceci Negra 2004–06 *Italian A1 (ind.)*. Team was owned by the Danesi, Ceci & Negri Energy Company.

4878 Cantine & Ceci Carpiparma 1999–2006 *Italian A1 (ind.)*. Cantine Wine Company and Ceci Energy Company owned the team. Double city name was added.

4879 CVS Cantine 2001–02 *Italian A1 (ind.)*. Cantine Wine Company was joined by CVS Security Services as dual owners of the team.

4880 Ceci & Negri de Parmacarpi 2007 to date *Italian A1*. Ceci merged with Negri to form the Ceci & Negri Energy Company, which owns the team. Owners changed the team name to represent Parma and the nearby city of Carpi. Home games continue to be played in Parma.

Parramatta, New South Wales, Australia

4881 Patriots 1989–90–90–91 *Australian (W)*. Moniker was appropriate because it honors the original English settlers who founded the city in 1788. New South Wales Governor Arthur Phillips, leading a militia and a company of surveyors, established the city in 1788.

Parras, Coahuila, Mexico

4882 Coahuila Saraperos 1974 *Mexican Center (A)*. Team was a farm club of the Saraperos de Saltillo. Mexico is noted for its beautiful blankets—known in Spanish as Sarapes. "Sarapero" means "blanket-maker." Team was known by the state name of Coahuila Saraperos.

Parsons, Kansas

4883 Preachers 1905 *Missouri Valley (C)*; 1906 *Kansas State (D)*; 1907x *Oklahoma–Arkansas–Kansas O.A.K. (D)*. Team disbanded June 2. As settlers reached Kansas, Baptist, Methodist, Quaker, Presbyterian and Jesuits missions were built throughout the state. Russian Mennonites arrived in Kansas in the 1870s and introduced hard winter wheat that stimulated farming. A parson is a Protestant minister or pastor in charge of a parish. With C. Pinkerton at the helm as manager in 1906, newspapers called the players "Pinkerton's Preachers."

4884 Parsons 1921m *Southwestern (D)*. Team moved to Cushing (OK) July 27. The shorter name was a spin-off from "Preachers."

Pasadena, California

4885 Silk Sox 1910x *South California Trolley (D)*. Team and league disbanded June 13. Players wore silk hose. In the era 1900–20 the city had textile mills manufacturing cotton, wool, linen and silk fabrics.

4886 Millionaires 1913m *South California (D)*. Team moved to Santa Barbara (CA) June 13. Millionaire owners of companies, galleries, factories, laboratories and Hollywood movie stars built expensive houses in Pasadena in this era. The city is known as the "Hub of the Fabulous Gulf Coast" and the "Crown City."

4887 Eagles 1918–19 *Southern California (W)*; 1922–23–24–25 *Southern California (W)*. The players of these integrated teams decided to call themselves the "Eagles."

Pasco-Kennewick-Richland, Washington

4888 Tri-City Posse 1995–2002 *Western (ind.)*. Team played its home games at Sanders-Jacobs Field in Pasco (WA) but could not compete with the NWL Dust Devils, who were playing in Gesa Stadium. Gold prospectors and fur trappers entered the region in 1880, which spurred the arrival of the Northern Pacific Railway. The train brought settlers to Washington and Oregon. Bandits, cattle rustlers and highwaymen began to prey on the settlers, prompting the deputizing of vigilante posses.

4889 Tri-City Dust Devils 2001 to date *Northwest (A)*. Team played its home games in Pasco (WA) at Gesa Stadium and later Pasco Stadium. Dusty wind storms plague southern Washington State, forcing farms to irrigate crops with water from the Columbia and Snake rivers. Farms near to these rivers were so well irrigated that Kennewick became known as the "Grassy Place."

Paterno, Catania, Italy

4890 Ragaina 2001 *Italian A1*. Team was owned by Ragaina Farm Machinery.

4891 Cittadei Normanni 2002–05 *Italian A1*. The Citta Monuments of St. Eta are located near the city in honor of the Norman warriors who established the city in the 11th century.

Paterson, New Jersey

4892 Silk Weavers 1896–98 *Atlantic (ind.)*. Paterson in the nineteenth century had silk textile mills and was nicknamed the "Silk City."

4893 Giants 1899 *Atlantic (ind.)*. Team had a loose affiliation with New York Giants. In the 1890s, some New Jersey minor league teams had loose affiliations with the NL New York Giants. Indeed, there have been loose affiliations between minor league teams and geographically near major league franchises dating to 1885.

4894 Intruders 1904, 1907 *Hudson River (C)*. Team had a loose affiliation with the New York AL club. The nickname was a spin-off of New York's "Invaders" moniker. Although the farm system devised by Branch Rickey did not arise until the 1920s and become universal until 1950, there were about fifty loose-affiliation "farm" teams with indirect dealings with big league teams in the era 1885–1920.

4895 Invaders 1905–06 *Hudson River (C)*. Team had a loose affiliation with AL New York "Invaders" (Yankees, used unofficially 1903–12, became official in 1913). In the era 1885–1920 teams in minor league cities close to a major league baseball team sometimes had a loose affiliation with the big league club, i.e., a working agreement in which minor league player contracts could be more easily purchased.

4896 Silk Citys 1914 *Atlantic (D)*. Moniker was a spin-off of the 1904 "Silk Weavers." Paterson, noted for its silk textiles industry for the era 1850–1920, is known as the "Silk City."

Patton, Pennsylvania

4897 Patton Baseball Club m1906 *Interstate (D)*. Team began season in Hornell (NY) and moved to Patton August 6. Team had no nickname.

Pauls Valley, Oklahoma

4898 Raiders 1948–54 *Sooner State (D)*. Oklahoma has historically had "raiders" of all types, i.e., Indians, outlaws, bandits, rustlers and robbers. With field manager Dutch Prather at the helm, newspapers during spring training started to call the players "Prather's Raiders." Management then ordered "Raiders" jerseys. Prather left the team after the 1948 season but the nickname was retained.

Pawhuska, Oklahoma

4899 Huskers 1920–22 *Western Assn. (D).* Moniker, arbitrarily assigned to the team by local reporters, was appropriate because there are corn farms in Oklahoma where kernels are husked from the cob. With field manager Rudy Hulswitt at the helm in 1921, local newspapers called the players "Hulswitt's Huskers."

4900 Osages 1922 *Western Assn. (D).* City was built along the Osage River. The Osage Indians originally inhabited Kansas but then were resettled in reservations in Oklahoma in the nineteenth century.

4901 Huskies m1924 *Oklahoma State (D).* Team started season in Ardmore (OK) and then moved to Pawhuska June 8. Reporters decided on a more "dashing" name than the "Huskers," so newspapers started using the obvious spin-off of "Huskies." With manager Drap Hayes at the helm, newspapers called the players "Hayes' Huskies."

Pawtucket, Rhode Island

4902 Secrets 1892x *New England. (ind.).* Team stumbled out of the gate en route to a terrible 17–47 record, which so dampened fan attendance that local newspapers jested the team "played in secret." The resulting depressed revenues caused the team to disband July 2.

4903 Clam-eaters 1894–95 *New England (ind.).* Fishing boats brought in seafood catches, i.e., fish, lobsters, crabs, oysters and clams, that were transported to city factories for cleaning, packing and shipping to market.

4904 Maroons 1894–96 *New England (ind.).* Players wore maroon hose.

4905 Phenoms 1897 *New England (ind.).* "Phenom" is an abbreviation for phenomenal. It refers to a promising young person displaying talent in a particular endeavor. Tag was used in baseball to describe a talented rookie. With manager John Smith at the helm, newspapers called the players "John Smith's Phenoms."

4906 Colts 1897–99 *New England (ind.);* 1908x *Atlantic Assn. (D).* Circuit and team disbanded May 19. With manager William Connors at the helm in 1908, newspapers called the players "Connors' Colts." These teams had numerous young players. Newspaper editors balked at using Pawtucket "Phenoms"—a name with 16 letters—and switched to "Colts," which in this era meant young players. The word "rookie"—a derivation of "recruit"—coined in 1895, came into popular usage in 1917 as U.S. Army recruits boarded ship to sail to Europe and fight in World War I.

4907 Tigers 1898 *New England (ind.);* 1914 *Colonial (C).* Players wore striped hose (1898) and stirrups (1914). More than ten professional baseball teams took the Tiger moniker in the 1890s when striped stockings became a fad among baseball, football and soccer teams. With field manager H. B. Whiting at the helm, local newspapers called the players "Whiting's Tigers."

4908 Rovers 1915 *Colonial (C).* With manager Jim Connor at the helm in 1915, newspapers called the players "Connor's Rovers." "Rover" is a term for an offensive position in soccer. In baseball, the position of "shortstop" was known as "rover" in the 1850s.

4909 Slaters 1946–49 *New England (B).* In 1790 Pawtucket resident Sam Slater built the first cotton mill in the United States. The mill was run by water power. Another mill, built by Slater in 1793, is today a museum in the city. The moniker has nothing to do with

slate mining. Slate miners are called "slaters" but the meaning doesn't apply here.

4910 Indians 1966–67 *Eastern (AA).* Team was a farm club of the Cleveland Indians.

4911 Red Sox 1970–72 *Eastern (AA);* 1973 to date *International (AAA)* The 1976 team went by the state name of **Rhode Island Red Sox.** The team was a farm club of the Boston Red Sox.

4912 PawSox 2002 to date *International (AAA).* Many teams named Sox use this style to uniquely identify themselves, i.e., Bo-Sox, Chi-Sox, Lyn-Sox, Paw-Sox, Sky Sox, Sun Sox, and even Cub-Sox.

Pearl, Mississippi

4913 Mississippi Braves 2005 to date *Southern (AA).* Team is a farm club of the Atlanta Braves.

Pearl City, West Oahu, Hawaii

4914 West Oahu Canefires 1995–97 *Hawaii Winter (W);* 2006–07 *Hawaii Winter (W).* Sugar plantations on Oahu Island grow sugar cane, which is burned before harvest to liquefy the sugar sap. Both teams went by the island name of West Oahu.

Pearlsburg, Virginia–Narrows, Virginia

4915 New River Rebels 1946–50 *Appalachian (D).* Pearlsburg is at the border of Virginia (Confederate state) and West Virginia (Union state). Several battles were fought here during the Civil War. Virginia is known as the "Battlefield of the Civil War."

Peekskill, New York

4916 Peekskill Base Ball Club 1888x *Hudson River (ind.).* Team and circuit disbanded in mid-season (date unknown); 1903 *Hudson River (D);* 1905 *Hudson River (C).* These teams had no nickname.

4917 Highlanders 1946–49 *North Atlantic (D).* City was built on the northern edge of the Blue Mountains.

Pekin, Illinois

4918 Celestials 1909–13x *Illinois–Missouri (D).* After its construction by Kubla Khan in the 13th century, the "Inner City" of Peking, China, contained the "Forbidden City" where the imperial palace was built near to the "Gate of Heavenly Peace." The imperial palace is known as the "Palace of Celestial Purity." From this name, the Inner City and then Peking itself became known as the "Celestial City." Pekin, Illinois—originally known as "Peking"—emulated its Chinese inspiration by also calling itself the "Celestial City." As the team captured the 1910 league championship, Pekin fans found themselves in the throes of "celestial happiness."

Pendleton, Oregon

4919 Pendleton Base Ball Club 1891 *Pacific Inter-State (ind.).* Team had no nickname.

4920 Pets 1908x *Inland Empire (D).* Team and league disbanded June 12 because of a dangerous summer heat wave. A baseball manager's players in this era were sometimes referred to as the so-and-so's "Pets," a precursor to our modern "Dogs" and "Dawgs." Local newspapers called the players Mr. "Lorimer's Pets" and Mr. "Hosier's Pets" after the franchise's two managers this year.

4921 Buckaroos 1913–14 *Western Tri-State (D).* The first "Pendleton Round-Up," a rodeo featuring riders, cowboys and Indians, was featured in 1912 and has since been held annually every September. Since that year Pendleton is known as the "Round-Up City." Founded in 1869 the city became a cattle center where herds were assembled to be driven across mountainous terrain into Idaho, Wyoming and Montana. "Buckaroo" is a slang that means "calf," particularly a stray. The name later came to mean "cowboy." With manager Terry McKune at the helm, the team was called "McKune's Buckaroos."

Penn Yan, New York

4922 Penn Yan Base Ball Club 1888 *New York State (ind.)*. Team had no nickname.

Pennington Gap, Virginia

4923 Lee Bears 1937–38 *Appalachian (D)*. Team played at Leeman Field.

4924 Bears 1939 *Appalachian (D)*. Newspapers shortened the name. The team continued to play in Leeman Field.

4925 Miners 1940 *Appalachian (D)*; 1948–51 *Mountain States (D)*. Coal deposits, discovered in the region in 1900, prompted the arrival of railroads to transport coal (and lumber) to city factories for processing and shipping.

Pensacola, Florida

4926 Pensacola Base Ball Club m1893 *Southern (ind.)*. Team started season in Birmingham (AL) and then moved to Pensacola May 28. Team had no nickname.

4927 Snappers 1913x *Cotton States (D)*. The Snapper is a tropical blue fish that swims off the coast of Florida.

4928 Pilots 1927 *Southeastern (B)*. 1927–30; 1941–42 *Southeastern (B)*. Pilot boats guide commercial and recreational traffic through Florida's largest landlocked harbor at Pensacola. The U.S. Naval Air Training School opened here in 1914. The city gained a reputation for both maritime and aerial "pilots." Pensacola is known as the "Annapolis of the Air." With manager Bill Holden at the helm in 1927, newspapers called the players "Bill Holden's Pilots." After Wally Dashiell left the team following the 1940 season, newspapers went back to "Pilots."

4929 Flyers 1928–30 *Southeastern (B)*; 1938–40 *Southeastern (B)*; 1946–50 *Southeastern (B)*. The Naval Education and Training Command, established here in 1927, was the first base to train U.S. Navy and U.S. Marine airplane pilots. Pensacola is known as the "Cradle of Naval Aviation." With manager Tom Pyle at the helm 1929–30, newspapers called the players "Pyle's Flyers." With manager Wally Dashiell at the helm, newspapers called the players "Wally's Flyers" as the team finished first and made the playoffs in 1938, won the league championship in 1939, and made the playoffs again in 1940. The Naval Aviation Museum was built here and opened its doors in 1946. Pensacola is home to the famous air show "Blue Angels." Pensacola is the site of the National Museum of Naval Aviation.

4930 Dons 1957–59 *Alabama–Florida (D)*. Spanish conquistador Don Tristan de la Luna founded a settlement here in 1559. Newspapers liked the four-letter name.

4931 Angels 1960 *Alabama–Florida (D)*. The Old Christ Church, built here in the sixteenth century, is the oldest original church in Florida. Pensacola is home to the famous air show "Blue Angels." Pensacola is the site of the National Museum of Naval Aviation. The team was not a farm club of the PCL Los Angeles Angels.

4932 Senators 1961–62 *Alabama–Florida (D)*. Team was a farm club of the Washington Senators.

4933 Pelicans 2002–03 *Southeast (ind.)*; 2004–05 *Central (ind.)*; 2006–10 *American Assn. (ind.)*. The brown pelican inhabits the coastal waters of the Gulf of Mexico. The team disbanded after the 2010 season.

Peoria, Arizona

4934 Padres 1988–2000 *Arizona (R)*; 2004 to date *Arizona (R)*. These teams were farm clubs of the San Diego Padres.

4935 Brewers 1989–91 *Arizona (R)*. Team was a farm club of the Milwaukee Brewers.

4936 Cardinals 1989–91 *Arizona (R)*. Team was a farm club of the St. Louis Cardinals.

4937 Mariners 1989 to date *Arizona (R)*. Team was a farm club of the Seattle Mariners.

4938 Saguaros 2003 to date *Arizona Fall (W)*. The Saguaro is a desert cactus found in Arizona and northern Mexico that yields wood and bears an edible fruit.

4939 Javelinas 2007 to date *Arizona Fall (W)*. The Javelina is a wild boar that inhabits the Rocky Mountains.

Peoria-Scottsdale, Arizona

4940 Brewers 1988 only *Arizona (R)*. Team was a farm club of the Milwaukee Brewers.

Peoria, Illinois

4941 Reds 1883–84 *Northwestern (ind.)*; 1888 *Central Inter-State (ind.)*; 1937 *Three-I (B)*. The nineteenth-century players wore red hose. Originally **Red Stockings**, newspapers shortened it to **Redlegs** and "Reds." The 1937 team was a farm club of the Cincinnati Reds.

4942 Canaries 1889 *Central Inter-State (ind.)*; 1890 *Western Inter-State (ind.)*; 1891 *Northwestern (ind.)*; 1892m *Illinois–Iowa (ind.)*. Team moved to Aurora (IL) June 7. Players wore yellow hose. The 1889 team had three managers this season: Charles Bartson, Charles Flynn and Charles Levis. As a result, newspapers called the yellow-hosed players "Charlie's Canaries." Teams that wore yellow stockings in the nineteenth century were sometimes called the "Canaries."

4943 Distillers 1894–96x Team disbanded July 25; *Western Assn. (ind.)* 1900 *Central (ind.)*; 1902–03 *Western (A)*; m1904m *Central (B)*. Team started season in Marion (IN), moved to Peoria June 1, and then returned to Marion July 31; 1905–17x *Three-I (Illinois–Iowa–Indiana)(B)*. Season ended July 8 because of U.S. entry into World War I, but the league did not disband. Established in 1845, the city had built seven distilleries by 1860, which produced whiskey, bourbon and gin. Hiram Walker & Sons Distillery became the world's largest whiskey distillery. Peoria is known as "Whiskey Town."

4944 Blackbirds 1897 *Western Assn. (ind.)*. Players wore black hose. In the era 1890–1910, some teams had a bird nickname based on the players' stocking colors, i.e., Blackbirds, Bluebirds, Blue Jays, Canaries, Cardinals, Crows, Doves and Ravens.

4945 Tractors 1919–32x *Three-I (B)*; 1933 *Mississippi Valley (B)*; 1934 *Central (B)*; 1935 *Three-I (B)*. Factories here built farm and mining tractors for Illinois farms and coal mines.

4946 Red Wings 1946–51 *All-American Girls Professional Baseball League (ind.)*. Players wore red trim. The name was chosen not only as a spin-off of the 1937 Peoria Reds but also because of the nearby red-trim uniforms of the St. Louis Cardinals, also known as the Redbirds.

4947 Chiefs 1953–57 *Three-I (B)*; 1984 to date *Midwest (A)*. Team in 1953 was a farm club of the Cleveland Indians. Although no longer a Cleveland farm club in 1954, the team retained the

Indians nickname. The current team logo is that of a Dalmatian, i.e., a fire dog wearing a firefighter's cap, which implies the image of a "fire chief" in an attempt to get away from the now politically incorrect image of an Indian chief.

4948 Suns 1983 *Midwest (A)*. Peoria is the "Bright Spot of America." The city has a planetarium at its Lakeview Park where solar studies are conducted. The name was switched to "Chiefs" in 1984 to avoid confusion with and a potential lawsuit from the National Basketball Association Phoenix Suns.

Perth, Western Australia, Australia

4949 Heat 1989–90–98–99 *Australian (W)*; 2010 to date *Australian (W)*. Western Australia is the most arid and sunny region of Australia. Summers here are warm and dry with numerous heat waves, although late afternoon sea breezes provide relief.

4950 Western Heelers 1999–2000 *International Baseball (W)*. The IBL was a circuit in Australia that replaced the Australian Baseball League but lasted only this one campaign. "Heelers" are dogs that were used in cattle drives in the nineteenth century and on ranches today.

Perth, Ontario, Canada

4951 Blue Cats 1936 *Canadian–American (C)*. Team was a farm club of the IL Montreal Royals, who in turn had a loose affiliation with the Brooklyn Dodgers. All three teams wore Dodger-blue trim uniforms. The blue catfish, i.e., the "Blue Cat," is found in nearby Murphy's Point Lake, Sharbot, Lake, Charleston Lake and Seeleys' Bay.

Perth-Cornwall, Ontario, Canada

4952 Braves 1936 *Canadian–American (C)*. The Iroquois battled French fur trappers, Ottawa-Cree, and Huron tribes in the seventeenth century. By 1850, waves of British and American settlers pushed the Iroquois into reservations scattered about Ontario. The team had a loose affiliation with the NL Boston Bees (nee Boston Braves), using the parent club's previous nickname.

4953 Bisons 1937 *Canadian–American (C)*. Team was a farm club of Buffalo Bisons. In the era 1950, some higher classification (AAA, AA) minor league teams had farm teams in the ranks of the lower classification (A, B, C, D) minor league teams.

Perth Amboy, New Jersey

4954 Pacers 1914 *Atlantic (D)*. Harness racing uses horses called "pacers" or "trotters." Monmouth Race Park hosted horse racing in New Jersey 1870–90 and 1892–93 but anti-gambling laws closed it in 1894. Before the park reopened in 1939, New Jersey racing fans went to Jerome Race Track in New York City. In the slang of this era, a winning sports team or standout athlete "sets the pace." Newspaper reporters, who also covered horse racing, called the team the "Pacers."

Peru, Indiana

4955 Peru Base Ball Club 1890 *Indiana State (ind.)*. Team had no nickname.

Petach Tikva, Israel

4956 Pioneers 2007 *Israeli (ind.)*. City was founded in 1878 by settlers known as "The Pioneers." The circuit disbanded after the 2007 season.

4957 Ra'anan Express 2007 *Israeli (ind.)*. The rapid transit train running between Petach Tokva and Tel Aviv is named the Ra'anan Express. The circuit disbanded after the 2007 season.

Petaluma, California

4958 Incubators 1910 *Central California (D)*. Team was sponsored by an egg production company. Young players on the team were sometimes called "Chicks." Nearby poultry farms utilize incubators to hatch poultry eggs. With manager Dennis Healey at the helm, newspapers called the players "Dennis Healy's Incubators." Petaluma is the "Egg Basket of the World."

Petersboro, Ontario, Canada

Note: City was spelled Petersborough in 1912.

4959 White Caps 1912 Canadian *(C 1912–13, B 1914)*. City is built along Lake Ontario and Georgia Bay whose stormy seas whip up a "white cap"—a wave with a foaming, broken white crest. Players wore all-white caps.

4960 Petes 1912 Canadian *(C 1913, B 1914)*. The moniker "Petes," not found in the dictionary, was a space-saving tag dreamed up by a local reporter for newspaper headlines, i.e., "Petes edge Tecumsehs, 3–2."

Petersburg, Virginia

4961 Petersburg Base Ball Club 1885–86 *Virginia (ind.)*. Team had no nickname.

4962 Champs 1894 *Virginia (ind.)*. The team won the 1894 league pennant.

4963 Farmers 1895–96m. Team moved to Hampton (VA) August 13. Farms in the region transport produce to city processing and packing houses.

4964 Goobers m1910–17x *Virginia (C)*. Team started the 1910 season in Portsmouth (VA) and then moved here July 5. In 1917, the team and circuit disbanded May 15 because of U.S. entry into World War I; 1918x *Virginia (C)*. City and team disbanded June 28 due to U.S. entry into World War II; 1919–21m *Virginia (C 1919, B 1920–21)*. Team moved to Tarboro (VA) August 2; 1924 *Virginia (B)*. Farms in the region transport peanuts to city processing and packing houses. With manager John J. Grim at the helm, newspapers called the players "Grim's Goobers."

4965 Hustlers 1911 *Virginia (C)*. "Hustlers" was a complimentary slang for "baseball players." In this era, there was no connotation of gambling. The emphasis was on players who played hard, i.e., "The players hustled and won the game." With manager Henry Busch at the helm, newspapers called the players "Henry Busch's Hustlers."

4966 Trunkmakers 1923 *Virginia (B)*. City had numerous luggage and trunk factories in the nineteenth and early twentieth century.

4967 Broncos 1926–28x *Virginia (B)*. Team and league disbanded June 3. With manager Charles Connolly at the helm, newspapers called the players "Connolly's Broncos." Tom Abbot took over in mid-season and the name became "Abbot's Broncos." With Olin Pratt at the managerial helm in 1927, the name became "Olin's Bronchos," and in 1928, with Earl Hanson as the field skipper, the name became "Hanson's Bronchos." In the era 1880–1930, baseball players were often referred to by Wild West names, i.e., Braves, Colts, Indians, Ponies, Rustlers, and Broncos.

4968 Rebels 1941–42 *Virginia (C)*. In June 1864, Robert E. Lee sent General Meade to lead 50,000 Confederate troops to defend the city of Petersburg against Ulysses S. Grant's 113,000 Union soldiers.

With manager Clarence Pickrel at the helm, newspapers called the players "Clarence Pickrel's Rebels." Steve Mizerak took over in 1942 and the name became "Mizerak's Rebels."

4969 Generals 1948–50 *Virginia (C).* General Benedict Arnold's British forces pillaged the city in 1780. In 1781, British general Charles Cornwallis attacked the city but was driven back to Yorktown where he surrendered to George Washington, ending the Revolutionary War. Robert E. Lee placed 50,000 Confederate troops here to defend against Ulysses Grant's 113,000 Union troops in June 1864. Grant won the battle and laid siege to the city.

Philadelphia, Pennsylvania

4970 Athletics 1870 *Independent;* 1871–75 *National Assn. (M);* 1876 *National (M);* 1877 *League Alliance (ind.);* 1881 *Eastern Championship Assn. (M);* 1882–91 *American Assn. (M);* 1892 *Eastern (ind.);* 1894 *Pennsylvania State (ind.);* 1896 *Pennsylvania State (ind.);* m1896–97 *Atlantic (ind.).* Team started 1896 season in New York and moved to Philadelphia July 13; 1900m *Atlantic (ind.).* Team moved to Harrisburg (PA) May 10; 1901–54 *American (M).* Starting in 1859 as the "Athletic Town Ball Club of Philadelphia," team switched to playing baseball in 1860 and re-named itself the "Athletic Baseball Club of Philadelphia." The team turned semi-professional in 1869, and went professional in 1870. The team joined the NA in 1871 and then switched to the NL in 1876. Over the years, nine other Philadelphia baseball franchises used the name.

4971 A's 1870 *Independent;* 1871–75 *National Assn. (M);* 1876 *National (M);* 1877 *League Alliance (ind.);* 1881 *Eastern Championship Assn. (M);* 1882–91 *American Assn. (M);* 1892 *Eastern (ind.);* 1894 *Pennsylvania State (ind.);* 1896 *Pennsylvania State (ind.);* m1896–97 *Atlantic (ind.).* Team started 1896 season in New York and moved to Philadelphia July 13; 1900m *Atlantic (ind.).* Team moved to Harrisburg (PA) May 10. 1901–54 *American (M).* Starting in 1870, all Philadelphia Athletic uniforms displayed a gothic "A" on the left breast of the jersey. In use for 142 years, it has since become the most famous "single-letter" identification for a baseball team.

4972 Blue Stockings 1871–75 *National Assn. (M).* Players wore blue stockings. Newspapers shortened it to **Blues** and **Blue Legs**. By the 1880s, the name was passé in Philadelphia, even if the players on a team there wore blue hose. Four big league teams today sport blue stirrups — the Blue Jays, Cubs, Dodgers and Royals.

4973 Quaker City 1873–75 *National Assn. (M).* Used alternatively with the plural Quaker Citys. In the 19th century many baseball teams slavishly used city nicknames, i.e., Capital City, Garden City, Gate City, Forest City, Monumental City, Flour City, Zephyr City and Quaker City. The newspaper-friendly spinoff became Quakers which is sometimes used even today.

4974 Pearls 1873–75 *National Assn. (M).* Players wore pearl white stockings.

4975 White Stockings 1873–75 *National Assn. (M).* With the Chicago White Stockings disbanded after the 1871 season, some newspapers called the white-hosed Philadelphia players the "White Stockings."

4976 Phillies 1873–75 *National Assn. (M);* 1881 *Eastern Assn. (M); 1882 League Alliance (ind.);* 1883 to date *National (M).* First used by an amateur Philadelphia baseball team in 1866, a "Phillie" means an inhabitant of the city of Philadelphia, but it was also a newspaper contraction of "Philadelphias." The city itself is often known as "Philly." With manager Horace Phillips at the helm in 1882, newspapers called the players "Phillips' Phillies." In 1883, player-manager Al Reach chose "Phillies"—a moniker used three times before to give the team a unique identity apart from the NA-NL-ECA-AA Philadelphia Athletics. Reach declared to reporters about the name: "It tells you who we are and where we're from." The moniker had its greatest emphasis in 1883 (Wright), 1890 (newspapers) and in 1933, when the tag finally became official and appeared for the first time as lettering on player jerseys.

4977 Fergy's Fillies 1873–75 *National Assn. (M).* Ferguson Malone managed the team.

4978 Snowballers 1874 *National Assn. (M).* In April 1874 several games in Philadelphia were "snowed out."

4979 Centennial 1875 *National Assn. (M).* Team was named in honor of the Philadelphia 1776–1876 Centennial Exhibition. The name was sometimes pluralized, i.e., **Centennials.**

4980 Chocolate Sox 1875 After two seasons wearing white stockings (1873–74), the players wore chocolate-brown hose.

4981 Blue Stockings 1876 *National (M);* 1883–91 *American Assn. (M).* Players wore blue hose. Newspapers shortened it to **Blue Legs** and **Blues.**

4982 Bastards 1876 *National (M).* Chicago club owner William Hulbert wrote a letter to Charles Fowle, owner of the St. Louis club, to complain about the "double-dealing bastards" in reference to the owners of the Philadelphia Athletics for trying to engage in shady business dealings.

4983 Phils 1883 to date *National (M).* Moniker was a newspaper abbreviation that actually became the franchise's official nickname for a few months in 1942 in an ill-advised effort to get away from the losing image of "Phillies." But the fans gagged on the now-official nickname as the 1942 team finished last with a 42–109 record, 62-and-a-half games behind first-place St. Louis. The moniker has been used in newspaper headlines since 1883, i.e., "Phils beat Nats, 5–3."

4984 Conquering Heroes 1883 *American Assn. (M).* The Athletics won the 1883 American Association pennant despite numerous player injuries. In a September cartoon in a Philadelphia newspaper the A's players were depicted as wounded soldiers of the Revolutionary War trudging home, bloodied, on crutches and wagons. The injuries may have prompted the A's management to decline playing the NL champion Boston Red Stockings in a NL-AA "World Series."

4985 Infants 1883 *National (M).* "Infants" was a nineteenth century generic name for a team of mostly young players who struggled to win games in a "fast" (i.e., competitive) league. The 1883 expansion Phillies struggled mightily, compiling a horrendous 17–81 record to finish last in the National League.

4986 Quakers 1883 to date *National (M);* 1890 *Players (M).* Used alternately with "Phillies" in the 1880s, the name persisted until well into the 1950s. By the 1960s, however, with University of Pennsylvania college teams starting to use "Quakers" more than their official team moniker of "Red and Blue," the use of Quakers with the NL baseball team in Philadelphia started to fade. The name does appear in newspaper by-lines here and there. Although some historians claim the team was "Quakers" in the 1880s and then "Phillies" in the 1890s, newspaper accounts show that both terms were interchangeably as far forward as 1910. A schism occurred in 1890, with newspapers favoring "Quakers" for the Players League team and "Phillies" for the National League team. Starting in 1891, "Phillies" became the quasi-official team name for the surviving NL team (the PL had disbanded), while "Quakers" became the permanent unofficial, alternate moniker.

4987 Fillies 1883–95 *National (M).* Tag was an alternate spelling that never caught on. When the Brooklyn team, managed by Dave Foutz in 1895, was called "Foutz' Fillies," the "Philadelphia Fillies" name faded away.

4988 Keystones 1884 *Union Assn. (M).* Pennsylvania is the "Keystone State." An amateur team called the Philadelphia Keystones began play in 1859. In baseball jargon, the "keystone" is second base and the second baseman and shortstop constitute the "keystone combination."

4989 Reds 1884 *Reserve (ind.).* The players wore red hose.

4990 Ice Wagon Gang 1886 *National (M).* Tag was slang that referred to either a very slow team, i.e., "plodding like a slow moving ice wagon," or a fast, base-stealing team, i.e., "racing like a runaway ice wagon." In this case, the latter meaning applied as the 1886 Phillies led the NL in stolen bases with 326 swipes. The tag was coined by the *Philadelphia North American* August 4, 1886.

4991 Gorhams 1888 *Independent Negro team*; 1887 *National League of Colored Baseballists (ind.).* Team played as a semi-professional outfit in Gorham (NY) in 1887, turned all-professional in this circuit (which disbanded May 23), and then moved to Philadelphia in 1888 to play as the all-professional Philadelphia Gorham Giants.

4992 Giants 1889 *Middle States (ind.)*; 1906 *International (ind.)* and *Independent Negro team.* Black teams of this season, i.e., Trenton Cuban-X-Giants and Philadelphia Giants, emulated the 1888–89 world champion New York Giants by selecting this nickname. The 1906 team, using the 1889 nickname, joined the International League of Independent Professional Baseball Clubs in August in between playing an independent schedule. When the team challenged Chicago AL in October 1906 to a "world's championship game," White Sox owner Charles Comiskey refused to play.

4993 Dismal Athletics 1890 *American Assn. (M).* A name used by baseball authors Gary Gillette and Pete Palmer to describe the 1890 A's club, already decimated by PL player raids, that lost its last 22 games to drop its 54–56 record to 54–78. They wound up in seventh place in the 1890 American Association.

4994 Ponies 1890 *National (M).* Just as the Chicago Colts, Cleveland Infants and Pittsburgh Innocents had young players because of the signing wars between the NL and Players League, the Philadelphia Nationals were called the "Ponies" (a generic name for young players) because of the numerous rookies and young players on the roster. Actually, the "Ponies" did quite well, going 84–57, good for a third-place finish in the weakened 1890 National League.

4995 Students 1890 *National (M).* Another generic moniker for young players. In the minor leagues of this era, college-age players often played spring games for their college team and then signed with the minor league professional baseball team located in their college town.

4996 Troubadours 1890 *American Assn. (M).* This season the Athletics finished seventh of eight American Association teams with a crummy 54–78 record, prompting Philadelphia newspapers to brand the players a bunch of "troubadours." A troubadour is an actor in mask and costume up on stage. Philadelphia fans and newspapers complained that the Athletic players were "masquerading as professional and even big league players," i.e., wearing uniforms, spikes and sporting big league equipment while actually performing like amateur players

4997 Red Quakers 1890, 1901–02, 1911–42 *National (M).* In 1890 Philadelphia had three teams—the blue-hosed AA Athletics, the red-hosed NL Phillies and the blue-hosed PL Quakers. Some newspapers called the NL club the "Red Quakers" to distinguish them from the other two clubs. The moniker reappeared in 1901, when the Philadelphia Phillies went back to red hose, while the Philadelphia Athletics used blue hose. The Athletics used blue trim annually, without exception, right up to their last season in Philadelphia in 1954. The Phillies used red trim (i.e., piping, letters and stirrups) with certain exceptions, i.e., 1903–10 and 1943–49. By 1942 the moniker "Red

Quakers" had become passé. The team switched to blue-trim in 1943 with a new nickname—the Blue Jays.

4998 Colts 1894 *Pennsylvania State (ind.).* Team had numerous young players on the team who, in the slang of the day, were known as "colts." The word "rookie" would not be coined until 1895 and enter into popular use until 1917. The team was a farm club of the Philadelphia Phillies.

4999 The Greatest Hitting Machine of All-Time 1894 *National (M).* Tag was coined by baseball author David Nemec to describe the 1894 Phillies, who had a major league record .349 *team* batting average. Billy Hamilton scored 192 runs on 220 hits, and there were *four* .400 hitters—Tuck Turner (.416), San Thompson (.407), Ed Delahanty (.407), and Billy Hamilton (.404). The hitters benefitted from the new 60'6" pitching distance.

5000 Mack's Braves 1901–11 *American (M).* "Braves" was a generic moniker for "baseball players" in this era. It was complimentary in praise of the "brave players" who garnered AL pennants in 1902, 1905, 1910 and 1911. "Braves" had first been used in 1877 and was a generic moniker until the Boston Nationals appropriated it in 1912.

5001 Mack's Red Men 1901–11 *American (M).* Tag was a spin-off from "Mack's Braves."

5002 Mack Men 1901–51 *American (M).* In the era 1895–1915 "manager nicknames" were pretty much a dime a dozen. By the time of the Athletics AL pennants 1929–31, the tag "Mack Men" was a proud title in Philadelphia. Mack managed the team for a record fifty years. Newspapers contracted the moniker to the still-shorter **Macks.**

5003 Blue Quakers 1901–54 *American (M).* In an era when team nicknames were not only unofficial but also quite nebulous, a typical newspaper gimmick was to assign a stocking color to a city nickname. Hence, starting in 1901 the AL Philadelphia Athletics were known as the **Blue Quakers** while the NL Philadelphia Phillies were called the **Red Quakers.** The Athletics maintained blue-trim uniforms and blue stirrups until their last season in Philadelphia in 1954. The Phillies mostly wore red-trim uniforms (i.e., red piping, red striped stirrups and red letters on the jersey) with a few gaps in the 1930s and 1940s. In 1955 the gimmick ended when the A's moved to Kansas City.

5004 Discards 1902 *National (M).* The 1902 team was called the "Discards" because they were raided by American League teams, forcing them to sign young players and washed-up veterans who had been "discarded" (i.e., given their unconditional release or not offered a contract) by other teams. The lack of talent showed as the "Discards" finished last with a 56–81 record. Only four regulars and one lone pitcher returned from the 1901 squad as management sifted through 31 players in 1902.

5005 Mack's Marvels 1902–14 *American (M).* This first edition of winning Athletic teams was called "Mack's Marvels"—in the style of the Brooklyn "Superbas," St. Louis "Perfectos," and Pittsburgh "Premiers." These "adoration nicknames" were common to this era and "Mack's Marvels" received this adoration by winning AL pennants in 1902, 1905, 1910–11 and 1913–14. The offense was provided by hitters Jimmy Collins (Hall of Fame), Lave Cross, Harry Davis, Dave Fultz, Topsy Hartsel, Matty McIntyre, Danny Murphy, Eddie Murphy, Simon Nicolls, Wally Schang, Socks Seybold and Ossee Shreckengost. The pitching was also "marvelous" with such hurlers as Chief Bender (Hall of Fame), Bill Bernhard, Boardwalk Brown, Joe Bush, Andy Coakley, Jack Coombs, Jimmy Dygent, Chick Fraser, Duke Houk, Bert Husting, Eddie Plank (Hall of Fame), Rube Waddell (Hall of Fame) and Snake Wittse.

5006 White Elephants 1902–54 *American (M).* During the 1902 season when a reporter asked then AL Baltimore Orioles player-manager John McGraw before a game against the A's what he thought of the Athletics, McGraw sneered, "They're a bunch of "White Elephants!" "White Elephant" refers to a person or animal that doesn't try very hard and is pampered. When Athletics manager Connie Mack saw McGraw's remarks in a newspaper story the next day, it so angered him that he ordered "White Elephant" mascot logos sewn onto the players' cold-weather sweaters. When the A's won AL pennants in 1902, 1905, 1910–11, 1913–14, Mack proudly called his charges the "White Elephants" as a moniker of pride. By 1918 a "White Elephant" logo appeared on the left sleeve of the players' uniforms. Although the logo was dropped after 1927, the moniker persisted in newsprint. White elephants of ancient Burma, Thailand, Laos and Cambodia were worshiped as divine beings. As the symbol of the monarchy, they were maintained near the royal palace and did no labor.

5007 Giants 1903–13 *Independent Negro team.* The tag "Giants" was popular for black teams. In October 1906, this team challenged the 1906 World Series champion Chicago White Sox to a game for the "world's title." Chicago rejected the bid. Led by player-manager Rube Foster between 1904 and 1909, the "Rube Foster's Giants" won five Eastern Negro championships.

5008 Misfits 1904 *National (M).* "Misfits" was a generic name of the era (1895–1905) given to a team that experienced a large number of defeats. Managed by Hugh Duffy, the "Misfits" had no .300 hitters and only one pitcher (Frank Corridon, posting six wins and five losses) with a winning record en route to a 52–100 mark and a last-place finish in 1904.

5009 Nod Boys October 1905 *American (M).* Although Athletic fans were delighted that the A's won the 1905 AL pennant, they accused the players of being "asleep on the field" during the 1905 World Series, easily won by the NL champion New York Giants of John McGraw, 4 games to 1.

5010 Professionals 1906 *International Independent (ind.).* An all-professional outfit playing against black teams in the ILIPBC, this team had only white players.

5011 Culture City Clan 1906–14 *American (M).* Philadelphia is nicknamed the "City of Culture." The Athletics of this era certainly were a ballclub of "high culture," winning AL pennants in 1910–11 and 1913–14 and World Series' championships in 1910–11 and 1913.

5012 Quaker Giants 1909 *Independent Negro team.* Philadelphia is the "Quaker City." In the era 1870–1920, all Philadelphia teams were identified by the generic tag of "Quakers."

5013 Black Phillies 1910 *Independent Negro team.* Moniker was a spinoff from the National League Phillies.

5014 Live Wires 1915 *National (M).* With America becoming wired for electricity, team owner William Baker, excited about his team contending for its first pennant ever (after 32 seasons in the NL), proposed calling the team the "Live Wires." But local newspapers and fans, already incredulous at the hideous names of Federal League teams, refused to use the moniker.

5015 The Little Girl with Curls 1915–54 *American (M).* Baseball writer Harry Robert and editor Ed Fitzgerald, in their 1959 book entitled *The American League,* described the Philadelphia Athletics as the "little girl with the curl in the middle of her forehead. When the A's were good (1902–14, 1927–33), they were very good, but when they were bad (1915–26, 1934–54) ... they were horrid!"

5016 Subterranean Denizens 1916 *American (M).* The 1916 Athletics set a modern AL record for fewest wins in a 154-game schedule with an appalling 36–117 record for a last-place finish. Only the 1899 Cleveland Spiders had a worse record, going 20–134 in the regular season. Owner-manager Connie Mack had completed a two-year gutting of the team because he was cash-strapped.

5017 Hilldale Daisies 1918–22 *Independent Negro team; Eastern Colored (M).* 1923–28; *American Negro (M);* 1932 *East–West (ind.);*

Negro National (M). 1934–37; 1945 *United States (ind.).* Team, established in 1910 as amateurs, wore daisy yellow hose 1910–17, then switched to red when they turned professional in 1918. Hilldale is a Philadelphia suburb.

5018 Phoolish Phillies 1919–30 *National (M).* By 1930, some Philadelphia newspapers started calling the team the "Phoolish Phillies," citing the bad trades and managerial hirings that owner William Baker had made in the preceding twenty seasons. The newspapers, at the time, were totally unaware that the Phillies fortunes were about to get much worse, i.e., the "Great Depression" and its poster child — the "Futile Phillies."

5019 Faltering Phillies 1919–49 *National (M).* Tag was a spinoff from the "Futile Phillies" (which started to appear in newspapers in 1941), coined by baseball author Richard Orodenker.

5020 Doormats of the National League 1919–49 *National (M).* In this thirty-one-year period, the Phillies finished last in the National League no less than sixteen times. The tag was coined by baseball writer Richard Orodenker.

5021 Hapless Phillies 1919–49 *National (M).* "Hapless" was a moniker applied to several MLB franchises that endured the misfortunes of chronic losing, i.e., the Hapless Browns, Hapless Senators, Hapless Red Sox (1920s), Hapless Braves and the Hapless Phillies. The adjective was popularized by a 1971 article in *Baseball Digest* and by baseball author W. Harrison Daniel in a 2003 baseball book.

5022 Madison Stars 1920 *Independent Negro team.* Team's home field was on Madison Avenue. "Stars" was the second-most popular nickname for black teams after "Giants."

5023 Stars 1923 *Independent Negro team.* After "Giants," the moniker "Stars" was the most popular nickname for black baseball teams. Newspapers liked it.

5024 Royal Giants 1925–31–32 *Southern California Winter (W);* 1937–38–39–40 *Southern California Winter (W).* The nucleus of the team came from the Brooklyn Royal Giants, playing summer and autumn games in Philadelphia before traveling to Los Angeles in November 1925.

5025 Famous Athletics 1927–32 *American (M).* This tag was given to the teams that won 596 games in the period 1927–32, including three straight AL pennants 1929–31. The "Famous Athletics" had such great hitters as Ty Cobb (Hall of Fame), Mickey Cochrane (Hall of Fame), Eddie Collins (Hall of Fame), Al Simmons (Hall of Fame), Zack Wheat (Hall of Fame), Jimmy Fox (Hall of Fame) and Jimmy Dykes and formidable pitchers Lefty Grove (Hall of Fame), John Quinn, George Earnshaw, Rube Walker and Waite Hoyt.

5026 Tigers 1928 *Independent Negro team.* Players wore striped stirrups.

5027 Bull Elephants 1929 *American (M).* Tag was a spin-off of "White Elephants" for the 1929 American League and World Series champions. The offense was as powerful as a Bull Elephant with Jimmy Foxx, Al Simmons, Mickey Cochrane, Al Simmons and Jimmy Dykes doing the hitting. The pitching arms of the hurlers were as strong as an elephant's trunk as George Earnshaw, Lefty Grove, Rube Walberg, Ed Rommel and Howard Ehmke helped produce 104 victories. The "Bull Elephants" trampled the NL champion Chicago Cubs in the seventh inning of Game 3 with 10 runs to turn an 8–0 deficit into a 10–8 victory en route to a 4 games to 1 World Series victory.

5028 Futile Phillies 1941 to date *National (M).* Probably the third-most famous unofficial team nickname in major league baseball (after "Bronx Bombers" and "Bums"), the retroactive tag was used by weary Phillies fans and Philadelphia newspapers to describe the perennially losing Phillies. In the period 1919–30 the "Futile Phillies" finished in last place eight of twelve years. Then in the years 1936–45, the Phillies finished last eight of ten seasons. Some success in the early 1950s quickly degenerated into "futile" eras in 1954–61, 1988–92, and 1996–2000 before the trio of pennants of 2008–09, 2011. As a historical name, it refers to the Phillies era of 1919–49, although it was used by demanding Philadelphia fans whenever their team experiences a lengthy losing streak. A 2005 historical spin-off was the rather lame alliteration Phailures. Phillie pennants in 1980, 1983, 1993, 2008–09 and a 102-win season in 2011 has shelved the sorry moniker for the time being.

5029 Blue Jays 1943–49 *National (M).* New team owner William Carpenter, stung by the Philadelphia fans' epithet of "Futile Phillies," held a name-the-team contest that chose to a new nickname — the "Blue Jays." Almost at once the nickname sunk into oblivion, bred of controversy. Students at Johns Hopkins University (whose own sports teams were the "Blue Jays") protested to Phillies owner Bob Carpenter Jr. about usurping their mascot. They berated the NL franchise for its 15 last-place finishes and its 12 100+ seasonal losses. Carpenter fired back in the press, "What about Johns Hopkins teams? They haven't won a ball game in 20 years, have they? I saw their team once. Boy! What a ragged outfit!" Newspaper reporters gleefully covered the screaming match, forcing Carpenter to lamely blurt out, "We're not changing the name from Phillies to Blue Jays — just changing the trim from red to blue and not the nickname." A little blue jay logo was sewn onto the left sleeve of the uniforms while the trim color was changed from red to blue. But the moniker "didn't fly" as the team kept right on losing, averaging 95 defeats per year through the 1948 season. In 1950 the uniform trim color switched back to red and "Phillies" was reinstalled as the official nickname while the team fortuitously improved from a decent 81 victories in 1949 to 91 victories in 1950 that clinched the NL pennant. One Phillie fan had the last laugh in any case. In 1943 that fan submitted an entry in the contest. His entry was "Stinkers." The winning entry of "Blue Jays" was submitted by Philadelphian Mrs. John L. Crooks. Strangely, the name "Blue Jays" never appeared on Philadelphia uniforms. The uniform blouse displayed "Philadelphia" and "Phila." The only identification of the moniker was a very small blue jay mascot logo on the left sleeve of the player uniform. The contest had 5,064 fans submitting their suggestions. Mrs. Crooks won a $100 war bond.

5030 Whiz Kids 1950 *National (M).* In 1950, the Phillies had one of the youngest rosters in the major leagues. Led by hitters Richie Asburn (Hall of Fame), Andy Seminick, Dick Sisler and Eddie Waitkus and pitchers Robin Roberts (Hall of Fame), Curt Simmons and Jim Konstanty, the "Whiz Kids" won the 1950 National League pennant. The name derives from a popular 1940s radio show called *Whiz Kids* — a contest in which high–IQ kids won prize money for answering general knowledge questions (sort of like the *Jeopardy* TV show of today).

5031 Cardiac Kids 1950 *National (M).* The Phillies, a young team with a sprinkling of veterans, won quite a few games this season with come-from-behind victories that left Phillies fans emotionally wrenched. The name is used in other sports.

5032 Fightin' Phillies 1950 to date *National (M).* As the Phillies won their first pennant in 35 seasons (and only their second NL flag in 67 years), excited Phillies fans praised their players as the "Fightin' Phillies." Indeed, the Phillies had to "fight" their way through a three-team pennant race as Brooklyn finished in second place, two games back with New York in third place, five games back. Although the name faded in the 1960s when the team started losing again, it has appeared sporadically in the media, especially in the subsequent pennant years of 1980, 1983, 1993 and 2008–09. The contracted **Fightin's** has also been used. Phighting Phillies and Phightin's. Phillies players have been noted for their "hard-nosed" play over the years.

5033 Fizz Kids 1958–61 *National (M).* In an unfriendly spin-off of "Whiz Kids," angry Philadelphia fans called this bunch of losers

the "Fizz Kids" as the team "fizzled" year-in and year-out to finish in last place four consecutive seasons with 69–85, 64–90, 59–95 and 47–107 records. In 1961, during the months of July and August, the Phillies and their fans had to endure a major league–record 23 consecutive defeats. Kids often shake a bottle or can of soda to watch it squirt all over their friends and then "fizzle out."

5034 El Foldo Phillies 1964 *National (M).* Tag was a Spanish-style moniker — both sympathetic and derogatory — for manager Gene Mauch's 1964 Phillies, who, bolstered by hitters Dick Allen, Johnny Callison and Wes Covington and along with capable pitching from Jim Bunning, Chris Short, Art Mahaffey and Jack Baldschun, were poised to capture the 1964 NL pennant with an excellent 90–60 record, placing them six-and-a-half games ahead with only 12 games to play in the schedule. The team then pulled off what newspapers called "El Foldo" as the Phils lost 10 games in a row, allowing the St. Louis Cardinals to take the pennant. The Phillies recovered to win their last two games but it was too late as the Cardinals (93–69) edged out the Phillies (92–70) by one game.

5035 Fizzle Phillies 1964 *National (M).* Tag was a spin-off of "Fizz Kids" to describe the team's catastrophic ten-game losing streak, which cost them the 1964 National League pennant.

5036 Phutile Phillies 1976–78 *National (M).* Although the Phillies won three consecutive N.L. Eastern Division titles these three seasons, each time they were defeated in the N.L. Championship Series by the Cincinnati Reds (1976) and the Los Angeles Dodgers (1977–78), prompting embittered Phillies fans and newspapers to brand the players as the "Phutile Phillies." This gaudy spelling gimmick was popular in the 1970s.

5037 Comeback Gang 1980 *National (M).* After a thirty-year drought, the Phillies won the National League pennant by staging repeated come-from-behind victories during regular season games. Led by hitters Pete Rose, Mike Schmidt (Hall of Fame), Greg Luzinski, Bob Boone, Manny Trillo, Garry Maddox and Bake McBride and pitchers Steve Carlton (Hall of Fame), Ken Brett, Jim Lonborg, Larry Christensen, Ron Reed, Dick Ruthven and Tug McGraw, the Phillies won the NL pennant and then defeated the AL champion Kansas City Royals in the 1980 World Series, 4 games to 2.

5038 The Team That Wouldn't Die 1980 *National (M).* Praising the Phillies players for their seeming endless comebacks, baseball author Hal Bodley wrote a book with the same title about the 1980 NL and World Series champion Phillies.

5039 Pillies 1981–82 *National (M).* Philadelphia newspapers did an exposé about Phillies players who were abusing amphetamines and called the pill-popping Phillies players the "Pillies."

5040 Wheeze Kids 1983 *National (M).* In a humorous play on words of the 1950 "Whiz Kids," a bunch of aging players (who no doubt gasped and wheezed as they ran the bases) fought off their arthritic aches and pains to win a surprise 1983 National League pennant. Led by such oldsters and veterans as Pete Rose (age 42), Joe Morgan (39), Garry Maddox (33), Mike Schmidt (33), Gary Mathews Sr. (32), Bo Diaz (age 30), and Ivan DeJesus (age 30), and pitchers Ron Reed (40), Steve Carlton (38), Tug McGraw (38), John Denny (30) and Al Holland (30), the Phillies won their third National League pennant.

5041 Quick-Change Phillies 1987–89 *National (M).* In the course of only three seasons, the Phillies had four field managers, had a 75 percent turnover of their player roster, and said goodbye to Mike Schmidt, who retired in May 1989. There were only four players on the roster in 1987 who appeared for the Phillies in 1989 — Schmidt, Von Hayes, Steve Jeltz and Chris James. There was 100 percent turnover of pitchers.

5042 The Softball Team 1993 *National (M).* The 1993 Phillies looked like a Saturday "beer and bratwurst" softball league team, as they won a surprise National League pennant in 1993. Led by hitters Greg Luzinski, Lenny Dykstra, John Kruk, Darrin Dalton, Mickey Morandini, Dave Hollins and Ricky Jordan and pitchers Terry Mulholland, Mitch Williams and Curt Schilling, the scraggly-bearded, big-bellied "softball team" won the NL Eastern Division and then defeated the Atlanta Braves in the NL Championship Series, 4 games to 2, to win the franchise's fourth National League pennant.

5043 Macho Row 1993 *National (M)*. If beer bellies, scruffy beards, and arm tattoos can be interpreted by women as "macho," then these guys were certainly a "Macho Row" in winning the 1993 NL pennant. The offense provided 156 home runs and a league-leading 297 doubles to score a league-high 877 runs, which spurred this spin-off tag from the old New York Yankees "Murderer's Row" of 1926–28.

5044 Broad Street Bellies 1993 *National (M)*. Tag was a humorous spin-off from the NHL Philadelphia Flyers' "Broad Street Bullies" of the 1970s. The Phillies hitters were conspicuous for their beards, raggedy locks and beer bellies—none of which impeded them from batting .274 and hitting 156 home runs en route to the National League pennant.

5045 The Good, Bad & Ugly Phillies 2008 *National (M)*. Tag was coined by Philadelphia sportswriter Todd Zolecki to describe the play of the Phillies—which varied from good to bad to ugly—as the Philly fans underwent emotional torture until the team played good enough in September to pull ahead of the Atlanta Braves, win the NL Eastern Division title, the 2008 NL pennant, and the 2008 World Series over the AL champion Tampa Bay Rays, 4 games to 1. Name reflected the famous Sergio Leone 1967 "Spaghetti Western" of the same title. Zolecki used the name in reflection of Phillies history since the franchise's inception in 1883. The "Good" eras were 1915, 1950, 1980–93, 2008–09; the "Bad" eras were 1883–1914, 1916–18, 1951–79, 1990–2007; and the "Ugly" era was 1919–49.

5046 Philthies 2008 to date *National (M)*. New York Mets fans reviled the 2008–09 back-to-back NL pennant winners by hurling this rather cleverly spelled epithet at the Philadelphians. Less inventive and more vulgar tags included the homophobic **Phags** and **Phaggots.**

5047 Sillies 2008 to date. With the team now an NL powerhouse, Mets fans and other detractors used this rather clever tag as a gesture of envious disrespect, which is a frequent exclamation of the Warner Brothers' cartoon star Daffy Duck.

5048 Phantastic Phillies 2008–09, 2011 *National (M)*. Coined by baseball writer Natalie King in her 2009 book of the same title, the tag praised the exploits of the back-to-back NL pennant-winning Phillies. The tag was also applied to the 2011 Phillies en route to their 105-win season.

Philipsburg, Montana

5049 Philipsburg Base Ball Club 1892 *Montana State (ind.)*. Team had no nickname.

Philipsburg, Pennsylvania

5050 Philipsburg Base Ball Club 1887 *Mountain League (ind.)*. Team had no nickname

Phoenix, Arizona

5051 Senators 1915 *Rio Grande Valley Assn. (D)*; 1928–30 *Arizona State (D)*; 1931–32 *Arizona–Texas (D)*; 1947–50 *Arizona–Texas (C)*; 1951 *Southwest International (C)*; 1952–53 *Arizona–Texas (C)*. Phoenix has been the state capital of Arizona since 1889. With man-

ager Herbert Hester at the helm in 1915, newspapers called the players "Hester's Senators."

5052 Stars 1954 *Arizona–Texas (C)*; 1955–57 *Arizona–Mexico (C)*. Team was a farm club of the Hollywood Stars. In the period 1900–50, some higher classification minor league teams (AAA and AA) maintained their own farm clubs in the lower classification minor leagues (A, B, C, D). From 1951 through 1957 the Pacific Coast League had an Open classification that allowed its teams (the Hollywood Stars included) to maintain their own farm clubs.

5053 Giants 1958–59 *Pacific Coast (AAA)*; 1966–85 *Pacific Coast (AAA)*. The teams were farm clubs of the San Francisco Giants.

5054 Firebirds 1986–97 *Pacific Coast (AAA)*. The Phoenix is a bird of Greek mythology who fell to Earth in flames and then magically rose again from its ashes. In 1867 Jack Swilling, a soldier and prospector, and Lord Darrell Dupa, an Englishman, rebuilt irrigation canals originally constructed by the Hohokam Indians. Duppa, predicting that a city would rise from the ruins of the Indian irrigation canals, named the site Phoenix. Phoenix, built in the Valley of the Sun, experiences many "fiery" days.

5055 Athletics 1988 *Arizona (R)*; 2011 to date *Arizona (R)*. Teams were farm clubs of the Oakland Athletics.

5056 Brewers 1988–95 *Gulf Coast (R)*. Team was a farm club of the Milwaukee Brewers.

5057 Diamondbacks 1996–97 *Arizona (R)*; 1998 to date *National (M)*. The 1996–97 team was a farm club of the expansion franchise Arizona Diamondbacks. Since 1993 major league expansion teams have fielded minor league teams for two or three seasons before the major league franchise began play to develop a ready-made farm club. The diamondback is a poisonous rattlesnake found in the southwest. The new team held a name-the-team contest. "Diamondbacks" was the winner. Some other entries included: Coyotes (already used by the NHL Phoenix Coyotes), Sauguros (used by a team in the Arizona Fall League), the Arizona Phoenix (after the mythical firebird known as the "Phoenix"), Scorpions (regional arthropod), and Rattlers (Diamondback Rattle Snake). The scientific name of the desert rattle snake is Crotalus Atrox. Team owner Jerry Colangelo chose Diamondbacks, explaining, "We wanted to put a little bite into our name."

5058 D-backs 1998 to date *National (M)*. Tag is used in newspaper headlines because "Diamondbacks" contains eleven letters, i.e., "D-Backs edge Mets, 4–3." The tag inspired Tampa Bay fans, starting in 2008, to stubbornly call their Florida team the "D-Rays" (after the defunct "Devil Rays") rather than the new, lame marketing moniker of "Tampa Bay Rays."

5059 Snakes 1998 to date *National (M)*. In the years 1895–1905 some baseball teams adopted "adoration nicknames," i.e., Superbas, Wonders, Premiers, Marvels and Perfectos. In other eras, baseball teams often preferred "low-down nicknames" like Field Rats, Gym Rats, Krazy Kats, Killers and Scrappers. As such, "Snakes" is a "low-down" moniker that has proven to be quite popular with Phoenix fans.

5060 White Sox 2001–02 *Arizona (R)*. Team was a farm club of the Chicago White Sox. The Arizona Rookie League is a complex league with teams playing in the greater Phoenix metropolitan area.

5061 Brewers 2001 to date *Arizona (R)*. Team was a farm club of the Milwaukee Brewers.

5062 Dodgers 2011 to date *Arizona (R)*. Team was a farm club of the Los Angeles Dodgers.

5063 Padres 2010 to date *Arizona (R)*. Team was a farm club of the San Diego Padres.

5064 Indians 2011 to date *Arizona (R)*. Team was a farm club of the Cleveland Indians.

5065 Rangers 2011 to date *Arizona (R)*. Team was a farm club of the Texas Rangers.

5066 Reds 2011 to date *Arizona (R)*. Team was a farm club of the Cincinnati Reds.

5067 Royals 2011 to date *Arizona (R)*. Team was a farm club of the Kansas City Royals.

Piedmont, West Virginia

5068 Piedmont Baseball Club m1906m *Pennsylvania–Ohio–Michigan (P.O.M.). (D)*. Team started season in Butler (PA), moved to Piedmont July 14, and then moved to Charleroi (PA) August 6; m1907m *Western Pennsylvania (D)*. Team started the 1907 season in Latrobe, moved Cumberland (MD) May 28, and then moved again to Piedmont June 27 before moving to Somerset July 5. The teams had no nickname.

5069 Drybugs 1916 *Potomac (D)*; 1918x *Blue Ridge (D)*. Although home games continued to be played in Piedmont, team went by the two-city name of Piedmont-Westernport Drybugs. Circuit and team disbanded June 16 because of U.S. entry into World War I. The city is built along the Potomac River, which attracts mosquitoes and other bugs. The "Dry Bugs" are insects that inhabit dusty fields. With manager Cy Harris at the helm, newspapers called the players "Cy's Drybugs." Dutch Kane took over in mid-season 1916 and the name became "Dutch's Dry Bugs."

Pikeville, Kentucky

5070 Brewers 1982 *Appalachian (R)*. Team was a farm club of the Milwaukee Brewers.

5071 Cubs 1983–84 *Appalachian I*. Team was a farm club of the Chicago Cubs.

5072 Rifles 1993–94 *Frontier (ind.)*. Tag refers to a famous firearm of the nineteenth century. First mentioned in a War of 1812 song, this rifle became the leading firearm in Kentucky by 1825 and was known as the "Kentucky Rifle."

Pinar del Rio, Pinar del Rio, Cuba

5073 Vequeros 1967–68–91–92 *Cuban National (S)*; 1992–93 to date *Cuban National (S)*. Plantations near the city transport tobacco to city factories for the production of tobacco products. Cuba is world famous for its cigars. Tobacco along with sugar is the island's leading cash crop. The name should not be confused with "Vaqueros" (cowboys). Vequeros means "cigar-makers."

5074 Forestales 1974–75–91–92 *Cuban National (S)*. Timber from nearby forests is transported to lumber mills in the city. Forestales means "Foresters."

5075 Isla de Pinos 1977–78 *Cuban National (S)*. Team's official name was "Isla de Pinos," anticipating a move of the team to Nueva Gerona on the Isla de Juventud off the southwest Cuban coast. Team disbanded after the season before the transfer could be realized.

5076 Pativerdes 1992–93 to date *Cuban National (S)*. Players wore green stirrups. "Los Pativerdes" means "Green Sox." The Cuban National Series and the Chinese Baseball Leagues play in communist countries where the players are "state subsidized," i.e., they are paid by the government to be equally competitive with professional players in capitalist countries.

Pine Bluff, Arkansas

5077 Infants 1887 *Southwest (ind.)*. Unlike Babes, Cubs, Colts, etc., "Infants" referred to a team of young players that struggled on the field and usually lost a lot of games. The term "rookie" (coined in 1892) became popular in 1917, and largely replaced all these tags in the 1920s.

5078 Lumbermen 1903–04 *Cotton States (D)*. Lumber is transported from the Quachita National Forest to wood mills. Wood mills here manufactured wood products from pine trees. With manager George Blackburn at the helm, newspapers called the players "Blackburn's Lumbermen."

5079 Barristers 1906x *Arkansas–Texas (D)*. Team and league disbanded August 26. Federal Judge Isaac Parker, born in Pine Bluff and known as "The Hanging Judge," from his court in Fort Smith (AR) had sole jurisdiction over Arkansas and the Indian Territory (later to become Oklahoma) from 1875–96. He and his deputy marshals, who ranged the plains on horseback, cleaned out this region of outlaws, bandits, rustlers, bank robbers and assorted cut-throats, hanging 79 men on the gallows in Fort Smith. Parker's marshals had 65 of their own men killed in pursuit. Barrister means "judge" or "lawyer."

5080 Pine Knotts 1908 *Arkansas State (D)*. Knotty Pine trees grow throughout Arkansas and in and around Pine Bluff. The pine knot is the joint between a branch and the tree trunk. The Ouachita National Forest, west of the city, is mostly a pine forest. A "knot" was a slang for a young man, usually a stupid one, which was quite descriptive of a typical baseball player in this era.

5081 Judges 1930–32x *Cotton States (D)*. Team and league disbanded July 13; m1933x *Dixie (R)*. Team started season in Waco (TX) and moved to Pine Bluff June 27, assuming the nickname of the 1932 club. Team disbanded August 22; 1934–35 *East Dixie (R)*; 1936–40 *Cotton States (R)*; 1950–55m *Cotton States (R)*. Team moved to Meridian (MS) June 16. Newspaper editors wanted a shorter spin-off from "Barristers." With LeRoy "Cowboy" Jones at the helm 1936–38, newspapers called the players "Jones' Judges." Jimmy Sherlin took over in 1939, and the name became "Jimmy's Judges." The name was retained in 1940 under Red Rollings as "Rolling's Judges."

5082 Cardinals 1948–49 *Cotton States (R)*. Team was a farm club of the St. Louis Cardinals.

5083 Locomotives 1996 *Big South (ind.)*. The St. Louis–Iron Mountain–Southern Railroad reached Little Rock in 1872 and Pine Bluff in 1874. By 1882, the Little Rock–Fort Smith Railroad started running. Minerals and coal were transported here by train for processing. The modern era of independent professional baseball began in 1993 with the arrival of the Frontier and Northern leagues.

Pine Tree, Maine

5084 Pine Tree Baseball Club 1907 *Maine State (D)*. Team had no nickname.

Ping-Tung, Taiwan

5085 Eagles 1993–97 *Chinese Professional (ind.)*. Circuit's official name is the Chinese Professional Baseball League. This circuit is distinct from the Chinese Baseball League of mainland People's Republic of China. The team owner—the *China Times* Newspaper Company—chose an English nickname for marketing purposes. The team's title was the "China Times Eagles." Popular monikers for Asian professional sports league teams include Bears, Dragons, Hawks, Lions, Tigers and Eagles. The Chinese Baseball League and the Cuban National Series are state-subsidized baseball leagues.

Piqua, Ohio

5086 Picks m1911 *Ohio State (D)*. Team started season in Newark (OH) and then moved to Piqua June 22. Reporters choose a diminutive of the city name to better fit into newspaper headlines, i.e., "Picks edge Gems, 5–4."

Pittsburg, California

5087 Diamonds 1948m *Far West (D)*. Team moved to Roseville (CA) July 3; 1949–51x *Far West (D)*. In the 1890s, the city became known as the "Black Diamond City" because of the coal and asphalt mine nearby. "Black diamond" is a slang term for coal, just as oil has the nickname "black gold." These nicknames demonstrate the great commercial value of oil and coal.

Pittsburg, Kansas

5088 Pittsburg Base Ball Club 1891 *Southwestern (ind.)*. Team had no nickname.

5089 Coal Diggers 1903–04 *Missouri Valley (D 1903, C 1904)*. With manager Claude East at the helm, newspapers called the players "Claude's Coal-diggers." John Kane took over in 1904 and the name became "Kane's Coal-diggers."

5090 Miners 1905 *Missouri Valley (D 1903, C 1904)*. Newspaper editors chose a shorter spin-off from "Coal Diggers."

5091 Champions 1906m *Kansas State (D)*. Team moved to Vinita (KS) June 6. Team won 1905 Missouri Valley League pennant.

5092 Pirates 1909 *Western Assn. (R)*; 1921 *Southwestern (D)*; m1952 *Kansas–Oklahoma–Missouri K.O.M. (D)*. Team started season as the Bartlesville Pirates and then moved to Pittsburg July 7. Monikers of the teams of 1909 and 1921 were named after the NL Pittsburgh (PA) Pirates. The farm system started in the 1920s. The 1952 team was a farm club of the NL Pittsburgh Pirates.

5093 Browns 1946–51 *K.O.M. (D)*. Team was a farm club of St. Louis Browns.

Pittsburgh, Pennsylvania

5094 Alleghenys 1876 *Independent*; 1877–78x *International Assn. (M)*. Team joined this major league in 1877. Team disbanded in June 29; 1882–86 *American Assn. (M)*; 1887–1911 *National (M)*. By 1887 the team was playing its home games in a ballpark within the Pittsburgh city limits. These teams were named after the Allegheny Mountains. Actually, the team's home ballpark was in Allegheny, Pennsylvania, a town just outside Pittsburgh that eventually became a suburb of Pittsburgh in the 1880s. Alternate spelling was the plural **Alleghenies**. Team's official name was the "Allegheny Baseball Club." Contemporary newspapers also called the team by the modern style "Pittsburgh Alleghenys." The name faded away in 1912 when "Pirates" became the team's official nickname. Newspapers often contracted the name to **Allies**.

5095 Slaughterhouse Nine 1882 *American Assn. (M)*. There was no screen to protect fans sitting in seats only 30 feet behind home plate and foul balls hit back into those seats caused fans to run and duck for life and limb. One newspaper complained there were so many "bloodied heads" back there that it was like a "slaughterhouse" for cattle.

5096 Brewers 1882–83 *American Assn. (M)*; 1884 *Union Assn. (M)*. Unlike Milwaukee teams, who were called the "Brewers" because of the beer industry there, this bunch of Pittsburgh players frequented pubs late into the night even before a game day. Baseball author David Nemec in his *Great Nineteenth Century Baseball Encyclopedia* called the 1883 Alleghenys the "Boozing, Brawling Bad Ass Alleghenies." In this context "Brewers" meant drunken players. The team started the season in Chicago and then moved to Pittsburgh August 20. The 1884 team, starting the season in Chicago, gained its nickname in the Windy City because the players were noted for their overindulgence in liquor at Chicago pubs. The name followed the team to Pittsburgh in August.

5097 Pratt's Lushers 1882–83 *American Assn. (M)*. One Pitts-

burgh newspaper called them (manager Al) "Pratt's Lushers." The tag "lusher" also referred to a hard-drinking person (originally "lush," coined in 1790).

5098 Smoky City 1882–86 *American Assn. (M)*; 1884 *Union Assn. (M)*; 1887–1920 *National (M)*. This was not a complimentary nickname. In the nineteenth century the factories in Pittsburgh had absolutely no state or federal guidelines to control their smoke output. The skies of Pittsburgh were dark with smoke and soot even on bright sunny days. Government-mandated reform did not reach Pittsburgh until 1910. Ironically, by the 1950s and 1960s, Pittsburgh had one of the best records for clean air in the country. Newspapers often pluralized the tag to **Smoky Citys**. In the 1920s the moniker became "politically incorrect" as social groups started to rally against Pittsburgh's air pollution.

5099 Stogies m1884 *Union Assn. (M)*. Team started the season in Chicago and moved to Pittsburgh August 20; 1890 *Players (M)*; 1914–15 *Federal (M)*. With many industrial smoke stacks polluting the air, Pittsburgh in the nineteenth century was known as the "Smoky City." The name, a spin-off from "Smoky City," was appropriate because baseball players in this era when dressed in street clothes almost always were seen in a saloon with a glass of beer in hand, while chewing a stogie (a long, roughly-made, thin cigar). The "stogie" was first produced at a tobacco factory in Conestoga (PA) in 1880. The 1914–15 teams, led by player-manager Rebel Oakes, were known as "Oakes' Stogies."

5100 Pittsburgh Base Ball Club 1884 *Reserve (ind.)*. Team had no nickname.

5101 Keystones 1887 *National Colored (ind.)*; 1921 *Independent Negro team*; 1922 *Independent Negro team*. Pennsylvania is known as the "Keystone State."

5102 Smoked Italians 1887–90 *National (M)*. Pittsburgh fans roared with laughter at the gauche and garish yellow and black-striped uniforms the ball players wore onto the field in 1887. They called the players the "Smoked Italians" because the colors were reminiscent of a "Smoked Italian" sandwich with dark beef on a bun dripping with mustard sauce. Amazingly, the uniform style was retained for four seasons.

5103 Potato Bugs 1887–90 *National (M)*. Again, fans howled in laughter at the yellow and black Pittsburgh uniforms, calling the players "Potato Bugs." A "potato bug" is a "June bug"—a black and yellow insect that frequents sandy beaches.

5104 Zulus 1887–90 *National (M)*. Tag was another nickname for the yellow and black Pittsburgh uniforms. The black and yellow colors resembled the colors of the costumes and shields of the Zulu warriors of Africa whose numerous revolts and conflicts with the colonial British frequently was big news in the 1880s.

5105 Lowlanders 1887–1911 *National (M)*. Allegheny Valley is known as the "Lowlands." The moniker of "Lowlanders" did not refer to the team's performance but rather it was a geographical moniker, much like the New York Highlanders playing at Highland Park in a hilly region of New York City.

5106 Gum Chewers 1889 *National (M)*. The team's three managers this season tried to curb the players' chewing of tobacco because of all the tobacco spit on the field. Pittsburgh fans laughed, as the managers practically forced the players to chew sticks of gum instead of wads of tobacco. It didn't work.

5107 Innocents 1890 *National (M)*. More than any other NL team, the Pirates were raided by Players League teams until there was only a shell of a team left. The team signed rookies and washed-up veterans and was simply not competitive, finishing with a horrendous 23–113 record for a last-place finish, 66-and-a-half games out of first place. In this era "Innocents" referred to a young team that is outplayed by older, more experienced teams.

5108 Burghers 1890 *Players (M)*. A resident of a city with -burgh as its suffix is known as a "burgher," i.e., Augsburg, Bloomsburg, Edinburg, Hamburg, and Pittsburgh.

5109 Troubadours 1890 *National (M)*. Except for outfielder Billy Sunday and catcher Doggie Miller, the entire roster of the 1889 team jumped to the Players League or to other NL and AA teams. The talent-depleted franchise signed minor leaguers and semi-pros who stumbled to a horrendous 23–113 record. Pittsburgh fans called these inadequate players "Troubadours"—which refers to an actor in a flashy costume—because although these players in major league uniforms looked like big leaguers, they were really minor leaguers and semi-pros impersonating big leaguers.

5110 Hecker's Kids 1890 *National (M)*. After losing 18 of 19 players from the 1889 roster, the team owners and manager Guy Hecker were forced to sign a dozen inexperienced ball players whose lesser talents assured the team's 23–113 last-place finish. With Guy Hecker at the helm as field skipper, newspapers called the players "Hecker's Kids."

5111 Hecker's School Boys 1890 *National (M)*. Whereas the average age of the 1889 team was nearly 30, the 1890 team included such youngsters as outfielder John Berger (age 23), third baseman Fred Roat (23), utility man Bill Wilson (23), and pitchers Fred Schmidt (24), John Sowders (24), Dave Anderson (22), Bill Phillips (22) and Kirtley Baker (21).

5112 Boobies 1891 *National (M)*. Although the Players League had disbanded and most ex–NL players had returned to the Senior Circuit, the newly named Pirates failed to get any hitters to improve on a feeble .239 team batting average. Lou Bierbauer, whose "pirating" away from the Athletics gave his new team their nickname, was a bust at second base, hitting a meager .206, and the rest the offense had no .300 hitters. Starters Mark Baldwin and Silver King combined to lose 57 games. The result was another last-place finish with a hardly improved record of 55–80. One newspaper declared, "This team wins the booby-prize!" prompting Pittsburgh fans to call the team the "Boobies."

5113 Ragglers 1891 *National (M)*. The team's "ragged play," i.e., 475 errors in the field and a .239 team batting average in finishing last with a 55–80 record, led to the moniker of "Ragglers." Name gave rise to the slang (coined in 1904) of "raggle-taggle," which means motley or foolish.

5114 Pirates 1891 to date *National (M)*. One of the most famous nicknames in team sports, "Pirates" had its origins in the interleague wars of 1890. After the Players League disintegrated following the 1890 season, the National League and American Association tried to restore order with regard to players contracts. Pittsburgh furtively signed infielder Lou Bierbauer, who had been the second baseman for the 1889 Philadelphia Athletics of the American Association. Despite the outcry, Bierbauer stayed with Pittsburgh. Philadelphia newspapers called the signing "piratical." The name quickly became popular and has been used now for nearly 120 years.

5115 Buccaneers 1892 to date *National (M)*. Tag is an alternate moniker to Pirates, which has lasted 120 years to the present day. Newspapers immediately shortened it to **Bucs** for headlines, i.e., "Bucs edge Jints, 4–3."

5116 Beer Blokes 1893 *National (M)*. Like the Pittsburgh "Brewer" players of the 1880s, this bunch of fellows loved to frequent saloons and beer halls. A "bloke" is a word used in England that means "fellow," and a "beer bloke" is a fellow who likes to frequent drinking establishments.

5117 Balanced Bucaneers 1900–13 *National (M)*. Tag was coined by baseball writer David Nemec to admiringly describe the Pittsburgh Pirates teams of this 14-year streak of winning seasons, four NL pennants and the 1909 world's championship. The Pirates were balanced

with good pitching, good hitting, steady fielding and speedy base running.

5118 Smoketowners 1900–20 *National (M)*. In this era baseball teams sometimes used "town" nicknames for themselves, i.e., Bean-towners (Boston), Red-towners (Cincinnati), Jungle-towners (Detroit) and Smoke-towners (Pittsburgh). Pittsburgh is the "Smoky City."

5119 Premiers 1901–03 *National (M)*. After losing the Telegraph Cup playoff to Brooklyn in October 1900, the Pirates rewarded their fans with three consecutive National League pennants, 1901–03. The "Premiers" were powered by hitters Honus Wagner (Hall of Fame), Fred Clarke (Hall of Fame), Clarence Beaumont, and Claude Ritchey and boosted by pitchers Jack Chesboro (Hall of Fame), Deacon Phillipe, Jesse Tannehill and Ed Doheny. The Pirates produced superior records of 90–34, 103–36 and 91–49 and the 1902 "Premiers" finished a then-record 27-and-a-half games ahead of second-place Brooklyn.

5120 Clarke's Corsairs 1901–15 *National (M)*. With player-manager Fred Clarke at the helm, newspapers called the players "Clarke's Corsairs"—a stirring moniker that was appropriate because the "Corsairs" enjoyed a "treasure hoard" of 13 straight winning seasons (1901–13) that included four National League pennants and the 1909 World Series title. The four pennants were "treasure chests" won by such steady hitters like Honus Wagner, Fred Clarke, Clarence Beaumont, Claude Ritchey, Tom Leach, and John Wilson and pitchers Jack Chesboro, Deacon Phillipe, Jesse Tannehill, Ed Dohenny, Vic Willis, Sam Camnitz, Nick Maddox, Babe Adams, Al Leifield and Claude Hendrix. The name was popularized by baseball author Fred Lieb. The moniker of "Corsairs" is used occasionally in newspapers and baseball magazines to this day.

5121 The Base Thieves 1902 *National (M)*. Tag was coined by baseball writer David Nemec to describe the 103–36 Pirate 1902 NL pennant-winners who led the major leagues with 226 stolen bases.

5122 Swashbucklers 1909 *National (M)*. Local newspapers praised the team for "swashbuckling" its way to the 1909 NL pennant led by Honus Wagner on offense (who led the NL with 100 RBIs) and pitchers Vic Willis and Howie Camnitz. The team was also called the **Skull & Cross Bones Club** because the team photo depicted the players on a pirate boat proudly flying the Skull and Cross Bones flag.

5123 Filipinos 1913 *United States (ind.)*. With manager Deacon Phillipe at the helm, newspapers called the players "Phillipe's Filipinos." The Philippines had been annexed by the United States in 1900 following the end of the Spanish-American War (1897–98). There were no Filipino players on the team.

5124 Rebels 1914–15 *Federal (M)*. Team was named in honor of player-manager Rebel Oakes.

5125 Colored Stars 1916–19 *Independent Negro team*. Stars was the second-most popular team nickname for black franchises that, like for "Giants," often employed an adjective in front of this noun.

5126 Pennsylvania Giants 1919–20 *Independent Negro team*. This team used the state name as the descriptive adjective for this popular black team nickname.

5127 Red Caps 1919–20 *Independent Negro team*. Players wore red caps. Players were recruited from the city's railroad porters who wore red caps on the job.

5128 Giants 1924 *Independent Negro team*. Tag was the most popular of black baseball team names. The team went by the city name of "Pittsburgh Giants" and not by the state name of "Pennsylvania Giants," as did the 1919–20 team, which also was based in Pittsburgh.

5129 Bill McKechnie's Marauders 1925 *National (M)*. Led by manager Bill McKechnie, the Pirates "marauded" their way to their first NL flag since 1909. Led by Pie Traynor, Paul "Big Poison" Waner and Lloyd "Little Poison" Waner, the Pirates raided opposing NL pitching, posting a league-high .305 team batting average.

5130 Pennant-harbor Pirates 1925, 1927 *National (M)*. Tag was coined by baseball author Fred Lieb in his description of the Pittsburgh Pirates of 1925 and 1927. The 1925 Pirates offense boasted nine regulars whose batting average ranged from .298 to the team-high .357 of Kiki Cuyler. Five Pirate starters won 15 to 19 games each. In 1927 Paul Waner's .380 batting average led an offense with six regulars batting over .300 for the season.

5131 Brash Buccaneers 1925–27 *National (M)*. Baseball writer Fred Lieb, in his 1948 history of the Pittsburgh Pirates, called the two-time (1925, 1927) NL flag winners the "Brash Buccaneers." The team was led by hitters like Clyde Barnhardt, Max Carey (Hall of Fame), Kiki Cuyler (Hall of Fame), George Grantham, Stuffy McInnis, Pie Traynor (Hall of Fame), and Forest Wright and pitchers Vic Aldridge, Carmen Hill, Henry Meadows and Emil Yde.

5132 Crawfords 1929–32 *Independent Negro team*; 1933–38 *Negro National (M)*; 1945–46 *United States (ind.)*. This USL was a "paper league," created by Brooklyn Dodgers GM Branch Rickey as a cover to sign black players for the Dodgers and the Brooklyn farm clubs. Only a few games were played. Jim Dorsey, director of the Crawford Recreational Center, formed a semi-professional baseball club called the "Crawford Colored Giants." Dorsey then helped solicit money to form the professional "Pittsburgh Crawfords" for the 1929 season. The team joined the NNL, a major circuit, in 1933.

5133 El Foldo Pirates 1938 *National (M)*. The Pirates led the Chicago Cubs by five games in a two-team battle for the 1938 NL pennant. The Pittsburghers lost seven of 10 decisions while the Cubs stormed to ten straight victories including a three game sweep in Wrigley Field to close out the regular season, Sportswriter Charles Doyle tagged Pittsburgh as the "El Foldo Pirates." The name would reappear in 1964 when the Phillies similarly blew the 1964 NL flag.

5134 Rickey Dinks 1952–57 *National (M)*. Despite the efforts of famed General Manager Branch Rickey (who enjoyed great success in developing farm talent with the St. Louis Cardinals and Brooklyn Dodgers), the Pirates finished last in five of six seasons, prompting disenchanted Pittsburgh fans to call the team the "Rickey Dinks." The name derives from "rinky-dink," which means something manufactured with poor quality resulting in a mediocre product.

5135 Beat'em Bucs 1960 *National (M)*. Originally a slogan, the phrase was converted into a nickname. Led by manager Danny Murtaugh, the Pirates, who had finished fourth in 1959, came out of nowhere in the summer of 1960 to win the 1960 National League pennant with a 95–59 record by seven games over second-place Milwaukee. Pirate fans started chanting "Beat'em Bucs!" as the team, led by hitters Roberto Clemente (Hall of Fame), Smoky Burgess, Dick Groat, Don Hoak, Bill Mazeroski (Hall of Fame), and Bob Skinner and pitchers Vernon Law, Bob Friend, Harvey Haddix, Wilmer "Vinegar Bend" Mizell and Roy Face, won the NL pennant and then edged the AL champion New York Yankees, 4 games to 3, in one of the most exciting Fall Classics in history.

5136 Proud Pirates 1960–79 *National (M)*. Tag was coined by baseball author Michael Oleksak in praise of the Pirates of 1960–79. In a 20-year period, the Pirates enjoyed 15 winning seasons, including five division titles, three pennants and three World Series championships.

5137 Buccos 1960 to date *National (M)*. Tag is a spin-off of Buccaneers that became popular during the Pirates' 1960 NL pennant and world championship season. Although Roberto Clemente and other Latin players were on the team throughout the 1960s, the moniker was not true "Spanish" but rather an English abbreviation for newspaper headlines, i.e., "Buccos edge Yanks, 10–9." "Buccaneers" in Spanish is "Los Bucaneros." The name has survived to date.

5138 Battling Bucs 1960 to date *National (M)*. Tag is a spin-off of the 1950 NL champion Philadelphia "Fightin' Phillies," the 1960 NL champion Pirates team went by the moniker "Battling Bucs."

5139 Murtaugh's Marauders 1971 *National (M)*. In a spin-off from war movies like *Merill's Marauders* and *Kelly's Heroes*, the 1971 Pirates became known as "Murtaugh's Marauders" (after manager Danny Murtaugh). Led by hitters Roberto Clemente (Hall of Fame), Willie Stargell (Hall of Fame), Al Oliver, Manny Sanguillen, and Rennie Stennet and pitchers Steve Blass, Dock Ellis, and Bob Moose the Pirates "marauded" the NL Eastern Division teams to compile a 97–65 record, good for first place, and then "keel-hauled" San Francisco in the NL Championship Series, 3 games to 1, before "capsizing" the powerful AL champion Baltimore Orioles, 4 games to 3, in the 1971 World Series.

5140 Pittsburgh Lumber Company 1971–79 *National (M)*. Much like the "Lumber Companies" of the AL Minnesota Twins, the Pirates had some feisty singles hitters and big home run boppers during their successful 1970s era when they won two NL pennants, four NL Eastern Division titles and World Series titles in 1971 and 1979. The Lumber Company was powered by Willie Stargell, Dave Parker, Bill Madlock, Al Oliver, Bill Robinson, Richie Zisk, Omar Moreno, Ed Ott , Tim Foli and Phil Garner.

5141 We Are Family 1979 *National (M)*. Originally a slogan, the phrase was converted into the nickname "The Family." Slugger Willie Stargell proclaimed to reporters "We Are Family," describing the camaraderie of the players on the team as the Pirates compiled a 98–64 record to win the NL Eastern Division and then defeated Cincinnati, 3–0, in a sweep of the NL Championship Series to set up a stirring comeback from a 1–3 deficit to the Baltimore Orioles with three straight victories to clinch the 1979 World Series, 4 games to 3. The "Family" included hitters Willie Stargell (Hall of Fame), Tim Foli, Phil Garner, Bill Madlock, Omar Moreno, Steve Nicosia, Ed Ott, Dave Parker, Bill Robinson and Rennie Stennet and pitchers Jim Bibby, Bert Blyleven, John Candelaria, Grant Jackson, Bruce Kison, Enrique Romo and Kent Tekulve.

5142 Sunken Pirates 1984–86 *National (M)*. When the Pirates "sunk" to three consecutive last-place finishes in the NL Eastern Division, baseball writer Charles Feeney called the team the "Sunken Pirates."

5143 Mutineers 1985 *National (M)*. As the Pirates sank to a 57–104 last-place finish, Pittsburgh fans wanted the players to "walk the plank" as though they were "mutineers." Actually, management feared the fans would "mutiny" and stay away from the ballpark.

5144 New Bucs 1986 *National (M)*. After a ruinous 57–104 record in 1985 that left the Bucs 43.5 games out of the lead, management promoted a new 1986 slogan, i.e., "The New Bucs— We Play Hardball!" However, the slogan fizzled as the Bucs improved by only seven games to 64–98 to once again finish last in the NL East again — this time a half-game farther behind at 44 games out of lead.

5145 Tumbling Pirates 1989 *National (M)*. After a second-place finish in 1988, the team "tumbled" to fifth place with a 74–88 record. The tag was coined by John Mehno.

5146 Small Market Sailors 1995 *National (M)*. Coined by George King of the *Trenton Tribune* who described how the city of Pittsburgh was only the twentieth-largest TV market in major league baseball, which severely hampers small-market teams like the Pirates from signing talent needed to be competitive.

5147 Losers 1995–2010 *National (M)*. Disillusioned Pittsburgh fans branded the team as "Losers "and the vulgar **Succos** and **Succaneers**. The term "to suck" was originally a sexual innuendo but it has evolved into a non-sexual term for a feeling of disgust describing miserable failure or a lack of effort producing shoddy work. These monikers were happily discarded early in the 2011 season, as the team got off to a good start. However, the team skidded during the summer to yet another losing season.

5148 The Pittsburgh Working Men 1996 *National (M)*. This moniker reflected how the team had low-paid but hard-working players— much like steelworkers in Pittsburgh and American workers throughout the United States. Based in a "small market" city, the Pirates have had one of the lowest player payrolls in the major leagues.

5149 Shipped-Out Bucs 1996 *National (M)*. Coined by baseball writer Mike Donovan, again in scrutiny of the team's dilemma in playing in a small TV market city, the name reflected the Pirates budget problems that forced management to trade, release, sell, or lose to free agency players like Denny Neagle, Tim Wakefield, Carlos Garcia, Jay Bell, Charlie Hayes, Bobby Bonilla and Barry Bonds.

5150 Sea Bandits 1996 *National (M)*. Coined by baseball writer Mike Donovan, tag was a spin-off from Pirates, Buccaneers and Corsairs.

Pittsfield, Berkshire, Massachusetts

5151 Hillies m1905x *Hudson River (R)*. Team started season in Saugerties (NY) and moved to Pittsfield (MA) July 4. Team disbanded July 25; 1919–30 *Eastern (A)*. City was built at the foot of Berkshire Hills located in western Massachusetts. With manager Joe Birmingham at the helm 1919–20, newspapers called the players "Birmingham's Hillies." Walter Hammond took over in 1921, changing the name to "Hammond's Hillies." Under other managers, the name was retained through 1930.

5152 Electrics 1913–14 *Eastern Assn. (B)*; 1941–42 *Canadian–American (C)*; 1946–48 *Canadian–American (C)*. The city's first hydroelectric power plant, the Turner's Falls Station, was built in 1866 near Turner's Falls, which feeds the nearby Housatonic River. The Cabot Station started operations in 1916 to fully electrify the city. With manager John Zeller at the helm 1913–14, newspapers called the players "Zeller's Electrics."

5153 Indians 1949–50 *Canadian–American (R)*. Team was a farm club of the Cleveland Indians

5154 Phillies 1951 *Canadian–American (R)*. Team was a farm club of the Philadelphia Phillies.

5155 Red Sox 1965–69 *Eastern (AA)*. Team was a farm club of the Boston Red Sox.

5156 Senators 1970–71 *Eastern (AA)*. Team was a farm club of the Washington Senators.

5157 Rangers 1972–75 *Eastern (AA)*. Team was a farm club of the Texas Rangers.

5158 Berkshire Brewers 1976 *Eastern (AA)*. Team went by the county name of "Berkshire Brewers." The team was a farm club of the Milwaukee Brewers.

5159 Cubs 1985–88 *Eastern (AA)*. Team was a farm club of the Chicago Cubs.

5160 Mets 1989–2000 *New York–Pennsylvania (A)*. Team was a farm club of the New York Mets

5161 Astros 2001 *New York–Pennsylvania (A)*. Team was a farm club of the Houston Astros

5162 Berkshire Black Bears 2002 *Northern East (ind.)*; 2003–04 *Northeast (ind.)*. Players wore black-trim uniforms. Black bears once roamed the nearby Berkshire Hills.

5163 Colonials 2010 to date *Can–Am (ind.)*. The *Berkshire Eagle* newspaper sponsored a name-the-team contest. The winning entry was "Colonials." Massachusetts is one of the thirteen original American colonies.

Plainview, Texas

5164 Ponies 1953–55 *West Texas–New Mexico (C 1953–54, B 1955)*; 1956–57 *Southwestern (D)*. Founded in 1886, the city was a "horse town" with ranches, horse drives and rodeos.

5165 Athletics 1958–59 *Sophomore (D)*. Team was a farm club of the Kansas City Athletics.

Plant City, Florida

5166 Reds 1984–90 *Gulf Coast (R)*; 1999–2009 *Gulf Coast (R)*. The teams were farm clubs of the Cincinnati Reds.

Plattsmouth, Nebraska

5167 Indians 1892 *Nebraska State (ind.)*. Team was named in honor of the "Six Tribes of Nebraska." The Missouri, Omaha, Oto, Pawnee, Ponca, and Sioux tribes inhabited Nebraska in the eighteenth century.

Pocatello, Bancock, Idaho

5168 Bannocks 1926–28 *Utah–Idaho (R)*; 1952–56, 1961 *Pioneer (R)*. The city is located in Bannock County, which is named after the original inhabitants of Idaho— the Bannock Indians. Chief Pocatello of the Bannock Indians ceded land to allow a railroad town to be built here. The Fort Hill Reservation, 10 miles north of the city, is home to the Bannock and Shoshoni Indians. With manager Al Bonner at the helm at the start of 1926, newspapers called the players "Bonner's Bannocks." Bert McIvor took over in mid-season 1926 and the name became "Bert's Bannocks." In 1928 Jack Roche took over and the name became "Jack's Bannocks."

5169 Cardinals 1939–42 *Pioneer (R)*; 1946–51 *Pioneer (R)*. Team was a farm club of the St. Louis Cardinals.

5170 Redbirds 1939–42 *Pioneer (R)*. Redbirds was used as an occasional alternate for Cardinals.

5171 Athletics 1957–59 *Pioneer (R)*. Team was a farm club of the Kansas City Athletics.

5172 Giants 1960 *Pioneer (R)*. Team was a farm club of the San Francisco Giants.

5173 Chiefs 1962–65 *Pioneer (R)*. Shoshoni Chief Pocatello helped settlers build a railroad through the Shoshoni and Bannock reservations. The city, established in 1881, was named after him.

5174 Gems 1984–85 *Pioneer (R)*. Idaho is the "Gem State." Gold was discovered in Idaho in 1863, but when miners arrived to this state, they discovered a treasure house of silver, lead, zinc and phosphate. Gem deposits were discovered later, including agate, garnet, jade, opal and even diamonds.

5175 Pioneers 1990–91 *Pioneer (R)*. Team was known as the "Gate City Pioneers" for the 1990 season. "Gate City" is the nickname for Pocatello, which is also known as the "Gate City of the Northwest." Soldiers and pioneers built Fort Hall in 1870 to open the region for granite and phosphorus miners. When the railroad reached this region, the city of Pocatello was founded in 1881.

5176 Posse 1993 *Pioneer (R)*. As settlers arrived by train starting in 1881, Fort Hall soldiers and civilians, appointed as deputies, formed vigilante "posses" to confront bandits, rustlers, and brigands.

Pocomoke City, Maryland

5177 Salamanders 1922–23x *Eastern Shore (D)*. Team disbanded August 23. Salamanders are half-lizard, half-frog amphibians that swim at the bottom of lakes and pools. The red-backed salamander is found in the nearby Pocomoke River. The team got off to a bad start under manager Jack Ryan, prompting newspapers to call the bottom-feeding players "Ryan's Salamanders." When Sam Frocke took over the fifth-place team in August, the name became "Sam's Salamanders." James Sharpe took over in 1923 and the name became "James Sharp's Salamanders." Pocomoke City is the "Home of the National Bass Roundup."

5178 Red Sox 1937–39 *Eastern Shore (D)*. Team was a farm club of the Boston Red Sox.

5179 Chicks 1940 *Eastern Shore (D)*. Team had numerous young players, known in the slang of the era as "chicks." City was founded in 1865 and had many poultry farms. The team's youthful inexperience showed as they went 50–75 to finish last in the league.

Point Pleasant–Gallipolis, Ohio

5180 Point Pleasant–Gallipolis Baseball Club 1910 *Virginia Valley (D)*; 1911m *Mountain States (D)*. Team moved to Middleport (OH)-Pomeroy (OH) July 1. These teams had no nickname.

Pomona, California

5181 Arabs m1929m *California (D)*. Team began season in Santa Ana (CA) and moved to Pomona May 8. Team then moved to San Diego May 15. In the sixteenth century Spanish conquistador Francisco Vasquez de Coronado wandered throughout the California deserts in a vain search for gold for so many years that he received the nickname of Coronado "El Arabe." "El Arabe" means the "Arab." Many Spaniards have some Arab blood because portions of Spain had been held by the Muslims for 400 years.

Pomona, Rockland, New York

5182 Rockland Boulders 2011 to date *Can–Am (ind.)*. Team goes by the county name of Rockland Boulders. Rockland County got its name because the landscape is strewn with rocks and boulders.

Pompano Beach, Florida

5183 Mets 1969–73 *Florida State (A)*. Team was a farm club of the New York Mets.

5184 Cubs 1976–78 *Florida State (A)*. Team was a farm club of Chicago Cubs.

Ponca City, Oklahoma

5185 Poncans m1923–24 *Oklahoma State (D)*. Team started the season in Drumright (OK) and then moved to Ponca City June 7; 1926m *Southwestern (D)*. Ponca City moved to Eureka (KS) June 22. Teams were named after the Ponca Indians. A member of this tribe and an inhabitant of Ponca City is known as a "Poncan."

5186 Angels 1934–38 *Western Assn. (R)*. Team was a farm of the PCL Los Angeles Angels. In the era 1900–50, some farm teams in higher classifications (AAA and AA) had farm teams in lower classification leagues (A, B, C, D).

5187 Dodgers 1947–52 *Kansas–Oklahoma–Missouri (K.O.M.) (D)*. Team was a farm club of the Brooklyn Dodgers.

5188 Jets 1954 *Western Assn. (R)*. The moniker has two origins. Crude oil from nearby rigs is transported to refineries in the city. Gushing oil is known as "oil jets." In 1911, oil was discovered at the Miller Brothers Ranch just outside of the city. The Marland Oil Company was established and then merged with Continental Oil in 1929 to form Conoco. The Ponca City Regional Airport and McConnell Air Force Base are located near the city.

5189 Cubs m1955–57 *Sooner State (D)*. Team started the season in Gainesville (OK) and moved to Ponca City May 19. The team was a farm club of the Chicago Cubs.

Ponce, Puerto Rico

5190 Leones 1941–42–2006–07 *Liga Puertoriquena (W)*; 2008–09 to date *Liga Puertoriquena* The 2007–08 season was cancelled due to a labor dispute between the owners and players. The league started play again in 2008–09. Juan Ponce de Leon y Loazya, the grandson of Spanish conquistador Ponce de Leon, founded this city in 1692 and named it in honor of his grandfather. The Spanish word "leon" means "lion." City's full name is Ponce de Leon, hence the nickname.

Pontiac, Michigan

5191 Indians 1912–13 *Border (D)*. Chief Pontiac, an Ottawa chief, led the Ottawa, Chippewa and Pottawatomi tribes against British troops in 1763. With manager Henry McIntoch at the helm in 1912–13, newspapers called the players "McIntoch's Indians."

Port Arthur, Texas

5192 Refiners 1932m *Cotton States (D)*. Port Arthur moved to DeQuincy (LA) June 19. Oil was discovered at the Spindletop Gusher in 1901, 10 miles north of the city. The processing of crude oil into petrochemicals is the city's major industry. The city sponsors an annual event — the CavOILcade — celebrating the oil industry. With manager Frank Meyers at the helm, newspapers called the players "Meyers' Refiners."

5193 Tarpons 1940–42 *Evangeline (D)*. Tarpon are large, silver-scaled game fish found in the Atlantic Ocean, the Gulf of Mexico, nearby Sabine Lake and the Neches River. With manager Ray Flood at the helm, newspapers called the players "Ray Flood's Tarpons." Harry Strohm took over in 1941 and the name became "Harry Strohm's Tarpons." In mid-season 1942, Carl Kott took over and the name became "Carl Kott's Tarpons."

5194 Sea Hawks 1950–53 *Gulf Coast (R)* 1950, B 1951–53); 1954 *Evangeline (R)*; 1955–56 *Big State (B)*. Pirates, buccaneers, privateers, Spanish galleons and the English "Sea Hawks."

Port Charlotte, Charlotte County, Florida

5195 Charlotte Rangers 1987–2002 *Gulf Coast (R)*; 1991–99 *Florida State (A)*. The teams went by the county name of "Charlotte Rangers." Teams were farm clubs of the Texas Rangers.

5196 Charlotte Blue Jays 1991–92 *Gulf Coast (R)*. Team was a farm club of the Toronto Blue Jays.

5197 Charlotte Redfish 2007 *South Coast (ind.)*. The Redfish is an ocean perch — a type of rockfish with reddish scales.

5198 Charlotte Stone Crabs 2009 to date *Florida State (A)*. The stone crab is an aquatic arthropod that hides amongst ocean bottom rocks.

5199 Rays *Gulf Coast (R)*. 2009 to date. Team is a farm club of the Tampa Bay Rays.

Port Chester, New York

5200 Clippers 1947–48 *Colonial (B)*. Clipper boats have sailed the Long Island Sound since 1845. A "clipper" is a tri-mast swift-sailing ship of the era 1845.

Port Huron, St. Clair, Michigan

5201 Port Huron Base Ball Club 1890x *Michigan State (ind.).* Circuit and team disbanded June 13; 1897x *Michigan State (ind.).* Team disbanded in mid-season (date unknown). These teams had no nickname.

5202 Marines 1895x *Michigan State (ind.).* Team disbanded September 3. Port Huron has been a maritime port for shipping traveling in and out of Lakes Huron and St. Clair since 1850. Michigan is the "Lake State."

5203 Tunnelites 1900x *International (ind.).* Team disbanded July 3. The first St. Clair Canal, aka Grand Trunk Western Railroad Tunnel, built under the St. Clair River in 1891, was a rail tunnel for trains that was in operation 104 years to 1994. The second St. Clair Canal was opened in 1995. The tunnels have connected Port Huron with Sarnia, Ontario, Canada. With manager Patsy Flaherty at the helm, newspapers called the players "Flaherty's Tunnelites."

5204 Independents 1912–13 *Border (D).* Fort St. Joseph was built by the French explorer, Duluth, in 1686. The English took over the city during the French and Indian War. Americans built Fort Gratiot on the site of the old fort in 1814. Port Huron finally won its independence in 1815 after 130 years of colonial rule. The city is "independent," i.e., autonomous in its political relationship with Port Huron Township, the local government of the region. Michigan is divided into numerous townships. With manager Bill Bowen at the helm, newspapers called the players "Bill Bowen's Independents."

5205 Saints 1921 *Michigan–Ontario (B)*; 1926 *Michigan–Ontario (B)*; 1926 *Michigan State (B).* Team was a member of the Class B Michigan Ontario League until that circuit merged with the Class C Central League to form the Class B Michigan League on June 15. City is located in St. Clair County. With manager Johnny Carlin at the helm, newspapers called the players "Carlin's Saints." Carlin continued to manage the team after it transferred to this circuit. "Carlin's Saints" finished a respectable second, eight games behind Bay City.

Port Huron, Michigan–Sarnia, Ontario, Canada

5206 Saints 1922 *Michigan–Ontario (B).* Team, keeping the 1921 nickname, went by the dual city name of "Port Huron–Sarnia Saints." The move was made to attract fans from Sarnia to increase attendance.

Port St. Lucie, Florida

5207 Mets 1983 *Gulf Coast (R)*; 1988 to date *Florida State (A)*; 1992–99 *Gulf Coast (R)*; 2004–05 *Gulf Coast (R).* Team were farm clubs of the New York Mets.

5208 Dodgers 1992 *Gulf Coast (R).* Team was a farm club of Los Angeles Dodgers.

5209 Cubs 1993 *Gulf Coast (R).* Team was a farm club of Chicago Cubs.

Portageville, Missouri

5210 Pirates 1935–36m *KITTY (D).* Team moved to Owensboro (KY) July 17. Team was a farm club of the Pittsburgh Pirates. With manager Pat Patterson at the helm, newspapers called the players "Pat Patterson's Pirates." Hugh Wise took over in 1936 and the name became "Wise's Pirates."

Porterville, California

5211 Orange-packers 1911 *San Joaquin Valley (D).* Citrus fruit is shipped to factories for cleaning, packing and shipment to market.

5212 Packers 1949–50 *Sunset (C).* Name was shortened from the 1911 moniker.

5213 Comets m1952x *Southwest International (C).* Team started playing all its home games in Porterville starting April 25 but also represented Riverside-Ensenada. Team began season as Riverside-Ensenada (CA) and then moved here April 25 before disbanding August 1. With manager Chet Brewer at the helm of the team after it arrived from Riverside-Ensenada, local newspapers, looking for a short but catchy name, started to call previously unnamed team "Chet's Comets."

Portland, Connecticut

5214 Portland Base Ball Club 1891x *Connecticut State (ind.).* Team and league disbanded in mid-season (date unknown). Team had no nickname.

Portland, Maine

5215 Hill Citys 1885–88m *New England (ind.).* Team moved to Portsmouth (NH) July 20. City is located near Bradbury Mountain. Circuit was also known as the New England Interstate League. Because the city is located near Bradbury Mountain, Portland is known as the "Hill City." With manager Harrison Spence at the helm, newspapers called the players "Harrison Spence's Hill Cites." Plural spelling of **Hill Cities** was also used.

5216 Forest Citys 1885–88m *New England (ind.).* Team moved to Portsmouth (NH) July 20. Circuit was also known as the New England Interstate League; 1891–96x *New England (ind.).* Team disbanded August 23. In the nineteenth century the city planted many trees along its streets, giving rise to the city nickname of "Forest City." With manager Frank Leonard at the helm 1891–96, newspapers called the players "Frank Leonard's Forest Citys." The White Mountain National Forest is located 50 miles northwest of the city.

5217 Portland Base Ball Club 1897 *Maine State (ind.).* Team had no nickname.

5218 Phenoms 1899–1901 *New England (ind.).* Team had good young players and thus was loaded with "phenomenal" young talent, winning the 1901 NEL pennant. "Phenom" is a term for a talented young person who shows promise. With manager John Smith at the helm, newspapers called the players "John Smith's Phenoms."

5219 Blue Sox 1907 *Maine State (D)*; 1908 *Atlantic Assn. (D)*; 1919 *New England (B).* Players wore blue hose. The color was a spin-off of the red stirrups worn by the Boston Red Sox, with whom the Portland teams maintained a loose affiliation.

5220 Duffs 1913–15 *New England (B)*; 1916 *Eastern (B).* Team was named in honor of manager Hugh Duffy.

5221 Paramounts 1917 *Eastern (B).* Maine is known as the "Switzerland of America." Maine is home to the following mountains: North Turner, Center, North Brother, Katadin, Pleasant Pond, Bald, Blue and White. Portland is known as the "Hill City." With manager Mike Garrity at the helm in 1917, newspapers called the players "Mike Garrity's Paramounts."

5222 Eskimos 1926–27 *New England (B).* Maine experiences cold winters and chilly spring weather. With manager George Faulkner at the helm, newspapers called the players "George Faulkner's Eskimos." Duffy Lewis took over in 1927 and the name became "Lewis' Eskimos."

5223 Mariners 1928 *New England (B)*. The city is a deep-water harbor port located along Casco Bay and is the nearest U.S. port to Europe. Portland is the "Beautiful City by the Sea." The city was an important shipbuilding center during World War I and World War II. With manager Duffy Lewis at the helm in 1928, newspapers called the players "Lewis' Mariners."

5224 Gulls 1946 *New England (B)*. Sea gulls inhabit the shores of nearby Casco Bay. Newspaper editors wanted a short moniker, prompting reporters to call the players "Gulls." Portland is the "Beautiful City by the Sea."

5225 Pilots 1947–49 *New England (B)*. Pilot boats guide ships in and out of Casco Bay. With manager Del Bisonette at the helm in 1947–48, newspaper called the players "Del Bisonette's Pilots." Skeeter Newsome took over in 1949 and the name became "Skeeter's Pilots."

5226 Sea Dogs 1994 to date *Eastern (AA)*. Pirate ships were sailing along the Maine coast since settlers first reached the region in 1632. Pirates raided the Atlantic coast of North America until about 1800. A "Sea Dog" is slang for a pirate or buccaneer.

Portland, Oregon

5227 Roses 1890 *Pacific Northwest (ind.)*. City has 140 parks and three gardens, including the International Rose Test Gardens at Washington Park. An annual Portland Rose Festival has been held since 1907. In 1888, the local Episcopal Church held a convention in the city. Visitors from all over the country commented on how many rose gardens the city had. From the publicity Portland became known as the "Rose City."

5228 Gladiators 1890–92 *Pacific Northwest (ind.)*; 1896 *New Pacific (ind.)*; 1898 *Pacific Northwest (ind.)*. Baseball players in the nineteenth century were rough, rowdy athletes who were sometimes gawked at by fans and bloodied on (and off) the field — much like Ancient Roman gladiators. Portland was noted for its metalworking in this era. Some companies in the city used a sword as their trademark. With manager Robert Glenalvin at the helm, newspapers called the players "Glenalvin's Gladiators."

5229 Webfeet 1891–92 *Pacific Northwest (ind.)*; 1901–02 Pacific *Northwest (ind. 1901, D 1902)*. Ducks and geese inhabit the nearby Willamette Lake and Willamette River. "Web-foot" is a term for a duck. Wild ducks inhabit the nearby Colombia and Willamette rivers. Oregon is known as the "Web-foot State."

5230 Green Gages 1903m *Pacific National (A)*. City has plum groves that feature the Green Gage Plum — named after eighteenth century English botanist William Gage, who first bred this green plum. With manager John Grim at the helm, newspapers called the players "Grim's Green Gages."

5231 Browns 1904 *Pacific Coast (A)*. Players wore brown hose.

5232 Giants 1905 *Pacific Coast (A)*. Local reporters called the team the "Portland Giants" in emulation of the 1904 NL champion New York Giants. With manager Walter McCredie at the helm, newspapers called the team "Walter McCredie's Giants."

5233 Beavers 1906–17 (A 1906–07, (AA). 1908–17); 1919–72 Pacific Coast (AA 1919–45, AAA 1946–72); 1978–93 *Pacific Coast (AAA)*. Beavers inhabit the nearby Willamette and Columbia rivers. Oregon is the "Beaver State." One of the earliest name-the-team contests in professional baseball history was held in Portland in 1906. The winning entry was "Beavers." In a 2001 name-the-team contest, fans overwhelming chose "Beavers." Management put a "Lucky Beavers" patch on the uniform sleeve in 2008. Unable to get a new stadium, the team moved to Tucson (AZ) for the 2011 season. The beaver is the state animal of Oregon.

5234 Colts 1909, 1912, 1914m *Northwestern (B)*. Team moved to Ballard (WA) July 20. With many young players on the team because the club was a farm club of the PCL Portland Beavers, newspapers called the players the "Colts." The term "colt" was a contemporary slang for "young player." With manager Perle Casey at the helm in 1909, local newspapers called the players "Perle Casey's Colts." Manager "Nick" Williams returned in 1912 with a young crew, and the name became "Nick Williams' Colts."

5235 Pippins 1911, 1913 *Northwestern (B)*. Fruit farms in Oregon and Washington State grow the famous Pippin apples. With manager Nick Williams at the helm, newspapers called the players "Nick's Pippins," and "Williams' Pippins."

5236 Buckaroos 1918 *Pacific Coast International (B)*. In the era 1880–1920 baseball players were often referred to by Wild West names, i.e., Braves, Bronchos, Cowboys, Rustlers, and Buckaroos. Buckaroo, derived from the Spanish "vaquero," means a cowboy and, originally, a lost calf that has strayed from the herd. Cattle were driven and herded to ranches in Oregon when the Alaska Gold Rush of the 1880s and 1890s brought settlers and prospectors into the region. With manager Bill Fisher at the helm, newspapers called the players "Bill Fisher's Buckaroos."

5237 Ducks 1929–39 *Pacific Coast (AA)*. Moniker was a spin-off from the 1902 "Webfeet" team. Newspapers liked it because it was only five letters in length.

5238 Lucky Beavers 1943–54 *Pacific Coast (AA 1943–45, AAA 1946–54)*. In 1943, team had its first winning season since 1937, hence the term "Lucky" Beavers. In 1943 the team sponsored a $300,000 fund drive to help finance the construction of the "Lucky Beaver" B-17 bomber to be used in the war effort.

5239 Rosebuds 1946x *West Coast Negro (ind.)*. Circuit was also known as the Pacific Coast Negro League. Team disbanded in mid-season (date unknown). The tag was a spin-off from the 1892 Portland "Roses" team.

5240 Mavericks 1973–77 *Northwest (A)*. Tag was a spin-off from Buckaroos. The team played without big league affiliation these years. "Maverick" is baseball slang for an owner who refuses to affiliate with a major league parent club. Both "maverick" and "buckaroo" refer to a stray calf.

5241 Rockies 1995–2000 *Northwest (A)*. Team was the farm club of Colorado Rockies.

Portsmouth, New Hampshire

5242 Lillies m1888 New England *(ind.)*. Team started the season in Portland (ME) and moved to Portsmouth June 9. The Lilly is a bell-shaped white flower that is popular in New Hampshire. Players wore all-white uniforms and hose, hence the moniker "lily white." After the debacle of 1882 when multi-colored uniforms were used by players in both major leagues (the NL and AA), teams catered to their fans' tastes by dressing the players in all-white uniforms — especially at home. Since uniform numbers had not yet been invented, fans knew the home team players by their all-white uniforms. Road teams gradually began to don gray uniforms for contrast. With Frank Leonard at the helm, local newspapers called the players the alliterative "Leonard's Lillies."

Portsmouth, Ohio

5243 Riversides 1884 *Ohio State Assn. (ind.)*; 1894x *Tri-State (ind.)*. Circuit and team disbanded mid-season (date unknown). Portsmouth was known as the "Riverside City." The city is known as the "City Where Southern Hospitality Begins on the Ohio River." The Ohio Canal, stretching from Portsmouth to Cleveland (OH), was completed here in 1832. With manager Daniel Spry at the helm, newspapers called the players "Spry's Riversides." Even at the dawn of minor league baseball in 1883–84, clever newspaper reporters were always ready to liven up a newspaper account by dreaming up a nickname for the hometown team.

5244 Cobblers m1908–15 *Ohio State (D)*. Portsmouth was well known for its shoe and boot manufacturing in the nineteenth century. Shoe cobblers often had their shops on boats in order to avoid thieves. With R. Quinn at the helm after the team settled in Portsmouth in June 1908, local newspapers called the players "Quinn's Cobblers." Bill Doyle took over in 1909 and the name became "Bill Doyle's Cobblers." John McAllister took over in mid-season and the name became "McCallister's Cobblers." Then Charles O'Day took over and the name became "Charlie's Cobblers." Pete Childs took over in 1910–14 and the name became "Childs' Cobblers." Chester Spencer took over in 1915 and the name became "Chester's Cobblers" and "Spencer's Cobblers."

5245 Truckers m1908–15 *Ohio State (D)*. Team started 1908 season in Springfield (OH) and moved to Portsmouth June 16. Reporters, looking for a moniker for the team, noted that gasoline engine trucks were making their first appearance on Ohio roads. Metal products from Portsmouth's iron and steel mills were now being "trucked" all over Ohio. Prior to 1900 boats "trucked" goods along the Ohio River prior to stopping into Portsmouth's maritime port.

5246 Pirates 1935–36 *Middle Atlantic (C)*. Team was a farm club of the Pittsburgh Pirates.

5247 Red Birds 1937–40 *Middle Atlantic (C)*. Team was a farm club of the St. Louis Cardinals.

5248 Athletics 1948–50 *Ohio–Indiana (D)*. Team was a farm club of the Philadelphia Athletics.

5249 Explorers 1993–95 *Frontier (ind.)*. Team was named in honor of the Portsmouth Police Department's "Police Explorers"— a community organization for city youth.

Portsmouth, Virginia

5250 Truckers 1895 *Virginia State (ind.)*; 1906–10m *Virginia (C)*. Team moved to Petersburg (VA) July 5; 1914–15, 1917x *Virginia (C)*. Circuit and team disbanded May 15 due to U.S. entry into World War I; 1919–28x *Virginia (C)* 1919, *B* 1920–28). Team and league disbanded June 3; 1935 *Piedmont (B)*. Cargo ships that "truck" cargo have sailed the Elizabeth River, Hampton Roads and Chesapeake Bay since 1750. In medieval English, to "truck" meant to deal in traffic. Portsmouth is the "Hub of Tidewater" and the "Industrial Center."

5251 Browns 1896 *Virginia State (ind.)*; 1901m *Virginia–North Carolina (ind.)*. Team moved to Tarboro (VA) June 21. Players wore brown hose.

5252 Olympics 1897 *Southeast Virginia (ind.)*. Local reporters decided to use a name more lofty than "Truckers" and more interesting than "Browns" so they switched to "Olympics," which had been used by the 1871–72 Washington Olympics.

5253 Pirates 1900 *Virginia–North Carolina (ind.)*; 1912–13 *Virginia (C)*; 1916 *Virginia (C)*. Pirate ships sailed the coast of southeast Virginia and the Carolinas from 1570 to 1820. The most famous of these corsairs was Blackbeard the Pirate. With manager Lou Castro at the helm, newspapers called the players "Castro's Pirates." Lee Garvin took over in 1913 and the name became "Lee Garvin's Pirates."

5254 Merrimacks 1901m *Virginia–North Carolina (ind.)*. Team moved to Tarboro (VA) June 21; 1953–55 *Piedmont (B)*. The city's Gosport Naval Yard rebuilt the wooden *Merrimack* into the iron-clad *Virginia*, which engaged in battle with the *U.S.S. Monitor* in the waters of Hampton Roads on March 9, 1862. With manager Win Clark at the helm, newspapers called the players "Win Clark's Merrimacks."

5255 Foxes 1916 *Virginia (C)*. Team was named in honor of manager James Fox.

5256 Firefighters 1930–33 *Independent Negro team*. In the siege of Portsmouth in April 1862 Union forces set fire to the city.

5257 Cubs 1936–52 *Piedmont (B)*. Team was a farm club of the Chicago Cubs.

5258 Tides *Carolina (D 1961–62, A 1963–65)*. Team went by the regional name of **Tidewater Tides** 1963–65. Tides of the Elizabeth, James and Lafayette bays strike the shores of Portsmouth. Portsmouth is the "Hub of the Tidewater Region."

5259 Explorers *Frontier (ind.)*. Long before the city was founded in 1803, English and French explorers sailed the coasts of Virginia in the sixteenth and seventeenth centuries. Shawnee and later French, English, and American pioneers explored the Ohio River Valley in the seventeenth, eighteenth and nineteenth centuries while traveling along the Ohio and Scioto rivers.

Portsmouth-Norfolk, Virginia

5260 Tides 1961–62 *South Atlantic (A)*. With the team's formal name Portsmouth-Norfolk, newspapers insisted on a short moniker, so management went with the name of "Portsmouth-Norfolk Tides." Tides from the waters of Hampton Roads and the Atlantic Ocean roll onto shore here. The team played its home games in Portsmouth. Portsmouth is the "Hub of the Tidewater Region."

Pottstown, Pennsylvania

Note: Not be confused with Pottsville, PA.

5261 Pottstown Base Ball Club 1896x *Schuykill Valley (ind.)*. Team disbanded in mid-season (date unknown). Team had no nickname.

5262 Legionnaires 1932 *Interstate (D)*. The American Legion of Pennsylvania holds its annual meeting here. With manager Earl Potteiger at the helm, newspapers called the players "Potteiger's Legionnaires."

Pottsville, Pennsylvania

Note: Not to be confused with Pottstown, PA.

5263 Anthracites 1883 *Interstate (ind.)*. In 1806, settler "Old John" Pott, who founded nearby Pottstown in 1754 as a young man 54 years earlier, discovered coal and built a small furnace. As more coal was discovered, coal miners and their families settled the region. Pottsville is the "Coal City."

5264 Coal-crackers 1883 *Interstate (ind.)*. "Coal-crackers" are refiners who heat oil to "crack" it into lighter fluids, such as gasoline and kerosene.

5265 Black Legs 1883 *Interstate (ind.)*. Players wore black stockings. "Black Leg" was not a slang for coal-miner but rather term for a strike-breaker or "scab," which originated in England, and came to refer to replacement coal miners who crossed a picket line. After several years the word came to mean a "coal miner" in general.

5266 Colts 1894–95m *Pennsylvania State (ind.)*. Team moved to Allentown (PA) July 27. Team had many young players who were called "phenoms" because manager John "Phenomenal" Smith was at the helm. As a result, newspaper reporters called the players "Phenomenal Smith's Phenoms." However, editors rebelled at the moniker and insisted that their reporters call the players the synonymous "Colts."

5267 Lambs 1896m *Pennsylvania State (ind.)*. Team moved to

Shamokin (PA) in mid-season (date unknown). Switching away from "Phenoms" and "Colts," fans and reporters called this group of mostly young players the "Lambs" when the team struggled on the field causing attendance to dip. The subsequent drop in revenue forced the team to leave town in mid-season. In this era, young teams that struggled on the field were known as "Innocents" and "Lambs."

Poughkeepsie, New York

5268 Poughkeepsie Base Ball Club 1885 *Interstate (ind.)*; 1886 *New York State (ind.)*; 1894 *New York State (ind.)*. These teams had no nickname.

5269 Colts 1903–07 *Hudson River (D 1903, C 1904–07)*. Team had many young players who in the contemporary slang of the era were known as "colts." With manager William McCabe at the helm, newspapers called the players "McCabe's Colts."

5270 Honey Bugs 1913 *New York–New Jersey (D)*; 1914 *Atlantic (D)*. City had numerous honey bee farms in the nineteenth century. By 1910, farm production had largely given way to industrial factories. With manager Eugene Ressique at the helm in 1913, the team was first called "Eugene Ressique's Bees," but the players then became "Eugene Ressique's Honey Bugs." Newspaper editors were happy because "Bugs" was just as short as "Bees." The name was used again in 1914.

5271 Giants 1947 *Colonial (B)*. Team had a loose affiliation with the NL New York Giants. In the era 1985–1930, most links between major and minor league teams were loose affiliations, especially between teams geographically close to one another. However, starting in 1946, most minor league teams became formal farm clubs of big league parent franchises.

5272 Chiefs 1948–50x *Colonial (B)*. Team and league disbanded July 16. When Dutch settlers arrived here in 1687, the region was inhabited by the Poughkeepsie and Wapanee Indians.

Poza Rica, Veracruz, Mexico

5273 Petroleros 1955–56–57–58 *Liga Veracruzana de Mexico (ind.)*; 1958–83 *Mexican (AA 1958–66, AAA 1967–83)*; 1996–97 *Mexican (AAA)*. Crude oil from nearby oil fields is transported to refineries in the city. "Petroleros" means "oilers."

Princeton, Indiana

5274 Infants 1905 *Kentucky–Illinois–Tennessee KITTY (D)*. Regular season was shortened to August 17 because of a yellow fever epidemic. The team had many young players who struggled on the field. Young and losing teams in this era were known as "Infants" or "Lambs."

Princeton, West Virginia

5275 Reds 1988, 1991–92 *Appalachian (R)*. Team was a farm club of the Cincinnati Reds.

5276 Pirates 1989 *Appalachian (R)*. Team was a farm club of the Pittsburgh Pirates.

5277 Patriots 1990 *Appalachian (R)*. The 1990 team played as an independent without affiliation to a major league team. During the Civil War Virginia split into the pro–Union West Virginia and the pro–Confederacy Virginia. The name honors the leaders and soldiers of both sides as "patriotic."

5278 Reds 1991–96 *Appalachian (R)*. Team was a farm club of the Cincinnati Reds.

5279 Devil Rays 1997–2007 *Appalachian (R)*. Team was a farm club of the Tampa Bay Devil Rays.

5280 Rays 2008 to date *Appalachian (R)*. Team was a farm club of the Tampa Bay Rays. In 2007 the Tampa Bay Devil Rays changed their team nickname to the Tampa Bay "Rays."

Providence, Rhode Island

5281 Rhode Islands 1877 *New England Assn. (M)*. Team played as the semi-professional "Rhode Island Base Ball Club" in 1876, and then joined this major league in 1877. In the nineteenth century, numerous teams used their home state as their monikers, i.e., Baltimore Marylands, Louisville Kentuckys, San Francisco Californias, Richmond Virginias and Providence Rhode Islands. The team had two alternate nicknames that appeared in newspapers, i.e., **Little Rhodys** (State of Rhode Island's nickname) and **Rhodys**.

5282 Grays 1878–85 *National (M)*; 1886 *Eastern (ind.)*; 1891x *Eastern Assn. (ind.)*. Team disbanded August 13; 1892–1904 and 1906–08, 1910–11 *Eastern (ind.)*. 1892–1901, A 1902–11); 1912–17 *International (AA)* The Eastern League reorganized, including a name change to International; 1918–19 *Eastern (B 1918, A 1919–25)*; m1925 *International (AA)*. Team began the season in Newark (NJ) and moved to Providence May 16; 1927–30x *Eastern (A)*. Team disbanded July 18; 1948–49x *New England (B)*. Team disbanded June 20. Actually, at the start of the 1878 season, the players wore blue hose and the team was known as the Providence **Blues**. However, constant washing of the blue hose in an era when color-fast dyes were unknown caused the stockings' blue color to fade to gray. In 1895, with manager William Murray at the helm, the players were known as "Murray's Grays." By this time, the players wore gray hose from the start of the season. Color-fast dyes were not developed until the 1960s.

5283 The Toast of Providence 1884 *National (M)*. The term "Toast of the Town" referred to an individual or group of people whose prowess and success was a "cause célèbre" in a city, nation, or the world. Providence earned that title by winning its second NL pennant this season and then sweeping the American Association pennant-winning New York Metropolitans in what many historians call the "first true World Series." Name was coined by baseball author David Nemec in his *Great 19th Century Baseball Encyclopedia*.

5284 Providence Base Ball Club 1884 *Reserve (ind.)*. The Reserve League was the attempt of the National League and American Association to keep players away from the rival Union Association, a new circuit of major league pretensions that ignored the reserve clause and raided both the NL and AA for players. Team had no nickname.

5285 Clamdiggers 1891x *Eastern Assn.(ind.)*. Team disbanded August 13; 1892–94, 1898–1901, 1905, 1909–11 *Eastern (A)*. Founded in 1636 at the head of the Providence River that leads to Narragansett Bay and the Atlantic Ocean, fishing boats have arrived at the city's excellent harbor with seafood catches since the seventeenth century. Clams are harvested along the sandy beaches of the city and transported to factories where they are cleaned, packed and sent to market. With manager Bill McGunnigle at the helm, newspapers called the players "McGunnigle's Clam-diggers." With manager Walter Burnham at the helm in 1892–93, newspapers called the players "Walter Burnham's Clam-diggers." In 1894 William Murray took over and the name became "William Murray's Clam-diggers." Jack Dunn took over in 1905 and the name became "Dunn's Diggers." Hugh Duffy took over in 1909 and the name became "Hugh Duffy's Diggers." Between 1891 and 1911, the names "Grays" and "Clam-diggers" were interchangeable.

5286 Rubes 1926 *Eastern (A)*. Team disbanded July 18. Team was named in honor of manager Rube Marquard.

5287 Chiefs 1946–47 *New England (B)*. Roger Williams founded the city in 1636 after buying the land from the chiefs of the Narragansett Indians.

Provo, Utah

5288 Angels 2001–04 *Pioneer (R)*. Team was a farm club of the Anaheim Angels.

Puebla, Puebla, Mexico

5289 Pericos 1942–48 *Liga Mexicana (ind.)*; 1955–56–58–59 *Liga Veracruzana (W)*; 1955–56–58–59 *Veracruzana (W)*; 1960–69 *Mexican (AA 1960–66, AAA 1967–69)*; 1972–75 *Mexicana (AAA)*; 1993–95 *Liga Mexicana (AAA)*; 2000 to date *Liga Mexicana (AAA)*. Parrots inhabit the Mexican rain forests.

5290 Angeles 1976–80 *Mexican (AAA)*. Puebla's formal name in Spanish is Puebla de los Angeles, i.e., "City of the Angels."

5291 Angeles Negros 1982–83 *Liga Nacional de Mexico (ind.)*; 1985–87 *Mexican (AAA)*. Players wore black trim. Los Angeles Negros means "Black Angels."

5292 Tigres de Angelopolis 2004–06 *Mexican (AAA)*. Team went by the name of Angelopolis Tigers. Angelopolis is ancient Greek for "City of the Angels." The Mexico City Tigres moved to Puebla for the 2004 season. The nickname was retained. For the seasons 2004–06 Puebla had two teams—the Parrots and the Tigers. The team moved to Cancun, Quintana Roo for the 2007 season.

Pueblo, Colorado

5293 Pastimes 1885 *Colorado State (ind.)*. Numerous nineteenth century sporting teams, baseball included, often went by such "sporty" names as Active, Alert, Contest, Endeavor, Friendship, Lightfoot, Olympic, Quickstep, Rough'n Ready and Pastime.

5294 Ponies 1887 *Colorado (ind.)*; 1889 *Colorado State (ind.)*. Team had many young players known in the slang of the era as "colts" and "ponies." Actually, "pony" refers to a new team — either an expansion team in an existing league or a charter franchise in a brand new league. Also, since there were many horse ranches in Colorado in this era, newspaper reporters decided to call the players on these two clubs the "Ponies."

5295 Rovers 1896 *Colorado State (ind.)*. Spanish explorers camped here in the eighteenth century. Later, trappers, traders and prospectors reached the area, leading to the establishment of Fort Pueblo in 1842. "Rover" is another name for "explorer" or "wanderer." Colorado is the "Buffalo Plains State." Buffalo herds roamed and roved across this region. "Rover" was also a nineteenth century slang for a baseball player.

5296 Gems 1898–99 *Colorado State (ind.)*. Mild climate at the foothills of the Rocky Mountains allowed the city to become a tourist center. First known as "Fountain City" (1858–59), the city was renamed Pueblo in 1860 and became known as the "Gem City of the Arkansas Valley."

5297 Indians 1900 *Western (ind.)*; m1905–09 *Western (A)*. Team started the 1905 season in Colorado Springs (CO) and moved to Pueblo July 15; m1911 *Western (A)*. Team began the season in Wichita (KS) and moved here May 22 The Apache and the Ute massacred the inhabitants of Fort Pueblo on December 23, 1854. With manager Billy Hulen at the helm, newspapers called the players "Billy Hulen's Indians." With manager Ed McKean at the helm, newspapers called the players "McKean's Indians." Frank Selee took over in 1906 and the name became "Frank Selee's Indians." Lewis Drill took over in mid-season 1907 and the name became "Drill's Indians." Hamilton Patterson took over in 1908 and the name became "Hamilton Patterson's Indians." Walter Carlisle took over in 1910 and the name became "Carlisle's Indians." With Frank Isbell at the helm in 1911, newspapers called the players "Isbell's Indians."

5298 Steelworkers 1928–29 *Western (A)*. City smelters manufacture steel and steel products, i.e., tubing, wires and bars. Pueblo is known as the "Steel City of the West." The city was home to the Colorado Fuel and Iron Corporation. With manager Spencer Abbott at the helm in 1928, newspapers called the players "Spencer Abbott's Steel-workers." Jim Tierney took over in 1929 and the name was "Tierney's Steelworkers."

5299 Braves 1930–32 *Western (A)*. Moniker was a spin-off of the 1911 name "Braves." With manager Jimmy Payton at the helm in 1930–31, newspapers called the players "Payton's Braves." The name was retained in 1932 under two other managers. The team was not a farm club of the Boston Braves.

5300 Rollers 1941 *Western (D)*. City factories manufacture steel wheels for tanks, farm machines and trucks. A steel wheel of this type is known as a "roller." Metal cylinders used to roll up, spread, crush or flatten an object are also known as a "rollers." Local reporters dreamed up this name.

5301 Dodgers 1947–58 *Western (A)*. Team was a farm club of the Brooklyn Dodgers.

5302 Big Horns 1995 *Texas–Louisiana (ind.)*. Big horns are wild sheep of the Rocky Mountains. The male has large, curving horns.

Puerto de la Cruz, La Romana, Dominican Republic

5303 Orientales del Caribe 1963–64 *Liga Invernal Dominicana (W)*. City is actually a suburb of La Romana on the eastern tip of the island. "Orientales del Caribe" means "Caribbean Easterns." Liga Invernal Dominicana means Dominican Winter League.

Puerto La Cruz, Anzoategui, Venezuela

5304 Orientales de Anzoategui 1956–57–62–63 *Liga Venezolana (W)*; 1963–64 *Venezuelan (W)*. Team went by the state name of "Orientales de Anzoantegui." City is located in northeast Venezuela on the shores of the Caribbean Sea.

5305 Caribes del Oriente 1991–92 to date *Liga Venezolana (W)*. Team's formal title is "Caribes del Oriente," without the inclusion of the city name. "Caribe del Oriente" means "Easterners of the Caribbean."

Puerto Mexico, Venezuela, Mexico

Note: Today the city is Coatzocoalcos.

5306 Portenos 1964–68 *Liga del Sureste Mexicana (A)*. City is a river port along the Coatzacoalcos River. "Los Portenos" means "port men."

5307 Charos 1964–68 *Liga del Sureste Mexicana (A)*. Team was a farm club of the "Charos" de Jalisco. Teams in larger cities of the Mexican League, i.e., Mexico City, Guadalajara and Monterrey, sometimes had farm clubs in the class A leagues in Mexico in the era 1956–78. "Los charos" means "cowboys."

Puerto Penasco, Sonora, Mexico

5308 Club de Beisbol de Puerto Penasco 1969 *Liga del Norte Mexicana (A)*. Team had no nickname. According to league president Horatio Lopez, none of the six teams in this circuit had a nickname.

Five of the league franchises were located in Sonora state between Mexicali and Ciudad Juarez near the U.S.-Mexican border.

Pulaski, Virginia

5309 Counts 1942 *Virginia (C)*; 1946–50 *Appalachian (D)*. Count Casimir Pulaski was a Polish military leader who led American troops in Pennsylvania against the British in 1779. He was killed in battle October 9, 1779. With manager Jack Crosswright at the helm in 1942, newspapers called the players "Jack's Counts" and "Crosswright's Counts."

5310 Phillies 1952–55 *Appalachian (D)*; 1969–77 *Appalachian (R 1969–76, Summer A 1977)*. These teams were farm clubs of the Philadelphia Phillies.

5311 Cubs 1957–58 *Appalachian (D)*. Team was a farm club of the Chicago Cubs.

5312 Braves 1982–92 *Appalachian (R)*. Team was a farm club of the Atlanta Braves.

5313 Rangers 1997–2002 *Appalachian (R)*. Team was a farm club of the Texas Rangers.

5314 Blue Jays 2003–06 *Appalachian (R)*. Team was a farm club of the Toronto Blue Jays.

5315 Mariners 2008 to date *Appalachian (R)*. Team was a farm club of the Seattle Mariners.

Punxsutawney, Pennsylvania

5316 Policemen 1906 *Inter-State (D)*. From 1880 to 1900, Pennsylvania was convulsed by coal miner, iron and steel worker, textile worker and railroad laborer strikes. Local sheriff departments found themselves overwhelmed. In exasperation, the corporations established the "Coal and Iron Police." This "police" force actually were "goons," recruited from the ranks of prison guards, hoodlums and adventurers who did very little more than rough up protesting or striking workers. The Great Anthracite Strike of May–October 1902 and subsequent unrest prompted the Pennsylvania state government to establish the Pennsylvania State Police in 1905. This police force consisted of four troops designated A, B, C, D. Stationed in Punxsutawney — a suburb of Pittsburgh — the "Troop D Policemen" controlled labor unrest in Pittsburgh and Punxsutawney.

Pusan, Southeast, South Korea

5317 Lotte Giants 1982 to date *Korean (ind.)*. The Lotte Confectionary Company, the team owner, has factories in Japan that supplies cookies, cakes, candies and other sweets to the Japanese market. The company also owned a Japanese PL team — the Tokyo Lotte Orions. Team's management, ever mindful of the need to market the team in English, chose the moniker of "Giants." The name has nothing to do with the San Francisco Giants or Tokyo Yomiuri Giants. The team's slogan is "National Unity."

Quakertown, Pennsylvania

5318 Lehigh Valley Black Diamonds 1999–2000 *Atlantic (ind.)*. Nearby coal mines transport coal to city factories for processing. "Black Diamond" is a slang for coal. The term should not be confused with "Black Gold," which is a slang for oil.

Quebec (City), Quebec, Canada

5319 Bulldogs 1923 *Eastern Canada (B)*; 1924 *Quebec–Ontario–Vermont (B)*. Baseball team was named after the Quebec Bulldogs

ice hockey team. Local newspapers praised the players for "fighting like Bulldogs" en route to a 66–40 record and the 1923 ECL pennant. With manager Bill Innes at the helm, newspapers called the players "Bill's Bulldogs."

5320 Athletics 1940 *Quebec Provincial (B)*; 1941–42 *Canadian–American (C)*. Team was a farm club of the Brooklyn Dodgers and not the Philadelphia Athletics. Although it was not a formal farm club, the team had a loose affiliation with the Philadelphia Athletics. The first ice hockey team in Quebec was the Quebec Athletic Hockey Club of 1889. This team eventually became the NHL Quebec Bulldogs who won the Stanley Cup twice (1912 and 1913). In the period 1935–40, Canadian teams of the Can–Am and Quebec Provincial leagues maintained a loose affiliation with major league teams of the Northeast United State, which included using major league nicknames like Braves, Red Sox, Dodgers and Athletics.

5321 Alouettes 1946–48 *Canadian–American (C)*. Alouette is French for thrush, finch or sparrow. These birds are found throughout North America.

5322 Braves 1949–50 *Canadian–American (C)*; 1951–55 *Provincial (C)*. The 1949–50 team had a loose affiliation with the NL Boston Braves. In 1951 the team became a farm club of the NL Boston Braves (1951–52) and then the NL Milwaukee Braves (1953–55).

5323 Carnivals 1971–75 *Eastern (AA)*. City has hosted an annual winter carnival here since 1953.

5324 Metros 1975–77 *Eastern (AA)*. Team was a farm club of the Montreal Expos. The tag was a spin-off from Expos.

5325 Capitals 1999–2003 *Northern (ind.)* 1999–2003; 2005 to date *Canadian–American (ind.)*. Settled in 1608, the city became the capital of New France 1663–1763, Lower Canada 1791–1841, United Canada 1851–55 and Quebec Province 1867 to date. The moniker in French is "Les Capitales."

Quincy, Illinois

5326 Browns 1883–84 *Northwestern (ind.)*. Players wore brown hose.

5327 Ravens 1889 *Central Inter-State (ind.)*; 1890 *Western Inter-State (ind.)*; 1891–92 *Illinois–Iowa (ind.)*; 1894 *Western Assn. (ind.)*. With manager Burt Merrifield at the helm, newspapers called the players "Merrifield's Ravens." Players wore black hose. Ravens are the largest bird of the family of North American crows. Ravens sometimes cause significant crop damage in Illinois. With manager George Brackett at the helm, newspapers called the black-hosed players "Brackett's Ravens."

5328 Browns 1895 *Western Assn. (ind.)*. Players wore brown hose. George Brackett returned and the team became known as "Brackett's Browns."

5329 Bluebirds 1896x *Western Assn. (ind.)*. Team disbanded July 16. Players wore blue hose. With George Brackett at the helm, newspapers called the players the "Bluebirds."

5330 Giants 1897 *Western Assn. (ind.)*. Because it is the commercial, industrial and distribution center of western Illinois, the city is nicknamed the "Giant of Western Illinois." The alternate name was **Little Giants**

5331 Gems 1897 *Western Assn. (ind.)*; 1907 *Iowa State (D)*; 1908 *Central Assn. (D)*; 1913–17x *Three-I (B)*. Quincy, like several other nineteenth century cities, was called the "Gem City" because of its economic success and beautiful buildings. Quincy is also known as the "Most Beautiful of All Western Cities." In 1917, newspapers praised the team for having a "gem of a season" as the players won the 1913 Three-I League championship. The 1917 season ended early (on July 8) due to U.S. entry into World War I, but the league did not disband.

5332 Quincy Base Ball Club 1899m *Western Assn. (ind.)*. Team moved to Dubuque (IA) May 19. Team had no nickname.

5333 Vets 1909–10 *Central Assn. (D)*. The Illinois Veterans Home was built in Quincy in 1890. "Vets" is short for "Veterans."

5334 Infants 1911 *Three-I (B)*. Three-I League represented Illinois, Indiana and Iowa. The team had many young players. A young team that struggled on the field was sometimes called the "Infants." However, this team was in the pennant race before finishing in third place, four-and-a-half games out.

5335 Crybabies 1911 *Three-I (B)*. Tag was a spin-off from Infants. The term "crybaby" describes a player who kicks, screams and otherwise argues with the umpire about a call that doesn't go his— or his team's— way. With manager Bade Myers at the helm, newspapers called the players "Bade Myers' Crybabies."

5336 Debutantes 1911 *Three-I (B)*. "Debutantes" was yet another word to describe young players in this era. In its more formal definition, the word means a young person, usually a teenager, especially a young lady making her "debut into society" at an elegant social function. With Bade Myers at the helm, newspapers called the players "Bade's Debutantes."

5337 Old Soldiers 1912 *Three-I (B)*. Tag was a spin-off from the 1910 moniker "Vets." The Illinois Veterans Home was built in Quincy in 1890.

Ra'anna, Israel

5338 Express 2008 *Israeli (ind.)*. Team went by the name of Ra'anna Express while playing its 2007 home games in Petach-Tikva (a suburb of Tel-Aviv). Circuit disbanded after the 2007 season. The team was named after the Tel-Aviv, Petach-Tikva & Ra'anna Rapid Express Transit train.

Racine, Wisconsin

5339 Malted Milks 1909–11, 1914 *Wisconsin–Illinois (C)*. Legend has it that malted milk was invented here in a soda shop in 1910. With manager William Armstrong at the helm 1909–10, newspapers called the players "William Armstrong's Malted Milks." Larry Hoffman took over in 1911 and the name became "Hoffman's Malted Milks." The name was used again in 1914 under manager Frank Reynolds. Wisconsin is known as the "Dairy State."

5340 Belles 1912–13 *Wisconsin–Illinois (C)*; 1915x *Bi-State (D)*. Bi-State League represented Illinois and Wisconsin. Team and league disbanded July 7; 1943–50 *All-American Girls Professional Baseball League (ind.)*. The circuit played under softball rules 1943–47 and baseball rules 1948–50. Racine is known as the "Belle City," which is French for "Beautiful City." With manager Billy Fox at the helm 1912–13, newspapers called the players "Billy's Belles." Frank Reynolds returned in 1915 to lead "Reynold's Belles." James Sheffield took over in mid-season to guide "Sheffield's Belles." [As for the 1943–50 team, "Belle" also means "beautiful woman," in French hence, "Les Belles" means "beautiful women."]

Radford, West Virginia

5341 Rockets 1946–50 *Blue Ridge (D)*. With the capture of German V-2 rockets (1946) and the Roswell UFO Crash (1947), the American public became fascinated with rockets. Radford was the site of the U.S. Army Ammunition Plant built there in 1940. By 1946 German V-2 rockets were housed there. Radford University constructed a planetarium on the campus in 1944–45.

Raleigh, North Carolina

5342 Senators 1901 *Virginia–North Carolina (ind.)*. Raleigh has been the capital of North Carolina since 1794.

5343 Redbirds 1902x *North Carolina (C)*; 1908–10 *Eastern Carolina (D)*; 1921 *Piedmont (D)*. Players wore red trim. With field manager R.C. River at the helm in 1902, newspapers called the players "River's Redbirds." With manager Richard Crozier at the helm in 1909–10, newspapers called the players "Richard Crozier's Redbirds." Joe Ward returned in 1921, and the name became "Joe Ward's Redbirds."

5344 Lobsters 1902x *North Carolina (C)*. Tag was a red trim spin-off name. Fishing ships drop off lobsters to city port for transport to market.

5345 Capitals 1913–17x *North Carolina State (D)*. Team disbanded May 18; 1922–28 *Piedmont (C)*; 1930–32 *Piedmont (C)*; 1945–53 *Carolina (C)* 1945–48, B 1949–53); 1958–62 *Carolina (B)*. Moniker was a spin-off from the 1901 nickname of "Senators."

5346 Nationals 1920 *Piedmont (D)*. With manager Joe Ward at the helm, newspapers called the players "Joe Ward's Nationals." Newspapers shortened name to **Nats**.

5347 Grays 1924 *Independent Negro team*. Players wore gray trim.

5348 Tigers 1948–50 *Independent Negro team*; 1951–52 *Negro American (ind.)*. Team joined this professional but non-major circuit. Players wore striped hose.

5349 Mets 1963, 1968 *Carolina (A)*. Team was a farm club of the New York Mets.

5350 Cardinals 1964–65 *Carolina (A)*. Team was a farm club of the St. Louis Cardinals.

5351 Pirates 1966–67 *Carolina (A)*. Team was a farm club of the Pittsburgh Pirates.

Raleigh-Durham, North Carolina

5352 Mets 1968 *Carolina (A)*. Team was a farm club of the New York Mets.

5353 Phillies 1969 *Carolina (A)*. Team was a farm club of the Philadelphia Phillies.

5354 Triangles 1970 *Carolina (A)*. Duke University and nearby University of North Carolina in 1960–61 constructed a block of research laboratories shaped like a triangle. The site is known as "The Research Triangle."

Rancho Cucamonga, California

5355 Quakes 1993 to date *California (A)*. The San Andreas Fault, which runs under the California Pacific Coastline, causes periodic tremors and earthquakes. Team owner Hank Stickney held a name-the-team contest in which 200 names were submitted. "Quakes," being both short and historic for the region, was chosen the winner. Other entries included Crushers, Dodgers, Lions, Orioles, Orions, Padres and Quakes.

Ranger, Texas

5356 Nitros 1920–21x *West Texas (D)*. Team disbanded July 9; 1922 *West Texas (D)*. Nitroglycerin is used to make dynamite. City factories manufacture nitroglycerin. Dynamite, i.e., TNT, is used to blow holes into the ground. Then oil well drills were inserted into the holes to start drilling. Ranger has so many oil wells that it is known as the "City of Flowing Gold." Oil is known as "black gold" and "flowing gold."

Raton, New Mexico

5357 Raton Baseball Club m1912x *Rocky Mountain (D)*. Team started season in Canon City (CO) and moved to Raton June 4. Team and league disbanded July 5. Team had no nickname.

Ravenna, Italy

5358 DeAngelis-Godo 2006–09 *Italian A1 (ind.)*. Team was owned by DeAngelis-Godo Hotels.

5359 DeAngelis Northeast Knights 2010 *Italian A1 (ind.)*. Ravenna is located in northeast Italy. Medieval knights, known as the Condottiere, fought as mercenaries throughout Italy.

5360 Russi DeAngelis Northeast Knights 2011 to date *Italian A1 (ind.)*. Russi Company bought a part-interest in the team.

Raymond, Washington

5361 Cougars 1910 *Washington State (D)*. Cougars, also called mountain lions, inhabit the Olympic, Rocky and Cascade mountains of the Pacific Northwest. With manager Fred Dunbar at the helm, newspapers called the players "Dunbar's Cougars."

5362 Venetians 1911 *Washington State (D)*. Venetian-style gondolas provide rides for tourists on the nearby Willapa Bay. Gondolas have sailed the canals of Venice, Italy, since the 12th century. With manager C. D. Wineholt at the helm, newspapers called the players "Wineholt's Venetians."

Rayne, Louisiana

5363 Ricebirds 1920x *Louisiana State (D)*. Team disbanded July 6; 1935–41 *Evangeline (D)*. Ricebirds is a generic term for birds, i.e., crows, bobolinks, that feed in rice fields. Farms in the region transport rice to city factories for cleaning and processing prior to packing and shipping to market.

5364 Red Sox 1934 *Evangeline (D)*. Team was a farm club of the Boston Red Sox.

Reading, Pennsylvania

5365 Actives 1883 *Interstate Assn. (ind.)*; 1884 *Eastern (ind.)*; 1892 *Pennsylvania State (ind.)*; m1893–94 *Pennsylvania State (ind.)*. Team began season in Danville (PA) and then moved here July 7; m1895x Team began season in Pottsville, moved to Allentown July 27, and then moved here August 10. Team disbanded July 20; 1896 *Pennsylvania State (ind.)*. "Energetic" nicknames were popular in the nineteenth century. Examples include Actives, Come-Ons, Defiance, Excelsiors, Eureka, Fleet-foots, Fly-Aways, Harmony, Perseverance, Rough'n Readys and Wide-Awakes.

5366 Anthracites 1887 *Pennsylvania State (ind.)*. Anthracite coal is shipped to Reading to be used as fuel for smelters to convert iron ore into metallic iron. Pennsylvania is the "Coal State." Anthracite is "hard coal," which burns much more cleanly than bituminous coal.

5367 Indians 1896x *Pennsylvania State (ind.)*. Team disbanded in mid-season (date unknown); 1952–61 *Eastern (A)*; 1965 *Eastern (A)*. The Delaware Indians sold Pennsylvania to William Penn in the seventeenth century. The city of Reading was founded in 1733. The teams, playing 1952–61 and 1965, were farm clubs of the Cleveland Indians.

5368 Coal Heavers 1897–1900 *Atlantic (ind.)*. Moniker was a spin-off from the 1887 team. Men with shovels, known as "coal heavers," pitched coal into city factories to stoke iron and steel furnaces. The coal and iron industries of Pennsylvania were dependent on each other. Coal was used to heat iron ore furnaces to produce iron and steel; iron and steel went into the manufacture of tractors, trains and later trucks to haul coal.

5369 Dutchmen m1907–09 *Tri-State (B)*. Dutch farmers established the Pennsylvania Dutch Farm Region in the eighteenth century. With Dutch-American Curt Weigand at the helm, newspapers called the players "Curt Weigand's Dutchmen."

5370 Pretzels m1907–11 *Tri-State (B)*. Team started 1907 season in York (PA) and moved to Reading July 24; m1912 *Tri-State (B)*; 1914 *Tri-State (B)*; m1916–17 *New York State (B)*. Team started 1916 season in Albany (NY) and moved to Reading August 21. The J.T. Adams Pretzel Bakery opened for business here in 1873. Soon more bakeries started making pretzels, leading to Reading being nicknamed the "Pretzel City." One of the owners of the bakery and a team sponsor in 1907 was William Yeitzel, which prompted newspapers to call the players "Yeitzel's Pretzels." Reading is also the "Brewing City," as German immigrants here drank beer and munched on pretzels.

5371 Reading Grooms 1912x *United States (ind.)*. Team disbanded June 6. Manager was Leo Groom.

5372 Reading Brewers 1912x *United States (ind.)*. Team disbanded June 6. Spinoff from "Pretzels." Reading is the "Brewing City."

5373 Marines 1920 *International (AA)*. The Schuylkill River Canal was built in 1825. Barges transported coal to Pennsylvania cities, including Reading. By 1900, however, trains made the Schuylkill River coal barges obsolete. With manager Jack Hummel at the helm, newspapers called the players "Hummel's Marines." Cargo boats have been sailing the Schuylkill River since 1750.

5374 Keystones 1923–32 *International (AA)*. Pennsylvania is known as the "Keystone State." Newspapers shortened the name to **Keys.**

5375 Red Sox 1933–34 *New York–Pennsylvania (A)*; 1963–64 *Eastern (AA)*. Team was a farm club of the Boston Red Sox.

5376 Brooks 1935m *New York–Pennsylvania (A)*. Team moved to Allentown July 9; 1940 *Interstate (B)*. Teams were farm clubs of the Brooklyn Dodgers. The 1936 Allentown Brooks and the 1933–35 and 1941 Reading Brooks, both farm clubs of the Brooklyn Dodgers, took the name "Brooks"— an unofficial alternate nickname of the parent Dodgers. The Brooklyn AA-NL club has been known as the "Brooks" since 1884.

5377 Chicks 1940 *Interstate (B)*. Team had many young players, known in the slang of the era as "chicks." With manager Tom Oliver at the helm, newspapers called the players "Oliver's Chicks."

5378 Phillies 1967 to date *Eastern (AA)*. Team was a farm club of the Philadelphia Phillies.

Red Cloud, Nebraska

5379 Indians 1910 *Nebraska State (D)*. Red Cloud, chief of the Oglala-Sioux, battled soldiers and settlers intent on building the Bozeman Trail, which threatened buffalo herds, until the Bozeman Trail was abandoned in 1868.

Red Deer, Alberta, Canada

5380 Eskimos 1912 *Western Canada (D)*. The Eskimos are Aleut and Inuit Indians who have inhabited Greenland, Canada, Alaska and Siberia since migrating from Asia into North America. With field manager Jerry Hurley at the helm, local newspapers called the players "Jerry Hurley's Eskimos."

Red Oak, Iowa

5381 Blue Indians 1903 *Southwest Iowa (D)*. In the era 1880–1910 "Indians" was a common slang for a team of baseball players. The Blackhawk, Cherokee, Chickasaw, Pottawatomi and Sioux Indians inhabited Iowa until the first settlers arrived in 1820. The somewhat-derogatory term "Red Indians"—used widely at this time—provided the play on words for this team's moniker of "Blue Indians" based on the players' blue uniform trim and blue stirrups. The term "Red Indian" was used to distinguish a native of North America from an "East Indian," i.e., a person from India in Central Asia.

Red Springs, North Carolina

5382 Red Robins 1947–49 *Tobacco State (D)*. The robin (also called the "red robin") is a red-breasted thrush common in North America. With manager "Red" Norris at the helm in 1947, management dressed the players in red trim and called the team "Red Robins."

5383 Twins 1969 *Carolina (A)*. Team was a farm club of the Minnesota Twins.

Red Springs–Laurinburg, North Carolina

5384 Red Robins 1950 *Tobacco State (D)*. Team sought to attract fans from neighboring Laurinburg by going to a dual-city name. All home games continued to be played in Red Springs. Manager Red Norris returned to the helm and the players again wore red-trim uniforms.

Red Wing, Minnesota

5385 Manufacturers 1910–11x *Minnesota–Wisconsin (C)*. Team disbanded June 26. For the period 1880–1920, city factories produced boats, bricks, buttons, furniture, pottery and shoes. The city is especially noted for footwear, i.e., shoes, boots, sandals, slippers and sneakers. With manager Mike Malloy at the helm, newspapers called the players "Malloy's Manufacturers."

Redding, California

5386 Browns 1948–51 *Far West (D)*. Team was a farm club of the St. Louis Browns.

Redfield, South Dakota

5387 Red Sox 1920 *South Dakota (D)*. Because of the city's name, players wore red stirrups. The team was not a farm club of the Boston Red Sox.

5388 Reds 1920 *South Dakota (D)*. Newspapers shortened the tag by mid-season. Players wore red trim uniforms.

5389 Redfield Baseball Club 1921 *Dakota (D)*. Team had no nickname.

Redondo Beach, California

5390 Sand-dabs 1910 *Southern California Trolley (D)*. The Sand Dab is a flatfish found in the Pacific Ocean.

5391 Redondo Beach Baseball Club 1925–26 *California Winter (W)*. Team had no nickname.

Refugio, Texas

5392 Oilers 1938 *Texas Valley (D)*. Oil was discovered in the region in 1928, converting the city into a "boomtown."

Reggio Emilia, Reggio Emilia, Italy

5393 Palfinger 2003 *Italian A1 (ind.)*; 2005 *Italian A1 (ind.)*. The team was owned by the Palfinger Cranes & Hydraulics Company these two seasons.

Regina, Saskatchewan

5394 Bone-pilers 1909–10 *Western Canada (D)*. Both nineteenth century Cree Indians and Canadian hunters skinned and butchered buffalo, leaving bones stacked in piles. The Cree Indians had a religious practice of piling buffalo bones in stacks to placate the Buffalo spirits to ensure plentiful hunting in the future. Originated as a hunting camp, the future city was called Pile O'Bones and then renamed Regina when the Canadian Pacific Railway arrived there in 1882. With manager Charles Blackburn at the helm in 1909, newspapers called the players the "Blackburn's Bone-pilers." Roxey Walters and then Thomas Letcher took over in 1910 and the name became "Walters' Pilers" and "Letcher's Pilers."

5395 Red Sox 1913–14 *Western Canada (D)*. Players wore red trim. Team was not a farm club of the Boston Red Sox as the farm system would not start until the 1920s.

5396 Senators 1919–21x *Western Canada (C 1919, D 1920–21)*. City has been the provincial capital since 1905.

5397 Cyclones 1994 *North Central (ind.)*; 1995–97 *Prairie (ind.)*. The Saskatchewan Prairie is barren of trees, which gives rise to dust cyclones. Grasslands National Park is located in southern Saskatchewan. On June 30, 1912, the deadliest tornado in Canadian history struck the city of Regina, killing 28 people and leaving 2,500 homeless. Five hundred buildings were destroyed.

Rehoboth Beach, Delaware

5398 Pirates 1947–48 *Eastern Shore (D)*. Team was a farm club of Pittsburgh Pirates. The 1949 team was independent but retained the name of Pirates. The tag was appropriate because the city was built just south of Delaware Bay where, starting in the seventeenth century, pirates weighed anchor in a shallow bay that became known as the "Pirates' Cove."

5399 Seahawks 1949 *Eastern Shore (D)*. Tag was a spin-off from Pirates. Team played as an independent in 1949. With manager William Sisler at the helm, newspapers called the players "William Sisler's Seahawks." John Watson took over in mid-season 1949 and the name became "Watson's Seahawks."

Reidsville, North Carolina

5400 Luckies 1935–40 *Bi-State (D)*. Bi-State League represented North Carolina and Virginia; 1947 *Tri-State (B)*; 1948–54 *Carolina (C 1948, B 1949–55)*. Reidsville was home of the American Tobacco Company (until 1994), which manufactured Lucky Strike Cigarettes, and became known as the "Lucky City."

5401 Phillies 1955 *Carolina (B)*. Team was a farm club of the Philadelphia Phillies.

Reno, Nevada

5402 Silver Sox 1947–49 *Sunset (C)*; 1950–51 *Far West (D)*; m1955–64 *California (C 1955–62, A 1963–64)*. Team began the 1955 season in Channel Cities (CA) and moved to Reno July 1; 1966–81, 1988–92 *California (A)*; 2006–08 *Golden (ind.)*. Gold and silver was discovered at the Comstock Lode in 1859. As Virginia City arose at Comstock, a railroad line was built to ship gold and silver ore to Reno for refining. From 1859 to 1880, nearly 50 percent of U.S. silver was mined at Virginia City and refined in Reno. Players wore silver-hued stirrups.

5403 Padres 1982–87 *California (A)*. Team was a farm club of the San Diego Padres.

5404 Chukars 1996–98 *Western (ind.)*. The Chukar is a partridge that inhabits mountains and prairies.

5405 Blackjacks 1999 *Western (ind.)*. Like Las Vegas, Reno is known for its gambling casinos. "Blackjack" is a gambling card game popular in Reno casinos.

5406 Aces 2009 to date *Pacific Coast (AAA)*. Reno, known as Nevada's "Little Las Vegas," has its own casinos where popular card games like poker and blackjack are played. Superlative players at card games are known as "aces." In baseball, "ace" began as a term in honor of old Cincinnati Reds pitcher Asa Brainard (career 1868–80), who was so consistently good that when some other pitcher tossed a good game, the fans shouted, "He's an Asa!" or "He pitched an Asa!" The word eventually evolved into "ace," a term that would also be applied to tennis.

Reynosa, Tamaulipas, Mexico

5407 Broncos 1963–71 *Liga Mexicana (AA 1963–66, AAA 1967–76)*; 1980–82 *Mexican (AAA)*; 1983 *Nacional de Mexico (ind.)*. Just before the 1981 major league baseball strike, the Mexican League experienced a players strike in 1980. Some players who didn't return to the Mexican League formed a six-team Liga Nacional de Mexico for the 1982–83 seasons that consisted of the following clubs: Cordoba Coffee-Growers (1982–83), Durango Scorpions (1982–83), Jalisco Cowboys (1982–83), Mexico City Metros (1982), Monclova Steelers (1982–83), Puebla Black Angels (1982–83) and Reynosa Broncos (1983). The circuit disbanded after the 1983 season when all outlaw players were invited back to the Liga Mexicana (Mexican league); 1995–2003 *Mexican (AAA)*; 2009 to date *Mexican (AAA)*. Mexican rodeos feature "bucking broncos."

5408 Bravos 1972–76 *Liga Mexicana (AAA)*. City was founded in 1749, and after the end of Spanish rule in 1821, highway and plains bandits prowled the region outside of the city shouting "Bravo, bravo!!" as a hostile shout to warn horse carriages and later trains to stop.

Richmond, California

5409 Merchants 1910–11x *Central California (D)*. Team and league disbanded July 9. Merchants here sold processed foods, wine, petroleum products, tile and electrical equipment. Goods enter and leave the city via the Richmond Harbor Port.

Richmond, Indiana

5410 Quakers 1908 *Indiana–Ohio (D)*; 1917 *Central (B)*. City was founded in 1806 by the Society of Friends, a Quaker settlement that emigrated from North Carolina to Indiana and settled here along the Whitewater River. City is home to Earlham College, a Quaker university. Richmond is known as the "Quaker City of the West."

5411 Roses 1930 *Central (B)*; 1946–47 *Ohio State (D)*. Hill's Roses, a florist, owned several greenhouses in the city. The city, which hosts the annual Rose Festival, became known as the "Rose Center of the United States." City ships 20 million roses annually to all parts of the country. With manager John McCloskey at the helm in 1930,

newspapers called the players "McCloskey's Roses." With Merle Settlemire at the helm in 1946, local newspapers called the players "Merle's Roses" and "Settlemire's Roses." Rex Carr took over in 1947 and the name became "Rex Carr's Roses."

5412 Braves 1948 *Ohio–Indiana (D)*. Team was a farm club of the Boston Braves.

5413 Tigers 1949–51 *Ohio–Indiana (D)*. Team was a farm club of the Detroit Tigers.

5414 Roosters 1995–2005 *Frontier (ind.)*. Farms in the region transport poultry products to city packing centers.

Richmond, Kentucky

5415 Pioneers 1908–12 *Blue Grass (D)*. Colonel John Miller, a soldier and pioneer, founded the city in 1798. With manager W. Parrish at the helm in 1908, newspapers called the players "Parrish's Pioneers." The moniker was retained through 1912 under four other managers. Kentucky is the "Pioneer Commonwealth."

Richmond, Virginia

5416 Virginia 1884t *Eastern (ind.)*; t1884 *American Assn. (M)*. Team jumped from the EL to this major circuit August 5. 1885–86 *Virginia (ind.)*; 1954–64 *International (AAA)*. The 1884–86 teams had the official name of the Virginia Baseball Club. Several nineteenth-century teams were named after the state they played in, i.e., Maryland (Baltimore), Hoosier (Indianapolis), California (San Francisco), Kentucky (Louisville) and Virginia (Richmond). The plural **Virginias** also appeared in newspapers. The 1954 franchise adopted the name as a "throw-back."

5417 Crows 1894 *Virginia (ind.)*. Team owner W.B. Bradley dressed his player in black uniforms and called them the Crows. In the era 1890–1910, some teams were called bird names corresponding to their stocking color, i.e., Blackbirds, Bluebirds, Canaries, Cardinals, Crows, Doves, Ravens and Redbirds.

5418 Colts 1894 *Virginia (ind.)*; 1900x *Virginia (ind.)*. Team disbanded June 13; 1906–14 *Virginia (C)*; 1918–28 *Virginia (B)*; 1932x *Eastern (A)*. Team and league disbanded July 17 due to the Great Depression; 1933–53 *Piedmont (B)*. These teams had many young players who were known in the slang of the era as "colts."

5419 Bluebirds 1895–96 *Virginia (ind.)*; 1897–99 *Atlantic (ind.)*; 1901x *Virginia–North Carolina (ind.)*. Team disbanded July 3. Players wore blue hose. In the era 1890–1910, some teams were called bird names corresponding to their stocking color, i.e., Blackbirds, Bluebirds, Canaries, Cardinals, Crows, Doves, Ravens and Redbirds.

5420 Johnny Rebs 1897–99 *Atlantic (ind.)*. Tag was a spin-off from the song "When Johnny Comes Marching Home," which refers to a Union soldier. "Johnny Reb" deliberately refers to a Confederate soldier. Richmond is the "Capital of the Confederacy."

5421 Rebels 1912x *United States (ind.)*. Team and league disbanded June 24. The Confederate capital moved from Montgomery (AL) to Richmond in June 1861. The city was the site of numerous battles between Union and Confederate troops. Richmond is the "Confederate Capital."

5422 Climbers 1915–16 *International (AA)*. Young players in this era were sometimes called "Young Climbers" and "Climbers." In this era, a young person was assumed to be a "social climber," i.e., moving his or her way up the "Ladder of Society." Sports teams that won early in the regular season were sometimes called "Climbers" and "Comets." However, this 1915 team stumbled at the start and wound up in seventh place, 22 games under .500.

5423 Virginians 1917 *International (AA)*. A "Virginian" is an inhabitant of Virginia.

5424 Giants 1920 *Negro Southern (ind.)*; 1921–22 *Southeast Negro (ind.)*; 1923–24 *Independent Negro team*; 1928 *Independent Negro team*. This name was popular with black teams. Some 30 professional black baseball teams in the era 1890–1950 assumed the tag of "Giants."

5425 Byrds 1931 *Eastern (A)*. Indian trader William Byrd obtained a land grant from the English crown in 1673 and built a fort here along James River. His son, William Byrd II, founded the city in 1737. With manager Cy Williams at the helm, the team was called "Cy's Byrds." Bobby Murray took over as manager in mid-season to lead "Bobby Murray's Byrds."

5426 Virginians 1954–64 *International (AAA)*. A "Virginian" is an inhabitant of Virginia. Newspapers sometimes shortened the moniker to the nineteenth-century style **Virginias.**

5427 Braves 1966–2008 *International (AAA)*. Team was a farm club of the Atlanta Braves. Team moved to Lawrenceville, Gwinnett County, Georgia in 2009.

5428 Flying Squirrels 2010 to date *Eastern (AA)*. The *Richmond Times-Dispatch* held a name-the-team contest and the winner was "Flying Squirrels." Team owner Claude Domino said to reporters: "We wanted an identity to appeal to fans of all ages." Other entries in the contest were Flat-heads, Ham-bones, Hush Puppies, Rhinos, and Rock-hoppers. The team's logo is quite different from the famous Jay Ward cartoon character "Rocky the Flying Squirrel."

Ridgway, Elk, Pennsylvania

5429 Ridgway Baseball Club 1887x *Mountain (ind.)*. Team and league disbanded in mid-season (date unknown); 1916 *Interstate (D)*. These teams had no nickname.

Rimini, Emilia-Romagna, Italy

5430 Semenzato 1999–2002 *Italian A1 (ind.)*. Team was owned by the Hotel Bernardi Semenzato through the 2002 season.

5431 Telemarket 2003 to date *Italian A1 (ind.)*. Team was purchased by the Rimini Telemarketing Company in 2003.

Rio Blanco, Veracruz, Mexico

5432 Cidosa 1937–38 *Mexican (ind.)*. Team was owned by Textilos Cidosa, a textile company named after the district in which it was built. Team played its home games in Estadio Colonia Cidosa.

Riverside, California

5433 Reds 1941 *California (C)*. Team was a farm club of the Cincinnati Reds.

5434 Dons 1947, 1949 *Sunset (C)*. Spanish Dons ruled California for the era 1550–1820.

5435 Rubes 1948, 1950 *Sunset (C)*. Mount Rubidoux is located just west of the city. Easter sunrise services have been held there since 1909.

5436 Red Wave 1988–90 *California (A)*. Team owner Bobby Brett held a name-the-team contest. The fans chose "Red Wave" in honor of nearby Mount Rubidoux and because of the summer heat waves in the city. The players wore red and white uniforms.

5437 Pilots 1993–95 *California (A)*. March Air Force Base, established in 1918 as Alessandro Flying Field, is located southwest of the city. The team was a farm club of the Seattle Mariners, a major aviation city, and the team logo was a fighter jet.

Riverside-Ensenada, California

5438 Padres 1952m *Southwest International (C)*. Team moved to Porterville (CA) April 25. The team was a farm club of the PCL San Diego Padres.

Riverside-Porterville, California

5439 Comets m1952m *Southwest International (C)*. At season's start, the team represented Riverside (CA)-Ensenada (MX), and then represented Riverside-Porterville April 18. Team started playing all its home games in Porterville as of April 25. With manager Chet Brewer at the helm, the club's general manager, Emmett Ashford, called the players "Chet's Comets." In earlier years, "Comets" referred to a team on a winning streak that was surging up the league standings.

Riverton-Palmyra, Pennsylvania

5440 Athletics 1906 *International Independent (ind.)*. Circuit's full name was International League of Independent Baseball Clubs. Despite playing against black teams in the IL, this was an all-white team that maintained a loose affiliation with the Philadelphia Athletics. The team purchased uniforms from the big league Athletics and then adopted the "Athletics" moniker.

Roanoke, Virginia

5441 Braves 1894–96 *Virginia (ind.)*. With field manager Bill Byrd at the helm, local newspapers called the players "Byrd's Braves." "Braves" was a common generic slang for baseball players in this era. By 1912 the Boston-Milwaukee-Atlanta National League franchise monopolized this moniker.

5442 Magicians 1895–96 *Virginia (ind.)*. In the nineteenth century, sixteen U.S. cities and one Canadian city (Toronto) were known as "Magic City" because of their swiftly built "magical" economic growth and architectural prowess. Newspapers would say "This beautiful city appeared as though by magic!" With the arrival of the Virginia & Tennessee, Shenandoah Valley Railroad, Atlantic, Mississippi & Ohio Railroad and the Norfolk & Western Railroads, 1880–83, the town quickly grew into a city by 1884.

5443 Tigers 1906–14 *Virginia (C)*. With manager J.R. "Con" Strouthers at the helm, newspapers called the players "Strouther's Tigers." Players wore striped hose and then striped stirrups. Team was not a farm club of the Detroit Tigers. In the era 1890–1905, striped stockings often led to a team choosing the nickname of "Tigers."

Roanoke Rapids, North Carolina

5444 Roanoke Rapids Baseball Club m1916x *Virginia (C)*. Team began season in Hopewell (VA) and moved to Roanoke Rapids (NC) August 14. The team played one game (a victory) and then was dropped by the Virginia League directors on August 16. Team had no nickname.

5445 Blue Jays 1947 *Coastal Plain (D)*. Team had a loose affiliation with the Philadelphia Blue Jays. The team wore blue-trim uniforms and blue stirrups in the style of the Philadelphia Blue Jays.

5446 Jays 1948–50 *Coastal Plain (D)*. Newspapers shortened the 1947 name.

Roanoke-Salem, Virginia

5447 Red Sox 1943–50 *Piedmont (B)*. Team was a farm club of the Boston Red Sox.

5448 RoSox 1951–53x *Piedmont (B)*. Team disbanded July 24. The "Sox" name is sometimes combined with the prefix of a city name, i.e., BoSox, ChiSox, KnoxSox, LynSox, PawSox and RoSox.

Robstown, Texas

5449 Cardinals m1949 *Rio Grande Valley (D)*. Team began season in Dobson (TX) and then moved to Robstown June 6. The team was a farm club of the St. Louis Cardinals.

5450 Rebels 1950x *Rio Grande Valley (C)*. Team disbanded May 13. The team was a farm club of the Texas League Dallas Rebels. For the era 1920–57 higher classification (AAA and AA) minor league teams sometimes had farm clubs among the lower classification (A, B, C, D) minor league teams.

5451 Central Bend Aviators 2003–05 *Central (ind.)*; 2006–07 *American Assn. (ind.)*. Near the city are Corpus Christi International Airport and the Corpus Christi Naval Air Base. Team logo depicts the famous "Clipper" boat plane of the 1930s and 1940s.

Rochester, Minnesota

5452 Roosters 1910 *Minnesota–Wisconsin (C 1910–11, D 1912)*. Farms in the region transport poultry products to the city. With manager Jack Corrigan at the helm, newspapers called the players "Corrigan's Roosters."

5453 Bears 1911 *Minnesota–Wisconsin (C)*. Team had a loose affiliation with the NL Chicago Cubs. With manager Ted Corbett at the helm, local newspapers called the players "Corbett's Bears."

5454 Bugs 1912x *Minnesota–Wisconsin (D)*. Team and league disbanded July 1. The nearby Zumbro River was often infested with mosquitoes in the summer. Today, vigorous spraying with insecticides controls the mosquito population.

5455 Athletics 1958 *Three-I (B)*. Team was a farm club of the Kansas City Athletics.

5456 Aces 1993 *Northern (ind.)*. Moniker was a spin-off from the 1958 Rochester A's, which sounds like Rochester "Aces." Rochester has three country club golf courses—Eastwood, Meadow Lakes and Rochester. A golfer who excels at the game is known as an "ace." The team's best player was University of Minnesota "ace" pitcher Bill Cutshall. The team logo was a hitter at the plate. In baseball, there is the term "pitching ace" but it is not associated with a batter.

Rochester, New Hampshire

5457 Rochester Base Ball Club 1888x *New England International (ind.)*. Team and circuit disbanded in mid-season (date unknown). Team had no nickname.

Rochester, New York

5458 Flour Citys 1877 *New York State (M)*; 1878 *International Assn. (M)*; 1885 *New York State (ind.)*; 1886–87 *International (ind.)*; 1890 *American Assn. (M)*; 1891 *Eastern Assn. (ind.)*; 1892 *Eastern (ind.)*. Colonel Nathaniel Rochester and two partners established a flour mill here in 1803. The town established here was called Rochesterville. In 1825, the city changed its name to Rochester. Farms in the region transported bushels of wheat to flour mills. Rochester soon became known as the "Flour City." The team switched leagues in 1878.

5459 Blue Stockings 1877 *New York State (M)*; 1878 *International Assn. (M)*. Players wore blue hose. Local newspapers shortened the moniker to **Blue Legs** and **Blues**. Unlike "Red Sox" and "White Sox," the nicknames "Blue Sox" and "Green Sox" never caught on in baseball's major leagues.

5460 Raws 1877 *New York State (M)*; 1878 *International Assn. (M)*; 1885 *New York State (ind.)*; 1886–87 *International (ind.)*; 1888–89 *International Assn. (ind.)*; 1890 *American Assn. (M)*; 1891 *Eastern Assn. (ind.)*; 1892 *Eastern (ind.)*; 1895–97m *Eastern (ind.)*; 1899–1911 *Eastern (A 1902–07, AA 1908–11)*. City name is pronounced by natives as "Raw-chester." Newspapers liked the name but it was discarded by 1911.

5461 Hop Bitters m1879–80 *National Assn. (M)*; 1890 *American Assn. (M)*; 1891 *Eastern Assn. (ind.)*; 1892 *Eastern (ind.)*. Team started the 1879 season in Albany (NY) when new owner, Asa Boule, bought the team and moved it to Rochester May 19. Boule, the owner of a brewery, developed a concoction — he called it a tonic — made of fermented barley and hops designed to be of medicinal value. The 1879 team uniform bore the red letters "H.B." Asa Boule's son, William Soule, owned the 1890–92 Rochester teams.

5462 Advertising Gang 1879–80 *National Assn. (M)*. The *Brooklyn Eagle* newspaper was quick to condemn the team's marketing ploy, calling the franchise the "Advertising Gang" and the **Advertising Quack Medicine Team**.

5463 Pets 1886 *International (ind.)*; 1889 *International Assn. (ind.)*; 1890 *American Assn. (M)*. In the era 1885–1900, baseball players, who already were known by a whole menagerie of animal names, were sometimes referred to as the field manager's "pets." Under 1886 managers Dave Bancroft and Alonzo Knight, the players were known as "Bancroft's Pets" and "Knight's Pets." With manager Pat Powers at the helm 1889–90, newspapers called the players "Pat Powers' Pets." By 1900, fans thought the tag "too cute," and its use faded.

5464 Maroons 1886–87 *International (ind.)*. Players wore maroon hose.

5465 Flower Citys 1886–87 *International (ind.)*; 1888–89 *International Assn. (ind.)*; 1890 *American Assn. (M)*; 1891 *Eastern Assn. (ind.)*; 1892 *Eastern (ind.)*; 1895–97m *Eastern (ind.)*. Team moved to Montreal July 16; 1898m *Eastern (ind.)*. Team moved to Ottawa July 7. In 1850, Rochester's Ellwanger & Barry Nursery Company in 1850 was the world's largest seed nursery, giving rise to the city nickname of "Flower City." Rochester is also known as the "World's Largest Lilac Center."

5466 Lambs 1886–87 *International (ind.)*; 1888–89 *International Assn. (ind.)*. The 1886–87 name was a spin-off from 1886 manager Dave Bancroft's "Pets." In the nineteenth century, a "pet lamb" was a popular domestic pet. The team had many young players, known in the slang of the era as "lambs." With manager Frank Leonard at the helm 1888–89, newspapers called the players "Leonard's Lambs."

5467 Jingoes 1888–89 *International Assn. (ind.)*. Famed British Prime Minister Benjamin Disraeli went to college at England's University of Rochester. In the 1860s Disraeli faced fierce opposition from a pro-war political party known as the "Jingoes." The term "jingo" literally means a palace guard at Buckingham Palace in London, England. It stems from "jingoism," which — like "Chauvinism"— means belligerent patriotism. In the 1880s the Communist Party of America set up offices in cities throughout New York. Anti-communists violently denounced them, prompting some left-leaning newspapers, i.e., *Rochester Democrat and Chronicle*, to criticize these anti–Leftists as "jingoistic." The moniker extended into baseball to describe hot-headed players who violently argued with umpires on a disputed call. Such players were known as "anarchists" as well as "jingoes." With manager Henry Leonard at the helm in 1888, newspapers called the players "Leonard's Jingoes." Pat Powers took over in mid-season 1889 and the name became "Powers' Jingoes." Rochester (NY) is also named after Rochester, England.

5468 Black Stockings 1890 *American Assn. (M)*. Players wore black hose. Newspapers shortened it to **Black Legs** and **Black Sox**.

5469 Bronchos 1890 *American Assn. (M)*; 1899–1911 *Eastern (A*

1902–07, *AA* 1908–11*). According to baseball historian Bill McCarthy, with manager Pat Powers at the helm, newspapers called the players "Powers' Bronchos." Horse nicknames for teams were popular in this era, i.e., Bronchos, Colts, Riders and Ponies. With manager Al "Buck" Buckenberger at the helm 1899–1901 and 1905–08, newspapers called the players "Buck's Bronchos." In the years 1899 and 1901, Buckenberger's players "bucked their way to the pennant." The name was retained through 1911.

5470 West Shores 1890 *American Assn. (M).* Rochester is located on the western shore of Lake Ontario.

5471 Brownies 1895–96 *Eastern (ind.).* The Eastman-Kodak Company of Rochester (NY) produced the first hand-held camera — a little brown box-camera that was immediately nicknamed "The Brownie." To capitalize on the publicity, management dressed the players in brown hose. Newspapers sometimes shortened the moniker to **Browns**.

5472 Blackbirds 1897 *Eastern (ind.).* Players wore black hose. In the era 1890–1910, some teams got bird nicknames based on stocking color, i.e., Blackbirds, Bluebirds, Blue Jays, Canaries, Cardinals, Crows, Doves, Ravens and Redbirds.

5473 Patriots 1898m *Eastern (ind.).* The Montreal Jingoes team — Jingoes being a pro–British name — moved to Rochester in mid-season. Local fans and newspapers didn't want the Jingos name again, i.e., 1888–89 Rochester Jingoes, so newspapers went to the pro-American "Patriots." Starting in 1861 the Rochester Light Guards, known as "Taylor's Patriots," fought in the Civil War.

5474 Beau Brummels 1903–08 *Eastern (A 1902–07, AA 1908).* George "Beau" Brummel was a somewhat foppish nineteenth century Englishman (born in London in 1778) noted for his excessive spending, drinking, womanizing and preoccupation with expensive and fashionable clothing and high society manners. Such men tended to shun exercise and sports, rendering them quite unathletic. Baseball players — young men often better paid than laborers — tended to dress in fancy duds, drink excessively and chase women. The name first referred to a young man around 1850 and later, around 1880, to a baseball player. Baseball players in this era were known variously as Bridegrooms, Ladies' Men, Mashers and Beau Brummels. In 1903–04 the Rochesters finished in last place both seasons while going 62–202, prompting newspapers to complain the team "played like beau brummels." One tabloid sneered: "It is a mystery why these 'Beau Brummels' are not sent to jail for masquerading as ball players!"

5475 Hustlers 1909–11 Eastern *(AA).* 1902–07; 1912–20 *International (AA).* Politically incorrect today (because of its connotation to gambling), the name was complimentary, i.e., "a player who hustles on the field." Newspapers and fans were delighted with manager "John Ganzel's Hustlers" as they "hustled their way" to three consecutive EL pennants, 1909–11. Moniker alternated with "Bronchos" through the 1911 season. The name was used under four other managers through 1920.

5476 Colts 1921–22 *International (AA).* Tag was a newspaper-friendly spin-off from "Bronchos." With George Stallings at the helm as manager, newspapers called the players "Stallings' Colts."

5477 Tribe 1922–26 *International (AA).* The Iroquois Five Nations inhabited New York State when successive waves of Dutch, French, English and American settlers drove them westward. With manager George Stallings at the helm 1922–26, newspapers called the players "Stallings' Tribe." Stallings had previously been the manager of the Boston Braves — hence the spin-off moniker of "Tribe." The tag had nothing to do with the Cleveland Indians, who, starting in 1915, were also were known as "The Tribe."

5478 Red Wings 1927 to date *International (AA).* St. Louis Cardinal general manager Branch Rickey established a loose affiliation with the 1927 Rochester club, which was named "Red Wings" as a spin-off from "Cardinals." In 1932 the Red Wings became an official farm club of the St. Louis Cardinals for the period 1932–60. In 1961 the team became a farm club of the AL Baltimore Orioles, but the Red Wings moniker has been retained to date.

5479 New York Black Yankees 1930–32 *Independent Negro team.* Tag was a spin-off from AL New York Yankees. The team name refers to the state of New York and not to New York City.

Rock Island, Illinois

5480 Rock Island Base Ball Club 1891 *Illinois–Iowa (ind.);* 1895 *Eastern Iowa (ind.).* These teams had no nickname.

5481 Twin Citys 1894 *Western Assn. (ind.).* Team represented the "Twin Citys" of Rock Island and Moline. Newspapers often shortened the name to **Twins**.

5482 Islanders 1894 *Western Assn. (ind.);* 1898–99 *Western Assn. (ind.);* 1901–11 *Three-I (ind.* 1901 *B* 1902–11); m1914m *Central Assn. (D).* Team started season in Ottumwa and then moved to Rock Island July 17. With the franchise invading the territory of the Davenport Blue Sox and Moline Plowboys of the Three-I League, the National Association (the administrative organization of the minor leagues) ordered the franchise moved to Galesburg (IL) on July 24; 1920–21 *Three-I (B);* 1922–33 *Mississippi Valley (D);* 1934–35x *Western (A).* Team disbanded July 17 because of the Great Depression. Rock Island and Moline occupy a peninsula on the Mississippi River. The city was built on the coast of the Mississippi River just south of the island — *Rock Island* — for which it was named.

5483 Rocks 1936x *Western (A).* Team disbanded August 17 because of the Great Depression. Newspapers adopted this contraction for their headlines, i.e., "Rocks edge Dubs, 4–3."

5484 Robin Hoods m1936 *Western (A).* Team started 1936 season as the Omaha "Robin Hoods" and then moved to Rock Island August 18 after the Rock Island Rocks folded. The "Robin Hoods" moniker was retained.

5485 Islanders m1937x *Western (A).* Fans didn't like "Robin Hoods" (Nebraska's forest rangers) because it had nothing to do with Iowa. Management, therefore, switched to the long-standing moniker of "Islanders."

Rock Island–Moline, Illinois

5486 Rock Island–Moline Twins 1892 *Illinois–Iowa (ind.).* Team represented both cities — the "Twin Cities."

5487 Rock Island–Moline Islanders 1893–94 *Western Assn. (ind.).* Rock Island, for which the city and county are named, is a limestone rock island formation on the Mississippi River.

Rock Rapids, Iowa

5488 Browns 1902 *Iowa–South Dakota (D).* Players wore brown hose. The team had a loose affiliation with the St. Louis Browns. In the era 1885–1930, minor league teams, in cities geographically close to a major league team, sometimes had informal ties with the major league club, i.e., receiving used equipment and uniforms and selling players to the big league club.

Rockford, Illinois

5489 Forest City 1870 *Independent;* 1871 *National Assn. (M);* 1879x *Northwestern (ind.);* 1888 *Central Inter-State (ind.);* 1895–98 *Western Assn. (ind.).* After the city was established in 1852, city fathers ordered the planting of trees to line the streets, giving rise to the moniker of "Forest City." The White Pines Forest State Park is located about 30 miles southwest of the city.

5490 Green Stockings 1870 *Independent*; 1871 *National Assn. (M).* Management dressed the players in green stockings, modeled after the 1869–70 New York Mutual Green Stockings. Newspapers shortened the name to **Green Legs** and **Green Sox.**

5491 White Stockings 1879x *Northwestern (ind.).* The players wore white hose. Local newspapers shortened the name to **White Sox, White Legs** and **Whites.**

5492 Hustlers 1891–92 *Illinois–Indiana (ind.)*; 1895–99 *Western Assn. (ind.).* Politically incorrect today because of its connotations with gambling, the moniker was complimentary, referring to players who hustled on the field. The moniker soon became synonymous with a baseball player. With manager Hugh Nicol at the helm, newspapers called the players the alliterative "Hugh's Hustlers."

5493 Nicol-platers 1895–96 *Western Assn. (ind.).* Moniker was a spin-off from manager Hugh Nicol. The technology of nickel electroplating had just been perfected. Electroplating uses an electric current to put a metal coating on another metal or a non-metallic conducting surface.

5494 Red Stockings 1895–99x *Western Assn. (ind.).* Team disbanded July 25, 1896; 1897–98 *Western Assn. (ind.).* Players wore red hose.

5495 Roughriders 1899 *Western Assn. (ind.).* Rockford had a loose affiliation with the Chicago Nationals, who were sometimes called the "Roughriders" in 1899 after training in the spring in Arizona in an era when that state was still mostly "Cowboy Country." A cowboy on horseback is known as a "Roughrider." Teddy "Roosevelt's Roughriders"—a cavalry unit with mostly cowboys among the recruits—fought in Cuba during the Spanish-American War in 1898–99. With manager Henry "Hunky" Hines at the helm, local newspapers called the players the "Henry Hines' Roughriders."

5496 Red Sox 1901–04 *Three-I (ind.1901, B 1902–04).* Players wore red hose. Actually, the moniker was a spin-off of the Chicago White Sox, with whom the Rockford team had a loose affiliation.

5497 Reds 1908–10 *Wisconsin–Illinois (D 1908–09, C 1910–14).* Players wore red-trim uniforms and stirrups. The team had a loose affiliation with the Chicago White Sox. The Rockford players' red stirrups was a spin-off from the white stirrups of the Chicago Americans. Newspapers shortened the 1904 "Red Sox" tag to "Reds." The team was not a farm club of the Cincinnati Reds.

5498 Wolverines 1911–13 *Wisconsin–Illinois (D 1908–09, C 1910).* Moniker was a spin-off of manager Orville Wolf. The team also had a loose affiliation with the AL Detroit Tigers (whose NL predecessor team was the Detroit Wolverines). After Wolf left the team following the 1911 season, the name was retained through 1914.

5499 Indignants 1913 *Wisconsin–Illinois (C).* Team had several argumentative players. In the era 1880–1920, players who argued often or vehemently with umpires were known as Kickers, Orators and Indignants. With manager Clarence Marshall at the helm, newspapers called the players "Clarence's Indignants."

5500 Wolves 1914 *Wisconsin–Illinois (C).* Clarence Wolf returned as manager. By this time the moniker "Wolverines" had been appropriated by the collegiate sports teams of the University of Michigan. The moniker was appropriate because wolves do inhabit some areas in Illinois.

5501 Rockfordites 1915 *Three-I (B).* A "Rockfordite" is an inhabitant of Rockford. Local newspapers rejected this overlong name and went to "Rox" and "Wakes."

5502 Wakes 1915–16 *Three-I (B).* Team was named after manager Howard Wakefield. In the era 1880–1920, quite a few teams had nicknames derived from their field managers, i.e., Macks (Connie Mack), McGraws (John McGraw), Seleeites (Frank Selee), Loftusites (Fred Loftus), etc.

5503 Rox 1917 *Three-I (B)*; 1919–23 *Three-I (B)*; 1947–49 *Central Assn. (C).* Newspaper editors used this contraction for headlines, i.e., "Rox edge Blue Sox, 4–3." In the nineteenth century, the word "Stockings" was routinely contracted as "Socks" and "Legs." By 1900, the X-style lettering of "Sox" had become commonplace, although it first appeared in newspapers as early as 1875. "Rox" was another similar contraction.

5504 Rocks 1919–23 *Three-I (B)*; 1947–49 *Central Assn. (C).* A variation of "Rox," the moniker was used for headlines, i.e., "Rocks beat Dubs, 6–3." Today's Colorado Rockies are also referred to as the "Rocks."

5505 Peaches 1943–54 *All-American Girls Professional Baseball League (ind.).* Farms here transport peaches and other fruit to packing houses. The circuit played by softball rules 1943–47 and then switched to baseball rules 1948–54.

5506 Expos 1988–92 *Midwest (A).* Team was a farm club of the Montreal Expos.

5507 Royals 1993–94 *Midwest (A).* Team was a farm club of the Kansas City Royals.

5508 Cubbies 1995–98 *Midwest (A).* Team was a farm club of the Chicago Cubs. "Cubbies," used since 1915, was complimentary when the Cubs were winning 1915–46 but soon became a sour and sarcastic appellation for the 1947–2011 losers. Rockford fans didn't like a nickname they considered to have a losing image. Cubbies actually meant "Little Cubs," i.e., a minor league farm team.

5509 Reds 1999 *Midwest (A).* Team was a farm club of the Cincinnati Reds.

5510 Riverhawks 2002–09 *Frontier (ind.).* City is located near the Rock River. The hawk is a small falcon found in North America. Some hawks migrate to Rock River in warmer weather.

Rockingham, North Carolina

5511 Eagles 1950 *Tobacco State (D).* Team was owned by the Eagle Tobacco Company. The city's first cotton mill was built here in 1867, but tobacco took over as the primary crop by 1900.

Rockland, Connecticut

5512 Rockland Base Ball Club 1884 *Connecticut State (ind.).* Team had no nickname.

Rockland, Maine

5513 Rockland Base Ball Club 1884 *Connecticut (ind.)*; 1897 *Maine State (ind.).* These teams had no nickname.

Rocky Mount, North Carolina

5514 Railroaders 1909–10 *Eastern Carolina (D).* The Raleigh & Gaston and Wilmington & Raleigh Railroads arrived here in 1840. Site was called the Rocky Mount Depot until it became the town of Rocky Mount in 1867. With manager W.B. Fenner at the helm, newspapers called the players "Fenner's Railroaders."

5515 Carolinians 1915 *Virginia (C).* Inhabitants of North and South Carolina are known as "Carolinians." With manager Ray Ryan at the helm, newspapers called the players "Ryan's Carolinians."

5516 Downhomers 1916 *Virginia (C).* Rocky Mount in this era was a city located in surrounding rural farms and towns. From the song "Down Home on the Farm," rural residents became known as "Down-homers."

5517 Tar Heels 1916–17x *Virginia (C).* Team disbanded May 15 because of U.S. entry into World War I; 1920–23 *Virginia (B).* North Carolina is the "Tar Heel State." With manager Al Bridwell at the helm, newspapers called the players "Al Bridwell's Tar Heels." Phifer Fullenwider took over in mid-season 1920 and the name became "Fullenwider's Tar Heels." Frank Walker took over in 1923 and the name became "Walker's Tar Heels."

5518 Black Swans 1922 *Independent Negro team.* The swan, larger than a goose, is found in North America. Since the players on the field were as graceful as swans, management called them the "Black Swans."

5519 Elks 1922 *Independent Negro team.* The elk is a large North American deer.

5520 Bronchos 1924–25 *Virginia (B).* Rocky Mount newspaper reporters selected "Bronchos" to build a rivalry with the Richmond "Colts." Manager Jim Viox (pronounced v-O) took over in 1925 and the name became the rhyming "Viox' Broncos." Bill Pike took over in mid-season 1925 and the name became "Bill's Broncos."

5521 Buccaneers 1927 *Piedmont (C);* 1928–29 *East Carolina (D).* Team had a loose affiliation with the Pittsburgh Pirates. Rocky Mount was built along the Tar River. In this era, some teams in cities near a river were called "Pirates" and "Buccaneers." With manager Lee Gooch at the helm in 1927, newspapers called the players "Lee's Buccaneers." With manager Charles McMilan at the helm, the name became "McMilan's Buccaneers." The name was retained in 1929 under Zip King and Charles Moore as "King's Buccaneers" and "Charles' Buccaneers." Buccaneers were seventeenth-century freebooters that preyed on Spanish ships in the waters off the Carolina coast.

5522 Red Sox 1936–40 *Piedmont (B).* Team was a farm club of the Boston Red Sox.

5523 Leafs 1941 *Coastal Plain (D);* 1947–52 *Coastal Plain (D);* 1962–63, 1965–72 *Carolina (B).* 1962, *(A).* 1963–72). City is home to the Bright Leaf Tobacco Market, one of the world's largest. The city has several tobacco re-drying plants as well as numerous tobacco auction houses. With manager Norm McCaskill at the helm, newspapers called the players "McCaskill's Leafs."

5524 Rocks 1942 *Bi-State (D);* 1946 *Coastal Plain (D).* Newspapers used this abbreviation for their headlines, i.e., "Rocks defeat Hornets, 3–1."

5525 Senators 1964 *Carolina (A).* Team was a farm club of the Washington Senators.

5526 Phillies 1973–75 *Carolina (A).* Team was a farm club of the Philadelphia Phillies.

5527 Pines 1980 *Carolina (A).* Timber from pine tree forests in the western Carolinas is shipped to lumber mills here.

Rogers, Arkansas

5528 Rustlers 1934 *Arkansas State (D).* "Rustler" was slang for baseball player in the period 1880–1940. Baseball players in this era had a reputation as being physically dirty cowboy types with unsavory reputations and occasional brushes with the law — much like cattle rustlers. The players "rustled victories" away from opponents as the team won the 1934 Arkansas States League championship. In the nineteenth century, vigilantes and posses hunted cattle rustlers in Arkansas as much as in Texas.

5529 Cardinals 1935 *Arkansas State (D).* Team was a farm club of the St. Louis Cardinals.

5530 Lions 1936–37 *Arkansas–Missouri (D).* With manager Doc Ledbetter at the helm in 1936, newspapers called the players "Ledbetter's Lions." Frank Stapleton took over in mid-season and the name became "Stapleton Lions." In 1937, Ted Mayer guided "Meyer's Lions."

5531 Reds 1938 *Arkansas–Missouri (D).* Team was a farm club of the Cincinnati Reds.

Rohnert Park, Sonoma County, California

5532 Redwood Pioneers 1980–85 *California (A).* American pioneers revolted against the Mexican garrison here in 1846 and proclaimed the establishment of the California Republic. Two years later, the region was flooded with pioneers, settlers and prospectors when gold was discovered at Sutter's Mill on January 24, 1848. The city is near the Redwood National Park. The Redwood is a tall Evergreen Sequoia tree found in California and is the state tree.

5533 Sonoma County Crushers 1995–2002 *Western (ind.).* Farms in the region transport grapes to city wineries where crushers produce grape juice for fermentation. Nearly 90 percent of U.S. wines are produced in Napa and Sonoma counties in California.

Roma, Italy

Note: Rome in English, Roma in Italian.

5534 Café Danesi Nettuno 1999 to date *Italian A1 (ind.).* Team plays in Nettuno, a suburb of Rome. Café Danesi owns the team.

Rome, Georgia

5535 Romans 1910, 1912 *Southeastern (D);* 1913 *Appalachian (D);* The inhabitants of any city named Rome are called Romans. Settlers founded the city in 1834 amidst the Seven Hills of the Piedmont Plateau near the Coosa River — reminiscent of Ancient Rome's Seven Hills along the Tiber River in Italy.

5536 Hillites 1911 *Southeastern (D).* Rome, Georgia, is the "City of the Seven Hills."

5537 Hillies 1911 *Southeastern (D).* Tag was shorter for newspapers.

5538 Romans 1913 *Appalachian (D);* 1914–17x *Georgia–Alabama (D).* Team went by the dual-city name of **Rome-Lindale Romans** in 1917. Home games in 1917 were played in Rome. Team and league disbanded May 23 due to U.S. entry into World War I. With manager Jack Reidy managing 1913–15, the team was "Reidy's Romans." The moniker was used through 1917.

5539 Rome Baseball Club 1920–21 *Georgia State (D).* Team had no nickname.

5540 Red Sox 1950–51 *Georgia–Alabama (D).* Team had a loose affiliation with the AL Boston Red Sox in 1950, who provided the players with Red Sox uniforms. In 1951, the team became a formal farm club of the AL Washington Senators while the players continued to wear Red Sox uniforms.

5541 Braves 2003 to date *South Atlantic (A).* Team is a farm club of the Atlanta Braves.

Rome, New York

5542 Noble Romans 1898 *New York State (ind.).* The Equestrian class of ancient Rome was known as the "Noble Romans."

5543 Romans 1898–1901 Newspapers shortened the name.

5544 Colonels 1937–42 *Canadian–American (C);* 1946–51 *Canadian–American (C).* Colonel John Stanwix, a British general who fought in the French and Indian War, built Fort Stanwix here in 1758. The fort's officers supplied troops in the Battle of Oriskany in August 1777. Stanwix died at sea in 1765. With manager Bill Buckley at the helm in 1937, newspapers called the players "Bill Buckley's Colonels." After Buckley left the team following the 1938 season, the name was retained through 1942. Griffiss Air Force Base is located close to the city. Starting in 1946, the name referred to U.S. Air Force colonels.

5545 Coppers 2007 *New York State (ind.).* Founded in 1819, the city by 1870 built metal mills to process copper, which was transported to the city from nearby copper mines into finished copper and brass products. The team and circuit disbanded after the 2007 season. Rome, which had one of every ten copper factories in the United States, is known as the "Copper City."

Romeoville, Will, Illinois

5546 Will County Claws 1995x *North Central (ind.)*. Team disbanded July 5. Clawed creatures such as the red fox, gray fox, raccoons and coyotes inhabit Illinois.

5547 Will County Cheetahs 1996–97 *Heartland (ind.)*. When the Will County Claws joined this circuit, management wanted a spin-off from Claws and a fan poll chose "Cheetahs."

Rosamond, California

5548 Antelope Valley Ravens 1995 *Golden State (ind.)*. Players wore black-trim uniforms and hose. The raven is a large North American blackbird or crow.

Roseburg, Oregon

5549 Shamrocks 1904 *Oregon State (D)*. With Irish-American "Turkey" Morrow at the helm as manager, newspapers called the players "Turkey Morrow's Shamrocks." Oregon is the "Cool, Green Vacationland."

Roseville, California

5550 Diamonds m1948 *Far West (D)*. Team started season as the Pittsburg (CA) Diamonds and moved to Roseville June 30. The nickname of Diamonds was retained. "Diamonds" refers to "Black Diamonds," i.e., coal, and not the traditional clear-crystal diamonds.

Roswell, New Mexico

5551 Giants 1923x *Panhandle Pecos Valley (D)*. Circuit and team disbanded August 15. Minor league teams in this era sometimes emulated a successful ML team by adopting the big league club's nickname. The 1922–23 New York Giants were the 1922 World Series champions. The name became sarcastic as the team finished in last place. Name was also chosen to build up a rivalry with the Clovis Cubs.

5552 Sunshiners 1937 *West Texas–New Mexico (D)*. New Mexico is known as the "Sunshine State" and the "Land of Sunshine."

5553 Rockets 1949–55 *Longhorn (D 1949–50, C 1951–55)*; 1956 *Southwestern (B)*. A UFO allegedly crashed here in the summer of 1947. The New Mexico White Sands Testing Range, near the city, fired captured German V-2 rockets from 1946 to 1957. New Mexico is the "Space Age Research Center for the Free World."

5554 Pirates m1959 *Sophomore (D)*. Team started season in San Angelo (TX) and moved to Roswell June 9. Team was a farm club of the Pittsburgh Pirates.

Rossland, British Columbia, Canada

5555 Rossland Base Ball Club 1897 *Washington State (ind.)*. Team had no nickname.

Rotterdam, South Holland, Netherlands (Holland)

5556 DOOR-Neptunus 1999 to date *Hoofdklasse (ind.)*. Team is owned by both the Neptunus Soccer Club and by DOOR Sports Training Equipment.

5557 Sparta-Feyenoord 1999 to date *Hoofdklasse (ind.)*. The team is owned jointly by the Sparta Fussball Club and the Feyenoord Fussball Club — two veteran soccer franchises of the Netherlands Fussball (Soccer) League.

Round Rock, Texas

5558 Express 2000–04 *Texas (AA)*; 2005 to date *Pacific Coast (AAA)*. City is a stopping point for the Round Rock Express of the Central Texas & Austin Railroad. One of the franchise owners was Hall of Fame pitcher Nolan "The Express" Ryan, who got the nickname for having a great 100-MPH fastball.

Rouse's Point, New York

5559 Rouse's Point Base Ball Club 1895 *Eastern International (ind.)*. Team had no nickname.

Royersford, Pennsylvania

5560 Royersford Base Ball Club 1896x *Schuylkill Valley (ind.)*. Team had no nickname.

Rushville, Indiana

5561 Rushville Base Ball Club 1896x *Indiana State (ind.)*. Team disbanded in mid-season (date unknown). Team had no nickname.

Rusk, Texas

5562 Governors 1916 *East Texas (D)*. James S. Hogg, served 1891–95, was the first Texas governor who was born in the Lone Star State (in Rusk in 1851). With manager Jack Ashton at the helm, newspapers called the players "Ashton's Governors."

Russellville, Alabama

5563 Miners 1921 *Alabama–Tennessee (D)*. Coal, iron ore and limestone is transported from mines just outside Russellville to city factories to be refined.

Russi, Ravenna-Godo, Ravenna, Italy

5564 Russi-Godo DeAngelis 2006 to date *Italian A1 (ind.)*. Team represents the cities of Russi and Godo. Team is owned by the Villa de Angelis Hotels. The name also honors famous Italian race-car driver Elio DeAngelis (b. 1958), who was killed in a test-run accident May 14, 1986.

Rutland, Vermont

5565 Rutland Base Ball Club 1887 *Northeastern (ind.)*; 1905 *Northern (D)*; 1907 *New Hampshire (D)*. These teams had no nickname.

5566 Sheiks 1924x *Quebec–Ontario–Vermont (B)*. Handsome and suave Hollywood actor Rudolph Valentino gained stardom as the lead in the 1921 silent movie *The Sheik*. American women were crazed for him. Rutland star player Buck "The Sheik" Fraser led the league in batting average (.404), hits (140) and home runs (15). Fraser joined Quebec after Rutland folded. Baseball players — young, vigorous, well-dressed, better paid than the average worker and alluring to women — were sometimes called "sheiks" in deliberate emulation of Valentino. With the team leading the league during the schedule's first 54 games, local newspapers called the players the "Sheiks of the League." However, money troubles caused the team to disband on July 15 while leading the league with a 34–20 record.

Sabetha, Kansas

5567 Sabetha Base Ball Club 1910 *Eastern Kansas (D)*. Team had no nickname.

Sabinas, Coahuila, Mexico

5568 Piratas 1971–73 *Liga Mexicana (AAA)*. Sabinas is located near the Cerro del Pirata, a mountain north of the city. The city is also near the Rio Salado. Sometimes, a baseball team, playing in a city near to a river, is called "Pirates" or "Buccaneers." The Spanish word "piratas" means "pirates."

5569 Mineros de Coahuila 1971–79 *Mexican (AAA)*. Spanish arrived here in the sixteenth century looking for silver. By 1910 iron ore mines sent the ore to city smelting factories. On February 21, 2006, a coal mine explosion in Coahuila killed 65 miners. "Mineros" means "miners."

Sacramento, California

5570 Altas 1887 *California (ind.)*; 1889–91 *California (ind.)*. City is located near Mount Shasta between the Sierra Nevada and Coastal Mountains. Alta is the Spanish word for "high." The Spanish word "alta" means "high," and was the nineteenth-century term for upper California. Baja California, meaning "low," was the term for the Mexican-held lower California. The team was also name in honor of a race horse of the day named "Alta." With manager Tom Gleeson at the helm, newspapers called the players "Gleeson's Altas." Charley Gagus and then Charles Schreiver took over and the name became "Charley's Altas."

5571 Senators 1889–91 *California (ind.)*; m1893 *California (ind.)*; 1901 *California (ind.)*; 1908 *California (ind.)*; 1910 *California State (D)*; 1918–35 *Pacific Coast (AA 1918–35)*. Tag was a spin-off from Capitals. With manager Steve Lang at the helm in 1889, newspapers called the players "Steve Lang's Senators." Charles Schreiver took over in mid-season 1889 and the name became "Charles Schreiver's Senators." The 1910 team was also called the **Baby Senators** because it had a loose affiliation with the 1910 PCL Sacramento club, which was sometimes called the "Senators." Almost all the players were very young, hence "baby."

5572 White Stockings 1890 *California (ind.)*. Players wore white hose. The team was not a farm club of the NL Chicago White Stockings (who had abandoned that moniker in 1888). In this era (1885–1900) there were only about a dozen loose-affiliation "farm clubs," all located in the midwestern (Chicago) and northeastern U.S. (New York, Boston and Philadelphia) and all geographically close to these major league cities. Newspapers shortened the name to **White Legs** and **White Sox.**

5573 Capitals 1891 *California (ind.)*; m1893 *California (ind.)*. Sacramento has been the state of California capital since 1854. With manager John McCloskey at the helm, newspapers called the players "McCloskey's Capitals." Tom McGuirk took over in mid-season 1891 and the name became "McGuirk's Capitals."

5574 Dukes m1893 *California (ind.)*. Before its entry into the U.S., Spanish Dukes— Los Duques de California— governed California.

5575 Pirates m1893 *California (ind.)*. Team started season in Stockton (CA) and moved to Sacramento July 6. The team stocked its 1893 roster with several players raided from other teams. This practice was branded by newspapers of this era as "piracy," i.e., NL Pittsburgh Pirates, PL Chicago Pirates, Pacific NL San Francisco Pirates. With manager John Moore at the helm, newspapers called the players "Moore's Pirates." Pirate ships roamed the California coastline from the middle of the sixteenth century until well into the nineteenth century.

5576 Gilt Edges m1897–1901 *California (ind.)*; 1897–98 *California Winter (W)*; 1902 *California (ind.)*. The teams were owned by Ruhstaller's Brewery, which manufactured "Gilt Edge Beer."

5577 Sacramento Base Ball Club 1898 *Pacific Coast (ind.)*. Team had no nickname.

5578 Brewers 1899–1900 *California (ind.)*. Team was owned by Ruhstaller Brewery. With manager Edward Kripp at the helm in 1899, newspapers called the players "Edward Kripp's Brewers." J. Butler and then Arthur Beebe were at the helm in 1900, making the names "Butler's Brewers" and "Beebe's Brewers."

5579 Sacts 1903 *Pacific Coast (ind.)*; 1907–09 *California (ind.)*; 1909–14m *Pacific Coast (AA)*. Team moved to San Francisco (Missions) September 6. Newspapers used this name for their headlines, i.e., "Sacts edge Oaks, 6–5."

5580 Cordovas 1907 *California (ind.)*. Grapes from the nearby Cordova Vineyards are shipped to wineries in the city. With manager Bill Curtain at the helm, newspapers called the players "Curtain's Cordovas."

5581 Solons 1936–60 *Pacific Coast (AA 1918–45, AAA 1946–60)*; 1974–76 *Pacific Coast (AAA)*. Tag was a spin-off from Senators. Newspapers preferred this shorter moniker, which also avoided confusion with the AL Washington Senators.

5582 Steelheads 1999 *Western (ind.)*. The silvery-scaled, spectrum-scattering "rainbow" trout swims in both the salty waters off the Pacific Coast and then migrates to freshwater rivers in California, Oregon and Washington. The "rainbow trout" is also called the "Steelhead."

5583 Rivercats 2000 to date *Pacific Coast (AAA)*. City was built at the confluence of the Sacramento and American rivers. Mountain lions and bobcats inhabit the coastal and Sierra Nevada mountains. These cats sometimes forage along these two rivers. "Kats" and "dawgs" were a trendy "gimmick" monikers used in the 1990s in response to Rap music lyrics.

Saginaw, Michigan

5584 Old Golds 1883–84x *Northwestern (ind.)*. Players wore golden hose.

5585 Grays 1883–84x *Northwestern (ind.)*. Repeated washings of the player's gold stockings faded them to gray. Players wore gray uniforms.

5586 Saginaw Base Ball Club 1889 *Michigan State (ind.)*. Team had no nickname.

5587 Alerts 1893x *Ohio–Michigan (ind.)*. Team disbanded in June 11. Energetic-sounding monikers, i.e., Active, Athletic, Defiance, Eureka, Excelsior, Expert, Fleet Foot, Light Foot, Meteor, Rough'n Ready, Resolute, Wide-Awake and Alert, were common among baseball teams in the nineteenth century.

5588 Lumbermen 1896 *Inter-State (ind.)*. Timber from the Huron and Manistee National Forests are shipped to Saginaw's city lumber mills for processing.

5589 Tigers 1897x *Michigan State (ind.)*. Team disbanded in mid-season (date unknown); 1900m *Canadian (ind.)*. Team moved to Chatham (ONT) in mid-season (date unknown). These teams had a loose affiliation with the Western League Detroit Tigers. Like their Detroit Western League "parent" club, the Saginaw players wore striped stockings.

5590 Saginaw Baseball Club 1900x *International (ind.)*. Team disbanded July 3. The team had no nickname.

5591 White Sox 1902m *Michigan State (D)*. Team moved to Jackson (MI) July 20. The team had a loose affiliation with the AL Chicago White Sox.

5592 Jack Rabbits 1906 *Southern Michigan (D)*. With manager Clarence Jessup at the helm, newspapers called the players "Jessup's Jackrabbits."

5593 Wa-was 1908–10 *Southern Michigan (D)*. With manager A.A. Burkhardt at the helm in 1909, reporters came up with the moniker "A.A.'s Wa-was." With managers William Smith and then Frank Wessell at the helm in 1910, the name became "William's Wa-was" and "Wessell's Wa-was."

5594 Krazy Kats 1911 *Southern Michigan (C)*. With manager Matt Kittridge at the helm, newspapers called the players "Kittridges's Krazy Kats." Baseball players in the era 1870–1920 were perceived by the public as drunken, womanizing, misbehaving ruffians and louts who "acted crazy." "Cat" is a jazz slang, coined in this era for an individual (usually a man) who was enthusiastic about jazz music. A popular newspaper comic strip was the *Katzenjammer Kids*, which prompted the fad spelling "cat" as "kat."

5595 Kittens 1911 *Southern Michigan (C)*. Tag was a spin-off from Krazy Kats. Newspapers preferred the shorter and more attractive moniker. The moniker was appropriate because the team had a loose affiliation with the AL Detroit Tigers.

5596 Trailers 1912 *Southern Michigan (D)*. The Sauk Indians developed a trading and transportation "trail" that consisted of footpaths throughout Michigan. In 1808, the Michigan Territorial Government constructed a road leading from Detroit to Saginaw, and later to Flint and Pontiac, Michigan. This road became known as the "Saginaw Trail." Teams that finished in last place were variously known as Innocents, Misfits and Trailers. The 1912 Saginaw team finished in last place with a horribly "trailing" 19–44 record.

5597 Ducks 1913–15x *Southern Michigan (D 1913, C 1914–15)* Circuit known as League 1908–09 and Association 1910–15. Circuit and team disbanded July 7. Team was named in honor of manager Howard "Ducky" Holmes. The name was appropriate because wild ducks inhabit the nearby Saginaw River.

5598 Aces 1919–26t *Michigan–Ontario (B)*. Team started season in the Michigan–Ontario League, which then merged with the Central League June 14 to form the Michigan State League; t1926 *Michigan State (B)*. Pennant winners in the era 1900–20 were often called Aces, Boosters, Champions and Giants. The 1919 team played "like aces" with a superior 77–32 record to clinch the 1919 Michigan–Ontario League pennant. Ray McKee took over in 1920–21 and the name became "Ray's Aces." Al Bashang took over in 1924 and the name became "Al's Aces." Les Nunamaker took over in 1925 and the name became "Les Nunamaker's Aces."

5599 Athletics 1940 *Michigan State (C)*. With manager Dallas Avery at the helm, newspapers called the players "Avery's Athletics" and then "Avery's A's." Team was not a farm team of the Philadelphia Athletics.

5600 White Sox 1941 *Michigan State (C)*. Team was a farm club of the Chicago White Sox.

5601 Bears 1948–50 *Central (A)*. The team had a loose affiliation with the NL Chicago Cubs, although it never became an official farm club of the Chicago NL team. With manager Bob Finley at the helm in 1948–49, newspapers called the players "Bob's Bears."

5602 Jacks 1951 *Central (A)*. In the era 1850–1900, Saginaw was a lumber town where timber was brought from the Huron and Manistee National Forests to be processed in city wood mills. "Jacks" is a contraction of "lumberjacks."

Saginaw–Bay City, Michigan

5603 Hyphens 1890 *International (ind.)*. The moniker was a newspaper gimmick reflecting the hyphen used when the Saginaw–Bay City spelling appeared in datelines. The same gimmick was used with the 1910 Central California League Alameda "Bracketts."

St. Albans, Vermont

5604 St. Albans Base Ball Club 1887x *Northeastern (ind.)*. Circuit and team disbanded in mid-season (date unknown); 1895x *Eastern International (ind.)*. Circuit and team disbanded in mid-season (date unknown) These teams had no nickname.

St. Augustine, Florida

5605 Cuban Giants 1887–88 *Independent Negro team*. The team, by now quite famous, played its summer schedule in New York–New Jersey but decided to play exhibitions this winter in Florida to earn extra money.

5606 St. Augustine Base Ball Club 1891–92 *Florida Winter (W)*; 1892 *Florida State (ind.)*. These teams had no nickname.

5607 Saints 1926–27m *Southeastern (B)*. Team moved to Waycross (GA) July 25; 1936–41 *Florida State (D)*; 1946–50 *Florida State (D)*; 1952x *Florida State (D)*. Team disbanded June 2. The city, oldest in North America above the Rio Grande, was named after Saint Augustine, the famous early Christian church father.

St. Boniface, Manitoba, Canada

5608 Saints 1915 *Northern (C)*. City was named after Boniface, the eighth-century Apostle of Germany. He was canonized as St. Boniface.

5609 Bonnies 1915 *Northern (C)*. Newspapers used this short derivative for headlines, i.e., "Bonnies defeat Canucks, 5–3."

St. Catherines, Ontario, Canada

5610 Brewers 1930 *Ontario (C)*. Canadian Breweries Limited, producers of Niagara's Best Beer, owned the team.

5611 Blue Jays 1986–95 *New York–Pennsylvania (A)*. Team was a farm club of Toronto Blue Jays.

5612 Stompers 1996–99 *New York–Pennsylvania (A)*. Summer grapes are used to make wine in city wineries. In olden days, grapes were stomped upon by bare-footed peasants. The logo character, a young man dressed as a baseball player, has a bare, blue-stained foot stomping on grapes. The Niagara Grape and Wine Festival is held in the city three times a year, in spring, summer and fall.

St. Clair, Pennsylvania

5613 Saints m1932m *Interstate (D)*. Team began season in Norristown (PA) and moved to St. Clair May 28. The city was named after Saint Clair (Clare) of Assisi, a 13th-century saint. Religious team names, i.e., Saints, Apostles, Padres, and Friars, have been popular in sports.

St. Cloud, Minnesota

5614 Rox 1946–71 *Northern (C 1946–62, A 1963–71)*. Colored granite quarries were discovered here in 1870. "Rox" is a newspaper contraction for "rocks." St. Cloud is known as the "Granite City."

St. Cloud–Brainerd, Minnesota

5615 St. Cloud–Brainerd Baseball Club 1905m *Northern (D)*. Team moved to Superior (WI) June 25. Team had no nickname.

St. George, Staten Island, New York

5616 Staten Island Yankees 1999 to date *New York–Pennsylvania (A)*. Team was a farm club of the New York Yankees.

St. George, Utah

5617 Pioneerzz 1999–2001 *Western (ind.)*. Team was known as the **Zion Pioneerzz** 1999–2000, and then was renamed "St. George Pioneerzz" in 2001. Brigham Young led Mormon pioneers to Utah in 1854. A trendy spelling gimmick of the 1990s was the substitution of z and zz for s. Examples of such gimmicks were the Ottawa Raipdz (baseball), Utah Starzz (basketball) and West Tennessee Diamond Jaxx (baseball). The gimmick also was used for the letter x.

5618 Roadrunners 2007–10 *Golden (ind.)*. With characteristics of a desert wren and a prairie cuckoo, this bird ranges from the southwest United States to Central America.

St. Helena, California

5619 St. Helena Baseball Club 1910m *Central California (D)*. Team moved to Fruitvale (CA) April 24. Team had no nickname.

St. Hyacinthe, Quebec, Canada

5620 Saints 1940 *Quebec Provincial (B)*; 1950–51 *Provincial (C)*. City was named after St. Hyacinthe, a Polish missionary of the 13th century. He was canonized in 1594.

5621 Athletics 1952–53 *Provincial (C)*. Team was a farm club of the Philadelphia Athletics.

St. Jean-Sur-Richelieu, Quebec, Canada

5622 Braves 1948–52 *Provincial (ind. 1948–49, C 1949–52)*. Team went by shorter name of St. Jean Braves. First fortified by the French in the 1600s, the fort was defended by out-manned British troops in 1775, who displayed great bravery against American troops that were trying to reach Montreal. The team had a loose affiliation with the NL Boston Braves. Canadian baseball teams, of the Can–Am and Quebec Provincial Leagues of 1935–55, maintained a loose affiliation with major league teams in New York, Philadelphia, Boston and Detroit.

5623 Canadians 1953–55 *Provincial (C)*. A "Canadian" is an inhabitant of Canada. Since 1900, about a dozen professional sports teams in Canada have gone by the moniker of "Canadians" and/or the French "Les Canadiens."

St. John, New Brunswick, Canada

5624 St. John Base Ball Club 1890 *New Brunswick (ind.)*. Team had no nickname.

5625 Marathons 1913x *New Brunswick–Maine (D)*. Team and league disbanded August 23. The city is the host to the annual boat race called the Royal St. John Regatta Marathon on Quidi Vidi Lake.

St. Joseph, Michigan

5626 Autos 1940–41 *Michigan State (C)*. Starting in 1910, Ford, General Motors, Chevrolet and other automobile manufacturers built cars here. Michigan is the "Auto State."

St. Joseph, Missouri

5627 Reds 1886–87x *Western (ind.)*. Team disbanded July 28. Players wore red hose. Originally **Red Stockings**, local newspapers shortened the name to Reds.

5628 Clay-eaters 1889 *Western Assn. (ind.)*. Missouri River clay deposits are transported to brick, tile and pottery factories. "Clay-eater" is slang for clay miner. With manager Charles Lord at the helm, newspapers called the players "Charles Lord's Clay-eaters."

5629 Saints 1893–96x *Western Assn. (ind.)*. Team disbanded July 18; 1897–98x *Western Assn. (ind.)*; 1898m *Western (ind.)*. Team moved to Omaha (NE) July 7; 1900–05 *Western (ind. 1900–01, A 1902–05)*; m1917–26 Team began 1917 season in Sioux City (IA) and moved to St. Joseph August 5; 1927m *Western Assn. (B May 1–July 7, C July 7–Aug.31)*. Team moved to Joplin (MO) July 7, which caused the league classification to drop from B to C; 1930–35 *Western (A)*; 1940 *Western Assn. (C)*; 1954 *Western Assn. (C)*. 1954. City was named after Saint Joseph, one of the Twelve Apostles.

5630 Josies 1900–05 *Western (ind. 1900–01, A 1902–05)*. Tag was an alternate moniker to "Saints." Newspapers used it for headlines, i.e., "Josies top Creams, 4–2."

5631 Packers 1906m *Western Assn. (C)*. Team moved to Hutchinson (KS) June 12. Established in 1843, the city became a livestock and meat-packing center by 1850.

5632 Drummers 1910–17m *Western (A)*. Team moved to Hutchinson (KS) July 24; 1933–35 *Western (A)*. The city celebrates St. Joseph's Day every March 19 with a marching and drum band known as the "Patron Cadets." With manager Dutch Zwilling at the helm, newspapers called the players "Dutch's Drummers." Saint Joseph is the Patron Saint of St. Joseph, Missouri.

5633 Angels 1939 *Western Assn. (C)*. Team was a farm club of the PCL Los Angeles Angels. The name was appropriate because it was a spin-off from Saints. With manager Goldie Holt at the helm, newspapers called the players "Goldie's Angels."

5634 Ponies 1939, 1941m *Western Assn. (C)*. Team moved to Carthage (MO) June 3. With manager Goldie Holt at the helm, newspapers called the players the "Goldie Holt's Ponies." The Pony Express began in this city in 1860. The city was the eastern terminus for the Pony Express 1860–61.

5635 Cardinals 1946–51 *Western Assn. (C)*; 1953 *Western Assn. (C)*. These teams were farm clubs of the St. Louis Cardinals.

5636 Blacksnakes 2006–07 *American Assn. (ind.)*. The North American "Racer snake" is a slender, non-poisonous, black-skinned snake found in the Midwest and the Plains. The team disbanded after the 2007 season.

St. Louis, Missouri

5637 Red Stockings 1875 *National Assn. (M)*; 1882 *American Assn. (M)*. Players wore red hose. Originally **Red Stockings**, newspapers shortened the name to Reds and **Redlegs**. The 1882 players wore red hose at the start of the season. However, constant washing of the socks faded them to brown, prompting newspapers to call the players the "Browns."

5638 Mound City 1875; 1876–77 *National Assn. (M)*. St. Louis is the "Mound City" because of the mounds constructed by the prehistoric native American tribes known as the "Mound Builders." Newspapers sometimes called the team the **Mound City Brown Stockings**.

5639 Browns 1875; 1876–77 *National Assn. (M)*; 1882–91 *American Assn. (M)*; 1892–98 *National (M)*; 1902–04, 1970–53 *American (M)*. Players wore brown hose. The team switched leagues in 1876 and again in 1892. By 1883, the hose were deliberately dyed brown at season's start. No red hose would again appear until 1899. Originally **Brown Stockings**, newspapers shortened name to "Browns." The term "Brown Legs" seems not to have been used.

5640 Pilgrims 1876 *National (M).* In 1876, the Chicago "Westerners" and St. Louis "Pilgrims" were the two Western-most cities in the new National League. Indeed, in this era, the expanse of land from Minnesota to Oklahoma and Indiana to Iowa was not known as the Midwest but rather the "West." The St. Louis Browns were so far from the Atlantic Coast that they were often called the St. Louis "Pilgrims" because of the long "pilgrimage" the team had to make by train to the East Coast to play New York, Boston and Philadelphia.

5641 The Browns Are Here! 1882 *American Assn. (M).* From the outset, team owner Chris Van der Ahe knew he had to market the team to make enough money, so he pasted posters all over town in St. Louis announcing: "The Browns are here! The Hardest Hitters, the Finest Fielders, the Best Base-runners, and the Coming Champions!" Although the Browns didn't win any titles in 1882, by 1885 they were on a run of four consecutive American Association pennants and the title in the 1886 World Series.

5642 Der Poys 1882–91 *American Assn. (M).* Team owner Chris Von der Ahe was a beer baron who owned the Browns and their ballpark, Sportsman Park. Of German descent, he sold beer and even liquor at his ballpark, allowed ladies into the stands for free on "Ladies Day," staged "Wild West" shows, built a water slide, and hosted night-time horse racing under primitive electric arc lights. He proudly called his ball players, in his thick German accent, "Der Poys."

5643 Der Boss Club 1882–91 *American Assn. (M).* All the players, coaches, office workers and reporters referred to Chris Van der Ahe as "Der Boss," and his team became known as "Der Boss Club."

5644 Original Comiskeys 1883–89 & 1891 *American Assn. (M).* In reference to the AL Chicago White Sox, known as the Comiskeys because ex–St. Louis Browns star Charles Comiskey and his family owned the Sox 1901–58 with the team playing in Comiskey Parks I & II 1910–97. Similarly, baseball writers coined as the "Original Comiskeys" the powerhouse St. Louis Browns of 1883–89 (4 AA pennants and one World Series title), who were led by player-manager Comiskey. The tag was coined by baseball writer John D. Cash.

5645 Maroons 1884 *Union Assn. (M);* 1885–86 *National (M).* Players wore maroon hose. In 1885, the team jumped leagues; 1899–1921 *National (M).* While "Cardinals" referred only to the color, i.e., the Cardinal red worn by the papal clergy of the Vatican, a popular alternate was "Maroons." But when the team's uniforms displayed two avian Cardinals perched on a tree branch as a logo across the jersey for the 1922 season, the Maroons moniker was dropped.

5646 Sluggers 1884 *Union Assn. (M).* The Maroons led the Union Association in team batting average (.292), on-base percentage (.321), slugging percentage (.394), home runs (32), hits (1,251) and runs scored (887).

5647 Giants 1884 *Union Assn. (M);* 1909–19 *Independent Negro team;* 1920–21 *Negro National (M);* 1924–25 *California Winter (W).* Tag was a generic moniker for a baseball team that "wins big." The St. Louis Unions compiled an overwhelmingly "gigantic" 91–16 record to win the UA pennant by 21 games over Cincinnati.

5648 Mound City Monsters 1884 *Union Assn. (M).* Coined by baseball writer David Nemec to describe the "monster team" that team owner and oilman Henry Lucas put together by raiding NL and AA teams for pitcher Charlie Sweeney, second baseman Fred Dunlap, outfielder Orator Shaffer, outfielder Buttercup Dickerson, third baseman Jack Gleason and outfielder Dave Rowe.

5649 Henry Lucas' One Ring Circus 1884 *Union Assn. (M).* Maroons owner Henry Lucas, an aggressive, flamboyant oil baron who

sometimes pulled off shady deals that got him in legal trouble, ran his team "like a circus," much in the same way George Steinbrenner ran his New York Yankees from 1975–2005. Tag was coined by baseball writer David Voight.

5650 Henry Lucas' Colossus 1884 *Union Assn. (M).* Coined by baseball writer David Voight, the Maroons were a "colossus" only in the inferior UA. When the Maroons joined the NL for the 1885 season, they were the weakest "ant" there, going 36–72 to finish eighth in 1885 and compiling a 43–79 record for a sixth-place finish in the NL in 1886 before disbanding.

5651 Henry Lucas' Millionaires 1884 *Union Assn. (M).* Coined by baseball author David Nemec, the moniker referred to oil millionaire Henry Lucas' lavish spending to sign the best available talent from the NL and AA for his UA club. Much like his twentieth-century counterpart, George Steinbrenner of the New York Yankees, Lucas spent big bucks to sign such players like second baseman Fred Dunlap, outfielder Orator Schaffer, outfielder Buttercup Dickerson, third baseman Jack Gleason and outfielder Dave Rowe. Like Steinbrenner's 1998 Yankee "Millionaires" (125–50 record including playoffs) Lucas' Millionaires went 91–16, which translated to a 137–25 mark in today's major league 162-game schedule.

5652 Blues 1884 *Reserve (ind.).* Players wore blue hose.

5653 Colts 1884 *Reserve (ind.).* In this era, rookie players were known as "colts." The word "rookie" would not be coined until 1892 and popularized until 1917. The Reserve League was an attempt to form a minor league to thwart outlaw UA player raids. Rookies along with young and injured veterans made up the rosters. Players could be called up to their parent club at any time, making it more like an NFL taxi squad than the first true minor league. The Japanese Eastern and Western minor leagues of 1953–2008 operate very closely to this early experiment.

5654 Ponies 1884 *Reserve (ind.).* Tag was a spin-off from "colts." Youthful baseball players prance about on the ball field like ponies prance about on a pasture. When syndicate owner John O'Day started to plunder his AA New York Mets of talent that was then sent to his other property — the NL New York Giants — newspapers started to call the remaining young Mets players the "Ponies."

5655 Black Diamonds 1885–86 *National (M).* Players on the team wore jerseys with black diamonds on them to protest the NL owners who had blacklisted them during the winter for jumping to the outlaw UA in 1884.

5656 Juggernauts 1885–88 *American Assn. (M).* Baseball writer David Nemec coined this moniker for the St. Louis Browns teams that won four consecutive American Association pennants 1885–88. The Browns were "juggernauts," capturing first place by wide margins of 16 games (1885), 12 games (1886), 14 games (1887) and six-and-a-half games (1888). Even though the Browns finished second to Brooklyn in 1889, they still compiled a sterling 90–45 mark. Historically, St. Louis was attacked and occupied by General Ulysses S. Grant's "Union Juggernaut" army in the Battle of Vicksburg, June 1–July 4, 1863. Also called the Mound City Juggernauts.

5657 Down & Dirty Browns 1885–91 *American Assn. (M).* Much like the Baltimore Orioles of the 1890s, the Browns of the 1880s were rough-and-tumble players who slid hard, got into fights, baited umpires, and got their uniforms just as dirty as the Gas House Gang Cardinals of the 1930s.

5658 Mound City Steamrollers 1885–91 *American Assn. (M).* Baseball author David Nemec, in his splendid book on the American Association, **The Beer and Whiskey League,** called the St. Louis Browns flag winners of 1885–88 by this moniker. The Browns never dipped below a .667 winning percentage during their four pennant years with records of 79–33, 93–46, 95–40 and 92–43 as they "steamrolled" AA opponents — an achievement that dampened AA attendance enough to keep the association with less income than that of their rivals in the National League. St. Louis is known as the "Mound City" because an ancient Indian tribe, the Mound Builders, constructed mysterious mounds, perhaps for religious purposes.

5659 Der Champeens 1886 *American Assn. (M).* Another adulteration of English into "Pidgeon German" by team owner Chris Van der Ahe when his St. Louis Browns defeated the NL champion Chicago White Stockings in the 1886 World Series, 4 games to 2. After the Browns won, Van der Ahe exclaimed to reporters about his players: "My Poys … Der Champeens!"

5660 White Stockings 1888 *Western (ind.).* Players wore white hose. Originally **White Stockings**, local newspapers shortened it to "White Legs" and "White Sox." Team was a farm club of the American Association St. Louis Browns, hence the white color was a spin-off from brown.

5661 Bad, Bad Browns 1896–98 *National (M).* The team set a major league record at the time by going 108–303 over three seasons (1896–98) for a record-low .263 winning percentage. Only when the 1962–64 New York Mets posted a .247 winning percentage (144–440) was the Browns' mark eclipsed. The tag was coined by baseball author David Nemec.

5662 Cardinals 1899 to date *National (M).* Players wore red hose, then later red-trim uniforms and stirrups. The Robison brothers, owners of the team, dressed the players in red trim, prompting one female fan to remark, "What a lovely shade of cardinal!" Sportswriter Willie McHale overheard the lady's exclamation and starting using it in his newspaper reports. The name became immediately popular. In 1922 players jerseys carried a cardinal bird image. For the period 1899–1921, Cardinals referred to the color, i.e., Cardinal red, and not the bird. Club GM Branch Rickey had attended a lady's social club meeting in the off-season and saw that their banner was two cardinals perched on a tree branch. Rickey immediately ordered uniforms with a logo of two redbirds sitting on a baseball bat. The logo was immediately popular with fans and has been used for the past 89 years,

5663 Perfectos 1899–1901 *National (M).* Brothers Stanley and Frank Robison, who were syndicate owners of both the wretched St. Louis Browns and the perennially contending Cleveland Spiders, decided to plunder the Cleveland roster after the 1898 season to bolster the Browns, whom they carelessly declared to be the "Perfectos" in imitation of the Brooklyn "Superbas" (who also shamefully plundered the Baltimore Orioles). Although improved, the "Perfectos" could only muster a fourth-place finish in the 12-team National League in 1899 with an 84–67 record. For the next two seasons the Perfectos could only finish one game over .500 for their combined two-season record. The Perfectos moniker was quickly dropped in favor of "Cardinals."

5664 Scarlets 1899–1901 *National (M).* A second spin-off (Maroons was the other) from the Cardinal red moniker, the name never caught on.

5665 Cards 1899 to date *National (M).* Newspapers quickly shortened "Cardinals" to "Cards" and the contraction had a neutral meaning until baseball cartoonist Willard Mullin dreamed up the "St. Louis Swifty" Southern gentleman/card shark in 1941. The "Swifty" moniker had a double meaning, referring both to the card game of Poker and to the swift St. Louis base runners and outfielders of the great St. Louis teams of the 1940s.

5666 Masqueraders 1900 *National (M).* After going 84–67, good for a fourth-place finish in 1899 (by pirating the Cleveland Spiders roster), the team skidded to a 65–75 mark in 1900 to finish a most "imperfect" sixth out of eight teams. Unhappy St. Louis fans and newspapers called the players the "Masqueraders," explaining, "They masquerade as good players in their fancy red-trim uniforms and then cannot play!"

5667 Folding Cards 1900 *National (M).* Baseball writer Rick Hummel called the "bad hand" St. Louisians of 1900 (who finished with a 65–75 record) the "Folding Cards" because owners James and Frank Robison gutted their other baseball property—the Cleveland Spiders—for its best players, plunging the Spiders to a record 134 losses in 1899—to produce a fairly good team, reaching 84 victories only to see their created "hand" fold in 1900 with a losing 65–75 mark.

5668 Brownies 1902–53 *American (M).* Used affectionately in the era 1902–36 even though the Browns suffered through numerous losing seasons, the moniker transformed into a derogatory tag when the team lost a horrendous 316 games over the three seasons of 1937–39. The nickname was used much like the Chicago "Cubbies" in the 1980s as fans in both cities tired of their respective teams' losing ways. "Cute" diminutives like Beanies, Cubbies, Phillies, and Brownies can be traced to the start of the twentieth century.

5669 First in Booze, First in Shoes and Last in the American League 1902–53 *American (M).* Coined by colorful baseball owner Bill Veeck in his 1962 book (co-written by Ed Linn) *Veeck: As in Wreck.* Less a nickname than a slogan, it mimicked the famous words about the AL Washington Senators of 1901–60, which goes: "First in War, First in Peace, First in the Hearts of Their Countrymen, and Last in the American League."

5670 Misfits 1903 *National (M).* Many unhappy St. Louis fans, with a notion for poetic justice, branded the last-place Cardinals of 1903 (43–94) as the "Misfits," which was the same moniker stuck on the woeful 1899 Cleveland Spiders, who had all their best players swiped by St. Louis team owners Stanley and Frank Robison.

5671 The Burlesque Club 1903 *National (M).* A burlesque club was a form of vaudeville where female strippers performed sometimes scandalizing segments of the audience. St. Louis fans were "scandalized" by the performance of the last-place 1903 Cardinals, particularly the pitching staff, which surrendered a major league–high 1,353 hits to opposing teams.

5672 Amateurs 1903 *National (M).* Four regular hitters failed to hit .250, the offensive squad hit eight home runs all season, and there was not a single pitcher with a winning record in an "amateurish" performance, leading to a last-place finish with a 43–94 mark.

5673 Ravens 1905–06 *American (M).* Players wore black stockings for the 1905–06 season but then switched to brown stirrup hose over white sanitary socks in 1907. It was in the period 1907–08 that baseball players started wearing white sanitary socks covered with colored stirrups.

5674 Gingersnaps 1909 *National (M).* The Cardinals finished a crummy seventh with an 54–98 mark in 1909, prompting St. Louis fans and newspapers to call them "Gingersnaps," which is a cookie made of ginger and molasses. The notion was that the 1909 Cardinals were about as sturdy as a crumbly cookie.

5675 Terriers 1913 *Federal (ind.);* 1914–15 *Federal (M).* With Irishman Jack O'Connor at the helm in 1913 as manager, newspapers called the players "O'Connor's Terriers." The Irish terrier is a popular breed of dog. The team was owned by brewer and banker Otto Steifel, prompting some newspapers to call the team "Steifel's Terriers." With manager Three-Finger Brown at the helm, newspapers called the players "Three-Finger Brown's Terriers."

5676 Miners 1914–15 *Federal (M).* Missouri has numerous lead, iron, zinc and copper mines. Metal ore was transported to processing factories in St. Louis.

5677 Sloufeds 1914–15 Tag was an amalgam of St. Louis and "Federals." Fans hated it, and the name was discarded by mid-season 1915.

5678 Mound City Blues 1916 *Independent Negro team.* Players wore blue-trim uniforms and stirrups. St. Louis is known as the "Mound City."

5679 Neptunes 1916 *National (M).* Cardinal fans, miffed with the team's eighth-place finish with a 60–93 record, laughed when newspapers called the team the "Neptunes." The newspapers said, "They might as well be playing at the bottom of the ocean!" Neptune (Poseidon in Greek) was the Roman god of the ocean and seas.

5680 Cubs 1920 *Independent Negro team.* With so many black teams calling themselves "Giants" and "Stars," management wanted a different and short moniker. The team purchased old Cubs jerseys from the Chicago Cubs and dressed their players in them, taking on the moniker of "Cubs." The team played its home games in suburban Compton Hill.

5681 All-Stars 1922–23–23–24 *California Winter (W).* Tag was a spin-off from "Stars." The best players of the 1922 St. Louis Stars, i.e., George Scales, Charlie Blackwell, C.A. Dudley, Dan Kennard and Branch Russell, went west as a team calling themselves the St. Louis "All-Stars." Traveling black teams sometimes called themselves the "All-Stars" to get publicity.

5682 Stars 1922–31 *Negro National (M);* 1937 *Negro American (M);* 1939, 1941 *Negro American (M);* 1940 *Independent Negro team;* 1943 *Negro National (M).* No less than three NNL teams in 1922 adopted the name "Stars," i.e., the Cuban Stars, Detroit Stars and the St. Louis Stars, as the name had become a fad for black teams in the 1920s.

5683 Redbirds 1922 to date *National (M).* Team General Manager Branch Rickey attended a ladies social event and when he saw a birdcage with Cardinals in it, he dressed his 1922 players in uniforms with a logo of two cardinals perched on a branch. Prior to this bird logo, the "Cardinals" moniker only referred to the Cardinal red color of the trim of the players' uniforms and stirrup hose. Newspapers sporadically have called the team the clumsy **Birds-on-the-Bat.**

5684 Home-grown Cardinals 1926, 1928, 1930–31, 1934 *National (M).* Coined by baseball authors Fred Lieb and Jerome Milear in reference to Cardinal GM Branch Rickey's innovative "farm system" to develop their own players. The franchise had not won an NL pennant since joining the league in 1892 and then proceeded to win six NL pennants and three World Series in only eight seasons. The farm system continued to boost the major league team's fortunes as the Cardinals won three pennants and two world titles during the war years and eight NL pennants and five World Series since 1946.

5685 Sparklers 1926–28 *National (M).* Led by such "sparkling" performers like hitters Jim Bottomley (Hall-of-Fame), Frankie Frisch (Hall of Fame), Rogers Hornsby (Hall of Fame), Rabbit Maranville (Hall of Fame), Les Bell, Ray Blades, Taylor Douthit, Chick Hafey, George Harper, Bob O'Farrell, and Billy Southworth and pitchers Grover Cleveland Alexander (Hall of Fame), Jesse Haines, Art Reinhart, Flint Rhem and Bill Sherdel, the Cardinals won two NL pennants (1926, 1928) and split two World Series with the New York Yankees. General manager Branch Rickey, who founded the major league baseball farm system, built a team of "sparkling performers."

5686 Spirits of St. Louis 1930–31 *National (M).* In honor of Charles "Lucky Lindy" Lindbergh who made the first solo trans–Atlantic air flight from America to France in his plane "The Spirit of St. Louis," the pennant-winning Cardinals of 1930–31 were given this moniker. The "Spirits of St. Louis" were led by hitters Jim Bottomley (Hall of Fame), Frankie Frisch (Hall of Fame), Sparky Adams, Taylor Douthit, Charles Gelbert, Chick Hafey, Pepper Martin, George Watkins, and Jim Wilson and pitchers Burleigh Grimes (Hall of Fame), Paul Derringer, Bill Hallahan and Flint Rhem.

5687 Clouting Cardinals 1934 *National (M).* The 1934 Cardinals led the National League in hits (1,582), doubles (.294), batting average (.288) and slugging percentage (.425).

5688 Comeback Cardinals 1934 *National (M).* The 1934 Cardinals won 20 games while coming from behind after the sixth inning.

5689 Gas House Gang 1934–35 *National (M).* Along with the Brooklyn "Bums" and New York "Bronx Bombers," the Gas House Gang was the most famous unofficial baseball team nickname. Ironically, the name was not used during the 1934 season, employed instead at the start of the 1935 season. The moniker refers to the dirty uniforms of the St. Louis players in 1934 and 1935. Knock-down pitches, slides and diving for catches dirtied up the players' uniforms so that they looked dirty overall, smeared with grease, gasoline and soot, for mechanics working at a "gas house"— a 1930s slang for "gasoline station." Legend has it that Cardinals shortstop Leo Durocher coined the moniker in a 1935 interview with a newspaper reporter. Some of the 1934 "Mechanics" were hitters Frankie Frisch (Hall of Fame), Pepper Martin, Leo Durocher (Hall of Fame) and Joe "Ducky" Medwick and pitchers Dizzy Dean (Hall of Fame), Jerome "Daffy" Dean and Bill Walker. Durocher said, "We'd get our uniforms dirty diving for the ball, sliding on the bases, and hitting the dirt on knockdown pitches so much so that we looked like a bunch of mechanics at a gas house!"

5690 Rowdy Redbirds 1935 *National (M).* Tag was a spin-off of the "Gas House Gang." It didn't catch on and was dropped by newspapers.

5691 Swifties 1941–49 *National (M).* With daring and dashing base runners and fleet outfielders patrolling the skies, the Cardinals got this moniker — which was then promoted by baseball cartoonist Willard Mullins— as they won NL pennants in 1942, 1943, 1944 and 1946. During those years the Cardinal hitters were near or at the top in the statistical categories of runs scored, extra-base hits, outfield putouts and infield assists, which reflected the players' speed and agility at the bat, on the bases and in the field. The Cardinals led the NL in doubles in 1942 (282), 1944 (274), 1946 (265) and hit 259 doubles (second in the NL) in 1943. Led by hitters Johnny Mize (Hall of Fame), Stan Musial (Hall of Fame), Enos Slaughter (whose mad dash for home plate in Game 7 won the 1946 World Series over the Boston Red Sox), Walker Cooper, Whitey Kurowski, Marty Marion and Red Schoendienst and pitchers John Beazley, Howie Krist, Max Lanier, Len Warneke and Ernie White, the St. Louis "Swifties" won four National League pennants and three World Series titles during the 1940s.

5692 Flying Redbirds 1941–49 *National (M).* Tag was a spin-off from the "St. Louis Swifties."

5693 Home-grown Cardinals-II 1942 *National (M).* An Associated Press news story on the 1942 World Series described the St. Louis participant in the Fall Classic as the Home-grown Cardinals.

5694 Cinderella Browns 1944 *American (M).* With a franchise boosted by the military draft of World War II, the Browns won their first and only AL pennant with an 89–65 record in 1944. Led by hitters Milt Byrnes, Don Gutteridge, Mike Kreevich, Vern Stephens and Al Zarilla and pitchers George Caster, Sig Jackucki, John Kramer, Bob Muncrief and Nelson Potter, the Browns met the cross-town St. Louis Cardinals in the only all–St. Louis World Series and actually held a 2–1 games lead before the midnight hour struck with the Cardinals winning the next three games to capture the Fall Classic, 4 games to 2. Aka **Cinderella Brownies.**

5695 Rags-to-Riches Boys 1944 *American (M).* A spin-off of Cinderella Browns, the Browns and their fans had endured thirteen losing campaigns in fourteen years prior to the 1944 pennant season.

5696 Sewell's Wonders 1944 *American (M).* With manager Jim Sewell at the helm, newspapers called the pennant-winning players "Sewell's Wonders."

5697 Keane's Opportunists 1964 *National (M).* Trailing the 90–60 first-place Phillies by six games with only 12 to go in the closing days of the 1964 National League regular season, the Cardinals' position seemed hopeless, but the Phillies lost 10 straight ball games while manager Johnny Keane's Cardinals opportunistically won nine of 12, games allowing them to edge out the Phillies (and the Cincinnati Reds) by one game and the San Francisco Giants by two games. After getting future Hall-of-Famer Lou Brock from the Chicago Cubs in mid-season, the Cardinals, led by hitters Brock, Curt Flood, Dick Groat, Julian Javier, Tim McCarver and Bill White and pitchers Bob Gibson (Hall of Fame), Curt Simmons and Ray Sadecki, the Cardinals jumped from fifth place on August 17 to the National League pennant on October 1. The "Opportunists" then won the World Series against the New York Yankees, 4 games to 3, as Bob Gibson won Game 7 by a 7–5 score.

5698 El Birdos 1967–68 *National (M).* Led by 1967 NL Most Valuable Player Orlando Cepeda (Hall of Fame), one of the best Latin players in the league at the time, St. Louis fans started to call the team "El Birdos." Cepeda led a potent offense that included Lou Brock (Hall of Fame), Curt Flood, Julian Javier, Del Maxvil, Roger Maris, and Mike Shannon and the strong pitching of Bob Gibson (Hall of Fame), Steve Carlton (Hall of Fame), Nelson Briles, Dick Hughes and Ray Washburn to two consecutive National League pennants and a World Series victory, 4 games to 3, over the Boston Red Sox in 1967. Only a Detroit Tigers' comeback from a 3–1 deficit in the 1968 Fall Classic derailed the "Birdos." It was Cepeda himself who coined the term.

5699 Consistent Cardinals 1982 *National (M).* Coined by baseball writer Rick Hummel, the 1982 Cardinals played steady baseball to compile a 92–70 mark for first place in the NL Eastern Division and then defeated the Atlanta Braves (for the NL pennant) and the AL Milwaukee Brewers, 4 games to 3, for the world's championship. The Cardinals pursued the Phillies until Philadelphia faded in September while the Cardinals played consistent .580 baseball, allowing them to take the lead on September 13. George Hendrick, Keith Hernandez, Dane Iorg, Lonnie Smith (68 steals) and Ozzie Smith were steady hitters while fine pitching was provided by Ken Dayley, Bob Forsch, Rickey Horton, Jeff Lahti and Bruce Sutter.

5700 Herzog's Jackrabbits 1985 *National (M).* The Cardinals, led by manager Whitey Herzog, won their second NL pennant in four years by stealing 314 bases, hitting 245 doubles and 59 triples, and taking many extra bases on a league-high .264 team batting average. The Cardinals sped to a 101–61 record for the NL Eastern Division title and then the NL pennant (4 games to 2 over the Los Angeles Dodgers). Only a controversial play in Game 6 (the first-base ump blew a call on a ground out) against the cross-state Kansas City Royals converted what seemed to be a 4 games to 2 World Series triumph into a 4 games to 3 Fall Classic defeat.

5701 Herzog's Greyhounds 1987 *National (M).* En route to their third National League pennant in six seasons, manager Whitey Herzog's Cardinals led the major leagues in stolen bases with 248 (no other team in either Major League even reached 200). Speedsters Ozzie Smith, Vince Coleman and Willie McGee were especially adept at scoring from first on extra-base hits. Led by hitters Tom Brunansky, Jack Clark, Pedro Guerrero, Tommy Herr and Terry Pendleton and pitchers Danny Cox, Ken Dayley, Ricky Horton, John Tudor and Todd Worrell, the Cardinals captured the NL Eastern Division with a 95–67 record and then bested the San Francisco Giants, 4 games to 2, for the National League pennant. They fell short against the AL champion Minnesota Twins, 4 games to 3, in a "homer" series where neither team could win a road game and the Cardinals' speed could not neutralize the Twins' home run power in Minneapolis' Hubert H. Humphrey Metrodome.

5702 Folding Cardinals 1990 *National (M).* Baseball writer Rick Hummel coined this moniker for the 1990 Cardinals, who "folded like a poker player with a bad hand" from 86 victories in 1989 to a "bad bet" 70–92 record in 1990. This poker game theme was also

used by cartoonist Willard Mullins in the 1940s and 1950s who depicted the Cardinal franchise as the "St. Louis Swifty"—a Civil War era, steamboat-traveling Land of Dixie card shark with a Snidely Whiplash moustache.

5703 Birds-on-the-Bat 2006 to date *National (M).* When the Cardinals won an unexpected NL pennant and World Series title in 2006, after winning only 83 games in the regular season, people realized that the "Birds-on-the-Bat" uniform logo had been in use for 85 years (since 1922) as the Cardinals won 17 NL pennants and 10 World Series titles.

5704 Dealing Cards 2009 *National (M).* Coined by *The Sporting News* to describe how team GM John Mozeliak "wheeled and dealed" like a poker player to boost the Cardinals to a 91–71 mark and the 2009 NL Eastern Division title.

St. Lucie, Florida

5705 Mets 2001 to date *Florida State (A).* Team is a farm club of the New York Mets.

St. Mary's, Pennsylvania

5706 Saints 1916 *Interstate (D).* This city in Elk County north-northeast of Dubois was named after Saint Mary.

St. Paul, Minnesota

5707 Red Caps 1877 *League Alliance (ind.);* 1883 *Northwest (ind.).* Players wore red caps.

5708 Vulcans m1884 *Union Assn. (M).* After the Wilmington UA club disbanded September 15, the St. Paul NWL club took their slot by joining the UA September 27. Established 1838–40, the city soon had numerous iron-forges and blast furnaces. Vulcan (known as Hephaestus in Greek mythology) was the Roman god of fire, metalworking and handicrafts. It was Vulcan who forged the swords, spears and shields for the Olympian gods.

5709 White Caps m1884 *Union Assn. (M).* After the Wilmington UA club disbanded September 15, the St. Paul NWL club took their slot by joining the UA September 27. Players wore white caps and white stockings.

5710 Saints 1884t *Northwestern (ind.).* After the Wilmington UA club disbanded September 15, the St. Paul NWL club took their slot by joining the UA September 27; t1884 *Union Assn. (M);* 1886 *Northwest (ind.);* 1888–91m *Western Assn. (ind.).* Team moved to Duluth June 8; 1892m *Western (ind.).* Team moved to Fort Wayne May 25; 1895–99 *Western (ind.);* 1901 *Western (ind.);* 1902–60 *American Assn. (A 1903–11, AA 1912–45, AAA 1946–60);* 1993–2005 *Northern (ind.);* 2006 to date *American Assn. (ind.).* The city, named in honor of Saint Paul, is known as the "Saintly City."

5711 Apostles 1884t *Northwestern (ind.).* After the Wilmington UA club disbanded September 15, the St. Paul NWL club took their slot by joining the UA September 27; t1884 *Union Assn. (M);* 1886 *Northwest (ind.);* 1888–91m *Western Assn. (ind.).* Team moved to Duluth June 8; 1892m *Western (ind.).* Team moved to Fort Wayne May 25; 1895–99 *Western (ind.);* 1907 *American Assn. (A).* Tag was a spin-off from "Saints." The city was named after Saint Paul, one of the Twelve Apostles. With manager Ed Ashebach at the helm in 1907, newspapers called the players "Ashebach's Apostles."

5712 Freezers 1886 *Northwest (ind.).* The weather in April in St. Paul is downright wintry with snow and 20-degree temperatures common. Playing baseball here in April is rugged. The Minnesota early spring in 1886 was particularly cold, causing several games to be cancelled because of weather conditions. In April 1885 a reporter for the *New York Times*, while visiting St. Paul, wrote: "St. Paul is another Siberia — unfit for human habitation." Undaunted, hardy Minnesotans visit the annual St. Paul Winter Festival, which was first held in 1886. St. Paul is known as the "Winter Sport Capital of the Nation."

5713 Barnie's Babies 1886 *Northwest (ind.)*. Team had many young players. With manager Bill Barnie at the helm, managers called the players "Barnie's Babies."

5714 Sluggers 1888–89 *Western Assn. (ind.)*. Team had numerous good hitters. "Slugger" is a baseball slang that goes back to 1860, referring to a hitter who is able to hit the ball very hard numerous times. St. Paul outfielder John Carroll led the Western Association with 16 home runs — an unheard of number in this era.

5715 Marquettes 1901 *Western (ind.)*. Jacques Marquette was the seventeenth-century explorer who traveled into Minnesota.

5716 Twin Cities Gophers 1909 *Independent Negro* team. Gophers inhabit the western U.S., from the Midwest to the Pacific Coast, the southern U.S., Mexico and Central America. Minnesota is nicknamed the "Gopher State." The team represented the "Twin Cities" of Minneapolis–St. Paul.

5717 St. Paul Baseball Club 1913m *Northern (C)*. Team moved to La Crosse (WI) July 23. Team had no nickname.

5718 Colored Gophers 1929 *Independent Negro team*. Tag was a spin-off from Gophers. Numerous black teams used "double nick-names" by adding the adjective "Black" and "Colored" to a noun like Giants, Yankees and Senators.

St. Petersburg, Florida

5719 Saints 1920–24x *Florida State (D 1920, C 1921–23, D 1924)*. Team and league disbanded August 8; 1925–27 *Florida State (D)*; m1928x *Florida State (D)*. Team started in Fort Lauderdale (FL) and moved to St. Petersburg May 24. Team and league disbanded July 4; 1947–54x *Florida International (C)*. 1947–48, *(B)*. 1949–54 Circuit and team disbanded July 27; 1955–65 *Florida State (D 1955–62, A 1963–65)*. The city was named after St. Petersburg, Russia. The name honors Saint Peter, who established the Roman Catholic Church in Rome in the first century A.D.

5720 Cardinals 1966–96 *Florida State (D 1955–62, A 1963–96)*; 1992–93 *Gulf Coast (R)*. These teams were farm clubs of the St. Louis Cardinals.

5721 Pelicans 1989–90x *Senior Assn. (W)*. 89–90x Circuit was officially known as the Senior Professional Baseball Association. Team and league disbanded January 5, 1990. The brown pelican, the state bird of Louisiana, also is indigenous to Florida.

5722 Devil Rays 1996–98 *Gulf Coast (R)*; 1997–2000 *Florida State (A)*. Team was a farm club of the Tampa Bay Devil Rays.

St. Thomas, Ontario, Canada

5723 Saints 1898–99 *Canadian (ind.)*; 1905 *Canadian (D)*; m1908 *International (D)*. Team began season in Guelph (ON) and moved here June 12; 1911–15 *Canadian (C 1911, D 1911, C 1912–14,, B 1914–15)*. Established in 1810, the city was named after Saint Thomas, one the Twelve Apostles.

5724 Blue Sox 1930 *Ontario (C)*. Players wore blue stirrups.

Saitama, Saitama, Japan

5725 Lotte Marines 2006 to date *Japanese Eastern (ind.)*. Team goes by the name of Urawa Lotte Marines. Home ballpark is in Urawa, a suburb of Saitama City. Team owner is the Lotte Baking Company of Seoul, South Korea. The team is a farm club of the Pacific League Chiba Lotte Marines.

5726 Seibu Lions 2007 to date *Japanese Western (ind.)*. Team goes by the name of Urawa Seibu Lions. The home ballpark is in Urawa, a suburb of Saitama City. Team owner was Seibu Ryutsu Railways. The team is a farm club of the Pacific League Seibu Lions.

5727 Yakult Swallows 2011 to date *Japanese Western (ind.)*. Team is a farm club of the Central League Tokyo Yakult Swallows.

Salamanca, Guanajuato, Mexico

5728 Petroleros 1960–62 *Mexican Center (D 1960, C 1961–62)*; 1975 *Mexican Center (A)*. Crude oil and natural gas is transported to petrochemical refineries. Los petroleros means "oilers."

5729 Tigres 1964–65 *Mexican Center (A)*. Team was a farm club of the Mexico City Tigers. From 1960 through 1975, there were four lower-classification (A) professional baseball leagues in Mexico. Some of these teams had working agreements with the two wealthiest Mexican League teams — the Mexico City Red Devils and the Mexico City Tigers.

Salem, Massachusetts

5730 Salem Base Ball Club 1884x *Massachusetts State Assn. (ind.)*. Team disbanded in mid-season (date unknown). Team had no nickname.

5731 Fairies m1887x *New England (ind.)*. Team started the 1887 season in Lawrence (MA) and moved to Salem July 26. Team disbanded July 9. Perhaps stemming from the Salem Witch Trials of 1692, a legend of "fairies" sprightly hovering in the night skies arose here in the eighteenth century. Salem is known as the "City of Witches" and "Witch City." Actually, the moniker arose because the team "played like fairies" en route to a hideous 10–45 record. "Fairies," in this context, mean a homosexual male that spins off to describe a man who plays as awkwardly as a girl, i.e., "Aw, he throws like a girl!" With manager Wallace Fessendon at the helm, newspapers called the players "Fessendon's Fairies." Ed Flanagan took over in mid-season and the name became "Flanagan's Fairies."

5732 Witches 1888x *New England (ind.)*. Team disbanded August 3; m1926–28 Team started 1926 season in Lowell (MA) before moving to Salem June 3; 1930 *New England (B)*. A mass hysteria of pre-teen girls in the town escalated into accusations of witchcraft against twenty women. A trial was held and seven of the women were hanged. Salem is now the "Witchcraft City." With Wallace Fessendon at the helm in 1888, newspapers called the players "Wally's Witches." With manager Thomas "Poke" Whalen at the helm 1926–28, newspapers called the players "Whalen's Witches."

5733 Salem Base Ball Club 1891–92 *New England (ind.)*; m1895x *New England Assn. (ind.)*. Team started season in Haverhill and moved to Salem June 20. Team and league disbanded July 8. These teams had no nickname.

Salem, Ohio

5734 Salem Base Ball Club 1898x *Ohio State (ind.)*. Circuit and team disbanded in mid-season (date unknown). Team had no nickname.

5735 Quakers 1912m *Ohio–Pennsylvania (D)*. Team moved to Fairmont (OH) July 9. Salem (OH) was established by Quaker settlers in 1801. Since that time, Salem has been known as the "Quaker City." Quakers settlers in America often chose Salem as the name of their municipality in such states as Massachusetts, New Jersey, Indiana and Ohio.

Salem, Oregon

5736 Raglans 1904x *Oregon (D)*. Circuit and team disbanded July 6. The "Raglan coat" is a British-style overcoat with loose sleeves. Founded in 1851, the city had several textile factories that manufactured men's clothing, including the popular nineteenth century "Raglan coat." Baseball players in cold weather wore either bulky woolen sweaters or "Raglan" coats.

5737 Senators 1940–42 *Western International (B)*; 1946–54 *Western International (B 1946–51, A 1952–54)*; 1946–54 *Western International (B 1946–51, A 1952–54)*; 1955–60 *Northwest (B)*; 1977–81 *Northwest (A)*. City was the Oregon territorial capital in 1851 and has been the state capital of Oregon since 1859. Salem is "Oregon's Beautiful Capital City" and the "Capital City." These teams were not farm clubs of the Washington Senators.

5738 Dodgers 1961–65 *Northwest (B 1961–62, A 1963–65)*; 1989 *Northwest (A)*. Team was a farm club of the Los Angeles Dodgers.

5739 Angels 1982–88 *Northwest (A)*. Team was a farm club of the California Angels.

Salem, Virginia

5740 Friends 1940 *Virginia (D)*. Team represented both Salem and Roanoke. The term "Friends," synonymous with "Twins," refers to a team that represents two cities. Sometimes a team will include both cities in its formal name, i.e., Ashland-Catlettsburg, Bangor-Berwick, Fargo-Moorhead, South Boston–Halifax, Sherman-Denison, etc. Other times only the home-field city will be included in the name, although fans from the companion city are encouraged to travel to the other's city's home field. Salem is a summer resort in the Blue Ridge Mountains. To attract tourists, the city announces itself as the "Friendly City." The "Quaker Friends" is a religious order here that provides many types of services for people.

5741 Rebels 1955 *Appalachian (D)*; 1957–59, 1961–63, 1967 *Appalachian (D 1957–62, R 1963–67)*; 1968–73 *Carolina (A)*. Roanoke was the site of several skirmishes and one major battle during the Civil War. Salem today is a suburb of Roanoke (VA). Although popular with the fans, the moniker was being used in a transition period in U.S. history when such names as "Indians" and "Rebels" were becoming "politically incorrect."

5742 Giants 1960 *Appalachian (D)*. Team was a farm club of the San Francisco Giants.

5743 Pirates 1964–66, 1974–79 *Appalachian (D)*. Team was a farm club of the Pittsburgh Pirates.

5744 Redbirds 1980–86 *Appalachian (D)*. Team was a farm club of the St. Louis Cardinals. "Redbirds" is a spin-off of Cardinals.

5745 Buccaneers 1987–94 *Appalachian (D)*. Team was a farm club of the Pittsburgh Pirates. The tag "Buccaneers" is a spin-off of Pirates.

5746 Avalanche 1995–2008 *Appalachian (D)*. Team was a farm club of the Colorado Rockies, whose location was in the Rocky Mountains where snowy avalanches sometimes occur. When the team switched affiliation to Houston in 2003, the Avalanche moniker was retained.

5747 Red Sox 2009 to date *Carolina (A)*. Team is a farm club of the Boston Red Sox.

Salem-Keizer, Oregon

5748 Volcanoes 1997 to date *Northwest (A)*. Nearby Mount St. Helens is an active volcano that erupted in 1983.

Salem-Roanoke, Virginia

5749 Friends 1939 *Virginia (D)*; 1941–42 *Virginia (C)*; 1946m *Blue Ridge (D)*. Team moved to Lenoir (NC) June 25. With quite a few double-city teams having already used the nickname of Twins since at least 1885, management chose the synonymous "Friends." The Quaker Friends is a religious order prominent in Quaker communities. In the Vietnam War era (1965–75), they counseled young men who had problems with the military draft.

Salina, Kansas

5750 Salina Base Ball Club 1887 *Kansas State (ind.)*; 1898 *Kansas State (ind.)*. These teams had no nickname.

5751 Blues 1898 *Kansas State (D)*. Players wore blue-trim uniforms and blue stirrups.

5752 Insurgents 1908–10 *Central Kansas (D)*; 1912 *Central Kansas (D)*; 1913 *Kansas State (D)*. Known as "Bleeding Kansas," the region was ravaged by pro-slavery gangs, abolitionist John Brown's anti-slavery raiders and guerrilla skirmishes at the border with Missouri. All of these raiders ignored civil authority and were branded as "Insurgents." With manager Bert Lamb at the helm in 1912, newspapers called the players "Bert's Insurgents." Lon Ury took over in 1913, changing the name to "Lon Ury's Insurgents."

5753 Trade-Winners 1908–10 *Central Kansas (D)*; 1913 *Kansas State (D)*. Founded in 1858, the city quickly became a wheat trade center that gave rise to annual farm product trade shows. Trade show winners were lionized by the press. Initially "Trade-Winners," local newspapers quickly shortened the moniker to **Winners**. Winning teams in this era were sometimes called Blue Ribbons, Champions, Trade Winners and Winners. With manager Frank Everhart at the helm in 1908, newspapers called the players "Frank Everhart's Trade-Winners." Ernest Quigley took over in 1909 and the name became "Ernest's Trade-Winners." Elmer Meredith took over in 1910 and the name became "Elmer Meredith's Trade-Winners."

5754 Coyotes 1914 *Kansas State (D)*. The coyote is a smallish wolf-like canine found mostly in central North America. With field manager Dick Robin at the helm, newspapers called the players "Dick Robin's Coyotes."

5755 Millers 1922–26 *Southwestern (C 1922–23, D 1924–26)*; 1938–41 *Western Assn. (C)*. Kansas is known as the "Wheat State" and the "Breadbasket of the Nation." The city receives wheat from nearby farms for processing in the city's wheat mills. Russian settlers brought a strain of "Hard Winter Wheat," i.e., wheat seeds that grow well in cooler temperatures, to Kansas in the 1870s. The result was a boom in wheat farming. With manager John McCloskey at the helm in 1922, newspapers called the players "McCloskey's Millers." Bennie Meyer took over in 1923 and the name became "Meyer's Millers." Floyd Dorland took over in 1924–25 and the name became "Dorland's Millers." Jimmy Payton took over in 1925 and the name became "Jimmy's Millers." Other manager-inspired names in 1938 were (Harry) "Sutter's Millers" and (Jack) "Calvey's Millers." Riley Parker took over in 1939 and the name became "Riley Parker's Millers." Jack Calvey returned in 1940. Russ Rollings took over in 1941 and the name became "Rollings' Millers."

5756 Blue Jays 1946–52 *Western Assn. (C)*. Team was a farm club of the Philadelphia Blue Jays. When the parent club reverted to Phillies in 1950, the minor league team's moniker of Blue Jays was retained for the 1950–51–52 seasons.

Salinas, California

5757 Colts 1949m *Sunset (C)*. Team moved to Tijuana (BC, Mexico) August 5. The team had numerous young players known in the common slang as "colts." The annual California Rodeo is held in Salinas. The rodeo features horses and colts.

5758 Packers 1954–58 *California (C)*; 1973–76 *California (A)*. Vegetable farms near the city transport this produce to city food processing factories to be cleaned, canned, packaged and shipped out. Farms in and around Salinas use hundreds of trucks to transport produce.

5759 Mets 1963–64 *California (A)*. Team was a farm club of the New York Mets.

5760 Salinas Valley Indians 1965 *California (A)*. Team was a farm club of the Cleveland Indians.

5761 Angels 1977–80 *California (A)*. Team was a farm club of the California Angels.

5762 Spurs 1982–87 *California (A)*; 1989–92 *California (A)*. Tag was an alliterative spin-off from Colts.

5763 Peppers 1995–98 *Western (ind.)*. Vegetable farms in the region grow lettuce, sugar beets and red and green peppers.

Salisbury, Maryland

5764 Indians 1922–28x *Eastern Shore (D)*. Circuit and team disbanded July 10; 1937–38 *Eastern Shore (D)*. The Potomac Indians, after whom the nearby Potomac River was named, inhabited this region until the eighteenth century. Harry Hoffman managed in 1922 and the name was "Hoffman's Indians." George Eichnor took over in mid-season 1922 and the name changed to "Eichnor's Indians." Burt Shipley managed in 1923 and the name was "Shipley's Indians." Alva Burris took over in 1924 and the name became "Burris' Indians." The name was retained through 1928 and again 1937–38 under four other managers. These teams were not farm clubs of the Cleveland Indians.

5765 Senators 1939 *Eastern Shore (D)*. Although their official nickname was "Nationals," the Washington AL team was popularly known as the "Senators." The switch to Senators stopped the fans' confusion with the Cleveland Indians.

5766 Cardinals 1940–41 *Eastern Shore (D)*; 1946–49 *Eastern Shore (D)*. Team was a farm club of the St. Louis Cardinals in 1940 and 1946–49. The team played with a loose affiliation with the St. Louis NL club in 1941.

5767 Athletics 1951 *Inter-State (B)*. Team was a farm club of the Philadelphia Athletics.

5768 Reds 1952 *Inter-State (B)*. Team was a farm club of the Cincinnati Reds.

5769 Delmarva Shorebirds 1996 to date *South Atlantic (A)*. Delmarva is an acronym for Delaware, Maryland and Virginia. A "shorebird" refers to sea gulls, pelicans, eagles, falcons and hawks that hunt and forage along the Mid-Atlantic coast.

5770 Rockfish 1998 *Maryland Fall (W)*. The Rockfish is a striped ocean bass that inhabits the rocky coastline waters here.

Salisbury, Rowan County, North Carolina

5771 Bees 1937–38 *North Carolina (D)*. Team was a farm club of the Boston Bees. With manager Otis "Blackie" Carter at the helm, newspapers called the players "Blackie's Bees" to distinguish them from the parent club NL Boston Bees.

5772 Giants 1939–42 *North Carolina (D)*. Team was a farm club of the New York Giants. With manager Johnny Heving at the helm, newspapers called the players "Heving's Giants" to distinguish them from the parent club NL New York Giants.

5773 Pirates 1945–52 *North Carolina (D)*.Team was a farm club of the Pittsburgh Pirates. Team was a formal farm club of the NL Pi-

rates 1945–51 and then played with a loose affiliation with the Pittsburgh NL club in 1952.

5774 Rocots 1953 *Tar Heel (D)*. Salisbury is located in Rowan County. Management combined the beginnings of Rowan and County.

5775 Braves 1960–62 Western Carolinas *(D 1960–62, A 1963–66)*. Team was a farm club of the Milwaukee Braves.

5776 Dodgers 1963–64 *Western Carolinas (A)*. Team was a farm club of the Los Angeles Dodgers.

5777 Astros 1965–66 *Western Carolinas (A)*. Team was a farm club of the Houston Astros.

5778 Senators 1968 *Western Carolinas (A)*. Team was a farm club of the Washington Senators.

Salisbury-Spencer, North Carolina

5779 Salisbury-Spencer Baseball Club 1905m *Virginia–North Carolina (D)*. Team moved to Winston-Salem July 17. Team had no nickname.

5780 Salisbury-Spencer Colonials 1925–29 *Piedmont (C)*. In 1778 British troops led by General Charles Cornwallis pursued American troops, led by Colonial Army General Nathaniel Greene, into Salisbury. With manager Pat O'Rourke at the helm, newspapers called the players "O'Rourke's Colonials." Rowdy Elliot took over in midseason and the name became "Elliot's Colonials." Moose Marhsall took over in 1926 and the name became "Moose Marshall's Colonials." The moniker was retained through 1929.

Salt Lake City, Utah

5781 Salt Lake City Baseball Club 1901 *Inter-Mountain (ind.)*. Team had no nickname.

5782 Elders m1903–04 *Pacific National (A 1903, B 1904)*. Team started 1903 season in Portland (OR) and moved to Salt Lake City July 2. The city has been the headquarters of the Mormon Church since 1847. The leadership council of the church is known as the "Church Elders." With manager John McCloskey at the helm in 1903, newspapers called the players "McCloskey's Elders." Frank "Dad" Gimlin took over in 1904 and the name became "Dad Gimlin's Elders."

5783 Mormons 1909m *Inter-Mountain (D)*. Team moved to Livingston (MT) July 10. Mormon settlers, led by Brigham Young, arrived here in 1847. Utah is now known as the "Land of the Mormons" and the "Mormon State." With manager E.S. Farnsworth at the helm, newspapers called the players "Farnsworth's Mormons."

5784 Skyscrapers 1911–14 *Union Assn. (D)*. City is located near the Wasatch Mountains. In the twentieth century a "skyscraper" began to mean a very tall building. Before 1900, the term skyscraper referred to a mountain. With manager Cliff Blankenship at the helm, newspapers called the players "Cliff Blankenship's Skyscrapers." Weaver took over in 1912 and the name became "A.C. Weaver's Skyscrapers." John McCloskey took over in 1913 and the name became "McCloskey's Skyscrapers." Harry Hester took over in 1914 and the name became "Harry Hester's Skyscrapers."

5785 Bees 1915–25 *Pacific Coast (AA)*; 1926–28 *Utah–Idaho (C)*; 1939–42 *Pioneer (C)*; 1946–57 *Pioneer (C)*; 1958–65 *Pacific Coast (AAA)*; 1969 *Pioneer (R)*; 1970 *Pacific Coast (AAA)*; 2006 to date *Pacific Coast (AAA)*. Mormon settlers first called the state "Deseret" and referred to it as the biblical "Land of Milk and Honey." From this reference, Utah (renamed in 1856) became known as the "Beehive State." There are honey bee farms in Utah. With manager Cliff Blankenship at the helm 1915–16, newspapers called the players "Blankenship's Bees." Bill Bernard took over in 1917 and the name became "Bernard's Bees." Walter McCreedie took over in 1918 and the name became "McCreedie's Bees." Edward Herr took over in 1919, and the name became "Eddie's Bees." Ernie Johnson took over in 1920 and the name became "Ernie's Bees." Duffy Lewis took over in 1922 and the name became "Duffy's Bees." Bud Orr managed at the start of 1926 and the name was "Bud's Bees." Bert Whaling took over in mid-season 1926 and the name became "Bert's Bees." Bob Coltrin took over in 1928 and the name became "Bob's Bees." By 1939 the "Bees" tag became traditional. The PCL franchise starting play in 2006 goes by the regional name of "Salt Lake" Bees.

5786 Giants 1967–68 *Pioneer (R)*. Team was a farm club of the San Francisco Giants.

5787 Angels 1971–74 *Pacific Coast (AAA)*. Team was a farm club of the California Angels.

5788 Gulls 1975–84 *Pacific Coast (AAA)*. Sea gulls inhabit the shorelines of the Great Salt Lake.

5789 Trappers 1985–92 *Pioneer (R)*. Team was named in honor of the Utah Trappers Association, which makes rules for the humane trapping of wolves, bobcats and other wildlife.

5790 Salt Lake Buzz 1994–2000 *Pacific Coast (AAA)*. When real-estate developer Joe Buzas bought the team, a fan poll chose the obvious "Buzz" as a spin-off from the old moniker of Bees.

5791 Salt Lake Stingers 2001–05 *Pacific Coast (AAA)*. Moniker was a spin-off of "Bees."

Saltillo, Coahuila, Mexico

5792 Pericos 1946x *Mexican National (B)*. Circuit withdrew from the National Assn. of Professional Baseball Leagues May 27. "Los Pericos" is Spanish for "parrots."

5793 Saraperos 1956–57 *Central Mexican (C)*; 1968–69 *Mexican Center (A)*; 1970 to date *Mexican (AAA)*. The 1980 players strike shut down Mexican League on July 3, 1980. However, the league did not go out of business. A "serape" is a long, colorfully striped, blanket-like shawl worn by Mexican men. Although American fashion has become popular in Mexico, many rural Mexican men still wear the serape. Spanish spelling is "sarape."

5794 Sultanes 1964 *Mexican Center (A)*. Team was a farm club of the Monterrey Sultans (Sultanes de Monterrey in Spanish).

San Angelo, Texas

5795 Bronchos 1921–22 *West Texas (D)*. Founded in 1869, the city had several horse ranches where "buckin' broncos" were tamed and trained. With manager Luke Robinson at the helm, newspapers called the players "Luke Robinson's Bronchos."

5796 Red Snappers 1928 *West Texas (D)*. Team was named after manager Earl "Red" Snapp. The moniker was appropriate because the city is located near O.C. Fisher Lake and the Concho River.

5797 Sheepherders 1929 *West Texas (D)*. Nearby sheep farms transport wool and mohair to city factories to be processed. The city has several wool textile mills for the manufacture of woolen clothing. With manager Walt Alexander at the helm, newspapers called the players "Alexander's Herders."

5798 Colts 1948–55 *Longhorn (D 1948–50, C 1951–55)*; m1957 *Southwestern (B)*. Team started season in Pampa (TX) and moved to San Angelo May 16; 2005 *Central (ind.)*; 2006–10 *United (ind.)*; 2011 to date *North American (ind.)*. The Colts spin-off from Bronchos was appropriate because all of the teams in the Longhorn League and in the subsequent circuits in which San Angelo franchises competed had many rookies and young players.

5799 Pirates 1958–59 *Sophomore (D)*. Team was a farm club of the Pittsburgh Pirates.

San Antonio, Texas

5800 Cowboys 1888x *Texas (ind.)*. Team disbanded May 24. Texas is the quintessential cowboy state. "Cowboys" was also slang for "baseball players." With manager John Cavanaugh at the helm, newspapers called the players "Cavanaugh's Cowboys."

5801 Missions m1888 *Texas (ind.)*. Team started season in Austin (TX) and moved to San Antonio July 4. This new San Antonio team took the name "Missions" and replaced the San Antonio "Cowboys," who disbanded May 24; 1892x *Texas (ind.)*. Team disbanded June 28; 1933–42 *Texas (A 1933–35, A1 1936–42)*; 1946–62, 1968–71, 1988 to date *Texas (AA)*. The city was founded as the Franciscan Mission of San Antonio de Valero in 1718. Since that time San Antonio has been known as the "Mission City." With manager John McCloskey at the helm in 1888, newspapers called the players "McCloskey's Missionaries" and "McCloskey's Missions." In the nineteenth century, newspapers used "Missions" and "Missionaries" alternately, but by 1900 "Missions" had become the exclusive name.

5802 Missionaries 1895–96 *Texas–Southern (ind.)*. With manager W.J. Clare at the helm in 1895, local newspapers called the players "Clare's Missionaries." Newspapers also used the shorter version of "Missions."

5803 Bronchos 1896–97 *Texas–Southern (ind.)*; 1898 *Texas (ind.)*; 1903–06 *South Texas (C)*; 1907–19 *Texas (C 1907–10, B 1911–19)*. City had several horse ranches in the vicinity to tame and train "buckin' bronchos." Baseball players in this era, noted for "horsing around," equine builds and prancing on the field, sometimes were called "bronchos." Newspapers started spelling the moniker, originally a Spanish word from 1850, as **Broncos**.

5804 Black Bronchos 1909 *Independent Negro team*; 1919 *Negro Texas (ind.)*. Moniker was a spin-off from the Texas League "Bronchos."

5805 Giants 1918 *Independent Negro team*. The tag "Giants" was popular for black teams.

5806 Bears 1920–28 *Texas (B 1920, A 1921–28)*. In 1794 the official city name became San Antonio de Bexar. Since that time San Antonio has been known as the "Free State of Bexar." Newspapers, starting in 1920, used "Bears" as a spin-off from "Bexar."

5807 Indians 1929–32 *Texas (A)*. The Tonkawa Indians were buffalo hunters who inhabited Central Texas. They were nearly wiped out by small pox and other European diseases.

5808 Bullets 1963–64 *Texas (AA)*. Team was a farm club of the Houston Colt .45's. The nickname "Bullets" was a spin-off of Colt .45's.

5809 Brewers 1972–76 *Texas (AA)*. Team was a farm club of the Milwaukee Brewers. The team was a Brewers farm club only in 1972. The team was a farm club of Cleveland (1973–75) and Texas (1976) but the popular Brewers moniker was retained.

5810 Dodgers 1977–87 Team was a farm club of the Los Angeles Dodgers.

5811 Tejanos 1994 *Texas–Louisiana (ind.)*. In today's "politically-correct" age, the moniker "Tejanos" was chosen to represent those people of Mexican heritage whose family line has lived north of the Rio Grande in Texas since the sixteenth century. In Spanish these people are known as "Los Tejanos." San Antonio is known as the "Gateway to Old Mexico."

San Benito, Texas

5812 Saints 1931 *Rio Grande Valley (D)*. City was named in honor of Saint Benito, in Spanish San Benito.

San Bernardino, California

5813 Kittens 1913 *Southern California (D)*. Team was named after manager Kitty Brashear.

5814 San Bernardino Baseball Club 1915–16 *California Winter (W)*. Team had no nickname.

5815 Padres 1929 *California State (D)*. Padre Francisco Dumetz founded a mission here in 1810. Father in Spanish is "padre." Team was not a farm club of the San Diego Padres, as the San Diego PCL franchise would not be established until 1936.

5816 Stars 1941x *California (C)*. Team disbanded June 29. Team was a farm club of the PCL Hollywood Stars.

5817 Valencias m1948 *Sunset (C)*. Team started 1948 season in Anaheim (CA) and moved to San Bernardino June 25. Valencia oranges from nearby fruit farms are transported to city factories for cleaning, packaging and shipping out to market.

5818 Pioneers 1949–50 *Sunset (C)*. Pioneering Mormon settlers arrived in 1851 and established the city here in 1854.

5819 Spirit 1987–95 *California (A)*. Founded in 1851 by Mormon settlers, the San Bernardino citizens are proud of their Mormon faith.

5820 Pride 1990–91x *Senior Assn. (W)*. Circuit and team disbanded January 5, 1991, due to low fan attendance. Fan poll chose "Pride" as an expression of the citizens' pride in their city, which has enjoyed fast growth in the last 25 years. Proud citizens nicknamed San Bernardino "The City on the Move."

5821 Stampede 1996–2002 *California (A)*. Founded by Mormon settlers in 1851, the city attracted many ranchers, who displaced the old Spanish ranchos with ranches for the horse and cattle drives of the era, 1860–1900. Elmore sports Group bought the "Spirits" franchise, renamed it the "Stampede," and built Fiscalini "The Ranch" Field as the team's home park.

5822 Sand Dragons 1999 *California Fall (W)*. San Bernardino Valley is a semi-arid region with desert-like patches. "Sand Dragon" is a nickname for a desert Gila Monster.

5823 Inland Empire 66ers 2003 to date *California (A)*. Highway 66 is a major highway leading into San Bernardino County. Southern California is the popular site to cruise the highways in a sports car.

Sandersville, Washington County, Georgia

5824 Wacos 1953–54 *Georgia State (D)*. Wacos is an amalgam of Washington County.

5825 Giants 1955–56 *Georgia State (D)*. Team was a farm club of the New York Giants.

San Diego, California

5826 San Diego Base Ball Club 1890–91 *California (W)*; 1915–16 *California Winter (W)*; 1930–31 *California Winter (W)*. These teams had no nickname.

5827 Bears 1913 *Southern California (D)*. With manager Spencer Abbot at the helm, newspapers called the players "Abbot's Bears." The moniker was appropriate because California is the "Golden Bear State." Marion Bear Park is located about 10 miles north of the city.

5828 Pantages 1915–16–16–17 *California Winter (W)*. Alexander Pantages, owner of Pantage Movie Theaters, also owned the team.

5829 Balboa Parks 1922–23–23–24 *California Winter (W)*. Team played at a stadium close to Balboa Park, a park in San Diego with eight gardens.

5830 Aces 1929 *California State (D)*. With manager Sam Agnew at the helm, newspapers called the players "Agnew's Aces." The name was appropriate because the North Island U.S. Naval Station started to fly airplanes in 1928 at the urging of General Billy Mitchell. San Diego is known as the "Air Capital of the West." Airplane "Flying Ace" barnstorming shows were popular in California in the 1920s.

5831 Merchants 1936–37 *California Winter (W)*. Team was sponsored by several city merchants who sold fish and farm produce.

5832 Gold Club 1936–37–37–38 *California Winter (W)*. Gold Club Bar owned the team.

5833 7-Up's 1936–37–39–40 *California Winter (W)*. Pepsi-Cola owned the team. Pepsi-Cola Company owns 7-Up. San Diego has a 7-Up bottling company.

5834 Padres 1936–68 *Pacific Coast (AA)*; 1969 to date *National (M)*. Franciscan padres founded the city as California's first mission in 1769. Major league baseball teams that used previous minor league monikers include Baltimore Orioles (IL Orioles), Detroit Tigers (WL Tigers), Los Angeles Angels (PCL Angels), Milwaukee Brewers (AA Brewers) and San Diego Padres (PCL Padres). San Diego newpapers often use **Pads** as a headline contraction, i.e., "Pads edege Cubs, 5–4."

5835 Paris Inn 1937–38 *California Winter (W)*. Paris Inn Restaurant owned the team.

5836 Farleys 1937–38–38–39 *California Winter (W)*. The Farley Real Estate Company owned the team.

5837 Tigers 1946 *Western Coast (ind.)*. Circuit was also called Pacific Coast Negro Baseball League. Players wore striped hose.

5838 Washington Padres 1974 *National (M)*. Businessman Joe Danzansky tried to buy the San Diego club and move it to Washington, D.C., for the 1974 season. The Topps Baseball Card Company was so sure that the deal was done that they printed baseball cards for Padre players that were labeled "Washington NL Club." Owner C. Arnholt Smith had a change of heart and decided not to sell to Daznansky and instead sold the team to McDonald's hamburger baron Ray Croc, who kept the team in San Diego.

5839 Ray Kroc's Hamburgers 1974–89 *National (M)*. Ray Kroc, who started and owned the McDonald's hamburger empire, owned the team from 1974 until he died in 1989. When the Padres would finish a season with a losing record (which was often), and especially when the team finished last in the NL Western Division, disgruntled San Diego fans would call the team "Kroc's Hambugers." The term "hamburger" is slang for a sloppy mess or an animal that has been slaughtered.

5840 Dick Williams' Men 1984 *National (M)*. People tend to forget that the 1984 National League champions were *not* the Chicago Cubs but rather manager Dick Williams' San Diego Padres. While "America's Team" from Wrigley Field was capturing the hearts of Americans in 1984, Williams led his Padres to the NL Western Division title with a 92–70 record to finish 12 games ahead of Atlanta in a division race that was over by the All-Star break, as the Padres got hot in June and July. "Williams' Men" were led by hitters Steve Garvey, Tony Gwynn (Hall of Fame), Terry Kennedy, Kevin McReynolds, Gene Richards, Luis Salazar and Garry Templeton and pitchers Rollie Fingers (Hall of Fame), Rich Gossage (Hall of Fame), Andy Hawkins, Tim Lollar, Eric Show, Mark Thurmond, and Ed Whitson. In the NL Championship Series, "Williams Men" looked beaten after losing the first two games in Chicago's Wrigley Field, 13–0 and 4–2, but they came back to win three straight games in San Diego to clinch the 1984 National League pennant.

5841 Friars 1998 to date *National (M)*. The name was a spin-off of Padres that became popular during the team's 1998 NL pennant season. However, with the college Providence Friars already using that moniker as their oficial nickname, the name is used only by local newspapers as an infrequent gimmick. Nevertheless, the "Swinging Friar" logo first appeared in 1958 for the San Diego PCL club. The NL Padres used the logo 1969–84, dropped it, and then restored it in 1996 and have used it to date. The logo is the only hint of brown on the now blue-trim uniforms after the brown-trim uniforms were finally discontinued after 27 years of use. Today, there is a "Swinging Friar" website for Padres fans to send in e-mails.

5842 Fathers 1998 to date *National (M).* The obvious English-language spin-off of "Los Padres." Moniker is used only by local newspapers and rather sparingly at that. **Dads** and **Daddies** are the obvious spin-off monikers for headlines, i.e., "Dads defeat Mets, 4–3." A 2005 newspaper article centered on the "San Diego Dads," i.e., San Diego men who were unemployed and would meet each other at San Diego baseball games for moral support.

5843 The Worst Division Winner Ever 2006 *National (M).* When the Padres won the 2006 NL Western Division with a meager 82–80 record, they "bested" the 82–79 mark of the 1973 NL Eastern Division champion New York Mets.

5844 Surf Dawgs 2005–06 *Golden (ind.).* Independent league baseball teams since 1993 have sometimes used trendy nicknames featuring dawg/dog and cat/katz monikers and other styles. A "surf dawg" is slang for a male surfer. The so-called San Diego Surf Dawgs (2007–08) of the Arizona Winter League played their home games in Yuma, Arizona.

5845 Dead-Ass Franchise 2011 *National (M).* Controversial sports broadcaster Mike North hurled this deprecatory tag against San Diego's management for failing to sign Adrian Gonzalez (who went to Boston) and other quality players, resulting in 71–91 record, dropping the team into last place in the National League West Division.

5846 Pesky Padres 2011 to date *National (M).* The official game program of the San Francisco Giants of July 7, 2011, described the San Diego players as the "Pesky Padres." The Padres had won the 2010 season series with the Giants, 12 games to 6. Regrettably, the term "pesky" has been a respectful, non-confrontational euphemism for "losing team." Diplomatic players and team officials, not wishing to bad-mouth the peers on another, non-competitive club, often coyly refer to the opponent as young but learning, struggling but still tough and pesky.

Sandusky, Ohio

5847 Maroons 1887 *Ohio State (ind.).* Players wore maroon hose.

5848 Sands 1887 *Ohio State (ind.).* Newspapers used this moniker in headlines, i.e., "Sands edge Stubs, 4–3."

5849 Suds 1887 *Ohio State (ind.).* Tag was another headline contraction, i.e., "Suds edge Gems, 5–4."

5850 Fish-eaters 1888x *Tri-State (ind.).* Team disbanded September 10. Fishing boats catch bass, catfish, perch and pike in Lake Erie. Sandusky is the "Gateway to Lake Erie." Some nineteenth century team nicknames described a ball player's and fans' culinary habits, i.e., Boston Beaneaters, Lima Beaneaters and Sandusky Fish-Eaters. With manager James Hever at the helm, newspapers called the players "James Hever's Fish-eaters."

5851 Sandies 1893 *Ohio–Michigan (ind.).* Newspapers used this moniker for headlines, i.e., "Sandies edge Daubers, 4–3."

5852 Sailors 1936–37m *Ohio–State (D).* Team moved to Marion (OH) June 22. Lake Erie cargo ships sail in and out of the "Gateway to Lake Erie," located on the coast of Sandusky Bay. With manager James "Chappie" Geygan at the helm, newspapers called the players "Geygan's Sailors."

San Fernando, Nicaragua

5853 Ferias 2004–05–07–08 *Nicaraguan (W)*; 2008–09 to date *Nicaraguan (W).* The Nicaraguan League suspended operations for the 2007–08 season because of financial problems but resumed play in 2008–09. The league went all-professional in the 2004–05 season but does not participate in the Caribbean World Series. Nicaragua's mountains, forests and swamps contain all sorts of wild animals, i.e., snakes, lizards, jaguars, eagles, hawks, bobcats and piranhas. "Las ferias" means "wild animals."

Sanford, Florida

5854 Celery-feds 1925 *Florida State (D).* Sanford is known as the "Celery City." With manager Nick Carter at the helm, newspapers called the players the "Carter's Celery-feds."

5855 Lookouts 1938 *Florida State (D).* Team was a farm club of the Chattanooga Lookouts. With manager Guy Lacy at the helm, newspapers called the players "Lacy's Lookouts."

Sanford, North Carolina

5856 Spinners 1941–42 *Bi-State (D)*; 1946–50 *Tobacco State (D).* Textile mills produce wearing apparel. With manager Zeb Harrington at the helm, newspapers called the players "Zeb Harrington's Spinners." After Frank Rogers took over in 1942, Zeb Harrington returned in 1946 as manager, and the name again became "Zeb's Spinners."

San Francisco, California

5857 Fog-eaters 1887 *California State (ind.)*; 1888–93 *California (ind.).* Circuit was the 1887 California State League and the 1888–93 California League; 1890–91–91–92 *California Winter (W).* San Francisco Bay is noted for its fogs, especially in the spring. A "fog-eater" is a pilot ship with bright lights and foghorns that sails San Francisco Bay guiding other boats. A soccer team in the 1980–81 Major Indoor Soccer league competed here and was called the "Fog."

5858 Pioneers 1887–88 *California (ind.).* Circuit was the California State League in 1887 and the California League in 1888; 1888–89–89–90 *California Winter (W).* Pioneers flooded California in 1848–49 after the Sutter Mills Gold Strike. With manager Mike Finn at the helm, newspapers called the players "Mike Finn's Pioneers."

5859 Haverlys 1887–90 *California (ind.)*; 1888–89–89–90 *California Winter (W).* The Haverly Theater of San Francisco owned the team. With manager Henry Harris at the helm in 1887, newspapers called the players "Henry's Haverlys" and "Harris' Haverlys." Although Harris managed the team in 1889, the Haverly name was dropped, and there was no new nickname.

5860 Knickerbockers 1888–89–89–90 *California Winter (W).* Numerous nineteenth century baseball teams, including this one on the Pacific coast, named themselves Knickerbockers, after Alexander Cartwright's original Knickerbockers Club, which first codified baseball rules in games played in New York and New Jersey in 1845.

5861 Californias 1888–89–90–91 *California Winter (W).* Several nineteenth century teams were named after their home state, i.e., Baltimore Marylands, Louisville Kentuckys, Manchester New Hampshirites, Richmond Virginias, and San Francisco Californias. The franchise's official name was the "California Base Ball Club."

5862 Bay Citys 1889 *California (ind.).* San Francisco is the "Bay City."

5863 Friscos 1891–93 *California (ind.)*; 1899–1900 *California (ind.).* Newspapers used the moniker for headlines, i.e., "Friscos edge Dukes, 4–3." With Henry Harris as manager for both teams, newspapers called the players "Harris' Friscos."

5864 Petalunas 1892–93 *Central California (W).* The petaluna is a flower found in the western U.S.

5865 Pacifics 1896 *California State (ind.).* Team was named after the Pacific Ocean.

5866 Olympics 1897–98 *California (ind.).* Hearkening back to the Ancient Greek Olympic games, numerous nineteenth century sporting teams called themselves the "Olympics." People in the nineteenth century were so fascinated by the ancient Olympic Games that the modern Olympic Games were first held in 1898. Franchise's official title was the "Olympic Base Ball Club."

5867 Athletics 1898–99 *California (ind.).* Franchise's official title was the "Athletic Base Ball Club of San Francisco."

5868 Wasps 1901–02 *California (ind.).* The sand wasp is regional to California, alighting on sandy beaches. *The Wasp* was a popular California magazine of this era that devoted its articles to politics and satire. Team "stung its opposition like sand wasps" en route to the 1901 California League championship. With manager Henry Harris at the helm in the 1901 pennant season, newspapers called the players "Harris' Wasps."

5869 Pirates 1903x *Pacific National (A).* Team disbanded August 21. This PNL team raided the roster of the PCL Seals for players. In this era any team that raided the roster of another team was sometimes branded by newspapers as "Pirates." California has had a colorful history of pirates roaming its coasts, i.e., Hippolyte de Bouchard, the Tres Marias Buccaneers and English privateers.

5870 Seals 1903–57 *Pacific Coast (A 1903–07, AA 1908–45, AAA 1946–51, Open 1952–57).* Fur seals swim the coastal waters of California.

5871 San Francisco Baseball Club 1907–08 *California (ind.);* m1915x *California State (ind.).* Team started season in Berkeley (CA) and moved to San Francisco April 28. Team and league disbanded May 30 due to heavy rain storms. These teams had no nickname.

5872 Orphans 1909m *California (ind.).* Team lost games often and early in 1909, driving fans to "abandon" the players by staying away from the park and forcing the team to move to Sacramento in mid-season. The team compiled a crummy 34–63 mark, prompting the move to Sacramento. Teams that disenchanted their home city fans like this were often called the Misfits, Orphans and Wanderers.

5873 Baby Seals 1910 *California State (D).* Team was a farm of the San Francisco Seals. The team was one of the earliest affiliates with a higher classification minor league team in minor league history.

5874 Missions m1914–15 *Pacific Coast (AA).* Team started 1914 season in Sacramento and moved to San Francisco September 6; 1926–36 *Pacific Coast (AA).* Spanish explorer Juan Bautista de Anza led soldiers and settlers here where a presidio (garrison) and a mission were built in 1777. Mission padres soon arrived and made an unsuccessful attempt to convert the natives to Christianity. Team was known as the **Mission Bells** (1926–27) and then the red-hosed **Mission Reds** (1928–36). Newspapers often shortened the name to **Monks** for headlines, i.e., "Monks edge Sacts, 4–3."

5875 Wolves 1915–17 *Pacific Coast (AA).* Team was named after manager Harry Wolverton.

5876 Bears 1923–26 *Pacific Coast (AA).* Moniker was a spin-off from the California Golden Bear, the symbol of the Californian flag. With manager Herbert Ellison at the helm, newspapers called the players "Herbert's Bears."

5877 Sea Lions 1946 *Western Coast (ind.).* Sea lions and seals swim along the coastal waters of California. The circuit had two names, known as the Western Coast Baseball Association and the Pacific Coast Negro Baseball League.

5878 Giants 1958 to date *National (M).* The New York Giants moved to San Francisco for the 1958 season. The moniker of "Giants" was retained.

5879 Bays 1962–67 *National (M).* A newspaper-friendly moniker derived from San Francisco Bay. The tag was abandoned when the Oakland Athletics arrived at the East Bay in 1968.

5880 Frisco 1958 *National (M).* An attempt to use a newspaper-friendly "Phillies"-style moniker went nowhere. "Frisco" is an abbreviation for San Francisco that is often used in non-sports talk.

5881 Jints 1958 to date *National (M).* An attempt to transfer this colorful "New Yorkese" moniker to the West Coast met with only lukewarm acceptance. People in California prefer not to talk like "Nu Yawkaas." The moniker is used mostly ad-lib by baseball commentators and used only infrequently in local newspapers to save line space, i.e., "Jints edge D-Backs, 4–3." The name rhymes with "pints" and not "mints."

5882 Gnats 1962 to date *National (M).* In the first of many heated pennant battles between the arch California rivals, Dodger fans "belittled" the Giants as "Gnats" during the 1962 season that culminated in a historic tie-breaking best 2-of-3 playoff for the 1962 NL pennant, which the Giants won, 2 games to 1. In later years, Giant fans, unhappy with a losing Giant team on the field, would hurl the same name onto Giant players as a sarcastic epithet, i.e., 1974, 1976–77, 1979–80, 1983, 1984–85, and 1995.

5883 Pumpkins 1985 *National (M).* The Giants, whose team colors are pumpkin orange and black, skidded to a miserable 62–100 record, dropping them into last place in the NL Western Division and prompting San Francisco fans to style them as the "Pumpkins." "Pumpkin," apart from its literal meaning for the vegetable (a pumpkin is not a fruit), is slang—derived from the Cinderella fairy tale wherein a sorceress converts an ordinary pumpkin into a carriage to transport Cinderella to the king's palatial ball—means something "extremely ordinary" and "unflattering." "Country bumkin" means an awkward and less-than-clever rural goof.

5884 Orange & Black 1989, 2000 to date *National (M).* During the 1989 NL pennant year, pleased Giants fans and newspapers started referring to the players—who wore uniforms of orange and black trim—as the "Orange & Black" in direct imitation of the NFL Oakland Raiders, who had styled themselves for years as the "Silver & Black." When the Giants started winning again in 2000 and then won the NL pennant in 2002, the name became popular again.

5885 Humm Babies 1989 *National (M).* San Francisco infielders would chatter (a traditional activity going back to Civil War baseball players) to fortify their pitcher's nerve. But Giant infielders Will Clark (first baseman), Robby Thompson (second baseman), Jose Uribe (shortstop) and Ernie Riles (third baseman) also hummed tunes to cheer on their teammate on the mound. When field manager Roger Craig noticed the humming, he immediately called his players the "Humm Babies."

5886 Stand-Tall Giants 1989 *National (M).* Giant fans were proud of the 1989 NL champions—the first pennant since 1962.

5887 Gay Area Giants 1990 to date *National (M).* In a war of words between Giant fans and their L.A. Dodger and Oakland Athletic antagonists, the latter often used this homophobic tag. Actually, the tag was metaphorical as "gay," in this sense, meant silly, inept and disappointing. Starting in the 1960s, San Francisco's gay (i.e., homosexual) community has become nationally known.

5888 Bay Area Blues 1996 *National (M).* Although the team colors were orange and black, San Francisco fans were feeling "blue" when the team finished last in the National League Western Division this season with a sad 68–94 record.

5889 Bay Bombers 2000–04 *National (M).* Led by Barry Bonds, Jeff Kent, Ellis Burks and other strong hitters, the Giants enjoyed five consecutive winning seasons and reached the World Series in 2002. Newspapers shortened the tag for headlines, i.e., "Bays edge Pads, 4–3." The tag vanished as the Giants slumped badly 2006–08, but returned 2010 as the Giant hitters powered the team in a 24-month trek to the World Series title on November 1, 2010.

5890 Barry Bonds & Company 2000–06 *National (M).* With

Barry Bonds, the most exciting San Francisco baseball player since Willie Mays, leading the way, the Giants franchise enjoyed eight straight winning seasons and reached the 2002 World Series. Bonds led the NL in batting average with .370 in 2002 and .362 in 2004 after slugging 73 home runs in 2001 to pass Mark McGwire's record of 70 (set in 1998). Bonds finished his career with the Giants by surpassing Henry Aaron for career major league home runs in 2008.

5891 Orange Nation 2002 to date *National (M).* In this era, fans of consistently winning sports franchises sometimes referred to their own large numbers of enthusiastic fans as "The Nation." Examples are the "Red Sox Nation" and the "Raider Nation." Powered by Barry Bonds, the Giants were consistent winners leading up to their 2002 NL pennant, which boosted attendance in San Francisco after it had sagged considerably in the 1980s. Although the team finished last in its division in 2007, management rebuilt the club to capture the 2010 World Series over the AL champion Texas Rangers, 4 games to 1.

5892 Los Gigantes 2005 to date *National (M).* With ever-increasing numbers of Spanish-speaking fans following the team, Spanish-language radio and TV broadcasters started to refer to the team as "Los Gigantes," which soon spilled over into English. The team held a special day honoring long-time star Giant pitcher Juan Marichal on May 25, 2005, with the Giant players wearing uniforms that spelled out "Gigantes" on the jersey blouses.

5893 Torture 2010 *National (M).* With the team grinding out one-run victories in the regular season and playoffs, players joked that they were "torturing" the fans, giving rise to the moniker San Francisco "Torture," which was touted by Giants broadcaster Duane Kulper. But the tortuous agony turned to ecstasy as the Giants won the NL pennant and the 2010 World Series over the Texas Rangers, 4 games to 1.

5894 Gyros 2010 to date *National (M).* With a slew of one-run games and come-from-behind victories, the Giants tortured their fans into spinning like a gyroscope from apprehension to elation and back again. Younger fans liked the flippant use of the tag.

5895 Bad News Bears 2010 *National (M).* Like the 1977 Walter Mathau movie *The Bad News Bears,* which was about a youth league team of misfits that won its regional tournament, the Giants won the NL pennant and the World Series with a collection of "castoffs" and "misfits" that gave no indication of an impending championship. Recognizing the contributions of players like Jose Guillen, Juan Uribe and Edgar Renteria — who had all been released from other teams — sports broadcaster Dave O'Brien coined the name. The California Golden Bear is the state symbol, hence the usage.

5896 Misfits 2010 *National (M).* Manager Bruce Bochy proudly called his players the "Misfits," a team with a lot of players signed who had been released by other teams, i.e., Jose Guillen, Juan Uribe and Edgar Renteria, en route to the NL pennant and a World Series triumph.

5897 Castoffs 2010 *National (M).* Tag was a spinoff of "Misfits," coined by sports broadcaster Dan Shulman. In the nineteenth century these two tags almost always referred to losing teams stocked with players of inferior talent.

San Francisco de Marcoris, Dominican Republic

5898 Club de San Francisco de Marcoris 1985 *Dominican Summer (R).* Team had no nickname.

5899 Gigantes del Noreste 1996–97–98–99 *Liga Dominicana (W).* Team was named in honor of Dominican baseball players Felipe Alou, Matty Alou, Jesus Alou and Juan Marichal — all of whom were players on the San Francisco Giants. "Los Gigantes" means "Giants."

San Francisco de Marcoris is located in the northeast of the Dominican Republic.

5900 Pollos Nacionales 1999–2000 to date *Liga Dominicana (W).* Regional farms ship poultry products to processing and packing houses. "Los Pollos Nacionales" means "National Chickens."

San Joaquin, Venezuela

5901 Piratas 2008 *Venezuela Summer (R).* Team was a farm club of the Pittsburgh Pirates. "Las Piratas" means "Pirates."

San Jose, California

5902 Gardeners 1891 *California (ind.).* The proliferation of gardens, both public and private, in the city in the nineteenth century led to San Jose becoming known as the "Garden City."

5903 Dukes 1891 *California (ind.).* Spanish dukes, i.e., "Los Duques de California," ruled the city from 1777 to 1848.

5904 San Jose Base Ball Club 1896 *California (ind.).* Team had no nickname.

5905 Beachcombers 1898 *Pacific States (ind.).* Originally meaning scavenger birds who feed at beaches and wharves (harbors), by 1890 the term referred to Eastern vacationers and tourists who flocked to San Jose in the winter, giving rise to a thriving winter tourist industry.

5906 Silver Stars 1898 *Pacific Coast (ind.).* Players wore silver hose and a cap with a silver star in the front over the bill. The name was originally used by the 1875 semi-professional San Jose "Silver Star" baseball club. In the Old West and nineteenth century California, the "silver star" was worn by sheriffs and U.S. marshals.

5907 Florists 1898–99 *California State (ind.).* The city's Municipal Rose Garden gave rise to its nickname of "The Garden City." The moniker was a spin-off of the 1891 San Jose "Gardeners" baseball team.

5908 Prune-pickers 1899 *Pacific States (ind.);* 1907–09 *California (ind.);* 1910 *California State (D).* The California Raisin Company was located here. By this time, the city had become a major fruit farming center. With manager W. F. McGraw (not John McGraw) at the helm, newspapers called the players "McGraw's Prune-pickers." With manager Emil Mayer at the helm in 1907, newspapers called the players "Emil Mayer's Prune-pickers." T. C. Barnett took over in 1909 and the name became "Barnett's Prune-pickers." With manager Willis Browne at the helm, newspapers called the players "Willis Browne's Prune-pickers." In 1899, San Jose also had a second professional baseball team — the "Florists" of the California State League.

5909 Bears 1913–15x *California State (D).* Team and league disbanded May 30 due to rain storms. The state animal of California is the golden bear. California is known as the Golden Bear State. With manager Walter Nagle at the helm in 1913, newspapers called the players "Walter's Bears." Mike Steffani took over in 1914 and the name became "Steffani's Bears."

5910 Owls 1942 *California (C).* With manager Goldie Holt at the helm, newspapers called the players the "Holt's Hoot Owls," which was shortened to "Holt's Owls." The Western Burrowing owl inhabits California and much of the western U.S.

5911 Red Sox 1947–55 *California (C).* The team was a farm club of the Boston Red Sox.

5912 JoSox 1956–57 *California (C).* Tag was a spin-off of Red Sox. Numerous teams combined city names with "Sox" at both the major and minor league levels, i.e., BoSox, ChiSox, LynSox, PawSox and JoSox.

5913 Pirates 1958m *California (C).* Team moved to Las Vegas in May 26. Team was a farm club of the Pittsburgh Pirates.

5914 Bees 1962–76 California (*C 1962, A 1963–69*); 1983–87 *California (A)*. After the city was founded in 1850, the first successful bee farm in the United States was established here in 1853.

5915 Royal Bees 1970–73 *California (A)*. Team was a farm club of the Kansas City Royals. The queen bee of a bee colony is also known as the "royal bee."

5916 Missions 1977–78 *Pacific Coast (AAA)*; 1979–81 *California (A)*. City was founded in 1777 as the San Jose Mission, or, in Spanish, La Mision de San Jose. The name was picked up from the PCL San Francisco Mission teams of 1914–15 and 1926–36. Numerous cities in the Spanish southwest started as missions.

5917 Expos 1982 *California (A)*. Team was a farm club of the Montreal Expos.

5918 Giants 1988 to date *California (A)*. Team was a farm club of the San Francisco Giants.

San Jose, Cuba

5919 San Jose Base Ball Club 1925–26 *Liga Cubana (W)*. Team had no nickname.

San Juan, Puerto Rico

5920 Senadores 1941–42–73–74 *Puerto Rico (W)*. Settled in 1508, the city was held by the Spanish, English and Dutch before the Americans made it the capital city in 1898.

5921 Marlins 1961m *International (AAA)*. The Miami Marlins moved to San Juan at the start of the 1961 season. The nickname was retained.

5922 Sunfans 1969x *Global (ind.)*. Fans use umbrellas, known as "sunfans" (sombrillos in Spanish) at the ballpark during sunny summers. The circuit and team disbanded in mid-season. The moniker was in English. In Spanish, the word "sunfan" is "sombrillo."

5923 Boricua 1979x *Inter-American (AAA)*. At the arrival of the Spaniards in the fifteenth and sixteenth centuries, the native people of Puerto Rico were the Boricuas. The team went by the regional name of "Boricuas de Puerto Rico."

5924 Metros 1983–84–95–96 *Liga Puertoriquiena (W)*. City, with a metropolitan area population of 1 million, is the largest city on the island.

San Leandro, California

5925 Cherry-pickers m1910–11 *Central California (D)*. Cherry farms transport fruit to processing factories in the city for cleaning, processing and packaging prior to shipping out to market. The team started 1910 season in Healdsburg (CA) and moved to San Leandro in mid-season.

San Luis Obispo, California

5926 San Luis Obispo 1929–30 *California Winter (W)*. Team had no nickname.

San Luis Potosi, Leon, Mexico

5927 Tuneros 1946–51 *Mexican (ind.)*; 1960–61 *Mexican Center (D 1960, A 1961)*; 1969–71 *Mexican Center (A)*;1982–83 *Nacional de Mexico (ind.)*; 1986–90 *Mexican (AAA)*; 2004–06 *Mexican (AAA)*. The Opuntia cactus of the arid regions of southwestern United States and northern Mexico yield an edible fruit called the prickly pear. Farms near the city transport the pears to city factories for cleaning, processing, packing and shipment to market.

5928 Reds 1962 *Mexican Center (A)*. Team was a farm club of the Mexico City Reds.

5929 Indians 1963 *Mexican Center (A)*. Team was a farm club of the Juarez Indians.

5930 Charos 1969–71 *Mexican Center (A)*. Team was a farm club of the Jalisco Cowboys. Los charos jeans "cowboys" or "riders."

5931 Reales 1991 *Mexican (AAA)*. City was founded in 1550 and named after King Louis IX of France.

San Luis Rio Colorado, Sonora, Mexico

5932 Algodoneros 1968–69 *Mexican Northern (A)*; 2009 to date *Norte de Mexico (ind.)*. Team was a farm club of the Union Laguna Cotton-Growers (Los Algodoneros) of the AAA Mexican League.

San Marino, Italy

5933 T & A 1999–2001 *Italian A1 (ind.)*; 2003 *Italian A1 (ind.)*. Teams were owned by the Technologie & Ambiente Company, a scientific research corporation. Minority owners included ITC (1999) and Factory Outlet (2000).

San Pedro, California

5934 San Pedro Baseball Club 1914–15 *California Winter (W)*; 1916–17–18–19 *California Winter (W)*. These teams had no nickname.

San Pedro de las Colonias, Coahuila, Mexico

5935 Algodoneros 1974 *Mexican Center (A)*. Team was a farm club of the Union Laguna Cotton Growers (Los Algodoneros) of the AAA Mexican League.

San Pedro de Marcoris, Dominican Republic

5936 Estrellas 1937 *Dominican (W)*. Team hired several U.S. Negro League stars.

5937 Estrellas Orientales 1951–61–62 *Dominican (W)*; 1963–64–64–65 *Dominican (W)*; The league suspended operations for the 1965–66 season because of political strife; 1966–67 to date *Dominican (W)*. Dominican League played a summer schedule 1951–55 before switching to a winter schedule starting with the 1955–56 season. The Dominican League suspended operations for the 1962–63 because of financial problems. The city is located on the eastern end of the island's southern coast. The "Stars" moniker is appropriate because the city has been noted for producing good and even "star" baseball players, many of whom have reached the major leagues, i.e., Rico Carty, Rafael Batista, Tony Fernandez, Pedro Guerrero, Rafael Ramirez and Juan Samuel.

5938 Astros-Cardinals 1990 *Dominican Summer (R)*. Team was a farm club of the Houston Astros and St. Louis Cardinals.

5939 Dodgers 1990–91 *Dominican Summer (R)*. Team was a farm club of the Los Angeles Dodgers.

5940 Rangers 1990–91 *Dominican Summer (R)*; 1997 *Dominican Summer (R)*; 2003 *Dominican Summer (R)*. Teams were farm clubs of the Texas Rangers.

5941 Giants 1990–92 *Dominican Summer (R)*; 1997 *Dominican Summer (R)*; 1999 *Dominican Summer (R)*. Teams were farm clubs of the San Francisco Giants.

5942 Orioles–White Sox 1990–93 *Dominican Summer (R)*. Team was a farm club of the Baltimore Orioles and Chicago White Sox.

5943 Astros 1991–93 *Dominican Summer (R)*; 1997–99 *Dominican Summer (R)*; 2003 *Dominican Summer (R)*. Teams were farm clubs of the Houston Astros.

5944 Angels 1993 *Dominican Summer (R)*; 1999 *Dominican Summer (R)*; 2005 *Dominican Summer (R)*. Teams were farm clubs of the Anaheim Angels.

5945 Astros-Giants-Phillies 1993 *Dominican Summer (R)*. Team was a farm club of the Houston Astros, San Francisco Giants and Philadelphia Phillies.

5946 Toyo Carp 1993–94 *Dominican Summer (R)*. Team was a farm club of the Hiroshima Toyo Carp of the Japanese Central League.

5947 Orioles 1997 *Dominican Summer (R)*; 2003 *Dominican Summer (R)*; 2005 *Dominican Summer (R)*. Teams were farm clubs of the Baltimore Orioles.

5948 Blue Jays 1997 *Dominican Summer (R)*; 2005 *Dominican Summer (R)*. Teams were farm clubs of the Toronto Blue Jays.

5949 Braves 1997–99 *Dominican Summer (R)*; 2003 *Dominican Summer (R)*. Teams were farm clubs of the Atlanta Braves.

5950 Red Sox 1997–99 *Dominican Summer (R)*. Team was a farm club of the Boston Red Sox.

5951 Athletics West 1998 *Dominican Summer (R)*. Team was a farm club of the Oakland Athletics.

5952 Dodgers II 1998–99 *Dominican Summer (R)*. Team was a farm club of the Los Angeles Dodgers.

5953 Pirates 2003 *Dominican Summer (R)*. Team was a farm club of the Pittsburgh Pirates.

San Rafael, California

5954 San Rafael Baseball Club 1910m *Central California (D)*. Team moved to Hayward (CA) June 12. Team had no nickname.

Santa Ana, Orange County, California

5955 Santa Ana Baseball Club 1907–08–09–10 *California Winter (W)*. Team had no nickname.

5956 Walnut-growers 1910x *Southern California Trolley (D)*. Team and league disbanded June 13. Founded in 1869, the city had packing houses for the cleaning and transport of fruits and nuts from nearby farms.

5957 Orange Countians 1929m *California State (D)*. Team moved to Pomona (CA) May 8. Santa Ana is located in Orange County.

Santa Ana, Sonora, Mexico

5958 Santos 2006–07 *Sonora del Norte (ind.)*. City was named after Saint Anne, which is "Santa Ana" in Spanish. Los Santos means "saints" in English.

Santa Barbara, California

5959 Barbareans m1913 *Southern California (D)*. Team started the season in Pasadena (CA) and moved to Santa Barbara June 13. Tag was a play on words of Barbarians. With manager Ed Householder at the helm, newspapers called the players "Householder's Barbareans." Kitty Brashear took over in mid-season and the name became "Brashear's Barbareans."

5960 Kittens m1913 *Southern California (D)*. Team started the season in Pasadena (CA) and moved to Santa Barbara June 13. Kitty Brashear took over as manager in mid-season and the name became "Kittens."

5961 Santa Barbara Baseball Club 1913–14 *California Winter (W)*. Team had no nickname.

5962 Stars 1941 *California (C)*. Team was a farm club of the Hollywood Stars of the Pacific Coast League.

5963 Saints 1942 *California (C)*. City was founded as the "Mission Santa Barbara," which was built here in 1786. "Stars" moniker was dropped as the team became a farm club of the San Francisco Seals. With manager John Clancy at the helm, newspapers called the players "Clancy's Saints." Santa Barbara is known as the "Queen of the Missions."

5964 Dodgers 1946–53 *California (C)*; 1964–67 *California (A)*. The 1946–53 teams were farm clubs of Brooklyn Dodgers. The 1964–67 teams were farm clubs of the Los Angeles Dodgers.

5965 Rancheros 1962–63 *California (A)*. During Spanish rule, 1790–1845, horse, cattle and sheep ranches, i.e., "rancheros," were established in and around the city.

Santa Barbara–Ventura, California

5966 Channel Cities Oilers 1954–55m *California (C)*. Team moved to Reno (NV) July 1. The "Channel Cities," i.e., Santa Barbara–Ventura, have ports for stopovers by oil tankers. Oil refineries in the city process the crude oil shipments that arrive here.

Santa Clara, California

5967 Padres 1979 *California (A)*. Playing as an independent, the team had a loose affiliation with the San Diego Padres.

Santa Clara, Villa Clara, Cuba

5968 Leopardos 1922–23–24–25 *Liga Cubana (W)*; 1929–30–30–31 *Liga Cubana (W)*; 1932–33 *Liga Cubana (W)*; 1935–36–39–40 *Liga Cubana (W)*. Jungle cat nicknames are popular in Latin America. Management decided to emulate the Havana Leones (Lions) and Marianao Tigres (Tigers). "Los Leopardos" means "leopards." Actually, leopards are found in Asia and Africa—but not in the Americas.

5969 Las Villas 1967–68–73–74 *Cuban National (S)*. Santa Clara is located in the province of Villa Clara. "Las Villas" is loosely translated as the "villagers."

5970 Naranjas 1967–68–73–74 *Cuban National (S)*. Regional farms transport oranges and other citrus fruit to packing houses in the city. "Naranjas" means "oranges,"

5971 Villa Clara 1980–81 to date *Cuban National (S)*. Team is named after the province.

Santa Cruz, California

5972 Santa Cruz Base Ball Club 1898 *Pacific States (ind.)*. Team had no nickname.

5973 Sand Crabs 1898 *Pacific Coast (ind.)*; 1908–09 *California (ind.)*. Fishing boats roam the coastal beaches where they harvest lobsters and crabs. The catch is transported to packing houses in the city. With manager H.R. Bradford at the helm in 1908, newspapers called the players "Bradford's Sand Crabs." Keating took over in mid-season 1908 and the name became "Keating's Sand Crabs." Fred Swanton took over in 1909 and the name became "Fred Swanton's Sand Crabs."

5974 Beachcombers 1899 *California (ind.)*. By 1895, California cities like San Jose and Santa Cruz were becoming tourist attractions for easterners escaping cold and snowy winters. "Beachcombers" by this time had become a nickname for beach resort vacationers. Santa Cruz is the "World's Most Famous Playground" and "California's Scenic Playground."

Santa Monica, California

5975 Santa Monica Baseball Club 1911–12 *California Winter (W)*; 1935–36–36–37 *California Winter (W)*. These teams had no nickname.

Santa Rosa, California

5976 Prune-pickers 1910m *Central California (D)*. Team moved to Alameda (CA) May 5. In addition to grapes, nearby farms also produce plums, which are shipped to city food processing factories where they are dried in prunes and canned.

5977 Pirates 1948 *Far West (D)*. Team was a farm club of the Pittsburgh Pirates.

5978 Cats 1949 *Far West (D)*. Team disbanded August 4. Since mountain lions inhabit numerous regions in California, management chose "Cats." The team was not a farm club of the Texas League Fort Worth Cats.

5979 Redwood Pioneers 1980–85 *California (A)*. In 1849 pioneers and prospectors flooded northern California in the search for gold. Cities such as San Francisco, Oakland, San Jose, Stockton, Modesto and Santa Rosa sprung up almost overnight. The state tree of California is the Redwood.

Santa Rosa, Mexico, Mexico

5980 Gallos 1937–38 *Mexican (ind.)*. Regional farms transport poultry products to packing houses. "Los Gallos" means "roosters."

Santiago, Dominican Republic

5981 Aguilas 1937 *Liga Dominicana (ind.)*; 1951–61–62 *Liga Dominicana (ind.)*. The Dominican League played a summer schedule 1951–55 and then switched to a winter schedule for the 1955–56 season. The Dominican League suspended operations for 1962–63 because of financial problems; 1963–64–64–65 *Dominican (W)*. The Dominican League suspended play in 1965–66 because of political strife; 1966–67 to date *Liga Dominicana (W)*. The team nickname of "Aguilas" (Eagles in English) is one of the most popular monikers among Latin American sports teams. The team, which plays at Cibao Stadium, went by the home park name of Cibao Eagles (Los Aguilas Cibaneas).

5982 Club de Besibol de Santiago 1985 *Dominican Summer (R)*. Team had no nickname.

5983 Dodgers II 1990 *Dominican Summer (R)*; 1992–94 *Dominican Summer (R)*. Teams were farm clubs of the Los Angeles Dodgers.

5984 Blue Jays–Brewers 1990–91 *Dominican Summer (R)*. Team was a farm club of the Toronto Blue Jays and the Milwaukee Brewers.

5985 Indians 1990–93 *Dominican Summer (R)*; 1995–98 *Dominican Summer (R)*; 1999 *Dominican Summer (R)*; 2003 to date *Dominican Summer (R)*. These teams were farm clubs of the Cleveland Indians.

5986 Angels-Dodgers-Padres 1991 *Dominican Summer (R)*. Team was a farm club of the California Angels, Los Angeles Dodgers and San Diego Padres.

5987 Royals-Cubs 1991 *Dominican Summer (R)*. Team was a farm club of the Kansas City Royals and Chicago Cubs.

5988 Co-Op 1992 *Dominican Summer (R)*; 1996 *Dominican Summer (R)*. These teams' actual nickname was the "Co-Ops"—which is short for "cooperative." In the modern meaning, "Co-Op" refers to an independent team. In the nineteenth century cooperative meant a team that was semi-professional.

5989 Cubs-Rockies-Royals 1992 *Dominican Summer (R)*. Team was a farm club of the Chicago Cubs, Colorado Rockies and Kansas City Royals.

5990 Rockies-Royals 1994–95 *Dominican Summer (R)*. Team was a farm club of the Colorado Rockies and Kansas City Royals.

5991 Cardinals 1995–98 *Dominican Summer (R)*. Team was a farm club of the St. Louis Cardinals.

5992 Brewers–White Sox 1996 *Dominican Summer (R)*. Team was a farm club of the Chicago White Sox and Milwaukee Brewers.

5993 Rangers 1996 *Dominican Summer (R)*. Team was a farm club of the Texas Rangers.

5994 Phillies 1996–97 *Dominican Summer (R)*; 1998–99 *Dominican Summer (R)*. These teams were farm clubs of the Philadelphia Phillies.

5995 Athletics West 1997 *Dominican Summer (R)*. Team was a farm club of the Oakland Athletics.

5996 Mets II 1997 *Dominican Summer (R)*. Team was a farm club of the New York Mets.

5997 Rangers II 1997 *Dominican Summer (R)*; 1999 only *Dominican Summer (R)*. Team was a farm club of the Texas Rangers.

5998 Royals 1997 *Dominican Summer (R)*; 1999 *Dominican Summer (R)*; 2003 to date *Dominican Summer (R)*. Team was a farm club of the Kansas City Royals.

5999 Rockies 1997–99 *Dominican Summer (R)*. Team was a farm club of the Colorado Rockies.

6000 White Sox 1999 *Dominican Summer (R)*; 2003 to date *Dominican Summer (R)*. These teams were farm clubs of the Chicago White Sox.

6001 Braves 2003 to date *Dominican Summer (R)*. Team was a farm club of the Atlanta Braves.

6002 Braves II 2003 to date *Dominican Summer (R)*. Team was a farm club of the Atlanta Braves.

6003 Indians II 2003 to date *Dominican Summer (R)*. Team was a farm club of the Cleveland Indians.

6004 Marlins 2003 to date *Dominican Summer (R)*. Team was a farm club of the Florida Marlins.

6005 Mariners 2003 to date *Dominican Summer (R)*. Team was a farm club of the Seattle Mariners.

Santiago de Cuba, Santiago de Cuba, Cuba

6006 Orientales 1917 *Liga Cubana (W)* Cuba (Winter); 1947–48 *Liga Nacional de Cuba*; 1961–62–66–67 *Cuban National (S)*. Santiago is located in the eastern region of the island. "Orientales" means "Easterns" or "Easterners."

6007 Azules del Oriente 1946–47 *Federacion Cubana (W)*. Players wore blue-trim uniforms and stirrups. Los Azules del Oriente means "Eastern Blues."

6008 Avispas 1977–78 to date *Cuban National (S)*. Wasps thrive in the tropical islands of the Carribean. Players wear wasp-brown trim uniforms. Los avispas means "wasps."

Santo Domingo, Dominican Republic

6009 Leones 1951–61–62 *Liga Dominican (W)*. The Dominican League played a summer schedule 1951–55 before switching to a winter schedule starting with the 1955–56 season. The Dominican League suspended operations for the 1962–63 season due to financial problems. 1963–64–64–65 *Liga Dominican (W)*. The Dominican Winter League suspended operations for the 1965–66 season due to political strife; 1966–67 to date *Liga Dominicana (W)*. With arch rival Licey choosing the alliterative "Tigres" (Tigers), Escogido went with the parallel "Leones" moniker. In 1910, the best semi-pro players on the island were chosen to form a "select" team. In Spanish "escogido" means "select." The "selects" were drafted from the three leading semi-professional teams on the island — San Carlos, Delco Light and Los Muchachos. Both teams became permanently professional in 1951.

6010 Tiburones Dominicanas 1969 *Global (ind.)*. Circuit and team disbanded in May 20. This league was sponsored by Oakland A's owner Charlie Finley. The circuit failed due to poor attendance in Third-World markets. "Los Tiburones Dominicanos" means "Dominican Sharks."

6011 Azucareros 1979x *Inter-American (AAA)*. Sugar plantations transport sugar cane to packing houses. Los "Azucareros" means "Sugarcane-pickers."

6012 Padres–Red Sox–Tigers 1990 *Dominican Summer (R)*. Team was a farm club of the San Diego Padres, Boston Red Sox and Detroit Tigers.

6013 Yankees 1990 *Dominican Summer (R)*. Team was a farm club of the New York Yankees.

6014 Athletics 1990 to date *Dominican Summer (R)*. Team was a farm club of the Oakland Athletics.

6015 Blue Jays I 1990–91 *Dominican Summer (R)*. Team was a farm club of the Toronto Blue Jays.

6016 Expos 1990–91 *Dominican Summer (R)*. Team was a farm club of the Montreal Expos.

6017 Pirates 1990–91 *Dominican Summer (R)*. Team was a farm club of the Pittsburgh Pirates.

6018 Mariners 1990–99 *Dominican Summer (R)*. Team was a farm club of the Seattle Mariners.

6019 Mets-Yankees 1991 *Dominican Summer (R)*. Team was a farm club of the New York Yankees and New York Mets.

6020 Brewers 1991–92 *Dominican Summer (R)*; 2000 to date *Dominican Summer (R)*. These teams were farm clubs of the Milwaukee Brewers.

6021 Cardinals-Tigers 1991–92 *Dominican Summer (R)*. Team was a farm club of the St. Louis Cardinals and Detroit Tigers.

6022 Angels 1992 *Dominican Summer (R)*. Team was a farm club of the California Angels.

6023 Marlins-Rangers 1992 *Dominican Summer (R)*. Team was a farm club of the Florida Marlins and Texas Rangers.

6024 Blue Jays West 1992–93 *Dominican Summer (R)*. Team was a farm club of the Toronto Blue Jays.

6025 Dodgers I 1992–97 *Dominican Summer (R)*. Team was a farm club of the Los Angeles Dodgers.

6026 Cubs-Rangers 1993 *Dominican Summer (R)*. Team was a farm club of Chicago Cubs and Texas Rangers.

6027 Padres-Yankees 1993 *Dominican Summer (R)*. Team was a farm club of the San Diego Padres and New York Yankees.

6028 Expos 1993–99 *Dominican Summer (R)*. Team was a farm club of Montreal Expos.

6029 Marlins 1993–99 *Dominican Summer (R)*. Team was a farm club of the Florida Marlins.

6030 Mets 1993 to date *Dominican Summer (R)*. Team was a farm club of the New York Mets.

6031 Pirates 1993 to date *Dominican Summer (R)*. Team was a farm club of the Pittsburgh Pirates.

6032 Astros-Brewers 1994 *Dominican Summer (R)*. Team was a farm club of the Houston Astros and Milwaukee Brewers.

6033 Blue Jays II 1994 *Dominican Summer (R)*. Team was a farm club of the Toronto Blue Jays.

6034 Braves-Rangers 1994 *Dominican Summer (R)*. Team was a farm club of the Atlanta Braves and Texas Rangers.

6035 Cardinals-Phillies 1994 *Dominican Summer (R)*. Team was a farm club of the St. Louis Cardinals and Philadelphia Phillies.

6036 Giants-Orioles 1994 *Dominican Summer (R)*. Team was a farm club of the San Francisco Giants and Baltimore Orioles.

6037 Cubs-Padres 1994–96 *Dominican Summer (R)*. Team was a farm club of the Chicago Cubs and San Diego Padres.

6038 Rockies-Royals 1994–96 *Dominican Summer (R)*. Team was a farm club of the Colorado Rockies and Kansas City Royals.

6039 Yankees 1994–96 *Dominican Summer (R)*. Team was a farm club of the New York Yankees.

6040 Tigers 1994–99 *Dominican Summer (R)*; 2000 to date *Dominican Summer (R)*. These teams were farm clubs of the Detroit Tigers.

6041 Cardinals 1995–98 *Dominican Summer (R)*; 2000 to date *Dominican Summer (R)*. These teams were farm clubs of the St. Louis Cardinals.

6042 Brewers–White Sox 1996 *Dominican Summer (R)*. Team was a farm club of the Milwaukee Brewers and Chicago White Sox.

6043 Diamondbacks 1996 to date *Dominican Summer (R)*. Team was a farm club of the Arizona Diamondbacks.

6044 Rangers 1996 *Dominican Summer (R)*. Team was a farm club of the Texas Rangers.

6045 Athletics West 1997 *Dominican Summer (R)*; 2000 to date *Dominican Summer (R)*. These teams were farm clubs of the Oakland Athletics.

6046 Royals 1997 *Dominican Summer (R)*; 1999 *Dominican Summer (R)*. These teams were farm clubs of the Kansas City Royals.

6047 Phillies 1997 *Dominican Summer (R)*; 2000 to date *Dominican Summer (R)*. These teams were farm clubs of the Philadelphia Phillies.

6048 Devil Rays II 1997–99 *Dominican Summer (R)*. The team was another farm club of the Tampa Bay Devil Rays.

6049 Devil Rays 1997–2007 *Dominican Summer (R)*. Team was a farm club of the Tampa Bay Devil Rays.

6050 Cubs 1997 to date *Dominican Summer (R)*. Team was a farm club of the Chicago Cubs.

6051 Padres 1997 to date *Dominican Summer (R)*. Team was a farm club of the San Diego Padres.

6052 Giants 1998 *Dominican Summer (R)*; 2000–06x Team disbanded July 6. *Dominican Summer (R)*. These teams were farm clubs of the San Francisco Giants.

6053 Orioles 1998 *Dominican Summer (R)*. Team was a farm club of the Baltimore Orioles.

6054 Angels–White Sox 1998 *Dominican Summer (R)*. Team was a farm club of the California Angels and Chicago White Sox.

6055 Rangers 1998–99 *Dominican Summer (R)*. Team was a farm club of the Texas Rangers.

6056 Twins Co-Op 1998–99 *Dominican Summer (R)*. Team was a farm club of the Minnesota Twins.

6057 Dodgers 1998 to date *Dominican Summer (R)*. Team was a farm club of the L.A. Dodgers.

6058 Reds 1998 to date *Dominican Summer (R)*. Team was a farm club of the Cincinnati Reds.

6059 Yankees 1998 to date *Dominican Summer (R)*. Team was a farm club of the New York Yankees.

6060 Mets Co-Op 1999 *Dominican Summer (R)*. Team was a farm club of the New York Mets.

6061 Diamondbacks–Red Sox 2000 *Dominican Summer (R)*.

Team was a farm club of the Arizona Diamondbacks and Boston Red Sox.

6062 Yankees 2000–01 to date *Dominican Summer (R)*. Team was a farm club of the New York Yankees.

6063 Diamondbacks 2000–06x *Dominican Summer (R)*. Team was a farm club of the Arizona Diamondbacks.

6064 Rockies 2000–06x *Dominican Summer (R)*. Team was a farm club of the Colorado Rockies.

6065 Mets 2000–09 *Dominican Summer (R)*. Team was a farm club of the New York Mets.

6066 Athletics North 2000 to date *Dominican Summer (R)*. Team was a farm club of the Oakland Athletics.

6067 Brewers 2000 to date *Dominican Summer (R)*. Team was a farm club of the Milwaukee Brewers.

6068 Dodgers East 2000 to date *Dominican Summer (R)*. Team was a farm club of the Los Angeles Dodgers.

6069 Dodgers North 2000 to date *Dominican Summer (R)*. Team was a farm club of the Los Angeles Dodgers.

6070 Padres 2000 to date *Dominican* Summer. Team was a farm club of the San Diego Padres.

6071 Phillies 2000 to date *Dominican Summer (R)*. Team was a farm club of Philadelphia Phillies.

6072 Reds 2000 to date *Dominican Summer (R)*. Team was a farm club of the Cincinnati Reds.

6073 Red Sox East 2000 to date *Dominican Summer (R)*. Team was a farm club of the Boston Red Sox.

6074 Red Sox North 2000 to date *Dominican Summer (R)*. Team was a farm club of the Boston Red Sox.

6075 Tigers 2000 to date *Dominican Summer (R)*. Team was a farm club of the Detroit Tigers.

6076 Twins 2000 to date *Dominican Summer (R)*. Team was a farm club of the Minnesota Twins.

6077 Nationals I 2006–08 *Dominican Summer (R)*. Team was a farm club of the Washington Nationals.

6078 Nationals II 2006–08 to date *Dominican Summer (R)*. Team was a farm club of the Washington Nationals.

Santo Domingo–Boca Chica, Dominican Republic

Note: These teams played at a ballpark in Boca Chica — a suburb of Santo Domingo.

6079 Blue Jays 1990–94 *Dominican Summer (R)*. Team was a farm club of the Toronto Blue Jays.

6080 Blue Jays II 1991, 1994 *Dominican Summer (R)*. Team was a farm club of Toronto Blue Jays.

6081 Cardinals 2000x *Dominican Summer (R)*. Team disbanded July 5; 2005 to date *Dominican Summer (R)*. These teams were farm clubs of the St. Louis Cardinals.

6082 Indians II 2000x *Dominican Summer (R)*. Team was a farm club of the Cleveland Indians.

6083 Phillies 2000x *Dominican Summer (R)*; 2005 to date *Dominican Summer (R)*. Team was a farm club of the Philadelphia Phillies.

6084 Red Sox 2000x *Dominican Summer (R)*; 2003 *Dominican Summer (R)*; 2005 to date *Dominican Summer (R)*. These teams were farm clubs of the Boston Red Sox.

6085 Twins 2000x *Dominican Summer (R)*. Team was a farm club of the Minnesota Twins.

6086 Athletics II 2000 to date *Dominican Summer (R)*. Team was a farm club of the Oakland Athletics.

6087 Dodgers 2000 to date *Dominican Summer (R)*. Team was a farm club of the Los Angeles Dodgers.

6088 Mariners 2000 to date *Dominican Summer (R)*. Team was a farm club of the Seattle Mariners.

6089 Yankees I 2002 to date *Dominican Summer (R)*. Team was a farm club of the New York Yankees.

6090 Yankees II 2002–05, 2007 to date *Dominican Summer (R)*. Team was a farm club of the New York Yankees.

6091 Diamondbacks 2003 *Dominican Summer (R)*; 2005–06x *Dominican Summer (R)*. These teams were farm clubs of the Arizona Diamondbacks.

6092 Padres 2003 *Dominican Summer (R)*. Team was a farm club of the San Diego Padres.

6093 Tigers 2003 *Dominican Summer (R)*. Team was a farm club of the Detroit Tigers.

6094 Twins 2003 *Dominican Summer (R)*. Team was a farm club of the Minnesota Twins.

6095 Giants 2003–06x *Dominican Summer (R)*. Team disbanded July 2. Team was a farm club of the San Francisco Giants.

6096 Rockies 2003–06x *Dominican Summer (R)*. Team was a farm club of the Colorado Rockies.

6097 Mets 2003 to date *Dominican Summer (R)*. Team was a farm club of the New York Mets.

6098 Nationals 2005x *Dominican Summer (R)*. Team was a farm club of the Washington Nationals.

6099 Devil Rays 2005–07 *Dominican Summer (R)*. Team was a farm club of the Tampa Bay Devil Rays.

6100 Athletics I 2005 to date *Dominican Summer (R)*. Team was a farm club of the Oakland Athletics.

6101 Cubs 2005 to date *Dominican Summer (R)*. Team was a farm club of the Chicago Cubs.

6102 Indians I 2005 to date *Dominican Summer (R)*. Team was a farm club of the Cleveland Indians.

6103 Marlins 2005 to date *Dominican Summer (R)*. Team was a farm club of the Florida Marlins.

6104 Mets 2005 to date *Dominican Summer (R)*. Team was a farm club of the New York Mets.

6105 Reds 2005 to date *Dominican Summer (R)*. Team was a farm club of the Cincinnati Reds.

6106 Royals 2005 to date *Dominican Summer (R)*. Team was a farm club of the Kansas City Royals.

6107 Twins 2005 to date *Dominican Summer (R)*. Team was a farm club of the Minnesota Twins.

6108 Padres-Yankees 2006 *Dominican Summer (R)*. Team was a farm club of the San Diego Padres and New York Yankees.

6109 Rays 2008 to date *Dominican Summer (R)*. Team was a farm club of the Tampa Bay Rays.

Sapporo, Hokkaido, Japan

6110 Hokkaido Nippon Ham Fighters 2004 to date *Japanese Central (ind.)*. Team goes by the company name of "Nippon Ham Fighters," which has owned the franchise in both Tokyo and Sapporo since 1974. The team also goes by the prefecture (equivalent to state in the U.S.) name of "Hokkaido Nippon Ham Fighters." The Tokyo Nippon Ham Fighters moved to Sapporo for the 2004 season. The team nickname was retained; 2004 to date *Japanese Eastern (ind.)*. Team moved to the Sapporo suburb of Kumagaya, starting in 2006, and goes by the name of "Kumayaga Nippon Ham Fighters."

Sapulpa, Oklahoma

6111 Oilers m1909–11 *Western Assn. (C 1909–10, D 1911)*. Team started 1909 season in Webb City (MO) and moved to Sapulpa July 18. Oil and natural gas deposits were discovered in the area in 1928.

Crude oil and natural gas is processed in city refining factories. With manager Larry Milton at the helm in 1910, newspapers called the players "Milton's Oilers." George McAvoy took over in 1911 and the name became "McAvoy's Oilers."

6112 Sappers 1921–22 *Southwestern (D* 1921, *C* 1922–23). Newspapers used this moniker for headlines, i.e., "Sappers edge Refiners, 5–4."

6113 Yanks 1923 *Southwestern (C).* Sapulpa native Denver Grigsby, a member of the 1921 Sapulpa roster, was signed by the New York Yankees in 1921 and sent to the minors. He became known as "Yank" Rigsby after leading the 1922 Sapulpa team with a .336 BA, 17 HR and a .604 slugging percentage. The 1923 Sapulpa team was then named "Yanks" even though Grigsby was playing with the Chicago Cubs in 1923. With manager Barney Cleveland at the helm, newspapers called the players "Barney Cleveland's Yanks."

Sarasota, Florida

6114 Gulls 1926 *Florida State (D).* Seagulls inhabit the coastlines of Florida. With manager Ivan Olson at the helm, newspapers called the team "Olson's Gulls."

6115 Tarpons 1927 *Florida State (D).* Tarpons swim the waters of the Caribbean and the Gulf of Mexico. With manager Harry Manush at the helm, newspapers called the players "Harry Manush's Tarpons."

6116 Sun Sox 1961–63 *Florida State (D* 1961–62, *A* 1963–65). Team was a farm club of the Chicago White Sox. Sarasota is the "Sunshine City," which gave rise to the moniker of "Sun Sox." The 1963 team was a farm club of the Houston Colt .45s but kept the Sun Sox moniker.

6117 Astros 1964 *Sarasota Rookie (R);* 1965 *Florida Rookie (R);* 1977–79 *Gulf Coast (R).* These teams were farm clubs of the Houston Astros.

6118 Braves 1964 *Sarasota Rookie (R);* 1965 *Florida Rookie (R);* 1966 *Gulf Coast (R);* 1976–87 *Gulf Coast (R).* The 1964–65 teams were farm clubs of the Milwaukee Braves. The 1976–87 teams were farm clubs of the Atlanta Braves.

6119 Cardinals 1964 *Sarasota Rookie (R);* 1965 *Florida Rookie (R);* 1966–76 *Gulf Coast (R).* These teams were farm clubs of the St. Louis Cardinals.

6120 White Sox 1964 *Sarasota Rookie (R);* 1965 *Florida Rookie (R);* 1966–97 *Gulf Coast (R);* 1983–97 *Gulf Coast (R).* These teams were farm clubs of the Chicago White Sox.

6121 Yankees 1964 *Sarasota Rookie (R);* 1965 *Florida Rookie (R);* 1966 *Gulf Coast (R);* 1986 *Gulf Coast (R);* 1988–91 *Gulf Coast (R).* These teams were farm clubs of the New York Yankees.

6122 Twins 1965 *Florida Rookie (R);* 1966–71 *Gulf Coast (R);* 1990 *Gulf Coast (R).* These teams were farm clubs of the Minnesota Twins.

6123 Pirates 1968 *Gulf Coast (R).* Team was a farm club of the Pittsburgh Pirates.

6124 Tigers 1968 *Gulf Coast (R);* 1970 *Gulf Coast (R).* These teams were farm clubs of the Detroit Tigers.

6125 Reds 1968 *Gulf Coast (R);* 1970 *Gulf Coast (R).* Team was a farm club of the Cincinnati Reds.

6126 Indians 1968–74 *Gulf Coast (R);* 1970 *Gulf Coast (R).* These teams were farm clubs of the Cleveland Indians.

6127 Expos 1969 *Gulf Coast (R).* Team was a farm club of the Montreal Expos.

6128 Tourists 1970 *Gulf Coast (R).* Team was a farm club of the Asheville Tourists. The team's big league parent club was the Baltimore Orioles, who stocked the team with players from the Orioles' Southern League farm team, the Asheville Tourists.

6129 Royals 1971–78 *Gulf Coast (R);* 1982–87 *Gulf Coast (R).* These teams were farm clubs of the Kansas City Royals.

6130 Redbirds 1972–73 *Gulf Coast (R).* Team was a farm club of the St. Louis Cardinals, whose unofficial alternate nickname is the "Redbirds."

6131 Royal Academy 1974 *Gulf Coast (R).* Team was a farm club of the Kansas City Royals. "Academy" is baseball slang for an all-rookie team.

6132 Royal Gold 1979–81 *Gulf Coast (R).* The parent club Kansas City Royals has two team colors—royal blue and royal gold. The parent Kansas City Royals fielded two GCL teams in this circuit for the years 1979–81, i.e., blue and gold.

6133 Royal Blue 1979–81 *Gulf Coast (R).* The parent club Kansas City Royals has two team colors—royal blue and royal gold. The parent Kansas City Royals fielded two GCL teams in this circuit for the years 1979–81, i.e., blue and gold.

6134 Astros Blue 1980–81 *Gulf Coast (R).* The parent club Houston Astros had two team colors—blue and orange. The parent club Houston Astros fielded two GCL teams in this circuit.

6135 Astros Orange 1980–81 *Gulf Coast (R).* The parent club Houston Astros had two team colors—blue and orange. The parent club Houston Astros fielded two GCL teams in this circuit for the years 1980–81, i.e., blue and orange.

6136 Mets 1983 *Gulf Coast (R);* 1988–90 *Gulf Coast (R).* These teams were farm clubs of the New York Mets.

6137 Phillies 1984 *Gulf Coast (R).* Team was a farm club of the Philadelphia Phillies.

6138 Reds 1984–90 *Gulf Coast (R);* 1999–2009 *Gulf Coast (R).* The Cincinnati Reds moved their GCL farm club to Phoenix to play in the 2011 Arizona Summer League. The team was a farm club of the Cincinnati Reds.

6139 Red Sox 1989–2004 *Gulf Coast (R).* Team was a farm club of the Boston Red Sox.

6140 Orioles 1991–2003 *Gulf Coast (R);* 2007 to date *Gulf Coast (R).* Team was a farm club of the Baltimore Orioles.

Sarasota-Bradenton, Florida

6141 Braves 1967 *Gulf Coast (R);* 1976–87 *Gulf Coast (R).* Team was a farm club of the Atlanta Braves.

6142 Indians 1967 *Gulf Coast (R);* 1975 *Gulf Coast (R).* Team was a farm club of the Cleveland Indians.

6143 Expos 1974 *Gulf Coast (R);* 1977–78 *Gulf Coast (R).* Team was a farm club of the Montreal Expos.

6144 Padres 1982 *Gulf Coast (R).* Team was a farm club of the San Diego Padres.

6145 Dodgers 1986–87 *Gulf Coast (R).* Team was a farm club of the Los Angeles Dodgers.

Saratoga Springs, New York

6146 Saratoga Base Ball Club 1886 *New York State (ind.);* 1886 *Hudson River (ind.).* These teams had no nickname.

Saskatoon, Saskatchewan, Canada

6147 Berry-pickers m1910–11 *Western Canada (D).* Team started 1910 season in Medicine Hat (ALB) and moved to Saskatoon July 23. The Cree Indians, who inhabited this region, grew sweet, violet berries known in English as "choke-berries." In the Cree language they were known as the Missakatoomina berries. The city name of Saskatoon is based on the name of Missakatoomina. With manager William Hamilton at the helm in 1910, newspapers called the players

"Bill's Berry-pickers." Frank Miley took over in 1911 and the name became "Frank's Berry-pickers."

6148 Quakers m1910–11 *Western Canada (D).* Team started 1910 season in Medicine Hat (ALB) and moved to Saskatoon July 23; 1913–14 *Western Canada (D);* 1919–21 *Western Canada (C 1919, B 1920–21).* After the city was founded in 1883 by Methodists from Toronto, Quaker settlers arrived here by 1890. As the railroad made connections, companies like Robin Hood Flour and Quaker Oats set up factories and stores here. With Frank Miley at the helm in 1911, newspapers called the players "Frank's Quakers." With manager Jerry Hurley at the helm in 1913, newspapers called the players "Hurley's Quakers." With manager George Brautigan at the helm in 1919, newspapers called the players "Brautigan's Quakers." Joe Kerman took over in 1920 and the name became "Kerman's Quakers." John Hummel took over in 1921 and the name became "Hummel's Quakers."

6149 Sheiks 1914 *Western Canada (D).* Local newspaper editors wanted a stylish and short name for the team. In response, reporters started calling the players the "Sheiks." The term "sheik" in this era also meant a "handsome young man" whom women found attractive. Many baseball players were athletic, muscular and good-looking with a fair amount of money in their pockets, hence the tag also meant "baseball player."

6150 Riot 1994 *North–Central (ind.);* 1995 *Prairie (ind.).* In 1953, in a semi-professional baseball tournament game in Rosetown, a city about 50 miles west of Saskatoon, between the North Battleford Beavers (about 80 miles northwest of Saskatoon) and a visiting Cuban all-star team, a beanball incident sparked a player fracas that soon escalated into the stands, bringing fans onto the field. Local newspapers the next day reported the incident as the "Rosetown Baseball Riot."

6151 Smokin' Guns 1996–97 *Prairie (ind.).* Saskatoon, in the era 1882–1900, was a "Wild West" town populated with settlers and outlaws. Cree Indians, stage-coach bandits, bank robbers, sheriffs, marshals, Royal Canadian Mounted Policemen, posses and vigilantes carried firearms. Half-breed (Cree and White) settlers staged two armed rebellions against the authorities during Saskatchewan's settlement era — the Red River Rebellion (1869–70) and the Northwest Rebellion (1885). The team logo was a little duck in a cowboy hat brandishing his six-shooters. Ducks are found throughout the Saskatchewan wilderness.

6152 Saskatchewan Silver Sox 2009–11 *Arizona Winter (W).* The 2009–11 team officially represented Saskatchewan but played its home games in Yuma, Arizona. The city of Saskatoon became a boomtown in 1901 when silver was discovered in the so-called "Canadian Shield" region of Manitoba and Saskatchewan.

6153 Legends 2011 to date *Canadian (ind.).* Flamelizard, Inc., the team's owner, chose the moniker to honor the legendary exploits of Saskatchewan Indians, explorers, pioneers, settlers, gold rushers, oil men and athletes during the last 200 years. [NASCAR race track, the Bristol Motor Speedway, in Saskatoon, hosts auto racing with racecars known as the "Legends of Alberta."]

Saugerties, New York

6154 Saugerties Base Ball Club 1903–05m *Hudson River (D 1903, C 1904–05).* Team moved to Pittsfield (MA) in July 4.

Sauget, Illinois

6155 Gateway Grizzlies 2001 to date *Frontier (ind.).* Team was given the regional name of "Gateway Grizzlies" because nearby St. Louis (MO) is the "Gateway to the West." Although the grizzly bear was driven out of Illinois by settlers and hunters in the 1840s, man-

agement chose the moniker because it was a spin-off from the Chicago Cubs. In the last 10 years, however, the incidence of wild bear sightings in Illinois and the Midwest has been increasing.

Sault Ste. Marie, Ontario, Canada

6156 Soos 1905 *Copper Country (D).* Newspapers used this tag for their headlines, i.e., "Soos defeat Calumet, 5–3." Moniker has nothing to do with the Sioux Indians. The French word "sault" (canal) is pronounced "soo."

Savannah, Georgia

6157 Broadways 1886 *Southern Colored (ind.).* Team played its home games at Broadway Avenue Park.

6158 Jerseys 1886 *Southern Colored (ind.).* Nearby dairy farms, which maintain Jersey cows, transport raw milk to city factories for pasteurization, dairy product manufacturing, bottling, canning, packaging and transporting to market.

6159 Lafayette 1886 *Southern Colored (ind.).* This all-professional circuit, baseball's first black professional league, was officially known as the Southern League of Colored Baseballists. French soldiers, assembled by French general Marquis de Lafayette, joined American colonial troops in a failed attack of the British garrison in this city in 1778.

6160 Forest Citys 1886–87 *Southern (ind.).* Founded in 1789 the city's settlers planted Moss-veil Oak trees along its streets. Savannah is the "Forest City of the South."

6161 Garden Citys 1886–87 *Southern (ind.);* 1896 *Southern (ind.).* City has many parks and gardens. Savannah is the "Garden City."

6162 White Feathers 1886–87 *Southern (ind.).* The Chippewas inhabited the region into the nineteenth century. Chippewa chiefs wore headdresses with white feathers. James Oglethorpe, the founder of Georgia, and a traveling party sailed the Savannah River to meet Chippewa Chief Tomichichi on February 10, 1773. The chief ordered a medicine man to present a ring of white feathers to Oglethorpe as a gift of greeting.

6163 Electrics 1893–94 *Southern (ind.).* City built its first hydroelectric plant along the Savannah River in 1892. The Savannah Electric Streetcar Company began running electrified trolley cars in 1872.

6164 Electricians 1894 *Southern (ind.).* Tag was a spin-off from Electrics. Newspaper editors rebelled against it, and reporters switched back to "Electrics."

6165 Modocs 1894 *Southern (ind.).* The Western Modoc Indians occupied California and the Pacific Northwest. The Eastern Modoc Indians occupied Florida and Georgia until the mid-nineteenth century.

6166 Indians 1898 *Southern (ind.);* 1906–12 *South Atlantic (C);* 1926–28x *Southeastern (B);* 1936–42 *South Atlantic (B);* 1946–54 *South Atlantic (A).* The Chippewa, Eastern Modoc and Klamath Indians inhabited Georgia. With manager Bill Hallman at the helm in 1906, newspapers called the players "Bill Hallman's Indians." The moniker was retained through 1912. Bill Holland managed in 1926 and the name was "Bill Holland's Indians." Joe Brennan took over in 1927 and the name became "Brennan's Indians." Ray Schmandt managed in 1928 and the name was "Schmandt's Indians." The 1936–42 and 1946–54 teams were not farm clubs of the Cleveland Indians.

6167 Pathfinders 1904–05 *South Atlantic (C).* General James Oglethorpe built Fort Pulaski in 1733, which became a city and the state capital in 1777. "Pathfinder" is a term for "pioneer" or "explorer."

6168 Scouts 1911–12 *South Atlantic (C)*. Indian scouts were employed by settlers and soldiers throughout U.S. history because they knew the land and were skilled horse riders. Moniker is a spin-off from "Pathfinders," and "Indians."

6169 Colts 1913–15 *South Atlantic (C)*. Team had many young players. The youthful inexperience of the players showed as the 1915 team finished in last place. With manager Joseph Herold at the helm in 1913, newspapers called the players "Herold's Colts."

6170 Athletics 1955 *South Atlantic (A)*. Team was a farm club of the Kansas City Athletics.

6171 Redlegs 1956–58 *South Atlantic (A)*. Team was a farm club of the Cincinnati Redlegs.

6172 Reds 1959 *South Atlantic (A)*. The Cincinnati parent club switched back to "Reds."

6173 Pirates 1960 *South Atlantic (A)*. Team was a farm club of the Pittsburgh Pirates.

6174 White Sox 1962 *South Atlantic (A)*. Team was a farm club of the Chicago White Sox.

6175 Senators 1968–69 *Southern (AA)*. Team was a farm club of the Washington Senators.

6176 Indians 1970 *Southern (AA)*. Team was a farm club of the Cleveland Indians.

6177 Braves 1971–83 *Southern (AA)*. Team was a farm club of the Atlanta Braves.

6178 Cardinals 1984–95 *South Atlantic (A)*. Team was a farm club of the St. Louis Cardinals.

6179 Sand Gnats 1996 to date *South Atlantic (A)*. Infesting the sandy shores of the Savannah River are these small, black, biting dipterian Midge flies. Management held a name-the-team contest in which "Sand Gnats" received 70 percent of the vote. The team's director of marketing, Nick Brown, declared "Sand Gnats" to be the winner. Other entries included Hammerheads, Sea Turtles, Shadow and Thrashers. Asked why he chose Sand Gnats as the winner, Brown said with exasperation, "Well, we've got all these gnats here!"

Schaumburg, Illinois

6180 Flyers 1999 to date *Northern (ind.)*. The Schaumburg Regional Airport is located just outside the city. Management held a name-the-team contest. With several thousand fans voting, the team, city and park district officials chose "Flyers" from following finalists: Bulldogs, Grovers, K-Nines, Nighthawks, Pioneers, Prairie Stars and Sparks.

Schenectady, New York

6181 Electrics 1895 *New York State (ind.)*. General Electric established a hydroelectric plant here in 1892 — one of the earliest in the United States. Soon after this time, Schenectady became known as the "City That Lights the World."

6182 Electricians 1899–1904 *New York State (ind. 1899–1901, B 1902–04)*. Moniker was a spin-off from "Electrics." The first home of the General Electric Company, Schenectady soon became known as the "Electric City."

6183 Frog Alley Bunch 1903 *New York State (B)*. French settlers in the city were given the derogatory nickname of "Frogs." French immigrants started stores and shops on Rotterdam Street (previously occupied by Dutch immigrants) and the street got the nickname of "Frog Alley." The 1903 team played its home games here. "Frog" is a derogatory nickname for a Frenchman.

6184 Mohawks 1912 *Independent Negro team*. Region was inhabited by the River Indians, i.e., Delawares, Manhattans and Mohawks. Dutch settlers bought the site of the future city from the Mohawks in 1661. The city is located near to the Mohawk River.

6185 Mohawk Giants 1912–13 *Independent Negro team*; 1940–43 *Independent Negro team*. The 1915 team played at Island Park, located on Schenectady Island on the Mohawk River. "Mohawk" was used as the adjective, preceding the noun "Giants," in a typical black team nickname style. Also known as the **Mohawk Colored Giants**, the team changed its name in mid-season to the **Colored Stars**.

6186 Stars 1924m *Independent Negro team*. Team moved to Amsterdam (NY) July 10. Moniker was a spin-off from the 1915 "Colored Stars."

6187 Blue Jays 1946–50 *Canadian American (C)*; 1951–57 *Eastern (A)*. The 1946–50 team was a farm club of Philadelphia Blue Jays. *American (C)*. Team was a farm team of the 1946–49 Philadelphia Blue Jays. When the parent club returned to "Phillies" in 1950, the farm team retained the now-distinctive "Blue Jays" moniker. By 1951, the parent club, after abandoning Blue Jays in 1950, was solidly entrenched as the "Phillies." However, the Schenectady team, now playing in the Eastern League, decided to retain the now unique "Blue Jays," which was not being used by any other team in professional baseball in 1951.

Schulenburg, Texas

6188 Giants 1915x *Middle Texas (D)*. Team disbanded June 7. Team was in first place on May 20, prompting the local newspaper, the *Schulenburg Sticker*, to report: "The Schulenburg 'Giants' have played 17 games this season, winning 14 and losing 3. They are at the top of the league." Teams in this era that were winning and near or in first place were sometimes called "Giants."

Scottdale, Pennsylvania

6189 Scottdale Base Ball Club 1889 *Western Pennsylvania Assn. (ind.)*. Team had no nickname.

6190 Giants 1907 *Western Pennsylvania (D)*. When the Butler "White Sox" chose the nickname of the 1906 world champion Chicago White Sox, and then the Greensburg "Red Sox" chose the nickname of the 1903–04 world champion Boston Red Sox, reporters in Scottdale, in a battle for prestige, chose the moniker of the 1905 world champion New York NL club — the "Giants."

6191 Millers 1908m *Pennsylvania–West Virginia (D)*. Team moved to Grafton (WVa) July 31. Nearby wheat farms sent grain to processing factories in the city.

6192 Scotties 1925–30 *Middle Atlantic (C)*. A "Scottie" means an inhabitant of Scotland or any city with the prefix "Scott" in its name, i.e., Scottdale, Scottsdale. Scottsboro. etc. Tag was used for newspaper headlines, i.e., "Scotties edge Colts, 4–3." The city was founded as Scotts' Dale in 1730 by Scottish settlers.

6193 Cardinals 1931 *Middle Atlantic (C)*. Team was a farm club of the St. Louis Cardinals.

Scottsdale, Arizona

6194 Padres 1981–82 *Arizona (R)*; 1988–92 *Arizona (R)*. These teams were farm clubs of the San Diego Padres.

6195 Brewers 1988–89 *Arizona (R)*. Team was a farm club of the Milwaukee Brewers.

6196 Athletics 1988–95, 1997 *Arizona (R)*. These teams were farm clubs of the Oakland Athletics.

6197 Giants 1991–94, 2000–07, 2011 to date *Arizona (R)*. These teams were farm clubs of the San Francisco Giants.

6198 Scorpions 1992–96 *Arizona Fall (W)*; 2008 to date *Arizona Fall (W)*. Scorpions are found in the Southwest and in the nearby Arizona and Sonora deserts.

6199 Valley Vipers 2000 *Western (ind.)*. Scottsdale is located in the "Valley of the Sun." The poisonous rattlesnake and sidewinder, found in the Arizona desert and prairie land, are vipers. Moniker was also a spin-off of the NL Arizona Diamondbacks, although the Valley Vipers were not a farm club of the Diamondbacks.

6200 Diamondbacks 2011 *Arizona (R)*. Team was a farm club of the Arizona Diamondbacks.

Scranton, Pennsylvania

6201 Indians 1886x *Pennsylvania State Assn. (ind.)*. Team and league disbanded in mid-season (date unknown); 1887 *International (ind.)*. Team began season in Oswego (NY) and moved to Scranton May 31. Oswego's 3–23 record was expunged and Scranton started with a clean slate; 1894m *Pennsylvania State (ind.)*. Team moved to Shenandoah (PA) August 2. The original inhabitants of Pennsylvania, the Lackawanna and Seneca Indians, were forced onto reservations by 1837. With manager Denny Mack at the helm in 1887, newspapers called the players "Denny Mack's Indians."

6202 Miners m1887 *International (ind.)*; 1888 *Central (ind.)*; 1889 *Eastern Interstate (ind.)*; 1892–93 *Pennsylvania State Assn. (ind.)*; 1896–97 *Eastern (ind.)*; 1899x *Atlantic (ind.)*. Team disbanded July 9. 1900x *Atlantic (ind.)*. Team and league disbanded June 12; m1904–17 *New York State (B)*. Team started 1904 season in Schenectady (NY) and moved to Scranton July 17; 1923–37 *New York–Pennsylvania (B)*. 1923–32 *(A)*. 1933–37; 1944–45, 1952–53 *Eastern (A)*. Settling here in the 1780s, the Scranton and Slocum pioneers built an ironworks in 1840 and 1845, respectively, which stimulated coal mining for fuel to stoke the furnaces. By 1866, when the city was established, coal mining was the leading industry until manufacturing took over in the 1920s. The Lackawanna Iron & Coal Company was established here in 1847. Scranton soon became known as the "Anthracite Capital of the World." With manager Michael McDermott at the helm in 1896, newspapers called the players "McDermott's Miners." With manager Sandy Griffin at the helm in 1897, newspapers called the players "Griffin's Miners." With manager Marty Swift at the helm in 1899, newspapers called the players "Marty's Miners."

6203 Quakers m1894 *Eastern (ind.)*. Team started 1894 season in Troy (NY) and moved to Scranton August 2. Quakers were among the first settlers here starting in the 1780s. With manager Thomas Cahill at the helm in 1894, newspapers called the players "Cahill's Quakers." Pennsylvania is the "Quaker State."

6204 Coal Heavers 1895 *Eastern (ind.)*. Scranton & Lackawanna Iron & Steel Company, one of the leading steel and iron mills in the United States in this era, was heavily dependent on coal shipments to power its furnaces. Coal heavers shoveled coal into iron-smelting furnaces.

6205 Electrics 1896 *Eastern (ind.)*. The nation's first electric trolley cars started running on Scranton streets in 1886. Scranton quickly became known as the "Electric City."

6206 Red Sox 1939–43, 1946–52 *Eastern (A)*. Team was a farm club of the Boston Red Sox.

6207 Red Barons 1989–2006 *International (AAA)*. Team nickname was an amalgam of Scranton Red Sox and Wilkes-Barre Barons. The original "Red Baron" was German World War I flying ace Baron von Richtoven. The team has never used as a logo cartoonist Charles Schultz' comic strip "Snoopy" in his Red Baron flying ace outfit.

6208 Yankees 2007 to date *International (AAA)*. Team was a farm club of New York Yankees.

Seaford, Delaware

6209 Eagles 1946–49 *Eastern Shore (D)*. Delaware is the "First State," whose representatives were first to ratify the U.S. Constitution on December 7, 1787. Team chose "Eagles" to celebrate this event. The eagle is the national symbol of the United States.

Seattle, Washington

6210 Queen Citys 1890 *Pacific Northwest (ind.)*. Seattle, the leading metropolis of the Pacific Northwest, is the "Queen City of the Pacific."

6211 Hustlers 1890–92 *Pacific Northwest (ind.)*. With manager Gil Hatfield at the helm in 1892, newspapers called the players "Hatfield's Hustlers." In this era, "hustler" was slang for "baseball player."

6212 Yannigans 1896x *Pacific (ind.)*. Circuit and team disbanded June 15. Team had numerous young players. "Yannigan," now obsolete, was nineteenth-century slang for an inexperienced newcomer. With manager Charles "Count" Campau at the helm, newspapers called the players "Count Campau's Yannigans."

6213 Rainmakers 1896x *Pacific (ind.)*. Circuit and team disbanded June 15. Team had numerous games postponed or cancelled because of rainy weather. Briefly during the period 1895–1910, teams that experienced a lot of cancelled games because of a stretch of rainy weather were sometimes called "Rainmakers." The Pacific Northwest is noted for its heavy rainfall.

6214 Babies 1896 *Pacific Northwest (ind.)*. Team had numerous young players. Young players in this era were known as "Babies," especially when the team struggled on the field.

6215 Clamdiggers 1901–02 *Pacific Northwest (ind. 1901, B 1902)*. Clams are found in the beach sand, along the shores of the nearby Puget Sound and Dawomish River. With manager Daniel Dugdale at the helm, newspapers called the players "Daniel Dugdale's Clamdiggers." Seattle, the "Boating Capital of the World," is noted for its clams and halibut.

6216 Chinooks 1903 *Pacific National (A)*. The Chinook Indians were inhabitants of the Pacific Northwest. With Daniel Dugdale returning, newspapers called the players "Daniel's Chinooks."

6217 Indians 1903 *Pacific National (A)*. The PNL Seattle Chinooks (Indians) and the PCL Seattle Siwashes played the same season in 1903, but they were two different franchises. The Pacific National League lost the attendance battle with the Pacific Coast League and disbanded after the 1903 season; 1922–32, 1934–38 *Pacific Coast (AA 1919–38)*. Tag was a spin-off from Chinooks. Team, managed by Daniel Dugdale, was also known as "Daniel's Indians." With manager Walt McCreedie at the helm in 1922, newspapers called the players "Walt McCreedie's Indians." The moniker was retained through 1938 under eight other managers.

6218 Siwashes 1903–06 *Pacific Coast (A)*; 1907–17 *Northwest (B)*. French settlers of the eighteenth and nineteenth centuries called the Chinooks "Les Sauvages" (savages in English), which soon transformed into "Siwashes." Originally referring to the Chinook and later to any Pacific Northwest Indian tribe, it eventually came to refer to any and all Americans, i.e., settlers, trappers, hunters, prospectors. Today, the name refers to any inhabitant of the Pacific Northwest. With manager Parke Wilson at the helm 1903–04, newspapers called the players "Parke Wilson's Siwashes." The moniker was retained under seven other managers through 1917.

6219 Turks 1909 *Northwest (B)*. Young players contributed to the team's first-place finish with a handsome 109–58 mark. Local newspapers praised the team for "playing like Young Turks." Capable and aggressive young men were known in this era as "Young Turks." The "Young Turks" were a reformist, nationalist, revolutionary group in Turkey, comprised mostly of young men—some of whom were military school students—who demanded an end to the Ottoman Empire.

6220 Giants 1910–17 *Northwest (B)*; 1918x *Pacific International*

(B). Team and league disbanded July 7 because of U.S. entry into World War I, Baseball teams that won a pennant were often praised for "playing like giants." The name, however, used for the team at the start of the 1910 season in the hopes of a repeat pennant bombed as the team skidded to last place in the league with a shoddy 61–99 record, prompting fans and newspapers to use the name "Giants" as a sarcastic barb, i.e., "Lynch's 'Giants' Lose Again!" Jack Tighe took over in 1911 and the name became "Jack Tighe's Giants." Frank Raymond took over in mid-season 1911 and the name became "Raymond's Giants." Raymond spurred his team to "play like Giants" in winning the 1915 Northwestern League pennant. Rube Gardner took over in 1917 and the name became "Gardner's Giants." The 1918 Seattle team was "playing like Giants," putting them in first place when the league disbanded July 7.

6221 Dry Dockers 1919x *Northwest International (B)*. As in 1903, the city of Seattle had two baseball teams—the NWIL Dry Dockers and the PCL Mariners. The Rainiers won the attendance battle, forcing the Dry Dockers and the entire Northwest International circuit to disband June 8. One reason for the disbandment was Canada was hard hit by the Spanish Influenza epidemic. Water is pumped out or shut off from a dock to allow workers to construct or repair ships. The Port of Seattle along Elliot Bay has numerous dry docks for ship repair. The dry docks were used to construct hundreds of ships for the U.S. Navy during World War II. With manager Joe Devine at the helm, newspapers called the players "Devine's Dry Dockers."

6222 Rainiers 1919–21, 1933, 1939–64 *Pacific Coast (AA 1919–45, AAA 1946–51 & 1958–68, Open 1952–57)*; 1972–76 *Northwest (A)*. Seattle is situated near Mount Rainier. Actually, the team was owned by the Rainier Brewery Company, which gave rise to an alternate unofficial moniker of **Suds** (1919–37). In 1919, ownership wanted to get away from "Indians" because of the confusion with the AL Cleveland Indians.

6223 Purple Sox 1919–37 *Pacific Coast (AA)* The moniker was another spin-off from Mount Rainier as the players wore purple-trim uniforms and stirrups after the purple-hued clouds of the nearby Cascade and Olympic mountains.

6224 Angels 1965–68 *Pacific Coast (AAA)*. Team was a farm club of the California Angels.

6225 Steelheads 1946 *West Coast Assn. (ind.)*. Team was a road team—the Harlem Globetrotters Baseball Club—that represented Seattle this season. Abe Saperstein, owner of the Harlem Globetrotters basketball team since 1925, founded this baseball team in 1933, using the same team nickname. Unlike the basketball team that has traveled worldwide, this baseball team only traveled in the continental U.S. Gray-headed fish known as "steelheads" swim in the nearby Puget Sound and Dawomish River.

6226 Pilots 1969 *American (M)*. Seattle is the largest seaport of the Pacific Northwest. Pilot ships guide cargo ships in and out of the city's harbor Elliot Bay. Hence, the city is known as the "Gateway to Alaska and the Orient." Seattle was during World War II a manufacturing center for B-17 bomber planes. Boeing has been building planes here since 1941, giving the city the biggest aero-space industry on the West Coast. Dewey Sariano, former ship pilot with the U.S. Coast Guard, was a minority owner of the team. The moniker referred to both airplane pilots and maritime ship pilots.

6227 Mariners 1977 to date *American (M)*. Founded in 1851, the city became a major maritime port in 1914 with the completion of the Panama Canal. Name was selected in a name-the-team Contest. The winning entry was submitted by Roger Szmodis of Bellevue (WA), who explained: "I've selected Mariners because of the natural association between the sea and Seattle and her people—who have been both challenged and rewarded by it." "Mariners" was selected out of 600 name suggestions, which included "Pilots" and

"Rainiers." Seattle is the "World's Port" and the "Boating Capital of the World."

6228 M's 1977 to date *American (M)*. Used primarily by Seattle newspapers as a space-saving device, the M's moniker is mostly met with disdain since it has none of the history and charm of the "A's" abbreviation that has traveled through Philadelphia, Kansas City and Oakland since 1860.

Sedalia, Missouri

6229 Goldbugs 1901–04 *Missouri Valley (ind. 1901, D 1902–03 c71104)*; 1905 *Western Assn. (D)*. Insects with yellow shells, "goldbugs," are found in the Midwest. "Goldbugs" was also a nickname for politicians who supported the gold standard, i.e., basing paper money on gold. Progressive politicians in Missouri supported the gold standard for Missouri farmers in the years 1865–1900. The players wore golden yellow hose. In 1901, the team ignored league salary ceiling rules to sign better players than other league teams, which produced three straight winning seasons and a pennant when the team finished the 1903 campaign with 51 victories in its last 69 contests for an overall 86–47 record to clinch the flag. In this context, "goldbug" meant someone who enjoyed "golden riches."

6230 Cubs 1911m *Missouri State (D)*. Team moved to Brookfield (MO) May 24. Team had a loose affiliation with the Chicago Cubs, allowing them to receive "Cubs" uniforms and equipment from the big league club.

Seguin, Texas

6231 Toros 1976 *Gulf States (A)*. In the nineteenth century cattle drives brought bulls, cows and steer to ranches in the city. The Spanish name for bull is "toro." The city was founded in 1838 and was a Mexican town until 1847.

Selma, Alabama

6232 Christians 1901 *South Atlantic (ind.)*. Baptists and Presbyterian settlers arrived here, founding the city in 1816.

6233 Centralites 1911–12 *Southeast (D)*; 1913 *Cotton States (D)*. City is located in Central Alabama. The league's Huntsville team was called the "Westerns."

6234 River Rats 1914 *Georgia–Alabama (C)*. U.S. rivers, as the Industrial Revolution progressed, had become polluted in this era. The Alabama River was infested with rats feeding on garbage. The problem was so prevalent that several sports teams playing in riverfront cities called themselves the "River Rats." The notion that North America was before 1900 a "pristine paradise" was untrue. Settlers and industry polluted North America's land and water for 200 years.

6235 Selmians 1927 *Southeastern (B)*. An inhabitant of Selma is known as a "Selmian."

6236 Clover Leafs 1928–30 *Southeastern (B)*; 1932x *Southeastern (B)*. Team and league disbanded May 21 due to the Great Depression; 1937–41 *Southeastern (B)*; 1946–47, 1949–50 *Southeastern (B)*; 1957–62 *Alabama–Florida (D)*; 2002–03r *Southeast (ind.)*. Team became a road team in mid-season and adopted the regional name of "Southeastern Clover Leafs." With Irishman Polly McLarry at the helm as manager in 1928, newspapers called the players "McLarry's Clover Leafs." The clover plant, also called the "Shamrock plant," is found not only in Ireland but also throughout the southern states in the Black Soil Belt. Many Irish immigrants came to Alabama and Selma in the era 1845–1900. Selma was home to the Cloverleaf Creamery & Butter Company. All Selma teams, except the 1948 club, were known as "Clover Leafs."

6237 Cubs 1948 *Southeastern (B)*. Team was a farm club of the Chicago Cubs.

Seminole, Oklahoma

6238 Oilers 1947–49 *Sooner State (D)*; 1954–57 *Sooner State (D)*. Eastern Oklahoma Oil Fields were built here in 1930 after oil and natural gas were discovered in the region in 1928. City refineries process the crude oil and gas.

6239 Ironmen 1950–51 *Sooner State (D)*. Iron and steel factories in the city convert iron ore into metal.

Seneca, Kansas

6240 Seneca Baseball Club 1910 *Eastern Kansas (D)*. Team had no nickname.

Seneca Falls, New York

6241 Maroons 1888–89 *New York State (ind.)*. Players wore maroon hose.

Seoul, Federal District, South Korea

6242 OB Bears 1982 to date *Korean (ind.)*. Oriental Breweries, owner of the baseball franchise, named the team the "Bears." The Doosan Forklift Company of Seoul bought the team from Oriental Breweries after the 1998 season. The team nickname was retained as the team's title became the **Doosan Bears**.

6243 MBC Blue Dragons 1982–89 *Korean (ind.)*. The Monhwa Broadcasting Company owned the team and chose the nickname of "Dragons." Management dressed the players in blue-trim uniforms. Dragons are an ancient Asian symbol of good luck.

6244 Twins 1990 to date *Korean (ind.)*. Team went by the owner name of LG Twins. LG are the initials of the Lucky & Goldstar Companies. The L & G Companies bought the franchise from MBC after the 1989 season. Lucky and Gold Star are "twin" manufacturing companies.

6245 Heroes 2008 to date *Korean (ind.)*. The Hyundai Company sold its Suwon team—the Unicorns—to the Woori Tobacco Company of Seoul, which moved the franchise from Suwon to Seoul and renamed the team as the "Heroes." Baseball players have always been "heroes" to fans, especially children.

Sevierville, Tennessee

6246 Tennessee Smokies 2000 *Southern (AA)*. The Knoxville Smokies moved to suburban Sevierville about 20 miles southeast of Knoxville.

Seward, Nebraska

6247 Statesmen 1910–13m *Nebraska State (D)*. Team moved to Beatrice (NE) July 21. William H. Seward (born in New York in 1801) was U.S. Secretary of State (1861–69). He legislated the Kansas-Nebraska Act (1854) and the Homestead Act, both of which helped settlers find land in Nebraska. In 1868, Seward negotiated with the Russian government for the purchase of Alaska, which became known as Seward's Folly until gold and oil were discovered there. This Nebraska city was named after him.

Shamokin, Pennsylvania

6248 Maroons 1887–88 *Central Pennsylvania (ind.)*. The players wore maroon hose.

6249 Shamokin Base Ball Club 1896m *Pennsylvania State (ind.)*. Team moved to Reading (PA) in mid-season (date unknown); m1897m *Central Pennsylvania (ind.)*. Team started season in Pottsville (PA), then moved here in mid-season (date unknown). Team moved Lock Haven (PA) later in the season (date unknown); 1905 *Tri-State (ind.)*. These teams had no nickname.

6250 Shammies 1925 *New York–Pennsylvania (B)*. Newspapers used the moniker for headlines, i.e., "Shammies edge Miners, 5–4." With manager Amos Strunk at the helm, newspapers called the players "Amos' Shammies" and "Strunk's Shammies."

6251 Indians 1926–27 *New York–Pennsylvania (B)*. Before European settlers arrived here, the region was inhabited by the Algonquin Indians. With manager Irvin Trout at the helm in 1927, newspapers called the players "Irvin's Indians."

Shanghai, Kiangsu, China

6252 Golden Eagles 2002 to date *Chinese (S)*. Circuit is officially known as the Chinese Baseball League. Players wore gold-trim uniforms and stirrups. The eagle, which inhabits Asia, is an ancient symbol in Asia.

Sharon, Pennsylvania

6253 Sharon Base Ball Club 1895m *Iron & Oil (ind.)*. Team moved to Elberon (PA) in mid-season (date unknown). Team had no nickname.

6254 Steels 1905–06 *Ohio–Pennsylvania (C)*. Established in 1802, the city built its first iron and steel mills in 1870. By 1900, city factories made finished steel products. With manager Frank Killen at the helm, newspapers called the players "Killen's Steels."

6255 Giants 1907–08 *Ohio–Pennsylvania (D)*. With the 1907 team going a poor 55–84, good for a seventh-place finish, disgruntled fans and newspapers sarcastically called the players the "Giants." The team improved to 62–56 and fourth place in 1908, but newspapers still taunted the players as "Giants." With manager Rudy Kling at the helm, newspapers called the players "Kling's Giants." Van Johnson took over in mid-season 1907 and the name became "Van's Giants" and "Johnson's Giants."

6256 Travelers 1911 *Ohio–Pennsylvania (D)*. Team started the 1911 season in Newcastle (PA) and moved to Sharon August 12. Teams of this era that moved in mid-season were sometimes called Orphans, Pilgrims, Wanderers and Travelers. With manager William Thomas at the helm, local newspapers called the players "Bill Thomas' Travelers."

6257 Giants 1912m *Ohio–Pennsylvania (D)*. Team moved to Fairmount (WV) July 9. With manager Charles Eichenberger at the helm, newspapers called the players "Charles Eichenberger's Giants."

Shawnee, Oklahoma

6258 Indians m1904mx *Southwestern (D)*. Team moved to Chickasha (OK) June 30 and then returned to Shawnee August 3. Team and league disbanded September 5; 1923–24x *Oklahoma State (D)*. Team and league disbanded July 8. The Shawnee Indian Mission was established in 1872 and became the city of Shawnee in 1894. The Shawnee were relocated from the Eastern U.S. to Oklahoma, starting in the 1870s. The Seminoles who inhabited the American Southwest fought two wars against American troops in 1817–18 and 1842–43, both in Florida, and then were relocated to Oklahoma. Oklahoma is the "Land of the Red Men."

6259 Browns m1904m Team moved to Chickasha (OK) June 30 and then returned to Shawnee August 3. Team and league disbanded September 5. When the team returned to Shawnee on August 3, the team name was changed from "Indians" to "Browns." The players wore brown hose.

6260 Blues 1906x *South Central (D)*. Circuit and team disbanded July 21. Players wore blue trim uniforms and hose.

6261 Braves m1925 *Southwestern (D)*. Team started season in Enid (OK) and moved to Shawnee June 17. Tag was a spin-off from Indians.

6262 Robins 1929–30 *Western Assn. (C)*. The robin is a type of thrush, with red breasts and feathers, found throughout North America. The players wore Robin red-trim uniforms and stirrups. With manager Ray Powell at the helm, newspapers called the players "Ray's Robins."

6263 Hawks m1950–57 *Sooner State (D)*. Team started 1950 season in Duncan (OK) and moved to Shawnee August 18. Management decided to name the team the "Hawks."

Sheffield-Tuscumbia, Alabama

6264 Twins 1926 *Tri-State (D)*. Team played home games in Sheffield but also represented Tuscumbia. Baseball teams since 1885 that represented two cities sometimes have been called "Twins."

Shelby, North Carolina

6265 Cardinals 1937–38m *North Carolina State (D)*. Team moved to Gastonia (NC) July 22. Team was a farm club of the St. Louis Cardinals.

6266 Nationals 1939 *Tar Heel (D)*. Team was a farm club of the Washington Nationals.

6267 Colonels 1940 *Tar Heel (D)*; 1960–63 *Western Carolina (D 1960–62, A 1963)*. Colonel Isaac Shelby was an American militia colonel who led colonial troops against the British in the Revolutionary War and led American troops into Canada in 1813. The city was named after Shelby, who was born in Maryland and served as governor of Kentucky (1792–96) in 1843. With manager Lou Haneles at the helm, newspapers called the players "Lou Haneles' Colonels."

6268 Cubs 1946 *Tri-State (B)*. Team was a farm club of the Chicago Cubs.

6269 Farmers 1948–52 *Western Carolina (D)*. Farms near the city send cotton, fruit, dairy products, wheat and beef to city factories for processing and transport to market. The city is known for the famous Shelby's Farmers' Market since 1930. With manager Rube Wilson at the helm in 1948, newspapers called the players "Rube's Farmers. "Rube" means a rustic person, i.e., a farmer. Wilson left the team after the 1948 season but the name was retained through 1952.

6270 Clippers 1953–54 *Tar Heel (D)*. Clipper ships have sailed the nearby Broad River since 1840. Railroad "Clipper" trains have also chugged in and out of the city since 1850. With manager David Coble at the helm in 1953, newspapers called the players the "David Coble's Clippers." Harold Kollar took over in 1954 and the name became "Kollar's Clippers."

6271 Yankees 1964 *Western Carolina (A)*. Team was a farm club of the New York Yankees.

6272 Rebels 1965 *Western Carolina (A)*. The tag of "Rebels" has been used by many teams. North Carolina withdrew from the Union by its Declaration of Mecklenburg on May 20, 1861. Many Civil War battles were fought in the Carolinas.

6273 Senators 1969 *Western Carolinas (A)*. Team was a farm club of the Washington Senators.

6274 Reds 1977–78 *Western Carolinas (A)*. Team was a farm club of the Cincinnati Reds.

6275 Pirates 1979 *Western Carolinas (A)*; 1980 *South Atlantic (A)*. Team was a farm club of the Pittsburgh Pirates.

6276 Mets 1981–82 *South Atlantic (A)*. Team was a farm club of the New York Mets.

Shelbyville, Illinois

6277 Queen Citys 1907–08x *Eastern Illinois (D)*. Team and league disbanded August 20. "Queen City" is a nickname given to cities, mostly in the nineteenth century, that built beautiful buildings and achieved rapid economic success, i.e., farming and coal mining here.

Shelbyville, Kentucky

6278 Grays 1908 *Blue Grass (D)*. Players wore gray uniforms.

6279 Shelbyville Baseball Club 1909–10m *Blue Grass (D)*. Team moved to Maysville (KY) August 24. Team had no nickname.

Sheldon, Iowa

6280 Sheldon Baseball Club 1902 *Iowa–South Dakota (D)*. Team had no nickname.

Sheldon-Primghar, Iowa

6281 Hyphens m1903 *Iowa–South Dakota (D)*. Team started season in Council Bluffs (IA) and moved to Sheldon June 25. "Hyphens" was a newspaper gimmick for the "twin city" teams of Bay City–Saginaw, Johnstown-Amsterdam-Gloverville, Matoon-Charleston and Springfield-Charleston. In this case, newspapers listed the team as "Sheldon-Primghar."

Shelton, Connecticut

6282 Shelton Baseball Club 1896–98x *Naugatuck Valley (ind.)*. Team and circuit disbanded in mid-season (date unknown). Team had no nickname.

Shenandoah, Iowa

6283 Shenandoah Baseball Club 1903x *Southwest Iowa (D)*. Team disbanded July 18. Team had no nickname.

6284 Pin Rollers 1910–11 *Missouri–Iowa–Nebraska–Kansas M.I.N.K. (D)*. In this era, the baseball bat was likened to a "pin roller," especially in Midwest baseball jargon. Hence, baseball players were sometimes called "pin rollers." Similarly, the baseball sphere has been likened to an apple, aspirin, pill and potato. Slang names for the bat include club, lumber, pin, stick, timber, tomahawk and wand. With manager Fred Wells at the helm in 1910, newspapers called the players "Fred Wells' Pin Rollers." Today, a "pin roller" is usually called a "rolling pin."

Shenandoah, Pennsylvania

6285 Hungarian Rioters 1888 *Central Pennsylvania (ind.)*; 1889 *Middle States (ind.)*. Circuit was also known as the Eastern Interstate League. During the Civil War, the Union Army quelled food riots in the Shenandoah Valley in 1864–65. In the same era, the Austrian-Hungarian Empire was experiencing riots in Budapest, Hungary, provoked by Hungarian, Croatian and Magyar separatists who wanted jobs, food and independence. In the 1880s, several Pennsylvania cities, including Shenandoah, were convulsed by iron and steel mill strikes, leading to riots. Newspapers likened the striking workers to the "Hungarian rioters" in Europe. In this era, newspaper reporters sometimes assigned nicknames to teams based on catastrophic events, i.e., Flood-Sufferers, Hungarian Rioters, Cyclones, Fever Germs and Insurgents.

6286 Huns m1894–95x *Pennsylvania State (ind.)*. Team started 1894 season in Scranton (PA) and then moved to Shenandoah August 2. Team disbanded May 20, 1895. Team also represented Mahanoy City, forcing newspapers editors of both cities to sometimes identify team as the Shenandoah–Mahanoy City "Huns." Eventually, the editors in both cities reduced the name to Shenandoah Huns when it was obvious that no home games would be played in Mahanoy City. The nickname has two origins. First, it was an obvious newspaper contraction of "Hungarian Rioters," which aggravated local newspaper editors. Fortunately, the "Huns" contraction, which is a derogatory slang for "Germans," was appropriate because most of the immigrants coming into this region of Pennsylvania were German. With the prospect of a team named the "Shenandoah–Mahony City Hungarian Rioters," local newspaper editors here would have surely rioted! With manager William Brennan at the helm, newspapers called the players "Brennan's Huns."

Sherbrooke, Quebec, Canada

6287 Braves 1940x *Quebec Provincial (B)*. Team was a farm club of the Boston Braves. Of the six teams in the league, four had loose affiliations with major league teams, i.e., the Drummondville Tigers, Granby Red Socks, Quebec Athletics and the Sherbrooke Braves. Team disbanded August 1.

6288 Canadians 1946 *Border (C)*. Along with Kingston (Ontario) and Granby (Quebec), the Sherbrooke team represented Canada while Auburn, Ogdensburg and Watertown were U.S. teams. The nickname in French was "Les Canadiens." With manager Dutch Proecher at the helm, newspapers called the players "Proecher's Canadians."

6289 Athletics 1950–51 *Provincial (C)*. Of the eight teams in the league, six of them had loose affiliations with major league teams—the Drummondville Cubs, Farnham Pirates, Granby Red Sox, Quebec Braves, St. Jean Braves and Sherbrooke Athletics.

6290 Indians 1953–55 *Provincial (C)*. Team was a farm club of Cleveland Indians. By 1953, six teams in the circuit established formal relationships with major league teams. The 1953 Three Rivers Yankees maintained a loose affiliation with New York AL and the Drummondville Royals were a farm club of the IL Montreal Royals (of the Brooklyn Dodgers farm system) in 1953 and Philadelphia AL in 1954.

6291 Pirates 1972–73 *Eastern (AA)*. Team was a farm club of Pittsburgh Pirates.

Sherman, California

6292 Merchants National 1926–27–27–28 *California Winter (W)*. Merchants National, a chain grocery store, sponsored the team.

Sherman, Texas

6293 Students 1895 *Texas–Southern (ind.)*. City is home to Stephen Austin College. Some of the players on the professional team were also players on the college team. With manager Russ Steinhoff at the helm, newspapers called the players "Steinhoff's Students."

6294 Orphans 1895–96m *Texas–Southern (ind.)*. En route to a 53–64 fifth-place finish in 1895, home attendance dropped, forcing the team onto extended road trips. The team did manage to finish the 1895 season. The next season, afflicted with the same attendance woes, the club moved to Austin June 10, 1896. Nicknames like Forlorns, Orphans, Travelers and Wanderers were typical monikers in the era 1895–1915 for teams forced to take to the road because of low attendance at home. Most of these "Orphans" disbanded in mid-season, although the Sherman club lasted longer than most. In a slight twist from the usual origin, Sherman fans and newspapers called the players "Orphans" because the team had four managers during the 1895 season — Llewellyn Legg, Mr. Ryan, Mike O'Connor ("O'Connor's Orphans") and Mr. Douglas. The players were "orphaned" three times by the departure of three "fatherly" managers before Mr. Douglas finished out the season.

6295 Sherman Base Ball Club 1898 *Southwest (ind.)*. Team had no nickname.

6296 Cubs 1912 *Texas–Oklahoma (D)*. The team had young players who, in this era, were known as "cubs." When the Ardmore club started being called "Giants" (after the 1904–05, 1911 NL champion New York Giants) and the Bonham club went with the "Tigers" (after the 1907–08–09 AL champion Detroit Tigers), reporters in Sherman, wanting an equally prestigious name for their players, started calling the team the "Cubs" (after the 1906–07–08 and 1910 NL champion Chicago Cubs). With Jimmy Humphries at the helm, newspapers called the players "Humphries' Cubs."

6297 Lions 1913–14x *Texas–Oklahoma (D)*. Team disbanded July 30; 1916 *Western Assn. (D)*; 1921 *Texas–Oklahoma (D)*. Just before the start of the 1913 season, the Texarkana entry in the league started being called the "Tigers." In response, Sherman's newspapers and fans called their team the "Lions." Stanley "Dolly" Gray managed in 1914 and the name was "Dolly's Lions." Charlie Moran took over in mid-season 1914 and the name became "Charlie Moran's Lions." With manager Walter Frantz at the helm in 1916, newspapers called the players "Walter Frantz' Lions." Jack Love succeeded him in mid-season, and the name became "Love's Lions." With Babe Peeples and then Curley Maloney at the helm in 1921, newspapers called the players "Peeble's Lions" and "Maloney's Lions." The name was appropriate because mountain lions inhabit Texas.

6298 Hitters 1915 *Western Assn. (D)*. With manager Dad Ritter at the helm, newspapers called the players the rhyming "Ritter's Hitters."

6299 Browns 1917 *Western Assn. (D)*. Team had a loose affiliation with the American League St. Louis Browns, receiving donated equipment and "Browns" uniforms. Donning these uniforms, the players became known as the "Browns." The team was not a formal farm club of the St. Louis Browns.

6300 Red Sox 1922 *Texas–Oklahoma (D)*. Players wore red stirrups. Team was not a farm club of the Boston Red Sox.

6301 Twins 1923 *Texas Assn. (D)*; 1946 *East Texas (C)*; 1952 *Sooner State (D)*. Although it did not include Denison (TX) in its name, the team encouraged neighboring Denison fans to attend home games of the team in Sherman. Baseball teams in this era that represented two cities were sometimes called "Twins."

6302 Snappers 1929 *Lone Star (D)*. The team was named after manager Earl "Red" Snapp. Snapping turtles are found in Texas, which made the name doubly appropriate.

Sherman-Denison, Texas

6303 Sherman-Denison Base Ball Club 1897 *Texas (ind.)*. Team had no nickname.

6304 Students 1902m *Texas (D)*. Team moved to Texarkana May

6. Sherman is the home of Stephen Austin College. Several players on the professional team also played with the college team.

6305 Twins 1947–51 *Bi-State (B)*; 1953 *Sooner (D)*. Although home games were played in Sherman, this team had Denison included in its official name as the "Sherman-Denison Twins." Since 1885, the moniker "Twins" has been used for some teams that represented two cities.

Shreveport, Louisiana

6306 Grays 1895x *Texas–Southern (ind.)*. Team disbanded August 6. Players wore gray hose.

6307 Creoles 1898x *Southwestern (ind.)*. Circuit and team disbanded in mid-season (date unknown). Creoles are people of Spanish or French descent who were born in Louisiana.

6308 Tigers 1899 *Southern (ind.)*. A Confederate Army Cannoner-Zouva military unit, known as the "Louisiana Tigers," distinguished themselves at the Battle of Shenandoah in 1864. The Louisiana State University "Fighting Tigers" was the name used for the school's football team starting in 1896, and was picked up by this baseball team three years later.

6309 Giants 1901–03 Southern Assn. *(ind. 1901, A 1902–07)*. With manager George Reed at the helm of the 1901–02 team, newspapers called the players "George's Giants." In 1903 Bob Gilk became the manager and the newspapers switched to "Gilk's Giants." The moniker "Giants," thanks to the success of the glamorous New York Giants, was a popular baseball team nickname in this era.

6310 Pirates 1904–07 Southern Assn. *(A)*; 1908–10 *Texas (C)*. Pirates, buccaneers and corsairs raided the coast of Louisiana from 1580 until 1830. Reporters wanted their players to emulate the NL Pittsburgh Pirates—winners of three straight NL pennants (1901–03). With manager Robert Gilks at the helm 1904–06, newspapers called the players "Robert Gilk's Pirates." Thomas Fisher took over in 1907, and the name became "Thomas Fisher's Pirates." With manager Dale Gear at the helm in 1908, newspapers called the players "Dale Gear's Pirates."

6311 Gassers 1915–24 Texas *(B 1915–20, A 1921–35)*. Oil and natural gas was discovered in 1906 at Caddo Lake near the Texas border, converting the city into an oil "boom-town." With manager Lee Garvin at the helm in 1915, newspapers called the players "Garvin's Gassers." Syd Smith took over in 1915 and the name became "Syd Smith's Gassers." Billy Smith took over 1919–22 and the name became "Smith's Gassers." Johnny Vann took over in mid-season 1922 and the name became "Vann's Gassers." Ira Thomas took over in 1923 and the name became "Ira Thomas' Gassers."

6312 Sports 1925–32m Texas *(A)*. Team moved to Tyler (TX) May 16. Texas League temporarily suspended operations July 7, 1918, due to World War I and the Spanish influenza, but then resumed play April 17, 1919; 1933 *Dixie (C)*; 1934m *East Dixie (C)*. Team moved to Greenwood (MS) July 13; 1935m *West Dixie (C)*. Team moved to Gladewater (TX) June 4; 1938–42 *Texas (A1)*; 1946–57 *Texas (AA)*; 1959–61 Southern Assn. *(AA)*; 2003–05 *Central (ind.)*; 2006–08 American Assn. *(ind.)*. Newspaper editors here wanted a nickname that was energetic and short. With manager Sid Smith at the helm, reporters started calling the players "Sid Smith's Sports." Fans liked the name, which was an obvious spin-off from the city name, so much so that it was used for the next 83 years. The team, playing exclusively as an independent, was the only Texas League franchise without a major league parent club, in large part due to segregation laws in Shreveport forbidding Negro baseball players to play in Shreveport's Texas League Park. To compensate for their inability to field badly needed African American players, the franchise resorted to grooming white players in lower classification minor league teams

in Sweetwater, Texas (1947–48), Bryan, Texas (1950), Monroe, Louisiana (1950–53), Monroe–West Monroe, Louisiana (1950–54), Concord, North Carolina (1951), Statesville, North Carolina (1953), and Hobbs, New Mexico (1955). The result was a first-place finish and a playoff berth in 1954 and a Southern Association championship in 1955. All these Shreveport farm teams used the team nickname "Sports."

6313 Acme Giants 1929–31 *Texas–Oklahoma (N)*; 1932–36 *Independent Negro team*. Black teams frequently used a complimentary, descriptive adjective in front of the Giants noun. "Acme" means a person or group of people who are talented and perform with top quality.

6314 Braves 1968–71 *Texas (AA)*. Team was a farm club of the Atlanta Braves.

6315 Captains 1972–2000 *Texas (AA)*. Captains have been steering boats along the Red River since city founder Captain Henry Shreve cleared the Red River of a driftwood jam in 1834. Ever October, the city hosts the Red River Revel where river captains parade their boats up the river. The team's logo is a pirate captain, which harkens the image of Caribbean pirates sailing off the coast of Louisiana in the seventeenth century.

6316 Giants 1986 *Texas (AA)*. Team was a farm club of the San Francisco Giants.

6317 Swamp Dragons 2001–02 *Texas (AA)*. Swampy shores of nearby Lakes Caddo and Bistineau and the Red River invoke fantasies of steamy Mesozoic swamps when dinosaurs once roamed here some 65 million years ago. A dragon is a dinosaur-like creature of legend. More than fifty swampy lakes and ponds are located near Shreveport. The Caddo Indians bandied about legends of a dinosaur-like creature that roamed the swampy regions here some 500 years ago. According to legend this dinosaur or dragon safeguarded the Caddo from swamp alligators. Mandalay Sports Entertainment bought the Shreveport team in 2000. Since MSE also owned the Dayton Dragons of the Midwest League, it was decided to use the "Dragons" name for the Shreveport franchise as well.

Shreveport-Bossier, Louisiana

6318 Sports 2006–08 *American Assn. (ind.)*. The 2008 franchise regionalized its name to Shreveport-Bossier while continuing to play its home games in Shreveport.

6319 Captains 2009 to date *American Assn. (ind.)*. The moniker of the 2000 team was revived.

Sichuan, Szechwan, China

6320 Dragons 2005 to date *Chinese (S)*. Circuit is known officially as the Chinese Baseball League. Both the CBL and the Cuban National Series League are state-subsidized sports circuits. The dragon is an ancient symbol of China dating to the Ming and Chi'n dynasties of 2000 years ago. The dragon was the symbol of the emperors of China.

Sidney Mines, Nova Scotia, Canada

6321 Ramblers 1937–39 Cape Breton *(D 1937–38, C 1939)*. City hosts the International Fisherman's Race, showcasing racing schooners known as "rovers" and "ramblers." The tag "ramblers" sometimes was used to describe soccer, rugby football, and baseball teams, i.e., the players "ramble" over the field. With manager Bill Buckley at the helm, newspapers called the players "Buckley's Ramblers." Fred Loftus took over in 1938 and the name became "Fred Loftus' Ramblers." Merle Settlemire took over in 1939 and the name became "Settlemire's Ramblers."

Silao, Guanajuato, Mexico

6322 Club de Beisbol de Silao 1978 *Mexican Center (A)*. Team had no nickname.

Siloam Springs, Arkansas

6323 Buffalos 1934 *Arkansas State (D)*. Team was a farm club of the Houston Buffalos. When an amendment was introduced in 1921 to the 1902 National Association of Professional Baseball Leagues agreement, which legalized the technique, several higher classification (AAA and AA) minor league teams developed their own farm teams among the lower classification (A, B, C, D) minor leagues.

6324 Travelers 1935 *Arkansas State (D)*; 1936–38 *Arkansas–Missouri (D)*. These team were farm clubs of the Little Rock Travelers of the Southern Association.

6325 Cardinals 1940 *Arkansas–Missouri (D)*. Team was a farm club of the St. Louis Cardinals.

Sincelejo, Sucre, Colombia

6326 Toros 2003–04 *Liga Colombiana (W)*. Bull fighting is popular in Columbia.

Sioux City, Iowa

6327 Explorers 1993–2005 *Northern (ind.)*; 2006 to date *American Assn. (ind.)*. Originally, the team was slated to be known as the Sioux City "Sioux," but Native American groups complained about the moniker. The name chosen in its place, "Explorers," referred to the explorers Meriwether Lewis and William Clark, who visited Iowa in the summer of 1804. One man of the Lewis and Clark expedition, Sgt. Charles Floyd, died here in 1804.

Sioux Falls, South Dakota

6328 Canaries 1902–03 *Iowa–South Dakota*; 1920–23 *Dakota*; 1924 *Tri-State*; 1933–38 *Nebraska State*; 1939–41 *Western*; 1942, 1946–53 *Northern*; 1993–2009 *American Assn. (ind.)*. The canary is a yellow finch that got its name when it was imported to the American continent from the Canary Islands near the northwest African coast. The players wore canary yellow hose.

6329 Packers 1966–71 *Northern (A)*. Nearby hog farms transport these animals to slaughterhouses. Meat products are then packed and transported to market.

6330 Fighting Pheasants 2010 to date. *American Assn. (ind.)*. Tag was often shortened to **Pheasants** in the newspaper. Originating in Europe, pheasants are found throughout North America. "Fighting" is an adjective used for some nicknames, i.e., "Fighting Phillies" and "Fighting Gamecocks," to impart an image of spirit and energy for the team.

Slippery Rock, Arkansas

6331 Midwest Sliders 2007–08 *Continental (ind.)*. Moniker was a play on words from "Slippery" Rock. Team became a road team in 2008, known as the Midwest Sliders.

Somerset, Pennsylvania

6332 Somerset Baseball Club m1907x *Western Pennsylvania (D)*. Team began the season in Latrobe (PA), then moved to Cumberland (PA), then to Piedmont (PA), and then to Somerset July 11. The team disbanded July 28. Team had no nickname.

Somerville, New Jersey

6333 West Ends 1892m *Central New Jersey (ind.)*. Team played on the west side of town at the West-End Ball Park.

South Bend, Indiana

6334 Green Stockings m1888 *Indiana State (ind.)*. Team started season in Lafayette (IN) and then moved to South Bend in mid-season; 1915x *Central (D)*. The players wore green hose. Newspapers shortened it to **Green Legs**. With manager Angus Grant at the helm, newspapers called the players "Grant's Green Stockings."

6335 Greens 1903–09 *Central (B)*. Players wore green-trim. Team was named after the 1878–81, 1886–87 and 1889–96 semi-professional baseball team — the South Bend Green Stockings. The tradition of green hose and green-trim uniforms originated with the University of Notre Dame Fighting Irish. The green shamrock is the symbol of Ireland. With manager Angus Grant at the helm in 1906 (eighteen years after his 1888 tour of duty) and 1909, newspapers called the players "Grant's Greens" and Grant's **Green Sox**.

6336 Bronchos 1910 *Central (B)*. As the players excited their fans by racing to an 88–50 mark en route to the 1910 Central League pennant, the team was "tossing off opponents like bucking bronchos." The term "bronchos" was "Wild West" slang for "baseball players."

6337 Benders 1911m *Central (B)*. Team moved to Grand Rapids (MI) July 13; 1912 *Central (D)*; 1914 *Southern Michigan Assn. (C)*; 1916–17m *Central (B)*. Team moved to Peoria (IL) July 8. Moniker was used by newspapers for its headlines, i.e., "Benders edge Brakies, 4–3." With manager Ben Kohler at the helm in 1914 and 1916, newspapers called the players "Ben's Benders." Moniker was used through 1917.

6338 Bux m1911 *Central (D)*. Team started season in Evansville (IN) and moved to South Bend August 11. The white tail deer, found throughout the Midwest, is a North American deer. "Bux" is a newspaper contraction for "bucks." In this era "X" spellings first began to appear, i.e., Sox, Rox and Bux.

6339 Indestructos 1915x *Southern Michigan Assn. (C)*. The team was awarded the pennant with a 44–24 mark when the circuit and team disbanded on July 5, 1915. Newspapers praised the players as "indestructible" in compiling a nine-and-a-half-game lead over second-place Battle Creek by July. Moniker was a spin-off of the 1899–1900 Brooklyn Superbas (who won two straight NL pennants those years) and the 1899 St. Louis Perfectos (who finished a mediocre fourth). In this era such immodest monikers as Superbas, Perfectos, Invincibles, Wonders, Champions and Indestructos were a fad. By 1920, these indiscreet names lost favor with fans and newspapers.

6340 Green Sox 1915x *Southern Michigan Assn. (C)*. Team and league disbanded July 7. Players wore green-trim stirrups. The team was a farm club of the Chicago White Sox. The green stirrups were a spin-off from the white stirrups of the Chicago Americans.

6341 Studebaker Athletics 1915x *Southern Michigan Assn. (C)*. Team and league disbanded July 7. The team was owned by the local Studebaker Automobile Company, which started manufacturing cars here in 1902. This double-moniker was one of the early attempts at a marketing nickname. The tag "Athletics" emulated the 1914 AL champion Philadelphia Athletics, and the team's title was the Studebaker Athletic Club. Local newspapers balked and switched to "Green Sox."

6342 Factors 1915x *Southern Michigan Assn. (C)*. Team and league disbanded July 7. The moniker was in honor of the Studebaker factory workers. Originally "Factory Workers," newspapers shortened it to "Factors."

6343 Twins 1932x *Central (B)*. Team disbanded July 21 because of the Great Depression. The team also represented Elkhart, Indiana, hence the moniker of "Twins."

6344 Studebakers 1932x *Central (B)*. Team disbanded July 21 because of the Great Depression. The Studebaker Automobile Company built a manufacturing plant in 1902 and made its headquarters here.

6345 Blue Sox 1943–54 *All-America Girls Professional Baseball League (ind.)*. The stirrup hue was a spin-off from the 1910 South Bend Green Sox and the nearby Chicago White Sox. The players wore blue-trim uniforms and blue stirrups.

6346 White Sox 1988–93 *Midwest (A)*. Team was a farm club of Chicago White Sox.

6347 Silver Hawks 1994 to date *Midwest (A)*. The Studebaker "Silver Hawk" was a popular automobile model in the 1920s and 1930s.

South Bend, Washington

6348 River Rats 1911 *Washington State (D)*. Rats infested the nearby Willapa Bay and River. In this era America's bays, lakes and rivers, much like the air, were horribly polluted because of the absence of any conservation and anti-pollution laws in the era of laissez-faire capitalism. Rats infested the waterways searching for food amongst the garbage. The slang-insult of "wet rat" appeared in this era. Unhappy fans and local newspapers lambasted the players' miserable, last-place 11–44 record by accusing the team of "playing like river rats."

South Boston, Virginia

6349 Wrappers 1940 *Bi-State (D)*. The team switched to a single city title while retaining the 1939 nickname.

South Boston–Halifax, Virginia

6350 Twins 1937 *Bi-State (D)*. Some teams that represented two cities were known as "Twins."

6351 Wrappers 1938–40 *Bi-State (D)*. Tobacco plantations transported tobacco leaves to city factories to be processed, packaged and shipped out. Tobacco has been cultivated in Virginia since 1700. The "wrapper" is the tobacco leaf used as the exterior sheath of a cigar. With tobacco nicknames already used by league rivals, i.e., the Reidsville Luckies and Danville Leafs, the South Boston newspaper reporters used "Wrappers" as a team moniker.

South McAlester, Oklahoma (Indian Territory 1905–06)

6352 Coal Miners 1905m *Missouri Valley (C)*. Team moved to Fort Smith (AR) August 30. Mines in the region transported coal to processing factories.

6353 Miners 1906 *South Central (D)*. Newspapers shortened the tag from "Coal Miners" to "Miners." With Mr. Smith at the helm as manager, newspapers called the players "Smith's Miners."

Sparta, Georgia

6354 Saints 1948–49 *Georgia State (D)*. Sparta was settled by families from New York who were adherents of the Church of Jesus Christ and the Latter Day Saints, which was founded by Joseph Smith in 1820. The moniker was a play on words, i.e., from pagan Greece to saintly Christianity.

Spartanburg, South Carolina

6355 Spartans 1907 *South Carolina (D)*; 1908–11 *Carolina Assn. (D)*; 1919, 1922–29 *South Atlantic Assn. (C)*. 1919–20, *(B)*. 1921–29; m1931x *Palmetto (D)*. Team began season in Anderson (SC) and then moved here June 29. Team and league disbanded July 23 because of the Great Depression; 1938–40m *South Atlantic (B)*. Team moved to Charleston (SC) July 15; 1946 *Tri-State (B)*. Nickname actually comes not from ancient Sparta, but from the Spartan Regiment of South Carolina militia that fought the British in the Revolutionary War at the Battles of Cowpens and Kings Mountain. The soldiers were so-named because they fought fearlessly and fiercely, like the ancient Spartans. The city, founded in 1785, was actually named after the Spartan Regiment. An inhabitant of Spartanburg is known as a "Spartan."

6356 Red Sox 1912 *Carolina Assn. (D)*. Players wore red stirrups. The team was not a farm team of the Boston Red Sox. The farm system was twenty years in the future.

6357 Pioneers 1920–21 *South Atlantic Assn. (B)*. After the Revolutionary War ended in 1781, the new U.S. government sent pioneer families here where they founded the city in 1785. French pioneers settled in South Carolina as early as 1562.

6358 Peaches 1947–55 *Tri-State (B)*. Farms in the region transport peaches and other fruit to packing houses in the city.

6359 Phillies 1963–79 *Western Carolinas (A)*; 1980, 1986–94 *South Atlantic (A)*. These teams were farm clubs of the Philadelphia Phillies.

6360 Traders 1981–82 *South Atlantic (A)*. The city has been a commercial, industrial and distribution center since 1800. Trading markets buy and sell cotton textiles and food products with numerous peach farms in the area as well as melons, poultry and feed crops.

6361 Spinners 1983 *South Atlantic (A)*. With cotton textiles serving as the state's leading industry since the 1880s, it was at this time in the 1980s that many textile mills closed in South Carolina because of competition from cheaper foreign textile mills.

6362 Suns 1984–85 *South Atlantic (A)*. Team was owned by Louis Eliopoulos. In ancient Greek, the word "helios" (also spelled "elios") means "sun." Mike Odina, the former general manager of the Jacksonville Suns, became the GM for the Spartanburg team. The team these two seasons was not a farm of the Class AA Jacksonville Suns.

6363 Alley Cats 1995x *Atlantic Coast (ind.)*. Team and league disbanded June 30. This independent franchise had a loose affiliation with the Charleston (WV) "Alley Cats." With manager Buzz Capra at the helm, management chose "Alley Cats." Local newspapers called the players "Capra's Alley Cats."

Spindale, Rutherford, North Carolina

6364 Rutherford County Owls 1949–52 *Western Carolina (D)*; 1960 *Western Carolina (D)*. Owls inhabit the trees of the nearby Pisgah National Forest and the peaks and caves of the Blue Ridge Mountains north of the city. With Rutherford County as part of the team's title, newspapers insisted on a short moniker like "Owls." With manager Rube Wilson at the helm 1949–51, newspapers called the players "Wilson's Owls." Cliff Bolton took over in 1952 and the name became "Bolton's Owls." With manager Jim Poole at the helm, newspapers called the players "Poole's Owls."

Spokane, Washington

6365 Spokes 1890–92 *Pacific Northwest (ind.)*. Newspapers used the moniker for headlines, i.e., "Spokes edge Tigers, 7–6."

6366 Bunchgrassers 1892 *Pacific Northwest (ind.)*. With manager

Ollie Beard at the helm in 1892, newspapers called the players "Beard's Bunch-grassers." Cattle, driven along the Oregon Trail in the 1850s, consumed the so-called "bunch grass" that grew on the plains there. "Bunch grass" is a type of prairie grass that grows in clumps and is used as cattle feed.

6367 Falls 1897x *Washington State (ind.)*. Circuit and team disbanded in mid-season (date unknown). Settled in 1871, the city was originally Spokane Falls, after the waterfall at the west terminus of the Spokane River. The name changed to Spokane in 1890. The moniker was used by newspapers in headlines, i.e., "Falls beat Tigers, 5–3."

6368 Blue Sox 1901 *Pacific Northwest (ind. 1901, B 1902)*. Originally **Blue Stockings**, newspapers shortened it to "Blue Sox." In this era, newspapers were transitioning away from "stockings" to "sox."

6369 Smoke-eaters 1902 *Pacific Northwest (B)*. Washington State consists of seven national forests: Colville, Gifford-Pinchot, Kaniksu, Mt. Baker–Snoqualmie, Okanogan, Olympic and Umatilla. When forest fires occur, firefighters and forest rangers known as the "Smoke-eaters" go in to battle the flames.

6370 Indians 1903–04 *Pacific National (A 1903, B 1904)*; m1905–07 *Northwestern (B)*. Team began 1905 season in Victoria (BC) and moved to Spokane July 11; 1918x *Pacific Coast International (B)*. Team disbanded May 26 and the league as well on July 7 because of U.S. entry into World War I; 1920 *Pacific Coast International (B)*; 1940–42 *Western International (B)*; 1946–54x *Western International (B 1946–51, A 1952–54)*. Team disbanded June 21; 1955–56 *Northwest (B)*; 1958–71 *Pacific Coast (AAA)*; 1972 *Northwest (A)*; 1973–82 *Pacific Coast (AAA)*; 1983 to date *Northwest (A)*. With Spokane some 400 miles inland from the Pacific coast, along the eastern border of Washington State, the name "Inlanders" was tried in April 1903. When a newspaper misprint spelled the moniker as "Indians," the new name caught on like wildfire, and by June 1903 the team was the Spokane "Indians." The moniker was appropriate because the coastal Indians, i.e., Lummi, Makah, and Yakima, arrived here across the Bering Straits about 9,000 years ago. With manager Charles McIntyre at the helm, newspapers called the players "McIntyre's Indians." E.E. Quinn took over in 1907 and the name became "Quinn's Indians." The moniker became traditional and has been used by nine Spokane franchises to date.

6371 Hawks 1937–39 *Western International (B)*. The hawk is a small falcon with curved talons that inhabits North America and hunts and nests in the forests and mountains of Washington State. Newspapers wanted a short and energetic moniker for the team.

Springdale, Arkansas

6372 Northwest Arkansas Naturals 2008 to date *Texas (AA)*. Arkansas is known as the "Natural State" because of its hills, rivers, springs, waterfalls and lightning storms, all of which are depicted in the team logo. Arkansas is home to more than 100 waterfalls—a remarkable scene in nature.

Springfield, Illinois

6373 White Stockings 1883 *Northwestern (ind.)*. Players wore white hose. At first **White Stockings**, newspapers shortened it to **White Legs**, **White Sox** and **Whites**. This minor league team was one of the first to form a loose affiliation with a major league team — in this case, the NL Chicago White Stockings. The Springfield team received donated equipment and uniforms, including white hose, from the Chicagoans, hence the team nickname.

6374 Senators 1889 *Central Inter-State (ind.)*; m1895m *Western Assn. (ind.)*. Team started season in Jacksonville (IL) and then moved

here in mid-season (date unknown). Team then moved to Burlington (IA) later in the season (date unknown); 1905–11m *Three-I (B)*. Team moved to Decatur (IL) May 31; 1912 *Three-I (B)*; 1925–32x *Three-I (B)*. Team disbanded July 12 due to the Great Depression; 1933 *Mississippi Valley (B)*; 1935 *Three-I (B)*. City has been the state capital of Illinois since 1837. Baseball teams playing in state capitals sometimes were called Senators, Capitals, Nationals and Solons.

6375 Capitals 1889 *Central Inter-State (ind.)*; m1895m *Western Assn. (ind.)*. Team started season in Jacksonville (IL) and moved here in mid-season (date unknown). Team then moved to Burlington (IA) later in the season (date unknown); 1996–2001 *Frontier (ind.)*. Tag was an alternate to Senators. *Frontier (ind.)*. The 1996 team revived this moniker, which had last been used here 101 years earlier.

6376 Reds 1900m *Central (ind.)*. Team moved to Jacksonville (IL) May 21. Players wore red hose. Originally **Red Stockings**, newspapers shortened it to "Reds."

6377 Foot-trackers m1903 *Three-I (B)*. Team started 1903 season in Joliet and moved to Springfield June 12. Before the city was founded in 1818, explorers roamed about the Sangamon River to map out the territory. These explorers were called "foot-trackers" and "trackers." With manager Frank Belt at the helm, newspapers called the players "Frank Belt's Foot-trackers."

6378 Hustlers 1904 *Three-I (B)*. The 1904 team finished first with a 74–48 record, prompting newspapers to praise the players for "hustling their way to the pennant." With manager Frank Donnelly at the helm in 1904, newspapers called the players "Frank Donnelly's Hustlers."

6379 Watchmakers 1913–14 *Three-I (B)*. City was home to the Waltham Watch Company. Under manager Howard Wakefield in 1914, the team was called "Wakefield's Watchmakers."

6380 Red Birds 1934 *Central (B)*; 1978–81 *American Assn. (AAA)*. These teams were farm clubs of the St. Louis Cardinals. In this era, some St. Louis Cardinal farm teams opted for "Redbirds" instead of "Cardinals" to distinguish their team from the parent club. Since "Redbirds" has been the unofficial alternate to "Cardinals" for the National League team since 1900, the moniker was appropriate.

6381 Browns 1938–42 *Three-I (B)*; 1946–49 *Three-I (B)*. These teams were farm clubs of the St. Louis Browns.

6382 Sallies 1948 *All-American Girls Professional Baseball League (ind.)*. In this era "Sally" was a semi-complimentary — but not derogatory — slang for a girl, i.e., "That 'sally' in the polka-dot dress sure is pretty!" In Australia, the corresponding term is "Sheila."

6383 Giants 1950 *Mississippi–Ohio Valley (D)*. Management wanted a solid, traditional moniker like "Giants." Team was not a farm club of the NL New York Giants.

6384 Cardinals 1982–93 *Midwest (A)*. Team was a farm club of the St. Louis Cardinals. The young team of players were often called the **Baby Birds**.

6385 Sultans 1994–95 *Midwest (A)*. New owners of the team, unable to get a consensus on the team nickname, looked for a name in the dictionary and chose "Sultans."

Springfield, Hampden, Massachusetts

6386 Blues 1877 *New England Assn. (M)*. Players wore blue hose. Originally **Blue Stockings**, local newspapers shortened it to "Blues."

6387 Pros 1878 *International Assn. (M)*; 1879 *National Assn. (M)*. In the era 1869–1880, the notion of professional, semi-professional and amateur, especially for a sport like baseball, continued to be vague in the minds of the sporting public. Thus, newspapers often emphasized that a baseball team was a group of professionals to distinguish it from the other baseball nines in town that were semi-professional or amateur. The tag was first used in the *New York Clipper* May 22, 1878. Newspapers also referred to the team as the **Professionals** and the **Springfield Professionals.**

6388 Capitals 1879 *National Assn. (M).* Springfield is the state capital of Massachusetts.

6389 Green Stockings 1879 *National Assn. (M).* Players wore green hose. Originally "Green Stockings," newspapers shortened it to **Green Legs.**

6390 Springfield Base Ball Club 1884 *Massachusetts State Assn. (ind.)*; 1885 *Southern New England (ind.).* These teams had no nickname.

6391 Hatters 1887 Eastern *(ind.).* Springfield was noted for its hat manufacturing, going back to colonial times, and was known as the "Hat City" as early as 1750.

6392 Ponies 1893–94 *Eastern (ind.)*; 1902–12 *Connecticut (D 1902–03, B 1904–12)*; 1913–14 *Eastern Assn. (B)*; 1916–19, 1922–31 *Eastern (B 1916–18, A 1919–31)*; 1934 *Northeastern (B).* While newspapers in Chicago were calling those 1893–94 players manager "Cap Anson's Colts," the local newspapers here called the 1893–94 Springfield team "Tom Burns' Ponies. The spin-off is understandable because Burns and Anson had been teammates for twelve years on the old Chicago White Stockings. For that reason, the 1893–94 teams had a loose affiliation this season with the Chicago Colts. The term "farm club" was unknown in the nineteenth century; the term "pony team" used instead. Springfield was also an expansion franchise in the Eastern League, which in this era also was known as a "pony team." The name "Ponies" was so popular that Springfield teams were known by this moniker until 1934.

6393 Maroons 1895 *Eastern (ind.).* Players wore maroon hose.

6394 Tips 1915 *Colonial (ind.).* Team was a farm club of the Brooklyn Tip-Tops of the Federal League. The Federal League, a third major league 1914–15, had several franchises that maintained farm teams.

6395 Green Sox 1917 *Eastern (B).* Players wore green stirrups. Players wore green-trim uniforms in honor of the 1879 Springfield Green Stockings but the color was a spin-off of the red stirrups of the Boston Red Sox, with whom the Springfield club had a loose affiliation.

6396 Hampdens 1920–22 *Eastern (A).* Springfield is located in Hamden County.

6397 Rifles 1932x *Eastern (A).* Circuit and team disbanded July 17 due to the Great Depression; 1942–43 *Eastern (A).* Developed in this city in 1855, the "Springfield Rifle" was a bolt-operated magazine-fed .30 caliber rifle favored by U.S. Army soldiers during World War I. During the Civil War, thousands of Springfield Rifles were manufactured here for the Union Army. With Bill Meyer at the helm in 1932, leading the team to first place, newspapers called the players "Meyer's Rifles." The 1932 team had a loose affiliation with the New York Yankees and were sometimes known as "Rupert's Rifles." The moniker was used again for the 1942–43 teams.

6398 Nationals 1939–41 *Eastern (A).* Team was a formal farm club of the Washington AL club in 1939, and then maintained a loose affiliation with the Washingtonians 1940–41. With manager Spencer Abbott at the helm, newspapers called the players "Spencer Abbott's Nationals." Rabbit Maranville took over in 1941 and the name became "Rabbit Maranville's Nationals."

6399 Cubs 1948–49 *New England (B)*; 1950–53 *International (AAA).* These teams were farm clubs of the Chicago Cubs.

6400 Giants 1957–65 *Eastern (A 1957–62, AA 1963–65).* Although the parent club New York Giants moved to San Francisco in 1958, they maintained a farm team here through the 1965 season.

Springfield, Missouri

6401 Indians 1887 *Southwestern (ind.).* The ancient Woodland peoples of Missouri were replaced by the Sauk, Fox, Illiniwek, Osage, Missouri, Iowa and Kansas tribes by the 1600s.

6402 Reds 1902 *Missouri Valley (D).* Players wore red hose. The team was not a farm club of the Cincinnati Reds.

6403 Midgets 1903–04 *Missouri Valley (D).* 1903, C 1904); 1906–09 *Western Assn. (C)*; 1921–30 *Western Assn. (C).* Team in 1903 was led by owner-manager Frank "Shorty" Hurlburt. Although standing at 5'5"— not that short of a height, especially in an era when a 6' man was considered to be a behemoth — reporters gleefully called the players "Shorty's Midgets." Hurlburt relinquished the managerial reins in 1904, but continued to own the franchise. Moniker was used again 1906–08 under other managers until Hurlburt took over as field skipper again in 1909. With manager "Runt" Marr at the helm in 1923, reporters returned to the use of the moniker, calling the players "Runt's Midgets" and "Marr's Midgets." Mark Purtell took over in 1925 and the name became "Mark's Midgets." Purtell led the team to the 1926 WA championship and fans endearingly called them "Midgets who play like giants." Joe Mathes took over in 1929 and the name became "Mathes' Midgets." Norman "Kid" Elberfeld took over in 1930 and the name became "Kid's Midgets."

6404 Highlanders 1905 *Western Assn. (C).* With owner-manager Frank Hurlburt again at the helm, reporters started calling the players "Hurlburt's Highlanders." After a while newspaper editors hated it. The city is built on rolling hills, 1,300 feet above sea level. The team was not a farm club of the AL New York Highlanders.

6405 Jobbers 1911x *Western Assn. (D).* Team disbanded May 10. "Jobber" is midwest slang for a merchant, especially a retail merchant. The city had numerous merchants buying and selling poultry, livestock and dairy products. With manager Lawrence Milton at the helm, local newspapers called the players "Lawrence Milton's Jobbers."

6406 Orioles 1920 *Western Assn. (D).* Similar to the Atlantic Coast Baltimore Oriole, the Midwestern oriole, which is found in Missouri, is known as the "golden robin." With manager Steve O'Rourke at the helm, newspapers called the players "O'Rourke's Orioles." The players wore yellow and black "oriole" stirrups. The team was not a farm team of the IL Baltimore Orioles.

6407 Merchants 1920 *Western Assn. (D).* The city by this time had a large market street for the purchase, sale and shipping of poultry, livestock, dairy products and grain.

6408 Red Wings 1931 *Western Assn. (C)*; 1934 *Western Assn. (C).* GM Branch Rickey's St. Louis Cardinals were establishing the farm system. The team had a loose affiliation with the NL St. Louis Cardinals and was a farm club of the Class AA International League Rochester Red Wings. The 1934 team also was a farm club of the Rochester Red Wings.

6409 Cardinals 1932 *Western Assn. (D)*; 1933 *Western (A)*; 1935–42 *Western Assn. (C)*; 2005 to date *Texas (AA).* During the Great Depression minor league teams would accept donated uniforms from their major league parent clubs. In this case the uniforms had Cardinals on the jersey, so the old name of Red Wings didn't match up. Moreover, with the Class AA Rochester Red Wings named since 1928, it was decided to go back to the parent club's Cardinals moniker. The team, playing 2005 to date, is a farm club of the St. Louis Cardinals.

6410 Cubs m1948 *Western Assn. (C).* Team began season in Hutchinson (KS) and moved to Springfield July 27; 1950 *Western Assn. (C).* These teams were farm clubs of the Chicago Cubs.

Springfield, Ohio

6411 Springfield Base Ball Club 1884 *Ohio State Assn. (ind.)*; 1885 *Inter-State (ind.)*; 1889–90x *Tri-State (ind.)*. Team disbanded July 10. These teams had no nickname.

6412 Governors 1897–98 *Inter-State (ind.)*. Springfield native and future president William Henry Harrison was Ohio's territorial governor in 1800.

6413 Wanderers m1899 *Inter-State (ind.)*. Team began season in Grand Rapids (MI) and moved to Columbus (OH) July 20. Attendance in both these cities was rock-bottom and the franchise was forced to "wander" yet again to Springfield, Ohio, July 30. Teams forced onto extended road trips and eventually transferring in mid-season to another city because of low attendance in the home city ballpark were called Exiles, Orphans or Wanderers. With manager Fred Torreyson at the helm in all three cities, Springfield newspapers called the players "Fred Torreyson's Wanderers."

6414 Babes 1905–07 *Central (B)*. Manager Jack Hendricks led a team of very young players, whom newspapers called "Jack Hendricks' Babes."

6415 Reapers 1908m *Ohio State (D)*. Team moved to Portsmouth (OH) June 16; 1911 *Ohio State (D)*; 1912–14x *Central (B)*. Team disbanded August 8; 1916–17 *Central (C)*. The reaper is a machine that cuts standing grain. Virginia inventor Cyrus McCormick invented the reaper in 1831. Large grain farms are located here that use reapers for corn, wheat and oats. With manager Ed Ransick at the helm, newspapers called the players "Ransick's Reapers." En route to a 1911 pennant-winning 84–55 record, manager Charles O'Day's players "cut down opponents like a reaper cutting wheat."

6416 Buckeyes 1928 *Central (B)*. Ohio is the Buckeye State. The name caused confusion with the Ohio State Buckeyes collegiate teams and was dropped by newspapers after this one year.

6417 Dunnmen 1929 *Central (B)*. Team was named after manager Jack Dunn.

6418 Blue Sox 1930 *Central (B)*. Team had a loose affiliation with the red-trimmed NL Cincinnati Reds. The Springfield players wore blue stirrups, which was a spin-off of the red stirrups worn by the Cincinnati Nationals.

6419 Chicks 1933 *Middle Atlantic (C)*. Team had many young players known in the slang of the era as "chicks." With manager Jake Pitler at the helm, newspapers called the players "Jake Pitler's Chicks."

6420 Pirates 1934 *Middle Atlantic (C)*. Team was a farm club of the Pittsburgh Pirates.

6421 Indians 1937–39 *Middle Atlantic (C)*. Team was a farm club of the Cleveland Indians.

6422 Cardinals 1941–42 *Middle Atlantic (C)*. Team was a farm club of the St. Louis Cardinals.

6423 Giants 1948–51 *Ohio–Indiana (D)*. Team was a farm club of the New York Giants.

Springfield, Tennessee

6424 Blanket-makers 1923m *Kentucky–Illinois–Tennessee (KITTY). (D)*. Team moved to Milan (TN) July 19. Textile factories in the city manufacture cushions, sheets and blankets. With manager Frank Stapleton at the helm, newspapers called the players "Frank Stapleton's Blanket-makers."

Springfield-Charleston, Vermont

6425 Hyphens 1911 *Twin States (D)*. "Hyphens" was a newspaper slang that was used at times instead of Twins. The gimmick faded by 1920 because most fans thought it was silly.

Springfield-Ozark, Missouri

6426 Mountain Ducks 2000–01 *Texas–Louisiana (ind.)*; 2002–04 *Central (ind.)*. Mountain ducks are flat-bill ducks that inhabit nearby Stockton Lake and the Ozark Mountains. The team switched leagues in 2002.

Stamford, Connecticut

6427 Stamford Base Ball Club m1888 *Connecticut State (ind.)*. Team began season in Bridgeport (CT) and moved to Stamford in mid-season (date unknown). Team had no nickname.

6428 Bombers 1947 *Colonial (B)*. Under the leadership of player-manager Zeke Bonura, who as a player bashed 119 homers while batting .307 in only seven big-league seasons for an average of 17 homers per year, newspapers called the players "Bonura's Bombers." Stamford, England, during World War II was a training site for RAF bomber pilots. The city is the home of the Stewart National Guard Air Force Base. Bombers such as the B-29, B-36 and B-47 flew in and out this base in the era 1946–56.

6429 Pioneers 1948–49x *Colonial (B)*. City was settled in 1641 by Puritan families from England. Zeke Bonura returned and guided "Bonura's Pioneers." The name was retained in 1949 under Joe Glenn, i.e., "Joe Glenn's Pioneers," and Herb Stein, i.e., "Herb Stein's Pioneers."

Stamford, Texas

6430 Colonels 1922 *West Texas (D)*. Edward House, born in Stamford, was an army colonel during the Indian Wars and the Spanish-American War who then served as an advisor in the Woodrow Wilson administration. With manager Poston Baker at the helm, newspapers called the players the "Poston's Colonels."

State College, Pennsylvania

6431 Spikes 2006 to date *New York–Pennsylvania (A)*. Occasionally a team nickname will refer to baseball equipment, i.e., Gloversville "Glovers," Louisville "Bats," Boston "Red Caps" and State College "Spikes." Team's logo, a leaping stag baring its antlers, is an oblique reference to the team nickname.

Statesboro, Georgia

6432 Pilots 1952–55x *Georgia State (D)*. Team disbanded July 1. City factories construct pilot boats that guide shipping on the nearby Savannah, Ogeechee and Canochee rivers.

Statesville, North Carolina

6433 Owls 1939–40 *Tar Heel (D)*; 1942 *North Carolina (D)*; 1947–52 *North Carolina (D)*; 1960–63 *Western Carolinas (D 1960–62, A 1963)*. Predatory night owls inhabit the Pisgah, Uwharrie and Croatan National Forests in North Carolina. Manager Stuffy McCrone in 1939 led "McCrone's Owls." Manager Jim Poole in 1942 led "Poole's Owls."

6434 Cubs 1945–46 *North Carolina (D)*. Team was a farm club of the Chicago Cubs.

6435 Blues 1953x *Tar Heel (D)*. Team disbanded July 11. Players wore blue-trim uniforms.

6436 Sports m1953 *Tar Heel (D)*. Team started season in Lincolnton (NC) and moved to Statesville July 12. Team was a farm club of the Shreveport Sports. The Class AA Shreveport Sports, barred from signing black players due to city segregation laws, were forced to stock their own farm clubs during the 1950s.

6437 Colts 1964 *Western Carolinas (A)*. Team was a farm club of the Houston Colt .45's.

6438 Tigers 1966–67 *Western Carolinas (A)*. Team was a farm club of the Detroit Tigers.

6439 Indians 1969m *Western Carolinas (A)*. Team moved to Monroe (NC) June 20. Team was a farm club of the Cleveland Indians.

Staunton, Illinois

6440 Infants m1908 *Eastern Illinois (D)*. Team began season in Danville (IL) and moved to Staunton July 17. With manager W.C. Dithridge at the helm guiding a young team to the pennant, newspapers called the players "Dithridge's Infants."

Staunton, Virginia

6441 Valleyites 1894 *Virginia (ind.)*. Staunton is located in the Shenandoah Valley, east of the Appalachian Mountains and west of the George Washington National Forest. Staunton is the "Queen City of the Shenandoah Valley."

6442 Hayseeds 1894 *Virginia (ind.)*. Literally referring to the seed shaken out of hay, the moniker was a slang at first used as an insult, i.e., an unsophisticated yokel or hick, and then affectionately as an affable rural person or a likeable fellow from farm country. Numerous such terms sprung up in this era, i.e., Hillbilly, Yokel, Hick, Farm Boy, Country Bumpkin and Country Boy.

6443 Presidents 1939–42 *Virginia (D)*. Staunton is the birthplace of the 28th president of the United States, Woodrow Wilson, who was born here in 1856. Staunton is known as the "Birthplace of Woodrow Wilson."

Sterling, Illinois

6444 Rag-chewers 1890m *Illinois–Iowa (ind.)*. Team moved to Galesburg (IL) in mid-season (date unknown). "Rag-chewer" is an old slang referring to someone "mad enough to chew a rag." The meaning evolved to denote an argumentative person. Baseball players in this era were much more brutal than today in their argumentative ways, which included kicking and punching umpires.

6445 Infants m1910 *Northern Assn. (D)*. Team began season in Joliet (IL) and moved to Sterling (IL) June 21. Team and league disbanded July 19. With manager Hunky Hines at the helm, newspapers called the players "Hines' Infants."

Steubenville, Ohio

6446 Stubs 1887 *Ohio State (ind.)*; 1895m *Western Inter-State (ind.)*. Team moved to Akron (OH) June 1; 1906–07 *Pennsylvania–Ohio–Michigan (P.O.M.) (D)*; 1909 *Ohio–Pennsylvania (C)*; 1911x *Ohio–Pennsylvania (C)*. Team disbanded August 20; 1913x *Inter-State (B)*. Team and league disbanded July 21. Moniker was used in newspaper headlines, i.e., "Stubs edge Suds, 4–3." With manager John Smith at the helm in 1906, newspapers called the players "Smith's Stubs." Percy Stetler took over in 1907 and guided the team to the pennant as newspapers called the players "Stetler's Stubs."

6447 Factory Men 1905 *Ohio–Pennsylvania (D)*. City has had factories to convert iron ore into steel and ferrous alloys. City also has factories for the production of chemicals.

Steubenville-Follansbee, Ohio

6448 Stubs 1912 *Ohio–Pennsylvania (D)*. Team disbanded September 5 just before the Stubs were to compete in the league playoffs.

The team represented both Steubenville and Follansbee. Home games were played in Steubenville. The moniker was used for newspaper headlines, i.e., "Stubs edge Nocks, 4–3."

Stillwater, Minnesota

6449 Stillwater Base Ball Club 1884 *Northwestern (ind.)*. Team had no nickname.

Stockton, California

6450 Colts 1888 *California (ind.)*. Manager J.P. Carroll managed "Carroll's Colts."

6451 River Pirates 1893m *California (ind.)*. Stockton is California's major inland seaport. It is located at the junction of the San Joaquin and Calaveras rivers, which merge into the Stockton Channel. Pirates, buccaneers, corsairs, privateers and "Sea Hawks" sailed the coast of California for three centuries, 1550–1850.

6452 Dukes 1893m *California (ind.)*. Team moved to Sacramento (CA) July 2. Long before the city was founded in 1847, the Spanish Dukes of New Spain governed California for 300 years.

6453 Stockton Base Ball Club 1896–97m *California (ind.)*. Nameless team moved to Sacramento (CA) on July 5, 1897.

6454 Millers 1898 *Pacific Coast (ind.)*; 1907–08 *California (ind.)*; 1910 *California State (ind.)* 1914–15 *California State (D)*. In this era, city was a milling center for oats, corn and wheat from nearby farms. With manager Cy Moreing at the helm, newspapers called the players "Moreing's Millers." With manager Jimmy McCall at the helm, newspapers called the players "McCall's Millers."

6455 Terrors 1898 *California (ind.)*. In the hopes of energizing fan interest (and subsequent newspaper sales) about a team that would "terrorize the opposition," local reporters at season's start called the players the Stockton "Terrors." The team terrorized none of their opponents as they finished in sixth place with a most non-threatening 17–23 record.

6456 Wasps 1900 *California (ind.)*. With manager George Harper at the helm, newspapers called the players "Harper's Wasps." The sand wasp is an insect found along the sandy beaches of California. A satirical political magazine entitled *The Wasp* was popular in this era among California readers.

6457 Tigers 1909 *California (ind.)*. With the success of the AL Detroit Tigers, management dressed the players in striped hose, which led newspapers to call the players the Tigers.

6458 Producers 1913 *California State (D)*. Nearby farms send fruits and vegetables to city packing factories. The city was the produce center of the San Joaquin Valley. Led by manager Jack Thomas, the team won the 1912 league championship with a productive 79–44 record, good for a six-game margin by "out-producing their opponents."

6459 Fliers 1941 *California (C)*. Stockton Air Field was completed December 5, 1941, where 2,000 pilots were trained by December 1942. City is also the site of the Sharpe Army Depot.

6460 Ports 1946–72 *California (C)*; 1979–99, 2002 to date. City is an inland deepwater port that is surrounded by 1,000 miles of waterways.

6461 Mariners 1978 *California (C)*. Team was a farm club of the Seattle Mariners.

6462 Mudville Nine 2000–01 *California (C)*. Writer Ernest Lawrence Thayer saw a baseball game here in 1888 and promptly penned the now-famous poem "Casey at the Bat." Casey's hometown team was the "Mudville Nine." The nineteenth-century city was nicknamed "Mudville" because of the muddy shores of its lengthy waterways. Alas, "Mighty Mudville struck out" in 2000, finishing with a losing record and then losing a 2001 semifinal playoff, 2 games to 1, to Bakersfield. Some historians denied Stockton was the setting for mythical Casey, so management went back to "Ports" for the 2002 season.

Stratford, Ontario, Canada

6463 Poets 1899m *Canadian (ind.)*. Team moved to Woodstock (ONT) June 8. The famed poet and theatrical writer William Shakespeare was born in Stratford, England.

Streator, Illinois

6464 Speed Boys 1912, 1914 *Illinois–Missouri (D)*. In the era 1900–10, as the automobile changed American ways, "Speed Boys" was slang for a winning baseball team, usually a pennant winner. Local reporters used the moniker for the team, i.e., the Streator "Speed Boys," in anticipation of a successful campaign, but the team skidded to 46–65 sixth-place finish.

6465 Boosters 1913–14 *Illinois–Missouri (D)*; 1915 *Bi-State (D)*. The Bi-State League represented Illinois and Wisconsin. Undaunted Streator fans switched from "Speed Boys" to "Boosters"—yet another moniker describing a first-place team. Alas, the team failed to win a pennant these two seasons, playing under a .500 pace in each campaign. Manager Bob Coyle at the helm in 1913 guided "Bob's Boosters." The name was retained in 1914 under two other managers. The Streator players under manager Jack Herbert finally justified their fans' enthusiasm in them by going 38–15 to finish first in the six-team league. Local newspapers called the players "Herbert's Boosters."

Strong City–Cottonwood Falls, Kansas

6466 Twin Citys 1909m *Kansas State (D)*. Team moved to Larned (KS) July 12. Occasionally, a baseball team that represented two cities was known as the "Twins."

Stroudsburg, Pennsylvania

6467 Poconos 1932x *Interstate (D)*. Team and league disbanded June 20 because of the Great Depression; 1946–50 *North Atlantic (D)*. Originally the site of Fort Penn in 1776, the city was built near the Pocono Foothills near the Blue Mountains.

Suffolk, Virginia

6468 Suffolk Base Ball Club 1897 *Southeast Virginia (ind.)*. Team had no nickname.

6469 Tigers 1915 *Virginia (C)*; 1918 *Independent Negro*. Because of striped yellow and black stockings of the Princeton University college football and Detroit Tigers baseball teams, "Tigers" became a favorite moniker for sports teams in the era 1890–1920. The Suffolk players on both teams wore striped stirrups. In the years 1905–08, stirrup hose arrived. Most of these stirrups were striped, which forced teams to choose "Tigers" for some other reason.

6470 Nuts 1919–20 *Virginia (C 1919, B 1920)*. The city has been home to the Planters' Peanut Company since 1912. Suffolk is nicknamed the "World's Largest Peanut Market." The moniker was used to challenge a league rival—the Petersburg Goobers.

6471 Sunbeams 1921 *Independent Negro team*. Suffolk is ringed by farm country that enjoys sunny summer weather.

6472 Wildcats 1921 *Virginia (B)*. Tag was a spin-off from Tigers. Players continued to wear striped stirrups, but this style no longer

automatically led to "Tigers" as a nickname. Moreover, with the glory days of 1907–11 gone, the 1920 Detroit Tigers struggled to a 60–93 record and a seventh-place finish. This decline prompted Suffolk to go to a spin-off name.

6473 Aces 1935–38 *Independent Negro team*. Team owner Johnny Robinson wanted an energetic, newspaper friendly moniker and chose "Aces."

6474 Goobers 1948–51 *Virginia (D)*. Moniker is a spin-off from "Nuts." The terms "goober" and "goober Pea" is a Southern slang for peanut.

Sulphur Springs, Texas

6475 Lions 1923 *East Texas (D)*. Mountain lions inhabit Texas. The league rival Mount Pleasant "Cats" influenced the selection of Lions. With manager Roy Eichord at the helm, newspapers called the players "Eichord's Lions."

6476 Saints 1924 *East Texas (D)*. After the Mexican-American War, Lutheran immigrants, Germans and Swedes settled in Texas. The city also has Roman Catholic churches from its Spanish era. With manager Johnny Meanor at the helm, newspapers called the players "Meanor's Saints."

6477 Spartans 1925x *East Texas (D)*. Team disbanded June 7. When Tyler newspaper reporters called their Tyler team the "Trojans," their counterparts in Sulphur Springs, looking for an equivalent moniker, started calling their team the "Spartans." The city was founded in 1855 because of its sulphur springs mineral waters just south of the city. Mineral water bath resorts were built and the resulting tourist industry helped the city develop. The moniker was appropriate because the ancient Greek city of Thermopoli also had hot sulphur springs, which attracted tourists 2,500 years ago. Thermopoli is only a short distance from the site of the ancient Greek city of Sparta. Thermopoli is the ancient Greek word for "hot springs." With manager Abe Bowman at the helm, newspapers called the players "Bowman's Spartans."

Sumter, South Carolina

6478 Gamecocks 1907–08 *South Carolina (D)*. With manager Guy Gunter at the helm in 1907, newspapers called the players "Guy Gunter's Gamecocks." Frank Dingle took over in 1908 and the name became "Frank's Gamecocks." Since 1680 fighting roosters—known as "gamecocks"—have been used in betting matches. Rooster fighting was a popular betting sport in the colonial Carolinas and in the nineteenth-century South.

6479 Chicks 1949–50 *Tri-State (B)*. Nearby farms send poultry, soybeans and cotton to city factories for processing. Farm teams at this level in this era almost always consisted of very young players, i.e., "Chicks."

6480 Indians 1970 *Western Carolinas (A)*. Team was a farm club of the Cleveland Indians.

6481 Astros 1971 *Western Carolinas (A)*. Team was a farm club of the Houston Astros.

6482 Flyers 1985–91 *South Atlantic (A)*. Shawn Air Force Base is located north of the city. Gull-like birds, known as "Royal Terns," are found on nearby Bull's Island. Swan Lake is located just west of the city.

Sun City, Arizona

6483 Rays 1989–90–90–91x *Senior Professional (W)*. The sun's rays in Sun City make for warm winters and baking summers. The tag was not related to the Tampa Bay Devil Rays.

6484 Solar Sox 1992–96 *Arizona Fall (W)*. Players wore solar yellow sanitary hose in the style of the Oakland Athletics. Most baseball teams wear white sanitary hose.

Sunbury, Pennsylvania

6485 Sunbury Base Ball Club 1887 *Central Pennsylvania (ind.)*. Team had no nickname.

6486 Senators 1939 *Inter-State (C)*. With manager Bill Kersetter at the helm in 1939, newspapers called the players "Kersetter's Senators." Team was not a farm club of the AL Washington Senators.

6487 Indians 1940 *Inter-State (B)*. City had its origins as Fort Augusta (built 1756) during the French & Indian War. The Shamokin and Nanticoke Indians inhabited this region in pre–Columbian times. With manager Dutch Dorman at the helm in 1940, newspapers called the players "Dorman's Indians." The team was not a farm club of the Cleveland Indians.

6488 Yankees 1946–47 *Inter-State (B)*. Team was a farm club of the New York Yankees.

6489 Reds 1948–49 *Inter-State (B)*. Team was a farm club of the Cincinnati Reds.

6490 Athletics 1948–49 *Inter-State (B)*. Team was a farm club of the Philadelphia Athletics.

6491 Giants 1951–52 *Inter-State (B)*. Team was a farm club of the New York Giants.

6492 Redlegs 1955 *Piedmont (B)*. Team was a farm club of the Cincinnati Redlegs.

Superior, Nebraska

6493 Brickmakers 1910–13 *Nebraska State (D)*. In this era, the city was noted for its brick manufacture because of the abundance of Portland and masonry cement, crushed stone, construction sand and gravel here. With manager Dennis Bockewitz at the helm 1910–13, newspapers called the players "Bockewitz' Brickmakers." F.H. Bigby took over in 1914 and the name became "Bigby's Brickmakers."

6494 Senators 1956–58 *Nebraska State (D)*. Team was a farm club of the Washington Senators.

Superior, Wisconsin

6495 Longshoremen 1903–04x *Northern (D)*. Team disbanded August 8; m1905 *Northern (D)*. Team began season in St. Cloud–Brainerd (MN) and moved to Superior June 25. Men who work on the wharf of a port unloading and loading cargo onto and from boats are known as "longshoremen." The city is a port of Lake Superior. Superior has been a lake port for all sorts of cargo, i.e., grain, iron ore, copper ore, manufactured goods, lumber, flour and oil since 1883. With manager John Lagger at the helm in 1903, newspapers called the players "Lagger's Longshoremen." Don Cameron took over in 1904 and the name became "Cameron's Longshoremen."

6496 Red Sox 1910–11 *Minnesota–Wisconsin (C)*; 1912 *Central International (C)*; 1913–15x *Northern (C)*. Team disbanded July 5. Players wore red stirrups. The hose color of the 1912 team was in response to the rival Duluth White Sox. These teams were not farm clubs of the AL Boston Red Sox.

6497 Blues 1933–42 Northern *(D 1933–40, C 1941–42)*; 1946–55 *Northern (C)*. Team had a loose affiliation with the blue-trim Brooklyn Dodgers 1933–36. The team became a farm club of the St. Louis Browns in 1937 but retained its blue-trim uniforms and nickname. In 1938 the team resumed a loose affiliation with the Dodgers until it became an official farm club of Brooklyn 1939–41. In 1942 the team, retaining its blue-trim and nickname, became a farm club of the nearby AL Chicago White Sox. The team, starting in 1946 and wearing the blue-trim style of its parent club, was an official farm club of the Brooklyn Dodgers.

Surprise, Arizona

6498 Royals 2003 to date *Arizona (R)*. Team was a farm club of the Kansas City Royals.

6499 Royals-2 2003 *Arizona (R)*. Team was a farm club of the Kansas City Royals.

6500 Rangers 2003 to date *Arizona (R)*. Team was a farm club of the Texas Rangers.

6501 Fightin' Falcons 2005 *Golden (ind.)*. Sports team nicknames since the 1990s are sometimes stylized like the Fightin' Phillies, Fighting Irish, Amazin' Mets, Angry A's, Running Redbirds, and Nasty Nationals. North American falcons are found in mountains, forests, prairies, and even deserts. The adjective "fighting," often shortened to "fightin'," originated as a title in military units.

Surrey, British Columbia, Canada

6502 Glaciers 1995 *Western (ind.)*. Although glaciers reached this region 10,000 years ago, the only glaciers in Canada today are located on the Northern Queen Elizabeth Islands. Surrey is a suburb of Vancouver (BC).

Sussex, New Brunswick, Canada

6503 Skyhawks 2008 *Canadian–American (ind.)*. Hawk nicknames for sports teams often use prefix-embellishments, such as Sparrowhawks, Nighthawks, Fighting Hawks, Predator Hawks and Skyhawks. Moniker is appropriate because hawks inhabit much of Canada, including the rivers, national parks and mountains of New Brunswick.

Suwon, Kyonggi, South Korea

6504 Raiders 1991–99 *Korean (ind.)*. Team was owned by the Ssangbang Wool Clothing Company, which chose the English-language nickname of "Raiders." The team's title was the "Ssangbang Wool Raiders."

6505 Wyvern 2000 to date *Korean (ind.)*. Team owner Son Kilseung chose "Wyvern" instead of the overused "Dragons" as a novelty for the team's fans. The "wyvern" is a dragon used in British medieval heraldry. Obviously, the dragon is an ancient symbol in Asia, representing courage, health and good fortune. The team's title of "SK Wyvern" represents the initials of the owner's name, i.e., "Son Kilseung Wyvern."

Sweetwater, Texas

6506 Swatters m1920–22 *West Texas (D)*. Team started 1920 season in Gorman (TX) before moving to Sweetwater August 7; 1949–51 *Longhorn (D)*. "Swatter" is baseball slang for batter or hitter, especially power hitters who "swat" lots of extra-base hits and home runs, i.e., "Babe Ruth swatted the ball over the fence." Incidentally, Babe Ruth had the moniker "Sultan of Swat." With manager Clarence "Pop Boy" Smith at the helm in 1921–22, newspapers called the players "Smith's Swatters" and "Pop Boy's Swatters." A hitter who has "pop" in his bat is able to "swat" the ball.

6507 Sports 1947–48 *Longhorn (D)*. Team was a farm club of the Shreveport Sports. In the era 1947–55, Class AA Shreveport had a half-dozen farm teams of its own — all named "Sports" — because of its segregation laws forbidding Negroes to play ball on its home baseball field. Major league teams, busy signing black players, could not send these black men to Shreveport, forcing independent Shreveport franchise to set up its own farm teams to siphon compensatory white talent up to this Class AA club.

6508 Braves 1952 *Longhorn (D)*. With Texas as a battleground, Apache and Comanche tribes battled Spaniards, Mexicans, Americans and each other in the eighteenth and nineteenth centuries. The team was not a farm club of the Boston Braves.

6509 Spudders m1954 *Longhorn (C)*. Team began season in Wichita Falls (TX) and moved to Sweetwater May 6. When the Wichita Falls "Spudders" moved here in mid-season, the nickname was retained to save the cost of manufacturing new home uniforms.

Sydney, New South Wales, Australia

6510 Metros 1989–90 *Australia (W)*. With a population of nearly 7 million (including suburbs), making it the largest city in the country of Australia, Sydney is a true metropolis.

6511 Waves 1989–90–91–92 *Australian (W)*. Founded in 1788 as a penal colony by the British, the city became the country's leading port because of a natural harbor that spurred commerce and manufacturing. The city has miles and miles of beaches.

6512 Blues 1991–92–96–97 *Australian (W)*. The baseball team adopted the "Blues nickname of the New South Wales Cricket Club. The cricketers didn't seem to mind until abruptly in 1997 they sued the baseball team for copyright infringement. The baseball team owners, rather than get soaked in court, simply switched the team nickname from "Blues" to "Storm."

6513 Hunter Eagles 1994–95–97–98 *Australia (W)*. Eagles are found worldwide and also in Australia. Management decided to call the team the "Hunter Eagles" to emphasize the bird's predatory nature and to distinguish the team from other teams named Eagles.

6514 Storm 1997–98–98–99 *Australian (W)*. Pacific squalls hit here.

6515 Blue Sox 2010 to date *Australia (W)*. Tag was a spin-off from the 1997 team. The New South Wales flag has blue trim. Players wear blue stirrups. The original Australian Baseball League played as a professional circuit from 1989–99 to 1999–2000 and then disbanded.

Sydney, Nova Scotia, Canada

Note: Not to be confused with Sydney Mines, Nova Scotia, Canada.

6516 Steel Citians 1937–38 *Cape Breton Colliery (D 1937–38, C 1939)*. City is known by the nickname of "Steel City." Founded in 1784 because of nearby coal mines, the city built iron and steel factories here in the 1880s. Inhabitants of Sydney are known as the "Steel Citians."

Sydney Mines, Nova Scotia, Canada

Note: Sydney Mines is located 10 miles N of Sydney and is a separate municipality.

6517 Ramblers 1937–39 *Cape Breton Colliery (D 1937–38, C 1939)*. The Workers Educational Association of the city has sponsored bird-watching and hiking clubs since the 1920s. The hikers have become known as "Ramblers."

Syracuse, New York

6518 Stars 1876 *Independent*; 1877 *New York State Assn. (M)*; 1877 *League Alliance (ind.)*; 1878 *International Assn. (M)*; 1879 *National (M)*; 1885 *New York State (ind.)*; 1886–89 *International (ind.)*; 1890 *American Assn. (M)*; 1891–92x *Eastern Assn. (ind.)*. Team disbanded July 22. 1894–1901m *Eastern (ind.)*. Team moved to Brockton (MA) July 25; 1902–17 *New York State (B)*; 1920–27 *International (AA)*; 1928–29 *New York–Pennsylvania (B)*. The 1876 team began play as the "Star Baseball Club" of Syracuse. The moniker "Star" was used quite frequently by baseball teams in the pre-professional era of 1845–70 and was traditional for Syracuse baseball teams for 64 years.

6519 Chiefs 1934–55 *International (AA 1934–45, AAA 1946–55)*; 1961–96, 2007 to date *International (AAA)*. With manager Bill Sweeney at the helm in 1934, newspapers called the players "Sweeney's Chiefs." Fans liked the name so much that management made it official in 1935. The moniker also referred to the Onondoga Indians — a branch of the Iroquois, who inhabited pre–Columbian New York State.

6520 Sky Chiefs 1997–2006 *International (AAA)*. The *Sky Chief* was a scouting airplane about the size of a Cessna or Piper Cub used by the authorities to monitor traffic, track illegal activities from the air, and scout for forest fires, earthquake damage, floods, etc. The moniker was chosen in 1997 because it was felt that Chiefs had become politically incorrect. In 2007 the team went back to Chiefs — but not an Indian name — rather the "Super Chief" railroad locomotive.

Tacoma, Washington

6521 Tigers 1890–92 *Pacific Northwest (ind.)*; 1896 *Pacific Northwest (ind.)*; 1901–02 *Pacific Northwest (ind. 1901, B 1902)*; 1903x *Pacific National (A)*. Team disbanded August 16; 1904–05 *Pacific Coast (A)*; 1906–17 *Northwestern (B)* Regular season shortened to July 15 due to U.S. entry into World War I; 1918x *Pacific Coast International (B)*. Team disbanded May 26; 1919x *Northwest International (B)*. Team and league disbanded June 5. 1920–21 *Pacific Coast International (B)*; 1922 *Western International (B)*; 1937–42 *Western International (B)*; 1946–51 *Western International (B)*; 1980–91 *Pacific Coast (AAA)*. Around 1890 there was a fashion trend, probably inspired by the University of Princeton Tigers football team, for sports team players to wear striped stockings. The trend first went to football teams and quickly jumped to baseball teams. Some teams whose players donned striped stockings were called "Tigers." By 1906 stirrups were introduced, and most of them were striped, ending the association between striped stockings and the nickname of "Tigers." However, "Tigers" was the traditional moniker for Tacoma baseball teams through 1991. In the years 1980–91, the Tacoma Tigers were a farm club of the Detroit Tigers.

6522 Daisies 1891–92 *Pacific Northwest (ind.)*. At the start of the 1891 season the *Tacoma Ledger* bubbled to its readers about the team's chances: "The Tacoma team, from all indications, will be a daisy!" Although the team became known as the "Daisies," the team finished in last place. The "Daisies" improved to second place in 1892. "Daisy" is a slang for a first-rate person or thing, i.e., "That new guy is a daisy!"

6523 Rabbits 1896 *New Pacific (ind.)*. With manager Charlie Strobel at the helm, newspapers called the players "Strobel's Rabbits." The nickname "Rabbits" referred less to a regional animal than it did to players who were speedy on the bases. In this era 1870–1919, speed on the bases was emphasized instead of home runs simply because this was the Dead-ball Era. More and more "lively" balls were introduced in 1909, 1920, and again in 1930 to boost sagging attendance in the professional game.

6524 Robbers 1896 *New Pacific (ind.)*. With manager Charlie Strobel at the helm, newspapers sometimes called the players "Strobel's Robbers." Baseball players in this era were often regarded by the public as uncouth, disreputable hooligans—hence such names as Rustlers, Savages, Pirates, Indians, Gladiators and Robbers.

6525 Colts 1896 *New Pacific (ind.).* Team had many young players, who were known in the slang of the era as "colts." With manager Charlie Strobel at the helm, newspapers called the players "Strobel's Colts."

6526 Cubs 1910x *Washington State (D).* Team disbanded July 18. With many young players on the roster, newspapers called the team the "Cubs," which was slang in this era for young players.

6527 Giants 1960–65 *Pacific Coast (AAA).* Team was a farm club of the San Francisco Giants.

6528 Cubs 1966–71 *Pacific Coast (AAA).* Team was a farm club of the Chicago Cubs.

6529 Twins 1972–77 *Pacific Coast (AAA).* Team was a farm club of the Minnesota Twins.

6530 Yankees 1978 *Pacific Coast (AAA).* Team was a farm club of the New York Yankees.

6531 Tugs 1979 *Pacific Coast (AAA).* Tug boats have been hauling cargo vessels in Puget Sound to city ports since 1900. The city was settled here in the 1860s along the coast of Puget Sound and quickly became a maritime port.

6532 Rainiers 1992 to date *Pacific Coast (AAA).* Team was named after nearby Mount Rainier. The moniker had been used by the old PCL Seattle Rainiers.

Taegu, North Kyun-Sang, South Korea (also spelled Daegu)

6533 Samsung Lions 1982 to date *Korean (ind.).* Franchise is named the "Samsung Lions" after its corporate sponsor, Samsung Electronics. With team owner Lee Kun-hee in charge of the franchise, the team is known as "Lee Kun's Lions." Samsung markets the team in Korean and English.

6534 MBC Blue Dragons 1982–89 *Korean (ind.).* The dragon is a symbol ubiquitous throughout Asia. It symbolizes courage, strength and good fortune. The team was owned by MBC Industries and went by the title, in English, of "MBC Blue Dragons." The players wore blue-trim uniforms and stirrups.

Taejeon, South Chungchong, South Korea (also spelled Daejon)

6535 Eagles 1986 to date *Korean (ind.).* From the league's inception in 1982, the team owners of the Korean Professional Baseball League realized the need to market in English. The original owner, Binggrae, chose the English language title of "Binggrae Eagles" for the 1986–93 seasons. The franchise was then purchased by the Hanwha Finance Company and, with the eagle mascot retained, the team became the "Hanwha Eagles" in 1994 to date. With team owner Kim seung-youn in charge of the franchise, the team is known as "Kim seung's Eagles."

Taft, Texas

6536 Cardinals 1938 *Texas Valley (D).* Team had a loose affiliation with the St. Louis Cardinals.

Taichung, West Central, Taiwan

6537 Jungo Bears 1993–95 *Chinese Professional (ind.).* Bears inhabit much of Asia, including China's famous Panda bears. Jungo-Chen Yiping Construction Company, owner of the team 1990–94, chose the nickname, and the team went by the title of "Jungo Bears." Circuit is officially the Chinese Professional Baseball League.

6538 Bulls 1996 to date *Chinese Professional (ind.).* Sinon Agrochemical Corporation bought the team in 1996 and changed the team's name to the "Sinon Bulls." Players wore red-trim uniforms, and the "Bulls" moniker referred to cattle farms found near the city.

6539 Robomen 1997–2002 *Taiwan Major (ind.).* The moniker was a spin-off from a popular TV cartoon called *Robo-Boy.* Robomen in Latin alphabet Chinese is "Agan." The team owner was First Securities Bank of China and the team's title was the "First Securities Robomen." The Taiwan Major League disbanded after the 1992 season.

Tainan, Southwest, Taiwan

6540 Lions 1990 to date *Chinese Professional (ind.).* The league's official name is the Chinese Professional Baseball League. Team owner Uni-President Bank chose "Lions" because it is a traditional symbol in Asia, much like tigers, elephants and dragons. The soft drink company 7-Up Beverages of Taiwan bought part ownership of the franchise in 2009. The nickname was retained. The players wear lion-tan trimmed uniforms.

Taipei, Taipei Province, Taiwan

6541 Elephants 1990 to date *Chinese Professional (ind.).* League's official name is the Chinese Professional Baseball League. Brother Hotels, the team's owner, chose in English the nickname of "Elephants." Elephants inhabit Asia and are a historic symbol there. The team's title is "Brother Hotels Elephants."

6542 Tigers 1990–99 *Chinese Professional (ind.).* Mercury Enterprises, the owner of a chain of restaurants and gift shops, owned the team and chose the English nickname of "Tigers." The famous Asian tiger is found throughout the continent. The revolutionaries of the notorious Boxer's Rebellion of 1899–1900 against European colonial powers were known as the "Tigers of Heaven." The American air squadron that helped fight the Japanese in 1940–41, before U.S. entry into the war, were known as the "Flying Tigers." The team was known as the plural "Mercuries Tigers."

6543 Taipei County Dragons 1990–99 *Chinese Professional (ind.).* Team, playing in a ballpark in Hsinjuang in suburban Taipei, represented Taipei County. Weichuan Foods owned the team and chose the English nickname of "Dragons." The title of the team was the "Weichuan Dragons." The dragon is a famous and ancient symbol in Asian countries.

6544 Eagles 1993–97 *Chinese Professional (ind.).* Settled by the mainland Chinese for a thousand years since the 7th century, the Chinese symbols of dragon, tiger and eagle were widely used in Taiwanese culture. The China Times Newspaper Company, owner of the team, chose the name in English of "Eagles." The team's official title was the "China Times Eagles."

6545 Taipei County Whales 1997 to date *Chinese Professional (ind.).* The team, playing in a ballpark in suburban Taipei, represented Taipei County. The China Trust Banking Company, owner of the team, chose the nickname in English of "Whales." Whales swim in the East China, South China and Philippine seas and the Strait of Taiwan. Japanese whaling ships routinely hunt whales in international waters in this region.

6546 Suns 1997–2002 *Taiwan Major (ind.).* Macoto Bank, the team's owner, chose the English nickname of "Suns." The aboriginal peoples of Taiwan, who settled the island 4,000 years ago, worshiped a "Sun God."

6547 Cobras 2003–07 *Chinese Professional (ind.).* Macoto Bank, the team's owner, moved the franchise to this circuit and renamed the team, in English, the "Cobras." The team's title was the "Macoto Cobras." The world's most famous snake, the cobra, is found throughout Asia.

6548 T-Rex 2008–10 *Chinese Professional (ind.).* GPS-OEM-ODM Company bought the baseball franchise from Macoto Bank and renamed the team, in English, the "T-Rex." Interest in dinosaurs has been high in Asia not only because of Hollywood and Japanese dinosaur movies but also because archeologists have discovered a treasure house of dinosaur fossils in Asia.

6549 Lamigo Monkeys 2011 to date *Chinese Professional (ind.).* Management, regarding the previous moniker of "T-Rex" as passé, chose a new nickname. The Lamigo monkey is found in the jungles of Asia.

Takayama, Gifu, Japan

6550 Junior Swallows 1962–97 *Japanese Eastern (ind.).* Team was a farm club of the Central League Tokyo Yakult Swallows. In this era, farm clubs of the Japanese senior professional circuits were sometimes called "Junior."

Talladega, Alabama

6551 Highlanders m1912 *Southeastern (D).* Team started season in Huntsville (AL) and moved to Talladega (AL) July 9. The city was settled in 1835 in the vicinity of the Appalachian Mountains in elevated terrain 560 feet above sea level. Irish and Scottish "Highlanders" arrived in Alabama, starting in 1814. With manager Arthur Riggs at the helm, newspapers called the players "Arthur Riggs' Highlanders." Talladega is the "Bride of the Mountains."

6552 Indians 1913–14 *Georgia–Alabama (D);* 1928 *Georgia–Alabama Assn. (D);* 1929–30x *Georgia–Alabama (D).* Team disbanded August 14 because of the Great Depression. The Choctaw and Chickasaw Indians inhabited Alabama. The Battle of Talladega in 1813 resulted in American forces, under Andrew Jackson, defeating the Creeks here. Both the Creeks and Choctaws were eventually driven west. With manager Earl Hawkins at the helm, newspapers called the players "Hawkins' Indians."

6553 Tigers 1915–17 *Georgia–Alabama (D).* With manager Tige Garrett at the helm 1915–16, newspapers called the players "Tige's Tigers." Ed Goosetree took over in 1917, and the name became "Goosetree's Tigers."

Tallahassee, Florida

6554 Capitols 1935–42 *Georgia–Florida (D).* City has been the state capital of Florida since 1823. Tallahassee is known as the "Capital City."

6555 Pirates 1946–50 *Georgia–Florida (D).* Team was a farm club of the Pittsburgh Pirates.

6556 Citizens 1951 *Alabama–Florida (D).* Tallahassee was the only significant rebel city not captured by Union troops. A "citizens' army" consisting of civilians and seminary students turned back the Union Army in February 1865 at the Battle of Natural Bridge.

6557 Rebels 1954 *Florida International (B).* The resolution for the secession of the Southern states was signed here in April 1861.

Tallassee, Alabama

6558 Indians 1939 *Alabama–Florida (D);* 1940–41 *Alabama State (D);* 1946–48 *Georgia–Alabama (D).* Choctaws, Creeks and Cherokees fought American troops led by Andrew Jackson in the Red Sticks

War of 1814 and lost. By 1840 all Alabama Indians had been relocated to Indian Territory in Oklahoma. With manager Rosy Gilhousen at the helm, newspapers called the players "Gilhousen's Indians." None of these teams were farm clubs of the Cleveland Indians. With manager John Heving at the helm in 1946, newspapers called the players "Heving's Indians." John Hill took over in 1947 and the name became "Hill's Indians." The name was retained through 1948 under two other managers.

6559 Cardinals 1949 *Georgia–Alabama (D).* Team was a farm club of the St. Louis Cardinals.

Tamagawa, Japan

Note: Tamagawa is a suburb of Tokyo.

6560 Nippon Ham Fighters 1974–2003 *Eastern (Japan).* Team was a farm club of the Central League Tokyo Nippon Ham Fighters. Nippon Ham owned both the CL and EL teams. The team moved to Chiba for the 2004 season.

Tamaqua, Pennsylvania

6561 Dukes 1932m *Interstate (D).* Team moved to Slatington (PA) June 8. English and French Dukes funded the settlement of Pennsylvania in the seventeenth and eighteenth centuries. i.e., the Marquis Duquesne founded nearby Fort Duquesne, later the city of Pittsburgh.

Tampa, Florida

6562 Tampa Base Ball Club 1890–91–91–92 *Florida (W);* 1892 *Florida State (ind.).* These teams had no nickname.

6563 Smokers 1919–27 *Florida State (D* 1919–20, *C* 1921–23, *D* 1924–27*);* 1929–30 *Southeastern (B);* 1946–54 *Florida International (C)* 1946–48, *(B)* 1949–54. Tobacco tycoon Vicente Martinez Ybor established a cigar factory here in 1870. Tobacco from plantations is shipped to city factories for the manufacture of cigars. "Smoker" is a slang or nickname for cigar. Tampa is the "Cigar City" and the "Cigar Capitol of America."

6564 Krewes 1928 *Southeastern (B).* Female pirates, masquerading as men, were led by the She-Pirates Anna Bonney and Mary Read along the Florida coast in the years 1702–22. These women named themselves the "Krewe of the Sisters of the Sword." Krewe is an old English spelling for crew.

6565 Tarpons 1957–87 *Florida State (D)* 1957–62, *(A)* 1963–88. The tarpon is a silvery-scaled fish of warm waters of the Atlantic, Caribbean and the Gulf of Mexico.

6566 Yankees 1984 to date *Gulf Coast (R);* 1988 *Florida State (D);* 1994 to date *Florida State (A).* These teams were farm clubs of the New York Yankees.

Tampa–St. Petersburg, Florida

6567 Devil Dogs 1998 to date *American (M).* With the popularity of "Dogs, Dawgs, Cats and Katz" for sports team nicknames in the 1990s inspired in large part by Rap music's popularity, Tampa–St. Petersburg fans tagged the team as the "Devil Dogs."

6568 Raymonds 1998 to date *American (M).* Named after the mascot Raymond the Devil Ray, the moniker was popular especially during the run of the popular Ray Romano TV show *Everybody Loves Raymond* (1996–2005). Even after the franchise switched to "Rays" in 2008, the moniker is still occasionally used.

6569 Tampa Bay Devil Rays 1998–2007 *American (M).* Team plays its home games in St. Petersburg (FL). The devil ray is a manta that inhabits the Caribbean Sea and the Gulf of Mexico. Name was selected as a second choice in a name-the-team contest. The winner was "Stingrays," which was the preference of team owner Vince Naimoli, but there was a Hawaiian Winter League team—the Honolulu Sting Rays—already using the name. Naimoli chose the runner-up, which was "Devil Rays." Some of the entries in the name-the-team contest included Back-Crackers, Big Feet, Fruit Blossoms, Manta Rays, Pterodactyls, Snowbirds and Toads.

6570 The Good, Bad & Ugly Devil Rays 1999 *American (M)*. Coined by Mark Topkin, who noted that the 1999 club had some good name players, i.e., third baseman–designated hitter Wade Boggs and pitcher Wilson Alvarez, bad defense and bad hitting and ugly luck when injuries battered the roster, all leading to a 69–93 mark and a fifth-place finish in the "Showdown Gunfight" that is known as the AL Eastern Division—a reference to the famous 1967 Sergio Leone Western movie *The Good, the Bad and the Ugly*. In September 2011, the Rays were really good, rallying to make up nine games and clinch the AL wild card over fading Boston. The name also used to describe the 2010 Philadelphia Phillies.

6571 Double-A's 2003 *American (M)*. Tag was a spinoff from "Devil Rays" to describe the team's impending sixth consecutive last-place finish in the A.L. Eastern Division. The term was coined by baseball author Steve Rushin, who implied that the team consisted of little better than Class AA minor leaguers competing against the likes of the Yankees and Red Sox. Detractors of the team referred to losing Tampa Bay teams as the **Gays**. In today's English, "gay" has developed a non-sexual meaning referring to negligent activity and insincere behavior.

6572 Tampa Bay Rays 2008 to date *American (M)*. Team plays its home games in St. Petersburg (FL). The Ray is an elasmo-branch, warm-water fish with ventral gills. Varieties of the ray include the Manta ray, the sting ray, the devil fish and the devil ray. However, the new name refers to the rays of the Florida sun and is represented on the players jerseys by a twinkling solar ray. Team co-owner Stuart Sternberg declared to reporters: "The new name is a beacon that radiates throughout Tampa Bay and across the state of Florida." But the team mascot continues to be a ray fish. On a less than enthralling note, fans, dreading years of losing baseball, made the following suggestions as follows: Fay Wrays (actress Fay Wray), Martha Rays (comedienne Martha Raye), Steve Rays (musician Stevie Ray) and Bill Rays (Bill Ray was a figure in a political scandal). Two alert Tampa Bay fans spent $87 to gain a copyright on three nicknames—Tarpons, Thunder and Thunderbolts—in an attempt to sell the monikers to co-owner Vince Naimoli for thousands of dollars. Although Naimoli complimented the two fellows for their capitalist savvy, he turned down their sales offer.

6573 D-Rays 2008 to date *American (M)*. Fans and newspapers didn't like what they considered to be crass commercialism in changing the team nickname from the uneasy adjective in "Devil Rays" to the more squeaky clean "Rays." They got around the switch by calling the team the "D-Rays," in the style of D-Backs (for the overlong Arizona Diamondbacks).

6574 Blue Mohawks October 2008 *American (M)*. Fans started dying their hair blue and cutting it into a Mohawk style to celebrate the team's playoff victories.

6575 Orlando Rays 2008 *American (M)*. Team opened the 2008 season vs. Toronto in a three game series in Orlando (FL).

6576 Gays 2008 to date *American (M)*. Yankee, Red Sox and Marlin fans, unhappy at being pushed out of the spotlight by the suddenly powerful St. Petersburg boys, lambasted the franchise as the "Gays." Not overtly homophobic, the term's secondary meaning of "frivolous, inept and ridiculous" applied in this case.

6577 Undaunted Underdogs 2011 *American (M)*. Coined August 5, 2011, by Stan McNeal of *The Sporting News*, the moniker refers to the hope and energy of the Tampa Bay players and fans as the team tried for its fourth consecutive winning season and a playoff berth in the American League Eastern Division.

Tampico, Tamaulipas, Mexico

6578 Alijadores 1937–48 *Mexican (ind.)*; 1967–68 *Mexican Center (A)*; 1971–79 *Mexican (AAA)*; 1982 *Nacional de Mexico (ind.)*; 1983–85 *Mexican (AAA)*. Founded in 1523, abandoned after its destruction by pirates in 1683 and resettled in 1823 as a Gulf of Mexico seaport, ship cargoes of farm produce, copper ore, oil, and livestock have been loaded and unloaded by dockworkers since 1825. Ships enter port from the Gulf of Mexico and the adjacent Pannuco River where Mexico's most modern port provides excellent loading facilities.

6579 Algodoneros *Mexican Center (A)* 1969–70 *Mexican Center (A)*. Team was a farm club of the Algodoneros de Gomez Palacio. Los algodoneros means "Cotton-growers" and "Cotton-packers." In the period 1964–76, the Class AAA Mexican League maintained its own farm system of leagues, i.e., Center (A), Pacific (A), Rookie (A) and Southeast (A). More than a few of these teams assumed the team nicknames of their parent clubs, i.e., Reds, Tigers, Dockworkers, Cactus Men and Cotton Men.

6580 Astros 1983–85 *Mexican (AAA)*. Several Mexican League teams have used so-called "big league" team monikers, i.e., Mexico City "Tigers," Puebla "Angels," Reynosa "Braves," Monclova "Pirates" and Tampico "Astros."

Tamuin, San Luis Potosi, Mexico

6581 Club de Beisbol de Tamuin 1973 *Mexican Center (A)*. Team had no nickname.

Tarboro, North Carolina

6582 Tarheels m1901x *Virginia–North Carolina (ind.)*. North Carolina is the "Tarheel State"—a name that was coined during the Civil War. North Carolina soldiers sometimes failed to hold their position, prompting critics to say that they should have "put tar on their heels to stick in their trenches."

6583 Tartars m1901x *Virginia–North Carolina (ind.)*. Team started season in Portsmouth (VA) and moved to Tarboro June 21. Team and league disbanded August 17. The Tartars were Mongolian warriors led by Genghis Khan who terrified much of Euro-Asia from 1350 to 1700. Since baseball players of this era were regarded by the public as savage and ill-tempered individuals—much like the image of the Tartars—the moniker was appropriate. With Win Clark at the helm as field manager, local newspapers called the players "Clark's Tartars." The nicknames "Tarheels" and "Tartars" were used interchangeably this year.

6584 Tarbabies m1921 *Virginia (B)*. Team began season in Petersburg (VA) and moved to Tarboro August 2. "Tar doll" is a character from the old Uncle Remus story written by Joel Chandler Harris. The term started as a derogatory epithet for black people, but then meant a difficult or even insoluble problem. As a baseball slang, it refers to young players from North Carolina or playing in North Carolina. With manager Bill Martin at the helm, newspapers called the players "Bill Martin's Tar-babies." Baseball players to get a better grip on their bats use tar on the bat handle—a practice that goes back to the nineteenth century.

6585 Serpents 1937–38 *Coastal Plain (D)*. With manager Fred

"Snake" Henry at the helm, newspapers called the players the "Snake's Serpents."

6586 Tars 1939 *Coastal Plain (D)*; 1946–48 *Coastal Plain (D)*; 1952 *Coastal Plain (D)*. Newspapers preferred this four-letter Phillies-style moniker.

6587 Cubs 1940 *Coastal Plain (D)*. Team was a farm club of the Chicago Cubs.

6588 Orioles 1941 *Coastal Plain (D)*. Team was a farm club of the Baltimore Orioles. In the era 1935–54 the International League Baltimore Orioles had an occasional farm team of its own.

6589 Athletics 1949–51x *Coastal Plain (D)*. Team disbanded June 6. Team was a farm club of the Philadelphia Athletics.

Taunton, Massachusetts

6590 Herrings 1897–99 *New England (ind.)*. The herring is a fish of the North Atlantic Ocean and the Taunton River. Although inland from the Atlantic coast, the city is a river port where fishing boats dock with their catch. With manager Bobby Moore at the helm, newspapers called the players "Moore's Herrings."

6591 Tigers m1905 *New England (B)*. The Lowell "Tigers" club moved here August 3. The team nickname was retained.

6592 Taunton Baseball Club 1908m *Atlantic Assn. (D)*. Team moved to Attleboro (MA) May 9; 1914 *Colonial (C)*. These teams had no nickname.

6593 Herrings 1915x *Colonial (ind.)*. Team disbanded July 10. With manager Thomas Gilroy at the helm, newspapers called the players "Gilroy's Herrings."

6594 Blues 1933 *New England (B)*. The Taunton club wore blue stirrups, whose blue color was a spin-off of the red stirrups worn by the Boston Red Sox.

Taylor, Texas

6595 Producers m1915m *Middle Texas (D)*. Team began season in Austin (TX) and then moved here May 1. Team moved to Brenham (TX) June 8. Farms nearby provide cotton, grain, sorghum, watermelons, cabbage, spinach and sheep wool for shipment to city factories to be cleaned, processed, packed and shipped to market.

Taylorville, Christian, Illinois

6596 Tailors 1907–08 *Eastern Illinois (D)*. Newspapers used the moniker for headlines, i.e., "Tailors edge Miners, 4–3." The name was appropriate because city had textile mills and tailor shops.

6597 Taylored Commies m1910m *Northern Assn. (ind.)*. Team started season as the Decatur Commies (short for Commodores) moved here where they became known by the awkward "Taylored Commies," and then after playing here for about a two weeks, moved back to Decatur. Some local newspaper writer coined it, probably to shorten the full name from an unmanageable "Taylorsville Commodores" to this still-overlong moniker. The moniker had nothing to do with "Communist" and its abbreviation of "Commies."

6598 Christians 1911 *Illinois–Missouri (D)*. City is the county seat of Christian County.

Tecate, Sonora, Mexico

6599 Cereveceros de Tecate 2009 to date *Norte de Mexico (ind.)*. Tecate Beer Company owned the team. "Los cervezero" means "brewers."

Tecumseh, Michigan

6600 Tecumseh Baseball Club 1906–08 *Southern Michigan (D)*. Team had no nickname.

Tegucigalpa, Francisco Morazon, Honduras

6601 Medias Verdes 1980–81 *Honduran (W)*. Players wore green stirrups. Los "medias verdes" means "Green Sox."

Tel Aviv–Jaffa, Tel-Aviv, Israel

6602 Lightning 2007 *Israeli (ind.)*. The Israeli League disbanded after the 2007 season. Thunder and lightning storms from the Mediterranean Sea roll over the coastlines here.

6603 Netanya Tigers 2007 *Israeli (ind.)*. The Israeli League disbanded after the 2007 season. The team played its home games in Tel-Aviv before a scheduled move to Netanya in 2008.

Tempe, Arizona

6604 Mariners 1989–92 *Arizona (R)*. Team was a farm club of the Seattle Mariners.

6605 Rafters 1993–96 *Arizona Fall (W)*. Rafting enthusiasts navigate the rapids of the Salt River. Rafts are canoe-like, kayak-like boats for vigorous and dangerous maneuvers down river rapids.

6606 Angels 2011 to date *Arizona (R)*. Team was a farm club of the Los Angeles Angels of Anaheim.

Temple, Texas

6607 Bollweevils 1905–07 *Texas (D 1905–06, C 1907)*. The bollweevil is a cotton beetle that eats the boll, i.e., pod, of the cotton plant. Cotton plantations near the city sent cotton to city textile mills. With manager Ben Shelton at the helm, newspapers called the players "Ben Shelton's Boll-Weevils."

6608 Tigers 1914 *Middle Texas (D)*. Players wore striped stirrups, prompting reporters to call the players the "Tigers."

6609 Governors 1915 *Middle Texas (D)*; 1916 *Central Texas (D)*; 1917m *Central Texas (D)*. Team moved to Corsicana (TX) June 1. James Hogg of Temple was the first native-born Texan to serve as Texas governor (1892–96).

6610 Surgeons 1924–26 *Texas Assn. (D)*. City has four hospitals — Scott & White, King's Daughters, Santa Fe and Veterans Administration. With manager Rankin Johnson at the helm in 1924, newspapers called the players "Rankin Johnson's Surgeons." The name was retained through 1926.

6611 Eagles 1949–54 *Big State (B)*. Team was a farm club of the Dallas Eagles. Both Dallas and the Houston Buffaloes of the Class AA Texas League occasionally maintained farm teams of their own from the ranks of Class A and B leagues during the era 1930–60.

6612 Redlegs m1957x *Big State (B)*. Team began season in Port Arthur (TX) and moved to Temple May 30. Team disbanded August 20. The team was a farm club of the Cincinnati Redlegs.

Teocalitche, San Luis Potosi, Mexico

6613 Chapulines 1977–78 *Mexican Center (A)*. Farms in San Luis Potopsi are often plagued by grasshoppers (Los chapulines in Spanish). At this time one of Mexican television's favorite comedy shows was *The Adventures of the Chapuline Colorado* — a spoof on Superman.

Terre Haute, Indiana

6614 Browns 1884 *Northwestern (ind.)*; 1919–20 *Three-I (B)*. The 1884 players wore brown hose. With manager Al Buckenberger at the helm in 1884, newspapers called the players "Buck's Browns." With famous pitcher Mordecai "Three-Finger" Brown at the helm in 1919 as manager, the team president dressed the players in brown-trim uniforms and brown stirrups, prompting local newspapers to call the players the "Browns." The team was not a farm club of the AL St. Louis Browns.

6615 Hoosiers m1888x *Central Inter-State (ind.)*. Team began season in Crawfordsville and moved to Terre Haute July 2. Team and league disbanded July 28; 1889 *Illinois–Indiana (ind.)*; 1890 *Western Interstate (ind.)*. A "Hoosier" is an inhabitant of Indiana. With manager George Hammerstein at the helm in 1888, newspapers called the players "Hammerstein's Hoosiers."

6616 Hottentots 1891x *Northwest (ind.)*. Team and league disbanded June 30; 1892x *Illinois–Indiana (ind.)*; m1895 *Western (ind.)*. Team began season in Toledo (OH) and moved here July 5; 1897 *Central (ind.)*; 1899 *Illinois–Indiana (ind.)*; 1900 *Central (ind.)*; 1901–02 *Three-I (ind.* 1901, *B* 1902); 1903–09 *Central (B)*. The Hottentots are an African people of Namibia and South Africa. The moniker had some aptness in this era because, with the Wild West becoming tame, the American public developed a fascination with "Dark Africa," i.e., the African treks of explorer Stanley Livingston and others. Some baseball historians link this team nickname with African American players Bud Fowler and Moses Fleetwood Walker who played on Terre Haute teams in 1888 and 1890, respectively.

6617 Stags 1910 *Central (B)*. The white-tailed deer inhabits Indiana. The male of the species is known as a "stag," and the female, a "doe." With manager George "Cuppy" Groeschow at the helm, newspapers called the players "George Groeschow's Stags."

6618 Miners 1911 *Central (B)*. Founded in 1853, city factories were soon built that processed gravel, limestone and sand to manufacture cement. Terre Haute is known as the "Pittsburgh of the Big West."

6619 Terriers 1912–14 *Central (B)*. Newspapers used the name, derived from the city name, for headlines, i.e., "Terriers edge Stogies, 4–3." In this era, 1900–20, dog names, i.e., bulldogs, greyhounds, huskies, and rovers, started to become popular with sports teams. With manager Angus Grant at the helm in 1912, newspapers called the players "Grant's Terriers." Larry Quinlan took over in 1914 and the name became "Larry's Terriers."

6620 Highlanders 1915–16 *Central (B)*. Between 1816 and 1853, the city was built on a bluff 500 feet above sea level. French explorers who discovered the region in the eighteenth century called the area "Terre Haute"— which is French for "High Land." Terre Haute is known as the "Switzerland of America." Several thousand German immigrants arrived here in the era 1865–1900. These immigrants were "Hochlander" from the Highlands of Germany. With manager R.W. Gilbert at the helm, newspapers called the players "Gilbert's Highlanders."

6621 Tots 1921–32x *Three-I (B)*. Team and league disbanded July 15 because of the Great Depression; 1935 *Three-I (B)*; 1937x *Three-I (B)*. Team disbanded July 3. By 1920, newspaper editors demanded short team nicknames. Hence, Stockings became Sox, Beaneaters became Braves, Highlanders became Yankees, Nationals became Nats and Solons, Buccaneers became Bucs, Commodores became Commies, Champions became Champs, and Hottentots became Tots. With manager Bob Coleman at the helm in 1921–22, the team was known as "Bob's Tots." Ernie Robertson took over in 1923 and the name became "Robertson's Tots." The name was used to 1937.

6622 Phillies 1946–54 *Three-I (B)*. Team was a farm club of the Philadelphia Phillies.

6623 Tigers 1955–56 *Three-I (B)*. Team was a farm club of the Detroit Tigers.

6624 Huts 1956 *Three-I (B)*. Although the 1956 team's official nickname was "Tigers," newspapers sometimes used "Huts" for headlines, i.e., "Huts edge Kernels." The moniker is a condensation of "Terre Haute Hottentots," using T-U-T-S.

Terrell, Texas

6625 Red Sox 1907 *North Texas (D)*. Players wore red-trim stirrups. It was at this time, 1905–07, the players started wearing color and stripped stirrups over white sanitary hose. The team was not a farm of the Boston Red Sox.

6626 Cubs 1915x *Central Texas (D)*. Team and league disbanded July 24. With the Corsicana Athletics (Philadelphia Athletics were AL champions 1914), Ennis Tigers (Detroit Tigers were AL champions 1907–09) and Waxahachie Athletics as 1915 rivals in the league, local newspapers, wanting a prestigious major league nickname, decided to go with the moniker of "Cubs" (Chicago Cubs were 1906–08, 1910 NL champions). The name was appropriate because the team had mostly young players known in the slang of the era as "cubs."

6627 Terrors 1916 *Central Texas (D)*; 1925–26 *Texas Assn. (D)*. Tag was probably a spin-off from Champions, Indestructos, Invincibles, Perfectos and Superbas. Yet, fans were getting weary of these boastful team nicknames of the period 1899–1925, a style that faded by 1930. Reporters also chose the moniker because Texas is a land of "terror," i.e., the Mexican-American War, Indian attacks, bank robbers, train robbers, outlaws, bandits, cattle rustlers, the Civil War, dust storms, tornadoes, and hurricanes. Much like "Tigers" and "Trojans," the moniker "Terrors" was used by teams with city names containing the letter T in its spelling, i.e., Stockton Terrors, Tulsa Terrors and Terrell Terrors. Fans here didn't care for it, especially since the team had two consecutive losing campaigns.

Texarkana, Texas

6628 Nobles 1897 *Arkansas (ind.)*. Team started the season as the Anniston (AR) Nobles and moved here in mid-season (date unknown). The nickname was retained. Anniston was named after Queen Anne of England, hence the city nickname of "Noble City."

6629 Twins 1898 *Southwest (ind.)*; 1924–26 *East Texas (D)*; 1927–29x *Lone Star (D)*. Team and league disbanded May 16; 1941 *Cotton States (C)*. Texarkana, although one metropolitan area, is actually two cities, i.e., Texarkana (TX) and Texarkana (AR), which are divided by the Texas-Arkansas state line. Texarkana is known as the "Twin Cities.

6630 Casket-makers m1902x *Texas (D)*. Team started the season in Sherman-Denison (TX) and then moved here May 6. Team disbanded July 8. In this era, four morbid nicknames were used for last-place teams, i.e., Undertakers, Grave-diggers, Pallbearers and Casket-makers. Newspapers played up the idea that the ruinous play of the players on a team wallowing in last place "killed and buried" their fans' hopes for a pennant or even a winning season. Even more, a team in last place was not merely in the cellar but in the grave yard. With manager Fred Cavender — which fans noted suggested "cadaver" — at the helm of the newly arrived team (already saddled with a macabre 1–10 record), local newspapers called the players who compiled a grisly 20–36 record in Texarkana "Cavender's Casket-makers."

6631 Shine-Oners 1906x *Arkansas–Texas (D)*. Team disbanded August 25. Team was named after the popular song of this era "Shine On Harvest Moon." With manager Cap Shelton at the helm, newspapers called the players "Shelton's Shine-Oners." The fall harvest moon is very impressive in the cool and clear autumn skies here.

6632 Texarkana Baseball Club 1909x *Arkansas State (D)*. Team and league disbanded July 7. Team had no nickname.

6633 Tigers 1912 *South Central (D)*; 1913–14 *Texas–Oklahoma (D)*. Players wore striped stirrups, prompting reporters to call the team the "Tigers." With manager Dad Ritter at the helm in 1913, newspapers called the players "Ritter's Tigers." The teams were not farm clubs of the Detroit Tigers.

6634 Liners 1937–40 *East Texas (C)*. Texarkana is built on the state line between Arkansas and Texas. With manager Bill Windle at the helm, newspapers called the players "Windle's Liners." Eph Lobaugh took over in 1939 and the name became "Eph Lobaugh's Liners." Abe Miller took over in 1940 and the name became "Miller's Liners." Clair Bates took over in mid-season 1940 and the name became "Clair Bates' Liners."

6635 Bears 1946 *East Texas (C)*; 1947–53 *Big State (B)*. Arkansas is the "Bear State." With manager Gabby Lusk at the helm, newspapers called the players "Gabby's Bears." The team in 1946 was not a farm team of the Chicago Cubs but, rather, the Chicago White Sox. The team was an independent 1947–53. Edward Borom managed "Borom's Bears" in 1948.

6636 Gunslingers 2008 *Continental (ind.)*. After the Civil War ended, the Texas-Arkansas border was stirred up by the advent of railroads, oil wells and lumber fields, which became a breeding ground for bandits and gun-slinging outlaws of all types. Isaac "Hanging Judge" Parker and his deputy marshals had jurisdiction over Indian Territory (now Oklahoma) and the northern Texas-southern Arkansas border. There were plenty of shoot-outs between marshals and gun-toting outlaws.

Texas City, Texas

6637 Texans 1952–53 *Gulf Coast (B)*; 1955 *Big State (B)*; m1956 *Big State (B)* After the Beaumont Exporters moved back to Beaumont July 8, the Lubbock Hubbers moved here July 9. An inhabitant of the state of Texas and the municipality of Texas City is a "Texan." With managers Bones Sanders and then Zane Skinner at the helm in 1952, newspapers called the players "Sanders' Texans" and "Zane's Texans."

6638 Pilots 1954m *Evangeline (C)*. Team moved to Thibodaux (LA) June 17. Pilot boats on Galveston Bay guide cargo boats carrying oil, chemicals and tin. The maritime organization, known as the "Galveston-Texas City Pilots," are described by the City of Galveston website as the "Sentinels of the Ports of Galveston County" since 1845. The pilots guide vessels safely to their berths and out to sea.

6639 Exporters m1956m *Big State (B)*. Team played only five games representing Texas City and then moved back to Beaumont (TX) July 8. The team began season as the Beaumont (TX) Roughnecks and then moved here July 2. Since earlier Beaumont teams had been called the Exporters, newspapers called the team both "Texans" and "Exporters" (after the old Beaumont team moniker). In April 1947 a shipload of ammonium nitrate exploded, killing 500 people and destroying more than half the city. Mournful but undaunted, the city rebuilt its port.

6640 Stars 1977 *Lone Star (A)*. Texas is the "Lone Star State." Choice was reinforced because the team was playing in the Lone Star League.

6641 Bay Area Toros 2007–09 *Continental (ind.)*. Team went to the regional name to attract fans from nearby Galveston (TX). The team name was originally the alliterative Texas City Toros but was changed to the regional "Bay Area Toros" at the start of the 2007 season. The city is located on the coast of Galveston Bay. Players wore bull red uniforms and stirrups.

Texas City–LeMarque, Texas

6642 Texans 1951 *Gulf Coast (B)*. Although team represented both cities, home games were played in Texas City. An inhabitant of the state of Texas and the municipality of Texas City is a "Texan." Although the franchise represented both cities, the team's official title was "Texas City Texans."

Thetford Mines, Quebec, Canada

6643 Mineurs 1953–55 *Provincial (C)*; 1975 *Eastern (AA)*. City was established in 1876 where asbestos minerals, i.e., amphibole and chrysotile, were shipped to city factories for processing. The French "les mineurs," in English, means "miners."

6644 Pirates 1974 *Eastern (AA)*. Team was a farm club of the Pittsburgh Pirates.

Thibodaux, Louisiana

6645 Giants 1946–53 *Evangeline (D 1946–48, C 1949–53)*. Team was named after Hall of Fame New York Giants outfielder Mel Ott, who was born in nearby Gretna, Louisiana, and 1939 New York Giants star Zeke Bonura, who batted .321 that season. Ott hit 511 home runs in his career and was still active in the major leagues in 1946. Bonura was the team's 1946 manager. With manager Sidney Gautreaux at the helm 1947–48, newspapers called the players "Sidney Gautreaux' Giants." Gus Ploger took over in 1949 and the name became "Gus Ploger's Giants." The name was retained through 1953 under two other managers. The team was not a farm club of the New York Giants.

6646 Pilots m1954 *Evangeline (C)*. Team began season in Texas City Pilots (ind.) and moved here June 17. The team nickname was retained.

6647 Senators 1956–57 *Evangeline (C)*. Team was a farm club of the Washington Senators.

Thomasville, Georgia

6648 Hornets 1913 *Empire State (D)*; 1914 *Georgia State (D)*. With manager Martin Dudley at the helm both years, newspapers called the players "Martin Dudley's Hornets." Yellow-jacket hornets, which are not bees, proliferate in Georgia's warm climate.

6649 Orioles 1935–39 *Georgia–Florida (D)*. The New World oriole is found in the Midwest and South. With manager Harry O'Donnell at the helm, newspapers called the players "O'Donnell's Orioles." Cy Morgan took over in 1939 and the name became "Morgan's Orioles." The Thomasville (GA) team was not a farm club of the IL Baltimore Orioles, who did have a farm club in Thomasville (NC) 1937–39.

6650 Tourists 1940 *Georgia–Florida (D)*. Thomasville's annual Rose Festival attracts thousands of visitors every year. Tourists also visit the region for quail hunting. The team was not a farm club of the Class B Asheville Tourists. Thomasville is known as the "Original Winter Resort of the South." Resorts were built here starting in 1895 to entice Northerners anxious to escape cold winters.

6651 Lookouts 1941 *Georgia–Florida (D)*. Team was a farm club of the Chattanooga Lookouts. Washington NL took over from IL Baltimore in 1940 as the team's parent club. In 1940, the team was a farm club of the Chattanooga Lookouts (part of the Washington farm system). In 1941 the team took on the Class A1 Chattanooga team's nickname.

6652 Tigers 1946–50 *Georgia–Florida (D)*; 1962–63 *Georgia–Florida (D 1962, A 1963)*. Team had a loose affiliation with the AL

Detroit Tigers in 1946. In 1947 the team became a formal farm club of the AL Tigers. In 1962–63, the team was a farm club of the Detroit Tigers.

6653 Tomcats 1952 *Georgia–Florida (D)*. A 1952 farm club of the Detroit Tigers, management wanted a name to both distinguish the team from the parent club Detroit but maintain a link to them as well.

6654 Dodgers 1953–58 *Georgia–Florida (D)*. Although the NL Dodgers moved to Los Angeles from Brooklyn in 1958, they maintained a farm team here for that 1958 campaign.

Thomasville, North Carolina

6655 Chairmakers 1937 *North Carolina State (D)*. The Thomasville Chair Company was established here in 1904. The city soon became known as the "Chair City" and the "Big Chair." The company changed its name in 1960 to Thomasville Furniture Industries.

6656 Orioles 1938 *North Carolina State (D)*. Team was a farm club of the International League Baltimore Orioles. This North Carolina team is not to be confused with the 1935–39 Class A Georgia-Florida Thomasville (GA) Orioles, who had nothing to do with the Baltimore IL club.

6657 Tommies 1939–42 *North Carolina State (D)*; 1945 *North Carolina State (D)*. Newspapers used this moniker for headlines, i.e., "Tommies defeat Moors, 5–3."

6658 Dodgers 1946–47 *North Carolina State (D)*. Team was a farm club of the Brooklyn Dodgers.

Thomasville–High Point, North Carolina

6659 Hi-Toms 1948–52 *North Carolina (D)*. The 1948–52 league and franchise are the same as the 1947 NCSL entry in Thomasville, except for a change to a double city name. No home games were played in High Point; 1953 *Tar Heel (D)*; 1954–58 *Carolina (B)*; 1965–66 *West Carolinas (A)*; 1968–69 *Carolina (A)*. Moniker was used by newspapers for headlines, i.e., "Hi-Toms edge Owls, 4–3."

Thomson, Georgia

6660 Orioles 1956 *Georgia State (D)*. Team was a farm club of the Baltimore Orioles.

Three Rivers, Quebec, Canada (Trois Rivieres in French)

6661 Trios 1922–23m *Eastern Canada (B)*. Team moved to Montreal (QUE) July 5. French explorer Samuel de Champlain in 1634 discovered three rivers in this region — the St. Lawrence, St. Maurice and the St. Francois.

6662 Renards 1940 *Quebec Provincial (B)*; 1941–42 *Canadian–American (C)*. The red fox and grey fox are found throughout the U.S. and Canada. "Le renard" is the French word for fox.

6663 Royals 1946–50 *Canadian–American (C)*; 1951 *Provincial (C)*. Teams were farm clubs of the International League Montreal Royals.

6664 Yankees 1952–53 *Provincial (C)*. Team had a loose affiliation with the New York Yankees but was not a formal farm club.

6665 Phillies 1954–55 *Provincial (C)*. Circuit aka Quebec Provincial League. Team was a farm club of the Philadelphia Phillies.

6666 Aigles 1971–77 *Eastern (AA)*. Eagles are found throughout Canada and in Quebec's numerous provincial reserves.

Thunder Bay, Ontario, Canada

6667 Whiskey Jacks 1993–98 *Northern (ind.)*. The Whiskey Jack is a sparrow-like bird of North America, and is also known as the Gray Jay and Canadian Jay. These birds often stay the winter months, searching for food at lumber camps.

Tianjin, Northeast, China

6668 Fierce Lions 2002 to date *Chinese (S)*. This circuit, known officially as the Chinese Baseball League, is subsidized by the government of the People's Republic of China. Unlike the Cuban League, the teams of the CBL play exhibition and tournament games with pro teams from Japan, South Korea and Taiwan. The lion was a heraldic symbol both for the Ming Dynasty (1368–1644) and British forces that occupied the city 1900 following the Boxer Rebellion. Unbelievably, the capitalist company, 7-Eleven Food Stores, bought the franchise in 2010.

Tiffin, Ohio

6669 Tiffin Base Ball Club 1889x *Ohio State (ind.)*. Team disbanded in mid-season. Team had no nickname.

6670 Mud Hens 1936–41 *Ohio State (D)*. Team was a farm club of the Toledo Mud Hens.

Tifton, Georgia

6671 Tifters 1917x *Dixie (D)* Circuit and team disbanded July 4 because of U.S. entry into World War I. Moniker was used for newspaper headlines, i.e., "Tifters edge Packers, 4–3." Usually, a "headline nickname" was shorter than the city name, especially when the city name had more than six letters.

6672 Blue Sox 1949–50 *Georgia State (D)*; 1951–53, 1955 *Georgia–Florida (D)*. With the rival Baxley-Hazlehurst Red Socks and the Dublin Green Sox in the circuit for the 1949 season, Tifton management decided to dress the players in blue stirrup socks and call them Blue Sox to create a three-way red, green and blue rivalry. The team was not a farm club of the blue-trimmed Brooklyn Dodgers, which had several "Blue Sox" minor league farm clubs in this era.

6673 Indians 1954 *Georgia–Florida (D)*. Team was a farm club of the Cleveland Indians.

6674 Phillies 1956 *Georgia–Florida (D)*. Team was a farm club of the Philadelphia Phillies.

Tijuana, Baja California, Mexico

6675 Potros m1949–50 *Sunset (C)*. Team started 1949 season as the Salinas (CA) Colts and moved here August 5. Following the transfer, the team nickname was retained but was translated into Spanish, i.e., the Salinas Colts became Los Potros de Tijuana; 1951–52 *Southwest International (C)*; 2007–08 *Mexican (AAA)*.

6676 Colts/Potros 1956 *Arizona–Mexico (C)*. English-speaking fans called the team the "Colts." Spanish-speaking fans called the team "Los Potros."

6677 Toros 2004–06 *Mexican (AAA)*. Bull fighting is a popular spectacle in Mexico.

6678 Truenos 2009 to date *Norte de Mexico (ind.)*. Thunder storms often strike Tijuana. Trueno means thunder.

6679 Cimarrones 2010m *Golden (ind.)*. Team moved to Yuma (AZ) in mid-season, although it maintained its Tijuana title. Team started season as the **Potros** (Colts) but the name was changed to **Cimarrones**. In Spanish "cimarrones" can mean cowboys, Indians, renegades, wild horses and rams (although the more common word in Spanish for a ram is "carnero"). The team moved to Yuma (AZ) in mid-season but maintained its Tijuana title, and is listed here as a Tijuana team.

Toda, Saitama, Japan

6680 Tamagawa Swallows 2006 to date *Japanese Eastern (ind.)*. Team was a farm club Central League Tokyo Yakult Swallows. The team is owned by the Tamagawa Company.

Tokorozawa, Saitama, Japan

6681 Lions 1979 *Japanese Pacific (ind.)* 1979 to date; 1979 to date *Japanese Western (ind.)*. Seibu Railways bought the Fukuoka Crown Lighter Lions franchise after the 1978 season, and moved the team to the city of Tokorozawa. Seibu renamed the team the "Seibu Lions." In 2008, the team went to the regional name of "Saitama Lions" after the prefecture (i.e., state or province) in which the city of Tokorozawa is located. The nickname "Lions" goes back to the old Tokyo "Lions" of the Japanese Professional League of 1938. Lions are found in both Africa and southeast Asia. Seibu Railways continues to own the Pacific League team. The Western League Lions have been known as the "Seibu Lions" (1979–2002), "Goodwill Lions" (2003) and "Invoice Lions" (2004 to date).

Tokyo, Tokyo Prefecture, Japan

6682 Greater Tokyo 1936–37 *Japanese Pro (ind.)*. Team played in a suburban park and represented "greater Tokyo" (Dai Tokyo in Japanese). A parallel in the United States was the 1903–04 New York Yankees, who were also known as the "Greater New Yorks."

6683 Senators 1936–39 *Japanese Professional (ind.)*; 1946 *Japanese Professional (ind.)*. During the years 1930–45, in this era of imperial rule, Japan had a legislative body, the Diet, with appointed and elected senators to compliment the executive rule of the Emperor Hirohito. The Japanese Diet is located in Tokyo. In 1946, General Douglas MacArthur allowed the Japanese to keep their emperor system but insisted on an American-style legislature with senators and representatives, which was promptly established in the capital city of Tokyo. MacArthur also insisted that professional baseball start up once again in Japan in 1946 — not only to help Japan's economy but also to provide the Japanese people with an entertainment that the Japanese had followed since 1920. The team had two logos: one of a lion; and, the other of a dragon. However, the team was known exclusively as "Senators." The 1946 team owner was Japanese statesman Kinkazu Sainjoji, which prompted the revival of the name of "Senators."

6684 Kyojin 1936–44 *Japanese Professional (ind.)*. When the New York Giants toured Japan in 1935, Giant outfielder Lefty O'Doul suggested that the Tokyo All-Star team assembled by Yomiuri newspaper owner Matsutaro Shoriki to play against them be nicknamed the Tokyo "Giants." Shoriki enthusiastically agreed and the team was named "Kyojin"— Japanese for Giants. O'Doul only played 11 years in the major leagues but compiled an amazingly high .349 career batting average. He is *not* in the Hall of Fame!

6685 Korakuen Eagles 1937–39 *Japanese Professional (ind.)*. The Korakuen Food Company, owner of the team, wanted a noble moniker and chose "Eagles." Even with tensions arising with the United States, Japanese owners realized the importance of marketing team nicknames in English as well as Japanese. Eagles are found in Asia.

6686 Lions 1938–40 *Japanese Professional (ind.)*. Nishitetsu Nip- pon Railways owned the team and chose the nickname of "Lions." The nickname was chosen in rivalry with the Osaka "Tigers."

6687 Wings 1940 *Japanese Professional (ind.)*. The Japanese were proud of their air force that had devastated China, especially the new Japanese Zero, which was regarded as superior to the German Messerschmidt and the British Spitfire. The team was also known as **Tsubasa**, which is the Japanese word for "Wings."

6688 Black Eagles 1940–41 *Japanese Professional (ind.)*. As was the case with the pro–British "Highlanders" being replaced by the pro–American "Yankees" in New York in 1903, this team, originally called the Tokyo Koprakuen Eagles — which many Japanese equated with the American governmental seal — was forced to change the moniker shortly after the start of the 1940 season to "Black Eagles." The name in Japanese is Kurowashi.

6689 Taiyo 1941–42 *Japanese Professional (ind.)*. Team was owned by Taiyo International Foods.

6690 Asahi 1941–44 *Japanese Professional (ind.)*. Team, owned by Asahi-Shimbun Newspapers, had no nickname.

6691 Daiwa 1942–43 *Japanese Professional (ind.)*. Team was owned by the Daiwa Property Company.

6692 Nishitetsu 1943 *Japanese Professional (ind.)*. Team was owned by Nishitetsu Hotels.

6693 Sangyo 1944 *Japanese Professional (ind.)*. Team was owned by Sangyo Bank.

6694 Gold Stars 1946 *Japanese Professional (ind.)*. Team was owned by Lucky Gold Star Telephones. The owner of LGS Telephones and the baseball team was Komajiro Tamura, who dressed the players in gold-trim uniforms with a gold star on the cap.

6695 Pacific 1946 *Japanese Professional (ind.)*. Team was named after the Pacific Ocean. In the nineteenth century, U.S. baseball teams that were named after the two great oceans included the Brooklyn Atlantics, Long Island Atlantics and San Francisco Pacifics.

6696 Giants 1947–49 *Japanese Professional (ind.)*; 1950 to date *Japanese Central (ind.)*; 1952–54 *Kansai (ind.)*; 1955 *Japanese Western (ind.)*; 1962–2005 *Japanese Eastern (ind.)*. In 1947, team resumed play after two years of inactivity. Although once again known as "Kyojin" (in Japanese), team owner Yomiuri Newspapers heavily emphasized marketing the team by its English name of "Yomiuri Giants." The team switched leagues from the JPL to the CL in 1950. In 1954, Yomiuri Newspapers established a minor league farm club with the moniker of "Giants" in the Kansai League for the Central League franchise. The minor league team joined the WL in 1955 but disbanded at season's close. Yomiuri established the **Junior Giants** in the Eastern League in 1962. The Junior Giants moved to Kawasaki in 2006.

6697 Robins 1947–49 *Japanese Professional (ind.)*; 1950–52 *Japanese Central (ind.)*. Team owner Taiyo Fishing Company chose the name "Robins" for the team, whose players wore uniforms with robin-red trim. In 1950 Shochiku Movies purchased the team, making the title the "Shochiku Robins." In 1953 the Taiyo Whales and Shochiku Robins merged and the franchise was moved to Kawasaki, a city just southwest of Tokyo. The franchise was dormant in 1954 and then began play in Kawasaki in 1955. Robins are birds that are found in North America and Asia.

6698 Stars 1947–49 *Japanese Professional (ind.)*; 1950–56 *Japanese Pacific (ind.)*. Komajiro Tamura, owner of Lucky Star Telephones, renamed his 1946 Gold Stars team for the 1947 season the bilingual "Kinsei Stars," which translates literally as the "Gold Star Stars." Daei Motion Pictures bought the franchise in 1949, retaining the nickname for the team, which was now known as the "Daiei Stars." The moniker, in honor of the acting stars of Japanese cinema, was marketed in both English and Japanese. The team jumped leagues in 1950, leaving the disbanded JPL for the new Pacific League.

6699 Tokyu 1948 *Japanese Professional (ind.)*. Team was owned by Tokyu Electric Railways.

6700 Flyers 1948 *Japanese Professional (ind.)*; 1950–74 *Japanese Pacific (ind.)*; 1955 *Japanese Eastern (ind.)*; 1962–73 *Japanese Eastern (ind.)*. Tokyu Electric Railway and Daiei Motion Pictures owned team in 1948 and chose the portmanteau nickname of "Kyuei Flyers." "Flyers" referred to the "Flyer" express train on the Tokyo-Osaka rail line. Tokyu Electric Railways owned a new franchise in 1950 (team was not related to the 1948 franchise), and reused the 1948 Flyer moniker. The 1950 team was formally known as the "Tokyu Flyers." In 1954, Toei Corporation bought both franchises, kept the nickname, and marketed the team as the "Toei Flyers." Toei started an EL farm club in 1955 (that lasted only one season). Nittaku Home Builders bought the teams in 1973 and named them the "Nittaku Home Flyers." The next season, 1974, Nippon Ham Foods Company bought the teams, now known as the "Nippon Ham Flyers." In 1975, the Flyers moniker, now conflicting with the NHL Philadelphia Flyers hockey team, was dropped in favor of "Fighters."

6701 Swallows 1950–65, 1970 to date *Japanese Central (ind.)*; 1955–65, 1970–2005 *Japanese Eastern (ind.)*. In 1950, the Kokutetsu National Railways named its new team the "Kokuketsu Swallows." The swallow is a swift bird that inhabits Japan. In 1955, Kokutetsu established an EL farm club with the same nickname. In 1965 Sankei Shimbun Newspapers bought both franchises and named the teams "Sankei Swallows." The teams became the "Sankei Atoms" in 1966 (see below), but then Sankei sold the teams to Yakult Beverages in 1970, which named them the "Yakult Atoms" for four seasons. The name for both teams was changed back to "Yakult Swallows" in 1974. The EL Swallows moved to the city of Toda in 2006.

6702 Orions 1950–91 *Japanese Pacific (ind.)*; 1955 *Japanese Eastern (ind.)*; 1962–68 *Japanese Eastern (ind.)*. *The Mainichi Daily News* chose "Orions" for its new team in 1950. In 1955 Mainichi established a farm club with the same name in the Eastern League. In 1958, Mainichi merged with Daiei Retail Stores, and the team was known by the amalgamated company name of "Damai Orions" (1958–63). For the years 1964–68, the team dropped company names and was known by the city name of "Tokyo Orions." In 1969, Lotte Confectionaries of Seoul, South Korea, bought the franchise and the team became the "Lotte Orions." The constellation of Orion is very prominent in the skies of Asian lands. One team logo portrayed stars on a shield. Another team logo portrayed stars on a flag. The stars represented the constellation of Orion. Lotte moved the team to the city of Chiba for the 1992 season and changed the name to the "Lotte Marines." The EL Orions moved to Kawasaki in 1969.

6703 Unions 1955 *Japanese Pacific (ind.)*; 1955 *Japanese Eastern (ind.)*. Ryutaro Takahashi, owner of the Tombo Pencil Company, established two franchises (in the PL and the EL) in 1955 and named the team the "Tombo Unions." The EL farm team played only this one season. The team switched to the name of the owner as the "Takahashi Unions" in 1956. Daiei Retail Stores bought the team in 1957 and the name became "Daiei Unions." In 1958, the Mainichi Newspaper Company became co-owner with Daiei and the team gained a new nickname, becoming the "Damai Orions," 1958–61. The team's logo under Tombo was a pencil-shaped dragon fly.

6704 Atoms 1966–69 *Japanese Central (ind.)*; 1966–73 *Japanese Western (ind.)*. From 1971 to 1972, the WL team played in the Tokyo suburb of Takayama. Sankei Shimbun Newspapers owned the CL and WL "Sankei Atoms" 1966–69, and, Yakult Beverages owned the CL and WL "Yakult Atoms" 1970–73. *Atom Boy* was a TV-cartoon show that was very popular in Japan in the 1960s. The collective Japanese psyche was traumatized by Hiroshima and Nagasaki — hence the fantasizing about it the form of *Godzilla, Atom Boy* and *Atomic Age Japanese* science-fiction movies. New episodes of *Atom Boy* have

been produced to the present day. The team's official title was the "Sankei Atoms," after team owner Sankei.

6705 Dragons 1969x *Global (ind.)*. The dragon is an ancient symbol of courage and good fortune in Asian cultures.

Toledo, Ohio

6706 Blue Stockings 1883 *Northwestern (ind.)*; 1884 *American Assn. (M)*. Newspapers shortened the name to **Blue Legs** and **Blues**.

6707 Maumees 1884 *American Assn. (M)*; 1888 *Tri-State (ind.)*; 1890 *American Assn. (M)*. Toledo was built along the shores of the Maumee River.

6708 Avengers 1885 *Western (ind.)*. In this era, teams that followed a slow start with a winning streak, allowing them to climb back into contention, were said to be "avenging" their earlier losses to league opponents. The 1884 UA Cincinnati club was also the "Avengers." With player-manager Dan O'Leary at the helm, newspapers called the players "O'Leary's Avengers." When he took over Toledo in 1885, the nickname followed him there.

6709 Black Pirates 1889 *International Assn. (ind.)*; 1890 *American Assn. (M)*; 1892 *Western (ind.)*. Team had a loose affiliation with the Pittsburgh Pirates. Players wore all-black jerseys and white stockings. Toledo is located near the Ohio and Maumee rivers. Teams that played in cities located adjacent to a river sometimes were called by the romanticized name of "Pirates." The real "river pirates" were crews of boat raiders who attacked ships sailing larger rivers in the seventeenth and eighteenth centuries in the Americas, Asia and Africa. "Black" also referred to Toledo's status as the "World's Largest Coal-shipping Port." With manager Charlie Morton at the helm, newspapers called the black-shirted players "Charlie Morton's Black Pirates."

6710 Swamp Angels 1890 *American Assn. (M)*; 1895m *Western (ind.)*. Team moved to Terre Haute June 30; 1896–1900 *Inter-State (ind.)*. Legend has it that "swamp angels," i.e., evil spirits, rise at night from the vapors of the swampy shores of the summertime Maumee River. With manager Dennis Long at the helm in 1895, newspapers called the players "Dennis Long's Swamp Angels." The 1896 team played in Bay View Park near marshlands of the Ohio River. With owner-manager Charles Strobel at the helm in 1896, newspapers called the players "Strobel's Swamp Angels."

6711 White Stockings 1894 *Western (ind.)*. Team had a loose affiliation with the Chicago Nationals, who had been known as the "White Stockings" 1870–71, 1874–87. Newspapers shortened the name to **White Legs, White Sox** and **Whites**. The team's home field was known as White Stocking Park 1894–95.

6712 Mud Hens 1897–1900 *Inter-State (ind.)*; 1901 *Western Assn. (ind.)*; 1902–13 *American Assn. (A 1902–07, AA 1908–13)*; 1914 *Southern Michigan Assn. (C)*; 1916–55 *American Assn. (AA 1916–45, (AAA) 1946–55)*; 1965 to date *International (AAA)*. The team played in Bay View Park near marshlands of the Ohio River. Marshland birds, nicknamed "mud hens," often flew onto the field. The "mud hen" is also known as a "coot-bird," although the latter was never used as a nickname. Toledo is the "Mud Hen City."

6713 Iron Men 1916–18 *American Assn. (AA)*. Toledo manager Roger Bresnahan was a veteran of seventeen big league seasons, playing the most grueling of all positions — catcher — squatting behind the plate, getting battered by foul balls in 974 major league contests and giving him the nickname of "Iron Man." Toledo is the city "Where Coal and Iron Meet."

6714 Rays 1945 *United States (ind.)*. Team was a charter franchise for Branch Rickey's proposed United State League, a Negro circuit. The USL played only a few games in 1945 and, apparently, none in 1946. The team had a "ray" logo, i.e., a beam of light, referring to the city's many glass factories. Toledo is the "Glass Capital of the World."

6715 Glass Sox 1954 *American Assn. (AA)*. Toledo had numerous glass manufacturing factories, giving rise to the city nickname of the "Glass City." The fans didn't like the moniker and it was dropped. Toledo was home to the Owens-Illinois, Ford and Libby Owens glass companies.

Toluca, Mexico, Mexico

6716 Osos Negros 1980 *Mexican (AAA)*. In 1938, a Hungarian circus visited Toluca to entertain the residents of the city. A pregnant female bear escaped into the countryside, had her cub, and they roamed the region for weeks. In 1977 a natural park was established by the city and was named "El Parque del Oso Bueno" (Good Bear Park) in honor of these creatures. The 1980 baseball team dressed its players in black trim and called the team "Los Osos Negros." The moniker in English was the Toluca "Black Bears."

6717 Truchas 1984 *Mexican (AAA)*. Rainbow trout inhabit rivers in central Mexico. "Trucha" means trout.

Topeka, Kansas

6718 Athletics 1886 *Western (ind.)*. Newspaper reporters called the team "Athletics," which was a popular baseball nickname in this era.

6719 Capitals 1886 *Western (ind.)*. Topeka has been the state capital of Kansas since 1861.

6720 Golden Giants 1887 *Western (ind.)*. With manager Walton Goldsby at the helm, newspapers called the players "Goldsby's Golden Giants." Players wore golden yellow stockings. The Golden Giants were as "good as gold," compiling a "golden" 90–25 record to win the 1887 WL pennant by 15 games over second-place Lincoln.

6721 Populists 1893 *Western (ind.)*. Angry over high taxes, mortgage foreclosures and low prices, Kansas farmers were instrumental in the birth of the Populist Party in the 1890s. The *Topeka Populist* newspaper championed the populist movement, which was fighting against monopoly ownership of Kansas railroads.

6722 Maroons 1896 *Kansas State (ind.)*. Players wore maroon hose.

6723 Giants 1897–98 *Kansas State (ind.)*; 1904–07 *Independent Negro*. The 1887 name was used again.

6724 Saints 1904 *Missouri Valley (C)*. In the first half of the nineteenth century, missionaries of the Church taught Christianity to the Kiowa, Kansa, Pawnee and Wichita tribes of Kansas. With manager John Shrant at the helm, team was called "Shrant's Saints." Spencer Abbot took over and the name became "Spencer Abbot's Saints."

6725 White Sox 1905–08 *Western Assn. (C)*. Team had a loose affiliation with the Chicago White Sox. Players wore white hose 1905–06 and white stirrups over white sanitary socks 1907–08.

6726 Jayhawks 1909–15 *Western (A)*; 1927–28 *Western Assn. (C)*; m1932x Team started season in Joplin (MO) and moved to Topeka May 6. Team disbanded July 18 due to the Great Depression. *Western Assn. (C)*. Kansas is the "Jayhawk State."

6727 Savages 1916 *Western (A)*. Baseball players in this era were often called Braves, Indians, Warriors, Rustlers and Savages. This "politically incorrect" term in our era hardly batted an eyelash in 1916. Kansas had many Indian tribes, i.e., Comanche, Kansa, Kiowa, Missouri, Pawnee, Osage, Otoe and Wichita. These Indians fought settlers and the U.S. Cavalry in savage battles. The Pawnee and Osage were noted for their "savagery." The state was known as "Bleeding Kansas," as pro-slavery forces (led by John Brown) and abolitionist

forces (led by William Quantrill) savagely clashed. The term for the American Indian, i.e., the "Noble Savage," was coined around 1830. With manager Bill Lattimore at the helm, newspapers called the players the "Latti's Savages." Clyde Engle took over in mid-season and the name became "Engle's Savages."

6728 Kaw-nees 1918x *Western (A)*. Team moved to Hutchinson (KS) June 2. With manager Johnny Nee at the helm, newspapers combined his last name with Kaw—a slang for Kansas Indians—to produce "Kaw-nees." The Kansa Indians spoke a language called "kaw."

6729 Kaws 1922–23 *Southwestern (C)*. "Kaw" is a slang word for a Kansas Indian. Local newspapers liked it. The name also refers to the nearby Kaw River.

6730 Senators 1924 *Western Assn. (C)*; 1925–26 *Southwestern (D)*; 1929–31 *Western (A)*; 1933–34 *Western (A)*. Topeka has been the state capital of Kansas since 1861. The moniker was a spin-off of the 1886 Topeka Capitals team.

6731 Owls 1939–42 *Western Assn. (C)*; 1946–54 *Western Assn. (C)*; 1956–58 *Western (A)*. With manager Bill Wilson at the helm in 1939, newspapers called the players "Wilson's Owls."

6732 Hawks 1959 *Three-I (B)*. Spin-off from "Jayhawks." Legend says that the name "Jayhawks" was an amalgamation of "jays" and "hawks"—two birds that inhabited Kansas. Jayhawks soon came to mean an inhabitant of Kansas.

6733 Reds 1960–61 *Three-I (B)*. Team was a farm club of the Cincinnati Reds.

Toronto, Ontario, Canada

6734 Canucks 1885 *Canadian (ind.)*; 1886–90 *International (ind.)*. Circuit was League 1886–87 and 1890 and Association 1888–89; 1895–m96m–1900 *Eastern (ind.)*. Originally, an offensive slur for French Canadian, the name has evolved into a neutral description of any Canadian. With manager Charles Maddock at the helm in 1895, newspapers called the players "Maddock's Canucks." Toronto played its home games in Albany (NY) July 9 to July 31, 1896.

6735 Canadians 1895 *Eastern (ind.)*. Team moved to Albany (NY) in mid-season 1896, played a few games there, and then moved back to Toronto. The name means an inhabitant of Canada. When John Chapman took over from Charles Maddock in mid-season 1895, newspapers switched to "Chapman's Canadians."

6736 Maple Leafs m1896m–1911 *Eastern (ind.)*. The Eastern League renamed itself the International League in 1912. Some internal reorganization occurred, so it could be said that the IL was a "new" league; 1912–67 *International (AA 1912–45, AAA 1946–67)*. The Maple tree is the national tree of Canada. Canada adopted the maple leaf as its national flag symbol in 1959. Toronto played its home games in Albany (NY) July 9–31, 1896.

6737 Beavers *Canadian (B 1914, C 1914)*. With manager Joe Keenan at the helm, newspapers called the players "Keenan's Beavers." When George "Knotty" Lee took over in mid-season, the newspapers went to "Lee's Beavers."

6738 Blue Jays 1977 to date *American (M)*. Nickname was chosen in a name-the-team contest. The "Blue Jays" name and mascot was chosen because blue was the traditional uniform color for the CFL Toronto Argonauts and the NHL Toronto Maple Leafs (the Toronto NHL club's logo is a blue maple leaf). But there was controversy about the choice. The franchise was originally owned by LaBlatt Breweries, who then sold it to R. Howard Webster. Allegedly, LaBlatt pressured Webster to call the team the Toronto "Blues" to boost sales of the LaBlatt "Blue Brand Beer," or at the very least to choose a nickname that contained "blue" in its spelling. A name-the-team contest was held and 30,000 fans participated. Webster chose "Blue Jays" as the winning entry to maintain a link with Maple Leafs, Argonauts and LaBlatt. Webster declared: "The Blue Jay is a North American bird, bright blue in color, with a white undercoating and a black neck ring. It is strong, aggressive and inquisitive. It dares to take on all-comers—yet it is down-to-Earth, gutsy and good-looking." Some of the entries in the contest were Beavers, Bobcats, Dragons, Grizzlies, Hogs (Toronto is known as "Hogtown"), Scorpions, T-Rex, Tarantulas, Terriers and Travelers.

6739 OK, OK Jays 1983 *American (M)*. Tag was coined by baseball writer John Robertson to celebrate the previously struggling 1977 expansion team's first winning season with an "okay" 89–73 record, good for a respectable fourth-place finish in a very tough AL Eastern Division.

6740 Blow Jays 1983, 2000 to date. *American (M)*. Reminiscent of the Philadelphia Phillies of 1964, the Blue Jays were poised to win the AL Western Division, having compiled a sterling 96–59 record, only to lose their last seven games in a row to allow the Detroit Tigers to grab first place on the last day of the season. Furious Toronto fans and newspapers berated the team as the "Blow Jays" because they "blew the lead." Tag reappeared around 2000, used by Yankees and Red Sox fans and disgruntled Blue Jay fans when the team was losing.

6741 Canada's Team 1985–93 *American (M)*. After finally outgrowing its expansion pains, the Blue Jays started to win in 1985. "Canada's Team" enjoyed nine consecutive winning seasons while copping five AL Eastern Division titles, two American League pennants and back-to-back World Series titles (1992–93). During this time the Blue Jays were paced by hitters Roberto Alomar, George Bell, Pat Borders, Kelly Gruber, Candy Maldonado, Fred McGriff, John Olerud, Devon White and Dave Winfield (Hall of Fame) and pitchers Juan Guzman, Tom Henke, Jimmy Key, Jack Morris, Dave Stieb, Todd Stottlemyre, David Wells and Duane Ward. The moniker "Canada's Team" was a spin-off from the "America's Team" marketing gimmicks for the NL Atlanta Braves (1982), the NL Chicago Cubs (1984) and the NFL Dallas Cowboys (1977).

6742 Dive Bombers 1987 *American (M)*. (1987) A spin-off from "Blow Jays" to describe the Blue Jays seven-game losing streak "nose dive" to let the AL Eastern Division title get away from them. Actually, it is an inaccurate tag since a dive bomber is supposed to successfully pull up from its dive. The 1987 Blue Jays were a dive bomber that couldn't pull up from its dive and crashed.

6743 Okay Blue Jays 1989 Coined by baseball author Peter Bjarkman for the 1989 team that won its second AL Eastern Division title with an "okay" 89–73 record.

6744 Soaring Blue Jays 1992–93 *American (M)*. The term was coined by baseball writer Neil MacCarl to honor the back-to-back world champion Blue Jays of 1992–93. Hitters Roberto Alomar, Joe Carter, Tony Fernandez, Paul Molitor, John Olerud and Dave Winfield (Hall of Fame) and pitchers Juan Guzman, Paul Hentgen, Jack Morris, Dave Stewart and Duane Ward helped to the team "soar" to two consecutive world titles. When Joe Carter hit a game-ending, World Series–winning home run against the Philadelphia Phillies in Game 6 of the 1993 World Series, he "soared" around the bases. The moniker was also used in 1989 when the team won the AL Eastern Division title with an 89–73 record.

6745 BJ's 2005 to date *American (M)*. Before the "Hippie Revolution" of 1967–72 and the appearance of such comedians as George Carlin and Andrew Dice Clay, obscene words were taboo in polite society and in the media. But starting in the 1970s, the liberalization of America extended itself into language, allowing coarser words into formal communications. In the 1990s there was an abrupt, but not unexpected, proliferation of derogatory nicknames that would have been considered obscene only a generation earlier. "BJ," of course, refers to a colloquial description of an oral sexual act and was meant to be an epithet. The tag was used mostly by detractors among arch-rival Yankee and Red Sox fans. An even coarser version is **Blow Gays**. Shunned by the press, the term has persisted. Originated by hostile Yankee and Red Sox fans, these tags are also used by disgruntled Toronto fans when the team is losing.

6746 Blue Yays 2006 to date *American (M)*. In 2006, Mexican president Vicente Fox noted that Mexican immigrants were taking up residence in Canada in large numbers. The Spanish-speaking population in Toronto has increased since 2000. As such, there is now a Spanish language broadcast for Blue Jay games. Spanish-speakers mangle the difficult-to-pronounce word as "blue yays." The tag is also spelled **Blue Hyahs**.

6747 Bluebirds 2009 to date *American (M)*. In a conscious attempt to emulate the St. Louis Nationals most popular unofficial team nickname of "Redbirds," this tag started to gain in usage. A bluebird is a thrush. The blue jay is a jay. The cardinal is a crested finch. "Redbird" is a synonym for cardinal.

Torreon, Coahuila, Mexico

6748 Algodoneros 1940–43 *Mexican (ind.)*; 1946 *Mexican (ind.)*; 1949–53 *Mexican (ind.)*; 1997–2002 *Mexican (AAA)*. Cotton picked in nearby farms is transported to city textile mills for the manufacture of fabrics and garments.

6749 Club de Beisbol de Torreon 1968 *Mexican Center (A)*. Team had no nickname.

6750 Vaqueros de Union Laguna 2003 to date *Mexican (AAA)*. In nineteenth century Mexico, much as in the United States and Canada, cattle was driven by cowboys to ranches.

Torreon–Gomez Palacio, Coahuila, Mexico

6751 Laguneros 1946 *Mexican National (B)*. City was settled and built at the junction of the Nazas and Santiago Grande rivers, which overflow to create swamps and small inland lakes known as lagoons (lagunas in Spanish). In Spanish and nineteenth century Mexican times, people used small boats and canoes to move about on these lagoons. They were called "Los Laguneros."

Torrington, Connecticut

6752 Demons 1897 *Connecticut (ind.)*. Moniker was a spin-off from "torrid." The word torrid in English means very hot, i.e., the torrid flames of Hell!

6753 Torrington Base Ball Club 1898 *Naugatuck Valley (ind.)*. Team had no nickname.

6754 Braves 1950 *Colonial (B)*. In 1950 the Hartford Chiefs, a farm club of the Boston Braves, maintained its own farm team here. Although Torrington was not a formal farm of the Boston Braves, Hartford provided them with equipment and uniforms, including jerseys with the Braves name.

Traverse City, Michigan

6755 Resorters 1910 *West Michigan (D)*; 1911–14x *Michigan State (D)* Low attendance forced the team onto the road July 8. Team disbanded September 1. The city is located at Grand Traverse Bay, which many tourists used for swimming and boating. The city built the Neahtawanta Resort for summer tourists. With manager Henry Collett at the helm, local newspapers called the players "Henry Collett's Resorters."

6756 Beach Bums 2006 to date *Frontier (ind.)*. Beach Bum is a twentieth-century slang for a young man who prefers surfing, cavorting and partying at an idyllic summertime beach rather than going to work. At first derogatory, the phrase is now used with admiration. Actually, the team logo portrays two "beach bum" bears who wear touristy hats and sunglasses with Hawaiian shirts rather than a tousled hair youth in a bathing suit riding the wave with his surf board.

Trenton, New Jersey

6757 Trenton Capitals 1883 *Inter-State (ind.)*. Trenton has been the state capital of New Jersey since 1890.

6758 Trentonians 1884–85 *Eastern (ind.)*. In the 1870s and 1880s "city inhabitant" nicknames, i.e., Phillies, Trentonians, Auburnians, New Yorkers, etc., were sometimes used by reporters. By the 1890s almost all professional baseball teams were christened with "mascot" nicknames from newspaper reporters. An inhabitant of Trenton is known as a "Trentonian."

6759 Pets 1884–85 *Eastern (ind.)*. With manager Pat Powers at the helm, newspapers rebelled against "Trentonians" and started to call the players "Powers' Pets."

6760 Cuban Giants 1886–88 *Independent Negro* team m1889 *Middle States (ind.)*. Team moved to Hoboken (NJ) July 7. The Cuban Giants, who played their home games in 1885 in Babylon (NY), now played their home games split between Hoboken (NJ) and Trenton (NJ) 1886–89. In 1889, the team played its home games in four cities: New York City, Johnston (PA), Trenton (NJ) and Hoboken. The team is listed under Trenton and Hoboken for the years 1886–89 because it played most of its home games in these two cities. With manager Stan Govern at the helm, the newspapers *Trenton American* and *Trenton Daily Times* called the players "Stan Govern's Giants," in accordance with the wishes of team owner Walter Cook, who didn't want the tag "Cubans" used in print. In 1888, team had a "gigantic season" while posting a 105–23–1 record. See Hoboken (NJ). As more black teams turned professional in the 1890s with quite a few of them also using the moniker "Giants," newspapers simply called this team the "Trenton Giants."

6761 Trenton Base Ball Club 1897 *New Jersey State (ind.)*. Team had no nickname.

6762 Tigers 1907–14 *Tri-State (B)*. Players wore striped hose. Popularized by the Princeton University football and Detroit Tigers baseball clubs, numerous sport teams in this era dressed their players in striped stockings.

6763 Senators m1936–37 *New York–Pennsylvania (A)*. Team began 1936 season in York (PA) and moved to Trenton (NJ) July 2; 1938 *Eastern (A)*; 1939–42 *Inter-State (C 1939, B 1940–41)* City has been the state capital of New Jersey since 1790. Coincidentally, team became a farm club of the AL Washington Senators in 1937. The team in 1938 was also a farm club of the Washington Senators. In 1939, the team dropped its affiliation with the Washington Senators but kept its "Senators" moniker for playing in the state capital of New Jersey. The moniker was a spin-off of the 1883 Trenton "Capitals."

6764 Packers 1943–44 *Inter-State (B)*. Corn, cranberries, peppers, and tomatoes from nearby farms are transported to city factories for cleaning, processing, packing and shipping out to market.

6765 Spartans 1945 *Inter-State (C)*. When Walter Alston, later manager of the Brooklyn and Los Angeles Dodgers, became player-manager here in 1945, newspapers called his players "Alston's Spartans." Alston had a "fighting Spartan" season, batting .313 in 128 games.

6766 Giants 1946–50 *Inter-State (C)*. Team was a farm club of the New York Giants.

6767 Thunder 1994 to date *Eastern (AA)*. Team held a name-the-team contest and the winner was "Thunder." Atlantic thunderstorms often batter the New Jersey area. At first a two-headed Slavic eagle, by 2000 the logo was a "Thor, the Thunder God" character, and now a storm cloud shaped like a baseball player.

Trenton, Tennessee

6768 Reds 1922 *Kentucky–Illinois–Tennessee KITTY (D)*. Players wore red-trim uniforms and stirrups. The team had a loose affiliation with the Cincinnati Reds.

6769 Twins m1923 *KITTY (D)*. Team joined the circuit earlier in the season as the Milan "Twins"(representing Milan and nearby Rock Island) and then moved here July 9 where the nickname was retained.

Trieste, Trieste, Italy

6770 Alpina-Tergeste 2005 *Italian A1 (ind.)*. Trieste was founded by the Romans c. 200 B.C. and was known as Tergeste Alpinae, i.e., Tergeste of the Alps. The Acegas Corporation owned the team.

6771 Potocco Rangers Redipuglia 2008 *Italian A1 (ind.)*. Team's home field was in Redipuglia, a suburb of Trieste. Potocco Furniture Company owned the team and chose the nickname of "Rangers." Fleet outfielders "range" across the grassy turf of the baseball outfield.

Troncero, Federal District, Venezuela

6772 Phillies 2008 to date *Venezuelan Summer (R)*. Troncero is a suburb of Caracas, Venezuela. The team was a farm club of the Philadelphia Phillies.

Troy, Alabama

6773 Trojans 1936–39 *Alabama–Florida (D)*; 1940–41 *Alabama State (D)*; 1946–47 *Alabama State (D)*. Whether it is ancient Troy 3,000 years ago, Troyes (France), Troy (New York) or Troy (Alabama), an inhabitant of a city named Troy is known as a "Trojan."

6774 Dodgers 1941 *Alabama State (D)*. Team moved to Tuskegee (AL) July 31. The team was a farm club of the Brooklyn Dodgers.

6775 Tigers 1948–49 *Alabama State (D)*. Team was a farm club of the Detroit Tigers.

Troy, New York

6776 Haymakers 1871–72 *National Assn. (M)*; 1879–82 *National (M)*. The moniker originated with the 1867 Troy "Haymakers" baseball team when a player of the visiting New York Mutuals, before a game with the Troy team in Troy, sniffed haughtily to a newspaper reporter, "We won't be beaten by a bunch of 'haymakers' from the farm!" The Troy fans took the derogatory name to heart and turned it into their battle cry. When the team turned professional in 1871, the moniker was retained.

6777 Green Stockings 1871–72 *National Assn. (M)*; 1879–82 *National (M)*. The players wore green hose. Newspapers shortened the moniker to "Green Legs."

6778 Trojans 1871–72 *National Assn. (M)*; 1878 *New York State Championship Assn. (M)*; 1879–82 *National (M)*; 1886x *Hudson River (ind.)*. Circuit and team disbanded in mid-season (date unknown); 1888 *International Assn. (ind.)*; 1890 *New York State (ind.)*; 1891–93 *Eastern (ind.)*; 1900–16m *New York State (ind. 1900–01, B 1902–16)*. Team moved to Harrisburg (PA) June 20, 1916. The inhabitants of

Ancient Troy of Homer's *Iliad* were known as "Trojans." Likewise, the inhabitants of Troy, New York, are also known as "Trojans."

6779 Unions 1871–72 *National Assn. (M)*; 1879–82 *National (M)*. The club, upon forming an amateur nine in 1865, was known as the Lansingburg Unions. Lansingburg and Troy were two neighboring towns that eventually merged into a single city.

6780 Washerwomen 1894m *Eastern (ind.)*. Team moved to Scranton (PA) August 2; 1899 *New York State (ind.)*. Team began 1899 season in Auburn (NY) and moved to Troy August 1. In the 1860s, newspapers reported that "washerwomen" in the U.S.— many of them foreign-born laborers— were being exploited at low salaries, i.e., $1 a week. Washerwomen in Troy (NY) petitioned for higher wages and won, increasing wages from $2 to $3 to $8 to $14 a week by 1890. However, they continued to work brutal hours— anywhere from 12 to 14 hours a day, including Saturdays. The moniker soon was applied to any laborer, including baseball players, who often complained that they were "overworked and underpaid." Baseball writer John Shiffert wrote that the 1894 Troy team "played like a bunch of old ladies," i.e., "washerwomen." In this meaning, apart from brutalizing work, "washerwoman" meant a somewhat frail and elderly woman. With manager Charles Van Arman at the helm, newspapers called the players "Arman's Washerwomen."

6781 Troy Base Ball Club 1895 *New York State (ind.)*. Team had no nickname.

6782 Tri-City Valley Cats 2002 to date *New York–Pennsylvania (A)*. Mountain cougars inhabit the nearby Adirondack and Catskill mountains. Troy, Albany and Schenectady occupy a valley bordered by the Adirondack Mountains to the north and the Catskill Mountains to the south. All home games were played in Troy (NY).

Tsuruse, Mie, Japan

6783 Orions 1971–80 *Japanese Eastern (ind.)*. Team was a farm club of the CL Tokyo Lotte Orions.

Tucson, Arizona

6784 Old Pueblos 1915 *Rio Grande Valley Assn. (D)*. City, founded in 1700 as the San Xavier del Bac Indian Mission, has the nickname of the "Old Pueblo" (El Pueblo Viejo).

6785 Cowboys 1928–30 *Arizona State (D)*; 1937–41 *Arizona–Texas (D 1937–39, C 1940–41)*; 1951 *Southwest International (C)*; 1952–54 *Arizona–Texas (C)*; 1955–58 *Arizona–Mexico (C)*. Founded in 1700, city soon became a ranching town for cattle drives of eighteenth century Spanish-America, nineteenth century Mexico, and finally the United States, from 1850 to date. The city was a territorial capital 1867–77. In 1928 former big leaguer George "Rube" Foster became manager. Foster, born in Lehigh (OK), also was known as "Cowboy" Foster. Based on his two personal nicknames, newspapers called the players "Rube's Cowboys." A "rube" means a rustic, unsophisticated young man. Cowboys were also regarded as rustic and unsophisticated— as were baseball players. With manager Harry Krause at the helm 1937–38, newspapers called the players "Krause's Cowboys." Bill Salkeld took over in 1939 and the name became "Salkeld's Cowboys." The name was retained through 1941 under Lester Patterson.

6786 Waddies 1928–30 *Arizona State (D)*. "Waddy" was slang for "cowboy" that came into use around 1895. The name also was used for cattle rustlers and thieves. Its origin may be the Australian prodding stick— the Wadi.

6787 Mission Bells 1931 *Arizona–Texas (D)*. Team was a farm club of the San Francisco Mission Bells. Starting in the 1930s, PCL teams like the Los Angeles Angels, Hollywood Stars, S.F. Seals and

S.F. Missions had an occasional loose affiliation or formal farm affiliation with lower classification (A, B, C, D) minor league teams.

6788 Lizards 1932x *Arizona–Texas (D)*. Circuit and team disbanded July 24 due to the Great Depression. Desert lizards abound in Arizona's Painted Desert.

6789 Baby Seals 1937–41 *Arizona–Texas (D 1937–39, C 1940–41)*. Team was a farm club of the PCL San Francisco Seals. With manager Lester Paterson at the helm, newspapers called the players "Les Patterson's Baby Seals."

6790 Toros 1969–97 *Pacific Coast (AAA)*; 2009–10 *Golden (ind.)*. Bullfighting was the premier spectator sport during the era of Spanish colonial rule. There is still bullfighting here today. The circuit, in which the 2009–10 team played, was called the Golden Baseball League

6791 Sidewinders 1998–2008 *Pacific Coast (AAA)*; 2009–10 *Golden (ind.)*. Team was a farm club of the Arizona Diamondbacks. Sidewinders is a spin-off from Diamondbacks. Also called the Horned Viper, this type of rattlesnake moves along the sand by coiling itself into sideways loops to propel itself. The franchise moved to Reno (NV) for the 2009 season and was renamed the Reno Aces.

6792 Padres 2011 to date *Pacific Coast (AAA)*. Team is a farm club of the San Diego Padres. San Diego Padres owner Jeff Moorad purchased the 2010 PCL Portland Beavers franchise and moved the team to Tucson (AZ) before the 2011 season.

Tulare, California

6793 Merchants 1910x *San Joaquin Valley (D)*. Team disbanded August 8. Produce from nearby farms is transported here to city markets. The South Pacific Railroad arrived here in 1871, allowing merchants to flourish. The city burned down three times between 1872 and 1895.

Tullahoma, Tennessee

6794 Tennessee Walkers 1997 *Big South (ind.)*. A "Walker" is a show-horse at rodeos that paces about in a dance-like display. The city is a resort area that sponsors horse shows featuring Walkers. Tennessee, like Kentucky, has always sponsored horse racing and horse shows. The Iroquois Steeplechase is held annually in Nashville (TN). The "walker" is a breed of riding horse, known as a "walking horse," dates back to the eighteenth century. The "walker" was bred for trail riding but not racing. With team owner Jeff McCall running the franchise, newspapers called the players "McCall's Walkers."

Tulsa, Oklahoma

6795 Oilers 1905 *Missouri Valley (C)*; 1906x *South Central (D)*. Team and league disbanded in August 22; 1907x *Oklahoma–Arkansas–Kansas O.A.K. (D)*. Team disbanded August 6; 1908 *Oklahoma–Kansas (D)*; 1910x *Western Assn.(C)*. Team disbanded July 22; 1914 *Western Assn. (D)*; 1932 *Western (A)*; 1933–42 *Texas (A 1933–35, A1 1936–42)*; 1946–65 *Texas (AA)*; 1966–68 *Pacific Coast (AAA)*; 1969–76 *American Assn. (AAA)*. The Glenn Pool Gusher was struck near Tulsa in 1905. By the 1920s Oklahoma led the U.S. in oil production. With Charlie Schaft at the helm in 1905, the team was called "Charlie's Oilers." The name became traditional, used by nine franchises over 72 seasons.

6796 Terriers 1912 *Oklahoma State (D)*. Dog names for sports teams, i.e., Bulldogs, Greyhounds, Huskies and Terriers became popular in this era. With manager Howard Price at the helm, newspapers called the players "Howard Price's Terriers."

6797 Terrors 1912 *Oklahoma State (D)*. "Terrors" was slang for baseball players who were often equated with Indians, Braves, Rustlers, Warriors, and Savages— all of whom "terrorized" their prey. Northern Texas, Oklahoma and southern Arkansas was a particularly lawless region in the years 1880–1900 with Indians, outlaws, bandits roaming over the land, striking "terror" into the hearts of pioneers, settlers and oil workers. Actually, the name was a spin-off from the "Terriers" nickname by which the team also was known.

6798 Producers 1915 *Western Assn. (D)*. Agricultural products from nearby farms are shipped to city factories for cleaning, processing, packing and shipping out to market.

6799 Drillers 1977 to date *Texas (AA)*. Tag was a spin-off from Oilers. With the NFL Houston Oilers and the NHL Edmonton Oilers using the "Oilers" name, management decided to go with the spin-off moniker of "Drillers."

Tupelo, Mississippi

6800 Wolves 1925–26 *Tri-State (D)*. The 1925 team played like "hungry wolves" as they went a fierce 67–39 to finish first in the 1925 regular season. O.V. Pressley took over as manager in 1926 and the name became "O.V. Pressley's Wolves."

6801 Tornado 1997 *Big South (ind.)*; 1998x *Heartland (ind.)*. Team disbanded June 20. The city is at the southern line of the notorious Tornado Alley where ferocious tornadoes are likely to develop, extending northward into Iowa.

Tuskegee, Alabama

6802 Airmen m1941 *Alabama State (D)*. Team began season in Troy (AL) and then moved here July 31. The Tuskegee Air Base, just outside the city, was the site where black U.S. Army–Air Force pilots trained before seeing distinguished service in the air battles of Europe. The base also trained white pilots. The two groups were segregated. A movie and two television documentaries were filmed about the black "Tuskegee Airmen."

Twin Falls, Idaho

6803 Bruins 1926–28x *Utah–Idaho (C)*. Team disbanded July 5. Black bears and grizzly bears inhabit the eleven national forests of Idaho.

6804 Cowboys 1939–42 *Pioneer (C)*; 1946–58 *Pioneer (C)*. Team went by the regional name of "Magic Valley Cowboys" 1952–58; 1961–71 *Pioneer (C 1961–62, A 1963, R 1964–70)*; 1968–71 *Pioneer (R)*. Team went by the regional name of "Magic Valley Cowboys." After gold was discovered in the region in 1860, numerous camps were built around the mines. When silver and lead were discovered, the mining camps grew into a city. Cattle drives along the Oregon Trail brought cattle into the city to meat packing houses.

Tyler, Texas

6805 Elbertas 1912 *South Central (D)*. Famous Elberta peaches are grown in nearby farm groves and then transported to city packing houses for cleaning and packing.

6806 Trojans 1924–26 *East Texas (D)*; 1927–29 *Lone Star (D)*; 1931x *East Texas (D)* Circuit and team disbanded May 5 because of the Great Depression; 1935 *West Dixie (C)*; 1936–40 *East Texas (C)*; 1946 *East Texas (C)*; 1947–48 *Lone Star (C)*; 1949–50 *East Texas (C)*. Reporters chose the moniker "Trojans" because of the successful college football team, the USC Trojans, the introduction of the "Trojan" tractor for U.S. farms in 1950, and the rivalry with league opponent the Sulphur Springs Spartans, i.e., Trojans vs. Spartans.

6807 Sports m1932 *Texas (A)*. Team began season as the Shreveport (LA) Sports and moved here May 16. The nickname was retained.

6808 Governors 1933 *Dixie (C)*; 1934 *West Dixie (C)*. City was settled in the 1840s and named after then–U.S. President (1841–45) John Tyler, who had been governor of Virginia and provided assistance that strengthened the then-independent Republic of Texas.

6809 Wildcatters 1994–97 *Texas–Louisiana (ind.)*. Crude oil and natural gas from nearby oil wells are transported to city refineries. Oil prospectors got the nickname "wildcatters" because they roam the prairies like a wildcat. The team logo is a black panther. Panthers inhabit Texas.

6810 Roughnecks 2001 *All-American (ind.)*. Working the oil and natural gas rigs is dirty, hard, rough and sweaty labor that requires the stamina and toughness of a "roughneck." Originally meaning a strong and muscular man, the term "roughneck" came to mean an oil field worker.

Union City, Tennessee

6811 Greyhounds 1935–42x *Kentucky–Illinois–Tennessee KITTY (D)*. Team and league disbanded June 19 due to U.S. entry into World War II; 1946–52 *KITTY (D)*. At the start of the 1935 season, management held a name-the-team contest for the fans. Winner Claude Botts chose "Greyhounds" because this dog is "powerful, sleek and fast-running." Dog track racing, especially greyhounds, was popular in the 1920s and 1930s.

6812 Dodgers 1953 *KITTY (D)*; 1954–55 *KITTY (D)*. Team was a farm club of the Brooklyn Dodgers.

Union Spring, Alabama

6813 Springers 1936–37 *Alabama–Florida (D)*. Moniker was used for newspaper headlines, i.e., "Springers edge Trojans, 4–3."

6814 Redbirds 1938 *Alabama–Florida (D)*. Team, with the players wearing red-trim uniforms and stirrups, was named after manager Red Lucas. The team had a loose affiliation with the St. Louis Cardinals.

Uniontown, Pennsylvania

6815 Coal Barons 1906–07 *Pennsylvania–Ohio–Michigan (P.O.M.) (D)*; 1908–09 *Pennsylvania–West Virginia (D)*; 1947–49 *Middle Atlantic (C)*. Teams in a city with an industry such as coal, lumber, cotton and oil were often referred to as Barons in the style of the nineteenth century phrase "Big Barons of Industry." Populists of this era were less admiring, calling such men the "Robber Barons." Nearby mines shipped anthracite and bituminous coal to city processing factories. Uniontown is known as the "City of Coal Kings." With manager James Groninger at the helm in 1906, newspapers called the players "James Groninger's Coal Barons." Alex Pearson took over in 1907 and the name became "Alex Pearson's Coal Barons." In 1908, field skipper Frank Sisley managed "Frank Sisley's Coal Barons."

6816 Cokers 1926 *Middle Atlantic (C)*. City factories burned coal in a process called distillation to produce coke, which is used as fuel and as a reducing agent in metallurgy. Uniontown is known as the "Coke City." With manager Lee King at the helm, newspapers called the players "Lee King's Cokers."

Uriangato, San Luis Potosi, Mexico

6817 Club de Uriangato 1975 *Mexican Center (A)*. Team had no nickname.

Utica, New York

6818 Pent-Ups m1878 *International Assn. (M)*; 1885 *New York State (ind.)*; 1889–90 *New York State (ind.)*; 1898–99 *New York State (ind.)*. Team began the 1878 season in Binghamton (NY) and moved here July 9, prompting local newspapers to report that the team has "pent-up here."

6819 Pretty Little Team m1878 *International Assn. (M)*. Team began season in Binghamton (NY) and then moved here July 9; 1879 *National Assn. (M)* The 1878 International Association changed its name to National Association in 1879 when the circuit's lone Canadian entry, London, disbanded after the 1878 season. After a winning performance in a game the day before, a reporter for the *New York Clipper* sports newspaper of April 27, 1878, wrote that the Utica club was a "pretty, little team." The "Pretty Little Team" from Utica lived up to its praise by having a winning season with a 38–26.

6820 Utes m1878 *International Assn. (M)*. Team began season in Binghamton (NY) and moved here July 9; 1879 *National Assn. (M)*; 1910–17 *New York State (B)*; 1924m *New York–Pennsylvania (B)*. Team moved to Oneonta (NY) August 7. The 1878 International Association changed its name to National Association in 1879 when the circuit's lone Canadian entry, London, disbanded after the 1878 season. Newspapers used the moniker for headlines, i.e., "Utes edge Allies, 4–3."

6821 Asylums 1900 *New York State (ind.)*. The name, appropriate because of the construction of the New York State Mental Hospital here in 1895, is a spin-off from "pent-up," which was a contemporary slang for being locked up in a looney bin.

6822 Indians 1911 *New York State (B)*. The team was named after the Ute Indians, who inhabited New York State in pre-colonial times.

6823 Braves 1939–42 *Canadian American (B)*; 1943 *Eastern (A)*. Team, in 1939, was a farm club of the Boston Braves. The team went independent in 1940 but retained the nickname of its 1939 parent club.

6824 Blue Sox 1944–50 *Eastern (A)*; 1981–95, 1997–2001 *New York–Pennsylvania (A)*. The 1944–50 team was a farm club of the Philadelphia Blue Jays. The parent club NL Blue Jays switched its nickname back to Phillies in 1950, but the Utica club stayed with Blue Sox to have its own distinctive moniker. The team played as an independent 1981–85 and switched to the old-time "Blue Sox" to avoid a change in the uniform color trim. The team became a farm club of the Phillies (1986–87), White Sox (1988–92), and then Red Sox (1993–95) but retained the traditional blue trim.

6825 Blue Jays 1977–80 *New York–Pennsylvania (A)*. Team was a farm club of the Toronto Blue Jays.

6826 Blue Marlins 1996 *New York–Pennsylvania (A)*. Team became a farm club of the Florida Marlins. The blue marlin is a blue-scaled bill fish found in tropical waters off the coast of Florida. The name didn't catch on and the team switched back to Blue Sox in 1997.

6827 Brewmasters 2007 *New York State (ind.)*. German immigrant Francis Xavier Matt established the Matt Brewing Company in Utica in 1888 to satiate the thirst of beer-drinking Welsh and German immigrants who arrived here in the era 1885–1920. German Americans here stage an annual Bavarian Beer Festival.

Utrecht, Netherlands (Holland)

6828 UVV Utrecht 2011 to date *Holland Honkball Hoofdklasse (ind.)*. Utrecht is a suburb of Amsterdam. The team was formed by players of the Utrecht Voetbal Vereniging (Utrecht Volleyball Club).

Vacaville, Solano, California

6829 Steelheads 2000–02 *Western (ind.)*. The Steelhead is a silver-scaled rainbow trout that migrates between salty ocean and inland fresh water.

Valdosta, Troup, Georgia

6830 Stars 1906 *Georgia State (D)*. With manager A.J. Starr at the helm, newspapers called the players Valdosta "Stars."

6831 Millionaires 1913 *Empire State (D)*; 1914 *Georgia State (D)*; 1915 *Florida–Louisiana–Alabama–Georgia (F.L.A.G.) (D)*; 1916 *Dixie (D)*. Tobacco and cotton plantations here made their owners rich. "Millionaires"—like "Barons"—was a common nickname for baseball teams playing in cities that were involved in prosperous industries like coal, steel and iron, lumber, oil, cotton and tobacco. With manager Dutch Jordan at the helm in 1913, newspapers called the players "Jordan's Millionaires." Whitey Moore took over in mid-season 1913 and the name became "Moore's Millionaires." With Frank Moffett at the managerial helm in 1914, newspapers called the players "Moffett's Millionaires." Joseph Herald took over in mid-season 1914 and the name became "Herald's Millionaires."

6832 Trojans 1939–42 *Georgia–Florida (D)*. Local newspaper editors wanted a name as energetic and formidable as the team's parent club—the Pittsburgh Pirates. In this era, the moniker was popular as the USC "Trojans" won five Rose Bowls in eleven college football seasons. Valdosta is located in Troup County, which partly inspired the "Trojan" nickname. With World War II approaching, newspapers wanted a name that also inspired defense and bravery. With manager Billy Morrell at the helm 1939–40, newspapers called the players "Morrell's Trojans." Stew Hofferth took over 1941–42 and the name became "Hofferth's Trojans."

6833 Dodgers 1946–52, 1957–58 *Georgia–Florida (D)*. Team was a farm club of the Brooklyn Dodgers.

6834 Browns 1953 *Georgia–Florida (D)*. Team was a farm club of the St. Louis Browns.

6835 Tigers 1954–56 *Georgia–Florida (D)*. Team was a farm club of the Detroit Tigers.

Valencia, Carabobo, Venezuela

6836 Navegantes 1946–1954–55 *Liga Venezolana (W)*; 1955–56 *Association Venezolana (W)*. Team went by the legendary name of "Magellan Navigators "(Los Navegantes Magallanes). The Dutch explorer Ferdinand Magellan sailed the coast of Venezuela in 1520. Cargo ships transported the city's many goods, i.e., textiles, paper, cement, furniture, dairy products, soap, vegetables, oils, pharmaceuticals and automobile parts.

6837 Magallanes 1955–56–61–62 *Liga Venezolana (W)*. Team was named after Dutch explorer Ferdinand Magellan. "Magallanes" is the Spanish spelling of "Magellans."

6838 Navegantes de Magallanes 1964–65–87–88 *Liga Venezolana (W)*; 1995–96 to date *Liga Venezolana (W)*. The nickname in English is the "Magellan Navigators."

Vallejo, California

6839 Vallejo Base Ball Club 1891–92 *California (ind.)*; 1910 *Central California (D)*. These teams had no nickname.

6840 Pastimes 1911 *Central California (D)*. Baseball teams of the era 1870–1920 sometimes used general sporting monikers like Athletic, Contest, Olympic and Pastime. Baseball, as early as 1855, was known as the "American Pastime."

6841 Marines 1913m *California State (D)*. Team moved to Watsonville (CA) July 6. Commercial, military and recreational boats have sailed here since 1850. Mare Island Naval Shipyard has been building ships here since 1900. Valdosta since then has been known as "Navy Town." The city is also home to the California Maritime Academy.

6842 Chiefs 1949 *Far West (D)*. With manager Louis Vezilich at the helm, newspapers called the players the "Vezilich's Chiefs."

Valley City, North Dakota

6843 Hi-Liners 1922m *Dakota (D)*. Team moved to Bismarck (ND) August 3; m1923 *North Dakota (D)*. Team began season as New Rockford–Carrington (ND) and moved here July 17. When the Dakota Territory was divided by the U.S. Congress into North and South Dakota in 1889, North Dakotans became known as "High-liners" while South Dakotans were called the "Low-liners." With manager Earl Pickering at the helm in 1923, newspapers called the players "Earl Pickering's High-liners."

Valley-Lanett, Alabama– West Point, Georgia

6844 Valley Rebels 1946–51 *Georgia–Alabama (D)*. Team went by the regional name of "Valley Rebels" to include West Point (GA). The Confederacy was organized in Montgomery, Alabama, in January 1861. Many Civil War battles were fought in Georgia.

Valleyfield, Quebec, Canada

6845 Valleyfield Baseball Club 1922m *Eastern Canada (B)*. Team moved to Cap de la Madeleine (QUE) July 29. Team had no nickname.

Vancouver, British Columbia, Canada

6846 Horse Doctors 1905 *Northwestern (B)*; 1907 *Northwestern (B)*. Manager John McCloskey fielded a team of veteran players who soon became known as the "Vets" in local newspapers. A playful newspaper reporter spun Vets into the much-too-long "Veterinarians," which then spun into "Horse Doctors." "Horse doctor" is slang for veterinarian.

6847 Beavers 1908–11, 1914, 1916–17 *Northwestern (B)*; 1918x *Pacific International (B)*. Team and league disbanded July 7 due to Canada's entry into World War I. Fans considered "Horse Doctors" to be silly, prompting a switch to Beavers. Beavers inhabit the lakes and rivers of British Columbia. With manager Bob Brown again at the helm, newspapers called the players "Bob Brown's Beavers."

6848 Champions 1912, 1915 *Northwestern (B)*. Team won NWL pennants in 1911 and 1914.

6849 Bees 1913 *Northwestern (B)*. Tag was a contraction of Beavers. At the season's start, newspapers started calling the team the Vancouver **B's** in order to save line space. Soon, fans and reporters lengthened it to "Bees." With manager Bob Brown at the helm, newspapers called the players "Brown's Bees" and "Bob's Bees."

6850 Maple Leafs 1937–38 *Western International (B)*. The maple leaf is the national symbol of Canada.

6851 Capilanos 1939–42 *Western International (B)*; 1946–54 *Western International (B 1946–51, A 1952–54)*. With manager John Kerr at the helm in 1939, the name was "Kerr's Capilanos." Jim Crandall took over in 1940 and the name became "Crandall's Capilanos." Don Osborne took over in 1941 and guided "Osborne's Capilanos."

6852 Mounties 1956–62 *Pacific Coast (AAA)*; 1965–69 *Pacific Coast (AAA)*; 1978–99 *Pacific Coast (AAA)*. The team was named in honor of the Royal Canadian Mounted Police, whose police officers are known as "Mounties."

6853 Canadians 1978–99 *Pacific Coast (AAA)*; 2000 to date *Northwest (A)*. Unlike the NHL Montreal Canadiens, this baseball team was named after the team owner — Molson Canadian Beer.

Vancouver, Washington

6854 Soldiers 1904m *Oregon State (D)*. Team moved to Albany (OR) May 18; 1918 *Pacific Coast International (B)*. The moniker's reference is not to be confused with Fort Victoria, B.C. Fort Vancouver Barracks was built here in 1848. In 1899 soldiers of the famous all-black U.S. Army 24th Infantry arrived in the city, not to pacify Indians but to quell labor strife. Some fans and newspaper reporters in 1918 felt that the Canadian origin of "Brown's Beavers" made the moniker inappropriate and preferred the 1904 name of "Soldiers."

6855 Beavers 1918 *Pacific Coast International (B)*. With the nickname "Beavers " available following the disbandment of the Vancouver BC Northwest League franchise in 1918 because of World War I, newspapers here called the players "Brown's Beavers." Brown was the former Vancouver, B.C., manager, and he crossed the border to manage this U.S. team.

6856 Soldiers 1918 *Pacific Coast International (B)*. Some fans and newspaper reporters felt that the Canadian origin of "Brown's Beavers" was inappropriate and preferred the 1899 name of "Soldiers."

Vandergrift, Pennsylvania

6857 Pioneers 1947–50x *Middle Atlantic (C)*. Team disbanded July 20. Eighteenth-century pioneers sailed along the Kiskiminetas River searching for suitable sites to settle. Immigrants included English Quakers and German Protestants. Jacob Vandergrift (after whom the city was named) established an oil company here that attracted people to settle here. Newspapers of the day hailed him as a "pioneer in the petroleum industry" because he constructed the Star Pipe Line, the first U.S. oil pipeline. With manager Floyd Patterson (no relation to the boxer of the same name) at the helm in 1947–48, newspapers called the players "Patterson's Pioneers." The name was retained through 1950 under three different managers.

Van Wert, Ohio

6858 Buckeyes 1908x *Indiana–Ohio (D)*. Team and league disbanded June 8. Ohio is nicknamed the "Buckeye State" after a tree known as the buckeye tree, which is a type of horse chestnut tree. Ohioans were known as Buckeyes dating to 1788. A common team nickname for nineteenth-century Ohio baseball teams, the Ohio State University football team picked up the moniker in 1912 when it joined the Big Ten Conference. Van Wert was the only Ohio team in the four-team circuit. The three other league teams played in Indiana. In the era 1885–1915, when a lone state representative played in a league, out-of-town newspapers would refer to the players by their state nickname, i.e., Hoosiers (Indiana), Wolverines (Michigan), Quakers (Pennsylvania) and Buckeyes (Ohio).

Venice, California

6859 Tigers 1913–15m *Pacific Coast (AA)*. Venice returned to Vernon July 11. The Vernon (CA) Tigers of 1912 moved to Venice at the start of the 1913 season. The team nickname was retained. The team was sometimes called Villagers, i.e., Village of Venice.

Venoco, Venezuela

6860 Astros 2008 *Venezuelan Summer (R)*. Team was a farm club of the Houston Astros.

6861 Orioles 2008 *Venezuelan Summer (R)*. Team was a farm club of the Baltimore Orioles.

Ventura, Ventura, California

6862 Yankees 1947–49 *California (C)*. Team was a farm club of the New York Yankees.

6863 Braves 1950–52 *California (C)*. Team was a farm club of the Boston Braves.

6864 Channel Cities Oilers 1953 *California (C)*. Ventura and its surrounding towns are known as the "Channel Cities." The Union Oil Company was established here in 1890. Drilling began at the Ventura Oil Fields in 1919.

6865 Ventura County Gulls 1986 *California (A)*. Seagulls inhabit the California coast.

6866 Pacific Suns 1998 *Western (ind.)*. Circuit was officially known as the Western Baseball League. California is the "Sunshine Empire."

Veracruz, Veracruz, Mexico

6867 Aguila 1937–39 *Liga Mexicana (ind.)*; 1941 *Liga Mexicana (ind.)*; 1949–57 *Mexican (ind.)*; 1949–54, *AA* 1955–57); 1959–74 *Liga Mexicana (AA)*; 1979–86 *Mexican (AAA)*; 1982–83 *Nacional de Mexico (ind.)*; 1992–95 *Liga Mexicana (AAA)*; 1999 *Liga Mexicana (AAA)*. The singular nickname and mascot referred not to the bird but to the eagle image on the Mexican flag.

6868 Azules 1940–51 *Mexican (ind.)*. Players wore blue-trim uniforms and stirrups.

6869 Aguilas Rojas 2000 to date *Liga Mexicana (AAA)*. Players switched from their traditional blue trim to red trim. Aguilas Rojas means "Red Eagles."

Vernon, California

6870 Tigers 1909–12 *Pacific Coast (AA)*; 1915–25 *Pacific Coast (AA)* After a two-year (1913–14) stay in Venice (CA), franchise moved back to Vernon (CA) in 1915; 1917–18 *California Winter (W)*; 1924–25 *California Winter (W)*. The players wore striped hose. With manager Happy Hogan at the helm in 1909, newspapers called the players "Hogan's Tigers." The player uniform had a Tiger logo on the left breast of the jersey.

6871 Villagers 1909–12 *Pacific Coast (AA)*. Vernon goes by the official title of "Village of Vernon." With manager W.L. "Happy" Hogan at the helm, newspapers called the players "W.L. Hogan's Villagers."

Vernon, Texas

6872 Dusters 1947–52 Longhorn *(D 1947–50, C 1951–5)*. Paralleling the famous Chisholm Trail was the Great Western Trail over which 7 million head of cattle were herded to Texas ranches during the era 1873–1903. The dust kicked up by the cattle was tremendous. Vernon is located in the Red River Valley, which itself is in the southern portion of "Tornado Alley." The region is periodically assailed by tornadoes and "Dust Devils." The largest ranch in Texas—Waggoner Ranch—is near Vernon. The ranch not only handles cattle but is also a farm region whose crops are dusted by "duster" airplanes with insecticide.

Vero Beach, Florida

6873 Dodgers 1980 to date *Florida State (A)*. Team was a farm club of the Los Angeles Dodgers.

Vicksburg, Mississippi

6874 Red Stockings 1893–94 *Mississippi (ind.)*. Players wore red hose. Originally Red Stockings, local newspapers shortened it to **Redlegs** and **Reds**.

6875 Hill-Climbers 1902–08 *Cotton States (D)*. Culminating at the Red Clay hills in the northeast Mississippi, the region in and around Vicksburg has many rolling hills, ranging from 200 to 800 feet above sea-level. Settled by the French in 1719, the city was built on these rolling hills. With manager Billy Earle at the helm in 1903–04 and 1906, newspapers called the players "Billy's Hill-Climbers." During the Siege of Vicksburg (July 4, 1862–July 10, 1863), Union and Confederate troops scrambled up and down the nearby Red Clay hills in retreat by day and at night to scout the opponent's battle formations.

6876 Hill Billies 1910–12x *Cotton States (D)*. Team disbanded August 13; 1922–23x *Cotton States (D)*. Circuit and team disbanded July 24; 1924–32m *Cotton States (D)*. Team moved to Jackson (MS) June 1; 1937 *Cotton States (C)*; 1941 *Cotton States (C)*; 1950 *Southeastern (B)*; 1955 *Cotton States (C)*. With manager Bruce Hayes at the helm in 1910, newspapers called the players "Hayes' Hillbillies." Otto Mills succeeded Hayes in mid-season 1910 and the name became "Mill's Hillbillies." Moniker actually was a spin-off from "Hill-Climbers." Ollie Mills returned for 1923–24, prompting local newspapers to again call the players "Mills' Hill-Billies." The name was retained through 1932 under fourteen other managers. With manager Pap Williams at the helm in 1955, newspapers called the players "Williams' Hill Billies."

6877 Billies 1946–49 *Southeastern (B)*. Management shortened the name to fit in newspaper headlines. With manager Louis Blair at the helm in 1946, local newspapers called the players "Blair's Billies."

Victoria, British Columbia, Canada

6878 Chappies 1896 *Pacific Northwest (ind.)*. "Chappies"—aka "Chaps"—are trouser-like leather leggings that were used by Canadian cowboys here after the city was founded in 1843. The name evolved into cowboy and from there further referred to a young man. Later it meant an athlete and then baseball player. "Pea Bushes," known as "Chaparral Bushes," i.e., Chappies, are bushy Evergreen-Oak trees that grow in the Pacific Northwest.

6879 Legislators 1905m *Northwestern (B)*. Team moved to Spokane (WA) July 11. Victoria, founded in 1843, has been the provincial capital of British Columbia since 1866. The First Legislative Council of Victoria drafted the Provincial Constitution here in 1853–54. With manager G.G. Howlett at the helm, newspapers called the players "G.G. Howlett's Legislatures." Canada, as a member of the British Commonwealth, uses an English parliamentary form of government with a king, prime minister, parliament and the royal courts.

6880 Bees 1911–15x *Northwestern (B)*. Team disbanded August 1 due to Canada's entry into World War I; 1921 *Pacific Coast International (B)* Circuit aka the International Northwestern League. Local newspapers started to call the 1911 team "Beavers," which Victoria fans quickly rejected since arch-rival Vancouver was also being called the "Beavers." The newspapers contracted it to **B's**—to save newspaper space—and the moniker evolved into "Bees." With manager William Holmes at the helm in 1911, newspapers called the players

"Bill's Bees." The same evolution from "Beavers to B's to Bees" happened in Vancouver in 1913 when both teams were called the "Bees." The moniker stemmed from the cities' province of British Columbia, which is referred to as B.C., i.e., "Bee-Sea." In 1914 Vancouver switched back to "Beavers." With manager Cliff Blankenship at the helm in 1920, newspapers called the players "Blankenship's Bees." The presence of the Vancouver Beavers in the league in 1921 did not affect the choice of Bees.

6881 Tyees 1919x *Northwest International (B)*. Team and league disbanded June 8 partly due to the Spanish Influenza; 1952–54x *Western International (B)*. Team disbanded August 2. Tyee is a Chinook Indian word for "chief." The Tyee salmon is a fish that swims in nearby Puget Sound. With manager Cecil Garriott at the helm 1952–53, newspapers called the players "Cecil Garriott's Tyees." Don Pries took over in 1954 and the name became "Prie's Tyees."

6882 Islanders 1920 *Pacific Coast International (B)*. City is located on Vancouver Island at the end of the Strait of Juan de Fuca. Vancouver Island is sometimes called Victoria Island.

6883 Athletics 1946–51 Western International *(B 1946–51, A 1952–54)*. Management marketed the team as the "Athletics." The team was not a farm club of the AL Philadelphia Athletics.

6884 Mussells 1978–80 *Northwest (A)*. Fishing ships bring in catches of fish and shellfish, called "mussel," which is cleaned, processed, packaged and canned in city food processing plants for shipment to market.

6885 Seals 2010 *Golden (ind.)*. Phocidae fur seals inhabit North America along the Pacific Coast, from the Arctic southward to California. Their presence along the California coast gave rise to the 1903–57 PCL San Francisco Seals team nickname.

Victoria (Ciudad Victoria), Tamaulipas, Mexico

6886 Club de Beisbol de Victoria 1971 *Mexican Center (A)*; 1973 *Mexican Center (A)*; 1976–78 *Mexican Center (A)*. These teams had no nickname.

6887 Henequereneros 1974 *Mexican Center (A)*. Agave in Spanish is henequeren. The agave plant is so fibrous that it is used to make ropes and coarse fabrics. "Los Henequereneros" means "Agave Planters." Agave in Spanish is El Henequeren.

Victoria, Texas

6888 Rosebuds 1910–11x *Southwest Texas (D)*. Team disbanded August 11; 1926m *Gulf Coast (D)*. Team moved to Edinburg (TX) August 24; 1957 *Big State (B)*; 1958–61m *Texas (AA)*. Team moved to Ardmore (TX) May 27; 1977 *Lone Star (A)*. Team's owners, the William Baird family, hailed from Pasadena, California, and named the team after the annual New Year's Day Rose Parade in Pasadena. The family had a rose garden planted just outside the Victoria ballpark. With manager Lou Rochelli at the helm in 1957, newspapers called the players "Rochelli's Rosebuds." The moniker, which was official in 1957, was appropriate because of the song "The Yellow Rose of Texas."

6889 Eagles 1956 *Big State (B)*. Team was a farm club of the Dallas Eagles. In the era 1900–50, some larger city population AAA and AA minor league franchises, i.e., Los Angeles, Baltimore and Dallas, occasionally maintained their own farm teams.

6890 Giants m1961 *Texas (AA)*. Team started the season in Rio Grande Valley and moved here June 10. The team was a farm club of the San Francisco Giants.

6891 Toros 1974 Texas (AA). The area was settled by Mexican cowboys in 1824 as a ranch for cattle drives. The city later built a bullfighting arena. "Toro" is the Spanish name for "bull." The city became American in 1850 but bullfighting persisted.

Victoria de las Tunas, Las Tunas, Cuba

6892 Espinosos 1977–78 to date *Cuban National (S)*. Espina, i.e., "spiny cactus," is a type of cactus found in Cuba. "Los Espinosos" means "Spiny Cactus Farmers." The Cuban National Championship is a state subsidized league in a communist country.

6893 Magos 1977–78 to date *Cuban National (S)*. Founded in 1759, the city had a church "Iglesia de los Magos," i.e., Church of the Magi. The Spanish word "Los Magos" means the "Magi." The Magi were the "Three Wise Men" of the Bible's Christmas story.

Vidalia, Georgia

6894 Indians 1952–56 *Georgia State (D)*. Team had a loose affiliation, in 1952–54, with the Cleveland Indians. The team became an official farm club of the Cleveland Indians, starting in 1955.

Vidalia-Lyons, Georgia

6895 Twins 1948–50 *Georgia State (D)*. The team, playing its home games in Vidalia, represented both cities.

Viera, Brevard, Florida

6896 Brevard County Manatees 1994 to date *Florida State (A)*. Similar to a walrus or a sea lion, the manatee swims in the warm coastal waters of west Africa and the Caribbean.

Villahermosa, Tabasco, Mexico

6897 Plataneros 1964–66, 1969–70 *Liga del Sureste de Mexico (A)*; 1977–80 *Liga Mexicana (AAA)*. Plantations in the region transport bananas and other fruit to city packing houses.

6898 Ganaderos 1967–68 *Liga del Sureste de Mexico (A)*. Cattle ranches transport livestock to city slaughterhouses. "Los Ganaderos" means "Cattlemen."

6899 Cardenales 1975–76 *Liga Mexicana (AAA)*. Players wore Cardinal red-trim uniforms and stirrups. The team was not a farm club of the St. Louis Cardinals. "Los Cardenales" means "Cardinals."

Vincennes, Indiana

6900 Reds 1904 *Kentucky–Illinois–Tennessee (KITTY) (D)*. Players wore red hose. The team was not known as the "Red Stockings."

6901 Alices 1905–06 *(KITTY) (D)*; 1908 *Eastern Illinois (D)*; 1910 *KITTY (D)*; 1913 *KITTY (D)*. Actress Alice Terry was born in Vincennes in 1899, appeared in local vaudeville as a child actress, 1903–15, and went to Hollywood in 1916 where she enjoyed an 18-year career, mostly in silent movies.

6902 Hoosiers 1911 *KITTY (D)*. The Vincennes team was the only Indiana entry in the league, prompting newspapers to call the players "Hoosiers." A "Hoosier" is an inhabitant of Indiana. With manager Charlie Gosnell at the helm in 1911, newspapers called the players "Charlie Gosnell's Hoosiers."

6903 Citizens 1950 *Mississippi Ohio Valley (M.O.V.) (D)*. Moniker was a spinoff from the city nickname, the "Citadel of the Old Northwest."

6904 Velvets 1951–52m *(M.O.V.) (D)*. Team moved to Canton (OH) June 7. In this meaning, "velvet" refers to "winnings, gain or profit." The more usual meaning refers to a soft fabric of silk and cotton. Sometimes, a winning team is said to be "making the plays like velvet."

Vinita, Oklahoma

6905 Cherokees 1905 *Missouri Valley (C)*. The Cherokees, driven west into Oklahoma, sided with the Confederacy and then skirmished with "Sooner" settlers in 1893, before finding themselves forced into reservations. With manager Ed Finney at the helm, newspapers called the players "Finney's Cherokees."

6906 Vinita Baseball Club m1906x *Kansas State (D)*. Team began season in Pittsburg (KS) and moved here June 6. Team disbanded July 5. The team had no nickname.

Virginia, Minnesota

6907 Ore Diggers 1913–16x *Northern (C)*. Team disbanded July 10. Iron ore from nearby mines is transported to city smelters to be converted into iron and steel. The city gained the nickname of the "Queen City of the Iron Range." With manager Billy Shannon at the helm, newspapers called the players "Shannon's Ore-diggers." Bobby Roth took over in mid-season 1913 and the name became "Bobby Roth's Ore-diggers." Edward Stewart took over and the name became "Edward Stuart's Ore-diggers." Kid Taylor took over in 1914 and the name became "Kid Taylor's Ore-diggers." The name was retained through 1916 under two more managers.

Visalia, California

6908 Pirates 1910x *San Joaquin Valley (D)*. Team and league disbanded September 12. With the city 200 miles inland, local newspapers chose the moniker "Pirates," not after any ocean or river-sailing buccaneers, but after the 1909 world champion Pittsburgh Pirates, in the hopes some winning pixie dust would rub off on the players. With manager Newt Young at the helm, newspapers called the players "Newt's Pirates."

6909 Cubs 1946–52, 1954–56 *California (C)*. Team was a farm club of the Chicago Cubs.

6910 Stars 1953 *California (C)*. Team was a farm club of the Hollywood Stars.

6911 Redlegs 1957–59 *California (C)*. Team was a farm club of the Cincinnati Redlegs.

6912 Athletics 1960–61 *California (C)*. Team was a farm club of the Kansas City Athletics.

6913 White Sox 1962 *California (C)*. Team was a farm club of the Chicago White Sox.

6914 Mets 1968–75 *California (A)*. Team was a farm club of the New York Mets.

6915 Oaks 1977–92, 1996–2008 *California (A)*. Oak trees are abundant in the Oakland-Visalia area. When the team started play in 1977, it took the old and newspaper-friendly name of "Oaks," used for more than 50 years by the old Oakland Oaks of the Pacific Coast League.

6916 Central Valley Rockies 1993–94 *California (A)*. Team was a farm club of the Colorado Rockies.

6917 Rawhide 2009 to date *California (A)*. Cowboys use whips made of rawhide to drive cattle. Holstein cows provide the region with milk and cowhide, which is used to make the famous "rawhide" whips used by cowboys to herd cattle dating to the 1870s in California. Visalia has been a cattle ranch center since 1880.

Wabash, Indiana

6918 Sycamores 1899 *Indiana–Illinois (ind.)*; 1900–01 *Indiana State (ind.)*. The city fathers of nineteenth century Wabash planted Sycamore trees along the city's lanes. Sycamore trees are found in the nearby Salomonie and Frances Slocum state forests.

6919 Browns 1899 *Indiana–Illinois (ind.)*; 1900–01 *Indiana State (ind.)*. Players wore brown hose.

6920 Rockeries 1909–11 *Northern State of Indiana (D)*. The nearby Wabash River has so many collectible rocks on its floor that many residents created beautiful rock gardens, each one known as a "rockery," throughout the city. Wabash soon became known as the "Rock City." With manager Eddie Pferferle at the helm, newspapers called the players "Eddie Pferferle's Rockeries."

Waco, Texas

6921 Babies 1889–90x *Texas (ind.)*. Team and league disbanded June 10. In this era a new (or expansion) franchise was sometimes called the "Baby," while the young players on such a team were called "Babies." This inexperienced "baby" team finished last in 1889. The moniker became associated with losing teams, insomuch as new teams were almost always outclassed by more experienced teams. With manager Charles Levi at the helm in 1890, newspapers called the players "Levi's Babies."

6922 Giants 1890 *Texas (ind.)*. Team and league disbanded June 10. With the players a year older, the team improved to a winning 24–20 record, pleasing fans and newspapers, who started calling them the "Giants"—a slang in this era for a winning team. With manager Charles Levis at the helm, newspapers called the players "Levi's Giants."

6923 Hubites 1892x *Texas (ind.)*. Team disbanded June 10. Because of its geographic and commercial importance, the city became known as the "Hub of Texas."

6924 Tigers m1897 *Texas (ind.)*. Team started season in Sherman (TX) and moved to Waco in mid-season (date unknown); 1902x *Texas (D)*. Team disbanded July 8. Team disbanded July 8; 1905 *Texas (C 1905, 1907–10, D 1906, B 1911–20)*. The 1897 team started the season as the Sherman-Denison "Tigers" (the players wore striped stockings) and moved here in mid-season. The striped hose and the nickname were retained. With field manager Emmitt Rogers at the helm in 1902, newspapers called the striped hose players "Emmitt Rogers' Tigers." With manager Don Curtis at the helm in 1905, newspapers called the players "Curtis' Tigers." In 1907, the players switched from striped woolen stockings to white cotton sanitary hose with a looped stirrup stocking over it. The stirrup stocking had brown and yellow stripes.

6925 Yellowjackets 1898–1901 *Independent Negro* team. Players wore yellow and black striped hose.

6926 Steers m1903 *Texas (D)*. Team began season in Paris (TX) and moved to Waco June 26. In 1897, Dallas newspapers called their team "Sullivan's Steers" in honor of manager Ted Sullivan. When Sullivan was named manager of the Waco team in 1903, the Waco newspapers, reviving the moniker from Sullivan's Dallas' days, called his Waco players "Sullivan's Steers."

6927 Navigators 1906–19 *Texas (C 1907–10, D 1906, B 1911–19)*. Cargo and pilot ships have navigated the Brazos River since the city was founded 1856. Waco is nicknamed the "Queen of the Brazos." The nickname was maintained under the managers as follows: Lee Dawkins' Navigators, Frederick Cavender's Navigators, Brooks Gordon's Navigators, Ellis Hardy's Navigators, and Archie Tanner's Navigators.

6928 Skippers 1912–13 *Texas (B)*. Moniker was a spin-off from

"Navigators." With Ellis Hardy and Thomas Carson as managers, players were called "Ellis' Skippers" and "Carson's Skippers."

6929 Indians 1923–24 *Texas Assn.* (*D*). The Waco (aka Hueco) and Cherokee Indians inhabited this region into the nineteenth century. The team was not a farm club of the Cleveland Indians.

6930 Cubs 1925–30 *Texas* (*A*); 1933m *Dixie* (*C*). Team moved to Pine Bluff (AR) June 27. Manager Del Pratt led the 1925–30 team, which had many young players who were known in the slang of the era as "cubs." The 1933 team also had young players.

6931 Dons 1947 *Big State* (*B*). Before Texas joined the U.S. in 1850, the city of Waco was ruled by the old Spanish Dons of the eighteenth century and the Mexican Dons of 1824–49.

6932 Pirates 1948–53m *Big State* (*B*). Team moved to Longview (TX) June 27, 1953, after a tornado destroyed Katy Park in Waco. The team was a farm club of the Pittsburgh Pirates.

6933 Pirates 1954–56 *Big State* (*B*). The team was a farm club of the Pittsburgh Pirates.

Wahpeton-Breckenbridge, Minnesota

6934 Twins 1921–22 *Dakota* (*D*). The team represented both cities. All home games were played in Wahpeton, but fans from Breckenbridge, which is in the same metropolitan area, were encouraged to attend—a common practice for a team representing two cities.

Wailuku, Maui, Hawaii

6935 Stingrays 1993–97 *Hawaii Winter* (*W*). The stingray swims the waters off the coasts of the Hawaiian Islands. The devil ray, aka manta and devil fish, of the family Mobulidae, is different than the stingray of the family Dasyatidae. The devil ray has wing-like fins while the stingray has a tail with a poisonous spine.

6936 Maui Strong Warriors 2010 *Golden* (*ind.*); 2011 *North American* (*ind.*). The Golden, Northern and United leagues of 2010 merged to form the North American League in 2011. The Polynesian warriors were known for their bravery and strength. The name in the Polynesian language is "Na Koa Ikaika." The team is also called **Maui Na Koa Ikaika.**

Waipahu, Oahu Island, Hawaii

6937 West Oahu Canefires 1995–97 *Hawaii Winter* (*W*). Sugar cane is routinely burned to extract sugar. The Oahu Sugar Company transports sugar to packing houses in the city.

6938 North Shore 2006–08 *Hawaii Winter* (*W*). The team plays in a park in Waipahu, which is located on the north shore of Pearl Harbor.

Walden, New York

6939 Hummingbirds m1946 *North Atlantic* (*D*). Team started the season as the Newburgh (NY) Hummingbirds and moved to Walden May 23. The nickname was retained. The Ruby-throated Hummingbird is found throughout the northeastern U.S.

Waldorf, Maryland

6940 Southern Maryland Blue Crabs 2008 to date *Atlantic* (*ind.*). The blue crab is an aquatic arthropod found in the Atlantic and Gulf coastal waters.

Walla Walla, Washington

6941 Walla Walla Base Ball Club *Pacific Interstate* (*ind.*). Team had no nickname.

6942 Walla Wallans 1908 *Inland Empire* (*D*). The Walla Walla (Little River People) Indians once inhabited the lower Walla Walla River region. Walla Wallans are inhabitants of the city of Walla Walla.

6943 Bears 1912–14 *Western Tri-State* (*C* 1912–13, *D* 1914); 1969–71, 1983 *Northwest* (*A*). With manager Gus Badz (also spelled Bade) at the helm in 1912, newspapers called the players "Badz' Bears." With a city name of ten letters and one space, newspaper editors loved "Bears." Brown bears, black bears and grizzly bears inhabit the Pacific Northwest of the U.S. and western Canada.

6944 Islanders 1972 *Northwest* (*A*). Team was a farm club of the PCL Hawaii Islanders.

6945 Rainbows 1972 *Northwest* (*A*). Washington State has a rainy climate, causing the appearance of many rainbows here. Walla Walla is the "Place of Many Waters."

6946 Padres 1973–82 *Northwest* (*A*). Team was a farm club of the San Diego Padres.

Waltham, Massachusetts

6947 Waltham Base Ball Club 1884 *Massachusetts State Assn.* (*ind.*). Team played several home games in Worcester (MA) in midseason. Team had no nickname.

6948 Rosebuds 1934m *Northeastern* (*B*). Team moved to Worcester (MA) May 24. The city was named after Waltham Abbey of England, whose city flag bears a red rose. Waltham (USA) also uses a red rose and hosts an annual garden and flower show every spring.

Wappinger Falls, New York

6949 Hudson Valley Renegades 1994–97 *New York–Pennsylvania* (*A*). The Wappinger Indians were the most prominent of the Hudson River Indians, who fought the Dutch in 1640–45 and then were driven along with the Delaware Indians northward. The team logo is a raccoon, whose image is sometimes used for sports teams named "Bandits" or "Renegades" because this animal's facial fur is usually dark around the eyes, giving the image of a bandit's mask. In the nineteenth century, the word "renegade" was interchangeable with bandit, robber, thief and burglar.

Warren, Minnesota

6950 Wanderers 1917x *Northern* (*C*). Team and league disbanded July 4 because of U.S. entry into World War I. As the team skidded to a 16–30 mark, which dropped them into last place, fans started refusing to show for games at the ballpark. Management then took the team on an extended road trip, prompting newspapers to brand the team with the typical contemporary slang of "Wanderers." With manager Frank Withrow at the helm, newspapers called the players "Withrow's Wanderers."

Warren, Pennsylvania

6951 Wonders 1895 *Iron & Oil* (*ind.*); 1898x *Iron & Oil* Circuit and city disbanded in mid-season (date unknown). The Brooklyn PL (1890) and Brooklyn NL (1891–92) teams, managed by John Montgomery Ward, were known as "Ward's Wonders." The moniker never caught on because they didn't win anything. The Warren team, assigned the "Wonders" moniker in April of this season by local newspapers in the hopes of a "wondrous" season, didn't win either and the fans and newspapers ditched it.

6952 Blues 1908x *Interstate (D)*. Team and league disbanded June 5. The team had a loose affiliation with the American League Cleveland Blues (also known as the Naps in 1908). Players wore blue-trim uniforms and stirrups. In the era 1885–1920, minor league teams geographically close to major league cities sometimes had a loose affiliation with the team.

6953 Bingos m1914–16x *Interstate (D)*. Team disbanded August 4. Team was a farm club of the Binghamton Bingos. The moniker was appropriate because Pennsylvania brandy drinkers (manufactured in Brandywine, PA) of the eighteenth and nineteenth centuries were known as "bingos." With manager William Webb at the helm, newspapers called the players "Bill's Bingos." George Bell took over in 1915 and the name became "Bell's Bingos." The term "bingo" is baseball jargon for a base hit.

6954 Redskins 1940–41 *Pennsylvania State Assn. (D)*. Team was a farm club of the Cleveland Indians. Just as the NFL 1933–36 Boston "Redskins" moniker was a spin-off from the NFL 1932 Boston "Braves," the Warren baseball team went with "Redskins," also in emulation of the NFL Washington "Redskins," who were winning the NFL Eastern Division in 1940. The "Redskins" nickname was not "politically incorrect" in this era. Selected words and images in American English only became "politically incorrect" in the 1960s and 1970s. With manager William Rhiel at the helm in 1940, newspapers called the players "Rhiel's Redskins." The name was retained in 1941 under Alex McColl.

6955 Buckeyes 1940–41 *Pennsylvania State Assn. (D)*. Oak trees are not only common in Ohio but also in Pennsylvania. The buckeye is the nut of the oak tree. Under manager William Rhiel, the team was called "Bill's Buckeyes."

Warsaw, North Carolina

6956 Red Sox 1947–48 *Tobacco State (D)*. Players wore red stirrups. The team was not a farm club of the AL Boston Red Sox.

Warwick, Rhode Island

6957 Rhode Island Tiger Sharks 1996 *Northeast (ind.)*. The city is located along the East Greenwich and Naragansett bays where tiger sharks swim near the coast.

Washington, District of Columbia

6958 Olympics 1871–72 *National Assn. (M)*. In the nineteenth century, sporting teams espoused the "Olympic Ideal" (although the first modern Olympic games were not held until 1898), which prompted numerous athletic clubs in various sports, i.e., baseball, lacrosse, rowing, town ball, rounders, cricket, etc., to refer to themselves as the Olympic Club.

6959 Blue Stockings 1871–72 *National Assn. (M)*. Manager Nick Young dressed his players in blue hose as a deliberate spin-off from the Boston Red Stockings, Brooklyn Orange Stockings, Chicago White Stockings, and New York Green Stockings. Originally "Blue Stockings," newspapers shortened it to **Blue Legs** and **Blues**.

6960 Nationals 1872–73 *National Assn. (M)*; 1879–80 *National Assn. (M)*; 1881x *Eastern Championship Assn. (M)*. Team disbanded June 7; 1884 *Union Assn. (M)*; 1885 *Eastern (ind.)*; 1886–89 *National (M)*; 1891 *American Assn. (M)*; 1905–56 *American (M)*; 2005 to date *National (M)*. The "National Baseball Club," manned by federal office clerks, was established in 1859. The team disbanded in 1861 because of the Civil War, reformed in 1865, and then turned professional in 1870. The moniker is based on the status of Washington, D.C., as the "Nation's Capital." "Nationals" was chosen in an April 1905 fan poll to get away from the losing image of Senators, but the moniker never

caught on. Newspapers invariably shortened it to "Nats." The longer version of "Nationals" was shunned by fans and newspapers. The first time the "Nationals" moniker appeared in print was in *The Sporting News* May 20, 1905.

6961 Black Stockings 1875 *National Assn. (M)*. Players wore black hose. Originally **Black Stockings**, newspapers shortened it to **Black Legs**. In this era, the term "Blackleg" meant a "gambler," but there was no "politically incorrect" sense of indignation in the nineteenth century.

6962 Southerners 1875 *National Assn. (M)*. In the 1870s, Washington was the southern-most major league baseball city.

6963 Senators 1884 *American Assn. (M)*; 1886–89 *National (M)*; 1890 *Atlantic Assn. (ind.)*; 1891 *American Assn. (M)*; 1892–99 *National (M)*; 1901–04 & 1957–60 *American (M)*; 1912x *United States (ind.)*. Team disbanded May 27. 1961–71 *American (M)*. As many as thirty professional baseball teams (not including farm clubs) playing their home games in a state capital or the national capital in Washington, D.C., 1884 to date have been called "Senators" after these federal legislators who meet in the U.S. Senate House. With manager Mike Scanlon at the helm in 1884, newspapers called the players "Scanlon's Senators." It was the first use of "Senators" for a Washington, D.C., professional baseball team.

6964 Statesmen 1884 *American Assn. (M)*; 1886–89 *National (M)*; 1891 *American Assn. (M)*. Tag was a spin-off from Senators.

6965 Capitals 1887x *National Colored (ind.)*. Circuit and team disbanded May 23. Tag was a spin-off from Nationals. Originally **Capital Citys**, newspapers shortened it to "Capitals."

6966 Hapless Senators 1901–11 *American (M)*. Joining the AL in 1901, the Hapless Senators forced their fans to suffer through their first eleven seasons with losing records. Over the next 12 seasons the Senators improved as the team posted six winning campaigns. The nickname was coined by baseball author Jeff Carroll.

6967 Solons 1901–60 *American (M)*; 1961–71 *American (M)*. An ancient name derived from the ancient Greek leader Solon, the term originally meant "politician" or "man of the government." By the nineteenth century, it had evolved into meaning a "senator." Newspapers used it eagerly because it had only six letters.

6968 Nats 1905–60 *American (M)*; 1961–71 *American (M)*; 2005 to date *National (M)*. The selection of "Nationals" as the Washington AL team's official nickname in 1905 was undone almost immediately as Washington fans yawned at it. But newspapers liked the diminutive, space-saving "Nats" spin-off tag so much that the "Nats" moniker became the automatic newspaper contraction for "Senators" for the next 67 years.

6969 First in War, First in Peace and Last in the American League 1909–60 *American (M)*. Phrase is not a nickname but rather a slogan — and one of the most famous baseball franchise slogans ever. The phrase arose in 1909 as the Washington club completed its fourth consecutive last-place finish in the American League. In 1955 the slogan was used again as the franchise finished last four times in six seasons, driving attendance down so low that owner Calvin Griffith (son of Clark) moved the franchise to Minneapolis–St. Paul in 1961. The phrase originated with U.S. Army General "Light Horse" Harry Lee's eulogy for George Washington in 1799 and praised Washington as "First in War, First in Peace, and First in the Hearts of His Country Men!" By 1910, the phrase was used in any season the team finished last.

6970 Griffs 1912–60 *American (M)*. When ex-pitcher Clark Griffith took the reins of field manager in 1912, newspapers started calling the Washington players the "Griffs." In 1920 Griffith had accumulated enough money to become part-owner, and later in the 1930s became sole owner of the team. As a result, the newspaper-friendly name of "Griffs" became permanent. Aka the **Griffmen**.

6971 Red Caps 1920 *Independent Negro team*. Players wore red caps.

6972 Braves 1921–22 *Independent Negro team*. Tag was a spin-off from "Red Caps." Originally "Red Braves," newspapers shortened the nickname of these red-capped players to "Braves."

6973 Black Sox 1922 *Independent Negro team*. Players wore black-trim hose. The moniker was a spin-off from the 1875 National Association Washington "Black Stockings."

6974 Potomacs 1923 *Independent Negro team*; 1924 *Eastern Colored (M)*. The city of Washington, D.C., is built along the banks of the Potomac River.

6975 Damn Senators 1924 *American (M)*. In a tongue-in-cheek spinoff from the "Damn Yankees" of the era 1949–64 (which gave rise to a Broadway play and a Hollywood movie), baseball author Mark Gavreau Judge wrote a book with this title on the exploits of the 1924 Washington Senators—the only World Series champion in the 155-year history of Washington D.C. baseball (1855–2010).

6976 First in War, First in Peace, First in Everything 1924 *American (M)*. Coined by *ESPN Baseball Magazine*, the term praised the 1924 AL and world champion Senators with a spin-off from "Light Horse" Harry Lee's 1799 eulogy for George Washington and the unflattering play on words of this phrase to describe chronically losing Senator teams.

6977 Grays 1928 *Independent Negro team*. Players wore gray-trim uniforms.

6978 Pilots 1932 *East–West (M)*; 1933–34 *Independent Negro team*. Pilot boats guide cargo traffic along the nearby Potomac River.

6979 The Wrecking Crew of '33 1933 *American (M)*. A spinoff of the Brooklyn Dodgers "Wrecking Crews" of the 1950s, baseball writer Gary Sarnoff used this moniker as the title of his 2009 book about the slugging Washington Senators, who won the city's last major league pennant in 1933. Although hitting only 60 home runs, the Senators hit 261 doubles (second in the AL), 86 triples (first) and batted .287 (first) en route to a splendid 99–53 record.

6980 Elite Giants 1936–37 *National Negro (M)*. The independent Nashville Elite Giants moved to Washington D.C. and then joined the National Negro League.

6981 Black Senators 1938 *Independent Negro team*. The team received uniforms and equipment donated to them by the American League Washington Senators. The team assumed the name on the Senators jerseys.

6982 Royals 1939 *Independent Negro team*. Tag was a spin-off from Senators. Bouncing away from American-style government, the team went for a nickname of the British monarchy—in this case "Royals." The moniker was also a spin-off from the Kansas City Monarchs and the Brooklyn Royal Giants.

6983 Homestead Grays 1939–48 *National Negro (M)*. Pittsburgh Homestead Grays moved to Washington D.C. for the 1939 season. The team name was retained.

6984 The Liveliest Corpse in the American League 1959 *American (M)*. Tag was coined by *Dell Baseball Magazine* in March 1960 because even though the Senators finished last in the American League in 1959 with a poor 63–81 mark, the team hit 163 home runs (second in the AL), including round-trippers hit by Harmon Killebrew (42), Jim Lemon (33), Bob Allison (30) and Roy Sievers (21).

6985 First of the Worst 1961–71 *American (M)*. Coined by historical baseball writer Bill Gilbert, it referred to this franchise's status as the first of eight granted an expansion franchise by the big leagues in the 1960s—the others being the Los Angeles Angels (1961), Houston Astros (1962), New York Mets (1962), Kansas City Royals (1969), Montreal Expos (1969), San Diego Padres (1969), and Seattle Pilots (1969). Before moving to Dallas–Fort Worth, Texas, in 1972, the team could only muster a single winning season (86–76 in 1969)

in eleven years in the nation's capital. Expansion teams in pro sports are notorious for being the worst teams in a given league during their early years, which usually lasts from three to 10 seasons. The Senators were a prime example by losing 100+ games four times and finishing last in the 10-club American League four times.

6986 Hapless Senators 1961–71 *American (M)*. The tag was coined by baseball writer Rich Westcott to describe this expansion team that produced 10 losing seasons in its 11-year existence. In their first four seasons, the "Hapless Senators" lost 407 games, including 100+ defeats each year.

6987 Nasty Nats 2005 to date *National (M)*. Tag was coined by baseball broadcaster Ken Harrelson. Harrelson is the "Master of Nicknames" with regard to his coinage of nicknames for players, i.e., Frank "The Big Hurt" Thomas, and for teams, i.e., Atlanta "Bravos," Boston "Carmines" and Texas "Wranglers." The Harrelson usage was mainly affectionate, but bitterly disillusioned D.C. fans have hurled it at the players as an epithet for producing one lousy season after another since moving here from Montreal in 2005.

6988 Gnats 2006 to date *National (M)*. When the team fell flat on its face with four consecutive losing seasons, including 205 losses in 2008–09, angry D.C. fans started spinning-off "Nats" into "Gnats." A gnat is a pesky, irritating mosquito-like insect, which also means something small and insignificant.

6989 Natinals 2009 *National (M)*. Two players—Adam Dunn and Ryan Zimmerman—wore uniforms with the team nickname misspelled on their jerseys as "Natinals." What would seem like a trivial incident was magnified by disgruntled fans and local newspapers as a symbol of the franchise's perennial negligence, which was blowing away the goodwill of D.C. fans, who seemingly have waited for a winner forever (last pennant was in 1933).

Washington, Indiana

6990 Washington Base Ball Club 1896 *Kentucky–Indiana (ind.)*. Team had no nickname.

Washington, New Jersey

6991 Potomacs 1932 *Interstate (D)*. Team and league disbanded June 20 because of the Great Depression. Even though the team is located in New Jersey near the Delaware River and is nowhere near the Potomac River, management of this Organized Baseball team chose "Potomacs" for the name recognition possessed by the 1923–24 Negro League teams of Washington, D.C.

Washington, Pennsylvania

6992 Little Senators 1896 *Interstate (ind.)*. Because this Pennsylvania city is the namesake of the nation's capital where the major league Senators were playing, local newspapers called these young minor league players the "Little Senators."

6993 Patriots 1905 *Ohio–Pennsylvania (C)*. Patriotic George Washington was the "Pater Patriae," which is Latin for the "Father of His Country."

6994 Washington Baseball Club 1906–07 *Pennsylvania–Ohio–Michigan (P.O.M.) (D)*. Team had no nickname.

6995 Generals 1934–35 *Pennsylvania State Assn. (D)*. With manager Benny Bengough at the helm, newspapers called the players "Benny Bengough's Generals."

6996 Redbirds 1939–42 *Pennsylvania State Assn. (D)*. Team was a farm club of the St. Louis Cardinals.

6997 Wild Things 2002 to date *Frontier (ind.)*. "Wild Thing" is slang for a wild animal, i.e., a wildcat. Indeed, the team logo is a wildcat. A new slant on this slang was popularized by the 1960s rock song "Wild Thing," i.e., an attractive young woman interested in passionate pleasures.

Waterbury, Connecticut

6998 Brass Citys 1884 *Connecticut (ind.)*. Known as the "Brass City" and the "Brass Center of the World," Waterbury was home to the Anaconda American Brass Company, Chase Brass & Company, and Scorill Brass Manufacturing Company.

6999 Waterbury Base Ball Club 1885 *Southern New England (ind.)*. Team jumped leagues, leaving the Southern New England League and joining the Eastern League September 4, 1885; 1891 *Connecticut State (ind.)*; 1894 *Connecticut State*. While a member of the SENL in 1885, team had no nickname. The 1891 and 1894 teams also had no nickname.

7000 W's 1885–86 *Eastern (ind.)*. Team jumped leagues, leaving the Southern New England League and joining the Eastern League September 4, 1885. The contraction was used in newspaper headlines, i.e., "W's edge Elms, 4–3."

7001 Giants 1888 *Connecticut State (ind.)*; 1966–67, 1977–78 *Eastern (AA)*. The 1888 team had a loose affiliation with the New York Giants. In the nineteenth century, some minor league teams that were only a 100 miles or so from a big league team would develop a very loose affiliation with the major league club involving players, contract purchases, equipment and uniforms with the minor league outfit adopting the "parent" club's team nickname. The 1966–67 and 1977–89 teams were farm clubs of the San Francisco Giants.

7002 Ponies 1897 *Connecticut State (ind.)*. "Ponies" was a nineteenth century baseball slang for: 1) an expansion team; 2) a syndicate club whose players were being stolen by the richer team of the syndicate; and 3) young players. In this case, the Waterbury team had a roster of many young players.

7003 Roughriders 1898–1900 *Connecticut State (ind.)*. With manager Roger Connor at the helm, newspapers called the players "Roger Connor's Roughriders." With Teddy Roosevelt's "Roughriders" making charges up and down San Juan Hill in Cuba during the Spanish-American War of 1897–98, some sports teams fancied themselves as "roughriders." The moniker was a spin-off from "Ponies." The name was also partly inspired by Fred Drew (born in Waterbury in 1829), who was an army doctor serving with the rough-riding "Pony Soldiers" of Fort Riley in the 1870s and 1880s.

7004 Braves 1900 *Connecticut State (ind.)*. "Braves" in this era was slang for baseball players. Baseball players were known by a plethora of cowboy and Indian names, i.e., Indians, Rustlers, Warriors, and Braves.

7005 Hustlers 1901 *Connecticut State (ind.)*. With manager Roger Connor at the helm, newspapers called the players "Roger's Hustlers" and "Connor's Hustlers." The tag "hustler" in this era was slang for baseball players. The connotation with gambling would not arise until the 1970s.

7006 Authors 1906–08 *Connecticut (B)*. By 1900 noted writer and author Eugene O'Neill, who grew up in Connecticut, was a celebrity. With manager Harry Durant at the helm, newspapers called the players "Durant's Authors." The rival Bridgeport club, managed by James "Orator" O'Rourke, was known as "O'Rourke's Orators"—which gave rise to an "Authors vs. Orators" rivalry.

7007 Invincibles 1909 *Connecticut (B)*. The period 1899–1920 was one where unjustifiably cocky team nicknames with no regard to their actual pennant chances were used, i.e., Superbas, Perfectos, Wonders and Invincibles. The rival New Britain team of this circuit went with "Perfectos," provoking the local Waterbury newspapers to call their players by the title of Michael "Doherty's Invincibles,"

which they felt was justified because manager Doherty was the first modern major league player to perform on two World Series–winning teams. The team was not at all invincible, however, producing a mediocre 64–61 record and finishing in fourth place. Moreover, the New Britain Perfectos also flopped, finishing 10 games out of the lead in third place.

7008 Finnegans 1910 *Connecticut (B)*. With manager Michael Finn at the helm, newspapers called the players the "Finnegans." In this era, a "Finnegan" was slang for an "Irishman," which was appropriate since a disproportionate number of baseball players were Irish. The 1910 Waterbury club also had some Irish-Americans on the team.

7009 Champs 1911 *Connecticut (B)*. Team won 1910 pennant. Started by manager John McGraw's "World Champions" lettering across the jerseys of his 1906 New York Giants (they had won the 1905 World Series), several teams called themselves "Champions" after winning the previous season's pennant. When Cleveland AL did it for the 1921 season, the fad was already waning as fans and newspapers felt it to be too pretentious.

7010 Spuds 1912m *Connecticut (B)*. Team moved to New Britain (CT) June 15. "Spud" was a nineteenth-century slang for "Irishman." Between 1850 and 1900, thousands of Irish immigrants settled in the city. The term "spud" derives from the Irish potato. Ireland's Great Potato Famine of 1840–49 drove thousands of Irish to immigrate to the United States.

7011 Contenders 1913 *Eastern Assn. (B)*. With manager Sam Kennedy at the helm, newspapers called the players "Kennedy's Contenders." Team struggled, though, finishing in third place, 13 games behind the lead. With the in-the-fad "Champions" much too audacious for an unproven team, the players were called by the hopeful but cautious moniker of "Contenders."

7012 Frolickers 1914 *Eastern Assn. (B)*. With manager Lee Fohl at the helm, newspapers called the players "Fohl's Frolickers." Baseball players—often called Colts, Bronchos, Ponies, Lambs, Rabbits, Cubs and Chicks—frolicked about the field before, after and during games.

7013 Huskies 1914 *Eastern Assn. (B)*. Tag derived from the University of Connecticut mascot. Because the school's abbreviation of "UConn" sounds like the Alaskan "Yukon," where the snow dogs known as huskies abound, the college team was called the "Huskies," which went straight to the city's professional baseball team this summer. With manager Lee Fohl at the helm, the players were known as "Lee Fohl's Huskies."

7014 Nattatucks 1918–19 Eastern *(B 1918, C 1919)*. The Indians who settled here hundreds of years ago called this region Mattatuck. They sold Mattatuck to the Pilgrims in 1657, which was founded as the city of Waterbury in 1673. Over a period of a hundred years, the name Mattatuck evolved into Nattatuck.

7015 Brasscos 1920–22 *Eastern (C)*. Moniker is a spin-off from the team's owner—the American Brass Company. The American Brass Companies formed in 1899 from the merger of Ansonia, Coe and Waterbury Brass companies. Later, ABC changed its name to ARCO Metals.

7016 Timers 1947–50 *Colonial (B)*. Waterbury was home to the Timex Watch Company. With manager James Acton at the helm in 1947, newspapers called the players "Jim Acton's Timers." The name was retained through 1950 under five other managers.

7017 Indians 1968–69 *Eastern (AA)*. Team was a farm club of the Cleveland Indians.

7018 Pirates 1970–71 *Eastern (AA)*. Team was a farm club of the Pittsburgh Pirates.

7019 Dodgers 1973–76 *Eastern (AA)*. Team was a farm club of the Los Angeles Dodgers.

7020 Giants 1977–78 *Eastern (AA)*. Team was a farm club of the San Francisco Giants.

7021 Athletics 1979 *Eastern (AA)*. Team was a farm club of the Oakland Athletics.

7022 Reds 1980–83 *Eastern (AA)*. Team was a farm club of the Cincinnati Reds.

7023 Angels 1984 *Eastern (AA)*. Team was a farm club of the California Angels.

7024 Indians 1985–86 *Eastern (AA)*. Team was a farm club of the Cleveland Indians.

7025 North Shore Spirit 1997–98 *Northeast (ind.)*; 1999–2000 *Northern (ind.)*. Team owner Nicholas Lopardo initially decided to name the team the Waterbury "Wizards," but the baseball Fort Wayne Wizards of the Midwest League threatened a copyright infringement lawsuit. Leopardo then switched to a patriotic motif, choosing as the team's mascot an eagle and naming the team the regional North Shore "Spirit," after the American "Spirit of '76," a phrase used to describe the American Revolutionary War of 1776–81. The team switched circuits in 1999. The team was also known as the Waterbury Spirits in 1997. Revolutionary hero Nathan Hale, executed by the British as a spy, was born in Connecticut. Connecticut privateers destroyed many British merchant boats.

Waterford, Oakland, Michigan

7026 Oakland County Cruisers 2010 *Frontier (ind.)*. Team played in suburban Detroit's Oakland County. Team disbanded after the 2010 season. By 1965, Ford (Mustang), Pontiac (Firebird) and Mercury (Cougar) were producing the popular "pony" cars. Today, these "pony" cars are known as "cruisers" — the driver and passengers can effortlessly "cruise the streets" in the pursuit of kicks.

Waterloo, Iowa

7027 Waterloo Base Ball Club 1895 *Eastern Iowa (ind.)*. Team had no nickname.

7028 Microbes 1904–06 *Iowa State (D)*. After the research of nineteenth-century microbiologists Louis Pasteur and Robert Koch convinced people of the existence of germs, the American public was becoming hygiene-conscious and insisted on clean drinking water. The connection between "microbes" and "water," as in "Waterloo," is obvious. The name was retained through 1906 under two other managers. The star pitcher of the 1904 team was Lawrence "Bugs" Raymond. He won 19 games (19–7) and became a major leaguer. With manager James Myers at the helm, newspapers also called the players "Myers' Microbes." In 1905 with new manager Harry Meeks at the helm, the name became "Meek's Microbes." The 1902 Chicago Nationals were called "Microbes" because the team had numerous short and puny fellows on the roster. There is no indication that the Waterloo team had diminutive fellows on the team.

7029 Cubs 1907 *Iowa State (D)*. Team had a loose affiliation with the Chicago Cubs. Local newspapers started calling the Waterloo players, who were very young, the "Cubs." A contemporary slang for young baseball players was "cubs."

7030 Lulus 1908–09 *Central Assn. (D)*. Moniker was used for newspaper headlines, i.e., "Lulus edge Bees, 4–3."

7031 Boosters 1910–11 *Three-I (B)*. With manager Frank Boyle at the helm, newspapers called the players "Boyle's Boosters." The moniker was popular in the era 1900–20, denoting a team that was contending for or winning a pennant, which often prompted fans to start a "booster club" to cheer on the players.

7032 Jays 1913–15 *Central Assn. (D)*. Team was named in honor of manager Jay Andrews.

7033 Shamrocks 1915–16 *Central Assn. (D)*. When Irish American manager Eddie Brennan took over in mid-season 1915, newspapers started calling the players the "Shamrocks." The shamrock, a three-leaf plant, is the national symbol of Ireland.

7034 Loons 1917 *Central Assn. (D)*. The yellow-billed loon is a duck-like water bird that inhabits nearby Loon Lake in wintertime.

7035 Hawks 1922–32 *Mississippi Valley (D)*; 1936 *Western (A)*; 1958–71 *Midwest (D 1958–62, A 1963–71)*. Moniker is a contraction of "hawkeye." Iowa is the "Hawkeye State." The name is appropriate because, although the state nickname derives from the Black Hawk chief "Hawkeye," the Midwest is inhabited by hawks.

7036 Reds 1937 *Western (A)*. The team had a loose affiliation with the NL Cincinnati Reds in 1937 before becoming a formal farm team with the NL Reds in 1938.

7037 Red Hawks 1938–39 *Three-I (B)*. Team, as in 1937, was a farm club of the Cincinnati Reds. Rather than continue with the "Reds" moniker, management combined "red" with "hawks" (the regional bird) and came up with "Red Hawks."

7038 White Hawks 1940–42 *Three-I (B)*. When the Chicago White Sox took over as the parent club, the nickname was changed from "Red Hawks" to "White Hawks."

7039 Royals 1972–76 *Midwest (A)*. Team was a farm club of the Kansas City Royals.

7040 Indians 1977–78 *Midwest (A)*. Team was a farm club of the Cleveland Indians.

7041 Diamonds 1989–93 *Midwest (A)*. Team was a co-operative operation in 1989 with players sent here by the Oakland A's, Baltimore Orioles and San Diego Padres. Management held a name-the-team contest and the winner was "Diamonds." The team logo was a baseball diamond of Riverside Park (the team's home field) capped with a14-carat gem. The diamond reflected the state of Iowa's stature as the "Brightest Star in the American Constellation." San Diego took over as the sole parent club 1990–93 but the name was retained. The National League Arizona Diamondbacks are also known as the "D-Backs" but they are never referred to as the "Diamonds."

Waterloo, New York

7042 Waterloo Base Ball Club 1888 *New York State (ind.)*. Team had no nickname.

Watertown, Massachusetts

7043 Townies 1888 *Eastern International (ind.)*; 1934 *Northeastern (A)*. A "townie" was a nineteenth-century slang for: 1) a person who lived his or her whole life in only one town; and, 2) a person who was an inhabitant of a city whose name ends in the suffix of "town," i.e., Allentown, Charlestown, Hagerstown, Pottstown and Watertown. Newspapers used the moniker for headlines, i.e., "Townies edge Belleville, 4–3." Spin-off tags for baseball teams from various types of municipalities include Burghers (Pittsburgh), Burros (Attleboro), Municipals (Monroe) and Villies (Holdenville).

Watertown, New York

7044 Watertown Base Ball Club 1886 *Central New York (ind.)*. Team had no nickname.

7045 Havana Red Sox 1913 *Independent Negro team*. Players wore red-trim stirrups. Several players on the team were black Cubans who played winter ball with the Havana Red Sox (Los Rojos de la Habana).

7046 Havana Black Sox 1920–25 *Independent Negro team*. Players wore black-trim stirrups. This team also had some players from Havana, Cuba — hence the name "Havana Black Sox."

7047 Grays m1936m *Canadian–American (C)*. The team played a series of home games in Massena (NY) between June 24 and July 12 before returning to Watertown July 13. The players wore gray uniforms.

7048 Athletics 1946–51 *Border (C)*. Team was a farm club of the Philadelphia Athletics.

7049 Pirates 1983–88 *New York–Pennsylvania (A)*. Team was a farm club of the Pittsburgh Pirates.

7050 Indians 1989–98 *New York–Pennsylvania (A)*. Team was a farm club of the Cleveland Indians.

Watertown, South Dakota

7051 Cubs 1921–22 *Dakota (D)*; 1923x *South Dakota (D)*. Circuit and team disbanded July 17. The team had numerous young players who were known in the slang of the era as "cubs." Brown bears and grizzly bears inhabit North and South Dakota. With manager John Mokate at the helm in 1922, newspapers called the players "Mokate's Cubs."

7052 Expos 1970–71 *Northern (A)*. Team was a farm club of the Montreal Expos.

Watsonville, California

7053 Infants 1898x *California (ind.)*. Team disbanded July 5. The team had mostly young players who showed their inexperience by struggling to a 6–13 record before disbanding July 5. A young team that struggled on the field was sometimes known by the contemporary slang of "Infants."

7054 Gardiners 1899 *California (ind.)*. Team was owned by Gardiner's Resort Hotel.

7055 Hayseeds 1899 *California (ind.)*. In this era "hayseed" was slang for a "farm boy." The name had a derogatory slant, meaning a bumpkin (unsophisticated) and a yokel (doltish). Since lots of baseball players in this era behaved like bumpkins and yokels, the slang was quite appropriate. Nearby apple and strawberry farms send fruit produce to city factories to be washed and packed. Watsonville is known as the "Strawberry Capital of the World." Strawberries used to be known as "hay-berries."

7056 Pippins m1913 *California State (D)*. Team started season in Vallejo (CA) and moved to Watsonville July 6. Apple orchards grow the famous Pippin apples, which are then transported to city packing houses. Martinelli's Apple Cider Company was located in the city.

Wausau, Wisconsin

7057 Lumberjacks 1905–07 *Wisconsin State (D)*; 1908 *Wisconsin–Illinois (D)*; 1909–11x *Minnesota–Wisconsin (C)* 1909–11, *(D)* 1912 Team disbanded June 26; 1912–14 *Wisconsin–Illinois (D)* 1912–13, *(C)* 1913–14; 1936–39, 1941 *Northern (C)*; 1946–53 *Wisconsin State (D)*; 1956–57 *Northern (C)*. Founded in 1839 by lumberman George Stevens, the city built wood mills to process pine trees transported here from Wisconsin forests. Up until 1900, Wisconsin was 80 percent forestland. The moniker was used with a line of managers as follows: Jack's [Corbett] Lumberjacks (1905), Jack's [Mott] Lumberjacks (mid-season 1905), Nick's [Malvern] Lumberjacks (1905–06), Mickey's [Malloy] Lumberjacks (1912), [Ernest] Landgraft's Lumberjacks (1913), [George] Bubsir's Lumberjacks (1914), Lute's [Boone] Lumberjacks (1936), Dickie Kerr's Lumberjacks (1937), Bunny Brief's Lumberjacks (1938) and Wally Gilbert's Lumberjacks (1941).

7058 Timberjacks 1940 *Northern (D)*, 1942 *Northern (C)*. Moniker was a spin-off from "Lumberjacks." With manager Walter Gilbert at the helm each year, newspapers called the players "Walter Gilbert's Timberjacks."

7059 Mets 1975–78 *Midwest (A)*. Team was a farm club of the New York Mets.

7060 Timbers 1979–90 *Midwest (A)*. Name was a spin-off from "Lumberjacks" and "Timberjacks."

Waverly, New South Wales, Australia

7061 Reds 1989–90–94–95 *Australian (W)*. Players wore red-trim uniforms and stirrups.

Waverly, New York

7062 Wagon-makers m1901 *New York State (ind.)*. Team began season as the Cortland (NY) "Wagon-Makers" and moved here July 11. The nickname was retained. With manager William A. Smith at the helm, newspapers called the players "Will's Wagon-makers." Wagon-making was in its last years in the United States, just prior to the start of the "Auto Age."

Waxahachie, Texas

7063 Buffaloes 1914 *Central Texas (D)*. Waxahachie is the Apache and Wichita Indian word for "Buffalo Creek. " Herds of buffaloes roamed this region for hundreds of years. By 1890 the surviving herds had been pushed out of the region. With manager Luther Burleson at the helm, newspapers called the players "Burleson's Buffaloes." The team had a loose affiliation with the Texas League Houston Buffaloes, receiving donated Buffaloes uniforms.

7064 Athletics 1915–16 *Central Texas (D)*. With manager Anson Cole at the helm in 1915, newspapers called the players "Anson's Athletics" and "Cole's Athletics." The name was retained in 1916 under Dee Poindexter.

Waycross, Ware, Georgia

7065 Machinists 1906 *Georgia State (D)*. With the advent of electricity, the city established machine shops to build mobile homes and manufacture furniture, crates, boxes, bricks and concrete. Machinists by the hundreds made the parts for the trains of the Atlantic Coast Line Railroad. After 1945 the city's machine shops manufactured airplane and missile parts.

7066 Blowhards 1913 *Empire State (D)*. Less than 100 miles from Georgia's southeast coast, the city is subject to the powerful winds of Atlantic storms. A slang for "braggart" since 1857, the word originally meant a windy storm. Baseball players in this era were often regarded as "blowhards," especially when they got drunk. With manager Charles Wahoo at the helm, local newspapers called the players "Charlie Wahoo's Blowhards."

7067 Grasshoppers 1914 *Georgia State (D)*. In this era, Georgia farms were periodically ravaged by grasshoppers, locusts and boll-weevils. More than thirty different types of grasshoppers plagued farms in the South. Newspapers shortened the name to **Hoppers**, i.e., "Hoppers edge Hornets, 4–3."

7068 Moguls 1914 *Georgia State (D)*; 1915 *Florida–Louisiana–Alabama–Georgia F.L.A.G. (D)*. Starting in 1874, freight locomotives, known as "Moguls," traveled in and out of Waycross' rail depot on the Atlantic Coast Line Railroad. With manager Langdon Clark at the helm in 1914, newspapers called the players "Langdon Clark's Moguls." With manager Hammond Reynolds at the helm, newspapers called the players "Hammond Reynolds' Moguls."

7069 Saints m1927m *Southeastern (B)*. The St. Augustine (FL) Saints played a series of home games here in mid-season, July 15–25, before returning to St. Augustine July 26.

7070 Bears 1939–42 *Georgia–Florida (D)*; 1946–55 *Georgia–Florida (D)*. The city of Waycross is located in Ware County. Like the San Antonio Bears (Bexar County), the team nickname was inspired by the county name, although the team nickname is listed with the city name. With manager Albert Leitz at the helm, newspapers called the players "Albert's Bears." Black bears inhabited the South until about 1740 when pioneers and settlers drove them westward. There are some bears today, however, found in the North Georgia Mountains and the Ocmulgee River.

7071 Braves 1956–58 *Georgia–Florida (D)*; 1963 *Georgia–Florida (A)*. Team was a farm club of the Milwaukee Braves.

Wayland, Massachusetts

7072 Birds m1934 *Northeastern (B)*. Team began season in Cambridge (MA) and moved to Wayland July 17. The most common wild bird here is the Northern Shrike, which occupies eastern North America. The Chickadee is the state bird of Massachusetts. With manager Bill Morrell at the helm, newspapers called the players "Bill Morrell's Birds."

Wayne, West Virginia

7073 West Virginia Coal Sox 1993x *Frontier (ind.)*. Team disbanded July 12.

Waynesboro, Pennsylvania

7074 Redbirds 1920, 1925, 1928–30 *Blue Ridge (D)*. Players wore red-trim uniforms. With league rivals Martinsburg (Blue Sox) using blue trim and Chambersburg (Maroons) using maroon trim, Waynesboro dressed its players in red trim for contrast. The team was not a farm club of the NL St. Louis Cardinals.

7075 Villagers 1921–23, 1926–27 *Blue Ridge (D)* Waynesboro is officially known as the Village of Waynesboro. With manager Bill Morris at the helm, newspapers called the players "Bill Morris' Villagers." The name was retained through 1924 under two other managers. Ed Greene took over in 1926 and the name became "Greene's Villagers."

Waynesburg, Pennsylvania

7076 Waynesburg Baseball Club 1906 *Pennsylvania–Ohio–Michigan (P.O.M.) (D)*. Team had no nickname.

Webb City, Missouri

7077 Missourians 1887 *Southwestern (ind.)*. Webb City was the only Missouri team in the league. An inhabitant of Missouri is known as a "Missourian."

7078 Webb City Base Ball Club 1891 *Southwestern (ind.)*. Team had no nickname.

7079 Goldbugs m1903 *Missouri Valley (D)*. Team started season in Nevada (MO) and moved here July 13. Team disbanded July 16; 1905 *Missouri Valley (C)*; 1906–07 *Western Assn. (C)*. When the Nevada club moved here on July 13, 1903, local newspapers didn't know what to call the yellow-hosed players. Since the Sedalia "Goldbugs," whose players also sported yellow stirrups, were in first place, the local newspaper called the new team the "Goldbugs" as well, in the hope that maybe some good luck would rub off on the new team.

The moniker may have been a jinx because the franchise, now bankrupt, disbanded only three days later. With the Sedalia Goldbugs now in the Western Association, the new Webb City club was emboldened to use the name again. The state of Missouri, long a hotbed of socialism and farmers' rights, supported the gold standard for U.S. dollar bills because it helped farmers and merchants against the banks. A supporter of the gold standard in Missouri was known as a "goldbug." With the Sedalia team disbanded in 1906, Webb City took sole possession of the "Goldbugs" name.

7080 Web-feet 1908–09m *Western Assn. (C)*. Ducks inhabit the nearby Grand Lake of the Cherokee southwest of the city and Stockton Lake northeast of the city. Although technically a reference to any web-footed aquatic bird, it is a usual slang for a "duck."

7081 Ducklings 1909m *Western Assn. (C)*. Team moved to Sapulpa (OK) July 18. The moniker was a spin-off from "Web-feet." With numerous young players on the 1909 team, the moniker of "Ducklings" was used. Local newspapers quickly shortened it to **Ducks**. In this era, a young player was sometimes called a "duckling."

Weir City, Missouri

7082 Browns 1891 *Southwestern (ind.)*. The team had a loose affiliation with the St. Louis Browns, who donated used equipment, uniforms and brown stockings to this team.

Welch, West Virginia

7083 Miners 1937–42 *Mountain State (D)*; 1946–55m *Appalachian (D)*. Team moved to Marion (VA) July 14. Coal mined from the nearby Pocahontas Coal Fields is transported to city factories to be processed.

Welland, Ontario, Canada

7084 Pirates 1989–94 *New York–Pennsylvania (A)*. Team was a farm club of the Pittsburgh Pirates.

7085 Aqua Ducks 1995–96 *North Atlantic (ind.)*. Water birds, i.e., ducks, inhabit the nearby Welland River. Ducks often swim the nearby Welland Canal.

Wellington, Kansas

7086 Wellington Base Ball Club 1887 *Kansas State (ind.)*. Team had no nickname.

7087 Dukes 1909–11x *Kansas State (D)*. Team played 10 home games in Wichita (KS) June 11–23, 1911. Team and league disbanded July 11, 1911. General Arthur Wellesley was a nineteenth century British statesmen who later became the first Duke of Wellington.

Wellsburg, West Virginia

7088 Wellsburg Base Ball Club 1891 *Ohio Valley (ind.)*. Team had no nickname.

Wellsville, New York

7089 Wellsville Base Ball Club 1890 *Western New York (ind.)*. Team had no nickname.

7090 Rainmakers 1914–16 *Interstate (D)*. In the era 1895–1920 teams that had several games cancelled due to rainy weather sometimes became known as the "Rainmakers." Rainy weather in this region produced an abundance of well water, which prompted the first settlers here to name their new city "Well's Ville."

7091 Yankees 1942–46 *Pennsylvania–Ohio–New York (P.O.N.Y.) (D)*. Team was a farm club of the New York Yankees.

7092 Nitros 1947, 1949 *P.O.N.Y. (D)*. Oil Springs (NY) in western New York State, one of the first U.S. oil fields, transported oil to the city for the manufacture of nitroglycerin, i.e., "nitro," to be used for "fracturing," i.e., blowing holes in the ground to facilitate the sinking of an oil rig drill.

7093 Red Sox 1948 *P.O.N.Y. (D)*. Team was a farm club of the Boston Red Sox.

7094 Senators 1950 *P.O.N.Y. (D)*. Team was a farm club of the Washington Senators.

7095 Rockets 1951–52 *P.O.N.Y. (D)*. Team owner Rocco Sgro, who took over as field manager in 1952, bought the team in 1951, prompting local newspaper to call the players "Rocco's Rockets." Sgro provided uniforms with the name "Rockets."

7096 Braves 1953–56 *P.O.N.Y. (D)*; 1957–61 *New York–Pennsylvania (D)*. Teams were farm clubs of the Milwaukee Braves.

7097 White Sox 1963–65 *New York–Pennsylvania (A)*. Team was a farm club of the Chicago White Sox.

Wenatchee, Washington

7098 Chiefs 1937–41 *Western International (B)*; 1946–54 *Western International (B)*; 1946–51 *(A)* 1952–54; 1955–65 *Northwest (B 1955–62, A 1963–65)*. The Pacific Northwest was once inhabited by the Chinook, Yakima, Wenatchee and other coastal Indians.

Wessington Springs, South Dakota

7099 Saints 1920 *South Dakota (D)*. City was founded in 1890 by Joseph Smith's Church of Jesus Christ and the Latter Day Saints (est. 1830).

West, Texas

7100 West Baseball Club 1914 *Central Texas (D)*. Team had no nickname.

West Baden, Indiana

7101 Sprudels 1910 *Central Texas (D)*; 1912–13 *Independent Negro team*. When the Central Texas team disbanded after the 1910 season, the 1912 black team picked up the nickname. West Baden has hot springs, which is named after the "Sprudel" hot springs found in the Czech Republic in Europe. "Sprudel" is the Czech word for "spring."

West Frankfort, Illinois

7102 Cardinals 1947–48 *Illinois State (D)*; 1949–50 *Missouri–Ohio Valley (M.O.V.) (D)*. Teams were farm clubs of the St. Louis Cardinals.

West Haven, New Haven, Connecticut

7103 West Haven Base Ball Club 1892 *Connecticut (ind.)*. Team had no nickname.

7104 Yankees 1972–79 *Eastern (AA)*. Team was a farm club of the New York Yankees.

7105 Whitecaps 1980 *Eastern (AA)*. Stormy weather causes the formation of white caps (breaking waves of white foam) in the nearby, appropriately named White River. Management dressed the players in all-white baseball caps.

7106 Athletics 1981–82 *Eastern (AA)*. Team was a farm club of the Oakland Athletics.

7107 New Haven County Cutters 2004 *Northeast (ind.)*; 2005–07 *Canadian–American (ind.)*. A "cutter" is a sailboat, which also uses oars, to transport light cargo and passengers on rivers and lakes. The city was built near the West River and the New Haven Harbor. The franchise disbanded after the 2007 season.

West Manchester, New Hampshire

7108 West Manchester Base Ball Club 1886 *New Hampshire (ind.)*. Team had no nickname.

West Palm Beach, Florida

7109 Sheriffs 1928 *Florida State (D)*. In 1928, a hurricane smashed into Florida and heavily damaged towns and cities, including West Palm Beach. The West Palm Beach Sheriff's Department dispatched police and deputy sheriffs to provide emergency relief to the city's inhabitants. To honor these officers, newspapers called the team the "Sheriffs." With manager Ernie Burke at the helm, newspapers called the players "Ernie's Sheriffs."

7110 Indians 1940–42x *Florida East Coast (D)*. Circuit and team disbanded May 14 because of U.S. entry into World War II; 1946–54x *Florida International (C)* 1946–48, *(B)* 1949–54. Circuit and team disbanded July 27; 1955 *Florida State (D)*. With manager Cecil Downs at the helm in 1940, newspapers called the players "Cecil Downs' Indians." Fans liked the name so much that even after Downs left the team in mid-season 1940, the moniker was retained through 1942. These teams were not farm clubs of the Cleveland Indians.

7111 Sun Chiefs 1956 *Florida State (D)*. After 14 years using "Indians" without being a farm club of the Cleveland Indians, management decided to avoid any further confusion with the Cleveland franchise. The new nickname combined "Sunshine State" (Florida's state nickname) and the Indians' spin-off of "Chiefs."

7112 Braves 1965–68 *Florida State (A)*; 1992–2006 *Gulf Coast (R)*. These teams were farm clubs of the Milwaukee (1965) and Atlanta (1966–68, 1992–2006) Braves.

7113 Expos 1969–77 *Florida State (A)*; 1992–97 *Gulf Coast (ind.)*. Teams were farm clubs of the Montreal Expos.

7114 Tropics 1989–90 *Senior Assn. (W)*. The Senior Professional Baseball Association was a "gimmick" league, limiting the rosters to pitchers and hitters over the age of 35 and catchers over the age of 30. Curious fans attended the games in 1989–90, but the gimmick wore off so quickly that the circuit disbanded midway in the 1990–91 season. The moniker refers to Florida's tropical weather.

West Plains, Missouri

7115 Badgers 1936m *Northeast Arkansas (D)*. Team moved to Caruthersville (MO) June 11. The badger is found in North America, including Missouri, but is not found in the "Badger State" of Wisconsin. The Wisconsin "badger" refers to lead miners.

West Warwick, Rhode Island

7116 Rhode Island Tiger Sharks 1996 *Northeast (ind.)*. City is built along the Pawtuxet River, which flows into Tiogue Lake. The moniker "Tiger Sharks" is an obvious spin-off from Tiogue Lake. Although some sharks do swim in Naragansett Bay to the east, the true Tiger Shark swims in the warmer waters of the Caribbean Sea and Pacific Ocean.

Westboro, Massachusetts

7117 W's 1878 *Independent.* Team joined the "New England Championship," which was a loose grouping of New England teams that was more a tournament than a true league. The tag was used for newspaper headlines, i.e., "W's edge Elms, 4–3."

Westfield, New Jersey

7118 Westfield Base Ball Club 1892x *Central New Jersey (ind.).* Circuit and team disbanded in mid-season (date unknown). Team had no nickname.

Wewoka, Oklahoma

7119 Wewoka Baseball Club m1924x *Oklahoma State (D).* Team began season in Guthrie (OK), moved to McAlester (OK) May 24, and then moved here June 8. Team and league disbanded July 8. The team had no nickname.

Wheeling, West Virginia

7120 Green Stockings 1887 *Ohio State (ind.).* Players wore green hose. Originally "Green Stockings," newspapers shortened it to **Green Legs.**

7121 Nailers 1888–90 *Tri-State (ind.);* 1891 *Ohio Valley (ind.);* 1894–97 *Interstate (ind.).* Iron and steel mills that sprang up here in the nineteenth century specialized in the manufacture of nails, screws, bolts and tacks. Wheeling became known as the "Nail City."

7122 Mountaineers 1895 *Iron & Oil (ind.).* West Virginia, in the heart of the Appalachian Mountains, is the "Mountain State."

7123 Stogies 1899–1900 *Interstate (ind.);* m1901 *Western Assn. (ind.).* Team began system in Grand Rapids (MI) and moved here June 3; 1903–12 *Central (B);* 1913 *Interstate (B);* 1915–16 *Central (B);* 1925–31 *Middle Atlantic (C);* 1933–34 *Mid-Atlantic (C).* In 1850, Mifflin Marsh, a Wheeling cigar manufacturer, created the "stogie"— a slender, cylindrical cigar that sold well because of its low price. Marsh named the cigar after the "Conestoga Wagons" of his boyhood pioneer days because these wagons, which came out of Conestoga (PA), kicked up a lot of smoky dust along the trail. Wheeling, like nearby Pittsburgh in this era, had numerous factories that belched black smoke out of their chimneys like a cigar. With manager C.S. "Pop" Shriver at the helm in 1915, local newspapers called the players "Shriver's Stogies." Harry Smith took over in 1916 and the name became "Smith's Stogies." With manager Jack Sheehan at the helm in 1933, newspapers called the players "Sheehan's Stogies."

Whiteville, North Carolina

7124 Tobs 1950 *Tobacco State (D).* North Carolina's tobacco industry dates to the eighteenth century. Officially **Tobacconists,** local newspapers shortened it to "Tobs."

Wichita, Kansas

7125 Braves 1887 *Western (ind.);* 1956–58 *American Assn. (AAA).* The tribes that inhabited Kansas before the nineteenth century included the Comanche, Cherokee, Cheyenne, Kiowa, Pottawatomie, Shawnee and the Wichita. The term "Braves" was a nineteenth-century slang for "baseball players." The 1956–58 team was a farm club of the Milwaukee Braves.

7126 Maroons 1891–92x *Kansas (ind.).* Players wore maroon hose.

7127 Jobbers 1905 *Western Assn. (C to June 1, D June 2, 1905);* 1909–11m *Western (A).* Team moved to Pueblo (CO) May 22; 1912–13 *Western (A);* 1918–20 *Western (A).* "Jobber" is slang for a wholesale merchant, the "middleman" who sells and buys goods. In Kansas, jobbers handled two major items: wheat and oil. Under the 1906 managers, the team was known as "Bill Kimmell's Jobbers" and "John Holland's Jobbers." With manager Frank Isbell at the helm, newspapers called the players "Isbell's Jobbers."

7128 Jabbers 1906 Western Assn. *(D).* "Jabbers" is another word for "cowpokes," i.e., cowboys who poked and prodded steers along the cattle drives of the old Chisholm Trail, starting in 1868, which contributed to the founding of the city of Wichita in 1870. Wichita soon became the "Cow Capital." The original team nickname in 1905 was "Jobber," but by 1906 it became "Jabber." In the April 22, 1907, the *Wichita Eagle,* a news story called the team the "Jabbers." Later in the season, the name had become "Jobber," indicating the two names were being used interchangeably. In 1907, the players "did the job," as they roared to a 98–35 record, 15-and-a-half games in front, to win their second pennant in three years. Even today the tag persists, i.e., the *Wichita Eagle* reported on a July 14, 2002, Wichita baseball team victory in a local amateur game that the Wichita boys "jabbed the opposing team like a boxer!"

7129 Witches m1911m *Kansas State (D).* After the Western League Jobbers left town, the Wellington (KS) Dukes KSL team moved here for a few games June 11–23, and then moved back to Wellington June 24. To avoid confusion with the "Jobbers," local newspapers called this team the obvious spin-off moniker of "Witches."

7130 Wolves 1914–16 *Western (A);* 1917, 1921–22 *Western (A).* Team moved to Colorado Springs (CO) September 10. The North American gray wolf is found in Kansas. With manager Clyde "Buzzy" Ware at the helm, local newspapers called the players "Clyde Ware's Wolves."

7131 Izzies 1923–36 *Western (A).* With manager Frank "Izzy" Isbell, former major leaguer and Wichita alumnus, at the helm, newspapers called the players "Isbell's Izzies."

7132 Larks 1927–28 *Western (A).* With manager Doc Crandall at the helm, newspapers called the players "Crandall's Larks." The moniker was appropriates because the lark and Old World songbird that now inhabits North America are found in Kansas.

7133 Aviators 1929–32 *Western (A).* In the 1920s Beech, Boeing and Cessna set up airplane manufacturing plants here. During World War II thousands of war planes were manufactured here. Wichita soon became known as the "World's Great Airplane Manufacturing Center" and the "Air Capital of the World." With manager Art Grigg at the helm, newspapers called the players "Art's Aviators." Jimmy Payton took over in 1932, making the name "Payton's Aviators."

7134 Oilers 1933m *Western (A).* Team moved to Muskogee (OK) June 6. Wichita is the "Petroleum Capital of Kansas." Kansas oil and natural gas wells transport oil and natural gas to city petrochemical factories.

7135 Indians 1950–55 *Western (A).* The Wichita Indians battled settlers starting in the eighteenth century until they were forced onto reservations in Oklahoma. The team had a loose affiliation with the AL Cleveland Indians in 1950 and then became a formal farm club of the AL Indians in 1951–52. The team became a farm of the AL St. Louis Browns in 1953 and then the Baltimore Orioles 1954–55 but retained the Indians moniker through 1955.

7136 Aeros 1970–84 *American Assn. (AAA).* Tag was a spin-off from Aviators.

7137 Pilots 1987 *Texas (AA).* Moniker was a spin-off from Aeros.

7138 Wranglers 1988–2007 *Texas (AA).* Cattle-driving cowboys—called "cattle wranglers"—pushed cattle along the Chisholm

Trail to ranches and meat-packing centers in Wichita during the era 1875–1900. "Wrangler" is derived from "wrestler," i.e., the cowboy had to wrestle a stray calf to the ground and rope him.

7139 Wingnuts 2008 to date *American Assn. (M)*. The "wing-nut" is a bolt has two flat projecting pieces, i.e., "wings," which can be readily tightened with the thumb and forefinger. The wing-nut has been used in the construction of airplanes here since the 1930s.

Wichita Falls, Texas

7140 Irish Lads 1911–13m *Texas–Oklahoma (D)*. With Irishman Fred Morris at the helm as manager, newspapers started calling the players "Morris' Irish Lads." Although Morris left the team after the 1911 season, the nickname was retained. With so many Irish Americans in professional baseball in the era 1890–1920, Irish team nicknames were not uncommon. Irish immigrants flooded into Texas after the Irish Potato Famine of 1840–50. Irish families in Wichita Falls went to work in the oil fields or planted potato farms.

7141 Drillers 1912–13m *Texas–Oklahoma (D)*. The first oil field in this area was discovered in 1901. The nearby Burkburnett Oil Boom followed in 1909, along with a third oil boom in 1937.

7142 Spudders 1920–32m *Texas (B 1920, A 1921–32)*. Team moved to Longview (TX) May 20; 1941–42m *West Texas–New Mexico (D)*. Team moved to Big Springs (TX) May 22; 1947–53 *Big State (B)*; 1954m *Longhorn (C)*. Team moved to Sweetwater (TX) May 6; 1956–57x *Big State (B)*. Team disbanded May 23. With manager Walt Salm at the helm 1920–24, newspapers called the players "Salm's Spudders." Irish immigrants, who didn't go to work in the oil fields or petrochemical factories, set up potato farms. With manager Sammy Hale at the helm in 1941, newspapers called the players "Sammy's Spudders." By 1947, the moniker had become official.

7143 Giants 1929–31 *Texas–Oklahoma (N)*. Tag was a popular black nickname dating back to 1885 and the Cuban Giants.

Wilkes-Barre, Pennsylvania

7144 Black Diamonds 1886–87x *Pennsylvania State (ind.)*. Team disbanded in mid-season and was replaced by the IA Coal Barons (date unknown); 1889x *Eastern Interstate (ind.)*. In the era 1870–1920, the city was the "Anthracite Capital of the World." The city was the world's leading producer of Anthracite coal until the 1920s, giving rise to the nickname the "Black Diamond City." The term "Black Diamond" is slang for coal because of its obvious economic value.

7145 Colts 1886–87x *Pennsylvania State (ind.)*. Team had many young players who were known in the slang of the era as "colts." Unhappy with "Black Diamonds" because it was too long, local newspapers often used "Colts" instead.

7146 Coal Barons 1887 *International Assn. (ind.)*; 1888 *Central (ind.)*; 1889x *Atlantic Assn. (ind.)*; 1890x *International (ind.)*; m1892x *Pennsylvania State (ind.)*. Team began season in Pittsburgh and then moved here May 8. Team and league disbanded June 23; 1893–98 *Eastern (ind.)*; 1899–1900 *Atlantic (ind.)*. The nineteenth-century "Robber Barons" made their million-dollar fortunes in oil, steel and iron, cotton, cattle, railroads, shipbuilding and coal, among other enterprises. Wilkes-Barre is known as the "Diamond City," which refers to coal. Not only does "black diamond" mean coal, but real diamonds are formed from coal that is subjected to millions of years of heat and pressure. Baseball teams, playing in cities whose economy was based on oil, steel and iron, cotton, cattle, railroads, shipbuilding and coal, were sometimes known as "Barons" or "Millionaires." With manager Dan Shannon at the helm in 1893–95, newspapers called the players "Shannon's Coal Barons." Jack Chapman took over in

1896 and the name became "Chapman's Coal Barons." Howard Earl took over in mid-season 1896 and the name became "Howard Earl's Coal Barons." Shannon returned to manage in 1897–1900 and the team became, once again, "Shannon's Coal Barons." In 1900, manager Billy Clymer guided "Billy Clymer's Coal Barons."

7147 Barons 1905–17 *New York State (B)*; 1923–37 *New York–Pennsylvania (B)*; 1938–48, 1950 *Eastern (A)*; 1953–55m *Eastern (A)*. Team moved to Johnstown (PA) July 1. Newspapers shortened "Coal Barons" to "Barons." The moniker was appropriate because the Wilkes-Barre region was originally known as the "Barony of Rose" when settled by William Penn in the seventeenth century. "Barony" is the land held by a baron.

7148 Indians 1949, 1951 *Eastern (A)*. Team was a farm club of the Cleveland Indians.

Williamson, West Virginia

7149 Williamson Baseball Club 1912 *Mountain States (D)*. Team had no nickname.

7150 Colts 1937–38 *Mountain States (C)*. Team had many young players, known in the slang of the era as "colts." Newspapers liked the short name. With manager Nat Hickey at the helm, newspapers called the players "Hickey's Colts."

7151 Redbirds 1939–42 *Mountain States (C)*. Team was a farm club of the St. Louis Cardinals.

Williamsport, Pennsylvania

7152 Williamsport 1885x *Interstate (ind.)*. Circuit and team disbanded June 1. Team had no nickname.

7153 Lumber Citys 1886–87 *Pennsylvania State (ind.)*. Lumber has been transported to city saw-mills since 1870, giving rise to Williamsport becoming known as "The Lumber City" and the "Sawdust City of America."

7154 Demarests 1897 *Central Pennsylvania (ind.)*. Founded by David Demarest, the Demarest Sewing Machine Company owned the team.

7155 Millionaires 1904–10 *Tri-State (D)*. The nineteenth century Barons of oil, iron and steel, lumber, railroads, cotton and coal built so many residential homes for themselves here that the city of Williamsport boasted it had the most millionaires in the world.

7156 Champions 1908 *Tri-State (D)*. Team won pennants in 1907–08. In the era 1900–20, a pennant-winning team would style itself as "Champions" at the start of the following season, sometimes even having the name emblazoned on the uniform's jersey.

7157 Billies 1923 *New York–Pennsylvania (B)*. Moniker was used by newspapers for headlines, i.e., "Billies edge Barons, 4–3."

7158 Grays 1924–37 *Pennsylvania (B)*; *New York–Pennsylvania (B)*; 1938–42 *Eastern (A)*; *Eastern (A)* 1944–46, 1954–56; 1958–62 *Eastern (A)*. Players wore gray uniforms.

7159 Tigers 1947–52 *Eastern (A)*. Team was a farm club of the Detroit Tigers.

7160 Athletics 1953 *Eastern (A)*. Team was a farm club of the Philadelphia Athletics.

7161 Mets 1964–67 *Eastern (AA)*. Team was a farm club of the New York Mets.

7162 Astros 1968–70 *New York–Pennsylvania (A)*. Team was a farm club of the Houston Astros.

7163 Red Sox 1971–72 *New York–Pennsylvania (A)*. Team was a farm club of the Boston Red Sox.

7164 Tomahawks 1976 *Eastern (AA)*. Team was a farm club of the Cleveland Indians. Moniker was a spinoff from "Indians." Although human rights activists in this era railed against the seemingly racist "tomahawk chop" used by Atlanta Braves fans, nobody seemed to care about this "politically incorrect" team nickname.

7165 Bills 1987–91 *Eastern (AA)*. Tag was a spin-off from the 1923 Billies.

7166 Cubs 1994–98 *New York–Pennsylvania (A)*. Team was a farm club of the Chicago Cubs.

7167 Cross-cutters 1999 to date *New York–Pennsylvania (A)*. Tag was a spin-off from "Lumber City." A "cross-cutter" is a long, curved, pliable saw used by lumbermen. It is used to cut across the grain.

Williamston, Martin, North Carolina

7168 Martins 1937–41 *Coastal Plain (D)*. Williamston is located in Martin County. Moreover, Williamston is the original home of the Lockheed-Martin Airplane Company. The city was named after the eighteenth-century commander of the Martin County Militia of the Revolutionary War era — Colonel Bill Williams.

Willimantic, Connecticut

7169 Colts 1910x *Connecticut Assn. (D)* Circuit and team disbanded August 4. The team had many young players, who in the slang of the era were known as "colts." Newspapers liked the short name because Willimantic has eleven letters.

Willows, California

7170 Cardinals 1948–50 *Far West (D)*. Team was a farm club of the St. Louis Cardinals.

Wilmington, Delaware

7171 Malone's Men 1883 *Interstate Assn.* Players were managed by Ferguson Malone.

7172 Quicksteps 1883 *Inter-State (ind.)*; 1884m *Eastern (ind.)*. The 1884 team jumped from the Eastern League to the Union Association August 12. Team disbanded September 15. m1884x *Union Assn. (M)*; 1885m *Eastern (ind.)*. Team moved to Atlantic City June 19. An amateur team in New Jersey in 1865 recruited players from the New York City Quickstep Firefighters Company. The nickname eventually went to an 1866 amateur club in Wilmington and became traditional in that city for its baseball teams. In the nineteenth century, baseball team nicknames were wont to emphasize some physical on-the-field skill the players had — hence Lightfoot, Active, Rough'n Ready, Alert, Wide-Awake, Ambidexter, Swiftfoot, Gymnast and Quickstep.

7173 Delawareans 1884m *Eastern (ind.)*. The 1884 team jumped from the Eastern League to the Union Association August 12. Team disbanded September 15. m1884x *Union Assn. (M)*; 1885 m *Eastern (ind.)*. Team moved to Atlantic City June 19. Inhabitants of Delaware are known as Delawareans.

7174 Purple Stockings 1884m *Eastern (ind.)*. The 1884 team jumped from the Eastern League to the Union Association August 12. Team disbanded September 15. m1884x *Union Assn. (M)*. The players wore purple stockings. Newspapers shortened it to Purple Legs.

7175 Blue Hens 1885m *Eastern (ind.)*. Team moved to Atlantic City June 19. Players wore blue hose and blue-trim uniforms in honor of Delaware's state bird — the Blue Hen. Blue hens, aka fighting game-cocks, have been used in cock-fighting here for 300 years. The Delaware Regiment of the Colonial Army in the Revolutionary War wore blue coats and became known as the "Blue Hens."

7176 Quakers 1889x *Middle States (ind.)*. Team disbanded in mid-season 1889 (date unknown). Contested for in the seventeenth century by the Swedish, Dutch and British, the region went into an economic decline until Quaker settlers simulated it using water power from the nearby Brandywine Creeks.

7177 Peach-growers 1890x *Atlantic Assn. (ind.)*. Team disbanded August 22. Farms in the region transported peaches and other fruits to city packing houses. Originally "Peach-growers," newspapers shortened it to **Peaches** and **Peach Blossoms**.

7178 Peaches 1896 *Atlantic (ind.)*; 1904–05 *Tri-State (ind.)*; 1907–08 *Tri-State (B)*. Name was a shorter version of "Peach-growers." Originally **Peach-growers**, local newspapers again shortened it to "Peaches." With photographs now appearing in newspapers, editors were extremely space-conscious.

7179 Giants 1906x *Independent Negro team (ind.)*. After playing briefly in the International Black League, team disbanded July 5. Moniker was popular with black teams. In 1906 alone, there were six black "Giants" teams, i.e., Brooklyn Royal Giants, Chicago Leland Giants, Famous Cuban Giants, Philadelphia Giants, Philadelphia X-Giants and the Wilmington Giants.

7180 Chicks 1911–14 *Tri-State (B)*. Team had many young players, who were known in the slang of the era as "chicks." With manager Pete Cassidy at the helm in 1911, newspapers called the players "Cassidy's Chicks." James Jackson took over in 1912 and the name became "Jackson's Chicks."

7181 Potomacs 1925 *Independent Negro team (ind.)*. Wilmington is located near the Potomac River.

7182 Hornets 1930 *Independent Negro team (ind.)*. Players wore black and yellow stirrups.

7183 Quaker Giants 1930 *Independent Negro team (ind.)*. Black teams often combined an adjective with Giants, i.e., American Giants, Royal Giants, Cuban Giants, Leland Giants and, for this team, Quaker Giants.

7184 Blue Rocks 1940–52 *Interstate (B)*; 1993 to date *Carolina (A)*. The Brandywine River, near to the city, is noted for its rock-bed of beautiful blue granite rocks.

7185 Stars 1998–99 *Maryland Fall (W)*. Delaware, a crucial site of battles of the American Revolutionary War and the first state to ratify the U.S. Constitution, is the "First State."

Wilmington, North Carolina

7186 Giants 1901 *Virginia–North Carolina (ind.)*. The team was in a fierce pennant battle with Raleigh and finished second by a half-game (58–46). Fans and newspapers admiringly called the players "Giants." The term "Giants" in this era described a winning team, i.e., "They played like 'Giants.'"

7187 Sailors 1902x *North Carolina (C)*. Team disbanded July 10; 1908–10 *East Carolina Assn. (D)*. City was built at the junction of the Cape Fear River and Atlantic Ocean. The city has North Carolina's most important deep-water port. Ships have been traveling to and from the city since 1730. With manager Dick Smith at the helm in 1908–09, newspapers called the players "Smith's Sailors." The name was retained in 1910 under two other managers.

7188 Pirates 1928–29 *Eastern Carolina (D)*; 1932–35 *Piedmont (B)*; 1946–50 *Tobacco State (D)*. Pirates, buccaneers, corsairs, privateers and even she-pirates sailed the North Carolina coast from 1550 to 1820. The terror brought by these pirates inspired the name of "Cape Fear." With manager Hal Weafer at the helm, newspapers called the players "Weafer's Pirates." The team was not a farm club of the Pittsburgh Pirates.

7189 Port City Roosters 1995–96 *Southern (AA)*. Wilmington is the "Port City" along the Cape Fear River and the Atlantic Ocean. Farms in the region transport poultry products to city packing houses.

Wilson, North Carolina

7190 Tobs 1908–10 *East Carolina (D)*; 1922–23 *Virginia (B)*; 1939–41 *Coastal Plain (D)*; 1942x *Bi-State (D)* Bi-State League represented Virginia and North Carolina; 1946–52 *Coastal Plain (D)*; 1956 *Carolina (B)*; m1957–68 *Carolina (B)*. Team started 1957 season in Kinston (NC) and moved here May 11. Wilson has auction houses in which bright-leaf tobacco is auctioned. Originally **Tobacconists**, local newspapers shortened it to "Tobs." With manager Earl Holt at the helm in 1908–09, newspapers called the players "Earl Holt's Tobacconists." The name was retained in 1910 under Charles McGeehan.

7191 Bugs 1920–21, 1924–27 *Virginia (B)*. The pine-gnawing beetle has been a pest to North Carolina's forests and the local lumber industry for more than 150 years. With manager Bunn Hearn at the helm in 1922 and 1926–27, newspapers called the players "Bunn's Bugs."

7192 Pennants 1973 *Carolina (A)*. Team was a farm club of the International League Peninsula Whips. "Pennants" is a spin-off of "Whips." In the nineteenth century, baseball teams that won their league championships were allowed to fly the "Whip Pennant."

Wilson, Oklahoma

7193 Drillers 1922 *Oklahoma State (D)*. Nearby oil and natural gas wells transport oil and gas to refineries in the city. The Glenn Pool Gusher, near Tulsa, was struck in 1905 and stimulated the construction of oil refineries here.

Winchester, Kentucky

7194 Hustlers 1908–12m *Blue Grass (D)*. Team moved to Nicholasville (KY) June 8. In this era "hustler" was a complimentary slang for a baseball player. Disappointed Winchester fans sarcastically called the 1908 players "hustlers" as the team finished last. With manager Harry Kunkel at the helm, newspapers called the players "Harry's Hustlers" and "Kunkel's Hustlers." When the 1909 players "hustled" to the 1909 pennant with a splendid 75–44 record, gratified fans and newspapers switched from sarcasm to admiration, as they called manager Daddy Horn's charges "Horn's Hustlers."

7195 Dodgers 1922–24 *Blue Grass (D)*. With manager Howard Camnitz at the helm in 1922, newspapers called the players "Howard's Dodgers." With manager Pat Devereaux at the 1923 helm, newspapers called the players "Devereaux's Dodgers." The team was not a farm of the Brooklyn Dodgers.

Winchester, Tennessee

7196 Tennessee Tomahawks 1996 *Big South (ind.)*; 1997–98 *Heartland (ind.)*. Settlers of the eighteenth century traveled here along the nearby "Warriors Trail," which got its name when Delaware, Susquehanna and Shawnee Indians, armed with tomahawks, attacked them.

7197 Tennessee T's 2001 *All-American (ind.)*. With the team going by the state name of Tennessee, management chose T's to compensate for the nine-letter state name. Management rejected using Winchester because it was even longer at ten letters.

Windsor, Ontario

7198 Windsor Baseball Club 1912–13 *Border (D)*. Team had no nickname.

Wink, Texas

7199 Spudders 1937–38 *West Texas–New Mexico (D)*. Farms in the region transport potatoes to city packing houses. With manager Joe Tate at the helm, newspapers called the players "Tate's Spudders." "Tater" is slang for "potato."

Winnipeg, Manitoba, Canada

7200 Winnipeg Base Ball Club 1891 *Red River Valley (ind.)*. Team had no nickname.

7201 Maroons 1902–05 *Northern (ind. 1902, D 1903–05)*; 1906–07 *Northern Copper Country (C)*; 1908 *Northern (D)*; 1909–11x *Western Canada (D)*. Team disbanded August 21; 1912 *Central International (C)*; 1913–17x *Northern (C 1913–16, D 1917)*. Circuit and team disbanded July 4 due to Canadian involvement in World War I; 1919–21 *Western Canada (C 1919, B 1920–21)*; 1933–42 *Northern (D 1933–40, C 1941–42)*. Players wore maroon hose.

7202 Peggers 1905 *Northern (D)*. Newspapers used the moniker for headlines, i.e., "Peggers edge Crooks, 4–3." A "peg" is a baseball term referring to a hard throw by a fielder to put out a base runner. A "pegger" (bad English) is sometimes used to refer to a baseball pitcher.

7203 Goldeyes 1954–64 *Northern (C 1954–62, A 1963–64)*; 1969 *Northern (A)*; 1994–2010 *Northern (ind.)*; 2011 to date *North American (ind.)*. The North American golden-eye duck inhabits the northern U.S. and Canada. In this case, the team mascot and logo is the Goldeye fish found in streams, rivers and lakes of North America.

7204 Whips m1970–71 *International (AAA)*. Team began season in Buffalo (NY) and moved to Winnipeg June 11. Management wanted a five-letter name to match up with the parent club Montreal "Expos" and chose "Whips" from a hastily arranged name-the-team contest.

Winona, Minnesota

7205 Clippers 1877 *League Alliance (ind.)*; 1884 *Northwestern (ind.)*. Clipper ships transported wheat and lumber up and down the Mississippi and Minnesota rivers to city processing factories from 1850 to 1900. The city was founded as a trading post for the lumber industry in 1851 by steamboat clipper captain Orren Smith. Today, the city hosts an annual "Steamboat Days" summer festival. Since 1860, the city has been a railroad depot for "clipper" express trains. A famous Civil War "clipper gun boat" of the U.S. Navy was the "Winona."

7206 Pirates 1909–12 *Minnesota–Wisconsin (C 1909, 1911, D 1910, 1912)*; 1913–14 *Northern (C)*. City is located close to the Mississippi River. In the era 1880–1910, teams playing in "river cities" sometimes assumed the name of "Pirates." In 1909–11, manager Joe Killian guided "Joe Killian's Pirates." Fred Curtis took over in 1912 to guide "Fred Curtis' Pirates." Winona hosts an annual "Steamboat Days Festival" every summer. In North America, in the period 1700–1850, there were actual river pirates who would attack cargo ships while looking for money, gold and valuable goods.

7207 Athletics m1958 *Three-I (B)*. Team started season in Rochester (MN) and moved here June 29. The team was a farm club of the Kansas City Athletics.

Winooski, Vermont

7208 Vermont Expos 1997–2005 *New York–Pennsylvania (A)*. Team was a farm club of the Montreal Expos.

7209 Vermont Lake Monsters 2006 to date *New York–Pennsyl-*

vania (A). Much like the "Loch Ness Monster" in Scotland, there have been tales and legends about a monster—"Nessie the Sea Dragon"—swimming in the waters of nearby Lake Champlain.

Winsted, Connecticut

7210 Winsted Base Ball Club 1898 *Naugatuck Valley (ind.).* Team had no nickname.

Winston-Salem, North Carolina

7211 Winston-Salem Base Ball Club 1892 *South Atlantic (ind.).* Team had no nickname.

7212 Twins m1905 *Virginia–North Carolina (D).* Team began season in Salisbury-Spencer (NC) and moved to Winston-Salem July 17; 1908–12 *Carolina Assn. (D)*; 1913–17x *North Carolina State (D)* Circuit and team disbanded May 30 because of U.S. entry into World War I; 1920–32m *Piedmont (D 1920, C 1921–31, B 1932).* Team was known as the "Winston Twins" in 1920 and then switched to Winston-Salem Twins in 1921. Team moved to High Point (NC) August 20; 1933 *Piedmont (B)*; 1937–42 *Piedmont (B)*; 1954–56 *Carolina (B).* In 1921, management realized that both cities had to be included in the team's name in order to attract Salem fans to the ballpark in Winston. A baseball team, which represented two cities, was sometimes called the "Twins." Winston-Salem is known as the "Twin Cities."

7213 Giants 1920 *Independent Negro team.* Tag was a popular Negro team moniker.

7214 Eagles 1938 *Independent Negro team.* Playing in a "Confederate" state, management chose a "pro North" mascot to inform fans that they were a club of black players. "Code word" nicknames like Giants, Stars and Eagles indicated a black team.

7215 Cardinals 1945–53 *Carolina (C 1945–48, B 1949–53).* Team was a farm club of the St. Louis Cardinals.

7216 Redbirds 1957–60 *Carolina (B).* Team was a farm club of the St. Louis Cardinals.

7217 Red Sox 1961–83 *Carolina (B 1961–62, A 1963–83).* Team was a farm club of the Boston Red Sox.

7218 Spirits 1984–94 *Carolina (A).* The direct origin of the name was the 1984 Olympic Games in Los Angeles. In the spring of 1984, team owner Dennis Bastien announced he was renaming the team from "Red Sox" to "Spirits" to capture the Spirit of the 1984 Olympic Games. The city was settled by Moravian pioneers who were very "spiritual" in establishing churches, hospitals and social agencies.

7219 Warthogs 1995–2009 *Carolina (A).* Although the true warthog is a type of swine native to Africa, there are numerous types of wild pigs found in North America. Team general manager Peter Fisch announced the new moniker by declaring to the media, "We wanted people here in the city to have something new and exciting to think about."

7220 Dash 2010 to date *Carolina (A).* The *Winston-Salem Journal* newspaper held a name-the-team contest and the winner was "Dash," which hearkens back to such goofy names of the early 1900s as "Brackets" and "Hyphens." Winston and Salem consolidated in 1913 and became known as the "Twin Cities." The name Winston-Salem bears a dash, just as the Alameda (CA) baseball club was printed in 1910 California newspapers as the Alameda [Santa Rosa] "Bracketts." Announced in December 2008, local newspapers liked its four letters, but its only genuine meaning is one that refers to a baseball player "dashing around the bases."

Winter Haven, Florida

7221 Sun Sox 1966 *Florida State (A).* Team was a farm club of the Chicago White Sox.

7222 Mets 1967 *Florida State (A).* Team was a farm club of the New York Mets.

7223 Red Sox 1969–92 *Florida State (A)*; 1989–92 *Gulf Coast (R).* These teams were farm clubs of the Boston Red Sox.

7224 Super Sox 1989–90 *Senior Assn. (W)* Circuit, officially known as the Senior Professional Baseball Association, was a "gimmick" league restricting rosters to batters and pitchers age 35 and older and catchers age 30 and older. With two previous franchises known as "Sun Sox" and "Red Sox," the team went with the somewhat-immodest Super Sox. The league drew well in 1989–90 because fans were curious, but interest then waned, forcing the circuit to disband in mid-season of 1990–01.

7225 Indians 1989–90 *Gulf Coast (R).* Team was a farm club of the Cleveland Indians.

Winters-Ballinger, Texas

7226 Eagles m1953x *Longhorn (C).* Team began the season in Lamesa (TX) and then moved here June 3. Team disbanded June 7. Team was a farm club of the Texas League Dallas Eagles. In the era 1910–50, some AA and AAA minor league clubs, i.e., Los Angeles, Baltimore and Dallas, maintained their own farm clubs of the A-B-C-D classifications and donated equipment and uniforms to these teams. The city newspaper, the *Ballinger Eagle*, was established in 1887. Near to the city are the Double Eagle Oil Fields. Also near to the city is Eagle Mountain, which includes Eagle Lake. With manager Harold Webb at the helm, newspapers called the players "Webb's Eagles." A previous local team, the Ballinger "Cats," was a farm club of the Texas League Fort Worth Cats, establishing a pattern of Class AA-C minor league affiliations.

Wisconsin Rapids, Wisconsin

7227 White Sox 1940–42 *Wisconsin State (D)*; 1946–50, 1952–53 *Wisconsin State (D).* Teams were farm clubs of the Chicago White Sox.

7228 Wisconsin Rapids Sox 1951 *Wisconsin State (D).* Team was a farm club of the Chicago White Sox.

7229 Senators 1963 *Midwest (A).* Team was a farm club of the Washington Senators.

7230 Twins 1964–83 *Midwest (A).* Team was a farm club of the Minnesota Twins.

Woodbridge, Prince William, Virginia

7231 Prince William Pirates 1984–86 *Carolina (A).* Team went by the county name of Prince William Pirates because the team represented both Woodbridge and nearby Daly City, although all home games were played in Woodbridge. The team was a farm club of the Pittsburgh Pirates.

7232 Prince William Yankees 1987–88 *Carolina (A).* Team was a farm club of the New York Yankees.

7233 Prince William Cannons 1989–98 *Carolina (A).* Virginia's native sons included George Washington, Harry "Light Horse" Lee, Robert E. Lee and Thomas "Stonewall" Jackson as the cannons blasted in the Revolutionary War (1776–81), the War of 1812 (1812–15) and the Civil War (1861–65).

7234 Potomac Cannons 1989–98 *Carolina (A).* Team went by the county name of "Prince William Cannons," 1989–98, and then switched to the river name of "Potomac Cannons" for the seasons of 1999–2004, to again represent both Woodbridge and Daly City.

7235 Potomac Nationals 2005 to date *Carolina (A).* Team goes by the river name of "Potomac Nationals." The team is a farm club of the Washington Nationals.

Woodstock, Ontario, Canada

7236 Bains m1899 *Canadian (ind.)*. Team began season in Stratford (ONT) and moved here June 8. A "bain" is a French-style hot bath that was offered in the hotels, resorts and spas that were first built here in 1895. Woodstock resident John Bain was the owner of the Bain Wagon Company here in the 1890s.

7237 Maroons 1905 *Canadian (C)*. Players wore maroon hose.

Woonsocket, Rhode Island

7238 Woonsocket Base Ball Club 1891 *New England (ind.)*. Team joined the league June 21; 1892 *New England (ind.)*. The teams had no nickname.

7239 Trotters 1908x *Atlantic Assn. (D)*. Team disbanded May 4 after playing only one game. Although the "Automobile Age" had arrived, the city's trotting horses still pulled street trolleys, carriages and wagons. Harness racing with trotting horses was popular in New England. By 1900–10, however, the street cars were becoming electrified. With manager John Leighton at the helm, newspapers called the players "Leighton's Trotters." Baseball teams often were identified with horses, i.e., Bronchos, Charley Horses, Colts, Mules, Ponies and Trotters.

7240 Tigers 1914 *Colonial (C)*. Players wore striped hose. In the era 1890–1920, some teams whose players wore striped hose or stirrups were called "Tigers." By 1920, nearly all stirrups were striped, making the "Tiger stripes" connection irrelevant.

7241 Speeders 1914 *Colonial (C)*. Team had a loose affiliation with the Boston Red Sox, whose unofficial, alternate tag was "Speed Boys." In the "dead ball" era of 1900–19, many if not most baseball teams emphasized base path speed for the hit and run, bunts, taking the extra base, and stealing bases. Teams like the Boston Red Sox that excelled at this type of strategy were called "Speed Boys" and "Speeders." The nickname derived ultimately from the automobile, which people called "speeders," and "speedsters."

7242 Woonsocket Baseball Club m1933 *New England (B)*. Team started season in Lawrence (MA) and moved here July 18. Team had no nickname.

Wooster, Ohio

7243 Trailers 1905 *Ohio–Pennsylvania (C)*. The team lost its first two games, prompting the local newspaper to call them the "Trailers." A lack of attendance convinced the team owners to fold the team May 6. Teams in this era that streaked early in the season into first place were called the "Comets." Losing teams that sank into the second division or last place were known as "Trailers," i.e., "The 1962 Mets were trailing, 60 games out of first." Mohican Indians in seventeenth and eighteenth century Ohio were good trackers, also known as "trailblazers" and "trailers."

Worcester, Massachusetts

7244 Red Stockings 1878 *International Assn. (M)*; 1879 *National Assn. (M)*. Players wore red hose. Originally "Red Stockings," newspapers shortened the moniker to **Redlegs**, **Red Sox** and **Reds**. None of these monikers were official nicknames and were used strictly as a gimmick for newspaper stories. The team never had an official nickname.

7245 Ruby Legs 1878 *International Assn. (M)*; 1879 *National Assn. (M)*; 1880–82 *National (M)*. Players wore ruby-red hose. Originally Red Stockings, Redlegs and Reds, the term "Ruby Legs" was used to avoid confusion with the "Boston Red Stockings" and the "Cincinnati Reds." Although newspapers started calling the Worcester players the "Ruby Legs," the nickname was unofficial. The team never had an official nickname.

7246 Irvings 1878 *International Assn. (M)*. Tag was used by some Worcester newspapers because the professional Worcester team had previously been an amateur club, known as the "Irving Baseball Club of Worcester." The team was owned by a Mr. Irving.

7247 Spindle Citys 1878 *International Assn. (M)*. Worcester, a major textile city from the eighteenth century to the 1920s, has the nickname of "Spindle City." Nearby Lowell (MA), also a textile center of the era, is also nicknamed the "Spindle City." Ironically, the arrival of automation in the 1920s drove textile mills out of New England to the Carolinas and elsewhere.

7248 Browns 1878 *International Assn. (M)*; 1879 *National Assn. (M)*; 1880–82 *National (M)*; 1888 *New England (ind.)*. Repeated washings of the players' stockings caused them to fade from red to brown. This happened to other teams as well, i.e., Chicago UA 1884 (gold to brown) and St. Louis AA 1882 (red to brown). The nickname was unofficial, used only in newspapers as a change-of-pace from the "Worcesters."

7249 Giants 1879 *National Assn. (M)*. When the team went on a six-game winning streak in July, *The New York Clipper* called the players the "Giants." The term "Giants" was slang for a "winning team," irrespective of the height, size and build of the players.

7250 Lame Ducks 1882 *National (M)*. As Worcester stumbled like a "lame duck" to a hideous 18–66 record, talk was rife in the local newspapers that ex–ball player and businessman Al Reach was going to buy the franchise and move it to Philadelphia. Hence, Worcester newspapers complained the team was a "lame duck." The term originated with American politicians who were finishing out a term in office without a chance for re-election.

7251 Worcester Base Ball Club 1884 *Massachusetts State (ind.)*; 1889–90m *Atlantic Assn.(ind.)*. Team moved to Lebanon (PA) July 28; 1891 *New England (ind.)*; 1894 *New England (ind.)*; m1898 *New England (ind.)*. Team started season in New Bedford (MA) and moved here June 14. These teams had no nickname.

7252 Farmers 1899–1900 *Eastern (ind.)*. Farms in central and western Massachusetts transport cranberries, corn, hay and tobacco to city processing plants.

7253 Clam-diggers 1899–1900 *Eastern (ind.)*. Clams collected at the Massachusetts coastal Moonhead-Squantum Mud Flats are transported to Worcester city food plants for cleaning, processing, packing and shipping off to market.

7254 Quakers 1901 *Eastern (ind.)*. With manager Matt Kittridge at the helm, newspapers called the players "Kittridge's Quakers." Quakers, persecuted by the Pilgrims in New England in the eighteenth century, arrived here around 1800.

7255 Hustlers 1902 *Eastern (ind.)*. "Hustler" was a complimentary slang for a "hustling" baseball team or "hustling players." The "politically incorrect" link that arose with gambling in the 1970s was not an issue in this era. With manager Frank Leonard at the helm, newspapers called the players "Leonard's Hustlers."

7256 Riddlers 1902–03m *Eastern (ind.)*. Team moved to Montreal (QUE) July 21, 1903. En route to a losing 25–39 record, local newspapers lamented that the fans' pennant hopes had been "riddled" by the team's repeated blunders. Fans also considered the team's inability to win to be a "riddle." With manager George Wrigley at the helm, newspapers called the players "Wrigley's Riddlers." Attendance plummeted, forcing the franchise to move July 21.

7257 Reds 1904m *Connecticut (B)*. Team moved to Norwich (CT) June 21. Players wore red hose. Newspapers did not call the team the "Red Stockings."

7258 Busters 1906–15 *New England (B)*; 1916–17 *Eastern (B)*.

With the franchise winning pennants in 1906, 1908, and 1909, local newspapers gushed that the team was "playing like gang-busters!" "Buster" was a contemporary slang for a robust youth — particularly an athlete. With manager Jesse Burkett at the helm for three pennants in four years, newspapers called the players "Burkett's Busters."

7259 Boosters 1918–21 *Eastern (B 1918, A 1919–21)*, m1922 *Eastern (A)*. Team started 1922 season in Fitchburg and moved here July 30. The moniker rhymes with Worcester's pronunciation of "wooster." In this era, a team that was supported by an enthusiastic "booster club" was sometimes known as the "Boosters."

7260 Panthers 1923–25 *Eastern (A)*. Tired of abstract names like "Boosters" and "Busters," local newspapers wanted an animal mascot and went with the "Panthers." With manager Jesse Burkett at the helm, newspapers called the players "Burkett's Panthers." In 1925, Ed Eayrs took over and the name became "Eayrs' Panthers."

7261 Coal Heavers 1924 *Eastern (A)*. Pennsylvania coal and iron-ore was hauled off of trucks and trains by "coal heavers," who dumped it onto conveyor belts running straight to the smelters.

7262 Chiefs 1933 *New England (B)*. Team was named in honor of manager "Chief" Were.

7263 Rosebuds m1934 *Northeastern (A)*. Team began season as the Waltham (MA) "Rosebuds" and moved here May 24. The team nickname was retained.

7264 Tornadoes 2005 to date *Canadian–American (ind.)*. Team held a name-the-team contest and the winning entry was "Tornadoes." On June 9, 1953, a terrible tornado struck the region and killed 94 people. In and around the city, 4,000 buildings were damaged and Assumption College was destroyed. The tornado also caused 10,000 people to become homeless.

Worthington, Minnesota

7265 Cardinals 1939–40 *Western (D)*. Team was a farm club of St. Louis Cardinals.

Wuxi, Jiangsu, China

7266 Hope Stars 2005–10 *Chinese (S)*. Circuit's official title is the Chinese Baseball League, subsidized by the government of the People's Republic of China, and is not to be confused with the Chinese Professional Baseball League of Taiwan. China's under–21 baseball playing "stars" are on this team, providing "hope" for the country's baseball future.

Wyandotte, Michigan

7267 Wyandotte Baseball Club 1912 *Border (D)*; 1913 *Border (D)*. These teams had no nickname.

Wytheville, Virginia

7268 Pioneers 1948 *Blue Ridge (D)*. English, Dutch, Swedish and German pioneer families settled here in the eighteenth century.

7269 Statesmen 1949–50m *Blue Ridge (D)*. Team moved to Bassett (VA) June 27 due to a polio outbreak; 1953–55 *Appalachian (D)*. George Wythe, for whom the city was named, was a Virginia statesmen who signed the Declaration of Independence.

7270 Cardinals 1957–59 *Appalachian (D)*. Team was a farm club of the St. Louis Cardinals.

7271 Senators 1960 *Appalachian (D)*. Team was a farm club of the Washington Senators.

7272 Twins 1961–63 *Appalachian (D)*. Team was a farm club of the Minnesota Twins.

7273 Athletics 1964 *Appalachian (D)*. Team was a farm club of the Kansas City Athletics.

7274 Reds 1967 *Appalachian (R)*. Team was a farm club of the Cincinnati Reds.

7275 Senators 1965 *Appalachian (R)*; 1969 *Appalachian (R)*. Team was a farm club of the Washington Senators.

7276 Braves 1971–73 *Appalachian (R)*. Team was a farm club of the Atlanta Braves.

7277 Cubs 1985–89 *Appalachian (R)*. Team was a farm club of the Chicago Cubs.

Yakima, Washington

7278 Indians 1920–21 *Pacific International (B)*. Team was named after the Yakima Indians. Pressured by settlers, pioneers and soldiers, the Yakima tribe attacked American troops in the Yakima War of 1855–58 but were defeated and forced back into reservations by 1861. The city was founded as Fort Simcoe. With manager Bob Vaughn at the helm in 1920, the team was called "Vaughn's Indians." Frank Raymond took over in 1921 to lead "Frank Raymond's Indians."

7279 Pippins 1937–41 *Western International (B)*. Washington State is the nation's leading producer of apples. Orchards in the region produce four types of apples— Delicious, Golden Delicious, Wine-Sap and Pippin. Yakima is known as the "Fruit Bowl of the Nation." With manager Raymond Jacobs at the helm, newspapers called the players "Raymond's Pippins."

7280 Stars 1946–47 *Western International (B)*. Team was a farm club of the Hollywood Stars.

7281 Packers 1948 *Western International (B)*. Farm produce, i.e., apples, grain, grapes, pears, sugar beets, vegetables and hops, are transported to city packing houses where they are cleaned and packed.

7282 Bears 1949–54 *Western International (B)*; 1955–64 *Northwest (B 1955–62, A 1963–64)*; *Northwest (A)* 1990 to date. The Black Bear roams both forests and mountains in Washington State.

7283 Braves 1965–66 *Northwest (A)*. Team was a farm club of the Atlanta Braves.

Yamagata, Honshu, Japan

7284 Golden Eagles 2007 to date *Japanese Eastern (ind.)*. Players wore gold-trim uniforms and stirrups. The team is a farm club of the Sendai Tohoku Golden Eagles. The Japanese Eastern and Western leagues consist of 12 farm clubs run by the 12 franchises of the Japanese Central and Pacific leagues.

Yazoo City, Mississippi

7285 Zoos 1904 *Delta (D)*; 1911 *Cotton States (D)*; m1912x *Cotton States (D)*. Team began the season in New Orleans (LA) and moved here May 9. Team disbanded August 3. Moniker was used in newspaper headlines, i.e., "Zoos edge Senators, 4–3."

7286 Zuzus 1910 *Cotton States (D)*. Tag was another headline moniker, i.e., "Zuzus beat Senators, 6–3."

Yokohama, Japan

7287 Taiyo Whales 1978–91 *Central (ind.)*; 1978–91 *Japanese Eastern (ind.)*. Japan is one of the few countries that engages in almost unrestricted whaling. The city has been a major seaport since 1880. The team was owned by the Taiyo Fish Packing Company. The Eastern League team was a farm club of the Central League Whales.

7288 Yokohama Bay Stars 1992 to date *Central (ind.)*; 1992–2004 *Japanese Eastern (ind.)*. "Stars" refers to "starfish." The team has a starfish mascot. The city was built on the shore of Tokyo Bay where starfish swim in nearby Yokohama Bay. The Eastern League team was a farm club of the Central League Stars.

7289 Shonan Sea Rex 2005 to date *Japanese Eastern (ind.)*. The whale is known as the "King of the Sea." Rex is the Latin word for king. Shonan Company owns the team.

Yonkers, New York

7290 Yonkers Base Ball Club 1888 *Hudson River (ind.)*; 1905x *Hudson River (C)*. Team disbanded June 1. These teams had no nickname.

7291 Hoot Owls 1995 *Northeast (ind.)*. Night owls inhabit the nearby Bear Mountain, Harriman and Roosevelt state parks. They also inhabit the Catskill Mountains to the east.

York, Nebraska

7292 Prohibitionists 1911–15x *Nebraska State (D)* Circuit and team disbanded July 18. The Prohibition Party (founded 1869) nominated B.L. Paine of Lincoln (NE) for U.S. president in 1912. The pro-agrarian Populist Party arose because of low farm prices, high railroad shipping charges and rising interest rates that were hurting Nebraska farmers. The populists and prohibitionists here were allied together. With manager Jim Pierce at the helm 1914–15, newspapers called the players "Pierce's Prohibitionists."

7293 Dukes 1928–31 *Nebraska State (D)*. The tag is a play on words for the English Dukes of York, whose line goes back to 1385.

York, Pennsylvania

7294 White Roses 1884x *Keystone Assn. (ind.)*. Circuit and team disbanded June 7; m1884 *Eastern (ind.)*. After the Keystone Association White Roses disbanded June 7, the Harrisburg EL team moved here, assuming the old nickname; 1893 *Pennsylvania State Association (ind.)*; 1905–07m *Tri-State (B)*. Team moved to Reading (PA) July 24; 1909–14m *Tri-State (B)*. Team moved to Lancaster (PA) July 8; 1923–33 *New York–Pennsylvania (B 1923–32, A 1933)*; 1936m *New York–Pennsylvania (A)*. Team moved to Trenton (NJ) July 2; 1943–52 *Inter-State (B)*; 1953–55 *Piedmont (B)*; 1958–59 *Eastern (A)*; 1962–67 *Eastern (A 1962, AA 1963–69)*. The fifteenth century English Civil War — known as the War of the Roses (1455–71) — between the House of York (symbol White Rose) and the House of Lancaster (symbol Red Rose) ended in 1471 with Edward the Duke of York crowned as English king Edward IV. York is known as the "White Rose City."

7295 Colored Monarchs 1886 *Independent Negro team*. Team was either professional (players received a salary) or semi-professional (players received a share of the gate receipts). The Cuban Giants (1885–99) were the first professional black baseball team. The first Duke of York eventually became the English monarch, King Edward IV in 1442.

7296 Hayseeders 1889 *Middle States (ind.)*. Founded in 1741, the city had numerous hay farms. "Hayseeder" was a slang or nickname for a farmer who was an inhabitant of rural America.

7297 Monarchs 1889 *Eastern Inter-State (ind.)*; The 1889 club, a team of white players, was named after the kings of the old English House of York; 1890 *Pennsylvania State (ind.)*. Cuban Giants, a black team, played in this league as the "York Monarchs." York is known as the "Castle City."

7298 Big Gorhams 1891 *Independent Negro team*. New York Gorhams moved here for the 1891 season. "Big Gorhams" referred to the team's presence in the "Big City" of New York. The team had

originated several years earlier in Gorham (NY), a town in western New York State.

7299 Yahoos 1896 *Pennsylvania State (ind.)*. A "yahoo" is a rude and boorish fellow (originally from Jonathon Swift's *Gulliver Travelers*). Throughout baseball history, there have been players who have been or are "yahoos."

7300 Penn Park Athletics 1903 *Independent Negro (ind.)*. This black team played in the Penn Park district of the city.

7301 Penn Parks 1904 *Tri-State (ind.)*. Team played its home games at a field in Penn Park, a neighborhood in the city.

7302 Genuine Cuban Giants 1908 *Independent Negro team*. After the Cuban Giants broke up in 1900, several black teams claimed to be the continuation of the franchise, leading to such names as Cuban-X-Giants, Original Cuban Giants and Genuine Cuban Giants. None of the players on the roster of the 1908 club played with the nineteenth-century Cuban Giants.

7303 Bees 1940 *Interstate (B)*. Team was a farm club of the Boston Bees.

7304 Pirates 1968–69 *Eastern (AA)*. Team was a farm club of the Pittsburgh Pirates.

7305 Revolution 2007 to date *Atlantic (ind.)*. The Continental Congress met here to ratify the Articles of Confederation during the Revolutionary War. During the war, York was the capital of the United States. The team logo is an eagle.

Youngstown, Ohio

7306 Youngstown Base Ball Club 1884 *Iron & Oil Assn. (ind.)*. Team had no nickname.

7307 Giants 1889 *Ohio State (ind.)*; 1890 *Tri-State (B)*; 1899–1900m *Inter-State (ind.)*. Team moved to Marion (OH) August 5. In the nineteenth century, several minor league teams emulated the glamour team of baseball — the New York "Giants." In the nineteenth century teams playing well and contending for their league's pennant were said by newspapers to be "playing like giants."

7308 Puddlers 1896–98 *Inter-State (ind.)*. The conversion of cast iron to wrought iron is known as "puddling." The Youngstown Sheet & Steel Tube Company was established here in 1895.

7309 Ohio Works 1905–06 *Ohio–Pennsylvania (C)*. The McDonald Ohio Iron & Steel Works owned the team. The Ohio Iron Works was founded by Daniel and James Heaton in 1803.

7310 Champs 1907–08 *Ohio–Pennsylvania (C)*. Team won three straight flags, 1905–07.

7311 Indians 1909 *Ohio–Pennsylvania (C)*. The Iroquois Indians inhabited Ohio in pre–Columbian times.

7312 Steelmen 1910–11 *Ohio–Pennsylvania (C)*; 1912 *Central (B)*; 1913 *Inter-State (B)*; 1915 *Central (B)*. Youngstown was the home of the McDonald Ohio Iron & Steel Works and the Ohio Iron Works (established 1803).

7313 Tubers m1931 *Middle Atlantic (C)*. Team began season in Hagerstown (MD), then moved to Parkersburg (WVa) and moved here July 12. "Tubing" is the manufacture of iron and steel tubes by workers known as "tubers." The city was home to the Youngstown Sheet and Steel Tube Company.

7314 Buckeyes 1932 *Central (B)*. Ohio is the "Buckeye State." Named after the Buckeye tree, inhabitants of Ohio are known as "Buckeyes."

7315 Browns 1939–41 *Middle Atlantic (C)*. Team was a farm club of St. Louis Browns.

7316 Gremlins 1946 *Middle Atlantic (C)*. The 1941 parent club St. Louis Browns had a little pixie-like gremlin as its mascot logo. In 1946, Youngstown's new owners, Bill Koval and Nick Andolina, didn't want to go with "Browns" again, particularly since the new

1946 team was now a farm club of the Philadelphia Athletics. The owners wanted keep the little pixie mascot, so they switched from "Browns" to "Gremlins." The tag was also a spin-off from head coach Paul Brown's AAFC Cleveland (Ohio) Browns, i.e., "Paul Browns' Browns." Local newspapers, noting that Paul Birch was the field manager, called the players "Paul Birch's Gremlins."

7317 Colts 1947–48 *Middle Atlantic (C)*. Team had many young players, known in baseball jargon as "colts." Newspapers liked the five-letter name.

7318 Athletics 1949–51m *Middle Atlantic (C)*. Team moved to Oil City (PA) June 2. The team was a farm club of the Philadelphia Athletics.

Ypsilanti, Michigan

7319 Ypsilanti Baseball Club 1913 *Border (D)*. Team had no nickname.

Yuma, Arizona

7320 Panthers 1950 *Sunset (C)*; 1951–52 *Southwest International (C)*. Mountain lions and North American jaguars inhabit Arizona's northern highlands and national parks.

7321 Sun Sox 1955–56 *Arizona–Mexico (C)*. Players wore solar yellow uniform trim and stirrups. Yuma, situated in the northwestern region of the Sonora Desert, is noted for its intensely sunny skies. The team, an independent in 1955 and a farm club of the Cincinnati Reds in 1956, had not been a farm club of either the Boston Red Sox or Chicago White Sox. Yuma is the "City of the Desert Sun." Yuma's newspaper is *The Yuma Sun*.

7322 Desert Dawgs 1995x *Golden State (ind.)*. Circuit and team disbanded July 4. In the 1990s, partly inspired by rap music, which used to invent such spellings as "dawg" and "katz," sports teams started using such monikers as Alley Cats, Cracker Cats, Diamond Kats, Diamond Dogs, Mud Dogs, Pioneerzz, Rail Cats, River Dogs, River Cats, Salt Dogs, Surf Dogs, Starzz and, for this team, Desert Dawgs. Moniker refers specifically to the desert coyote, which inhabits western Arizona's Sonora desert. The coyote is a wolf-like creature and a member, like dogs and wolves, of the Canidae (canine) family. Yuma is built near the Coyote Wash River.

7323 Bullfrogs 2000–02 *Western (ind.)*. The bullfrog is a large deep-voice frog found in the waters of the nearby Colorado, Gila and Coyote Wash rivers.

7324 Scorpions 2005–07 *Golden (ind.)*; 2007 to date *Arizona Winter (W)*. Poisonous scorpions inhabit the Sonora Desert, south and east of the city.

7325 Snow Falcons 2007 *Arizona Winter (W)*. Team revived the name of the 2005 Surprise "Fightin' Falcons" of the Golden Baseball League. Snow falcons are found in the Grand Canyon State Park in northwest Arizona.

7326 Canada Miners 2007–08 *Arizona Winter (W)*. Arizona Winter League disbanded after this single season. The team revived the name of the 2005 Mesa (AZ) Canada Miners of the Golden Baseball League, a summer circuit. Both teams were stocked with Canadian players. Arizona is noted for its copper mining, but the players on the team hailed from western Canada, which is also noted for its mining industry. Logo shows a miner looking for Canadian gold.

7327 Surf Dogs 2007 to date *Arizona Winter (W)*. Team was a farm club of the 2007 San Diego "Surf Dawgs" of the Golden Baseball League. When San Diego disbanded after the 2007 season, this Yuma team retained the nickname.

7328 Sonora Pilots 2008 *Arizona Winter (W)*. Team is named in

honor of the Marines Corps Air Station of Yuma. The team had a fighter jet logo and a winged–S insignia.

7329 Team Canada 2009 to date *Arizona Winter (W)*. Franchise dropped its "Miners" nickname and was renamed "Team Canada." The players are from Canada.

7330 Team Mexico 2011 to date *Arizona Winter (W)*. Team has Mexican players

Zacatecas, Zacatecas, Mexico

7331 Pericos de Zacatecas 1965–67 *Mexican Center (A)*. Team went by the state name of "Zacatecas Parrots." The team, known as "Parrots" in English, was a farm club of the Class AAA Mexican League Puebla Parrots (Los Pericos de Puebla). Parrots inhabit the tropical rain forests of Mexico.

7332 Petroleros de Zactecas 1968–70 *Mexican Center (A)*. Team, known as "Oilers" in English, was a farm club of the Class AAA Mexican League Poza Rica Oilers (Los Petroleros de Poza Rica).

7333 Tuzos de Zacatecas 1971–73 *Mexican Center (A)*; 1982–83 *Nacional de Mexico (ind.)*. Gophers are burrowing rodents found in the southwest U.S. and Mexico (known as "tuzos" in Spanish).

7334 Club de Beisbol de Zacatecas 1976–78 *Liga Central de Mexico (A)*. Team had no nickname and used the state name of Zacatecas in its title.

Zanesville, Ohio

7335 Kickapoos 1887 *Ohio State (ind.)*; 1888 *Tri-State (ind.)*. The Kickapoo, Shawnee and Miami Indian tribes led by Chief Little Turtle were defeated at the Battle of Fallen Timbers by American troops led by Genera "Mad Anthony" Wayne and eventually were forced onto reservations in Kansas and Oklahoma by the 1840s. With manager Patrick Welsh at the helm in 1887, newspapers called the players "Patrick's Kickapoos." When Pete McShannick succeeded Welsh in mid-campaign 1887, the newspapers switched to "McShannick's Kickapoos."

7336 Zanesville Base Ball Club 1897 *Ohio–West Virginia (ind.)*; 1898 *Ohio State (ind.)*; 1907 *Pennsylvania–Ohio–Michigan (P.O.M.) (D)*. These teams had no nickname.

7337 Moguls 1905–06 *Ohio–Pennsylvania (C)*. The city's most famous son, Zane Grey, a noted author of fictional Wild West tales, became a "movie mogul," i.e., a movie producer, who formed his own motion picture company and then sold it to Paramount Pictures. The moniker also referred to the "Mogul" freight trains that traveled along the Ohio Railroad through Zanesville starting in the 1850s. With manager Fred Drumm at the helm in 1905, newspapers called the players "Drumm's Moguls."

7338 Infants 1908–09 *Central (B)*. Team had many young players, known in the baseball jargon of the time as "infants." With manager Martin Hogan at the helm, newspapers called the players "Martin Hogan's Infants." Robert Montgomery took over 1909–10 and the name became "Montgomery's Infants."

7339 Potters 1910–12 *Central (B)*. Zanesville is known as the "Pottery City." Clay from the eastern Ohio clayfields is transported to city ceramics factories to make bricks, tile and pottery.

7340 Flood Sufferers 1913x *Interstate (B)*. Team disbanded July 13 because of the Ohio Flood of 1913. The Ohio Flood of 1913 hit Zanesville particularly hard—five of seven city bridges were destroyed by the flood waters. The disaster was known as the Miami River Flood of 1913, which killed 361 people and severely damaged Dayton and Zanesville. Some baseball reporters in this era named teams after catastrophic events, i.e., Louisville Cyclones, Memphis

Fever Germs, Salina Insurgents, Shenandoah Hungarian Rioters, and Zanesville Flood-Sufferers.

7341 Grays 1933–37 *Middle Atlantic (D)*; 1993–95 *Frontier (ind.)*. Besides writing "Wild West" stories and making movies, Zanesville native Zane Grey played college baseball. His brother, R.C. Grey, played professional baseball in Newark (NJ) and Wheeling (WVa). Players wore gray-trim uniforms and stirrups. Alternate spelling in 1933–37: **Greys**

7342 Cubs 1941–42 *Middle Atlantic (C)*. Team was a farm club of the Chicago Cubs.

7343 Dodgers 1944–47 *Ohio State (D)*; 1948 *Ohio–Indiana (D)*. These teams were farm clubs of the Brooklyn Dodgers.

7344 Indians 1949–50 *Ohio–Indiana (D)*. Team was a farm club of the Cleveland Indians.

Zebulon, North Carolina

7345 Carolina Mudcats 1991 date *Southern (AA)*. The 1990 Columbus (GA) Mudcats moved to Zebulon for the 1991 season. The team nickname was retained.

Zhengzhou, Henan, China

7346 Henan Elephants 2009 to date *Chinese Baseball (S)*. Team goes by the provincial name of "Henan Elephants." The team is sponsored by the Henan Elephants Machinery Company, Ltd.

Zion, Lake, Illinois

7347 Lake County Fielders 2010 *Northern (ind.)*; 2011 to date *North American (ind.)*. The Golden, Northern and United leagues merged to form the North American League. Actor Kevin Costner is a part-owner of the team. Costner is famous for his popular 1989 movie *Field of Dreams*, which was filmed in Zion, Illinois. Management held a name-the-team contest and the winner was "Fielders." Other entries were Comets, Cowpokes, Luckies and Skippers.

Zion, Utah

7348 Pioneerz 1999–2000 *Western (ind.)*. Since about 1990, there has been a trendy fad of using household pet names like "dog" and "cat," not only because they represent old Jazz slang, i.e., "cat" (a street-smart young man) or "hep cat" (a young man who appreciates Jazz music) but also newer "Rap" and "Hip-hop" slang, i.e., "dog" (which parallels "cat") and dawg (an anti-establishment spelling form). Another spelling trend, again partly due to Rap and Hip-hop music, is the substitution of the letter **Z** for the letter S. Examples include the "Utah Starzz" and "Zion Pioneerz." The Mormon Pioneers arrived in Utah in the 1840s.

APPENDICES

I: Barnstorming and League-Affiliated Road Teams

These teams started the regular season without a home city and barnstormed throughout the year. Teams that started the regular season with a home city and then went on barnstorming road trips because of low attendance at home are not included here but are instead listed under the cities for which they began the year.

Famous Cuban Giants 1905 *Independent Negro team.* Invoking the name of the old Cuban Giants of 1885–99, the team signed several contemporary Cuban players and two players who had actually played with the 19th-century namesake, Pop Watkins (1B) and pitcher Sampson.

Pop Watkins' Stars 1907-08 *Independent Negro team.* Pop Watkins was a player/promoter who signed some of the black stars of this era, such as Sol White, John Henry Llyod, Charlie Grant, Home Run Johnson, Jose Munoz and Chappie Johnson, to barnstorm on this team.

Smart Set 1912–15 *Independent Negro team.* With no official leagues or regular season schedule yet established, this team barnstormed each summer for four years. "Smart set" was a contemporary slang for well-dressed, elegant and sophisticated people who gathered at ostentatious parties or upper-class social functions.

Bill Peter's Union Giants 1915–23 *Independent Negro team.* Bill Peters was a 19th century first baseman for the Chicago Unions, as early as 1890, who later became a manager. When the Chicago Union Giants disbanded after the 1915 season, he formed a barnstorming team using the name "Union Giants."

Pete Gilkerson's Union Giants 1915–34 *Independent Negro team.* Pete Gilkerson, a baseball promoter, formed this barnstorming team. At the start of the 1915 season, some players of the old Chicago Union Giants joined Bill Peter's team while others joined this team.

Henry Gray Baseball Club 1916 *Independent Negro team.* Henry Gray was a baseball promoter who organized this team to travel around the eastern U.S.

Silas Green Baseball Club 1921 *Independent Negro team.* Silas Green was a baseball promoter.

Florida Minstrels 1921 *Independent Negro team.* The team as named after a touring Negro minstrel show of the 1880s known as the "Florida Minstrels."

Georgia Minstrels 1921 *Independent Negro team.* The team was named after a touring Negro minstrel show of the 1860s known as the "Georgia Minstrels."

Bustin' Babes 1927 *Independent team.* This group was a barnstorming team that toured the U.S. from Rhode Island to California after the 1927 season. Its most famous member was Babe Ruth — who was noted for "bustin' the baseball."

Jack Johnson's All-Stars 1927 *Independent Negro team.* Topeka Jack Johnson was a baseball player and boxer who formed the Topeka (KS) Giants in 1917. In 1927 he formed a barnstorming team — the "All-Stars." The tag "All-Stars" was a popular name for barnstorming teams to attract the attention of fans looking for top-flight baseball competition.

Larrupin' Lous 1927 *Independent team.* A companion club, headed by Yankee great Lou Gehrig, traveled across the U.S. playing games against the Bustin' Babes. Sometimes Gehrig joined Ruth on a combined team during this tour. Gehrig named the team after his own personal nickname of "Larrupin Lou" — given to him by fans and reporters. "Larrup" means to thrash or beat someone or something, i.e. "The cowboy larruped the bucking bronco."

New York All-Stars 1928 *Independent Negro team.* The team traveled throughout New York State.

Texas Colored Giants 1929–31 Independent team. Founded by Canadian businessman Red Whitman, team assumed a popular adjective, i.e. "colored" and noun "Giants" — commonly used by black baseball teams in this era. Note: Another barnstorming outfit of this era — the Texas Black Spiders (players wore black trim uniforms) — seems to have been only semi-professional.

Cuban House of David 1931 *Independent Negro team.* The team, a spin-off of the famous House of David baseball team, consisted of both American blacks and Cubans.

John Davidson's All-Stars 1931-32 *Independent Negro team.* John Davidson was a baseball promoter looking to earn barnstorming money during the Great Depression.

Lou Santop's Broncos 1931-32 *Independent Negro team.* Louis Santop was a hard-hitting catcher who played in the black leagues in the 1920s and 1930s. He organized this barnstorming team to make a little money during the worst days of the Great Depression.

Ramiro Ramirez' Stars 1933 *Independent Negro team.* Ramiro Ramirez was a Cuban pitcher who played winter ball in Cuba and played in the summer on such U.S.–based teams as the Cuban Stars and New York Cubans. Ramirez signed star players like Josh Gibson, Rap Nixon, Otis Starks and Bill Casey to barnstorm and to earn a little extra money during the depths of the Great Depression.

Baltimore Silver Moons 1934 *Independent Negro team.* The team had been the independent Baltimore Pirates (1932-33) and was renamed as the "Silver Moons" as a marketing ploy to attract more fans. Although the team's home base was Baltimore, the team spent almost the entire season on the road. The team logo was a "Baseball Man in the Moon." Reinforcing the "Silver Moon" image was the many night games the team played this season

Zulu Cannibal Giants 1934–37 *Independent Negro team.* This moniker was the nadir of Negro League baseball team nicknames. The players called themselves "Zulu Cannibals," painting their faces and wearing grass skirts to the mirth of many white and black fans who attended the team's contests. Whether the players were trying to pass themselves off as real Africans or were just pandering to the fans' visions of stereotypes is hard to say.

Caribbean Kings 1935–45 *Independent team.* Stocked with black and white Cuban players, the team was founded and named by sports promoter Dempsey Hovland. Cuba is located in the Caribbean Sea.

Negro National League All-Stars 1936 *Independent team.* Team was a barnstorming club that traveled the U.S. after the conclusion of the 1936 regular season. Team deserved its moniker of "All-Stars" because of the star players on the roster, including Josh Gibson, Cool Papa Bell, Buck Leonard, Ray Brown, and pitcher Satchel Paige.

Satchel Paige's All-Stars 1936–37, 1946 *Independent team.* Sport's promoter Johnny Barton hired star pitcher Satchel Paige to form a barnstorming team which Barton called "Satchel Paige's All Stars." Team toured the U.S. in 1936 and then the Dominican Republic in 1937. Team reformed after the 1947 regular season as a black team to tour along Bob Feller's All-Stars—a group of major leaguers.

Ethiopian Clowns 1937–63 *Independent Negro team.* An attempt to combine the name of a distinguished African country, Ethiopia, with "clowning around" on the field resulted in the "Ethiopian Clowns." The team barnstormed mostly but also played league ball in Cincinnati and Indianapolis during World War II. Haille Selassie was the leader of Ethiopia when it was invaded and sacked by Mussolini in 1938. After World War II, Selassie once again became Ethiopia's leader.

Satchel Paige's All-Stars 1939–46 *Independent Negro team.* With Paige as the Negro League's most glamorous star, he organized Satchel Paige's All-Stars to barnstorm and to compete with in particular barnstorming major league teams. Most games were played in Southern California, particularly Los Angeles. Buck Leonard, Cool Papa Bell, Buck O'Neil and other black All-Stars, who were fixtures in the Negro All-Star Game every summer in Chicago, were on this team.

Colorado Silver Bullets 1995–97 *Independent team.* The first and only all-professional women's baseball club, the team was sponsored by Coors Brewing Company — brewers of Coor "Silver Bullet" Light Beer, so known because the rounded silver aluminum can in which this light beer was sold had a slight bullet shape. Since the team hearkened back to Colorado the name also referred to the "silver bullets" that some gunslingers used in the days of the Old West — a lot of that silver coming from Colorado silver mines. Note: The Texas Cowgirls, who competed 1949–77 as an all-women's barnstorming baseball team, were strictly a semi-professional club.

Southern Nomadic Miners 1995x *Golden State (ind.)* Circuit and team disbanded July 4. The team played all its games on the road, prompting the regional name of Southern Nomadic Miners. Nomadic game hunters roamed Arizona from 12,000 B.C. to about 500 A.D. when farming first appeared. Although settlers came to Arizona in the period 1850–90 after gold and silver were discovered in the region, it was copper that by 1890 became Arizona's biggest asset. Copper ore is shipped to city factories for smelting and processing.

Western Warriors 1998 *Western (ind.).* The moniker was a spin-off from "Road Warriors." The team toured the cities of the Western League.

Black Diamonds 1999–2001 *Atlantic (ind.).* The team played its 1998 home games in Easton as the "Lehigh Valley Black Diamonds," but low attendance forced the franchise to barnstorm, starting in 1999. The nickname "Black Diamonds" is slang for "coal miners." Coal mining was Pennsylvania's major industry in the 19th century.

Pennsylvania Road Warriors 2002–04 *Atlantic (ind.).* Originally meaning a person who travels extensively, the motorcycle gangs of the era 1950–80 and the Mad Max movies of actor Mel Gibson, "Road Warrior" evoked the image of an armed individual on a motorcycle. In sports, the moniker refers to a team that wins many road games. The team toured the cities of the Atlantic League all three seasons.

Japan Samurai Bears 2005 *Golden (ind.).* The nickname was a combination of the "Bad News Bears" of the 1976 Hollywood movie and the ancient symbol of Japan — the Samurai warrior. The Japanese public venerates the historical legends of their ancient Samurai and Ninja, but they also are aficionados of kids' cartoons and logos, showing kids at play. The team toured the cities of the Golden Baseball League.

Road Warriors 2006–07 *Atlantic (ind.); Atlantic (ind.)* 2011 to date. The 2004 Pennsylvania Road Warriors returned in 2006–07 — minus the state name. Another similarly named team started play in 2011.

Grays 2007 *Canadian-American (ind.).* Players wore gray-trim uniforms.

Texas Heat 2007 *Continental (ind.).* Texas is noted for its hot summers.

Team China 2007 to date *Arizona Fall (W).* The team played its "home" games in Phoenix, Mesa, Scottsdale and Yuma. The team's players all come from China.

Team USA 2007 to date *Arizona Fall (W).* The team played its "home" games in Phoenix, Mesa, Scottsdale and Yuma. A rival of Team China, the team had American-born players.

Sliders 2008 *Frontier (ind.).* Playing the 2007 season as the Slippery Rock (PA) Sliders, the team was forced to barnstorm in 2008. The team moved to a new home ballpark in Waterford Township (MI) in 2009 and became known as the Oakland County Cruisers.

Coastal Kingfish 2009 *Continental (ind.).* The kingfish is a type of drum fish that inhabits the warm waters of the Gulf of Mexico and the Caribbean Sea.

New York Federals 2011 to date *Can-Am (ind.).* The team travels throughout New York State. After the Civil War, "federal" meant "Northerner."

II: Major League Team Nicknames Year-by-Year, 1871–1900

Legend

Italics = Most popular unofficial name for that particular season (almost always coined by the fans, newspaper reporters, or a team owner).

BOLD = Official team nickname

(Name) = refers to an individual or group of individuals who coined the name.

(h) = historical, i.e. refers to a name that appeared gradually over the years without a specific origin.

1871 National Association

Philadelphia	Athletic, *Athletics*, Blues, Blue Legs
Chicago	White Legs, Whites, *White Stockings*
Boston	Bostonians, Down-Easters, Reds, Redlegs, *Red Stockings*
Washington	Blues, Blue Legs, Blue Stockings, *Olympics*
Troy	Green Legs, Green Stockings, Haymakers, Trojans, Unions
New York	Green Legs, Green Stockings, Mutes, Mutual, *Mutuals*, Unruly Bad Boys of Baseball (Neil McDonald)

Cleveland	Blues, Blue Legs, Blue Stockings, Forest City, *Forest Citys*
Fort Wayne	Kekinoga, *Kekiongas*
Rockford	Forest City, *Forest Citys,* Green Legs, Green Stockings
Brooklyn	Eckford, *Eckfords,* Orange Legs, Yellow Legs

1872 National Association

Boston	Bostonians, Champions, Down-Easters, Reds, Redlegs, *Red Stockings*
Philadelphia	Athletic, *Athletics,* Blues, Blue Legs
Baltimore	Canaries, *Lord Baltimores,* Mustard Sox, Striped Legs, Yellow Legs
New York	Green Legs, Green Stockings, Mutes, Mutual, *Mutual,* Unruly Bad Boys of Baseball (McDonald)
Troy	Green Legs, Green Stockings, Haymaker, Haymakers, Trojans, Unions
Cleveland	Blues, Blue Legs, Forest City, *Forest Citys*
Brooklyn	Atlantic, *Atlantics*
Washington	Blues, Blue Legs, Blue Stockings, Olympic, *Olympics*
Middletown	Mansfield, *Mansfields*
Brooklyn	Eckford, *Eckfords,* Orange Legs
Washington	National, *Nationals*

1873 National Association

Boston	Bostonians, Champions, Down-Easters, Noble Red Men (*New York Clipper*), Reds, Redlegs, *Red Stockings*
Philadelphia	Fillies, Pearls, Pirates, *Phillies,* Power-house, Quaker, Quakers, Raiders, Whites, White Legs, White Stockings
Baltimore	Canaries, Lord Baltimore, *Lord Baltimore,* Mustard Sox, Yellow Legs
Philadelphia	Athletic, *Athletics,* Blues, Blue Legs
New York	Green Legs, Green Stockings, Mutes, Mutual, *Mutuals,* Unruly Bad Boys of Baseball (McDonald)
Brooklyn	Atlantic, *Atlantics*
Washington	National, *Nationals*
Elizabeth	Growlers, Jersey Nine, Resolute, *Resolutes*

1874 National Association

Boston	Down-Easters, Champions, Reds, Redlegs, *Red Stockings*
New York	Green Legs, Green Stockings, Mutes, Mutual, *Mutuals,* Unruly Bad Boys of Baseball (McDonald)
Philadelphia	Athletic, *Athletics,* Blues, Blue Legs
Philadelphia	Fillies, Pearls, *Phillies,* Quaker, Quakers, Snow-ballers, Whites, White Legs, White Stockings
Chicago	Whites, White Legs, *White Stockings*
Brooklyn	Atlantic, *Atlantics*
Hartford	Blues, Charter Oaks, *Dark Blues,* Nutmeggers
Baltimore	Canaries, *Lord Baltimores,* Lords, Mustard Sox, Yellow Legs

1875 National Association

Boston	Giants from the East, Greeks, Reds, Redlegs, *Red Stockings*
Hartford	Blues, Charter Oaks, *Dark Blues,* Nutmeggers
Philadelphia	Athletic, *Athletics,* Blues, Blue Legs
St. Louis	*Browns,* Brown Stockings, Mound City Nine, Mound Citys

Philadelphia	Fillies, Pearls, *Phillies,* Quaker, Quakers, Whites, White Legs, White Stockings
New York	Green Legs, Green Stockings, Mutes, Mutual, *Mutuals,* Unruly Bad Boys of Baseball (McDonald)
Chicago	Whites, White Legs, *White Stockings*
New Haven	Elm City, *Elm Citys,* Elms, Warriors
Washington	Blacks, Black Legs, Black Stockings, Southerners, Southern Nine
St. Louis	Reds, Redlegs, *Red Stockings*
Philadelphia	Centennial, *Centennials*
Brooklyn	Atlantic, *Atlantics*
Keokuk	Western, *Westerns*

1876 National League

Chicago	Big White Machine (David Nemec), Chicagos, Giants, Mighty Nine, Whites, White Legs, *White Stockings*
St. Louis	*Browns,* Brown Stockings, Pilgrims
Hartford	Blues, *Dark Blues,* Yankees
Boston	Bay Staters, Bostons, Red Caps, Reds, Red Legs, *Red Stockings*
Louisville	Blues, Falls City, Falls Citys, *Grays,* Kentuckians, Kentucky Cracks, Kentucky Leaguers
New York	Chocolate Sox, Mutual, *Mutuals,* Unruly Bad Boys of Baseball (McDonald)
Philadelphia	Athletic, *Athletics,* Bastards, Blues, Blue Legs
Cincinnati	Buckeyes, Ponies, Porkopolitans, Queen Citys, *Reds,* Red Legs, *Red Stockings*
New Haven	Elm Citys, Elms
Binghamton	**Cricket**
Columbus	**Buckeyes, BucSyracuse**

1877 National League

Boston	Bostons, Hubs, Red Caps, Reds, Red Legs, *Red Stockings*
Louisville	Falls City, Falls City, *Grays,* Kentuckians
Brooklyn	Hartford, *Hartfords*
St. Louis	*Browns,* Brown Stockings
Chicago	Chicagos, Whites, White Legs, *White Stockings*
Cincinnati	Reds, Red Legs, *Red Stockings* (Owner) Si Keck's Stinker Nine

1877 New England Association

Lowell	Brethern (Harry Wright), Ladies' Men, Lowells, Spindle Citys
Manchester	New Hampshirites, *Reds,* Red Legs, Red Stockings
Fall River	Braves, Cascades
Providence	Little Rhodys, Rhode Island, *Rhode Islands,* Rhodies
Lynn	Live Oaks, Oaks

1877 New York State Association

Syracuse	Salt Citys, *Stars,* Twinklers
Binghamton	*Crickets,* Chirpers
Auburn	Auburnians
Rochester	Blue Legs, Blues. Blue Stockings, Flour Citys
Buffalo	Bisons, Buffalos, Buffern

1877 International Association

Columbus	Buckeyes, Bucks

Guelph	Maple Leafs
London	Canadian Indians, Tecumsehs
Lynn	Live Oaks, Oaks
Manchester	New Hampshirites, Spindle Cities
Pittsburgh	Alleghenies, Alleghenys, Allies
Rochester	Blue Stockings, Blue Legs, Blues, Flour Cities

1878 National League

Boston	Bostons, The Hub, Red Caps, Reds, Red Legs, *Red Stockings*
Cincinnati	Porkopolitans, Queen Citys, *Reds*, Red Legs, Red Stockings
Providence	Big Nine, *Grays*, Little Rhodys, Rhode Island, Rhode Islands, Yankees
Chicago	Chicagos, Whites, White Legs, *White Stockings*
Indianapolis	Blues, Capital Citys, Capitals, Homeless Browns, Hoosiers, Indians
Milwaukee	Brewers, Bulls, Cream City, Cream Citys, Grays

1878 International Association

Binghamton	*Crickets*, Chirpers
Brooklyn	*Blues*, True Blues
Buffalo	Bisons, Buffalos
Columbus	Buckeyes
Hartford	Charter Oaks
Hornellsville	*Hornells*, Railroad Men, Tourists
London	Canadian Indians, Indians, *Tecumsehs*
Lowell	Lowells, Spindle Citys
Manchester	New Hampshirites, Pros, Red Stockings, *Reds*, Wranglers
New Bedford	Blue Stockings, Blues, *Whalers*
New Haven	Connecticut Cracks, *Elm Citys*, Professionals
Pittsburgh	Alleghenys, Allies
Rochester	Flour Citys
Springfield	Professionals, Pros
Syracuse	Salt Citys, *Stars*, Twinklers
Utica	*Pent-Ups*, Red Stockings, Redlegs, Reds, Utes
Worcester	Giants, Irvings, Red Stockings, *Reds*, Ruby Legs

1879 National League

Providence	Dark Blues, *Grays*, Rhode Islanders, Rhode Island Nine, Rhode Islands, Yankees
Boston	Bostons, Red Caps, Red Legs, Red Stockings
Buffalo	*Bisons*, Blues
Chicago	Chicagos, Whites, White Legs, *White Stockings*
Cincinnati	Pioneers, Porkopolitans, Queen Citys, Reds, Red Legs, *Red Stockings*
Cleveland	*Blues*, Forest Citys
Syracuse	*Stars*, Twinklers, Twinks
Troy	Haymakers, Trojans, Unions

1879 National Association

Albany	Blue Stockings, Blue Legs, Blues
Albany	Capital Citys, Capitals
Holyoke	Gentlemen, Gents, Hard Hitters, Malone's Men, Nationalists
Washington	Nationalists, Nationals, Nats
Springfield	Bob Ferguson's Men, Gentlemen, Professionals, Pros

Manchester	New Hampshirites, Professionals, Pros, Red Stockings, Redlegs, Reds, Wranglers
Rochester	The Advertising, Flour Citys, Hop Bitters
Utica Utes	Kickers, Pent-Ups, Red Stockings, Redlegs, Reds, Utes

1880 National League

Chicago	Chicagos, Whites, White Legs, *White Stockings*
Providence	*Grays*, Rhode Islands, Yankees
Cleveland	*Blues*, Forest Citys
Troy	Haymakers, Trojans, Unions
Worcester	Reds, Ruby Legs, Browns
Boston	*Beaneaters*, Bostons, Red Caps, Red Legs, Red Stockings
Buffalo	*Bisons*, Buffalos, Scarlets
Cincinnati	Porkopolitans, Reds, Red Legs, *Red Stockings*

1880 National Association

Albany	Capital Citys, Capitals
Baltimore	Green Stockings, Green Legs, Greens
Philadelphia	Athletics
Rochester	The Advertising Team, Flour Citys, Hop Bitters
Washington	Nationals

1881 National League

Chicago	Chicagos, Whites, White Legs, *White Stockings*
Providence	*Grays*, Rhode Islands, Yankees
Buffalo	Bisons, Buffalos, Grays
Detroit	Detroits, Straits City, Straits Citys, *Wolverines*
Troy	Haymakers, Trojans, Unions
Boston	*Beaneaters*, Bostons, Red Caps, Red Legs, Red Stockings
Cleveland	*Blues*, Forest Citys
Worcester	Ruby Legs (occasional newspaper use), Browns (occasional newspaper use)

1881 Eastern Championship Association

Albany	Capital Citys, Capitals
Baltimore	Lord Baltimores, Marylands, Monumental Citys, Monumentals, Red Stockings, Redlegs, Reds
Brooklyn	Atlantics
New York	Brown Stockings, Browns
New York	Metropolitans, Mets
New York	Quicksteps
Philadelphia	Athletics
Philadelphia	Red Quakers, Red Stockings, Red Legs, Reds

1882 National League

Chicago	Chicagos, Whites, White Legs, *White Stockings*
Providence	*Grays*, Light Blues, Rhode Islands, Yankees
Boston	*Beaneaters*, Beanies, Bostons, Reds, Red Legs, Red Stockings
Buffalo	*Bisons*, Buffalos, Grays
Cleveland	*Blues*, Blue Legs, Forest Citys
Detroit	Detroits, Old Golds, Straits City, Straits Citys, *Wolverines*, Wolves
Troy	Green Legs, Haymakers, Trojans, Unions
Worcester	(Mgr. Freeman) Brown's Browns, Lame Ducks (h), Reds, Red Legs, Red Stockings, Ruby Legs

1882 American Association

Cincinnati	Maroons, Porkers, Porkopolitans, Rainbows, *Reds*, Red Legs, Red Stockings, Scarlets, Silkshirts, Zebra Stockings
Philadelphia	Athletic, *Athletics*, Maroons
Louisville	Bourbonville, Colonels, *Eclipse*, Falls Citys, Kaintucks, Red Legs
Pittsburgh	*Alleghenys*, Allies, Brewers, The Brewery, Lowlanders (Mgr. Al) Pratt's Lushers, Slaughterhouse Nine, Smoky Citys
St. Louis	*Browns*, Brown Stockings, Der Boss Club, Der Poys
Baltimore	Birdlings, Birds, Canaries, Lambs, Lord Baltimores, Mgr. Henry Myers' Martyrs, Marylands, Oyster-Openers, Yellow Legs

1883 National League

Boston	*Beaneaters*, Beanies, Blue Caps, Reds, Red Legs, Red Stockings
Chicago	Lake City, Lake Citys, Whites, White Legs, *White Stockings*
Providence	*Grays*, Light Blues, Yankees
Cleveland	*Blues*, Blue Legs, Dark Blues, Forest Citys
Buffalo	*Bisons*, Grays, Sluggers
New York	*Gothams*, Leaguers, Maroons, New Yorks
Detroit	Browns, Detroits, Reds, Red Legs, Ponies, Straits Citys, Wolverines, Wolves
Philadelphia	Fillies, Infants, Leaguers, *Phillies*, Quakers, Red Quakers

1883 American Association

Philadelphia	Associations, Athletic, *Athletics*, Blues, Blue Legs, Conquering Heroes
St. Louis	*Reds*, Red Legs, *Browns*, Der Boss Club, Der Poys
Cincinnati	Maroons, Porkers, Porkopolitans, Queen Citys, *Reds*, Red Legs, Red Stockings, Scarlets
New York	Associations, Hustlers (August), Metropolitan, *Metropolitans* (Mets), Ponies
Louisville	Blues, Blue Legs, Bourbonville, Colonels, *Eclipse*
Columbus	Buckeyes, Colts, Discoverers, Pearl-Grays, Senators, Solons
Pittsburgh	Alleghanys, *Alleghenys*, Allies, Brewers, Lowlanders, Sluggers (April), Smoky Citys
Baltimore	Birdlings, Birds, Blue Legs, Bill Barnie's Boys, Lord Baltimores, *Orioles*, Oyster-Openers

1884 National League

Providence	Clam-Eaters, *Grays*, Rhode Islands, Yankees
Boston	Bostons, *Beaneaters*, Reds, Red Legs, Red Stockings
Buffalo	*Bisons*, Buffalos, Giants
Chicago	Chicagos, Giants, Rough'n'Toughs, Whites, White Legs, *White Stockings*
New York	*Gothams*, Leaguers, Maroons
Philadelphia	Fillies, Leaguers, *Phillies*, Quakers, Whites, White Legs
Cleveland	*Blues*, Blue Legs, Forest Citys
Detroit	Detroits, Wolverines

1884 American Association

New York	Associations, Metropolitan, *Metropolitans*, Mets, Ponies

Columbus	Buckeyes, Colts, Discoverers, Pearl-Grays, Senators, Solons
Louisville	Bourbonville, Colonels, *Eclipse*
St. Louis	Browns, Der Boss Club, Der Poys
Cincinnati	Maroons, Pioneers, Porkers, Porkopolitans, *Reds*, Red Legs, Red Stockings, Scarlets
Baltimore	Birdlings, Birds, Bill Barnie's Boys, Lord Baltimores, Orioles, Oysterville
Philadelphia	Associations, *Athletics*, Blues, Blue Legs
Toledo	*Blues*, Blue Legs, Blue Stockings
Brooklyn	Atlantics, Brooks, Church Citys, Grays, Polka Dots, *Trolley Dodgers*
Richmond	Virginia, *Virginias*
Pittsburgh	Allegheny, *Alleghenys*, Allies, Lowlanders
Indianapolis	Blue Legs, Blues, Blue Stockings, *Hoosier*, Indians
Washington	Statesmen

1884 Union Association

St. Louis	(Team owner Henry) Lucas' Colossus (David Voight), Fred Dunlap's Giants, Hirelings, Lucas' One Ring Circus (David Nemec), *Maroons*, Lucas' Millionaires (David Nemec), Mound City Monsters (Nemec), Onions, Sluggers, Unions
Milwaukee	Blues, Brewers, Cream Citys, Grays
Cincinnati	Avengers, Cannonballs, Hirelings, Dan O'Leary's Grabs, Onions, *Outlaw Reds*, Unions
Baltimore	Maroons, Monumental Citys, *Monumentals*
Boston	Beaneaters, *Blues*, Blue Legs, Dark Blues, Leaguers, Nationals
Chicago	Browns, Ed Hengle's Brewers, Browns, *Gold Stockings*, Old Golds
Washington	Nationals, Onions, Unions
Pittsburgh	Brewers, Onions, Smoky Citys, *Stogies*, Unions
Philadelphia	Keystones, Onions, Unions
St. Paul	Apostles, Saints, Vulcans, White Caps
Altoona	*Famous Altoonas*, Infants, Mountain Citys, Pride, Unfortunates
Kansas City	Cowboys
Wilmington	Purple Stockings, *Quicksteps*

1885 National League

Chicago	Cap Anson's Kickers, Terrors, Whites, White Legs, *White Stockings*
New York	*Giants*, Jints, Leaguers, Maroons (Mgr. Jim) Mutrie's Men, Nationals
Philadelphia	Fillies, Leaguers, *Phillies*, Quakers, Red Quakers,
Providence	*Grays*, Yankees
Boston	*Beaneaters*, Hub Team, Leaguers, Nationals, Reds, Red Legs, Red Stockings, Yankees
Detroit	Detroits, Reds, Red Legs, *Wolverines*, Wolves
Buffalo	Bisons, Buffalos
St. Louis	Black Diamonds, Leaguers, Harry Lucas' Tribe, Lucas Club, *Maroons*, Nationals

1885 American Association

St. Louis	Associations, *Browns*, Brown Stockings, Der Boss Club, Der Poys, Mound City Steamrollers (Nemec), Original Comiskey Men (Nemec)
Cincinnati	Porkers, Porkopolitans, Queen Citys, *Reds*, Red Legs, Red Stockings, Scarlets, Scarlet Stockings

Pittsburgh   Alleghenys, Allies, Lowlanders, Smoky Citys
Philadelphia   Associations, *Athletics*, Blues, Blue Legs
Brooklyn   Atlantics, Boodle-Grabbers, Church Citys, Red Legs,
               Trolley Dodgers
Louisville   Bourbonville, *Colonels*, Dark Reds, *Eclipse*, Red Caps
New York   Associations, *Metropolitans*, Mets, Ponies, Pony Team,
               Staten Island Indians, Whites, White Legs
Baltimore   Birdlings, Birds, Bill Barnie's Boys, Lord Baltimores,
               Orioles, Oysterville, Red Legs

Cincinnati   *Reds*, Red Legs, Red Stockings, Sluggers
Baltimore   Birdlings, Birds, Kickers, Lord Baltimores, Maroons,
               Orioles, Oyster-Openers
Louisville   *Colonels*, Eclipse, Falls Citys
Philadelphia   *Athletics*, Mail-Carriers
Brooklyn   Church Citys, Grays, *Trolley Dodgers*
New York   Metropolitan, Metropolitans
Cleveland   Babies, Baby, Blues, Blue Legs, Forest Citys, Remnants,
               Spiders

1886 National League

Chicago   Chicagos, Cap Anson's Kickers, Record-Breakers, Ter-
               rors, Whites, White Legs, *White Stockings*, Windy
               Citys
Detroit   Big-Four Team, Fred Dunlap's Daiseys, Giants, Record-
               Makers, Sluggers, *Wolverines*
New York   Blues, Blue Legs, Evaporating Giants, *Giants*, Jim
               Mutrie's Men, Jints, Nickel Plates, Real Things
Philadelphia   Fillies, *Phillies*, Quakers, Red Quakers
Boston   *Beaneaters*, Hub Team, Reds, Red Legs, Red Stockings
St. Louis   Black Diamonds, George Lucas' Tribe, Lucas Club,
               Maroons, Traveling Hospital
Kansas City   Babies, Baby, *Blues*, Blue Legs, *Cowboys*, Dave Rowe's
               Revengers, Stormy Petrels
Washington   Capitols, Capitol Citys, *Senators*, Statesmen

1886 American Association

St. Louis   *Browns*, Der Boss Club, Der Champeens, Der Poys,
               Juggernauts (Nemec), Mound City Steamrollers
               (Nemec), Original Comiskey Men (John D. Cash)
Pittsburgh   Alleghenys, Allies, Lowlanders, Smoky Citys
Brooklyn   Charlie Byrne's Boys, Church Citys, *Trolley Dodgers*
Louisville   Bourbonville, *Colonels*, *Eclipse*, Falls Citys
Cincinnati   (Mgr. Opie) Caylor's Crabs, Maroons, Porkers, Pork-
               opolitans, *Reds*, Red Legs, Red Stockings, Scarlets
Philadelphia   Athletics
New York   Blues, Blue Legs, *Metropolitans*, Staten Island Indians
Baltimore   Birdlings, Birds, Bill Barnie's Boys, Lord Baltimores,
               Orioles, Oyster-Openers, Worst Hitters Ever (Mar-
               shall Wright)

1887 National League

Detroit   Big-Four Team, Giants, Record-Makers, Sluggers,
               Wolverines
Philadelphia   Fillies, *Phillies*, Quakers, Red Quakers
Chicago   Whites, White Legs, *White Stockings*
New York   Giants, Jints (Mgr. Jim) Mutrie's Men, Mutrie Men
Boston   Bay States, *Beaneaters*, Down-Easters, Mike Kelly's
               Satellites, Hub Team, Reds, Red Legs, Red Stock-
               ings
Pittsburgh   *Alleghenys*, Allies, Potato Bugs, Smoky Citys, Smoked
               Italians, Zulus
Washington   Capitols, Capitol Citys, *Senators*, Statesmen
Indianapolis   Hapless Hoosiers, Hoosiers

1887 American Association

St. Louis   *Browns*, Der Boss Club, Juggernauts (Nemec), Mound
               City Steamrollers (Nemec), Original Comiskey
               Men (Cash)

1888 National League

New York   Blacks, Black Legs, *Giants*, Gotham Giants, Jim Mutrie's
               Men, Mutrie Men, Jints
Chicago   Blacks, Black Legs, *Black Stockings*, Cap Anson's Colts,
               Swallowtails, Windy Citys
Philadelphia   Fillies, *Phillies*, Quakers, Red Quakers
Boston   *Beaneaters*, Hub Team, Reds, Red Legs, Red Stockings
Detroit   Sluggers, Whites, White Legs, White Stockings, *Wolver-
               ines*
Pittsburgh   *Alleghenys*, Allies, Gas Citys, Lowlanders, Potato Bugs,
               Smoked Italians, Smoky Citys, Stogies, Zulus
Indianapolis   Blue Licks, Hapless Hoosiers (h), *Hoosiers*
Washington   Capitols, Capitol Citys, *Senators*

1888 American Association

St. Louis   *Browns*, Brown Stockings, Der Boss Club, Der Cham-
               peens, Der Poys
Brooklyn   *Bridegrooms*, Church Citys
Philadelphia   Athletics
Cincinnati   Queen Citys, Pioneers, *Reds*, Red Legs, Red Stockings,
               White Nadjies
Baltimore   Birdlings, Bill Barnie's Birdlings, Lord Baltimores, *Ori-
               oles*, Oysterville
Cleveland   Blues, Forest Citys, *Spiders*
Louisville   Bourbonville, *Colonels*, *Eclipse*, Falls Citys, Red-Shirts
Kansas City   Babies, Baby, Blues, *Cowboys*, Ice Wagon Gang, Ma-
               roons, Reds, Red Legs

1889 National League

New York   Blacks, Black Legs, *Giants*, Homeless Giants, Jints
               (Mgr. Jim) Mutrie's Men, Mutrie Men, Nadjies
               (owner) Nick Engel's Nickels, Nick Engels Nickle-
               Platers, Staten Islanders, White Nadjies
Boston   *Beaneaters*, Blue Ribbons, Blue Ribbon Boys, Reds,
               Red Legs, Red Stockings
Chicago   Blacks, Black Legs, *Black Stockings*, Dickey Birds, Laven-
               ders, Windy Citys
Philadelphia   Fillies, Giants, *Phillies*, Quakers
Pittsburgh   *Alleghenys*, Allies, Potato Bugs, Smoky Citys, Smoked
               Italians, Zulus
Cleveland   Babies, Baby, Castoffs, Forest Citys, Hand-Me-Downs,
               Rebels, *Spiders*
Indianapolis   Hoosiers, Hustling Hoosiers (August)
Washington   Capitols, Capitol Citys, *Senators*

1889 American Association

Brooklyn   *Bridegrooms*, Church Citys
St. Louis   *Browns*, Brown Stockings, Der Poys
Philadelphia   Athletics

Cincinnati   Hospital Team, Pioneers, Porkers, Porkopolitans, Queen Citys, *Reds*, Red Stockings, Red Legs, White Nadjies

Baltimore   Birdlings, Birds, Bill Barnie's Boys, Canaries, Lord Baltimores, *Orioles*, Oysterville, Yellow Leg

Columbus   Babies, Baby, Blues, Buckeyes, Al Buckenberger's Buckeyes, Ohio Men, Senators, Solons

Kansas City   Blues, Blue Legs, *Cowboys*, Ice Wagon Gang

Louisville   Blue Jays, Blue Legs Bourbonville, Clan-Na-Gaels, *Colonels*, Falls Citys, Jays, Liables, Lillies, Loseville, Record-Breakers, Unfortunates

1890 National League

Brooklyn   *Bridegrooms*, Whiskerless Heroes

Chicago   Babes, Blacks, BlackLegs, Bronchos, Broncos, Cap Anson's Colts, Chicks, *Colts*, Cubs (April), Recruits

Philadelphia   George Wright's Phillies, George Wright's Quakers, *Phillies*, Ponies, Quakers, Red Quakers, Students

Cincinnati   Babies, Baby, Dealers, Porkopolitans, Queen Citys, *Reds*, Red Legs, Red Stockings, Rhinelanders

Boston   *Beaneaters*, Frank Selee's Beaneaters, Reds, Red Legs, Red Stockings

New York   *Giants* (Mgr. Jim) Mutrie's Colts, Mutrie's Giants, Mutrie's Mules, *Mules*, Young Giants

Cleveland   Blacks, Black Legs, Dark Blues, *Kids*, Gus Schmeltz' Kids, Schmeltz' Spiders, Spiders

Pittsburgh   *Alleghenys*, Allies, Colts, Guy Hecker's Boobies, Hecker's Kids, Hecker's School Boys, Innocents, Lowlanders, Nomads, Potato Bugs, School Boys, Smoked Italians, Smoky Citys, Stogies, Troubadours, Wanderers, Zulus

1890 American Association

Louisville   Bourbon City, Bourbon Citys, Bourbonville, *Colonels*, Cyclones, Distillery Delegates, Eclipse, Sour-Mashes, The Wonder of the Age

Columbus   (Mgr. Al) Buckenberger's Bad Actors, Buckenberger's Buckeyes, Blues, Blue Legs, Buckenberger's Buckyes, Buckenberger's Bucks, Bucks, Capitals, Capital Citys, Colts, Ohio Men, Senators, Solons

St. Louis   *Browns*, Brown Socks, Brown Stockings

Toledo   Black Pirates, Maumees, Swamp Angels

Rochester   Flour Citys, Flower Citys, Pat Power's Pets

Syracuse   Salt Citys, *Stars*, Twinklers, Twinks

Philadelphia   *Athletics*, Blues, Blue Legs, Blue Quakers, Troubadors

Brooklyn   Castaways, *Gladiators*, Kennedy's Kids

Baltimore   Birdlings, Birds, Lord Baltimores, *Orioles*, Oysterville

1890 Players League

Boston   Braves, Mike "King" Kelly's Beaneaters, Kelly's Braves, Kelly's Warriors, Kelly's Red Legs, Kelly's Warriors

Brooklyn   Blues, Blue Legs, Monte Ward's Galaxy of Stars, Ward's Men. *Ward's Wonders*

New York   Blacks, Black Legs, Buck Ewing's Braves, Ewing's Charley Horses (spinoff from Jim Mutrie's Mules), Ewing's Giants, Ewing's Warriors, Giants

Chicago   Buccaneers, Bucks, Charlie Comiskey's All-Stars, Comiskey's Stars, *Pirates*, Whites, White Legs, White Stockings

Philadelphia   Fillies, Harry Wright's Ponies, Wright's Students, Phillies, Ponies, *Quakers*, Red Quakers

Pittsburgh   *Maroons*, Ned Hanlon's Crew

Cleveland   Babes, Grays, Infants, Kickers (August), Spiders

Buffalo   Bisons, Browns, Home for Respectable Old Men, Reds, Red Legs, Browns

1891 National League

Boston   Bay States, *Beaneaters*, Frank Selee's Beaneaters, Reds, Red Legs, Red Stockings

Chicago   Blacks, Black Legs, Black Stockings, Cap Anson's Chicks, Chicks, Cap Anson's Colts, *Colts*, Garden Citys

New York   *Giants*, Jints (Mgr. Jim) Mutrie's Mugs, Sleepy Giants

Philadelphia   *Phillies*, Quakers

Cleveland   Blues, Bolivar's Blues, Forest Citys, *Spiders*

Brooklyn   Bridegrooms, Monte Ward's Wonders, *Trolley Dodgers*, Wonders

Cincinnati   Porkopolitans, Queen Citys, *Reds*, Red Legs, Red Stockings, Rhines, Rhinelanders

Pittsburgh   All-Stars, Boobies, Lowlanders, *Pirates*, Quitters, Ragglers, Smoky Citys, Smoked Italians

1891 American Association

Boston   All-Stars, Clock-work Team (Fred Lieb), Reds, Red Legs, *Red Stockings* (Mgr. Frank) Selee's Selects, Sluggers, Speed Boys

St. Louis   Boozy Browns, *Browns*, Sluggers (Mgr. Charlie) Comiskey's Warriors

Baltimore   Bill Barnie's Birdlings, Birds, *Orioles*, Oysterville

Philadelphia   Athletics

Cincinnati   Mike "King" Kelly's Braves, Kelly's Green Legs, *King Kelly's Killers*, Kelly's Klippers, King Kelly's Royals, King Kelly's Subjects

Milwaukee   Babies, Baby, *Brewers*, Cream Citys

Columbus   Buckeyes, Colts, Senators, Solons

Louisville   Bourbonville, Colonels, Cyclones, Distillery Delegates, Eclipse, Giants, Loseville, Sour Mashes

Washington   Giants, Nationals, *Senators*

1892 National League

Boston   All-Stars, *Beaneaters*, Scientific Beaneaters (Steven Riess), Frank Selee's Men, Seleeites

Cleveland   Spiders, Forest Citys

Brooklyn   Bridegrooms, Church Citys, Monte Ward's Wonders, Trolley Dodgers

Philadelphia   *Phillies*, Quakers

Cincinnati   Porkopolitans, Queen Citys, *Reds*, Red Legs, Red Stockings, Rhinelanders

Pittsburgh   Al Buckenberger's Buccaneers, Buccaneers, Bucs, Gas Citys, *Pirates*, Smoky Citys

Chicago   *Colts*, Cap Anson's Colts

New York   Giants, Jints

Louisville   Bourbonville, *Colonels*, Falls Citys, Loseville, Night Riders, Wanderers

Washington   Capital Citys, Nationals, *Senators*

St. Louis   Boozy Browns (h), *Browns*, Brown Stockings

Baltimore   Birdies, Birdlings, Birds, Bombers, Maroons, *Orioles*, Oysterville, Sparrows, Young-Bloods

1893 National League

Boston   All-Stars, *Beaneaters*, Scientific Beaneaters (Riess), Frank Selee's Men, Seleeites

Pittsburgh	Al Buckenberger's Buccaneers, Buccaneers, Bucs, Gas Citys, *Pirates*, Smoky Citys
Cleveland	Forest Citys, Hospital Team, Rainmakers, Scrappy Spiders (Mgr. Patsy) Tebeau's Tartars, *Spiders*
Philadelphia	*Phillies*, Quakers
New York	*Giants*, Jints (Mgr. Monte) Ward's Weepers
Cincinnati	Barnstormers, Queen Citys, Porkopolitans, *Reds*, Red Legs, Red Stockings, Rhinelanders
Brooklyn	Bridegrooms, Church Citys, Dave Foutz' Fillies, Trolley Dodgers
Baltimore	Birdies, Birdlings, Birds, Bombers, *Orioles*, Oysterville, Sparrows, Young-Bloods
Chicago	*Colts*, Cap Anson's Colts
St. Louis	*Browns*, Brown Stockings
Louisville	(Mgr. Jim Barnie's) Boobies, Bourbonville, *Colonels*, Falls Citys, Kings of Losers (h), Loseville, Night Riders, Wanderers
Washington	Capital Citys, Nationals, *Senators*

1894 National League

Baltimore	Birdies, Birdlings, Birds, Bombers, Diamond Thieves (Dennis Purdy), Greatest Team of the Gay Nineties (Steve Goldman, Ted Patterson), Guys in the Black Hats (Purdy) (Mgr. Ned) Hanlon's Machine (David Pietrusza), Juggernauts (Ted Patterson), Masters of Inside Baseball (Fred Lieb), Notorious Orioles (Steven Riess), Old Orioles (Ned Hanlon), *Orioles*, Oysterville, Rowdy Orioles (David Pietrusza), Scientific Orioles (Fred Lieb), Baseball's Scientists (Fred Lieb), Scrappy Orioles (Pittsburgh Commercial Gazzette), Rough and Resourceful Orioles (Joe Kiernan),Rowdy Orioles (Steven Riess), Soaring Birds (Michael Gesker), Team That Gave Birth to Modern Baseball (Burt Solomon), Tricksters (J. Raymond "Jim" Price)
New York	*Giants*, Jints
Boston	All-Stars, *Beaneaters*, Frank Selee's Men, Scientific Beaneaters (Riess), Seleeites
Philadelphia	*Phillies*, Quakers
Brooklyn	Bridegrooms, Church Citys, Dave Foutz' Fillies, Trolley Dodgers
Cleveland	Spiders
Pittsburgh	Al Buckenberger's Buccaneers, Buccaneers, Bucs, Gas Citys, *Pirates*, Smoky Citys
Chicago	*Colts*, Cap Anson's Colts
St. Louis	*Browns*, Brown Stockings
Cincinnati	(Mgr. Charlie) Comiskey's Chumps, Porkopolitansm Queen Citys, *Reds*, Red Legs, Red Stockings, Rhinelanders
Brooklyn	Bridegrooms, Church Citys, Dave Foutz' Fillies, Pussycats, Trolley Dodgers
Washington	Capital Citys, Nationals, *Senators*
Louisville	Bourbonville, *Colonels*, Falls Citys, Loseville, Night Riders, Wanderers

1895 National League

| Baltimore | Birdies, Birdlings, Birds, Bombers, Diamond Thieves (Purdy), Greatest Team of the Gay Nineties (Goldman, Patterson), Guys in the Black Hats (Purdy) (Mgr. Ned) Hanlon's Machine (Pietruzsa), Juggernauts (Patterson), Masters of Inside Baseball |

	(Lieb), Notorious Orioles (Riess), Old Orioles (Hanlon), *Orioles*, Oysterville, Rowdy Orioles (Riess), Scientific Orioles (Lieb), Baseball's Scientists (Lieb), Scrappy Orioles (American Film Institute), Rough and Resourceful Orioles (Kiernan), Soaring Birds (Gesker), Team That Gave Birth to Modern Baseball (Solomon), Tricksters (J. Raymond "Jim" Price)
Cleveland	Scrappy Spiders (h), Spiders
Philadelphia	*Phillies*, Quakers
Chicago	*Colts*, Cap Anson's Colts
Brooklyn	Bridegrooms, Church Citys, Dave Foutz' Fillies, Foutz' Furies, Trolley Dodgers
Boston	All-Stars, *Beaneaters*, Frank Selee's Men, Seleeites
Pittsburgh	Al Buckenberger's Buccaneers, Buccaneers, Bucs, Gas Citys, *Pirates*, Smoky Citys
Cincinnati	(Mgr. Charlie) Comiskey's Chumps, Porkopolitans, Queen Citys, *Reds*, Red Legs, Red Stockings, Rhinelanders
New York	*Giants*, Jints
Washington	Capital Citys, Nationals, *Senators*
St. Louis	*Browns*, Brown Stockings
Louisville	Bourbonville, *Colonels*, Falls Citys, Loseville, Night Riders, Wanderers

1896 National League

Baltimore	Birdies, Birdlings, Birds, Bombers, Greatest Team of the Gay Nineties (Goldman, Patterson), Guys in the Black Hats (Purdy) (Mgr. Ned) Hanlon's Machine (Pietruzsa), Juggernauts (Patterson), Masters of Inside Baseball (Lieb), Notorious Orioles (Riess), Old Orioles (Hanlon), *Orioles*, Oysterville, Rowdy Orioles (Riess), Scientific Orioles (Lieb), Baseball's Scientists (Lieb), Scrappy Orioles (American Film Institute), Rough and Resourceful Orioles (Kiernan), Soaring Birds (Gesker), Team That Gave Birth to Modern Baseball (Solomon), Tricksters (J. Raymond "Jim" Price)
Cleveland	Forest Citys, Scrappy Spiders, *Spiders*
Cincinnati	Porkopolitans, Queen Citys, *Reds*, Red Legs, Red Stockings, Rhinelanders
Boston	All-Stars, *Beaneaters*, Frank Selee's Men, Seleeites
Chicago	*Colts*, Cap Anson's Colts
Pittsburgh	All Buckenberger's Buccaneers, Buccaneers, Bucs, Gas Citys, *Pirates*, Smoky Citys
New York	*Giants*
Philadelphia	*Phillies*, Quakers
Washington	Capital Citys, Nationals, *Senators*
Brooklyn	Bridegrooms, Church Citys, Dave Foutz' Fillies, Trolley Dodgers, Foutz' Warriors
St. Louis	*Browns*, Brown Stockings
Louisville	Bourbonville, *Colonels*, Falls Citys, Loseville, Night Riders, Wanderers

1897 National League

| Boston | All-Stars, *Beaneaters*, Good-Guy Beaneaters (Rory Costello), Frank Selee's Men, Seleeites Baltimore Birdies, Birdlings, Birds, Bombers, Diamond Thieves (Purdy), Greatest Team of the Gay Nineties (Goldman, Patterson) (Mgr. Ned) Hanlon's Machine (Pietruzsa), Juggernauts (Masterson), Mas- |

ters of Inside Baseball (Lieb), Notorious Orioles (Riess), Old Orioles (Hanlon), *Orioles*, Oysterville, Rowdy Orioles (Riess), Scientific Orioles (Lieb), Baseball's Scientists (Lieb), Scrappy Orioles (American Film Institute), Rough and Resourceful Orioles (Kiernan), Soaring Birds (Gesker), Team That Gave Birth to Modern Baseball (Solomon), Tricksters (J. Raymond "Jim" Price)

New York	*Giants*
Cincinnati	Porkopolitans, Queen Citys, *Reds*, Red Legs, Red Stockings, Rhinelanders
Cleveland	Spiders
Brooklyn	Bridegrooms, Church Citys, Dave Foutz' Fillies, Trolley Dodgers
Washington	Capital Citys, Nationals, *Senators*
Pittsburgh	Al Buckenberger's Buccaneers, Buccaneers, Bucs, Gas Citys, *Pirates*, Smoky Citys
Chicago	*Colts*, Cap Anson's Colts
Philadelphia	*Phillies*, Quakers
Louisville	Bourbonville, *Colonels*, Falls Citys, Loseville, Night Riders, Wanderers
St. Louis	*Browns*, Brown Stockings

1898 National League

Boston	All-Stars, *Beaneaters*, Frank Selee's Men, Seleeites
Baltimore	Birdies, Birdlings, Birds, Bombers, Diamond Thieves (Purdy), Greatest Team of the Gay Nineties (Goldman, Patterson) (Mgr. Ned) Hanlon's Machine (Pietruzsa), Masters of Inside Baseball (Lieb), Notorious Orioles (Riess), Old Orioles (Hanlon), *Orioles*, Oysterville, Rowdy Orioles (Riess), Scientific Orioles (Lieb), Baseball's Scientists (Lieb), Scrappy Orioles (American Film Institute), Rough and Resourceful Orioles (Kiernan), Soaring Birds (Gesker), Team That Gave Birth to Modern Baseball (Solomon), Tricksters (J. Raymond "Jim" Price)
Cincinnati	Porkopolitans, Queen Citys, *Reds*, Red Legs, Red Stockings, Rhinelanders
Chicago	*Colts*, Cap Anson's Colts
Cleveland	Spiders
Philadelphia	*Phillies*, Quakers

New York	*Giants*
Pittsburgh	Al Buckenberger's Buccaneers, Buccaneers, Bucs, Gas Citys, *Pirates*, Smoky Citys
Louisville	Bourbonville, *Colonels*, Falls Citys, Loseville, Night Riders, Wanderers
Brooklyn	Bridegrooms, Church Citys, Dave Foutz' Fillies, Trolley Dodgers
Washington	Capital Citys, Nationals, *Senators*
St. Louis	*Browns*, Brown Stockings

1899 National League

Brooklyn	Bridegrooms, Church Citys, Dave Foutz' Fillies, Trolley Dodgers
Boston	All-Stars, *Beaneaters*, Frank Selee's Men, Seleeites
Philadelphia	*Phillies*, Quakers
Baltimore	Birdies, Birdlings, Birds, Bombers, Mgr. John McGraw's Men, *Orioles*, Oysterville
St. Louis	*Browns*, Brown Stockings
Cincinnati	Porkopolitans, Queen Citys, *Reds*, Red Legs, Red Stockings, Rhinelanders
Pittsburgh	Al Buckenberger's Buccaneers, Buccaneers, Bucs, Gas Citys, *Pirates*, Smoky Citys
Chicago	*Colts*, Cap Anson's Colts
Louisville	Bourbonville, *Colonels*, Falls Citys, Loseville, Night Riders, Wanderers
New York	*Giants*
Washington	Capital Citys, Nationals, *Senators*
Cleveland	Barnstormers, Exiles, Forest Citys, Forlorns, Leftovers, Misfits, Rejects, *Spiders*, Wanderers

1900 National League

Brooklyn	Bridegrooms, Church Citys, Dave Foutz' Fillies, Kickers, Trolley Dodgers
Pittsburgh	Al Buckenberger's Buccaneers, Buccaneers, Bucs, Gas Citys, *Pirates*, Smoky Citys
Philadelphia	*Phillies*, Quakers
Boston	All-Stars, *Beaneaters*, Frank Selee's Men, Seleeites
Chicago	*Colts*, Cap Anson's Colts
St. Louis	*Browns*, Brown Stockings
Cincinnati	*Reds*, Red Legs, Red Stockings, Rhinelanders
New York	*Giants*

III: Major League Team Nicknames Year-by-Year, 1901 to Date

Legend:

Italics = Most popular unofficial name for that particular season (almost always coined by the fans, newspaper reporter, or a team owner).

BOLD = Official team nickname

(Name) = refers to an individual or group of individuals who coined the name.

(h) = historical, i.e. refers to a name that appeared gradually over the years without a specific origin.

1901 National League

Pittsburgh — Balanced Buccaneers (David Nemec), Buccaneers (Bucs) (Mgr. Fred) Clarke's Corsairs, *Pirates*, Premiers, Smoke-towners

Philadelphia — Discards, Nationals, *Phillies*, Quakers, Red Quakers

Brooklyn — Bridegrooms (Grooms), Brooks, Dodgers, So-Called Superbas

St. Louis — *Cardinals*, Maroons, Masqueradors, Nationals, Scarlets (Mgr. Patsy) Tebeau's Tebeauites, Hanlon's Superbas, Suburbas, Trolley Dodgers

Boston — *Beaneaters* (Beanies) (Mgr. Al) Buckeberger's Galaxy, Nationals, Red Stockings Redville

Chicago — Colts, *Cubs,* Nationals, Remnant (Mgr. Frank Selee) Seelites, West-siders, Youngsters

New York — *Giants*, Jints, Nationals

Cincinnati — Lobsters, Queen Citys, *Reds*, Red Legs, Red Stockings, Red Towners, Rhinelanders

1901 American League

Chicago — Americans, Champions, Comiskeyites (Mgr. Cal Griffith) Griffith's Go-Go-Sox (David Nemec & Scott Flatow), Griffith Men, Invaders, Lake-shores, Original Go-Go-Sox (Nemec & Flatow), Pennant-Grabbers, Pale Hose (Mgr. Clark) Griffith's Satellites, White Sox (Sox), *White Stockings*

Boston — Americanos, Americans, Beantowners, (Mgr. Jimmy) Collins' Bostons, Collins' Crew, Invaders, New Englanders, Pilgrims (informal newspaper), Plymouth Rocks (informal newspaper), Puritans (informal newspaper), Somerites, Somersets

Detroit — Bengals, Man-eaters, Michiganders, Rowdies, *Tigers*, Wolverines

Philadelphia — Americans, Athletics (A's), Blue Quakers, Mackites, Mack Men

Baltimore — Birdies, Birdlings, Canaries, (Mgr. John) McGraw's Flock, *Orioles*, McGraw's Roughnecks (Fred Lieb), Roughneck Orioles (Lieb), Yellow Legs

Washington — Capital Citys, Capitals, Griffs, Nationals, *Senators*, Capitals, Capitols, Solon

Cleveland — *Blues,* Bluebirds, Blue Jays, Bronchos, Buckeyes, Forest Citys, Infants, McAleer Men, Spiders

Milwaukee — *Brewers*, Beermakers

1902 National League

Pittsburgh — Balanced Buccaneers (Nemec), Base Thieves (Nemec), Buccaneers (Bucs), (Mgr. Fred) Clarke's Corsairs, *Pirates*, Premiers, Smoke-towners

Brooklyn — Bridegrooms (Grooms), Brooks, Dodgers, So-Called Superbas, (Mgr. Ned) Hanlon's Superbas, Suburbas, Trolley Dodgers

Boston — *Beaneaters* (Beanies), Beantowners, (Mgr. Al) Buckeberger's Galaxy, Nationals, Red Stockings

Cincinnati — Lobsters, Queen Citys, *Reds*, Red Legs, Red Stockings, Red Towners, Redville, Rhinelanders

Chicago — Colts, *Cubs,* (Mgr. Tom Loftus') Legion, Microbes, Nationals, Recruits, Remnants, (Mgr. Frank Selee) Seelites, West-siders, Youngsters

St. Louis — *Cardinals*, Maroons, Nationals, Scarlets, (Mgr. Patsy) Tebeau's Tebeauites

Philadelphia — Discards, Nationals, *Phillies*, Quakers, Red Quakers

New York — *Giants*, Jints, Nationals

1902 American League

Philadelphia — *Athletics* (A's), Blue Quakers, (Mgr. Connie) Mack's Marvels, Mack Men, White Elephants

St. Louis — Americans, *Browns*, Brownies

Boston — Beantowners, (Mgr. Jimmy Collins) Collinsites, Invaders, Nationalists, Nationals, Pilgrims, Plymouth Rocks, Puritans (owner William Somers) Somerites, Somersets, Speed Boys

Chicago — Americans, Champions, Comiskeyites, Lake-shores, Pale Hose, *White Sox* (Sox), White Stockings

Cleveland — Blues, Bluebirds, Blue Jays, *Bronchos*, Forest Citys, Giants, Injunction Dodgers

Washington — Capital Citys, Capitals, Griffs, Nationals (Nats), *Senators*, Statesmen

Detroit — Bengals, Man-eaters, *Tigers*, Wolverines

Baltimore — Birdies, Birdlings, Canaries, (Mgr. John) McGraw's Flock, *Orioles*, McGraw's Roughnecks (h), Yellow Legs

1903 National League

Pittsburgh — Balanced Buccaneers (Nemec), Buccaneers (Bucs), (Mgr. Fred) Clarke's Corsairs, Clarke's Crew, Premiers, Smoke-towners

New York — Bulldozers, *Giants*, Jayhawks, Nationals, Possibilities, Real-Things Rowdies

Chicago — Colts, *Cubs*, Nationals, Panamahatmas, Panamas, West-siders

Cincinnati — *Reds*, Red Legs, Red Stockings, Red Towners, Rhinelanders Lobsters

Brooklyn — Bridegrooms (Grooms), Brooks, Dodgers, (Mgr. Ned) Hanlon's Superbas, Suburbas, Trolley Dodgers

Boston — Beaneaters (Beanies), Beantowners, Nationals, Red Stockings

Philadelphia — Nationals, *Phillies*, Quakers, (Mgr. Charles) Zimmer's Zimmerites

St. Louis — Amateurs, Burlesque Club, *Cardinals*, Maroons, Misfits, Nationals, Sclarlets, (Mgr. Patsy Tebeau) Tebeauites.

1903 American League

Boston — Americans, Americanos, Beantowners, (Mgr. Jimmy) Collins' Canned Cods, Collins' Stars, Collinsites, Collins' Conquerors, Collins' Crew, Collins' Gentlemen, Giants, Hub Team. Invaders, (General Manager Frank) Killea's Killeaites, Old Timers, Pilgrims, Plymouth Rocks, Puritans, Speed Boys

Philadelphia — *Athletics* (A's), (Mgr. Connie) Mack's Freaks, Mack's Hustlers, White Elephants, Mack's Braves, Mack's Tribe

Cleveland — All Stars, Babes, Blues, Bluebirds, Blue Jays, Hard Hitters, (player-manager Nap) Lajoie's Pets

New York — Americans, Burglars, Gothamites, Greater New Yorks, Invaders, *Highlanders*, Hilltoppers, Metropolitans (October 1902), Porch-Climbers, Yankees (Yanks)

Detroit — Bengals, Man-eaters, *Tigers*, Wolverines

St. Louis — Americans, *Browns*, Brownies

Chicago — Americans, Invaders, Pale Hose, White Stockings, White Socks, *White Sox* (Sox), White Stockings, Windy Citys

Washington — Capital Citys, Capitals, Griffs, Hapless Senators (Jeff Caroll), Nationals (Nats), Orphans (April only), *Senators*

1904 National League

New York	Celtics, *Giants*, Gothams, Jints, (Mgr. John) McGraw's Men, Nationals, Real Things
Chicago	Colts, *Cubs*, Nationals, West-siders
Cincinnati	*Reds*, Red Legs, Red Stockings, Rhinelanders
Pittsburgh	Allegheny Citys, Buccaneers, *Pirates*, Pittsburghers, Smoky Citys, Smoke-towners
St. Louis	*Cardinals*, Maroons, Nationals, (Mgr. Kid) Nichols' Nicholites, Scarlets
Brooklyn	Bridegrooms, Brooks, Dodgers, (Mgr. Ned) Hanlon's Real Things, Hanlon's Superbas, Trolley Dodgers
Boston	Beaneaters, Beantowners, (Mgr. Al) Buckenberger's Boys, Buck's Boys, Luckless Bostons, Nationals, Red Stockings, Southenders
Philadelphia	Misfits, Nationals, *Phillies*, Quakers

1904 American League

Boston	Americans, Baked Bean Bunch, Beantowners, (Mgr. Jimmy Collins') Collinsites, Collins' Conquerors, Invaders, Pilgrims, Plymouth Rocks, Puritans
New York	All-Stars, Americans, Burglars, Greater New Yorks, Highlanders, Hilltoppers, Husky Highlanders, Invaders, *Yankees* (Yanks) All-Stars
Chicago	Americans, Pale Hose, *White Sox* (Sox), White Stockings, Windy Citys
Cleveland	Blues, Forest Citys, *Naps*
Philadelphia	Athletics (A's), (Mgr. Connie) Mack's Braves, Culture City Clan, Mack Men, Mack's Red Men, Mack's Tribe, White Elephants
St. Louis	Americans, *Browns*, Brownies
Detroit	Bengals, Man-eaters, *Tigers*, Wolverines
Washington	Americans, Griffs, Hapless Senators (Carroll), Nationals (Nats), Orphans, *Senators*

1905 National League

New York	Celtics, Giants, Jints, (Mgr. John McGraw) McGraw Men, Nationals
Pittsburgh	Balanced Buccaneers (Nemec), Buccaneers (Bucs), *Pirates*, Smoke-towners
Chicago	Colts, *Cubs*, Nationals, Spuds (*Chicago Tribune*), West-siders, Zephyrs
Philadelphia	Nationals, *Phillies*, Quakers
Cincinnati	*Reds*, Red Legs, Red Stockings, Redville, Rhinelanders
St. Louis	Cardinals, *Maroons*, Nationals, Scarlets
Boston	Beaneaters, Beantowners, Luckless Bostons, Nationals, Red Stockings, (Mgr. Fred Tenny's) Tennyites
Brooklyn	Bridegrooms (Grooms), Brooks, Disappointing Dodgers, Dismal Dodgers (Glenn Stout & Richard Johnson), Dodgers, Drowsy Dodgers (Fred Lieb), (Mgr. Ned) Hanlon's Superbas, Suburbas, Trolley Dodgers

1905 American League

Philadelphia	Americans, *Athletics*, (Mgr. Connie Mack) Mack Men, Mack's Marvels, White Elephants, Nod Boys (October)
Chicago	Americans, Hitless Wonders (Charles Dreyden & Hughie Fullerton), Pale Hose, *White Sox* (Sox), White Stockings
Detroit	Bengals, *Tigers*, Wolverines

Boston	Americans, Beantowners, Pilgrims, Plymouth Rocks, Puritans
Cleveland	Blues, *Naps*
New York	Americans, Highlanders, Hilltoppers, *Yankees*
Washington	Americans, Griffs, **NATIONALS** (Nats), *Senators*, Solons, (Mgr. Jake) Stahl Stalwarts
St. Louis	Americans, *Browns*, Brownies

1906 National League

Chicago	Big Bad Bears (Glenn Dickey), Bears, Colts, Cub Machine (Gil Bogan), *Cubs*, Giant-Killers, Killers, (Mgr. Frank) Chance Men, Nationals, Spuds (*Chicago Tribune*), Windy City Crew, Sluggers, Terrors, (Mgr. Frank) Chance's Warriors, Chance-Men, West-siders, Wonders
New York	*Giants*, Jayhawks, Jints, (Mgr. John McGraw) McGraw Men, McGraw's Rowdies
Pittsburgh	*Pirates*, Buccaneers (Bucs), Smoky Citys, Smoke-towners, Smokes
Philadelphia	Nationals, *Phillies*, Quakers
Brooklyn	Beaver Hats, Bridegrooms (Grooms), Brooks, Dodgers (Mgr. Patsy) Donovan's Cohorts, Donovan's Coop, Donovan's Dodgers, Superbas, Trolley Dodgers
Cincinnati	*Reds*, Red Legs, Red Shirts, Red Stockings, Redville, Rhinelanders
St. Louis	*Cardinals*, Maroons, (Mgr. John) McCloskey's Men, Nationals, Scarlets
Boston	Beaneaters, Beantowners, Luckless Bostons, Nationals, Reds, Red Legs, Red Stockings, South-Enders, (Mgr. Fred) Tenney's Human Limits, Tenney's Youngsters, Tennyites

1906 American League

Chicago	Americans (owner) Charles Comiskey's Men, Comiskeyites, Hitless Wonders, Pale Hose, Peerless White Sox, *White Sox* (Sox), Whirlwinds, White Stockings
New York	Americans, Highlanders, Hilltoppers, *Yankees*
Cleveland	Blues, Lajoieville, *Naps*
Philadelphia	Americans, Athletics, (Mgr. Connie) Mack's Men, Culture City Clan, Mack Men, White Elephants, Mack's Clan
St. Louis	Americans, (Mgr. Jimmy) McAleer's Men, McAleerites, *Ravens*
Detroit	Bengals, Mgr. Hugh Jennings' Jungletowners, Man-eaters, Microbes, *Tigers*, Wranglers
Washington	Americans, Griffs, (Mgr. Jake), Stahl's Stalwarts, **NATIONALS** (Nats), *Senators*, Solons
Boston	Americans, Beantowners, (Mgr. Jimmy) Collins' Crew, Collinsites, Jokes, Pilgrims, Plymouth Rocks, Puritans

1907 National League

Chicago	Bear Cubs, Bears, Big Bad Bears (Dickey), Bruins, (Mgr. Frank Chance) Chance Men, Cub Machine (Bogan), *Cubs*, Fleet Bear Cubs, Nationals, West-Siders
Pittsburgh	Balanced Buccaneers (Nemec), Buccaneers (Bucs), *Pirates*, Smoke-towners
Philadelphia	Nationals, *Phillies*, Quakers

New York	Giants, Jints, (Mgr. John) McGraw's Celtics, McGraw Men, Nationals
Brooklyn	Bridegrooms (Grooms), Dodgers, (Mgr. Patsy) Donovan's Dodgers, Superbas, Suburbas, Trolley Dodgers
Cincinnati	(Mgr. Ned) Hanlon's Kids, *Reds*, Red Legs, Red Stockings, Redville, Rhinelanders
Boston	Beantowners, *Doves*, Nationals, White Legs
St. Louis	*Cardinals*, Maroons, Nationals, Scarlets

1907 American League

Detroit	Bengals, Dazzling Tigers, (Mgr. Hugh) Jennings' Braves, Jungletowners, Maneaters, Pride of Michigan, Prowling Tigers, *Tigers*
Philadelphia	Americans, *Athletics* (A's), (Mgr. Connie Mack) Mack Men, Culture City Clan, Macks, White Elephants
Chicago	Americans, (Mgr. Fielder) Jones' Cohorts, Hitless Wonders, Pale Hose, Southsiders, *White Sox* (Sox)
Cleveland	Blues, (Mgr. Nap) Lajoie's Braves Napkins, *Naps*
New York	Americans, Burglars, Highlanders, Hilltoppers, *Yankees* (Yanks)
St. Louis	Americans, *Ravens*
Boston	Americans, Beantowners, Pilgrims, Plymouth Rocks, Puritans, (General manager John) Taylorites
Washington	Americans, (Mgr. Clark) Griffith's Griffs, Hapless Senators (Carroll), **NATIONALS** (Nats), *Senators*, Solons

1908 National League

Chicago	Bear Cubs, Bears, Big Bad Bears (Dickey), Bruins, Cubbies, Cub Machine (Bogan), **CUBS**, Fleet Cubs, Nationals, Chance Men, (Mgr. Frank) Chance's Warriors
New York	*Giants*, Jints, (Mgr. John) McGraw's Men, Nationals
Pittsburgh	Balanced Buccaneers (Nemec), Buccaneers (Bucs), Clarke's Crew, *Pirates*, Smoke-towners
Philadelphia	Nationals, *Phillies*, Quakers
Cincinnati	*Reds*, Red Legs, Red Stockings, Redville, Rhinelanders
Boston	Beantowners, *Doves*, Nationals, Red Stockings, Redlegs, Reds
Brooklyn	Brooks, Dodgers, (Mgr. Patsy) Donovan's Dodgers, Drowsy Dodgers (Lieb), Superbas, Suburbas
St. Louis	*Cardinals*, Flame Reds, Flames, Flaming Bunch, Maroons, (Mgr. Jim) McCloskey's Men, McCloskey Men, Nationals, Scarlets

1908 American League

Detroit	Bengals, Dazzling Tigers, (Mgr. Hugh) Jennings' Jungle-Towners, Kitties, Maneaters, *Tigers,* Pride of Michigan, Prowling Tigers
Cleveland	Blues, Lajoieville, Napkins, *Naps*, Sluggers
Chicago	Americans, Bees, (Mgr. Fielder) Jones' Hose, Stingers, White Legs, *White Sox*, White Stockings
St. Louis	Americans, *Browns*, Brownies
Boston	Americans, Beantowners, BoSox, Crimson Hose, Hub Hose, **RED SOX**
Philadelphia	Americans, *Athletics* (A's), (Mgr. Connie) Mack's Men, Culture City Clan, Mack Men, White Elephants
Washington	Americans, Griffs, Hapless Senators (Carroll), **NATIONALS** (Nats), *Senators*, Solons
New York	All-Stars, Americans, *Highlanders*, Hilltoppers, Yankees (Yanks)

1909 National League

Pittsburgh	Balanced Buccaneers (Nemec), Buccaneers (Bucs), (Mgr. Fred) Clarke's Corsairs, Clarke's Crew, *Pirates*, Skull & Crossbones Club, Smoke-towners, Swashbucklers
Chicago	Big Bad Bears (Dickey), Bruins, (Mgr. Franch Chance) Chance Men, Cubbies, Cub Machine (Bogan), **CUBS**, Nationals
New York	*Giants*, Jints, (Mgr. John) McGraw's Men, McGraw Men, Nationals
Cincinnati	(Mgr. Clark Griffith) Griffs, *Reds*, Red Legs, Red Stockings, Redville, Rhinelanders
Philadelphia	Nationals, *Phillies*, Quakers
Brooklyn	Brooks, Dodgers, Superbas, Suburbas, Trolley Dodgers
St. Louis	*Cardinals*, Flame Reds, Flames, Flaming Bunch, Gingersnaps, Nationals, Scarlets
Boston	Beantowners, Doves, Nationals, Pilgrims, Red Legs

1909 American League

Detroit	Bengals, Dazzling Tigers, (Mgr. Hugh) Jennings' Jungle-Towners, Kitties, Man-eaters, McGraw Men, Nationals, Pride of Michigan
Philadelphia	Americans, *Athletics* (A's), (Mgr. Connie) Mack's Men, Culture City Clan, Mack Men, White Elephants.
Boston	Americans, Beantowners, BoSox, Crimson Hose, Hub Hose, **RED SOX**
Chicago	Americans, (owner Charles) Comiskey's Clan, White Legs, *White Sox*, White Stockings, (Mgr. Billy) Sullivan's Warriors
New York	Americans, *Highlanders*, Hilltoppers, *Yankees* (Yanks)
Cleveland	Blues, (Mgr. Deacon) McGuire's Molly Maguires, Napkins, *Naps*
St. Louis	Americans, *Browns*, Brownies
Washington	Americans, Grifs, Hapless Senators (Carroll), Misfits, **NATIONALS** (Nats), *Senators*, Solons

1910 National League

Chicago	Big Bad Bears (Dickey), Bruins, (Mgr. Frank Chance) Chance Men, Cubbies, Cub Machine (Bogan), **CUBS,** Nationals, West-Siders
New York	Giants, Jints, (Mgr. John) McGraw's Men, McGraw Men, Nationals
Pittsburgh	Buccaneers (Bucs), Clarke's Crew, *Pirates*, Smoke-towners
Philadelphia	(Mgr. Red) Dooin's Men, Live Wires, Nationals, *Phillies*, Quakers
Cincinnati	(Mgr. Clark Griffith) Griffs, *Reds*, Red Legs, Red Stockings, Redville, Rhinelanders
Brooklyn	Brooks, (Mgr. Bill) Dahlen's Dodgers, Dodgers, Infants, Superbas, Suburbas, Trolley Dodgers
St. Louis	*Cardinals*, Maroons, Nationals, Scarlets
Boston	Beantowners, Doves, Heps, Nationals, Pilgrims, Rustlers

1910 American League

Philadelphia	Americans, *Athletics* (A's), (Mgr. Connie) Mack's Men, Culture City Clan, Mack's Marvels, Mack Men, White Elephants
New York	Americans, Highlanders, Hilltoppers, *Yankees* (Yanks)

Detroit   Bengals (Mgr. Hugh) Jennings' Jungle-Towners, Man-eaters, Kitties, Prowling Tigers, *Tigers*

Boston   Americans, Beantowners, BoSox, Crimson Hose, Hub Hose, **RED SOX**

Cleveland   Blues, (Mgr. Deacon) McGuire's Molly Maguires, *Naps*

Chicago   Americans, Comiskeys, South-siders, White Legs, **WHITE SOX** (*Spalding Guide* drops "White Stockings")

Washington   Americans, Griffs, Hapless Senators (Carroll), **NATIONALS** (Nats), *Senators*

St. Louis   Americans, *Browns*, Brownies

1911 National League

New York   *Giants*, (Mgr. John) McGraw's Men, McGraw Men, Nationals

Chicago   Bruins, (Mgr. Frank Chance) Chance Men, Cubbies, Cub Machine (Bogan), **CUBS**, Nationals, West-siders

Pittsburgh   Buccaneers (Bucs), (Mgr. Fred) Clarke's Crew, **PIRATES** ("Pirates" written on players' jerseys) Smoke-towners

Philadelphia   Nationals, *Phillies*, Quakers, Mgr. Red Dooin's Men, Red's Quakers

St. Louis   *Cardinals*, Maroons, Nationals, Scarlets

Cincinnati   (Mgr. Clark Griffith) Griffs, **REDS** ("Reds" C-logo appears on players' jersey for the first time), Red-landers, Red Legs, Red Stockings, Rhinelanders

Brooklyn   Blues, Brooks, (Mgr. Bill) Dahlen's Dodgers, Infants, Trolley Dodgers

Boston   Beantowners, Heps, Nationals, Pilgrims, Rustlers

1911 American League

Philadelphia   Americans, *Athletics* (A's), (Mgr. Connie) Mack's Men, Culture City Clan, Mack Men, Macks' Marvels, Mack's Red Men, White Elephants

Detroit   Bengals, (Mgr. Hugh) Jennings' Jungle-Towners, Kitties, Maneaters, Prowling Tigers, *Tigers*

Cleveland   Blues, (Mgr. Deacon) McGuire's Molly McGuires, *Naps*

Chicago   Americans, Comiskeys, South-siders, White Legs, *White Sox*

Boston   Americans, Beantowners, BoSox, Crimson Hose, Hub Hose, **RED SOX**

New York   Americans, Highlanders, Hilltoppers, Pinstripers (first use of pinstripe uniforms), *Yankees* (Yanks)

Pittsburgh   Buccaneers (Bucs), (Mgr. Fred) Crew, **PIRATES**, Smoke-towners

Washington   Americans, Griffs, Hapless Senators (Carroll) **NATIONALS** (Nats), Senators

St. Louis   Americans, *Browns*, Brownies

1912 National League

New York   *Giants*, Jints, (Mgr. John) McGraw's Men, McGraw Men, Nationals

Pittsburgh   Buccaneers (Bucs), (Mgr. Fred) Crew, **PIRATES**, Smoke-towners

Chicago   Bruins, (Mgr. Franck Chance) Chance Men, Cubbies, **CUBS**, Nationals, West-siders

Cincinnati   *Reds*, Red-landers, Red Legs, Red Stockings, Redville, Rhinelanders

Philadelphia   Nationals, *Phillies*, Quakers

St. Louis   *Cardinals*, Maroons, Nationals, Scarlets

Brooklyn   Brooks, (Mgr. Bill) Dahlen's Dodgers, Dodgers, Infants, Trolley Dodgers

Boston   **BRAVES**, Nationals, Rustlers, Tribesmen

1912 American League

Boston   Beantowners, Crimson Hose, Hub Hose, **RED SOX** (Sox)

Washington   Americans, Griffs, **NATIONALS** (Nats), Senators

Philadelphia   Americans, *Athletics* (A's), (Mgr. Connie) Mack's Men, Culture City Clan, Mack Men, White Elephants

Chicago   Americans, Comiskeys, Pale Hose, Southsiders, White Legs, **WHITE SOX** ("White Sox" appears on players' uniforms & *Spalding Guide* discouraged the use of "White Stockings") (Sox).

Cleveland   Blues, *Naps*

Detroit   Bengals, (Mgr. Hugh) Jennings' Jungle-Towners, Kitties, Maneaters, *Tigers*

St. Louis   Americans, *Browns*, Brownies

New York   Americans, Highlanders, Hilltoppers, *Yankees*

1913 National League

New York   *Giants*, Jints, (Mgr. John) McGraw's Men, McGraw Men, Nationals

Philadelphia   Nationals, *Phillies*, Quakers, Red Quakers

Chicago   Bruins, Cubbies, **CUBS**, (Mgr. Johnny) "Trojan" Evers' Trojans, Nationals, West-siders

Pittsburgh   Buccaneers (Bucs), (Mgr. Fred) Clarke's Crew, **PIRATES**, Smoke-towners

Boston   **BRAVES**, Tribesmen

Brooklyn   Brooks, (Mgr. Bill) Dahlen's Dodgers, Dodgers, Infants, Trolley Dodgers

Cincinnati   **REDS** (*Spalding Guide* declared "Reds" as the team's official name and discredited the use of "Red Stockings"), Red-landers, Red Legs, Red Towners, Rhinelanders

St. Louis   *Cardinals*, Maroons, Nationals, Scarlets

1913 American League

Philadelphia   Americans, *Athletics* (A's), (Mgr. Connie) Mack's Marvels, Mack's Men, Culture City Clan, Mack Men, White Elephants

Washington   Americans, Griffs, **NATIONALS** (Nats), *Senators*

Cleveland   Blues, *Naps*

Boston   Americans, Beantowners, Crimson Hose, Hub Hose, **RED SOX** (Sox)

Chicago   Americans, (Mgr. Nixey Callahan) Callahans, Comiskeys, Pale Hose, Southsiders, White Legs, **WHITE SOX** (Sox)

Detroit   Bengals, (Mgr. Hugh) Jenning's Jungle-Towners, Kitties, Man-eaters, *Tigers*

New York   Americans, (Mgr. Frank) Chance's Men, Chance Men, **YANKEES** (Yanks)

St. Louis   Americans, *Browns*, Brownies

1914 National League

Boston   **BRAVES**, Darlings of the Press, Freight Train, Miracle Braves, Miracle Men, Steady Climbers, Tidal Waves, Tribesmen, Whirlwinds

New York   *Giants*, Jints, (Mgr. John) McGraw's Men, McGraw Men
St. Louis   *Cardinals*, Maroons, Nationals, Scarlets
Chicago   Bruins, Cubbies, **CUBS**, Nationals, West-siders
Brooklyn   Brooks, Dodgers, Infants, (Mgr. Wilbert) Robinson's Flock, *Robins*
Philadelphia Nationals, *Phillies*, Quakers, Red Quakers
Pittsburgh Buccaneers (Bucs), (Mgr. Fred) Clarke's Crew, Nationals, **PIRATES**, Smoke-towners
Cincinnati (Mgr. Buck Herzog) Herzogs, **REDS** (*Spalding Guide* discouraged use of "Red Stockings"), Red-landers, Red Legs, Rhinelanders

1914 American League

Philadelphia Americans, *Athletics* (A's), (Mgr. Connie) Mack's Marvels, Mack's Men, Culture City Clan, Mack Men, White Elephants
Boston   Americans, Beantowners, BoSox, Crimson Hose, Hub Hose, **RED SOX** (Sox)
Washington Americans, Griffs, **NATIONALS** (Nats), *Senators*
Detroit   Bengals, (Mgr. Hugh) Jennings' Jungle-Towners, Kitties, Man-eaters, *Tigers*
St. Louis   Americans, *Browns*, Brownies
Chicago   Americans, ChiSox, Comiskeys, Pale Hose, Polar Cubs, Southsiders, White Legs, **WHITE SOX** (Sox)
New York   (Mgr. Frank) Chance's Men, **YANKEES** (Yanks)
Cleveland   (Mgr. Joe) Birmingham's Tribe (No mention of "Indians" this year), Blues, *Naps*

1914 Federal League

Indianapolis Federals (Feds), Hoo-Feds, *Hoosiers*
Chicago   Blue Sox, Browns, Chifeds, Federals (Feds) (C-Feds logo on jersey)
Baltimore   Balt-Feds, Federals, *Terrapins*
Buffalo   Buf-Feds, Federals
Brooklyn   Brook-Feds, Federals, *Tip Tops*
Kansas City Federals, Kawfeds, **PACKERS**
Pittsburgh Federals, Pitt-Feds, *Rebels*
St. Louis   Federals, Slou-Feds

1915 National League

Philadelphia Live Wires (William Baker), Nationals, *Phillies*, Quakers, Red Quakers
Boston   **BRAVES**
Brooklyn   Brooks, Dodgers, Innocents, (Mgr. Wilbert) Robinson's Flock, *Robins*
Chicago   Bruins, Cubbies, **CUBS**, Nationals, West-siders
Pittsburgh Buccaneers (Bucs), (Mgr. Fred) Clarke's Crew, Nationals, **PIRATES**, Smoke-towners
St. Louis   *Cardinals*, Maroons, Nationals, Scarlets
Cincinnati **REDS** (*Sporting News Guide* discredits use of "Red Stockings"), Red Legs, Rhinelanders
New York   *Giants*, Jints, (Mgr. John) McGraw's Men, McGraw Men

1915 American League

Boston   Beantowners, BoSox, Crimson Hose, Hub Hose, **RED SOX** (Sox)
Detroit   Bengals, (Mgr. Hugh) Jennings Jungle-Towners, Kitties, Man-eaters, *Tigers*
Chicago   Americans, ChiSox, Comiskeys, Pale Hose, (Mgr.

Clarence Rowland) Rowlanders, Rowlands, Southsiders, White Legs, **WHITE SOX** (Sox)
Washington Americans, Griffs, **NATIONALS** (Nats), Senators
New York   Knickerbockers (proposed but not used), **YANKEES** (Yanks)
St. Louis   Americans, *Browns*, Brownies
Cleveland   (Mgr. Joe) Birmingham's Tribe, Blues, Featherbrains (Terry Pluto), Featherheads (Terry Pluto), **INDIANS**, (sleeping) Naps, Squaws, The Tribe
Philadelphia *Athletics* (A's), (Mgr. Connie) Mack's Men, Mack Men

1915 Federal League

Chicago   **WHALES** (Whale logo on the players' jerseys)
St. Louis   **TERRIERS** (Terrier logo on uniform sleeve)
Pittsburgh Rebels
Kansas City **PACKERS**
Newark   **PEPPERS** (Peps)
Buffalo   Blues, Electrics
Brooklyn   **TIP-TOPS** (Tip-Top logo on uniform)
Baltimore   **TERRAPINS** (Terrapin logo on jersey)

1916 National League

Brooklyn   Brooks, Castoffs, Dodgers, Mercuries, (Mgr. Wilbert) Robinson's Flock, Robins, Superbas, Well-Orchestrated Castoffs
Philadelphia *Phillies*, Quakers, Red Quakers, The One-Man-Team
Boston   **BRAVES**
New York   *Giants*, Jints, (Mgr. John) McGraw's Men, McGraw Men, Meteoric Giants, Meteors
Chicago   Bruins, Cubbies, **CUBS**, Jovians, Northsiders, Wrigleys
Pittsburgh Buccaneers (Bucs), **PIRATES**, Rings-of-Fire, Smoke-towners
Cincinnati **REDS**, Red-landers, Red Legs, Rhinelanders
St. Louis   *Cardinals*, Maroons, Neptunes, Scarlets

1916 American League

Boston   Beantowners, BoSox, Crimson Hose, Hub Hose, **RED SOX** (Sox)
Chicago   ChiSox, Comiskeys, Pale Hose, Southsiders, White Legs, **WHITE SOX** (Sox)
Detroit   Bengals, (Mgr. Hugh) Jennings' Jungle-Towners, Kitties, Man-eaters, *Tigers*
New York   **YANKEES** (Yanks)
St. Louis   Americans, *Browns*, Brownies
Cleveland   **INDIANS**, The Tribe
Washington Americans, Griffs, **NATIONALS** (Nats), *Senators*
Philadelphia *Athletics* (A's), (Mgr. Connie) Mack's Men, Mack Men, Subterranean Denizens, White Elephants

1917 National League

New York   *Giants*, Jints, (Mgr. John) McGraw's Men, McGraw Men
Philadelphia *Phillies*, Quakers, Red Quakers
St. Louis   *Cardinals*, Maroons, Scarlets
Cincinnati **REDS**, Red Legs, Rhinelanders
Chicago   Bruins, Cubbies, **CUBS,** Northsiders
Boston   **BRAVES**
Brooklyn   Brooks, Dodgers, (Mgr. Wilbert) Robinson's Flock, Rainmakers, *Robins*, Superas
Pittsburgh Bucanners (Bucs), **PIRATES**, Smoke-towners

1917 American League

Chicago   ChiSox, Comiskeys, Cuboard of Hitters, Pale Hose, **WHITE SOX** (Sox)
Boston   Beantowners, BoSox, Crimson Hose, Hub Hose, **RED SOX** (Sox)
Cleveland   **INDIANS**, The Tribe
Detroit   Bengals, (Mgr. Hugh) Jennings' Jungle-Towners, Kitties, Man-eaters, *Tigers*
Washington Americans, Griffs, **NATIONALS** (Nats), *Senators*
New York   **YANKEES** (Yanks)
St. Louis   Americans, *Browns*, Brownies
Philadelphia *Athletics* (A's), Blue Quakers.(Mgr. Connie) Mack's Men, Mack Men, Subterranean Denizens, White Elephants

1918 National League

Chicago   Bruins, Cubbies, **CUBS**, Northsiders
New York   *Giants*, Jints, (Mgr. John) McGraw's Men, McGraw Men
Cincinnati   **REDS**, Red Legs, Rhinelanders
Pittsburgh   Buccaneers (Bucs), **PIRATES**, Smoke-towners
Brooklyn   Brooks, Dodgers, (Mgr. Wilbert) Robinson's Flock, *Robins*, Superbas
Philadelphia *Phillies*, Quakers, Red Quakers
Boston   **BRAVES**, Futile Braves (Mike LeBlanc)
St. Louis   *Cardinals*, Maroons, Scarlets

1918 American League

Boston   Beantowners, BoSox, Crimson Hose, Hub Hose, **RED SOX** (Sox)
Cleveland   **INDIANS**, The Trine
Washington Americans, Grifs, **NATIONALS** (Nats), *Senators*
New York   (Mgr. Miller Huggins") Hug Men, **YANKEES** (Yanks)
St. Louis   Americans, Brownies, *Browns*
Chicago   ChiSox, Comiskeys, Pale Hose, **WHITE SOX** (Sox)
Detroit   Benglas, (Mgr. Hugh) Jennings' Jungle-Towners, Kitties, *Tigers*
Philadelphia *Athletics* (A's), Blue Quakers, (Mgr. Connie) Mack's Men, Mack Men, Subterranean Denizens, White Elephants

1919 National League

Cincinnati Brainy Bunch, (Mgr. Pat) Mortan's Machine, **REDS**, Red Legs, Rhinelanders, The Well-Oiled Machine
New York   **GIANTS**, Jints, (Mgr. John) McGraw's Men, McGraw Men
Chicago   Bruins, Cubbies, **CUBS**, Northsiders
Pittsburgh Buccaneers (Bucs), **PIRATES**, Smoke-towners
Brooklyn   Brooks, Dodgers, (Mgr. Wilbert) Robinson's Flock, *Robins*, Superbas
Boston   **BRAVES**, Futile Braves (LeBlanc)
St. Louis   *Cardinals*, Maroons, Scarlets
Philadelphia Faltering Phillies (Richard Orodenker), Doormats of the NL (Orodenker), *Phillies*, Phoolish Phillies, Quakers, Red Quakers

1919 American League

Chicago   ChiSox, Comiskeys, (Mgr. Bill Gleason) Gleasonites, Pale Hose, **WHITE SOX** (Sox)
Cleveland   **INDIANS**, The Tribe

New York   (Mgr. Miller Huggins') Hug Men. **YANKEES** (Yanks)
Detroit   Bengals, (Mghr. Hugh) Jennings' Jungle-Towners, Kitties, *Tigers*
St. Louis   Americans, Brownies, *Browns*
Boston   Beantowners, BoSox, Crimson Hose, Hub Hose, **RED SOX** (Sox)
Washington   Americans, Griffs, **NATIONALS** (Nats), *Senators*
Philadelphia *Athletics* (A's), Blue Quakers, (Mgr. Connie) Mack's Men, Mack Men, Subterranean Denizens, White Elephants

1920 National League

Brooklyn   Brooks, (Mgr. Wilbert) Robinson's Flock, *Robins*, Sluggers, Superbas
New York   **GIANTS**, Jints, (Mgr. John) McGraw's Men, McGraw Men
Cincinnati   **REDS**, Red Legs, Rhinelanders
Pittsburgh   Buccaneers (Bucs), **PIRATES**, Smoke-towners
Chicago   Bruins, Cubbies, **CUBS**, Northsiders
Boston   **BRAVES**, Futile Braves (LeBlanc)
Philadelphia Doormats of the NL (Orodenker), Faltering Phillies (Orodenker), *Phillies*, Phoolish Phillies, Quakers, Red Quakers

1920 American League

Cleveland   **INDIANS**, The Tribe, Mighty Warriors (Mike LeBlanc)
Chicago   ChiSox, Comiskeys, (Mgr. Bill Gleason) Gleasonites, Pale Hose, Southsiders, **WHITE SOX** (Sox)
New York   (Mgr. Miller Huggins') Hug Men, **YANKEES** (Yanks)
St. Louis   Americans, **BROWNS**, Brownies
Boston   Beantowners, BoSox, Crimson Hose, Hub Hose, **RED SOX** (Sox)
Washington   Americans, Griffs, **NATIONALS** (Nats), *Senators*
Detroit   Bengals, (Mgr. Hugh) Jennings's Jungle-Towners, Kitties, **TIGERS**
Philadelphia **ATHLETICS** (A's), Blue Quakers, (Mgr. Connie) Mack's Men, Mack Men, Subterranean Denizens, White Elephants

1921 National League

New York   **GIANTS**, Jints, (Mgr. John) McGraw's Men, McGraw Men
Pittsburgh   Buccaneers (Bucs), **PIRATES**
St. Louis   **CARDINALS**, Maroons, Scarlets
Boston   **BRAVES**
Brooklyn   Brooks, Dodgers, (Mgr. Wilbert) Robinson's Flock, *Robins*, Superbas
Cincinnati   **REDS**, Red Legs, Rhinelanders
Chicago   Bears, Bruins, Cubbies, **CUBS**, Northsiders
Philadelphia Doormats of the NL (Orodenker), Faltering Phillies (Orodenker), *Phillies*, Phoolish Phillies, Quakers

1921 American League

New York   (Mgr. Miller Huggins) Hug Men, Huggins' Sluggers, (Team owner Jacob) Rupert's Rifles, **YANKEES** (Yanks)
Cleveland   **INDIANS**, The Tribe, World's Champions
St. Louis   Americans, **BROWNS**, Brownies
Washington   Americans, Griffs, **NATIONALS** (Nats), *Senators*

Boston — Beantowners, BoSox, Crimson Hose, Hub Hose, **RED SOX** (Sox)

Detroit — Bengals, Ty Cobb's Tygers, Kitties, **TIGERS**

Chicago — ChiSox, Comiskeys, (Mgr. Bill Gleason) Gleasonites, Pale Hose, Southsiders, White-Legged Crew, **WHITE SOX** (Sox)

Philadelphia — **ATHLETICS** (A's), (Mgr. Connie) Mack's Men, Mack Men, Subterranean Denizens, White Elephants

1922 National League

New York — **GIANTS**, Jints, (Mgr. John McGraw) McGraw Men

Cincinnati — **REDS**, Red Legs, Rhinelanders

Pittsburgh — Buccaneers (Bucs), **PIRATES**, Smoke-towners

St. Louis — **CARDINALS** (Cards), Redbirds (1st year)

Chicago — Bears, Bruins, Cubbies, **CUBS**, Northsiders

Brooklyn — Brooks, Dodgers, (Mgr. Wilbert) Robinson's Flock, *Robins*, Superbas

Philadelphia — Faltering Phillies (Orodenker), *Phillies*, Quakers, Red Quakers

Boston — **BRAVES**, Futile Braves (LeBlanc)

1922 American League

New York — (Mgr. Miller Huggins) Hug Men, (Team owner Jacob) Rupert's Rifles, Huggin's Sluggers **YANKEES** (Yanks)

St. Louis — Americans, **BROWNS**, Brownies

Detroit — Bengals, Ty Cobb's Tygers, Kitties, **TIGERS**

Cleveland — **INDIANS**, The Tribe

Chicago — ChiSox, Comiskeys, Pale Hose, Southsiders, **WHITE SOX** (Sox)

Washington — Griffs, **NATIONALS** (Nats), *Senators*

Philadelphia — **ATHLETICS** (A's), (Mgr. Connie Mack) Mack Men, Subterranean Denizens, White Elephants

Boston — Beantowners, BoSox, Crimson Hose, Dead Sox (h), Hub Hose, **RED SOX** (Sox)

1923 National League

New York — **GIANTS**, Jints, (Mgr. John McGraw) McGraw Men

Cincinnati — **REDS**, Red Legs, Rhinelanders

Pittsburgh — Buccaneers (Bucs), **PIRATES**

Chicago — Bears, Bruins, Cubbies, **CUBS**, Northsiders

St. Louis — **CARDINALS** (Cards), Redbirds

Brooklyn — Brooks, Dodgers, (Mgr. Wilbert) Robinson's Flock, *Robins*, Superbas

Boston — **BRAVES**, Futile Braves (LeBlanc)

Philadelphia — Doormats of the NL (Orodenker), Faltering Phillies (Orodenker), Phoolish Phillies, *Phillies*, Quakers

1923 American League

New York — (Mgr. Miller Huggins) Huggins' Men, Huggins' Sluggers, Hug Men, (Team owner Jacob) Rupert's Rifles, **YANKEES** (Yanks)

Detroit — Bengals, Kitties, **TIGERS**, Mgr. Ty Cobb's Tygers

Cleveland — **INDIANS**, The Tribe

Washington — Americans, Griffs, **NATIONALS** (Nats), *Senators*

St. Louis — Americans, **BROWNS**, Brownies

Philadelphia — **ATHLETICS** (A's), (Mgr. Connie Mack) Mack Men, White Elephants

Chicago — Bump Sox, ChiSox, Comiskeys, Pale Hose, Southsiders, **WHITE SOX** (Sox)

Boston — Beantowners, BoSox, Crimson Hose, Dead Sox (h), Hub Hose, **RED SOX** (Sox)

1924 National League

New York — Giant Machine, **GIANTS**, Jints, (Mgr. John McGraw) McGraw Men

Brooklyn — Brooks, Dodgers, (Mgr. Wilbert) Robinson's Flock, *Robins*, Superbas

Pittsburgh — Buccaneers (Bucs), **PIRATES**

Cincinnati — **REDS**, Red Legs, Rhinelanders

Chicago — Bears, Bruins, Cubbies, **CUBS**, Northsiders

St. Louis — **CARDINALS** (Cards), Redbirds

Philadelphia — Faltering Phillies (Orodenker), *Phillies*, Quakers

Boston — (Mgr. Dave) Bancroft's Braves, **BRAVES**, Futile Braves (LeBlanc)

1924 American League

Washington — Americans, Damn Senators (Mike Gavreaux), First in War, First in Peace and First in Everything (*ESPN Magazine*), Griffs, **NATIONALS** (Nats), *Senators*

New York — (Mgr. Miller Huggins) Hug Men, Huggins' Sluggers, (Team owner Jacob) Rupert's Rifles, **YANKEES** (Yanks)

Detroit — Bengals, Kitties, **TIGERS**, Mgr. Ty Cobb's Tygers

St. Louis — Americans, **BROWNS**, Brownies

Philadelphia — **ATHLETICS** (A's), (Mgr. Connie Mack) Mack Men, White Elephants

Cleveland — **INDIANS**, The Tribe

Boston — Beantowners, BoSox, Crimson Hose, Hub Hose, **RED SOX** (Sox)

Chicago — ChiSox, Comiskeys, Pal Hose, Southsiders, **WHITE SOX** (Sox)

1925 National League

Pittsburgh — Brash Buccaneers (Fried Lieb), Buccaneers (Bucs), (Mgr. Bill) McKechnie's Boys, McKechnie's Marauders, Pennant-harbor Pirates (Fred Lieb), **PIRATES**

New York — **GIANTS**, Jints, (Mgr. John McGraw) McGraw Men, Muggsy McGraw Men

Cincinnati — **REDS**, Red Legs, Rhinelanders

St. Louis — **CARDINALS** (Cards), Redbirds

Boston — **BRAVES**

Brooklyn — Brooks, Daffiness Boys, Daffy Dodgers, (Mgr. Wilbert) Robinson's Flock, *Robins*, Superbas

Philadelphia — Faltering Phillies (Orodenker), *Phillies*, Quakers

Chicago — Bears, Bruins, Cubbies, **CUBS**, (Mgr. Bill) Killefer's Men, Northsiders

1925 American League

Washington — Americans, Griffs, **NATIONALS** (Nats), *Senators*

Philadelphia — **ATHLETICS** (A's), (Mgr. Connie Mack) Mack Men, White Elephants

St. Louis — Americans, **BROWNS**, Brownies

Detroit — Bengals, Kitties, **TIGERS**, Mgr. Ty Cobb's Tygers

Chicago — ChiSox, Comiskeys, Pale Hose, Southsiders, **WHITE SOX** (Sox)

Cleveland — **INDIANS**, The Tribe

New York — (Mgr. Miller Huggins) Hug Men, Huggins' Sluggers, **YANKEES** (Yanks)

Boston   Beantowners, BoSox, Crimson Hose, Dead sox (h),
              Hub Hose, **RED SOX** (Sox)

1926 National League

St. Louis   **CARDINALS** (Cards), Home-grown Cardinals (Fred
              Lieb & Whitney Martin), Redbirds, Sparklers
Cincinnati   **REDS**, Red Legs, Rhinelanders
Pittsburgh   Buccaneers (Bucs), **PIRATES**
Chicago   Bears, Bruins, Cubbies, **CUBS**, Northsiders, Wrigley's
              Chicago Branch, Wrigleys (Weegham Park re-
              named Wrigley Field)
New York   **GIANTS**, Jints, (Mgr. John McGraw) McGraw Men
Brooklyn   Brooks, Daffiness Boys, Daffy Dodgers, (Mgr. Wilbert)
              Robinson's Flock, *Robins*, Superbas
Boston   **BRAVES**, Futile Braves (LeBlanc)
Philadelphia Doormats of the NL (Orodenker), Faltering Phillies
              (Orodenker), Phoolish Phillies, *Phillies*, Quakers

1926 American League

New York   (Mgr. Miller Huggins) Hug Men, Murderers' Row,
              Huggins' Sluggers, **YANKEES** (Yanks), Window-
              Breakers
Cleveland   **INDIANS**, The Tribe
Philadelphia **ATHLETICS** (A's), (Mgr. Connie Mack) Mack Men,
              White Elephants
Washington   Americans, Griffs, **NATIONALS** (Nats), *Senators*
Chicago   ChiSox, Comiskeys, Pale Hose, Southsiders, **WHITE
              SOX** (Sox)
St. Louis   Americans, **BROWNS**, Brownies
Detroit   Bengals, Kitties, **TIGERS**, Mgr. Ty Cobb's Tygers
Boston   Beantowners, BoSox, Crimson Hose, Dead Sox (h),
              Hub Hose, **RED SOX** (Sox)

1927 National League

Pittsburgh   Brash Buccaneers (Lieb), Buccaneers (Bucs), Pennant-
              harbor Pirates (Lieb), **PIRATES**
St. Louis   **CARDINALS** (Cards), Redbirds, Sparklers
New York   **GIANTS**, Jints, (Mgr. John McGraw) McGraw Men
Chicago   Bears, Bruins, Cubbies, **CUBS**, Northsiders, Wrigleys
Cincinnati   **REDS**, Red Legs, Rhinelanders
Brooklyn   Brooks, Daffiness Boys, Daffy Dodgers, (Mgr. Wilbert)
              Robinson's Flock, *Robins*, Superbas
Boston   **BRAVES**, Futile Braves (LeBlanc)
Philadelphia Doormats of the NL (Orodemker), Faltering Phillies
              (Orodenker), Phoolish Phillies, *Phillies*, Quakers

1927 American League

New York   Gehrig & Ruth, Inc. (Warren Wilbert), The Greatest
              Team of All-Time (MLB 1999 vote), (Mgr. Miller
              Huggins) Hug Men, Murderers' Row, Huggins'
              Sluggers, Steamrollers, **YANKEES** (Yanks), Win-
              dow-Breakers, Wonder Team
Cleveland   **INDIANS**, The Tribe
Philadelphia **ATHLETICS** (A's), (Mgr. Connie Mack) Mack Men,
              White Elephants
Washington   Americans, Griffs, **NATIONALS** (Nats), *Senators*
Chicago   ChiSox, Comiskeys, Pale Hose, Southsiders, **WHITE
              SOX** (Sox)
St. Louis   Americans, **BROWNS**, Brownies
Detroit   Bengals, Kitties, **TIGERS**, Mgr. Ty Cobb's Tygers

Boston   Beantowners, BoSox, Crimson Hose, Dead Sox (h),
              Hub Hose, **RED SOX** (Sox)

1928 National League

St. Louis   **CARDINALS** (Cards), Home-grown Cardinals (Lieb
              & Martin), Redbirds, Sparklers
New York   Fighting Giants (*Sporting News Guide*), **GIANTS**,
              Jints, (Mgr. John McGraw) McGraw Men
Chicago   Bears, Bruins, Cubbies, **CUBS**, Northsiders, Wrigleys
Pittsburgh   Buccaneers (Bucs), **PIRATES**
Cincinnati   **REDS**, Red Legs, Rhinelanders
Brooklyn   Brooks, Daffiness Boys, Daffy Dodgers, Dodgers,
              (Mgr. Wilbert) Robinson's Flock, *Robins*, Super-
              bas
Boston   **BRAVES**, Futile Braves (LeBlanc)
Philadelphia Doormats of the NL (Orodenker), Faltering Phillies
              (Orodenker), Phoolish Phillies, *Phillies*, Quakers

1928 American League

New York   (Mgr. Miller Huggins) Hug Men, Millionaires, Mur-
              derers' Row, Huggins' Sluggers, Steamrollers,
              YANKEES (Yanks), Window-Breakers
Philadelphia **ATHLETICS** (A's), (Mgr. Connie Mack) Mack Men,
              White Elephants
St. Louis   **BROWNS**, Brownies, (Mgr. Dan) Howley's Sensations
              (*Sporting News Guide*)
Washington   Americans, Griffs, **NATIONALS** (Nats), *Senators*,
              Solons
Chicago   ChiSox, Comiskeys, Pale Hose, Southsiders, **WHITE
              SOX** (Sox)
Detroit   Bengals, Kitties, (Mgr. George) Moriarty's Man-
              Eaters, **TIGERS**
Cleveland   **INDIANS**, The Tribe
Boston   Beantowners, BoSox, Crimson Hose, Dead Sox (h),
              Hub Hose, **RED SOX** (Sox)

1929 National League

Chicago   Bears, Bruins, Cubbies, **CUBS**, (Mgr. Joe McCarthy)
              McCarthy Men, Northsiders, Wrigleys
Pittsburgh   Buccaneers (Bucs), **PIRATES**
New York   Fighting Giants (*Sporting News Guide*), **GIANTS**,
              Jints, (Mgr. John McGraw) McGraw Men
St. Louis   **CARDINALS** (Cards), Redbirds
Philadelphia *Phillies*, Quakers
Brooklyn   Brooks, Daffiness Boys, Daffy Dodgers, Dodgers, (Mgr.
              Wilbert) Robinson's Flock, *Robins*, Superbas
Cincinnati   **REDS**, Red Legs, Rhinelanders
Boston   **BRAVES**, Futile Braves (LeBlanc)

1929 American League

Philadelphia **ATHLETICS** (A's), Bull Elephants, Famous Athletics
              (h), (Mgr. Connie Mack) Mack Men, Shining A's,
              White Elephants
New York   (Mgr. Miller Huggins) Hug Men, Millionaires, Mur-
              derers' Row, Huggins' Sluggers, **YANKEES** (Yanks),
              Window-Breakers
Cleveland   **INDIANS**, The Tribe
St. Louis   Americans, **BROWNS**, Brownies
Washington   Americans, Griffs, **NATIONALS** (Nats), *Senators*,
              Solons

Detroit	Bengals, Kitties, **TIGERS**
Chicago	ChiSox, Comiskeys, Pale House, Southsiders, **WHITE SOX** (Sox)
Boston	Beantowners, BoSox, Crimson Hose, Dead Sox (h), Hub Hose, **RED SOX** (Sox)

1930 National League

St. Louis	**CARDINALS** (Cards), Home-grown Cardinals (Lieb & Martin), Redbirds, Spirits of St. Louis (h), Steady-Climbers, Steady-Pluggers
Chicago	Bruins, Cubbies, **CUBS**, (Mgr. Joe McCarthy) McCarthy Men, Northsiders, Wrigleys
New York	Fighting Giants (*Sporting News Guide*), **GIANTS**, Jints, (Mgr. John McGraw) McGraw Men
Brooklyn	Brooks, Dodgers, (Mgr. Wilbert) Robinson's Flock, *Robins*, Superbas
Pittsburgh	Buccaneers (Bucs), **PIRATES**
Boston	**BRAVES**, Futile Braves (LeBlanc)
Cincinnati	**REDS**, Red Legs, Rhinelanders
Philadelphia	Doormats of the NL (Orodenker), Faltering Phillies (Orodonker), Phoolish Philiies, *Phillies*, Quakers

1930 American League

Philadelphia	**ATHLETICS** (A's), Famous Athletics (h), (Mgr. Connie Mack) Mack Men, White Elephants
Washington	Americans, Griffs, **NATIONALS** (Nats), *Senators*, Solons
New York	**YANKEES** (Yanks)
Cleveland	**INDIANS**, The Tribe
Detroit	Bengals, **TIGERS**
St. Louis	Americans, **BROWNS**, Brownies
Chicago	ChiSox, Comiskeys, Pale Hose, Southsiders, **WHITE SOX** (Sox)
Boston	Beantowners, BoSox, Crimson Hose, Dead Sox (h), Hub Hose, **RED SOX** (Sox)

1931 National League

St. Louis	**CARDINALS** (Cards), Home-grown Cardinals (Lieb & Martin), Redbirds, Spirits of St. Louis
New York	**GIANTS**, Jints, (Mgr. John McGraw) McGraw Men
Chicago	Bruins, Cubbies, **CUBS**, (Mgr. John McGraw) McGraw Men, Northsiders, Wrigleys
Brooklyn	Breooks, Dodgers, (Mgr. Wilbert) Robinson's Flock, *Robins*, Superbas
Pittsburgh	Buccaneers (Bucs), **PIRATES**
Philadelphia	*Phillies*, Quakers
Boston	**BRAVES**, Fuitile Braves (LeBlanc)
Cincinnati	Depression Era Reds (Lee Allen), **REDS**, Red Legs, Rhinelanders

1931 American League

Philadelphia	**ATHLETICS** (A's), Famous Athletics (h), (Mgr. Connie Mack) Mack Men, White Elephants
New York	(Mgr. Joe) McCarthy Men, **YANKEES** (Yanks)
Washington	Americans, Griffs, **NATIONALS** (Nats), *Senators*
Cleveland	**INDIANS**, The Tribe
St. Louis	Americans, **BROWNS**, Brownies
Boston	Beantowners, BoSox, Crimson Hose, Hub Hose, **RED SOX** (Sox)
Detroit	Bengals, **TIGERS**

| Chicago | ChiSox, Comiskeys, Pale Hose, Southsiders, **WHITE SOX** (Sox) |

1932 National League

Chicago	Bruins, Cubbies, **CUBS**, Northsiders, Wrigleys
Pittsburgh	Buccaneers (Bucs), **PIRATES**
Brooklyn	Brooks, (Mgr. Max) Carey's Canaries, Kings, **DODGERS**
Philadelphia	*Phillies*, Quakers
Boston	**BRAVES**
New York	**GIANTS**, Jints, (Mgr. John McGraw) McGraw Men
St. Louis	**CARDINALS** (Cards), Redbirds
Cincinnati	Depression Reds (Allen), **REDS**, Red Legs, Rhinelanders

1932 American League

New York	(Mgr. Joe) McCarthy Men, **YANKEES** (Yanks)
Philadelphia	**ATHLETICS** (A's), Famous Athletics (h), (Mgr. Connie Mack) Mack Men, White Elephants
Washington	Americans, Griffs, **NATIONALS** (Nats), *Senators*, Solons
Cleveland	**INDIANS**, The Tribe
Detroit	Bengals, **TIGERS**
St. Louis	Americans, **BROWNS**, Brownies
Chicago	ChiSox, Comiskeys, Pale Hose, Southsiders, **WHITE SOX** (Sox)
Boston	Beantowners, BoSox, Crimson Hose, Dead Sox (h), Hub Hose, **RED SOX** (Sox)

1933 National League

New York	**GIANTS**, G-Men, Jints, (Mgr. Bill Terry) Terry Men
Pittsburgh	Buccaneers (Bucs), **PIRATES**
Chicago	Bruins, Cubbies, **CUBS**, Northsiders, Wrigleys
Boston	**BRAVES**
St. Louis	**CARDINALS** (Cards), Redbirds
Brooklyn	Brooks, **DODGERS**
Philadelphia	**PHILLIES** (Phils), Quakers
Cincinnati	Depression Reds (Lee Allen), **REDS**, Red Legs, Rhinelanders

1933 American League

Washington	Americans, Griffs, **NATIONALS** (Nats), *Senators*, Solons, Wrecking Crew of '33 (Gary Sarnoff)
New York	(Mgr. Joe) McCarthy Men, **YANKEES** (Yanks)
Philadelphia	**ATHLETICS** (A's), (Mgr. Connie Mack) Mack Men, White Elephants
Cleveland	**INDIANS**, The Tribe
Detroit	Bengals, **TIGERS**
Chicago	ChiSox, Comiskeys, Pale Hose, Southsiders, **WHITE SOX** (Sox)
Boston	Beantowners, BoSox, Crimson Hose, Hub Hose, **RED SOX** (Sox)
St. Louis	Americans, **BROWNS**, Brownies

1934 National League

St. Louis	**CARDINALS** (Cards), Clouting Cardinals, Comeback Cardinals, Gas-House Gang, Home-grown Cardinals (Lieb & Martin), Redbirds
New York	**GIANTS**, Jints, G-Men, (Mgr. Bill Terry) Terry Men
Chicago	Bruins, Cubbies, **CUBS**, Northsiders, Wrigleys

Boston	**BRAVES**
Pittsburgh	Buccaneers (Bucs), **PIRATES**
Brooklyn	Brooks, **DODGERS**
Philadelphia	**PHILLIES** (Phils), Quakers, Slugfest City
Cincinnati	Bristling Reds, Depression Reds (h), **REDS**, Red Legs, Rhinelanders, Roughhouse Reds

1934 American League

Detroit	Bengals, G-Men, Roaring Tigers, **TIGERS**
New York	(Mgr. Joe) McCarthy Men, **YANKEES** (Yanks)
Cleveland	**INDIANS**, The Tribe
Boston	Beantowners, BoSox, Crimson Hose, Hub Hose, **RED SOX** (Sox)
Philadelphia	**ATHLETICS** (A's), (Mgr. Connie Mack) Mack Men
St. Louis	Americans, **BROWNS**, Brownies
Washington	Americans, Griffs, **NATIONALS** (Nats), *Senators*, Solons
Chicago	ChiSox, Comiskeys, Pale Hose, Southsiders, **WHITE SOX** (Sox)

1935 National League

Chicago	Bruins, Comeback Cubs, Cubbies, **CUBS**, Northsiders, Wrigleys
St. Louis	**CARDINALS** (Cards), Redbirds, Rowdy Redbirds
New York	**GIANTS**, Jints, G-Men, (Mgr. Bill Terry) Terry Men
Pittsburgh	Buccaneers (Bucs), **PIRATES**
Brooklyn	Brooks, **DODGERS**
Cincinnati	**REDS**, Red Legs, Rhinelanders
Philadelphia	**PHILLIES** (Phils), Quakers
Boston	America's Depression Team (Steven Riess), **BRAVES**, Futile Braves (LeBlanc), Innocents

1935 American League

Detroit	Bengals, G-Men, Roaring Tigers, **TIGERS**
New York	(Mgr. Joe) McCarthy Men, **YANKEES** (Yanks)
Cleveland	**INDIANS**, The Tribe
Boston	Beantowners, BoSox, Crimson Hose, Hub Hose, **RED SOX** (Sox)
Chicago	ChiSox, Comiskeys, Pale Hose, Southsiders, **WHITE SOX** (Sox)
Washington	Americans, Griffs, **NATIONALS** (Nats), *Senators*, Solons
St. Louis	Americans, **BROWNS**, Brownies
Philadelphia	**ATHLETICS** (A's), (Mgr. Connie Mack) Mack Men, White Elephants

1936 National League

New York	**GIANTS**, G-Men, Jints, (Mgr. Bill Terry) Terry Men
Chicago	Bruins, Cubbies, **CUBS**, Northsiders, Wrigleys
St. Louis	**CARDINALS** (Cards), Redbirds
Pittsburgh	Buccaneers (Bucs), **PIRATES**
Cincinnati	**REDS**, Red Legs, Rhinelanders Boston **BEES**
Brooklyn	Brooks, **DODGERS**, Dreary Dodgers (Fred Lieb)
Philadelphia	Doormats of the NL (Orodenker), Faltering Phillies (Orodonker), Futile Phillies (Orodenker), **PHILLIES** (Phils), Phoolish Phillies, Quakers

1936 American League

New York	Bronx Bombers, Dominators (Gary Gillette & Pete Palmer), Magnificent Yankees (Meany), (Mgr. Joe) McCarthy Men, **YANKEES** (Yanks)

Detroit	Bengals, **TIGERS**
Chicago	Bronx Bombers, ChiSox, Comiskeys, Pale Hose, Southsiders, **WHITE SOX** (Sox)
Washington	Americans, Griffs, **NATIONALS** (Nats), *Senators*, Solons
Cleveland	**INDIANS**, The Tribe
Boston	Beantowners, BoSox, Crimson Hose, Hub Hose, **RED SOX** (Sox)
St. Louis	Americans, **BROWNS**, Brownies
Philadelphia	**ATHLETICS** (A's), (Mgr. Connie Mack) Mack Men, White Elephants

1937 National League

New York	**GIANTS**, G-Men, Jints, (Mgr. Bill Terry) Terry Men
Chicago	Bruins, Cubbies, **CUBS**, Northsiders, Wrigleys
Pittsburgh	Buccaneers (Bucs), **PIRATES**
St. Louis	**CARDINALS** (Cards), Redbirds
Boston	**BEES**
Brooklyn	Brooks, **DODGERS**
Cincinnati	**REDS**, Red Legs, Rhinelanders
Philadelphia	Doormats of the NL (Orodenker), Faltering Phillies (Orodonker), Futile Phillies (Orodenker), **PHILLIES** (Phils), Phoolish Phillies, Quakers

1937 American League

New York	Bronx Bombers, Magnificent Yankees (Meany), (Mgr. Joe) McCarthy Men, Snow White (& The Seven Dwarfs), **YANKEES** (Yanks)
Detroit	Bengals, **TIGERS**
Chicago	ChiSox, Comiskeys, Pale Hose, Southsiders, **WHITE SOX** (Sox)
Cleveland	**INDIANS**, The Tribe
Boston	Beantowners, BoSox, Crimson Hose, Hub Hose, **RED SOX** (Sox)
Washington	Americans, Griffs, **NATIONALS** (Nats), *Senators*, Solons
Philadelphia	**ATHLETICS** (A's), (Mgr. Connie Mack) Mack Men, White Elephants
St. Louis	Americans, **BROWNS**, Brownies

1938 National League

Chicago	Bruins, Cubbies, **CUBS**, Northsiders, Wrigleys
Pittsburgh	Buccaneers (Bucs), **PIRATES**
New York	**GIANTS**, G-Men, Jints, (Mgr. Bill Terry) Terry Men
Cincinnati	**REDS**, Red Legs, Rhinelanders
Boston	**BEES**
St. Louis	**CARDINALS** (Cards), Redbirds
Brooklyn	Brooks, Bums, **DODGERS**, Dem Bums, Dreary Dodgers (Stout & Johnson), Our Bums
Philadelphia	Doormats of the NL (Orodenker), Faltering Phillies (Orodonker), Futile Phillies (Orodenker), **PHILLIES** (Phils), Phoolish Phillies, Quakers

1938 American League

New York	Bronx Bombers, Magnificent Yankees (Meany), (Mgr. Joe) McCarthy Men, Snow White (& the Seven Dwarfs), **YANKEES** (Yanks)
Boston	Beantowners, BoSox, Crimson Hose, Hub Hose, **RED SOX** (Sox)
Cleveland	**INDIANS**, The Tribe
Detroit	Bengals, **TIGERS**
Washington	Americans, Griffs, **NATIONALS** (Nats), *Senators*, Solons

Chicago	ChiSox, Comiskeys, Pale Hose, Southsiders, **WHITE SOX** (Sox)
St. Louis	Americans, **BROWNS**, Brownies
Philadelphia	**ATHLETICS** (A's), (Mgr. Connie Mack) Mack Men, White Elephants

| Washington | Americans, Griffs, **NATIONALS** (Nats), *Senators*, Solons |
| Philadelphia | **ATHLETICS** (A's), (Mgr. Connie Mack) Mack Men, White Elephants |

1939 National League

Cincinnati	(Mgr, Bill "Deacon" McKechnie) Deacon Boys, Niners, Queen City Renaissance, **REDS**, Red Legs, Rhinelanders, Vine Street Victors
St. Louis	**CARDINALS** (Cards), Redbirds
Brooklyn	Brooks, Bums, Dem Bums, **DODGERS**, Our Bums
Chicago	Bruins, Cubbies, **CUBS**, Northsiders, Wrigleys
New York	**GIANTS**, Jints, (Mgr. Bill Terry) Terry Men
Pittsburgh	Buccaneers (Bucs), **PIRATES**
Philadelphia	Doormats of the NL (Orodenker), Futile Phillies (Orodenker), **PHILLIES** (Phils), Phoolish Phillies, Quakers

1939 American League

New York	Bronx Bombers, Irresistible Yankees, Magnificent Yankees (h), (Mgr. Joe) McCarthy Men, Snow White (& the Seven Dwarfs), **YANKEES** (Yanks)
Boston	Beantowners, BoSox, Crimson Hose, Hub Hose, **RED SOX** (Sox)
Cleveland	**INDIANS**, The Tribe
Chicago	ChiSox, Comiskeys, Pale Hose, Southsiders, **WHITE SOX** (Sox)
Detroit	Bengals, **TIGERS**
Washington	Americans, Griffs, **NATIONALS** (Nats), *Senators*, Solons
Philadelphia	**ATHLETICS** (A's), (Mgr. Connie Mack) Mack Men, White Elephants
St. Louis	Brownies, **BROWNS**, Little Brownies

1940 National League

Cincinnati	Red Legs, **REDS**, Rhinelanders, Vine Street Victors
Brooklyn	Brooks, Bums, Dem Bums, **DODGERS**, Our Bums
St. Louis	**CARDINALS** (Cards), Redbirds
Pittsburgh	Buccaneers (Bucs), **PIRATES**
Chicago	Bruins, Cubbies, **CUBS**, Northsiders, Wrigleys
New York	**GIANTS**, Jints, (Mgr. Bill Terry) Terry Men
Boston	**BEES**
Philadelphia	Doormats of the NL (Orodenker), Faltering Phillies (Orodenker), Futile Phillies (Orodenker), **PHILLIES** (Phils), Phoolish Phillies, Quakers

1940 American League

Detroit	Bengals, Good Ol' Boys (Dizzy Trout), Slow-Sluggers, **TIGERS**
Cleveland	Cry-babies, **INDIANS**, The Tribe
New York	Bronx Bombers, (Mgr. Joe McCarthy) McCarthy Men, **YANKEES** (Yanks)
Boston	Beantowners, BoSox, Crimson Hose, Hub Hose, **RED SOX** (Sox)
Chicago	ChiSox, Comiskeys, Pale Hose, Southsiders, **WHITE SOX** (Sox)
St. Louis	Brownies, **BROWNS**

1941 National League

Brooklyn	(Mgr. Leo) Durocher's Battlers, Brooks, Bums, Dem Bums, **DODGERS**, Flatbush Flock, Our Bums
St. Louis	**CARDINALS** (Cards), Flying Redbirds, Redbirds, Swifties
Cincinnati	Red Legs, **REDS**, Rhinelanders
Pittsburgh	Buccaneers (Bucs), **PIRATES**
New York	**GIANTS**, Jints, (Mgr. Bill Terry) Terry Men
Chicago	Bruins, Cubbies, **CUBS**, Northsiders, Wrigleys
Boston	**BRAVES**, Futile Braves (Kaese)
Philadelphia	Doormats of the NL (Orodenker), Faltering Phillies (Orodenker), Futile Phillies (contemporary by 1941), Hapless Phillies (*Baseball Digest* 1971, W. Harrison Daniel & Christopher Threston), **PHILLIES** (Phils), Quakers

1941 American League

New York	Bronx Bombers, (Mgr. Joe McCarthy) McCarthy Men, **YANKEES** (Yanks)
Boston	Beantowners, BoSox, Crimson Hose, Hub Hose, **RED SOX** (Sox)
Chicago	ChiSox, Comiskeys, Pale Hose, Southsiders, **WHITE SOX** (Sox)
Cleveland	**INDIANS**, The Tribe
Detroit	Bengals, **TIGERS**
St. Louis	Brownies, **BROWNS**
Washington	Americans, Griffs, **NATIONALS** (Nats), *Senators*, Solons
Philadelphia	**ATHLETICS** (A's), (Mgr. Connie Mack) Mack Men, White Elephants

1942 National League

St. Louis	**CARDINALS** (Cards), Flying Redbirds, Home-grown Cardinals, Redbirds. Swifties
Brooklyn	(Mgr. Leo) Durocher's Battlers, Brooks, Bums, Dem Bums, **DODGERS**, Our Bums
New York	**GIANTS**, Jints, (Mgr. Mel) Ott Men
Cincinnati	Red Legs, **REDS**, Rhinelanders
Pittsburgh	Buccaneers (Bucs), **PIRATES**
Chicago	Bruins, Cubbies, **CUBS**, Northsiders, Wrigleys
Boston	**BRAVES**
Philadelphia	Doormats of the NL (Orodenker), Faltering Phillies (Orodenker), Futile Phillies, Hapless Phillies (*Baseball Digest* 1971, Daniel & Threston), **PHILLIES** (Phils), Quakers

1942 American League

New York	Bronx Bombers, (Mgr. Joe McCarthy) McCarthy Men, **YANKEES** (Yanks)
Boston	Beantowners, BoSox, Crimson Hose, Hub Hose, **RED SOX** (Sox)
St. Louis	**BROWNS**, Brownies
Cleveland	**INDIANS**, The Tribe
Detroit	Bengals, **TIGERS**

Chicago	ChiSox, Comiskeys, Pale Hose, Southsiders, **WHITE SOX** (Sox)
Washington	Americans, Griffs, **NATIONALS** (Nats), *Senators*, Solons
Philadelphia	**ATHLETICS** (A's), (Mgr. Connie Mack) Mack Men, White Elephants

1943 National League

St. Louis	**CARDINALS** (Cards), Flying Redbirds, Redbirds. Swifties
Cincinnati	Red Legs, **REDS**, Rhinelanders
Brooklyn	Brooks, Bums, Dem Bums, **DODGERS**, Our Bums
Pittsburgh	Buccaneers (Bucs), **PIRATES**
Chicago	Bruins, Cubbies, **CUBS**, Northsiders, Wrigleys
Boston	**BRAVES**
Philadelphia	Faltering Phillies (Orodenker), Futile Phillies, Hapless Phillies (*Baseball Digest*, Daniel & Threston), **PHILLIES** (Phils), Quakers
New York	**GIANTS**, Jints, (Mgr. Mel) Ott Men

1943 American League

New York	Bronx Bombers, (Mgr. Joe McCarthy) McCarthy Men, **YANKEES** (Yanks)
Washington	Americans, Griffs, **NATIONALS** (Nats), *Senators*, Solons
Cleveland	**INDIANS**, The Tribe
Chicago	ChiSox, Comiskeys, Pale Hose, Southsiders, **WHITE SOX** (Sox)
Detroit	Bengals, **TIGERS**
St. Louis	Brownies, **BROWNS**
Boston	Beantowners, BoSox, Crimson Hose, Hub Hose, **RED SOX** (Sox)
Philadelphia	**ATHLETICS** (A's), (Mgr. Connie Mack) Mack Men, White Elephants

1944 National League

St. Louis	**CARDINALS** (Cards), Flying Redbirds, Redbirds, Swifties
Pittsburgh	Buccaneers (Bucs), **PIRATES**
Cincinnati	Red Legs, **REDS**, Rhinelanders
Chicago	Bruins, Cubbies, **CUBS**, Northsiders, Wrigleys
New York	**GIANTS**, Jints, (Mgr. Bill Terry) Terry Men
Boston	**BRAVES**
Brooklyn	Brooks, Bums, Dem Bums, **DODGERS**, Our Bums
Philadelphia	Doormats of the NL (Orodenker), Faltering Phillies (Orodenker), Futile Phillies, Hapless Phillies (*Baseball Digest*, Daniel & Threston), **PHILLIES** (Phils), Quakers

1944 American League

St. Louis	Americans, **BROWNS**, Cinderella Boys, Cinderella Brownies (Richard Peterson), Cinderella Browns, Rags-to-Riches Boys, Sackcloth Brownies (October) (Peterson) Mgr. (Jim) Sewell's Wonders
Detroit	Bengals, Slow-Sluggers, **TIGERS**
New York	Bronx Bombers, (Mgr. Joe McCarthy) McCarthy Men, **YANKEES** (Yanks)
Boston	Beantowners, BoSox, Crimson Hose, Hub Hose **RED SOX** (Sox)

Cleveland	Cry-babies, **INDIANS**, The Tribe
Philadelphia	**ATHLETICS** (A's), (Mgr. Connie Mack) Mack Men, White Elephants
Chicago	Bruins, **CUBS**, Northsiders, Wrigleys
Washington	Americans, Griffs, Hapless Senators (Carroll), **NATIONALS** (Nats), *Senators*, Solons

1945 National League

Chicago	Bruins, Cubbies, **CUBS**, Northsiders, Wrigleys
St. Louis	**CARDINALS** (Cards), Flying Redbirds, Nationals, Redbirds, Swifties
Brooklyn	Brooks, Bums, Dem Bums **DODGERS**, Our Bums
Pittsburgh	Buccaneers (Bucs), **PIRATES**
New York	**GIANTS**, Jints, (Mgr. Mel) Ott Men
Boston	**BRAVES**
Cincinnati	Red Legs, **REDS**, Rhinelanders,
Philadelphia	Doormats of the NL (Orodenker), Faltering Phillies (Orodenker), Futile Phillies, Hapless Phillies (*Baseball Digest*, Daniel & Threston), **PHILLIES** (Phils), Quakers

1945 American League

Detroit	Bengals, Slow-Sluggers, **TIGERS**
Washington	Americans, Griffs, **NATIONALS** (Nats), *Senators*, Solons
St. Louis	Americans, Brownies, **BROWNS**
New York	Bronx Bombers, (Mgr. Joe McCarthy) McCarthy Men, **YANKEES** (Yanks)
Cleveland	**INDIANS**, The Tribe
Chicago	Bruins, **CUBS**, Northsiders, Wrigleys
Boston	Beantowners, BoSox, Crimson Hose, Hub Hose, **RED SOX** (Sox)
Philadelphia	**ATHLETICS** (A's), (Mgr. Connie Mack) Mack Men, White Elephants

1946 National League

St. Louis	**CARDINALS** (Cards), Flying Redbirds, Redbirds, Swifties
Brooklyn	Brooks, Bums, Dem Bums, **DODGERS**, Our Bums
Chicago	Bruins, Cubbies, **CUBS**, Northsiders, Wrigleys
Boston	**BRAVES**
Philadelphia	Futile Phillies, Hapless Phillies (*Baseball Digest*, Daniel & Threston), **PHILLIES** (Phils), Quakers
Cincinnati	Red Legs, **REDS**, Rhinelanders, Vine Street Victors
Pittsburgh	Buccaneers (Bucs), **PIRATES**
New York	**GIANTS**, Jints

1946 American League

Boston	Beantowners, BoSox, Crimson Hose, Hub Hose, **RED SOX** (Sox), Slam Bang Sox
Detroit	Bengals, Slow-Sluggers, **TIGERS**
New York	Bronx Bombers, (Mgr. Joe McCarthy) McCarthy Men, **YANKEES** (Yanks)
Washington	Americans, Griffs, **NATIONALS** (Nats), *Senators*, Solons
Chicago	ChiSox, Comiskeys, Pale Hose, Southsiders, **WHITE SOX** (Sox)
Cleveland	**INDIANS**, The Tribe, Wahoos
St. Louis	Brownies, **BROWNS**

Philadelphia	ATHLETICS (A's), (Mgr. Connie Mack) Mack Men, White Elephants	Chicago	ChiSox, Comiskeys, Pale Hose, Southsiders, **WHITE SOX** (Sox)

1947 National League

Brooklyn	Brooks, Bums, Dem Bums, **DODGERS,** Our Bums
St. Louis	**CARDINALS** (Cards), Flying Redbirds, Redbirds, Swifties
Boston	**BRAVES**
New York	**GIANTS.** Jints
Cincinnati	Red Legs, **REDS,** Rhinelanders, Vine Street Victors
Chicago	Bruins, Cubbies, **CUBS,** Northsiders, Wrigleys
Philadelphia	Faltering Phillies (Orodenker), Futile Phillies, Hapless Phillies (*Baseball Digest*, Daniel & Threston), **PHILLIES** (Phils), Quakers
Pittsburgh	Buccaneers (Bucs), **PIRATES**

1947 American League

New York	Bronx Bombers, (Mgr. Joe McCarthy) McCarthy Men, **YANKEES** (Yanks),
Detroit	Bengals, Slow-Sluggers, **TIGERS**
Boston	Beantowners, BoSox, Crimson Hose, Hub Hose, **RED SOX** (Sox)
Cleveland	Chief Wahoo's Tribe (Thomas Altherr & Alvin Hall), **INDIANS,** The Tribe, Wahoos
Philadelphia	ATHLETICS (A's), (Mgr. Connie Mack) Mack Men, White Elephants
Chicago	ChiSox, Comiskeys, Pale Hose, Southsiders, **WHITE SOX** (Sox)
Washington	Americans, Griffs, **NATIONALS** (Nats), *Senators,* Solons
St. Louis	Brownies, **BROWNS**

1948 National League

Boston	**BEES,** Futile Braves (Kaese), Mohawk Tribe, (Mgr. Billy) Southworth's Mohawks
St. Louis	**CARDINALS** (Cards), Flying Redbirds, Redbirds
Brooklyn	Brooks, Bums, Dem Bums, **DODGERS,** Our Bums
New York	**GIANTS,** Jints
Pittsburgh	Buccaneers (Bucs), **PIRATES**
Philadelphia	Futile Phillies, Hapless Phillies (*Baseball Digest*, Daniel & Threston), **PHILLIES** (Phils), Quakers
Cincinnati	Red Legs, **REDS,** Rhinelanders, Vine Street Victors
Chicago	Basement Bruins (h), Bruins, Cubbies, **CUBS,** Hibernating Cubs (h), Northsiders, Wrigleys

1948 American League

Cleveland	Arrowhead Tribe, Boys of the Summer of '48 (Russell Schneider), Chief Wahoo's Tribe (Altherr & Hall), **INDIANS,** The Tribe, Wahoos
Boston	Beantowners, BoSox, Crimson Hose, Hub Hose, **RED SOX** (Sox)
New York	Bronx Bombers, (Mgr. Joe McCarthy) McCarthy Men, **YANKEES** (Yanks)
Philadelphia	ATHLETICS (A's), (Mgr. Connie Mack) Mack Men, White Elephants
Detroit	Bengals, **TIGERS**
St. Louis	Brownies, **BROWNS**
Washington	Americans, Griffs, **NATIONALS** (Nats), *Senators,* Solons

1949 National League

Brooklyn	Brooks, Bums, Dem Bums **DODGERS,** Our Bums
St. Louis	**CARDINALS** (Cards), Flying Redbirds, Redbirds, Swifties
Philadelphia	Futile Phillies, Hapless Phillies (*Baseball Digest*, Daniel & Threston), **PHILLIES** (Phils), Quakers
Boston	**BEES,** Futile Braves (h)
New York	**GIANTS,** Jints
Pittsburgh	Buccaneers (Bucs), **PIRATES**
Cincinnati	Red Legs, **REDS,** Rhinelanders, Vine Street Victors
Chicago	Basement Bruins (h), Bruins, Cubbies, **CUBS,** Hibernating Cubs (h), Northsiders, Wrigleys

1949 American League

New York	Bronx Bombers (Bombers), Damn Yankees (Douglas Wallop & Thomas Gilbert), (Mgr. Joe McCarthy) Magnificent Yankees (Tom Meany), McCarthy Men, Men of Autumn (Dom Forker), **YANKEES** (Yanks)
Boston	Beantowners, BoSox, Chief Wahoo's Tribe, Crimson Hose, Hub Hose, **RED SOX.**
Cleveland	Chief Wahoo's Tribe (Altherr & Hall), **INDIANS,** The Tribe, Wahoos
Detroit	Bengals, Slow-Sluggers, **TIGERS**
Philadelphia	ATHLETICS (A's), (Mgr. Connie Mack) Mack Men, White Elephants
Chicago	ChiSox, Comiskeys, Pale Hose, Southsiders, **WHITE SOX** (Sox)
St. Louis	Brownies, **BROWNS**
Washington	Americans, Griffs, Hapless Senators (Carroll), **NATIONALS** (Nats), *Senators,* Solons

1950 National League

Philadelphia	Fightin' Phillies, (Mgr. Bill) Carpenter's Kids, **PHILLIES** (Phils), Quakers, Whiz Kids
Brooklyn	Blue Wrecking Crew, Boys of Summer (Roger Kahn), Brooks, Bums, Dem Bums, **DODGERS,** Methodical Maulers, Our Bums
New York	**GIANTS,** Jints
Boston	**BRAVES**
St. Louis	**CARDINALS** (Cards), Redbirds
Cincinnati	Red Legs, **REDS,** Rhinelanders
Chicago	Bruins, Cubbies, **CUBS,** Northsiders, Wrigleys
Pittsburgh	Buccaneers (Bucs), Fifty-Fifty Team, **PIRATES,** (GM Branch Rickey) Rickey-Dinks

1950 American League

New York	Bronx Bombers (Bombers), Bronx Juggernaut (h), Damn Yankees (Gilbert & Wallop), Lordly Bombers (h), Men of Autumn (Forker), Magnificent Yankees (Meany), Rampaging Yankees (h), **YANKEES** (Yanks)
Detroit	Bengals, **TIGERS**
Boston	Beantowners, BoSox, Crimson Hose, **RED SOX** (Sox)
Cleveland	Chief Wahoo's Tribe (Altherr & Hall), **INDIANS,** The Tribe, Wahoos.

Washington	Americans, Griffs, **NATIONALS** (Nats), *Senators*, Solons
Chicago	ChiSox, Comiskeys, Pale Hose, Southsiders, **WHITE SOX** (Sox)
St. Louis	Brownies, **BROWNS**
Detroit	Bengals, **TIGERS**
Philadelphia	**ATHLETICS** (A's), (Mgr. Connie Mack) Mack Men, White Elephants.

1951 National League

New York	Comeback Giants, **GIANTS**, Jints
Brooklyn	Blue Wrecking Crew, Boys of Summer (Roger Kahn), Brooks, Bums, Dem Bums, **DODGERS**, Methodical Maulers, Our Bums
St. Louis	**CARDINALS** (Cards), Redbirds
Boston	**BRAVES**
Philadelphia	Fizz Kids, **PHILLIES** (Phils), Quakers
Cincinnati	**REDS**, Red Legs, Rhinelanders
Pittsburgh	Buccaneers (Bucs), Fifty-Fifty Team, **PIRATES**, (General manager Branch Rickey) Rickey-Dinks
Chicago	Basement Bruins (h), Cubbies, **CUBS**, Hibernating Cubs (h), Northsiders, Wrigleys

1951 American League

New York	Bronx Bombers (Bombers), Bronx Juggernaut (h), Damn Yankees (Gilbert & Wallop), Lordly Bombers (h), Magnificent Yankees (Meany), Men of Autumn (Forker), Rampaging Yankees (h), **YANKEES** (Yanks)
Cleveland	Chief Wahoo's Tribe (Altherr & Hall), **INDIANS**, The Tribe, Wahoos
Boston	Beantowners, BoSox, Crimson Hose, **RED SOX** (Sox)
Chicago	ChiSox, Comiskeys, Go-Go-Sox, Pale Hose, Southsiders, **WHITE SOX** (Sox)
Detroit	Bengals, **TIGERS**
Philadelphia	**ATHLETICS** (A's), Mack Men, Macks, White Elephants
Washington	Americans, Griffs, **NATIONALS** (Nats), *Senators*, Solons
St. Louis	Brownies, **BROWNS**

1952 National League

Brooklyn	Blue Wrecking Crew, Boys of Summer (Kahn), Brooks, Bums, Dem Bums, **DODGERS**, Methodical Maulers (h), Our Bums
New York	**GIANTS**, Jints
St. Louis	**CARDINALS** (Cards), Redbirds
Philadelphia	Fightin' Phillies, **PHILLIES** (Phils), Quakers
Chicago	Bruins, Cubbies, **CUBS**, Northsiders, Wrigleys
Cincinnati	**REDS**, Red Legs, Rhinelanders
Boston	**BRAVES**
Pittsburgh	Buccaneers (Bucs), Fifty-Fifty Team, **PIRATES**, (Mgr. Branch Rickey) Rickey-Dinks

1952 American League

New York	Bronx Bombers (Bombers), Bronx Juggernaut (h), Damn Yankees, Lordly Bombers (h), Magnificent Yankees (Meany), Men of Autumn (Forker), Rampaging Yankees (h), **YANKEES** (Yanks)

Cleveland	**INDIANS**, Chief Wahoo's Tribe (Altherr & Hall), The Tribe, Wahoos.
Chicago	ChiSox, Comiskeys, Go-Go-Sox, Pale Hose, Southsiders, **WHITE SOX** (Sox)
Philadelphia	**ATHLETICS** (A's), Mack Men, Macks, White Elephants
Washington	Americans, Griffs, **NATIONALS** (Nats), *Senators*, Solons
Boston	Beantowners, BoSox, Crimson Hose, **RED SOX** (Sox)
St. Louis	Brownies, **BROWNS**
Detroit	Bengals, **TIGERS**

1953 National League

Brooklyn	Artful Dodgers (Jack Dawkins), Blue Wrecking Crew, Boys of Summer (h), Brooks, Bums, Dem Bums, **DODGERS**, Methodical Maulers, Our Bums
Milwaukee	Beer-makers, **BRAVES**, Miracle Boys (William Sunners), Miracle Braves
Philadelphia	Fightin' Phillies, **PHILLIES** (Phils), Quakers
St. Louis	**CARDINALS** (Cards), Redbirds
New York	**GIANTS**, Jints
Cincinnati	**REDLEGS**, Reds, Rhinelanders
Chicago	Bruins, Cubbies, **CUBS**, Northsiders, Wrigleys
Pittsburgh	Buccaneers (Bucs), Fifty-Fifty Team, **PIRATES**, (Mgr. Branch Rickey) Rickey-Dinks

1953 American League

New York	Bronx Bombers (Bombers), Bronx Juggernaut (h), Damn Yankees (contemporary), Lordly Bombers (h), Men of Autumn (Forker), Rampaging Yankees (h), **YANKEES** (Yanks)
Cleveland	Chief Wahoo's Tribe (Altherr & Hall), Indians, The Tribe, Wahoos.
Chicago	ChiSox, Comiskeys, Go-Go-Sox, Pale Hose, Southsiders, **WHITE SOX** (Sox)
Boston	Beantowners, BoSox, Crimson Hose, **RED SOX** (Sox)
Washington	Americans, Griffs, **NATIONALS** (Nats), *Senators*, Solons
Detroit	Bengals, **TIGERS**
Philadelphia	**ATHLETICS** (A's), White Elephants
St. Louis	Brownies, **BROWNS**, U-Boats

1954 National League

New York	**GIANTS**, Incredible Giants (Tom Meany), Jints, Willie Mays & Company
Brooklyn	Blue Wrecking Crew, Boys of Summer (Kahn), Brooks, Bums, Dem Bums, **DODGERS**, Methodical Maulers, Our Bums
Milwaukee	Beer-makers, **BRAVES**
Philadelphia	Fightin' Phillies, **PHILLIES** (Phils), Quakers
Cincinnati	**REDLEGS**, Reds, Rhinelanders
St. Louis	**CARDINALS** (Cards), Redbirds
Chicago	Bruins, Cubbies, **CUBS**, Northsiders, Wrigleys
Pittsburgh	Buccaneers (Bucs), Fifty-Fifty Team, **PIRATES**, (Mgr. Branch Rickey) Rickey- Dinks

1954 American League

Cleveland	(Mgr. Al) Lopez Limited, Chief Wahoo's Tribe (Altherr & Hall), **INDIANS**, The Tribe, Wahoos
New York	Bronx Bombers, Bronx Juggernaut (h), Damn Yan-

kees, Lordly Bombers (h), Rampaging Yankees (h), **YANKEES** (Yanks)

Chicago	ChiSox, Comiskeys, Go-Go-Sox, Pale Hose, South-siders, **WHITE SOX** (Sox)
Boston	Beantowners, BoSox, Crimson Hose, **RED SOX** (Sox)
Detroit	Bengals, **TIGERS**
Washington	Americans, Griffs, **NATIONALS** (Nats), *Senators*, Solons
Detroit	Bengals, **TIGERS**
Baltimore	Baby Birds, Birds, **ORIOLES** (O's)
Philadelphia	**ATHLETICS** (A's), White Elephants

1955 National League

Brooklyn	Blue Wrecking Crew, Boys of Summer (Kahn), Brooks, Bums, Dem Bums, Determined Dodgers (h), **DODGERS**, Frolicking Dodgers, Methodical Maulers, Our Bums
Milwaukee	Beer-makers, **BRAVES**
New York	**GIANTS**, Jints, Willie Mays & Company
Philadelphia	Fightin' Phillies, **PHILLIES** (Phils), Quakers
Cincinnati	**REDLEGS**, Reds, Rhinelanders
Chicago	Bruins, Cubbies, **CUBS**, Northsiders, Wrigleys
St. Louis	**CARDINALS** (Cards), Redbirds
Pittsburgh	Buccaneers (Bucs), **PIRATES**, (Mgr. Branch Rickey) Rickey-Dinks

1955 American League

New York	Bronx Bombers, Bronx Juggernaut, Damn Yankees, Lordly Bombers (h), Rampaging Yankees (h), **YANKEES** (Yanks)
Cleveland	Chief Wahoo's Tribe (Altherr & Hall), **INDIANS**, The Tribe, Wahoos.
Chicago	ChiSox, Comiskeys, Go-Go-Sox, Pale Hose, South-siders, **WHITE SOX** (Sox)
Boston	Beantowners, BoSox, Crimson Hose, **RED SOX** (Sox)
Detroit	Bengals, **TIGERS**
Kansas City	**ATHLETICS** (A's), White Elephants, Underdog Athletics (Janet Bruce), Yankees' Farm Club
Baltimore	Baby Birds, Birds, (Mgr. Paul) Richards' Flock, **ORIOLES** (O's)
Washington	Americans, Griffs. Hapless Senators (Carroll), **NATIONALS** (Nats), *Senators*, Solons

1956 National League

Brooklyn	Blue Wrecking Crew, Boys of Summer (Kahn), Brooks, Bums, Dem Bums, Determined Dodgers, **DODGERS**, Methodical Maulers, Our Bums
Milwaukee	Beer-makers, **BRAVES**
Cincinnati	**REDLEGS**, Reds, Rhinelanders
St. Louis	**CARDINALS** (Cards), Redbirds
Philadelphia	Fightin' Phillies, **PHILLIES** (Phils), Quakers
New York	**GIANTS**, Jints, Willie Mays & Company
Pittsburgh	Buccaneers (Bucs), **PIRATES**, (Mgr. Branch Rickey) Rickey-Dinks
Chicago	Basement Bruins (h), Bruins, Cubbies, **CUBS**, Hibernating Cubs, Northsiders, Wrigleys

1956 American League

New York	Bronx Bombers (Bombers), Bronx Juggernaut (h), Damn Yankees, Lordly Bombers (h), **YANKEES** (Yanks)

Cleveland	Chief Wahoo's Tribe (Altherr & Hall), **INDIANS**, The Tribe, Wahoos
Chicago	ChiSox, Comiskeys, Go-Go-Sox, Pale Hose, South-siders, **WHITE SOX** (Sox)
Boston	Beantowners, BoSox, Crimson Hose, **RED SOX** (Sox)
Detroit	Bengals, **TIGERS**
Baltimore	Baby Birds, Birds, **ORIOLES** (O's)
Washington	Americans, Griffs, **NATIONALS** (Nats), *Senators*, Solons
Kansas City	**ATHLETICS** (A's), White Elephants, Underdog Athletics (Bruce), Yankees' Farm Club

1957 National League

Milwaukee	Beer-makers, **BRAVES**
St. Louis	**CARDINALS** (Cards), Redbirds
Brooklyn	Blue Wrecking Crew, Boys of Summer (Kahn), Brooks, Bums, Dem Bums, **DODGERS**, Methodical Maulers, Our Bums
Cincinnati	**REDLEGS**, Reds, Rhinelanders
Philadelphia	Fightin' Phillies, **PHILLIES** (Phils), Quakers
New York	**GIANTS**, Willie Mays & Company
Chicago	Bruins, Cubbies, **CUBS**, Northsiders, Wrigleys
Pittsburgh	Buccaneers (Bucs), **PIRATES**, (Mgr. Branch Rickey) Rickey-Dinks

1957 American League

New York	Bronx Bombers (Bombers), Bronx Juggnernaut (h), Damn Yankees, Lordly Bombers (h), Rampaging Yankees (h), **YANKEES** (Yanks)
Chicago	ChiSox, Comiskeys, Go-Go-Sox, Guerrilla Attack Team, Pale Hose, Southsiders, **WHITE SOX** (Sox)
Boston	Beantowners, BoSox, Crimson Hose, **RED SOX** (Sox)
Detroit	Bengals, **TIGERS**
Baltimore	Baby Birds, Birds, **ORIOLES** (O's)
Cleveland	Chief Wahoo's Tribe, **INDIANS**, Subdued Indians, The Tribe, Wahoos
Kansas City	**ATHLETICS** (A's), White Elephants, Underdog Athletics (Bruce), Yankees' Farm Club
Washington	Griffs, Hapless Senators (Carroll), Nats, **SENATORS**, Solons

1958 National League

Milwaukee	Beer-makers, **BRAVES**
Pittsburgh	Buccaneers (Bucs), **PIRATES**, (Mgr. Branch Rickey) Rickey-Dinks
San Francisco	**GIANTS**, Frisco, Jints, Willie Mays & Company
Cincinnati	**REDLEGS**, Reds, Rhinelanders
Chicago	Bruins, Cubbies, **CUBS**, Northsiders, Wrigleys
St. Louis	**CARDINALS** (Cards), Redbirds
Los Angeles	**DODGERS**, Hollywood Bums (Willard Mullin)
Philadelphia	Fightin' Phillies, Fizz Kids, Futile Phillies, **PHILLIES** (Phils), Quakers

1958 American League

New York	Bronx Bombers (Bombers), Bronx Juggernaut (h), Damn Yankees, Lordly Bombers (h), Rampaging Yankees (h), **YANKEES** (Yanks)
Chicago	ChiSox, Comiskeys, Go-Go-Sox, Pale Hose, South-siders, **WHITE SOX** (Sox)

Boston   Beantowners, BoSox, Crimson Hose, **RED SOX** (Sox)
Detroit   Bengals, **TIGERS**
Baltimore   Baby Birds, Birds, **ORIOLES** (O's)
Cleveland   Chief Wahoo's Tribe (Altherr & Hall), **INDIANS**, The Tribe, Wahoos.
Kansas City   **ATHLETICS** (A's), White Elephants, Underdog Athletics (Bruce), Yankees' Farm Club
Washington   Griffs, Hapless Senators (Carroll), Nats, **SENATORS**, Solons

1959 National League

Los Angeles   **DODGERS**, Hollywood Heroes, Sun-kissed Dodgers (Gary Gillette & Pete Palmer)
Milwaukee   **BRAVES**
San Francisco   **GIANTS**, Jints
Pittsburgh   Buccaneers (Bucs), **PIRATES**
Chicago   Bruins, Cubbies, **CUBS**, Northsiders, Wrigleys
Cincinnati   **REDS**, Rhinelanders
St. Louis   **CARDINALS** (Cards), Redbirds
Philadelphia   **PHILLIES** (Phils), Fizz Kids

1959 American League

Chicago   ChiSox, Comiskeys, Go-Go-Sox, Pale Hose, Southsiders, **WHITE SOX** (Sox)
Cleveland   Chief Wahoo's Tribe (Altherr & Hall), **INDIANS**, The Tribe, Wahoos
New York   Bronx Bombers (Bombers), **YANKEES** (Yanks)
Detroit   Bengals, **TIGERS**
Boston   Beantowners, BoSox, Crimson Hose, **RED SOX** (Sox)
Baltimore   Baby Birds, Birds, **ORIOLES** (O's)
Kansas City   **ATHLETICS** (A's), White Elephants, Underdog Athletics (Bruce), Yankees' Farm Club
Washington   Griffs, Hapless Senators (Carroll), Liveliest Corpse in the American League (*Dell Baseball Magazine*), Nats, **SENATORS**, Solons

1960 National League

Pittsburgh   Battlin' Bucs, Beat 'em Bucs (slogan), Buccaneers (Bucs), Buccos, (Mgr. Danny) Murtaugh's Marauders, **PIRATES**, Proud Pirates (Michael Oleksak)
Milwaukee   **BRAVES**
St. Louis   **CARDINALS** (Cards), Redbirds
Los Angeles   **DODGERS**
San Francisco   **GIANTS**, Jints
Cincinnati   **REDS**, Redlegs, Rhinelanders
Chicago   Bruins, Cubbies, **CUBS**, Northsiders, Wrigleys
Philadelphia   **PHILLIES** (Phils), Fizz Kids

1960 American League

New York   Bronx Bombers (Bombers), Bronx Juggernaut (h), Lordly Bombers (h), Rampaging Yankees (h), **YANKEES** (Yanks)
Baltimore   Baby Birds, Birds, **ORIOLES** (O's)
Chicago   ChiSox, Comiskeys, Go-Go-Sox, Pale Hose, So-So Sox (Michael LeBlanc), Southsiders, **WHITE SOX** (Sox)
Cleveland   Chief Wahoo's Tribe (Altherr & Hall), **INDIANS**, The Tribe, Wahoos

Washington   Americans, Griffs, **NATIONALS** (Nats), *Senators*, Solons
Detroit   Bengals, **TIGERS**
Boston   Beantowners, BoSox, Crimson Hose, **RED SOX** (Sox)
Kansas City   **ATHLETICS** (A's), White Elephants, Underdog Athletics (h), Yankees' Farm Club

1961 National League

Cincinnati   Ragamuffins, **REDS**, Red Legs, Rhinelanders
Los Angeles   **DODGERS**
San Francisco   **GIANTS**, Willie Mays & Company
Milwaukee   **BRAVES**, (Mgr. Birdie) Tebbett's Tribe
St. Louis   **CARDINALS** (Cards), Redbirds
Pittsburgh   Buccaneers (Bucs), **PIRATES**
Chicago   Bruins, Cubbies, **CUBS**, Northsiders, Wrigleys
Philadelphia   **PHILLIES** (Phils), Fizz Kids

1961 American League

New York   B-52 Bombers, Bronx Bombers (Bombers), (Mgr. Ralph) Houk's High-Altitude Bombers, **YANKEES** (Yanks)
Detroit   Bengals, **TIGERS**
Baltimore   Baby Birds, Birds, **ORIOLES** (O's)
Chicago   ChiSox, Comiskeys, Go-Go-Sox, Pale Hose, So-So Sox (LeBlanc), Southsiders, **WHITE SOX** (Sox)
Cleveland   Chief Wahoo's Tribe (Altherr & Hall), **INDIANS**, The Tribe, Wahoos
Boston   Beantowners, BoSox, Crimson Hose, **RED SOX** (Sox)
Minnesota   **TWINS**, Win! Twins! (slogan)
Los Angeles   **ANGELS**, Halos, Seraphs
Kansas City   **ATHLETICS** (A's), White Elephants, Underdog Athletics (Bruce), Yankees' Farm Club
Washington   First of the Worst (Bill Gilbert), Hapless Senators (Rich Westcott), Nats, New Senators, **SENATORS**, Solons

1962 National League

San Francisco   Bay Area Blasters, **GIANTS**, (Mgr. Alvin) Dark's Gladiators, Willie Mays & Company
Los Angeles   **DODGERS**
Cincinnati   **REDS**, Rhinelanders
Pittsburgh   Buccaneers (Bucs), Buccos, **PIRATES**, Proud Pirates (Oleksak)
Milwaukee   **BRAVES**, (Mgr.) Birdie Tebbett's Tribe
St. Louis   **CARDINALS** (Cards), Redbirds
Philadelphia   **PHILLIES** (Phils)
Houston   **COLT .45's**, Colts
Chicago   Bruins, Cubbies, **CUBS**, Northsiders, Wrigleys
New York   (Mgr. Casey) Stengel's Amazin's, Amazing Mets, Babies, Casey's Loveable Losers, **METS**

1962 American League

New York   Bronx Bombers (Bombers), **YANKEES** (Yanks)
Minnesota   (Mgr. Sam) Mele's Muscle-men, Minnesota Lumber Company, **TWINS**
Los Angeles   **ANGELS**, Cherubs, Halos, Seraphs
Detroit   Bengals, **TIGERS**
Chicago   ChiSox, Comiskeys, Go-Go-Sox, Pale Hose, So-so Sox (LeBlanc), Southsiders, **WHITE SOX** (Sox)

Cleveland	Chief Wahoo's Tribe (Altherr & Hall), **INDIANS**, The Tribe, Wahoos
Baltimore	Baby Birds, Birds, **ORIOLES** (O's)
Boston	Beantowners, BoSox, Crimson Hose, **RED SOX** (Sox)
Kansas City	**ATHLETICS** (A's), White Elephants, Underdog Athletics (Bruce), Yankees' Farm Club
Washington	Hapless Senators (Westcott), Nats, **SENATORS**, Solons

1963 National League

Los Angeles	**DODGERS**, Roger Dodgers (Gillette & Palmer), Sandy Koufax & Company
St. Louis	**CARDINALS** (Cards), Redbirds
San Francisco	**GIANTS**, Jints
Philadelphia	Fightin' Phillies, **PHILLIES** (Phils)
Cincinnati	**REDS**, Rhinelanders
Milwaukee	**BRAVES**
Chicago	Bruins, Cubbies, **CUBS**, Northsiders, Wrigleys
Pittsburgh	Buccaneers (Bucs), Buccos, **PIRATES**
Houston	**COLT .45's**, Colts
New York	Amazin's, Amazing Mets, Casey's Loveable Losers, **METS**

1963 American League

New York	Bronx Bombers (Bombers), B-52 Bombers, **YANKEES** (Yanks)
Chicago	ChiSox, Comiskeys, Go-Go-Sox, Pale Hose, Southsiders, **WHITE SOX** (Sox)
Minnesota	Minnesota Lumber Company, **TWINS**
Baltimore	Baby Birds, Birds, **ORIOLES** (O's)
Cleveland	Chief Wahoo's Tribe (Altherr & Hall), **INDIANS**, The Tribe, Wahoos
Detroit	Bengals, **TIGERS**
Boston	Beantowners, BoSox, Crimson Hose, **RED SOX** (Sox)
Kansas City	**ATHLETICS** (A's), Flashy Athletics, White Elephants, Underdog Athletics (Bruce)
Los Angeles	**ANGELS**, Halos, Seraphs
Washington	Hapless Senators (Westcott), Nats, **SENATORS**, Solons

1964 National League

St. Louis	**CARDINALS** (Cards), (Mgr. Johnny) Keane's Opportunists, Redbirds
Cincinnati	(Mgr. Fred) Hutchinson's Horses, **REDS**, Rhinelanders
Philadelphia	El Foldo Phillies, Fightin' Phillies, Fizzle Phillies, **PHILLIES** (Phils)
San Francisco	Bay Area Blasters, **GIANTS**, Willie Mays & Company
Milwaukee	**BRAVES**
Los Angeles	**DODGERS**
Pittsburgh	Buccaneers (Bucs), Buccos, **PIRATES**
Chicago	Bruins, Cubbies, **CUBS**, Northsiders, Wrigleys
Houston	**COLT .45's**, Colts
New York	(Mgr. Casey) Stengel's Amazin's, Amazing Mets, Casey's Loveable Losers, **METS**

1964 American League

New York	Baseball's Roman Empire, Bronx Bombers (Bombers), Dynastic Yankees, **YANKEES** (Yanks)

Chicago	ChiSox, Comiskeys, Go-Go-Sox, Pale Hose, Southsiders, **WHITE SOX** (Sox)
Baltimore	Baby Birds, Birds, **ORIOLES** (O's)
Detroit	Bengals, **TIGERS**
Los Angeles	**ANGELS**, Halos, Seraphs
Cleveland	Chief Wahoo's Tribe, **INDIANS**, The Tribe, Wahoos
Minnesota	Minnesota Lumber Company, **TWINS**
Boston	Beantowners, BoSox, Crimson Hose, **RED SOX** (Sox)
Washington	Hapless Senators (Westcott), Nats, **SENATORS**, Solons
Kansas City	**ATHLETICS** (A's), Flashy Athletics, White Elephants, Underdog Athletics (Bruce)

1965 National League

Los Angeles	**DODGERS**, Sandy Koufax & Company
San Francisco	Bay Area Blasters, **GIANTS**, Willie Mays & Company
Pittsburgh	Buccaneers (Bucs), **PIRATES**, Pride Pirates (Oleksak)
Cincinnati	**REDS**, Rhinelanders
Milwaukee	**BRAVES**, Lame Duck Braves, Vagabond Braves
Philadelphia	**PHILLIES** (Phils)
St. Louis	**CARDINALS** (Cards), Redbirds
Chicago	Bruins, Cubbies, **CUBS**, Northsiders, Wrigleys
Houston	**ASTROS**
New York	Amazin's, Amazing Mets, Casey's Loveable Losers, **METS**

1965 American League

Minnesota	Minnesota Lumber Company, Paul Bunyon's Team, **TWINS**
Chicago	ChiSox, Comiskeys, Go-Go-Sox, Pale Hose, Southsiders, **WHITE SOX** (Sox)
Baltimore	Baby Birds, Birds, **ORIOLES** (O's)
Detroit	Bengals, **TIGERS**
Cleveland	Chief Wahoo's Tribe (Altherr & Hall), **INDIANS**, The Tribe, Wahoos
New York	Bronx Bombers, Fallen Empire, **YANKEES** (Yanks)
California	**ANGELS**, Halos, Seraphs
Washington	Hapless Senators (Westcott), Nats, **SENATORS**, Solons
Boston	Beantowners, BoSox, Crimson Hose, Hub Hose, **RED SOX** (Sox)
Kansas City	**ATHLETICS** (A's), Flashy Athletics, White Elephants, Underdog Athletics (h)

1966 National League

Los Angeles	**DODGERS**, Sandy Koufax & Company
San Francisco	Bay Area Blasters, **GIANTS**, Willie Mays & Company
Pittsburgh	Buccaneers (Bucs), Buccos, **PIRATES**, Pittsburgh Lumber Company, Proud Pirates (Oleksak)
Philadelphia	Fightin' Phillies, **PHILLIES** (Phils)
Atlanta	**BRAVES**
St. Louis	**CARDINALS** (Cards), Redbirds
Cincinnati	**REDS**, Rhinelanders
Houston	**ASTROS**
New York	Amazin's, Amazing Mets, **METS**
Chicago	Basement Bruins (h), Bruins, Cubbies, **CUBS**, Hibernating Bears (h), Northsiders, Wrigleys

1966 American League

Baltimore	Amazing Orioles, Baby Birds, Birds, Birds-on-a-Wing, O-O-Orioles!, **ORIOLES** (O's), Rare Birds

Minnesota	Paul Bunyon's Team, **TWINS**
Detroit	Bengals, **TIGERS**
Chicago	ChiSox, Comiskeys, Go-Go-Sox, Pale Hose, Southsiders, **WHITE SOX** (Sox)
Cleveland	Chief Wahoo's Tribe (Altherr & Hall), **INDIANS**, The Tribe, Wahoos
California	**ANGELS**, Halos, Seraphs
Kansas City	**ATHLETICS** (A's), Flashy Athletics, White Elephants, Underdog Athletics (h)
Washington	Hapless Senators (Westcott), Nats, **SENATORS**, Solons
Boston	Beantowners, BoSox, Crimson Hose, Hub Hose, **RED SOX** (Sox)
New York	The Best Last Place Team in History (Jim Bouton), Bronx Bombers, **YANKEES** (Yanks)

1967 National League

St. Louis	El Birdos (Orlando Cepeda), **CARDINALS** (Cards), Orlando Cepeda & Company, Redbirds
San Francisco	**GIANTS**, Jints, Willie Mays & Company
Chicago	Bruins, Cubbies, **CUBS**, (Mgr. Leo) Durochers Dandies, Leo's Lions, Northsiders, Wrigleys
Cincinnati	**REDS**, Rhinelanders
Philadelphia	**PHILLIES** (Phils)
Pittsburgh	Buccaneers (Bucs), Buccos, **PIRATES**
Atlanta	**BRAVES**
Los Angeles	**DODGERS**
Houston	**ASTROS**
New York	Amazin's, Amazing Mets, **METS**

1967 American League

Boston	Beantowners, BoSox, Cinderella Red Sox, Crimson Hose, Hub Hose, Impossible Dream Red Sox, **RED SOX** (Sox)
Detroit	Bengals, **TIGERS**
Minnesota	Paul Bunyon's Team, **TWINS**
Chicago	ChiSox, Comiskeys, Go-Go-Sox, Hitless Wonders II, Pale Hose, Southsiders, (Mgr. Eddie) Stanky's Mouse, Stanky's Vultures, **WHITE SOX** (Sox)
California	**ANGELS**, Halos, Seraphs
Baltimore	Baby Birds, Birds, **ORIOLES** (O's)
Washington	Hapless Senators (Westcott), Nats, **SENATORS**, Solons
Cleveland	Chief Wahoo's Tribe (Altherr & Hall), Feather-Heads, **INDIANS**, The Tribe, Wahoos
New York	Bronx Bombers, **YANKEES** (Yanks)
Kansas City	**ATHLETICS** (A's), White Elephants, Underdog Athletics (h)

1968 National League

St. Louis	El Birdos (Cepeda), **CARDINALS** (Cards), Bob Gibson & Company, Redbirds
San Francisco	(Mgr. Herman) Franks' Bridesmaids, **GIANTS**, Willie Mays & Company
Chicago	Bruins, Cubbies, **CUBS**, (Mgr. Leo) Durocher's Dandies, Leo's Lions, Northsiders, Wrigleys
Cincinnati	**REDS**, Rhinelanders
Philadelphia	**PHILLIES** (Phils)
Pittsburgh	Buccaneers (Bucs), Buccos, **PIRATES**
Atlanta	**BRAVES**

Los Angeles	**DODGERS**
Houston	**ASTROS**
New York	Amazin's, Amazing Mets, **METS**

1968 American League

Detroit	Bengals, Good Ol' Boys (Paul Hemphill), Second Gas House Gang, Sock It to 'Em Tigers (Mark Patterson), **TIGERS**
Baltimore	Baby Birds, Birds, **ORIOLES** (O's)
Cleveland	**INDIANS**, The Tribe
Boston	Beantowners, BoSox, Crimson Hose, Hub Hose, **RED SOX** (Sox)
New York	Bronx Bombers, **YANKEES** (Yanks)
Oakland	**ATHLETICS** (A's), Green & Gold, White Elephants, Yankees' Farm Club
Minnesota	**TWINS**
California	**ANGELS**, Halos, Seraphs
Chicago	ChiSox, Comiskeys, Falling Hose (h), Go-Go-Sox, Pale Hose, Sagging Sox, Southsiders, **WHITE SOX** (Sox)
Washington	Hapless Senators (Westcott), Nats, **SENATORS**, Solons

1969 National League

EASTERN DIVISION

New York	Amazin's, Amazing Mets, Magical Mystery Mets, **METS**, Mets Machine, Miracle Mets
Chicago	Big Bad Bears (*NY Daily Herald*), Bruins, Cubbies, **CUBS**, (Mgr. Leo) Durocher's Dandies, Leo's Lions, Northsiders, Wrigleys
Pittsburgh	Buccaneers (Bucs), Buccos, **PIRATES**
St. Louis	**CARDINALS** (Cards), Redbirds
Philadelphia	**PHILLIES** (Phils)
Montreal	**EXPOS**, Les Expos, Les Tri-Colores, The Red, White & Blue

WESTERN DIVISION

Atlanta	**BRAVES**
San Francisco	**GIANTS**, Jints, Willie Mays & Company
Cincinnati	Big Red Machine, **REDS**, Rhinelanders
Los Angeles	**DODGERS**
Houston	**ASTROS**
San Diego	**PADRES** (Pads), Dads, Fathers, Missionaries

1969 American League

EASTERN DIVISION

Baltimore	Big Bad Birds, Birds, Century Crew, **ORIOLES** (O's)
Detroit	Bengals, **TIGERS**
Boston	Beantowners, BoSox, Crimson Hose, Hub Hose, **RED SOX** (Sox)
Washington	Nats, **SENATORS**, Solons
New York	Bronx Bombers, **YANKEES** (Yanks)
Cleveland	Feather-Brains, Feather-Heads, **INDIANS**, The Lost Tribe (h), The Tribe, Wandering Tribe (h)

WESTERN DIVISION

Minnesota	(Mgr. Billy) Martin's Hard-Hitters, Minnesota Lumber Company, **TWINS**
Oakland	**ATHLETICS** (A's), Green & Gold

California	ANGELS, Halos, Seraphs
Kansas City	Boys in Blue, ROYALS, R's
Chicago	ChiSox, Comiskeys, Falling Hose, Pale Hose, Southsiders, WHITE SOX (Sox)
Seattle	PILOTS

1970 National League

EASTERN DIVISION

Pittsburgh	Buccaneers (Bucs), Buccos, Pittsburgh Lumber Company, PIRATES, Proud Pirates (Oleksak), Roberto Clemente & Company
Chicago	Bruins, Cubbies, CUBS, Northsiders, Wrigleys
New York	Amazin's, Amazing Mets, METS, Miracle Mets
St. Louis	CARDINALS (Cards), Redbirds
Philadelphia	PHILLIES (Phils)
Montreal	EXPOS, Les Expos, Les Tri-Colores, The Red, White & Blue

WESTERN DIVISION

Cincinnati	Big Red, Big Red Machine, REDS, Rhinelanders
Los Angeles	DODGERS
San Francisco	GIANTS, Jints, Willie Mays & Company
Houston	ASTROS
Atlanta	BRAVES
San Diego	PADRES (Pads), Dads, Fathers

1970 American League

EASTERN DIVISION

Baltimore	Big Bad Birds, Birds, Century Crew, ORIOLES (O's)
New York	Bronx Bombers, YANKEES (Yanks)
Boston	Beantowners, BoSox, Crimson Hose, Hub Hose, RED SOX (Sox)
Detroit	Bengals, TIGERS
Cleveland	INDIANS, Lost Tribe (h), Tribe, Wandering Tribe (h)
Washington	Nats, SENATORS, Solons

WESTERN DIVISION

Minnesota	(Mgr. Bill) Rigney's Hard-Hitters, Minnesota Lumber Company, TWINS
Oakland	ATHLETICS (A's), Green & Gold
California	ANGELS, Halos, Seraphs
Kansas City	Boys in Blue, Men in Blue, ROYALS, R's
Milwaukee	BREWERS
Chicago	ChiSox, Comiskeys, Falling Hose, Pale Hose, Southsiders, Stop-Stop Sox, WHITE SOX (Sox)

1971 National League

EASTERN DIVISION

Pittsburgh	Buccaneers (Bucs), Buccos, Pittsburgh Lumber Company, PIRATES, Proud Pirates (Oleksak)
St. Louis	CARDINALS (Cards), Redbirds
Chicago	Bruins, Cubbies, CUBS, Northsiders, Wrigleys
New York	Amazin's, Amazing Mets, METS, Miracle Mets
Montreal	EXPOS, Les Expos, Les Tri-Colores, The Red, White & Blue
Philadelphia	Futile Phillies, PHILLIES (Phils)

WESTERN DIVISION

San Francisco	GIANTS, Jints, Willie Mays & Company
Los Angeles	DODGERS
Atlanta	BRAVES
Cincinnati	The Big Red Machine, REDS, Rhinelanders
Houston	ASTROS
San Diego	PADRES (Pads), Dads, Fathers

1971 American League

EASTERN DIVISION

Baltimore	Big Bad Birds, Birds, Century Crew, ORIOLES (O's)
Detroit	Bengals, TIGERS
Boston	Beantowners, BoSox, Crimson Hose, Hub Hose, RED SOX (Sox)
New York	Bronx Bombers, YANKEES (Yanks)
Washington	Nats, SENATORS, Solons
Cleveland	Feather-Brains, Feather-Heads, INDIANS, The Lost Tribe (h), The Tribe, Wandering Tribe (h)

WESTERN DIVISION

Oakland	ATHLETICS (A's), Green & Gold, Swinging A's
Kansas City	Men in Blue, ROYALS
Chicago	ChiSox, Comiskeys, Pale Hose, Rising Sox, Southsiders, WHITE SOX (Sox)
California	ANGELS, Halos, Seraphs
Minnesota	Minnesota Lumber Company, TWINS
Milwaukee	BREWERS, Brew Crew

1972 National League

EASTERN DIVISION

Pittsburgh	Buccaneers (Bucs), Buccos, Pittsburgh Lumber Company, PIRATES, Proud Pirates (Oleksak)
Chicago	Bruins, Cubbies, CUBS, Northsiders, Wrigleys
New York	Amazin's, Amazing Mets, METS, Miracle Mets
St. Louis	CARDINALS (Cards), Redbirds
Montreal	EXPOS, Les Expos, Les Tri-Colores, The Red, White & Blue
Philadelphia	Futile Phillies, PHILLIES (Phils)

WESTERN DIVISION

Cincinnati	Big Red, Big Red Machine, REDS, Rhinelanders
Houston	ASTROS
Los Angeles	DODGERS
San Francisco	GIANTS, Willie Mays & Company
Atlanta	BRAVES
San Diego	PADRES (Pads), Dads, Fathers

1972 American League

EASTERN DIVISION

Detroit	Bengals, Billy Martin's Half-Game Champs (Todd Masters), TIGERS
Boston	Beantowners, BoSox, Crimson Hose, Hub Hose, RED SOX (Sox)
Baltimore	Big Bad Birds, Birds, ORIOLES (O's)
New York	Bronx Bombers, YANKEES (Yanks)
Cleveland	INDIANS, The Lost Tribe, The Tribe, Wandering Tribe
Milwaukee	BREWERS

WESTERN DIVISION

Oakland	Angry Athletics, **ATHLETICS** (A's), Best from the West, Champagne and Baloney A's (Tom Clark), Dynastic A's, Fighting A's, (Team owner Charley) Finley's Moustache Brigade, Green & Gold, Moustache Gang, Swinging Athletics
Chicago	ChiSox, Comiskeys, Pale Hose, Rising Sox, Southsiders, **WHITE SOX** (Sox)
Minnesota	Minnesota Lumber Company, **TWINS**
Kansas City	**ROYALS**, Men in Blue
California	**ANGELS**, Halos, Seraphs
Texas	**RANGERS**, Strangers

1973 National League

EASTERN DIVISION

New York	Amazin's, Amazing Mets, Leap-frog Mets, **METS**, Miracle Mets
St. Louis	**CARDINALS** (Cards), Redbirds
Pittsburgh	Buccaneers (Bucs), Buccos, **PIRATES**
Montreal	**EXPOS**, Les Expos, Les Tri-Colores, The Red, White & Blue
Chicago	Bruins, Cubbies, **CUBS**, Northsiders, Wrigleys
Philadelphia	Futile Phillies, **PHILLIES** (Phils)

WESTERN DIVISION

Cincinnati	Big Red, Big Red Machine, **REDS**, Rhinelanders
Los Angeles	**DODGERS**
San Francisco	**GIANTS**, Jints
Houston	**ASTROS**
Atlanta	**BRAVES**
San Diego	**PADRES** (Pads), Dads, Fathers

1973 American League

EASTERN DIVISION

Baltimore	Big Bad Birds, Birds, **ORIOLES** (O's)
Boston	Beantowners, BoSox, Crimson Hose, Hub Hose, **RED SOX** (Sox)
Detroit	Bengals, **TIGERS**
New York	Bronx Bombers, **YANKEES** (Yanks)
Milwaukee	**BREWERS**, Brew Crew
Cleveland	Feather-Brains, Feather-Heads, **INDIANS**, The Lost Tribe, The Tribe, Wandering Tribe

WESTERN DIVISION

Oakland	Angry Athletics, **ATHLETICS** (A's), Best from the West, Champagne and Baloney (Clark) A's, Dynastic A's, Fighting A's, Green & Gold, Moustache Gang, Swinging Athletics
Kansas City	**ROYALS**, Men in Blue
Minnesota	Minnesota Lumber Company, **TWINS**
California	**ANGELS**, Halos, Seraphs
Chicago	ChiSox, Comiskeys, Pale Hose, Pallid Hose (h), Southsiders, **WHITE SOX** (Sox)
Texas	Corralled Rangers, **RANGERS**

1974 National League

EASTERN DIVISION

Pittsburgh	Buccaneers (Bucs), Buccos, Pittsburgh Lumber Company, **PIRATES**, Proud Pirates (Oleksak)

St. Louis	**CARDINALS** (Cards), Redbirds
Philadelphia	**PHILLIES** (Phils)
Montreal	**EXPOS**, Les Expos, Les Tri-Colores, The Red, White & Blue
New York	Amazin's, Amazing Mets, **METS**
Chicago	Basement Bruins (h), Bruins, Cubbies, **CUBS**, Northsiders, Wrigleys

WESTERN DIVISION

Los Angeles	Babes of Summer, **DODGERS**, Little Blue Wrecking Crew
Cincinnati	Big Red, The Big Red Machine, **REDS**, Rhinelanders
Atlanta	**BRAVES**
Houston	**ASTROS**
San Francisco	**GIANTS**, Jints
San Diego	**PADRES** (Pads), Dads, Fathers, (owner Ray) Kroc's Hamburgers, Washington Padres

1974 American League

EASTERN DIVISION

Baltimore	Big Bad Birds, Birds, **ORIOLES** (O's)
New York	Bronx Bombers, **YANKEES** (Yanks)
Boston	Beantowners, BoSox, Crimson Hose, Hub Hose, **RED SOX** (Sox)
Cleveland	**INDIANS**, The Lost Tribe, The Tribe, Wandering Tribe
Milwaukee	**BREWERS**, Brew Crew
Detroit	Bengals, Dull Claws, **TIGERS**

WESTERN DIVISION

Oakland	Angry Athletics, **ATHLETICS** (A's), Best from the West, Champagne and Baloney A's (Clark), Dynastic A's, Green & Gold, Rugged A's, Swinging Athletics
Texas	**RANGERS**
Minnesota	Minnesota Lumber Company, **TWINS**
Chicago	ChiSox, Comiskeys, Pale Hose, Southsiders, **WHITE SOX** (Sox)
Kansas City	**ROYALS**
California	**ANGELS**, Halos, Seraphs

1975 National League

EASTERN DIVISION

Pittsburgh	Buccaneers (Bucs), Buccos, Pittsburgh Lumber Company, **PIRATES**, Proud Pirates (Oleksak)
Philadelphia	Fightin' Phillies, **PHILLIES** (Phils)
New York	Amazin's, Amazing Mets, Left-field Mets, **METS**
St. Louis	**CARDINALS** (Cards), Redbirds
Chicago	Bruins, Cubbies, **CUBS**, Northsiders, Wrigleys
Montreal	**EXPOS**, Les Expos, Les Tri-Colores, Phase-Two Expos, The Red, White & Blue

WESTERN DIVISION

Cincinnati	Big Red, Big Red Machine, **REDS**, Rhinelanders, Sparky Anderson's Destroyers (Warren Wilbert)
Los Angeles	Babes of Summer, **DODGERS**, Little Blue Wrecking Crew
San Francisco	**GIANTS**, Jints
San Diego	**PADRES** (Pads), Dads, Fathers

Atlanta   **BRAVES**
Houston   **ASTROS**, Disastros, Lastros, Rainbows, Yellow 'Stros of Texas
Los Angeles   Babes of Summer, **DODGERS**, Little Blue Wrecking Crew

1975 American League
EASTERN DIVISION

Boston   Beantowners, BoSox, Crimson Hose, Hub Hose, Over-the-Wall Gang, **RED SOX** (Sox), Super Sox
Baltimore   Big Bad Birds, Birds, **ORIOLES** (O's)
New York   Bronx Bombers, **YANKEES** (Yanks)
Cleveland   **INDIANS**, The Lost Tribe (h), The Tribe, Wandering Tribe (h)
Milwaukee   **BREWERS**, Stop-Fast Brewers
Detroit   Bengals, Docile Tigers (Jim Hawkins), (Mgr. Ralph) Houk's Sad Sacks, **TIGERS**

WESTERN DIVISION

Oakland   **ATHLETICS** (A's), Green & Gold, Over-30 Gang
Kansas City   Bridesmaids, **ROYALS**
Texas   **RANGERS**
Minnesota   Minnesota Lumber Company, **TWINS**
Chicago   ChiSox, Comiskeys, Pale Hose, Southsiders, **WHITE SOX** (Sox)
California   **ANGELS**, Halos, Seraphs

1976 National League
EASTERN DIVISION

Philadelphia Fightin' Phillies, **PHILLIES** (Phils), Phutile Phillies (October)
Pittsburgh   Buccaneers (Bucs), Buccos, **PIRATES**
New York   Amazin's, Amazing Mets, **METS**, Miracle Mets
Chicago   Bruins, Cubbies. **CUBS**, Northsiders, Wrigleys
St. Louis   **CARDINALS** (Cards), Redbirds
Montreal   **EXPOS**, Fizz-Two Expos, Les Expos, Les Tri-Colores, The Red, White & Blue

WESTERN DIVISION

Cincinnati   Big Red, Big Red Machine, **REDS**, Rhinelanders, Sparky Anderson's Destroyers (Wilbert)
Los Angeles   Babes of Summer, **DODGERS**, Little Blue Wrecking Crew
Houston   **ASTROS**, Rainbows, Yellow 'Stros of Texas
San Francisco **GIANTS**, Jints
San Diego   **PADRES** (Pads), Dads, Fathers
Atlanta   **BRAVES**, Peach State Lemons (*The Sporting News*)

1976 American League
EASTERN DIVISION

New York   Bronx Bombers, Bronx Zoo (Sparky Lyle), Damnable Yankees (Moss Klein & Bill Madden), (owner George) Steinbrenner's Millionaires, **YANKEES** (Yanks)
Baltimore   Big Bad Birds, Birds, **ORIOLES** (O's)
Boston   Beantowners, BoSox, Crimson Hose, Crunch Bunch, Hub Hose, Over-the-Wall Gang, **RED SOX** (Sox)
Cleveland   **INDIANS**, The Lost Tribe (h), The Tribe, Wandering Tribe (h)

Detroit   Bengals, **TIGERS**
Milwaukee   **BREWERS**

WESTERN DIVISION

Kansas City   Blue Thunder, Men-in-Blue, **ROYALS**
Oakland   **ATHLETICS** (A's), Green & Gold
Minnesota   Minnesota Lumber Company, **TWINS**
California   **ANGELS**, Halos, Seraphs
Texas   **RANGERS**
Chicago   ChiSox, Comiskeys, Pale Hose, Pallid Hose, Southsiders, **WHITE SOX** (Sox)

1977 National League
EASTERN DIVISION

Philadelphia Fightin' Phillies, **PHILLIES** (Phils), Phutile Phillies (October)
Pittsburgh   Buccaneers (Bucs), Buccos, **PIRATES**
St. Louis   **CARDINALS** (Cards), Redbirds
Chicago   Bruins, Cubbies, **CUBS**, Grizzly Bears, Northsiders, Water-Beetles, Wrigleys
Montreal   **EXPOS**, Les Expos, Les Tri-Colores, The Red, White & Blue
New York   Amazin's, Amazing Mets, **METS**, Miracle Mets, Mutts

WESTERN DIVISION

Los Angeles   Babes of Summer, (Mgr. Tommy) Lasorda's Blue-bloods, **DODGERS**, Little Blue Wrecking Crew
Cincinnati   Big Red Machine, **REDS**, Rhinelanders
Houston   **ASTROS**, Rainbows, Yellow 'Stros of Texas
San Francisco **GIANTS**, Jints
San Diego   **PADRES** (Pads), Dads, Fathers
Atlanta   **BRAVES**, Peach State Lemons (*The Sporting News*)

1977 American League
EASTERN DIVISION

New York   The Best Team Money Could Buy, Bronx Bombers, Bronx Zoo (Lyle), Damnable Yankees (Klein & Madden), Quarreling Yankees, (Team owner George) Steinbrenner's Millionaires, **YANKEES** (Yanks)
Baltimore   Big Bad Birds, Birds, No-Name Orioles, **ORIOLES** (O's), Baseball's Rocky
Boston   Beantowners, BoSox, Crimson Hose, Crunch Bunch, Hub Hose, **RED SOX** (Sox)
Detroit   Bengals, **TIGERS**
Cleveland   **INDIANS**, The Lost Tribe (h), The Tribe, Wandering Tribe (h)
Milwaukee   **BREWERS**, Brew Crew
Toronto   **BLUE JAYS** (Jays)

WESTERN DIVISION

Kansas City   Blitz, Blue Thunder, Men-in-Blue, **ROYALS** (R's), Streakers
Texas   **RANGERS**
Chicago   ChiSox, Comiskeys, Little White Machine, Pale Hose, Southside Hitmen, Southsiders, **WHITE SOX** (Sox)
Minnesota   Minnesota Lumber Company, **TWINS**
California   **ANGELS**, Halos, Seraphs

Seattle   MARINERS, M's
Oakland   ATHLETICS (A's), F's, Triple-A's

1978 National League

EASTERN DIVISION

Philadelphia   Fightin' Phillies, PHILLIES (Phils), Phutile Phillies (October)
Pittsburgh   Buccaneers (Bucs), Buccos, PIRATES
Chicago   Bruins, Cubbies, CUBS, Northsiders, Wrigleys
Montreal   EXPOS, Les Expos, Les Tri-Colores, The Red, White & Blue
St. Louis   CARDINALS (Cards), Redbirds
New York   Amazin's, Amazing Mets, METS, Miracle Mets, Mutts

WESTERN DIVISION

Los Angeles   Babes of Summer, (Mgr. Tommy) Lasorda's Blue-bloods, DODGERS, Little Blue Wrecking Crew
Cincinnati   Big Red Machine, REDS, Rhinelanders
San Francisco   GIANTS, Jints
San Diego   PADRES (Pads), Dads, Fathers
Houston   ASTROS, Disastros, Rainbows, Yellow 'Stros of Texas
Atlanta   BRAVES

1978 American League

EASTERN DIVISION

New York   Bronx Bombers, Bronx Zoo (Lyle), October Men (Roger Kahn), Quarreling Yankees, (Team owner George) Steinbrenner's Millionaires, YANKEES (Yanks)
Boston   Beantowners, BoSox, Crimson Hose, Hub Hose, RED SOX (Sox)
Milwaukee   (Mgr. George Bamberger) Bambi's Bombers, BREW-ERS, Brew Crew, Wrecking Crew
Baltimore   Birds, ORIOLES (O's)
Detroit   Bengals, TIGERS
Cleveland   INDIANS, The Lost Tribe (h), The Tribe, Wandering Tribe (h)
Toronto   BLUE JAYS (Jays)

WESTERN DIVISION

Kansas City   Blue Thunder, Deja-Vu Royals (October), Men-in-Blue, ROYALS (R's)
California   ANGELS, Halos, Seraphs
Texas   RANGERS
Minnesota   Minnesota Lumber Company, TWINS
Chicago   ChiSox, Comiskeys, Pale Hose, Southsiders, WHITE SOX (Sox)
Oakland   ATHLETICS (A's), F's, Triple A's
Seattle   MARINERS, M's

1979 National League

EASTERN DIVISION

Pittsburgh   Buccaneers (Bucs), Buccos, PIRATES, Proud Pirates (Oleksak), We Are Family (Willie Stargell)
Montreal   EXPOS, Les Expos, Les Tri-Colores, The Red, White & Blue
St. Louis   CARDINALS (Cards), Redbirds
Philadelphia   PHILLIES (Phils)

Chicago   Bruins, Cubbies, CUBS, Northsiders, Wrigleys
New York   Amazin's, Amazing Mets, METS

WESTERN DIVISION

Cincinnati   Big Red Machine, REDS, Rhinelanders
Houston   ASTROS, First-Place Renters, Rainbows, Yellow 'Stros of Texas
Los Angeles   (Mgr. Tommy) Lasorda's Blue Bloods, DODGERS, Little Blue Wrecking Crew
San Francisco   GIANTS, Jints
San Diego   PADRES (Pads), Dads, Fathers
Atlanta   BRAVES

1979 American League

EASTERN DIVISION

Baltimore   Big Bad Birds, Birds, ORIOLES (O's)
Milwaukee   (Mgr. George Bamberger) Bambi's Bombers, BREW-ERS, Brew Crew
Boston   Beantowners, BoSox, Crimson Hose, Hub Hose, RED SOX (Sox)
New York   Bronx Bombers, (Team owner George) Steinbrenner's Millionaires, YANKEES (Yanks)
Detroit   Bengals, TIGERS
Cleveland   INDIANS, The Lost Tribe (h), The Tribe, Wandering Tribe (h)
Toronto   BLUE JAYS

WESTERN DIVISION

California   ANGELS, Cherubs, Cloud Nine Angels, Glitter Gang, Halos, Seraphs
Kansas City   Blue Thunder, Men-in-Blue, ROYALS
Texas   RANGERS
Minnesota   Minnesota Lumber Company, TWINS
Chicago   ChiSox, Comiskeys, Pale Hose, Southsiders, WHITE SOX (Sox)
Seattle   MARINERS, M's
Oakland   ATHLETICS (A's), F's, Triple-A's

1980 National League

EASTERN DIVISION

Philadelphia   Comeback Gang, Fightin' Phillies, PHILLIES (Phils), The Team That Wouldn't Die (Hal Bodley)
Montreal   EXPOS, Les Expos, Les Tri-Colores, The Red, White & Blue
Pittsburgh   Buccaneers (Bucs), Buccos, PIRATES
St. Louis   CARDINALS (Cards), Redbirds
New York   Amazin's, Amazing Mets, METS, Mutts
Chicago   Basement Bruins, Bruins, Cubbies, CUBS, North-siders, Wrigleys

WESTERN DIVISION

Houston   ASTROS ('Stros), (Mgr. Bill) Virdon's No-Names, The Orange, Rainbows, Yellow 'Stros of Texas
Los Angeles   (Mgr. Tommy) Lasorda's Bluebloods, DODGERS, Little Blue Wrecking Crew
Cincinnati   REDS, Rhinelanders
Atlanta   BRAVES
San Francisco   GIANTS
San Diego   PADRES (Pads), Dads, Fathers, (owner Ray) Kroc's Hamburgers

1980 American League
EASTERN DIVISION

New York	Bronx Bombers, (Team owner George) Steinbrenner's Millionaires, **YANKEES** (Yanks)
Baltimore	Birds, **ORIOLES** (O's)
Milwaukee	(Mgr. George Bamberger) Bambi's Bombers, **BREWERS**, Brew Crew
Boston	Beantowners, BoSox, Crimson Hose, Hub Hose, **RED SOX** (Sox)
Detroit	Bengals, **TIGERS**
Cleveland	**INDIANS**, The Lost Tribe (h), The Tribe, Wandering Tribe (h)
Toronto	**BLUE JAYS** (Jays)

WESTERN DIVISION

Kansas City	Boys in Blue, Middle America's Team, **ROYALS** (R's)
Oakland	**ATHLETICS** (A's)
Minnesota	**TWINS**, Twinkies
Texas	**RANGERS**
Chicago	ChiSox, Comiskeys, Pale Hose, Southsiders, **WHITE SOX** (Sox)
California	**ANGELS**, Halos, Seraphs
Seattle	**MARINERS**, M's

1981 National League
EASTERN DIVISION

Montreal	**EXPOS**, Les Expos, Les Tri-Colores, 'Spos, The Red, White & Blue
Philadelphia	Fightin' Phillies, **PHILLIES** (Phils), Pillies
St. Louis	**CARDINALS** (Cards), Redbirds
Pittsburgh	Buccaneers (Bucs), Buccos, **PIRATES**
New York	Amazin's, Amazing Mets, **METS**, Mutts
Chicago	Basement Bears (h), Bruins, Cubbies, **CUBS**, Hibernating Bears (h), Loveable Losers, Northsiders, Scrubs, Spiders, Wrigleys

WESTERN DIVISION

Los Angeles	Babes of Summer, (Mgr. Tommy) Lasorda's Bluebloods, **DODGERS**, Little Blue Wrecking Crew, The Rat-pack
Houston	**ASTROS** ('Stros), (Mgr. Bill Virdon's No-Names), Rainbows, Yellow Stro's of Texas
Cincinnati	Baseball's Best Team, **REDS**, Rhinelanders
San Francisco	**GIANTS**
Atlanta	**BRAVES**
San Diego	**PADRES** (Pads), Dads, Fathers, (owner Ray) Kroc's Hamburgers

1981 American League
EASTERN DIVISION

New York	Bronx Bombers, (Team owner George) Steinbrenner's Millionaires, **YANKEES** (Yanks)
Milwaukee	(Mgr. George Bamberger) Bambi's Bombers, **BREWERS**, Brew Crew
Baltimore	Birds, **ORIOLES** (O's)
Detroit	Bengals, **TIGERS**
Boston	Beantowners, BoSox, Crimson Hose, Hub Hose, **RED SOX** (Sox)
Cleveland	**INDIANS**, The Lost Tribe (h), The Tribe, Wandering Tribe (h)
Detroit	Bengals, **TIGERS**

WESTERN DIVISION

Oakland	**ATHLETICS** (A's), (Mgr. Billy Martin) Billy-Ball (style of play), Buds
Kansas City	Boys in Blue, Middle America's Team, **ROYALS** (R's)
Texas	**RANGERS**
Chicago	ChiSox, Comiskeys, Pale Hose, Southsiders, **WHITE SOX** (Sox)
California	**ANGELS**, Halos, Seraphs
Seattle	**MARINERS**, M's
Minnesota	**TWINS**, Twinkies

1982 National League
EASTERN DIVISION

St. Louis	**CARDINALS** (Cards), Consistent Cardinals, High-Flying Cardinals, Redbirds, Running Redbirds
Philadelphia	Fightin' Phillies, **PHILLIES** (Phils), Pillies
Montreal	**EXPOS**, Les Expos, Les Tri-Colores, The Red, White & Blue
Pittsburgh	Buccaneers (Bucs), Buccos, **PIRATES**
Chicago	Bruins, Cubbies, **CUBS**, Loveable Losers, Northsiders, Wrigleys
New York	Amazin's, Amazing Mets, **METS**, Mutts

WESTERN DIVISION

Atlanta	America's Team (Ted Turner), **BRAVES**
Los Angeles	(Mgr. Tommy) Lasorda's Bluebloods, **DODGERS**
San Francisco	**GIANTS**
San Diego	**PADRES** (Pads), Dads, Fathers
Houston	**ASTROS** ('Stros), Disastros, Rainbows, Yellow 'Stros of Texas
Cincinnati	Big Red Lemon, Red-Faced Reds, **REDS**, Rhinelanders

1982 American League
EASTERN DIVISION

Milwaukee	Beer-makers, **BREWERS**, Brew Crew, Mighty Brewers, True Blue Crew, (Mgr. Harvey Kuenn) Harvey's Wallbangers
Baltimore	Birds, **ORIOLES** (O's)
Boston	Beantowners, BoSox, Crimson Hose, Hub Hose, **RED SOX** (Sox)
Detroit	Bengals, **TIGERS**
New York	Bronx Bombers, **YANKEES** (Yanks)
Cleveland	**INDIANS**, The Lost Tribe (h), The Tribe, Wandering Tribe (h)
Toronto	**BLUE JAYS** (Jays)

WESTERN DIVISION

California	**ANGELS**, Glitter Gang, Halos, Seraphs
Kansas City	Boys in Blue, M*A*S*H Royals, Middle America's Team, **ROYALS** (R's)
Chicago	ChiSox, Comiskeys, Good News-Bad News Sox, Pale Hose, Southsiders, **WHITE SOX** (Sox)
Seattle	**MARINERS**, M's
Oakland	**ATHLETICS** (A's)
Texas	**RANGERS**
Minnesota	**TWINS**, Twinkies

1983 National League
EASTERN DIVISION

Philadelphia	Fightin' Phillies, **PHILLIES** (Phils), Wheeze Kids

Pittsburgh	Buccaneers (Bucs), Buccos, **PIRATES**
Montreal	**EXPOS**, Frustrated Expos, Les Expos, Les Tri-Colores, The Red, White & Blue
St. Louis	**CARDINALS** (Cards), Redbirds
Chicago	Basement Bears, Bruins, Cubbies, **CUBS**, Loveable Losers, Northsiders, Wrigleys
New York	Amazin's, Amazing Mets, **METS**, Mutts

WESTERN DIVISION

Los Angeles	(Mgr. Tommy) Lasorda's Bluebloods, **DODGERS**
Atlanta	**BRAVES**
Houston	**ASTROS** ('Stros), Rainbows, Yellow 'Stros of Texas
San Diego	**PADRES** (Pads), Dads, Fathers
San Francisco	**GIANTS**, Jints
Cincinnati	**REDS**, Rhinelanders

1983 American League
EASTERN DIVISION

Baltimore	Birds, Cry-Baby Orioles (October), High-Flying Orioles, **ORIOLES** (O's)
Detroit	Bengals, **TIGERS**
New York	Bronx Bombers, **YANKEES** (Yanks)
Toronto	**BLUE JAYS** (Jays), OK-OK Jays (John Robertson)
Milwaukee	**BREWERS**, Brew Crew
Boston	Beantowners, BoSox, Crimson Hose, Hub Hose, **RED SOX** (Sox)
Cleveland	Feather-Brains, Feather-Heads, **INDIANS**, The Lost Tribe (h), The Tribe, Wandering Tribe (h)

WESTERN DIVISION

Chicago	ChiSox, Comiskeys, Pale Hose, Southsiders, **WHITE SOX** (Sox), Winning Ugly White Sox (Doug Rader)
Kansas City	Blue Thunder (Steve Cameron), Boys in Blue, Middle America's Team, **ROYALS** (R's)
Texas	**RANGERS**
Oakland	**ATHLETICS** (A's)
California	**ANGELS**, Halos, Seraphs
Minnesota	**TWINS**, Twinkies
Seattle	**MARINERS** (M's)

1984 National League
EASTERN DIVISION

Chicago	America's Team, Bruins, Cubbies, **CUBS**, Northsiders, Wrigleys
New York	Amazin's, Amazing Mets, **METS**
St. Louis	**CARDINALS** (Cards), Redbirds
Philadelphia	**PHILLIES** (Phils)
Montreal	**EXPOS**, Les Expos, Les Tri-Colores, The Red, White & Blue
Pittsburgh	Buccaneers (Bucs), Buccos, **PIRATES**, Sunken Pirates (Charles Feeney)

WESTERN DIVISION

San Diego	Dads, Fathers, **PADRES** (Pads), (Mgr. Dick) Williams Men
Atlanta	**BRAVES**
Houston	**ASTROS** ('Stros), (Mgr. Bill Virdon's No-Names), Rainbows, Yellow 'Stros of Texas
Los Angeles	(Mgr. Tommy) Lasorda's Bluebloods, **DODGERS**
Cincinnati	**REDS**, Rhinelanders
San Francisco	**GIANTS**, Gnats

1984 American League
EASTERN DIVISION

Detroit	Bengals, Bless You Boys (slogan), Hungry Felines, Roaring Tigers, **TIGERS**
Toronto	**BLUE JAYS** (Jays), Blue Jays Rising (h)
New York	Bronx Bombers, **YANKEES** (Yanks)
Boston	Beantowners, BoSox, Crimson Hose, Hub Hose, **RED SOX** (Sox)
Baltimore	Birds, **ORIOLES** (O's)
Cleveland	**INDIANS**, The Lost Tribe (h), The Tribe, Wandering Tribe (h)
Milwaukee	**BREWERS**, Brew Crew

WESTERN DIVISION

Kansas City	Baseball's Most Successful Expansion Team (Tracy Ringolsby), Blue Thunder (Cameron), Boys in Blue, Gamers (Jim Sundberg), Middle America's Team, Missouri's Finest, Never Say Die Royals (Ringolsby), Royal Finishers (Alan Eskew), **ROYALS** (R's)
California	**ANGELS**, Halos, Seraphs
Chicago	ChiSox, Comiskeys, Pale Hose, Southsiders, **WHITE SOX** (Sox)
Minnesota	**TWINS**, Twinkies
Oakland	**ATHLETICS** (A's)
Seattle	**MARINERS** (M's)
Texas	**RANGERS**

1985 National League
EASTERN DIVISION

St. Louis	**CARDINALS** (Cards), High-Flying Cardinals, Jackrabbits, Racing Redbirds, Redbirds, Running Redbirds
New York	Amazin's, Amazing Mets, **METS**
Montreal	**EXPOS**, Les Expos, Les Tri-Colores, The Red, White & Blue
Chicago	Black and Blue Bears, Bruins, Bruins-in-Ruins, Cubbies, **CUBS**, Loveable Losers, Northsiders, Wrigleys
Philadelphia	Futile Phillies, **PHILLIES** (Phils)
Pittsburgh	Buccaneers (Bucs), Buccos, Mutineers, **PIRATES**, Sunken Pirates (Feeney)

WESTERN DIVISION

Los Angeles	Artful Dodgers, (Mgr. Tommy) Lasorda's Bluebloods, **DODGERS**
Cincinnati	**REDS**, Rhinelanders, (Mgr. Pete) Rose's Rosy Reds
Houston	**ASTROS** ('Stros), Mgr. Bill Virdon's No-Names, Rainbows, Yellow 'Stros of Texas
San Diego	**PADRES** (Pads), Dads, Fathers
Atlanta	**BRAVES**
San Francisco	**GIANTS**, Murphy's Law Giants, Pumpkins

1985 American League
EASTERN DIVISION

Toronto	**BLUE JAYS** (Jays), Canada's Team, Fungo Blues
New York	Bronx Bombers, **YANKEES** (Yanks)
Detroit	Bengals, **TIGERS**
Baltimore	Birds, **ORIOLES** (O's)
Boston	Beantowners, BoSox, Crimson Hose, Hub Hose, **RED SOX** (Sox)

Milwaukee   **BREWERS**, Brew Crew
Cleveland   Feather-Brains, Feather-Heads, **INDIANS**, The Lost Tribe (h), The Tribe, Wandering Tribe (h)

Western Division

Kansas City Blue Thunder, Boys in Blue, Middle America's Team, No-Quits (October), Relentless Royals (h), Re-markable Royals (h), Resilient Royals (Jeffrey Spi-vak), **ROYALS** (R's) Royal-finish Royals
California   **ANGELS**, Halos, Seraphs
Chicago   ChiSox, Comiskeys, Pale Hose, Southsiders, **WHITE SOX** (Sox)
Minnesota   **TWINS**, Twinkies
Oakland   **ATHLETICS** (A's)
Seattle   **MARINERS** (M's)
Texas   **RANGERS**

1986 National League
Eastern Division

New York   Amazin's, Amazing Mets, The Bad Guys (Jeff Pearl-man), Dominating Mets, Kings of Queens, Loco-motives, Methodical Mets (Tracy Ringolsby), **METS**, Miraculous Mets, The Other New York Team
Philadelphia **PHILLIES** (Phils)
St. Louis   **CARDINALS** (Cards), Redbirds
Montreal   **EXPOS**, Les Expos, Les Tri-Colores, The Red, White & Blue
Chicago   Bruins, Cubbies, **CUBS**, (Mgr. Dallas Green) Green Kids, Little Bears, Loveable Losers, Northsiders, Wrigleys
Pittsburgh   Buccaneers (Bucs), Buccos, **PIRATES**, Sunken Pirates (Feeney), Mutineers

Western Division

Houston   **ASTROS** ('Stros), Fast-Lane Astros, Mgr. Bill Virdon's No-Names, Rainbows Yellow 'Stros of Texas
Cincinnati   **REDS**, Rhinelanders
San Francisco **GIANTS**
San Diego   **PADRES** (Pads), Dads, Fathers
Los Angeles (Mgr. Tommy) Lasorda's Bluebloods, **DODGERS**
Atlanta   **BRAVES**, Peach State Lemons (*The Sporting News*)

1986 American League
Eastern Division

Boston   Beantowners, BoSox, Cubs of the American League (October), Crimson Hose, Hub Hose, Near Miss Sox (October), Red Hot Sox, **RED SOX** (Sox), Surprise Sox, Sweet Sox
New York   Bronx Bombers, The Other Team from New York, **YANKEES** (Yanks)
Detroit   Bengals, **TIGERS**
Toronto   **BLUE JAYS** (Jays)
Cleveland   (Mgr. Pat) Corrales' Cast-Offs, **INDIANS**, Misfits, Rejects, The Tribe
Milwaukee   **BREWERS**, Brew Crew
Baltimore   Birds, **ORIOLES** (O's)

Western Division

California   **ANGELS**, Cherubs, Halos, Last Chance Gang, Seraphs
Texas   **RANGERS**

Oakland   **ATHLETICS** (A's)
Kansas City Boys in Blue, **ROYALS** (R's)
Chicago   ChiSox, (General manager Ken) Harrelson's Circus, Comiskeys, Mismatched Sox, Pale Hose, Runless Hose, Southsiders, Strange Sox (Dan Van Dyck), Team Chaos, **WHITE SOX** (Sox)
Minnesota   **TWINS**, Twinkies
Seattle   **MARINERS** (M's)

1987 National League
Eastern Division

St. Louis   **CARDINALS** (Cards), High-Flying Cardinals, (Mgr. Whitey) Herzog's Greyhounds, Redbirds
New York   Amazin's, Amazing Mets, **METS**
Montreal   **EXPOS**, Expos Express, Les Expos, Les Tri-Colores, The Red, White & Blue
Philadelphia **PHILLIES** (Phils), Quick-change Phillies
Pittsburgh   Buccaneers (Bucs), Buccos, **PIRATES**
Chicago   Basement Bruins (h), Bruins, Cubbies, **CUBS**, Flubs, Gilligan Islanders (April), Loveable Losers (h), Northsiders, Smurfs, Wrigley Field Money Machine, Wrigleys

Western Division

San Francisco Bay Area Bombers, **GIANTS**, Stand-Tall Giants
Cincinnati   (Mgr. Pete) Rose's Bridesmaids, **REDS**, Rhinelanders
Houston   **ASTROS** ('Stros), Rainbows, Yellow 'Stros of Texas
Los Angeles (Mgr. Tommy) Lasorda's Bluebloods, **DODGERS**, Wait Till Next Year Dodgers
Atlanta   **BRAVES**, Peach State Lemons (*The Sporting News*)
San Diego   **PADRES** (Pads), Dads, Fathers, (owner Ray) Kroc's Hamburgers

1987 American League
Eastern Division

Detroit   Bengals, **TIGERS** Sleeping Tigers (October)
Toronto   Blow Jays, **BLUE JAYS** (Jays), Blue Jays Jazz, Dive Bombers, Sleeping Giants
Milwaukee   Black & Blues, **BREWERS**, Brew Crew, Grown-Up Brewers, Suds City Streakers Team Streak
New York   Bronx Bombers, (Team owner George) Steinbrenner's Amazin's, **YANKEES** (Yanks)
Boston   Beantowners, BoSox, Crimson Hose, Hub Hose, **RED SOX** (Sox)
Baltimore   Birds, Low-Flying Birds, **ORIOLES** (O's)
Cleveland   Erie Sensation, Feather-Brains, Feather-Heads, **INDIANS**, The Lost Tribe, The Tribe, Jeff Torborg's Tumblers, Wandering Tribe

Western Division

Minnesota   Jekyll & Hyde Twins, Lumber-jacks, Metrodome Mir-acle, Midwest Revival, Minnesota Lumber Com-pany, Turn-about Twins, **TWINS**, Twinkies
Kansas City Boys in Blue, **ROYALS** (R's)
Oakland   **ATHLETICS** (A's)
Seattle   **MARINERS** (M's)
Chicago   ChiSox, Comiskeys, Pale Hose, Southsiders, Swoon Sox (June), **WHITE SOX** (Sox)
California   **ANGELS**, Halos, Seraphs
Texas   **RANGERS**

1988 National League
EASTERN DIVISION

New York	Amazin's, Amazing Mets, **METS**
Pittsburgh	Buccaneers (Bucs), Buccos, **PIRATES**
Montreal	Derailed Express, **EXPOS**, Les Expos, Les Tri-Colores, The Red, White & Blue
Chicago	Bruins, Cubbies, **CUBS**, Loveable Losers, Northsiders, Smurfs, Wrigleys
St. Louis	**CARDINALS** (Cards), Redbirds
Philadelphia	Futile Phillies, **PHILLIES** (Phils), Quick-change Phillies

WESTERN DIVISION

Los Angeles	Artful Dodgers (Gordon Verell), Baseball's Top Dogs, (Mgr. Tommy) Lasorda's Bluebloods, **DODGERS**, Cinderella Dodgers, Destiny's Darlings, Over-achievers, Top Dogs, Unexpected Guests
Cincinnati	**REDS**, Rhinelanders, (Mgr. Pete) Rose's Runner-Ups
San Diego	**PADRES**
San Francisco	**GIANTS**
Houston	**ASTROS** ('Stros), Mgr. Bill Virdon's No-Names, Rainbows, Up & Down Astros, Yellow 'Stros of Texas
Atlanta	**BRAVES**, Futile Braves (Joe Strauss), Peach State Lemons (*The Sporting News*)

1988 American League
EASTERN DIVISION

Boston	Beantowners, BoSox, Crimson Hose, Hub Hose, (Mgr. Joe) Morgan's Magic Sox, Old Towne Team, **RED SOX** (Sox), Teasers
Detroit	Bengals, **TIGERS**
Milwaukee	**BREWERS**, Brew Crew, (Mgr. Tom) Treblehorn's Chargers, Mission Impossible Brewers
Toronto	**BLUE JAYS** (Jays), Boo Jays
New York	Bronx Bombers, **YANKEES** (Yanks)
Cleveland	**INDIANS**, The Lost Tribe (h), The Tribe, Wandering Tribe (h)
Baltimore	Birds, Low-Flying Birds, Murmurers' Row, Pigeons, **ORIOLES** (O's), Spaghetti-O's, UniO's, WhO's, Zeros, Zer'O's

WESTERN DIVISION

Oakland	Amazing A's, **ATHLETICS** (A's), Bay Area Bashers, Juggernauts, Rugged A's, Straight-A's (Tom Kurkijan), White Elephants
Minnesota	**TWINS**, Twinkies
Kansas City	Boys in Blue, **ROYALS** (R's)
California	**ANGELS**, Halos, Seraphs
Chicago	ChiSox, Comiskeys, (Mgr. Jim) Fregosi's Forlorns, Pale Hose, St. Petersburgh Sailors, St. Petersburg Sox, Southsiders, Vancouver White Sox, **WHITE SOX** (Sox)
Texas	**RANGERS**
Seattle	**MARINERS** (M's)

1989 National League
EASTERN DIVISION

Chicago	Boys of Zimmer, Bruins, Cubbies, **CUBS**, Good Chemistry Cubs, Northsiders, Wrigleys
New York	Amazin's, Amazing Mets, Fall-Short Mets, **METS**
St. Louis	**CARDINALS** (Cards), Redbirds
Montreal	Derailed Express, **EXPOS**, Les Expos, Les Tri-Colores, The Red, White & Blue
Pittsburgh	Buccaneers (Bucs), Buccos, **PIRATES**, Tumbling Pirates (John Mehno)
Philadelphia	Futile Phillies, **PHILLIES** (Phils), Quick-change Phils

WESTERN DIVISION

San Francisco	**GIANTS**, (Mgr. Roger) Craig's Humm-Babies, Stand-Tall Giants
San Diego	Agony & Ecstasy Padres, Dads, Fathers, **PADRES** (Pads)
Houston	**ASTROS** ('Stros), Mgr. Bill Virdon's No-Names, Rainbows, Yellow 'Stros of Texas
Los Angeles	(Mgr. Tommy) Lasorda's Bluebloods, **DODGERS**, Punchless Dodgers
Cincinnati	Distracted Reds, **REDS**, Rhinelanders
Atlanta	**BRAVES**, Futile Braves, Peach State Lemons (*The Sporting News*)

1989 American League
EASTERN DIVISION

Toronto	**BLUE JAYS** (Jays), Okay Blue Jays (Peter Bjarkman), Soaring Blue Jays (Neal McCarl)
Baltimore	Birds, Near-Miracle Orioles, **ORIOLES** (O's)
Boston	Beantowners, BoSox, Crimson Hose, Hub Hose, Old Towne Team, **RED SOX** (Sox)
Milwaukee	**BREWERS**, Brew Crew
New York	Bronx Bombers, (owner George) Steinbrenner's Sputterers, **YANKEES** (Yanks)
Cleveland	**INDIANS**, The Lost Tribe (h), The Tribe, Wandering Tribe (h)
Detroit	Bengals, Tame Tigers, **TIGERS**

WESTERN DIVISION

Oakland	**ATHLETICS** (A's), Bay Area Bashers, Juggernauts, Rugged A's, Straight-A's, White Elephants
Kansas City	Boys in Blue, **ROYALS** (R's)
California	**ANGELS**, Halos, Seraphs
Texas	**RANGERS**
Minnesota	**TWINS**, Twinkies, Yo-Yo Twins
Seattle	**MARINERS** (M's)
Chicago	ChiSox, Comiskeys, Pale Hose, Southsiders, **WHITE SOX** (Sox), Struggling Sox

1990 National League
EASTERN DIVISION

Pittsburgh	Buccaneers (Bucs), Buccos, **PIRATES**
New York	Amazin's, Amazing Mets, Fall-Short Mets, **METS**
Montreal	Derailed Express, **EXPOS**, Les Expos, Les Tri-Colores, The Red, White & Blue
Chicago	Bruins, Cubbies, **CUBS**, Loveable Losers, Northsiders, Wrigleys
Philadelphia	Futile Phillies, **PHILLIES** (Phils)
St. Louis	**CARDINALS** (Cards), Folding Cards (Rick Hummel), Redbirds

WESTERN DIVISION

Cincinnati	Distracted Reds, Little Red Machine, Red October Reds, **REDS**, Red October Reds, Wire-to-Wire Reds
Los Angeles	(Mgr. Tommy) Lasorda's Bluebloods, **DODGERS**

San Francisco GIANTS, Jints
Houston   ASTROS ('Stros), Rainbows, Yellow 'Stros of Texas
San Diego   PADRES (Pads), Dads, Fathers
Atlanta   BRAVES, Futile Braves, Peach State Lemons

1990 American League
EASTERN DIVISION

Boston   Beantowners, BoSox, Crimson Hose, Hub Hose, Il-
           logical Sox, Old Towne Team, RED SOX (Sox)
Toronto   BLUE JAYS (Jays), Soaring Blue Jays (McCarl)
Detroit   Bengals, TIGERS, Michigan's Team
Cleveland INDIANS, The Lost Tribe (h), The Tribe, Wandering
           Tribe (h)
Baltimore Birds, ORIOLES (O's)
Milwaukee BREWERS, Brew Crew
New York   Bronx Bombers, Bronx Bunnies, Bronx Bomb, YAN-
           KEES (Yanks), New York's Other Team, (Team
           owner George) Steinbrenner's Stutterers

WESTERN DIVISION

Oakland   ATHLETICS (A's), Bay Area Bashers, Juggernauts,
            Rugged A's, Straight-A's F's (October), White Ele-
            phants
Chicago   Black Sox, ChiSox, Comiskeys, Good Guys Who Wear
            Black, Pale Hose, Southsiders, WHITE SOX (Sox),
Texas   RANGERS, Wranglers (Ken Harrleson)
California ANGELS, Halos, Seraphs
Seattle   MARINERS (M's)
Kansas City Boys in Blue, ROYALS (R's)
Minnesota   TWINS, Twinkies

1991 National League
EASTERN DIVISION

Pittsburgh   Buccaneers (Bucs), Buccos, Killer Bees, PIRATES
St. Louis   CARDINALS (Cards), Redbirds
Chicago   Bruins, Cubbies, CUBS, Loveable Losers, Northsiders,
              Wrigleys
Philadelphia PHILLIES (Phils)
New York   Amazing Mets, Amazin's, METS
Montreal   Derailed Express, EXPOS, Les Expos, Les Tri-Colores,
              The Red, White & Blue

WESTERN DIVISION

Atlanta   BRAVES, Bravos (Ken Harrelson), Cinderella Braves
Los Angeles   (Mgr. Tommy) Lasorda's Bluebloods, DODGERS,
              Punchless Dodgers
San Diego   Agony & Ecstasy Padres, PADRES
San Francisco GIANTS, Jints
Cincinnati   Distracted Reds, REDS, Rhinelanders
Houston   ASTROS ('Stros), Disastros, Lastros. Rainbows, Yellow
              'Stros of Texas

1991 American League
EASTERN DIVISION

Toronto   BLUE JAYS (Jays), Canada's Team, Soaring Blue Jays
          (McCarl)
Boston   Beantowners, BoSox, Carmines (Ken Harrelson),
          Crimson Hose, Hub Hose, Old Towne Team,
          RED SOX (Sox)
Detroit   Bengals, TIGERS

Milwaukee BREWERS, Brew Crew
New York   Bronx Bombers, Bronx Bunnies, YANKEES (Yanks)
Baltimore Birds, Near-Miracle Orioles, ORIOLES (O's)
Cleveland Feather-Brains, Feather-Heads, INDIANS, The Lost
           Tribe (h), The Tribe, The Wandering Tribe (h)

WESTERN DIVISION

Minnesota   Armored Twins, Cinderella Twins, (Mgr. Tom) Kelly's
             Heroes, On-Top-of-the-World Twins, Team-of-
             Destiny Twins, TWINS, Twinkies, Worst-to-First
             Twins (h), Yo-Yo Twins
Chicago   ChiSox, Comiskeys, Good Guys Who Wear Black,
             Pale Hose, Southsiders, WHITE SOX (Sox)
Texas   RANGERS, Wranglers (Ken Harrelson)
Oakland   ATHLETICS (A's), Bay Area Bashers, Juggernauts,
             Rugged A's, Straight-A's, White Elephants
Seattle   MARINERS (M's)
Kansas City Boys in Blue, ROYALS (R's)
California   ANGELS, Halos, Seraphs

1992 National League
EASTERN DIVISION

Pittsburgh   Buccaneers (Bucs), Buccos, PIRATES
Montreal   Derailed Express, EXPOS, Les Expos, Les Tri-Colores,
              The Red, White & Blue
St. Louis   CARDINALS (Cards), Redbirds
Chicago   Bruins, Cubbies, CUBS, Northsiders, Wrigleys
New York   Amazin's, Amazing Mets, METS, Worst Team That
              Money Can Buy (Klapisch-Harper)
Philadelphia Futile Phillies, PHILLIES (Phils)

WESTERN DIVISION

Atlanta   Blessed Braves, BRAVES, Bravos
Cincinnati   Distracted Reds, REDS, Rhinelanders
San Diego   Agony & Ecstasy Padres, PADRES
Houston   ASTROS ('Stros)
San Francisco GIANTS, Jints
Los Angeles   (Mgr. Tommy) Lasorda's Bluebloods, DODGERS,
              Punchless Dodgers

1992 American League
EASTERN DIVISION

Toronto   BLUE JAYS (Jays), Soaring Blue Jays (McCarl)
Milwaukee BREWERS, Brew Crew
Baltimore Birds, Near-Miracle Orioles, ORIOLES (O's)
Cleveland INDIANS, The Lost Tribe (h), The Tribe, Wandering
          Tribe (h)
New York Bronx Bombers, Bronx Bunnies, YANKEES (Yanks)
Detroit   Bengals, TIGERS
Boston   Beantowners, BoSox, Carmines, Crimson Hose, Dead
          Sox, Hub Hose, Old Towne Team, RED SOX (Sox)

WESTERN DIVISION

Oakland   ATHLETICS (A's), White Elephants
Minnesota   TWINS, Twinkies
Chicago   ChiSox, Comiskeys, Good Guys Who Wear Black,
            Pale Hose, Southsiders, WHITE SOX (Sox)
Texas   RANGERS
California ANGELS, Halos, Seraphs
Kansas City Boys in Blue, ROYALS (R's)
Seattle   MARINERS (M's)

1993 National League
EASTERN DIVISION

Philadelphia	Broad Street Bellies, Comeback Gang, Fightin' Phillies, **PHILLIES** (Phils), Quick-change Phils, The Softball Team
Montreal	Derailed Express, **EXPOS**, Les Expos, Les Tri-Colores, The Red, White & Blue
St. Louis	**CARDINALS** (Cards), Redbirds
Chicago	Bruins, Cubbies, **CUBS**, Loveable Losers, Northsiders, Wrigleys
Pittsburgh	Buccaneers (Bucs), Buccos, **PIRATES**
Florida	The Fins, The Fish, Florida's Team, **MARLINS**
New York	Amazin's, Amazing Mets, Fall-Short Mets, **METS**

WESTERN DIVISION

Atlanta	**BRAVES**, Futile Braves, Peach State
San Francisco	**GIANTS**, Jints
Houston	**ASTROS** ('Stros)
Los Angeles	(Mgr. Tommy) Lasorda's Bluebloods, **DODGERS**, Punchless Dodgers
Cincinnati	Distracted Reds, **REDS**, Rhinelanders
Colorado	**ROCKIES**, Rocks, Rox
San Diego	**PADRES** (Pads), Dads, Fathers

1993 American League
EASTERN DIVISION

Toronto	**BLUE JAYS** (Jays), Soaring Blue Jays (MacCarl)
New York	Bronx Bombers, **YANKEES** (Yanks),
Baltimore	Birds, **ORIOLES** (O's)
Detroit	Bengals, **TIGERS**
Boston	Beantowners, BoSox, Crimson Hose, Dead Sox, Hub Hose, Old Towne Team, **RED SOX** (Sox)
Cleveland	**INDIANS**, The Lost Tribe (h), The Tribe, Wandering Tribe (h)
Milwaukee	**BREWERS**, Brew Crew

WESTERN DIVISION

Chicago	ChiSox, Comiskeys, Good Guys Who Wear Black, Pale Hose, Southsiders, **WHITE SOX** (Sox)
Texas	**RANGERS**
Kansas City	Boys in Blue, **ROYALS** (R's)
Seattle	**MARINERS** (M's)
California	**ANGELS**, Halos, Seraphs
Minnesota	**TWINS**, Twinkies
Oakland	**ATHLETICS** (A's), White Elephants

1994 National League
EASTERN DIVISION

Montreal	Derailed Express, **EXPOS**, Les Expos, Les Tri-Colores, The Red, White & Blue
Atlanta	**BRAVES**, Buffalo Bills of Baseball, Futile Braves, Peach State Lemons
New York	Amazin's, Amazing Mets, Fall-short Mets, **METS**
Philadelphia	Comeback Gang, **PHILLIES** (Phils), Quick-change Phils
Florida	The Fins, The Fish, **MARLINS**

CENTRAL DIVISION

Cincinnati	**REDS**, Red Legs, Rhinelanders
Houston	**ASTROS** ('Stros)

Pittsburgh	Buccaneers (Bucs), Buccos, **PIRATES**
St. Louis	**CARDINALS** (Cards), Redbirds
Chicago	Bruins, Cubbies, **CUBS**, Flubs, Loveable Losers, Northsiders, Wrigleys

WESTERN DIVISION

Los Angeles	(Mgr. Tommy) Lasorda's Bluebloods, **DODGERS**, Punchless Dodgers
San Francisco	**GIANTS**, Jints
Colorado	Blake Street Bombers, Blake Street Bullies, **ROCKIES**, Rocks, Rox
San Diego	Agony & Ecstasy Padres, Dads, Fathers, **PADRES** (Pads)

1994 American League
EASTERN DIVISION

New York	Bronx Bombers, **YANKEES** (Yanks)
Baltimore	Birds, Jurassic Park Orioles, **ORIOLES** (O's)
Toronto	**BLUE JAYS** (Jays), Soaring Blue Jays, Jays Blue
Boston	Beantowners, BoSox, Carmines (Harrelson), Crimson Hose, Dead Sox, Hub Hose, Old Towne Team, **RED SOX** (Sox)
Detroit	Bengals, Declawed Tigers, **TIGERS** Kitties

CENTRAL DIVISION

Chicago	ChiSox, Comiskeys, Good Guys Who Wear Black, Pale Hose, Southsiders, **WHITE SOX** (Sox), Good Guys Who Wear Black
Cleveland	**INDIANS**, The Tribe
Kansas City	Boys in Blue, **ROYALS** (R's)
Minnesota	**TWINS**, Twinkies
Milwaukee	**BREWERS**, Brew Crew

WESTERN DIVISION

Texas	Dangers, **RANGERS**, Strangers, Wranglers (Harrelson)
Oakland	**ATHLETICS** (A's), White Elephants
Seattle	**MARINERS** (M's)
California	**ANGELS**, Halos, Seraphs

1995 National League
EASTERN DIVISION

Atlanta	**BRAVES**, Pride of the South, Team of the 1990s (World Series ring)
New York	Amazin's, Amazing Mets, Fall-Short Mets, **METS**
Philadelphia	Comeback Gang, **PHILLIES** (Phils), Quick-change Phils
Florida	The Fins, The Fish, **MARLINS**
Montreal	**EXPOS**, Les Expos, Les Tri-Colores, The Red, White & Blue, Bon Voyage Expos

CENTRAL DIVISION

Cincinnati	**REDS**, Red Legs, Rhinelanders
Houston	**ASTROS** ('Stros), (Mgr. Terry) Collins' Grinders
Chicago	Bruins, Cubbies, **CUBS**, Loveable Losers, Northsiders, Wrigleys
St. Louis	**CARDINALS** (Cards), Redbirds
Pittsburgh	Buccaneers (Bucs), Buccos, **PIRATES**, Shipped-Out Bucs (Mike Donovan), Small Market Sailors (George King), The Working Men (Scott Tolley)

WESTERN DIVISION

Los Angeles	(Mgr. Tommy) Lasorda's Bluebloods, **DODGERS**, Punchless Dodgers Jigsaw Puzzle Dodgers
Colorado	Blake Street Bombers, Blake Street Bullies, **ROCKIES**, Rocks, Rox
San Diego	Agony & Ecstasy Padres, Dads, Fathers, **PADRES** (Pads)
San Francisco	**GIANTS**, Gnats

1995 American League

EASTERN DIVISION

Boston	Beantowners, BoSox, Carmines (Ken Harrelson), Crimson Hose, Hub Hose, Old Towne Team, **RED SOX** (Sox)
New York	Bronx Bombers, **YANKEES** (Yanks)
Baltimore	**ORIOLES** (O's)
Detroit	Bengals, Declawed Tigers, **TIGERS** Kitties
Toronto	Asterisk Blue Jays, **BLUE JAYS** (Jays), Jays Blue, Soaring Blue Jays

CENTRAL DIVISION

Cleveland	AL's Creme de la Creme, AL's Coronation Team, **INDIANS**, Joy Riders, Oakland Raiders of Baseball, Rampaging Indians, The Tribe
Kansas City	**ROYALS** Men in Blue
Chicago	ChiSox, Comiskeys, Pale Hose, Southsiders, **WHITE SOX** (Sox), Struggling Sox Revolving-Doors, Titanics
Milwaukee	**BREWERS**, Brew Crew
Minnesota	**TWINS**, Twinkies,

WESTERN DIVISION

Seattle	**MARINERS** (M's)
California	**ANGELS**, Halos, Seraphs
Texas	**RANGERS**, Strangers, Wranglers
Oakland	**ATHLETICS** (A's), Oakland F's, White Elephants

1996 National League

EASTERN DIVISION

Atlanta	**BRAVES**
Montreal	Bon Voyage Expos, Deja Vu Expos, **EXPOS**, Les Expos, Mirrors, Les Tri-Colores, The Red, White & Blue
Florida	The Fins, The Fish, **MARLINS**
New York	Amazin's, Amazing Mets, Fall-Short Mets, **METS**
Philadelphia	**PHILLIES** (Phils), Quick-change Phils

CENTRAL DIVISION

St. Louis	**CARDINALS** (Cards), Redbirds
Houston	**ASTROS** ('Stros), (Mgr. Terry) Collins' Grinders
Cincinnati	**REDS**, Red Legs, Rhinelanders
Chicago	Bruins, Cubbies, **CUBS**, Keystone Kubs, Loveable Losers, Northsiders, Wrigleys
Pittsburgh	Buccaneers (Bucs), Buccos, **PIRATES**, Sea Bandits (Mike Donovan), Small Market Sailors (King), Working Men (Tolley)

WESTERN DIVISION

| San Diego | Agony & Ecstasy Padres, Dads, Fathers, Missionaries, **PADRES** (Pads) |
| Los Angeles | (Mgr. Tommy) Lasorda's Bluebloods, **DODGERS**, Punchless Dodgers, Jigsaw Puzzle Dodgers |

| Colorado | Blake Street Bombers, Blake Street Bullies, **ROCKIES** Rocks, Rox |
| San Francisco | Bay Area Blues, **GIANTS**, Jints |

1996 American League

EASTERN DIVISION

New York	(Mgr Joe) Torre's Battlers, Bronx Bombers, **YANKEES** (Yanks), New-Look Yankees, Lovable Underdogs (Team owner George) Steinbrenner's Battlers
Baltimore	Birds, Near-Miracle Orioles, **ORIOLES** (O's)
Boston	Beantowners, BoSox, Crimson Hose, Hub Hose, Old Towne Team, **RED SOX** (Sox)
Toronto	**BLUE JAYS** (Jays), Soaring Blue Jays, Jays Blue
Detroit	Bengals, Declawed Tigers, Tabby Cats, **TIGERS**, Toothless Tabbies

CENTRAL DIVISION

Cleveland	**INDIANS**, The Tribe
Chicago	ChiSox, Comiskeys, Pale Hose, Southsiders, **WHITE SOX** (Sox)
Minnesota	**TWINS**, Twinkies
Milwaukee	**BREWERS**, Brew Crew
Kansas City	**ROYALS**, Men in Blue

WESTERN DIVISION

Texas	**RANGERS**, Wranglers (Harrelson)
Seattle	**MARINERS** (M's)
Oakland	**ATHLETICS** (A's), White Elephants
California	**ANGELS**, Halos, Mickey Mouse Club, Seraphs

1997 National League

EASTERN DIVISION

Atlanta	**BRAVES**
Florida	The Fins, The Fish, **MARLINS**, Men of Teal, Millionaire Marlins
New York	Amazin's, Amazing Mets, Fall-Short Mets, **METS**
Montreal	**EXPOS**, Les Expos, Les Tri-Colores, The Red, White & Blue
Philadelphia	**PHILLIES** (Phils)

CENTRAL DIVISION

Houston	**ASTROS** ('Stros)
Pittsburgh	Buccaneers (Bucs), Buccos, **PIRATES**, Small-Market Sailors (King), Steel City's Team, Working Men (Tolley)
Cincinnati	**REDS**, Red Legs, Rhinelanders
St. Louis	**CARDINALS** (Cards), Redbirds, Stand Pat Cards, Unshuffled Cards
Chicago	Bruins, Cubbies, **CUBS**, Flubs, Gilligan's Islanders, Loveable Losers, Northsiders, Team Tribune (Jay Marrioti), Wrigleys

WESTERN DIVISION

San Francisco	**GIANTS**, Jints
Los Angeles	Blues, **DODGERS**
Colorado	Black Street Bombers, Blake Street Bullies, **ROCKIES**, Rocks, Rox
San Diego	Agony & Ecstasy Padres, Dads, Fathers, Missionaries, **PADRES**

1997 American League

EASTERN DIVISION

Baltimore	Birds, **ORIOLES** (O's)
New York	Bronx Bombers, **YANKEES** (Yanks)
Detroit	Bengals, **TIGERS**, Changing-Stripes Tigers, Tiger-Lilies
Boston	Beantowners, BoSox, Crimson Hose, Hub Hose, Old Towne Team, **RED SOX** (Sox)
Toronto	Bluebirds, **BLUE JAYS** (Jays)

CENTRAL DIVISION

Cleveland	**INDIANS**, The Tribe
Chicago	ChiSox, Comiskeys, Light Sox, Pale Hose, Southsiders, **WHITE SOX** (Sox), White Flag White Sox, White Towels, Team Angst, Team Surrender, No Mas Sox Left-overs, Remnants, Team Reinsdorf, Baseball's Oakland Raiders
Milwaukee	**BREWERS**, Brew Crew, Budget Brewers (Bill Mazeroski), Termites (Frank Thomas)
Minnesota	**TWINS**, Twinkies
Kansas City	**ROYALS** Revamped Royals

WESTERN DIVISION

Seattle	**MARINERS** (M's)
Texas	**RANGERS**
Oakland	(Mgr. Art Howe) Art's Acorns, **ATHLETICS** (A's), White Elephants
California	**ANGELS**, Halos, Seraphs

1998 National League

EASTERN DIVISION

Atlanta	**BRAVES**
New York	Amazin's, Amazing Mets, Fall-Short Mets, **METS**
Philadelphia	Comeback Gang, **PHILLIES** (Phils)
Montreal	**EXPOS**, Les Expos, Les Tri-Colores, The Red, White & Blue
Florida	The Fins, Fire-sale Marlins, The Fish, **MARLINS**

CENTRAL DIVISION

Houston	**ASTROS** ('Stros)
Chicago	Bruins, Cubbies, **CUBS**, Northsiders, (Mgr. Jimmy) Riggleman's Rigglers, Wrigleys
St. Louis	**CARDINALS** (Cards), Redbirds
Cincinnati	**REDS**, Red Legs, Rhinelanders
Milwaukee	**BREWERS**, Brew Crew, Termites (Frank Thomas)
Pittsburgh	Buccaneers (Bucs), Buccos, **PIRATES**, Shipped-Out Bucs (Mike Lopreseti), Small Market Sailors (King)

WESTERN DIVISION

San Diego	Agony & Ecstasy Padres, Dads, Fathers, Missionaries, **PADRES**
San Francisco	**GIANTS**, Jints
Los Angeles	**DODGERS**, Punchless Dodgers
Colorado	Blake Street Bombers, Blake Street Bullies, **ROCKIES**, Rocks, Rox
Arizona	**DIAMONDBACKS** (D-Backs)

1998 American League

EASTERN DIVISION

New York	Bronx Bombers, (owner George) Steinbrenner's Warriors, **YANKEES** (Yanks)
Boston	Beantowners, BoSox, Crimson Hose, Hub Hose, Old Towne Team, **RED SOX** (Sox)
Toronto	**BLUE JAYS** (Jays)
Baltimore	Birds, **ORIOLES** (O's)
Tampa Bay	**DEVIL RAYS** (Rays)

CENTRAL DIVISION

Cleveland	**INDIANS**, The Tribe
Chicago	ChiSox, Comiskeys, Pale Hose, Southsiders, **WHITE SOX** (Sox)
Kansas City	Men in Blue, **ROYALS**
Minnesota	**TWINS**, Twinkies
Detroit	Bengals, Declawed Tigers, **TIGERS**

WESTERN DIVISION

Texas	**RANGERS**, Wranglers (Harrelson)
Anaheim	**ANGELS**, Halos, Seraphs
Seattle	**MARINERS** (M's)
Oakland	**ATHLETICS** (A's), Oakland F's, White Elephants

1999 National League

EASTERN DIVISION

Atlanta	**BRAVES**
New York	Amazin's, Amazing Mets, Fall-Short Mets, **METS**
Philadelphia	**PHILLIES** (Phils)
Montreal	**EXPOS**, Les Expos, Les Tri-Colores, The Red, White & Blue
Florida	The Fins, The Fish, **MARLINS**

CENTRAL DIVISION

Houston	**ASTROS** ('Stros)
Cincinnati	**REDS**, Red Legs, Rhinelanders, Upstart Reds
Pittsburgh	Buccaneers (Bucs), Buccos, **PIRATES**, Shipped Out Bucs (Lopreseti), Small Market Sailors (King)
Chicago	Bruins, Cubbies, **CUBS**, Cubs, Northsiders, Wrigleys
St. Louis	**CARDINALS** (Cards), Redbirds
Milwaukee	**BREWERS**, Brew Crew

WESTERN DIVISION

Arizona	**DIAMONDBACKS** (D-Backs)
San Francisco	**GIANTS**, Jints
Los Angeles	**DODGERS**, Punchless Dodgers
San Diego	Agony & Ecstasy Padres, Dads, Fathers, Missionaries, **PADRES**
Colorado	Blake Street Bombers, Blake Street Bullies, **ROCKIES**, Rocks, Rox

1999 American League

EASTERN DIVISION

New York	Bronx Bombers, **YANKEES** (Yanks), Team of The Century
Boston	Beantowners, BoSox, Crimson Hose, Hub Hose, Old Towne Team, Overachievers, **RED SOX** (Sox)
Toronto	**BLUE JAYS** (Jays)
Baltimore	Birds, Near-Miracle Orioles, **ORIOLES** (O's)
Tampa Bay	**DEVIL RAYS** (Rays)

CENTRAL DIVISION

Cleveland	**INDIANS**, The Tribe
Chicago	ChiSox, Comiskeys, The Kids Can Play (slogan), Pale Hose, Southsiders, **WHITE SOX** (Sox)

Detroit	Bengals, **TIGERS**
Kansas	City Bulls, **ROYALS**
Minnesota	**TWINS**, Twinkies

WESTERN DIVISION

Texas	**RANGERS**, Wranglers (Harrelson)
Oakland	**ATHLETICS** (A's), White Elephants
Seattle	**MARINERS** (M's)
Anaheim	**ANGELS**, Halos, Seraphs

2000 National League
EASTERN DIVISION

Atlanta	**BRAVES**, Bravos
New York	Amazin's, Amazing Mets, **METS**
Florida	The Fins, The Fish, **MARLINS**
Montreal	Derailed Express, **EXPOS**, Les Expos, Les Tri-Colores, The Red, White & Blue
Philadelphia	**PHILLIES** (Phils)

CENTRAL DIVISION

St. Louis	**CARDINALS** (Cards), Redbirds
Cincinnati	**REDS**, Red Legs, Rhinelanders
Milwaukee	**BREWERS**, Brew Crew
Houston	Disastros, **ASTROS** ('Stros)
Pittsburgh	Buccaneers (Bucs), Buccos, **PIRATES**
Chicago	Basement Bears, Bruins, Cubbies, **CUBS**, Flubs, Loveable Losers, Northsiders, Wrigleys

WESTERN DIVISION

San Francisco	Barry Bonds & Company, **GIANTS**, (Mgr. Dusty) Baker's G-Men, Jints, Los Gigantes, Orange & Black, Orange Nation
Los Angeles	Bluebloods, Blues, **DODGERS**
Arizona	**DIAMONDBACKS** (D-Backs), Snakes
Colorado	Blake Street Bombers, Blake Street Bullies, **ROCKIES**, Rocks, Rox
San Diego	**PADRES** (Pads), Dads, Fathers, Missionaries

2000 American League
EASTERN DIVISION

New York	Bronx Bombers, **YANKEES** (Yanks)
Boston	Beantowners, BoSox, Carmines, Crimson Hose, Hub Hose, Old Towne Team, **RED SOX** (Sox), Sawks
Toronto	**BLUE JAYS** (Jays), Blue Ox
Baltimore	Birds, **ORIOLES** (O's)
Tampa Bay	**DEVIL RAYS** (Rays)

CENTRAL DIVISION

Chicago	ChiSox, Comiskeys, Cream of the American League (David & Michael Neft and Richard M. Cohen), Go-Go-Sox, The MOB, Monsters of Baseball, Pale Hose, Pros (Joe Torre), Southside Hitmen, Southsiders, White Hot Sox, **WHITE SOX** (Sox)
Cleveland	**INDIANS**, The Tribe
Detroit	Bengals, Kitties, **TIGERS**
Kansas City	Men in Blue, **ROYALS**
Minnesota	**TWINS**, Twinkies

WESTERN DIVISION

Oakland	**ATHLETICS** (A's), White Elephants
Seattle	**MARINERS** (M's)
Texas	**RANGERS**, Wranglers
Anaheim	**ANGELS**, Halos, Los Angelitos, Seraphs

2001 National League
EASTERN DIVISION

Atlanta	**BRAVES**, Bravos
Philadelphia	**PHILLIES** (Phils)
New York	Amazin's, Amazing Mets, **METS**
Florida	The Fins, The Fish, **MARLINS**
Montreal	Bon Voyage Expos, **EXPOS**, Les Expos, Les Tri-Colores, The Red, White & Blue

CENTRAL DIVISION

Houston	**ASTROS** ('Stros), Yellow 'Stros of Texas
St. Louis	**CARDINALS** (Cards), Redbirds
Chicago	Bruins, Cubbies, **CUBS**, Loveable Losers, Northsiders, Wrigleys
Milwaukee	**BREWERS**, Brew Crew
Cincinnati	**REDS**, Red Legs, Rhinelanders
Pittsburgh	Buccaneers (Bucs), Buccos, **PIRATES**, Shipped Out Bucs (Lopreseti), Small Market Sailors (King)

WESTERN DIVISION

Arizona	**DIAMONDBACKS** (D-Backs), Snakes, Snazzy Snakes
San Francisco	Barry Bonds & Company, **GIANTS**, G-Men, Jints, Los Gigantes, Orange & Black, Orange Nation
Los Angeles	Bluebloods, **DODGERS**
San Diego	**PADRES** (Pads), Dads, Fathers, Missionaries
Colorado	**ROCKIES**, Rocks, Rox

2001 American League
EASTERN DIVISION

New York	Bronx Bombers, **YANKEES** (Yanks)
Boston	Beantowners, BoSox, Crimson Hose, Hub Hose, Old Towne Team, **RED SOX** (Sox)
Toronto	**BLUE JAYS** (Jays)
Baltimore	Birds, **ORIOLES** (O's)
Tampa Bay	**DEVIL RAYS** (Rays)

CENTRAL DIVISION

Cleveland	**INDIANS**, The Tribe
Minnesota	**TWINS**, Twinkies
Chicago	ChiSox, Comiskeys, Pale Hose, Southsiders, **WHITE SOX** (Sox)
Detroit	Bengals, Declawed Tigers, Kitties, **TIGERS**
Kansas City	Men in Blue, Rock-bottom Royals, **ROYALS**

WESTERN DIVISION

Seattle	**MARINERS** (M's)
Oakland	**ATHLETICS** (A's), White Elephants
Anaheim	**ANGELS**, Halos, Los Angelitos, Seraphs
Texas	**RANGERS**, Wranglers

2002 National League
EASTERN DIVISION

Atlanta	**BRAVES**, Bravos
Montreal	**EXPOS**, Les Expos, Les Tri-Colores, The Red, White & Blue
Philadelphia	**PHILLIES** (Phils)
Florida	The Fins, The Fish, **MARLINS**
New York	Amazin's, Amazing Mets, **METS**

CENTRAL DIVISION

St. Louis	**CARDINALS** (Cards), Redbirds
Houston	**ASTROS** ('Stros)

Cincinnati   **REDS**, Red Legs, Rhinelanders
Pittsburgh   Buccaneers (Bucs), Buccos, **PIRATES**
Chicago   Bruins, C.U.B.S. (Completely Useless by September), Cubbies, **CUBS**, Loveable Losers, Northsiders, Wrigleys
Milwaukee   **BREWERS**, Brew Crew, Traders

Western Division

Arizona   **DIAMONDBACKS** (D-Backs), Snakes
San Francisco   Barry Bonds & Company, **GIANTS**, G-Men, Jints, Los Gigantes, Orange & Black, Orange Nation
Los Angeles   Bluebloods, **DODGERS**
Colorado   **ROCKIES**, Rocks, Rox
San Diego   **PADRES** (Pads), Dads, Fathers, Missionaries

2002 American League
Eastern Division

New York   Bronx Bombers, Evil Empire (Larry Luchino), **YANKEES** (Yanks)
Boston   Beantowners, BoSox, Crimson Hose, Hub Hose, Old Towne Team, **RED SOX** (Sox)
Toronto   **BLUE JAYS** (Jays)
Baltimore   Birds, **ORIOLES** (O's)
Tampa Bay   **DEVIL RAYS** (Rays)

Central Division

Minnesota   **TWINS**, Twinkies, Yo-Yo Twins
Chicago   ChiSox, Comiskeys, Pale Hose, Southsiders, **WHITE SOX** (Sox), Struggling Sox
Cleveland   **INDIANS**, The Tribe
Kansas City   **ROYALS**
Detroit   Bengals, Declawed Tigers, **TIGERS**

Western Division

Oakland   **ATHLETICS** (A's), White Elephants
Anaheim   **ANGELS**, Halos, Seraphs, Wings
Seattle   **MARINERS** (M's)
Texas   **RANGERS**

2003 National League
Eastern Division

Atlanta   **BRAVES**, Bravos
Florida   The Fins, The Fish, **MARLINS**, (Manager) Jack McKeon's Fighting Warriors.
Philadelphia   **PHILLIES** (Phils)
Montreal   **EXPOS**, Les Expos, Les Tri-Colores, The Red, White & Blue
New York   Amazin's, Amazing Mets, **METS**

Central Division

Chicago   Bruins, Cubbies, **CUBS**, Loveable Losers, Northsiders, Wrigleys
Houston   **ASTROS** ('Stros)
St. Louis   **CARDINALS** (Cards), Redbirds
Pittsburgh   Buccaneers (Bucs), Buccos, **PIRATES**
Cincinnati   **REDS**, Red Legs, Rhinelanders
Milwaukee   **BREWERS**, Brew Crew, Traders

Western Division

San Francisco   Barry Bonds & Company, **GIANTS**, G-Men, Jints, Los Gigantes, Orange & Black, Orange Nation
Los Angeles   Bluebloods, **DODGERS**

Arizona   **DIAMONDBACKS** (D-Backs), Snakes
Colorado   **ROCKIES**, Rocks, Rox
San Diego   **PADRES** (Pads), Dads, Fathers, Missionaries

2003 American League
Eastern Division

New York   Bronx Bombers, **YANKEES** (Yanks)
Boston   Beantowners, BoSox, Crimson Hose, Hub Hose, Old Towne Team, **RED SOX** (Sox)
Toronto   **BLUE JAYS** (Jays)
Baltimore   Birds, **ORIOLES** (O's)
Tampa Bay   **DEVIL RAYS** (Rays)

Central Division

Minnesota   **TWINS**, Twinkies
Chicago   ChiSox, Pale Hose, Southsiders, **WHITE SOX** (Sox)
Kansas City   Men in Blue, **ROYALS**
Cleveland   **INDIANS**, The Tribe
Detroit   Bengals, Declawed Tigers, Motor City Kitties, **TIGERS**

Western Division

Oakland   **ATHLETICS** (A's), White Elephants
Seattle   **MARINERS** (M's)
Anaheim   **ANGELS**, Halos, Seraphs
Texas   **RANGERS**, Wranglers (Harrelson)

2004 National League
Eastern Division

Atlanta   **BRAVES**, Bravos
Philadelphia   **PHILLIES** (Phils)
Florida   The Fins, The Fish, **MARLINS**
New York   Amazin's, Amazing Mets, **METS**
Montreal   **EXPOS**, Les Expos, Les Tri-Colores, The Red, White & Blue

Central Division

St. Louis   **CARDINALS** (Cards), Redbirds
Houston   **ASTROS** ('Stros)
Chicago   Bruins, Cubbies, **CUBS**, Loveable Losers, Northsiders, Wrigleys
Cincinnati   **REDS**, Red Legs, Rhinelanders
Pittsburgh   Buccaneers (Bucs), Buccos, **PIRATES**
Milwaukee   **BREWERS**, Brew Crew, Traders

Western Division

Los Angeles   Bluebloods, **DODGERS**
San Francisco   Barry Bonds & Company, **GIANTS**, G-Men, Los Gigantes, Orange & Black, Orange Nation
San Diego   **PADRES** (Pads), Dads, Fathers, Missionaries
Colorado   **ROCKIES**, Rocks, Rox
Arizona   **DIAMONDBACKS** (D-Backs)

2004 American League
Eastern Division

New York   Bronx Bombers, **YANKEES** (Yanks), (Team owner George) Steinbrenner's Stutterers
Boston   Beantowners, BoSox, Crimson Hose, Hub Hose, Idiots (Johnny Damon), Old Towne Team, **RED SOX** (Sox)
Baltimore   Birds, **ORIOLES** (O's)
Tampa Bay   **DEVIL RAYS** (Rays)
Toronto   **BLUE JAYS** (Jays)

CENTRAL DIVISION

Minnesota	**TWINS**, Twinkies
Chicago	ChiSox, Pale Hose, Southsiders, **WHITE SOX** (Sox)
Cleveland	**INDIANS**, The Tribe
Detroit	Bengals, Kitties, Tabbies. **TIGERS**
Kansas City	Men in Blue, Rock-bottom Royals, **ROYALS**

WESTERN DIVISION

Anaheim	**ANGELS**, Halos, Seraphs
Oakland	**ATHLETICS** (A's), White Elephants
Texas	**RANGERS**, Wranglers (Harrelson)
Seattle	**MARINERS** (M's)

2005 National League
EASTERN DIVISION

Atlanta	Baby Braves, **BRAVES**, Bravos
Philadelphia	**PHILLIES** (Phils)
Florida	The Fins, The Fish, **MARLINS**
New York	Amazin's, Amazing Mets, Los Mets, **METS**
Washington	Nasty Nats, **NATIONALS** (Nats)

CENTRAL DIVISION

St. Louis	**CARDINALS** (Cards), Redbirds
Houston	**ASTROS** ('Stros)
Milwaukee	**BREWERS**, Brew Crew, Youngen's
Chicago	Bruins, Cubbies, **CUBS**, Loveable Losers, Northsiders, Wrigleys
Pittsburgh	Buccaneers (Bucs), Buccos, **PIRATES**
Cincinnati	**REDS**, Red Legs, Rhinelanders

WESTERN DIVISION

Arizona	**DIAMONDBACKS** (D-Backs)
San Francisco	Barry Bonds & Company, **GIANTS**, G-Men, Los Gigantes, Orange & Black
Los Angeles	Azul, Bluebloods, **DODGERS**, Los Doyers
San Diego	**PADRES** (Pads), Dads, Fathers, Missionaries
Colorado	**ROCKIES**, Rocks, Rox, Todd and the Toddlers

2005 American League
EASTERN DIVISION

New York	Bronx Bombers, Emperors (Mike Vaccaro), **YANKEES** (Yanks)
Boston	Beantowners, BoSox, Boys of Summer (Chris Snow), Crimson Hose, Hub Hose, Old Towne Team, **RED SOX** (Sox)
Toronto	**BLUE JAYS** (Jays)
Baltimore	Birds, **ORIOLES** (O's)
Tampa Bay	**DEVIL RAYS** (Rays)

CENTRAL DIVISION

Chicago	ChiSox, Pale Hose, Southsiders, **WHITE SOX** (Sox), Wizards of Ozzie
Cleveland	**INDIANS**, The Tribe
Minnesota	**TWINS**, Twinkies
Detroit	Bengals, Kitties, Tabbies, **TIGERS**, Tiggs
Kansas City	Men in Blue, Rock-bottom Royals, **ROYALS**

WESTERN DIVISION

Anaheim	**ANGELS**, Halos, Los Angeles Angels of Orange County of California of the United States of America of the Northern Hemisphere of the Planet Earth of the Solar System of the Milky Way Galaxy of the Universe, Seraphs
Oakland	**ATHLETICS** (A's), White Elephants
Texas	Lamers, **RANGERS**, Wranglers (Harrelson)
Seattle	**MARINERS** (M's)

2006 National League
EASTERN DIVISION

New York	Amazin's, Amazing Mets, Los Mets, **METS**
Philadelphia	**PHILLIES** (Phils)
Atlanta	**BRAVES**, Bravos
Florida	The Fins, The Fish, **MARLINS**
Washington	**NATIONALS** (Nats)

CENTRAL DIVISION

St. Louis	**CARDINALS** (Cards), Redbirds
Houston	**ASTROS** ('Stros)
Cincinnati	**REDS**, Red Legs, Rhinelanders
Milwaukee	**BREWERS**, Brew Crew, Cerveceros
Pittsburgh	Buccaneers (Bucs), Buccos, **PIRATES**
Chicago	Basement Bears, Bruins, Cubbies, **CUBS**, Flubs, Loveable Losers, Northsiders, Wrigleys

WESTERN DIVISION

San Diego	**PADRES** (Pads), Dads, Fathers, Missionaries, Worst Division Winner Ever
Los Angeles	Azul, Bluebloods, **DODGERS**, Los Doyers
San Francisco	Barry Bonds & Company, **GIANTS**, Gnats, Jints
Arizona	**DIAMONDBACKS** (D-Backs), Snakes
Colorado	**ROCKIES**, Rocks, Rox, Todd and the Toddlers

2006 American League
EASTERN DIVISION

New York	Bronx Bombers, **YANKEES** (Yanks)
Toronto	**BLUE JAYS** (Jays)
Boston	Beantowners, BoSox, Crimson Hose, Hub Hose, Old Towne Team, **RED SOX** (Sox)
Baltimore	Birds, **ORIOLES** (O's)
Tampa Bay	**DEVIL RAYS** (Rays)

CENTRAL DIVISION

Minnesota	**TWINS**, Twinkies
Detroit	Bengals, Team of Destiny, **TIGERS**
Chicago	ChiSox, Pale Hose, Southsiders, **WHITE SOX** (Sox), Struggling Sox
Cleveland	**INDIANS**, The Tribe
Kansas City	Men in Blue, Rock-bottom Royals, **ROYALS**

WESTERN DIVISION

Oakland	**ATHLETICS** (A's), White Elephants
Anaheim	**ANGELS**, Halos, Seraphs
Texas	**RANGERS**, Wranglers (Harrelson)
Seattle	**MARINERS** (M's)

2007 National League
EASTERN DIVISION

Philadelphia	**PHILLIES** (Phils)
New York	Amazin's, Amazing Mets, Meltdown Melts, **METS**
Atlanta	**BRAVES**, Bravos
Washington	**NATIONALS** (Nats)
Florida	The Fins, The Fish, **MARLINS**

Colorado	**ROCKIES**, Rocks, Rox
San Francisco	**GIANTS**, Gnats, Jints
San Diego	**PADRES** (Pads), Dads, Fathers, Missionaries

CENTRAL DIVISION

Chicago	Bruins, Cubbies, **CUBS**, Loveable Losers, Northsiders, Wrigleys
Milwaukee	**BREWERS**, Brew Crew, Cerveceros
St. Louis	**CARDINALS** (Cards), Redbirds
Houston	**ASTROS** ('Stros)
Cincinnati	**REDS**, Red Legs, Rhinelanders
Pittsburgh	Buccaneers (Bucs), Buccos, **PIRATES**, Shipped Out Bucs (Lopreseti), Small Market Sailors (Kings)

WESTERN DIVISION

Arizona	**DIAMONDBACKS** (D-Backs)
Colorado	**ROCKIES**, Rocks, Rocktober (slogan), Rox
San Diego	**PADRES** (Pads), Dads, Fathers, Missionaries
Los Angeles	Azul, Bluebloods, **DODGERS**, Los Doyers
San Francisco	**GIANTS**, Gnats, Jints

2007 American League

EASTERN DIVISION

Boston	Beantowners, BoSox, Carmines, Crimson Hose, Hub Hose, Old Towne Team, **RED SOX** (Sox)
New York	Bankees, Bronx Bombers, **YANKEES** (Yanks)
Toronto	**BLUE JAYS** (Jays)
Baltimore	Birds, **ORIOLES** (O's)
Tampa Bay	**DEVIL RAYS** (Rays)

CENTRAL DIVISION

Cleveland	**INDIANS**, The Tribe
Detroit	Bengals, **TIGERS**
Minnesota	**TWINS**, Twinkies
Chicago	ChiSox, Pale Hose, Southsiders, **WHITE SOX** (Sox)
Kansas City	Men in Blue, Rock-bottom Royals, **ROYALS**

WESTERN DIVISION

Los Angeles	**ANGELS**, Halos, Seraphs
Seattle	**MARINERS** (M's)
Texas	**RANGERS**, Wranglers (Harrelson)
Oakland	**ATHLETICS** (A's), Un-athletics, White Elephants

2008 National League

EASTERN DIVISION

Philadelphia	Good, Bad & Ugly Phillies (Todd Zolecki), **PHILLIES** (Phils)
New York	Amazin's, Amazing Mets, Meltdown Melts, **METS**
Florida	The Fins, The Fish, **MARLINS**
Atlanta	**BRAVES**, Bravos
Washington	**NATIONALS** (Nats)

CENTRAL DIVISION

Chicago	Bruins, Cubbies, **CUBS**, Loveable Losers, Northsiders, Wrigleys
Milwaukee	**BREWERS**, Brew Crew, Brewhas (ESPN)
Houston	**ASTROS** ('Stros)
St. Louis	**CARDINALS** (Cards), Redbirds
Cincinnati	**REDS**, Red Legs, Rhinelanders
Pittsburgh	Buccaneers (Bucs), Buccos, **PIRATES**, Shipped Out Bucs (Lopreseti), Small Market Sailors (King)

WESTERN DIVISION

Los Angeles	Azul, Bluebloods, **DODGERS**, Los Doyers
Arizona	**DIAMONDBACKS** (D-Backs)

2008 American League

EASTERN DIVISION

Tampa Bay	**DEVIL RAYS** (Rays)
Boston	Beantowners, BoSox, Carmines, Crimson Hose, Hub Hose, Old Towne Team, **RED SOX** (Sox)
New York	Bronx Bombers, **YANKEES** (Yanks)
Toronto	**BLUE JAYS** (Jays)
Baltimore	Birds, **ORIOLES** (O's)

CENTRAL DIVISION

Chicago	ChiSox, Pale Hose, Southsiders, **WHITE SOX** (Sox)
Minnesota	Piranhas (Ozzie Guillen), **TWINS**, Twinkies
Cleveland	**INDIANS**, The Tribe
Kansas City	Men in Blue, **ROYALS**
Detroit	Bengals, Declawed Tigers, **TIGERS**

WESTERN DIVISION

Los Angeles	**ANGELS**, Halos, Seraphs
Texas	**RANGERS**, Wranglers (Harrelson)
Oakland	**ATHLETICS** (A's), Un-athletics, White Elephants
Seattle	**MARINERS** (M's)

2009 National League

EASTERN DIVISION

Philadelphia	**PHILLIES** (Phils)
Florida	The Fins, The Fish, **MARLINS**
Atlanta	**BRAVES**, Bravos
New York	**METS**, Amazin's, Amazing Mets
Washington	**NATIONALS** (Nats)

CENTRAL DIVISION

St. Louis	**CARDINALS** (Cards), Dealing Cards, Redbirds
Chicago	Bruins, Cubbies, **CUBS**, Hibernating Cubs, Loveable Losers, Northsiders, Wrigleys
Milwaukee	**BREWERS**, Brew Crew, Milwaukee's Worst
Cincinnati	**REDS**, Red Legs, Rhinelanders
Houston	**ASTROS** ('Stros)
Pittsburgh	Buccaneers (Bucs), Buccos, **PIRATES**, Shipped Out Bucs (Lopreseti), Small Market Sailors (King)

WESTERN DIVISION

Los Angeles	Azul, Bluebloods, **DODGERS**, Los Doyers
Colorado	**ROCKIES**, Rocks, Rox
Arizona	**DIAMONDBACKS** (D-Backs)
San Francisco	**GIANTS**, Jints
San Diego	**PADRES** (Pads), Dads, Fathers, Missionaries

2009 American League

EASTERN DIVISION

New York	Bronx Bombers, Team America Love to Hate, **YANKEES** (Yanks)
Boston	Beantowners, BoSox, Carmines, Crimson Hose, Hub Hose, Old Towne Team, **RED SOX** (Sox)
Tampa Bay	**RAYS**
Toronto	**BLUE JAYS** (Jays)
Baltimore	Birds, **ORIOLES** (O's)

CENTRAL DIVISION

Minnesota	Piranhas (Guillen), Sharks (Ozzie Guillen), **TWINS**, Twinkies
Detroit	Bengals, Tamed Tigers, **TIGERS**
Chicago	ChiSox, Pale Hose, Southsiders, **WHITE SOX** (Sox)
Cleveland	**INDIANS**, Lost Tribe by the Lake, The Tribe
Kansas City	Men in Blue, Rock-bottom Royals, **ROYALS**

WESTERN DIVISION

Los Angeles	**ANGELS**, Halos, Seraphs
Texas	**RANGERS**, Wranglers (Harrelson)
Seattle	**MARINERS** (M's)
Oakland	**ATHLETICS** (A's), Un-athletics, White Elephants

2010 National League

EASTERN DIVISION

Philadelphia	Good, Bad & Ugly Phillies (Todd Zolecki), **PHILLIES** (Phils)
Atlanta	**BRAVES**, Bravos
Florida	The Fins, The Fish, **MARLINS**
New York	Amazin's, Amazing Mets, **METS**
Washington	**NATIONALS** (Nats)

CENTRAL DIVISION

Cincinnati	New Sheriff in Town (Jim Memolo), **REDS**, Red Legs, Rhinelanders, Sheriffs (Memolo)
St. Louis	**CARDINALS** (Cards), Redbirds
Houston	**ASTROS** ('Stros)
Milwaukee	**BREWERS**, Brew Crew
Chicago	British Petroleum Cubs (Len Grabstein), Bruins, Cubbies, **CUBS**, Loveable Losers, Northsiders, Wrigleys
Pittsburgh	Buccaneers (Bucs), Buccos, **PIRATES**, Shipped Out Bucs (Lopreseti), Small Market Sailors (King)

WESTERN DIVISION

San Francisco	Bad News Bears, Castoffs, **GIANTS**, Jints, Misfits, Torture
Colorado	**ROCKIES**, Rocks, Rox
San Diego	**PADRES** (Pads), Dads, Fathers, Missionaries
Los Angeles	Azul, Bluebloods, **DODGERS**, Los Doyers
Arizona	**DIAMONDBACKS** (D-Backs), Snakes

2010 American League

EASTERN DIVISION

Tampa Bay	**RAYS**
New York	Bottomless Pit Yankees (*Sporting News*), Bronx Bombers, **YANKEES** (Yanks)
Boston	Beantowners, BoSox, Carmines (Harrelson), Crimson Hose, Hub Hose, Old Towne Team, **RED SOX** (Sox)
Toronto	**BLUE JAYS** (Jays)
Baltimore	Birds, **ORIOLES** (O's)

CENTRAL DIVISION

Minnesota	Killer Bees (Guillen), Piranhas (Guillen), Sharks (Guillen & Joe Cowley), **TWINS**, Twinkies
Chicago	British Petroleum White Sox (Len Grabstein), ChiSox, Dow-Jones Sox (Len Grabenstein), Pale Hose, Sad Sox (Toni Ginneti), Schizophrenic Sox (Granetsein), Southsiders, **WHITE SOX** (Sox)
Detroit	Bengals, **TIGERS**

Cleveland	**INDIANS**, Lost Tribe by the Lake, The Tribe
Kansas City	Men in Blue, Rock-bottom Royals, **ROYALS**, Trey's Boys

WESTERN DIVISION

Texas	**RANGERS**, Wranglers (Harrelson), Yard-bangers
Los Angeles	**ANGELS**, Halos, Reloaded Halos, Seraphs
Oakland	**ATHLETICS** (A's), White Elephants
Seattle	**MARINERS** (M's)

2011 National League

EASTERN DIVISION

Philadelphia	**PHILLIES** (Phils)
Atlanta	**BRAVES**, Bravos
Florida	The Fins, The Fish, **MARLINS**
New York	Amazin's, Amazing Mets, **METS**
Washington	**NATIONALS** (Nats)

CENTRAL DIVISION

Milwaukee	**BREWERS**, Brew Crew
St. Louis	**CARDINALS** (Cards), Redbirds
Cincinnati	**REDS**, Red Legs, Rhinelanders
Pittsburgh	Buccaneers (Bucs), Buccos, **PIRATES**,
Chicago	Bruins, Cubbies, **CUBS**, Dead-Ass Team (Bob Brenly), Loveable Losers, Northsiders, Wrigleys
Houston	**ASTROS** ('Stros)

WESTERN DIVISION

Arizona	**DIAMONDBACKS** (D-Backs), Snakes
San Francisco	**GIANTS**, Jints
Colorado	**ROCKIES**, Rocks, Rox
Los Angeles	Azul, Bluebloods, **DODGERS**, Los Doyers
San Diego	**PADRES** (Pads), Dads, Dead Ass Team (Mike North), Fathers, Missionaries

2011 American League

EASTERN DIVISION

New York	Bronx Bombers, **YANKEES** (Yanks)
Tampa Bay	**RAYS**
Boston	Beantowners, BoSox, Carmines (Harrelson), Crimson Hose, Hub Hose, Old Towne Team, **RED SOX** (Sox)
Toronto	**BLUE JAYS** (Jays)
Baltimore	Birds, **ORIOLES** (O's)

CENTRAL DIVISION

Detroit	Bengals, **TIGERS**
Cleveland	**INDIANS**, Cockroaches (Les Grobstein), The Tribe
Chicago	British Petroleum White Sox (Len Grobstein), ChiSox, Cockroaches (Les Grobstein), Dow-Jones Sox (Les Grobenstein), Pale Hose, Sox-a-tanics (Joe Cowley), Slopfest Sox (Rick Morrisey) Southsiders, **WHITE SOX** (Sox)
Kansas City	Men in Blue, **ROYALS**, Trey's Boys
Minnesota	Piranhas (Guillen), **TWINS**, Twinkies

WESTERN DIVISION

Texas	**RANGERS**, Wranglers (Harrelson)
Los Angeles	**ANGELS**, Halos, Seraphs
Oakland	**ATHLETICS**, (A's), White Elephants
Seattle	**MARINERS**, (M's)

BIBLIOGRAPHY

Alexander, Gerard, and Joseph Kane, editors. *Nicknames of U.S. Cities and States*. Metuchen, N.J.: Scarecrow, 1970.

Benson, Michael. *Ballparks of North America*. Jefferson, North Carolina: McFarland, 1989.

Bjarkman, Peter. *Baseball with a Latin Beat: A History of the Latin American Game*. New York: Carroll and Graf, 2000.

Chrisman, David. *The History of the International League*. 1983.

Davids, L. Robert, ed. *Minor League Stars*: vols. I, II & III. Cleveland: Society for American Baseball Research, 1992.

Filichia, Peter. *Professional Baseball Franchises: From the Abbeville Athletics to the Zanesville Indians*. New York: Facts on File, 1993.

Finch, Robert, H. Addington, and Ben Morgan. *The Story of Minor League Baseball: History of the Game of Professional Baseball in the United States with Particular Reference to Its Growth and Development in the Smaller Cities and Towns of the Nation. The Record of Championship Professional Leagues from 1901 to 1952*. Columbus, Ohio: National Association of Professional Leagues, 1952.

Garcia, Miguel Angel y hijo. *Momentos Inolvidables de Besibol Profesional Venezolano, 1946–84*.

Hurth, Charles A. *Baseball Records. The Southern Association, 1901–47*. New Orleans: The Southern Association, 1947.

James, Bill. *The New Bill James Historical Baseball Abstract*. The Free Press, 2001.

Johnson, Arthur. *Minor League Baseball and Local Economic Development*. Champaign: University of Illinois Press, 1993.

Johnson, Daniel E. *Japanese Baseball: A Statistical Handbook*. Jefferson, North Carolina: McFarland, 1998.

Johnson, W. Lloyd. *Minor League Register*. Durham, North Carolina: Baseball America, 1994.

Lange, Fred W. *History of Baseball in California and Pacific Coast Leagues, 1847–1938*. Oakland: privately published, 1938.

Mackey, R. Scott. *Barbary Baseball: The Pacific Coast League of the 1920's*. Jefferson, North Carolina: McFarland, 1995.

Madden, W.C. *The All-American Girls Professional Baseball League Record Book*. Jefferson, North Carolina: McFarland, 2000.

McNeil, William F. *Baseball's Other All-Stars: The Greatest Players From the Negro Leagues, Japanese Leagues, Mexican League and the Pre–1960 Winter Leagues in Cuba, Puerto Rico and the Dominican Republic*. Jefferson, North Carolina: McFarland, 2001.

Merriam Webster's Biographical Dictionary. Springfield, MA. Merriam Webster, Inc. 1995.

Merriam Webster's Geographical Dictionary. Springfield, MA. Merriam Webster, Inc. 1995.

Moss, Earle W. *The Leagues and League Cities of Professional Baseball, 1910–41*. Fort Wayne: Heilbroner Baseball Bureau, 1941.

Nemec, David. *The Beer and Whiskey League: The Illustrated History of The American Association — Baseball's Renegade Major League*. New York: Lyons & Burford, 1994.

_____, and Dave Zeman. *The Baseball Rookies Encyclopedia*. Brassey's, 2004.

Objoski, Robert. *Bush League: A Colorful, Factual Account of Minor League Baseball from 1877 to the Present*. New York: MacMillan 1975.

Oleksak, Michael. *Beisbol: Latin Americans and the Grand Old Game*. Masters, 1991.

O'Neal, Bill. *The International League, A Baseball History: 1884–1992*. Austin, Texas: Eakin, 1991.

O'Neal, Bill. *The Pacific Coast League, 1903–1988*. Austin, Texas: Eakin, 1990.

O'Neal, Bill. *The Southern League: Baseball in Dixie, 1885–1994*. Austin, Texas: Eakin, 1994.

O'Neal, Bill. *The Texas League: A Century of Baseball 1888-1987*. Austin, Texas: Eakin, 1987.

Perez, Medina y Ramon G., *Historia de Beisbol Panameno*. Panama City: Dutigrafia, S.A.

Pietrusza, David. *Baseball's Canadian-American League: A History of Its Inception, Franchises, Participants, Locales, Statistics, Demise and Legends, 1936–1951*. Jefferson, North Carolina: McFarland, 1990.

Pina, Tony. *Los Grandes Finales*. Quisqueyana, D.R.: S.D. Editora Colegial.

Random House Webster College Dictionary. New York, N.Y. Random House, 1997.

The Road Atlas. Chicago, Illinois. Rand McNally 2011.

Rucker, Mark, and Peter C. Bjarkman. *Smoke: The Romance and Lore of Cuban Baseball*. Total Sports Illustrated, 1998.

Ruggles, William B. *The History of the Texas League of Professional Baseball Clubs, 1888–1951*. Dallas: The Texas League, 1951.

Schlossberg, Dan. *The New Baseball Catalogue*. Jonathon David, 1998.

Siwoff, Seymour, ed. *The Elias Book of Baseball Records, 2009*. New York: Seymour Siwoff.

Snelling, Dennis. *The Pacific Coast League: A Statistical History, 1903–1957*. Jefferson, North Carolina: McFarland, 1995.

Spalding, Albert. *America's National Game*. University of Nebraska Press, Reprinted edition 1992 (original edition 1911).

Sumner, Benjamin Barrett. *Minor League Baseball Standings: All North American Leagues Through 1999*. Jefferson, North Carolina: McFarland, 2000.

Sumner, Jim, and Dave Kemp, ed. *Minor League History Journal*, vol. I. Cleveland: Society for American Baseball Research, 1991.

Torres, Angel. *La Historia de Beisbol Cubano, 1876–1976*. Havana, Cuba: Libros L.A.

Van Hyning, Thomas E. *Puerto Rico's Winter Leagues*. New York: 1983.

_____. *The Santurce Crabbers: Sixty Seasons of Puerto Rican Baseball*. Jefferson, North Carolina: McFarland, 1998.

Guides, Serials, Encyclopedias and Official Publications

American Association Record Book. Published by the American Association, 1996.

Archivo de Beisbol.

Baseball Blue Book. 1909–1996. Lexington, Kentucky: Sportsource.

Baseball Blue Book: Minor League Digest, 1997–2002. St. Petersburg, FL: National Association of Professional Baseball Leagues.

Baseball America Almanac, 1985–2009. Durham: Baseball America.

Baseball America Directory, 1990–2009. Durham: Baseball America.

Baseball America Statistics Report, 1983–1987. Durham: Baseball America.

Baseball Digest, published 10 times a year, 1997–2010. Evanston, Illinois: Century Sports.

Baseball Research Journal, 1972–1996. Cleveland: Society for American Baseball Research.

Compilaciones Oficiales de la Liga de Beisbol Profesional de Puerto Rico, 1967/68 hasta 1997/98. San Juan, P.R.: Liga de Beisbol Profesional de Puerto Rico, 1998.

Enciclopedia de Beisbol: Ponce Leones, 1938–1987. San Juan, P.R.: Editoria Corripio, 1989.

Enciclopedia del Beisbol Mexicano, 1996. Monterrey, Mexico: Revista Deportivas, S.A. de C.V. (REDSA)

Encyclopedia of Minor League Baseball, Second Edition. Llyod Johnson and Miles Wolff, ed. Baseball America, 1997.

Gracyzk, Wayne. *Japan Pro Fan Hanbook, 1996–2000.* Tokyo: Japanese Professional Baseball, 1997.

Jiminez, O., and Jose D. Jesus, ed. Santiago, D.R.: Amigo de Hogar, 1977.

King, Dick. *Baseball '76: Official Bi-Centennial Edition* (NAPBBL). St. Petersburg: National Association of Professional Baseball Leagues, 1976.

Official American Association Baseball Guide, 1883–1891. Philadelphia: Alfred J. Reach. Cleveland, Ohio: SABR Microfilm Lending Library.

Official American League Baseball Guide, 1901–1939. Philadelphia: Alfred J. Reach.

Official Baseball Guide, 1877–1900. New York: American Sports Publishing. Cooperstown, New York: Baseball Hall of Fame Library.

Official Baseball Guide, 1940–2010. St. Louis: The Sporting News.

Players National League Guide, 1890. Cleveland, Ohio: SABR Microfilm Lending Library.

Reichler, Joseph L. ed. *The Baseball Encyclopedia, 1969–1988.* New York: MacMillan.

Spalding's Minor League Guide, 1889–1902. New York & Chicago: American Sports Publishing. Cleveland, Ohio: SABR Microfilm Lending Library.

The Sports Encyclopedia: Baseball, 21st Edition. New York: St. Martin's Griffin, 2001.

Thorn, John, and Pete Palmer, ed. *Total Baseball IV: The Official Encyclopedia of Major League Baseball.* New York: Viking, 1997.

Wolff, Rick ed. *The Baseball Encyclopedia.* New York: MacMillan.

Newspapers On Microfilm

Chicago Tribune, 1876–1902. Harold Washington Public Library, Chicago.

New York Clipper, 1853–1924. DeKalb, Illinois: Governor's State University Library. Cleveland, Ohio: SABR Microfilm Lending Library.

The Sporting Life (Philadelphia, PA), 1883–1892. Cleveland, Ohio: SABR Microfilm Lending Library.

The Sporting News (St. Louis, MO), 1886–1902. Cleveland, Ohio: SABR Microfilm Lending Library.

Websites

Australian Baseball History

Baseball America

Baseball Chronology

Baseball Cube

Baseball Reference

Demitry, Steve. Steve Dimitry's Old Time Baseball Web Page.

Japanese Central League

Japanese Pacific League

Korean Baseball Organization

LIDOM Beisbol de la Republica Dominicana

Liga del Pacifico de Mexico

Liga Mexicana del Beisbol

Liga Profesional de Beisbol de Colombia

Liga Profesional de Beisbol de Nicaragua

Liga Profesional de Beisbol de Panama

Liga Puertoriquena de Beisbol.

Liga Serie A de Baseball Italiano

Liga Venezolana de Beisbol Profesional.

Logo Server

Major League Baseball

Minor League Baseball

Netherlands Baseball Website

Skilton, John. John Skilton's Baseball Links.

Wikipedia Sports—Baseball

INDEX

References are to entry numbers.